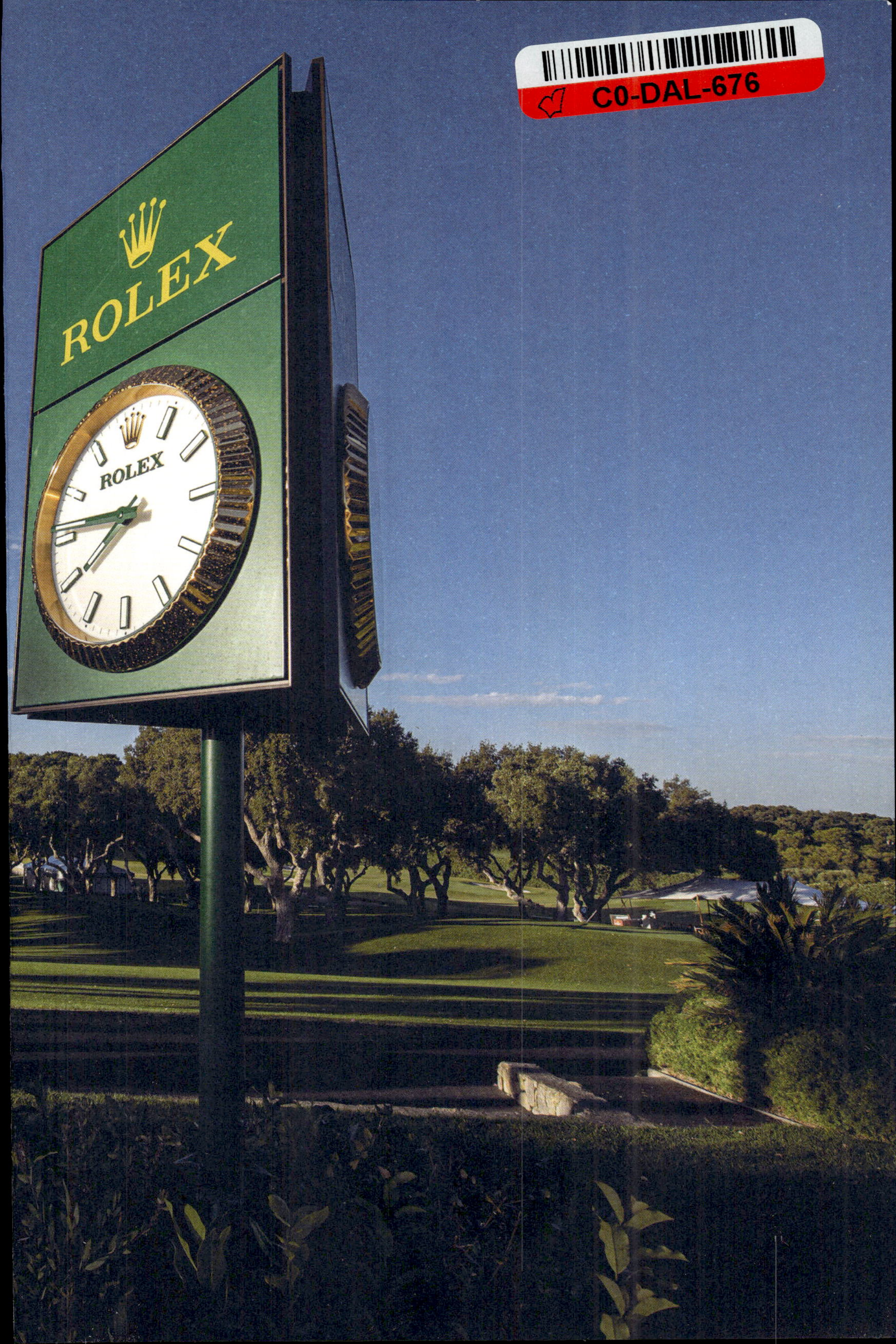
ROLEX
ROLEX

THE WORLD OF PROFESSIONAL GOLF
2023

ROLEX

PRESENTS

THE WORLD OF PROFESSIONAL GOLF 2023

Founded By Mark H McCormack

IMG

Contributors
Matt Cooper
Doug Ferguson
Bill Fields
Donald "Doc" Giffin
Lewine Mair
Beth Ann Nichols
Marino Parascenzo
Mitchell Platts

Editor
Andy Farrell

Managing Editor
Sarah Wooldridge

Photography
Getty Images

Producer, official video
Sian Bayliss

First published 2023

Designed and produced by TC Communications Ltd.

ISBN 978-0-9914858-9-5

Printed and bound in England

To view the official video of
The World of Professional Golf 2023,
which reviews the highlights of the 2022 year in golf,
please go to:
www.rwopg2023.com and enter the password: **Rolex2023**

Rolex Presents
The World of Professional Golf
is available online at:
worldofprofessionalgolf.com

Explore the Year in Retrospect alongside a collection of feature articles from years gone by. This truly archival platform showcases the colourful and captivating stories as lived by the game's biggest names.

Contents

THE TOURS

Preface

In a year when an intriguing mix of new names and resurgent forces claimed golf's biggest prizes, it is a privilege to be able to present a first-person account of her incredible 2022 season by one of the latter group. Lydia Ko returned to the top of the Rolex Rankings after a gap of over five years and finished as the Rolex LPGA Player of the Year after her third win of the year at the CME Group Tour Championship. One of the most eloquent voices in the game, still only in her mid-20s, Ko writes compellingly on how standards in the women's game are rapidly becoming higher and higher, which drives her own desire to keep improving. Sadly, as the year drew to a close, there was the news of the death of Kathy Whitworth, the winner of more LPGA titles than anyone else and a true giant of the game. The year also saw the passing of Tom Weiskopf, who is remembered in a poignant tribute by our longtime contributor Marino Parascenzo.

Ko and Rory McIlroy, the year-end world number ones, have much in common, being as articulate behind a microphone as they are with golf clubs in hand. But neither was a winner at the 2022 major championships, which saw many amazing and uplighting moments, from Scottie Scheffler's masterclass at Augusta National to Ashleigh Buhai's late-night playoff win at Muirfield. Yet the most historic week of the year came at The 150th Open at St Andrews, crowned by Cameron Smith's incredible inward half on the Old Course during the final round.

Founded by IMG's Mark H McCormack in 1967, and known as Rolex Presents *The World of Professional Golf* since 2006, this annual continues to chronicle the deeds of the finest professional golfers. This 57th edition was made possible by the generous support Arnaud Laborde, of Rolex and arrives after the publication saw a significant development with an online presence at www.worldofprofessionalgolf.com. A selection of archive material is available to view and more will be added over time.

As the landscape of professional golf gets ever more complex, a note is in order on how to find tournaments in the book. Co-sanctioned events may generally found in the geographical host tour's chapter, while an event being played outside a tour's traditional borders, but not co-sanctioned with a local tour, can be found in that tour's section. With the rise of mixed events, which is to be welcomed, the gender of the winner may indicate where the report may be found, with historic victories for Hannah Green and Linn Grant in the WPGA Tour of Australasia and the Ladies European Tour sections respectively. The schedule at the start of each tour chapter indicates were the report is to be found.

It should also be noted that it was not always possible to obtain full prize money breakdowns with results on certain tours. Where tours have switched to publishing only points with results, that is indicated by a lack of a currency symbol.

Mighty thanks are due to Tim Leney and his team at TC Communications for masterminding the production of this edition, and to Peter Dixon, who brought patience, rigour and a keen eye to the role of proofreading the publication. A sincere tip of the cap to all the reporters, broadcasters, photographers and television staff who provide coverage of professional golf, and to all the dedicated communications staff at the leading organisations and tours.

Thanks in particular to: Melanie Roux, Alexandra Gasser, Julie Wittig, and Paul Bouteloup of Rolex; Sian Bayliss; Matt Cooper; Vicky Cuming; Doug Ferguson; Mary Flanagan, Ed Hodge and Mike Woodcock of The R&A; Bill Fields; Sasha Forster of the OWGR; Tony Greer; Doc Giffin; Ross Hallett; Sean Harry and Andrew Reddington of Getty Images; Alastair Johnston; Bethan Jones and Eva-Lotta Strömlid of the LET; Tim Lacy; Christina Lance and Amy Mills of the LPGA; Laury Livsey of the PGA Tour; Lewine Mair; Michele Mair; Adrian Mitchell; Jonathan Montague; Beth Ann Nichols; Marino Parascenzo; Mitchell Platts; Brian Poe; Alistair Tait; Yoshiko Tsukamoto of the JLPGA; Henry Watt; and Sarah Wooldridge.

Andy Farrell
Editor
January 2023

Foreword

It has long been my feeling that a sport as compelling as professional golf is deserving of a history, and by history I do not mean an account culled years later from the adjectives and enthusiasms of on-the-spot reports that have then sat in newspaper morgues for decades waiting for some patient drudge to paste them together and call them lore. Such works can be excellent when insight and perspective are added to the research, but this rarely happens. What I am talking about is a running history, a chronology written at the time, which would serve both as a record of the sport and as a commentary upon the sport in any given year — an annual, if you will …

When I embarked on this project two years ago (the first of these annuals was published in Great Britain in 1967), I was repeatedly told that such a compendium of world golf was impossible, that it would be years out of date before it could be assembled and published, that it would be hopelessly expensive to produce and that only the golf fanatic would want a copy anyway. In the last analysis, it was that final stipulation that spurred me on. There must be a lot of golf fanatics, I decided. I can't be the only one.

And then one winter day I was sitting in Arnold Palmer's den in Latrobe, Pennsylvania, going through the usual motions of spreading papers around so that Arnold and I could discuss some business project, when Arnold happened to mention that he wanted to collect a copy of each new golf book that was published from now on, in order to build a golf library of his own.

"It's really too bad that there isn't a book every year on the pro tour," he said.

"Ah," I thought. "Another golf fanatic. That makes two of us."

So I decided to do the book. And I have. And I hope you like it. If so, you can join Arnold and me as golf fanatics.

Mark H McCormack
Cleveland, Ohio
January 1968

Clive Brunskill/Getty Images

Mark H McCormack 1930—2003

In 1960, Mark Hume McCormack shook hands with a young golfer named Arnold Palmer. That historic handshake established a business that would evolve into today's IMG, the world's premier sports and lifestyle marketing and management company — representing hundreds of sports figures, entertainers, models, celebrities, broadcasters, television properties, and prestigious organisations and events around the world. With just a handshake Mark McCormack had invented a global industry.

Sean McManus, President of CBS News and Sports, reflects, "I don't think it's an overstatement to say that like Henry Ford and Bill Gates, Mark McCormack literally created, fostered and led an entirely new worldwide industry. There was no sports marketing before Mark McCormack. Every athlete who's ever appeared in a commercial, or every right holder who sold their rights to anyone, owes a huge debt of gratitude to Mark McCormack."

Mark McCormack's philosophy was simple. "Be the best," he said. "Learn the business and expand by applying what you already know." This philosophy served him well, not only as an entrepreneur and CEO of IMG, but also as an author, a consultant and a confidant to a host of global leaders in the world of business, politics, finance, science, sports and entertainment.

He was among the most-honoured entrepreneurs of his time. *Sports Illustrated* recognised him as "The Most Powerful Man in Sports". In 1999, ESPN's Sports Century listed him as one of the century's 10 "Most Influential People in the Business of Sport".

Golf Magazine called McCormack "the most powerful man in golf" and honoured him along with Arnold Palmer, Gerald Ford, Dwight D Eisenhower, Bob Hope and Ben Hogan as one of the 100 all-time "American Heroes of Golf". *Tennis* magazine and *Racquet* magazine named him "the most powerful man in tennis".

Tennis legend Billie Jean King believes, "Mark McCormack was the king of sports marketing. He shaped the way all sports are marketed around the world. He was the first in the marketplace, and his influence on the world of sports, particularly his ability to combine athlete representation, property development and television broadcasting, will forever be the standard of the industry."

The London *Sunday Times* listed him as one of the 1,000 people who influenced the 20th century. Alastair Cooke on the BBC said simply that "McCormack was the Oracle; the creator of the talent industry, the maker of people famous in their profession famous to the rest of the world and making for them a fortune in the process ... He took on as clients people already famous in their profession as golfer, opera singer, author, footballer, racing car driver, violinist — and from time to time if they needed special help, a prime minister, or even the Pope."

McCormack was honoured posthumously by the Golf Writers Association of America with the 2004 William D Richardson Award, the organisation's highest honour, "Given to recognise an individual who has consistently made an outstanding contribution to golf".

Among McCormack's other honours were the 2001 PGA Distinguished Service Award, given to those who have helped perpetuate the values and ideals of the PGA of America. He was also named a Commander of the Royal Order of the Polar Star by the King of Sweden (the highest honour for a person living outside of Sweden) for his contribution to the Nobel Foundation.

Journalist Frank Deford states, "There have been what we love to call dynasties in every sport. IMG has been different. What this one brilliant man, Mark McCormack, created is the only dynasty ever over all sport."

Through IMG, Mark McCormack demonstrated the value of sports and lifestyle activities as effective corporate marketing tools, but more importantly, his lifelong dedication to his vocation — begun with just a simple handshake — brought enjoyment to millions of people worldwide who watch and cheer their heroes and heroines.

That is his legacy.

Written and first published in 2004

ROLEX

Rolex's partnership with golf dates back almost 60 years, during which time our brand has championed the sport's constant quest for excellence and commitment to upholding its finest traditions. Throughout this journey we have shared many milestone moments and 2022 was no exception.

Our Testimonees shone on the world stage, displaying a determination to push back the boundaries of performance and achievement that is fundamental to Rolex's own core philosophy. Among these exceptional athletes, Scottie Scheffler was a standout performer. One of several new brand ambassadors across all our sporting associations, the American won four titles, including his first Major, at the Masters in Augusta. He also claimed the World No. 1 ranking and was named the PGA TOUR Player of the Year.

Englishman Matt Fitzpatrick also secured a first Major victory, at the U.S. Open, while American Justin Thomas collected his second, winning the PGA Championship five years after his maiden triumph in the same tournament. Spaniard Jon Rahm, meanwhile, completed a hat-trick of victories at the prestigious DP World Tour Championship, Dubai.

Rolex Testimonees were also at the forefront of women's golf in 2022. Canadian Brooke Henderson won her second Major, adding The Amundi Evian Championship title to her long list of honours, while Lydia Ko was named Rolex Player of the Year for a second time. The New Zealander's victory at the LPGA Tour's season finale, the CME Group Tour Championship, was her third of the year and clinched the year-long Race to the CME Globe title.

In team events, the United States maintained their dominance of the Presidents Cup, securing victory over the International team for a 12th time at the 14th edition of the biennial tournament, held in September at Quail Hollow Club in Charlotte, North Carolina. The Palmer Cup, the annual Ryder Cup-style competition for elite university golfers from around the world – it is named after our first golf Testimonee, the legendary Arnold Palmer – was successfully staged at the Geneva Golf Club, with the International selection prevailing over the United States.

The World of Professional Golf, which Rolex has been presenting since 2006, provides a comprehensive review of these and all the other season highlights, and I know that you, like me, will enjoy reliving them.

As you savour all the thrilling action from 2022, may I take this opportunity to wish you all the best for 2023 when we anticipate another year of fruitful partnership with the sport, one that reaches every corner of the globe. As always, we look forward to being present at all the Majors as well as The Ryder Cup, which will be staged in Italy for the first time at the Marco Simone Golf and Country Club on the outskirts of Rome.

Jean-Frédéric Dufour
Rolex SA
Chief Executive Officer

Rolex and Golf

Rolex is committed to the permanent quest for excellence in all its endeavours and has been a long-term supporter of golf in its pursuit of the same. The brand's enduring relationship with the sport began almost 60 years ago, in 1967, when Arnold Palmer, joined by Jack Nicklaus and Gary Player, became Rolex's first golfing Testimonees. Known together as The Big Three, these legendary players changed the face of golf forever, and their partnership with the brand marked the start of a relationship based on the shared commitment to continuous improvement and unwavering precision. Since then, the affiliation has grown and flourished, permeating every level of the game worldwide. From elite players and golf legends, to all the game's Major championships – where success represents the pinnacle of achievement in the sport – as well as the foremost professional tours and worldwide amateur championships, Rolex is ever-present. The Swiss manufacturer's support for the game is built on a strong sense of integrity and respect for tradition that promote the continuity of expertise and transfer of knowledge, and an understanding of the importance of investing in the sport's development for future generations.

Kevin C. Cox / Getty Images

Scottie Scheffler - Masters Tournament

Ezra Shaw/Getty Images

Justin Thomas - PGA Championship

Andrew Redington/Getty Images

Matt Fitzpatrick - U.S. Open

Jon Rahm - DP World Tour Championship

Thomas Pieters - Abu Dhabi HSBC Championship

Stuart Franklin/Getty Images

Brooke Henderson - The Amundi Evian Championship

Michael Reaves/Getty Images

Lydia Ko - CME Group Tour Championship

Gregory Shamus/Getty Images

Hideki Matsuyama - Sony Open

@LETgolf

Lexi Thompson - Aramco Team Series - New York

Kevin C. Cox/Getty Images

Jordan Spieth - RBC Heritage

Dean Mouhtaropoulos/Getty Images

Victor Perez - Dutch Open

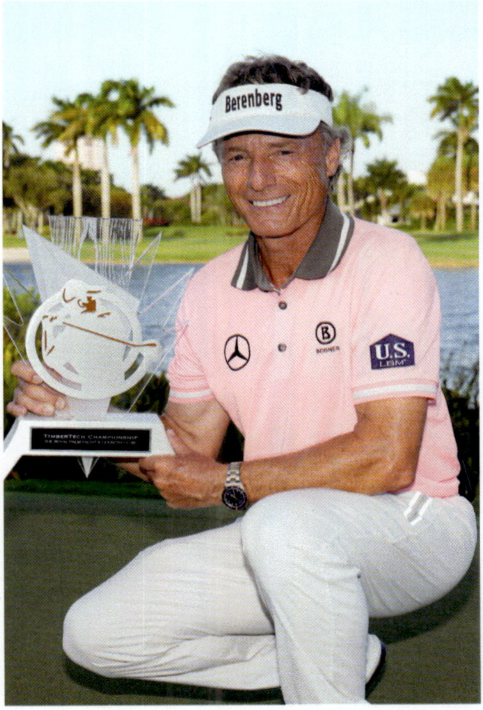

Raj Mehta/Getty Images

Bernhard Langer - TimberTech Championship

Eakin Howard/Getty Images

Fred Couples - SAS Championship

1 Lydia Ko

Michael Reaves/Getty Images

2 Nelly Korda

Douglas P. DeFelice/Getty Images

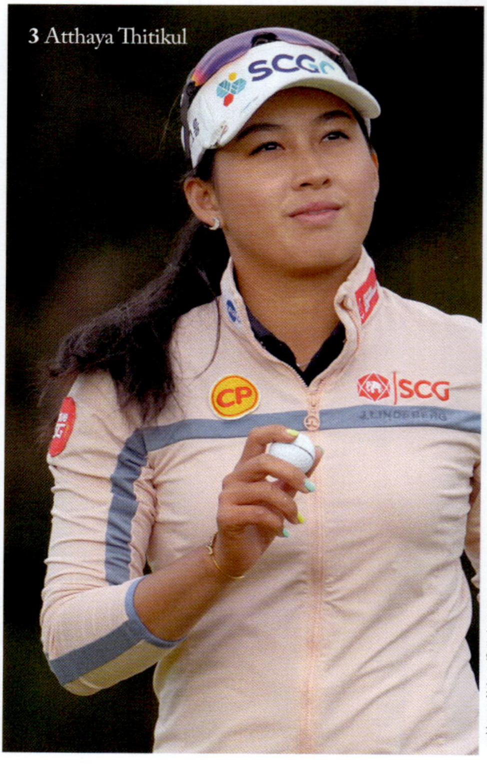

3 Atthaya Thitikul

oshimasa Nakano/Getty Images

The Year In Prospect

Tiger Woods on the way to winning the 100th US Open at Pebble Beach.

Jonathan Ferrey/Getty Images

Venues like Pebble matter to the game

By Andy Farrell

Pebble Beach, one of the most spectacular venues in championship golf, will stage a US Open for the seventh time in 2023. The one difference from the previous versions will be who is playing — not the leading male players, who were last there in 2019 and who also have the opportunity of playing in an annual PGA Tour event on the Monterey Peninsula, but the best women golfers in the world. This will be a first US Women's Open at Pebble Beach Golf Links, one of the highlights of the season's championship golf, and that matters, according to two-time champion Juli Inkster. "If you can win a US Women's Open on a course where Nicklaus, Watson, Woods and Kite won, it matters," Inkster said.

Jack Nicklaus called the 18th tee at Pebble, jutting out into the Pacific Ocean, with the par-five fairway doglegging around the pounding breakers of not-always-so-still Stillwater Cove, to a green framed by the hills of the Del Monte Forest behind, "one of the greatest places in golf". John Bodenhamer, the chief championships officer of the United States Golf Association, said of the scene: "Arguably, the greatest walk in golf." Residents of St Andrews on the east coast of Scotland may beg to differ, but on the west coast of America he has a point. Here, a women's major champion will be declared for the first time.

The evolution of the women's majors continues apace in two areas. One is prize money, with purses having risen dramatically in recent years, including to $10 million at the US Women's Open. The other is to do with the stage upon which those championships are being held. More and more of the traditional major venues are being used to host both men's and women's championships. The KPMG Women's PGA has been upgrading its roster in recent years, the AIG Women's Open first visited the Old Course at St Andrews in 2007 and, in 2022, Muirfield hosted for a first time.

Both these strands come together in Mina Harigae. In the US Women's Open at Pine Needles last summer, Harigae became the first woman golfer to earn over $1 million for not winning. No one could stop a dominant Minjee Lee from claiming the trophy, but Harigae came closer than anyone else. After her runner-up finish there, it would be understandable if the 33-year-old American was looking forward to trying her luck again the following year. But Harigae has been looking forward to the 2023 US Women's Open ever since it was announced in 2017 that Pebble Beach was going to be the venue.

"Hearing that Pebble Beach was going to be the site of our US Open in 2023 was the most exciting news I had heard about women's golf," Harigae said. "I immediately started thinking of how hard the USGA would set up the course and how it might differ from the men's US Opens there."

Harigae grew up in Monterey and first picked up a golf club at an after-school clinic put on by the Salvation Army at the Bayonet and Black Horse Club. Her high school golf team played home matches at Spyglass Hill, she won the first of four California Women's Amateur titles aged 12 and was taught by the professional at Cypress Point, Jim Langley. Asked how often she has played Pebble Beach, she said: "Oh, people will be jealous, but I think over, like, 30 times." Her best score is a 65 and she was runner-up in the 2018 TaylorMade Pebble Beach Invitational, which features a mixed field of PGA Tour, Champions and LPGA players. Inkster won the unofficial event in 1990, long before the victories of Hannah Green and Linn Grant in 2022.

Harigae's parents have run a Japanese restaurant in Monterey for more than three decades. It should get good business early in July when Harigae's fellow LPGA players are in town. "My dad is the sushi chef and my mom is the kitchen chef, so hopefully my friends will go there when we play this next year," Harigae said at Pine Needles. "I think about it all the time, returning to Pebble Beach for the Women's US Open. That's my dream tournament for sure. I'm so proud to be from there. I have so many great memories at Pebble Beach. It's my favourite place on earth, so I'm really looking forward to it."

Harigae is far from the only person to feel this way about her hometown. Australian painter Francis McComas is reputed to have called the Monterey Peninsula the "greatest meeting of land and water". The phrase, or its corruption "most felicitous", is often attributed to Robert Louis Stevenson, who passed by and wrote about the area, just not that line, apparently. Pebble Beach, just along from Carmel, was founded by Samuel Morse, an environmentalist and the nephew of the inventor of the telegraph. It was his vision to move the planned housing into the hills and instead build a public golf course with as many holes as possible on the clifftops. Two California state amateur champions, Jack Neville and Douglas Grant, laid out the original course in 1919, with two-time US Amateur champion Chandler Egan later making a few refinements, such as extending the 18th into the exciting par five it is today.

JONES AT A LOOSE END

Although a remote location, 120 miles south of San Francisco, the course got the attention of the USGA, who awarded Pebble the first US Amateur to be played west of the Mississippi. The year was 1929 and Bobby Jones was at the height of his career, a year away from the Grand Slam. It was his first visit to California and he attracted crowds wherever he went. He broke Pebble's course record with a 67 in practice and was the co-medallist in qualifying. He had won the title for four of the previous five years and had just won a third US Open. Yet, in a monumental shock, he lost in the first round to a 19-year-old from Omaha, Nebraska. Johnny Goodman was hardly known at that point, but would become the last amateur to win the US Open four years later.

Suddenly at a loose end, Jones played at Cypress Point, a newer course nearby. Jones had been impressed by Pebble, but was completely smitten by Cypress and spent most of the week following matches at the Amateur while conversing with its architect, Dr Alister Mackenzie. When Jones decided to build his own course at Augusta a few years later, he knew the man he wanted to design it. The person who brought them together was Marion Hollins, who had engaged Mackenzie for the job at Cypress Point. Hollins was a champion in her own right. She won the 1921 US Women's Amateur and would become America's first Curtis Cup captain in 1932. When the Pebble Beach Championship for Women began in 1923, Hollins won six times in a row, seven in all, and finished runner-up on another six occasions.

Pebble played host to the US Women's Amateur for the first time in 1940, when Betty Jameson retained her title. Jameson would become the second ever US Women's Open champion in 1947 and a founder member of the LPGA in 1950. In 1961, Nicklaus won his second US Amateur in three years, playing 112 holes in 20 under par. "I fell in love with it immediately," he said of Pebble. "It remains my favourite among the 600 or so courses I have played around the world." Decades later, when a plot of land became available to bring the short fifth hole onto the shorefront, Nicklaus designed it. Now the fourth through the 10th hug the clifftop, as well as the last two holes.

The US Open did not arrive until 1972. There had still been doubts within the USGA about the remote location. But television loved it, and the viewers, too. Coverage was extended to 13 of the 18 holes, the most ever, and there was even a back-nine duel.

2023 SCHEDULE

January 19-22	Abu Dhabi HSBC Championship	Yas Links
January 26-29	Hero Dubai Desert Classic	Emirates
February 2-5	PIF Saudi International	Royal Greens
February 16-19	Genesis Invitational	Riviera
March 2-5	HSBC Women's World Championship	Sentosa
March 2-5	Arnold Palmer Invitational	Bay Hill
March 9-12	Players Championship	TPC Sawgrass
March 22-26	WGC Dell Technologies Match Play	Austin CC
April 6-9	Masters Tournament	Augusta National
April 2-23	Chevron Championship	Carlton Woods
May 4-7	Hanwha Lifeplus International Crown	TPC Harding Park
May 11-14	Cognizant Founders Cup	Upper Montclair
May 18-21	PGA Championship	Oak Hill
Mar 25-28	KitchenAid Senior PGA Championship	Fields Ranch East
June 1-4	Memorial Tournament	Muirfield Village
June 15-18	US Open Championship	Los Angeles CC (North)
June 22-25	KPMG Women's PGA Championship	Baltusrol (Lower)
June 29-July 2	US Senior Open	Sentry World
July 6-9	US Women's Open	Pebble Beach
July 13-16	Genesis Scottish Open	Renaissance Club
July 20-23	The 151st Open	Royal Liverpool, Hoylake
July 27-30	Amundi Evian Championship	Evian
July 27-30	Senior Open presented by Rolex	Royal Porthcawl
August 3-6	Trust Golf Women's Scottish Open	Dundonald
August 10-13	AIG Women's Open	Walton Heath
August 10-13	FedEx St Jude Championship	TPC Southwind
August 17-20	BMW Championship	Olympia Fields
August 24-27	Tour Championship	East Lake
August 24-27	US Senior Women's Open	Waverley
September 14-17	BMW PGA Championship	Wentworth
September 22-24	Solheim Cup	Finca Cortesin
Sept 29-Oct 1	Ryder Cup	Marco Simone
November 16-19	DP World Tour Championship	Jumeirah Estates
November 16-19	CME Group Tour Championship	Tiburon
November 23-26	Andalucia Costa del Sol Open de Espana	Las Brisas

If Arnold Palmer had holed his birdie putt at the 14th and Nicklaus had missed his bogey putt at the 12th, Palmer would have overtaken the longtime leader. Neither happened. Nicklaus became Pebble's first champion when his one-iron at the 17th hit the flagstick and finished six inches away. Until Matt Fitzpatrick at Brookline in 2022, the Bear was the only player to win a US Amateur and a US Open at the same venue.

In 1982, there was another memorable shot at the same hole, Tom Watson chipping in to deny Nicklaus a repeat victory. Ten years on and Tom Kite chipped in at the short seventh amid a gale and went on to win a longed for major title. Earlier, Nicklaus had congratulated Colin Montgomerie on winning after the Scot set a clubhouse target that looked unlikely to be beaten. Even earlier, on Saturday, Gil Morgan became the first player ever to reach double digits under par in a US Open. He went 12 under at the seventh, the

107-yard beauty, and then played the beastly string of par fours, the eighth, ninth and 10th, in six-five-six. He was 17 over for his last 29 holes.

The future of Pebble Beach was assured when it was bought from the previous Japanese owners by a consortium led by Peter Ueberroth, of 1984 LA Olympics fame, and including Palmer and Carmel mayor Clint Eastwood. By 2000, there was nowhere else the USGA wanted to go for its 100th US Open. This time Tiger Woods was playing the Nicklaus role, a multiple winner of the Crosby Clambake, and the best player in the game. He won by 15 strokes, on 12 under par, to start his famous Tiger Slam. The only moment of jeopardy came in the third round at the 18th and was known only to Tiger's then caddie Steve Williams, who handed his player a ball for the reload after Tiger had snap-hooked his drive into the Pacific and realised it was the last ball in the bag. Woods kept it on dry land this time. History was set in motion.

Graeme McDowell in 2010 and Gary Woodland in 2019 added to the US Open folklore at Pebble, which will not be the only new venue for the women in 2023. After 51 years in Palm Springs, the Chevron Championship moves to The Club at Carlton Woods in The Woodlands outside Houston. The KPMG Women's PGA will be played on the Lower course at Baltusrol, a regular men's major venue, and the AIG Women's Open goes to Walton Heath, south of London. The classic heathland course, where James Braid was the pro for almost half a century, has hosted many prestigious events but never a major before. The winner will add her name to an eclectic roll of honour that includes Harry Vardon, George Duncan, Cecil Leitch, Henry Cotton, Jean Donald, Peter Thomson, Marley Spearman, Michael Bonallack, Tom Kite, Paul Way and the American Ryder Cup team, rather convincingly, from 1981.

While the Solheim Cup heads to Spain and the Ryder Cup to Italy, both for the first time, the men's majors are mostly on familiar terrain, albeit with a new tee on the 13th hole at Augusta National. The PGA Championship returns to Oak Hill, and the Open Championship to Royal Liverpool at Hoylake, where the last two winners were Woods in 2006 and Rory McIlroy in 2014. Each won in their own way in very different conditions. Tiger steered his way around a burnt out links with precise iron play; McIlroy put on a driving masterclass, thrillingly making two eagles in the last three holes on Saturday moments before a huge thunderstorm hit.

The US Open, however, will be played for the first time on the North course at Los Angeles Country Club, where America won the Walker Cup in 2017 with a team including Collin Morikawa, Scottie Scheffler and Will Zalatoris. The Beverly Hills course, chiefly designed by George Thomas and restored by Gil Hanse, will host the city's first US Open for 75 years, since Ben Hogan won at Riviera in 1948. It held the first LA Open, now the Genesis Invitational, in 1926, won by Harry Cooper, and hosted the US Women's Amateur in 1930, when Glenna Collett Vare won the fifth of her record six titles. The US Women's Open will arrive in 2032, but visits Riviera in only three years' time, while the long list of future sites includes America's finest venues.

Said the USGA's Bodenhamer: "We like to think of them as the cathedrals of the game. Places like Pebble Beach and Riviera and Oakmont and Oakland Hills and Merion and Inverness. The great women players will be able to make their own history like Jack and Tom and Tiger did at Pebble, and Ben Hogan and Bob Jones did at Merion. They're going to make those memories at the game's greatest places as we go into the future, and we're really proud of that.

"It's important where players win a US Open, for men and women. The ghosts of the past, those moments that are made, they do matter."

The Year In Retrospect

Scottie Scheffler and Rory McIlroy.

Sam Greenwood/Getty Images

Much to celebrate and much to talk about

By Doug Ferguson

Relative unknowns became household names in a matter of months. Good players suddenly were looked upon as great ones in a matter of weeks. And when the Saudi Arabian riches of LIV Golf were involved, a "no" became a "yes" in a matter of days. For a sport reputed to move slowly, the fractured world of golf in 2022 seemed to change by the minute.

Scottie Scheffler was but one example. He qualified for the 2020 Masters in his rookie season on the PGA Tour without having won, a rare feat. The next year, he was the only American on a dominant Ryder Cup team at Whistling Straits who had not won a tournament. So, the talent was there, just not the trophies. Scheffler was winless in 65 tries on the PGA Tour when he arrived at the WM Phoenix Open in February. Six tournaments later, he walked off the 18th green at Augusta National with his fourth victory, which included a Masters green jacket, a World Golf Championship and the number one world ranking. "I don't feel like number one in the world. I feel like the same guy I was four months ago, and I hope that doesn't change," Scheffler said.

Scheffler wasn't the only rising star, just the biggest. There was a fresh face from South Korea known by his given name, Joohyung Kim, a 20-year-old who had won the Singapore International in his first tournament of 2022. He was given a sponsor's exemption to the Genesis Scottish Open, and he was tied for the lead until a bogey on the final hole. That was only the start. Four weeks later, despite a quadruple-bogey eight on the opening hole of the Wyndham Championship, Kim won his first PGA Tour event. And then he was simply known as "Tom Kim", a nickname he had as a boy because of his fascination with the cartoon character Thomas the Tank Engine. In just three months, Kim went from contending against a strong field to winning his first PGA Tour event and then shining on the stage at the Presidents Cup with a two-iron into seven feet and a winning putt that prompted him to slam his cap to the turf in a wild celebration. All aboard!

And then there was Cameron Young, who was 490th in the world when he won his first Korn Ferry Tour event. One year later, he was on the verge of winning the PGA Championship until a late double bogey derailed his chances. He missed a playoff by one shot at Southern Hills. Two months later, he shot 31 on the back nine at St Andrews only to finish one shot behind Cameron Smith in The 150th Open. By the end of the year, the 25-year-old Young was the easy choice as PGA Tour Rookie of the Year on the strength of five runner-up finishes. He started the year 134th in the world ranking. He ended the year at number 16.

Change was just as swift outside the ropes.

Rory McIlroy was holding court below the clubhouse at Riviera Country Club in Los Angeles in February. Most of the buzz that week at the Genesis Invitational was caused by rumours about Greg Norman's bid to start a rival league funded by the Saudi Arabia sovereign wealth fund. But then Phil Mickelson served up damaging remarks that insulted all sides — Norman's project, the Saudis who were paying for it and the PGA Tour for how they operated. That led top players from Dustin Johnson to Bryson DeChambeau to state their allegiance to established tours. McIlroy referred to Mickelson's comments as "naive, selfish, egotistical, ignorant", and he said LIV Golf was "dead in the water". He said Norman would have to play for LIV Golf to fill the field. "I mean, seriously, who else is going to do it?" Turns out he was dead wrong. Just over three months later, Norman had signed up 42 players — Johnson's was the biggest name — and LIV Golf was up and running.

During a corporate function the week of the US Open in June, Brooks Koepka huddled with a group of top players and encouraged them to stand together against this new Saudi-funded league. A week later, Koepka became the latest to join. PGA Tour commissioner Jay Monahan had scheduled a press conference at the Travelers Championship the week after the US Open to announce a new alliance between the PGA Tour and the DP World Tour. Monahan was 10 minutes into his press conference when LIV Golf announced the Koepka deal.

Throw out the threat of LIV Golf, and 2022 had more than enough to offer.

Tiger Woods added to his legend despite playing only three times. He made a stunning return to the Masters just over a year after he shattered bones in his right leg from a horrific car crash in Los Angeles. He has never missed the cut as a pro at Augusta National, and even limping around the hilly terrain didn't change that. Just to see him in his Sunday red shirt hobbling up the hill on the 18th felt like a victory. Far more poignant was Woods crossing the Swilcan Bridge at St Andrews for what likely will be the final time. It was Friday, not Sunday, but no less special as thousands upon thousands filled every inch of space behind the ropes, behind a fence, in balconies and rooftops to witness the moment.

Four different players in their 20s won the men's major championships, the first time that has ever happened. McIlroy had his most consistent year, minus a major championship. His year was made even more remarkable by willingly speaking out against the rival league, all while joining Henrik Stenson as the only players to win the FedEx Cup and the DP World Tour Points race in the same season. The LPGA Tour saw the resurgence of Lydia Ko and the arrival of another teenager, Atthaya Thitikul of Thailand, who was among four players who reached number one in the Rolex Women's World Rankings in 2022. Neither won a major, though women's golf has shown to be deeper and more balanced in talent each year. This was the third consecutive year no one won multiple majors in women's golf, and the last 16 majors dating to 2019 have been won by 15 players. Jennifer Kupcho, perhaps best known for winning the inaugural Augusta National Women's Amateur, captured her first major at the Chevron Championship in its final staging at Mission Hills in California. The other first-time major champion was Ashleigh Buhai in the AIG Women's Open, the first South African in 43 years to claim a woman's major. The biggest turnaround in golf might have been Steven Alker. He was the quintessential journeyman, playing 556 times on six tours that received world ranking points. He qualified for only three seasons on the PGA Tour, two in Europe. His biggest year financially was $261,901 on the Korn Ferry Tour in 2014. He never was higher than 191st in the world. And in his first full year on the PGA Tour Champions, the New Zealander won four times, made over $3.5 million and captured the Charles Schwab Cup.

But there was no escaping the biggest rivalry in golf — the Establishment against LIV Golf, played out in sound bites and press releases and, sadly, in court rooms. The celebration of The 150th Open at St Andrews was still fresh when 10 players with LIV Golf filed an antitrust lawsuit against the PGA Tour alleging monopolist behaviour. The PGA Tour filed a countersuit. Smith still had the words "champion golfer of the year" ringing in his ears when he was asked in his press conference at St Andrews about rumours he was going to defect to the new league. "I just won the British Open, and you're asking about that. I think that's pretty ... not that good," he replied. When the PGA Tour season ended, Smith was with LIV Golf.

One popular refrain for the year was "Saudi fatigue". Everyone was tired of it. And yet that's all anyone wanted to talk about.

SCHEFFLER SHOWS HIS METTLE

Scheffler certainly did his part to put the attention squarely back on golf. He looked to be headed for another runner-up finish in the WM Phoenix Open when Patrick Cantlay stood over a 10-foot birdie putt in a playoff. Cantlay missed, and Scheffler seized on the opportunity by winning for the first time on the PGA Tour. Three weeks later, on a Bay Hill course in Florida that was so crusty and yellow it felt like US Open conditions, Scheffler showed his mettle down the stretch by closing with four tough pars to win. And then in the WGC Dell Technologies Match Play, the Texan had to emerge from a group of European Ryder Cup players — Ian Poulter, Tommy Fleetwood and Matt Fitzpatrick — and then take down Dustin Johnson in the semi-finals before cruising to a third win in five starts. This one took him to number one in the world, replacing Jon Rahm.

Scheffler was born in New Jersey before his mother took a job running a law firm in Dallas, and they took out a golf membership at Royal Oaks to work with Randy Smith. The pro recalls a boy who sat for hours on an empty bucket of range balls to watch tour players work magic with their short game, often challenging them to contests. In the Texas heat, Scheffler wore long pants at junior tournaments because that's how tour players dressed, and that's what he wanted to be. That was his dream. Reaching number one in the world in just three years on the PGA Tour? "I never really got that far in my dreams," he said. Surely, the big run would have to end at some point. Golf is filled with players who get on hot streaks until they eventually fade. Next up was the Masters, and so much attention was on the return of Woods and the hopes of McIlroy getting the last leg of the career Grand Slam or Smith, fresh off his bold win at the Players Championship. That changed when Scheffler posted a 67 on Friday in a raging wind that plays with the mind among the Georgia pines. He built a five-shot lead, and no one caught him.

Now there was no denying the number one player in golf, even if it was still fresh enough not to feel real to Scheffler. It was his final victory of the year, and it would be easy to suggest that he finally faded into the background. But consider how close he came to making 2022 one of the great years in golf. He lost in a playoff at the Charles Schwab Challenge at Colonial when his close friend, Sam Burns, holed a 45-foot birdie putt to win. He was one putt away from a playoff with Matt Fitzpatrick in the US Open at The Country Club. He was lurking at St Andrews until a boil developed on the weekend, making it painful for him to walk. Scheffler didn't disclose that injury until later.

SCOTTIE SCHEFFLER

The American Express	T25
Farmers Insurance Open	T20
WM Phoenix Open	W
Genesis Invitational	T7
Arnold Palmer Invitational	W
Players Championship	T55
WGC Dell Technologies Match Play	W
Masters Tournament	W
AT&T Byron Nelson	T15
PGA Championship	MC
Charles Schwab Challenge	2
RBC Canadian Open	T18
US Open	T2
Travelers Championship	T13
Genesis Scottish Open	MC
The 150th Open	T21
Fedex St Jude Championship	MC
BMW Championship	T3
Tour Championship	T2
CJ Cup	T45
World Wide Technology Championship	T3
Cadence Bank Houston Open	T9
Hero World Challenge	2

His season ended by finishing one shot behind McIlroy in the Tour Championship, costing him the FedEx Cup and its $18 million bonus. The Tour Championship has gone to a staggered start based on a player's position in the FedEx Cup, meaning Scheffler started with a two-shot lead against the 30-man field, and a six-shot lead to start against McIlroy. He still led by six going into the final round when McIlroy chased him down for the win. "I've had a really great year and I wanted to finish it off with a win here," Scheffler said. He had to settle for leading the world money list at $14,323,704, more than $3 million ahead of McIlroy, not including the FedEx Cup bonus. He was voted the PGA Tour Player of the Year for his four victories, his first major and for holding the number one ranking longer than anyone else in 2022. It wasn't all bad.

Smith had five victories and could have made a strong case for PGA Tour Player of the Year, and even though he left to join LIV Golf, he remained on the ballot. The strife was such that Smith most certainly wasn't given much consideration. His play spoke volumes, though. Renowned as a pure putter who could be wild off the tee, Smith devoted himself to fitness to become stronger, not so much for added distance but greater control of his swing. When he was keeping the ball in play, he was a threat. And with that sure-fire putter, the Australian showed how explosive he could be. Smith sent out an early indication at the Sentry Tournament of Champions on the Plantation course at Kapalua, a par 73 that is suited for power. He wound up setting a PGA Tour record to par at 34 under to beat Rahm, who entered the year as the number one player in the world.

CAMERON SMITH

Sentry Tournament of Champions	W
Sony Open	MC
PIF Saudi International	T4
Genesis Invitational	T33
The Players Championship	W
Masters Tournament	T3
RBC Heritage	MC
PGA Championship	T13
Memorial Tournament	T13
RBC Canadian Open	T48
US Open	MC
Genesis Scottish Open	T10
The 150th Open	W
Fedex St Jude Championship	T13
Tour Championship	20
Boston Invitational	T4
Chicago Invitational	W
Bangkok Invitational	T41
Jeddah Invitational	T21
Fortinet Australian PGA Championship	W
ISPS Handa Australian Open	T47

And then Smith elevated his game even higher at the Players Championship, which PGA Tour players consider to be the next best thing to a major. It certainly was the wildest week of weather, with rain, wind and near-freezing temperatures. The third round wasn't completed until Monday morning. The most difficult day was Saturday, when players faced 40 mph gusts when playing to the nefarious par-three 17th with the island green. Smith battled his way into contention, going into the final round just two shots behind. He had only one par through 13 holes. He one-putted eight of the last nine greens. With the tournament on the line and the pin on the island green tucked to the right, Smith hit nine-iron onto the 12 feet of grass separating the pin from the water. And after punching out of the trees into the water on the final hole, he calmly hit wedge to three feet to secure the win. That defined him as a player — tough as nails, a product of growing up in Queensland. "I grew up watching rugby league and watching the Queenslanders come from behind. And even when it got gritty, they'd somehow manage to win. I think that's kind of instilled in all of us," he said.

It was plenty gritty at St Andrews, where his 30 on the back nine for a 64 and a one-shot victory will be remembered as one of the greatest closing rounds in Open Championship history. It was his first major, and Smith added two more victories — one in LIV Golf, the other at the Australian PGA Championship during his first trip home in three years because of travel restrictions from the Covid-19 pandemic.

With practically every stop along the way, LIV Golf remained a topic, even at the majors. "You can't go anywhere without somebody bringing it up," Justin Thomas said at Brookline. "This is the US Open, and this is an unbelievable venue, a place with so much history, an unbelievable field, so many storylines, and yet that seems to be what all the questions are about. That's not right for the US Open. That's not right for us players. But that's, unfortunately, where we're at right now."

Part of that was speculation of who was going to join, and a big part of the conversation centred around one player no one saw. Mickelson disappeared from public view after his comments exposed his intentions of working with the Saudis — a once-in-a-lifetime chance to get leverage against the PGA Tour and change the way it operates. It wasn't until Mickelson and other players filed the lawsuit in August was it disclosed Monahan had suspended him for two months — March 22 to May 22 — for recruiting players to a rival league. Mickelson was a no-show at the Masters, and he chose not to defend his title at the PGA Championship. By the time the US Open arrived, he was suspended for the rest of the year for playing in a LIV Golf event. He offered no real insight in an awkward press conference at Brookline, and he was gone by the weekend. He missed the cut in both majors he played, the US Open and The Open. Mickelson finished his second round at St Andrews about two hours after Woods, and only a few hundred spectators remained in the grandstands offering polite applause. A year before, he became the oldest major champion by winning the PGA at age 50. He ended 2022 outside the top 200 in the world for the first time since July 1992 — a year before Jordan Spieth was born.

McILROY NEVER FAILS TO DELIVER

As much as Mickelson was at the centre of the LIV Golf discussion, so was McIlroy. One of the most popular players in the game today, he used his platform not only to declare his allegiance to the PGA Tour and DP World Tour, but to speak out against the rival league. His opinion was sought more than any other, and McIlroy never failed to deliver. Behind the scenes, he was working with Woods and other top players to devise a new schedule for the PGA Tour that would make prize money at least competitive with LIV Golf and its $25 million purses and to bring the top players together more often. And when he put his hands on a golf club, he still performed at a remarkably high level. McIlroy won three times in 2022, and while none was the major he so dearly covets, all were significant because of the timing.

The first was the RBC Canadian Open a week before the US Open. McIlroy was the defending champion from 2019 — golf's fourth-oldest national championship had been cancelled the previous two years because of the pandemic — and the title sponsor was reeling from having lost three corporate ambassadors to LIV Golf, including Dustin Johnson. The Canadian gallery was out in full force and McIlroy delivered a brilliant show, holding off Justin Thomas and Tony Finau down the stretch, while Justin Rose narrowly missed out on a 59. During the telecast, Monahan gave his first interview since LIV Golf began and defended his right to suspend players who joined the rival league. He also subtly challenged the source of funding when he said, "I would ask any player that has left, or any player that would ever consider leaving, 'Have you ever had to apologise for being a member of the PGA Tour?'" McIlroy took a dig at Norman after winning, saying it was a day he would remember for a long time because it was his 21st title on the PGA Tour and that was "one more than someone else. That gave me a little bit of extra incentive today." It didn't take long to check the PGA Tour records and see Norman was on 20 career wins.

The standard for McIlroy is such that he is measured by the majors, and his last Grand Slam title was in 2014. He holed a bunker shot for birdie on the 18th at Augusta National for a 64 to tie the Masters record for lowest closing round. He was runner-up, though he was never in the mix to win. He opened with a 65 to lead the PGA Championship only to stall out and tie for eighth. He was one shot out of the lead at the US Open and tied for fifth. Nothing haunted him more than The 150th Open at St Andrews, where he was tied for the 54-hole lead with Viktor Hovland. McIlroy managed only two birdies on Sunday and finished third, later weeping in the arms of his wife, Erica. That didn't make the year a failure.

RORY McILROY	
Abu Dhabi HSBC Championship	T12
Slync.io Dubai Desert Classic	3
Genesis Invitational	T10
Arnold Palmer Invitational	T13
The Players Championship	T33
Valero Texas Open	MC
Masters Tournament	2
Wells Fargo Championship	5
PGA Championship	8
Memorial Tournament	T18
RBC Canadian Open	W
US Open	T5
Travelers Championship	T19
The 150th Open	3
Fedex St Jude Championship	MC
BMW Championship	T8
Tour Championship	W
BMW PGA Championship	T2
DS Automobiles Italian Open	4
Alfred Dunhill Links Championship	T4
CJ Cup	W
DP World Tour Championship	4

A tumultuous season on the PGA Tour ended at the Tour Championship. This came one week after McIlroy and Woods led a private, players-only meeting during the BMW Championship to outline changes for the PGA Tour going forward. Monahan announced those changes on the eve of the Tour Championship, with McIlroy listening from the back of the room. The biggest change was creating "elevated events" that would offer $20 million in prize money and require the top players to compete in them. On the course at East Lake, McIlroy started the tournament six shots behind based on his FedEx Cup standing. McIlroy birdied the final two holes of the third round for a 63 that put him in the final group with Scheffler, still six shots back. And then he delivered to win the $18 million bonus by one shot over Scheffler and Sungjae Im. "This is the best place in the world to play golf. It's the most competitive. It's got the best players. It's got the deepest fields. I don't know why you'd want to play anywhere else," McIlroy said, getting in the final word with his clubs.

His year wasn't over. McIlroy won the CJ Cup in South Carolina — the tournament moved from South Korea for the third straight year because of travel restrictions brought on by the pandemic — and returned to number one in the world for the first time since 2020. It was the ninth time McIlroy had ascended to the top of the world ranking, the first occasion coming 10 years earlier. The record belongs to Woods and Norman, who each went to number one in the world 11 times.

McIlroy stayed there for the rest of the year, though competition was tight with Scheffler right behind. Since the dominance of Woods — number one for a record 683 weeks — McIlroy joined Dustin Johnson as the only two players to be at number one for 100 weeks or more. Not since Woods in 2009 has anyone stayed at number one the entire calendar year, and it doesn't figure to be easy for McIlroy going forward. Competition is getting younger and deeper and tougher with each passing year.

Between wins at the Tour Championship and the CJ Cup, McIlroy returned to Europe for three DP World Tour events. He was runner-up at the BMW PGA Championship to good friend Shane Lowry, finished fourth in the Italian Open and tied for fourth in the Alfred Dunhill Links Championship. He returned after the CJ Cup for the DP World Tour Championship in Dubai, and capturing the DP World Tour points list was not a foregone conclusion. McIlroy tied for fourth, that was enough when Ryan Fox faltered. It was the fourth time McIlroy had finished as Europe's number one player, this one with an exception: it was his first such title without winning on the DP World Tour. His points came from the majors, and for finishing in the top 10 at five of the six regular DP World Tour events he played. His worst result was a tie for 12th in the Abu Dhabi HSBC Championship to start his remarkable year.

McIlroy played the Italian Open for the first time with a purpose — Marco Simone is hosting the Ryder Cup in 2023. For an off year in the Ryder Cup, there was plenty of activity. Zach Johnson, who captured his two majors at Augusta National (2007) and St Andrews (2015), was selected in late February to be the US captain for the 2023 match. Europe typically announces its captain at the start of the year during the Middle East swing. But with so much speculation caused by LIV Golf — who was going, who was staying — it delayed the decision until March. Henrik Stenson accepted the job and pledged his support of the DP World Tour and to win back that precious gold trophy.

By the middle of July, however, Stenson had decided to join LIV Golf and Europe removed him as captain, handing the reins to Luke Donald. Still to be determined is who would be playing for Donald. Tensions were running so high among players who joined LIV Golf and those who stayed that McIlroy had a falling out with Sergio Garcia, once among his closest friends in golf. Jon Rahm, a strong supporter of the PGA Tour and DP World Tour, felt the Ryder Cup should not consider on which tour someone belonged, only that Team Europe had its best 12 players to face the Americans. US Open champion Matt Fitzpatrick felt the same way. The DP World Tour also faced a legal challenge from players it punished for joining LIV, and a decision was not expected until 2023. In the meantime, there was the reality of an ageing European team. Stalwarts such as Garcia and Lee Westwood, Ian Poulter and Paul Casey, were all in their 40s and on the downside of their best golf.

LIV Golf took its toll on another cup. The Presidents Cup is run by the PGA Tour and dates to 1994 as an opportunity for non-Europeans to compete in team matches. Trevor Immelman of South Africa was captain of the International team, which had been getting closer to changing a competition so one-sided that the Americans had lost only one time, all the way back in 1998. The Internationals lost its best Presidents Cup player in Louis Oosthuizen of South Africa, who along with Branden Grace were among the first to play LIV Golf events and thus be suspended. A month before the match at Quail Hollow Club in North Carolina, Cameron Smith and Marc Leishman of Australia, and Joaquin Niemann of Chile had defected. That meant Immelman had to face the daunting US team with eight players who had never played in the Presidents Cup. Only three of his 12 players had won tournaments in 2022 and only two — Adam Scott and Hideki Matsuyama — had won majors. The plucky team did its best to keep it close, particularly the dazzling play of Tom Kim, only to fall well short again. Next up is to see who Europe brings to Italy, although the core of Europe was still intact with US Open champions Rahm and Fitzpatrick, four-time major winner McIlroy and Open champion Lowry, Tommy Fleetwood, Viktor Hovland and Tyrrell Hatton. Rahm appeared to be well-suited to be the emotional spark for Europe, just as fellow Spaniards like Garcia, Jose Maria

Olazabal and the great Seve Ballesteros were before him.

Rahm began the year at number one in the world and he started off by finishing at 33 under par at the Sentry Tournament of Champions, a PGA Tour record any other time except this one because Smith was one better. Rahm had a cold putter in the early months, and he lost the number one ranking when Scheffler won the Dell Match Play. Most disturbing to the Spaniard was his performance in the majors. A year after he captured the US Open and finished in the top 10 in the other three majors, he didn't feature in any of them. That didn't make it a lost a year, of course. Rahm won the Mexico Open and the Spanish Open, and he capped off his year with a victory in the DP World Tour Championship. He finished the year at number four on the world money list with $9,941,545.

The player one spot ahead of him on the world money list was Patrick Cantlay with $10,081,605. Cantlay isn't always flashy, but he took another step toward being one of the top American players through sheer consistency. Cantlay won the Zurich Classic team event with Xander Schauffele, his best friend in golf. He won the BMW Championship for the second straight year with a brilliant eight-iron from a sidehill lie in the bunker on the final hole at Wilmington Country Club in Delaware. The majors remain a glaring hole in his otherwise solid game, with only one top 10 in 2022 (Open Championship) and no serious chance at winning. But he was never far away. Cantlay twice lost in a playoff, to Scheffler in the WM Phoenix Open and to Jordan Spieth in the RBC Heritage at Hilton Head when both found a bunker short of the green. Spieth had a clean lie, Cantlay's shot was plugged. He also was runner-up in the Rocket Mortgage Classic and the Shriners Children's Open in Las Vegas when he hooked a tee shot into a ravine on the final hole and lost to Tom Kim. He remained among the top 10 in the world ranking the entire year.

The Official World Golf Ranking was in the news more than usual, and not just because three players occupied the number one position during the year. Officials from the six main tours had been working on trying to develop a system that would properly rank each field from top to bottom. Their solution was to get away from minimum points (24 points to the winner of a PGA Tour or DP World Tour tournament, less for some of the smaller tours). The strength of field calculation involved a statistical evaluation of every player in the field, not just players among the top 200. The change took place in August and led to some confusion during the transition from the old model to the new one. Smaller fields, no matter how strong at the top, received fewer points than they once did and some tournaments on the DP World Tour were particularly hurt without top players. Officials believe it will take until the middle of 2023 for the new system to be fully integrated.

The greater debate, of course, involved LIV Golf. The new league, which officially launched in early June, did not apply to be part of the OWGR system until July 6 after it had played two tournaments. Peter Dawson, the former R&A chief executive who now is chairman of the OWGR, responded with a statement that simply said, "Examination of the application will now commence". LIV Golf faced a few hurdles with its format of 54 holes, no cut after 36 holes and no clear path of qualifying to join the 48-man league. Among the guidelines for OWGR inclusion is a 36-hole cut for tournaments with 54 holes, and an average of 75-player fields over the course of the season. New tours asking for OWGR inclusion also typically must comply with guidelines for at least one year. Norman, however, suggested the deck was stacked against him because the eight-member panel includes executives from the DP World Tour and the PGA Tour. He wanted Monahan and DP World Tour chief Keith Pelley to recuse themselves.

Norman also tried to get points through the MENA Tour (acronym for Middle East,

North Africa). LIV Golf already had infused $300 million into the Asian Tour and had aligned itself with that circuit. The MENA Tour provides a pathway to the Asian Tour with 54-hole tournaments that have $75,000 prize funds. Mickelson, Dustin Johnson, Brooks Koepka and the rest of LIV Golf players became part of the MENA Tour. The OWGR didn't accept it and the year ended with no world ranking points for LIV Golf and no indication when — or if — the league would join the OWGR system. The effect was noticeable. Johnson was number 13 in the world when he signed with LIV Golf. He ended the year at number 41, and that included points he earned from his tie for 24th in the US Open and his tie for sixth in the Open Championship. Bryson DeChambeau went from number 24 when he joined to number 67. Brooks Koepka fell out of the top 50 for the first time since 2014. He finished the year at number 52, down from 19th when he joined.

Koepka and Johnson were among the winners in the seven individual tournaments that were part of the LIV Golf Invitational Series. The tournaments featured shotgun starts, but the big attraction was money. LIV Golf offered $4 million to the winner from the $20 million prize fund, with an additional $5 million for the team competition. Johnson led the way with $13,637,767 in seven tournaments — $10,575,267 of that from individual play — and with team results and bonuses, he topped $35 million. No one won more than one tournament.

FOX IN THE RUNNING ON DP WORLD TOUR

On the DP World Tour five players claimed two victories apiece. That included Thriston Lawrence of South Africa, who won the Sir Henry Cotton Award as the Rookie of the Year helped by his win at the Omega European Masters in Switzerland, and then added the Investec South African Open. The best performance came from Ryan Fox of New Zealand, who picked up wins in the Ras Al Khaimah Classic and Alfred Dunhill Links Championship and was still in the running to win the DP World Tour points race until he fell short in the final tournament of the year. Even so, Fox finished the year 28th in the world ranking, tops among those who did not have PGA Tour membership. The breakthrough belonged to Adrian Meronk of Poland, who already is used to being introduced as the "first Polish player" in various feats — first to earn a DP World Tour card, the first in the Olympics, first to appear in the Open Championship and the US Open. With his victory in the Horizon Irish Open, he became the first Polish player to win on tour. Meronk added another victory in the ISPS Handa Australian Open to finish the year at number 48 in the world. That will make him the first Pole to play in the Masters.

The other big development with the DP World Tour was its expanded alliance with the PGA Tour. That already was evident in 2022 with the Genesis Scottish Open being co-sanctioned by both tours for the first time, and two American tournaments — the Barbasol Championship in Kentucky held the same week as the Scottish Open, and the Barracuda Championship in California held the same week as The Open — being part of the DP World Tour schedule. The expanded partnership that goes through 2035 also provides the leading 10 players from the DP World Tour not already eligible to have PGA Tour cards.

Xander Scahuffele won the Genesis Scottish Open at The Renaissance Club, one of five Rolex Series events during the season. Thomas Pieters won the Abu Dhabi HSBC Championship and Viktor Hovland the Dubai Desert Classic at the start of the year, while Shane Lowry held off McIlroy and Rahm in a dramatic finish at Wentworth in the BMW PGA Championship. Then Rahm took the season-ending DP World Tour Championship in Dubai.

Schauffele's win in Scotland capped off a big summer on the PGA Tour. He had gone some three years without winning on the PGA Tour. They weren't exactly lean years. Schauffele had the lowest 72-hole score at the Tour Championship in 2020, the year Dustin Johnson started with a big lead as the FedEx Cup's top seed. He won the Olympic gold medal in 2021 in Tokyo, where his mother was raised and grandparents still live. But the lack of a tour title was gnawing at him. Schauffele received credit for an official PGA Tour victory by teaming with Cantlay at the Zurich Classic in New Orleans, and then he came into his own. At the Travelers Championship the week after the US Open, he was in the final group with Cantlay and had to hold off a late charge from PGA Tour rookie Sahith Theegala. The unofficial win came in Ireland when he won the JP McManus Pro-Am, which had one of the strongest fields of the year in a cause for charity. And then he held off the charging pack at the Scottish Open and was in fine form for St Andrews. Much like his good friend Cantlay, Schauffele has established himself as one of the premier American players except for winning a major.

JOOHYUNG KIM	
Singapore International	W
SNBC Singapore Open	T2
PIF Saudi International	T45
Royal's Cup	17
International Series — Thailand	T23
Commercial Bank Qatar Masters	MC
Trust Golf Asian Mixed Cup	2
Trust Golf Asian Mixed Stableford Challenge	T4
GS Caltex Maekyung Open	T5
AT&T Byron Nelson	T17
PGA Championship	MC
International Series — England	5
US Open	23
Genesis Scottish Open	3
The 150th Open	T47
3M Open	T26
Rocket Mortgage Classic	7
Wyndham Championship	W
Fedex St Jude Championship	T13
BMW Championship	T54
Shriners Children's Open	W
Zozo Championship	T25
CJ Cup	T11
Dunlop Phoenix	T4
Hero World Challenge	T10

Theegala was among two players who reached the Tour Championship in their first year on the PGA Tour without ever winning. He had a chance in the WM Phoenix Open until his tee shot on the par-4 17th went over the green and into the water. He had a one-shot lead on the 18th hole at the Travelers when he took two shots to get out of a fairway bunker and closed with a double bogey. He was a runner-up in the tour's final event of the year at the RSM Classic on the Georgia coast. It was a great start to his career, and not even the best among newcomers. That distinction goes to Cameron Young, the quiet but talented American who was a product of the Covid-19 pandemic.

Young chose to finish his degree in economics at Wake Forest and then went through qualifying in 2019. He was the medalist for the PGA Tour Canada qualifying tournament, but the Canadian season doesn't start until the summer, and the pandemic arrived in the spring. Young had nowhere to play for six months — the Canadian tour was for domestic players only — and he kept missing out in Monday qualifiers for the Korn Ferry Tour. He finally got status for 2021 and won twice to get his PGA Tour card, and then he took off. Young not only had five runner-up finishes his rookie season, but he was also contending in the biggest tournaments with a big game. His swing is reminiscent of Hideki Matsuyama with a pause at the top, and then enormous speed that makes him among the longest hitters. The rest of his game is fundamentally sound, a product of his father, David Young, a longtime head professional at Sleepy Hollow in New York. His father recalls a trip to

Scotland when Cameron was 13. They played Carnoustie, North Berwick and the Old Course. The weather wasn't great. "It rained like the first four days we were there, and I have these pictures of him wearing my raingear down to his knees, soaking wet," David Young said. "I'm thinking, 'After this trip, this kid is never going to want to play golf again.' But it did just the opposite. It got him excited about it." His return to St Andrews nearly brought him a silver Claret Jug. Instead, he ended 2022 still searching for his first professional victory with a game that suggests a trophy is not too far away.

Theegala and Young failed to win this year, and they had company among top players. Most notable was Collin Morikawa, who already had two majors and a World Golf Championship in the two years since he graduated from university. He ended 2021 on the cusp of reaching number one in the world, needing to win his final event at the Hero World Challenge and instead losing a five-shot lead on the final day. And then he started 2022 by closing with an 11-under-par 62 to tie for fifth at the Sentry Tournament of Champions. That turned out to be one of the highlights. Morikawa shared the 36-hole lead at the US Open until ballooning to a 77 in the third round. He missed the cut in his title defence at the Open Championship. He was among three players who started the year in the top 10 and fell out at the end. The others were Johnson and DeChambeau, neither of whom had access to ranking points the final seven months after joining LIV Golf.

So much was happening in the world of golf, and Tiger Woods was hardly visible, at least inside the ropes. His effect on the sport was evident in the weeks before he returned at the Masters. He flew up to Augusta National for a practice round and to test his right leg on the hills of Augusta National. The Internet came to life with fans tracking the flight of his private jet to Augusta, photos of him getting off the plane. The PGA Tour came up with a "Player Impact Program" to offer a $50 million bonus pool to those who generated interest in the tour and themselves. Woods won the inaugural year of the program by playing only two rounds at the PNC Championship with his son. And he won in 2022 by playing only slightly more, though he was constantly in the news just by playing in the three majors.

The year wasn't without reason to celebrate for Woods. He was among four inducted into the World Golf Hall of Fame at PGA Tour headquarters in Ponte Vedra Beach, Florida. Also inducted were former PGA Tour commissioner Tim Finchem, three-time US Women's Open champion Susie Berning Maxwell and Marion Hollins, a visionary and developer, a confidante of Alister Mackenzie and the brains behind Cypress Point, the iconic American course near Pebble Beach. But that night was all about Woods and his family, particularly allowing 14-year-old daughter Sam to introduce him.

By now, his feats are legendary from his 93 victories worldwide that count toward the Official World Golf Ranking, his 15 majors and the 82 career titles on the PGA Tour that tie him with Sam Snead for the record. Woods didn't talk about any of his achievements, or the multiple surgeries on his legs and back that cut short his career. Instead, he spoke of his parents taking out a loan on their house to pay for junior golf, and he choked up talking about his late father who told him he would have to earn everything he wanted. "If you don't go out there and put in the work, you don't go out and put in the effort, one, you're not going to get the results. But two, and more importantly, you don't deserve it. You need to earn it. So that defined my upbringing. That defined my career," he said in an emotional speech.

Most telling was the number of top PGA Tour players, some of them major champions in their 20s, who sat in the audience or leaned over the balcony on the third floor to watch. The ripple effect of Woods seems unending.

LYDIA KO BACK AT THE TOP

Women's golf had some rising stars of their own, as usual, this time on both sides of the Atlantic Ocean and coming from all corners of the world. Atthaya Thitikul is a 19-year-old from Thailand whose career was decided early when her parents offered her a chance to play either golf or tennis. She watched YouTube videos of both sports and chose golf, and never looked back. At age 14, she played her first LPGA Tour event in Thailand and finished in 37th from a 66-player field. She won the Ladies European Tour money title and was Rookie of the Year in 2021, earned her LPGA Tour card through the qualifying tournament and a year later reached number one in the Rolex Women's World Rankings. She won twice on the LPGA Tour and won the Louise Suggs Rolex Rookie of the Year. She lost the number one ranking after two weeks to Nelly Korda and then Lydia Ko, two of the best in golf. She finished fifth on the women's world money list with $2,205,167.

Linn Grant, the Swede with Scottish heritage, played her college golf at Arizona State and within six months of turning professional in the summer of 2021, she had status on the LPGA Tour and the Ladies European Tour. She chose to play most of her golf in Europe, and it paid off in a big way, and an historic way at one tournament. Grant won six times, the most of any woman around the world. Four of those victories were on the Ladies European Tour, and that included the Volvo Car Scandinavian Mixed at Halmstad Golf Club in Sweden. The tournament was co-sanctioned with the DP World Tour with a field of 78 men and 78 women playing from different tees for the same trophy and equal prize money. Grant closed with a 64 to win by nine shots ahead of the nearest men — Henrik Stenson and Marc Warren — and 14 ahead of the closest woman. It was the second time a woman had won against a mixed field, with Hannah Green winning the TPS Murray River in Australia by four shots.

LINN GRANT

Dimension Data Ladies Challenge	W
SuperSport Ladies Challenge	T3
Jabra Ladies Classic — Sunshine	W
Joburg Ladies Open	W
Investec South African Women's Open	T7
Madrid Ladies Open	7
Jabra Ladies Open	T13
Mithra Belgian Ladies Open	W
Volvo Car Scandinavian Mixed	W
Aramco Team Series — London	3
Amundi German Masters	T4
Amundi Evian Championship	T8
Trust Golf Women's Scottish Open	MC
AIG Women's Open	T19
ISPS Handa World Invitational	T4
Aramco Team Series — Sotogrande	T7
Skafto Open	W
VP Bank Swiss Ladies Open	2
KPMG Women's Irish Open	T19
BMW Ladies Championship	T8
Toto Japan Classic	3
Andalucia Costa del Sol Open de Espana	3

But the world of women's golf was largely about a return of the old guard. If it seems as though Lydia Ko has been around forever, maybe that's because she won her first LPGA Tour event 10 years ago when she was 15, the youngest ever to win on the LPGA Tour. She was 17 when she reached number one in the Rolex Women's World Rankings for the first time in 2015. She was still 18 and already had won two majors. But it wasn't long before her game began to lag behind, and the New Zealand great went three years without winning before she slowly began to turn it around last year. And then 2022 brought her back to the top of golf.

Ko won the Gainbridge LPGA at Boca Rio in January by one shot over Danielle Kang, who had won the LPGA season opener. And while Ko didn't win again until the latter

LYDIA KO

Hilton Grand Vacations Tournament of Champions	T10
Gainbridge LPGA	W
HSBC Women's World Championship	T23
JTBC Classic	T12
Chevron Championship	T25
Lotte Championship	T18
Palos Verdes Championship	T3
Cognizant Founders Cup	T12
US Women's Open	5
ShopRite LPGA Classic	T4
Meijer LPGA Classic	4
KPMG Women's PGA Championship	T46
Amundi Evian Championship	T3
Trust Golf Women's Scottish Open	T5
AIG Women's Open	T7
CP Women's Open	4
Dana Open	T16
Walmart NW Arkansas Championship	T5
The Ascendant LPGA	3
BMW Ladies Championship	W
Pelican Women's Championship	T26
CME Group Tour Championship	W

portion of the year, her consistency was astonishing. She had 14 finishes in the top 10, three of them in the majors. Ko won the BMW Ladies Championship in South Korea, and then she closed out her big year in the best way. By capturing the season-ending CME Group Tour Championship, Ko not only claimed the biggest prize in women's golf at $2 million, but she also returned to number one in the world for the first time in more than five years and swept all the biggest honours, such as the Rolex Player of the Year and the Vare Trophy for the lowest scoring average. And if all that wasn't enough, she ended 2022 by getting married. Ko led the women's world money list with $4,364,403, with $2 million of that coming from the final event.

That it took so long for Ko to return to the top of the world ranking was not so much about how far back she started, rather how deep the competition continues to become in women's golf. She was the fourth player to reach number one for the year, but really the one player who outperformed all the others, some of that because of injury. Nelly Korda, coming off a monumental year of five wins, a major and an Olympic gold medal, started the year at number one. It wasn't long before her season came to a halt. She felt pain in her right arm during a visit to the Players Championship, and it was diagnosed as a blood clot. She had surgery and was out for four months, not returning until the US Women's Open. She didn't feature in any of the four majors she played. Korda won an Aramco Series event on the Ladies European Tour, and then finally got on track — and returned to number one in the world — by repeating her victory at the Pelican Women's Championship. "Going through what I've been through this year and regaining that world number one ranking is really special," she said.

Jin Young Ko was at number one for the most weeks (39), though it wasn't the South Korean's best year. It started well enough with a victory in the HSBC Women's World Championship in Singapore. That turned out to be her only victory of the year. Most telling that something was wrong were the majors. She had a pair of top 10s without being in serious contention. But as her wrist injury worsened, so did her results. She missed the cut in the AIG Women's Open, and after another missed cut at her next start in Canada, she took two months off. Returning on home soil in the BMW Ladies Championship, she had to withdraw after two rounds.

Minjee Lee was number two on the world money list at $3,855,946, and she cashed in at what is considered the biggest prize in women's golf. She overwhelmed the field in the US Women's Open, which this year offered the biggest prize fund in women's golf history at $10 million. This was three weeks after the Australian won the Cognizant Founders Cup, and Lee added to her breakthrough year by finishing runner-up at the KPMG Women's PGA Championship. She finished the year fourth in the Rolex Women's World Rankings.

Money became a big talking point in women's golf this year, including the source of it — the corporate world, becoming increasingly sensitive toward giving women their due. Cognizant entered the golf sponsorship world by joining both tours. It was a corporate partner for the Presidents Cup, and a title sponsor for an LPGA Tour event. All the majors raised their prize funds. A year ago, the five LPGA majors combined to offer $23.4 million in prize money. In 2022, the total prize fund for the majors was $37.8 million. Throw in CME offering a $7 million purse — with $2 million for the winner — and it was another indicator of women's golf on the rise. At the final tournament of the year, LPGA Tour commissioner Mollie Marcoux Samaan announced a 2023 schedule in which prize money tops $100 million for the first time in history.

WHITWORTH'S LEGACY OF WINNING

If there was a moment for sadness in women's golf, it was the passing of one of the all-time greats. Kathy Whitworth set a benchmark in American golf that no one ever touched. Not Sam Snead or Tiger Woods on the PGA Tour, not even Mickey Wright and Annika Sorenstam on the LPGA Tour. Among the numbers that stand out in golf are the 18 professional majors won by Jack Nicklaus and 59 — still the magic number of a scorecard, even if it's no longer the record. Add to that list the number 88, which is how many titles Whitworth won in her career. She died on Christmas Eve at the age of 83, leaving behind a legacy of simply winning. She was the first woman to earn $1 million for her career on the LPGA. Her only regret was her six majors didn't include a US Women's Open. Whitworth was the LPGA player of the year seven times in an eight-year span (1966 through 1973). She won the Vare Trophy for the lowest scoring average seven times, and she was the leading money winner in eight seasons. But it was that number, 88, that came to define her through the years. Snead and Woods each won 82 times on the PGA Tour, while Wright won 82 times on the LPGA. Internationally, Jumbo Ozaki won 94 times on the Japan Golf Tour.

Golf also lost Tom Weiskopf, a blend of high golf intelligence, enormous talent, great vision and endless candour. He won the Open Championship in 1973 at Troon for his only major and was four times a runner-up at the Masters. Weiskopf's notorious temper was merely a product of high expectations for his game. That was just the golf. Jack Nicklaus once said of him, "Tom Weiskopf had as much talent as any player I've ever seen play the tour." He was magnificent in the television booth, most famously at the 1986 Masters when he was asked what was going through Nicklaus's mind during that famous charge to win a sixth green jacket. "If I knew the way he thought, I would have won this championship," Weiskopf said. He partnered with Jay Moorish for his entry into golf architecture and designed 80 courses, most notably Loch Lomond. He died in August, and one comment seemed to capture why he succeeded in so many areas of the game. "I love the game. I love talking about it and thinking about it and to me it is endlessly fascinating," Weiskopf said.

Dow Finsterwald, who won the 1958 PGA Championship when it switched from match play to medal play, was another player whom the golf world mourned in 2022. Argentina lost another giant when Eduardo Romero — "El Gato" — died in February. He won eight times on the European Tour and five on the PGA Tour Champions, with two senior majors. He also won more than 50 times in Latin America. Also gone from golf was Bart Bryant, killed in a freak car accident in Florida. Bryant went 18 years and six trips to qualifying school before finally winning on the PGA Tour, and two of those wins were memorable. He beat Tiger Woods down the stretch at the Memorial and the Tour Championship.

Meanwhile, global professional golf became more important than ever. Joohyung Kim emerged from the Asian Tour to become the new star known as Tom Kim on the PGA Tour. After he departed, no one dominated the Asian Tour in terms of wins but American Sihwan Kim claimed his first victory after 11 years as a pro and then won again to claim the Order of Merit title. Another new star may be on the way in the form of Thailand's Ratchanon Chantananuwat, who as an amateur, and still at school, won the Trust Golf Asian Mixed Cup, birdieing five of the last eight holes, to become, at the age of 15 years and 37 days, the youngest male player to win on a major tour. Ryo Ishikawa was 15 years and eight months when he first won in Japan.

The Japan Golf Tour continues to produce young talent. Hideki Matsuyama certainly isn't the first big star from the Land of the Rising Sun, though his impact has been profound even before he won the 2021 Masters. Following in his footsteps was Keita Nakajima, who turned professional last year after reaching number one in the amateur ranking. Next up might be Taiga Semikawa, who won twice on the Japan Golf Tour while still an amateur in college and turned professional by the end of the year. The biggest star for 2022 was Kazuki Higa, who won four times on the Japan Tour at age 27. Higa finished the year 68th in the world, and Augusta National was impressed enough to award him a special invitation to the Masters.

Higa was among several players from all corners of the world who posted multiple-win seasons. Linn Grant on the Ladies European Tour collected six victories across various tours, while Min Ji Park dominated the Korea LPGA Tour, winning six times for the second straight year. Manu Gandas won six times on the Professional Golf Tour of India. On the Japan LPGA, Mao Saigo looked like she might top them all when she won five times in the first 12 tournaments on the schedule, though no more the rest of the year. Miyuu Yamashita took over from there on the Japan LPGA and matched her with five wins by the end of the year. On the developmental Step Up tour in Japan, Kokona Sakurai also won five times. The most amazing of the seasons might have belonged to Prayad Marksaeng of Thailand. Not only did he win six times on the Japan Senior PGA Tour, but he actually won six consecutive tournaments.

MIN JI PARK

Mediheal Hankook Ilbo Championship	T28
Nexen Saint Nine Masters	WD
CreaS F&C KLPGA Championship	T4
Kyochon Honey Ladies Open	T8
NH Ladies Championship	W
Doosan Match Play Championship	T9
Lotte Open	T28
Celltrion Queens Masters	W
DB Group Korea Women's Open	3
BC Card Hankyung Ladies Cup	W
Daebo hausD Open	T10
Amundi Evian Championship	T37
Jeju Samdasoo Masters	T25
Dayouwinia MBN Ladies Open	T27
HighOne Resort Ladies Open	T28
Hanwha Classic	2
KB Financial Group Star Championship	W
OK Financial Group Se Ri Pak Invitational	T23
Hana Financial Group Championship	WD
Hite Jinro Championship	W
SK Networks Seoul Economics Ladies Classic	T25
S-Oil Championship	T35
SK Shieldus SK Telecom Championship	W
Hana Financial Group Singapore Women's Open	T9

While the PGA Tour and DP World Tour created a partnership that provided the leading 10 players from Europe to have PGA Tour cards, the end of the year saw lines being drawn. It was at the end of 2010 when Tim Finchem, the commissioner of the PGA Tour, spoke about the potential of a world tour. "I think that at some point in time, men's professional golf will become integrated globally. Golf generally is a splintered sport, multi-organisational at every level. But there's movement," he said. How swiftly it's moving is up for debate all these years later, and there still is no idea how it would look. But this year brought some interesting developments.

The DP World Tour and the Sunshine Tour in South Africa have had an alliance for a quarter-century and that was renewed in 2021. Much already has been said about the partnership between the PGA Tour and the DP World Tour. Toward the end of the year, the PGA Tour and DP World Tour announced a new partnership with Japan. The top three players on the Japan Golf Tour Order of Merit would earn membership in Europe the following year, along with both tours working on business development. Europe has long been regarded the true world tour considering the countries and continents in which it plays. It announced a new tournament in old territory — Japan. The JGTO chairman, Isao Aoki, spoke of the "rich tradition" of men's golf and Japan over 40 years. "This development is the next step in the journey of our organisation," he said.

Then, the PGA Tour and DP World Tour widened their global reach by including the Korean PGA and the Professional Golf Tour of India to their alliance. Under those terms, the leading player from those tours will have access to the DP World Tour. Ultimately, all paths lead to the PGA Tour because of the earlier partnership that allows the leading 10 from Europe to come to America. Meanwhile, the Asian Tour received that massive boost at the start of the year from LIV Golf and its $300 million infusion, and it became clear the Asian Tour was aligned more with LIV Golf. The PGA Tour already added the Genesis Scottish Open to its schedule, while the DP World Tour had two US-based events on its schedule.

STEVEN ALKER	
Mitsubishi Electric Championship	2
Chubb Classic	T5
Cologuard Classic	T20
Hoag Classic	T15
Rapiscan Systems Classic	W
ClubCorp Classic	T2
Insperity Invitational	W
Regions Tradition	T3
KitchenAid Senior PGA Championship	W
Principal Charity Classic	T3
US Senior Open	T11
Bridgestone Senior Players Championship	T3
The Senior Open Presented by Rolex	T3
Boeing Classic	5
Dick's Sporting Goods Open	T37
Ally Challenge	T9
Ascension Charity Classic	T5
Sanford International	T58
Pure Insurance Championship	T2
SAS Championship	2
Dominion Energy Charity Classic	W
TimberTech Championship	T6
Charles Schwab Cup Championship	3

Where will it all lead? As fractured as men's golf was in 2022, there was some question when or if it ever could be made whole again. The sport always has had separate tours on all six continents, and that's unlikely to change. The difference this year was partnerships popping up all over. And the major championships still wielded most of the interest. Augusta National, while expressing frustration in the state of professional golf, said the Masters would keep the same qualifying criteria going forward. The R&A and USGA both said it was important to keep the heritage of its majors — The Open and the US

Open — by keeping an open line of qualifying.

Adam Scott is an Australian who lives in Switzerland, so perhaps that made it easy for him to keep such a neutral role. He listened as the war of words seemed to increase. Rory McIlroy and Tiger Woods said the only path to reconciliation was for Greg Norman to no longer be part of LIV Golf. Sergio Garcia wondered why no one was asking for the removal of PGA Tour commissioner Jay Monahan. That led Scott to wonder what there was to even talk about, especially with lawsuits in play. "I genuinely feel like LIV should get on with what they're doing, and the PGA Tour should get on with what they're doing and it will all sort out. Whether that's together or not, I have no clue. But I don't necessarily think that it has to be together or not together for the good of the game. I think the good of the game will prevail, but it's a big shake-up and we're not used to that," he said.

Indeed, this was a memorable year for the feats on the golf course and the disruption and acrimony away from it. It brought the emergence of Scottie Scheffler and the return of Rory McIlroy. Three players won majors for the first time. The race for the season points title on the PGA Tour, the DP World Tour and the LPGA Tour were not decided until the final round, sometimes the final hole. There was much to celebrate, and that always leaves fans curious about what's in store for the following year. That much stays the same. The end of the year is just like any other, looking ahead to who might be golf's biggest winner, with the hope being it is more memorable on the golf course than in the court room.

Doug Ferguson is golf correspondent of the Associated Press

Lydia Ko with the Rolex Player of the Year, the Vare Trophy and the CME Globe.

Prepare to be amazed — the level is so high

By Lydia Ko

What an incredible year 2022 turned into. So many exciting things happened in my life, culminating in my wedding. Nothing could be more special than that, though the golf was not too bad, either! I could not have asked for anything more. Winning the Gainbridge so early in the year was the perfect start. Winning the BMW Ladies Championship in Korea in front of my family was a real bucket-list moment. Then finishing the season with the victory at the CME Group Tour Championship, with the Rolex Player of the Year and the Vare Trophy on the line, obviously meant so much, aside from the $2 million first prize, a landmark development for women's golf for which we are all so grateful. Later I also got back to the top of the Rolex Rankings for the first time since 2017. To be honest, I wasn't sure if I'd ever be back there again. It was a dream come true, one I was able to truly savour during my time off before enjoying the preparations for my wedding.

Perhaps the most special thing about the CME was winning in front of my fiancé Jun for the first time. To be able to celebrate such a special moment with my loved ones made it extra meaningful. When I won in Korea, he wasn't there. He sent me a text while I was going up the 18th hole because I had enough of a lead that he thought I would win. I called him after my round, and I just started bawling. I was in tears because I wished I could celebrate that special moment with him.

Jun is a very special person in my life. He motivates and inspires me to become a better person and a better player. When I first met him, it was just before my win in Hawaii in 2021, when I'd gone three years without winning. A few of the girls said, "Hey, he is your lucky charm." I was, like, "Yeah, I've got to keep him around." He puts a smile on my face, and I know that no matter if I shoot 79, like I did at Congressional, or I shoot 65, as I did in the final round in Korea, he will always love me and talk to me the same way. My golf really is not how he perceives me. I am so thankful for meeting him.

For a while, when things weren't going great in my career, my identity felt so connected to my golf. After meeting him, I've actually wanted to work harder during the times that I am working, and then also enjoy time off. I probably had a few more breaks than I did a few years ago, but that's helped me be more focused when I am at work.

When I was a teenager, I was a little bit more carefree. I was just going around playing golf, and golf was all I thought about. If I had a bad day on the golf course, I didn't feel like a good person. I felt like golf was reflecting who I was. I don't think that is a healthy position to be in for your mental health. Now I think I have a better perspective that this is what I do, it is my work, and I'm very grateful to be able to do what I love. If I don't have a good day, I do get frustrated and wish it was better, but it doesn't take away my self-esteem. In that way, I'm able to get over it. My goal is to play without fear.

A lot of things have happened since I first won the CME as a 17-year-old in 2014. For a start, I don't miss wearing the big glasses I used to have and having to clean my lenses all the time! I've gone through my share of ups and downs, but all of those moments make the good times feel even better. It felt like a long three years before I won again in Hawaii. But all those times build you up to the player you are now. I hope that I've grown more as an individual since then. I think golf is very relatable to life in general. It's a continuous learning journey. At 25, I'm excited with where I am at in life and golf.

Last year was the best, most consistent golf I've played throughout a season. To have my first win in my second event was definitely an extra bonus because going into the season I wasn't feeling super confident about my game and wasn't really sure how it was going to go. It caught me by surprise, but I was able to take good rhythm from that. And I think, from the US Open onwards, I played really consistently, and those last two wins were more than I could have ever asked for.

Playing alongside the best women golfers in the world, I know I need to keep improving because everyone else is. You can see it by the scores each week. You can't afford even one day with just an okay score. I think people underestimate what the level of the LPGA is right now. It is so high. The cuts are getting lower and lower, keeping your card is really hard. To win is on a whole new level, it's very, very difficult. It's not like the courses are getting easier. They are getting longer and the Rules officials have their minds to try and make it as hard as possible for us. Even then the play is still so good.

OH, MY GOD, THEY'RE SO GOOD

I kept saying it but the years Jin Young Ko and Nelly Korda had in 2021 were absolutely incredible. We are all pushing each other to be the best versions of ourselves. Last year we had both young stars like 19-year-old Atthaya Thitikul reach number one in the world and Jennifer Kupcho win the Chevron in dominating fashion, and a veteran like Ashleigh Buhai finally make her breakthrough at the AIG Women's Open. Minjee Lee was unstoppable at the US Open, In Gee Chun was superb at the KPMG Women's PGA and Brooke Henderson won her second major at the Evian. All special performances. Sometimes I wish more people would come out and watch us play. Then I think they would be amazed at how talented these players are. There are times when I am playing alongside them, I am, like, "Oh, my God, they're so good".

In 2023 the prize money on the LPGA is due to pass $100 million for the first time and that shows how much our partners believe in us. We have so many big events that continue to grow and that's really cool to see. It's not only great for those of us that are playing right now, but for future generations. I feel the LPGA Tour is making a stance not just in women's golf but in women's sports about how everybody should see female athletes. There is so much to look forward to in 2023. Getting to play a US Women's Open at Pebble Beach will be special, as will going to great courses such as Baltusrol and Walton Heath, while the Chevron Championship is going to a super new venue in Houston. And I always love going to Evian, where I enjoy catching up with my partners at Rolex.

Someone who was instrumental to my recent success was Sean Foley. Everybody that really knows Sean, knows that he is more than just a golf instructor. He helped me at a point in my career when I had so many questions in my head that I really wasn't sure where I was heading. He was able to lift me up, and sometimes our conversations were very non-technique or golf-related. It was just about the mind or breathing or just other stuff outside the golf course. He helped me so much with that. It was not an easy decision when we stopped working together formally, but it was a decision we both made. Sean said, "hey, I'm always a text or a call away". He said, we're friends, but for me, he is more than a friend. He is like a mentor and somebody that I really look up to. I know that if I ever need to reach out and ask for his advice, he is always going to be there for me. I think to have somebody like that in your life, not only just in work, is something that you should be very thankful for. Sean is such an incredible person. Everybody needs a Sean in their life.

I know one of the things I will be asked about from now on is the Hall of Fame, being only a few points away from the qualifying mark. It would be a huge honour to join all the legends of the game, but it is not my biggest goal in the short term. I just try to focus on my game. I know that if I play good golf and keep putting myself in contention, all of those other things are going to follow. My drive and motivation are to be the best player I can be and I don't want to lose that passion.

That passion helped me win the BMW in the land of my birth, one of the most emotional moments of my career. Having the background I have is something I am very proud of and embrace. I have these shoes that we collaborated on with ECCO that shows who I am — with the silver fern and the hibiscus flower. New Zealand is where I grew up, learned to play golf and the country I am so happy to represent. It was such an exciting year for Kiwi golf. Ryan Fox pushed Rory McIlroy all the way on the DP World Tour, Steven Alker won the Charles Schwab Cup on the PGA Tour Champions, and Momoka Kobori got her LET card by winning a couple of times on the Access Series in Europe. We're from far down under and for us to be flying the New Zealand flag on all these different tours shows how much golf in our country has grown. Hopefully this will inspire more juniors to take it up and want to be the next Alker or Foxy or me.

And yet, although I play under the New Zealand flag, I was born in Seoul. It was a hometown to my parents and where I lived my early years in Korea. I'm proud of my Korean heritage, I speak Korean. It is my birth country and that's always going to be a special place to anyone. Every time I go back there, I'm super excited and there was definitely a yearning to win at least once in the country. I teared up right after I dropped the putt on the 18th hole, though I really didn't have any time to cry. Suddenly, my extended family, my parents, my sister, my brother-in-law, aunts, cousins were all there. We don't get a lot of opportunity to win in front of family. I really wanted to win for them, and especially my dad. Due to Covid, it was the first time in two-and-a-half years that he had seen me play an LPGA event. Just thinking about it again now makes me want to tear up.

Actually, I was going to the first tee for the final round and I felt butterflies in my stomach. I was quite nervous. That was when I realised I really wanted to win in Korea. My sister was with me and she gave me some very wise advice. She told me that a little nerves are always a good thing, and I think that also. Life on tour is not easy and I'm very thankful that my mom and my sister travel with me. They make it so much more fun.

My family have been through this journey with me. I remember coming over to the US for the first time with my mom to play the Callaway Junior Worlds in San Diego. And I might sound like I was born in the 1960s, but at that time navigation wasn't as good as we have now. She printed five pieces of paper of how to get from LAX to San Diego. If you missed one exit, you had to go back to find your route again. Back in New Zealand, she would drive eight hours for me to play in junior events. I know that she might be one of my toughest critics — she sometimes jokes, "You played so much better when you were, like, 15" — but at the same time I know that she says that because she wants me to just keep growing, and I think she keeps me really humble.

I should say "thank you" more often. I don't end up saying it enough. So now, after my last win as a single lady, with a new phase of my life beginning, thank you to everyone who has helped me to chase my dreams, thank you to my family for your belief and love, and, especially, thank you, Mom!

Lydia Ko is a Rolex Testimonee. On the LPGA in 2022 she won the CME Globe, the Rolex Player of the Year, the Vare Trophy, the money list and returned to the top of the Rolex Rankings.

Gary Player watches intently as Monique Kalkman putts during The R&A's Celebration of Champions.

A major step to making golf more inclusive

By Lewine Mair

Everyone knows the drill with Lee Trevino. On the golf course, at least, it is a case of he talks and you listen. Or appear to listen, it is all the same to the so-called Merry Mex. So imagine the surprise of Kipp Popert when Trevino asked to sit next to him at breakfast and started to enquire about his game. The occasion was The R&A's Celebration of Champions at St Andrews. Trevino was among the stars invited to appear in the exhibition that was one of the highlights of The 150th Open, alongside the likes of Tiger Woods, Rory McIlroy, Sir Nick Faldo, Georgia Hall and Dame Laura Davies.

Also included were a number of amateur champions and four players from the European Disability Golf Association, who preside over one of the game's most rapidly growing areas. Popert, who ended the year as the world number one for golfers with disabilities, has cerebral palsy and the 23-year-old Englishman has undergone operations on an almost annual basis to reconstruct his feet as and when the condition demands.

Trevino was keen to find out how Popert played this and that shot, while it was typical of him that he went on to regale his companion with a few of his own tricks of the trade. All of the above, in turn, led to a series of Open contestants wanting to be introduced to Popert, with the situation turning into one more illustration of how the professionals, to a man, were embracing the EDGA brigade.

The whole occasion was the stuff of dreams for Popert and his colleagues. Julian Postigo Arco, the swashbuckling Spaniard who casts aside his crutches to play one-legged golf to a handicap of 0.4 was the other man in the group, while there were two Dutch representatives in Jennifer Straga and Monique Kalkman. The teenage Straga plays to three in spite of the fact that her condition — she has short arms and legs — stops her from hitting a useful distance, while Kalkman plays to a single-figure handicap from a wheelchair.

Never before had such a bright spotlight been shone on the skills possessed by these golfers. As Tony Bennett, the president of EDGA, said proudly of his payers, they all bring the right kind of attention to their disability and people look at it and go, "Wow, I didn't realise someone in a wheelchair could hit it 150 yards and play off a nine handicap, or that guy that plays off one leg hits it 270 yards".

To think that it was no longer ago than 2019 that Keith Pelley, the CEO of the DP World Tour, came to the British Masters at Hillside to outline the link he had in mind for EDGA players and his own. Then and there, he announced a couple of 36-hole tournaments for EDGA players, these to be held on the same courses and in the same week as DP World Tour events. The first of them was to be run in conjunction with the Scottish Open, and the second at the end-of-year DP World Tour Championship in Dubai.

Caroline Mohr was one of three players who Pelley introduced to the media that day at Hillside. And when Pelley invited her to the microphone, this former LET professional, who had lost her right leg to cancer, silenced everyone in the room with an account of how she had coped with the terrible conditions in the morning pro-am. Early on, she had been complaining to herself about the wintry cold. Then she changed tack: "Suddenly, I stopped all the nonsense and said, 'No, no. I'm here! I get to be here!'"

Talk about a lesson in adhering to the message in that familiar old lyric, "Ac-Cent-Tchu-Ate the Positive": "You've got to accentuate the positive, Eliminate the negative, Latch on to the affirmative, Don't mess with Mister In-Between."

To Pelley's credit, and despite the difficulties of the Covid era, what is now known as the G4D Tour has continued to grow with seven events in its first full season in 2022, of which Popert won four, from a total of 97 EDGA tournaments. For 2023 there will be an Order of Merit winner and a schedule of nine G4D events, the first of which was the Australian All Abilities Championship in December 2022, where Popert took the title at Victoria Golf Club alongside ISPS Handa Australian Open champions Adrian Meronk and Ashleigh Buhai as, in a world first, the three national championships were played concurrently.

"I firmly believe that golf has the potential to be the most inclusive sport in the world and the G4D Tour is a major step in realising this ambition," Pelley said. "We have seen unprecedented numbers enquire about playing, thanks to the ability for these inspirational players to play Tour level courses next to the best players on the DP World Tour."

Bennett added: "The G4D Tour is the visible manifestation of EDGA's development of golf for the disabled, a process that started 22 years ago. Since our first collaboration with the European Tour, there has been exponential growth at all levels. The G4D Tour has created greater awareness and resulted in a cascade effect with more tournaments at every level, more national federations building accessible activities, and more grassroots programmes than ever before."

PARALYMPICS BID

For a next step, the players would love for their sport to be included in the Paralympics. Golf was turned down for 2024, but EDGA have put in a bid for 2028 and fingers are crossed. "Hopefully," said Popert, who qualified for last year's Amateur Championship, "it will happen and I will be ready. As golfers we play for ourselves a lot of the time. The biggest honour is to represent your country and when I watched cerebral palsy football at London in 2012, I was blown away."

Mind you, 2028 may be too far away for a player whose ultimate aim is to do as the four-foot, 11-inch Brendan Lawlor has done and turn professional. The Irishman has been a key figure in the world of golf for the disabled since he won the tournament run in conjunction with the 2019 Scottish Open, even though he was hitting long irons into the par fours where the regular tour players were using wedges.

Lawlor, who has teed up on the DP World Tour, is accruing plenty of sponsorships via Niall Horan, the manager of Modest Golf, while Australia's Geoff Nicholas, 62, is a longtime PGA professional from Sydney who has won tournaments for golfers with disabilities all around the world. Nicholas was born with a leg deformity caused by the morning-sickness drug Thalidomide and had his right leg amputated when he was a young boy. Meanwhile, it is often overlooked that Ladies European Tour winner Diksha Digar has a hearing impairment that has required the use of hearing aids since the age of six. In 2022 the Indian won gold at the Deaflympics, having won silver as a 16-year-old in 2017, and by appearing at Tokyo in 2021, became the first golfer to represent her country at both the Olympics and the Deaflympics.

But the question currently going the rounds in EDGA circles is whether players could eventually make a living by playing as professionals among the amateurs in their and the G4D events. Last year, the prize money that was handed out at five EDGA events was in line with The R&A guidelines for amateur status. These events, which were sponsored by RSM, a multinational network of accounting firms, had prize funds which, depending on the size of the field, went up to £1,350, with the maximum single prize being £700. Whether the professionals may see more in the way of monetary rewards is something that does not seem to have been ruled out.

A second question relates to someone like Popert who has ambitions to play on the DP World Tour itself. Since he has stated that it would be tough for him to walk too many 72-hole tournaments in a row, would he be allowed to use a buggy?

Here, the name Casey Martin has been invoked. Initially, Martin, who suffered from a circulatory issue known as Klippel-Trenaunay Syndrome in his right leg, was denied permission to use a buggy by the PGA Tour, but he successfully won a lawsuit in 1998 that overturned the decision. After qualifying for that year's US Open at Olympic Club, the former Stanford team-mate of Woods finished in a share of 23rd place. The case eventually went all the way to the Supreme Court, which ruled in Martin's favour in 2001.

When the buggy question was raised with the DP World Tour, who have played so big a part in raising standards among golfers with disabilities, the hierarchy indicated that they will be judging each case on its merits when the time comes.

Popert, in the meantime, has been working on making himself fitter and stronger while improving his short game to the extent where it would be a match for the best of the professionals. "The modern game is going a certain way because of distance," said Popert, "but I can still work extremely hard at the other parts of my game. An elite player from 120 yards in is going to score well."

Where he and his peers are light years ahead of more ordinary mortals is when it comes to the mind game. Like a Tiger, a Seve or a Trevino, they have what it takes to do the seemingly impossible.

Lewine Mair is a senior European writer for Global Golf Post

THE
OPEN

EVERYTHING HAS LED TO THIS
EVERYTHING HAS LED TO THIS
THE OPEN
18

St Andrews salutes the Tiger

By Andy Farrell

Would he stop? What would it mean if he did, or didn't? Tiger Woods approached the Swilcan Bridge. No one quite knew what was about to happen, but everyone wanted to be here. Every grandstand seat behind the 18th hole, along the first fairway and by the 17th hole was taken. The Links, the street to the right of the fairway, was packed with spectators craning for a view. Above them, in the hotels and golf clubs and apartments, people filled the balconies and hung out of windows. Every vantage point was occupied. St Andrews, filled to the brim with a record number of fans for The 150th Open, had turned out in force. Whatever was about to happen, no one wanted to miss it. As they walked off the 18th tee at the start of one of the most famous walks in golf — framed by the buildings of the auld grey town, presided over by The R&A's clubhouse at the head of golf's original course, the West Sands and the North Sea not far away, the ancient setting transformed into a unique amphitheatre for a modern major championship — the others in Tiger's group hung back, including his caddie Joe LaCava and playing partners Max Homa and Matt Fitzpatrick. Homa had to tug back the US Open champion. "He was, like, you were a little bit too close," said Fitzpatrick. "I'm, like, was I? I was panicking, but we were all good. We knew what we were doing."

Woods had targeted an appearance in this Open — "the most historic one we've ever had," he said — during the long rehabilitation after his near-fatal car crash in 2021. "I was just hoping to play this one event this year," he said. As it had turned out, he had also made it to the Masters. All the old skills were still there, but it was a painful walk up and down the hills of Augusta National, a triumph of determination to complete four rounds. At Southern Hills, for the PGA Championship, he managed three rounds but then needed another operation. He skipped the US Open and arrived at St Andrews under the weather, Rory McIlroy worried that he had given Tiger Covid when they were together in Ireland.

For one of the latest honorary members of the Royal and Ancient Golf Club of St Andrews, Woods did not get a kind member's bounce off the first tee on Thursday. He had to play his approach shot from a divot and landed in the burn. His scores made it inevitable he would miss the cut, but the spectators had cheered him out to the Loop and back again for two days running by the time he reached the 18th on Friday afternoon. The ovation was only going to grow larger and larger as his stiff-legged walk came to its conclusion.

The old stone bridge over the burn has become the place to acknowledge a St Andrews farewell. Only that same morning Mark Calcavecchia had waved and shed a tear. Into his 60s now, the 1989 champion should have played his last Open in 2020, but it was cancelled that year and in 2021 he was injured. A special invitation was issued and gratefully accepted. "I'm not sure what I was expecting, but I felt it," Calc said. "I felt the emotions. They were cheering for me, aware it was my last Open. So that was pretty cool. It means a lot."

In 2015, it had been Sir Nick Faldo, the 1990 winner at the home of golf, and Tom Watson. Due to weather delays, Watson finished in the gloaming of a late Scottish summer evening, fans coming back from the town after dinner, the R&A members spilling out of the clubhouse to salute the five-time champion.

Watson played alongside Jack Nicklaus in 2005. Nicklaus had had a couple of trial farewells in previous St Andrews Opens but this was really it. He proved it with a birdie on the 18th green which would have raised any roof that could have stretched over the joyous scene. "I knew the hole would move wherever I hit the ball," said the Golden Bear. He and Watson, friends and rivals, left the green with their arms around each other's shoulders. There was not a dry eye in the house.

Ten years earlier it had been Arnold Palmer's turn. If anyone deserved a protracted ovation from the Swilcan Bridge it was Palmer, the man who reinvigorated the Open Championship, first missing out to Kel Nagle at the Centenary Open at St Andrews in 1960, then returning to capture the Claret Jug with his thrilling escapades the next two years. "When I came up the 18th I kept thinking about 1960 and what that led to," said the King. "A lot of great years and happy times. Looking at all the people and the buildings going up 18, it was very warming, a happy time."

Faldo, who had already finished his round, stayed at the back of the 18th green while Palmer finished. "What he's done for The Open is everything," Faldo said. "But for Arnold Palmer in 1960, who knows where we'd be; probably in a little shed on the beach."

Woods was a 19-year-old amateur in 1995 making his debut in The Open. "I watched Arnold hit his first tee shot on the second day, and that was quite special," Woods recalled early in the week in 2022. "I was going to the range and next thing I hear, 'On the tee, from the USA, Arnold Palmer'. He gets up there and gives it the big ol' waggle and hits it up the middle of the fairway and his head is bobbing all over the place.

"And I played probably four or five holes behind Jack and Tom when Jack retired in '05. Hearing the roars get louder and louder and louder as we came towards the finish. Then the roar because, obviously, he made the putt. I mean, he wasn't going to miss that putt. Everyone has seemed to have made their farewell here."

NO STOPPING ON THE BRIDGE

Woods did not stop on the Swilcan Bridge. He was not about to retire on the spot, as some of the wilder speculation had it. He did remove his cap and waved in appreciation of all the applause and cheering. He kept moving and the sound kept washing over him.

"This is my favourite golf course," Woods said of the Old. "I fell in love with it back in 1995. I remember my very first practice round, I couldn't believe how stupidly hard this place is because I played every hole into the wind. I happened to have the tide change. All of a sudden the wind changes, and, see, these bunkers are now in play. It's amazing the ingenuity that they had then that this golf course has stood the test of time. It's still a challenge. I love how it can be played in so many different ways."

A photograph of Woods from that first practice round at St Andrews still has pride of place in his office. He visited what was then called the British Golf Museum and ended up in a tie for 68th place, enjoying himself on the last day with a putt from 60 yards short of the sixth green. Along with the Scottish Open the previous week at Carnoustie, it was his first experience of links golf and played a part in his record-shattering victory in the 1997 Masters. "Those two weeks were a strong introduction to links golf," Woods wrote in his book *Unprecedented*. "I loved it, and could see the relationship between the type of golf you wanted to play there, and at Augusta, especially if it was playing firm. Augusta in '97 played like the inland links the designers intended.

Woods returned to the Old Course for his only visit outside The Open in 1998, as part of an American dream team at the Alfred Dunhill Cup, along with Mark O'Meara, that year's Masters and Open champion, and John Daly, the 1995 Open winner. In cold and blustery conditions, Woods played four rounds in 14 under par with a pair of 66s, but did lose to Santiago Luna, ranked 190th in the world, as Spain beat the USA in the semi-finals.

Ahead of the Millennium Open in 2000 at St Andrews, Woods said. Every time you come here, you learn something new and you experience a piece of history. That's so neat. It's not often in sport you can go back in time on a golf course that is almost identical to how it started."

Woods was the overwhelming favourite, having just won the US Open at Pebble Beach by 15 strokes. He was at the zenith of his powers. And he was not relying on old myths. Precision was everything. "People say around the world that St Andrews is an easy course because all you have to do is aim left," he said. "That's not the case. With the fairways being as fast as they are, you need to position your ball off the tee. You have to be very careful. Too far left and there are all those pot bunkers coming at you on the shared fairways. Run into those and you can only pitch out."

He did not run into any of them — and all 112 bunkers had had their faces sharply revetted specially for the occasion — over the four days. He also did not three-putt on the huge double greens. He won by eight strokes with a new record total for a major of 19 under par. He also, at the first opportunity, completed the career Grand Slam, only the fifth man after Gene Sarazen, Ben Hogan, Gary Player and Nicklaus to claim all four of the modern majors. With that in mind, Woods said: "This venue means a lot to me." No one has joined the elite group since.

Woods won again at St Andrews by five strokes in 2005. Only Nicklaus had also won back-to-back Opens at the home of golf in modern times. In 2010, Woods opened with a 67 but it was to be his last sub-par round on Old Course. He finished 23rd, missed the cut in 2015 and would do so again in 2022. With no date set for the next Open at St Andrews, who knew if the 46-year-old would be back for a seventh crack.

As he continued his walk up the 18th fairway, Woods exchanged nods with McIlroy, walking down the first fairway, and Justin Thomas, still waiting to tee off. "It was a cool moment to be on that fairway when that was happening," McIlroy said of the Tiger salute. "Everyone hopes it's not the end of his Old Course career. I think he deserves, we deserve, him to have another crack at it."

Fitzpatrick, still walking behind Woods, said: "Just looking around, seeing everyone stood up and giving him a standing ovation, it was incredible. It gave me goosebumps. It's something that will live with me forever. It's thoroughly deserved and, I think towards the end of it, you could see he was a little bit emotional as well. It was a big deal."

Woods pulled his cap down over his face. "I had a few tears," he said. "I'm not one who gets very teary-eyed very often about anything. The warmth of the ovation got to me. It's something I'll always remember. The ovations got louder as I was coming in. I felt the respect. I've always respected the traditions of the game. I've put my heart and soul into this event over the years and people appreciated my play. I've won it three times. Life moves on. People know my circumstances. I've been coming here since 1995 and I don't know if I'll be physically able to play by the next time if it's 2030. I feel I'll be able to play future British Opens, but it felt like this might be my last one here at St Andrews. I understand what Jack and Arnold had gone through in the past. I was kind of feeling that way at the end."

Last seen, at the end of the year, Woods and son Charlie were parading synchronised limps at the PNC Championship. There may not be any more Opens at St Andrews, but the honorary R&A member will return. "I'm sure my son will probably want me to come back and play," he said. "I have my locker here right when you walk into the clubhouse on the left. That's pretty neat."

Whatever happened that Friday afternoon, that we witnessed and he experienced, we all experienced — a farewell, a salute, a celebration — fittingly, it was uniquely Tigeresque, and will live long in the memory once much else of 2022 has faded to dust.

A life of towering achievement in golf

By Marino Parascenzo

Through the final stretch of his treatment, Tom Weiskopf was still working on three projects — one in Utah, one in Montana and one in Idaho — and his wife Laurie said that just a week ago, the week before he died, he was doing some work over at Spanish Peaks, the mountain course he'd designed near their Montana home. "He worked to the end," she said. "It was amazing. He had a big life."

And perhaps golf course architecture finally was the key to understanding one of the most baffling golfers ever on the PGA Tour. Weiskopf, an imposing six-foot-three — brilliant, gifted, tormented — strode through golf history, blazing a trail with fiery golf and a fiery temper. He came to course architecture after his playing days. With partners, and solo, he did some 80 courses, and was the champion of the driveable par four. In architecture, maybe at last he'd found something in this maddening game that he could control. Now there was nothing to rage against. No more perfect tee shots hitting a hard spot and ricocheting into the deep rough, no more meticulous putts lipping out off an invisible bump. Now there were the drawing board and the vast reaches of the mind.

If golf ever had a truly tragic figure, it was Weiskopf — blessed with a talent that allowed him to soar, but cursed with a temperament that dragged him down.

"I could not accept failure when it was my fault," he said after winning the US Senior Open in 1995. "It just used to tear me up."

This sort of turbulence won him criticism, contempt and a nickname, "Towering Inferno". From a movie about a burning skyscraper. Tommy Bolt, famed club thrower of the previous generation, at least got something catchy — "Terrible Tommy" and "Thunder Bolt" — but as a temper he wasn't even in Weiskopf's class. Bolt eventually admitted that a lot of his blow-ups were merely showmanship. There was no showmanship in Weiskopf. "Sure I threw clubs," Weiskopf was quoted as saying. "Just absolute frustration … directed internally to me. I'm not a mean guy, not an angry guy. I am a moody person, though …"

His eruptions seemed random and spontaneous. In one incident, insignificant except as an example, a golf writer recalled wanting to write a pre-tournament story on Weiskopf at a US Open, and was waiting in the locker room, the best place for player interviews. Weiskopf, finished with practice, had changed his shoes and was checking his locker. The writer had opted to remain silent and stand aside till he was through. Finally, Weiskopf stood up, lifted some envelopes off the top shelf, then suddenly wheeled and snapped, "Well, you gonna let me check my goddamned mail or what?" The writer apologised and left.

Weiskopf died at age 79 on 20 August 2022, at his home in Big Sky, Montana. He is survived by his wife Laurie and by his daughter from his first marriage, Heidi. He was preceded in death by his first wife, Jeanne, whom he divorced, and by their son Eric. He was diagnosed with pancreatic cancer late in 2020. He underwent an aggressive treatment that allowed him to resume some of his design work and he had an encouraging period late in 2021, but the cancer returned in April. "He really fought it for a long, long time, and he did so bravely," his wife Laurie said.

Weiskopf, the son of a railroad worker, was born 9 November 1942, in precisely the wrong place and at the wrong time — in Massillon, Ohio, some three years after fellow Ohioan Jack Nicklaus, and thus, for all of the excellence of his play, he was constantly reminded that he wasn't as good as Nicklaus.

"I know he always felt like he was sort of in my shadow because he followed me at Ohio State, and he shouldn't have felt that way," Nicklaus told golf writer Dave Shedloski. "He was a great player in his own right. He was impressive ... one of the four or five most talented players I've ever seen, one of the top-five ball-strikers I've ever known."

But Weiskopf had a fatalist's view when it came to Nicklaus, offering it with famous and brutal candour: "Jack knew he was going to beat you. You knew Jack was going to beat you. And Jack knew you knew he was going to beat you."

There were some notable exceptions. True, Nicklaus beat Weiskopf five times, including twice at the Masters. But then, Weiskopf beat Nicklaus four times — in the 1972 Inverrary Classic by a shot, the 1975 Canadian Open in a playoff, the 1978 Doral-Eastern Open by one, and the 1995 US Senior Open by four.

Weiskopf had an even tougher foe than Nicklaus that he also beat — alcohol. He left the tour in his early 40s, and said if it hadn't been for alcohol, he could have had 10 more good years. He gave it up in the early days of 2000.

By any measure, Weiskopf had an extraordinary career. He won a major, the 1973 Open Championship, won 15 other PGA Tour events, finished second in the Masters four times, second in a US Open, and won four times on the Senior PGA Tour, then returned to an acclaimed career in course architecture. And in a grand irony — for all of his accomplishments, he once turned down a chance to play in the Ryder Cup in order to go hunting and ended up branded as the guy who didn't want to play for his country. It was a specious claim and, in the vernacular, a bum rap. And it was ironic because Weiskopf, though inadvertently, helped save the Ryder Cup.

Weiskopf had played in two Ryder Cups, going 3-2-1 on his debut in 1973, a 19-13 American win, and 4-0-0 in the Americans' 21-11 runaway in 1975, when he turned Laurel Valley into a 16-hole course. He never played the 17th and 18th. And he became the lightning rod for the 1977 Ryder Cup without even hitting a ball.

Earlier in 1977, the news he'd been waiting for so anxiously had finally arrived — his hunt was on. Weiskopf, an avid outdoorsman, was going for the Grand Slam of North American bighorn sheep, the wild sheep with those big, curled horns. Weiskopf already had the Bighorn, the Stone and the Desert. He needed the Dall, from far up in the forbidding Yukon. Weiskopf's permit, for 21 days, came with a serious coincidence. It fell at Ryder Cup time.

"I had booked my hunt two years in advance," he said. "It was the only date I could get." So in March, he wrote to the PGA of America, which conducts the American side of the Ryder Cup, informing officials of his situation and instructing them to remove his name from consideration for the team. Then six months later, at the World Series of Golf in September, the Ryder Cup team was announced for the match two weeks later. Weiskopf was stunned and angered to hear his name. He had not been taken off the list and he'd made the team on performance points. And so he made it clear he wasn't going to play. Let the outrage begin. Critics accused him of something akin to treason.

"They said I didn't want to play for my country," Weiskopf said. "That really hurt. That killed me." Some 45 years later, though the treason smear had faded, it was in all his obituaries — he had skipped the Ryder Cup to go hunting.

Weiskopf did go up into the Yukon and get his Grand Slam Dall, and Lanny Wadkins replaced him and the Americans won again, this time by 12½-7½, and there hung a grim tale. Great Britain & Ireland's best showing was a 5-5 tie in singles, and the US now led the biennial series 18-3-1. Players, fans, media — everybody was weary of it all. The Ryder Cup was dying of disinterest. So much so that after this latest debacle, Lord Derby, then president of the British and Irish PGA, had an urgent talk with Nicklaus. Could the Ryder Cup be saved?

Nicklaus's answer: expand the team immediately, from Great Britain and Ireland, to Europe. Get fresh and real muscle. The bold and brilliant young Spaniard, Seve Ballesteros, for example.

So in the 1979 Ryder Cup, it was USA versus Europe. And some impressive British talent was beginning to emerge. Ballesteros was joined by Sandy Lyle and Nick Faldo. The US still won easily, 17-11, but the good old days of the Ryder Cup were over.

And Tom Weiskopf's role? In their chat, Nicklaus was pressing the point of interest in the Ryder Cup dying. He slipped His Lordship one final elbow in the ribs. Some of our guys, Nicklaus reminded him, would rather go hunting.

Marino Parascenzo was the golf correspondent of the Pittsburgh Post-Gazette *for 37 years and is a longtime contributor to* The World of Professional Golf

IN MEMORIUM

Among those professional golfers, and those who impacted professional golf, who died in 2022 were:

Bob Shearer, 73, January 9

A stalwart of the Melbourne golf scene, Bob Shearer won the 1969 Australian Amateur, then had 27 victories as a professional in a career stretching to four decades. In 1982 he won the Australian Open by four strokes from Jack Nicklaus and Payne Stewart at The Australian, a Nicklaus-designed course, and added the Australian PGA at Royal Melbourne in 1983. Four times he won the Australasian Order of Merit, as well as posting two victories in Europe in 1975, one on the PGA Tour in 1982 and four on the European Seniors Tour. He became a golf course architect and was a life member of the PGA of Australia. His wife, Kathie, is a longtime media official at tournaments in Australia.

Dick Ferris, 85, January 16

Dick Ferris was awarded a lifetime achievement award by the World Golf Hall of Fame but died two months prior to ceremony at the Players Championship in March. Chair of the PGA Tour Policy Board for 13 years from 1994, he joined with Arnold Palmer, Clint Eastwood and former Major League Baseball commissioner Peter Ueberroth to purchase the Pebble Beach Company from Japanese owners in 1999.

Bob Goalby, 92, January 20

A three-iron to six feet for an eagle at the 15th hole was the highlight of a closing 66 at Augusta National that won Bob Goalby the Masters in 1968. There should have been a playoff but Roberto de Vicenzo signed for a four, instead of the three he plainly made, at the 17th and finished one behind. Goalby got little credit at the time for his victory, but acted with great class, spending the presentation ceremony consoling the unfortunate Argentinian. He took heart from the letter he received from Masters founder Bobby Jones, who wrote: "I ask you to always remember that you won the tournament under the Rules of Golf and by superlative play." Goalby won 11 times on the PGA Tour, was a runner-up at the US Open and the PGA Championship, was a Ryder Cup player, a television commentator and one of the pioneers of the Champions Tour. He was uncle to Jay and Jerry Haas, and a great uncle to Bill Haas. Jay said: "He was a hard guy, but he had a huge heart."

Tomoo Ishii, 98, January 24

One of the first Asian players to play in the Masters in the mid-1960s, making the cut on two of his three appearances, Tomoo Ishii twice represented Japan at the Canada Cup. He claimed nine victories in Japan and Asia, outscoring Peter Thomson by four shots, after they were tied after 54 holes, to win the 1964 Capitol Hills Open in Manila, Philippines.

Eduardo Romero, 67, February 13

Known affectionately by his nickname of "El Gato" — The Cat — Eduardo Romero stalked the fairways of the world with both fun and success. The son of a club professional, and a protege of Roberto de Vicenzo, he won over 80 times in South America, as well as eight times on the European Tour, including the national Opens of France, Scotland and Spain, between 1989 and 2002, when he was 48. A fine senior career was highlighted by his victory at the 2008 US Senior Open. He frequently represented Argentina at the Alfred Dunhill Cup and the World Cup, finishing second with Angel Cabrera in the latter on home soil in Buenos Aires in 2000, behind only Tiger Woods and David Duval. He also became the mayor of his home city of Villa Allende in the province of Cordoba.

Kyi Hla Han, 61, February 19

A professional golfer from Myanmar whose career stretched to 25 years, Kyi Hla Han won the 1994 Singapore Open and the 1999 Volvo China Open, the year he finished as number one on the Asian Tour. One of the first from Asia regularly to travel internationally, he was a travelling companion of, and "big brother" to, a young Vijay Singh. He became the executive chairman of the Asian Tour in 2006, holding the post for a decade. Current commissioner Cho Minn Thant said: "Asian golf has lost one of its greatest players, its greatest personalities and its greatest leaders." From 2023, selected rookies on the Asian Tour will receive funding from the Kyi Hla Han Future Champions Programme.

Lu Liang-huan, 83, March 15

Taiwan's Lu Liang-huan charmed the galleries at Royal Birkdale in 1971, bowing to them in acknowledgement of their applause and doffing his distinctive pork pie hat, and earning the nickname "Mr Lu". It was his first appearance in The Open and he took Lee Trevino, a golfing friend from the days Trevino was in the US Marine Corps and Lu in the Chinese Air Force, to the 72nd hole. Both birdied as Trevino won by one, but Lu benefitted from a shot rebounding off the forehead of a woman spectator. She was concussed but he later paid for her family to holiday in his homeland. The following week, Lu won the French Open. A caddie from his schooldays, he won the inaugural Hong Kong Open in 1959 at Fanling, where he was briefly the club pro, and the same title again in 1974. Olympic bronze medallist CT Pan said:"Not only did he have high-end ball skills, but because of his sharpness and coolness, Mr Lu is the teacher I looked up to most in my childhood. Thank you, teacher Lu, for your contributions to golf."

Joan Joyce, 81, March 26

A multi-sport wizard, Joan Joyce played for 19 years on the LPGA and held the record for the fewest number of putts in a round, 17, at the 1982 Lady Michelob event. Previously, she had been a successful softball pitcher, with 50 perfect games and Ted Williams and Hank Aaron among her strikeout victims in exhibition games. She also played basketball and volleyball and was a member of 20 different Halls of Fame. At her death, she was in her 28th season as softball coach at Florida Atlantic University, where she had also been the women's golf coach for 18 years.

Shirley Spork, 94, April 12

A Detroit public school teacher, Shirley Spork became a founding member of the LPGA in 1950. She had grown up on the 17th hole at Bonnie Brook and would sneak onto the course with her only club, a putter she bought for a dollar from her earnings reselling lost balls. Her true passion was teaching and she took a club pro job in Palm Springs in the winter and played the tour in the summer. A pioneer twice over, she drove the founding of the LPGA Teaching & Club Pro division in 1959. "There are many things I admire about Shirley," noted Karrie Webb, "but one, in particular, is her passion to continue to learn and stay involved with the game." A regular attendee at the Founders Cup and at Mission Hills, it was at the 2022 Chevron Championship, shortly before her death, that she was awarded honorary membership of the LPGA Hall of Fame.

Jack Newton, 72, April 15

"Once I got my tail up, I wasn't afraid of anybody," said Jack Newton, the 1979 Australian Open champion, who won once on the PGA Tour and three times in Europe. He was runner-up to Tom Watson in the 1975 Open at Carnoustie, in a playoff, and to Seve Ballesteros at the 1980 Masters. Newton's playing career ended in July 1983, at the age of 33, when he walked into a plane's spinning propeller during a rainstorm. Given only a 50-50 chance of surviving, he lost his right arm, his right eye and had severe abdominal injuries, and spent two months in intensive care. After a long rehabilitation, he taught himself to play one handed to a handicap of around 12, became a forthright television pundit, a golf course designer and set up the Jack Newton Junior Golf Foundation.

Bart Bryant, 59, May 31

Bart Bryant, who died in a car accident in Polk City, Florida when a truck ran into his own stationary vehicle, endured many injuries and trips to the Qualifying School to make it to the PGA Tour, where he won three times in his 40s. In 2005 he won the Memorial ahead of Fred Couples and the Tour Championship by six from Tiger Woods. Older brother Brad also won on the PGA Tour and both were winners on the Champions Tour. Growing up, the brothers had dominated junior and high school golf in Alamogordo, New Mexico.

Mac McLendon, 76, July 4

After playing golf at Louisiana State University, Mac McLendon struggled for form as a professional and with the weekly Monday qualifying for non-exempt players on the PGA Tour. He almost quit before teaming up with Hubert Green to win the National Team Championship in 1974. "I had some really bad times," he said. "But I'm not a quitter." He won three more times, twice in 1978, before retiring to work in financial services.

Dale Douglass, 86, July 6

Dale Douglass grew up in Colorado and won three times on the PGA Tour, all within nine months from April 1969. He won 11 times on the PGA Tour Champions, including four in his rookie season of 1986, the highlight coming with a one-shot win over Gary Player in the US Senior Open at Scioto in Columbus, Ohio. He also won the Liberty Mutual Legends of Golf four times with Charles Coody.

Tommy Jacobs, 87, July 11

Tommy Jacobs, older brother of John Jacobs, had the distinction for 58 years of being the youngest competitor at the Masters. In 1951 he won the US Junior Amateur and then reached the semi-finals of the US Amateur, which earned him an invitation to the 1952 Masters when he was 17. Matteo Manassero broke the record in 2010. A four-time PGA Tour winner who played in the 1965 Ryder Cup, Jacobs was runner-up by four shots to Ken Venturi at the 1964 US Open and, along with Gay Brewer, lost an 18-hole playoff to Jack Nicklaus at the 1966 Masters.

Tom Weiskopf, 79, August 20

With a majestic swing and a fiery temper, at six-foot-three he was nicknamed the "Towering Inferno". Tom Weiskopf won 16 times on the PGA Tour but only one major championship, the 1973 Open at Troon. He followed Jack Nicklaus as Ohio's next big star but endured many near-misses in majors, including four runner-up finishes at the Masters. During his broadcasting career, he was asked what Nicklaus was thinking on the 16th tee of the 1986 Masters. He replied: "If I knew the way he thought, I would have won this tournament." He later found great acclaim as a golf course designer, with Troon North, TPC Scottsdale, and Loch Lomond among his 80 or so creations.

Herb Kohler Jr, 83, September 9

Having hugely expanded the family plumbing and manufacturing business, Herb Kohler created major championship venues Blackwolf Run and Whistling Straits, where the USA regained the Ryder Cup in 2021, in Sheboygan County, Wisconsin next to Lake Michigan. He also owned the Old Course Hotel and redeveloped Hamilton Hall behind the 18th green at St Andrews.

Russell Weir, 71, September 21

Known as the "Tartan Tour Chieftain" for winning over 100 times on the Scottish PGA circuit, Russell Weir won the Scottish Boys title in 1968, but never attempted to play full time on the European Tour. Instead, he became the longtime professional at his home club of Cowal in Dunoon, on the western shore of the Firth of Clyde. He played eight times for GB&I in the PGA Cup between 1986-2000, captained the team twice and was made an honorary member of the PGA.

Titiya Plucksataporn, 39, October 22

One of the first Thai golfers to play on the Ladies European Tour, Titiya Plucksataporn, known as "Tobby" and for an ever-present smile, turned professional in 2005 and was a member of the circuit for 14 years. She started golf at the age of 12 and was coached by her father, Tarat, before she, too, took up coaching in Thailand. She died from cancer at the age of 39.

Dow Finsterwald, 93, November 4

Dow Finsterwald might have gone down in history as the last losing finalist at the PGA Championship (to Lionel Hebert in 1957). Instead, he returned the following year and won the first strokeplay version ahead of Billy Casper and Sam Snead. Originally from Ohio, he won 11 times on the PGA Tour before acting as head pro at the Broadmoor Resort in Colorado Springs for 28 years. He played on four Ryder Cup teams and was a victorious non-playing captain in 1977. A lifelong friend of Arnold Palmer after they met playing college golf, he missed out to the King in both the 1960 and '62 Masters. He served as a vice-president of the PGA of America, on various USGA committees and as a rules official at the Masters. "He did all he could for the game," said his son, Dow Finsterwald Jr, Colonial's head pro.

Sandy Jones, 75, November 28

Sandy Jones served the Professional Golfers' Association for 37 years, the two-handicapper from Mount Ellen Golf Club previously having become president of the Lanarkshire Golf Association at the age of 32. In 1980 he became secretary of the Scottish Region and more than quadrupled prize money on the Tartan Tour before moving to the PGA's national headquarters at The Belfry as chief executive in 1991. His successor Robert Maxfield said: "Sandy led the PGA for more than 25 years, instigating significant change and improvement. Through his work with the Ryder Cup, the PGA World Alliance, and PGAs of Europe, he was a significant figure in the world of golf." Jones, a proud Scot, charming colleague and visionary leader, was also president of the Golf Foundation. Guy Kinnings, the DP World Tour's Ryder Cup director added: "In terms of the Ryder Cup, he played an integral role in helping it become the global sporting occasion it is today. He was hugely respected and his passion for our sport was obvious to all."

Kathy Whitworth, 83, December 24

Golf saw one of its greatest rivalries in the 1960s when Mickey Wright and Kathy Whitworth were contending for LPGA titles. Wright, who retired full-time from the tour in 1969, ended with 82 victories; Whitworth achieved a record 88 wins over a span of 23 years from 1962. She won 11 times in 1968 and claimed at least one win for an amazing 17 consecutive years. While Wright won 13 major championships, Whitworth claimed six, including three LPGA Championships, but never the US Women's Open. As Louise Suggs said: "Mickey was the greatest golfer, but Kathy was the greatest winner."

Whitworth started playing golf at the age of 15 on a nine-hole course built for the employees of the El Paso Natural Gas company in her hometown of Jal, New Mexico. "Golf just grabbed me by the throat," she recalled. "I can't tell you how much I loved it." She learnt the game on the course, not at a practice range, and that extended to her early days on the LPGA, learning as she went along from the lowest of bases. "I almost quit because I was playing so bad." It took her three and a half years to get the first win and she had been a runner-up 11 times — out of a career total of 93 — before her second win arrived by four strokes from Wright. Then she was off and running. "Winning never got old," she said.

"I'm glad when I look back on it that I didn't succeed right away. When it happened, I was ready. I think some people win without even knowing how they won. I had lost some playoffs. I had come close a few times. You have to learn how to win. You learn by making mistakes and analysing the round after the tournament and thinking back and saying, 'Ah, I should have ...'"

In 1981 she was the first LPGA player to pass $1 million in career earnings, which did not make up for the lack of a US Open, but "it was a consolation which took some of the sting out of not winning". The following year she was inducted into the World Golf Hall of Fame and in 1990 she was the US captain at the first Solheim Cup. She died suddenly, celebrating Christmas Eve with family and friends. Her partner, Bettye Odle, wrote: "Kathy left this world the way she lived her life, loving, laughing and creating memories."

Barry Lane, 62, December 31

One of the finest ball-strikers of his generation on the European Tour, Barry Lane was also one of the most popular playing partners among his peers. He won five times on the circuit, including the 1988 Scottish Open ahead of Sandy Lyle, the 1992 German Masters from Bernhard Langer and Ian Woosnam, and the 1993 European Masters by one from Seve Ballesteros. The fifth came in 2004 after a 10-year gap. He played in the 1993 Ryder Cup, won the inaugural Andersen Consulting World Championship, a precursor to the WGC Match Play, in 1995 and claimed eight victories on the European Legends Tour. In December 2022, he presented the newly renamed Barry Lane Rookie of the Year award to Adilson Da Silva at the season-ending MCB Tour Championship in Mauritius.

Leona Maguire, Ireland's first LPGA winner.

Douglas P. DeFelice/Getty Images

Notes from the year in curiosities

By Matt Cooper

It seems it has become as important for a future major champion to have **experience of contending in a recent major** as it is for a climber of Mount Everest to venture into the thin air above base camp before the final ascent.

The numbers are persuasive. Since the start of the 2017 season there have been 23 men's major championships and no fewer than 21 of the winners had finished in the top eight, or been in the top four after 54 holes, in one of their previous three major starts. In other words, they had experience of the final day drama and/or of sleeping with the knowledge that the next day might transform their lives.

Perhaps no golfer more vividly exemplifies this trend than the year's US Open champion Matt Fitzpatrick, whose major record ahead of the PGA Championship was unquestionably poor, including just one top 10 in 27 starts (and that courtesy of very late birdies on Sunday). At Southern Hills, however, he was fourth and just a month later he was putting the lessons learned into practice.

His victory at The Country Club was not only vindication of his own talent and capacity to learn quickly, it was also a long-awaited first taste of elite level triumph for his caddie Billy Foster, whose success with the likes of Severiano Ballesteros, Darren Clarke and Lee Westwood had always lacked major championship sparkle.

The blow that clinched Fitzpatrick's first major triumph found the heart of the 18th green in the final round from a bunker 160 yards down the fairway, an effort his playing partner Will Zalatoris granted odds of one-in-20 ("at best") and just one of **many crucial shots in 2022 that were executed from sand**.

There was the sensational par save from the doughnut bunker on Muirfield's 18th that sealed victory for Ashleigh Buhai in the AIG Women's Open play-off; Rory McIlroy's unlikely birdie conversion from a greenside bunker at the 18th in the final round of the Masters; the Northern Irishman's eagle two from more sand on the 10th at the Old Course during the third round of The Open that vaulted him into a solo lead; and you might even argue that Cameron Smith's nerveless putt around (rather than from) the Road Hole Bunker at the 17th the very next day added to the year's tale of sand trap excellence, not least because without it he would not have lifted the Claret Jug.

The Monaco Grand Prix is famous for both taking place in the middle of Monte Carlo and being a difficult circuit to overtake on. Is St Andrews the golfing equivalent? It needs no repeating that the Old Course starts and ends in the town, but it is less well-appreciated that Open winners on the course make fast starts and it is a **tricky business passing** them. Ahead of The 150th Open the previous 15 Old Course winners — a run heading all the way back to 1939 — had been within three shots of the lead after the first round and Smith maintained the trend. To put this unlikely run of stubborn pacesetters into perspective, in major championships held away from St Andrews in the 21st century, 53 of 86 winners were within three shots after the first round. A rate of 62 per cent against 100 per cent.

Buhai's first major championship triumph in the AIG Women's Open came just in the nick of time after she and playoff opponent In Gee Chun had found themselves journeying up and down Muirfield's 18th hole deep into the gathering gloom of Sunday night. Perhaps we can give the organisers some leeway in what, on the face of it, seems to have been an imprudent decision to start the final round in late afternoon. How so? Well, the other four women's majors have frequently required extra holes, yet this was the very first time the Women's Open wasn't settled in 72 holes since it became a major championship in 2001 and, in very stark contrast, since the start of that year there have been no fewer than 21 playoffs in the other 71 women's majors contested.

South Africa's Thriston Lawrence hit the heights in the DP World Tour's 2022 season claiming two victories on his way to being crowned Rookie of the Year and rarely has a phrase been quite so apt because the vast majority of the South African's **best golf came at altitude**.

On the high veldt around Johannesburg he claimed a win and another three top 15 finishes, he added victory in Crans-sur-Sierre at the European Masters, second place in Nairobi at the Kenyan Open and even a top 10 in the Czech Masters (only 388m above sea level but a factor).

In all, he made 22 starts at "normal" height earning six top 20s, two of them top 10s. But at altitude? Nine appearance, seven of them top 20s, six of those top 10s, including both wins. His adjusted stroke average was over five shots per tournament better in thin air (69.66 against 71.00). As if to rubber-stamp his preferences he opened the 2023 season with yet another win at altitude back in Johannesburg at the South African Open.

When Ireland's **Leona Maguire completed her breakthrough** victory on the LPGA Tour in February's Drive On Championship she pushed Lexi Thompson into second place. On the face of it, that one-two may not be especially noteworthy, but quietly the pair have been more closely linked throughout their careers than is often acknowledged.

They were born a mere three months apart either side of New Year 1995, made debuts in professional events at the age of 12, were on opposite sides at both the 2008 Junior Ryder Cup and 2009 Junior Solheim Cup, competed against each other at the 2010 Curtis Cup and were paired together in the first round of the 2011 Irish Open when 16 years old.

Their respective paths to the top of the game separated shortly after. Thompson won on the LPGA while still at school and then left the education system while Maguire took the alternative route of completing four years at Duke University. That they have both ultimately become LPGA winners is perhaps proof that there is no one set path to the top of the game.

"It was awesome," said Canada's Aaron Cockerill after he aced the par-three 13th hole in the DP World Tour's European Masters in August, adding: **"I've not had a hole-in-one in years."** Just seven days later, however, he had notched another, this time on the short 16th in the Made in Himmerland tournament.

Those bare details, extraordinary as they are, tell only half the story because fate was playing peculiar games with the card-chasing 30-year-old. After his first perfect blow, for example, he jokingly asked: "Where's the car?!" His actual prize was a rather underwhelming contribution to a life insurance policy. Worse was to come when his second ace left him bewildered and, ultimately, bereft.

He'd played the front nine of his first round in Denmark in three under but had lurched to one over before the hole-in-one, and after it he finished with a quadruple bogey and a bogey, whereupon "after some hole-in-one chatter in the recording area I forgot to sign my card and got DQ'd". So much for a hole-in-one representing good luck.

And so much for the notion that all elements of farce had been drained from Cockerill's end-of-season. Six weeks later he was preparing to play in Mallorca but his clubs were lost in Madrid. His six-month pregnant wife not only flew to the Spanish capital to fetch them the day before the first round, she even posted a video on Twitter of the clubs being loaded. "Refused to board the plane until I saw this," she wrote adding a crying-with-laughter emoji. The tears and the drama were all worth it. The lucky/unlucky Cockerill made the cut and with it confirmed his playing rights for 2023.

He might also reconsider his disappointment about the hole-in-one prize if he ever hears of the record five aces recorded at the KLPGA's Mediheal Hankook Ilbo Championship. Jae Hee Kim won a Maserati, Ree An Kim ₩20 million worth of jewellery and Jin Seon Han a set of golf clubs, but Yea Lin Kang and Seo Yeon Kwon got nothing because the sponsors had under-estimated the field's accuracy and ran out of prizes.

When Guido Migliozzi headed into the weekend of the Open de France 13 strokes behind the leader Rasmus Hojgaard he is unlikely to have been overly hopeful of lifting the trophy. However, the Dane's collapse, his own brilliant final round of 62 and the tricky nature of the course combined to permit exactly that scenario. It was the **largest 36-hole deficit overcome** on the DP World Tour in the 21st century and the first double-digit example since Ricardo Gonzalez in the 2003 Open de Madrid. There have been 21 instances of winners being eight or more strokes behind at the halfway stage of four-round events in the 21st century on the tour and Le Golf National has witnessed — or perhaps provoked — four of them. Not so much romantic as frantic weekends in Paris.

A notable comeback was also achieved on the PGA Tour when Canada's Adam Svensson emerged from outside the top 100 after 18 holes to win the RSM Classic. He was the first winner to overcome such a first-round leaderboard position handicap on the PGA Tour since Ian Poulter won the 2018 Houston Open.

What were the rounds of the year? The statistics reveal that we've already discussed one: Migliozzi's closing round in France which gained 9.83 strokes on the field making it the joint second best of 2022 on the DP World Tour (alongside Haotong Li's second-round 63 in the Dutch Open). They were only bettered by Cameron Tringale's 61 that gained 10.81 strokes on the field in the PGA Tour co-sanctioned Scottish Open; it was the year's best effort on both circuits. The data overlooks the second-round 67 which Justin Thomas posted on his way to victory in the PGA Championship, an effort that defied the wind and saw him maintain his challenge when the vast majority of morning starters fell from contention.

In the women's game, numbers and memories are in agreement because In Gee Chun's first-round eight-under-par 64 in the KPMG PGA Championship stood tall, gaining an enormous 11.02 strokes on the field. When she walked off the course the field average score was 76.01 and she bettered the next best morning-wave total by seven. It earned her a five-shot lead which she extended to an advantage of six by halfway, allowing her the rare privilege of taking 150 blows at the weekend (two 75s) and yet still claim a major championship (her third).

Campbell Rawson is **not your average halfway leader** of a professional tour event. The 34-year-old New Zealander relocated to Adelaide in his youth to take up Australian Rules Football, later turned to golf, was good enough to win the 2019 Victorian PGA

Championship on the PGA Tour of Australasia, but when that result failed to kickstart his career he turned in another direction entirely and became a stockbroker.

Perhaps inspired by the fine year his good friend Ryan Fox had enjoyed in Europe, Rawson took a few days leave in November to play in the 2022 edition of the Vic PGA yet his expectations were understandably low. "I get to play once a week, practise two hours a week if I'm lucky when my son's asleep on a Sunday, and this is just a privilege to be here and playing okay," he explained after surprising himself and the field with a nine-under-par 63 second round at Moonah Links which vaulted him into the halfway lead.

Alas, he closed 80-79 to end the week T51st but all was not lost. In April he is heading to Augusta National to follow Fox in his Masters debut. "Eight of us are going," he said. "All the boys who grew up together."

Be careful what you wish for? The Challenge Tour event named the Indoor Golf Group Challenge had to be reduced to 54 holes as a **consequence of inclement weather**.

Matt Cooper is a freelance golf journalist

The Rankings

Lydia Ko

Rolex Rankings

In 2020 Lydia Ko briefly dropped out of the top 50 on the Rolex Women's World Rankings for the first time in her professional career. Her renaissance since then has been remarkable. The Kiwi ended that year ranked 29th, moved up to third at the end of 2021 and returned to the world number one spot in November 2022. She first became the best player in the world as a 17-year-old in 2015 and, in two stints, was the number one for 104 weeks until June 2017. No one has regained the number one title after such a long gap since the Rankings began. "I'm very grateful to be world number one again," Ko said. "To be honest, I wasn't sure if I'd ever be back here again."

Ko won three times in 2022, including the CME Group Tour Championship, and was the Rolex LPGA Player of the Year. By entering 2023 at the top of the list, Ko overtook Inbee Park (106) and Yani Tseng (109) for total weeks as number one and lies behind only Lorena Ochoa (158) and Korea's Jin Young Ko (152). While Nelly Korda started the year as number one before suffering a blood clot in her left arm, Jin Young Ko returned to the top spot for 38 weeks although her form suffered due to a persistent wrist injury.

Atthaya Thitikul, at the age of 19, spent two weeks as world number one, the 16th player to achieve the feat, the second Thai after Ariya Jutanugarn, and the second youngest after Lydia Ko. Korda resumed top spot for a fortnight following her win at the Pelican Women's Championship before Lydia Ko usurped the American. Thitikul, with two wins as an LPGA rookie, had the biggest net points gain in 2022, followed by Miyuu Yamashita, a five-time winner in Japan, and In Gee Chun, who won the KPMG Women's PGA and had the biggest jump into the top 10. Sweden's Linn Grant, with six worldwide wins, moved from 259th to 26th over the year. Jin Young Ko and Nelly Korda were among those to lose most points over the year, along with Inbee Park and Sei Young Kim, who both fell out of the top 10.

The Rolex Rankings — developed at the World Congress of Women's Golf in May 2004 — is sanctioned by the main professional women's tours: the Ladies Professional Golf Association (and Symetra Tour); the Ladies European Tour (and Access Series); the Japan LPGA Tour (and Step Up Tour); the Korea LPGA Tour (and Dream Tour); the WPGA Tour of Australasia; the China LPGA Tour; and the Chinese Taipei LPGA Tour; as well as The R&A and the United States Golf Association. In 2023 the Thai LPGA will also be included.

The Rolex Rankings are updated and released weekly. The major golf tours developed the rankings and the protocol that governs it, while R2IT, an independent software development company, was retained to develop the software and maintain the rankings on a weekly basis.

Official events from all the tours are taken into account and points awarded according to strength of field, with the exception of the five major championships on the LPGA Tour, which have a fixed points distribution. The players' points averages are determined by taking the number of points awarded over a 104-week rolling period, with points awarded in the most recent 13-week period carrying a strong value, and then dividing by the number of tournaments played, with a minimum divisor of 35.

MOST WEEKS AT NUMBER ONE BY YEAR

			Weeks
2006	SWE	Annika Sorenstam	45
2007	MEX	Lorena Ochoa	37
2008	MEX	Lorena Ochoa	52
2009	MEX	Lorena Ochoa	52
2010	KOR	Jiyai Shin	19
2011	TPE	Yani Tseng	46
2012	TPE	Yani Tseng	53
2013	KOR	Inbee Park	38
2014	KOR	Inbee Park	31
2015	NZL	Lydia Ko	29
2016	NZL	Lydia Ko	52
2017	NZL	Lydia Ko	23
2018	CHN	Shanshan Feng	16
2019	KOR	Jin Young Ko	35
2020	KOR	Jin Young Ko	52
2021	KOR	Jin Young Ko	27
2022	KOR	Jin Young Ko	38

Final 2022 Rolex Women's World Golf Rankings

				Average Points	Events	Total Points	2022 Net Points
1	(3)	NZL	Lydia Ko	**7.60**	52	395.11	88.33
2	(1)	USA	Nelly Korda	**7.13**	41	292.30	-156.37
3	(19)	THA	Atthaya Thitikul	**6.37**	46	292.88	178.57
4	(7)	AUS	Minjee Lee	**6.17**	53	326.95	34.93
5	(2)	KOR	Jin Young Ko	**5.86**	44	257.72	-218.11
6	(12)	USA	Lexi Thompson	**5.24**	46	241.10	34.12
7	(10)	CAN	Brooke M Henderson	**5.15**	53	272.84	23.32
8	(35)	KOR	In Gee Chun	**4.65**	50	232.31	104.55
9	(9)	KOR	Hyo Joo Kim	**4.32**	49	211.84	-33.77
10	(6)	JPN	Nasa Hataoka	**4.05**	55	222.49	-60.39
11	(40)	IRL	Leona Maguire	**3.66**	55	201.39	77.44
12	(28)	FRA	Celine Boutier	**3.45**	57	196.80	18.85
13	(42)	USA	Jennifer Kupcho	**3.39**	56	189.71	66.12
14	(18)	KOR	Min Ji Park	**3.37**	58	195.37	-7.78
15	(57)	CHN	Xiyu Lin	**3.32**	50	166.13	68.09
16	(11)	USA	Danielle Kang	**3.28**	47	154.23	-71.14
17	(33)	ENG	Charley Hull	**3.17**	53	168.02	39.03
18	(21)	USA	Jessica Korda	**3.17**	41	129.82	-14.93
19	(26)	AUS	Hannah Green	**3.14**	52	163.43	13.19
20	(55)	KOR	Hye-Jin Choi	**3.10**	64	198.66	60.85
21	(4)	KOR	Sei Young Kim	**2.91**	50	145.26	-165.98
22	(14)	JPN	Ayaka Furue	**2.90**	74	214.88	-14.02
23	(64)	JPN	Miyuu Yamashita	**2.89**	78	225.38	134.05
24	(84)	RSA	Ashleigh Buhai	**2.87**	57	163.83	79.89
25	(29)	ENG	Georgia Hall	**2.77**	53	146.74	-12.29
26	(259)	SWE	Linn Grant	**2.74**	26	95.82	80.87
27	(44)	SWE	Madelene Sagstrom	**2.72**	53	144.14	26.74
28	(36)	USA	Megan Khang	**2.62**	51	133.59	13.78
29	(38)	JPN	Mao Saigo	**2.60**	73	189.89	56.18
30	(15)	SWE	Anna Nordqvist	**2.58**	57	147.27	-62.67
31	(136)	USA	Andrea Lee	**2.48**	49	121.56	90.74
32	(8)	JPN	Yuka Saso	**2.42**	56	135.55	-67.54
33	(81)	KOR	Su Ji Kim	**2.39**	64	152.86	62.30
34	(16)	JPN	Mone Inami	**2.39**	81	193.34	-58.38
35	(22)	USA	Ally Ewing	**2.31**	49	112.99	-51.66
36	(5)	KOR	Inbee Park	**2.29**	42	96.22	-197.65
37	(54)	MEX	Gaby Lopez	**2.25**	53	119.29	9.86
38	(17)	KOR	Jeongeun Lee[6]	**2.22**	55	122.08	-73.29
39	(546)	JPN	Haruka Kawasaki	**2.18**	34	76.26	72.19
40	(68)	USA	Marina Alex	**2.17**	47	102.06	21.04
41	(90)	SWE	Maja Stark	**2.13**	38	81.11	36.16
42	(37)	JPN	Hinako Shibuno	**2.13**	61	129.73	-26.89
43	(244)	USA	Lilia Vu	**2.13**	49	104.14	88.17
44	(43)	JPN	Yuna Nishimura	**2.11**	78	164.73	22.93
45	(323)	KOR	Yewon Lee	**2.06**	45	92.82	81.96
46	(49)	KOR	So Mi Lee	**2.06**	67	138.18	2.55
47	(47)	KOR	A Lim Kim	**2.02**	60	121.38	-10.26
48	(—)	USA	Allisen Corpuz	**2.02**	24	70.62	70.62
49	(31)	KOR	Hae Ran Ryu	**1.96**	67	131.01	-23.79
50	(20)	USA	Lizette Salas	**1.95**	52	101.49	-68.29

Figure in brackets indicates final position of 2021

				Average Points	Events	Total Points	2022 Net Points
51	(48)	USA	Mina Harigae	**1.94**	53	102.77	-2.58
52	(46)	ESP	Carlota Ciganda	**1.92**	62	119.21	-1.97
53	(50)	DEN	Nanna Koerstz Madsen	**1.89**	54	102.29	-9.93
54	(13)	THA	Patty Tavatanakit	**1.89**	51	96.60	-96.36
55	(72)	JPN	Minami Katsu	**1.88**	79	148.57	23.89
56	(32)	KOR	Hee Jeong Lim	**1.88**	66	123.75	-56.75
57	(77)	KOR	Eun-Hee Ji	**1.83**	50	91.66	14.54
58	(214)	RSA	Paula Reto	**1.83**	56	102.24	73.76
59	(123)	KOR	Ji Young Park	**1.78**	66	117.66	53.91
60	(111)	ENG	Jodi Ewart Shadoff	**1.75**	52	90.90	38.66
61	(89)	USA	Alison Lee	**1.74**	56	97.68	33.00
62	(61)	KOR	Narin An	**1.73**	58	100.47	-14.65
63	(71)	USA	Ryann O'Toole	**1.70**	52	88.59	6.55
64	(86)	JPN	Yuri Yoshida	**1.59**	84	133.78	59.14
65	(115)	KOR	Chella Choi	**1.59**	53	84.34	26.30
66	(51)	KOR	Hyun Kyung Park	**1.57**	66	103.56	-30.87
67	(106)	SLO	Pia Babnik	**1.56**	45	70.07	29.38
68	(53)	KOR	Jiyai Shin	**1.54**	59	91.12	-32.83
69	(62)	JPN	Sakura Koiwai	**1.54**	84	129.40	-19.97
70	(85)	KOR	Jung Min Hong	**1.52**	57	86.80	39.99
71	(70)	JPN	Momoko Ueda	**1.50**	68	101.97	-7.24
72	(319)	SCO	Gemma Dryburgh	**1.50**	50	74.82	59.11
73	(24)	THA	Ariya Jutanugarn	**1.47**	60	87.90	-91.40
74	(34)	THA	Moriya Jutanugarn	**1.46**	61	89.07	-55.65
75	(128)	USA	Cheyenne Knight	**1.46**	56	81.67	26.16
76	(379)	USA	Sophia Schubert	**1.44**	50	72.14	61.01
77	(100)	KOR	So Young Lee	**1.42**	64	91.14	11.28
78	(25)	KOR	So Yeon Ryu	**1.38**	50	69.24	-81.69
79	(121)	KOR	Yunji Jeong	**1.38**	66	91.32	47.28
80	(52)	GER	Caroline Masson	**1.35**	55	74.37	-38.15
81	(105)	KOR	Ga Young Lee	**1.35**	68	91.85	12.32
82	(60)	KOR	Amy Yang	**1.35**	49	65.94	-29.16
83	(131)	USA	Sarah Schmelzel	**1.34**	55	73.87	21.08
84	(102)	KOR	Han Sol Ji	**1.34**	66	88.54	9.35
85	(463)	JPN	Chisato Iwai	**1.34**	49	65.48	59.79
86	(294)	KOR	Ina Yoon	**1.30**	30	45.66	32.49
87	(76)	THA	Pajaree Anannarukarn	**1.30**	61	79.56	-5.00
88	(229)	FRA	Pauline Roussin	**1.30**	33	45.51	28.57
89	(133)	JPN	Kotone Hori	**1.28**	73	93.76	40.21
90	(209)	JPN	Nana Suganuma	**1.28**	70	89.61	51.69
91	(139)	KOR	Jin Hee Im	**1.24**	61	75.37	31.11
92	(58)	FIN	Matilda Castren	**1.20**	54	65.00	-25.06
93	(152)	JPN	Saiki Fujita	**1.19**	74	87.94	31.90
94	(79)	JPN	Sayaka Takahashi	**1.18**	81	95.20	-19.17
95	(118)	ENG	Bronte Law	**1.13**	59	66.56	6.95
96	(119)	JPN	Erika Kikuchi	**1.08**	74	80.27	7.65
97	(75)	AUS	Stephanie Kyriacou	**1.08**	58	62.65	8.33
98	(80)	KOR	Jenny Shin	**1.08**	55	59.21	-19.55
99	(59)	KOR	Da Yeon Lee	**1.07**	41	43.92	-63.13
100	(467)	JPN	Amiyu Ozeki	**1.06**	39	41.16	35.66

				Average Points	Events	Total Points	2022 Net Points
101	(65)	USA	Brittany Altomare	**1.04**	54	56.07	-40.66
102	(110)	KOR	Ji Hyun Oh	**1.04**	61	63.23	-6.01
103	(151)	KOR	Ye Rim Choi	**1.03**	69	70.76	18.25
104	(108)	MEX	Maria Fassi	**1.00**	50	50.08	-2.73
105	(372)	JPN	Miyu Sato	**0.99**	41	40.71	32.48
106	(82)	KOR	Ga Eun Song	**0.96**	66	63.31	12.56
107	(590)	KOR	Ji U Ko	**0.95**	41	39.13	35.64
108	(39)	USA	Yealimi Noh	**0.95**	60	57.06	-59.58
109	(66)	JPN	Ai Suzuki	**0.95**	71	67.30	-48.76
110	(125)	JPN	Nozomi Uetake	**0.94**	74	69.84	10.97
111	(94)	TPE	Wei-Ling Hsu	**0.94**	55	51.77	-21.70
112	(117)	JPN	Kana Mikashima	**0.94**	77	72.33	-6.52
113	(141)	KOR	A Yean Cho	**0.94**	68	63.87	3.59
114	(160)	JPN	Serena Aoki	**0.93**	81	75.48	18.31
115	(104)	KOR	Min Young Lee[2]	**0.93**	70	65.12	-19.68
116	(484)	KOR	Seo Yeon Kwon	**0.93**	45	41.64	36.47
117	(198)	KOR	Jin Seon Han	**0.93**	67	61.99	20.34
118	(69)	KOR	Seon Woo Bae	**0.92**	70	64.64	-52.95
119	(120)	THA	Wichanee Meechai	**0.92**	55	50.67	1.30
120	(196)	THA	Pornanong Phatlum	**0.91**	58	52.97	19.13
121	(265)	JPN	Akie Iwai	**0.91**	44	40.12	25.63
122	(857)	KOR	Min Ju Kim	**0.91**	40	36.37	35.13
123	(147)	KOR	Yu Jin Sung	**0.90**	67	60.36	9.63
124	(193)	CHN	Haruka Morita	**0.88**	72	63.66	19.49
125	(233)	SWE	Caroline Hedwall	**0.87**	43	37.23	15.32
126	(74)	DEN	Emily Kristine Pedersen	**0.86**	55	47.30	-27.62
127	(92)	JPN	Erika Hara	**0.86**	74	63.42	-33.15
128	(56)	USA	Stacy Lewis	**0.86**	52	44.50	-49.80
129	(127)	SUI	Albane Valenzuela	**0.85**	54	45.66	12.20
130	(598)	GER	Chiara Noja	**0.84**	27	29.44	26.01
131	(91)	USA	Lauren Stephenson	**0.83**	53	44.14	-22.25
132	(344)	SUI	Morgane Metraux	**0.83**	54	44.77	35.07
133	(144)	NIR	Stephanie Meadow	**0.83**	53	43.86	0.88
134	(390)	JPN	Rio Takeda	**0.83**	24	28.93	21.09
135	(27)	KOR	Ha Na Jang	**0.82**	61	50.19	-125.40
136	(174)	KOR	Min Song Ha	**0.81**	69	56.19	10.15
137	(97)	GER	Esther Henseleit	**0.81**	59	47.70	-17.17
138	(95)	USA	Angel Yin	**0.81**	56	45.16	-21.96
139	(279)	USA	Lucy Li	**0.81**	45	36.24	22.32
140	(99)	KOR	Jung Min Lee	**0.80**	65	52.28	-25.44
141	(513)	JPN	Shuri Sakuma	**0.80**	47	37.69	33.13
142	(614)	ESP	Ana Pelaez Trivino	**0.79**	23	27.51	24.34
143	(258)	KOR	Jeong Mee Hwang	**0.78**	68	53.12	32.90
144	(327)	JPN	Kana Nagai	**0.78**	80	62.43	38.36
145	(114)	USA	Lindsey Weaver-Wright	**0.78**	56	43.65	-11.67
146	(355)	CAN	Maude-Aimee Leblanc	**0.78**	47	36.59	26.07
147	(98)	JPN	Momoko Osato	**0.77**	84	64.40	-35.85
148	(155)	GER	Leonie Harm	**0.76**	40	30.23	3.43
149	(83)	USA	Elizabeth Szokol	**0.75**	42	31.44	-38.17
150	(308)	CHN	Yuting Shi	**0.75**	68	50.74	29.90

				Average Points	Events	Total Points	2022 Net Points
151	(405)	CHN	Ruoning Yin	**0.74**	26	25.96	18.70
152	(132)	JPN	Ayaka Watanabe	**0.74**	75	55.61	-8.06
153	(30)	USA	Austin Ernst	**0.73**	33	25.61	-114.30
154	(—)	JPN	Kokona Sakurai	**0.72**	24	25.14	25.14
155	(113)	KOR	Mi-Jeong Jeon	**0.71**	76	54.11	-22.41
156	(192)	KOR	Su Yeon Jang	**0.71**	64	45.55	5.77
157	(138)	KOR	Hee Ji Kim	**0.70**	59	41.22	10.68
158	(185)	JPN	Ayako Kimura	**0.70**	77	53.68	3.95
159	(263)	CZE	Klara Spilkova	**0.69**	43	29.48	14.10
160	(149)	KOR	Ye Sung Jun	**0.68**	67	45.49	9.66
161	(274)	KOR	Ah-Reum Hwang	**0.68**	67	45.26	18.42
162	(96)	CHN	Yu Liu	**0.67**	55	36.85	-36.32
163	(210)	KOR	Ji Won Hong	**0.66**	59	38.91	18.81
164	(103)	THA	Jasmine Suwannapura	**0.66**	59	38.82	-37.24
165	(177)	JPN	Mao Nozawa	**0.66**	82	53.88	6.71
166	(270)	USA	Lauren Coughlin	**0.66**	50	32.85	12.98
167	(306)	JPN	Kumiko Kaneda	**0.65**	64	41.89	17.53
168	(206)	RSA	Lee-Anne Pace	**0.65**	52	33.78	9.35
169	(253)	BEL	Manon De Roey	**0.65**	54	34.99	12.44
170	(194)	USA	Emma Talley	**0.65**	56	36.27	3.30
171	(195)	KOR	So Hyun Bae	**0.65**	66	42.72	21.05
172	(275)	SWE	Johanna Gustavsson	**0.65**	56	36.23	16.24
173	(285)	KOR	Sun Ju Ahn	**0.65**	33	22.60	8.90
174	(137)	GER	Olivia Cowan	**0.64**	48	30.84	-6.96
175	(429)	KOR	Da Som Ma	**0.64**	47	30.07	23.61
176	(218)	USA	Jennifer Chang	**0.64**	47	29.93	11.19
177	(460)	SWE	Frida Kinhult	**0.64**	52	33.10	27.37
178	(109)	FRA	Perrine Delacour	**0.62**	46	28.63	-30.67
179	(188)	USA	Annie Park	**0.62**	48	29.77	-0.95
180	(135)	KOR	Jeongeun Lee[5]	**0.62**	48	29.76	-10.04
181	(646)	AUS	Grace Kim	**0.62**	32	21.53	18.72
182	(428)	JPN	Momoko Kishibe	**0.60**	62	37.50	28.73
183	(45)	USA	Amy Olson	**0.60**	51	30.63	-89.58
184	(88)	AUS	Su Oh	**0.60**	59	35.33	-41.31
185	(199)	KOR	Haeji Kang	**0.59**	49	29.15	-0.69
186	(122)	KOR	Ju Young Pak	**0.59**	43	25.56	-39.36
187	(165)	AUS	Sarah Kemp	**0.59**	52	30.84	-5.34
188	(93)	KOR	Ji Yeong Kim[2]	**0.59**	69	40.76	-45.63
189	(175)	TPE	Pei-Ying Tsai	**0.59**	79	46.55	-4.14
190	(473)	JPN	Sae Ogura	**0.59**	47	27.65	22.26
191	(223)	KOR	Seung Yeon Lee	**0.59**	68	39.91	5.83
192	(87)	USA	Brittany Lincicome	**0.58**	36	20.75	-25.81
193	(126)	IND	Aditi Ashok	**0.58**	61	35.13	-21.58
194	(464)	JPN	Miyu Goto	**0.57**	65	37.24	31.09
195	(391)	ECU	Daniela Darquea	**0.56**	49	27.61	17.64
196	(568)	JPN	Shiho Kuwaki	**0.56**	45	25.31	21.53
197	(178)	TPE	Teresa Lu	**0.56**	68	38.00	-8.38
198	(142)	JPN	Ritsuko Ryu	**0.56**	76	42.43	-17.01
199	(328)	KOR	Hyo Ju You	**0.56**	57	31.81	21.18
200	(107)	KOR	Sung Hyun Park	**0.55**	47	25.90	-28.30

				Average Points	Events	Total Points	2022 Net Points
201	(572)	JPN	Miyuu Abe	**0.55**	50	27.49	23.74
202	(249)	JPN	Mami Fukuda	**0.55**	74	40.49	8.88
203	(201)	KOR	Yeun Jung Seo	**0.54**	66	35.35	-4.49
204	(1067)	MAR	Ines Laklalech	**0.53**	18	18.69	18.12
205	(157)	JPN	Shina Kanazawa	**0.53**	73	38.93	-13.85
206	(264)	JPN	Shoko Sasaki	**0.53**	77	40.75	9.67
207	(241)	KOR	Eun Woo Choi	**0.53**	68	35.87	5.33
208	(124)	ENG	Alice Hewson	**0.52**	55	28.65	-4.61
209	(191)	USA	Gerina Piller	**0.52**	44	22.81	-10.30
210	(318)	ENG	Liz Young	**0.52**	47	24.26	12.47
211	(603)	KOR	Chae Eun Lee[2]	**0.52**	55	28.38	23.78
212	(—)	NZL	Momoka Kobori	**0.52**	25	18.05	18.05
213	(377)	USA	Amanda Doherty	**0.51**	47	24.20	16.02
214	(112)	JPN	Eri Okayama	**0.50**	76	38.28	-40.83
215	(197)	KOR	Jae Hee Kim	**0.50**	61	30.47	8.98
216	(359)	SWE	Jessica Karlsson	**0.50**	33	17.48	8.74
217	(256)	KOR	Seul Gi Jeong	**0.50**	64	31.84	4.00
218	(217)	KOR	Bo Mi Kwak	**0.49**	66	32.52	-1.29
219	(—)	JPN	Kotoko Uchida	**0.49**	41	20.11	20.11
220	(63)	ENG	Melissa Reid	**0.49**	43	21.05	-66.96
221	(246)	USA	Caroline Inglis	**0.49**	47	22.79	7.01
222	(497)	JPN	Nanako Ueno	**0.48**	51	24.66	19.67
223	(204)	MAS	Kelly Tan	**0.48**	47	22.60	-5.22
224	(606)	KOR	Carrie Park	**0.48**	32	16.82	13.51
225	(649)	KOR	Uh Jin Seo	**0.48**	45	21.54	18.75
226	(370)	KOR	Hee Won Na	**0.48**	64	30.60	15.50
227	(148)	KOR	Se Lin Hyun	**0.47**	68	32.03	-4.04
228	(363)	KOR	Eun Hye Jo	**0.47**	48	22.54	12.23
229	(262)	ARG	Magdalena Simmermacher	**0.47**	55	25.74	4.77
230	(162)	JPN	Lala Anai	**0.47**	82	38.35	-21.43
231	(159)	JPN	Yui Kawamoto	**0.47**	72	33.62	-17.01
232	(869)	JPN	Haruka Amamoto	**0.47**	36	16.78	15.59
233	(458)	JPN	Fumika Kawagishi	**0.46**	74	34.32	25.28
234	(171)	KOR	Seung Hui Ro	**0.46**	68	31.50	-0.05
235	(298)	TPE	Peiyun Chien	**0.46**	54	24.89	5.09
236	(166)	KOR	Song Yi Ahn	**0.46**	64	29.46	-15.13
237	(407)	RSA	Nicole Garcia	**0.46**	42	19.31	12.15
238	(212)	SWE	Linnea Strom	**0.46**	59	27.01	-5.41
239	(331)	AUS	Whitney Hillier	**0.46**	57	25.99	11.98
240	(129)	TPE	Min Lee	**0.45**	50	22.72	-19.53
241	(134)	KOR	Da Been Heo	**0.45**	65	29.32	-29.98
242	(248)	CHN	Muni He	**0.45**	47	21.20	2.36
243	(245)	CHN	Ruixin Liu	**0.45**	46	20.68	1.17
244	(855)	KOR	Seo Yeon Yoo[2]	**0.45**	32	15.69	14.45
245	(41)	GER	Sophia Popov	**0.45**	48	21.41	-97.92
246	(—)	THA	Jaravee Boonchant	**0.44**	23	15.56	15.56
247	(296)	FIN	Ursula Wikstrom	**0.44**	50	22.00	6.27
248	(230)	KOR	Min Kyung Choi	**0.44**	62	27.18	-2.73
249	(228)	KOR	Hana Lee	**0.44**	63	27.55	10.58
250	(164)	KOR	Hae Rym Kim	**0.43**	64	27.44	-19.83

				Average Points	Events	Total Points	2022 Net Points
251	(657)	CZE	Sara Kouskova	**0.43**	20	14.99	12.27
252	(184)	KOR	Jee Hyun Ahn	**0.42**	57	24.15	-9.54
253	(404)	ENG	Charlotte Thomas	**0.42**	33	14.57	7.30
254	(227)	JPN	Nanoko Hayashi	**0.42**	65	26.99	-2.21
255	(202)	NED	Anne van Dam	**0.41**	48	19.75	-14.02
256	(749)	KOR	Yebeen Sohn	**0.41**	40	16.36	14.36
257	(220)	JPN	Yuka Yasuda	**0.41**	71	28.94	2.94
258	(189)	JPN	Shiho Oyama	**0.41**	39	15.83	-19.36
259	(101)	USA	Jennifer Song	**0.41**	50	20.30	-42.06
260	(412)	CHN	Xiaowen Yin	**0.41**	24	14.20	7.12
261	(314)	JPN	Sakura Yokomine	**0.40**	42	17.01	2.41
262	(647)	ITA	Virginia Elena Carta	**0.40**	28	14.15	11.34
263	(349)	KOR	You Min Hwang	**0.40**	17	14.04	4.65
264	(281)	KOR	Ji Min Jung[2]	**0.40**	60	23.88	8.86
265	(153)	KOR	Ji Hyun Kim	**0.40**	70	27.66	-24.21
266	(1254)	KOR	Hyejun Park	**0.40**	30	13.83	13.58
267	(395)	ENG	Meghan MacLaren	**0.39**	56	22.10	10.74
268	(261)	JPN	Chie Arimura	**0.39**	69	27.06	-1.52
269	(146)	AUS	Gabriela Ruffels	**0.39**	43	16.82	-11.37
270	(205)	JPN	Miki Sakai	**0.39**	82	31.88	-15.76
271	(705)	USA	Gina Kim	**0.39**	26	13.59	11.28
272	(254)	USA	Lindy Duncan	**0.39**	50	19.36	-2.68
273	(219)	USA	Dana Finkelstein	**0.39**	44	17.03	-8.05
274	(388)	CHN	Liqi Zeng	**0.39**	15	13.54	5.65
275	(329)	JPN	Mizuki Oide	**0.39**	71	27.45	6.79
276	(291)	AUT	Christine Wolf	**0.38**	42	16.03	-1.95
277	(232)	WAL	Lydia Hall	**0.38**	54	20.56	-1.06
278	(653)	KOR	Su Yeon Bae	**0.38**	49	18.61	15.86
279	(156)	DEN	Nicole Broch Estrup	**0.38**	48	18.15	-21.47
280	(1063)	JPN	Mirai Hamasaki	**0.38**	31	13.13	12.56
281	(187)	FIN	Sanna Nuutinen	**0.37**	58	21.69	-16.73
282	(143)	ESP	Azahara Munoz	**0.37**	36	13.44	-35.09
283	(208)	KOR	Woo Jeong Kim	**0.37**	67	24.88	-11.93
284	(172)	SWE	Pernilla Lindberg	**0.37**	50	18.47	-18.45
285	(302)	KOR	Gyeol Park	**0.37**	66	24.34	1.31
286	(180)	KOR	Chae Yoon Park	**0.37**	67	24.68	-16.75
287	(236)	TPE	Chia Yen Wu	**0.37**	24	12.83	-3.67
288	(315)	JPN	Rumi Yoshiba	**0.36**	80	28.99	3.00
289	(536)	KOR	Jeongmin Moon	**0.36**	37	13.39	9.12
290	(378)	ENG	Gabriella Cowley	**0.36**	52	18.78	8.06
291	(282)	KOR	Joo Mi Lee	**0.36**	62	22.30	8.51
292	(382)	AUS	Karis Davidson	**0.36**	27	12.50	3.16
293	(299)	KOR	Yeon Ju Jung	**0.36**	64	22.79	0.06
294	(222)	KOR	Ji Su Kim	**0.36**	67	23.85	0.13
295	(396)	FIN	Tiia Koivisto	**0.35**	54	19.02	7.72
296	(703)	WAL	Becky Brewerton	**0.35**	36	12.67	10.35
297	(335)	JPN	Hana Wakimoto	**0.35**	69	24.24	3.23
298	(268)	JPN	Hina Arakaki	**0.35**	73	25.57	-3.83
299	(284)	KOR	Hye Lim Jo	**0.35**	60	20.98	3.74
300	(190)	JPN	Asuka Kashiwabara	**0.35**	80	27.95	-23.21

YEAR-END TOP 10s

2006
1 Sorenstam
2 Ochoa
3 Webb
4 Kerr
5 Inkster
6 A Miyazato
7 Creamer
8 J Jang
9 Ohyama
10 Hurst

2007
1 Ochoa
2 Pettersen
3 Webb
4 Sorenstam
5 Creamer
6 Kerr
7 Jy Shin
8 Inkster
9 MH Kim
10 Pak

2008
1 Ochoa
2 Tseng
3 Sorenstam
4 Creamer
5 Pettersen
6 Jy Shin
7 Kerr
8 Alfredsson
9 Stanford
10 Webb

2009
1 Ochoa
2 Jy Shin
3 Pettersen
4 Kerr
5 Tseng
6 Creamer
7 Nordqvist
8 A Miyazato
9 Stanford
10 Wie

2010
1 Jy Shin
2 Kerr
3 Pettersen
4 NY Choi
5 Tseng
6 A Miyazato
7 IK Kim
8 SJ Ahn
9 SH Kim
10 Wie

2011
1 Tseng
2 Pettersen
3 NY Choi
4 Kerr
5 Creamer
6 SJ Ahn
7 Jy Shin
8 IK Kim
9 A Miyazato
10 Lewis

2012
1 Tseng
2 NY Choi
3 Lewis
4 I Park
5 Feng
6 Pettersen
7 SY Ryu
8 Jy Shin
9 A Miyazato
10 M Miyazato

2013
1 I Park
2 Pettersen
3 Lewis
4 L Ko
5 SY Ryu
6 Feng
7 NY Choi
8 Webb
9 Thompson
10 IK Kim

2014
1 I Park
2 L Ko
3 Lewis
4 Pettersen
5 Feng
6 Wie
7 SY Ryu
8 HJ Kim
9 Webb
10 Thompson

2015
1 L Ko
2 I Park
3 Lewis
4 Thompson
5 SY Ryu
6 Feng
7 SY Kim
8 A Yang
9 IK Kim
10 Chun

2016
1 L Ko
2 A Jutanugarn
3 Chun
4 Feng
5 Thompson
6 SY Kim
7 HN Jang
8 Henderson
9 SY Ryu
10 SH Park

2017
1 Feng
2 SH Park
3 SY Ryu
4 Thompson
5 Chun
6 A Jutanugarn
7 Nordqvist
8 IK Kim
9 L Ko
10 Kerr

2018
1 A Jutanugarn
2 SH Park
3 SY Ryu
4 I Park
5 Thompson
6 Mj Lee
7 Hataoka
8 Hall
9 Henderson
10 JY Ko

2019
1 JY Ko
2 SH Park
3 N Korda
4 Kang
5 SY Kim
6 Hataoka
7 J Lee[6]
8 Henderson
9 Mj Lee
10 Thompson

2020
1 JY Ko
2 SY Kim
3 I Park
4 N Korda
5 Kang
6 Henderson
7 Hataoka
8 Mj Lee
9 HJ Kim
10 SH Park

2021
1 N Korda
2 JY Ko
3 L Ko
4 SY Kim
5 I Park
6 Hataoka
7 Mj Lee
8 Saso
9 HJ Kim
10 Henderson

2022
1 L Ko
2 N Korda
3 Thitikul
4 Mj Lee
5 JY Ko
6 Thompson
7 Henderson
8 Chun
9 HJ Kim
10 Hataoka

Official World Golf Ranking

Rory McIlroy's third win of the year at the CJ Cup in October took him back to world number one for the first time since 2020 and the ninth time in his career. Only Tiger Woods and Greg Norman, with 11 times each, have had more stints in top spot. "I've worked so hard over the last 12 months to get back to this place," said McIlroy, whose consistency across the year included top-10 finishes at each of the major championships.

Earlier in the year Scottie Scheffler became the 25th different player to become world number one with his third win in five starts at the WGC Dell World Match Play. The American went on to win the Masters and stayed number one for 30 weeks, earning him the McCormack Award as the player who had most weeks on top of the OWGR during the year.

Scheffler had the biggest net gain in points in 2022, ahead of Cameron Young and exciting Korean Joohyung Kim, who both rose from the 130s at the start of the year into the top 20. Cameron Smith, the Open and Players champion, jumped from 21st to third, although many of his colleagues who joined the LIV Golf Invitational Series fell down the Ranking. The OWGR accepted an application to join from LIV Golf, although whether a league only operating limited-field events over 54 holes with no cut, and no open qualifying system, could meet the Ranking's criteria was being evaluated.

The McCormack Award was first presented to Tiger Woods in 1998, who kept it to himself for 13 years. The idea to reward the player who spent most weeks as the number one in any given year was proposed by then PGA Tour Commissioner Tim Finchem, with the name recognising the late Mark H McCormack's vision and dedication in establishing and administering the World Ranking system.

The Ranking was launched at the 1986 Masters, since when 25 players have been the number one. There is a minimum divisor of 40 events and a maximum divisor of 52 events. Enhancements to the strength of field calculation and the points distribution for each tournament were announced in 2021 for implementation in August 2022. Strokes gained data from every player is now used to evaluate each tournament's Total Field Rating, with minimum values removed for all but the major championships and The Players.

A forerunner world ranking appeared in *Mark H McCormack's World of Professional Golf* prior to 1986.

MOST WEEKS AT NUMBER ONE BY YEAR

			Weeks				Weeks
1986	ESP	Seve Ballesteros	20	2005	USA	Tiger Woods	38
1987	AUS	Greg Norman	51	2006	USA	Tiger Woods	52
1988	AUS	Greg Norman	44	2007	USA	Tiger Woods	52
1989	ESP	Seve Ballesteros	31	2008	USA	Tiger Woods	52
1990	AUS	Greg Norman	46	2009	USA	Tiger Woods	52
1991	WAL	Ian Woosnam	39	2010	USA	Tiger Woods	43
1992	ENG	Nick Faldo	25	2011	ENG	Luke Donald	32
1993	ENG	Nick Faldo	52	2012	NIR	Rory McIlroy	28
1994	AUS	Greg Norman	27	2013	USA	Tiger Woods	41
1995	AUS	Greg Norman	29	2014	NIR	Rory McIlroy	22
1996	AUS	Greg Norman	52	2015	NIR	Rory McIlroy	34
1997	AUS	Greg Norman	40	2016	AUS	Jason Day	41
1998	USA	Tiger Woods	43	2017	USA	Dustin Johnson	46
1999	USA	Tiger Woods	38	2018	USA	Dustin Johnson	35
2000	USA	Tiger Woods	52	2019	USA	Brooks Koepka	33
2001	USA	Tiger Woods	52	2020	USA	Dustin Johnson	19
2002	USA	Tiger Woods	52	2021	ESP	Jon Rahm	27
2003	USA	Tiger Woods	52	2022	ESP	Scottie Scheffler	30
2004	USA	Tiger Woods	35				

Known as the McCormack Award since 1998

Final 2022 Official World Golf Ranking

				Average Points	Events	Total Points	2022 Net Points	Strokes Gained Rating
1	(9)	NIR	Rory McIlroy	**8.6456**	46	397.70	121.18	2.5724
2	(12)	USA	Scottie Scheffler	**8.4072**	52	437.17	173.07	2.1270
3	(21)	AUS	Cameron Smith	**7.5653**	39	302.61	104.27	1.9278
4	(4)	USA	Patrick Cantlay	**7.2630**	38	290.52	32.04	2.2583
5	(1)	ESP	Jon Rahm	**6.5331**	44	287.46	-112.95	2.3581
6	(6)	USA	Xander Schauffele	**6.1889**	43	266.12	-21.38	2.0769
7	(34)	USA	Will Zalatoris	**5.8026**	44	255.31	118.55	1.7863
8	(7)	USA	Justin Thomas	**5.4133**	45	243.60	-55.98	1.9529
9	(24)	ENG	Matt Fitzpatrick	**5.2688**	50	263.44	50.00	1.7458
10	(8)	NOR	Viktor Hovland	**5.2280**	52	271.86	-57.52	1.7636
11	(2)	USA	Collin Morikawa	**4.9248**	46	226.54	-211.33	1.4842
12	(15)	USA	Tony Finau	**4.8125**	52	250.25	-3.79	1.8194
13	(11)	USA	Sam Burns	**4.4873**	49	219.88	-24.13	1.5845
14	(14)	USA	Jordan Spieth	**4.4049**	44	193.82	-26.66	1.2756
15	(131)	KOR	Joohyung Kim	**4.2657**	44	187.69	135.67	1.1253
16	(134)	USA	Cameron Young	**3.9516**	50	197.58	146.08	1.2972
17	(35)	USA	Max Homa	**3.8992**	48	187.16	42.94	1.4582
18	(23)	USA	Billy Horschel	**3.7573**	50	187.87	-28.14	1.2822
19	(26)	KOR	Sungjae Im	**3.5801**	56	186.17	-21.01	1.6548
20	(44)	IRL	Shane Lowry	**3.5152**	49	172.24	45.44	1.3924
21	(18)	JPN	Hideki Matsuyama	**3.4908**	47	164.07	-80.45	1.4605
22	(31)	CHI	Joaquin Niemann	**3.3011**	46	151.85	-7.44	1.5370
23	(40)	ENG	Tommy Fleetwood	**3.0115**	52	156.60	30.23	1.2881
24	(61)	USA	Brian Harman	**3.0089**	51	153.46	50.22	1.2233
25	(87)	USA	Keegan Bradley	**2.8246**	45	127.11	48.03	1.2450
26	(22)	ENG	Tyrrell Hatton	**2.7977**	48	134.29	-58.38	1.3443
27	(214)	AUT	Sepp Straka	**2.7196**	62	141.42	98.99	0.1850
28	(213)	NZL	Ryan Fox	**2.6927**	47	126.56	89.40	0.6256
29	(72)	IRL	Seamus Power	**2.6904**	48	129.14	57.03	1.1116
30	(57)	USA	Russell Henley	**2.5340**	45	114.03	15.10	1.1956
31	(42)	USA	Kevin Kisner	**2.5166**	46	115.76	-7.03	0.3440
32	(17)	MEX	Abraham Ancer	**2.5051**	46	115.24	-137.16	1.1108
33	(66)	USA	Aaron Wise	**2.4670**	46	113.48	28.66	1.2954
34	(38)	CAN	Corey Conners	**2.4347**	52	126.60	-10.82	1.2849
35	(46)	AUS	Adam Scott	**2.4278**	43	104.40	8.26	1.0277
36	(110)	USA	Tom Hoge	**2.3928**	62	124.43	50.89	0.9487
37	(65)	BEL	Thomas Pieters	**2.3921**	41	98.08	22.58	0.9957
38	(63)	KOR	Kyoung-Hoon Lee	**2.3452**	55	121.95	22.79	0.7961
39	(71)	SWE	Alex Noren	**2.3384**	50	116.92	22.48	1.3495
40	(32)	USA	Talor Gooch	**2.2381**	43	96.24	-54.53	1.2014
41	(3)	USA	Dustin Johnson	**2.2092**	32	88.37	-196.44	1.4901
42	(250)	USA	Kurt Kitayama	**2.1950**	50	109.75	78.61	0.4352
43	(381)	USA	Sahith Theegala	**2.1793**	53	113.32	96.28	0.6999
44	(98)	CHI	Mito Pereira	**2.1255**	50	106.28	26.48	1.1246
45	(94)	USA	Harold Varner III	**2.1180**	45	95.31	14.55	1.0988
46	(39)	CAN	Mackenzie Hughes	**1.9680**	55	102.34	-30.59	0.5694
47	(20)	USA	Jason Kokrak	**1.9645**	41	80.55	-131.22	0.8258
48	(163)	POL	Adrian Meronk	**1.9417**	49	95.14	44.96	0.5047
49	(29)	USA	Kevin Na	**1.9305**	37	77.22	-99.73	0.9704
50	(10)	RSA	Louis Oosthuizen	**1.9138**	31	76.55	-151.41	1.4431

Figure in brackets indicates final position of 2021

				Average Points	Events	Total Points	2022 Net Points	Strokes Gained Rating
51	(19)	USA	Daniel Berger	**1.8864**	32	75.46	-110.86	1.5282
52	(16)	USA	Brooks Koepka	**1.8849**	33	75.40	-119.66	0.6733
53	(174)	USA	JT Poston	**1.8010**	56	93.65	42.83	0.5777
54	(193)	USA	Scott Stallings	**1.7760**	54	92.35	48.62	0.6531
55	(67)	RSA	Dean Burmester	**1.7675**	56	91.91	-5.63	0.6031
56	(49)	AUS	Min Woo Lee	**1.7400**	48	83.52	-10.95	0.3742
57	(13)	USA	Harris English	**1.7311**	40	69.25	-166.94	0.4832
58	(28)	ENG	Paul Casey	**1.7241**	31	68.96	-107.20	1.3116
59	(89)	USA	Keith Mitchell	**1.7225**	50	86.13	3.92	0.9579
60	(41)	AUS	Lucas Herbert	**1.6912**	48	81.18	-18.91	0.6221
61	(69)	USA	Maverick McNealy	**1.6768**	50	83.84	-8.23	1.0947
62	(361)	USA	Taylor Montgomery	**1.6719**	47	78.58	59.97	0.9379
63	(230)	RSA	Thriston Lawrence	**1.6215**	50	81.08	49.89	0.1443
64	(359)	USA	Davis Riley	**1.6171**	57	84.09	60.12	0.5467
65	(181)	CAN	Adam Svensson	**1.5878**	57	82.57	37.81	0.3790
66	(51)	USA	Cameron Tringale	**1.5741**	48	75.56	-30.84	0.6674
67	(5)	USA	Bryson DeChambeau	**1.5739**	30	62.96	-200.72	0.8445
68	(172)	JPN	Kazuki Higa	**1.5605**	52	81.15	38.71	-0.0314
69	(48)	RSA	Christiaan Bezuidenhout	**1.5517**	52	80.69	-40.90	0.9028
70	(55)	SCO	Robert MacIntyre	**1.5382**	52	79.99	-21.26	0.4896
71	(79)	AUS	Cam Davis	**1.5328**	52	79.71	-5.35	0.7698
72	(25)	USA	Patrick Reed	**1.5294**	49	74.94	-135.86	0.5990
73	(198)	ESP	Adrian Otaegui	**1.5244**	54	79.27	34.31	0.3820
74	(150)	CAN	Adam Hadwin	**1.5229**	52	79.19	22.66	0.7818
75	(362)	ESP	Pablo Larrazabal	**1.5223**	42	63.94	43.05	-0.3692
76	(43)	ENG	Justin Rose	**1.5178**	37	60.71	-44.43	0.8338
77	(141)	ESP	Adri Arnaus	**1.5067**	50	75.34	17.52	-0.1025
78	(246)	ENG	Jordan Smith	**1.4984**	51	76.42	38.37	0.8117
79	(156)	USA	Andrew Putnam	**1.4980**	60	77.90	21.39	0.7290
80	(179)	USA	Denny McCarthy	**1.4806**	57	76.99	28.05	0.8748
81	(59)	COL	Sebastian Munoz	**1.4775**	54	76.83	-27.87	0.7789
82	(52)	KOR	Si Woo Kim	**1.4703**	59	76.46	-35.90	0.7313
83	(91)	BEL	Thomas Detry	**1.4659**	54	76.23	-5.45	0.4020
84	(36)	AUS	Marc Leishman	**1.4580**	44	64.15	-62.15	0.6543
85	(92)	ARG	Emiliano Grillo	**1.4572**	55	75.77	-5.83	0.6378
86	(291)	USA	JJ Spaun	**1.4560**	57	75.71	44.53	0.6170
87	(114)	USA	Matt Kuchar	**1.4481**	43	62.27	-3.79	0.9208
88	(90)	USA	Joel Dahmen	**1.4451**	51	73.70	-5.00	0.6039
89	(95)	USA	Chris Kirk	**1.4239**	50	71.19	3.00	0.6527
90	(74)	ENG	Richard Bland	**1.4022**	41	57.49	-25.41	0.1090
91	(109)	ZIM	Scott Vincent	**1.3949**	45	62.77	-11.00	-0.0997
92	(321)	USA	Alex Smalley	**1.3942**	46	64.13	42.15	0.6898
93	(205)	ENG	Callum Shinkwin	**1.3526**	43	58.16	22.48	0.1140
94	(278)	IND	Anirban Lahiri	**1.3513**	45	60.81	34.90	0.4023
95	(151)	USA	Luke List	**1.3453**	56	69.96	11.85	0.2802
96	(126)	ENG	Danny Willett	**1.3370**	52	69.52	0.79	0.2699
97	(251)	USA	Matthew NeSmith	**1.3342**	55	69.38	31.75	0.4705
98	(105)	USA	Troy Merritt	**1.3127**	57	68.26	-6.65	0.4746
99	(117)	USA	Gary Woodland	**1.3030**	48	62.54	-2.54	0.5964
100	(252)	USA	Trey Mullinax	**1.2844**	53	66.79	37.86	0.0936

				Average Points	Events	Total Points	2022 Net Points	Strokes Gained Rating
101	(223)	THA	Sadom Kaewkanjana	**1.2725**	28	50.90	19.08	0.0756
102	(96)	DEN	Rasmus Hojgaard	**1.2639**	51	64.46	-6.65	0.4111
103	(85)	USA	Rickie Fowler	**1.2607**	44	55.47	-14.15	0.4132
104	(159)	RSA	Oliver Bekker	**1.2472**	59	64.86	11.71	-0.0854
105	(120)	USA	Lucas Glover	**1.2457**	53	64.78	-4.17	0.0715
106	(226)	CAN	Taylor Pendrith	**1.2433**	46	57.19	17.02	0.6796
107	(81)	FRA	Victor Perez	**1.2376**	48	59.41	-18.17	0.0945
108	(127)	USA	Brendon Todd	**1.2310**	50	61.55	-7.07	0.6334
109	(97)	JPN	Rikuya Hoshino	**1.2301**	51	62.73	-1.88	0.1080
110	(104)	AUS	Matt Jones	**1.2272**	43	52.77	-23.58	0.2579
111	(115)	ENG	Sam Horsfield	**1.2126**	33	48.51	-13.03	0.4871
112	(123)	AUS	Jason Day	**1.1870**	39	47.48	-9.02	0.8228
113	(45)	ESP	Sergio Garcia	**1.1860**	38	47.44	-69.61	1.1002
114	(1744)	USA	Ben Griffin	**1.1754**	33	47.01	47.01	0.1214
115	(675)	USA	Justin Suh	**1.1621**	43	49.97	43.12	0.1989
116	(577)	JPN	Yuto Katsuragawa	**1.1581**	45	52.11	42.96	-0.1828
117	(358)	CHN	Carl Yuan	**1.1549**	42	48.51	29.65	0.2455
118	(99)	JPN	Yuki Inamori	**1.1469**	54	59.64	-1.07	-0.2810
119	(162)	USA	Hudson Swafford	**1.1446**	43	49.22	-2.18	0.0444
120	(102)	USA	Brendan Steele	**1.1369**	44	50.02	-18.34	0.4966
121	(121)	USA	Taylor Moore	**1.1229**	54	58.39	-1.01	0.4469
122	(64)	RSA	Erik van Rooyen	**1.1151**	48	53.52	-45.11	-0.0689
123	(58)	AUT	Bernd Wiesberger	**1.1067**	40	44.27	-52.58	0.5850
124	(73)	RSA	Shaun Norris	**1.1050**	49	54.14	-34.81	-0.4223
125	(27)	USA	Webb Simpson	**1.1015**	40	44.06	-111.83	0.5710
126	(88)	ITA	Guido Migliozzi	**1.0873**	54	56.54	-19.63	-0.4978
127	(139)	JPN	Shugo Imahira	**1.0861**	51	55.39	2.69	-0.5201
128	(257)	KOR	Bio Kim	**1.0795**	47	50.73	22.73	-0.4709
129	(197)	USA	Chez Reavie	**1.0792**	55	56.12	10.90	0.0898
130	(83)	VEN	Jhonattan Vegas	**1.0726**	43	46.12	-33.08	0.7338
131	(384)	USA	Will Gordon	**1.0699**	56	55.63	37.44	0.0739
132	(147)	JPN	Mikumu Horikawa	**1.0672**	49	52.29	2.33	-0.3044
133	(77)	USA	Kevin Streelman	**1.0660**	55	55.43	-35.91	0.3353
134	(93)	DEN	Nicolai Hojgaard	**1.0583**	50	52.91	-17.68	-0.4176
135	(101)	ENG	Aaron Rai	**1.0548**	58	54.85	-19.58	0.4844
136	(290)	GER	Yannik Paul	**1.0443**	51	53.26	28.21	0.0614
137	(303)	SCO	Ewen Ferguson	**1.0322**	55	53.68	24.57	-0.2782
138	(659)	ENG	Benjamin Taylor	**1.0258**	50	51.29	44.18	-0.0480
139	(207)	KOR	Seonghyeon Kim	**1.0228**	47	48.07	14.60	-0.0095
140	(138)	JPN	Tomoharu Otsuki	**1.0187**	52	52.97	-2.34	-0.5337
141	(558)	JPN	Kaito Onishi	**1.0175**	40	40.70	31.19	-0.3919
142	(116)	FRA	Antoine Rozner	**1.0162**	54	52.84	-13.90	0.1332
143	(54)	ENG	Ian Poulter	**1.0150**	43	43.64	-66.68	0.6098
144	(432)	DEN	Thorbjorn Olesen	**1.0102**	42	42.43	28.12	-0.0706
145	(62)	USA	Chan Kim	**1.0101**	46	46.47	-32.51	-0.0671
146	(460)	CHN	Haotong Li	**1.0022**	38	40.09	26.31	-0.8803
147	(82)	USA	Bubba Watson	**0.9961**	26	39.84	-26.76	0.8648
148	(897)	RSA	MJ Daffue	**0.9954**	39	39.82	36.08	0.0274
149	(196)	USA	Patrick Rodgers	**0.9915**	63	51.56	6.32	0.6777
150	(351)	AUS	Brad Kennedy	**0.9892**	44	43.53	24.19	-0.1871

				Average Points	Events	Total Points	2022 Net Points	Strokes Gained Rating
151	(30)	USA	Matthew Wolff	**0.9753**	31	39.01	-93.94	-0.1280
152	(368)	SCO	Richie Ramsay	**0.9750**	53	50.70	28.67	0.1489
153	(50)	JPN	Takumi Kanaya	**0.9636**	50	48.18	-41.34	-0.2654
154	(53)	USA	Stewart Cink	**0.9586**	50	47.93	-48.64	0.1621
155	(84)	USA	Cameron Champ	**0.9562**	45	43.03	-30.23	-0.1634
156	(60)	RSA	Garrick Higgo	**0.9554**	56	49.68	-53.97	-0.6818
157	(354)	USA	Paul Haley II	**0.9531**	51	48.61	29.62	-0.0952
158	(494)	ENG	Callum Tarren	**0.9511**	55	49.46	36.02	0.1968
159	(408)	USA	Tyson Alexander	**0.9472**	49	46.41	30.37	-0.6067
160	(86)	ENG	Laurie Canter	**0.9455**	41	38.77	-35.55	-0.0672
161	(129)	GER	Stephan Jaeger	**0.9452**	58	49.15	-13.50	0.3862
162	(240)	ITA	Francesco Molinari	**0.9443**	39	37.77	7.71	0.2083
163	(249)	USA	Wyndham Clark	**0.9430**	56	49.03	11.30	0.4912
164	(37)	ENG	Lee Westwood	**0.9410**	36	37.64	-82.39	0.2017
165	(264)	USA	Mark Hubbard	**0.9399**	58	48.88	13.54	0.5838
166	(108)	RSA	Charl Schwartzel	**0.9341**	39	37.36	-25.13	-0.2996
167	(119)	RSA	Justin Harding	**0.9302**	48	44.65	-25.84	0.0985
168	(170)	GER	Marcel Schneider	**0.9294**	49	45.54	0.65	-0.0718
169	(429)	USA	Robby Shelton	**0.9274**	58	48.23	29.23	-0.0029
170	(70)	JPN	Ryosuke Kinoshita	**0.9222**	52	47.95	-26.66	-0.4167
171	(380)	USA	Beau Hossler	**0.9049**	52	47.05	24.77	0.2846
172	(154)	USA	Adam Schenk	**0.9027**	62	46.94	-10.02	0.1798
173	(199)	THA	Phachara Khongwatmai	**0.9005**	26	36.02	1.58	-0.5825
174	(1038)	USA	Davis Thompson	**0.9000**	36	36.00	33.38	-0.1331
175	(321)	GER	Hurly Long	**0.8998**	56	46.79	22.07	-0.1776
176	(107)	USA	Lanto Griffin	**0.8969**	45	40.36	-33.63	0.5596
177	(47)	USA	Ryan Palmer	**0.8962**	44	39.43	-67.59	0.2336
178	(80)	DEN	Marcus Helligkilde	**0.8907**	45	40.08	-27.38	-0.2104
179	(219)	RSA	Hennie du Plessis	**0.8887**	46	40.88	3.73	-0.1149
180	(284)	USA	John Huh	**0.8858**	52	46.06	20.60	-0.1400
181	(68)	RSA	Branden Grace	**0.8785**	45	39.53	-57.03	0.3027
182	(78)	ENG	Matt Wallace	**0.8771**	58	45.61	-43.16	-0.1706
183	(296)	USA	Lee Hodges	**0.8741**	57	45.45	16.67	0.2613
184	(133)	SWE	Alexander Bjork	**0.8676**	44	38.18	-18.82	0.3120
185	(336)	USA	Nick Hardy	**0.8639**	52	44.92	20.78	0.4267
186	(144)	USA	Sean Crocker	**0.8604**	56	44.74	-14.32	-0.9902
187	(299)	SCO	Russell Knox	**0.8603**	59	44.73	14.03	0.3639
188	(404)	CHN	Zecheng Dou	**0.8568**	48	41.13	24.99	-0.1281
189	(395)	ENG	Richard Mansell	**0.8553**	44	37.63	21.61	0.0152
190	(155)	USA	Greyson Sigg	**0.8533**	56	44.37	-10.30	0.3267
191	(436)	USA	Sihwan Kim	**0.8477**	45	38.15	23.62	-0.8063
192	(463)	TPE	Chun-an Yu	**0.8474**	42	35.59	22.63	-0.2415
193	(334)	USA	Brandon Wu	**0.8473**	56	44.06	21.83	-0.0929
194	(111)	RSA	Dylan Frittelli	**0.8472**	59	44.06	-29.26	0.0951
195	(167)	JPN	Hiroshi Iwata	**0.8411**	51	42.90	1.63	-0.9535
196	(306)	SCO	Connor Syme	**0.8400**	51	42.84	14.00	-0.2301
197	(182)	SWE	Henrik Stenson	**0.8372**	38	33.49	-5.63	0.0716
198	(132)	SCO	Martin Laird	**0.8358**	47	39.28	-12.57	0.6082
199	(637)	SWE	David Lingmerth	**0.8313**	48	39.90	32.35	-0.1640
200	(276)	FRA	Matthieu Pavon	**0.8302**	54	43.17	10.00	-0.4042

				Average Points	Events	Total Points	2022 Net Points	Strokes Gained Rating
201	(285)	JPN	Ryo Hisatsune	**0.8279**	50	41.39	15.96	-0.3878
202	(589)	ENG	Paul Waring	**0.8269**	39	33.08	24.25	-0.4107
203	(168)	USA	Hayden Buckley	**0.8263**	58	42.97	-0.04	0.1372
204	(113)	WAL	Jamie Donaldson	**0.8243**	45	37.09	-24.80	-0.4797
205	(152)	JPN	Yuta Ikeda	**0.8180**	46	37.63	-6.94	-0.7525
206	(124)	JPN	Jinichiro Kozuma	**0.8153**	50	40.76	-13.98	-0.8046
207	(183)	USA	David Lipsky	**0.8108**	56	42.16	-5.11	0.3855
208	(148)	AUS	Jason Scrivener	**0.8052**	43	34.62	-14.12	-0.2111
209	(246)	SWE	Sebastian Soderberg	**0.8016**	55	41.68	7.29	-0.5708
210	(176)	USA	Chad Ramey	**0.7974**	57	41.46	-5.26	-0.1512
211	(277)	USA	Pat Perez	**0.7934**	42	33.32	-0.48	0.7681
212	(103)	USA	Johannes Veerman	**0.7925**	47	37.25	-27.70	-0.2516
213	(33)	USA	Phil Mickelson	**0.7818**	26	31.27	-82.92	-0.7325
214	(394)	ENG	Eddie Pepperell	**0.7803**	49	38.24	21.41	0.0214
215	(374)	USA	Justin Lower	**0.7777**	55	40.44	21.73	0.1816
216	(231)	JPN	Tomoyo Ikemura	**0.7768**	49	38.06	6.98	-1.0971
217	(177)	RSA	George Coetzee	**0.7758**	50	38.79	-6.82	0.1872
218	(304)	RSA	JC Ritchie	**0.7738**	56	40.24	11.72	-0.5853
219	(128)	JPN	Hideto Tanihara	**0.7708**	37	30.83	-21.66	-0.8366
220	(122)	FRA	Julien Brun	**0.7698**	49	37.72	-16.10	0.0054
221	(391)	CHN	Ashun Wu	**0.7673**	45	34.53	18.03	-0.1343
222	(145)	TPE	CT Pan	**0.7626**	49	37.37	-22.67	0.0631
223	(236)	GER	Maximilian Kieffer	**0.7621**	49	37.34	1.55	-0.2797
224	(153)	ESP	Rafa Cabrera Bello	**0.7606**	56	39.55	-17.52	-0.6621
225	(999)	JPN	Aguri Iwasaki	**0.7552**	36	30.21	27.27	-0.2934
226	(203)	KOR	Sanghyun Park	**0.7551**	40	30.20	-3.93	-0.5533
227	(480)	USA	Austin Eckroat	**0.7451**	35	29.80	17.59	-0.0582
228	(653)	JPN	Riki Kawamoto	**0.7425**	33	29.70	22.49	-0.8673
229	(180)	FIN	Kalle Samooja	**0.7418**	48	35.61	-6.38	-0.7538
230	(56)	MEX	Carlos Ortiz	**0.7307**	42	30.69	-78.88	-0.1495
231	(287)	KOR	Byeong Hun An	**0.7279**	53	37.85	6.37	-0.2044
232	(195)	USA	Joseph Bramlett	**0.7274**	60	37.83	-7.54	-0.0305
233	(275)	IND	Shubhankar Sharma	**0.7268**	55	37.79	3.97	-0.8098
234	(255)	PRY	Fabrizio Zanotti	**0.7266**	40	29.06	0.45	0.1067
235	(248)	FIN	Tapio Pulkkanen	**0.7236**	52	37.63	2.02	-0.3214
236	(143)	USA	Patton Kizzire	**0.7219**	55	37.54	-21.57	0.1071
237	(454)	SWE	Jens Dantorp	**0.7192**	54	37.40	23.35	-0.7866
238	(185)	FIN	Mikko Korhonen	**0.7121**	41	29.20	-6.39	0.1137
239	(149)	ENG	Marcus Armitage	**0.7052**	53	36.67	-19.91	-0.1918
240	(171)	JPN	Naoyuki Kataoka	**0.7031**	50	35.16	-5.32	-1.2720
241	(253)	GER	Matti Schmid	**0.7012**	46	32.26	3.54	-0.4012
242	(490)	RSA	Ockie Strydom	**0.6977**	50	34.89	22.55	-0.8337
243	(261)	ENG	Harry Hall	**0.6971**	56	36.25	8.55	-0.3212
244	(100)	ESP	Santiago Tarrio	**0.6931**	56	36.04	-23.92	-0.6340
245	(221)	THA	Jazz Janewattananond	**0.6895**	64	35.85	-5.81	-0.5054
246	(328)	NOR	Kristian Krogh Johannessen	**0.6865**	44	30.21	9.00	-0.2449
247	(76)	RSA	Daniel van Tonder	**0.6850**	58	35.62	-50.64	-0.5205
248	(234)	SWE	Joakim Lagergren	**0.6835**	53	35.54	-0.29	-0.6996
249	(370)	RSA	Louis de Jager	**0.6800**	54	35.36	14.25	-0.4536
250	(280)	RSA	Jaco Ahlers	**0.6790**	46	31.23	4.89	-0.7400

				Average Points	Events	Total Points	2022 Net Points	Strokes Gained Rating
251	(556)	AUS	Anthony Quayle	**0.6756**	56	35.13	25.60	-1.2553
252	(699)	ENG	Nathan Kimsey	**0.6733**	45	30.30	23.92	-0.5794
253	(241)	ESP	Jorge Campillo	**0.6722**	61	34.96	-4.00	-0.1645
254	(286)	ITA	Edoardo Molinari	**0.6704**	55	34.86	6.46	-0.0201
255	(479)	KOR	Minkyu Kim	**0.6667**	32	26.67	14.44	-0.9698
256	(312)	FRA	Romain Langasque	**0.6657**	56	34.61	6.48	-0.0717
257	(222)	CAN	Nick Taylor	**0.6604**	56	34.34	-3.99	0.1740
258	(142)	USA	Adam Long	**0.6564**	56	34.13	-28.35	0.3385
259	(487)	MAS	Gavin Green	**0.6520**	57	33.90	18.50	-0.6991
260	(137)	USA	Harry Higgs	**0.6494**	58	33.77	-31.30	-0.5883
261	(204)	USA	Scott Piercy	**0.6474**	52	33.67	-6.36	-0.0344
262	(157)	SCO	Grant Forrest	**0.6472**	56	33.66	-18.14	-0.5728
263	(903)	DEN	Oliver Hundeboll Jorgensen	**0.6449**	41	26.44	22.81	-1.2362
264	(184)	JPN	Ryo Ishikawa	**0.6432**	42	27.01	-9.29	-0.5720
265	(206)	USA	Charles Howell III	**0.6390**	31	25.56	-10.92	0.7700
266	(227)	USA	Doug Ghim	**0.6383**	52	33.19	-3.82	-0.0299
267	(237)	USA	Sam Ryder	**0.6382**	60	33.18	-6.31	0.2112
268	(952)	THA	Nitithorn Thippong	**0.6329**	34	25.32	22.08	-1.2976
269	(158)	DEN	Jeff Winther	**0.6304**	48	30.26	-17.87	-0.5742
270	(639)	ENG	Steve Lewton	**0.6282**	28	25.13	17.58	-0.6656
271	(428)	KOR	Eunshin Park	**0.6280**	35	25.12	10.50	-1.1986
272	(412)	SCO	David Law	**0.6236**	56	32.43	12.27	-0.3607
273	(258)	NZL	Daniel Hillier	**0.6192**	56	32.20	4.25	-1.0947
274	(266)	USA	Max McGreevy	**0.6176**	55	32.12	0.83	-1.0001
275	(420)	TPE	Chan Shih-chang	**0.6144**	22	24.58	9.78	-1.0096
276	(1127)	KOR	Junggon Hwang	**0.6140**	22	24.56	22.37	-0.8648
277	(611)	RSA	Deon Germishuys	**0.6121**	55	31.83	23.48	-1.2332
278	(548)	USA	Brandon Matthews	**0.6113**	40	24.45	14.78	-0.7750
279	(146)	POR	Ricardo Gouveia	**0.6107**	51	31.15	-14.65	-0.5362
280	(136)	USA	Kramer Hickok	**0.6103**	55	31.74	-27.55	-0.3163
281	(169)	JPN	Masahiro Kawamura	**0.6061**	58	31.52	-21.65	-0.4370
282	(320)	USA	Chesson Hadley	**0.6052**	53	31.47	4.90	-0.2149
283	(112)	SVK	Rory Sabbatini	**0.6033**	48	28.96	-44.29	-0.2145
284	(271)	USA	Chase Hanna	**0.5996**	57	31.18	4.89	-0.8565
285	(178)	USA	Michael Thompson	**0.5989**	49	29.35	-14.17	0.0539
286	(130)	USA	John Catlin	**0.5972**	56	31.05	-36.65	-0.2333
287	(125)	USA	Robert Streb	**0.5946**	58	30.92	-36.95	-0.1069
288	(173)	ENG	Daniel Gavins	**0.5884**	57	30.59	-10.73	-0.7262
289	(691)	ENG	Todd Clements	**0.5870**	47	27.59	20.99	-1.0114
290	(1140)	NIR	Tom McKibbin	**0.5854**	40	23.42	21.31	-0.7574
291	(106)	DEN	Joachim B Hansen	**0.5843**	58	30.38	-44.35	-1.0848
292	(160)	AUT	Matthias Schwab	**0.5833**	52	30.33	-22.69	0.0255
293	(337)	SCO	Scott Jamieson	**0.5830**	49	28.57	5.67	-0.1703
294	(217)	JPN	Ryuko Tokimatsu	**0.5769**	50	28.85	-3.57	-0.7264
295	(307)	JPN	Satoshi Kodaira	**0.5766**	64	29.98	1.22	-0.1631
296	(703)	FRA	Clement Sordet	**0.5752**	51	29.34	22.75	-0.7677
297	(899)	GER	Marc Hammer	**0.5733**	38	22.93	19.21	-1.9493
298	(305)	USA	Ryan Armour	**0.5652**	49	27.70	-2.51	0.0763
298	(1744)	JPN	Taiga Semikawa	**0.5652**	13	22.61	22.61	0.2068
300	(282)	NED	Wil Besseling	**0.5646**	49	27.67	-1.86	-0.6182

YEAR-END TOP 10s

	1968	1969	1970	1971	1972	1973
1	Nicklaus	Nicklaus	Nicklaus	Nicklaus	Nicklaus	Nicklaus
2	Palmer	Player	Player	Trevino	Player	Weiskopf
3	Casper	Casper	Casper	Player	Trevino	Trevino
4	Player	Palmer	Trevino	Palmer	Crampton	Player
5	Charles	Charles	Charles	Casper	Palmer	Crampton
6	Boros	Beard	Devlin	Barber	Jacklin	Miller
7	Coles	Archer	Coles	Crampton	Weiskopf	Oosterhuis
8	Thomson	Trevino	Jacklin	Charles	Oosterhuis	Wadkins
9	Beard	Barber	Beard	Devlin	Heard	Heard
10	Nagle	Sikes	Huggett	Weiskopf	Devlin	Brewer

	1974	1975	1976	1977	1978	1979
1	Nicklaus	Nicklaus	Nicklaus	Nicklaus	T Watson	T Watson
2	Miller	Miller	Irwin	T Watson	Nicklaus	Nicklaus
3	Player	Weiskopf	Miller	Green	Irwin	Irwin
4	Weiskopf	Irwin	Player	Irwin	Green	Trevino
5	Trevino	Player	Green	Crenshaw	Player	Player
6	M Ozaki	Green	T Watson	Marsh	Crenshaw	Aoki
7	Crampton	Trevino	Weiskopf	Player	Marsh	Green
8	Irwin	Casper	Marsh	Weiskopf	Ballesteros	Crenshaw
9	Green	Crampton	Crenshaw	Floyd	Trevino	Ballesteros
10	Heard	T Watson	Geiberger	Ballesteros	Aoki	Wadkins

	1980	1981	1982	1983	1984	1985
1	T Watson	T Watson	T Watson	Ballesteros	Ballesteros	Ballesteros
2	Trevino	Rogers	Floyd	T Watson	T Watson	Langer
3	Aoki	Aoki	Ballesteros	Floyd	Norman	Norman
4	Crenshaw	Pate	Kite	Norman	Wadkins	T Watson
5	Nicklaus	Trevino	Stadler	Kite	Langer	Nakajima
6	Pate	Ballesteros	Pate	Nicklaus	Faldo	Wadkins
7	Ballesteros	Graham	Nicklaus	Nakajima	Nakajima	O'Meara
8	Bean	Crenshaw	Rogers	Stadler	Stadler	Strange
9	Irwin	Floyd	Aoki	Aoki	Kite	Pavin
10	Player	Lietzke	Strange	Wadkins	Peete	Sutton

	1986	1987	1988	1989	1990	1991
1	Norman	Norman	Ballesteros	Norman	Norman	Woosnam
2	Langer	Ballesteros	Norman	Faldo	Faldo	Faldo
3	Ballesteros	Langer	Lyle	Ballesteros	Olazabal	Olazabal
4	Nakajima	Lyle	Faldo	Strange	Woosnam	Ballesteros
5	Bean	Strange	Strange	Stewart	Stewart	Norman
6	Tway	Woosnam	Crenshaw	Kite	Azinger	Couples
7	Sutton	Stewart	Woosnam	Olazabal	Ballesteros	Langer
8	Strange	Wadkins	Frost	Calcavecchia	Kite	Stewart
9	Stewart	McNulty	Azinger	Woosnam	McNulty	Azinger
10	O'Meara	Crenshaw	Calcavecchia	Azinger	Calcavecchia	R Davis

	1992	1993	1994	1995	1996	1997
1	Faldo	Faldo	N Price	Norman	Norman	Norman
2	Couples	Norman	Norman	N Price	Lehman	Woods
3	Woosnam	Langer	Faldo	Langer	Montgomerie	N Price
4	Olazabal	N Price	Langer	Els	Els	Els
5	Norman	Couples	Olazabal	Montgomerie	Couples	Love
6	Langer	Azinger	Els	Pavin	Faldo	Mickelson
7	Cook	Woosnam	Couples	Faldo	Mickelson	Montgomerie
8	N Price	Kite	Montgomerie	Couples	M Ozaki	M Ozaki
9	Azinger	Love	M Ozaki	M Ozaki	Love	Lehman
10	Love	Pavin	Pavin	Elkington	O'Meara	O'Meara

1998	**1999**	**2000**	**2001**	**2002**	**2003**
1 Woods	1 Woods	1 Woods	1 Woods	1 Woods	1 Woods
2 O'Meara	2 Duval	2 Els	2 Mickelson	2 Mickelson	2 Singh
3 Duval	**3** Montgomerie	**3** Duval	3 Duval	3 Els	3 Els
4 Love	4 Love	4 Mickelson	4 Els	4 Garcia	4 Love
5 Els	5 Els	5 Westwood	5 Love	5 Goosen	5 Furyk
6 N Price	6 Westwood	6 Montgomerie	6 Garcia	6 Toms	6 Weir
7 Montgomerie	7 Singh	7 Love	7 Toms	7 Harrington	7 Goosen
8 Westwood	8 N Price	8 Sutton	8 Singh	8 Singh	8 Harrington
9 Singh	9 Mickelson	9 Singh	9 Clarke	9 Love	9 Toms
10 Mickelson	10 O'Meara	10 Lehman	10 Goosen	10 Montgomerie	10 Perry

2004	**2005**	**2006**	**2007**	**2008**	**2009**
1 Singh	1 Woods	1 Woods	1 Woods	1 Woods	1 Woods
2 Woods	2 Singh	2 Furyk	2 Mickelson	2 Garcia	2 Mickelson
3 Els	3 Mickelson	3 Mickelson	3 Furyk	3 Mickelson	3 Stricker
4 Goosen	4 Goosen	4 Scott	4 Els	4 Harrington	4 Westwood
5 Mickelson	5 Els	5 Els	5 Stricker	5 Singh	5 Harrington
6 Harrington	6 Garcia	6 Goosen	6 Rose	6 R Karlsson	6 Furyk
7 Garcia	7 Furyk	7 Singh	7 Scott	7 Villegas	7 Casey
8 Weir	8 Montgomerie	8 Harrington	8 Harrington	8 Stenson	8 Stenson
9 Love	9 Scott	9 Donald	9 KJ Choi	9 Els	9 McIlroy
10 Cink	10 DiMarco	10 Ogilvy	10 Singh	10 Westwood	10 Perry

2010	**2011**	**2012**	**2013**	**2014**	**2015**
1 Westwood	1 Donald	1 McIlroy	1 Woods	1 McIlroy	1 Spieth
2 Woods	2 Westwood	2 Donald	2 Scott	2 Stenson	2 J Day
3 Kaymer	3 McIlroy	3 Woods	3 Stenson	3 Scott	3 McIlroy
4 Mickelson	4 Kaymer	4 Rose	4 Rose	4 B Watson	4 B Watson
5 Furyk	5 Scott	5 Scott	5 Mickelson	5 Garcia	5 Stenson
6 McDowell	6 Stricker	6 Oosthuizen	6 McIlroy	6 Rose	6 Fowler
7 Stricker	7 D Johnson	7 Westwood	7 Kuchar	7 Furyk	7 Rose
8 Casey	8 J Day	8 B Watson	8 Stricker	8 J Day	8 D Johnson
9 Donald	9 Schwartzel	9 Dufner	9 Z Johnson	9 Spieth	9 Furyk
10 McIlroy	10 W Simpson	10 Snedeker	10 Garcia	10 Fowler	10 Reed

2016	**2017**	**2018**	**2019**	**2020**	**2021**
1 J Day	1 D Johnson	1 B Koepka	1 B Koepka	1 D Johnson	1 Rahm
2 McIlroy	2 Spieth	2 Rose	2 McIlroy	2 Rahm	2 Morikawa
3 D Johnson	3 Thomas	3 D Johnson	3 Rahm	3 Thomas	3 D Johnson
4 Stenson	4 Rahm	4 Thomas	4 Thomas	4 McIlroy	4 Cantlay
5 Spieth	5 Matsuyama	5 DeChambeau	5 D Johnson	5 DeChambeau	5 DeChambeau
6 Matsuyama	6 Rose	6 Rahm	6 Woods	6 W Simpson	6 Schauffele
7 Scott	7 Fowler	7 F Molinari	7 Cantlay	7 Morikawa	7 Thomas
8 Reed	8 B Koepka	8 McIlroy	8 Rose	8 Schauffele	8 Hovland
9 Noren	9 Stenson	9 Finau	9 Schauffele	9 Cantlay	9 McIlroy
10 B Watson	10 Garcia	10 Schauffele	10 Fleetwood	10 Hatton	10 Oosthuizen

2022
1 McIlroy
2 Scheffler
3 Smith
4 Cantlay
5 Rahm
6 Schauffele
7 Zalatoris
8 Thomas
9 Fitzpatrick
10 Hovland

Data from World of Professional Golf 1968–1985; World Ranking 1986–2022

World Money Lists

Scottie Scheffler surpassed the mark set by Tiger Woods in 2006 when the Masters champion set a new record for official prize money with his earnings of $14.3 million in 2022. Scheffler, who spent much of the year as the world number one, won four times in all, including the WGC Dell Match Play as well as at Augusta National. Rory McIlroy finished second on the men's World Money List despite winning both the FedEx Cup and the DP World Tour points list.

Lydia Ko won the biggest first-place prize ever in women's golf of $2 million at the CME Group Tour Championship to overtake US Open champion Minjee Lee at the top of the Women's World Money List. Ko's total of $4,364,403 was only $591 short of Lorena Ochoa's record annual total in 2007. A total of 36 female players passed $1 million in earnings compared to 22 in 2021. Padraig Harrington, who continued to play regular tour events in 2022, led the Seniors list ahead of Champions Tour number one Steven Alker.

The lists are compiled from the results of all the official tournaments on the main tours featured in this book, as well as other events where reliable figures could be obtained. For events to qualify, a minimum of 36 holes and four players are required, while exhibition matches, skins games and skill contests are excluded. Annual performance bonuses such as for the FedEx Cup and the Race to Dubai are also excluded, so McIlroy's $18 million for winning the Tour Championship was not included as the PGA Tour do not award official prize money for the event. Prize money on the LIV Golf Invitational Series was not considered.

In more than five decades that the Men's World Money List has been compiled, the earnings of the player finishing in 200th position have risen from $3,326 in 1966 to $802,338 in 2022. The top 200 players in 1966 earned a total of $4,680,287. In 2022, the comparable total was $485,267,548.

The conversion rates used for 2022 were: Euro = US$1.06; Australian dollar = US$0.67; Japanese yen = US$0.0075; South African rand = US$0.059; South Korean Won = US$0.00079; Canadian dollar = US$0.73.

The Career World Money List, which has been led by Tiger Woods since 2000, is compiled from the regular and senior lists that have been published in all previous editions of this book, as well as a table prepared for a companion book, *The Wonderful World of Professional Golf* (atheneum, 1973). Additional records were taken from official records of major golf associations.

MEN'S WORLD MONEY LIST LEADERS

1966	USA	Jack Nicklaus	$168,088
1967	USA	Jack Nicklaus	276,166
1968	USA	Billy Casper	222,436
1969	USA	Frank Beard	186,993
1970	USA	Jack Nicklaus	222,583
1971	USA	Jack Nicklaus	285,897
1972	USA	Jack Nicklaus	341,792
1973	USA	Tom Weiskopf	349,645
1974	USA	Jonny Miller	400,255
1975	USA	Jack Nicklaus	332,610
1976	USA	Jack Nicklaus	316,086
1977	USA	Tom Watson	358,034
1978	USA	Tom Watson	384,388
1979	USA	Tom Watson	506,912
1980	USA	Tom Watson	651,921
1981	USA	Johnny Miller	704,204
1982	USA	Raymond Floyd	738,699
1983	ESP	Seve Ballesteros	686,088
1984	ESP	Seve Ballesteros	688,047
1985	GER	Bernhard Langer	860,262
1986	AUS	Greg Norman	1,146,584
1987	WAL	Ian Woosnam	1,793,268
1988	ESP	Seve Ballesteros	1,261,275
1989	RSA	David Frost	1,650,230
1990	ESP	Jose Maria Olazabal	1,633,640
1991	GER	Bernhard Langer	2,186,700
1992	ENG	Nick Faldo	2,748,248
1993	ENG	Nick Faldo	2,825,280
1994	RSA	Ernie Els	2,862,854
1995	USA	Corey Pavin	2,746,340
1996	SCO	Colin Montgomerie	3,071,442
1997	SCO	Colin Montgomerie	3,366,900
1998	USA	Tiger Woods	2,927,946
1999	USA	Tiger Woods	7,681,625
2000	USA	Tiger Woods	11,034,530
2001	USA	Tiger Woods	7,771,562
2002	USA	Tiger Woods	8,292,188
2003	FJI	Vijay Singh	8,499,611

2004	FJI	Vijay Singh	11,638,699
2005	USA	Tiger Woods	12,280,404
2006	USA	Tiger Woods	13,325,949
2007	USA	Tiger Woods	12,902,706
2008	FJI	Vijay Singh	8,025,128
2009	USA	Tiger Woods	10,998,054
2010	NIR	Graeme McDowell	7,371,586
2011	ENG	Luke Donald	9,730,870
2012	NIR	Rory McIlroy	11,301,228
2013	USA	Tiger Woods	9,490,217
2014	NIR	Rory McIlroy	10,526,012
2015	USA	Jordan Spieth	12,477,758
2016	USA	Dustin Johnson	9,347,352
2017	USA	Justin Thomas	10,300,894
2018	USA	Bryson DeChambeau	9,231,811
2019	NIR	Rory McIlroy	10,820,759
2020	USA	Dustin Johnson	9,385,820
2021	USA	Collin Morikawa	11,262,648
2022	USA	Scottie Scheffler	14,323,704

2022 MEN'S WORLD MONEY LIST

1	USA	Scottie Scheffler	$14,323,704
2	NIR	Rory McIlroy	11,091,906
3	USA	Patrick Cantlay	10,081,605
4	ESP	Jon Rahm	9,941,545
5	AUS	Cameron Smith	9,884,937
6	USA	Will Zalatoris	9,203,920
7	NOR	Viktor Hovland	8,972,526
8	ENG	Matt Fitzpatrick	8,161,621
9	USA	Xander Schauffele	7,858,855
10	USA	Tony Finau	7,850,637
11	USA	Justin Thomas	6,586,000
12	USA	Cameron Young	6,291,800
13	USA	Sam Burns	6,067,105
14	USA	Billy Horschel	5,988,944
15	USA	Max Homa	5,941,509
16	AUT	Sepp Straka	5,768,057
17	IRL	Shane Lowry	5,681,177
18	USA	Keegan Bradley	5,677,669
19	KOR	Joohyung Kim	5,290,390
20	USA	Jordan Spieth	5,174,120
21	USA	Brian Harman	5,090,635
22	USA	Tom Hoge	5,068,445
23	ENG	Tommy Fleetwood	4,943,028
24	ENG	Tyrrell Hatton	4,867,650
25	CHI	Joaquin Niemann	4,771,948
26	USA	Sahith Theegala	4,733,843
27	KOR	Sungjae Im	4,438,252
28	IRL	Seamus Power	4,385,269
29	CAN	Corey Conners	4,175,337
30	USA	Kevin Kisner	4,160,097
31	USA	Collin Morikawa	4,105,694
32	KOR	Kyoung-Hoon Lee	4,029,293
33	USA	Kurt Kitayama	3,914,241
34	JPN	Hideki Matsuyama	3,880,588
35	USA	Russell Henley	3,876,422
36	SWE	Alex Noren	3,848,788
37	USA	Scott Stallings	3,737,282
38	NZL	Ryan Fox	3,582,813
39	USA	JT Poston	3,469,384
40	USA	Aaron Wise	3,293,897
41	USA	Davis Riley	3,235,740
42	IND	Anirban Lahiri	3,205,968
43	USA	JJ Spaun	3,132,844
44	USA	Andrew Putnam	3,045,389
45	USA	Harold Varner III	2,976,531
46	AUS	Adam Scott	2,963,489
47	ARG	Emiliano Grillo	2,852,515
48	CAN	Adam Hadwin	2,831,220
49	USA	Denny McCarthy	2,823,452
50	CAN	Adam Svensson	2,806,922
51	USA	Keith Mitchell	2,686,499
52	CAN	Mackenzie Hughes	2,634,497
53	RSA	Christiaan Bezuidenhout	2,625,337
54	CHI	Mito Pereira	2,618,719
55	USA	Matthew NeSmith	2,554,950
56	POL	Adrian Meronk	2,547,988
57	USA	Matt Kuchar	2,525,679
58	BEL	Thomas Pieters	2,515,778
59	USA	Maverick McNealy	2,481,911
60	USA	Joel Dahmen	2,460,102
61	USA	Dustin Johnson	2,368,866
62	USA	Trey Mullinax	2,363,565
63	USA	Chris Kirk	2,274,171
64	AUS	Cam Davis	2,245,590
65	USA	Alex Smalley	2,214,092
66	USA	Luke List	2,137,390
67	CAN	Taylor Pendrith	2,130,446
68	BEL	Thomas Detry	2,097,538
69	KOR	Si Woo Kim	2,078,756
70	USA	Brendon Todd	2,019,665
71	AUS	Jason Day	1,997,855
72	USA	Troy Merritt	1,988,449
73	USA	Gary Woodland	1,981,557
74	USA	Lucas Glover	1,972,723
75	AUS	Lucas Herbert	1,957,599
76	USA	Beau Hossler	1,950,463
77	USA	Taylor Montgomery	1,950,292
78	USA	Wyndham Clark	1,888,564
79	ENG	Callum Tarren	1,887,669
80	USA	Daniel Berger	1,883,539
81	ENG	Danny Willett	1,860,191
82	ENG	Paul Casey	1,846,950
83	RSA	Thriston Lawrence	1,813,472
84	AUS	Matt Jones	1,797,514
85	USA	Taylor Moore	1,796,261
86	USA	Chez Reavie	1,781,539
87	ESP	Adrian Otaegui	1,774,832
88	SCO	Russell Knox	1,771,363

89	USA	Lee Hodges	1,763,713
90	DEN	Rasmus Hojgaard	1,753,200
91	ENG	Jordan Smith	1,748,793
92	USA	Rickie Fowler	1,739,727
93	COL	Sebastian Munoz	1,723,001
94	ENG	Aaron Rai	1,710,025
95	USA	Patrick Rodgers	1,708,244
96	USA	Brendan Steele	1,697,308
97	USA	Cameron Tringale	1,684,191
98	USA	Brandon Wu	1,667,745
99	USA	Hudson Swafford	1,663,339
100	SCO	Robert MacIntyre	1,660,844
101	USA	Kevin Na	1,619,390
102	ENG	Justin Rose	1,590,098
103	MEX	Abraham Ancer	1,587,864
104	USA	David Lipsky	1,542,465
105	USA	Mark Hubbard	1,517,062
106	USA	John Huh	1,480,404
107	ENG	Richard Bland	1,473,139
108	GER	Stephan Jaeger	1,467,421
109	USA	Kevin Streelman	1,459,016
110	USA	Jason Kokrak	1,442,000
111	USA	Ryan Palmer	1,438,169
112	USA	Hayden Buckley	1,436,355
113	USA	Patrick Reed	1,428,697
114	AUS	Min Woo Lee	1,426,356
115	USA	Talor Gooch	1,425,696
116	JPN	Kazuki Higa	1,416,605
117	AUS	Marc Leishman	1,416,196
118	RSA	Dean Burmester	1,400,497
119	ESP	Adri Arnaus	1,396,931
120	USA	Brooks Koepka	1,375,224
121	USA	Adam Long	1,364,131
122	SCO	Ewen Ferguson	1,345,234
123	USA	Justin Lower	1,339,335
124	USA	Sam Ryder	1,336,673
125	USA	Nick Hardy	1,289,040
126	USA	Cameron Champ	1,281,458
127	RSA	Dylan Frittelli	1,279,302
128	ESP	Pablo Larrazabal	1,270,191
129	USA	Greyson Sigg	1,268,920
130	SCO	Richie Ramsay	1,248,510
131	RSA	Erik van Rooyen	1,243,815
132	USA	Doug Ghim	1,242,269
133	USA	Ben Griffin	1,241,230
134	USA	Chesson Hadley	1,234,210
135	USA	Bubba Watson	1,228,149
136	USA	Adam Schenk	1,221,839
137	USA	Tyson Alexander	1,220,630
138	RSA	Garrick Higgo	1,220,262
139	IND	Shubhankar Sharma	1,218,395
140	ENG	Callum Shinkwin	1,205,515
141	USA	Harris English	1,185,434
142	GER	Yannik Paul	1,184,334
143	FRA	Antoine Rozner	1,178,226
144	CAN	Nick Taylor	1,177,000
145	ITA	Guido Migliozzi	1,170,533
146	USA	Lanto Griffin	1,155,274
147	USA	Patton Kizzire	1,147,422
148	SCO	Martin Laird	1,139,748
149	FRA	Victor Perez	1,136,789
150	USA	Chad Ramey	1,123,769
151	USA	Stewart Cink	1,112,466
152	ENG	Sam Horsfield	1,103,445
153	MAS	Gavin Green	1,099,827
154	ENG	Ben Taylor	1,089,439
155	ITA	Francesco Molinari	1,073,422
156	ESP	Rafa Cabrera Bello	1,072,625
157	DEN	Thorbjorn Olesen	1,064,302
158	USA	Will Gordon	1,045,852
159	GER	Hurly Long	1,044,481
160	USA	Pat Perez	1,040,539
161	RSA	Oliver Bekker	1,039,316
162	USA	James Hahn	1,036,532
163	USA	Scott Piercy	1,018,587
164	USA	Peter Malnati	1,011,545
165	USA	Michael Thompson	1,009,462
166	USA	Max McGreevy	1,007,916
167	AUT	Matthias Schwab	985,175
168	SWE	David Lingmerth	974,434
169	SCO	Connor Syme	964,675
170	TPE	CT Pan	964,558
171	USA	Charles Howell III	959,280
172	ENG	Matt Wallace	951,668
173	ESP	Jorge Campillo	951,164
174	THA	Sadom Kaewkanjana	943,909
175	GER	Maximilian Kieffer	937,054
176	USA	Robby Shelton	920,591
177	JPN	Yuto Katsuragawa	910,218
178	CHN	Haotong Li	908,250
179	CHN	Ashun Wu	906,344
180	JPN	Rikuya Hoshino	885,720
181	USA	Austin Smotherman	875,074
182	JPN	Mikumu Horikawa	870,907
183	ENG	Oliver Wilson	870,629
184	PAR	Fabrizio Zanotti	868,570
185	ENG	Richard Mansell	866,495
186	JPN	Satoshi Kodaira	860,704
187	SCO	David Law	853,826
188	FRA	Matthieu Pavon	851,208
189	SWE	Sebastian Soderberg	849,576
190	KOR	Seonghyeon Kim	845,679
191	USA	Ryan Brehm	842,986
192	FRA	Romain Langasque	841,961
193	USA	Doc Redman	840,467
194	SWE	Joakim Lagergren	839,299
195	USA	Brian Stuard	835,181
196	KOR	Byeong Hun An	830,790
197	ENG	Ian Poulter	824,396
198	RSA	Charl Schwartzel	823,179
199	USA	Joseph Bramlett	816,761
200	ENG	Eddie Pepperell	802,338

200	ENG	Eddie Pepperell	802,338
201	RSA	Justin Harding	801,199
202	USA	Nate Lashley	800,263
203	TPE	Chun-an Yu	799,247
204	USA	Chan Kim	798,488
205	VEN	Jhonattan Vegas	795,206
206	SWE	Henrik Stenson	782,221
207	THA	Jazz Janewattananond	781,030
208	ESP	Sergio Garcia	778,779
209	GER	Marcel Schneider	777,629
210	ZIM	Scott Vincent	762,264
211	JPN	Hiroshi Iwata	749,679
212	JPN	Aguri Iwasaki	747,237
213	USA	Davis Thompson	746,519
214	USA	Webb Simpson	737,055
215	SCO	Scott Jamieson	732,797
216	USA	Ryan Armour	724,957
217	USA	Charley Hoffman	721,249
218	ENG	Paul Waring	720,977
219	RSA	Branden Grace	712,013
220	USA	Tyler Duncan	711,965
221	JPN	Ryo Hisatsune	709,936
222	ENG	Lee Westwood	707,296
223	CAN	Michael Gligic	695,196
224	USA	Vince Whaley	694,631
225	USA	Sihwan Kim	689,958
226	KOR	Bio Kim	679,739
227	ITA	Edoardo Molinari	667,182
228	AUT	Bernd Wiesberger	665,461
229	USA	Ben Martin	663,474
230	USA	Paul Haley II	662,918
231	ENG	Matthew Southgate	657,364
232	JPN	Takumi Kanaya	656,948
233	JPN	Tomoharu Otsuki	656,606
234	USA	Robert Streb	652,509
235	ENG	Dale Whitnell	648,417
236	USA	Cameron Percy	645,889
237	USA	Kelly Kraft	642,430
238	RSA	George Coetzee	639,699
239	FIN	Tapio Pulkkanen	639,472
240	NIR	Graeme McDowell	636,368
241	ENG	Marcus Armitage	635,292
242	USA	Justin Suh	625,222
243	USA	Bryson DeChambeau	624,928
244	USA	Chris Gotterup	624,010
245	CHN	Zecheng Dou	623,635
246	USA	Brice Garnett	609,410
247	USA	Harry Higgs	607,035
248	ENG	Matthew Jordan	595,592
249	FIN	Kalle Samooja	595,167
250	USA	Sean O'Hair	594,546

WOMEN'S WORLD MONEY LIST LEADERS

1989	USA	Betsy King	$675,964	2006	MEX	Lorena Ochoa	2,656,310
1990	USA	Beth Daniel	963,578	2007	MEX	Lorena Ochoa	4,364,994
1991	USA	Pat Bradley	763,118	2008	MEX	Lorena Ochoa	2,763,193
1992	USA	Dottie Mochrie (Pepper)	819,895	2009	KOR	Jiyai Shin	2,179,908
1993	JPN	Mayumi Hirase	757,712	2010	KOR	Jiyai Shin	2,150,256
1994	ENG	Laura Davies	1,006,143	2011	TPE	Yani Tseng	3,806,713
1995	SWE	Annika Sorenstam	1,043,121	2012	KOR	Inbee Park	3,185,020
1996	ENG	Laura Davies	1,383,003	2013	KOR	Inbee Park	2,508,811
1997	SWE	Annika Sorenstam	1,460,252	2014	USA	Stacy Lewis	2,574,039
1998	SWE	Annika Sorenstam	1,170,898	2015	NZL	Lydia Ko	2,859,771
1999	AUS	Karrie Webb	1,641,959	2016	THA	Ariya Jutanugarn	2,583,428
2000	AUS	Karrie Webb	2,111,213	2017	KOR	Sung Hyun Park	2,346,664
2001	SWE	Annika Sorenstam	2,105,868	2018	THA	Ariya Jutanugarn	2,791,449
2002	SWE	Annika Sorenstam	2,997,812	2019	KOR	Jin Young Ko	3,126,955
2003	SWE	Annika Sorenstam	2,159,050	2020	KOR	Jin Young Ko	1,911,762
2004	SWE	Annika Sorenstam	2,746,824	2021	KOR	Jin Young Ko	3,502,161
2005	SWE	Annika Sorenstam	2,756,540	2022	NZL	Lydia Ko	4,364,403

2022 WOMEN'S WORLD MONEY LIST

1	NZL	Lydia Ko	$4,364,403	35	USA	Megan Khang	1,025,005
2	AUS	Minjee Lee	3,855,946	36	USA	Jessica Korda	1,010,540
3	KOR	In Gee Chun	2,673,860	37	ESP	Carlota Ciganda	937,214
4	CAN	Brooke M Henderson	2,454,190	38	JPN	Sakura Koiwai	927,606
5	THA	Atthaya Thitikul	2,205,167	39	USA	Lilia Vu	918,939
6	USA	Lexi Thompson	2,105,345	40	JPN	Yuri Yoshida	881,158
7	KOR	Hye-Jin Choi	2,083,408	41	KOR	Su Ji Kim	857,774
8	USA	Jennifer Kupcho	1,975,632	42	ENG	Jodi Ewart Shadoff	857,128
9	JPN	Miyuu Yamashita	1,884,133	43	KOR	Eun-Hee Ji	835,642
10	IRL	Leona Maguire	1,866,629	44	RSA	Paula Reto	808,130
11	USA	Nelly Korda	1,685,164	45	MEX	Gaby Lopez	800,239
12	KOR	Hyo Joo Kim	1,584,102	46	JPN	Yuka Saso	784,128
13	RSA	Ashleigh Buhai	1,553,004	47	USA	Sophia Schubert	771,054
14	ENG	Georgia Hall	1,436,379	48	USA	Cheyenne Knight	768,975
15	JPN	Nasa Hataoka	1,404,576	49	USA	Lizette Salas	762,032
16	AUS	Hannah Green	1,317,114	50	KOR	A Lim Kim	747,851
17	CHN	Xiyu Lin	1,310,499	51	KOR	So Mi Lee	727,327
18	JPN	Mao Saigo	1,295,167	52	KOR	Ji Young Park	721,192
19	USA	Mina Harigae	1,293,471	53	USA	Allisen Corpuz	721,135
20	FRA	Celine Boutier	1,272,941	54	KOR	Jeongeun Lee[6]	702,979
21	KOR	Jin Young Ko	1,260,471	55	JPN	Haruka Kawasaki	692,578
22	KOR	Min Ji Park	1,211,053	56	USA	Marina Alex	691,583
23	JPN	Yuna Nishimura	1,208,255	57	USA	Alison Lee	688,430
24	ENG	Charley Hull	1,169,407	58	KOR	Yewon Lee	668,857
25	SWE	Madelene Sagstrom	1,160,922	59	SCO	Gemma Dryburgh	662,000
26	SWE	Anna Nordqvist	1,147,470	60	USA	Ally Ewing	660,511
27	USA	Andrea Lee	1,142,433	61	JPN	Kotone Hori	653,272
28	JPN	Ayaka Furue	1,134,618	62	JPN	Hae Ran Ryu	653,260
29	SWE	Linn Grant	1,121,021	63	JPN	Nana Suganuma	648,539
30	KOR	Sei Young Kim	1,083,246	64	KOR	Narin An	646,686
31	JPN	Mone Inami	1,048,829	65	KOR	Chella Choi	642,856
32	JPN	Hinako Shibuno	1,040,882	66	DEN	Nanna Koerstz Madsen	640,191
33	USA	Danielle Kang	1,039,239	67	SWE	Maja Stark	632,887
34	JPN	Minami Katsu	1,029,076	68	KOR	Hee Jeong Lim	619,060

69	USA	Ryann O'Toole	616,600
70	KOR	Yun Ji Jeong	615,113
71	THA	Moriya Jutanugarn	615,048
72	THA	Pajaree Anannarukarn	612,297
73	JPN	Momoko Ueda	606,460
74	JPN	Saiki Fujita	594,668
75	KOR	Jiyai Shin	594,576
76	USA	Sarah Schmelzel	584,376
77	JPN	Ayako Kimura	582,717
78	KOR	Jung Min Hong	581,955
79	ENG	Bronte Law	578,800
80	JPN	Erika Kikuchi	573,178
81	JPN	Kana Nagai	560,805
82	AUS	Stephanie Kyriacou	551,824
83	FIN	Matilda Castren	537,701
84	KOR	So Young Lee	536,821
85	JPN	Serena Aoki	533,657
86	JPN	Sayaka Takahashi	527,225
87	KOR	Ga Young Lee	508,886
88	KOR	Hyun Kyung Park	498,536
89	KOR	Han Sol Ji	496,334
90	SLO	Pia Babnik	489,473
91	THA	Patty Tavatanakit	464,593
92	JPN	Haruka Morita	459,518
93	AUS	Amy Yang	439,097
94	THA	Pornanong Phatlum	438,951
95	KOR	Jin Hee Im	436,995
96	FRA	Caroline Masson	429,219
97	THA	Ariya Jutanugarn	421,503
98	KOR	A Yean Cho	421,052
99	JPN	Nozomi Uetake	419,730
100	KOR	Inbee Park	417,530
101	JPN	Ayaka Watanabe	411,753
102	KOR	Jenny Shin	411,558
103	JPN	Chirei Iwai	409,613
104	KOR	Au-Reum Hwang	404,992
105	JPN	Shoko Sasaki	404,142
106	USA	Stacy Lewis	399,412
107	KOR	Min Young Lee[2]	393,036
108	KOR	Ye Rim Choi	386,899
109	USA	Angel Yin	384,589
110	JPN	Miyu Sato	375,222
111	NIR	Stephanie Meadow	373,874
112	KOR	So Yeon Ryu	373,482
113	MAS	Kelly Tan	372,479
114	USA	Brittany Altomare	368,174
115	JPN	Yuting Seki	365,970
116	KOR	Jeong Mee Hwang	361,560
117	FRA	Pauline Roussin	353,906
118	KOR	Jin Seon Han	353,704
119	KOR	Yu Jin Sung	351,416
120	KOR	Min Song Ha	346,764
121	JPN	Ai Suzuki	345,208
122	SWI	Albane Valenzuela	340,107
123	KOR	Seon Woo Bae	336,975
124	JPN	Kana Mikashima	336,842
125	DEN	Emily Kristine Pedersen	335,889
126	KOR	Ji Hyun Oh	332,858
127	KOR	Ga Eun Song	329,321
128	SWE	Frida Kinhult	327,017
129	SWI	Morgane Metraux	326,312
130	MEX	Maria Fassi	323,927
131	USA	Jennifer Chang	309,667
132	KOR	Seo Yeon Kwon	306,141
133	THA	Wichanee Meechai	303,651
134	KOR	Ina Yoon	303,341
135	JPN	Mao Nozawa	303,161
136	USA	Lauren Coughlin	299,990
137	KOR	Ji Won Hong	295,117
138	JPN	Momoko Osato	293,126
139	ECU	Daniela Darquea	292,306
140	GER	Esther Henseleit	286,421
141	JPN	Amiyu Ozeki	286,187
142	TPE	Wei-Ling Hsu	282,242
143	JPN	Miyu Goto	281,700
144	JPN	Shuri Sakuma	279,183
145	JPN	Erika Hara	278,583
146	SWE	Johanna Gustavsson	273,577
147	USA	Lindsey Weaver-Wright	271,241
148	KOR	Mi-Jeong Jeon	269,027
149	TPE	Pei-Ying Tsai	266,847
150	JPN	Ritsuko Ryu	266,838
151	AUS	Sarah Kemp	265,648
152	JPN	Fumika Kawagishi	265,391
153	CAN	Maude-Aimee Leblanc	260,509
154	USA	Lauren Stephenson	257,842
155	JPN	Momoko Kishibe	254,041
156	JPN	Kumiko Kaneda	252,930
157	JPN	Mami Fukuda	249,021
158	KOR	Ji U Ko	248,540
159	JPN	Akie Iwai	247,995
160	TPE	Peiyun Chien	243,857
161	AUS	Su Oh	243,275
162	KOR	Minju Kim	239,843
163	JPN	Yui Kawamoto	238,646
164	KOR	Seung Yeon Lee	237,217
165	KOR	So Hyun Bae	237,026
166	KOR	Chae Eun Lee[2]	236,337
167	RSA	Lee-Anne Pace	234,612
168	KOR	Su Yeon Jang	234,257
169	BEL	Manon De Roey	232,636
170	JPN	Miyuu Abe	229,595
171	SWE	Caroline Hedwall	226,687
172	USA	Yealimi Noh	226,398
173	KOR	Ye Sung Jun	226,060
174	THA	Jasmine Suwannapura	225,737
175	KOR	Hyo Ju You	222,161
176	JPN	Sae Ogura	222,154
177	USA	Amanda Doherty	219,674
178	USA	Emma Talley	219,367
179	KOR	Eun Woo Choi	217,276
180	KOR	Haeji Kang	213,640

181	TPE	Teresa Lu	208,091
182	SWE	Linnea Strom	208,022
183	USA	Annie Park	204,363
184	KOR	Song Yi Ahn	204,354
185	KOR	Hee Ji Kim	203,573
186	JPN	Lala Anai	202,292
187	KOR	Jeongeun Lee[5]	202,277
188	KOR	Sung Hyun Park	199,659
189	JPN	Chie Arimura	197,776
190	JPN	Shiho Kuwaki	195,371
191	JPN	Mizuki Ooide	194,931
192	ESP	Ana Pelaez Trivino	193,395
193	KOR	Bo Mi Kwak	193,150
194	AUS	Grace Kim	192,132
195	KOR	Hee Won Na	191,543
196	CHN	Yu Liu	190,305
197	KOR	Dasom Ma	188,092
198	RSA	Ashleigh Buhai	184,378
199	USA	Caroline Inglis	183,483
200	JPN	Yuka Yasuda	183,244
201	KOR	Jung Min Lee	183,217
202	KOR	Hana Lee	182,666
203	GER	Leonie Harm	182,192
204	GER	Olivia Cowan	180,622
205	USA	Jill McGill	180,000
206	IND	Aditi Ashok	178,900
207	KOR	Se Lin Hyun	177,646
208	AUS	Whitney Hillier	177,534
209	JPN	Shina Kanazawa	177,081
210	KOR	Jae Hee Kim	174,748
211	KOR	Yeun Jung Seo	173,568
212	JPN	Rumi Yoshiba	171,990
213	JPN	Miki Sakai	171,273
214	JPN	Nanako Ueno	171,130
215	CHN	Ruoning Yin	170,140
216	CHN	Ruixin Liu	167,061
217	JPN	Saki Nagamine	166,281
218	FRA	Perrine Delacour	166,256
219	KOR	Eun Hye Jo	165,171
220	KOR	Seul Gi Jeong	163,948
221	ENG	Liz Young	162,152
222	CZE	Klara Spilkova	161,424
223	JPN	Rio Takeda	160,242
224	JPN	Nanoko Hayashi	160,103
225	JPN	Kotoko Uchida	158,795
226	KOR	Seung Hui Ro	158,612
227	KOR	Ji Yeong Kim[2]	157,798
228	ENG	Mel Reid	157,432
229	KOR	Min Kyung Choi	157,159
230	KOR	Uh Jin Seo	156,675
231	KOR	Sun Ju Ahn	155,989
232	KOR	Gyeol Park	153,894
233	JPN	Rio Ishii	153,630
234	ENG	Meghan MacLaren	153,546
235	JPN	Eri Okayama	152,289
236	USA	Gerina Mendoza	152,172
237	AUS	Karis Davidson	149,252
238	JPN	Asuka Ishikawa	149,044
239	ARG	Magdalena Simmermacher	147,445
240	NED	Anne van Dam	146,263
241	KOR	In-Kyung Kim	145,412
242	KOR	Da Yeon Lee	144,203
243	ENG	Alice Hewson	141,271
244	KOR	Chae Yoon Park	139,926
245	JPN	Hikaru Yoshimoto	139,471
246	JPN	Seira Oki	138,756
247	GER	Isi Gabsa	138,662
248	NED	Dewi Weber	137,749
249	KOR	Ji Su Kim	135,714
250	KOR	U Ree Jun	134,674

2022 SENIOR WORLD MONEY LIST

1	IRL	Padraig Harrington	$3,752,266
2	NZL	Steven Alker	3,544,425
3	USA	Steve Stricker	2,576,225
4	USA	Jerry Kelly	2,364,329
5	ESP	Miguel Angel Jimenez	2,247,749
6	GER	Bernhard Langer	1,880,423
7	THA	Thongchai Jaidee	1,701,452
8	CAN	Stephen Ames	1,587,725
9	RSA	Ernie Els	1,581,708
10	GER	Alex Cejka	1,413,305
11	USA	Steve Flesch	1,112,578
12	RSA	Retief Goosen	1,018,199
13	ENG	Paul Broadhurst	1,008,017
14	USA	David Toms	999,629
15	NIR	Darren Clarke	995,918
16	USA	Doug Barron	920,312
17	USA	Scott Parel	888,789
18	AUS	Rod Pampling	882,122
19	KOR	KJ Choi	875,155
20	USA	Paul Goydos	868,875
21	USA	Ken Duke	855,163
22	USA	Brian Gay	830,081
23	USA	Brett Quigley	827,832
24	USA	Kirk Triplett	789,315
25	USA	Lee Janzen	785,673
26	SWE	Robert Karlsson	779,163
27	USA	Brandt Jobe	772,936
28	USA	Gene Sauers	767,470
29	USA	Marco Dawson	755,156
30	USA	Jim Furyk	736,411
31	KOR	YE Yang	711,596
32	SCO	Colin Montgomerie	687,351
33	USA	Rocco Mediate	673,438
34	USA	Tim Petrovic	654,807
35	USA	Kevin Sutherland	651,737
36	USA	John Huston	610,961
37	FJI	Vijay Singh	610,642
38	USA	Woody Austin	602,157
39	CAN	Mike Weir	579,859
40	USA	Fred Couples	562,475
41	USA	Shane Bertsch	560,669
42	USA	Rob Labritz	539,173
43	USA	Joe Durant	535,343
44	AUS	Stuart Appleby	506,343
45	USA	Tom Pernice Jr	501,916
46	THA	Prayad Marksaeng	485,929
47	USA	Paul Stankowski	482,552
48	AUS	Mark Hensby	476,814
49	USA	Jeff Maggert	465,648
50	JPN	Ken Tanigawa	447,797
51	USA	Billy Andrade	445,555
52	USA	Scott Dunlap	441,373
53	USA	Bob Estes	407,049
54	USA	Harrison Frazar	389,421
55	USA	Scott McCarron	366,741
56	USA	David Branshaw	341,625
57	USA	Tim Herron	340,442
58	AUS	David McKenzie	328,717
59	JPN	Hiroyuki Fujita	328,403
60	RSA	James Kingston	326,293
61	USA	Dicky Pride	313,015
62	USA	Wes Short Jr	309,187
63	USA	Jay Haas	302,670
64	USA	John Daly	272,938
65	BRA	Adilson Da Silva	248,959
66	AUS	Glen Day	246,973
67	USA	Mario Tiziani	245,937
68	USA	Tom Gillis	241,468
69	DEN	Thomas Bjorn	232,126
70	USA	Corey Pavin	230,654
71	SCO	Paul Lawrie	230,614
72	USA	Cameron Beckman	228,119
73	USA	Billy Mayfair	212,236
74	USA	Clark Dennis	210,580
75	KOR	Charlie Wi	206,422
76	JPN	Katsumasa Miyamoto	204,587
77	ARG	Mauricio Molina	200,111
78	USA	Chris DiMarco	199,603
79	SWE	Joakim Haeggman	199,269
80	JPN	Takashi Kanemoto	197,537
81	USA	Duffy Waldorf	196,209
82	JPN	Keiichiro Fukabori	193,077
83	USA	Michael Allen	171,357
84	USA	Jeff Sluman	170,607
85	ARG	Ricardo Gonzalez	164,207
86	USA	Mark Walker	161,260
87	JPN	Toru Suzuki	154,628
88	THA	Thaworn Wiratchant	151,378
89	USA	Kent Jones	150,964
90	WAL	Stephen Dodd	147,094
91	USA	Tom Lehman	145,175
92	USA	Olin Browne	144,803
93	AUT	Markus Brier	142,692
94	JPN	Mitsuhiro Watanabe	140,251
95	USA	Davis Love III	139,514
96	ENG	Phillip Archer	138,210
97	AUS	Richard Green	133,368
98	USA	David Duval	131,634
99	SCO	Euan McIntosh	128,190
100	JPN	Yoshinobu Tsukada	127,276

CAREER WORLD MONEY LIST

1	USA	Tiger Woods	$145,282,836
2	USA	Phil Mickelson	104,563,016
3	NIR	Rory McIlroy	96,568,873
4	RSA	Ernie Els	93,555,153
5	FJI	Vijay Singh	91,319,608
6	USA	Jim Furyk	87,437,338
7	ENG	Justin Rose	81,115,259
8	ESP	Sergio Garcia	80,149,527
9	USA	Dustin Johnson	79,294,084
10	AUS	Adam Scott	74,140,790
11	ENG	Lee Westwood	69,795,696
12	GER	Bernhard Langer	66,527,943
13	USA	Matt Kuchar	63,454,220
14	IRL	Padraig Harrington	60,767,164
15	RSA	Retief Goosen	59,103,952
16	ENG	Paul Casey	59,066,449
17	USA	Steve Stricker	57,669,217
18	ENG	Luke Donald	56,534,711
19	USA	Davis Love III	55,907,242
20	USA	Jordan Spieth	55,768,774
21	ENG	Ian Poulter	55,431,285
22	AUS	Jason Day	54,300,747
23	SCO	Colin Montgomerie	54,130,425
24	USA	Zach Johnson	53,076,416
25	USA	David Toms	51,699,267
26	ESP	Jon Rahm	50,922,308
27	USA	Justin Thomas	49,001,316
28	USA	Bubba Watson	48,673,074
29	USA	Kenny Perry	48,572,414
30	USA	Rickie Fowler	48,113,621
31	ESP	Miguel Angel Jimenez	47,407,187
32	USA	Stewart Cink	47,186,575
33	NIR	Graeme McDowell	47,055,611
34	USA	Fred Couples	46,466,373
35	USA	Webb Simpson	46,363,081
36	JPN	Hideki Matsuyama	44,993,287
37	SWE	Henrik Stenson	44,911,734
38	USA	Charles Howell III	44,365,006
39	USA	Patrick Reed	42,813,008
40	USA	Brooks Koepka	42,472,096
41	USA	Jerry Kelly	42,409,707
42	USA	Tom Lehman	40,888,306
43	KOR	KJ Choi	40,522,321
44	SVK	Rory Sabbatini	40,418,200
45	USA	Kevin Na	40,328,481
46	ITA	Francisco Molinari	40,151,221
47	RSA	Charl Schwartzel	38,640,198
48	AUS	Mark Leishman	38,526,655
49	USA	Billy Horschel	38,464,459
50	USA	Brandt Snedeker	37,988,391
51	RSA	Nick Price	37,980,341
52	USA	Hale Irwin	37,825,229
53	USA	Keegan Bradley	37,808,471
54	USA	Jay Haas	37,804,688
55	USA	Justin Leonard	37,643,582
56	USA	Mark Calcavecchia	37,523,822
57	NIR	Darren Clarke	37,519,342
58	RSA	Louis Oosthuizen	37,434,896
59	AUS	Robert Allenby	37,042,566
60	USA	Fred Funk	36,928,988
61	USA	Tony Finau	35,205,642
62	AUS	Geoff Ogilvy	35,028,726
63	AUS	Stuart Appleby	34,712,135
64	USA	Charley Hoffman	34,662,469
65	USA	Ryan Palmer	34,327,652
66	USA	Jeff Sluman	34,234,261
67	USA	Gary Woodland	33,895,086
68	CAN	Mike Weir	33,864,200
69	USA	Ryan Moore	33,490,841
70	USA	Bill Haas	33,139,776
71	USA	Patrick Cantlay	32,986,655
72	USA	Nick Watney	32,463,097
73	GER	Martin Kaymer	32,392,709
74	ENG	Matt Fitzpatrick	32,293,429
75	USA	Xander Schauffele	32,175,604
76	USA	Mark O'Meara	31,987,701
77	USA	Tom Kite	31,623,817
78	USA	Jason Dufner	31,677,983
79	ENG	Tommy Fleetwood	31,509,570
80	IRL	Shane Lowry	31,285,472
81	USA	Scott Verplank	30,874,701
82	ENG	Tyrrell Hatton	30,815,504
83	USA	Kevin Kisner	30,754,173
84	DEN	Thomas Bjorn	30,194,815
85	USA	Loren Roberts	29,856,976
88	USA	Lucas Glover	29,701,504
89	USA	Tom Watson	29,614,942
90	AUS	Tim Clark	29,582,750
91	SWE	Robert Karlsson	29,485,711
92	USA	Scott Hoch	29,043,940
93	CAN	Stephen Ames	28,704,833
94	USA	Jimmy Walker	28,658,474
95	USA	Chad Campbell	28,562,338
96	USA	Chris DiMarco	28,438,987
97	USA	Pat Perez	28,394,367
98	RSA	David Frost	28,392,012
99	SWE	Alex Noren	28,330,984
100	USA	Bryson DeChambeau	28,171,274

World's Winners of 2022

Number in brackets shows eg second win of the year; the first of two numbers pertains to that particular tour

MAJORS CHAMPIONSHIPS

Chevron Championship	**Jennifer Kupcho**	*LPGA*
Masters Tournament	**Scottie Scheffler (4)**	*PGA Tour/DP World Tour*
PGA Championship	**Justin Thomas**	*PGA Tour/DP World Tour*
US Women's Open	**Minjee Lee (2)**	*LPGA*
US Open Championship	**Matt Fitzpatrick**	*PGA Tour/DP World Tour*
KPMG Women's PGA Championship	**In Gee Chun**	*LPGA*
The 150th Open	**Cameron Smith (3)**	*PGA Tour/DP World Tour*
Amundi Evian Championship	**Brooke Henderson (2)**	*LET/LPGA*
AIG Women's Open	**Ashleigh Buhai**	*LET/LPGA*

PGA TOUR

Sentry Tournament of Champions	**Cameron Smith**	
Sony Open	**Hideki Matsuyama**	
The American Express	**Hudson Swafford**	
Farmers Insurance Open	**Luke List**	
AT&T Pebble Beach Pro-Am	**Tom Hoge**	
WM Phoenix Open	**Scottie Scheffler**	
Genesis Invitational	**Joaquin Niemann**	
Honda Classic	**Sepp Straka**	
Arnold Palmer Invitational	**Scottie Scheffler (2)**	
Puerto Rico Open	**Ryan Brehm**	
The Players Championship	**Cameron Smith (2)**	
Valspar Championship	**Sam Burns**	
WGC Dell Technologies Match Play	**Scottie Scheffler (3)**	*DP World Tour*
Corales Puntacana Championship	**Chad Ramey**	
Valero Texas Open	**JJ Spaun**	
RBC Heritage	**Jordan Spieth**	
Zurich Classic	**Patrick Cantlay/Xander Schauffele**	
Mexico Open	**Jon Rahm**	
Wells Fargo Championship	**Max Homa**	
AT&T Byron Nelson	**Kyoung-Hoon Lee**	
Charles Schwab Challenge	**Sam Burns (2)**	
Memorial Tournament	**Billy Horschel**	
RBC Canadian Open	**Rory McIlroy**	
Travelers Championship	**Xander Schauffele (2)**	
John Deere Classic	**JT Poston**	
Barbasol Championship	**Trey Mullinax**	*DP World Tour*
Barracuda Championship	**Chez Reavie**	*DP World Tour*
3M Open	**Tony Finau**	
Rocket Mortgage Classic	**Tony Finau (2)**	
Wyndham Championship	**Joohyung Kim (1,2)**	
FedEx St Jude Championship	**Will Zalatoris**	
BMW Championship	**Patrick Cantlay (2)**	
Tour Championship	**Rory McIlroy (2)**	
Fortinet Championship	**Max Homa (2)**	
Presidents Cup	**USA**	
Sanderson Farms Championship	**Mackenzie Hughes**	
Shriners Children's Open	**Joohyung Kim (2,3)**	
Zozo Championship	**Keegan Bradley**	
CJ Cup	**Rory McIlroy (3)**	

Butterfield Bermuda Championship	**Seamus Power**	
World Wide Technology Championship	**Russell Henley**	
Cadence Bank Houston Open	**Tony Finau (3)**	
RSM Classic	**Adam Svensson**	
TaylorMade Pebble Beach Invitational*	**Parker Coody (1,2)**	
Hero World Challenge*	**Viktor Hovland (1,2)**	
QBE Shootout*	**Tom Hoge (2)/Sahith Theegala**	
PNC Championship*	**Vijay Singh/Qass Singh** [(A)]	*PGAT Champions*

**unofficial event*

KORN FERRY TOUR

Bahamas Great Exuma Classic	**Akshay Bhatia**
Bahamas Great Abaco Classic	**Brandon Harkins**
Panama Championship	**Carson Young**
Astara Golf Championship	**Brandon Matthews**
Lecom Suncoast Classic	**Byeong Hun An**
Chitimacha Louisiana Open	**Carl Yuan**
Lake Charles Championship	**Trevor Werbylo**
Club Car Championship	**TJ Vogel**
Veritex Bank Championship	**Tyson Alexander**
Huntsville Championship	**Harrison Endycott**
Simmons Bank Open	**Brent Grant**
Visit Knoxville Open	**Anders Albertson**
AdventHealth Championship	**Trevor Cone**
NV5 Invitational	**Harry Hall**
Rex Hospital Open	**Davis Thompson**
BMW Charity Pro-Am	**Robby Shelton**
Wichita Open	**Norman Xiong**
Live and Work in Maine Open	**Pierceson Coody**
The Ascendant	**Zecheng Dou**
Memorial Health Championship	**Paul Haley II**
Price Cutter Charity Championship	**David Kocher**
Utah Championship	**Andrew Kozan**
Pinnacle Bank Championship	**Robby Shelton (2)**
Albertsons Boise Open	**Will Gordon**
Nationwide Children's Hospital Championship	**David Lingmerth**
Korn Ferry Tour Championship	**Justin Suh**

PGA TOUR CANADA

Royal Beach Victoria Open	**Scott Stevens**
ATB Classic	**Wil Bateman**
Prince Edward Island Open	**Brian Carlson**
Osprey Valley Open	**Danny Walker**
Sotheby's International Realty Canada Ontario Open	**Noah Goodwin**
Quebec Open	**Ryan Gerard**
CentrePort Canada Rail Park Manitoba Open	**Parker Coody**
CRMC Championship	**Jake Knapp**
GolfBC Championship	**Noah Goodwin (2)**
Fortinet Cup Championship	**Wil Bateman (2)**

PGA TOUR LATINOAMERICA

Estrella del Mar Open	**Matt Ryan**
Termas de Rio Hondo Invitational	**Kevin Velo**
Abierto del Centro memorial Eduardo "Gato" Romero	**Alejandro Tosti**
JHSF Aberto do Brasil	**Jamie Lopez Rivarola**
Diners Club Peru Open	**Jose Toledo**

Quito Open	**Manav Shah**	
Jalisco Open GDL	**Jose de Jesus Rodriguez**	
Volvo Golf Championship	**Cristobal Del Solar**	
Fortox Colombia Classic	**Tommy Cocha**	
Bupa Tour Championship	**Jesus Montenegro**	
Visa Open de Argentina	**Zack Fischer**	
Neuquen Argentina Classic	**Cristobal Del Solar (2)**	
Scotia Wealth Management Chile Open	**Matt Ryan (2)**	

DP WORLD TOUR

Abu Dhabi HSBC Championship	**Thomas Pieters**	
Slync.io Dubai Desert Classic	**Viktor Hovland**	
Ras al Khaimah Championship	**Nicolai Hojgaard**	
Ras al Khaimah Classic	**Ryan Fox**	
Magical Kenya Open	**Ashun Wu**	
Commercial Bank Qatar Masters	**Ewen Ferguson**	
ISPS Handa Championship Spain	**Pablo Larrazabal (2)**	
Catalunya Championship	**Adri Arnaus**	
Betfred British Masters	**Thorbjorn Olesen**	
Soudal Open	**Sam Horsfield**	
Dutch Open	**Victor Perez**	
Porsche European Open	**Kalle Samooja**	
BMW International Open	**Haotong Li**	
Horizon Irish Open	**Adrian Meronk**	
Genesis Scottish Open	**Xander Schauffele (1,3)**	*PGA Tour*
Cazoo Classic	**Richie Ramsay**	
Hero Open	**Sean Crocker**	
Cazoo Open	**Callum Shinkwin**	
ISPS Handa World Invitational	**Ewen Ferguson (2)**	
D+D Real Czech Masters	**Maximilian Kieffer**	
Omega European Masters	**Thriston Lawrence**	
Made in HimmerLand	**Oliver Wilson**	
BMW PGA Championship	**Shane Lowry**	
DS Automobiles Italian Open	**Robert MacIntyre**	
Cazoo Open de France	**Guido Migliozzi**	
Alfred Dunhill Links Championship	**Ryan Fox (2)**	
Acciona Open de Espana	**Jon Rahm (1,2)**	
Estrella Damm Andalucia Masters	**Adrian Otaegui**	
Mallorca Golf Open	**Yannik Paul**	
Portugal Masters	**Jordan Smith**	
Nedbank Golf Challenge	**Tommy Fleetwood**	
DP World Tour Championship	**Jon Rahm (2,3)**	

CHALLENGE TOUR

Challenge de Espana	**Jens Dantorp**
Farmfoods Scottish Challenge	**Javier Sainz**
D+D Real Czech Challenge	**Nicolai B Kristensen**
Emporda Challenge	**Liam Johnston**
Kaskada Golf Challenge	**Martin Simonsen**
Blot Open de Bretagne	**Alfie Plant**
Italian Challenge Open	**Kristian Krogh Johannessen**
Le Vaudreuil Golf Challenge	**Nathan Kimsey**
Euram Bank Open	**Marc Hammer (1,2)**
Big Green Egg German Challenge	**Alejandro Del Rey**
Irish Challenge	**Todd Clements**
Vierumaki Finnish Challenge	**Velten Meyer**

Frederikshavin Challenge	**Freddy Schott**
Dormy Open	**Emilio Cuartero Blanco**
Indoor Golf Group Challenge	**Mikael Lindberg**
B-NL Challenge Trophy	**Alexander Knappe (2)**
Open de Portugal	**Pierre Pineau**
Swiss Challenge	**Daniel Hillier**
Hopps Open de Provence	**Joel Sjoholm**
British Challenge	**Euan Walker**
English Trophy	**Jeremy Freiburghaus**
Rolex Challenge Tour Grand Final	**Nathan Kimsey (2)**

ALPS TOUR

Ein Bay Open	**Stefano Mazzoli**
Red Sea Little Venice Open	**Oihan Guillamoundeguy** (A)
New Giza Open	**Tomas Guimaraes Bessa**
Winter Series Terre dei Consoli	**Adrien Pendaries**
Winter Series Golf Nazionale	**Mathias Eggenberger**
Abruzzo Alps Open	**Manuel Morugan**
Molinetto Alps Open	**Koen Kouwenaar**
Goesser Open	**Markus Brier**
Memorial Giorgio Bordoni	**Gregorio De Leo**
Open de la Mirabelle d'Or	**Tom Vaillant** (A)
Aravell Golf Open	**Tom Vaillant** (A) **(2)**
Alps de Andalucia	**Gary Hurley**
Hauts de France-Pas de Calais Golf Open	**Davey Porsius**
Alps de Las Castillas	**Gregorio De Leo (2)**
Fred Olsen Alps de La Gomera	**Vince van Veen**
Roma Alps Open	**Gregorio De Leo (3)**
Castelconturbia Alps Open	**Ben Schmidt**
Emilia Romagna Alps Tour Grand Final	**Jonathan Yates**

EUROPRO TOUR

Cubefunder Shootout	**James Allan**
Ignis Management Championship	**Josh Hilleard**
World Snooker & Jessie May Championship	**Nick Cunningham**
IFX Payments Championship	**Jake Ayres**
Bendac Championship	**Ryan Brooks**
PDC Golf Championship	**Pavan Sagoo**
CPG Classic	**Dermot McElroy**
Glal.uk Worcestershire Masters	**Brandon Robinson-Thompson**
Q Hotels Collection Championship	**Nicholas Poppleton**
Dell Technologies Championship	**James Allan (2)**
Lancer Scott Open	**Jack Davidson**
Northern Ireland Masters	**Sam Broadhurst**
Spey Valley Golf Resort	**Stuart Grehan**
Eagle Orchid Scottish Masters	**Michael Stewart**
Wright-Morgan Championship	**Josh Hilleard (2)**
Matchroom Tour Championship	**James Allan (3)**

NORDIC GOLF LEAGUE

GolfStar Winter Series I	**John Axelsen**
GolfStar Winter Series II	**Marcus Kinhult**
Ecco Tour Spanish Masters	**Sebastian Friedrichsen**
PGA Catalunya Resort Championship	**Jeppe Kristian Andersen**
Bravo Tours Open	**Frederik Birkelund** (A)

Barncancerfonden Open	**Nicolai Tinning**	
Rewell Elisefarm Challenge	**Axel Boasson**	
Stora Hotellet Fjallbacka Open	**Simon Forsstrom**	
Moss & Rygge Open	**August Thor Host**	
Thisted Forsikring Championship	**Nicolai Nohr Madsen**	
Thomas Bjorn Samso Classic	**Mathias Gladbjerg**	
Junet Open	**Jesper Hagborg Asp**	
Unicef Championship	**Christian Jacobsen**	
PGA Championship Landeryd Masters	**Rasmus Holmberg**	
Big Green Egg Swedish Matchplay Championship	**Mathias Gladbjerg (2)**	
Holtsmark Open	**Tobias Ruth**	
Goteborg Open	**Jeppe Kristian Andersen (2)**	
Timberwise Finnish Open	**Viktor Edin**	
Esbjerg Open	**Christian Jacobsen (2)**	
Greatdays Trophy	**Rasmus Holmberg (2)**	
BMW Onsjo Open	**Frederik Severin Tottenborg**	
Trust Forsikring Championship	**August Thor Host (2)**	
Great Northern Challenge	**Frederik Birkelund (A) (2)**	
Gumbalde Open	**Adam Andersson**	
Race to Himmerland	**John Axelsen (2)**	
MoreGolf Mastercard Tour Final	**John Axelsen (3)**	
Sydbank Road to Europe Final	**Jeppe Kristian Andersen (3)**	

PRO GOLF TOUR

Dreamland Pyramids Classic	**Alan De Bondt**	
Allegria Open	**Victor Veyret**	
New Giza Pyramids Challenge	**Maximilian Herrmann**	
Red Sea Ain Sokhna Classic	**Jan Cafourek**	
Red Sea Egyptian Classic	**Yente Van Doren**	
Haugschlag NO Open	**Dario Antonisse**	
Gradi Polish Open	**Michael Hirmer**	
Raiffeisen Pro Golf Tour St Polten	**Jean Bekirian**	
Weihenstephan Open	**Marc Hammer**	
Richter+Frenzel Open	**Alexandre Liu**	
Altepro Trophy	**Jean Bekirian (2)**	
FaberExposize Gelpenberg Open	**Floris de Haas**	
Castanea Resort Championship	**Jannik de Bruyn**	

SUNSHINE TOUR

Vodacom Origins of Golf Final	**Martin Rohwer**	
Dimension Data Pro-Am	**Alexander Knappe**	*Challenge Tour*
Bain's Whisky Cape Town Open	**JC Ritchie**	*Challenge Tour*
Jonsson Workwear Open	**JC Ritchie (2)**	*Challenge Tour*
Mangaung Open	**Oliver Hundeboll**	*Challenge Tour*
MyGolfLife Open	**Pablo Larrazabal**	*DP World Tour*
Steyn City Championship	**Shaun Norris**	*DP World Tour*
SDC Open	**Clement Sordet**	*Challenge Tour*
Limpopo Championship	**Mateusz Gradecki**	*Challenge Tour*
Stella Artois Players Championship	**Jaco Ahlers**	
Sunshine Tour Championship	**Tristen Strydom**	
Lombard Insurance Classic	**Herman Loubser**	
FBC Zim Open	**Albert Venter**	
Sishen Classic	**Deon Germishuys**	
SunBet Challenge	**Rourke van der Spuy**	
Kit Kat Group Pro-Am	**Dylan Mostert**	
FNB Eswatini Nkonyeni Challenge	**Jaco Prinsloo**	

Vodacom Origins of Golf — De Zalze	**George Coetzee**	
Bain's Whisky Ubunye Championship	**Merrick Bremner/Martin Rohwer (2)**	
SunBet Challenge — Time Square	**Albert Venter (2)**	
Vodacom Origins of Golf — Highland Gate	**Anthony Michael**	
Gary & Vivienne Player Challenge	**Jaco Van Zyl**	
Vodacom Origins of Golf — San Lameer	**Wynand Dingle**	
SunBet Challenge — Wild Coast Sun	**MJ Viljoen**	
Vodacom Origins of Golf — St Francis Links	**Ruan Korb**	
Fortress Invitational	**Pieter Moolman**	
Blue Label Challenge	**Stephen Ferreira**	
SunBet Challenge — Sun Sibaya	**Dylan Naidoo**	
Vodacom Origins of Golf Final	**Combrinck Smit**	
PGA Championship	**George Coetzee (2)**	
Joburg Open	**Dan Bradbury**	*DP World Tour*
Investec South African Open	**Thriston Lawrence (1,2)**	*DP World Tour*
Alfred Dunhill Championship	**Ockie Strydom**	*DP World Tour*
AfrAsia Bank Mauritius Open	**Antoine Rozner**	*DP World Tour*

ALTRON BIG EASY TOUR

Blue Valley	**Christiaan Maas** (A)
Huddle Park	**Dongkwan Kim**
Reading	**Gregory Mckay**
Randpark	**Adam Breen**
Houghton	**Ricky Hendler**
Kyalami	**Casey Jarvis** (A)
Soweto	**Gerhard Pepler**
ERPM	**Ruan de Smidt**
Tour Playoff	**Gerhard Pepler (2)**
Tour Final	**Gerhard Pepler (3)**

ASIAN TOUR

Singapore International	**Joohyung Kim**	
SMBC Singapore Open	**Sadom Kaewkanjana**	*Japan Tour*
PIF Saudi International	**Harold Varner III**	
Royal's Cup	**Chan Shih-chang**	
International Series — Thailand	**Sihwan Kim**	
DGC Open	**Nitithorn Thippong**	*PGT India*
Trust Golf Asian Mixed Cup	**Ratchanon Chantananuwat** (A)	*LET*
Trust Golf Asian Stableford Challenge	**Sihwan Kim (2)**	*LET*
GS Caltex Maekyung Open	**Bio Kim**	*KPGA Tour*
International Series — England	**Scott Vincent (1,2)**	
Kolon Korea Open	**Minkyu Kim**	*KPGA Tour*
Mandiri Indonesia Open	**Gaganjeet Bhullar**	
International Series — Singapore	**Nitithorn Thippong (2)**	
International Series — Korea	**Taehoon Ok**	
Yeangder TPC	**Travis Smyth**	
Mercuries Taiwan Masters	**Chan Shih-chang (2)**	
International Series — Morocco	**Jazz Janewattananond**	
International Series — Egypt	**Andy Ogletree**	
Bangabandhu Cup Bangladesh Open	**Danthai Boonma**	
BNI Indonesian Masters	**Sarit Suwannarut**	

ASIAN DEVELOPMENT TOUR

Gurugram Challenge	**Dodge Kemmer**	*PGT India*
Laguna Phuket Challenge	**Thomas Sloman**	
Laguna Phuket Cup	**Sarun Sirithon**	
Blue Canyon Classic	**Chen Guxin**	

Blue Canyon Open	**Settee Prakongvech (1,2)**
OB Golf Invitational	**Naraajie E Ramadhanputra**
Indo Masters	**Harrison Gilbert**
Gunung Geulis Golf Invitational	**Chonlatit Chuenboonngam**
BNI Ciputra Golfpreneur Tournament	**Suteepat Prateeptienchai**
BRG Open	**Chen Guxin (2)**
OB Golf Invitational Jababeka	**Suteepat Prateeptienchai (2)**
Combiphar Players Championship	**Suteepat Prateeptienchai (3)**
PKNS Selangor Masters	**Shahriffudin Ariffin**
PIF Saudi Open	**Naraajie E Ramadhanputra (2)**
Aramco Invitational	**Varanyu Rattanaphiboonkij (1,2)**
Taifong Open	**Hung Chien-Yao**

ALL THAILAND GOLF TOUR

Boonchu Ruangkit Championship	**Settee Prakongvech**
Singha E-San Open	**Atiruj Winaicharoenchai**
Singha All Thailand Memorial	**Atiruj Winaicharoenchai (2)**
Singha Classic	**Varanyu Rattanaphiboonkij**
Singha Laguna Phuket Open	**Witchayanon Chothirunrungrueng**
Singha All Thailand Premier Championship	**Denwit David Boriboonsub**
Singha Pattaya Open	**Settee Prakongvech (2,3)**
Singha Championship	**Gunn Charoenkul**
Singha Chiang Mai Open	**Warun Ieamgaew**
Thailand Open	**Kwanchai Tannin**
Singha Bangkok Open	**Nitithorn Thippong (1,3)**
Singha Thailand Masters	**Poom Saksansin**

CHINA TOUR

Hangzhou International Championship	**An Tong** (A)
Shenyang International Open	**She Zihan**
Hengdian Championship	**Ma Chengyao**
Mitsubishi Electric Open	**Xiao Bowen**
Hainan Golf Open	**Bai Bobby Zhengkai**
CGA Championship	**Zhou Ziqin** (A)
Chongqing Open	**Zhou Yanhan** (A)

KPGA KOREAN TOUR

DB Damage Insurance Promy Open	**Sanghyun Park**
Woori Financial Group Championship	**Heemin Chang**
Descente Korea Munsingwear Match Play	**Eunshin Park**
KB Finance LIIV Championship	**Jiho Yang**
SK Telecom Open	**Bio Kim (2)**
KPGA Championship	**Sanghun Shin**
Hana Bank Invitational	**Junseok Lee**
Asiad CC Busan Open	**Junggon Hwang**
Honors K Sollago Han Jangsang Invitational	**Yongjun Bae**
Woosung Construction Open	**Yonggu Shin**
Bodyfriend Phantom Rovo Gunsan Open	**Yoseop Seo**
LX Championship	**Yoseop Seo (2)**
Bizplay-Electronic Times Open	**Jinho Choi**
DGB Financial Group Open	**Doyeob Mun**
Hyundai Insurance KJ Choi Invitational	**Hyungjoon Lee**
Genesis Championship	**Yeongsu Kim**
Golfzone-Toray Open	**Eunshin Park (2)**
LG Signature Players Championship	**Yeongsu Kim (2)**

MENA TOUR

Tournament 3	**Bailey Gill**	
Tournament 4	**Aron Zemmer**	

PROFESSIONAL GOLF TOUR OF INDIA

Gujarat Open	**Karandeep Kochhar**	
Glade One Masters	**Manu Gandas**	
Mujib Borsho Chattogram Open	**Kshitij Naveed Kaul**	
Tata Steel PGTI Players — Tollygunge	**Yuvraj Singh Sandhu**	
Tata Steel PGTI Players — Chandigarh	**Yuvraj Singh Sandhu (2)**	
Delhi-NCR Open	**Manu Gandas (2)**	
Tata Steel PGTI Players — KGISL	**Khalin H Joshi**	
Impiger Technologies Chennai Open	**Manu Gandas (3)**	
J&K Open	**Yuvraj Singh Sandhu (3)**	
Rajasthan Tourism Jaipur Open	**Om Prakash Chouhan**	
Kapil Dev Grant Thornton Invitational	**Varun Parikh**	
Tata Steel PGTI Players — American Express	**Yuvraj Singh Sandhu (4)**	
Jeev Milkha Singh Invitational	**Gaganjeet Bhullar (1,2)**	
Pune Open	**Veer Ahlawat**	
Telangana Golconda Masters	**Manu Gandas (4)**	
Indianoil Servo Masters	**Yuvraj Singh Sandhu (5)**	
Dream Valley Vooty Masters	**Manu Gandas (5)**	
SSP Chawrasia Invitational	**Manu Gandas (6)**	
Tata Steel Tour Championship	**Chikkarangappa S**	

JAPAN TOUR

Token Homemate Cup	**Jinichiro Kozuma**	
Kansai Open	**Kazuki Higa**	
ISPS Handa Championship Japan	**Yuto Katsuragawa**	
The Crowns	**Yuki Inamori**	
Asia Pacific Diamond Cup	**Shugo Imahira**	*Asian Tour*
Golf Partner Pro-Am	**Shugo Imahira (2)**	
Gateway to The Open Mizuno Open	**Scott Vincent**	
BMW Japan Tour Championship	**Kazuki Higa (2)**	
Aso Iizuka Challenge	**Tomoyo Ikemura**	
Japan Players Championship	**Yuki Inamori (2)**	
Japan PGA Championship	**Mikumu Horikawa**	
Shigeo Nagashima Invitational Sega Sammy Cup	**Hiroshi Iwata**	
Sansan KBC Augusta	**Riki Kawamoto**	
Fujisankei Classic	**Kaito Onishi**	
Shinhan Donghae Open	**Kazuki Higa (3)**	*Asian Tour/KPGA Tour*
ANA Open	**Tomoharu Otsuki**	
Panasonic Open	**Taiga Semikawa (A) (1,2)**	
Vantelin Tokai Classic	**Riki Kawamoto (2)**	
For The Players By The Players	**Shintaro Kobayashi**	
Japan Open Championship	**Taiga Semikawa (A) (2,3)**	
Heiwa PGM Championship	**Rikuya Hoshino**	
Mynavi ABC Championship	**Mikumu Horikawa (2)**	
Mitsui Sumitomo Visa Taiheiyo Masters	**Ryo Ishikawa**	
Dunlop Phoenix	**Kazuki Higa (4)**	
Casio World Open	**Chan Kim**	
Golf Nippon Series JT Cup	**Hideto Tanihara**	

ABEMA TV TOUR

Novil Cup	**Yuto Soeda**	
iGolf Shaper Challenge	**Hiroki Tanaka**	
Taiheiyo Club Challenge	**Taisei Yamada**	

Landic Challenge 9	**Taiko Nishiyama**	
Japan Create Challenge	**Taiga Semikawa (A)**	
Daisendori Cup	**Shota Matsumoto**	
Japan Players Championship Challenge	**Chisato Takamiya (A)**	
Minami Akita Michinoku Challenge	**Takashi Ogiso**	
Dunlop Phoenix Challenge	**Masayuki Yamashita (A)**	
PGM Challenge	**Yujiro Ohori**	
ISPS Handa Hero ni Nare Challenge	**Masanori Kobayashi**	
Elite Grips Challenge	**Takashi Ogiso (2)**	
Ryo Ishikawa Everyone Project Challenge	**Takuya Higa**	
Delight Works JGTO Final	**Yujiro Ohori (2)**	

ISPS HANDA PGA TOUR OF AUSTRALASIA

Fortinet Australian PGA Championship	**Jediah Morgan**	
Queensland PGA Championship	**Anthony Qualye**	
TPS Victoria	**Todd Sinnott**	*WPGA Australasia*
Vic Open	**Dimitrios Papadatos**	
TPS Sydney	**Jarryd Felton**	*WPGA Australasia*
TPS Hunter Valley	**Aaron Pike**	*WPGA Australasia*
Golf Challenge NSW Open	**Harrison Crowe (A)**	
The National PGA Classic	**Derek Ackerman**	
CKB WA PGA Championship	**Jay Mackenzie**	
Nexus Advisernet WA Open	**Braden Becker**	
Tailor-Made Building Services NT PGA Championship	**Austin Bautista**	
CKB WA PGA Championship	**David Micheluzzi**	
Nexus Advisernet WA Open	**Deyen Lawson**	
Victorian PGA Championship	**Andrew Martin**	
Queensland PGA Championship	**Aaron Wilkin**	
Fortinet Australian PGA Championship	**Cameron Smith (1,5)**	*DP World Tour*
ISPS Handa Australian Open	**Adrian Meronk (1,2)**	*DP World Tour*
Cathedral Invitational	**Nick Flanagan**	
Gippsland Super6	**Tom Power Horan**	
Sandbelt Invitational	**Cam Davis**	

LIV GOLF INVITATIONAL SERIES

London Invitational	**Charl Schwartzel**	
Portland Invitational	**Branden Grace**	
Bedminster Invitational	**Henrik Stenson**	
Boston Invitational	**Dustin Johnson**	
Chicago Invitational	**Cameron Smith (1,4)**	
Bangkok Invitational	**Eugenio Lopez-Chacarra**	*MENA Tour*
Jeddah Invitational	**Brooks Koepka**	*MENA Tour*
Miami Team Championship	**Four Aces**	

LPGA TOUR

Hilton Grand Vacations Tournament of Champions	**Danielle Kang**
Gainbridge LPGA	**Lydia Ko**
LPGA Drive On Championship	**Leona Maguire**
HSBC Women's World Championship	**Jin Young Ko**
Honda LPGA Thailand	**Nanna Koerstz Madsen**
JBTC Classic	**Atthaya Thitikul**
Lotte Championship	**Hyo Joo Kim**
Dio Implant LA Open	**Nasa Hataoka**
Palos Verdes Championship	**Marina Alex**
Cognizant Founders Cup	**Minjee Lee**
Bank of Hope LPGA Match Play	**Eun-Hee Ji**
ShopRite LPGA Classic	**Brooke Henderson**

Meijer LPGA Classic	**Jennifer Kupcho (2)**	
Dow Great Lakes Bay Invitational	**Jennifer Kupcho (3)/Lizette Salas**	
CP Women's Open	**Paula Reto (1,2)**	
Dana Open	**Gaby Lopez**	
Kroger Queen City Championship	**Ally Ewing**	
AmazingCre Portland Classic	**Andrea Lee (1,2)**	
Walmart NW Arkansas Championship	**Atthaya Thitikul (2)**	
The Ascendant LPGA	**Charley Hull**	
LPGA Mediheal Championship	**Jodi Ewart Shadoff**	
BMW Ladies Championship	**Lydia Ko (2)**	
Pelican Women's Championship	**Nelly Korda (1,2)**	
CME Group Tour Championship	**Lydia Ko (3)**	

EPSON TOUR

Florida's Natural Charity Classic	**Kum-Kang Park**	
Carlisle Arizona Women's Golf Classic	**Fatima Fernandez Cano**	
IOA Championship	**Linnea Strom**	
Casino del Sol Golf Classic	**Andrea Lee**	
Copper Rock Championship	**Dottie Ardina**	
Garden City Charity Classic	**Gabriella Then**	
IOA Golf Classic	**Grace Kim**	
Inova Mission Inn Championship	**Gina Kim**	
Carolina Golf Classic	**Lucy Li**	
Ann Arbor's Road to the LPGA	**Kiira Riihijarvi**	
Island Resort Championship	**Ssu-Chia Cheng**	
Twin Bridges Championship	**Lucy Li (2)**	
FireKeepers Casino Hotel Championship	**Xiaowen Yin**	
French Lick Charity Classic	**Xiaowen Yin (2)**	
Four Winds Invitational	**Yan Liu**	
Circling Raven Championship	**Jillian Hollis**	
Wildhorse Ladies Golf Classic	**Daniela Iacobelli**	
Guardian Championship	**Maria Torres**	
Murphy USA El Dorado Shootout	**Britney Yada**	
Tuscaloosa Toyota Classic	**Celine Borge**	
Epson Tour Championship	**Jaravee Boonchant**	

LADIES EUROPEAN TOUR

Magical Kenya Ladies Open	**Esther Henseleit**	
Aramco Saudi Ladies International	**Georgia Hall**	
Joburg Ladies Open	**Linn Grant (1,3)**	*Sunshine Ladies Tour*
Investec SA Women's Open	**Lee-Anne Pace**	*Sunshine Ladies Tour*
Madrid Ladies Open	**Ana Pelaez Trivino**	
Aramco Team Series — Bangkok	**Manon De Roey**	
Jabra Ladies Classic	**Tiia Koivisto**	
Mithra Belgian Ladies Open	**Linn Grant (2,4)**	
Ladies Italian Open	**Morgane Metraux**	
Volvo Car Scandinavian Mixed	**Linn Grant (3,5)**	
Aramco Team Series — London	**Bronte Law**	
Tipsport Czech Ladies Open	**Jana Melichova** (A)	
Amundi German Masters	**Maja Stark (2)**	
Estrella Damm Ladies Open	**Carlota Ciganda**	
Big Green Egg Open	**Anna Nordqvist**	
Trust Golf Women's Scottish Open	**Ayaka Furue**	*LPGA*
ISPS Handa World Invitational	**Maja Stark (3)**	*LPGA*
Aramco Team Series — Sotogrande	**Nelly Korda**	
Skafto Open	**Linn Grant (4,6)**	
Aland 100 Ladies Open	**Anne-Charlotte Mora**	

VP Bank Swiss Ladies Open	**Liz Young**
Lacoste Ladies Open de France	**Ines Laklalech**
KPMG Women's Irish Open	**Klara Spilkova**
Aramco Team Series — New York	**Lexi Thompson**
Hero Women's Indian Open	**Olivia Cowan**
Aramco Team Series — Jeddah	**Chiara Noja (1,2)**
Andalucia Costa del Sol Open de Espana	**Caroline Hedwall**

LET ACCESS SERIES

Terre Blanche Ladies Open	**Lucrezia Colombotto Rosso**
Flumserberg Ladies Open	**Lauren Holmey**
PGA Championship Trelleborg	**Meja Ortengren**
Amundi Czech Ladies Challenge	**Chiara Noja**
Montauban Ladies Open	**Momoka Kobori**
Smorum Ladies Open	**Cecilie Leth-Nissen** (A)
Golf Vlaanderen LETAS Trophy	**Kristalle Blum**
Hauts de France – Pas de Calais Golf Open	**Momoka Kobori (2)**
Trust Golf Links Series — Ramside Hall	**Chanettee Wannasaen**
Trust Golf Links Series — Musselburgh	**Arpichaya Yubol**
Santander Golf Tour Malaga	**Sara Kouskova**
Vasteras Open	**Sara Ericsson** (A)
Big Green Egg Swedish Match Play Championship	**Patricia Schmidt**
Goteborg Open	**Nastasia Nadaud**
Elite Hotels Open	**Sara Kouskova (2)**
ASGI Lavaux Ladies Open	**Sara Kouskova (3)**
Rose Ladies Open	**My Leander**
Santander Golf Tour — Burgos	**Verena Gimmy**
Calatayud Ladies Open	**Amy Taylor**

SUNSHINE LADIES TOUR

Vodacom Origins of Golf Final Pro-Am	**Lejan Lewthwaite**
SunBet Cape Town Ladies Open	**Nadia van der Westhuizen**
Dimension Data Ladies Challenge	**Linn Grant**
SuperSport Ladies Challenge	**Paula Reto**
Jabra Ladies Classic — Sunshine	**Linn Grant (2)**

KOREA LPGA TOUR

Lotte Rent a Car Ladies Open	**Su Yeon Jang**
Mediheal Hankook Ilbo Championship	**Ji Young Park**
Nexen Saint Nine Masters	**Hae Ran Ryu**
CreaS F&C KLPGA Championship	**A Lim Kim**
Kyochon Honey Ladies Open	**A Yean Cho**
NH Ladies Championship	**Min Ji Park**
Doosan Match Play Championship	**Jung Min Hong**
E1 Charity Open	**Yunji Jeong**
Lotte Open	**Yu Jin Sung**
Celltrion Queens Masters	**Min Ji Park (2)**
DB Group Korea Women's Open	**Hee Jeong Lim**
BC Card Hankyung Ladies Cup	**Min Ji Park (3)**
McCol Mona Park Open	**Jin Hee Im**
Daebo hausD Open	**Ga Run Song**
Ever Collagen Queens Crown	**Ina Yoon**
Hoban Seoul Shinmun Women's Classic	**A Yean Cho (2)**
Jeju Samdasoo Masters	**Han Sol Ji**
Dayouwinia MBN Ladies Open	**So Young Lee**
HighOne Resort Ladies Open	**Jin Seon Han**
Hanwha Classic	**Ji Won Hong**

KG Edaily Ladies Open	**Jeong Mee Hwang**
KB Financial Group Star Championship	**Min Ji Park (4)**
OK Financial Group Se Ri Pak Invitational	**Su Ji Kim**
Hana Financial Group Championship	**Su Ji Kim (2)**
Hite Jinro Championship	**Min Ji Park (5)**
Dongbu Koreit Championship	**Ga Young Lee**
Wemix Championship	**Hyo Ju You**
SK Networks Seoul Economics Ladies Classic	**So Mi Lee**
S-Oil Championship	**So Mi Lee (2)**
SK Shieldus SK Telecom Championship	**Min Ji Park (6)**
Hana Financial Group Singapore Women's Open	**Ji Young Park (2)**
PLK Pacific Links Championship	**Jung Min Lee**

KOREAN DREAM TOUR

Torbist Phoenix 3	**Seoyoon Kim^{2}**
MC2 Gunsan 6	**Ka Bin Choi**
QCapital Partners Norangtongdak Challenge 1	**Hani Kim**
Muan-All For You 8	**Ka Bin Choi (2)**
Muan-All For You 10	**Yeonseo Hwang**
Qcapital Partners Norangtondak Challenge 2	**Hye Lim Jo**
Torbist Phoenix 12	**Hye Lim Jo (2)**
Qcapital Partners Dream Tour Grand Final	**Seoyoon Kim2 (2)**

LPGA OF TAIWAN TOUR

Hitachi Ladies Classic	**Pei-Ying Tsai**
WPG Ladies Open	**Hsin Lee**
Jing Mao Ladies Open	**Hsin Lee (2)**
Grin Cup Charity Open	**Juliana Hung**
BGC Thailand Ladies Masters	**Patcharajutar Kongkraphan**
Da Da Digital Ladies Open	**Yu-Ju Chen**
Sampo Ladies Open	**Tsai-Ching Tseng**
Party Golfers Ladies Open	**Peng-Shan Liu**
Wistron Ladies Open	**Ya-Chun Chang**
Taiwan Mobile Ladies Open	**Chia Yen Wu**
CTBC Invitational	**Peiyun Chien**

CHINA LPGA TOUR

Hangzhou International Championship	**Tong An (A)**
Golf Liquor Challenge	**Zixin Ni (A)**
CTBC Ladies Classic	**Jiaze Sun**
Beijing Ladies Open	**Jiaze Sun (2)**
Zhangjiagang Shuangshan Challenge	**Liqi Zeng**
CGA Ladies Championship	**Liqi Zeng (2)**
Guowie Centre Plaza Zhuhai Challenge	**Xiang Sui**

JAPAN LPGA TOUR

Daikin Orchid Ladies	**Mao Saigo**
Meiji Yasuda Ladies Yokhama Tire	**Pei-Ying Tsai (1,2)**
T-Point Eneos Tournament	**Kotone Hori**
AXA Ladies	**Mao Saigo (2)**
Yamaha Ladies Open	**Mao Saigo (3)**
FujiFilm Studio Alice Ladies Open	**Momoko Ueda**
KKT Cup Vantelin Ladies Open	**Nozomi Uetake**
Fujisankei Ladies Classic	**Sayaka Takahasi**
Panasonic Ladies Open	**Mao Saigo (4)**
World Ladies Championship Salonpas Cup	**Miyuu Yamashita**

Hoken no Madoguchi Ladies	**Ayaka Watanabe**	
Bridgestone Ladies Open	**Mao Saigo (5)**	
Resort Trust Ladies	**Sakura Koiwai**	
Richard Mille Yonex Ladies	**Mone Inami**	
Ai Miyazato Suntory Ladies Open	**Miyuu Yamashita (2)**	
Nichirei Ladies	**Yuna Nishimura**	
Earth Mondahmin Cup	**Ayako Kimura**	
Shiseido Ladies Open	**Serena Aoki**	
Nippon Ham Ladies Classic	**Yuna Nishimura (2)**	
Daito Kentaku Eheyanet Ladies	**Erika Kikuchi**	
Rakuten Super Ladies	**Minami Katsu**	
Hokkaido Meiji Cup	**Min Young Lee2**	
NEC Karuizawa 72	**Chisato Iwai**	
CAT Ladies	**Chisato Iwai (2)**	
Nitori Ladies	**Mone Inami (2)**	
Golf5 Ladies	**Yuting Seki**	
JLPGA Championship Konica Minolta Cup	**Haruka Kawasaki (1,2)**	
Sumitomo Life Vitality Ladies Tokai Classic	**Amiyu Ozeki**	
Miyagi TV Cup Dunlop Ladies Open	**Miyuu Yamashita (3)**	
Japan Women's Open Championship	**Minami Katsu (2)**	
Stanley Ladies Honda	**Sakura Koiwai (2)**	
Fujitsu Ladies	**Ayaka Furue (1,2)**	
Nobuta Ladies Masters	**Haruka Kawasaki (2,3)**	
Mitsubishi Electric Hisako Higuchi Ladies	**Kumiko Kaneda**	
Toto Japan Classic	**Gemma Dryburgh**	*LPGA*
Itoen Ladies	**Miyuu Yamashita (4)**	
Daio Paper Elleair Ladies Open	**Saiki Fujita**	
JLPGA Tour Championship Ricoh Cup	**Miyuu Yamashita (5)**	

JAPAN STEP UP TOUR

Rashink Ningineer RKB Ladies	**Mayu Hosaka**	
Hanasaka Ladies Yanmar Tournament	**Hana Wakimoto**	
Fundokin Ladies	**Nao Obayashi**	
KCFG Madonoume Cup	**Satsuki Kuwayama**	
Twin Field Ladies	**Onnarin Sattayabanphot**	
ECC Ladies	**Kokona Sakurai**	
Shizuoka Shimbun & SBS Ladies	**Hsuan-Yu Yao**	
Castrol Ladies	**Ami Hirai**	
San-In Goenmusubi Ladies	**Haruka Kawasaki**	
Sanyo Shimbun Ladies Cup	**Kokona Sakurai (2)**	
Chugoku Shimbun Chupea Ladies Cup	**Kokona Sakurai (3)**	
Sky Ladies ABC Cup	**Misaki Miyazawa**	
Kanehide Miyarabi Open	**Kokona Sakurai (4)**	
Udon-Ken Ladies	**Kokona Sakurai (5)**	*LPGA Taiwan*
Shishido Hills Ladies Mori Building Cup	**Mana Shinozaki**	
Yamaguchi Shunan Ladies Cup	**Miyu Shinkai**	
Kyoto Ladies Open	**Hina Arakaki**	

WPGA TOUR OF AUSTRALASIA

Fortinet Australian WPGA Championship	**Su Oh**	
Drummond Melbourne International	**Karis Davidson**	
Vic Open	**Hannah Green**	*PGAT Australasia*
TPS Murray River	**Hannah Green (2)**	
Australian Women's Classic	**Meghan MacLaren**	*LET*
Women's NSW Open	**Maja Stark**	*LET*
ISPS Handa Australian Open	**Ashleigh Buhai (1,2)**	

PGA TOUR CHAMPIONS

Mitsubishi Electric Championship	**Miguel Angel Jimenez**	
Chubb Classic	**Bernhard Langer**	
Cologuard Classic	**Miguel Angel Jimenez (2)**	
Hoag Classic	**Retief Goosen**	
Rapiscan Systems Classic	**Steven Alker**	
ClubCorp Classic	**Scott Parel**	
Insperity Invitational	**Steven Alker (2)**	
Mitsubishi Electric Classic	**Steve Flesch**	
Regions Tradition	**Steve Stricker**	
KitchenAid Senior PGA Championship	**Steven Alker (3)**	*European Legends*
Principal Charity Classic	**Jerry Kelly**	
American Family Insurance Championship	**Thongchai Jaidee**	
US Senior Open	**Padraig Harrington**	*European Legends*
Bridgestone Senior Players Championship	**Jerry Kelly (2)**	
Shaw Charity Classic	**Jerry Kelly (3)**	
Boeing Classic	**Miguel Angel Jimenez (3)**	
Dick's Sporting Goods Open	**Padraig Harrington (2)**	
Ally Challenge	**Steve Stricker (2)**	
Ascension Charity Classic	**Padraig Harrington (3)**	
Sanford International	**Steve Stricker (3)**	
Pure Insurance Championship	**Steve Flesch (2)**	
Constellation Furyk & Friends	**Steve Stricker (4)**	
SAS Championship	**Fred Couples**	
Dominion Energy Charity Classic	**Steven Alker (4)**	
TimberTech Championship	**Bernhard Langer (2)**	
Charles Schwab Cup Championship	**Padraig Harrington (4)**	

EUROPEAN LEGENDS TOUR

Riegler & Partner Legends	**Euan McIntosh**	
Jersey Legends	**Richard Green**	
Farmfoods European Legends Links Championship	**Paul Lawrie**	
Swiss Seniors Open	**James Kingston**	
Winston Golf Senior Open	**Richard Green (2)**	
The Senior Open Presented by Rolex	**Darren Clarke**	*PGAT Champions*
JCB Championship	**Alex Cejka**	
Irish Legends	**Phillip Price**	
Staysure PGA Seniors Championship	**Adilson Da Silva**	
WCM Legends Open de France	**Gary Marks**	
Farmfoods European Senior Masters	**Paul Lawrie (2)**	
Italian Senior Open	**Ricardo Gonzalez**	
MCB Tour Championship — Seychelles	**Joakim Haeggman**	
MCB Tour Championship — Mauritius	**Thomas Bjorn**	

JAPAN PGA SENIOR TOUR

Kinshu Senior Okinawa Open	**Yoshinobu Tsukada**
Nojima Champions Cup	**Takashi Kanemoto**
Sumaiida Senior Cup	**Kiyoshi Maita**
Starts Senior	**Hiroyuki Fujita**
Fancl Classic	**Toru Suzuki**
Maruhan Cup Taiheiyo Club Senior	**Hiroyuki Fujita (2)**
Komatsu Open	**Keiichiro Fukabori**
Japan Senior Open Championship	**Prayad Marksaeng**
Japan PGA Senior Championship	**Prayad Marksaeng (2)**
Sasebo Senior Trust Group Cup	**Prayad Marksaeng (3)**
ISPS Handa After All Interesting Senior	**Prayad Marksaeng (4)**
Fukuoka Senior Open	**Prayad Marksaeng (5)**

Cosmo Health Senior Cup	**Prayad Marksaeng (6)**
Iwasaki Shiratsuyu Senior	**Mitsuhiro Watanabe**

LEGENDS OF THE LPGA

Legends Tour Challenge	**Jackie Gallagher-Smith**
Senior LPGA Championship	**Karrie Webb**
Land O'Lakes Legends Classic	**Juli Inkster**
US Senior Women's Open	**Jill McGill**
BJ's Charity Championship	**Pat Bradley/Jamie Fischer**

Multiple Winners of 2022

6 — Manu Gandas	Glade One Masters	*PGT India*
	Delhi-NCR Open	
	Impiger Technologies Chennai Open	
	Telangana Golconda Masters	
	Dream Valley Vooty Masters	
	SSP Chawrasia Invitational	
6 — Linn Grant	Dimension Data Ladies Challenge	*Sunshine Ladies*
	Jabra Ladies Classic — Sunshine	*Sunshine Ladies*
	Joburg Ladies Open	*Sunshine Ladies/LET*
	Mithra Belgian Ladies Open	*LET*
	Volvo Car Scandinavian Mixed	*LET/DP World*
	Skafto Open	*LET*
6 — Prayad Marksaeng	Japan Senior Open Championship	*Japan Seniors*
	Japan PGA Senior Championship	
	Sasebo Senior Trust Group Cup	
	ISPS Handa After All Interesting Senior	
	Fukuoka Senior Open	
	Cosmo Health Senior Cup	
6 — Min Ji Park	NH Ladies Championship	*Korea LPGA*
	Celltrion Queens Masters	
	BC Card Hankyung Ladies Cup	
	KB Financial Group Star Championship	
	Hite Jinro Championship	
	SK Shieldus SK Telecom Championship	
5 — Mao Saigo	Daikin Orchid Ladies	*Japan LPGA*
	AXA Ladies	
	Yamaha Ladies Open	
	Panasonic Ladies Open	
	Bridgestone Ladies Open	
5 — Kokona Sakurai	ECC Ladies	*Japan Step Up*
	Sanyo Shimbun Ladies Cup	
	Chugoku Shimbun Chupea Ladies Cup	
	Kanehide Miyarabi Open	
	Udon-Ken Ladies	
5 — Yuvraj Singh Sandhu	Tata Steel PGTI Players — Tollygunge	*PGT India*
	Tata Steel PGTI Players — Chandigarh	
	J&K Open	
	Tata Steel PGTI Players — American Express	
	Indianoil Servo Masters	

5 — Cameron Smith	Sentry Tournament of Champions	*PGA Tour*
	The Players Championship	*PGA Tour*
	The 150th Open	*Majors*
	Chicago Invitational	*LIV Golf*
	Fortinet Australian PGA Championship	*PGAT Australasia*
5 — Miyuu Yamashita	World Ladies Championship Salonpas Cup	*Japan LPGA*
	Ai Miyazato Suntory Ladies Open	
	Miyagi TV Cup Dunlop Ladies Open	
	Itoen Ladies	
	JLPGA Tour Championship Ricoh Cup	
4 — Steven Alker	Rapiscan Systems Classic	*PGAT Champions*
	Insperity Invitational	
	KitchenAid Senior PGA Championship	
	Dominion Energy Charity Classic	
4 — Padraig Harrington	US Senior Open	*PGAT Champions*
	Dick's Sporting Goods Open	
	Ascension Charity Classic	
	Charles Schwab Cup Championship	
4 — Kazuki Higa	Kansai Open	*Japan Tour*
	BMW Japan Tour Championship	
	Shinhan Donghae Open	
	Dunlop Phoenix	
4 — Scottie Scheffler	WM Phoenix Open	*PGA Tour*
	Arnold Palmer Invitational	*PGA Tour*
	WGC Dell Technologies Match Play	*PGA Tour*
	Masters Tournament	*Majors*
4 — Steve Stricker	Regions Tradition	*PGAT Champions*
	Ally Challenge	
	Sanford International	
	Constellation Furyk & Friends	
3 — James Allan	Cubefunder Shootout	*EuroPro*
	Dell Technologies Championship	
	Matchroom Tour Championship	
3 — Jeppe Kristian Andersen	PGA Catalunya Resort Championship	*Nordic*
	Goteborg Open	
	Sydbank Road to Europe Final	
3 — John Axelsen	GolfStar Winter Series I	*Nordic*
	Race to Himmerland	
	MoreGolf Mastercard Tour Final	
3 — Gregorio De Leo	Memorial Giorgio Bordoni	*Alps Tour*
	Alps de Las Castillas	
	Roma Alps Open	
3 — Tony Finau	3M Open	*PGA Tour*
	Rocket Mortgage Classic	
	Cadence Bank Houston Open	
3 — Miguel Angel Jimenez	Mitsubishi Electric Championship	*PGAT Champions*
	Cologuard Classic	
	Boeing Classic	
3 — Haruka Kawasaki	San-In Goenmusubi Ladies	*Korean Dream*
	JLPGA Championship Konica Minolta Cup	*Korea LPGA*
	Nobuta Ladies Masters	*Korea LPGA*
3 — Jerry Kelly	Principal Charity Classic	*PGAT Champions*
	Bridgestone Senior Players Championship	
	Shaw Charity Classic	

3 — Joohyung Kim	Singapore International	*Asian Tour*
	Wyndham Championship	*PGA Tour*
	Shriners Children's Open	*PGA Tour*
3 — Lydia Ko	Gainbridge LPGA	*LPGA*
	BMW Ladies Championship	
	CME Group Tour Championship	
3 — Sara Kouskova	Santander Golf Tour Malaga	*LET Access*
	Elite Hotels Open	
	ASGI Lavaux Ladies Open	
3 — Jennifer Kupcho	Chevron Championship	*LPGA*
	Meijer LPGA Classic	
	Dow Great Lakes Bay Invitational	
3 — Rory McIlroy	RBC Canadian Open	*PGA Tour*
	Tour Championship	
	CJ Cup	
3 — Gerhard Pepler	Soweto	*Big Easy*
	Tour Playoff	
	Tour Final	
3 — Settee Prakongvech	Boonchu Ruangkit Championship	*All Thailand*
	Blue Canyon Open	*Asian Development*
	Singha Pattaya Open	*All Thailand*
3 — Suteepat Prateeptienchai	BNI Ciputra Golfpreneur Tournament	*Asian Development*
	OB Golf Invitational Jababeka	
	Combiphar Players Championship	
3 — Jon Rahm	Mexico Open	*PGA Tour*
	Acciona Open de Espana	*DP World Tour*
	DP World Tour Championship	*DP World Tour*
3 — Xander Schauffele	Zurich Classic	*PGA Tour*
	Travelers Championship	*PGA Tour*
	Genesis Scottish Open	*DP World /PGA Tour*
3 — Taiga Semikawa (A)	Japan Create Challenge	*Abema Tour*
	Panasonic Open	*Japan Tour*
	Japan Open Championship	*Japan Tour*
3 — Maja Stark	Women's NSW Open	*LET/WPGA*
	Amundi German Masters	*LET*
	ISPS Handa World Invitational	*LET*
3 — Nitithorn Thippong	DGC Open	*Asian/PGT India*
	International Series — Singapore	*Asian Tour*
	Singha Bangkok Open	*All Thiland*
2 — Wil Bateman	ATB Classic	*PGAT Canada*
	Fortinet Cup Championship	
2 — Jean Bekirian	Raiffeisen Pro Golf Tour St Polten	*Pro Golf*
	Altepro Trophy	
2 — Gaganjeet Bhullar	Mandiri Indonesia Open	*Asian Tour*
	Jeev Milkha Singh Invitational	*PGT India*
2 — Frederik Birkelund (A)	Bravo Tours Open	*Nordic*
	Great Northern Challenge	
2 — Ashleigh Buhai	AIG Women's Open	*Majors*
	ISPS Handa Australian Open	*WPGA*
2 — Sam Burns	Valspar Championship	*PGA Tour*
	Charles Schwab Challenge	
2 — Patrick Cantlay	Zurich Classic	*PGA Tour*
	BMW Championship	
2 — A Yean Cho	Kyochon Honey Ladies Open	*Korea LPGA*
	Hoban Seoul Shinmun Women's Classic	

2 — Ka Bin Choi	MC2 Gunsan 6	*Korean Dream*
	Muan-All For You 8	
2 — George Coetzee	Vodacom Origins of Golf — De Zalze	*Sunshine*
	PGA Championship	
2 — Parker Coody	CentrePort Canada Rail Park Manitoba Open	*PGAT Canada*
	TaylorMade Pebble Beach Invitational	*unofficial*
2 — Cristobal Del Solar	Volvo Golf Championship	*Latinoamerica*
	Neuquen Argentina Classic	
2 — Ewen Ferguson	Commercial Bank Qatar Masters	*DP World Tour*
	ISPS Handa World Invitational	
2 — Steve Flesch	Mitsubishi Electric Classic	*PGAT Champions*
	Pure Insurance Championship	
2 — Ryan Fox	Ras al Khaimah Classic	*DP World Tour*
	Alfred Dunhill Links Championship	
2 — Hiroyuki Fujita	Starts Senior	*Japan Seniors*
	Maruhan Cup Taiheiyo Club Senior	
2 — Ayaka Furue	Trust Golf Women's Scottish Open	*LPGA/LET*
	Fujitsu Ladies	*Japan LPGA*
2 — Mathias Gladbjerg	Thomas Bjorn Samso Classic	
	Big Green Egg Swedish Matchplay Championship	
2 — Noah Goodwin	Sotheby's International Realty Canada Ontario Open	*PGAT Canada*
	GolfBC Championship	
2 — Hannah Green	Vic Open	*WPGA*
	TPS Murray River	*WPGA/PGAT Australasia*
2 — Richard Green	Jersey Legends	*European Legends*
	Winston Golf Senior Open	
2 — Chen Guxin	Blue Canyon Classic	*Asian Development*
	BRG Open	
2 — Marc Hammer	Weihenstephan Open	
	Euram Bank Open	
2 — Brooke Henderson	ShopRite LPGA Classic	*LPGA*
	Amundi Evian Championship	*Majors*
2 — Josh Hilleard	Ignis Management Championship	*EuroPro*
	Wright-Morgan Championship	
2 — Rasmus Holmberg	PGA Championship Landeryd Masters	*Nordic*
	Greatdays Trophy	
2 — Tom Hoge	AT&T Pebble Beach Pro-Am	*PGA Tour*
	QBE Shootout	
2 — Max Homa	Wells Fargo Championship	
	Fortinet Championship	
2 — Mikumu Horikawa	Japan PGA Championship	
	Mynavi ABC Championship	
2 — August Thor Host	Moss & Rygge Open	*Nordic*
	Trust Forsikring Championship	
2 — Viktor Hovland	Slync.io Dubai Desert Classic	*DP World Tour*
	Hero World Challenge	*PGA Tour*
2 — Shugo Imahira	Asia Pacific Diamond Cup	*Japan Tour/Asian Tour*
	Golf Partner Pro-Am	*Japan Tour*
2 — Mone Inami	Richard Mille Yonex Ladies	*Japan LPGA*
	Nitori Ladies	
2 — Yuki Inamori	The Crowns	*Japan Tour*
	Japan Players Championship	
2 — Chisato Iwai	NEC Karuizawa 72	*Japan LPGA*
	CAT Ladies	
2 — Christian Jacobsen	Unicef Championship	*Nordic*
	Esbjerg Open	

2 — Hye Lim Jo	Qcapital Partners Norangtondak Challenge 2	*Korean Dream*
	Torbist Phoenix 12	
2 — Minami Katsu	Rakuten Super Ladies	*Japan LPGA*
	Japan Women's Open Championship	
2 — Riki Kawamoto	Sansan KBC Augusta	*Japan Tour*
	Vantelin Tokai Classic	
2 — Bio Kim	GS Caltex Maekyung Open	*Asian Tour*
	SK Telecom Open	
2 — Seoyoon Kim[2]	Torbist Phoenix 3	*Korean Dream*
	Qcapital Partners Dream Tour Grand Final	
2 — Sihwan Kim	International Series — Thailand	*Asian Tour*
	Trust Golf Asian Stableford Challenge	*Asian Tour/LET*
2 — Su Ji Kim	OK Financial Group Se Ri Pak Invitational	*Korea LPGA*
	Hana Financial Group Championship	
2 — Yeongsu Kim	Genesis Championship	*KPGA Tour*
	LG Signature Players Championship	
2 — Nathan Kimsey	Le Vaudreuil Golf Challenge	*Challenge Tour*
	Rolex Challenge Tour Grand Final	
2 — Alexander Knappe	Dimension Data Pro-Am	*Sunshine/Challenge*
	B-NL Challenge Trophy	*Challenge*
2 — Momoka Kobori	Montauban Ladies Open	*LET Access*
	Hauts de France – Pas de Calais Golf Open	
2 — Sakura Koiwai	Resort Trust Ladies	*Japan LPGA*
	Stanley Ladies Honda	
2 — Nelly Korda	Aramco Team Series — Sotogrande	*LET*
	Pelican Women's Championship	*LPGA*
2 — Bernhard Langer	Chubb Classic	*PGAT Champions*
	TimberTech Championship	
2 — Pablo Larrazabal	MyGolfLife Open	*Sunshine/DP World*
	ISPS Handa Championship Spain	*DP World Tour*
2 — Thriston Lawrence	Omega European Masters	*DP World Tour*
	Investec South African Open	*Sunshine/DP World*
2 — Paul Lawrie	Farmfoods European Legends Links Championship	*European Legends*
	Farmfoods European Senior Masters	
2 — Andrea Lee	Casino del Sol Golf Classic	*Epson*
	AmazingCre Portland Classic	*LPGA*
2 — Hsin Lee	WPG Ladies Open	*LPGA Taiwan*
	Jing Mao Ladies Open	
2 — Minjee Lee	Cognizant Founders Cup	*LPGA*
	US Women's Open	*Majors*
2 — So Mi Lee	SK Networks Seoul Economics Ladies Classic	*Korea LPGA*
	S-Oil Championship	
2 — Lucy Li	Carolina Golf Classic	*Epson*
	Twin Bridges Championship	
2 — Adrian Meronk	Horizon Irish Open	*DP World Tour*
	ISPS Handa Australian Open	*Australasia/DP World*
2 — Chiara Noja	Amundi Czech Ladies Challenge	*LET Access*
	Aramco Team Series — Jeddah	*LET*
2 — Yuna Nishimura	Nichirei Ladies	*Japan LPGA*
	Nippon Ham Ladies Classic	
2 — Takashi Ogiso	Minami Akita Michinoku Challenge	*Abema Tour*
	Elite Grips Challenge	
2 — Yujiro Ohori	PGM Challenge	*Abema Tour*
	Delight Works JGTO Final	
2 — Eunshin Park	Descente Korea Munsingwear Match Play	*KPGA Tour*
	Golfzone-Toray Open	

2 — Ji Young Park	Mediheal Hankook Ilbo Championship	*Korea LPGA*
	Hana Financial Group Singapore Women's Open	
2 — Naraajie E Ramadhanputra	OB Golf Invitational	*Asian Development*
	PIF Saudi Open	
2 — Varanyu Rattanaphiboonkij	Singha Classic	*All Thailand*
	Aramco Invitational	*Asian Development*
2 — Paula Reto	SuperSport Ladies Challenge	*Sunshine Ladies*
	CP Women's Open	*LPGA*
2 — JC Ritchie	Bain's Whisky Cape Town Open	*Sunshine/Challenge*
	Jonsson Workwear Open	
2 — Martin Rohwer	Vodacom Origins of Golf Final	*Sunshine*
	Bain's Whisky Ubunye Championship	
2 — Matt Ryan	Estrella del Mar Open	
	Scotia Wealth Management Chile Open	
2 — Yoseop Seo	Bodyfriend Phantom Rovo Gunsan Open	*KPGA Tour*
	LX Championship	
2 — Robby Shelton	BMW Charity Pro-Am	*Korn Ferry Tour*
	Pinnacle Bank Championship	
2 — Chan Shih-chang	Royal's Cup	*Asian Tour*
	Mercuries Taiwan Masters	
2 — Jiaze Sun	CTBC Ladies Classic	*China LPGA*
	Beijing Ladies Open	
2 — Atthaya Thitikul	JBTC Classic	*LPGA*
	Walmart NW Arkansas Championship	
2 — Pei-Ying Tsai	Hitachi Ladies Classic	*LPGA Taiwan*
	Meiji Yasuda Ladies Yokhama Tire	*Japan LPGA*
2 — Tom Vaillant (A)	Open de la Mirabelle d'Or	*Alps Tour*
	Aravell Golf Open	
2 — Albert Venter	FBC Zim Open	*Sunshine*
	SunBet Challenge — Time Square	
2 — Scott Vincent	Gateway to The Open Mizuno Open	*Japan Tour*
	International Series — England	*Asian Tour*
2 — Atiruj Winaicharoenchai	Singha E-San Open	*All Thailand*
	Singha All Thailand Memorial	
2 — Xiaowen Yin	FireKeepers Casino Hotel Championship	*Epson*
	French Lick Charity Classic	
2 — Liqi Zeng	Zhangjiagang Shuangshan Challenge	*China LPGA*
	CGA Ladies Championship	

Chronology of 2022

	CHAPTER
JANUARY	
Cameron Smith sets new PGA Tour record of 34 under par in pipping Rahm at Kapalua	10
Jediah Morgan scores record 11-stroke victory in the Australian PGA at home club	19
Su Oh puts her name on the Karrie Webb Cup at the inaugural Australian WPGA	26
Joohyung Kim claims second Asian Tour win as the 19-year-old tops Order of Merit	17
A three-wood to two feet for eagle hands Hideki Matsuyama playoff win in Hawaii	10
Second win in three starts for Belgium's Thomas Pieters with Abu Dhabi triumph	14
Danielle Kang opens LPGA season with three-shot win at Tournament of Champions	21
Viktor Hovland beats Bland in a playoff for Dubai title, his third win in five events	14
Kang, hoping for back-to-back wins, finishes a shot behind Lydia Ko at Gainbridge	21
At the age of 37, Luke List wins first PGA Tour title in playoff over Zalatoris	10
FEBRUARY	
Harold Varner makes 90-foot eagle putt at the 18th to win the Saudi International	17
Ireland sees first LPGA victory as Leona Maguire beats Thompson by three at the Drive On	21
Kiwi Ryan Fox goes wire-to-wire for a five-stroke win at the Ras Al Khaimah Classic	14
Hannah Green wins for the first time in Australia with six-shot Vic Open triumph	26
A 25-foot putt on the third extra hole against Cantlay gives Scottie Scheffler first win	10
With second win in a row, Hannah Green is first woman to claim a mixed event title	26
In the footsteps of Hogan, Joaquin Niemann is fourth to win wire-to-wire at Riviera	10
JC Ritchie goes back-to-back in South Africa at Dimension Data and Jonsson Open	16
MARCH	
A first win for Sihwan Kim 11 years after turning pro at International Series Thailand	17
Jin Young Ko wins on her first start of the year, her sixth in 10 events, at HSBC WWC	21
Scottie Scheffler comes from nine behind at halfway for second win in three at Bay Hill	10
Aaron Pike beats Momoka Kobori at third extra hole in TPS Hunter Valley mixed event	19
An eagle at the second extra hole in Thailand for Nanna Koerstz Madsen's first LPGA win	21
Cameron Smith becomes the fifth Aussie to win The Players with putting masterclass	10
Harrison Crowe, 20, is fifth to hold NSW Amateur and Open titles together since 1930s	19
Georgia Hall handles the windy conditions for five-stroke win at Saudi International	23
Sam Burns successfully defends his title at Valspar in playoff win over Riley	10
Linn Grant wins first LET event as a member and third title on the Sunshine Tour	23
LPGA rookie Atthaya Thitikul, 19, scores 64 and wins Aviara in playoff over Madsen	21
It's three wins in five and world number one for Scottie Scheffler at WGC Match Play	10
APRIL	
Jennifer Kupcho makes last leap into Poppies Pond with maiden victory at Chevron	1
Lee-Anne Pace wins SA Open for fifth time in six-hole playoff against Simmermacher	23
Ratchanon Chantananuwat, 15-year-old amateur, is youngest to win on Asian Tour	17
In first start as world number one, Scottie Scheffler, 25, dominates at Masters	2
Sihwan Kim survives double at last to beat Stark by two at Asian Mixed Stableford	17
Hyo Joo Kim gets back into world's top 10 with two-shot Lotte win in Hawaii	21
Jordan Spieth beats Cantlay in a playoff to win RBC Heritage at Harbour Town	10
Meghan MacLaren wins third LET title — all three in Australia — at Bonville	26
Nasa Hataoko wins LA Open by five after Jin Young Ko quadruple bogey in third round	21
Patrick Cantlay and Xander Schauffele combine for wire-to-wire win in New Orleans	10

MAY

Braden Becker gets lucky bounce off amateur Hopewell's ball to win WA Open 19
A Lim Kim comes from three behind Hyo Joo Kim to win Korea LPGA Championship 24
Tristen Strydom, 2020 Q School winner, scores record six-shot Tour Championship victory 16
Jon Rahm goes wire-to-wire for seventh PGA Tour win at Mexico Open by one stroke 10
Thorbjorn Olesen ended four-year winless drought with eagle-birdie finish at The Belfry 14
A two-shot win for Max Homa at Wells Fargo three years after he first took the title 10
England's Sam Horsfield returns from three-month injury layoff with Soudal Open win 14
Minjee Lee back to winning ways beating Thompson by two shots at Founders Cup 21
Steve Stricker recovers from mystery illness to win Regions Tradition 27
Kyoung-Hoon Lee successfully defends at Byron Nelson pipping Spieth by one 10
Justin Thomas beats Zalatoris in three-hole playoff for second win at PGA Championship 3
Victor Perez beats Fox at fourth extra hole to win Dutch Open for second title 14
Mao Saigo wins for the fifth time in 10 starts in Japan at the Bridgestone Open 25
Linn Grant claimed her second LET win of the year wire-to-wire in Belgium 23
New Zealand's Steven Alker claims Senior PGA for third win of the season 27
At Colonial Sam Burns beats world number one Scheffler in playoff for second 2022 win 10

JUNE

Commanding Minjee Lee joins Webb as second Aussie to win USWO at Pine Needles 4
A week after winning in Japan, Scott Vincent wins International Series event in England 17
Billy Horschel takes the Memorial by four at Muirfield Village for seventh win 10
Linn Grant first woman to win on DP World Tour by nine shots at Scandinavian Mixed 23
Brooke Henderson eagles the first playoff hole to beat Weaver-Wright at ShopRite 21
Charl Schwartzel, winless since 2016, claims inaugural LIV Golf event in London 20
Rory McIlroy claims his 21st PGA Tour win by defending his 2019 Canadian Open title 10
Bronte Law holes huge putt for eagle on 18 to beat Hall by one at Aramco London 23
Hee Jeong Lim wins Korea Women's Open by six with record 19-under-par total 24
Jennifer Kupcho wins for second time with playoff success over Maguire at Meijer Classic 21
At scene of 2013 US Amateur win, Matt Fitzpatrick wins thrilling US Open at Brookline 5
Haotong Li makes 40-footer to win playoff over Pieters at BMW International 14
Padraig Harrington wins first Champions title at US Senior Open by one from Stricker 27
Travelers win for Xander Schauffele is his first individual PGA Tour title since 2019 10
After brilliant start, In Gee Chun hangs on for first major win for six years at KPMG 6

JULY

With a three-shot win over Fox, Adrian Meronk claims Poland's first DP World Tour win 14
Maja Stark came from three behind with birdies at the last two holes for German win 23
Xander Schauffele wins second start in a row at co-sanctioned Scottish Open 14
Carlota Ciganda wins for third time in Spain with wire-to-wire effort at Estrella Damm 23
Jennifer Kupcho claims third win of the year with Lizette Salas at Great Lakes Bay 21
Major winner Anna Nordqvist wins first regular LET title at Bog Green Egg Open 23
With 64, Cameron Smith wins historic 150th Open at St Andrews to deny Young and McIlroy 7
Eleven years after claiming the Claret Jug, Darren Clarke wins the Senior Open 28
Brooke Henderson wins her second major six years after the first with Evian triumph 8
Richie Ramsay wins fourth DP World title seven years after the third at Cazoo Classic 14
Karrie Webb wins the Senior LPGA on debut by four from old rival Sorenstam 30
Turning his form around, Sean Crocker won the Hero wire-to-wire for his maiden title 14
A stunning last-day charge gives Ayaka Furue her first LPGA title at Scottish Open 23
Tony Finau goes back-to-back at 3M Open and Rocket Mortgage Classic 10

AUGUST

Ashleigh Buhai wins AIG Open at fourth extra hole in fading light with bunker magic	9
He started with a quad but Joohyung Kim closes with a 61 for maiden US win by five	10
Ewen Ferguson goes wire-to-wire, Maja Stark goes 10 under for World Invitational wins	14/23
Will Zalatoris gets his first win after numerous near-misses in playoff at St Jude	10
Nelly Korda, after blood-clot surgery, earns first win of the year at Aramco Sotogrande	23
Patrick Cantlay retains his title at the BMW Championship with one-shot win	10
Thriston Lawrence claims his second DP World title and first in Europe at Crans	14
Linn Grant with fourth LET win and sixth in all at Skafto Open a year on from pro debut	23
Jill McGill gains maiden pro victory on debut in the US Senior Women's Open	30
Rory McIlroy stuns Scheffler to win Tour Championship and scoop FedEx Cup $18m bonus	10

SEPTEMBER

Oliver Wilson, 41, wins in Himmerland for second title, eight years after the first	14
Gaby Lopez rallies from four back with 63 and three closing birdies for third title	21
Dustin Johnson cans long putt to win a playoff for first LIV Golf win in Boston	20
Shane Lowry beats McIlroy and Rahm with birdie at 18th to win BMW PGA at Wentworth	14
Win at the Gary & Vivienne Player Challenge is Jaco van Zyl's first for six years	16
Liz Young, 39-year-old mother, pips Grant to finally land first LET win in Switzerland	23
At 2023 Ryder Cup venue, Robert MacIntyre beats Fitzpatrick in playoff at Marco Simone	14
Ines Laklalech is first Moroccan, Arab and north African to win on LET at French Open	23
After starting the season on Epson Tour, Andrea Lee claims first LPGA title in Portland	21
As PGA Tour season begins, Max Homa chips in at 18th to defend his Fortinet title	10
Cameron Smith switches to LIV but keeps winning, takes Chicago title on second start	20
Brilliant birdie at the 18th gives Guido Migliozzi a 62 and victory at Open de France	14
Klara Spilkova makes crucial par from a pond on her way to a playoff win at Irish Open	23
Taiga Semikawa, 21-year-old amateur, birdies five in a row on way to Panasonic win	18
Atthaya Thitikul defeats Danielle Kang in Walmart playoff for the 19-year-old's second win	21
Joohyung Kim stars for Internationals but America claim Presidents Cup once again	10

OCTOBER

Ryan Fox wins Alfred Dunhill Links paying tribute to his late partner Shane Warne	14
Minami Katsu defends title at the Japan Women's Open beating Shin by one	25
New cowboy boots for Charley Hull as Englishwoman wins second LPGA title in Texas	21
Jon Rahm wins Open de Espana for third time in four attempts finishing six clear	14
Win number five for Min Ji Park in Korea with playoff success at Hite Jinro	24
Back-to-back English wins on the LPGA as Jodi Ewart Shadow claims maiden title	21
Third win of the year and second in the US for Joohyung Kim at the Shriners	10
Lexi Thompson wins for the first time since 2019 at the Aramco Team Series New York	23
Keegan Bradley, who last won in 2018, pips Fowler and Putnam for Zozo win in Japan	10
Taiga Semikawa becomes the first amateur to win the Japan Open for 95 years	18
Lydia Ko wins in the land of her birth at the BMW Ladies Championship in Korea	21
Rory McIlroy makes it back to world number one with CJ Cup win, his third of the year	10

NOVEMBER

George Coetzee wins second SA PGA Championship for second win of the year	16
Birdie-par-eagle-birdie finish brings Jazz Janewattananond victory in Morocco	17
Prayad Marksaeng wins for the sixth time in a row on the Japan Senior PGA Tour	29
Gemma Dryburgh stuns locals with four-shot win at Toto Japan Classic for maiden title	25
At 65 and two months Bernhard Langer extends own record as the oldest Champions winner	27
Emotional Tommy Fleetwood defends title at Nedbank Golf Challenge from 2019	14
Min Ji Park makes it six wins in Korea for the second year running at season-ender	24
Nelly Korda back to world number one with successful defence at Pelican event	21

Padraig Harrington wins for fourth time on Champions Tour but Alker is number one	27
Tony Finau finishes four clear in Houston for third win of the year and fifth in all	10
Jon Rahm wins the DP World Tour Championship for third time; McIlroy the number one	14
Kazuki Higa claims Dunlop Phoenix for fourth win of the year on Japan Tour	18
Lydia Ko scoops biggest first prize in women's golf and sweeps LPGA awards at CME	21
Victorious homecoming in Brisbane for Cameron Smith at Australian PGA	19
Japan's new number one Miyuu Yamashita wins season-ender for her fifth title	25
Caroline Hedwall wins for the first time in four years at Andalucia Open de Espana	23

DECEMBER

Adrian Meronk and Ashleigh Buhai claim twin Australian Open titles in Melbourne	19/26
Thriston Lawrence holds on at Blair Atholl to win his national title at SA Open	16
Antoine Rozner provides cheer for France in Mauritius on day they lose World Cup final	16

Chevron Championship

Harry How/Getty Images

With her first major title, Jennifer Kupcho (top) became the last champion at Mission Hills after 51 years, winning by two strokes from Jessica Korda (left), with Slovenia's 18-year-old Pia Babnik in third.

David Cannon/Getty Images

Scottie Scheffler enjoys the rare luxury of teeing off at Augusta National's 18th hole on Sunday of the Masters Tournament with a five-stroke lead.

SCHEFFLER

Masters Tournament

Jamie Squire/Getty Images

Andrew Redington/Getty Images

Clockwise from top: Rory McIlroy created great excitement by holing his bunker shot at the final hole but Scheffler still won by three; Tiger Woods returned to competition for the first time since 2020.

PGA Championship

Richard Heathcote/Getty Images

Clockwise from top: Chile's Mito Pereira led going to the 72nd hole at Southern Hills but missed out on the playoff in which Will Zalatoris was pipped by Justin Thomas, who won the PGA for a second time.

US Women's Open

Jared C. Tilton/Getty Images

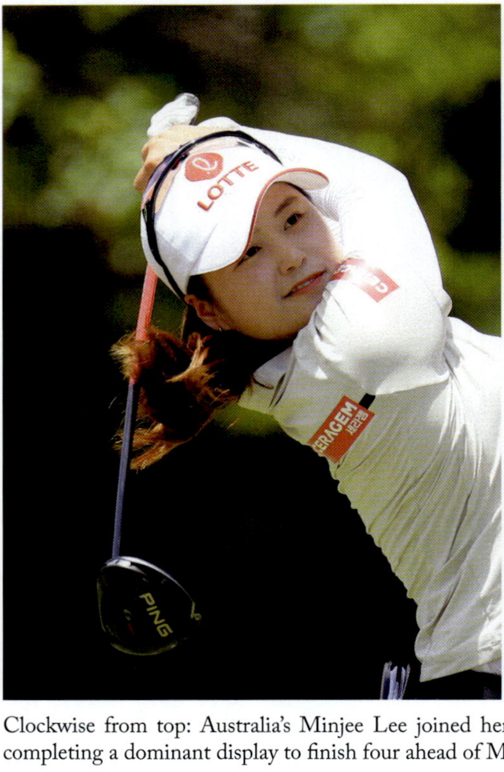

David Cannon/Getty Images

Clockwise from top: Australia's Minjee Lee joined her compatriot Karrie Webb in winning at Pine Needles, completing a dominant display to finish four ahead of Mina Harigae with Hye-Jin Choi in third place.

US Open Championship

Rob Carr/Getty Images

Clockwise from top: Matt Fitzpatrick, the 2013 US Amateur champion, celebrates another win at Brookline with caddie Billy Foster after beating Masters winner Scheffler and PGA runner-up Zalatoris by one stroke.

Fitzpatrick and Foster discuss the Englishman's second shot from a bunker on the 18th at The Country Clu
where the lie, he said, forced him to aim left with a big cut to find the heart of the green.

Andrew Redington/Getty Images

KPMG Women's PGA

Rob Carr/Getty Images

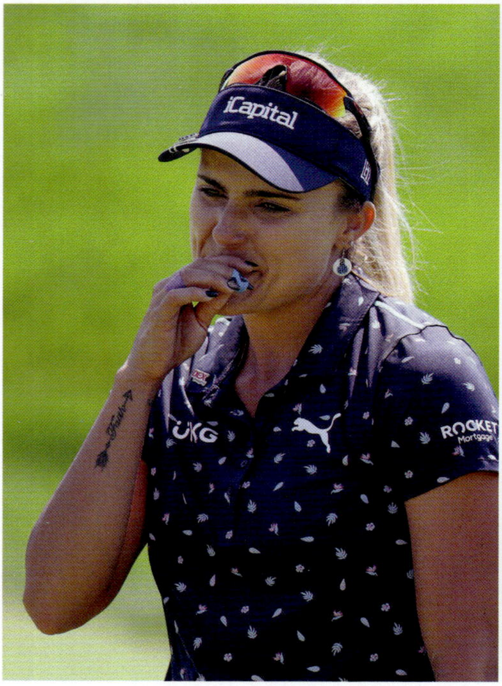

Rob Carr/Getty Images

Clockwise from top: Korea's In Gee Chun started fast and held on to win her third major title at Congressional by one stroke from US Open champion Lee and Lexi Thompson, who was two ahead with three to play.

The 150th Open

Richard Heathcote/R&A/R&A via Getty Images

Clockwise from top: Cameron Smith putted around the Road Hole Bunker for a vital par at the 17th to claim the Claret Jug with a closing 64; Cameron Young was the runner-up, while McIlroy slipped to third place.

Richard Heathcote/R&A/R&A via Getty Images

A final farewell? Tiger Woods acknowledges the gallery's ovation from the Swilcan Bridge during The 150th Oper
He said it hit him walking up the 18th that it might be his last Open at St Andrews.

THE

Amundi Evian Championship

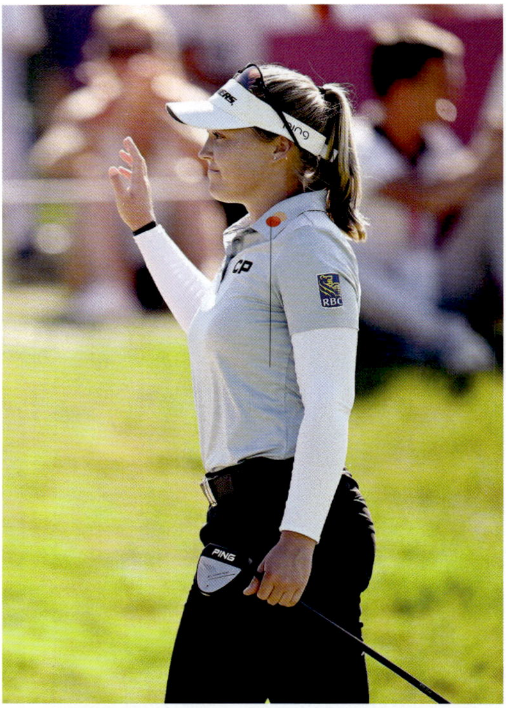

Stuart Franklin/Getty Images

Clockwise from top left: Six years after her first major victory, Canada's Brooke Henderson birdied the 18th at Evian to win by a stroke from Sophia Schubert, with young Japanese star Mao Saigo tying for third.

AIG Women's Open

Oisin Kenny/R&A/R&A via Getty Images

Octavio Passos/Getty Images

Clockwise from top: Ashleigh Buhai seals a first major victory over KPMG winner Chun in fading light on the fourth playoff hole at an historic first Women's Open at Muirfield; Hinako Shibuno was a stroke behind.

Stuart Franklin/R&A/R&A via Getty Images

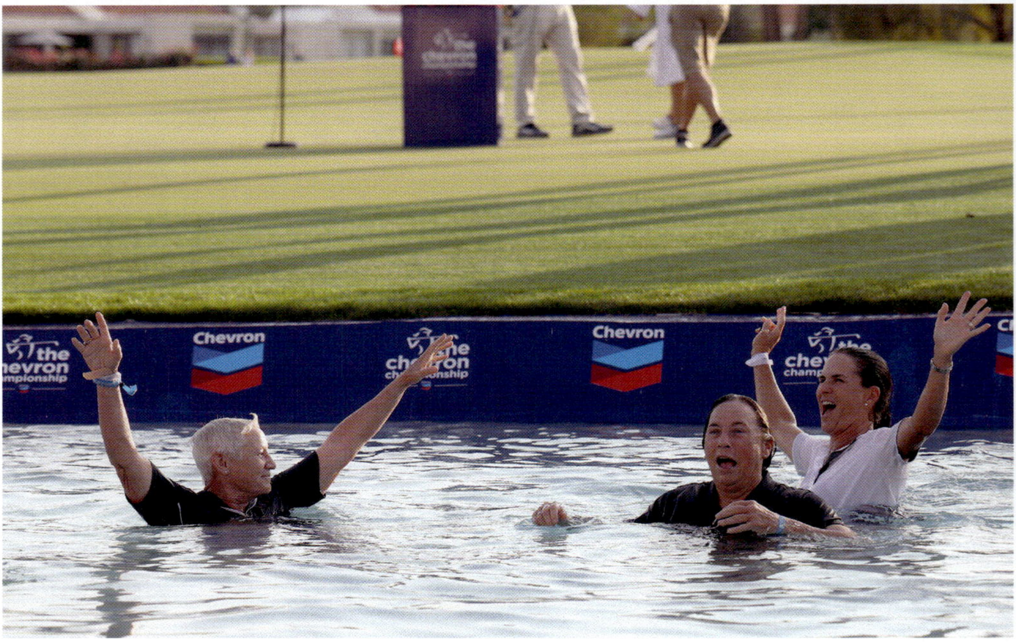

Harry How/Getty Images

Top: Champions all: Woods, McIlroy, Jack Nicklaus, Lee Trevino and Georgia Hall. Bottom: Amy Alcott, who started the tradition, makes the last jump into Poppie's Pond with Patty Sheehan and Patricia Meunier-Lebouc.

The Majors

CHEVRON CHAMPIONSHIP

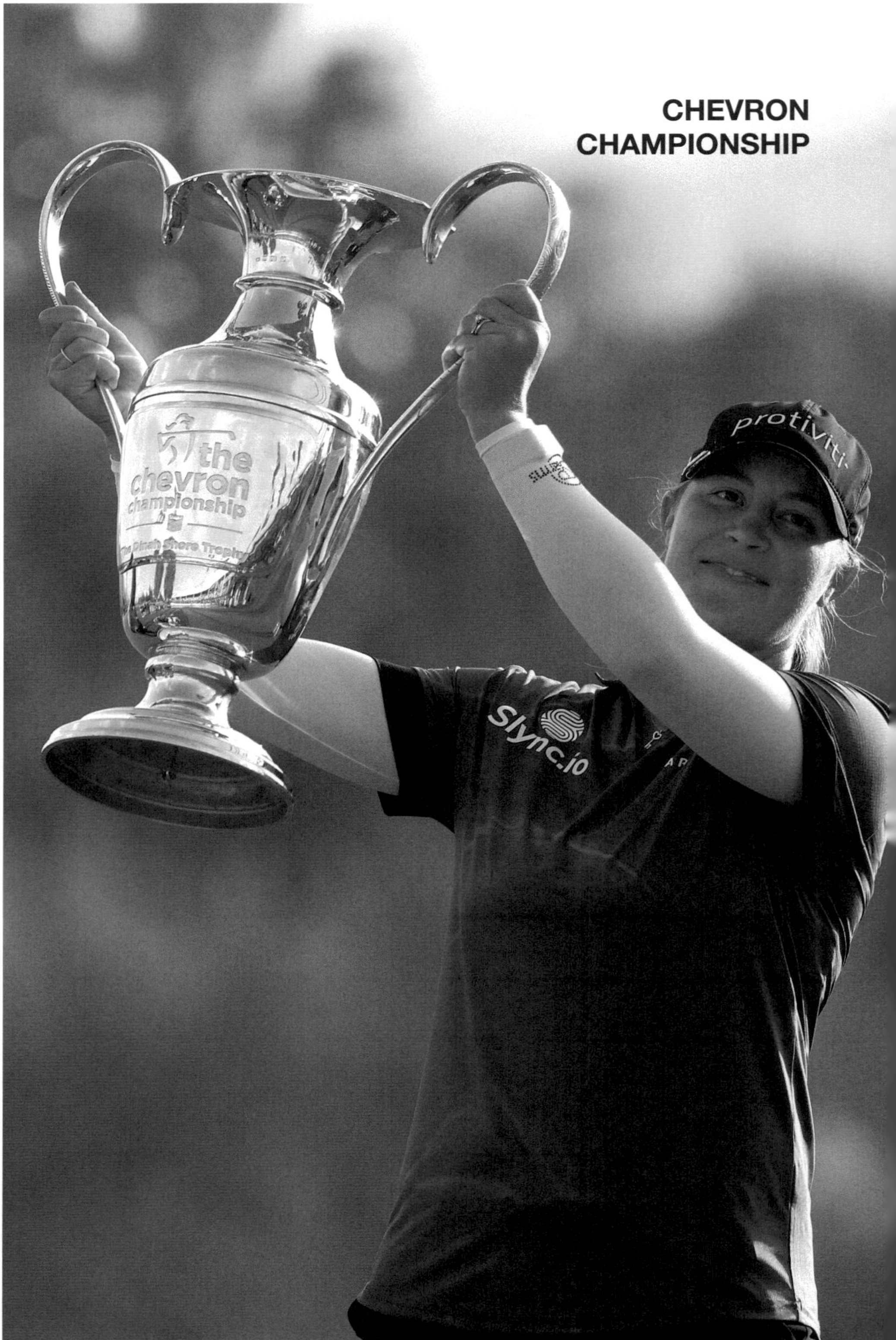

A bittersweet goodbye as Kupcho arrives

By Beth Ann Nichols

Bittersweet. It was the word of the week at the Chevron Championship, where players welcomed a new blue-chip sponsor and elevated purse and said goodbye to tradition. Goodbye to an icon they'd known but never met. Goodbye to a shimmering pond they'd spent years dreaming about.

With the Chevron Championship, for so long named for founding host Dinah Shore, moving to Texas in 2023, this would be the final leap into Poppie's Pond. When asked what she'd miss the most, former champion Stacy Lewis talked about a place fans don't even see — the locker room. Specifically, a bench she sat down on in 2011 after she took down world number one Yani Tseng to win her first major.

"I sat on that bench and called my college coaches," said an emotional Lewis, "and it was like it all hit me there."

Wistfully, she added, from now on, "We don't get to do that."

Lewis, of course, was referring to the five decades of tradition at Mission Hills Country Club. Five decades worth of memories that generations can share. No event on the LPGA schedule carries so much history in one place.

World number one Jin Young Ko can't swim, but she fought hard to keep a smiling face as she jumped into what she called a "swimming pool" for the first time after her 2019 victory. She wasn't the first non-swimmer to win, however, joined by a wading Pat Hurst and Tseng. Even so, Ko was eager for a second try.

Weren't they all?

Amy Alcott started this tradition back in 1988, back when the pond was a murky mess. American Jennifer Kupcho wasn't even born then, but she knows what it's like to own a part of history. In 2019, Kupcho became the first woman to hoist a trophy at Augusta National when she won the inaugural Augusta National Women's Amateur.

The 24-year-old from Colorado added another important piece of women's golf history to her résumé when her first major title came at the final championship ever held at the Dinah Shore Tournament Course.

"I think it's surreal," said Kupcho of her desert victory. "To be a major winner is really special, and to be the last person here at Mission Hills to jump into Poppie's Pond, it's all really special."

Before the first shot was ever struck that week, history was honoured as the LPGA announced all 13 founders would be placed in its Hall of Fame. Prior to that, only five founders were in the Hall. New inductees included local resident Shirley Spork, Alice Bauer, Bettye Danoff, Helen Dettweiler, Helen Hicks, Opal Hill, Sally Sessions and Marilynn Smith.

"Oh, my, what a tremendous surprise," said Spork, "and so, so welcomed for all our founders to be honoured and inducted into the tour's Hall of Fame." Spork, who was the spark behind the creation of the LPGA Teaching & Club Pro Division, died two weeks after the announcement at age 94. That she was finally honoured and celebrated for her life's work so close to home shortly before death was sad, but fitting.

The LPGA also eliminated a 10-year-minimum rule that allowed former Chevron champion Lorena Ochoa into the tour's Hall of Fame. Ochoa, who drew massive crowds in the California desert in her prime, was on hand early in the week to celebrate the honour. She even visited with the maintenance crew to thank them, as was her tradition as a player.

Ochoa said her jump into Poppie's Pond in 2008 was the video her kids enjoy watching the most. A couple dozen friends and family joined Ochoa for that celebratory swim, making it especially memorable. "I told them, look, 'All the friends are there'," she said. "We broke the record of many friends, and especially Mexicans, swimming there."

For Kupcho, there was one person in particular she was thrilled to have on hand for her celebration — new husband Jay Monahan (no relation to the PGA Tour commissioner). After carding an eight-under 64 on Saturday, Kupcho led by six heading into the final round. What looked like a runaway early on Sunday, got closer than Kupcho had hoped thanks to a final-round 74. She held on to ultimately finish two shots ahead of fellow American Jessica Korda.

Kupcho became the seventh player to make the Chevron Championship her first win on the LPGA. She also became the first American to jump into Poppie's Pond since Brittany Lincicome in 2015. "Honestly, I think one of the biggest things I've fought over the last year and a half is everyone is out here cheering for Nelly (Korda) or Lexi (Thompson) or someone else I'm playing with. I don't ever hear, 'Go, Jennifer.' That was really special today, to have that. To have my caddie and his friends and all of my friends out here supporting me, it's really special."

FIRST ROUND

Back on Wednesday, Kupcho started grinding hard after another disappointing round with her driver. Never mind that it was pro-am day at the Chevron Championship, Kupcho knew that she had to get one of the strongest parts of her game situated to have a chance.

The work paid off early as Kupcho carded nine birdies in Thursday's opening round to take the first-round lead with Minjee Lee after both shot 66. It marked the first time either player had held the first-round lead in a major championship.

"I haven't been hitting my driver super well the last couple weeks," said Kupcho, "so just wanted to come out here and try to hit the fairways. I mean, they're pretty narrow and the rough is really long. It's definitely a big advantage to be in the fairway."

Kupcho, a Wake Forest grad who won the 2018 NCAA Championship, made her Chevron debut in 2020 as a pro and took a share of 22nd. The Dinah Shore course suits her eye, she said, and she feels comfortable on the Desmond Muirhead layout. She hit 11 fairways, 14 greens and took 24 putts in her opening round.

"I love this place," Kupcho said, repeatedly.

Australia's Lee headed to the California desert with more belief in herself after finally shedding the best-player-without-a-major title at the 2021 Amundi Evian Championship. The Aussie, armed with added distance and a chill demeanour, suddenly seemed ripe to win majors in bunches. "I know I have one under my belt," she said, "but I do want a little bit more."

Lee's bogey-free 66 marked her second-lowest score on the Dinah Shore Tournament Course in nine appearances. Her best finish, T-3, came in 2017, and she was low amateur at the Chevron in 2014. "It was perfect," Lee said of the day's conditions. "Not a breath of wind when we played."

Defending champion Patty Tavatanakit kept the momentum rolling at Mission Hills with an opening 67, one back of the leaders. It marked the lowest opening round for a reigning champion at the event since it became a major in 1983. Only Annika Sorenstam has successfully defended the title (2001-2002).

Tavatanakit said she was proud of the effort and credited her work with the Vision54 coaching team for helping take her game to another level as a professional. "I think I was just calm," she said. "Something about this place just keeps me really calm, just really present. I think that's how I was able to turn my momentum mid-round."

Gabriela Ruffels gets to sleep in her own bed during Chevron week and the young pro played her way into the 2022 field by finishing in the top 20 the year prior. Ruffels, a 22-year-old Epson Tour player, tied for 15th at the 2020 Chevron as an amateur. She began her third appearance at the spring major with a 68, good for a share of fourth.

Ruffels' parents, both tennis players, live about 20 minutes away from Mission Hills at Toscana Country Club, so it feels like a home event for the former US Women's Amateur champion, though this was her first year playing in front of a crowd. "I feel comfortable out here," said Ruffels. "I feel like I practise on similar courses."

Annie Park, among those on 69, was the last player in the field at the Chevron, by virtue of her top 25 the week before. The former college star went out solo, without a marker, in the first round and called it "weird" but fun. "It was really peaceful," said Park. "I was taking my time out there and then saw the group behind me catch up to me and I'm like, I've got to start picking up the pace by myself."

It wasn't all that long ago that Park felt anything but peace inside the ropes. In fact, she was miserable. Park withdrew from four tournaments in the summer of 2021, including two majors, and hit the reset button with a two-month break. "It was interesting," she said. "The first couple weeks, because our schedule gets really packed, it felt weird being home during the season.

"Just kind of figured out, like, 'What are my hobbies? Let's start there.' Had a lot of perspectives and introspection, and I think without that, I wouldn't be here today." The former NCAA champion and LPGA winner played the last four events of 2021, which she called "really stressful", and barely kept her card. Yet she managed to play her way into the year's first major and onto the early leaderboard.

"Last week was the first time I actually enjoyed playing golf," she said.

After 18 holes: 66 (-6) Kupcho, Mj Lee; **67** Tavatanakit; **68** Ruffels, L Ko, Hall, Nordqvist, Masson, Anannarukarn

SECOND ROUND

Hinako Shibuno dazzled British fans when she shocked the world by winning the 2019 AIG Women's Open, her first LPGA event and first time playing outside her native Japan. Shibuno didn't feel quite so comfortable, however, the first time she teed it up at Mission Hills in 2020. "It was a hard course for me," she said, laughing. "I couldn't even imagine I could play here."

Much has changed in a short time for the Japanese superstar, except for her sparkling personality, of course. A second-round 66 catapulted the player known as the "Smiling Cinderella" to the top of the board at the halfway point, marking her second time at the top through 36 holes at a major, the first coming at the 2020 US Women's Open.

Shibuno opened up both sides of the Dinah Shore Tournament Course with tap-in birdies on numbers 1 and 10, carding a total of seven birdies on the day to get to nine under for the tournament. When asked if she'd fallen in love with the place yet, Shibuno laughed again. "It's better than that time," she said, "a little bit better."

Park continued her solid solo play with a second-round 67 to take a share of second place with Kupcho and 2021 champion Tavatanakit, one behind Shibuno. "I mean, I am by myself out there," said Park, who for the second day chose not to play with a marker. "There is a lot of talking to myself and I've been stuck with my caddie's dad jokes."

For Park, playing in her sixth Chevron, the eight-under total marked her career-best 36-hole score in a major championship. The 2018 ShopRite LPGA Classic winner made par on the 72nd hole of the JTBC Classic the week prior to snag the last spot in the Chevron field. Because there were 115 players in the field and Park was the last one in, she went off on her own.

Park recently switched to a new Scotty Cameron putter, added new iron shafts and a new TSi3 driver. In addition to all the tangible changes, Park once again touched on the large mental shift that only recently occurred. "I think last week was the first time I started to enjoy it again," she said. "Just not with golf, but just in general, like being able to see the spectators again and just having, I think, this newfound passion for golf."

Tavatanakit ended the day on a high note with birdies on numbers 17 and 18. It was good, she said, to have that moment with the fans on 18 again, something she hadn't experienced since her amateur days. The Thai player feels a special connection to this West Coast major having gone to school at UCLA, where she won seven times. Even though she now makes her base in Florida, Tavatanakit still considers herself to be a "Cali girl" at heart. "To not play this event next year in California," she said, "is just kind of a bittersweet goodbye."

Kupcho's second-round 70 was a grind, with 15 consecutive pars to start the round. "I wouldn't say I stayed very patient," said Kupcho. "I definitely got a little angry."

The former Wake Forest star took out a piece of chewing gum at the turn to help "chill" her out a bit. It also helped playing alongside her Solheim Cup partner Lizette Salas in the first two rounds. The pair became fast friends through their experience together at Inverness the previous September.

"I'm sure the fans out here saw that I am definitely a different person when I'm playing with a really good friend," said Kupcho. "It's more fun and I can just be myself with someone that I know really well."

Kupcho, long known as a strong ball-striker, said she simply wasn't hitting the ball hard enough on the greens to keep it on line Friday, but felt that her stroke was in good shape and that the work she'd done in the off season was beginning to show. She took 31 putts in Friday's round but remained positive. "I think my putting has been great this week," she said.

The cutline fell at one over par and, for a while, it looked like Rolex Rankings leader Jin Young Ko might not be around for the weekend after an opening 74. The South Korean claimed to have been rather nonchalant about an early exit, though she rebounded strongly with a 68 and was among the 74 players to make the cut. "If I'm eliminated, I can just go back home to Texas," said Ko, who explained that she was physically tired. "If not, it's just two more days of extension. So, I don't have pressure."

Stanford's Brooke Seay was the only amateur to make the cut.

After 36 holes: 135 (-9) Shibuno 66; **136** A Park 67, Tavatanakit 69, Kupcho 70; **137** SY Kim 67, HJ Kim 67; **138** Koerstz Madsen 67, Ewing 68

THIRD ROUND

Kupcho birdied four of the first five holes on Saturday, and it set the tone for the rest of the championship. In all, the American posted nine birdies in a career-best eight-under 64 to jump out to a six-stroke advantage over Tavatanakit. "Honestly it's all a blur," said Kupcho. "I mean, I hit the fairways, hit the greens, and really was just trying to put smooth putting strokes on them.

"That's what I did, and they fell."

Prior to her third round at Mission Hills, Kupcho watched the final round of the Augusta National Women's Amateur, which she won in 2019 in riveting fashion. The morning show provided a welcome distraction to the third-year pro. She even caught the end of Anna Davis's victory on her phone while parked at stoplights.

"I mean, it's awesome for a 16-year-old to go there and win," said Kupcho, who was a senior at Wake Forest when she triumphed at Augusta. "I mean, I can't even imagine what I was doing at 16, so props to her, that's awesome."

Kupcho played alongside Tavatanakit on Saturday. The pair played in plenty of college tournaments together and the friendly grouping helped keep things comfortable for both.

At the 2019 ANWA, Kupcho's final-round pairing with good friend Maria Fassi became an instant classic as their sportsmanship was talked about as much as their clutch shot-making. So much of that now iconic final round was memorable. A debilitating migraine came over Kupcho in the middle of the final round at Augusta that left her partially blind on the 10th hole. She played the final six holes at Augusta National in five under, highlighted by a spectacular hybrid off a hanging lie on the par-five 13th to six feet. She sank the putt for eagle to solidify one of the greatest moments in Amen Corner history.

Surely all of those good vibes came flooding back as she watched the third edition of the tournament unfold on her drive to the course. Kupcho's best finish at a major coming into the Chevron was a share of second at the 2019 Evian.

Tavatanakit, looking to become the seventh multiple winner of the championship, shot a 70 alongside Kupcho that must have felt like a million with four bogeys sprinkled throughout her card. Kupcho's 16-under 200 total set a new 54-hole record for the championship, and Tavatanakit would need something special to make Kupcho sweat. "I like chasing," said Tavatanakit. "Yeah, for sure. Better feeling. You play without fear and I love doing that."

The biggest deficit that anyone has ever stormed back from in a women's major is seven strokes. Minjee Lee was the most recent to accomplish the feat at the 2021 Evian in a playoff, joining Hall of Famers Patty Sheehan and Karrie Webb. It's also worth pointing out that Lydia Ko shot the best final round in LPGA major championship history at the Chevron in 2021, with her 10-under-par 62. The Kiwi was nine under through 11 holes, and Tavatanakit had watched it all unfold in front of her.

Jessica Korda, a six-time winner who is arguably the best player on tour without a major, sat alone in third, seven strokes back after a third-round 67. Her best finish in a major, a tie for fourth, came at both the 2018 Chevron and KPMG Women's PGA. Korda planned to stay aggressive on Sunday, noting that as the greens get crusty, her high ball flight would be even more of an advantage.

"It's a major," said Korda, "so you know the girls up front are going to be nervous, and we're kind of chasing them down and they know that. You've always just kind of got to think that you have a chance no matter what, and that's kind of the mentality you've got to go in there with."

This marked the first week that Brooke Henderson, one of the best drivers in women's golf, had to put a new driver in play after the LPGA adopted the new Model Local Rule, which forced the Canadian star to switch from a 48-inch driver to 46. Henderson had used a 48-inch driver since junior golf.

For months, Henderson tried dozens of different shafts leading up to the Chevron, ultimately going with the same shaft and Ping G400 driver head as before, but 2 inches shorter with a little extra weight in the grip. She hit 11 of 14 fairways in a third-round 67 and continued to hit driver off the deck. "It's been working so well," said Henderson, "and I feel like because it is firm and fast, I really haven't lost that much distance, and that's nice."

For Kupcho, the shortest club in the bag would likely determine her fate and so far, she couldn't be more pleased. "I mean, seriously this week I think my putting is definitely the props," said Kupcho, who took 24 putts in the first round and 25 in the third. "I have putted really well, and you've got to make putts in a major championship."

After 54 holes: 200 (-16) Kupcho 64; **206** Tavatanakit 70; **207** J Korda 67; **209** A Park 73; **210** Henderson 67, H Green 68, Thompson 71, Ruffels 71, Koerstz Madsen 72, HJ Kim 73

FOURTH ROUND

Kupcho woke up Sunday in picturesque Coachella Valley with a six-stroke lead and a date with destiny. But when she stepped on the 15th tee that afternoon, victory suddenly seemed so very fragile.

With now only a two-stroke lead over Jessica Korda and four holes to play, Kupcho began the final stretch with a couple of deep breaths. Once she got to the fairway of the 15th and realised that her second shot looked exactly like the approach shot she'd had two years prior — that she holed out for eagle! — happy memories flooded her mind.

A Korda bogey, coupled with Kupcho birdie on the 15th, put an end to any question about how this last lap around the Dinah Shore Tournament Course might end. "Then, I was able to just coast in," said Kupcho, who after leading by as many as seven on Sunday, ultimately finished two shots ahead of Korda.

After recording four bogeys in the first three rounds, Kupcho made seven on Sunday, including numbers 17 and 18, for a final-round 74 and a 14-under-par total of 274. It did little to diminish the celebration. "Honestly, I came out just trying to shoot a couple under," said Kupcho. "I mean, I had a six-stroke lead and I shot eight under yesterday, so I figured if someone can do that, then they deserve to be in a playoff.

"That was my mentality and what I was fighting for all day. Obviously didn't get there, but still pulled it out."

Kupcho earned a paycheck of $750,000 for her first LPGA title and the largest in the event's 51-year history. Korda's second-place finish was her best major showing to date. Not bad for being three over par through her first seven holes, she said. "Sometimes you've got to be lucky to win majors," she added, "and I still haven't found that yet."

While 18-year-old Slovenian Pia Babnik took third place on her debut by matching the Sunday best of 66, past champion Pernilla Lindberg enjoyed one last hurrah at the Dinah when the Swede aced the par-three fifth hole with a seven-iron. "We know we have done it in the past," said Lindberg, "and it's the perfect club from there."

All those special memories on one piece of property. On the 10th hole Sunday, Lindberg faced almost an identical putt to what she holed in 2018 on the eighth playoff hole to beat Inbee Park. "I almost holed it again," she said.

Lexi Thompson birdied the 18th to shoot 68 and finish tied for fourth. It's nothing that will go down in the record books, but to have one more feel-good moment with the fans meant the world to the past champion. "Hearing the cheers and the amount of fans that were out to support us," said Thompson, "there is nothing like it."

Kupcho felt that she had matured quite a lot in the last year. That, combined with improved putting, helped her finally break through with her first LPGA title at a major championship. "I've been able to calm myself down a lot better," she said. "Obviously I still have my spurts of anger, but I think that's how I get it out quickly and then move on. I think my whole mental game has gotten stronger."

Kupcho said she didn't want to get too far ahead of herself and went into the champion's leap without much of a plan. While her jump is the one that will be shown for decades to come, it technically wasn't the last.

After Kupcho had her moment in the pond, several legends in the game made their way to the water's edge. Past champion Sheehan, 65, led them off with a remarkable front flip into the pond. Alcott, the one who started this tradition back in 1988 with the "splash heard 'round the world", lifted up a rose in memory of her longtime caddie Bill Curry before diving in headfirst. France's Patricia Meunier-Lebouc was carried in by her husband when she won in 2003 but jumped in on her own this time. And while Sandra Palmer gave the crowd a scare when she took a tumble on her way into the pond, she had them all in stitches as she waded out with a little shimmy.

One last celebration for the ages, and the aged.

As for Kupcho, well, she couldn't be happier to have something else to talk about besides Augusta National. Even though she did paint her fingernails green for the occasion, hoping to draw on some good ANWA vibes, deep down she wanted the questions to turn to what she has accomplished on the LPGA.

"It's like, have you not seen what I've been doing out here?" said Kupcho. "Not that Augusta is not special, but now I'm a major champion.

"To add that to the list is something I've been wanting for a few years now."

Beth Ann Nichols is a senior writer at GolfWeek/USA Today

Mission Hills Country Club (Dinah Shore), Rancho Mirage, California — April 1-4
Par 72 (36-36); 6,884 yards — Purse: $5,000,000

1	**Jennifer Kupcho**	66	70	64	74	274	$750,000
2	**Jessica Korda**	71	69	67	69	276	461,757
3	**Pia Babnik**	70	70	71	66	277	334,972
4	Hinako Shibuno	69	66	77	66	278	195,295
	Celine Boutier	70	69	72	67	278	195,295
	Lexi Thompson	69	70	71	68	278	195,295
	Patty Tavatanakit	67	69	70	72	278	195,295
8	Alison Lee	71	70	72	67	280	108,708
	Hannah Green	70	72	68	70	280	108,708
	Nanna Koerstz Madsen	71	67	72	70	280	108,708
	Hyo Joo Kim	70	67	73	70	280	108,708
12	Minjee Lee	66	73	73	69	281	88,481
13	Georgia Hall	68	71	74	69	282	75,841
	Ryann O'Toole	73	69	69	71	282	75,841
	Madelene Sagstrom	71	70	70	71	282	75,841
	Brooke Henderson	72	71	67	72	282	75,841
17	Nasa Hataoka	71	74	71	67	283	57,388
	Danielle Kang	73	71	71	68	283	57,388
	Hye-Jin Choi	72	71	72	68	283	57,388
	Xiyu Lin	72	72	70	69	283	57,388
	Caroline Masson	68	71	73	71	283	57,388
	Yuka Saso	75	70	66	72	283	57,388
	Atthaya Thitikul	74	68	69	72	283	57,388
	Sei Young Kim	70	67	74	72	283	57,388
25	In Gee Chun	71	71	75	67	284	40,702
	Matilda Castren	71	69	75	69	284	40,702
	Wichanee Meechai	72	70	71	71	284	40,702
	Paula Reto	71	71	71	71	284	40,702
	Wei-Ling Hsu	72	69	72	71	284	40,702
	Charley Hull	71	71	69	73	284	40,702
	Lydia Ko	68	73	70	73	284	40,702
	Sarah Schmelzel	69	71	71	73	284	40,702
	Gabriela Ruffels	68	71	71	74	284	40,702
	Annie Park	69	67	73	75	284	40,702
35	Marina Alex	70	72	75	68	285	30,464
	Inbee Park	75	69	70	71	285	30,464
	Pauline Roussin	69	75	70	71	285	30,464
	Stephanie Meadow	73	72	67	73	285	30,464
39	Lizette Salas	74	69	74	69	286	25,281
	Leona Maguire	72	69	74	71	286	25,281
	Eun-Hee Ji	71	71	72	72	286	25,281
	Amy Yang	73	68	73	72	286	25,281
	Brittany Altomare	76	68	69	73	286	25,281
44	Lauren Stephenson	69	75	76	67	287	19,297
	Sophia Popov	71	74	72	70	287	19,297
	Narin An	72	70	75	70	287	19,297
	Giulia Molinaro	73	68	76	70	287	19,297
	Mel Reid	74	71	70	72	287	19,297
	Pornanong Phatlum	71	70	73	73	287	19,297
	Moriya Jutanugarn	73	71	69	74	287	19,297
	Ayaka Furue	71	71	71	74	287	19,297
	Ally Ewing	70	68	75	74	287	19,297
53	Austin Ernst	71	73	75	69	288	13,980
	Chella Choi	73	72	72	71	288	13,980
	Pernilla Lindberg	73	71	73	71	288	13,980
	Jin Young Ko	74	68	74	72	288	13,980
	Albane Valenzuela	70	74	71	73	288	13,980
	Jasmine Suwannapura	71	72	72	73	288	13,980
	Lindsey Weaver-Wright	72	70	73	73	288	13,980
	Ariya Jutanugarn	71	72	71	74	288	13,980
	Brittany Lincicome	72	69	72	75	288	13,980
	Pajaree Anannarukarn	68	71	73	76	288	13,980
63	Charlotte Thomas	71	71	77	70	289	11,757
	Perrine Delacour	75	69	74	71	289	11,757
65	Cheyenne Knight	74	71	73	72	290	10,997
	Alana Uriell	74	71	72	73	290	10,997
	Brooke Seay (A)	72	70	75	73	290	
	Jaye Marie Green	70	72	75	73	290	10,997
	Anna Nordqvist	68	74	71	77	290	10,997
70	Jodi Ewart Shadoff	71	72	76	72	291	10,365
71	So Yeon Ryu	76	68	76	72	292	9,986
	Aditi Ashok	76	69	74	73	292	9,986
	Bronte Law	71	71	76	74	292	9,986
74	Mi Hyang Lee	73	71	75	74	293	9,732
	MISSED THE 36-HOLE CUT						
	Bohyun Park (A)	77	69			146	
	Kelly Tan	77	69			146	
	In-Kyung Kim	75	71			146	
	Jeongeun Lee[5]	75	71			146	
	Cydney Clanton	73	73			146	

Isabella Fierro (A)	73 73	146
Sarah Kemp	73 73	146
Min Lee	71 75	146
A Lim Kim	70 76	146
Jenny Coleman	75 72	147
Amy Olson	75 72	147
Natasha Andrea Oon (A)	74 73	147
Angel Yin	74 73	147
Yu Liu	72 75	147
Su Oh	74 74	148
Gaby Lopez	72 76	148
Lilia Vu	72 76	148
Emily Kristine Pedersen	70 78	148
Angela Stanford	77 72	149
Sung Hyun Park	75 74	149
Sakura Yokomine	75 74	149
Stacy Lewis	73 76	149
Gurleen Kaur (A)	72 77	149
Megan Khang	72 77	149
Jennifer Song	76 74	150
Emma Talley	75 75	150
Carlota Ciganda	74 76	150
Hee Jeong Lim	71 79	150
Esther Henseleit	75 76	151
Mirim Lee	75 76	151
Mina Harigae	74 78	152
Maude-Aimee Leblanc	74 78	152
Ashleigh Buhai	73 79	152
Christina Kim	79 74	153
Hee Young Park	79 74	153
Jeongeun Lee[6]	78 75	153
Yealimi Noh	75 78	153
Yaeeun Hong	79 75	154
Janie Jackson	76 80	156
Allison Emrey	77 80	157
Jenny Shin	73 69	DQ

ROLL OF HONOUR

1972	Jane Blalock	Mission Hills
1973	Mickey Wright	Mission Hills
1974	Jo Ann Prentice*	Mission Hills
1975	Sandra Palmer	Mission Hills
1976	Judy Rankin	Mission Hills
1977	Kathy Whitworth	Mission Hills
1978	Sandra Post*	Mission Hills
1979	Sandra Post	Mission Hills
1980	Donna Caponi	Mission Hills
1981	Nancy Lopez	Mission Hills
1982	Sally Little	Mission Hills
1983	Amy Alcott	Mission Hills
1984	Juli Inkster*	Mission Hills
1985	Alice Miller	Mission Hills
1986	Pat Bradley	Mission Hills
1987	Betsy King*	Mission Hills
1988	Amy Alcott	Mission Hills
1989	Juli Inkster	Mission Hills
1990	Betsy King	Mission Hills
1991	Amy Alcott	Mission Hills
1992	Dottie Mochrie (Pepper)*	Mission Hills
1993	Helen Alfredsson	Mission Hills
1994	Donna Andrews	Mission Hills
1995	Nanci Bowen	Mission Hills
1996	Patty Sheehan	Mission Hills
1997	Betsy King	Mission Hills
1998	Pat Hurst	Mission Hills
1999	Dottie Pepper	Mission Hills
2000	Karrie Webb	Mission Hills
2001	Annika Sorenstam	Mission Hills
2002	Annika Sorenstam	Mission Hills
2003	Patricia Meunier-Lebouc	Mission Hills
2004	Grace Park	Mission Hills
2005	Annika Sorenstam	Mission Hills
2006	Karrie Webb*	Mission Hills
2007	Morgan Pressel	Mission Hills
2008	Lorena Ochoa	Mission Hills
2009	Brittany Lincicome	Mission Hills
2010	Yani Tseng	Mission Hills
2011	Stacy Lewis	Mission Hills
2012	Sun Young Yoo*	Mission Hills
2013	Inbee Park	Mission Hills
2014	Lexi Thompson	Mission Hills
2015	Brittany Lincicome*	Mission Hills
2016	Lydia Ko	Mission Hills
2017	So Yeon Ryu*	Mission Hills
2018	Pernilla Lindberg*	Mission Hills
2019	Jin Young Ko	Mission Hills
2020	Mirim Lee*	Mission Hills
2021	Patty Tavatanakit	Mission Hills
2022	Jennifer Kupcho	Mission Hills

**won in playoff*

Designated an LPGA major since 1983

MASTERS TOURNAMENT

Green jacket completes Scottie's dream outfit

By Bill Fields

On a stage brimming with youth, Scottie Scheffler showed he was ready to play the lead. The 25-year-old's journey to the top spot on the Official World Golf Ranking was swift. There were only 42 days between his first PGA Tour victory — at the WM Phoenix Open in early February 2022 — and his becoming number one after winning the Dell Technologies Match Play. That ascent was far faster than the previous record of 252 days set by Tiger Woods in the 1990s and put Scheffler in the spotlight as he arrived for the 2022 Masters with three wins in his last five starts.

Although Scheffler would candidly admit to having had a brief crisis of confidence on Sunday morning before leaving his rental home to play the final round at Augusta National Golf Club, it turned out that the lofty perch suited him just fine.

Scheffler left Georgia with a green jacket, earning the distinctive champion's attire with sublime shotmaking buttressed by a mature composure under pressure. His skills were supported by his experienced caddie, Ted Scott, who worked for Bubba Watson during his Masters victories in 2012 and 2014. Scheffler's wife, Meredith, was instrumental in helping her husband ease his pre-final round jitters.

"I cried like a baby this morning," Scheffler said after his three-stroke victory over Rory McIlroy. "I was so stressed out. I didn't know what to do. I was sitting there telling Meredith, 'I don't think I'm ready for this. I'm not ready, I don't feel like I'm ready for this kind of stuff,' and I just felt overwhelmed."

Invoking their faith and stressing that life would be okay regardless of how he played the last 18 holes, Meredith calmed down Scottie. "My identity isn't a golf score," he said later.

But his scores of 69, 67, 71 and 71 identified him as champion in just his 10th major appearance as he built on three major top 10s in 2021, and a tie for fourth place in the 2020 PGA Championship. At a Masters in which Woods was a huge story in his latest comeback to competition, and McIlroy, another multiple major champion, charged into the picture with a closing 64, Scheffler accomplished what he had been building toward since he was a child not much taller than his set of clubs.

Scheffler was born in New Jersey, but his family moved to Texas when he was six. Under the tutelage of instructor Randy Smith at Royal Oaks Country Club in Dallas, he dominated junior golf circles around Dallas, winning 90 of 136 starts on the North Texas PGA Junior Tour. Smith taught a number of tour pros — including Justin Leonard, winner of the Open Championship in 1997 — and Scheffler absorbed the talent he was around at Royal Oaks.

"I grew up around so many guys out there, just watching them and learning from them," Scheffler said. "I wore long pants when I was a kid at Royal Oaks because I wanted to play on the PGA Tour. I would wear pants and a collared shirt to third-grade class and get made fun of, rightfully so. I always wanted to be out here."

Scheffler is a graduate of Highland Park High School, alma mater of Los Angeles Dodgers ace pitcher Clayton Kershaw and Matthew Stafford, quarterback of the Los Angeles Rams. Hours after Scheffler broke through at the Phoenix Open, Stafford led the Rams to a Super Bowl victory.

A victory in the 2013 US Junior Amateur put Scheffler's name on a trophy won by stars such as Johnny Miller, David Duval, Woods and Jordan Spieth. That same summer, Scheffler advanced to the quarter-finals of the US Amateur at The Country Club at Brookline, the first reigning US Junior champion to go that deep into match play in 27 years. Scheffler followed Spieth to the University of Texas, where two-time Masters champion Ben Crenshaw, 1992 US Open winner Tom Kite and Leonard also attended. Scheffler was a member of the victorious 2017 US Walker Cup team.

"He just continues to work hard and to be prepared when the bell rings," Leonard said of Scheffler. "He does not spend much time thinking about results, he just tries to get better every day. He talks about being the same player he was just a few weeks before winning. I believe it."

Scheffler believed in himself over four important days at Augusta National. "I dreamed of having a chance to play in this golf tournament," he said. "I teared up the first time I got my invitation in the mail. We were fortunate enough to play here in college, and I love this place."

He was speaking to reporters on Sunday evening, a young man in long pants and a collared shirt, this time with a green jacket to complete his outfit. The place had loved him back in a big way.

FIRST ROUND

A major plot for the first round of the 86th Masters was virtually assured two days earlier when Tiger Woods met with reporters in the interview room. After a couple of days of practice at Augusta National, the verdict of whether he was healthy enough to compete was in.

"As of right now, I feel like I am going to play," Woods said.

Woods's presence, less than 14 months since a single-vehicle crash that caused severe injuries to his lower right leg, foot and ankle, was the talk of the tournament. Thousands swarmed his nine-hole practice rounds, the galleries resembling those of a Sunday afternoon, as Woods prepared for his first official event since the pandemic-delayed Masters of November 2020.

He had appeared in the PNC Championship with son Charlie in December 2021, but that was 36 holes riding in a cart. Woods played surprisingly well that weekend given what he had been through — gruelling rehabilitation following months in bed and the spectre of amputation — but the Masters was much different.

"I don't have to worry about the ball-striking or the game of golf," Woods said. "It's actually just the hills out here. That's going to be the challenge, and it's going to be a challenge of a major marathon."

With Augusta being pounded by heavy rain from Tuesday through early Thursday morning — more than three inches — first-round starting times were delayed by 30 minutes. The Honorary Starters got things started, with Tom Watson joining mainstays Jack Nicklaus and Gary Player in getting the tournament under way.

Many eyes were on Woods, in a grouping at 10:34am with Louis Oosthuizen and Joaquin Niemann. Twenty-five years after the historic first of his five Masters titles, Woods has surgical hardware supporting bones shattered in the accident. His gait looks different. He doesn't squat fully to read putts.

But the play of the 82-time PGA Tour winner was surprisingly solid in his first round back more than 500 days since his last official competition. A 10-foot putt to save par on the first was a good beginning. He hit a wonderful tee shot at the par-three sixth within two feet of the flagstick. Woods had 27 putts, including a 29-footer for birdie on the 16th, hit eight of 14 fairways and nine of 18 greens in regulation.

Woods has won so often that he usually isn't interested in moral victories. But he said his opening 71 was a triumph. "Yes, if you would have seen how my leg looked to where it's at now," he said. "To see where I've been — to get from there to here — was no easy task."

The one-under score left him tied for 10th place after a first round in which one of the game's best young players made some history of his own. Sungjae Im, of the Republic of Korea, began with three consecutive birdies and went on to shoot a five-under 67, one better than Cameron Smith, in what was a banner day for the joint runners-up in the 2020 Masters.

It marked the first time that a Korean had led any round at the Masters. "I'm excited and happy about the hot start," Im said, "but I want to be humble. I still have three days to play. I want to stay composed and hopefully continue this."

Smith, who arrived having won the recent Players Championship, had a strange scorecard that included double bogeys at numbers one and 18. "I think one and 18 was obviously frustrating," Smith said. "I think it'll motivate me the next few days."

With 18 players breaking par, four men shot 69: Scheffler, Niemann and past Masters champions Dustin Johnson and Danny Willett. Some marquee names didn't fare as well, with McIlroy, Spieth, Collin Morikawa, Jon Rahm, Justin Thomas and Brooks Koepka shooting over-par scores as Im, whose tie for second two years earlier came in his Masters debut, led the way.

"Because of that experience, I feel comfortable when I come to Augusta," Im said. "I feel like I can play well every time."

Smith, who teed off one grouping ahead of Woods, was like most people looking on, in person or more afar, as an unlikely comeback began. "You can't not watch him," Smith said. "He's unreal."

After 18 holes: 67 (-5) Im; **68** Smith; **69** Scheffler, D Johnson, Willett, Niemann; **70** Conners, Kokrak, Cantlay

SECOND ROUND

Scheffler had gone low before, coming into the 86th Masters having shot the most recent 59 on the PGA Tour, at The Northern Trust in 2020. He didn't need to come up with that kind of number in the second round at Augusta National. A five-under 67, matching Thomas for the day's low score, was just what he needed.

Conditions were more challenging than the day before, a gusty breeze pushing up the scoring average by almost a stroke to 74.607 with only six players — Scheffler, Thomas, Shane Lowry, defending champion Hideki Matsuyama, Charl Schwartzel and Hudson Swafford — shooting in the 60s.

Scheffler, teeing off in the last grouping of the afternoon, had the benefit of playing part of his round after the wind calmed down. But no one got off easy.

"I definitely feel like I was in a fight today," said Scheffler, who bogeyed two of the first three holes but birdied six of his last 12. "Today was important. I want to put myself in positions to win tournaments, and that's what's fun for me. That's what I've done the first two days here."

And how. Scheffler, at eight-under 136, built a five-stroke lead over Im, Lowry, Matsuyama and Schwartzel, matching the largest 36-hole margin in Masters history held by Harry Cooper (1936), Herman Keiser (1946), Jack Nicklaus (1975), Raymond Floyd (1976) and Spieth (2015). Cooper was the only one unable to convert such a comfortable lead into a victory.

"I'm looking forward to the challenges of tomorrow, but I wouldn't say much changes," Scheffler said. "I'm still playing the golf course. There's still 50 guys, or something like that, in the field and I can't worry about what those guys are doing. I'm just going to go out and play my game and just keep doing what I'm doing."

As CBS announcer Dottie Pepper appraised Scheffler, "There's a peaceful process about this young man." He demonstrated the easy command he had over his game on the 18th hole Friday, when he made par after a poor drive and a punch shot through the trees. With a dancing right foot on his downswing, a quirk that recalls the actions of Greg Norman and Mark Calcavecchia, Scheffler's swing, like his mindset, is distinctive.

"I feel like I've been very committed to my shots," Scheffler said of his approach. "I've done a really good job mentally of just setting up to the shots and accepting hitting bad ones and being fully committed to hitting good ones."

Woods, again drawing a dozen-deep gallery, didn't give his supporters much to cheer early as he bogeyed four of his first five holes, putting him in peril of missing the cut. But Woods steadied his play the rest of the way on the blustery day, shooting 74 to finish 36 holes in a tie for 19th.

"I could have easily kicked myself out of the tournament today, but I kept myself in it," said Woods, who made the cut for the 22nd consecutive time at the Masters. "It was a good fight. I got back in the ball game."

Other marquee names didn't fare as well and missed the cut, which came at four-over 148. Among those failing to advance to the weekend were Spieth, Koepka, Bryson DeChambeau and Xander Schauffele. Stewart Cink had a short week, too, but it was marked by a special moment. With son Reagan, on his birthday, alongside as caddie, Cink made a hole-in-one with an eight-iron from 166 yards on the 16th, the 24th ace there in Masters history. "This was exactly the way I would have drawn it up," Cink said. "It was like a dream shot."

It was the kind of Masters highlight that Scheffler, a golf junkie, has watched growing up around the game. "I've seen tons of highlights and plenty of stuff, and I feel like I'm constantly learning about this place."

Rounds with Woods and three-time champion Phil Mickelson in his previous appearances at Augusta National also had been educational. "I learned a lot just by watching those guys manage their way around the course," said Scheffler, who had proven to be a good student.

After 36 holes: 136 (-8) Scheffler 67; **141** Im 74, Schwartzel 69, Matsuyama 69, Lowry 68; **142** Smith 74, D Johnson 73, Na 71, Varner 71

THIRD ROUND

Major championships haven't been won on Saturdays for a long time — the Open Championship having gone away from such a conclusion in 1980 — but they certainly can still be lost on the first day of the weekend. Scheffler had such a commanding lead through 36 holes, and had been playing so well for a couple of months, that he didn't figure to vanish from the leaderboard in the third round. It was an unfamiliar position, though, the type of situation that could have made a golfer uncomfortable and vulnerable to a collapse.

During an unseasonably cool and breezy third round, Scheffler proved steady and remained in control, his advantage just reduced by two strokes after the challenging afternoon.

The temperature didn't rise out of the low 50s, the chill accompanied by a persistent wind that meant layers were as necessary as patience. Golfers used gloves, ski caps and neck gaiters to keep warm. Scheffler wore a vest between shots over his sweater, and his game didn't cool off much.

The tall Texan shot a 71, one of just nine under-par scores, which allowed him to maintain some distance between the rest of the field as he finished at nine-under 207. His margin at day's end was three shots over Smith, who fashioned Saturday's only sub-70 score, 68. Smith's prowess came after excelling in a cool and windy final round of the Players Championship in March and put him in position to better his joint runner-up finish in the 2020 Masters, where he broke 70 each day in much more hospitable conditions.

"Had hand warmers all day, but I don't think they helped to be honest," Smith said. "It was brutal."

Smith had company from the 2020 leaderboard in the form of fellow runner-up Im, who played the last 11 holes without a bogey and in five under to shoot 71 and move into third place at 212. Lowry and 2011 Masters champion Schwartzel also played capably, shooting 73s to finish at 214 in a tie for fourth. Schwartzel's card was highlighted by an eagle-two on the formidable 10th hole, where he sank his approach from 136 yards.

As for Woods, he struggled on Saturday, shooting the first of two weekend 78s, after exceeding what many thought possible when he made the cut in his first official tournament since his 2021 car crash.

Scheffler extended his lead to six strokes on the front nine, but four bogeys on the back narrowed his margin. His five on the 18th hole could have turned into a worse outcome if Scheffler hadn't utilised his poise and talent. His tee shot on the final hole darted quickly left, flying into the trees. The ball wasn't found immediately before being spotted under a holly. Scheffler had to take an unplayable lie and faced an uphill third shot from 242 yards. He powered a three-iron that flew onto the green before rolling long. He got up and down to lose only one stroke.

"We saw the guy with the flag that always finds the balls kind of panicking. I was like, oh, crap, wonder what's going on here," Scheffler said of the anxiety after his wayward tee shot. "Fortunately, they found the ball. And then all I was trying to do was figure out how I was going to get it on the green for my third shot. And fortunately, I was able to take an unplayable out of the bush and still have a swing."

Scheffler's late damage control left him in excellent shape to do what a small cadre of golfers have achieved at Augusta National since the inception of the Official World Golf Ranking in 1986: arrive at the Masters number one in the world and win a green jacket. Only Ian Woosnam (1991), Fred Couples (1992), Woods (2001,'02) and Dustin Johnson (2020) had pulled off the feat.

There were similarities between Scheffler and Couples, who claimed the top spot just before winning at Augusta. "Scottie's doing the same thing," said Woods. "He took care of it from the West coast through Florida. We all wish we had that two, three-month window when we get hot, and hopefully majors fall somewhere along in that window. We take care of it in those windows."

Through 54 holes, Scheffler was doing just that while getting admiration from his peers. "The golf he's played the last couple months, it's nuts," said Thomas, whose 72 left him eight shots back. "It seems effortless, at least when I've watched. It's not like anything he's doing is like, 'Oh, my gosh, that's unbelievable.' It's just he gets it around so well and he's so mature in his golf age."

After 54 holes: 207 (-9) Scheffler 71; **210** Smith 68; **212** Im 71; **214** Schwartzel 73, Lowry 73; **215** Conners 72, Thomas 72; **216** Willett 73; **217** D Johnson 75, Morikawa 74, Kokrak 71, McIlroy 71, Fleetwood 70

FOURTH ROUND

In the spring of 2014, when he was 17 years old, Scottie Scheffler won the Junior Invitational at Sage Valley Golf Club in Graniteville, South Carolina, just 15 miles from Augusta National. It's a prestigious tournament for young golfers. Scheffler finished one shot ahead of Cameron Champ, now a fellow member of the PGA Tour, and he received a yellow jacket given to the champion.

The stakes were much higher for Scheffler on Masters Sunday in 2022 as he competed for a coat of a different colour, the most famous garment in sports on the line. The Texan's nervousness in the hours before he got to the course was evidence of the enormity of the moment and belied the consummate calm that he had displayed in building a three-stroke lead over Australia's Smith through 54 holes. "I've felt at peace on the golf course," Scheffler said. "It's off the course that's hard for me."

The jitters were justified. Scheffler was in prime position to do something very special: win his first major championship and fourth tournament of 2022. How rare was that air? The last player to travel down Magnolia Lane on a Sunday night in April with four victories on the season, including the Masters, was Arnold Palmer in 1960. A victory would make Scheffler the 10th Texan to slip into a green jacket, joining such golf luminaries from the Lone Star State as Ben Crenshaw, Jimmy Demaret, Ben Hogan, Byron Nelson and Jack Burke Jr.

Scheffler was tested from the outset in the final round, which was played in warmer and less windy weather than the previous day. Smith started with two consecutive birdies, holing a 13-footer on the first and two-putting from 45 feet on the second hole. Meanwhile, Scheffler scrambled for a par on the first after missing the fairway and green. When he failed to make a 12-foot birdie on the second, his comfortable advantage was down to a single stroke.

Moments later, having yanked his tee shot into the left trees on the tempting yet testy 350-yard, par-four third hole, and seeing his pitch fail to make it on to the green, Scheffler was in jeopardy of losing command. He faced a 29-yard third shot with a steep slope between his ball and the green, with the flagstick not far beyond the edge of the putting green.

Scheffler had displayed a world-class short game throughout the Masters, causing CBS analyst and three-time Masters champion Sir Nick Faldo to say he "reminds me of Seve [Ballesteros] very much". The game's hottest player came through in dramatic fashion, bumping a pitch into the hill that rolled squarely into the cup for an unlikely birdie. When Smith bogeyed number three after a poor drive and weak approach, Scheffler's margin was back to three, a cushion that would grow later in the round.

"What is most pivotal was getting that ball up-and-down," Scheffler said of his third shot at number three. "To have it go in was obviously off the charts. Parring four and five was huge as well. After that I just started cruising. I felt comfortable with pretty much most of the aspects of my game. My swing maybe felt a little bit off, but other than that, I felt like I wasn't ever really going to make a bogey."

Until the final hole — where he arrived with a five-stroke lead, and a lapse of concentration led to two putts missed from close range and an inconsequential double bogey — Scheffler had only one blemish on his closing scorecard, a bogey on the difficult 10th hole.

Importantly, Scheffler got through the vexing 12th hole with a par, getting down in two from the left fringe. Smith wasn't so fortunate. After a wonderful birdie on the 11th to pull back within three, the Aussie let the tournament slip away from him on the hole that has bitten many contenders including Spieth, Koepka and Francesco Molinari in recent years.

The devilish hole named "Golden Bell" was ready to wreak more havoc. Smith's nine-iron didn't come close to hitting land, a "really bad swing at the wrong time", his ball splashing into Rae's Creek and leading to a triple bogey. "Wasn't even trying to go near that pin," Smith added. "It was just a terrible swing."

Smith fought back, making birdies at 15 and 16. He shot 73 and tied for third with Lowry at 283, five strokes behind Scheffler. "I was obviously very frustrated after the 12th hole but just hung in there and tried to finish off on a positive," said Smith, still the only player to shoot four rounds in the 60s at the Masters. "I feel I've played some of my best golf around here. It's quite frustrating, I guess, to not walk away with a win yet, but I look forward to the challenge of coming back here next year and trying to do it again."

McIlroy could relate, especially since a Masters victory would allow him to complete a career Grand Slam. In his 14th Masters, he didn't break 70 through three rounds and found himself 10 shots behind Scheffler going into Sunday. He then produced some final-round fireworks with birdies on five of the first 10 holes. An eagle on the par-five 13th briefly got him within three strokes of Scheffler, but he couldn't capitalise on the par-five 15th, where he drove left and had to lay up short of the pond.

Trailing by four when he got to the 18th, McIlroy produced one of the week's spectacular shots — and loudest roars — by holing a 54-foot shot from the right greenside bunker, his ball tracking perfectly down a steep slope for a birdie and a 64, his best score in 52 career rounds at Augusta National. Playing companion Morikawa then holed his shot from the same bunker, giving him a 67 and moving the American into fifth place.

"I thought if I could shoot 63 today, it would give me a shot," said McIlroy, now with a runner-up finish to go with three previous top fives at the Masters. "I didn't quite get there, but I gave it a good shot."

As Smith and McIlroy battled, Scheffler kept the lead and his focus, channeling Woods' historic victory in 1997. "I tried not to look up," Scheffler said. "I tried to keep my head down and just keep doing what I was doing because I didn't want to break my concentration. When I finally got to the last and I had a five-shot lead, I was like, 'All right, now I can enjoy this.' And you saw the results of that. Thanks, Tiger."

With four victories in six starts, Scheffler was on a Tiger-like roll. And like Woods, as a Masters champion had earned his way back for many years.

"It's such a fun golf course. It's such a fun piece of property. It's so fun to play," Scheffler said. "I can't believe I get to come back for a lifetime and get to enjoy this golf course."

It was one of the spoils of a career taking off, perhaps on target for greatness.

Bill Fields writes about golf in his newsletter, TheAlbatross.Substack.com

Augusta National Golf Club, Augusta, Georgia — April 7-10

Par 72 (36-36); 7,510 yards — Purse: $15,000,000

1	**Scottie Scheffler**	69	67	71	71	278	$2,700,000
2	**Rory McIlroy**	73	73	71	64	281	1,620,000
3	**Shane Lowry**	73	68	73	69	283	870,000
	Cameron Smith	68	74	68	73	283	870,000
5	Collin Morikawa	73	70	74	67	284	600,000
6	Corey Conners	70	73	72	70	285	521,250
	Will Zalatoris	71	72	75	67	285	521,250
8	Sungjae Im	67	74	71	75	287	450,000
	Justin Thomas	76	67	72	72	287	450,000
10	Cameron Champ	72	75	71	70	288	390,000
	Charl Schwartzel	72	69	73	74	288	390,000
12	Dustin Johnson	69	73	75	72	289	330,000
	Danny Willett	69	74	73	73	289	330,000
14	Matt Fitzpatrick	71	73	76	70	290	225,333
	Tommy Fleetwood	75	72	70	73	290	225,333
	Talor Gooch	72	74	73	71	290	225,333
	Harry Higgs	71	75	73	71	290	225,333
	Jason Kokrak	70	76	71	73	290	225,333
	Min Woo Lee	73	75	72	70	290	225,333
	Hideki Matsuyama	72	69	77	72	290	225,333
	Kevin Na	71	71	79	69	290	225,333
	Lee Westwood	72	74	73	71	290	225,333
23	Sergio Garcia	72	74	74	71	291	138,000
	Robert MacIntyre	73	73	76	69	291	138,000
	JJ Spaun	74	70	75	72	291	138,000
	Harold Varner III	71	71	80	69	291	138,000
27	Viktor Hovland	72	76	71	73	292	111,000
	Seamus Power	74	74	74	70	292	111,000
	Jon Rahm	74	72	77	69	292	111,000
30	Lucas Glover	72	76	72	73	293	93,150
	Russell Henley	73	74	76	70	293	93,150
	Marc Leishman	73	75	71	74	293	93,150
	Sepp Straka	74	72	76	71	293	93,150
	Hudson Swafford	77	69	73	74	293	93,150
35	Tony Finau	71	75	74	74	294	75,563
	Joaquin Niemann	69	74	77	74	294	75,563
	Patrick Reed	74	73	73	74	294	75,563
	Webb Simpson	71	74	73	76	294	75,563
39	Patrick Cantlay	70	75	79	71	295	63,000
	Tom Hoge	73	74	75	73	295	63,000
	Si Woo Kim	76	70	73	76	295	63,000
	Bubba Watson	73	73	78	71	295	63,000
43	Billy Horschel	74	73	79	70	296	55,500
44	Christiaan Bezuidenhout	73	71	77	76	297	51,000
	Kevin Kisner	75	70	75	77	297	51,000
46	Cam Davis	75	73	79	73	300	46,500
47	Tiger Woods	71	74	78	78	301	43,500
48	Max Homa	74	73	77	78	302	40,050
	Adam Scott	74	74	80	74	302	40,050
50	Daniel Berger	71	75	77	80	303	37,350
	Mackenzie Hughes	73	75	77	78	303	37,350
52	Tyrrell Hatton	72	74	79	80	305	36,000
	MISSED THE 36-HOLE CUT						
	Sam Burns	75	74			149	
	Brian Harman	74	75			149	
	Padraig Harrington	74	75			149	
	Zach Johnson	74	75			149	
	Takumi Kanaya	75	74			149	
	Kyoung-Hoon Lee	74	75			149	
	Lucas Herbert	74	76			150	
	Brooks Koepka	75	75			150	
	Ryan Palmer	75	75			150	
	Jordan Spieth	74	76			150	
	Mike Weir	74	76			150	
	Abraham Ancer	72	79			151	
	Stewart Cink	76	75			151	
	Austin Greaser (A)	74	77			151	
	Keita Nakajima (A)	72	79			151	
	Xander Schauffele	74	77			151	
	Bernhard Langer	76	76			152	
	Luke List	77	75			152	
	Guido Migliozzi	75	77			152	
	Francesco Molinari	78	74			152	
	Justin Rose	76	76			152	

Erik van Rooyen	73 79	152
Gary Woodland	75 77	152
Fred Couples	75 79	154
Cameron Young	77 77	154
Garrick Higgo	72 83	155
Aaron Jarvis (A)	81 74	155
Larry Mize	77 78	155
James Piot (A)	81 74	155
Bryson DeChambeau	76 80	156
Sandy Lyle	82 76	158
Vijay Singh	78 80	158
Thomas Pieters	79 80	159
Matthew Wolff	81 78	159
Stewart Hagestad (A)	79 81	160
Jose Maria Olazabal	77 84	161
Laird Shepherd (A)	81 85	166
Louis Oosthuizen	76	WD
Paul Casey		WD

ROLL OF HONOUR

1934	Horton Smith	Augusta National
1935	Gene Sarazen*	Augusta National
1936	Horton Smith	Augusta National
1937	Byron Nelson	Augusta National
1938	Henry Picard	Augusta National
1939	Ralph Guldahl	Augusta National
1940	Jimmy Demaret	Augusta National
1941	Craig Wood	Augusta National
1942	Byron Nelson*	Augusta National
1946	Herman Keiser	Augusta National
1947	Jimmy Demaret	Augusta National
1948	Claude Harmon	Augusta National
1949	Sam Snead	Augusta National
1950	Jimmy Demaret	Augusta National
1951	Ben Hogan	Augusta National
1952	Sam Snead	Augusta National
1953	Ben Hogan	Augusta National
1954	Sam Snead*	Augusta National
1955	Cary Middlecoff	Augusta National
1956	Jack Burke Jr	Augusta National
1957	Doug Ford	Augusta National
1958	Arnold Palmer	Augusta National
1959	Art Wall	Augusta National
1960	Arnold Palmer	Augusta National
1961	Gary Player	Augusta National
1962	Arnold Palmer*	Augusta National
1963	Jack Nicklaus	Augusta National
1964	Arnold Palmer	Augusta National
1965	Jack Nicklaus	Augusta National
1966	Jack Nicklaus*	Augusta National
1967	Gay Brewer	Augusta National
1968	Bob Goalby	Augusta National
1969	George Archer	Augusta National
1970	Billy Casper*	Augusta National
1971	Charles Coody	Augusta National
1972	Jack Nicklaus	Augusta National
1973	Tommy Aaron	Augusta National
1974	Gary Player	Augusta National
1975	Jack Nicklaus	Augusta National
1976	Raymond Floyd	Augusta National
1977	Tom Watson	Augusta National
1978	Gary Player	Augusta National
1979	Fuzzy Zoeller*	Augusta National
1980	Seve Ballesteros	Augusta National
1981	Tom Watson	Augusta National
1982	Craig Stadler*	Augusta National
1983	Seve Ballesteros	Augusta National
1984	Ben Crenshaw	Augusta National
1985	Bernhard Langer	Augusta National
1986	Jack Nicklaus	Augusta National
1987	Larry Mize*	Augusta National
1988	Sandy Lyle	Augusta National
1989	Nick Faldo*	Augusta National
1990	Nick Faldo*	Augusta National
1991	Ian Woosnam	Augusta National
1992	Fred Couples	Augusta National
1993	Bernhard Langer	Augusta National
1994	Jose Maria Olazabal	Augusta National
1995	Ben Crenshaw	Augusta National
1996	Nick Faldo	Augusta National
1997	Tiger Woods	Augusta National
1998	Mark O'Meara	Augusta National
1999	Jose Maria Olazabal	Augusta National
2000	Vijay Singh	Augusta National
2001	Tiger Woods	Augusta National
2002	Tiger Woods	Augusta National
2003	Mike Weir*	Augusta National
2004	Phil Mickelson	Augusta National
2005	Tiger Woods*	Augusta National
2006	Phil Mickelson	Augusta National
2007	Zach Johnson	Augusta National
2008	Trevor Immelman	Augusta National
2009	Angel Cabrera*	Augusta National
2010	Phil Mickelson	Augusta National
2011	Charl Schwartzel	Augusta National
2012	Bubba Watson*	Augusta National
2013	Adam Scott*	Augusta National
2014	Bubba Watson	Augusta National
2015	Jordan Spieth	Augusta National
2016	Danny Willett	Augusta National
2017	Sergio Garcia*	Augusta National
2018	Patrick Reed	Augusta National
2019	Tiger Woods	Augusta National
2020	Dustin Johnson	Augusta National
2021	Hideki Matsuyama	Augusta National
2022	Scottie Scheffler	Augusta National

**won in playoff*

PGA CHAMPIONSHIP

A matter of belief for doubting Thomas

By Doug Ferguson

Rare is the player from this generation who has a deep appreciation of golf history, at least history that dates beyond Tiger Woods and his Sunday red shirt and the way he ruled the sport. Justin Thomas is no exception. So there was little reason to be surprised when he was asked what he knew of John Mahaffey.

"Who?" he replied.

After an uncomfortable pause, the 29-year-old Thomas gave up. He was nonetheless pleased to know the purpose of this enquiry. They now share space in the record book for the greatest final-round comeback in PGA Championship history, both winning in a playoff. And that's where the similarities end.

Mahaffey stormed from seven shots behind in 1978 at Oakmont with a closing 66, and then he dispatched major champions Tom Watson and Jerry Pate in a sudden-death playoff with a birdie on the second hole. That was as close as Watson came to the final leg of the career Grand Slam. Thomas had a 67 on the final day at Southern Hills and had to fend off Will Zalatoris in a three-hole aggregate playoff. It was the second silver medal for Zalatoris at a major in as many years, though he had yet to win gold even at a regular PGA Tour event. Three of the leading four players — Zalatoris, Mito Pereira and Cameron Young — were still without a victory on a major tour.

For Thomas, it was his second Wanamaker Trophy in five years, always special when the champion comes from PGA stock. His father, Mike Thomas, was a career professional at Harmony Landing outside Louisville, Kentucky who once served as a PGA of America officer. His grandfather also was a club professional in Ohio who had competed in the PGA Championship and the US Open.

But this was far different from his first PGA Championship title in 2017 at Quail Hollow Club in North Carolina. Thomas began that year by winning both Hawaii tournaments, posting a 59 in the Sony Open and setting the PGA Tour's 72-hole record at 253. How to sum up his week at Southern Hills? He was so sick early in the week that he had to reduce his practice. He was on the bad end of the draw and had to face the worst of the Oklahoma wind on Friday morning. He started seven shots behind on Sunday and hit a shank on the par-three sixth hole. And he won the tournament.

It was on the range late Saturday evening when he was on the verge of losing his cool until wiser heads — his father, his caddie — prevailed and urged him to look at the big picture. There was nothing wrong with his game. There was nothing to fix.

"I've learned well enough now that you need to wait as long as you can until it's truly over, especially at a major," Thomas said in reflection. "Even though I was that far back, I probably was better off seven shots back with six people in front me than four back with 12 people in front of me. That's a huge difference. I got a little lucky."

The walk to the 18th green at Southern Hills, in regulation or a playoff, is an uphill climb, and it capped an improbable journey in so many ways. The course, a classic Perry Maxwell design built during the Depression and recently restored by Gil Hanse, wasn't even supposed to host the PGA Championship until 2030. That changed shortly after 6 January 2021, when rioters stormed the US Capitol as the presidential election was being certified and kept President Donald Trump as polarising as ever. The 2022 PGA Championship was scheduled for Trump National in Bedminster, New Jersey. The PGA of America felt it had no choice but to relocate. Southern Hills was the best option.

A new venue wasn't the only surprise. No one could have imagined going into the year that the field at the PGA Championship would have Tiger Woods, who once feared he would lose his right leg to amputation from a serious car crash, but that it would not have Phil Mickelson, the defending champion.

Mickelson, who a year earlier at Kiawah Island became the oldest player at age 50 to win a major, had been out of sight for three months. He stepped away after his inflammatory comments regarding the Saudi-funded rival league he supported were published in February. It was the first time since 2008 this major did not have its reigning champion.

His absence would have been more glaring without Woods to fill the void. Woods already did the unthinkable when he played the Masters — this just 14 months after shattering his right leg and ankle — and made it 72 holes. The Open Championship at St Andrews was the only other certainty, and then he felt good enough to give the PGA Championship a try. He made another cut, even if he only lasted three days.

The PGA Championship was more about the future. Another major for Thomas, a sign of more to come from challengers like Zalatoris, Young and Matt Fitzpatrick, and more major disappointment for Rory McIlroy. As for Southern Hills, it was the first time hosting a major since the 2007 PGA Championship, back when it was held in August and the heat was suffocating. Even amidst a change in season, one thing didn't change. Six of the seven previous major champions at Southern Hills are in the World Golf Hall of Fame. Thomas surely is headed there one day.

FIRST ROUND

Even though just five weeks had passed since the Masters, the next major couldn't arrive quickly enough — for golf and for McIlroy. LIV Golf was still on schedule to start its rival league and was becoming a mighty distraction. Woods weighed in by saying that while he appreciates a different point of view, "I believe in legacies. I believe in major championships. I believe in big events, comparisons to historical figures of the past."

For McIlroy, the immediate past was a 64 in the final round of the Masters for a runner-up finish. He was approaching eight years since his last major, and it was starting to weigh on him. And then he played as though he was ready to change that. The feature group Thursday morning was Woods, McIlroy and Jordan Spieth, who had won a month earlier at the RBC Heritage and thought this might be his best course to complete the career Grand Slam. Woods plotted his way around Southern Hills. McIlroy was all guns blazing, taking driver over the trees and challenging every inch of the course.

He opened with a five-under 65 for a one-shot lead over Zalatoris and Tom Hoge, who had won for the first time earlier in the year at the AT&T Pebble Beach Pro-Am. It was McIlroy's lowest start at a major since his five-under 66 at Valhalla in the 2014 PGA Championship, the last major he won. More than the score alone was how he achieved it, and it was clear playing alongside Woods their games were in a different place. Woods went with iron and position. McIlroy went with power and wedge play. That was most evident on the par-four 12th hole, their third of the round. Woods hit iron and left himself 178 yards for his second. McIlroy took driver over the trees down the left side and had 86 yards left, a lob wedge to a foot for the first of four consecutive birdies. Was this the year? These are questions only someone like McIlroy will get on a Thursday at a major.

"Yeah, look, it was a great start. I've been carrying some good form," McIlroy said. "I think when your game is feeling like that, it's a matter of sticking to your game plan, executing as well as you possibly can, and staying in your own little world."

Woods was limping at the end of his 72 holes at Augusta National and at the start of the PGA Championship. He had won that previous PGA Championship at Southern Hills in 2007, a year before his left knee gave out and well before the five back surgeries and one horrific car crash. A good start was wasted by three bogeys in the middle of his round. Two bogeys at the end gave him a 74 and he already was nine shots behind before limping away for a treatment of ice baths. "Loading hurts, pressing off it hurts, and walking hurts, and twisting hurts. If I don't do that, then I'm all right," he said.

Late in the afternoon, Thomas was still feeling sluggish and couldn't find the centre of the club face as often as he would have liked. The greens were getting crusty from a long day of heat and traffic. He made bogeys from the bunkers to close the front nine and erase a good start, but he cleaned up his game and felt like he stole one at the difficult 18th for a birdie and a 67. The biggest concern was his health.

"It was weird. I had some kind of bug. I had no energy. I had to be as efficient as I possibly could," Thomas said. He hadn't practised as much as he normally would but, within two shots of the lead, he would start the second round the next morning, when conditions typically are calmer and the greens are fresh and smooth. This was not going to be a typical Friday, however.

After 18 holes: 65 (-5) McIlroy; **66** Zalatoris, Hoge; **67** Thomas, Ancer, Kuchar; **68** Pereira, Riley, Fitzpatrick, Kirk, Smith, Niemann, Na, Herbert, Schauffele

SECOND ROUND

They could have belted out the title song to *Oklahoma!* even before players arrived at Southern Hills in the morning. The notorious wind, indeed, came sweeping down the plain and gave the course — any course, really — its best defence. Gusts topped 30mph in the morning, making it a challenge over every shot, from the tee through the green. Only 22 players remained under par after 36 holes, only five of them from late-early side of the draw — the side Thomas was on.

Thomas did his part with another 67, remarkable considering the wind. He was at six-under 134 and in the lead when he signed his card and headed to his rental house to watch on television to see how everyone else handled the conditions. Also playing Friday morning was Englishman Fitzpatrick, who had a reputation of playing his best golf in the toughest conditions. He had a 69 and was at three-under 137.

And then the hollow sound of wind raging through the trees grew silent. Cloud cover moved in, taking some of the sheen off the putting surfaces. Just like that, Southern Hills became vulnerable. The golf course Thomas saw on television was nothing like the course he had just played. "I was fuming on Friday afternoon," Thomas said. "I felt like I had played the best golf I had all year. I felt if everybody had played the same conditions, I'd be leading the golf tournament hands down. I wasn't. I was so agitated that everybody didn't have to deal with the same conditions I did. I had to turn the golf off."

There was some personal history to this for Thomas. "At The Players, he gets the crazy bad end of the draw. We got to the Masters, we get the crazy bad end of the draw. And you're like, 'What is going on here?' You're looking for something good to happen," said Jim "Bones" Mackay, the caddie for Thomas.

Plenty of good happened to those on the course Friday afternoon. Bubba Watson, the two-time Masters champion, had never scored better than a 68 in his 49 previous rounds at the PGA Championship. On this day, he dropped nine birdies and stood over a 25-foot birdie putt on the 18th hole with a chance to tie the major championship record of 62. He missed and had to settle for a 63, the 18th such score in the PGA, his name in the record book with Woods (2007) and Raymond Floyd (1982) at Southern Hills. Both went on to win. That would not be the case for Watson.

Pereira, of Chile, had a seven-foot birdie putt that would have been the 19th score of 63 or better in the PGA. He missed and shot 64, and the consolation was getting into the last group with Zalatoris, who had a 65 to lead by one.

It didn't work out all that well for everyone. McIlroy was on the good end of the draw and failed to take advantage. He didn't make a birdie until his 13th hole, and that was his only one of the afternoon in a round of 71. Even so, he was still in the mix. Never mind Watson, Pereira or Zalatoris. The excitement came from a familiar source. Woods looked certain to miss the cut when he butchered the par-three 11th hole and made double bogey, leaving him outside the cut line. And then he summoned a little more magic and revved up thousands in the gallery. He played the final seven holes with two birdies and a pair of 15-foot par putts. That gave him a 69 and allowed him to make it to the weekend. He was 12 shots behind, but he was still playing, and that felt like a victory. Woods had played only two tournaments because of his leg, both majors, and he made the cut both times.

Zalatoris was a daunting figure for someone who had never won on the PGA Tour or any other major tour in golf. Coming out of the Covid-19 pandemic, he got a spot in the US Open at Winged Foot and tied for sixth. At the Masters the following year, he wound up as a runner-up to Hideki Matsuyama. He had another top 10 at the PGA Championship in 2021 at Kiawah Island, and another at the Masters in April. He already was developing a reputation for being tough in the majors, a product of his iron game. Zalatoris uses the arm-lock putting stance, and he had worked extraordinary long hours with coach Josh Gregory going into Southern Hills. The work was paying off. He was at nine-under 131 headed into the weekend. "We lucked out with the draw, for sure," he said.

After 36 holes: 131 (-9) Zalatoris 65; **132** Pereira 64; **134** Thomas 67; **135** Watson 63; **136** McIlroy 71, Ancer 69, Riley 68; **137** Fitzpatrick 69, Cink 68; **138** Kirk 70, Hatton 68, Kuchar 71, Smith 70, Young 67, Burns 67, Woodland 68

THIRD ROUND

The third round brought the essence of Oklahoma weather, which in a word is "unpredictable". Scorching heat at the start of the week gave way a cold that made May feel like late autumn. Calm one afternoon, limb-shaking wind the next. The action inside the ropes was just as fickle.

The crowd got a full day of entertainment, even if it was at times painful to watch. Woods made the cut with one shot to spare, but that meant a breakfast tee time with Shaun Norris, the burly South African in a short-sleeved shirt. Woods had reason to wonder if making the cut was worth it. He was clutch again, but under different circumstances. His five-foot par putt on the final hole enabled him to break 80, though the 79 was by two shots his worst score since he began playing this major in 1997. It left him another early start for the final round, only suspicions were confirmed by the end of the day. He wasn't walking well, he wasn't playing well, and he chose to withdraw.

With that, he turned the stage over the unlikely cast of contenders, starting with Pereira. Not since Keegan Bradley in 2011 had a PGA Tour rookie won the PGA Championship, and the Chilean looked to be up to the task. With a pair of early birdies, and four bogeys in seven holes for Zalatoris, suddenly Pereira had a five-shot lead and was threatening to turn this into a runaway. Instead, he joined the parade of blunder with four bogeys in a five-hole stretch around the turn that rattled him and brought a dozen or so players back into the fold.

That list did not include McIlroy, whose opening 65 was starting to feel like a distant memory. After opening with five straight pars, McIlroy played the next six holes with two double bogeys, two bogeys and a birdie. Only a strong finish allowed him to salvage a 74. That left him even par for the championship, nine shots behind, even if the leader was a tour rookie.

Also left with little hope was Thomas. He had looked forward to Saturday as a fresh start, with everyone facing the same test. Except Thomas couldn't get anything going. He three-putted. When he laid up to the right number on the par-five 13th, he landed in a divot. He took bogey from the rough on the 18th, after trying to play conservatively off the tee with a fairway metal, and he signed for a 74 that would have seemed to signal an end to his chances. It felt that way as he got in a cart and drove to the range.

Pereira showed his mettle with a string of birdies after his stretch of bogeys, and one last birdie on the 18th gave him a 69. That put him at nine-under 201 and gave him a three-shot lead. He had passed his first test. "It's by far the biggest tournament I play, the biggest round of golf. And tomorrow is going to be even bigger," he said.

Fitzpatrick birdied his last two holes for a 67 to get into the final group for the first time in a major. He was the most battle-tested of the contenders with his seven DP World Tour titles and two Ryder Cup appearances. Young also had a 67, only a year on from winning for the first time on the Korn Ferry Tour. This stage was new to him. And then there was Zalatoris. As bad of a start as he had, the Texan played the last 11 holes with eight pars, one bogey and to birdies. It felt better than the 73 on his card.

"I was pretty frustrated with the start, but I would rather have a frustrating start and a good finish. It's good momentum heading into tomorrow," Zalatoris said.

The final round was starting to take shape down on the range. Thomas was starting a post-round practice session, still running hot in the chilly temperatures over a round — and possibly a tournament — that had gotten away from him. Mackay, the caddie, doesn't recall who spoke up first among his putting coach, his father and the caddie. But it was an intervention badly needed. "It was a collaborative effort to remind him, 'You still have a great chance to win. You can't let what happened today affect how you drive out of here.' The rallying cry was, 'There's nothing you need to practise down here. All you need to think about is getting rest and getting after it tomorrow'."

Thomas must have listened. He stopped after hitting about 20 balls, his shortest post-round session of the year. Seven shots behind, yes, but only six players in front of him. None had won a major. Four had yet to win on American soil.

After 54 holes: 201 (-9) Pereira 69; **204** Fitzpatrick 67, Zalatoris 73; **205** Young 67; **206** Ancer 70; **207** Power 67; **208** Cink 71, Thomas 74, Watson 73; **209** Simpson 65, Herbert 68, Homa 70, Burns 71, Woodland 71, Kirk 71, Riley 73

FOURTH ROUND

McIlroy in the majors is like an action hero who keeps arriving too late to save himself. He began the final round with four straight birdies to get within five, trying to put pressure on the untested leaders, then threw it into reverse himself and finished eighth.

As for Thomas, an early bogey was erased by a birdie, and one shot would have seemed to seal his doom. It was a five-iron on the par-three sixth hole over the water that he cold shanked into a tree on the right. "I've never won a tournament shanking a ball on Sunday, so that was a first," he later said. "And man, I would really like it to be a last." So much about his resolve centred around that shot. His second to the par three hit a branch and left him 100 yards away in a bunker. He hit a low, cutting gap wedge to 20 feet for perhaps the craziest bogey of his life. The real challenge came on the next hole. Still smarting, Thomas blasted his tee shot down the middle and Mackay's heart sank when he walked off the yardage. It was 197 yards, and with the cold air and wind, it was a perfect five-iron, the club Thomas had just shanked. He hit it to 10 feet, one of the more under-appreciated moments.

Even so, he was going nowhere, and neither was anyone else. Pereira traded bogeys with birdies. Zalatoris followed two birdies with two bogeys, including his own adventurous bogey on the par-three sixth when his tee shot bounded off the back slope and into the hedges, leading to a penalty drop. It looked to be a battle for survival, who could hang in the longest, who could avoid the key mistakes. And then Thomas began to make his move, starting with a pedestrian seven-iron to the front of the green on the par-three 11th with the pin all the way in the back. He would have been happy to escape with a two-putt par and couldn't stop smiling when the 65-foot putt with plenty of steam found the back of the cup and fell for birdie.

That was the spark he needed. He smashed his drive down the 12th to set up another birdie. He saved par from the bunker on the 14th and the 16th. And then he added a final birdie on the reachable par-four 17th with a bold play from the bunker to four feet. But when he missed a good birdie chance on the final hole, there was a part of Thomas that felt it might cost him. It nearly did, except those other contenders also lamented missed opportunities. For Young, it was a double bogey on the tough 16th. For Zalatoris, it was a shocking three-putt bogey on the same hole.

Save a thought for Pereira, who looked like the winner all the way. He had a chance to build a two-shot lead going to the last hole, but he chipped weakly from short of the green on the 17th, and his birdie putt needed one more turn. Still leading by one, playing quickly, he lashed at driver on the daunting finishing hole and over-cut it into the water. A playoff at this point was all but certain.

Thomas (67) and Zalatoris (71) already were in at five-under-par 275. Pereira looked certain to make bogey and join them, right up until his third shot went just long enough to bounce into the rough, and his par chip ran off the back of the green. He took double bogey and finished one shot out of the playoff. Not since Mickelson in the 2006 US Open at Winged Foot had a player come to the final hole of a major with a one-shot lead and made double bogey. "On Monday, I just wanted to make the cut. On Sunday, I wanted to win," he said, searching for perspective and finding only heartache after his 75.

In the three-hole playoff, Thomas and Zalatoris each made birdie on the 13th. And then, at the 17th with the wind off the left, his least favourite direction, Thomas delivered the shot of the tournament. "I pretty much aimed at the left bunker and hit a normal, cut three-wood. Aim at the left one, cut it to the second one. And if the wind wants to take up that gap, great," he said. "As soon as it came off, it was a perfect shot."

It set up a two-putt birdie. Zalatoris, who made eight-foot putts for birdie on the 17th and for par on the 18th in regulation to tie Thomas, couldn't deliver from about the same range in the playoff. Thomas, finally, had the lead with one hole to play. He closed with a par and Zalatoris couldn't catch him. And even as Thomas stood on the 18th as the PGA champion, there was a sense of disbelief how it all unfolded. His illness during practice. The wrong side of the draw. The 74 on Saturday. The seven-shot comeback. The Wanamaker Trophy.

He was more emotional the second time around, perhaps because he had gone 14 months without winning, nearly five years since he first won a major. "It's easy to start letting some doubt creep in, just kind of like, 'What's going to happen? When is it going to happen? Is it going to happen?'" he said.

Good thing he didn't ask how it was going to happen. Even he would have had a hard time explaining that one.

Southern Hills Country Club, Tulsa, Oklahoma
Par 70 (35-35); 7,556 yards

May 19-22
Purse: $15,000,000

1	**Justin Thomas**	67	67	74	67	275	$2,700,000
2	**Will Zalatoris**	66	65	73	71	275	1,620,000
	Thomas (4-3-4) defeated Zalatoris (4-4-X) in three-hole playoff						
3	**Mito Pereira**	68	64	69	75	276	870,000
	Cameron Young	71	67	67	71	276	870,000
5	Matt Fitzpatrick	68	69	67	73	277	530,417
	Tommy Fleetwood	71	70	69	67	277	530,417
	Chris Kirk	68	70	71	68	277	530,417
8	Rory McIlroy	65	71	74	68	278	436,600
9	Abraham Ancer	67	69	70	73	279	357,813
	Tom Hoge	66	74	70	69	279	357,813
	Seamus Power	71	69	67	72	279	357,813
	Brendan Steele	70	72	69	68	279	357,813
13	Tyrrell Hatton	70	68	74	68	280	253,750
	Lucas Herbert	68	73	68	71	280	253,750
	Max Homa	70	69	70	71	280	253,750
	Davis Riley	68	68	73	71	280	253,750
	Justin Rose	71	70	71	68	280	253,750
	Xander Schauffele	68	73	69	70	280	253,750
	Cameron Smith	68	70	73	69	280	253,750
20	Sam Burns	71	67	71	72	281	191,250
	Talor Gooch	69	70	74	68	281	191,250
	Webb Simpson	69	75	65	72	281	191,250
23	Stewart Cink	69	68	71	74	282	129,768
	Rickie Fowler	71	70	71	70	282	129,768
	Lucas Glover	75	69	68	70	282	129,768
	Shane Lowry	70	72	71	69	282	129,768
	Kevin Na	68	71	72	71	282	129,768
	Joaquin Niemann	68	71	72	71	282	129,768
	Aaron Wise	69	72	71	70	282	129,768
30	Adria Arnaus	72	68	70	73	283	83,750
	Tony Finau	69	72	74	68	283	83,750
	Bubba Watson	72	63	73	75	283	83,750
	Bernd Wiesberger	72	67	74	70	283	83,750
34	Brian Harman	74	70	71	69	284	61,607
	Matt Kuchar	67	71	73	73	284	61,607
	Marc Leishman	72	71	73	68	284	61,607
	Keith Mitchell	72	72	72	68	284	61,607
	Patrick Reed	69	70	73	72	284	61,607
	Jordan Spieth	72	69	74	69	284	61,607
	Gary Woodland	70	68	71	75	284	61,607
41	Viktor Hovland	70	70	75	70	285	43,839
	Kyoung-Hoon Lee	69	73	71	72	285	43,839
	Luke List	74	70	71	70	285	43,839
	Troy Merritt	73	70	72	70	285	43,839
	Adam Schenk	71	72	72	70	285	43,839
	Kevin Streelman	71	72	75	67	285	43,839
	Cameron Tringale	72	68	72	73	285	43,839
48	Keegan Bradley	72	70	73	71	286	32,146
	Laurie Canter	72	70	70	74	286	32,146
	Cam Davis	72	72	72	70	286	32,146
	Denny McCarthy	73	68	74	71	286	32,146
	Jon Rahm	73	69	76	68	286	32,146
	Harold Varner III	71	71	72	72	286	32,146
54	Ryan Fox	70	70	70	77	287	29,250
55	Jason Day	71	72	72	73	288	27,925
	Brooks Koepka	75	67	72	74	288	27,925
	Francesco Molinari	70	72	75	71	288	27,925
	Collin Morikawa	72	72	74	70	288	27,925
	Sebastian Munoz	74	70	69	75	288	27,925
60	Lanto Griffin	72	69	75	73	289	26,125
	Russell Henley	70	73	70	76	289	26,125
	Rikuya Hoshino	74	70	69	76	289	26,125
	Si Woo Kim	71	72	76	70	289	26,125
	Jason Kokrak	74	68	77	70	289	26,125
	Hideki Matsuyama	72	72	72	73	289	26,125
	Louis Oosthuizen	73	71	73	72	289	26,125
	Charl Schwartzel	71	73	73	72	289	26,125
68	Billy Horschel	75	69	77	69	290	25,000
69	Kramer Hickok	71	71	75	74	291	24,625
	Beau Hossler	69	71	78	73	291	24,625
71	Adam Hadwin	73	71	75	73	292	24,250
	Justin Harding	71	72	75	74	292	24,250
	Shaun Norris	71	72	74	75	292	24,250
	Thomas Pieters	69	73	77	73	292	24,250
75	Patton Kizzire	69	75	78	73	295	23,950
	Maverick McNealy	73	71	78	73	295	23,950
77	Robert MacIntyre	70	71	80	76	297	23,800
78	Sepp Straka	71	72	79	76	298	23,700
	Tiger Woods	74	69	79		WD	
	MISSED THE 36-HOLE CUT						
	Branden Grace	73	72			145	
	Harry Higgs	74	71			145	
	Chan Kim	72	73			145	
	Kevin Kisner	72	73			145	
	Min Woo Lee	73	72			145	
	Ryan Palmer	73	72			145	
	Ian Poulter	76	69			145	
	JJ Spaun	72	73			145	
	Henrik Stenson	72	73			145	
	Christiaan Bezuidenhout	73	73			146	
	Dustin Johnson	73	73			146	
	Russell Knox	74	72			146	
	Jinichiro Kozuma	73	73			146	
	Anirban Lahiri	73	73			146	
	Alex Noren	70	76			146	
	Scottie Scheffler	71	75			146	
	Lee Westwood	75	71			146	
	YE Yang	71	75			146	
	Rich Beem	73	74			147	
	Matthew Borchert	73	74			147	
	Dean Burmester	69	78			147	
	Jason Dufner	72	75			147	
	Sergio Garcia	73	74			147	
	Sadom Kaewkanjana	75	72			147	
	Adam Scott	77	70			147	
	John Daly	72	76			148	
	Yuki Inamori	72	76			148	
	Bio Kim	76	72			148	
	Scott Stallings	78	70			148	
	Hudson Swafford	74	74			148	
	Ryan Brehm	76	73			149	
	Corey Conners	76	73			149	
	Joel Dahmen	73	76			149	
	Sam Horsfield	74	75			149	
	Mackenzie Hughes	77	72			149	
	Daniel van Tonder	74	75			149	
	Oliver Bekker	78	72			150	
	Richard Bland	74	76			150	
	Cameron Champ	74	76			150	
	Tyler Collet	79	71			150	
	Garrick Higgo	74	76			150	
	Matt Jones	73	77			150	
	Jesse Mueller	72	78			150	
	Alexander Beach	73	78			151	
	Michael Block	78	73			151	
	Patrick Cantlay	76	75			151	
	Alex Cejka	72	79			151	
	Zach Johnson	74	77			151	
	Ryosuke Kinoshita	79	72			151	
	Chad Ramey	77	74			151	
	Erik van Rooyen	75	76			151	

Ryan Vermeer	75 76	151
Padraig Harrington	77 75	152
Kyle Mendoza	75 77	152
Jhonattan Vegas	73 79	152
Daniel Berger	73 80	153
Brandon Bingaman	78 75	153
Nicolai Hojgaard	78 75	153
Nic Ishee	78 75	153
Takumi Kanaya	77 76	153
Martin Kaymer	76 77	153
Shaun Micheel	76 77	153
Dylan Newman	78 75	153
Matthew Wolff	76 77	153
Joohyung Kim	78 76	154
Pablo Larrazabal	77 77	154
Carlos Ortiz	79 75	154
Wyatt Worthington II	77 77	154
Paul Dickinson	78 77	155
Colin Inglis	78 77	155
Jared Jones	79 78	157
Casey Pyne	79 78	157
Shawn Warren	78 79	157
Tim Feenstra	77 81	158
Austin Hurt	78 81	159
Sean McCarty	82 79	161
Zac Oakley	81 82	163

ROLL OF HONOUR

1916	Jim Barnes	Siwanoy
1919	Jim Barnes	Engineers
1920	Jock Hutchison	Flossmoor
1921	Walter Hagen	Inwood
1922	Gene Sarazen	Oakmont
1923	Gene Sarazen	Pelham
1924	Walter Hagen	French Lick Springs
1925	Walter Hagen	Olympia Fields
1926	Walter Hagen	Salisbury
1927	Walter Hagen	Cedar Crest
1928	Leo Diegel	Five Farms
1929	Leo Diegel	Hillcrest
1930	Tommy Armour	Fresh Meadows
1931	Tom Creavy	Wannamoisett
1932	Olin Dutra	Keller
1933	Gene Sarazen	Blue Mound
1934	Paul Runyan	The Park
1935	Johnny Revolta	Twin Hills
1936	Denny Shute	Pinehurst (No 2)
1937	Denny Shute	Pittsburgh Field Club
1938	Paul Runyan	Shawnee
1939	Henry Picard	Pomonok
1940	Byron Nelson	Hershey
1941	Vic Ghezzi	Cherry Hills
1942	Sam Snead	Seaview
1944	Bob Hamilton	Manito
1945	Byron Nelson	Moraine
1946	Ben Hogan	Portland
1947	Jim Ferrier	Plum Hollow
1948	Ben Hogan	Norwood Hills
1949	Sam Snead	Hermitage
1950	Chandler Harper	Scioto
1951	Sam Snead	Oakmont
1952	Jim Turnesa	Big Spring
1953	Walter Burkemo	Birmingham
1954	Chick Harbert	Keller
1955	Doug Ford	Meadowbrook
1956	Jack Burke Jr	Blue Hill
1957	Lionel Hebert	Miami Valley
1958	Dow Finsterwald	Llanerch
1959	Bob Rosburg	Minneapolis
1960	Jay Hebert	Firestone
1961	Jerry Barber*	Olympia Fields
1962	Gary Player	Aronimink
1963	Jack Nicklaus	Dallas Athletic Club
1964	Bobby Nichols	Columbus
1965	Dave Marr	Laurel Valley
1966	Al Geiberger	Firestone
1967	Don January*	Columbine
1968	Julius Boros	Pecan Valley
1969	Raymond Floyd	NCR
1970	Dave Stockton	Southern Hills
1971	Jack Nicklaus	PGA National
1972	Gary Player	Oakland Hills
1973	Jack Nicklaus	Canterbury
1974	Lee Trevino	Tanglewood Park
1975	Jack Nicklaus	Firestone
1976	Dave Stockton	Congressional (Blue)
1977	Lanny Wadkins*	Pebble Beach
1978	John Mahaffey*	Oakmont
1979	David Graham*	Oakland Hills
1980	Jack Nicklaus	Oak Hill
1981	Larry Nelson	Atlanta Athletic Club (Highlands)
1982	Raymond Floyd	Southern Hills
1983	Hal Sutton	Riviera
1984	Lee Trevino	Shoal Creek
1985	Hubert Green	Cherry Hills
1986	Bob Tway	Inverness
1987	Larry Nelson*	PGA National
1988	Jeff Sluman	Oak Tree
1989	Payne Stewart	Kemper Lakes
1990	Wayne Grady	Shoal Creek
1991	John Daly	Crooked Stick
1992	Nick Price	Bellerive
1993	Paul Azinger*	Inverness
1994	Nick Price	Southern Hills
1995	Steve Elkington*	Riviera
1996	Mark Brooks*	Valhalla
1997	Davis Love III	Winged Foot (West)
1998	Vijay Singh	Sahalee
1999	Tiger Woods	Medinah (No 3)
2000	Tiger Woods*	Valhalla
2001	David Toms	Atlanta Athletic Club (Highlands)
2002	Rich Beem	Hazeltine National
2003	Shaun Micheel	Oak Hill
2004	Vijay Singh*	Whistling Straits
2005	Phil Mickelson	Baltusrol (Lower)
2006	Tiger Woods	Medinah (No 3)
2007	Tiger Woods	Southern Hills
2008	Padraig Harrington	Oakland Hills
2009	YE Yang	Hazeltine National
2010	Martin Kaymer*	Whistling Straits
2011	Keegan Bradley*	Atlanta Athletic Club (Highlands)
2012	Rory McIlroy	Kiawah Island (Ocean)
2013	Jason Dufner	Oak Hill
2014	Rory McIlroy	Valhalla
2015	Jason Day	Whistling Straits
2016	Jimmy Walker	Baltusrol (Lower)
2017	Justin Thomas	Quail Hollow
2018	Brooks Koepka	Bellerive
2019	Brooks Koepka	Bethpage (Black)
2020	Collin Morikawa	TPC Harding Park
2021	Phil Mickelson	Kiawah Island (Ocean)
2022	Justin Thomas*	Southern Hills

**won in playoff*
Contested as match play until 1957

US WOMEN'S OPEN

Cream rises at Pine Needles with Lee dominant

By Marino Parascenzo

In taking the 77th US Women's Open to Pine Needles, in the Sandhills of North Carolina, the US Golf Association was celebrating Donald Ross yet again. Another Beethoven encore. Ross, a genius of a golf course architect, came from Scotland to the United States late in the 1800s, landing with $2 in his pocket, a head full of ideas and determination in his heart, and he would come to observe, "The Lord made golf courses, golf course architects simply discover them."

Some 400 courses bear the Ross stamp, and many have hosted championships, among them Pine Needles, established in 1927 and venue to three previous US Women's Opens. Annika Sorenstam won in 1996 by six shots, Australia's Karrie Webb in 2001 by eight, and American Cristie Kerr in 2007 by two. This fourth visit was the record for any course to hold the Women's Open.

Sorenstam, a Hall-of-Famer, was the only player in this field who had played in all four. She followed the win with a tie for 16th in 2001 and a tie for 32nd in 2007. She would be playing a different course this time. Pine Needles had been renovated, reopening in 2019 with wider fairways, rebuilt bunkers, some new ones, greens switched from bentgrass to Bermudagrass, and much wiregrass and native hardpan in place of rough. It was a par 71 and still playing at 6,600 yards, but it required a different game of her now, at 51. "I'm not in a spot right now in my career where I can attack these hole locations," she said. The keys to the course now were the approach shots and solving Ross's tricky greens.

The Women's Open had a presenting sponsor for the first time ever — ProMedica, a healthcare organisation based in Toledo, Ohio. The purse rocketed by $4.5 million to a record $10 million, and the first prize was now a record $1.8 million. For some in the field of 156 this was more than a national championship. It was a pivotal point in careers in transition.

For the legendary Sorenstam, it was something of a hail-and-farewell, returning to a landmark in her career. She had retired from the LPGA Tour in 2008. Her win in the 2021 US Senior Women's Open, an eight-shot lark, qualified her for this Women's Open. Sorenstam had no illusions about trying to restart her career. "I'm a lot more content in my life," she said, and noted she was there with her husband, Mike McGee, her caddie, and her kids — daughter Ava, 12, and son Will, 11. "One of the reasons I'm here," she said. "They want me to play and we're doing this together."

Michelle Wie West, 32, teen whiz of the early 2000s, was winding down her career — not retiring but "stepping away" from playing the LPGA Tour full time. She cited injuries and the demands of practice and rehabilitation. "I have zero regrets in my career," said Wie West, who joined the tour in 2009 and had five career wins, including the 2014 Women's Open.

Nelly Korda, world number two, had not played since early February after undergoing surgery for a blood clot in her left arm. "To tee it up and to hit my first shot, that is as far as I'm looking right now," she said.

Rose Zhang, 19, Stanford University freshman, the number one amateur in the world and owner of a bulging portfolio, was fresh from winning the NCAA Championship and leading Stanford to the team championship. Was she going to turn pro? Said Zhang: "I think for now, I'm definitely staying for at least another year at Stanford."

World number one Jin Young Ko, seeking her third major, arrived at Pine Needles on something of a high note. She took the HSBC Women's Champions early in March, following a sensational five wins in 2021 that brought her the Player of the Year Award. But her pre-tournament outlook was subdued. "I think I have a lot of problems in my swing," she said.

On the other hand, world number four Minjee Lee, arrived in a brighter frame of mind. "I just feel like I've kind of been trending," the Australian said. She'd won her first major the previous July, the 2021 Evian Championship, and just two weeks before won the Cognizant Founders Cup.

Defending champion Yuka Saso, of the Philippines, who beat Japan's Nasa Hataoka on the third playoff hole in 2021, was having a rewarding 2022. She'd had two top-six finishes and four other top-20s. What part of her game did she work on for Pine Needles? "Everything," she said. "In the US Open, you need everything."

FIRST ROUND

If a round in championship golf can be described as "charming", Sorenstam's first round in the 2022 US Women's Open was it. There were a lot things on her mind at Pine Needles that hot June morning. Hit five-iron or six-iron? (Drink more water! she ordered the kids over in the gallery.) How much is this putt going to break? (Put on more sunscreen! she signalled.) Where's Will? (Is he OK? Is he climbing some tree somewhere?) Dad McGee, as mom's caddie, could help inside the ropes, but not outside.

The spirit was strong, the nostalgia rich, the fans warm but the scorecard, as always, was pitiless. Sorenstam was even par through her 13th, then bogeyed three of her last five for a 74. She was graceful. "I'm a lot more content in my life," Sorenstam said. "My playing days are over. I'm not here to create a new career. I'm here to enjoy what I've done."

Someone with a sense of drama and history made the groupings for this 77th Women's Open, pairing a departing Swedish legend, Sorenstam, with a bright new Swedish amateur talent on the rise, Ingrid Lindblad, 22, the number two amateur in the world and a star at Louisiana State University. She was the 2022 Southeastern Conference champion and was fresh from finishing third in the NCAA national championship. And next she found herself paired with Sorenstam. "I was like, in shock," Lindblad said. "I was like, this cannot be true! Then on the first tee box I get her scorecard. I'm like, I have Annika's scorecard in my hands."

Lindblad soon enough discovered Sorenstam was real. Those fist bumps for birdies did the trick. Lindblad, needing just 26 putts, went on to take the lead with an amateur record of 65. "She was fearless," Sorenstam said. Lindblad birdied her first (the ninth), bogeyed her second, and made six birdies from there, including three straight from her 11th (the first). She was told that she could become only the second amateur to win the Women's Open, after France's Catherine Lacoste in 1967. "Yeah," she said, "it's possible."

Soon enough, her chances got a bit longer when winless LPGA veteran Mina Harigae, 32, made two late birdies for a seven-under 64 and the first tournament lead she ever had. "I just I hit a lot of good shots, but I made more good putts," she said. "I was putting really well out there today. Right off the get-go, number one and two, I made gettable putts. You know, seven-to-10 feet. That really got my confidence going."

Harigae opened with a sprint — five birdies and a front-nine 30. Coming in she had two bogeys and four birdies, the last two of which, at 15 and 16, tied Lindblad, then passed her. Next Harigae, in her 12th US Women's Open, would call on her mental approach to the game. "Kind of weird," she said. "Varies between one shot at a time, just trying to stay in the moment, just trying to listen to my surroundings a little bit more."

Beyond Lindblad, the traffic began to thicken, led by a trio at 67, three off the lead — Sweden's Anna Nordqvist, the 2021 AIG Women's Open champion, Ryann O'Toole, 2021 Women's Scottish Open champion, and Minjee Lee, the 2021 Evian champion, who had seven birdies, including three twos.

Elsewhere in the field: Nelly Korda, in her first outing for four months after surgery for the blood clot in her left arm, smoothed out an anxious start and shot a 70. "I kind of felt sick, how much adrenaline I was feeling," she said, "and then calmed myself down." Saso struggled to a 77, and Wie West shot 73. Amateur Zhang bounced back from a double bogey at 14 with birdies at 15 and 18 for a 72. Lexi Thompson, battered runner-up in 2021, eagled the par-five first and jumped into this chase with a 68. On losing a five-shot lead down the final nine last year: "It's over with," she said. "I took it, I learned from it, and I moved on."

After 18 holes: 64 (-7) Harigae; **65** Lindblad; **67** Mj Lee, Nordqvist, O'Toole; **68** Thompson, Ewing; **69** JY Ko, M Jutanugarn, SY Kim, Law, SH Park, Olson, Corpuz, A Park, Castren

SECOND ROUND

If Donald Ross was beaming over the success of his subtleties at Pine Needles, he had to be gnashing his teeth at the liberties the field took with his gem in the second round. Observers checked the book on the previous three Women's Opens at Pine Needles and noted: in 1996, after 36 holes, one player was under par. In 2001, there were three, and in 2007, five. That's a total of nine. And for 2022 —

26. After a sweltering first round, temperatures fell to more comfortable 80s for the second and an overnight shower made the course more approachable. It led to some movement on the leaderboard.

Most notably, Minjee Lee made up a three-stroke deficit with a five-under 66 to catch first-round leader Harigae, who fought some bumps and bruises for a 69. Tied at nine-under 133, they led by two.

"Today was fun ... a little more stressful, for sure, and things got a little shaky there," Harigae said. "But I was really happy with the way I hung in there and made some good birdies coming in." That would be her rousing finish: birdie-birdie-bogey-birdie. Encouraging, but she'd had her disappointments. Harigae was shaking off memories of the 2021 AIG Women's Open at Carnoustie, when she was tied for the second-round lead, then shot 76 in the third.

Harigae said she felt like a changed golfer, one with more confidence. "I think I'm just a completely different person and golfer in general," said the 32-year-old. "I'm much more mature. It took me a little bit, but I feel like I'm a lot more mature than I was in my 20s."

Lee, who won her first LPGA title at 18, bolted out of the starting gate, opening the front nine with two birdies and closing it with two more for a 31. After a three-putt bogey on 14, she birdied 15 and 16 to move alongside Harigae at the top of the leaderboard. "The golf course can really catch up to you quickly, so just trying to take whatever I have in front of me, as I go," said Lee. "Whenever I have a birdie opportunity, I try to take advantage of that."

Hye-Jin Choi, who was a 17-year-old amateur whiz when she was the runner-up in 2017, made a strong pitch with a nine-birdie 64 to tie for third with Nordqvist (68) at 135, two off the lead. How could she attack the greens for nine birdies? "My putting was much better today, and also thanks to the rain I think the greens were working for me," she said. "And so I think that's how I was able to attack birdies."

Top-ranked Jin Young Ko surged into the picture with a stunning birdie-eagle for a 67, tying her for fifth with amateur Lindblad (71) at 136, three off the lead. Ko birdied the par-four 14th on a long putt, and eagled the par-five 15th on a longer one, a 65-footer. "I don't think about winning," said Ko. "I just focus on my game ... and have fun."

Lindblad, Louisiana State University star, was getting this crash course in pressure golf: her opening 65 was good enough for the amateur record but not good enough for the lead; playing alongside Sorenstam and dealing with the emotional galleries; trying to solve the many demands of Pine Needles, and facing a midnight deadline on schoolwork due at LSU. "I have a quiz that I'm trying to get 38 out of 38 on, but I only have a 37 out of 38," she said. And the Open: "I think you're just going to have to follow your game plan."

The halfway cut came in at three-over 145, leaving 66 pros and four amateurs and taking defending champion Saso and such former winners as Brittany Lang (2016) and Ariya Jutanugarn (2018). The cut also took two historic figures. Wie West, famously "stepping away" from the LPGA, seemed to welcome the cut, as though liberated. She said she wanted to play one more event, the 2023 Women's Open at Pebble Beach. And she spoke of various projects she wanted to do. "So I'm just going to dive into those. I'm so excited."

And Sorenstam, winner of three US Women's Opens, had no illusions about her chances, at 51. But the spirit was ever young. She suffered eight bogeys and a double in an 81. "I was shooting for par or better," Sorenstam said. "Not really sure what happened today." The family was there to hug her on the 18th. No, Sorenstam wasn't hanging them up. Next was her Scandinavian Mixed in her native Sweden.

After 36 holes: 133 (-9) Harigae 69, Mj Lee 66; **135** HJ Choi 64, Nordqvist 68; **136** JY Ko 67, Lindblad 71; **137** M Jutanugarn 68, SY Kim 68; **138** Law 69, M Khang 67, O'Toole 71, SH Park 69, An Lee 68

THIRD ROUND

The statistical profile of Minjee Lee through the first three rounds of this Open — approach shots, putting — tempted even the most jaded golf observer to a certain conclusion: that the tournament was over, the Yogi Berra Proclamation notwithstanding. It was Berra, New York Yankees's legendary catcher and resident philosopher, who once proclaimed of a badly lopsided competition, "It ain't over till it's over."

Still, the way Lee was playing through 54 holes — for example, just five bogeys to date on Pine Needles's turtleback greens — the sentiment was that this tournament was over. And she was showing no effects from the pressure. She had just come through a head-to-head battle with Harigae, shot 67 and would take a three-stroke lead into the final round. "I'm just going to stick to what I know," said Lee. "I've been to plenty of US Opens and been in pressure situations like this before. Just take my experience … and try and get it done tomorrow."

Lee under pressure: in winning her one major, the 2021 Evian, she closed with 65-64, came from seven strokes behind in the final round to tie Jeongeun Lee6 and beat her on the first playoff hole. In her seven LPGA victories, five final rounds were in the 60s and two were at 70. This third round was a classic mano-a-mano battle. Lee and Harigae were tied, paired and playing each other.

First advantage, Harigae. She burst into a two-stroke lead at the fifth on her birdie and Lee's bogey. Lee got a stroke back with a birdie at six and they were tied again when Harigae bogeyed the seventh. Harigae birdied number eight and led by one. Then came an entry for USGA and LPGA history.

Lee entered a four-hole stretch, from the ninth, trailing by one and emerged, at the 12th, leading by four at 13 under. She had birdied all four, and no gimmes. From 12, 12, eight and six feet. Harigae matched Lee at nine to keep her lead. Lee drew level at the next. Harigae bogeyed the 11th for a two-shot swing to the Australian, and the same again at the 12th.

Lee parred home, while Harigae coolly stuck her tee shot at the par-three 16th to two feet and birdied, shot 70 and cut her deficit to three.

And it seemed Lee was playing alone. "I didn't really think about how Mina was playing," Lee said. "I was just trying to make as many birdies as I could. I didn't really notice her playing that much because I was in my zone."

Said Harigae of the bumpy stretch: "Obviously it wasn't good. The outcome I didn't like. But I didn't get too down on myself."

Lee's 54-hole total of 200 was a new US Women's Open record. She was leading the field in putting with 1.63 per green, and made 10 of 21 tries from 10-to-20 feet. Was this Open over? "My approach is going to be the same as the last three days," Lee offered. "I'm just going to try and make as many birdies as I can. Play safe when I need to and just take one shot at a time."

Bronte Law worked her way to the threshold of contention, six behind, with a 68 to sit in third place at seven under. Her key to Pine Needles: "As long as you can swallow your pride and know that you're going to be aiming away from a lot of flags," she said, "then I'm sure that you'll be more successful."

Six tied for fourth at a near-hopeless seven strokes off the lead: Nordqvist battled back for a 72 after opening with a double bogey. Xiyu Lin scattered six birdies for a 67. World number one Ko bogeyed 11, 13 and 14 and shot 71. "I think I was getting tired," she said. Choi bogeyed four of the first seven, then settled down for a 72. "I think in the beginning I was kind of shaky," she said. Lydia Ko finally hit a good drive at 15, bogeyed anyway and shot 66. Amateur Lindblad started with three birdies in four holes, ran into baffling bogeys and shot 71.

It was rub-of-the-green for these golfers. For Nelly Korda, it was cruel.

Newly back after four months off for surgery, she was encouraged. Through the 15th she was four under for the day and eight under for the championship. Then she bogeyed the last three holes, shot 70 and fell a hopeless nine behind. Call it Nelly's Anthem: "That was tough. But yeah, I'm just happy to be out here … I'm doing what I love and I'm out here competing at the US Women's Open, and a couple months back I wasn't sure if I was going to be doing that. So I'm just grateful to be out here."

After 54 holes: 200 (-13) Mj Lee 67; **203** Harigae 70; **206** Law 68; **207** L Ko 66, Lin 67, Lindblad 71, JY Ko 71, Nordqvist 72, HJ Choi 72; **208** Maguire 68, Ji 69, M Khang 70, M Jutanugarn 71

FOURTH ROUND

In the long and rich history of golf, where does Minjee Lee fit with the greatest Australian women, Karrie Webb and Jan Stephenson? Actually, she's not in the same conversation with those Hall-of-Famers, in terms of sheer numbers. But with her performance and victory in the 2022 US Women's Open, she's right at home.

Most immediately, Lee, at age 26, joined them as the third Australian woman to have won multiple majors. This was Lee's second, after the 2021 Evian. Webb has seven, Stephenson three.

"It's such a great honour just to be amongst those two names," Lee said. "It's just really, really special." A fitting acceptance after a lark of a win. In a field of 70 finishers, there was Lee and then 69 others. Lee crushed a world-class field.

Lee's numbers: 67-66-67-71 for a 13-under-par total of 271, a new championship record. Untouched and unruffled, Lee, number four in the world rankings, won by four over Harigae. World number one Jin Young Ko finished seven shots behind, number two Nelly Korda, 11, and number three Lydia Ko, eight. Under the USGA's heftier prize policy, Lee also won a record $1.8 million.

There are other ways to judge the strength of her play. Only two players broke Pine Needles's par of 71 in the final round — Hye-Jin Choi shot 70 and finished third, six strokes back, and Jeongeun Lee6, a 69, tied for 28th. And only three golfers shot par 71, Lee herself after a meaningless bogey at the last, Jin Young Ko, who finished fourth, and Jennifer Kupcho, tying for 40th.

Pine Needles had been primed for this conclusion. The course was firm and the hole locations were vexing. Sweden's Lindblad, the Louisiana State star, after taking low-amateur honours with a closing 76 for one-under 283, said: "After 12 holes I had hit 12 greens and was three over par." Nordqvist, three-major winner, on the closing 73 that tied her for sixth: "I shot two over, but it's probably one of the best two overs I've had." Korda, closing with 73 to tie for eighth after her medical layoff: "I actually had my best finish in the Women's Open, so maybe I should just keep that going."

There was drama and tension in this final round. It was at the last hole, the 422-yard, par-four 18th. Lee had already handled it routinely with three pars on the first three days. She came to it leading by a huge five shots. There was only one matter of doubt left. Lee had already broken the 54-hole record with her 200. Could she break the 72-hole record? And to do so, she needed a bogey or less at 18. She fired her tee shot down the left side of the fairway, in perfect position to come into the pin. Then she lifted her approach safely to the notorious Donald Ross green. "I just said to myself, 'This is pretty amazing'," Lee said. "This is pretty cool, just looking at the whole crowd and just everybody down the fairway."

Next, that may have been a touch of nerves showing at the 18th. Her approach was safe, some 35 feet from the flag, but she left her first putt five feet short, and then knocked that one 30 inches past. Then she braced herself and holed that one for a bogey, a par 71, and the US Women's Open championship on a record total of 271.

That record had stood for 26 years, set by Sorenstam in winning here at Pine Needles in 1996.

It was an awkward but efficient final round that Lee authored. It looked at first as though she would torch Pine Needles, birdieing the first hole, on two putts from 30 feet, and the second, on a long putt, and she was leading by five. But then she bogeyed the fifth and the seventh. Next, she birdied 12 and 15, then bogeyed 16 and 18. She also saved par four times — at nine from nine feet; 11 from eight, 13 from 13 feet and 14 from seven. "I didn't hit it that well," Lee insisted. "I had really good saves, up-and-downs from a lot of places. And then finishing, I had a couple birdies and a couple bogeys. I think that was enough to get it done."

Harigae, the emerging veteran, wasn't crushed that her best chance at that first win had sputtered out. She led in the first round, was tied with Lee at halfway, and spent the weekend as the closest Lee had to a challenger. She finished a commanding second, four behind with a two-bogey, one-birdie 72 for nine-under 275. "This is definitely top one or two highlights of my career," said Harigae. And the richest. The USGA's boost of the prize money put her second-place cheque at $1.08 million.

Finally, what was left was for Lee to see whether Webb had checked in. "Yeah, she texted me yesterday and the day before," Lee said, "and probably today, as well." Actually, Webb's finest compliment had come, in a way, some 20 years earlier. Lee was just a kid at the time, and had she even touched a club yet?

It was at the 2001 US Women's Open at Pine Needles. Webb had just won it and was in her champion's media interview. She was answering questions. "Well," Webb was saying, "you have to look at all the names on this trophy. Most of them are legends in their own right. And the cream always comes to the top in this tournament."

Pine Needles Lodge & Golf Club, Southern Pines, North Carolina — June 2-5
Par 71 (35-36); 6,638 yards — Purse: $10,000,000

1	**Minjee Lee**	67	66	67	71	271	$1,800,000
2	**Mina Harigae**	64	69	70	72	275	1,080,000
3	**Hye-Jin Choi**	71	64	72	70	277	685,043
4	Jin Young Ko	69	67	71	71	278	480,225
5	Lydia Ko	72	69	66	72	279	399,982
6	Anna Nordqvist	67	68	72	73	280	337,198
	Bronte Law	69	69	68	74	280	337,198
	Nelly Korda	70	69	70	73	282	261,195
	Megan Khang	71	67	70	74	282	261,195
	Leona Maguire	70	70	68	74	282	261,195
11	Moriya Jutanugarn	69	68	71	75	283	209,056
	Ingrid Lindblad (A)	65	71	71	76	283	
	Xiyu Lin	71	69	67	76	283	209,056
14	Sei Young Kim	69	68	75	72	284	187,166
15	Cheyenne Knight	74	71	69	72	286	151,731
	In Gee Chun	72	73	69	72	286	151,731
	Brooke Henderson	72	73	68	73	286	151,731
	Andrea Lee	70	68	72	76	286	151,731
	Eun-Hee Ji	70	69	69	78	286	151,731
20	Pajaree Anannarukarn	70	73	72	72	287	113,850
	Sakura Koiwai	70	71	73	73	287	113,850
	Charley Hull	75	68	70	74	287	113,850
	Lexi Thompson	68	71	72	76	287	113,850
24	Ally Ewing	68	74	74	72	288	87,248
	Frida Kinhult	73	70	73	72	288	87,248
	Atthaya Thitikul	71	73	71	73	288	87,248
	Allisen Corpuz	69	74	71	74	288	87,248
28	Jeongeun Lee[6]	73	70	77	69	289	67,899
	Ryann O'Toole	67	71	79	72	289	67,899
	Sung Hyun Park	69	69	77	74	289	67,899
	Carlota Ciganda	74	69	72	74	289	67,899
	Nasa Hataoka	71	72	72	74	289	67,899
	Hannah Green	70	71	72	76	289	67,899
34	Lizette Salas	71	70	74	75	290	51,040
	Celine Boutier	71	71	73	75	290	51,040
	A Lim Kim	74	70	71	75	290	51,040
	Marissa Steen	72	71	71	76	290	51,040
	Georgia Hall	72	71	71	76	290	51,040
	Lilia Vu	71	69	71	79	290	51,040
40	Jennifer Kupcho	72	71	77	71	291	41,409
	Rose Zhang (A)	72	71	75	73	291	
	Alison Lee	72	72	73	74	291	41,409
	Amanda Doherty	70	72	71	78	291	41,409
44	Brittany Altomare	73	69	77	73	292	33,209
	Matilda Castren	69	74	74	75	292	33,209
	Mao Saigo	70	72	75	75	292	33,209
	Pia Babnik	72	71	74	75	292	33,209
	So Mi Lee	73	68	69	82	292	33,209
49	Saki Baba (A)	73	72	70	78	293	
	Bailey Shoemaker (A)	72	70	72	79	293	
51	Linnea Johansson	71	73	76	74	294	24,103
	Marina Alex	73	72	75	74	294	24,103
	Lauren Hartlage	71	69	78	76	294	24,103
	Isi Gabsa	74	69	74	77	294	24,103
	Caroline Masson	72	73	72	77	294	24,103
	In-Kyung Kim	71	72	73	78	294	24,103
	Angel Yin	71	74	71	78	294	24,103
58	Yealimi Noh	72	72	76	75	295	21,734
	Narin An	72	70	76	77	295	21,734
60	Allison Emrey	71	73	78	74	296	21,219
	Sofia Garcia	72	73	77	74	296	21,219
	Amy Olson	69	72	75	80	296	21,219
63	Tiffany Chan	72	72	77	76	297	20,498
	Grace Kim	73	72	75	77	297	20,498
	Danielle Kang	71	74	73	79	297	20,498
	Jessica Korda	72	70	74	81	297	20,498
67	Annie Park	69	74	78	77	298	19,983
68	Bianca Pagdanganan	75	70	72	82	299	19,777
69	Yuna Takagi	74	68	77	84	303	19,571
70	Maude-Aimee Leblanc	72	73	79	81	305	19,369

MISSED THE 36-HOLE CUT

Pernilla Lindberg	75	71	146
Bohyun Par (A)	73	73	146
Stephanie Meadow	72	74	146
Nanna Koerstz Madsen	74	72	146
Yuna Nishimura	73	73	146
Ami Gianchandan (A)	71	75	146
Gemma Dryburgh	73	73	146
Sarah Kemp	76	70	146
Madelene Sagstrom	69	77	146
Beth Wu	71	75	146
Robynn Ree	73	74	147
Muni He	73	74	147
Michelle Wie West	73	74	147
Hyo Joo Kim	72	75	147
Britney Yada	74	73	147
Ilhee Lee	71	76	147
Catherine Park (A)	74	73	147
Dottie Ardina	78	69	147
Auston Kim	78	69	147
Lauren Kim (A)	75	73	148
Sara Im (A)	74	74	148
Brittany Lang	76	72	148
Lucy Li	74	74	148
Smilla Sonderby	75	73	148
Nicole Garcia	73	75	148
Mariel Galdiano	75	73	148
Ariya Jutanugarn	73	75	148
Stacy Lewis	74	74	148
Gaby Lopez	72	76	148
Mayu Hamada	74	74	148
Gabriela Ruffels	74	75	149
Momoko Ueda	78	71	149
Paula Reto	74	75	149
Patty Tavatanakit	71	78	149
Ayaka Furue	74	75	149
Alicia Joo	73	76	149
Anna Morgan (A)	76	73	149
Lauren Kim	70	79	149
Jensen Castle (A)	74	75	149
Alexa Pano	76	74	150
Na Yeon Choi	75	75	150
Hinako Shibuno	76	74	150
Sophia Popov	71	79	150
Hae Ran Ryu	74	76	150
Amy Yang	79	71	150
Kathleen Scavo	73	77	150
Ingrid Gutierrez	73	77	150
Mel Reid	75	75	150
So Yeon Ryu	74	76	150
Daniela Darquea	74	76	150
Laney Frye (A)	76	75	151
Yunxuan Michelle Zhang (A)	77	74	151
Angela Stanford	75	76	151
Yuka Saso	77	74	151
Mirim Lee	75	76	151
Maja Stark	74	77	151
Pornanong Phatlum	77	74	151
Kylee Choi (A)	75	76	151
Wenbo Liu	77	75	152
Yuri Onishi	75	77	152
Karen Kim	77	75	152

Jillian Hollis	74 78	152
Minsol Kim (A)	76 76	152
Lauren Gomez (A)	74 78	152
Anna Davis (A)	81 72	153
Louise Duncan (A)	75 78	153
Jaye Marie Green	75 78	153
Lydia Hall	73 81	154
Annabell Fuller (A)	79 75	154
Melanie Green (A)	76 78	154
Karissa Kilby (A)	77 78	155
Julianne Alvarez	74 81	155
Emma McMyler (A)	74 81	155
Annika Sorenstam	74 81	155
Alyaa Abdul	81 74	155
Jeonghyun Lee (A)	78 78	156
Alexandra Forsterling (A)	80 77	157
Natsumi Hayakawa	81 76	157
Lauren Miller (A)	80 77	157
Nika Ito (A)	80 78	158
Malak Bouraeda (A)	79 81	160
Blakesly Brock (A)	80 81	161
Bailey Davis (A)	87 74	161
Pauline Roussin	81 81	162
Gabby Lemieux	82 81	163
Ai Suzuki	78	WD

ROLL OF HONOUR

1946	Patty Berg	Spokane
1947	Betty Jameson	Starmount Forest
1948	Babe Didrikson Zaharias	Atlantic City
1949	Louise Suggs	Prince Georges
1950	Babe Didrikson Zaharias	Rolling Hills
1951	Betsy Rawls	Druid Hills
1952	Louise Suggs	Bala
1953	Betsy Rawls*	CC of Rochester
1954	Babe Didrikson Zaharias	Salem
1955	Fay Crocker	Wichita
1956	Kathy Cornelius*	Northand
1957	Betsy Rawls	Winged Foot (East)
1958	Mickey Wright	Forest Lake
1959	Mickey Wright	Churchill Valley
1960	Betsy Rawls	Worcester
1961	Mickey Wright	Baltusrol (Lower)
1962	Murle Lindstrom	Dunes
1963	Mary Mills	Kenwood
1964	Mickey Wright*	San Diego
1965	Carol Mann	Atlantic City
1966	Sandra Spuzich	Hazeltine National
1967	Catherine Lacoste (A)	Virginia Hot Springs (Cascades)
1968	Susie Maxwell Berning	Moselem Springs
1969	Donna Caponi	Scenic Hills
1970	Donna Caponi	Muskogee
1971	JoAnne Gunderson Carner	Kahkwa Club
1972	Susie Maxwell Berning	Winged Foot (East)
1973	Susie Maxwell Berning	CC of Rochester
1974	Sandra Haynie	LaGrange
1975	Sandra Palmer	Atlantic City
1976	JoAnne Gunderson Carner*	Rolling Green
1977	Hollis Stacy	Hazeltine National
1978	Hollis Stacy	CC of Indianapolis
1979	Jerilyn Britz	Brooklawn
1980	Amy Alcott	Richland
1981	Pat Bradley	LaGrange
1982	Janet Alex	Del Paso
1983	Jan Stephenson	Cedar Ridge
1984	Hollis Stacy	Salem
1985	Kathy (Baker) Guadagnino	Baltusrol (Upper)
1986	Jane Geddes	NCR
1987	Laura Davies*	Plainfield
1988	Liselotte Neumann	Baltimore (East)
1989	Betsy King	Indianwood (Old)
1990	Betsy King	Atlanta Athletic Club (Riverside)
1991	Meg Mallon	Colonial
1992	Patty Sheehan*	Oakmont
1993	Lauri Merten	Crooked Stick
1994	Patty Sheehan	Indianwood (Old)
1995	Annika Sorenstam	The Broadmoor (East)
1996	Annika Sorenstam	Pine Needles
1997	Alison Nicholas	Pumpkin Ridge (Witch Hollow)
1998	Se Ri Pak*	Blackwolf Run
1999	Juli Inkster	Old Waverly
2000	Karrie Webb	The Merit Club
2001	Karrie Webb	Pine Needles
2002	Juli Inkster	Prairie Dunes
2003	Hilary Lunke*	Pumpkin Ridge (Witch Hollow)
2004	Meg Mallon	Orchards
2005	Birdie Kim	Cherry Hills
2006	Annika Sorenstam*	Newport
2007	Cristie Kerr	Pine Needles
2008	Inbee Park	Interlachen
2009	Eun-Hee Ji	Saucon Valley (Old)
2010	Paula Creamer	Oakmont
2011	So Yeon Ryu*	The Broadmoor (East)
2012	Na Yeon Choi	Blackwolf Run
2013	Inbee Park	Sebonack
2014	Michelle Wie	Pinehurst (No 2)
2015	In Gee Chun	Lancaster
2016	Brittany Lang*	CordeValle
2017	Sung Hyun Park	Trump National (Old)
2018	Ariya Jutanugarn*	Shoal Creek
2019	Jeongeun Lee[6]	CC of Charleston
2020	A Lim Kim	Champions
2021	Yuka Saso*	Olympic (Lake)
2022	Minjee Lee	Pine Needles

**won in playoff*

US OPEN CHAMPIONSHIP

Fitzpatrick adds to his Brookline memories

By Marino Parascenzo

The US Open was returning to the site of some of its richest history, The Country Club, at Brookline, near Boston. Another chapter would be added, but this one was unexpected, in some regards unwanted, but elegantly accomplished.

It used to be a lot easier than this. It used to be that the brains of the US Golf Association, when preparing a course for its flagship event, the US Open, would huddle up like a bunch of monks in a medieval library, immerse themselves in such philosophies as the speed of the greens, the depth of the rough, hole locations and the like. Not this time. This time, while wrestling with the mechanics of staging and conducting the national championship, the USGA brass also faced other questions. LIV Golf had played its inaugural event in London the week before the US Open, and the PGA Tour suspensions had taken effect, thus raising a kind of no-way-out problem. This was the crucial question: would tour members who were already exempt into the US Open and now were no longer members still be permitted to play? The answer, in graceful logic, came the week before the Open. Said Mike Whan, in his first US Open as USGA CEO: "We pride ourselves in being the most open championship in the world. Our field criteria were set prior to entries opening earlier this year, and it's not appropriate, nor fair to competitors, to change criteria once established." So Phil Mickelson and Dustin Johnson and 12 other LIV golfers were able to play in the 2022 US Open.

And so The Country Club had another page for its legacy. It had played a role in two major developments early in American golf. In 1894, TCC joined Newport Country Club, Saint Andrew's Golf Club of Yonkers, New York, Chicago Golf Club and Shinnecock Hills Golf Club in forming the USGA, an organisation to set rules, conduct championship events and in general govern the game. And American golf took real root with the 1913 US Open at TCC, after Francis Ouimet — 20, amateur, former caddie and son of a relatively poor family living across the street from the club — beat the two best golfers of the day, British pros Harry Vardon and Ted Ray. Ouimet, the first amateur to win the Open, tied them in regulation and beat them in an 18-hole playoff the next day. Before that, golf was considered a game for the wealthy at private clubs. His stunning win lifted golf into the American mainstream of sports.

Brookline went on to host six US Amateurs, three US Women Amateurs and a Ryder Cup, as well as two other US Opens, Julius Boros winning in 1963 and Curtis Strange in 1988. Strange beat Nick Faldo in a playoff. It was beginning to look as if Matt Fitzpatrick needed to avoid a playoff if he wanted to avenge the defeats of compatriots Vardon, Ray and Faldo, yet his chances of doing so were not good after finding a fairway bunker at the 72nd hole.

As John Bodenhamer, the USGA's chief championships officer, had previously said of the club's traditional Open composite course, recently renovated by Gil Hanse: "This will be a good old-fashioned US Open with rough, and we'll see how they navigate that and what they use off the tee. I am telling you — with these small greens and the firmness, they're going to need to be in the fairway."

Fitzpatrick had already won at TCC, claiming the US Amateur title in 2013. But now on offer was a purse of $17.5 million, a record for the four majors and up $5m from 2021. The first prize was $3.15 million, up from $2.25m, and to claim it the Englishman would have to add to the US Open's treasury of jewels, those monumental shots that include Arnold Palmer driving the first green in 1960 at Cherry Hills, and Tom Watson chipping in at the 17th at Pebble Beach in 1982.

FIRST ROUND

The 2022 US Open began on an agreeable mid-June Thursday and true to its history it headed right for that dimension of the completely unexpected, totally hard-to-imagine and mostly difficult to believe — the Twilight Zone. Such as Rory McIlroy and his two fits of pique in the first round. And Jon Rahm, number two in the world and the defending champion, finding himself in an alley brawl just to crack par. And Scottie Scheffler, the hottest golfer on the planet, with four victories in almost no time and rated number one in the world, having to birdie his last two holes just to shoot par. And Mickelson scoring a 78. The numbers add up fast when you have a 12-footer for birdie and you four-putt for double bogey.

Emerging from such tremors, The Country Club had a leaderboard best described as not uncharacteristic of the US Open. Consider: a Canadian was leading, and tied just a stroke behind were an Englishman, a Swede, an Irishman, a South African and an American.

First, there was the Canadian, Adam Hadwin, the unlikeliest leader of all. He rated that dubious distinction because at the start of the week he wasn't even in the US Open. Hadwin, 34, was the first alternate out of the Dallas qualifier, and got in on Monday after an ailing back forced Paul Casey to withdraw. And then teeing off just after 2pm Hadwin jolted the leaderboard with five birdies over his last six holes (from the fourth) for a four-under-par 66 and a one-stroke lead. "I don't think that you can ask for a much better start to a US Open," said Hadwin.

Next came the five others at 67, among them McIlroy, the hugely popular Northern Irishman, winner of the Canadian Open the week before, winner of four career majors, and the 10-1 favourite. "It's been eight years since I won a major," he said, "and I just want to get my hands on one again." He hit only eight of 14 fairways, but 13 of 18 greens, and he had two brief outbursts. At number five (his 14th), a driveable par four, he was frustrated by the thick rough at a bunker and so gave the sand a couple of rebuking whacks. "You're thinking of making birdie on it, and all of a sudden you're scrambling for par," he said, which he did with a 20-foot putt. Then, miffed at missing the green at his final hole, the ninth, he gave his club a back-handed fling, maybe 15 feet. Certainly not one of his more expressive launches. But he made his point. Then made his only bogey.

Also at 67: Joel Dahmen birdied three of his last five holes and was tied for the lead before Hadwin finished. "I love being nervous, I love my hands shaking," he said; England's Callum Tarren, PGA Tour rookie, was in his first US Open. He hit 13 of 18 greens and needed just 28 putts. "I'm kind of pinching myself," he said; Sweden's David Lingmerth, also in as an alternate, made three birdies and no bogeys. At a US Open everybody has to dig, he said, "and inevitably something bad might happen"; South Africa's MJ Daffue, in his first major, made a spectator's day. "Some guy over there," Daffue said, speaking of someone who had made a proposition bet, "I made him $600 by making a putt. He was loving it."

Quite apart from the eclectic leaderboard, Mickelson was the centre of attention. Back in February, after drawing criticism for certain comments about the PGA Tour and the Saudis, he withdrew into a self-imposed silent exile for some four months. He emerged to play in the inaugural LIV tournament in London, then came to the US Open. He found the fans sympathetic, yelling "Go, Phil!" Also, "Happy Birthday!" on turning 52 on Thursday. He'd won six majors and needed a US Open to fill out his career Grand Slam, and he'd been tantalised by six seconds. But hope wilted fast this time. He had six bogeys, two double bogeys, one birdie, and did not to speak to the media. Johnson, the 2016 US Open champion, fared best of the LIV golfers, finishing in 24th at the end of the week after opening with a four-birdie, two-under 68, tying with Fitzpatrick, who birdied three of the final five holes on the front nine, and Justin Rose, author of a wild first nine in which he parred just one hole.

Fitzpatrick was the English kid who won the 2013 US Amateur at Brookline as a teenager. He was now 27, on the PGA Tour and a two-time Ryder Cupper. "I've tried to have no expectations coming into the week," said Fitzpatrick of his return to Brookline. "I feel I do have a chance because, A, I've had success here before, and, B, I've been playing well." Staying with the same family he was billeted with nine years earlier, he was enjoying homecookin' and hearing "Fitzy!" yelled from the galleries. "It just feels a bit more like a home game this week, that's why it feels different and for the better," he said.

He played in the afternoon, and raced to birdies at the fifth, eighth and ninth holes, but cooled off with a choppy back nine — bogeys at 11, 15 and 18, birdies at 12 and 17. "I've got great memories of the place," he added. And what was that he said back when they handed him the trophy at the 2013 US Amateur? "I guess it's great to go down in history," he said. "That's sort of what everyone wants to achieve in golf."

After 18 holes: 66 (-4) Hadwin; **67** Daffue, Tarren, Lingmerth, McIlroy, Dahmen; **68** Buckley, NeSmith, Harman, Wise, Fitzpatrick, D Johnson, Rose

SECOND ROUND

All in all, the second round of the US Open went swimmingly, especially after the anticipated dangerous weather didn't materialise. The worst of it was some heavy wind late in the morning followed by relative calm on a course not to be trifled with. There was the huge upheaval on the leaderboard, perhaps unusually thorough considering that of the top six in the first round, only two made it into the top seven in the second round.

Collin Morikawa wasn't troubled by his one-handed finishes. That is, by his right hand coming off the club. "It just shows maybe I'm not hitting it in the centre, but it doesn't mean I can't play well," he said, "and it doesn't mean the misses aren't going to be good."

And who's to argue with a five-birdie, one-bogey 66. It tied him at five-under 135 for a one-stroke lead with Joel Dahmen, whose 68 would force him to change his dinner plans. For the first time in his six years on the PGA Tour, he would be playing in the final group in a major. "We don't tee off until 3:45 tomorrow," Dahmen said. "I typically have to be home at five for dinner, so this will be different, for sure."

Morikawa, 25, who listed the 2020 PGA Championship and the 2021 Open Championship among his five wins, was four under before stumbling to a bogey at his 13th (the fourth), then birdied his 17th. "It's the US Open," he said. "No one has taken it deep so far and kind of run away."

Dahmen, 35, a cancer survivor with one win, had considered withdrawing from the qualifier. Now he was trying to collect himself. "It's kind of been a whirlwind," he said. "It's all kind of a blur, really."

And the second round ended with five tied for third at four-under 136, including the good-natured and immensely popular McIlroy, who said: "For a little part of the day, it seemed like I was going to be a few more behind, but I dug deep and played the last eight holes really, really well." This after needing three chops to get out of deep greenside rough at the third, then having to sink a 25-foot putt to save double bogey in his 69.

Alongside him were: Rahm (67), admiring the leaderboard: "I think it's great for golf that the highest ranked players and the best players are up there";

Beau Hossler (67): "If I had made 18 pars today, I would have been quite happy, as well"; Aaron Wise (68): "I feel my game is in a spot where all facets of it are pretty good"; Hayden Buckley (68): "The biggest thing is just patience. Missing six and seven cuts, it's hard to have patience."

Former US Amateur champion Fitzpatrick crafted a routine-looking par 70 that actually was a minor masterpiece for those who enjoy a good scare. Fitzpatrick started at the 10th, made the turn at one under, and stumbled to three straight bogeys starting home. He was inching toward the cut line, then birdied his 14th and 17th to be two under, three off the lead. "Played really, really well," Fitzpatrick said. "Three of my four bogeys were all three-putts, so that kind of sums up the day."

The second round also offered two episodes worthy of a place in the US Open archives. In one, South African Daffue, leading at the time, hit perhaps the craziest shot of the tournament — a four-wood second 280 yards off the carpeted deck of a hospitality facility at the par-five 14th, through a kind of tunnel — railing to the right, big tree and fans on the left, leafy branch overhead. He just missed the green, then flubbed the chip shot and bogeyed. He limped home with a 72, falling four off the lead. "I think it was an awesome shot," Daffue said, "but a birdie would have been better."

The second episode: Who was that guy and why was he running? That was Patrick Rodgers, and he was trying to outrun the law of gravity. At the par-five, 576-yard eighth (his 17th), Rodgers had hit his second to the false front of the green from where, as so many had learned, the ball would roll back off and keep on rolling, 30 yards back down the sloping fairway. So Rodgers ran the last 180 yards to get his ball marked before it could break free from the tight lie and start rolling. He got there in time. And he got an ovation from the gallery. Said Rodgers, through a big smile, "I'm a seasoned athlete." (He birdied, by the way. And for the week played the eighth hole in birdie-birdie-eagle-birdie.)

After 36 holes: 135 (-5) Morikawa 66, Dahmen 68; **136** Buckley 68, Rahm 67, McIlroy 69, Wise 68, Hossler 67; **137** Hardy 68, Scheffler 67, NeSmith 69, Rodgers 68, Harman 69

THIRD ROUND

Dahmen said it all in 18 words. "I knew it was going to be hard. I didn't know it was going to be that hard."

It was a day that stood a groggy leaderboard on its head again, ending up with Fitzpatrick and Will Zalatoris tied for the lead at four-under 206. On a day when bogeys were flying like so many crows, Zalatoris was the wonder of the leaderboard. Of the 64 who made the cut, he was the only player to make just one bogey. He also shot the day's low, a 67. "Felt," he said, "like I shot a 61."

Fitzpatrick got a shock. "I put my sun cream on before the round, thinking, oh, it's going to get nice and warm," he said. Then the winds hit. "You had to be switched on with the way you were hitting it, where you were missing it," he said. He shot a five-birdie, two-under 68. "Really happy with my score," he said.

And so it went in the third round of the US Open on a Saturday when the temperatures fell into the 60s and the winds climbed into the 20s (mph). Eight different players either led or shared the lead, and three of them didn't even finish in the top 10 for the day. Only seven broke TCC's par of 70 and only three others matched it.

The damage started at the top. Morikawa and Dahmen, co-leaders at the start of the round, were sent sprawling. Morikawa, two-time major champion, took two double bogeys, escaped a third with a 25-foot bogey putt, and shot a crippling 77. Dahmen, playing in the final group in a major for the first time, took four bogeys on the front nine and parred all the way home for a no-birdie 74. "It was way harder today," he said. "But it was a true US Open setup, that's for sure."

Zalatoris played cautiously, even defensively. "We didn't aim at a single flag, even with some wedges," he said. Three of his four birdies came on the front, along with that single bogey at the seventh. Fitzpatrick made the turn in one under, bogeyed the 10th, then birdied 14, 15 and 17, and bogeyed the 18th to tie Zalatoris for the lead.

Rahm, the sombre Spaniard and defending champion, got knocked out of the lead by two extraordinarily bizarre events and yet was almost beaming. At the par-five eighth, his tee shot left him at the base of a tall tree. He had to hit backward and one-handed to escape. He bogeyed. At the par-four 18th, he drove into a fairway bunker. His first shot out hit the lip and came back to him. His second soared ahead into a greenside bunker and a plugged lie. He double-bogeyed for a 71 and marvelled, "I'm only one shot back."

Scheffler, the Masters champion, was caught by TCC at its fiendish best. After a birdie-bogey start, Scheffler eagled the false-front par-five eighth, holing out from 80 yards, and was on his way. But at the par-three 11th, a mere 141 yards, his tee shot bounced off the green and into deep rough beyond, and he needed two to get on and two more to get down and double-bogeyed. He was out of the lead. Then he bogeyed 12, 13 and 14. "After 13," he said, "I just kept trying to pretend that what was happening wasn't happening." He finished birdie-par for a 71, and was two under and two off the lead.

McIlroy laboured to a one-birdie 73 and announced with relief, "Just kept myself in the tournament. That's all I was trying to do. Just keep hanging around." He was one under and three behind.

And underlining the capriciousness of the day: one of the seven under-par rounds came from Denny McCarthy. In only his third US Open, having just made the cut right on the number, he shot 68 before the leaders had even arrived. At day's end, he would be tied for 11th and five behind. "I think I blacked out," McCarthy cracked. "I don't even remember anything."

After 54 holes: 206 (-4) Zalatoris 67, Fitzpatrick 68; **207** Rahm 71; **208** Bradley 69, Hadwin 70, Scheffler 71; **209** Burns 71, McIlroy 73, Dahmen 74; **210** Hardy 73

FOURTH ROUND

If the 2022 US Open came down to a war of nerves, Fitzpatrick didn't seem to have any. Not on that cross-country birdie putt at the 13th, not on that do-or-die five-iron at the 15th and certainly not on that bunker shot at the 18th. The boyish Fitzpatrick, age 27 now and grinning through dental braces, just rolled along. He did miss the birdie putt at the 18th, but not by much. The tap-in filled out his card of 68-70-68-68 for a six-under-par total of 274, ending a three-way battle a stroke ahead of Zalatoris, who shot 69, and Scheffler, 67.

"Unbelievable," Fitzpatrick said. "It is so cliché, but it's stuff you dream of as a kid. I can retire a happy man tomorrow."

Zalatoris was suffering a different kind of cliché — runner-up in three majors: the 2021 Masters, the PGA Championship a month ago, and now here. "It stings," he said. "I'd pay a lot of money for about an inch and a half, and I'd probably be a three-time major champion at this point." And to Fitzpatrick: "My hat's off to him. He played great all week and gave a solid round today."

Scheffler, with a first and a second in the three 2022 majors so far, was miffed at his putting. "A few breaks here or there, and I would be the one holding the trophy," he said. "Tip of the hat to Fitzy. He definitely deserved to win."

For the record: it was Fitzpatrick's first victory in a major, his first pro win in the US, his eighth worldwide, and he was the first Englishman to win the US Open since Justin Rose in 2013. He also was the second man to win the US Amateur and US Open at the same course, after Jack Nicklaus at Pebble Beach.

The Country Club's historic acres were littered with broken dreams, none more so than McIlroy's. He'd won four majors, but none since 2014. The pre-tournament favourite this time, he challenged, sputtered, closed with a 69 and tied for fifth, four behind. There was a sadness in his farewell. "When I look back, will I remember the fifth place I had at Brookline?" McIlroy wondered. "Probably not."

Defending champion Rahm, knocked out of the lead by a closing double bogey the day before, never regained his footing. He shot a five-bogey 74 and tied for 12th. However, Hideki Matsuyama, the 2021 Masters champion, started the last round six behind and made a spirited run with a flawless, tournament-low 65. He finished fourth, three behind.

The field shook itself out fast in the final round. Fitzpatrick and Zalatoris were leading at four under. Rahm had a two-bogey front nine. Keegan Bradley, from two behind, bogeyed the first three holes; Hadwin was one over through six, and Scheffler birdied four of the first six to take the lead — briefly — and turn it into a three-man chase down the stretch.

Two early bogeys put Zalatoris a scary four behind, but he recovered with three birdies over the last four holes of the front nine. Fitzpatrick had three birdies and a bogey, and at six under was a stroke ahead of Zalatoris through the turn. This US Open was starting to perk.

Scheffler, two groups ahead, came stumbling out of the turn with two bogeys. "I look at those bogeys on 10 and 11," he said, "and really didn't hit a bad shot." Fitzpatrick matched him with bogeys at 10 and 11. Zalatoris birdied the 11th from 18 feet, went two ahead, then back to one on a bogey at 12.

Then came an unreal moment at the par-four 13th. Fitzpatrick rolled in a cross-country 50-footer for birdie. Zalatoris parred from 15 feet and they were tied again at five under. The par-four 15th became the pivotal hole. It's where the gods of golf played perhaps their merriest prank.

Zalatoris missed the fairway by just a few yards and found himself in ankle-deep rough. Fitzpatrick missed the fairway by yards and yards to the right, and found his ball "sitting perfectly". The galleries had trampled the thick grass flat. From there: "One of the best shots I hit all day," he said — a five-iron from 220 yards to 18 feet. He got his birdie, and Zalatoris bogeyed out of that rough. The two-shot swing had Fitzpatrick leading by two with three to play. Zalatoris snapped back immediately with a birdie at the par-three 16th, holing a six-footer, and both parred 17, which Scheffler had birdied just ahead.

Fitzpatrick immediately got himself into a mess at the 18th, hooking his tee shot into a fairway bunker. With Zalatoris safely down the fairway and within reach of a birdie, Fitzpatrick ignored the lay-up and opted to go for the green. Zalatoris, passing by, cringed in admiration. Fitzpatrick would have to get out of the bunker, carry a patch of rough, then carry a gaping bunker in front of the green. "Around 160-170 yards," Zalatoris said. "And to get it to be just past pin high ... the fact he had a look was just awesome."

Fitzpatrick pulled his nine-iron, squirmed down into the sand, and hit away. The ball soared obediently — a "squeezy fade" he called it — and dropped to the green, 18 feet from the flag. The fans erupted. Fitzpatrick narrowly missed his birdie putt, then calmly tapped in. Zalatoris stepped up to his 14-footer. It grazed the left edge of the cup. Fitzpatrick, 2013 US Amateur champion, had won the 2022 US Open. The impact of that miss dropped Zalatoris almost to his knees.

"It was kind of just a bit of hit-and-hope," Fitzpatrick said of the bunker shot. "One thing that I've been really struggling with this year is fairway bunker play. Still not 100 percent out of it." Well, all in all, he seemed to be getting the hang of it.

The Country Club (Open composite), Brookline, Massachusetts — June 16-19
Par 70 (35-35); 7,254 yards — Purse: $17,500,000

1	**Matt Fitzpatrick**	68	70	68	68	274	$3,150,000
2	**Scottie Scheffler**	70	67	71	67	275	1,557,687
	Will Zalatoris	69	70	67	69	275	1,557,687
4	Hideki Matsuyama	70	70	72	65	277	859,032
5	Collin Morikawa	69	66	77	66	278	674,953
	Rory McIlroy	67	69	73	69	278	674,953
7	Denny McCarthy	73	70	68	68	279	515,934
	Adam Hadwin	66	72	70	71	279	515,934
	Keegan Bradley	70	69	69	71	279	515,934
10	Gary Woodland	69	73	69	69	280	407,220
	Joel Dahmen	67	68	74	71	280	407,220
12	Seamus Power	71	70	70	70	281	347,058
	Jon Rahm	69	67	71	74	281	347,058
14	Guido Migliozzi	72	70	74	66	282	241,302
	Xander Schauffele	70	69	75	68	282	241,302
	Marc Leishman	70	71	73	68	282	241,302
	Adam Scott	69	73	72	68	282	241,302
	Cameron Tringale	71	71	71	69	282	241,302
	Patrick Cantlay	72	71	70	69	282	241,302
	Sebastian Munoz	74	69	69	70	282	241,302
	Hayden Buckley	68	68	75	71	282	241,302
	Nick Hardy	69	68	73	72	282	241,302
23	Joohyung Kim	72	68	73	70	283	171,732
24	Mackenzie Hughes	72	69	73	70	284	150,849
	Adam Schenk	70	70	73	71	284	150,849
	Dustin Johnson	68	73	71	72	284	150,849
27	Thomas Pieters	72	68	73	72	285	127,002
	Min Woo Lee	73	70	69	73	285	127,002
	Aaron Wise	68	68	75	74	285	127,002
	Sam Burns	71	67	71	76	285	127,002
31	MJ Daffue	67	72	78	69	286	100,331
	Callum Tarren	67	72	78	69	286	100,331
	Todd Sinnott	71	71	74	70	286	100,331
	Andrew Putnam	72	68	74	72	286	100,331
	Patrick Rodgers	69	68	75	74	286	100,331
	Davis Riley	72	67	73	74	286	100,331
37	Kyoung-Hoon Lee	71	72	73	71	287	75,916
	Justin Rose	68	73	74	72	287	75,916
	Joseph Bramlett	71	72	72	72	287	75,916
	Justin Thomas	69	72	72	74	287	75,916
	Jordan Spieth	72	70	71	74	287	75,916
	Matthew NeSmith	68	69	74	76	287	75,916
43	Chris Gotterup	73	69	75	71	288	59,332
	Travis Vick (A)	70	69	76	73	288	
	Richard Bland	70	72	72	74	288	59,332
	Brian Harman	68	69	75	76	288	59,332
47	Joaquin Niemann	71	70	76	72	289	50,672
	Max Homa	69	73	75	72	289	50,672
49	Sam Bennett (A)	70	73	74	73	290	
	Patrick Reed	70	71	75	74	290	44,038
	Sam Stevens	71	72	72	75	290	44,038
	David Lingmerth	67	72	74	77	290	44,038
53	Sebastian Soderberg	71	70	78	72	291	40,630
	Beau Hossler	69	67	78	77	291	40,630
55	Brooks Koepka	73	67	75	77	292	39,432
56	Wil Besseling	71	71	77	74	293	38,511
	Chris Naegel	73	69	77	74	293	38,511
	Tyrrell Hatton	72	71	76	74	293	38,511
	Bryson DeChambeau	71	71	76	75	293	38,511
60	Brandon Matthews	71	69	79	77	296	37,589
61	Harris English	73	69	78	77	297	37,221
	Austin Greaser (A)	72	70	76	79	297	
63	Grayson Murray	75	67	76	80	298	36,843
64	Stewart Hagestad (A)	73	70	79	77	299	

MISSED THE 36-HOLE CUT

Sergio Garcia	74	70	144
Sungjae Im	72	72	144
Mito Pereira	70	74	144
Corey Conners	71	73	144
Webb Simpson	70	74	144
Shane Lowry	72	72	144
Jason Kokrak	69	75	144
Jim Furyk	74	70	144
Erik Barnes	71	73	144
Matt McCarty	71	73	144
Wyndham Clark	70	74	144
James Piot	69	75	144
Billy Horschel	73	71	144
Kevin Kisner	73	71	144
Cameron Young	72	72	144
Stewart Cink	73	71	144
Kalle Samooja	77	67	144
Taylor Montgomery	72	73	145
Brian Stuard	73	72	145
Talor Gooch	74	71	145
Tom Hoge	73	72	145
Kevin Na	75	70	145
Tony Finau	73	72	145
Luke List	72	73	145
Nick Taylor	73	72	145
Ryan Fox	74	71	145
Si Woo Kim	76	69	145
Daniel Berger	70	75	145
Harold Varner III	72	73	145
Chan Kim	73	72	145
Branden Grace	76	69	145
Satoshi Kodaira	74	71	145
Ben Silverman	72	73	145
Sam Horsfield	73	73	146
Cameron Smith	72	74	146
Louis Oosthuizen	77	69	146
Davis Shore	74	72	146
Michael Thorbjornsen (A)	77	69	146
Troy Merritt	75	71	146
Scott Stallings	74	72	146
Russell Henley	76	70	146
Alex Noren	73	73	146
Francesco Molinari	73	73	146
Roger Sloan	76	70	146
Andrew Novak	73	74	147
Maxwell Moldovan (A)	75	72	147
Adri Arnaus	76	71	147
Viktor Hovland	70	77	147
Tommy Fleetwood	72	75	147
Adrien Dumont de Chassart (A)	72	75	147
Jonas Blixt	75	72	147
Bo Hoag	72	75	147
Ryan Gerard	74	73	147
Kurt Kitayama	74	73	147
Victor Perez	73	74	147
Lanto Griffin	72	75	147
Shaun Norris	70	78	148
Patton Kizzire	74	74	148
Keita Nakajima (A)	73	75	148
Rikuya Hoshino	77	71	148
Kevin Chappell	73	76	149
Chase Seiffert	74	75	149
Brady Calkins	76	73	149
William Mouw (A)	75	74	149
Sepp Straka	77	72	149
Andrew Beckler	78	71	149
Yannik Paul	77	73	150

Erik van Rooyen	78 72	150
Daijiro Izumida	73 77	150
Thorbjorn Olesen	75 76	151
Phil Mickelson	78 73	151
Danny Lee	76 75	151
Charles Reiter (A)	76 75	151
Laird Shepherd (A)	75 76	151
Harry Hall	74 77	151
Richard Mansell	77 74	151
Nick Dunlap (A)	78 74	152
Fred Biondi (A)	79 73	152
Tomoyasu Sugiyama	74 78	152
Lucas Herbert	74 79	153
Ben Lorenz (A)	77 76	153
Fran Quinn	76 77	153
Jinichiro Kozuma	76 77	153
Jesse Mueller	80 74	154
Isaiah Salinda	79 75	154
Jediah Morgan	82 74	156
Luke Gannon	76 80	156
Marcel Schneider	78 79	157
Caleb Manuel (A)	83 74	157
Sean Crocker	83 75	158
Sean Jacklin	78 80	158
Keith Greene	83 81	164

ROLL OF HONOUR

1895	Horace Rawlins	Newport
1896	James Foulis	Shinnecock Hills
1897	Joe Lloyd	Chicago
1898	Fred Herd	Myopia Hunt
1899	Willie Smith	Baltimore
1900	Harry Vardon	Chicago
1901	Willie Anderson*	Myopia Hunt
1902	Laurence Auchterlonie	Garden City
1903	Willie Anderson*	Baltusrol
1904	Willie Anderson	Glen View
1905	Willie Anderson	Myopia Hunt
1906	Alex Smith	Onwentsia
1907	Alex Ross	Philadelphia
1908	Fred McLeod*	Myopia Hunt
1909	George Sargent	Englewood
1910	Alex Smith*	Philadelphia
1911	John McDermott*	Chicago
1912	John McDermott	CC of Buffalo
1913	Francis Ouimet* (A)	Brookline
1914	Walter Hagen	Midlothian
1915	Jerome D Travers (A)	Baltusrol
1916	Charles Evans Jr	Minikahda
1919	Walter Hagen	Brae Burn
1920	Ted Ray	Inverness
1921	James Barnes	Columbia
1922	Gene Sarazen	Skokie
1923	Bobby Jones* (A)	Inwood
1924	Cyril Walker	Oakland Hills
1925	William Macfarlane*	Worcester
1926	Bobby Jones (A)	Scioto
1927	Tommy Armour*	Oakmont
1928	Johnny Farrell*	Olympia Fields
1929	Bobby Jones* (A)	Winged Foot (West)
1930	Bobby Jones (A)	Interlachen
1931	Billy Burke*	Inverness
1932	Gene Sarazen	Fresh Meadow
1933	Johnny Goodman (A)	North Shore
1934	Olin Dutra	Merion
1935	Sam Parks Jr	Oakmont
1936	Tony Manero	Baltusrol (Upper)
1937	Ralph Guldahl	Oakland Hills
1938	Ralph Guldahl	Cherry Hills
1939	Byron Nelson*	Philadelphia
1940	Lawson Little*	Canterbury
1941	Craig Wood	Colonial
1946	Lloyd Mangrum*	Canterbury
1947	Lew Worsham*	St Louis
1948	Ben Hogan	Riviera
1949	Cary Middlecoff	Medinah
1950	Ben Hogan*	Merion
1951	Ben Hogan	Oakland Hills
1952	Julius Boros	Northwood
1953	Ben Hogan	Oakmont
1954	Ed Furgol	Baltusrol (Lower)
1955	Jack Fleck*	Olympic (Lake)
1956	Cary Middlecoff	Oak Hill
1957	Dick Mayer*	Inverness
1958	Tommy Bolt	Southern Hills
1959	Billy Casper Jr	Winged Foot (West)
1960	Arnold Palmer	Cherry Hills
1961	Gene Littler	Oakland Hills
1962	Jack Nicklaus*	Oakmont
1963	Julius Boros*	Brookline
1964	Ken Venturi	Congressional (Blue)
1965	Gary Player*	Bellerive
1966	Billy Casper Jr*	Olympic (Lake)
1967	Jack Nicklaus	Baltusrol (Lower)
1968	Lee Trevino	Oak Hill
1969	Orville Moody	Champions
1970	Tony Jacklin	Hazeltine National
1971	Lee Trevino*	Merion
1972	Jack Nicklaus	Pebble Beach
1973	Johnny Miller	Oakmont
1974	Hale Irwin	Winged Foot (West)
1975	Lou Graham*	Medinah (No 3)
1976	Jerry Pate	Atlanta Athletic Club (Highlands)
1977	Hubert Green	Southern Hills
1978	Andy North	Cherry Hills
1979	Hale Irwin	Inverness
1980	Jack Nicklaus	Baltusrol (Lower)
1981	David Graham	Merion
1982	Tom Watson	Pebble Beach
1983	Larry Nelson	Oakmont
1984	Fuzzy Zoeller*	Winged Foot (West)
1985	Andy North	Oakland Hills
1986	Raymond Floyd	Shinnecock Hills
1987	Scott Simpson	Olympic (Lake)
1988	Curtis Strange*	Brookline
1989	Curtis Strange	Oak Hill
1990	Hale Irwin*	Medinah
1991	Payne Stewart	Hazeltine National
1992	Tom Kite	Pebble Beach
1993	Lee Janzen	Baltusrol (Lower)
1994	Ernie Els*	Oakmont
1995	Corey Pavin	Shinnecock Hills
1996	Steve Jones	Oakland Hills
1997	Ernie Els	Congressional (Blue)
1998	Lee Janzen	Olympic (Lake)
1999	Payne Stewart	Pinehurst (No 2)
2000	Tiger Woods	Pebble Beach
2001	Retief Goosen*	Southern Hills
2002	Tiger Woods	Bethpage (Black)
2003	Jim Furyk	Olympia Fields
2004	Retief Goosen	Shinnecock Hills

2005	Michael Campbell	Pinehurst (No 2)
2006	Geoff Ogilvy	Winged Foot (West)
2007	Angel Cabrera	Oakmont
2008	Tiger Woods*	Torrey Pines (South)
2009	Lucas Glover	Bethpage (Black)
2010	Graeme McDowell	Pebble Beach
2011	Rory McIlroy	Congressional (Blue)
2012	Webb Simpson	Olympic (Lake)
2013	Justin Rose	Merion
2014	Martin Kaymer	Pinehurst (No 2)
2015	Jordan Spieth	Chambers Bay
2016	Dustin Johnson	Oakmont
2017	Brooks Koepka	Erin Hills
2018	Brooks Koepka	Shinnecock Hills
2019	Gary Woodland	Pebble Beach
2020	Bryson DeChambeau	Winged Foot (West)
2021	Jon Rahm	Torrey Pines (South)
2022	Matt Fitzpatrick	Brookline

**won in playoff*

KPMG WOMEN'S PGA CHAMPIONSHIP

A win for smiling at game's highs and lows

By Bill Fields

Congressional Country Club has been a fixture in big-time golf for a long time, the site of multiple US Opens and a PGA Championship, US Senior Open and quite a few regular PGA Tour events. Congressional's Blue course is where a down-on-his-luck Ken Venturi (1964) and an up-and-coming Rory McIlroy (2011) broke through for memorable major triumphs.

But the Blue course that hosted the 2022 KPMG Women's PGA Championship didn't look much like the layout upon which the previous elite tournaments were contested. Congressional, originally designed by Devereux Emmet in the 1920s and subsequently worked on by Robert Trent Jones Sr and later his son, Rees Jones, was drastically remodelled in 2019-20 by architect Andrew Green. Only the routing and par of the holes stayed the same as Green transformed the property by removing trees, widening fairways, altering green complexes and putting in 40 acres of natural areas.

On Tuesday of championship week at a course that had seen so much change, it was only fitting that the event would have some important news. Whether players were on the practice tee or having a bite to eat, there was a buzz in the air when KPMG — the title sponsor since 2014 — and the PGA of America announced that the purse was increasing from $4.5 million to $9 million, with the winner receiving $1.35 million.

"We really wanted to make sure we utilised the event to showcase the best women's players in the game and to do that with one of the biggest purses," Jim Richerson, president of the PGA of America said, reflecting on the beginning of the partnership with KPMG. "We've seen that play out in the announcement today."

Fifty years ago, there was only a $50,000 purse for what was then called the LPGA Championship, with champion Kathy Ahern taking home $7,500.

Over 72 holes on the revitalised Blue course, playing for double the prize money as in 2021, it was fitting that the winner was a player who has gone through some changes herself.

In Gee Chun, of the Republic of Korea, splashed onto the global golf scene in 2015, winning the US Women's Open at Lancaster Country Club, in Pennsylvania, as a 20-year-old, impressing with her play and charming with a smiling demeanour that belied tough family circumstances growing up in South Korea. "But I still made it," Chun said at Lancaster through her coach and translator, Won Park. "My family tried everything not to make me feel any financial difficulties."

In addition to the US Women's Open victory, Chun won two 2015 events in both Korea and Japan that are considered majors on those circuits. Chun followed up with another LPGA major, the 2016 Amundi Evian Championship, as she opened with a 63 and posted a 72-hole score of 21 under, the lowest score to par in men's or women's major championship history.

That flurry of success led to a lot of high expectations followed by a period during which Chun couldn't match her earlier achievements. She was stung by criticism but played on. "When I got in a slump, some people said I should retire because my game was not good. But no matter what they said, I believed I could win again. I knew if I keep working hard, then I have a chance to win."

At times Chun also was unhappy about being away from her home country. She has been candid about dealing with depression.

Although Chun hadn't won on the LPGA Tour since 2018, she entered the Women's PGA trying to be less of a perfectionist, to seek to win while still enjoying herself. "That's how I got a lot of pressure from my golf," she said. "I just wanted to make a perfect shot and another perfect shot. Now I don't want to get more stressed. I just want to enjoy my golf game. I believe it's the key."

Chun rode a rollercoaster of highs and lows at Congressional, from a stunning 64 in the opening round to third and fourth-round scores of 75 that tested her patience and resolve.

"Before I started today," Chun said on Sunday evening, "my coach told me, 'In Gee, if you enjoy your game, this trophy is yours.' I really tried hard to keep smiling. Sometimes that's hard, but I hung in there. I'm so proud."

It had been a long journey from the time when she took her first swings as a fourth grader on a visit to a driving range with her father and a friend of his. Chun got teased for not hitting her first shots well. "I got fired up and felt I could do it," she once said. "I decided to spend some time in golf and fell in love with it."

FIRST ROUND

A great round is not judged solely by a score but the circumstances surrounding it. By that standard, what Chun achieved on the first day of the KPMG Women's PGA Championship was a stunning tour de force.

Not only was Congressional Country Club's Blue course measuring 6,809 yards on Thursday, more than two inches of rain fell overnight, making holes play even longer. Inbee Park, who counts consecutive victories in the Women's PGA Championship from 2013-15 among her seven major titles, called the course "a beast", feeling as if the soft conditions made it play about 7,200 yards. Park was unable to reach the 441-yard fourth hole with a three-wood second shot. The par-five ninth was stretched to 587 yards and played as one of the longest three-shot holes anyone could recall, with some players having to hit woods to reach the green on their third shot. Light precipitation continued in the morning, giving the early groups another factor to contend with and exacerbating the challenge.

Chun was in the morning wave — teeing off on the 10th hole at 8:22 with compatriot Narin An and South African Ashleigh Buhai — which made her performance that much more impressive. Even though it occurred at the start of the championship rather than at the pressure-paced finish, Chun produced one of the finest rounds in major history.

Laser focused on making the shots that the difficult setup and trying conditions demanded, Chun stayed in the moment and tried to have a good time by keeping things light with longtime veteran caddie Dean Herden. She admitted that she was unaware of how she stood throughout the morning. "I felt like I had a good focus on the course because I didn't know I made that many birdies," Chun said. "I'm trying to make the focus on every tee shot and every chip, putt."

Chun put together a magnificent, eight-under 64 thanks to pure ball-striking (hitting 14 of 14 fairways and 15 of 18 greens) and excellent work on the greens (25 putts). "I don't know what golf course In Gee is playing," marvelled long-hitting American Nelly Korda, who had one of the six 71s Thursday morning, the only under-par scores in addition to Chun's masterpiece, which quickly drew attention across the golf world.

"I can't stop staring at the leaderboard," PGA Tour star Justin Thomas tweeted after Chun had finished. "Leading by 7 halfway thru day 1!!!!"

When Chun finished her round at midday, the scoring average was 76.01. By day's end — when she held a five-stroke lead over Korea's Hye-Jin Choi and Pornanong Phatlum, of Thailand, who each had 69 in the afternoon — Chun had gained 11.38 strokes on the field.

For Chun, a pre-tournament scouting trip to Congressional paid dividends. Seeing the rigours of the course, particularly some long approach shots to vexing greens, she decided to put a seven-wood in her bag. Chun used the club effectively in the opening round, four times setting up birdies inside 10 feet. Along with her nine-wood, the fairway metals, which replaced three- and four-hybrids in her set, were lethal weapons.

"I made a lot of birdies with the seven-wood and the nine-wood," said Chun, whose round had similarities with the opening 65 by McIlroy in the 2011 US Open at Congressional that spotted him a three-shot cushion en route to a comfortable victory.

Chun, who carded only one bogey, did most of her damage in an eight-hole stretch from the 15th through the fourth. She reeled off four straight birdies starting at the 15th and then birdied three consecutive holes beginning at number two.

"I'm trying to make the focus on the course for the process, not the result," Chun said. "That helps a lot."

Still, the result tied the lowest opening round in Women's PGA Championship history, and the five-stroke advantage was the largest first-round lead in a women's major. It also was the lowest score shot on the Blue course since the extensive changes to the design.

Chun's 64 was two higher than her career low, a 62 in the third round of the 2016 Kingsmill Championship, and one off her lowest major score, 63 in the opening round of the 2016 Amundi Evian

Championship. Her opening round was one shot off the all-time Women's PGA mark of 63 by five players: Patty Sheehan, 1984; Meg Mallon, 1999; Kelly Shon, 2017; Sei Young Kim, 2020; and Nelly Korda, 2021.

Those closest to Chun after 18 holes, Choi and Phatlum, followed the leader's playbook in hitting lots of fairways and greens. Each required five more putts than Chun. Phatlum didn't need any putts on the 199-yard second hole, where she made a hole-in-one with a three-hybrid, the sixth ace of her career. "I didn't see it go in," she said, "but I just saw everyone clapping. It was a very happy moment."

Anyone who broke par in the opening round — 14 golfers did so — had reason to be pleased. Thirty-three of the previous 35 women's major champions opened the week with an under-par score in the first round. But Chun's stunner stood out like a neon sign on an otherwise dark street.

"She's just on fire," Brooke Henderson, who had a 71, said of the leader. "Sometimes, In Gee does that. Sometimes she just plays so well, and nothing bothers her. And it's really cool to see."

After 18 holes: 64 (-8) Chun; **69** Phatlum, HJ Choi; **70** Chang, Reto; **71** AL Kim, H Green, Hataoka, Kupcho, N Korda, Henderson, Furue, IK Kim, SY Kim

SECOND ROUND

The increasingly international makeup of the LPGA Tour during the 21st century can be seen clearly through the winners of the KPMG Women's PGA Championship. Coming into the event's 68th edition at Congressional Country Club, 17 of the previous 20 champions hailed from outside the United States. And with nine international golfers among the top 13 on the leaderboard through 36 holes, the odds were in favour of that trend continuing.

On Friday, Chun couldn't replicate the magic of the previous morning, but she was more than up to the task of staying in control. Far from following a great score with a mediocre or poor number — as often tends to happen in professional golf — Chun shot a three-under 69 that extended her lead to six strokes halfway through the championship.

Chun finished 36 holes at 11-under-par 133 with Lydia Ko, of New Zealand, and American Jennifer Kupcho the closest pursuers at 139. Chun got off to a fast start with birdies on three of the opening five holes then bogeyed seven and eight. She offset those mistakes with back-nine birdies at the 10th and 18th to become the only golfer to shoot in the 60s on Thursday and Friday.

"Honestly, before I started today, I felt a little pressure after I had a great first round," Chun said. "Everyone was talking about the five-shot lead. Everyone's expectations are really high. So, it was a little tough to focus. I want to see the big picture; I just want to enjoy the next two days.

A reporter asked Chun if her 69 felt like a disappointment in the wake of what she did the day before. "No, I think it's still a great score," she said. That certainly was the case, as only a half dozen players put up a better number on Friday.

That the pair of 25-year-olds, Ko (67) and Kupcho (68) were among that select group was no surprise. Ko came to Congressional with top-five finishes in her last three starts, including the US Women's Open, although she was looking for her first victory since the Gainbridge LPGA at Boca Rio in January, her 17th career LPGA victory. Kupcho arrived after a playoff victory the previous Sunday at the Meijer LPGA Classic after breaking through for her maiden win in high style at the Chevron Championship in April.

"The last couple of weeks it was a few silly mistakes, a few shots where I lost focus a little bit," Ko said. "Other than that, I feel my game is in a pretty solid place. At the same time, I think it is very difficult to win. The level of play on our tour is incredible. I'm just trying to put myself more in that kind of position. When you keep knocking on the door, you hope one day it will open."

Kupcho didn't seem to mind trailing going into the weekend. "I think just in general, being back is a lot better," she said, "whether it's with a lot of people or not. I think being behind and trying to catch up is better."

Lexi Thompson tied Ko for low score of the second round, and the American's five-under scorecard (seven better than Thursday's no-birdie 74) was marked by a hole-out for eagle on the par-four 17th hole. From 102 yards on her uphill second shot, Thompson hit a 50-degree wedge that landed 15 feet past the flagstick and spun back into the cup to the loud delight of the greenside gallery.

"We couldn't see anything from where we were," Thompson said. "I just went off the crowd. The more people, the better. I love playing in front of big crowds."

Thompson, 27, an 11-time winner on the LPGA Tour, hadn't hoisted a trophy since the 2019 ShopRite LPGA Classic and is stuck on one major victory, the 2014 Kraft Nabisco (now Chevron Championship). She was trying to break the drought with an attitude adjustment.

"My mental approach toward the game in general over this last year has changed," Thompson said. "I was hard on myself in majors. Now, I'm just going into every week knowing I have put in the hard work. It's just a matter of coming out here and trusting the process. And if it happens, amazing. If it doesn't, there's not much else I can do. Today went really well. Going into the weekend, if I go out and play like I did today — just solid and committing to my shots and the process of my routine — we'll see where it takes me."

After 36 holes: 133 (-11) Chun 69; **139** L Ko 67, Kupcho 68; **140** Inglis 68, SY Kim 69, Chang 70, Henderson 69, H Green 69; **141** Mj Lee 68, Lin 68, HJ Choi 72, Thompson 67

THIRD ROUND

Although Chun cruised through the opening two days at difficult Congressional Country Club, finishing off the championship wasn't going to be a cakewalk. The golfers chasing her had 36 holes to catch up. If that were to happen, it would have to be a two-part equation: those who were trailing needed to cut into the margin on Saturday with good play and hope that Chun cooled off.

With the Blue course drying out from the heavy rain earlier in the week, players were getting a bit more run on their tee shots, affording shorter approaches. But the greens also had more fire, with many pins tucked in difficult spots. On top of that challenge, temperatures rose into the 90s, the heat making for an endurance contest.

"I was sweating a lot in my warmup, and I was like, 'Oh, this is not what I want,'" said 2019 KPMG champion Hannah Green, of Australia. "The breeze picked up so that made it a little bit cooler, but it was pretty hot out there. Hydration was really important. The first day I barely drank any water because it was raining. Today, I was just guzzling water."

On a day when only two players shot in the 60s — Atthaya Thitikul (68) and Jenny Shin (69) — the challenge was to get in with a score around par. Chun wasn't able to do that, shooting a three-over 75 to finish 54 holes at eight-under 208. Choi (70), Sei Young Kim (71) and Thompson (70) had solid performances to cut Chun's lead to three, with Green another stroke further back.

At one point early in her third round, Chun extended her lead to seven strokes, the exact cushion when she reached the clubhouse after her opening 64. But the plot deviated from there, with the South Korean making four bogeys (after making just three through 36 holes) and a double bogey. She had to par the last two holes to salvage a 75, a finish that allowed her to leave the course on a good note.

"Absolutely, it was a little tough out there," Chun said. "I'm so proud of myself because I hung in there after I had double bogey on 16."

It had been a double bogey on the 16th hole in the final round of the 2017 US Women's Open that sabotaged Choi's bid for a major title as a 17-year-old amateur. Bidding to become only the second amateur to win that championship, after Catherine Lacoste in 1967, Choi was runner-up to Sung Hyun Park. Leading up to the Women's PGA, Choi had again been in the mix at the US Women's Open, finishing third at Pine Needles, six strokes behind winner Minjee Lee.

"It was very hot today, so it was difficult, but I'm glad to have finished with a good round," said Choi, playing in her debut Women's PGA. "My goal was to not be too aggressive and play safe. And I think that led to a good result."

Kim, the 2020 Women's PGA winner at Aronimink Golf Club outside Philadelphia, 140 miles northeast of Congressional, saved par on the long, par-four 18th after a three-putt bogey on the 17th to shoot her third consecutive sub-par round. "It took a lot of energy today," Kim said of playing in the heat. "It wasn't easy to keep focus on every single shot, especially after I made the turn to the back nine."

In Kim and Thompson, the leaderboard featured a pair of proven winners on the LPGA Tour. Kim had one major among 12 career titles, Thompson one major among her 11 victories. The two powerful players also have something else in common: neither tends to pay much attention to scoreboards when they're on the course. "I just try to ignore the scoreboard," Kim said.

"I honestly have been trying not to watch leaderboards at all any more," Thompson said. "I've just been trying to focus on my own game, my emotions. I'm sure my caddie will keep an eye on it. If I have to go for a shot, he'll let me know."

But there was no doubt that they knew where they stood with 18 holes to go — with ground to make up on Chun, who didn't play her best on Saturday but maintained a nice lead.

"I'm so excited and looking forward to an exciting final round," Chun said. "If it's going to be too easy, then I feel it is boring. I just want to enjoy another day tomorrow. I'm ready to go. I just want to keep being positive."

More than anyone else in the field, Chun sure had a right to feel that way.

After 54 holes: 208 (-8) Chun 75; **211** HJ Choi 70, Thompson 70, SY Kim 71; **212** H Green 72; **213** Thitikul 68, Henderson 73, Chang 73, Kupcho 74; **214** Meadow 72, Mj Lee 73

FOURTH ROUND

Sport psychologist Dr Bob Rotella utilised as the title of a book about the mental side of golf one of its absolutes: Golf Is Not a Game of Perfect. The final round of the KPMG Women's PGA Championship offered hours of evidence that Rotella was right.

On a Sunday of ups and downs by the eventual winner, Chun, and those who challenged her in a showdown at Congressional Country Club — most notably Thompson, who finished tied for second place with US Open champion Minjee Lee — it was clear that success amid major championship stress is largely about minimising and managing the mistakes that inevitably occur.

Chun prevailed, steadying herself after an outward 40 that caused her three-stroke lead after 54 holes to disappear quickly, and finding herself two behind Thompson making the turn. "I believe if I stick to my game plan, then I believe I have a chance in the back nine," said Chun, who rallied with an inward 35 for her second straight 75. "I try to hang in there. I'm so happy I made it. My body is still shaking, though."

Chun finished 72 holes at five-under-par 283, one ahead of Thompson and Lee, with Thitikul (72) in fourth, one further back on 285.

Thompson, who was trying to win for the first time in 51 starts, offered no critique of her closing round, declining to talk to the media after a disastrous finish that was painfully similar to how she struggled over the late stages of the fourth round in the 2021 US Women's Open at Olympic Club. There, after holding a five-stroke advantage late in the front nine, she came home in 41, missing out on a playoff won by Yuka Saso over Nasa Hataoka.

At Congressional, it was Thompson's often vulnerable short game that again sealed her fate. After missing good birdie chances late in the front nine that could have given her a more comfortable advantage, she missed a two-footer for par on the 14th hole.

With Chun failing to find the kind of groove she enjoyed over a fantastic opening 36 holes, Thompson still led by two with three holes left following a birdie on the 15th. But on the par-five 16th, after leaving herself just a 20-yard pitch for her third shot, Thompson badly misplayed her wedge, thinning it beyond the green. Her bogey combined with Chun's birdie from nine feet put them tied at the top with two to play.

Chun recaptured the lead on the 17th, making par as Thompson three-putted for bogey from 20 feet, failing to touch the cup on her three-foot par attempt. Thompson hit a good shot from the rough on her approach at the 18th hole, hitting it within 15 feet of the flagstick. But she was unable to convert it. Chun's second shot took a bad bounce and scooted just over the green, but she was able to make a five-footer for par to edge Thompson (73) and Lee, who closed with a birdie and a 70 in a strong bid to win a second straight major title. Only Hataoka, with 69 for a share of fifth place, had a better Sunday score than Lee.

"The wind was up, and it was quite a lot firmer than the first three days," said Lee. "We definitely didn't get the zip-back from any of our shots today. Definitely different conditions."

In contrast to the strategy of Thompson and Sei Young Kim (76 and tied for fifth), Lee was paying attention to where she stood during the round. "I pretty much had my eye on the leaderboard the whole day. I followed it pretty much every single hole when I could see, so I knew exactly which position I was in. I knew coming down 18 that maybe a birdie would get me close. I gave it a good shot today."

Indeed, she did. But Chun did just enough to stave off all challengers.

"I want to tell the truth," Chun said, recounting her struggles early on Sunday. "I couldn't control all the pressure. This is why I had four bogeys. Sometimes my golf is not perfect. When I got to the last putt on the 18th green, I tried to give myself a talk: 'In Gee, you've made a lot of putts of this distance. You have controlled the pressure already, so you can make it'."

They weren't empty words, because Chun's ball soon filled the bottom of the cup. In that important moment, her golf was perfect.

Congressional Country Club (Blue), Bethesda, Maryland — June 23-26
Par 72 (36-36); 6,894 yards — Purse: $9,000,000

1	**In Gee Chun**	64	69	75	75	283	$1,350,000
2	**Minjee Lee**	73	68	73	70	284	718,827
	Lexi Thompson	74	67	70	73	284	718,827
4	Atthaya Thitikul	73	72	68	72	285	467,580
5	Nasa Hataoka	71	72	75	69	287	274,166
	Hyo Joo Kim	73	72	71	71	287	274,166
	Hannah Green	71	69	72	75	287	274,166
	Hye-Jin Choi	69	72	70	76	287	274,166
	Sei Young Kim	71	69	71	76	287	274,166
10	Lilia Vu	75	70	73	70	288	156,315
	Eun-Hee Ji	74	70	72	72	288	156,315
	Stephanie Kyriacou	72	72	72	72	288	156,315
	Jessica Korda	74	70	71	73	288	156,315
	Stephanie Meadow	73	69	72	74	288	156,315
	Jennifer Chang	70	70	73	75	288	156,315
16	Lauren Coughlin	74	69	73	73	289	114,045
	Anna Nordqvist	75	69	71	74	289	114,045
	Chella Choi	72	72	71	74	289	114,045
	Brooke M Henderson	71	69	73	76	289	114,045
	Jennifer Kupcho	71	68	74	76	289	114,045
21	Georgia Hall	74	69	75	72	290	95,799
	Peiyun Chien	77	70	70	73	290	95,799
	Ashleigh Buhai	72	71	74	73	290	95,799
	In-Kyung Kim	71	72	73	74	290	95,799
25	Madelene Sagstrom	73	74	71	73	291	80,744
	Inbee Park	72	73	73	73	291	80,744
	Jeongeun Lee[5]	73	72	72	74	291	80,744
	Jenny Shin	74	73	69	75	291	80,744
	Angel Yin	72	70	73	76	291	80,744
30	Pajaree Anannarukarn	73	74	73	72	292	59,987
	Mao Saigo	74	70	76	72	292	59,987
	Mel Reid	72	72	74	74	292	59,987
	Caroline Inglis	72	68	78	74	292	59,987
	Paula Reto	70	77	70	75	292	59,987
	Nelly Korda	71	74	72	75	292	59,987
	Allisen Corpuz	72	72	72	76	292	59,987
	Alison Lee	76	67	73	76	292	59,987
	Jin Young Ko	72	72	71	77	292	59,987
	Yuka Saso	72	70	73	77	292	59,987
40	Gaby Lopez	74	72	74	73	293	42,957
	Aditi Ashok	76	71	72	74	293	42,957
	Wei-Ling Hsu	74	73	72	74	293	42,957
	Sarah Kemp	73	74	72	74	293	42,957
	Kelly Tan	76	70	70	77	293	42,957
	Matilda Castren	76	67	73	77	293	42,957
46	Xiyu Lin	73	68	77	76	294	36,037
	Cheyenne Knight	72	72	73	77	294	36,037
	Lydia Ko	72	67	76	79	294	36,037
49	So Yeon Ryu	78	69	71	77	295	33,299
50	Emily Kristine Pedersen	78	68	77	73	296	30,563
	Stacy Lewis	76	68	75	77	296	30,563
	A Lim Kim	71	72	76	77	296	30,563
	Mirim Lee	73	74	71	78	296	30,563
54	Leona Maguire	74	72	77	74	297	26,002
	Moriya Jutanugarn	72	72	79	74	297	26,002
	Elizabeth Szokol	74	73	75	75	297	26,002
	Ariya Jutanugarn	74	73	73	77	297	26,002
	Pornanong Phatlum	69	72	78	78	297	26,002
	Ryann O'Toole	72	73	73	79	297	26,002
60	Muni He	73	71	77	77	298	22,583
	Brittany Altomare	75	72	71	80	298	22,583
62	Sung Hyun Park	75	68	79	77	299	21,667
	Brianna Do	73	72	75	79	299	21,667
64	Narin An	74	73	73	80	300	20,987
65	Bianca Pagdanganan	74	73	76	78	301	20,072
	Robynn Ree	73	70	78	80	301	20,072
	Sophia Schubert	73	74	72	82	301	20,072
68	Jennifer Song	73	74	78	78	303	18,929
	Gerina Mendoza	79	68	77	79	303	18,929
70	Cydney Clanton	74	70	79	83	306	18,250
71	Maude-Aimee Leblanc	73	73	84	78	308	18,023
	Hinako Shibuno	72	75			WD	17,787
	MISSED THE 36-HOLE CUT						
	Brittany Lang	78	70			148	
	Jaye Marie Green	77	71			148	
	Amanda Doherty	76	72			148	
	Perrine Delacour	75	73			148	
	Charley Hull	75	73			148	
	Andrea Lee	75	73			148	
	Jenny Coleman	74	74			148	
	Megan Khang	74	74			148	
	Patty Tavatanakit	74	74			148	
	Morgane Metraux	73	75			148	
	Pauline Roussin	73	75			148	
	Alana Uriell	73	75			148	
	Ayaka Furue	71	77			148	
	Sandra Changkija	78	71			149	
	Jeongeun Lee[6]	78	71			149	
	Maria Fassi	77	72			149	
	Gina Kim	76	73			149	
	Ruixin Liu	76	73			149	
	Angela Stanford	76	73			149	
	Jodi Ewart Shadoff	75	74			149	
	Pernilla Lindberg	75	74			149	
	Amy Olson	75	74			149	
	Albane Valenzuela	75	74			149	
	Ruoning Yin	75	74			149	
	Carlota Ciganda	78	72			150	
	Frida Kinhult	78	72			150	
	Amy Yang	78	72			150	
	Marina Alex	77	73			150	
	Pia Babnik	77	73			150	

Dottie Ardina	76	74	150
Alisa Rodriguez	76	74	150
Mo Martin	75	75	150
Su Oh	75	75	150
Dana Finkelstein	74	76	150
Katherine Kirk	74	76	150
Agathe Laisne	74	76	150
Yealimi Noh	74	76	150
Celine Boutier	73	77	150
Katherine Perry-Hamski	81	70	151
Cristie Kerr	80	71	151
Lindsey Weaver-Wright	80	71	151
Meaghan Francella	79	72	151
Christina Kim	78	73	151
Sarah Jane Smith	78	73	151
Mariah Stackhouse	78	73	151
Ana Belac	77	74	151
Esther Henseleit	77	74	151
Haeji Kang	77	74	151
Sophia Popov	81	71	152
Min Lee	80	72	152
Sanna Nuutinen	80	72	152
Lizette Salas	80	72	152
Jasmine Suwannapura	79	73	152
Janie Jackson	78	74	152
Brittany Lincicome	78	74	152
Linnea Johansson	77	75	152
Ally Ewing	76	76	152
Isi Gabsa	76	76	152
Rachel Rohanna	76	76	152
Kaitlyn Papp	75	77	152
Giulia Molinaro	80	73	153
Bronte Law	79	74	153
Allison Emrey	78	75	153
Dewi Weber	75	78	153
Marissa Steen	81	73	154
Nanna Koerstz Madsen	79	75	154
Wichanee Meechai	78	76	154
Sarah Schmelzel	78	76	154
Emma Talley	78	76	154
Gemma Dryburgh	77	77	154
Charlotte Thomas	77	77	154
Stephanie Connelly Eiswerth	81	74	155
Jenny Suh Thompson	79	76	155
Caroline Masson	76	79	155
Ashley Tait-Wengert	81	75	156
Mina Harigae	80	76	156
Annie Park	80	76	156
Yu Liu	76	80	156
Nuria Iturrioz	83	75	158
Yaeeun Hong	80	78	158
Allie Knight	85	82	167
Ashley Grier	85	85	170
Jennifer Borocz	89	82	171
Lauren Stephenson	78		WD

ROLL OF HONOUR

1955	Beverly Hanson	Orchard Ridge
1956	Marlene Hagge*	Forest Lake
1957	Louise Suggs	Churchill Valley
1958	Mickey Wright	Churchill Valley
1959	Betsy Rawls	Sheraton Hotel
1960	Mickey Wright	Sheraton Hotel
1961	Mickey Wright	Stardust
1962	Judy Kimball	Stardust
1963	Mickey Wright	Stardust
1964	Mary Mills	Stardust
1965	Sandra Haynie	Stardust
1966	Gloria Ehret	Stardust
1967	Kathy Whitworth	Pleasant Valley
1968	Sandra Post*	Pleasant Valley
1969	Betsy Rawls	Concord
1970	Shirley Englehorn*	Pleasant Valley
1971	Kathy Whitworth	Pleasant Valley
1972	Kathy Ahern	Pleasant Valley
1973	Mary Mills	Pleasant Valley
1974	Sandra Haynie	Pleasant Valley
1975	Kathy Whitworth	Pine Ridge
1976	Betty Burfeindt	Pine Ridge
1977	Chako Higuchi	Bay Tree
1978	Nancy Lopez	Jack Nicklaus Sports Center
1979	Donna Caponi	Jack Nicklaus Sports Center
1980	Sally Little	Jack Nicklaus Sports Center
1981	Donna Caponi	Jack Nicklaus Sports Center
1982	Jan Stephenson	Jack Nicklaus Sports Center
1983	Patty Sheehan	Jack Nicklaus Sports Center
1984	Patty Sheehan	Jack Nicklaus Sports Center
1985	Nancy Lopez	Jack Nicklaus Sports Center
1986	Pat Bradley	Jack Nicklaus Sports Center
1987	Jane Geddes	Jack Nicklaus Sports Center
1988	Sherri Turner	Jack Nicklaus Sports Center
1989	Nancy Lopez	Jack Nicklaus Sports Center
1990	Beth Daniel	Bethesda
1991	Meg Mallon	Bethesda
1992	Betsy King	Bethesda
1993	Patty Sheehan	Bethesda
1994	Laura Davies	DuPont
1995	Kelly Robbins	DuPont
1996	Laura Davies	DuPont
1997	Christa Johnson*	DuPont
1998	Se Ri Pak	DuPont
1999	Juli Inkster	DuPont
2000	Juli Inkster*	DuPont
2001	Karrie Webb	DuPont
2002	Se Ri Pak	DuPont
2003	Annika Sorenstam*	DuPont
2004	Annika Sorenstam	DuPont
2005	Annika Sorenstam	Bulle Rock
2006	Se Ri Pak*	Bulle Rock
2007	Suzann Pettersen	Bulle Rock
2008	Yani Tseng*	Bulle Rock
2009	Anna Nordqvist	Bulle Rock
2010	Cristie Kerr	Locust Hill
2011	Yani Tseng	Locust Hill
2012	Shanshan Feng	Locust Hill
2013	Inbee Park*	Locust Hill
2014	Inbee Park*	Monroe
2015	Inbee Park	Westchester
2016	Brooke Henderson*	Sahalee
2017	Danielle Kang	Olympia Fields
2018	Sung Hyun Park*	Kemper Lakes
2019	Hannah Green	Hazeltine National
2020	Sei Young Kim	Aronimink
2021	Nelly Korda	Atlanta Athletic Club (Highlands)
2022	In Gee Chun	Congressional (Blue)

**won in playoff*

Known as the LPGA Championship until 2014

THE 150TH OPEN

Smith claims golf's holy grail for Oz

By Andy Farrell

And so to St Andrews, the Home of Golf, for the centrepiece of the season, a chance to celebrate the game's rich history amidst a turbulent present and uncertain future. "The 150th Open is a true milestone for our sport," said Martin Slumbers, chief executive of The R&A, "and it calls for celebration in so many ways."

It was quite the memorial to a championship that came about after the death of Allan Robertson, the supreme player of his age, and the need, from 1860, to find a new Champion Golfer of the Year. Prestwick was the original home but the auld grey town of St Andrews has long since become the pre-eminent venue. The Old Course, created by nature with a helping hand from Robertson and Old Tom Morris, was staging The Open for the 30th time. With the array of champions that have lifted the Claret Jug on this ancient links no wonder Rory McIlroy declared: "It's the holy grail of our sport, one of the highest achievements you can have in golf."

St Andrews had hosted previous significant occasions such as the Centenary Open in 1960, the Millennium Open in 2000 and the 150th anniversary Open in 2010. Tiger Woods had been at the peak of his powers in 2000 and a record crowd of 239,000 had attended. Such was the anticipation for The 150th — delayed by a year due to the St George's Open being postponed by the pandemic in 2020 — that ticket sales reached 290,000 for the week. "It's history every time we get to play here," said Woods, "and it's hard to believe it is more historic than normal, but it really is. This does feel it's the biggest Open Championship we've ever had."

Part of the celebrations included a four-hole exhibition where the marquee fourball contained Woods, McIlroy, Lee Trevino and Georgia Hall. "It was a pinch yourself moment," McIlroy said. Also among those playing were Gary Player, Sir Bob Charles, Sir Nick Faldo, Dame Laura Davies, Catriona Matthew and some of the leading golfers with disability, including Kipp Popert, who had played in the Amateur Championship a month earlier. Jack Nicklaus was also present for pictures on the Swilcan Bridge, before becoming the third American after Bobby Jones and Benjamin Franklin to receive an honorary citizenship of St Andrews. A total of 28 past champions attended the traditional dinner in the clubhouse of the Royal and Ancient, although not Phil Mickelson or Greg Norman.

Background chatter about rebel golf leagues became muted as Paul Lawrie, along with Woods and McIlroy newly installed as an honorary member of the Royal and Ancient, hit the first tee shot on Thursday. After the last putt on Sunday, it was a kid from Wantima Country Club in the northern suburbs of Brisbane, where his dad Des was club captain, and who became the Australian Amateur champion, worked his way through the Australasian and Asian professional circuits to the PGA Tour, where in 2022 he won the Sentry Tournament of Champions and the Players Championship, who prevailed at The 150th Open. Cameron Smith, possessed of both a shaggy mullet and a blessed putting touch, made his mark on the history of the game with a scintillating closing round of 64 that included five birdies in a row from the turn to win by one stroke from American Cameron Young and by two from the grail-denied McIlroy.

"To win an Open Championship in itself is probably going to be a golfer's highlight in their career," Smith said. "To do it around St Andrews, I think it's just unbelievable. This place is so cool. I love the golf course. I love the town."

On a Sunday that had begun with the ashes of five-time Open winner Peter Thomson scattered on the edge of the 18th green at dawn, it had been the Centenary Open that had been the pointer to this particular Australia Day. Some 62 years earlier, Kel Nagle, making a vital putt at the 17th, had held off fan favourite Arnold Palmer. Amid the roars for McIlroy, Smith now also produced heroics at the 17th on the way to collecting the Claret Jug, the third Australian after Thomson and Nagle to do so at the Home of Golf. "This one's for Oz," Smith concluded his winner's speech.

FIRST ROUND

Lawrie, the 1999 champion, hit one of the best shots of the day, not from the first tee but when he returned to the magnificent amphitheatre — a unique mix of modern grandstands and the old grey stone buildings — at the 18th. The 53-year-old from Aberdeen drove the green and made an eagle from only five feet. It was an illustration of how fast and firm, straw-coloured fairways were running. "I kid you not, I think the fairways are faster than the greens in some spots," said world number one Scottie Scheffler after a 68. Told they were, the Masters champion added: "They are? I'm glad I'm not losing my mind."

With the wind picking up throughout the day, it was an advantage to be off early in the morning. Smith posted a five-under-par 67 and claimed the first of six birdies by holing a 55-footer on the second green. The 28-year-old Queenslander had played a practice round alongside Marc Leishman and Adam Scott that was watched by 2021 Wimbledon champion Ashleigh Barty, who had retired after winning the Australian Open earlier in the year. Smith immediately found the speed of the greens to his liking, despite not having played at the Old Course since his amateur days. This was his fifth Open and first at St Andrews.

"It was probably some of the best lag putting I've ever done," he said. "My putt on the second managed to go in from a fair distance, that was pretty decent, but I seemed to have so many 80, 90, 100-footers out there today and I did a good job of getting down in two."

Although qualifier Robert Dinwiddie, who helps out part-time at a friend's construction company, matched Smith's 67 late in the day, only two players went lower in the first round. Young, a rookie on the PGA Tour who came close to winning the PGA Championship in May, made a stunning Open debut with an eight-birdie 64. Seven of them came in the first 12 holes, plus an almost regulation three at the last.

Young had played the Old Course once before, as a 13-year-old when his father, the professional at Sleepy Hollow Country Club in New York where Cameron grew up, had to get special permission for the teenager to play off the back tees. Young has always been a long hitter. He drove the ninth green and two-putted to be out in 31 and over the 12th green, chipping back and making a simple three. About his only blemish was three-putting the 14th for a par. "You could play every day here for a year," Young said, "and you would just scratch the surface of what you can know about this place."

Young was the 11th player to score 64 or better in the first round of The Open, and was to become the 11th who ended up not winning. McIlroy suffered the same fate in 2010, when he followed a 63 on Thursday with an 80 in the gale of Friday. After winning at Hoylake in 2014, McIlroy was unable to defend his title at St Andrews the following year after he injured himself playing football. There was no football this time, just a win at the Canadian Open. He had finished no worse than eighth in the year's three earlier majors.

A 66 left him two behind Young in second place. "It's another good start at a major. Three in a row for me now," he said. The world number two holed a birdie putt of 55 feet on the first green and made three birdies in a row from the fifth. He had a three at 12, bogeyed the 13th, then hit a drive of 380 yards at the 14th on the way to a four. With a three at the last he moved ahead of Smith. "I did everything that you're supposed to do around St Andrews," McIlroy said. "I birdied the birdie holes and made pars at the holes where you're looking to make a par and move to the next tee."

Of the conditions, he added: "This is the fiddliest Open that I've played. It's the only way I can describe it. And fiddly hasn't really been my forte over the years, but I'm hopefully going to make it my forte this week."

As for Woods, in only his third start since his near-fatal car crash in 2021, he was cheered from the first hole to the last, but right from the start nothing went his way. His opening tee shot found a divot and his second the burn. Double bogey. He went out in 41 and ended up with a 78. Returning to his favourite course, where he won in 2000 and 2005, had been the goal of his latest comeback. "This was always on the calendar to hopefully be well enough to play," Woods said. "And I am. I just didn't do a very good job of it."

After 18 holes: 64 (-8) Young; **66** McIlroy; **67** Smith, Dinwiddie; **68** Brown, Kitayama, Westwood, Kennedy, Hovland, Gooch, D Johnson, Scheffler

SECOND ROUND

Was it farewell to Woods? That was the question on Friday afternoon as the three-time champion walked up the 18th fairway. He was missing the cut — would sign for a 75 — but would he ever play in an Open at St Andrews again? No one was taking any chances. Every vantage point was taken. Crossing the bridge, Woods did not break stride. But the cap came off in acknowledgement of the ovation from the gallery. There were nods of respect exchanged with McIlroy, walking down the first fairway, and Justin Thomas, on the first tee.

On the cheers went, all the way to the green, Tiger hiding the emotion behind his cap. A proper St Andrews salute. "The fans, the ovation and the warmth, it was an unbelievable feeling," Woods said. "I feel like I will be able to play future Open Championships, but I don't know if I'll be able to play long enough for when it comes back around here."

"It was a cool moment to be on that fairway when that was happening," McIlroy said. "Everyone hopes it's not the end of his Old Course career." But the Northern Irishman had other things to think about. "Like the wind switch I got on the wedge shot on the first," he said. "Then that 60-footer back towards the burn, and you're thinking it wouldn't really look good if you putted one into the water."

He was saved from that fate but with his late tee-off, he was now playing catch up. The man everyone was chasing was Smith, who at the same moment had just been helped by the change in direction of the wind to drive the green at the 10th. Smith's drive went 396 yards to the back edge and he two-putted for his sixth birdie of the day.

The Australian's lag-putting was still in good shape, but he was also holing more than his share, totalling an astonishing 253 feet of holed putts during the round. He set off by birdieing the first three holes with putts of 47, 17 and 12 feet. A wedge to six feet took care of the seventh, then he holed from 30 feet at the eighth. The highlight of the round was still to come. At the 14th he reached the green in two and holed an eagle putt of 64 feet to get to 13 under par. "Once it started breaking pretty good, I thought it would have a chance," Smith said. "It was not really one you're trying to hole, you're just trying to get a nice easy birdie. Nice of it to pop in the side there."

By matching Young's score of 64 from the previous day, Smith became the "low Cameron", eventually holding a two-shot lead over the American, who birdied the last for a 69. Smith's total for 36 holes of 131 was a new record for St Andrews, one better than Faldo and Norman in 1990, and Louis Oosthuizen in 2010, while 13 under par for the first two rounds was a new Open record anywhere.

Hovland lit up the evening play by holing his second shot for an eagle at the 15th. The Norwegian also birdied the 18th for a 66 to get to 10 under par, alongside McIlroy, whose 68 included a three at the 17th on a 23-foot putt. The fans roared their support and McIlroy was feeling confident. "I know I've got the game. That's all I need," he said. "If Cam Smith goes out and shoots another two rounds like he did the first two days, I'm going to have a hard time to win. So I've just got to do the best I can do and worry about myself, and hopefully it's good enough."

After 36 holes: 131 (-13) Smith 64; **133** Young 69; **134** McIlroy 68, Hovland 66; **135** D Johnson 67; **136** Scheffler 68, Hatton 66; **137** Gooch 69, Scott 65, Cantlay 67, Theegala 68

THIRD ROUND

Friday evening's entertainment was only a preview of the drama that played out on Saturday. With Smith and Young, in the final twoball, unable to continue in the same vein as the previous two days, it was McIlroy and Hovland who became the centre of attention. And particularly a certain Northern Irishman who had made no secret of his desire to win a first Open — or any major — for eight years. Even without doing anything spectacular, like holing a bunker shot at the 10th hole, the fans were on his side. "The support I've got this week has been absolutely incredible," said McIlroy. "I appreciate it and feel it out there. The galleries have been massive."

McIlroy and Hovland both scored 66 to reach 16 under par and share a four-stroke lead. With Smith missing a four-footer for par on the opening hole, the door was open for the two European Ryder Cup players. Hovland went ahead by holing a succession of long putts on the way to four birdies in a row. The 24-year-old holed from 38 feet at the third and from 42 feet at the fourth, two-putted the fifth and then made a 20-footer at the sixth to lead The Open by two shots. So far his quest to become the first male major champion from Norway had yet to yield a top 10 finish but he was already a proven tour winner.

McIlroy had kept in touch with three birdies in five holes, then exploded into brilliance as he is wont. One behind playing the 10th, he drove into the little circular bunker in front of the green, the hole 27 yards away on a raised tier. "I was just trying to get it somewhat close," McIlroy said. "Anything inside 10 feet was going to be a really good shot. It just came out perfectly." He carried his ball onto the tier and then saw it spin to the right and into the hole for an eagle two. "It was skill to put it somewhere close, but it was luck that it went in. You need a little bit of luck now and again." Or, as Hovland put it, "That's just a filthy bunker shot. That was sick."

McIlroy punched the air but, unlike on the 72nd hole of the Masters, he cut his celebration short. There was still so much work to do. Hovland holed a putt of 14 feet for a birdie and the pair were tied at 15 under par. McIlroy went ahead at the 14th, then dropped a shot at the 17th, which was back to its fearsome worst after two relatively benign days. Only 8.4 per cent of the field hit the green and McIlroy and Hovland, who got down in two putts, were both over the back. After a pair of birdies at the last, Hovland, who had now collected six sub-70 scores in seven rounds in The Open, said: "That was pretty cool, I'm not going to forget this day too quickly."

McIlroy said: "We fed off each other. I was watching Viktor hole a couple of long ones, then I was rewarded for my patience around the turn with a couple of birdies and that hole-out on 10. It's unbelievably cool to have a chance to win The Open at St Andrews. It's what dreams are made of. I'm going to try and make a dream come true tomorrow."

The two Camerons finished tied in third place at 12 under, Young after a 71 marred by a double bogey at the 16th, Smith with a 73, his double coming at the 13th. His tee shot ended on the edge of a bunker and, with his feet in the sand, Smith tried to play a waist-high shot that never had a chance to carry the wild terrain in front of the green. He took two more hacks in the heather and two putts.

"The golfing gods weren't with me today," Smith said. "I hit a lot of good putts, just nothing was really dropping. The opposite to the first two days, which is pretty hard to take on the chin." He did get up and down neatly from the left of the 17th green, and still had hope for the following day. "I love making birdies. I love making putts. That's what I need to go out there and do tomorrow. I need to stay aggressive and make a ton of birdies."

After 54 holes: 200 (-16) Hovland 66, McIlroy 66; **204** Young 71, Smith 73; **205** SW Kim 67, Scheffler 69; **206** D Johnson 71; **207** Fleetwood 66, Fitzpatrick 69, Scott 70; **208** Spieth 68, Cantlay 71

FOURTH ROUND

Smith had talked the talk about making birdies, and on Sunday he walked in the putts to do just that. In the previous 149 Opens, no one had played the last nine holes in as few as 30 strokes to win. Nothing less was good enough for Smith now to claim his first major title after near misses at the Masters in 2020, when he became the first player to score four rounds in the 60s at Augusta National, and in 2022. With rounds of 67-64-73-64, Smith set a new record total for Opens at St Andrews of 268, beating the 269 of Woods in 2000, while his score of 20 under par tied Henrik Stenson's record at Royal Troon in 2016.

He was pushed all the way by Young, who eagled the last to finish one behind, while McIlroy had led for two-thirds of the round. It was incredibly tense. As he had been all week, McIlroy was the favourite of the huge gallery. He hardly did anything wrong, but it was Smith who found the spark of genius under pressure with five birdies in a row from the 10th.

McIlroy and Hovland, now in the final pairing, did little to energise each other. McIlroy's putt at the first green rolled over the left edge of the hole. That was to happen a lot. He missed a good chance at the third from five feet. Hovland three-putted the fourth to fall one behind. "It was a little anti-climactic after yesterday," said the Norwegian. He finished with a 74 to tie for fourth with Tommy Fleetwood, who closed with a 67. McIlroy went in front by two with a two-putt birdie at the fifth, but chances at the sixth and the ninth slid by again.

After a third round when his putter had been uncharacteristically cool, Smith rekindled the magic in a late-night putting session. He started collecting birdies again on Sunday at the third, from eight feet. Then he two-putted from 88 feet for a four at the fifth. He reached the turn three behind, out in 34 as was Young, despite driving into the gorse at the ninth. "I knew I had to be patient," Smith said. "I felt good all day. When those putts started going in on the back nine, it gave me a lot of momentum."

A delightful chip, off one mound and then another, set up a five-footer at the 10th. At the dangerous 11th, he hit a nine-iron almost pin high and a 16-footer went in there. "When that one dropped, I could see the hole getting a lot bigger, for sure." At the 12th, Smith threaded his drive between the mounds and the big bunker onto the front of the green, then putted up the tier to 11 feet and made that one. With McIlroy having two-putted the 10th from long range for his second and last birdie of the round, Smith was still one behind. That soon changed at the 13th with a drive and a six-iron to 18 feet. "Those two shots were two of the best all week," he said. "My second shot was when I thought we could really win this thing."

Holing the putt put him to 18 under par and tied for the lead with McIlroy. Two big blows at the par-five 14th put Smith just off the back of the green. He then hit the most gorgeous lag putt, from almost 30 yards, to within tap-in range. He now led by one at 19 under par.

Young also birdied the 10th, the 13th and the 14th to be two behind. McIlroy went close at 12, saw his putt at 13 pull up just short of the hole, and then took three putts from short of the 14th green. He was trying to stay patient, the crowd were still supportive, but now he realised he had fallen behind.

As ever in an Open at St Andrews, there was still the 17th to be negotiated. Smith's second shot with a nine-iron stalled at the front of the green, running off to the left to leave the bunker between himself and the flagstick. At the point of maximum danger, Smith relied on his putter. He swung the first effort off the contours to the right of the bunker, within inches of the cliff face, and onto the green, 10 feet right of the hole. "I was just trying to get it somewhere in there where I'd be able to give it a go. Managed to get away with a four."

Young said: "For him to accept he was going to have a 10-12-footer for par, obviously he hit a great first putt. There was no guarantee of having a par putt that short. It's another example of why he is one of the very best. He made a really good decision and executed it perfectly."

It was a vital par for the Australian and now McIlroy needed to respond. His approach at the 17th finished 18 feet away and generated a huge roar. His putt missed by only a couple of inches and engendered a collective sigh. McIlroy would need a two at the last to tie, took four and finished third. He hit every green in regulation and took 36 putts. He had only previously scored in the 60s in Opens at St Andrews, barring one round of 80, and now a 70 was not quite enough. "It's one I feel I let slip away," said McIlroy, his quest for golf's grail thwarted. "Of course, you have to let yourself dream. I'm only human. I'm not a robot. The putter went a little cold today, but, look, I got beaten by a better player this week."

Young made things interesting at the last by driving the green and holing from 17 feet for an eagle, a 65 and 19 under par. "It probably hurts a little worse to come up one shot short," admitted the 25-year-old New Yorker. "To watch Cameron shoot what he did, it was pretty amazing. I had a front-row seat to I'm sure one of the better rounds that's been played this year."

Two putts from just in front of the final green gave Smith his eighth birdie of the day and the Claret Jug. It had been a bravura performance that deserves its place in history but, in a sign of the times, Smith was asked about his future and replied: "I don't know, mate. I'm here to win golf tournaments." He had just won the biggest of them all.

St Andrews Links (Old), St Andrews, Fife, Scotland — July 14-17

Par 72 (36-36); 7,313 yards — Purse: $14,000,000

1	**Cameron Smith**	67	64	73	64	268	$2,500,000
2	**Cameron Young**	64	69	71	65	269	1,455,000
3	**Rory McIlroy**	66	68	66	70	270	933,000
4	Tommy Fleetwood	72	69	66	67	274	654,000
	Viktor Hovland	68	66	66	74	274	654,000
6	Brian Harman	73	68	68	66	275	469,500
	Dustin Johnson	68	67	71	69	275	469,500
8	Patrick Cantlay	70	67	71	68	276	325,667
	Bryson DeChambeau	69	74	67	66	276	325,667
	Jordan Spieth	71	69	68	68	276	325,667
11	Abraham Ancer	71	68	73	65	277	231,000
	Dean Burmester	71	73	67	66	277	231,000
	Tyrrell Hatton	70	66	73	68	277	231,000
	Sadom Kaewkanjana	71	67	74	65	277	231,000
15	Lucas Herbert	70	68	73	67	278	165,583
	Si Woo Kim	69	69	67	73	278	165,583
	Francesco Molinari	73	71	66	68	278	165,583
	Anthony Quayle	74	69	68	67	278	165,583
	Xander Schauffele	69	70	72	67	278	165,583
	Adam Scott	72	65	70	71	278	165,583
21	Matt Fitzpatrick	72	66	69	72	279	120,286
	Billy Horschel	73	69	70	67	279	120,286
	Kevin Kisner	74	70	65	70	279	120,286
	Min Woo Lee	69	69	73	68	279	120,286
	Shane Lowry	72	68	69	70	279	120,286
	Trey Mullinax	71	73	66	69	279	120,286
	Scottie Scheffler	68	68	69	74	279	120,286
28	Corey Conners	71	71	71	67	280	90,917
	Tony Finau	73	71	70	66	280	90,917
	Dylan Frittelli	70	71	69	70	280	90,917
	Thomas Pieters	75	67	67	71	280	90,917
	Harold Varner III	73	67	72	68	280	90,917
	Will Zalatoris	73	67	71	69	280	90,917
34	Thomas Detry	70	69	74	68	281	68,906
	Talor Gooch	68	69	75	69	281	68,906
	Robert MacIntyre	70	74	69	68	281	68,906
	Victor Perez	71	69	71	70	281	68,906
	Jon Rahm	73	67	71	70	281	68,906
	Sahith Theegala	69	68	74	70	281	68,906
	Lee Westwood	68	71	73	69	281	68,906
	Aaron Wise	72	67	71	71	281	68,906
42	Sam Burns	72	69	77	64	282	51,000
	Chris Kirk	75	68	69	70	282	51,000
	Jason Kokrak	72	70	72	68	282	51,000
	Thriston Lawrence	69	71	73	69	282	51,000
	Adrian Meronk	75	68	70	69	282	51,000
47	Garrick Higgo	72	69	76	66	283	40,600
	Yuto Katsuragawa	71	68	75	69	283	40,600
	Joohyung Kim	69	71	72	71	283	40,600
	Patrick Reed	72	68	76	67	283	40,600
	Jordan Smith	73	71	72	67	283	40,600
	Filippo Celli (A)	74	67	71	71	283	
53	Paul Casey	71	72	71	70	284	35,656
	Robert Dinwiddie	67	77	71	69	284	35,656
	Nicolai Hojgaard	73	67	71	73	284	35,656
	Brad Kennedy	68	72	72	72	284	35,656
	Joaquin Niemann	69	74	73	68	284	35,656
	Jason Scrivener	72	71	71	70	284	35,656
	Justin Thomas	72	70	72	70	284	35,656
	Lars van Meijel	74	70	71	69	284	35,656
	Danny Willett	69	73	73	69	284	35,656
62	David Carey	72	67	73	73	285	33,625
	Russell Henley	70	72	68	75	285	33,625
	Sebastian Munoz	73	71	71	70	285	33,625
	John Parry	69	74	70	72	285	33,625
	Ian Poulter	69	72	70	74	285	33,625
	Cameron Tringale	71	71	74	69	285	33,625
68	Christiaan Bezuidenhout	73	71	68	74	286	32,525
	Sergio Garcia	75	66	72	73	286	32,525
	Richard Mansell	73	71	68	74	286	32,525
	Hideki Matsuyama	71	72	76	67	286	32,525
72	Kurt Kitayama	68	73	73	73	287	32,013
	David Law	72	69	77	69	287	32,013
74	Marcus Armitage	71	72	71	74	288	31,763
	Justin De Los Santos	71	73	7074		288	31,763
76	Adria Arnaus	74	70	73	72	289	31,513
	Wyndham Clark	71	73	76	69	289	31,513
	Aaron Jarvis (A)	75	69	72	73	289	
79	Laurie Canter	72	70	74	74	290	31,325
	Barclay Brown (A)	68	70	77	75	290	
81	Sungjae Im	71	73	74	74	292	31,200
	Sam Bairstow (A)	72	72	79	69	292	
83	Jamie Rutherford	73	70	78	75	296	31,075

MISSED THE 36-HOLE CUT

Ben Campbell	74	71	145
Jamie Donaldson	76	69	145
Ernie Els	70	75	145
Justin Harding	74	71	145
Max Homa	73	72	145
Takumi Kanaya	74	71	145
Zander Lombard	77	68	145
Keith Mitchell	76	69	145
Collin Morikawa	72	73	145
Louis Oosthuizen	71	74	145
Webb Simpson	71	74	145
Henrik Stenson	75	70	145
Scott Vincent	69	76	145
Brandon Wu	71	74	145
Alexander Bjork	75	71	146
Richard Bland	78	68	146
Ryan Fox	71	75	146
Matthew Griffin	74	72	146
Emiliano Grillo	78	68	146
Matthew Jordan	74	72	146
Chan Kim	74	72	146
Kyoung-Hoon Lee	69	77	146
JT Poston	73	73	146
Keegan Bradley	76	71	147
John Catlin	74	73	147
John Daly	73	74	147
Matt Ford	71	76	147
Padraig Harrington	69	78	147
Zach Johnson	72	75	147
Guido Migliozzi	73	74	147
Keita Nakajima(A)	72	75	147
Shaun Norris	74	73	147
Aaron Rai	75	72	147
Ashley Chesters	75	73	148
Mingyu Cho	75	73	148
Rikuya Hoshino	75	73	148
Mackenzie Hughes	73	75	148
Brooks Koepka	73	75	148
Kevin Na	72	76	148
Seamus Power	73	75	148
Bernd Wiesberger	72	76	148
Stewart Cink	78	71	149
Kazuki Higa	73	76	149
Sihwan Kim	76	73	149
Haotong Li	73	76	149
Luke List	76	73	149
Phil Mickelson	72	77	149
Marco Penge	76	73	149

Mito Pereira	75 74	149
Fabrizio Zanotti	72 77	149
Harris English	76 74	150
Oliver Farr	76 74	150
Tom Hoge	74 76	150
Minkyu Kim	73 77	150
Marc Leishman	76 74	150
Aldrich Potgieter (A)	74 76	150
Gary Woodland	74 76	150
Stephen Dodd	77 74	151
Jorge Fernandez Valdes	74 77	151
Paul Lawrie	74 77	151
Ronan Mullarney	73 78	151
Dimitrios Papadatos	77 74	151
Sam Horsfield	76 76	152
Shugo Imahira	80 72	152
Sepp Straka	81 72	153
Tiger Woods	78 75	153
Darren Clarke	79 75	154
Jack Floydd	75 79	154
Jediah Morgan	79 76	155
Alex Wrigley	82 73	155
David Duval	82 74	156
Pablo Larrazabal	75 81	156
Mark Calcavecchia	83 82	165

ROLL OF HONOUR

1860	Willie Park Sr	Prestwick
1861	Tom Morris Sr	Prestwick
1862	Tom Morris Sr	Prestwick
1863	Willie Park Sr	Prestwick
1864	Tom Morris Sr	Prestwick
1865	Andrew Strath	Prestwick
1866	Willie Park Sr	Prestwick
1867	Tom Morris Sr	Prestwick
1868	Tom Morris Jr	Prestwick
1869	Tom Morris Jr	Prestwick
1870	Tom Morris Jr	Prestwick
1872	Tom Morris Jr	Prestwick
1873	Tom Kidd	St Andrews (Old)
1874	Mungo Park	Musselburgh
1875	Willie Park Sr	Prestwick
1876	Bob Martin*	St Andrews (Old)
1877	Jamie Anderson	Musselburgh
1878	Jamie Anderson	Prestwick
1879	Jamie Anderson	St Andrews (Old)
1880	Bob Ferguson	Musselburgh
1881	Bob Ferguson	Prestwick
1882	Bob Ferguson	St Andrews (Old)
1883	Willie Fernie*	Musselburgh
1884	Jack Simpson	Prestwick
1885	Bob Martin	St Andrews (Old)
1886	David Brown	Musselburgh
1887	Willie Park Jr	Prestwick
1888	Jack Burns	St Andrews (Old)
1889	Willie Park Jr*	Musselburgh
1890	John Ball (A)	Prestwick
1891	Hugh Kirkaldy	St Andrews (Old)
1892	Harold Hilton (A)	Muirfield
1893	William Auchterlonie	Prestwick
1894	JH Taylor	St George's
1895	JH Taylor	St Andrews (Old)
1896	Harry Vardon*	Muirfield
1897	Harold Hilton (A)	Royal Liverpool
1898	Harry Vardon	Prestwick
1899	Harry Vardon	St George's
1900	JH Taylor	St Andrews (Old)
1901	James Braid	Muirfield
1902	Sandy Herd	Royal Liverpool
1903	Harry Vardon	Prestwick
1904	Jack White	Royal St George's
1905	James Braid	St Andrews (Old)
1906	James Braid	Muirfield
1907	Arnaud Massy	Royal Liverpool
1908	James Braid	Prestwick
1909	JH Taylor	Royal Cinque Ports
1910	James Braid	St Andrews (Old)
1911	Harry Vardon*	Royal St George's
1912	Ted Ray	Muirfield
1913	JH Taylor	Royal Liverpool
1914	Harry Vardon	Prestwick
1920	George Duncan	Royal Cinque Ports
1921	Jock Hutchison*	St Andrews (Old)
1922	Walter Hagen	Royal St George's
1923	Arthur Havers	Troon
1924	Walter Hagen	Royal Liverpool
1925	Jim Barnes	Prestwick
1926	Bobby Jones (A)	Royal Lytham & St Annes
1927	Bobby Jones (A)	St Andrews (Old)
1928	Walter Hagen	Royal St George's
1929	Walter Hagen	Muirfield
1930	Bobby Jones (A)	Royal Liverpool
1931	Tommy Armour	Carnoustie
1932	Gene Sarazen	Prince's
1933	Denny Shute*	St Andrews (Old)
1934	Henry Cotton	Royal St George's
1935	Alf Perry	Muirfield
1936	Alf Padgham	Royal Liverpool
1937	Henry Cotton	Carnoustie
1938	Reg Whitcombe	Royal St George's
1939	Dick Burton	St Andrews (Old)
1946	Sam Snead	St Andrews (Old)
1947	Fred Daly	Royal Liverpool
1948	Henry Cotton	Muirfield
1949	Bobby Locke*	Royal St George's
1950	Bobby Locke	Troon
1951	Max Faulkner	Royal Portrush
1952	Bobby Locke	Royal Lytham & St Annes
1953	Ben Hogan	Carnoustie
1954	Peter Thomson	Royal Birkdale
1955	Peter Thomson	St Andrews (Old)
1956	Peter Thomson	Royal Liverpool
1957	Bobby Locke	St Andrews (Old)
1958	Peter Thomson*	Royal Lytham & St Annes
1959	Gary Player	Muirfield
1960	Kel Nagle	St Andrews (Old)
1961	Arnold Palmer	Royal Birkdale
1962	Arnold Palmer	Troon
1963	Bob Charles*	Royal Lytham & St Annes
1964	Tony Lema	St Andrews (Old)
1965	Peter Thomson	Royal Birkdale
1966	Jack Nicklaus	Muirfield
1967	Roberto de Vicenzo	Royal Liverpool
1968	Gary Player	Carnoustie
1969	Tony Jacklin	Royal Lytham & St Annes
1970	Jack Nicklaus*	St Andrews (Old)
1971	Lee Trevino	Royal Birkdale
1972	Lee Trevino	Muirfield
1973	Tom Weiskopf	Troon
1974	Gary Player	Royal Lytham & St Annes
1975	Tom Watson*	Carnoustie
1976	Johnny Miller	Royal Birkdale
1977	Tom Watson	Turnberry

1978	Jack Nicklaus	St Andrews (Old)
1979	Seve Ballesteros	Royal Lytham & St Annes
1980	Tom Watson	Muirfield
1981	Bill Rogers	Royal St George's
1982	Tom Watson	Royal Troon
1983	Tom Watson	Royal Birkdale
1984	Seve Ballesteros	St Andrews (Old)
1985	Sandy Lyle	Royal St George's
1986	Greg Norman	Turnberry
1987	Nick Faldo	Muirfield
1988	Seve Ballesteros	Royal Lytham & St Annes
1989	Mark Calcavecchia*	Royal Troon
1990	Nick Faldo	St Andrews (Old)
1991	Ian Baker-Finch	Royal Birkdale
1992	Nick Faldo	Muirfield
1993	Greg Norman	Royal St George's
1994	Nick Price	Turnberry
1995	John Daly*	St Andrews (Old)
1996	Tom Lehman	Royal Lytham & St Annes
1997	Justin Leonard	Royal Troon
1998	Mark O'Meara*	Royal Birkdale
1999	Paul Lawrie*	Carnoustie
2000	Tiger Woods	St Andrews (Old)
2001	David Duval	Royal Lytham & St Annes
2002	Ernie Els*	Muirfield
2003	Ben Curtis	Royal St George's
2004	Todd Hamilton*	Royal Troon
2005	Tiger Woods	St Andrews (Old)
2006	Tiger Woods	Royal Liverpool
2007	Padraig Harrington*	Carnoustie
2008	Padraig Harrington	Royal Birkdale
2009	Stewart Cink*	Turnberry
2010	Louis Oosthuizen	St Andrews (Old)
2011	Darren Clarke	Royal St George's
2012	Ernie Els	Royal Lytham & St Annes
2013	Phil Mickelson	Muirfield
2014	Rory McIlroy	Royal Liverpool
2015	Zach Johnson*	St Andrews (Old)
2016	Henrik Stenson	Royal Troon
2017	Jordan Spieth	Royal Birkdale
2018	Francesco Molinari	Carnoustie
2019	Shane Lowry	Royal Portrush
2021	Collin Morikawa	Royal St George's
2022	Cameron Smith	St Andrews (Old)

**won in playoff*

AMUNDI EVIAN CHAMPIONSHIP
SKECHERS
UKG
CP

Brooke gets the breaks for second major

By Andy Farrell

When Brooke Henderson launched her tee shot with a four-hybrid club at the 210-yard downhill 14th hole on Sunday at Evian, things could, very much, go either way. She was not entirely looking like the player who had led for the previous two days. In the final round, Henderson had bogeyed the first, four-putted the sixth for a double, made only one birdie to date and, after a bogey at the 11th, was three over par for the day.

She had not yet lost the lead, or at least a share of it. But it was just about to happen as a host of other players came into contention for the fourth women's major championship of the year. So it was a good moment for her tee shot at the 14th to pitch into the shallow bank on the left of the green, killing its forward momentum, take a right-hand turn and roll gently down to within four feet of the hole.

That was her first bit of good fortune on the hole. By the time Henderson had walked down to the green, Japan's Mao Saigo had birdied the 18th for a 64 to join two other players, Sei Young Kim and Sophia Schubert, ahead of Henderson at 15 under par. Her second break came when her ball did a complete 360-degree circuit of the hole and still fell between the lip and the flagstick.

It was not the only time that Henderson would wobble a putt around the circumference of the hole and live to tell the tale. "It's the little breaks that you get that make the difference in holding the trophy or finishing second or worse," said the new holder of the Amundi Evian Championship.

After the ragged first two-thirds of her final round, Henderson rallied in the most impressive fashion with three birdies in the final five holes to win by one stroke from Schubert, a young rookie left with tears of happiness after the performance of her short career so far. Henderson, after twin opening rounds of 64 followed by a 68 on Saturday to lead by two from So Yeon Ryu after 54 holes, may not have been so sanguine after finishing second. A 71 was good enough for the winning total of 267 for 17 under par.

Schubert, with a Sunday 68, did little wrong down the stretch, coming home in three under par. She held the lead in a major for the first time on the back nine and did not drop a shot. Over the last five holes, she was only one under compared to Henderson's three under but others had fared worse. Kim, a major winner, lost her chance with a double bogey at the 16th. Ryu, a double major champion, had her second double bogey of the day at the 15th in a closing 73.

Earlier, Nelly Korda had briefly tied for the lead with an eagle at the ninth, but played the last five in one over par. England's Charley Hull (67) had four birdies and two bogeys on the back nine, while Spain's Carlota Ciganda was bogey-free in a 68 but did not quite threaten. As ever, the hillside course overlooking Lake Geneva offered riches for those relaxed enough to take advantage, with Saigo and former winners Lydia Ko (66) and Hyo Joo Kim (67), all playing those five holes in three under. But Henderson had done it when it appeared her first major title for six years was slipping through her fingers.

"Yeah, when I was three over through 11 holes, it was like, this could go either way," Henderson said. "I really need to buckle down, because people are playing well. If I want to be at the top of the leaderboard again and if I want to contend, I really need to get it in gear here and hit as many good shots as I can and get as many birdie looks coming down the stretch. To make three of those in the last five holes was really big. It felt really nice to have the patience pay off and then to make the comeback."

Henderson, already her country's most prolific winner in professional golf with her 12th title here, became the first Canadian player, male or female, to become a two-time major champion. She won the KPMG Women's PGA Championship as an 18-year-old in 2016. Like In Gee Chun at this year's KPMG, she had waited six years for that second major.

"Winning the first major changed my life," she said. "My world ranking shot up and I just received a ton more attention from fans and media. It also made me feel like I really belonged out here, and that I could contend for big, major championships and compete against the best in the world, which is an amazing feeling.

"It has been a long time, and getting off to a fast start early this week, it just felt great to be at the top of the leaderboard at a major. I just tried to take that excitement as far as I could. To be sitting here a two-time major champion is just an unreal feeling."

Henderson had not won at all in 2020 and only once in 2021 before she claimed the ShopRite LPGA Classic in June. She had had to adapt to using a 46-inch driver, having spent all her career using a 48-inch model, and had worked on her putting with her coach, going left-hand low and improving her green-reading skills with her caddie-sister Brittany. But more than anything a spring break back home in Smiths Falls, Ontario, her first return in more than two years, was rejuvenating. "Sometimes you just need to take a step back, and being able to spend time with family and just connect back to where I grew up and relax for a couple weeks was really key," she said. "Then I was able to come back out and get two victories pretty quick and some top finishes. I think I just really needed it earlier this year."

FIRST ROUND

Wednesday's rain that brought to an end the recent heatwave left the course slightly softer — relatively — than might have been expected and in perfect condition for the onslaught of scoring in round one. It even got hot enough in the afternoon for Korda to dip her toes into the pond at the 18th, but first thing in the morning the hottest thing around was Schubert. In the first group of the day off the first tee, the youngster from Tennessee had a double bogey. "I know, I know," she lamented after an opening 69. "But then I just kept my head in it, tried to make myself forget about it, which was hard, and ended well." Holing a long putt on the second green helped a lot.

Japan's Ayaka Furue led the way on eight-under-par 63, while Korda and Henderson finished a stroke behind on 64. Neither the American nor the Canadian had scored better than 67 previously, and neither had enjoyed great success in France's major. Korda's best result in four starts was 19th in 2021, while Henderson's best in six appearances was ninth in 2016. Both got to grips with the slopey greens better than in the past.

Henderson led the morning wave thanks to her monster putt for eagle at the ninth, her finishing hole. "Definitely a bonus," she admitted. She had begun the day with birdies at the 10th and 11th, had four in five holes after the turn, but then dropped her only shot of the day at the eighth. "I feel my ball-striking gave me a lot of really great opportunities, which is always good, and then I was able to make some putts."

Korda also claimed a long putt to get to seven under, with a two at the eighth. Her route to that point was a little different. She had four birdies in the bag when she reached the 18th, her ninth, and came up short in the pond for her second shot. She had been between a six-iron and a seven for the approach to the par five. "I didn't really want to go long, but didn't really think about if I didn't hit that seven good it would go in the water," said the world number three.

With her ball only just on the edge of the water, Korda removed her shoes and socks and found her stance in the pond was "very slimy on the bottom". Nevertheless, she popped her ball up the bank to the front of the green and then two-putted for her par. "I had a decent chance of getting it out on the green, so I just went for it," she said. "Better than taking a drop, that's for sure."

In her fifth event back after suffering a blood clot, Korda was wearing a compression sleeve on her left arm, as well as sun sleeves on both. "I haven't had too much success on this golf course, so I try not to get the numbers too in my head, just go out and have fun."

Furue said she had "positive vibes" about the course from her debut performance in 2021 when she finished fourth. Already a runner-up at the Bank of Hope Match Play in her rookie season on the LPGA, the 22-year-old from Kobe was not dispirited by a bogey at the 13th, her fourth hole, and made nine birdies in the remaining 14, chipping to five feet for a four at the ninth to take the lead on her own. "I like the course, and with the good vibes from last year, I thought I would play good, and I played very well today," Furue said after her lowest LPGA score. "I had good rhythm. I hit it close a lot. My putting was very good also today."

American Cheyenne Knight set off fast with four birdies in her first five holes to lie fourth on 65, while five players were on five-under 66, including world number one Jin Young Ko and also Lydia Ko. The pair were playing together, alongside another former Evian champion, Anna Nordqvist, who had a 67 and the only bogey of the entire group as they finished on a collective 14 under. "Our whole group played really well," said the New Zealander Ko. "We all have like different games, but it's cool how we're all able to break down the course even though we have different ball flights, hit different distances.

There is always something to learn from them, especially Jin Young, her being the number one."

After 18 holes: 63 (-8) Furue; **64** Henderson, N Korda; **65** Knight; **66** Delacour, Hull, Nishimura, JY Ko, L Ko

SECOND ROUND

As well as the weather hotting up on Friday, the pin positions were also a notch harder for the second round. None of that could halt Henderson in her tracks as the 24-year-old Canadian opened up a three-shot lead. But that was not until the afternoon. In the morning, Korda herself was three ahead as the American contemplated some lunch and a nap — jet lag was to blame for a lousy night's sleep.

Perhaps that explained the 10 pars to start her round. Fortunately, from her point of view, the first-round leader, Furue, was not making much progress either. The Japanese player saw her tee shot at the 14th pull up two feet short of a hole-in-one. She made the two for only her second birdie of the day but by three-putting the next, symptomatic of a poor day on the greens, she ended up with a one-over-par 72 and drifted back to seven under.

Korda finally got going in the right direction with a birdie at the 11th, then dropped her first shot of the championship two holes later. She added two more birdies and then took revenge on the 18th by making an eagle. There was no flirting with the water this time as she hit a five-hybrid from 192 yards onto the green, the ball swirling off the slopes to two-and-a-half feet. "Yesterday I was struggling with the ball below my feet," she explained. "I was hitting it out right, so I told myself to aim a little bit more left, and thank God. It just turned out perfect."

A 67 gave Korda a halfway total of 11 under par, while no one else in the morning was better than eight under, including France's Perrine Delacour making the cut at the Evian for the first time. For Korda, prior to her nap, a first time contending at the major was a cause for plaudits. "Honestly, it's super good. A little pat on my back after two days and hopefully it keeps going that way."

Knowing that one former KPMG champion had backed up a strong opening round was the cue for another to follow suit. And then some. Henderson followed her long eagle putt from the previous day to close her first round by starting her second with a birdie at the first from almost 40 feet. "I noticed that Nelly had finished really well and was right up there," she said. "I was just trying to continue what I did yesterday: hit the ball in good places and try to make some putts."

Henderson also birdied the second, had a bogey at the next, her only dropped shot of the day, and added three more birdies to draw level with Korda at the 12th. It was her finish that set the Canadian apart as she birdied the last three holes, all with putts from 10-12 feet. It all added up to a second successive 64 — the first time a player at a women's major had opened with two scores of 64 or better — and a 14-under-par total of 128, one outside the record set by Jeongeun Lee[6] in 2021. With her left-low grip working a treat, she was finally taking advantage of her ball-striking. For the season to date, Henderson was ranked second for strokes gained ball-striking (off the tee and approach shots) behind only Minjee Lee, the US Women's Open champion, whose defence of her Evian title was not really hotting up until an eagle at the last got the Australian to three under par.

"To get it this far under par is really awesome," Henderson said. "I feel like I'm hitting the ball really well, which is nice. The putter has been hot for me the last couple of months, and it's a really great feeling. It's nice to have a little bit of momentum. This is a great position after two days, but it's only half over."

Koreans Sei Young Kim and Ryu both birdied the last four holes for rounds of 65 and 66 respectively to be nine under par, two behind Korda. Lydia Ko got to 10 under before missing the green at the short 16th and taking a five and then having a six at the last. She was back to seven under, alongside Furue and namesake Jin Young, both Kos having matching 69s.

There were two other 65s, from Andrea Lee and Schubert, who joined the group at eight under which also included Thai prodigy Atthaya Thitikul, whose 66 included a triple bogey on her third hole. Schubert, the 2017 US Amateur champion, played in that year's Evian and made the cut. Here, she again struggled on her opening hole with a bogey at the 10th, then holed a 20-footer at the next and was off and running. Six more birdies followed. She said of the indifferent start: "I just have to tell myself to stay positive. Just keep trucking along. Don't change anything. Don't try to force anything. A lot of the time people force making a birdie. I just had to really make sure that I wasn't doing that."

After 36 holes: 128 (-14) Henderson 64; **131** N Korda 67; **133** SY Kim 65, SY Ryu 66; **134** An Lee 65, Schubert 65, Thitikul 66, HJ Kim 66, Ciganda 67, Delacour 68

THIRD ROUND

Defending champion Minjee Lee squandered the momentum from an eagle to finish on Friday with a triple bogey at the first hole on Saturday. Easily done. When the leaders got onto the course, both Henderson and Korda bogeyed the opening hole. Two players looking for their second major title. While Henderson did not drop another shot all day, it turned into a topsy turvy affair for Korda, who birdied the 18th for a 71.

Both players had four birdies but Henderson posted a 68 to move to 17 under par. Not only was Korda six behind, along with a host of others on 11 under, but four players had gone past her. Ryu had a 65 to be 15 under, two behind the leader; Schubert had a 66 to be four back; and Ciganda (67) and Sei Young Kim (68) were on 12 under.

"A little disappointing honestly. I didn't hit it very good," Korda said. The plan for Sunday: "Trying to get my shit back together. Kidding. Just trying to stay a little bit more consistent off the tee, be a little bit more aggressive. Not even aggressive, a little smarter on the par fives. Hopefully drain some putts."

While Korda spent the day grinding to get back to level par for the round, Henderson made three birdies going out and another at the short 14th. Yet as she threatened to pull away from the field, there were only pars on the last four holes. There were some good up-and-downs but she also missed a chance at the last when a short putt lipped out. Frustrating, but there was solace to be found in the crêpes that had been fuelling her all week.

"Yeah, it was wasn't as good as the first two days, but I really hung in there. I felt the course is playing a little bit tougher for me today. Sometimes I tried to be aggressive and it worked out pretty well; other times I had to play safer, hit to the wide part of the greens. So a little bit of a mixed bag today. Hopefully clean some things up and finish strong tomorrow."

Ryu cut into the Canadian's lead by birdieing three of the last four holes for a 65. Two behind, the Korean could dream of adding to her major successes even if they were 11 years ago (US Women's Open) and five years ago (what is now the Chevron). "For sure, I haven't played really well and haven't been in contention for, I don't know, maybe over a year, so I'm really excited to be in this position," she said. "At the same time, I'm a little bit nervous. But all I can do is focus on what I can do."

At least Ryu had been there, and done it. This was all new to Schubert, who graduated from the Epson Tour in 2021 and was playing in only her second major as a professional. There was another double bogey, this time at the short fifth after finding the water. But once again showing her resilience, Schubert came home in 31, with birdies at the 11th and the last four holes, for a 66.

One thing making the rookie from East Tennessee feel at home was the course being on the side of a hill with all the uneven lies. "It definitely feels like it with the hills and the lakes and the mountains. I'm used to being on a bunch of undulation, used to hitting those shots, whether it be above your feet, below your feet. You have to know how to adjust."

So far her best result on tour was 12th place so three rounds in the 60s at a major were definitely uncharted territory. "This is what I've worked so hard for, to be at this point. I'm just trying not to think about it. I get to play with some of the best golfers in the world and I think to myself that I deserve to be here."

The low round of the day belonged to Switzerland's Albane Valenzuela, who scored 64 after going out in 30. Evian is a special place for her as it was not only where she played her first major as an amateur but where her Swiss-Mexican parents met. "It means the world. I love this place so much," she said. "To have my friends, family, and the support from Swiss people who are right across the lake, it means a lot."

After 54 holes: 196 (-17) Henderson 68; **198** SY Ryu 65; **200** Schubert 66; **201** Ciganda 67, SY Kim 68; **202** JY Ko 67, Hull 67, HJ Kim 68, Thitikul 68, N Korda 71

FOURTH ROUND

After one hole on Sunday Henderson and Ryu were tied. Henderson three-putted the first after coming up 12 feet short from long range, while Ryu birdied from 15 feet. But the Korean drifted out of contention with a bogey at the third and a double at the fifth. She took four putts and it was catching, as Henderson had her own problems a hole later.

After driving into a bunker, she was left with a long putt at the green. "The bunker was definitely not the best place to be. It was a pretty great shot, unfortunately I had like 30 yards of a putt left." She discussed chipping it with sister Brittany. "In hindsight, I feel like, yes, I should've chipped it. I feel I would've gotten closer." She still had 20 feet left for the par and took three more putts for a double. "I tried not to let it bother me too much, but obviously that does shake you up a little bit. But I was able to bounce back and birdie the next hole."

Before Henderson recovered one of the lost shots at the seventh, she was briefly tied for the lead by Korda. The American had set out with intent, birdieing the first two holes. At the sixth a spectator picked up her ball, which was replaced, but the problem was that she was well short and right of the green in trees for two shots. A double bogey followed, but Korda responded with a birdie at the seventh and an eagle at the ninth to get to 14 under par, the same score as Henderson after six holes. That was it for Korda, however, as she came home with eight pars and a bogey for a 69.

Elsewhere, Schubert was avoiding the mistakes of earlier rounds and, despite being more nervous than the day before, went out in 34 with a birdie at the sixth. Then she birdied the 11th and 12th and when Henderson bogeyed the 11th, Schubert was one ahead.

Next into the frame was Sei Young Kim, who had birdied the fourth and ninth going out and added another at the 14th to tie Schubert at 15 under. Saigo, the star of the Japanese LPGA in 2022 with five wins, closed out her weekend 65-64 to also get to 15 under par, where she would ultimately be joined by Lydia Ko, Hyo Joo Kim, Hull and Ciganda.

But not Sei Young Kim, who was finishing an alarming number of shots one-handed and came to grief when she missed the green at the 17th and ended up with a double bogey. At 13 under, she was alongside Ryu, Korda, Jin Young Ko, Thitikul, Georgia Hall and Linn Grant, the Scandinavian Mixed winner who as a professional had only ever finished in the top 10, except for 13th on the same course at the Jabra Ladies Open earlier in the season.

Schubert added a fourth birdie at the 15th by getting up and down from a bunker but missed for a four at the last and finished on 16 under. The runner-up said: "I want to cry. I want to cry tears of happiness. I'm proud of myself, proud of everyone that's helped me get to this point. It came just short, but I know that I'll be back, so I'm really happy."

Henderson played the last five holes in three under to claim the $1 million first prize out of a record Evian purse of $6.5m. After the two at the 14th, she hit two great shots onto the 15th green and two-putted. At the difficult par-three 16th, she hit one of the best tee shots of the day and made par. She was intending to go for the green in two at the last but her drive finished in the rough and she laid up. The wedge gave her the chance of ending it in regulation with a 12 foot putt.

"Over that putt, you know, really I just did not want to go to a playoff. Did not want to play that hole again. So I was like, please go in," Henderson said. "Obviously, to make that putt was a huge relief. It was really close the whole day. I think just having such a poor start and then staying patient and knowing that I was never really out of it, and to be able to climb back really means a lot."

Evian Resort Golf Club, Evian-les-Bains, France
Par 71 (35-36); 6,527 yards

July 21-24
Purse: $6,500,000

1	**Brooke M Henderson**	64	64	68	71	267	$1,000,000
2	**Sophia Schubert**	69	65	66	68	268	586,262
3	**Mao Saigo**	70	70	65	64	269	283,420
	Lydia Ko	66	69	68	66	269	283,420
	Charley Hull	66	69	67	67	269	283,420
	Hyo Joo Kim	68	66	68	67	269	283,420
	Carlota Ciganda	67	67	67	68	269	283,420
8	Linn Grant	67	71	69	64	271	124,079
	Georgia Hall	69	71	66	65	271	124,079
	Jin Young Ko	66	69	67	69	271	124,079
	Atthaya Thitikul	68	66	68	69	271	124,079
	Nelly Korda	64	67	71	69	271	124,079
	Sei Young Kim	68	65	68	70	271	124,079
	So Yeon Ryu	67	66	65	73	271	124,079
15	Yuna Nishimura	66	73	68	66	273	86,021
	Nasa Hataoka	69	66	72	66	273	86,021
	Ashleigh Buhai	68	70	67	68	273	86,021
	Andrea Lee	69	65	70	69	273	86,021
19	Cheyenne Knight	65	73	70	66	274	73,825
	Amy Yang	70	68	69	67	274	73,825
	Ayaka Furue	63	72	71	68	274	73,825
22	Brittany Altomare	69	69	70	67	275	63,746
	Hye-Jin Choi	71	68	67	69	275	63,746
	Anna Nordqvist	67	69	70	69	275	63,746
	In Gee Chun	67	72	66	70	275	63,746
	Jodi Ewart Shadoff	68	69	68	70	275	63,746
27	Esther Henseleit	70	71	69	66	276	53,522
	Gaby Lopez	70	70	66	70	276	53,522
	Madelene Sagstrom	70	69	66	71	276	53,522
	Albane Valenzuela	70	69	64	73	276	53,522
31	Stephanie Kyriacou	70	71	70	66	277	43,812
	Hannah Green	72	68	69	68	277	43,812
	Moriya Jutanugarn	70	70	69	68	277	43,812
	Pornanong Phatlum	71	69	68	69	277	43,812
	Jennifer Kupcho	71	70	65	71	277	43,812
	A Lim Kim	70	68	67	72	277	43,812
37	Amanda Doherty	69	70	72	67	278	36,270
	Xiyu Lin	70	70	69	69	278	36,270
	Min Ji Park	67	69	70	72	278	36,270
40	Stephanie Meadow	71	69	71	68	279	32,739
	Matilda Castren	68	73	68	70	279	32,739
42	Eun-Hee Ji	67	72	69	72	280	30,816
43	Caroline Masson	73	69	73	66	281	26,365
	Megan Khang	71	70	72	68	281	26,365
	Minjee Lee	70	69	73	69	281	26,365
	Lizette Salas	71	70	70	70	281	26,365
	Jasmine Suwannapura	70	67	74	70	281	26,365
	Yu Liu	69	72	69	71	281	26,365
	Kelly Tan	69	68	72	72	281	26,365
50	Morgane Metraux	72	68	71	71	282	21,505
	Olivia Cowan	73	66	71	72	282	21,505
	Jeongeun Lee[5]	71	69	69	73	282	21,505
	Alison Lee	71	67	67	77	282	21,505
54	Pia Babnik	70	70	71	72	283	18,937
	Ally Ewing	69	70	71	73	283	18,937
	Sarah Kemp	69	67	74	73	283	18,937
	Perrine Delacour	66	68	70	79	283	18,937
58	Wei-Ling Hsu	73	69	72	70	284	17,012
	Jenny Shin	73	66	73	72	284	17,012
60	Jennifer Chang	71	71	73	70	285	15,568
	Chella Choi	70	71	74	70	285	15,568
	Gemma Dryburgh	71	70	72	72	285	15,568
	Johanna Gustavsson	68	73	69	75	285	15,568
	Rachel Heck [A]	70	71	68	76	285	
65	Leona Maguire	70	71	74	71	286	14,604
	Anna Davis [A]	70	69	74	73	286	
	Rose Zhang [A]	70	68	74	74	286	
	Sarah Schmelzel	71	70	69	76	286	14,604
69	Agathe Laisne	72	70	76	69	287	13,802
	Marina Alex	72	68	74	73	287	13,802
	Haeji Kang	70	71	72	74	287	13,802
72	Pauline Roussin	71	70	73	79	293	13,160
73	Isi Gabsa	71	70	80	75	296	12,841
	MISSED THE 36-HOLE CUT						
	Manon De Roey	74	69			143	
	Pajaree Anannarukarn	73	70			143	
	Aline Krauter [A]	73	70			143	
	Annie Park	73	70			143	
	Celine Boutier	72	71			143	
	Wichanee Meechai	72	71			143	
	Inbee Park	72	71			143	
	Lauren Stephenson	72	71			143	
	Aditi Ashok	71	72			143	
	Mel Reid	71	72			143	
	Lindsey Weaver-Wright	71	72			143	
	Tiia Koivisto	70	73			143	
	Lilia Vu	70	73			143	
	Cristie Kerr	69	74			143	
	Ariya Jutanugarn	77	67			144	
	Peiyun Chien	74	70			144	
	Jessica Korda	74	70			144	
	Jennifer Song	74	70			144	
	Amy Olson	73	71			144	
	Yuka Saso	71	73			144	
	Ruixin Liu	70	74			144	
	Emma Talley	70	74			144	
	Mina Harigae	69	75			144	
	Ryann O'Toole	68	76			144	
	Sung Hyun Park	67	77			144	
	In-Kyung Kim	75	70			145	
	Jenny Coleman	74	71			145	
	Yealimi Noh	73	72			145	
	Marianne Skarpnord	73	72			145	
	Lauren Coughlin	72	73			145	
	Paula Reto	71	74			145	
	Allisen Corpuz	70	75			145	
	Nanna Koerstz Madsen	67	78			145	
	Maude-Aimee Leblanc	75	71			146	
	Maja Stark	72	74			146	
	Narin An	76	71			147	
	Valery Plata [A]	76	71			147	
	Patty Tavatanakit	74	73			147	
	Su Oh	73	74			147	
	Alana Uriell	72	75			147	
	Jensen Castle [A]	74	74			148	
	Janie Jackson	73	75			148	
	Meghan MacLaren	72	76			148	
	Charlotte Thomas	71	77			148	
	Mizuki Hashimoto [A]	74	75			149	
	Bronte Law	74	75			149	
	Magdalena Simmermacher	74	75			149	
	Lee-Anne Pace	73	76			149	
	Yaeeun Hong	72	77			149	
	Sophia Popov	70	79			149	
	Frida Kinhult	77	73			150	
	Jeongeun Lee[6]	71	79			150	
	Jess Emma Baker [A]	74	77			151	
	Gina Kim	74	77			151	
	Hinako Shibuno	74	77			151	
	Angela Stanford	73	78			151	
	Benedetta Moresco [A]	76	76			152	
	Sanna Nuutinen	79	78			157	
	Angel Yin	74				WD	

ROLL OF HONOUR

1994	Helen Alfredsson	Evian Resort
1995	Laura Davies	Evian Resort
1996	Laura Davies	Evian Resort
1997	Hiromi Kobayashi*	Evian Resort
1998	Helen Alfredsson	Evian Resort
1999	Catrin Nilsmark	Evian Resort
2000	Annika Sorenstam*	Evian Resort
2001	Rachel Teske	Evian Resort
2002	Annika Sorenstam	Evian Resort
2003	Juli Inkster	Evian Resort
2004	Wendy Doolan	Evian Resort
2005	Paula Creamer	Evian Resort
2006	Karrie Webb	Evian Resort
2007	Natalie Gulbis*	Evian Resort
2008	Helen Alfredsson*	Evian Resort
2009	Ai Miyazato*	Evian Resort
2010	Jiyai Shin	Evian Resort
2011	Ai Miyazato	Evian Resort
2012	Inbee Park	Evian Resort
2013	Suzann Pettersen	Evian Resort
2014	Hyo Joo Kim	Evian Resort
2015	Lydia Ko	Evian Resort
2016	In Gee Chun	Evian Resort
2017	Anna Nordqvist*	Evian Resort
2018	Angela Stanford	Evian Resort
2019	Jin Young Ko	Evian Resort
2021	Minjee Lee*	Evian Resort
2022	Brooke Henderson	Evian Resort

**won in playoff*

Designated an LPGA major since 2013

AIG WOMEN'S OPEN
SRIXON
FTI
CONSULTING
CUTTER & BUCK

Buhai in command at historic Muirfield

By Andy Farrell

Muirfield, the name drips with golfing history. Majestic setting on the shores of the Firth of Forth, Edinburgh to the west, the Kingdom of Fife to the north. Home to the Honourable Company of Edinburgh Golfers, who codified the first widely distributed rules of the game in 1744 and joined with Prestwick and the Royal and Ancient to re-start The Open with the Claret Jug in 1872.

After outgrowing first Leith Links and then Musselburgh, the club moved to its present home in 1891 and staged the first of its 16 men's Opens the following year. Of the champions crowned at Muirfield, all but one are multiple major winners and their number include two members of the Great Triumvirate, Harry Vardon and James Braid; two English knights, Sir Henry Cotton and Sir Nick Faldo; two great South Africans, Gary Player and Ernie Els; and a few celebrated Americans: Walter Hagen, Jack Nicklaus, Lee Trevino, Tom Watson and, most recently in 2013, Phil Mickelson. Braid and Faldo both won two Opens here, while Watson added a Senior Open title.

"I love the place," Watson said. "I love the feel of it, the smell of it, the taste of it. I love the links turf, the feel of my spikes in it. I love everything about it." Others hold Muirfield similarly in their affections. Nicklaus named his great course in Columbus, Ohio, after it; Player his house, and Braid used "Muirfield" for his son's middle name. Of why the greats prevail at Muirfield, golf writer Pat Ward-Thomas said: "The straight, bold stroke rarely, if ever, is in any way seriously punished, but the timid, the gutless and the wayward as rarely will escape retribution."

Els said simply: "Every links shot you can imagine, you're going to play it here." Scottish Walker Cup player Sam McKinlay wrote he would want to play a match for his life here as it is "the best and fairest of courses". Not that he would want to play it every day — "too fierce, too long, too exposed to the winds" for that. He added: "But a man who is in command of his game and himself will fare better at Muirfield than almost any other course I know."

And a woman who is in command of her game and herself, how would she fare at Muirfield? We finally found out when Ashleigh Buhai defeated In Gee Chun at the fourth extra hole of a playoff at the 2022 AIG Women's Open.

Not long after Mickelson's victory, a stunning performance played out against a controversy surrounding the club's history of having an all-male membership, a vote was held to rectify the situation. The resolution failed to pass and Muirfield was struck off the men's Open rota. A year later, in 2017, another vote was held and this time it was successful.

A more progressive attitude at the club meant that an opportunity to stage its first championship in the women's professional game was accepted enthusiastically. Lindsey Garden, a new member — there are no women members per se, "it's the same as it is for a man. We're equal" — and former Scottish international who acted as a playing marker at the weekend, said of hosting the best female golfers on the planet: "I think all the girls are loving playing our golf course, and that's what we want, just that opportunity to play here just as the men have had for years and years."

Dame Laura Davies, who played as an amateur on the second occasion the course hosted the Curtis Cup in 1984, was finally able to return. And local legend Catriona Matthew, the 2009 Women's Open champion and Solheim Cup star from nearby North Berwick, got to play at a course where she had been a teenage litter picker before progressing to being a walking scorer, accompanying runner-up John Cook in the penultimate group of the 1992 Open.

"I think it's going to be a great experience," Matthew said on the eve of the championship. "To have a chance to play Muirfield in a Women's Open, I think all the players will have watched the men play here over the years, and they, too, are delighted to have that opportunity to play their own Open here. For me personally, obviously growing up and living along road, I never would have imagined ever playing a major so close to home."

Along with an announcement that the prize purse was rising to $7.3 million, an increase of $1.5m on 2021, other players were delighted to be making history at the new venue. Defending champion

Anna Nordqvist: "I've heard a lot about Muirfield. I know the guys have played here over the years, so I think it's an amazing opportunity for us to have Muirfield added to our Open rotation. I would say it's going to be a challenge, but I think it's an amazing venue."

Nelly Korda, 2021 Olympic champion: "It's a beautiful golf club, beautiful golf course, and so far everyone has been really welcoming. It's going to be a great test, you have to strike it well. I think they have hosted 16 Open Championships, so it's going to be special to finally host a Women's, too, this week."

Jennifer Kupcho, 2022 Chevron winner: "I think it's great for women's golf. We're going to great golf courses, both here and at the US Open, and it's great we're able to play in the same places that the men play."

Georgia Hall, 2018 Women's Open champion: "I didn't really know what to expect. I've heard really good things about the course and it is really good. I think it's so important that the women are here this week. It makes such a mark on women's golf, and AIG and The R&A have done a fantastic job working together to get the championship here. It just keeps elevating this tournament. I think everyone wants to win the first women's professional event here. It's definitely a good one to win this year."

FIRST ROUND

During the practice days, Muirfield offered the competitors plenty of exposure to the ever-shifting winds, which came in handy during a first round when scoring was better than had been predicted. There was also some early morning rain for the first starters, including Matthew, who had the honour of hitting the opening tee shot. A 76 was not how the former champion had hoped to start, but she had the pleasure of watching playing partner Louise Duncan compile a four-under-par 67, with four birdies and an eagle at the 17th.

"It was worth the 4.30 alarm," Duncan said. The 22-year-old Scot was the leading amateur in 2021 at Carnoustie and a tie for 10th place earned her a spot in the field here. She had only turned professional the previous week at the Trust Golf Scottish Open but missed the cut so was still awaiting a first pay cheque. That would arrive at the end of the week with a top 20 finish, but for now the former Amateur champion was appreciating playing alongside Matthew. "She's really inspiring to all Scottish girls rising through the ranks, so it was really good to play with her. Just quite calming."

Duncan finished the day in third place, alongside Mexico's Gabby Lopez, who went bogey-free for the entire round, and behind only Hinako Shibuno on 65 and Jessica Korda on 66. Famously, Shibuno won on her major championship debut at the 2019 AIG Women's Open, having arrived expecting a links and actually finding herself feeling at home among the parkland pines of Woburn. She missed the cut on the defence of her title at Royal Troon, her first encounter with true links conditions. "Two years ago at Troon, the wind completely overtook my shots," she recalled. "I wasn't thinking about how to use this to my advantage. However, this tournament I could adapt my style to the elements. I imagined my swing, if the wind was coming from the right, I could play by feel how far from the pin I needed to aim for."

Or, as the Japanese player put it more succinctly: "I was hoping that I can be a friend with the wind." The Smiling Cinderella was beaming after her six-under start, her lowest score in a major, beating her opening 66 at Woburn and the two 66s she posted at the Chevron Championship earlier in the year. Four birdies in the first five holes proved she was indeed making friends with the elements. There were only two bogeys and birdies at the 16th and 17th holes put her out in front. "It has been a long time since I've played this well, especially putting," Shibuno said.

Korda was wearing a Muirfield hat, not to ingratiate herself with the locals but out of necessity. The suitcase with all her clothes was still stuck at Zurich airport. Friends and sponsors were helping out. "Monday, I wore Megan Khang's pants. Tuesday, I wore my sister's pants and Wednesday, I wore Alison Lee's pants. Today, I'm wearing FootJoy pants."

But the American's golf had arrived on time, a bogey at the second forgotten after adding four birdies, including with a wedge to two feet at the 12th, and an eagle at the 17th from 20 feet. "It's nice, at the end I looked at the leaderboard, but to be honest I was zoned in to what was going on," reflected the Chevron runner-up. "You have to stay on it here at all times. There's so much going on on the golf course with the crosswinds, trying to figure out where you want to land the ball. There's a lot of trust.

Almost like being willing to fail on every single shot."

It turned out this was Jess Korda's best round of the week by seven strokes, such is the fickle nature of Muirfield. She played alongside former winner Hall, who had a 70, and Chun, the KPMG Women's PGA champion, who was among those on 68, a group that also included US Open champion Minjee Lee. Lexi Thompson, a runner-up to Chun at Congressional, stumbled to a 75 and world number one Jin Young Ko made only one birdie in a 76.

Lee and Ko were joined by Nelly Korda (70) in an afternoon round featuring wind gusts of up to 30mph on a day when the scoring average increased by almost two strokes between the first and second halves of the draw. With Muirfield's idiosyncratic layout of two concentric circles going in opposite directions, Korda had the classic links experience of hitting an eight-iron 190 yards and a four-iron 180 yards. "Every hole you get a different wind direction, that's the course's defence," Nelly said. "You really have to concentrate. It's pretty mentally draining, for sure."

But fun, too. Brooke Henderson, the Amundi Evian champion, had her only bogey of an opening 70 at the 18th and said: "I really love this course. It's special to play here. I enjoyed the first round and I'm excited to play three more." Also on 70 were eventual winner Buhai and Finland's Madelene Sagstrom, who said of the course: "You have to be creative and you have to stay really patient. It really demands every part of your game. It demands the whole brain. It demands everything."

After 18 holes: 65 (-6) Shibuno; **66** J Korda; **67** Duncan, Lopez; **68** Stark, Chun, Boutier, Mj Lee, Ewart Shadoff; **69** HJ Choi, Yamashita, I Park

SECOND ROUND

Sagstrom, one of the runners-up to Nordqvist at Carnoustie in 2021, had not liked links golf when she first encountered it at the British Amateur in Wales, calling it "mega hate at first sight". Buhai, who played with Shibuno in the final pairing at Woburn in 2019, finishing fifth after being the 36-hole leader, has always loved links golf. "It's my favourite tournament of the year," said the South African, who had won three times on the Ladies European Tour, the first of them coming at the age of 18 in her third event as a professional.

Both Sagstrom and Buhai followed their Thursday 70s with 65s on Friday, matching Shibuno's de facto course record, to get to seven under par and lie one behind Korea's Chun. The morning starters still had the wind, and it was distinctly chilly, but when Sagstrom finished with three birdies in the last four holes in mid-afternoon conditions were improving. "It's beautiful out there right now. We've still got a little breeze, but it calmed down a little bit in the end. I didn't hit in the bunkers today, which helps, and I did miss two quite short putts but I putted really, really well. That helped my momentum."

Buhai was one of the later starters and shot up the leaderboard by going out in 30. The 33-year-old from Johannesburg birdied the second and the fourth, then holed a putt from over 40 feet for an eagle at the fifth. "It was a nice bomb to hole," she said. Then she birdied the sixth and the ninth, plus the 11th to get to eight under.

She knew all about the South African heritage at Muirfield, especially Els's victory in 2002. During a practice round, she looked up a video clip of Ernie's famous bunker shot at the 13th hole in the final round and tried to replicate it. "He was my hero growing up," Buhai said. "It's pretty cool to be able to play well for the first two rounds here and try to follow in his footsteps."

Buhai continued on her way with pars as the back nine progressed, while Shibuno dropped back with a 73, which contained just one birdie. Jessica Korda was going along steadily until four bogeys in a row from the 13th. She finished with a 74, the same score Nelly posted in the morning. Jess's playing partner Chun played the first eight holes in level par and then made five birdies in the last 10 holes. The elder Korda sister told Chun during the round that she loved the sound of the Korean's swing and, at the end, that she wanted a putting lesson from Chun.

There was also a moment of luck when a gust of wind blew her putt on the 13th into the hole after it had sat on the lip for three seconds. "Now I can enjoy more the Scottish greens," Chun joked. About the only thing that did not go the way of the three-time major winner was her bet with caddie Dean Herden. After studying the course in practice, her goal became to play a bogey-free round, in which case Herden would buy dinner and throw in $100 on top. So far, the Korean had dropped one shot each day. "I want to keep trying to make a bogey-free round the next two days," Chun said.

There were no bogey-free rounds on Friday. Buhai was the fourth player to reach the 18th without having dropped a shot but succumbed to the same fate as the others on the hardest hole on the course for round two. It was unlucky, though. Her drive finished in a divot. From there, she found a bunker, ran over the green with her third before getting up and down for a five. "Obviously disappointed to end with a bogey," said Buhai after dropping one behind Chun, "but I'm super chuffed with how I played today." She also noted that she had received a kind bounce off the bank of a bunker at the short 16th which led to a safe two-putt par, so not everything went against her.

Two off the lead was former champion Inbee Park, after a 67, while Hannah Green had a 66 to join Miyuu Yamashita, who almost holed her second at the fifth for an albatross, on five under. Lower down the leaderboard, Rose Zhang, the 2020 US Amateur champion, was the only non-professional to make the cut, the 19-year-old Stanford star guaranteeing herself the Smyth Salver, and two more rounds on the famous links. That was a prize not available to world number one Ko, despite a 71 highlighted by an eagle at the fifth, Thompson or reigning champion Nordqvist.

After 36 holes: 134 (-8) Chun 66; **135** Sagstrom 65, Buhai 65; **136** I Park 67; **137** Yamashita 68, H Green 66; **138** Boutier 70, Mj Lee 70, Shibuno 73, Kyriacou 68

THIRD ROUND

What a time for Buhai to play the round of her life. There was some good scoring on this Saturday, but it was a day when the wind kept getting stronger and those with the late afternoon tee-times suffered the worst. Shibuno, playing with a noticeably shorter backswing than when she won three years earlier, appeared to have made up again with the conditions — "I could be friends with the wind," said the Japanese star after a 66. But it was Buhai's 64 for a new course record that stole the show and gave the South African a five-shot lead over Shibuno and halfway leader Chun.

Once again Buhai dominated the front nine, this time going out in 31. She birdied the second, then hit her tee shot to two feet at the fourth for the first of four birdies in a row. At 12 under par at the turn, she was back at the top of the leaderboard and had not finished yet. Even as the wind intensified, she kept her tempo beautifully. She birdied the 10th from 18 feet and hit a five-wood into the strengthening wind at the 14th to 10 feet for another. She was out of position at the par-five 17th and yet chipped in for a four, shades of Trevino from 1972. At 15 under par she led by six.

Only, for the second day running, Buhai bogeyed the 18th, this time coming out of her five-wood approach, which ran over the green. She took three to get down for her only bogey but at 14 under par was still comfortably in front. "To be able to shoot that score in those conditions, you have to be able to pat yourself on the back," said the South African, who could not quite keep up with herself, thinking she was six under for the day and not seven under. "It's probably one of the best rounds of golf I've ever played," Buhai added. "I think I'm most proud of the way I just stayed focused and calm, and that's all I try to control. I wasn't thinking of the outcome."

Park, the 2015 champion at Turnberry, was playing alongside Buhai in the penultimate pairing and called the back nine "monstrous" due to the wind, which was again gusting up to 32mph into the evening as play concluded. Of Buhai, the seven-time major winner said: "The golf she's played today was just phenomenal. She played perfect today. I don't remember her making any mistakes. We are going to have to play some good golf tomorrow to catch her."

Park returned a 70, while in the final pairing Chun had a 70 and Sagstrom a 71. "I wish I could have played the golf course she played today," the Swede said of Buhai. "I could not see a seven-under out there today." Buhai's total of 129 for the middle two rounds (65-64) was a new record for the championship and her 54-hole total of 199 was one behind Karrie Webb's record from 1997 at Sunningdale. The only round lower in an Open Championship at Muirfield was Isao Aoki's 63 in the third round in 1980.

Chun had started brightly with birdies at the second and fifth holes, but the chance of a free dinner from her caddie disappeared with her first dropped shot at the par-five ninth. A bogey at 15 and a birdie at 17 comprised the Korean's back nine. "It was not easy and it was a bit windy out there. I think my game was really good today."

Buhai, yet to win on the LPGA Tour, let alone a major, said: "I don't think you can ever be comfortable in a major whether you're coming from behind or leading. It's going to be another tough day. The wind is going to blow, which is good. I prefer it that way. They say big leads are often more difficult, and I think because you try maybe to play defensively. But I think I'll just keep doing what I'm doing."

After 54 holes: 199 (-14) Buhai 64; **204** Shibuno 66, Chun 70; **206** I Park 70, Sagstrom 71; **208** Kyriacou 70; Mj Lee 70, Yamashita 71; **209** SH Park 68, Henderson 69, Thitikul 69, HJ Kim 70, Stark 70, HJ Choi 70

FOURTH ROUND

Big leads at Muirfield are never a sure thing. Faldo had one in 1992, fell behind and had to play the "best four holes of my life" to win. In 1959, Player took a double bogey at the 18th and had an agonising wait to see if he would lift the Claret Jug for the first time. And in 2002, Buhai's hero Els took a double bogey at the 16th and only won at the fifth playoff hole. It was a formula Buhai copied rather too closely for comfort — a late triple bogey, then four extra holes against Chun, with some bunker mastery thrown in for good measure.

It was Chun who came closest to wiping out Buhai's advantage. Looking for her second major of the year, and fourth in all, the KPMG winner hit her approach at the second to six inches and then holed long putts at the fourth and the sixth to be out in 33. Buhai dropped a shot at the second and Chun was within one until the South African got her four at the fifth via a fine bunker shot. Buhai took a six at the ninth after driving into a trap, but then Chun bogeyed the 10th, also in sand off the tee, and the 12th.

The gap was three shots. No one else was close. Leona Maguire compiled an early 66 and tied for fourth with Sagstrom (71) and Minjee Lee (69). Shibuno had an adventurous 71 with an eagle and a double bogey, three birdies and three bogeys. Ultimately, she was only one shot out of the playoff but she happily applauded Buhai's putts as Buhai had Shibuno's winning effort in 2019.

But, first, Buhai had her "other" at the 15th. Her drive finished under the lip of a bunker and in trying to play out backwards she ended up in thick rough. Her third only went a few yards, her fourth with a wood was still short of the green and she took three to get down for a seven. Now Buhai and Chun were tied at 10 under par. "It was very easy to panic and probably come home in an ambulance," Buhai said.

She did not panic, making three good pars to finish off with a 75, the score with which Hagen won an Open at Muirfield in 1929. A fine bunker shot at the 17th was crucial, while her second putt at the last was greeted with rousing applause by her husband David Buhai, formerly her caddie before their 2016 wedding, now the caddie of Jeongeun Lee6. Chun closed with a 70 having seen putts just miss on the 14th, after a superb long approach, from distance at the 16th, and at the 17th.

As the playoff at the 18th progressed, darkness began to fall. Here were two players refusing to be timid or gutless, remaining straight and bold. Chun played a lovely bunker shot on the first extra hole to save par, while the second was halved in bogey fives. Both parred the third time around, Buhai's birdie try just slipping by. Next time, Chun found a bunker off the tee and was only on the green in three. Buhai found the fairway yet again but pushed her approach into the right-hand portion of the bunker on the right. It was time for more South African bunker magic. Buhai put it to little more than a foot, and when Chun made her five, the Korean could only smile in resignation. "Almost close, I don't want to give up," Chun said. "But Ashleigh made a great up-and-down to win."

David Buhai was bursting with excitement as he forgivably stormed the green to embrace his wife. "He's so supportive," said the winner. "I saw him on the back nine and he told me to keep doing what I'm doing, just do me. To play the 18th, that tough tee shot, so many times, I'm just very happy how I managed the situation." Eight times in all Buhai hit the 18th fairway, a woman in command of her game and herself.

As for joining Player and Els as South African champions at Muirfield, she said: "It's a huge honour. To follow those two greats, two of my idols growing up, and for us to play here for the first time at Muirfield, making history, I'm very honoured and very proud to be South African right now." She joined Sally Little as a women's major winner from her country, while Alison Sheard won the Women's Open long before it was a worldwide major in 1979.

Buhai was the first major winner of 2022, male or female, not in their 20s, ironically for a player who first came to prominence as a young prodigy under the name of Ash Simon. "It's been a long journey," she reflected. "I turned pro when I was 18. There were a lot of things expected of me. I won straight off the bat on the Ladies European Tour. But this game has a way of giving you a hard time. I'm just so proud of how I've stuck it out. I have said the last four or five years, I've finally started to find my feet on the LPGA and felt I could compete, and although I'm 33 now, I feel I'm playing the best golf of my career.

"It's been a long journey, but man, it's all worth it right now."

After such a supreme display of ball-striking, especially with the long clubs in exacting conditions, from the final two and all those on the leaderboard, plus every links shot you can imagine, the same could be said of Muirfield and its embrace of women's golf.

Muirfield, Gullane, East Lothian, Scotland — August 4-7

Par 71 (36-35); 6,680 yards — Purse: $7,300,000

1	**Ashleigh Buhai**	70	65	64	75	274	$1,095,000
2	**In Gee Chun**	68	66	70	70	274	673,743
	Buhai won playoff at fourth extra hole						
3	**Hinako Shibuno**	65	73	66	71	275	488,285
4	Leona Maguire	71	69	71	66	277	309,546
	Minjee Lee	68	70	70	69	277	309,546
	Madelene Sagstrom	70	65	71	71	277	309,546
7	Celine Boutier	68	70	74	67	279	160,700
	Lydia Ko	71	70	70	68	279	160,700
	Nasa Hataoka	71	69	71	68	279	160,700
	Atthaya Thitikul	71	69	69	70	279	160,700
	Brooke M Henderson	70	70	69	70	279	160,700
	Stephanie Kyriacou	70	68	70	71	279	160,700
13	A Lim Kim	70	71	69	70	280	115,890
	Miyuu Yamashita	69	68	71	72	280	115,890
15	Kotone Hori	72	68	72	69	281	99,867
	Alison Lee	74	69	67	71	281	99,867
	Hyo Joo Kim	73	66	70	72	281	99,867
18	Sei Young Kim	74	70	67	71	282	90,006
19	Linn Grant	72	70	73	68	283	83,350
	Louise Duncan	67	73	74	69	283	83,350
	Jodi Ewart Shadoff	68	73	70	72	283	83,350
22	Georgia Hall	70	72	70	72	284	70,407
	Emily Kristine Pedersen	70	70	72	72	284	70,407
	Jeongeun Lee[6]	71	68	72	73	284	70,407
	Eun-Hee Ji	70	72	68	74	284	70,407
	Charley Hull	71	70	69	74	284	70,407
	Inbee Park	69	67	70	78	284	70,407
28	Ariya Jutanugarn	71	73	71	70	285	55,306
	Xiyu Lin	72	70	72	71	285	55,306
	Megan Khang	74	69	70	72	285	55,306
	Rose Zhang (A)	72	70	70	73	285	
	Andrea Lee	72	67	72	74	285	55,306
	Sung Hyun Park	72	69	68	76	285	55,306
	Hye-Jin Choi	69	70	70	76	285	55,306
35	So Yeon Ryu	70	72	70	74	286	46,554
	Hannah Green	71	66	74	75	286	46,554
37	Jennifer Kupcho	73	72	71	71	287	41,007
	Jessica Korda	66	74	73	74	287	41,007
	Cheyenne Knight	75	70	67	75	287	41,007
	Mel Reid	73	68	70	76	287	41,007
41	Nelly Korda	70	74	72	72	288	32,475
	Angela Stanford	73	72	70	73	288	32,475
	Leonie Harm	73	70	72	73	288	32,475
	Lilia Vu	76	68	70	74	288	32,475
	Narin An	75	68	70	75	288	32,475
	Marina Alex	70	69	72	77	288	32,475
	Maja Stark	68	71	70	79	288	32,475
48	Bronte Law	73	71	71	74	289	26,399
	Sarah Schmelzel	73	71	70	75	289	26,399
	Whitney Hillier	72	69	73	75	289	26,399
51	Mo Martin	73	69	76	72	290	23,442
	Jennifer Chang	72	73	72	73	290	23,442
	Ally Ewing	76	67	72	75	290	23,442
54	Esther Henseleit	73	70	76	72	291	20,852
	Lizette Salas	71	70	77	73	291	20,852
	Albane Valenzuela	73	70	74	74	291	20,852
	Brittany Altomare	70	71	76	74	291	20,852
58	In-Kyung Kim	71	74	74	73	292	17,600
	Lydia Hall	73	72	71	76	292	17,600
	Wichanee Meechai	70	74	72	76	292	17,600
	Paula Reto	74	70	69	79	292	17,600
	Gaby Lopez	67	73	73	79	292	17,600
63	Gemma Dryburgh	75	69	77	73	294	16,043
64	Ryann O'Toole	71	73	71	80	295	15,676
65	Lee-Anne Pace	71	73	75	77	296	15,309
	MISSED THE 36-HOLE CUT						
	Yuna Nishimura	77	69			146	
	Nanna Koerstz Madsen	76	70			146	
	Maude-Aimee Leblanc	76	70			146	
	Annie Park	76	70			146	
	Emma Talley	76	70			146	
	Ayaka Furue	75	71			146	
	Johanna Gustavsson	75	71			146	
	Sophia Popov	75	71			146	
	Jenny Shin	75	71			146	
	Nicole Broch Estrup	74	72			146	
	Anna Nordqvist	74	72			146	
	Sanna Nuutinen	74	72			146	
	Jung Min Hong	73	73			146	
	Caroline Masson	73	73			146	
	Mina Harigae	71	75			146	
	Alice Hewson	71	75			146	
	Ana Pelaez Trivino	71	75			146	
	Olivia Cowan	78	69			147	
	Mariajo Uribe	78	69			147	
	Diksha Dagar	77	70			147	
	Stacy Lewis	77	70			147	
	Jin Young Ko	76	71			147	
	Aditi Ashok	73	74			147	
	Chella Choi	72	75			147	
	Mao Saigo	72	75			147	
	Casandra Alexander	71	76			147	
	Pajaree Anannarukarn	71	76			147	
	Moriya Jutanugarn	77	71			148	
	Meghan MacLaren	77	71			148	
	Stephanie Meadow	76	72			148	
	Yuka Saso	75	73			148	
	Amy Yang	75	73			148	
	Amy Olson	74	74			148	
	Janie Jackson	73	75			148	
	Ursula Wikstrom	73	75			148	
	Sayaka Takahashi	72	76			148	
	Perrine Delacour	71	77			148	

Pia Babnik	79	70	149	Su Oh	77	75	152
Marianne Skarpnord	79	70	149	Morgane Metraux	76	76	152
Celine Herbin	77	72	149	Kelly Tan	76	76	152
Valery Plata (A)	77	72	149	Allisen Corpuz	75	77	152
Tiia Koivisto	76	73	149	Lexi Thompson	75	77	152
Catriona Matthew	76	73	149	Savannah De Bock (A)	74	78	152
Wei-Ling Hsu	75	74	149	Minami Katsu	74	78	152
Yealimi Noh	75	74	149	Magdalena Simmermacher	82	71	153
Mizuki Hashimoto (A)	73	76	149	Jeongeun Lee[5]	78	75	153
Liz Young	73	76	149	Lauren Coughlin	79	75	154
Carlota Ciganda	72	77	149	Chanettee Wannasaen	78	76	154
Peiyun Chien	77	73	150	Lauren Stephenson	76	78	154
Lindsey Weaver-Wright	77	73	150	Becky Brewerton	75	79	154
Michele Thomson	76	74	150	Hayley Davis	80	75	155
Patty Tavatanakit	75	75	150	Jess Emma Baker (A)	79	76	155
Ingrid Lindblad (A)	74	76	150	Laura Davies	75	81	156
Caley McGinty (A)	82	69	151	Manon De Roey	78	79	157
Sophia Schubert	79	72	151	Carmen Alonso	83	75	158
Angel Yin	79	72	151	Saiki Fujita	80	81	161
Anna Davis (A)	76	75	151	Jana Melichova	78	83	161
Jasmine Suwannapura	74	77	151	Matilda Castren	75		WD

ROLL OF HONOUR

1976	Jenny Lee Smith (A)	Fulford	2001	Se Ri Pak	Sunningdale (Old)
1977	Vivien Saunders	Lindrick	2002	Karrie Webb	Turnberry
1978	Janet Melville (A)	Foxhills	2003	Annika Sorenstam	Royal Lytham & St Annes
1979	Alison Sheard	Southport & Ainsdale	2004	Karen Stupples	Sunningdale (Old)
1980	Debbie Massey	Wentworth (East)	2005	Jeong Jang	Royal Birkdale
1981	Debbie Massey	Northumberland	2006	Sherri Steinhauer	Royal Lytham & St Annes
1982	Marta Figueras-Dotti (A)	Royal Birkdale	2007	Lorena Ochoa	St Andrews (Old)
1984	Ayako Okamoto	Woburn (Duke's)	2008	Jiyai Shin	Sunningdale
1985	Betsy King	Moor Park	2009	Catriona Matthew	Royal Lytham & St Annes
1986	Laura Davies	Royal Birkdale	2010	Yani Tseng	Royal Birkdale
1987	Alison Nicholas	St Mellion	2011	Yani Tseng	Carnoustie
1988	Corinne Dibnah*	Lindrick	2012	Jiyai Shin	Royal Liverpool
1989	Jane Geddes	Ferndown	2013	Stacy Lewis	St Andrews (Old)
1990	Helen Alfredsson*	Woburn (Duke's)	2014	Mo Martin	Royal Birkdale
1991	Penny Grice-Whittaker	Woburn (Duke's)	2015	Inbee Park	Turnberry
1992	Patty Sheehan	Woburn (Duke's)	2016	Ariya Jutanugarn	Woburn (Marquess)
1993	Karen Lunn	Woburn (Duke's)	2017	In-Kyung Kim	Kingsbarns
1994	Liselotte Neumann	Woburn (Duke's)	2018	Georgia Hall	Royal Lytham & St Annes
1995	Karrie Webb	Woburn (Duke's)	2019	Hinako Shibuno	Woburn (Marquess)
1996	Emilee Klein	Woburn (Duke's)	2020	Sophia Popov	Royal Troon
1997	Karrie Webb	Sunningdale (Old)	2021	Anna Nordqvist	Carnoustie
1998	Sherri Steinhauer	Royal Lytham & St Annes	2022	Ashleigh Buhai*	Muirfield
1999	Sherri Steinhauer	Woburn (Duke's)			
2000	Sophie Gustafson	Royal Birkdale			

**won in playoff*

Designated an LPGA major since 2001

Major Records

MOST VICTORIES
18 Jack Nicklaus; **15** Tiger Woods; **11** Walter Hagen; **9** Ben Hogan, Gary Player; **8** Tom Watson; **7** Harry Vardon, Bobby Jones, Gene Sarazen, Sam Snead, Arnold Palmer

15 Patty Berg; **13** Mickey Wright; **11** Louise Suggs; **10** Babe Zaharias, Annika Sorenstam; **8** Betsy Rawls; **7** Juli Inkster, Karrie Webb, Inbee Park

MOST VICTORIES IN A YEAR
3 Ben Hogan — 1953 (Masters, US Open, Open Championship); Tiger Woods — 2000 (US Open, Open Championship, PGA Championship)

3 Babe Zaharias* — 1950 (Titleholders, Western Open, US Open); Mickey Wright — 1961 (Titleholders, US Open, LPGA Championship); Pat Bradley — 1986 (Nabisco Dinah Shore, LPGA Championship, du Maurier Classic); Inbee Park — 2013 (Kraft Nabisco, LPGA Championship, US Open)
**Zaharias won all three of the LPGA majors contested in 1950*

CONSECUTIVE MAJOR VICTORIES
4 Tiger Woods (US Open, Open Championship, PGA Championship, 2000, Masters, 2001)

4 Mickey Wright (US Open, LPGA Championship, 1961, Titleholders, Western Open, 1962)

VICTORIES IN DIFFERENT MAJORS
4 Gene Sarazen, Ben Hogan, Gary Player, Jack Nicklaus, Tiger Woods; **3** Walter Hagen, Jim Barnes, Tommy Armour, Byron Nelson, Sam Snead, Arnold Palmer, Lee Trevino, Tom Watson, Ray Floyd, Phil Mickelson, Rory McIlroy, Jordan Spieth

5 Karrie Webb; **4** Louise Suggs, Mickey Wright, Pat Bradley, Annika Sorenstam, Inbee Park

MOST VICTORIES IN THE SAME MAJOR
6 Harry Vardon (Open Championship); Jack Nicklaus (Masters)

7 Patty Berg (Titleholders, Western Open)

LOWEST SCORES
62 Branden Grace (R3, Open Championship, Royal Birkdale, 2017)
63 Johnny Miller (R4, US Open, Oakmont, 1973); Bruce Crampton (R2, PGA Championship, Firestone, 1975); Mark Hayes (R2, Open, Turnberry, 1977); Jack Nicklaus (R1, US Open, Baltusrol, 1980); Tom Weiskopf (R1, US Open, Baltusrol, 1980); Isao Aoki (R3, Open, Muirfield, 1980); Raymond Floyd (R1, PGA, Southern Hills, 1982); Gary Player (R2, PGA, Shoal Creek, 1984); Nick Price (R3, Masters, Augusta National, 1986); Greg Norman (R2, Open, Turnberry, 1986); Paul Broadhurst (R3, Open, St Andrews, 1990); Jodie Mudd (R4, Open, Royal Birkdale, 1991); Nick Faldo (R2, Open, Royal St George's, 1993); Payne Stewart (R4, Open, Royal St George's, 1993); Vijay Singh (R2, PGA, Inverness, 1993); Michael Bradley (R1, PGA, Riviera, 1995); Brad Faxon (R4, PGA, Riviera, 1995); Greg Norman (R1, Masters, Augusta National, 1996); Jose Maria Olazabal (R3, PGA, Valhalla, 2000); Mark O'Meara (R2, PGA, Atlanta Athletic Club, 2001); Vijay Singh (R2, US Open, Olympia Fields, 2003); Thomas Bjorn (R3, PGA, Baltusrol, 2005); Tiger Woods (R2, PGA, Southern Hills, 2007); Rory McIlroy (R1, Open, St Andrews, 2010); Steve Stricker (R1, PGA, Atlanta Athletic Club, 2011); Jason Dufner (R2, PGA, Oak Hill, 2013); Hiroshi Iwata (R2, PGA, Whistling Straits, 2015); Phil Mickelson

(R1, Open, Royal Troon, 2016); Henrik Stenson (R4, Open, Royal Troon, 2016); Robert Streb (R2, PGA, Baltusrol, 2016); Justin Thomas (R3, US Open, Erin Hills, 2017); Haotong Li (R4, Open, Royal Birkdale, 2017); Tommy Fleetwood (R4, US Open, Shinnecock Hills, 2018); Brooks Koepka (R2, PGA, Bellerive, 2018); Charl Schwartzel (R2, PGA, Bellerive, 2018); Brooks Koepka (R1, PGA, Bethpage Black, 2019); Shane Lowry (R3, Open, Royal Portrush, 2019); Bubba Watson (R2, PGA, Southern Hills, 2022)

61 Hyo Joo Kim (R1, Evian Championship, Evian, 2014); Jeongeun Lee[6] (R2, Evian Championship, Evian, 2021); Leona Maguire (R4, Evian Championship, Evian, 2021)
62 Minea Blomqvist (R3, Women's British Open, Sunningdale, 2004); Lorena Ochoa (R1, Kraft Nabisco, Mission Hills, 2006); Mirim Lee (R1, Women's British Open, Woburn, 2016); Lydia Ko (R4, ANA Inspiration, Mission Hills, 2021)

LOWEST TOTALS
264 Henrik Stenson (Open Championship, Royal Troon, 2016); Brooks Koepka (PGA Championship, Bellerive, 2018)
265 David Toms (PGA Championship, Atlanta Athletic Club, 2001); Collin Morikawa (Open Championship, Royal St George's, 2021)

263 In Gee Chun (Evian Championship, Evian, 2016)
266 Minjee Lee (Evian Championship, Evian, 2021); Jeongeun Lee[6] (Evian Championship, Evian, 2021)

LOWEST TOTALS TO PAR
20 under par — Jason Day (PGA Championship, Whistling Straits, 2015); Henrik Stenson (Open Championship, Royal Troon, 2016); Dustin Johnson (Masters, Augusta National, 2020); Cameron Smith (Open Championship, St Andrews, 2022)
19 under par — Tiger Woods (Open Championship, St Andrews, 2000)

21 under par — In Gee Chun (Evian Championship, Evian, 2016)
19 under par — Dottie Pepper (Nabisco Dinah Shore, Mission Hills, 1999); Karen Stupples (Women's British Open, Sunningdale, 2004); Cristie Kerr (LPGA Championship, Locust Hill, 2010); Yani Tseng (LPGA Championship, Locust Hill, 2011); Inbee Park (KPMG Women's PGA, Westchester, 2015); Nelly Korda (KPMG Women's PGA, Atlanta Athletic Club, 2021)

LARGEST WINNING MARGINS
15 Tiger Woods (US Open, Pebble Beach, 2000); **13** Tom Morris Sr (Open Championship, Prestwick, 1862)

14 Louise Suggs (US Open, Prince George's, 1949); **12** Babe Zaharias (US Open, Salem, 1954); Cristie Kerr (LPGA Championship, Locust Hill, 2010)

OLDEST CHAMPIONS
50 years, 11 months, 7 days — Phil Mickelson (PGA Championship, 2021)

45 years, 7 months, 11 days — Fay Crocker (Titleholders, 1945)

YOUNGEST CHAMPIONS
17 years 5 months 3 days — Tom Morris Jr (Open Championship, 1868)

18 years 4 months 20 days — Lydia Ko (Evian Championship, 2015)

RYDER CUP — ROLL OF HONOUR

1927	GB&I	2½–9½	USA	Worcester
1929	GB&I	7–5	USA	Moortown
1931	GB&I	3–9	USA	Scioto
1933	GB&I	6½–5½	USA	Southport & Ainsdale
1935	GB&I	3–9	USA	Ridgewood
1937	GB&I	4–8	USA	Southport & Ainsdale
1947	GB&I	1–11	USA	Portland
1949	GB&I	5–7	USA	Ganton
1951	GB&I	2½–9½	USA	Pinehurst (No 2)
1953	GB&I	5½–6½	USA	Wentworth (West)
1955	GB&I	4–8	USA	Thunderbird
1957	GB&I	7½–4½	USA	Lindrick
1959	GB&I	3½–8½	USA	Eldorado
1961	GB&I	9½–14½	USA	Royal Lytham & St Annes
1963	GB&I	9–23	USA	Atlanta Athletic Club
1965	GB&I	12½–19½	USA	Royal Birkdale
1967	GB&I	8½–23½	USA	Champions
1969	GB&I	16–16	USA	Royal Birkdale
1971	GB&I	13½–18½	USA	Old Warson
1973	GB&I	13–19	USA	Muirfield
1975	GB&I	11–21	USA	Laurel Valley
1977	GB&I	7½–12½	USA	Royal Lytham & St Annes
1979	Europe	11–17	USA	The Greenbrier
1981	Europe	9½–18½	USA	Walton Heath
1983	Europe	13½–14½	USA	PGA National
1985	Europe	16½–11½	USA	The Belfry
1987	Europe	15–13	USA	Muirfield Village
1989	Europe	14–14	USA	The Belfry
1991	Europe	13½–14½	USA	Kiawah Island (Ocean)
1993	Europe	13–15	USA	The Belfry
1995	Europe	14½–13½	USA	Oak Hill
1997	Europe	14½–13½	USA	Valderrama
1999	Europe	13½–14½	USA	Brookline
2002	Europe	15½–12½	USA	The Belfry
2004	Europe	18½–9½	USA	Oakland Hills
2006	Europe	18½–9½	USA	K Club
2008	Europe	11½–16½	USA	Valhalla
2010	Europe	14½–13½	USA	Celtic Manor
2012	Europe	14½–13½	USA	Medinah (No 3)
2014	Europe	16½–11½	USA	Gleneagles Hotel
2016	Europe	11–17	USA	Hazeltine National
2018	Europe	17½–10½	USA	Le Golf National
2021	Europe	9-19	USA	Whistling Straits

SOLHEIM CUP — ROLL OF HONOUR

1990	Europe	4½–11½	USA	Lake Nona
1992	Europe	11½–6½	USA	Dalmahoy
1994	Europe	7–13	USA	The Greenbrier
1996	Europe	11–17	USA	St Pierre
1998	Europe	12–16	USA	Muirfield Village
2000	Europe	14½–11½	USA	Loch Lomond
2002	Europe	12½–15½	USA	Interlachen
2003	Europe	17½–10½	USA	Barseback
2005	Europe	12½–15½	USA	Crooked Stick
2007	Europe	12–16	USA	Halmstad
2009	Europe	12–16	USA	Rich Harvest Farms
2011	Europe	15–13	USA	Killeen Castle
2013	Europe	18–10	USA	Colorado
2015	Europe	13½–14½	USA	St Leon-Rot
2017	Europe	11½–16½	USA	Des Moines
2019	Europe	14½–13½	USA	Gleneagles Hotel
2021	Europe	15-13	USA	Inverness

The Tours

PGA Tour

Nothing summed up the 2021-22 PGA Tour season better than its last day: take nothing for granted. Scottie Scheffler, world number one, had been leading the FedEx Cup standings for 24 weeks. He was the number one seed for the Tour Championship and led by six strokes with one round to play. Then Rory McIlroy happened to him. McIlroy scored 66, Scheffler 73. The Northern Irishman won by one from Scheffler and Sungjae Im, claiming the $18 million bonus. "Incredible," McIlroy said. Under the starting strokes scoring system, he had started six behind Scheffler, then had a triple bogey at his opening hole of the tournament and a bogey at the next. "I was 10 behind on the third tee on Thursday," McIlroy marvelled, "I guess it just shows you anything's possible."

Graciously, he apologised to Scheffler's parents for stealing the FedEx Cup away from their son. "He deserves it," McIlroy said of Scheffler. "He's had an unbelievable year." Scheffler's dad, Scott, replied: "So did you. Good playing."

Both had a point. This was McIlroy's second win of the season. He had defended his title at the RBC Canadian Open from 2019 after the event was cancelled for two years due to the Covid pandemic. And he went on to defend at the CJ Cup later in the year. He was close in all the majors, but without winning, or necessarily having a chance to win. But the consistency was back and, so too, his ability to generate excitement. After that CJ Cup win, he regained the world number one title and went on to win the DP World Tour points list, doing a double that only Henrik Stenson had previously achieved.

Yet when the players of the PGA Tour came to vote for their Player of the Year for 2021-22, from McIlroy, Scheffler and Cameron Smith, the Players and Open champion, it was Scheffler, as McIlroy had intimated, who ended up with the Jack Nicklaus Award. It made a unique treble for Scheffler that demonstrated the Texan's rapid rise. He was the Korn Ferry Tour Player of the Year in 2019 and won the Arnold Palmer Award as the Rookie of the Year on the PGA Tour in 2020. In 2021 he was unbeaten on his Ryder Cup debut at Whistling Straits, taking down Europe's hottest player, Jon Rahm, in the singles.

So it was a surprise that he had not yet won entering 2022. He had been a runner-up four times before holing a 25-footer at the third playoff hole to beat Patrick Cantlay, the 2021 FedEx Cup winner, at the WM Phoenix Open. It was his 71st event on the PGA Tour and he had trailed by nine strokes going into the weekend. It started the run of his life. Four wins in six starts. He won the Arnold Palmer Invitational at Bay Hill, then the WGC World Match Play, where he became the world number one. He had gone from contender to the world's best in barely more than a month, no wonder he could hardly believe what was happening to him. He was running out of dreams to fulfil, but not of wins, donning the green jacket after a dominant performance at Augusta National.

Then, after the four runners-up, and the four wins, four more runners-up. He lost a playoff to Sam Burns at Colonial, was a stroke shy of Matt Fitzpatrick at the US Open, then to McIlroy at East Lake. He ended the year finishing second to Viktor Hovland at the unofficial Hero World Challenge. On the 2021-22 season as a whole, he had 11 top-10 finishes and topped the money list with a record $14 million, not including various bonuses.

Cameron Young, the son of a club pro from New York, attended Wake Forest, Palmer's alma mater, so it was fitting he received the Palmer Award after being voted the Rookie of the Year. Finally, he had won something. He had so many near misses. No one had had as many as five runner-up finishes since Vijay Singh in 2003. He was also third twice, including at the PGA Championship. At St Andrews, he eagled the 72nd hole to finish second to Smith in The 150th Open. Young was 19th in the FedEx Cup, but finished 10th on the money list, even with a "W". Sahith Theegala also made it to the Tour Championship as a rookie, and also came close to winning, particularly in Phoenix, then finishing runner-up to Xander Schauffele at the Travelers Championship.

That was a relief for Schauffele as he had not won an individual PGA Tour event for over three years. He did win Olympic gold in 2021 in Tokyo, then joined with Cantlay to claim the Zurich Classic as a pair. Schauffele also won the Genesis Scottish Open, co-sanctioned with the DP World Tour for the first time, as were the Barbasol and Barracuda tournaments. Third place at the Scottish helped Joohyung Kim become a temporary member of the PGA Tour and he recovered from a quadruple bogey at the first hole of the Wyndham Championship to win. At the Shriners later in the year, he became the first player since Tiger Woods to have two victories before the age of 21.

By then he was known as "Tom", from a childhood nickname, and had helped spark a Saturday revival for the International team at the Presidents Cup. It was not enough to stop yet another USA victory, but Kim was becoming a new star. The International team was not helped by losing their best player, Smith, just weeks ahead of the event after the Australian opted to join LIV Golf. It was still an historic year for Smith. He set a new PGA Tour record of 34 under par in winning the Sentry Tournament of Champions to start the year. He produced an incredible display of short-game prowess in winning the Players Championship, then conjured up a scintillating back nine of 30 on the Old Course to win at St Andrews.

Jay Monahan, commissioner of the PGA Tour, suspended all players who joined LIV Golf, while some resigned their membership. Those players that remained met in a Delaware hotel during the week of the BMW Championship and Monahan later announced a raft of significant changes to the PGA Tour season. The leading players committed to appearing in a series of what became known as "designated" events, starting with the Sentry Tournament of Champions and including the Genesis Invitational, the Arnold Palmer Invitational and the Memorial Tournament, the WGC Dell Match Play, the WM Phoenix Open, the RBC Heritage, Wells Fargo Championship, Travelers Championship, and the FedEx St Jude Championship, the BMW Championship and the Tour Championship. Purses would be in the region of $20 million, while the Players Championship was set to increase to $25 million. Players agreed to appear in them all bar one of their own choosing. Monahan also stated that from 2024 the FedEx Cup would run from January to August, in a change from the current wraparound season. Monahan went on to describe changes to the Player Impact Program, and introduced an earnings assurance scheme for members.

"Our top players are firmly behind the tour," Monahan said, "helping us deliver an unmatched product to our fans, who will be all but guaranteed to see the best players competing against each other in 20 events or more throughout the season. Every single member of the PGA Tour is going to benefit from the changes that we're going to be making."

2022 SCHEDULE

Sentry Tournament of Champions	**Cameron Smith**	
Sony Open	**Hideki Matsuyama**	
The American Express	**Hudson Swafford**	
Farmers Insurance Open	**Luke List**	
AT&T Pebble Beach Pro-Am	**Tom Hoge**	
WM Phoenix Open	**Scottie Scheffler**	
Genesis Invitational	**Joaquin Niemann**	
Honda Classic	**Sepp Straka**	
Arnold Palmer Invitational	**Scottie Scheffler (2)**	
Puerto Rico Open	**Ryan Brehm**	
The Players Championship	**Cameron Smith (2)**	
Valspar Championship	**Sam Burns**	
WGC Dell Technologies Match Play	**Scottie Scheffler (3)**	
Corales Puntacana Championship	**Chad Ramey**	
Valero Texas Open	**JJ Spaun**	
Masters Tournament	**Scottie Scheffler (4)**	*See chapter 2*
RBC Heritage	**Jordan Spieth**	
Zurich Classic	**Patrick Cantlay/Xander Schauffele**	
Mexico Open	**Jon Rahm**	
Wells Fargo Championship	**Max Homa**	
AT&T Byron Nelson	**Kyoung-Hoon Lee**	
PGA Championship	**Justin Thomas**	*See chapter 3*
Charles Schwab Challenge	**Sam Burns (2)**	
Memorial Tournament	**Billy Horschel**	

RBC Canadian Open	**Rory McIlroy**	
US Open	**Matt Fitzpatrick**	*See chapter 5*
Travelers Championship	**Xander Schauffele (2)**	
John Deere Classic	**JT Poston**	
Genesis Scottish Open	**Xander Schauffele (3)**	*See chapter 14*
Barbasol Championship	**Trey Mullinax**	
The 150th Open	**Cameron Smith (3)**	*See chapter 7*
Barracuda Championship	**Chez Reavie**	
3M Open	**Tony Finau**	
Rocket Mortgage Classic	**Tony Finau (2)**	
Wyndham Championship	**Joohyung Kim (1,2)**	
FedEx St Jude Championship	**Will Zalatoris**	
BMW Championship	**Patrick Cantlay (2)**	
Tour Championship	**Rory McIlroy (2)**	
Fortinet Championship	**Max Homa (2)**	
Presidents Cup	**USA**	
Sanderson Farms Championship	**Mackenzie Hughes**	
Shriners Children's Open	**Joohyung Kim (2,3)**	
Zozo Championship	**Keegan Bradley**	
CJ Cup	**Rory McIlroy (3)**	
Butterfield Bermuda Championship	**Seamus Power**	
World Wide Technology Championship	**Russell Henley**	
Cadence Bank Houston Open	**Tony Finau (3)**	
RSM Classic	**Adam Svensson**	
TaylorMade Pebble Beach Invitational*	**Parker Coody (1,2)**	
Hero World Challenge*	**Viktor Hovland (1,2)**	
QBE Shootout*	**Tom Hoge (2)/Sahith Theegala**	
PNC Championship*	**Vijay Singh/Qass Singh** (A)	
**unofficial event*		

Sentry Tournament of Champions

A no-cut shootout for 38 PGA Tour winners, the Sentry Tournament of Champions was an absolute thrashing in paradise. Consider that big-hitting Jason Kokrak shot a seven-under 285 at the par-73 Kapalua's Plantation course, and finished 38th and dead last. This when the leaders were shooting subterranean lows. Consider that Spain's Jon Rahm, world number one and in his first competition since October, made a tournament-high 32 birdies, shot 33-under 259 — and finished second.

And then there was Australia's Cameron Smith, who led for three rounds, tied with Rahm for the lead in the third, then beat him by a stroke. Smith shot 65-64-64-65 for 258, 34 under, and the frustrated Rahm 66-66-61-66. "Mate, it was intense," said Smith. "It was pretty crazy." It was his second individual tour victory, to go with two team wins.

"Those first six holes today," Rahm said (five pars, one birdie), "should have been a little bit better." Only three times in tour history had anyone posted 30 under or lower. Ernie Els shot 31 under, winning by eight in 2003, and Jordan Spieth, 30 under, winning by eight in 2016, both in the TOC at Kapalua, and Dustin Johnson, 30 under and winning by 11 in the 2020 Northern Trust at Liberty National. Three broke 30 under this time alone: Smith, Rahm, and Matt Jones, third at 32-under 260 with a stunning 62-61 finish.

The scoring feast began with the opening bell, with 22 of the 38 players breaking 70, led by Smith's 65 sparked by eagles at two par-fives, from 44 feet at the fifth and 37 at 15. "Yeah, I just needed those two eagles to get a really low one happening," he said. He led by one over Rahm and Patrick Cantlay.

Smith started the second round bogey-bogey, eagled number five again, this time from 35 feet, and birdied nine of the last 13 holes for a 64, and led by three over Rahm and Daniel Berger. The third round was merely incandescent. Smith played his last 14 holes in nine under, shot a flawless 64, and gave up three shots. "We had a fun battle today," is the way Rahm put it. After two early birdies and a bogey, Rahm birdied five straight from the seventh, then from 14 finished birdie-eagle-birdie-birdie-birdie for a 12-under 61, tying Smith for the lead at 26 under. Berger, with a third 66, was five behind.

As things turned out, the decisive point in the final round was Smith holing a five-footer for birdie at the fourth. That would be the stroke he won by. It put him one ahead of Rahm, and he led the rest of the way. They matched birdies at 13, 14 and 15, and pars at 16 and 17. At the par-five 18th, both barely missed the green. Smith, putting from 90 feet, came up three feet short, and Rahm's eagle putt from 50 feet missed on the high side. Both birdied, Rahm for a 66, Smith for a 65. And to shoot 33 under and lose? "I have every reason to be smiling," Rahm said. "It's a bittersweet moment." Said Smith: "Unreal round. Something I'll never forget."

Kapalua Resort (Plantation), Maui, Hawaii — January 6-9
Par 73 (36-37); 7,596 yards — Purse: $8,200,000

1	**Cameron Smith**	65	64	64	65	258	$1,476,000
2	**Jon Rahm**	66	66	61	66	259	810,000
3	**Matt Jones**	70	67	62	61	260	515,000
4	Patrick Cantlay	66	67	66	67	266	400,000
5	Daniel Berger	66	66	66	69	267	286,000
	Collin Morikawa	68	70	67	62	267	286,000
	Justin Thomas	74	67	61	65	267	286,000
8	Sungjae Im	67	67	65	69	268	217,500
	Kevin Kisner	69	68	66	65	268	217,500
10	Cam Davis	69	68	66	66	269	188,000
	Marc Leishman	69	67	65	68	269	188,000
12	Xander Schauffele	69	67	68	66	270	170,000
13	Hideki Matsuyama	69	65	68	69	271	155,000
	Kevin Na	67	68	68	68	271	155,000
15	Talor Gooch	68	70	67	67	272	132,500
	Max Homa	72	67	65	68	272	132,500
	Seamus Power	71	65	69	67	272	132,500
	Patrick Reed	74	64	66	68	272	132,500
19	Sam Burns	72	64	68	69	273	123,000
	Tony Finau	70	69	69	65	273	123,000
21	Stewart Cink	69	67	67	71	274	119,000
	Jordan Spieth	71	69	68	66	274	119,000
23	Billy Horschel	72	67	70	66	275	115,500
	Si Woo Kim	71	65	69	70	275	115,500
25	Bryson DeChambeau	69	68	67	72	276	113,000
	Garrick Higgo	68	69	69	70	276	113,000
	Erik van Rooyen	67	70	70	69	276	113,000
28	Joel Dahmen	68	69	69	71	277	110,500
	Brooks Koepka	68	68	72	69	277	110,500
30	Harris English	73	70	68	67	278	108,000
	Viktor Hovland	69	69	73	67	278	108,000
	Phil Mickelson	71	69	70	68	278	108,000
33	Branden Grace	69	69	74	67	279	105,500
	Kyoung-Hoon Lee	72	71	69	67	279	105,500
35	Abraham Ancer	72	69	71	70	282	103,500
	Lucas Glover	74	69	70	69	282	103,500
37	Lucas Herbert	69	73	68	74	284	102,000
38	Jason Kokrak	72	70	72	71	285	101,000

Sony Open

Hideki Matsuyama got off one final shot in the Sony Open, and it had to be described, inevitably, as one of the best shots he never saw. And it set up his victory. It came on the first hole of a playoff against Russell Henley at Waialae's par-five 18th. Matsuyama had hit his three-wood off the tee and then came the shot in question. He hit the three-wood again for his approach, a cut shot from 276 yards, "following the wind," he said, but dead into a dazzling January sun that he couldn't block even with a raised hand. But the erupting gallery told him where his ball ended up: three feet from the flag. Henley caught a fairway bunker and bogeyed. Matsuyama made the eagle and had his eighth win on the PGA Tour, tying Korea's KJ Choi for the most by an Asian-born player.

But first, there was something else Matsuyama couldn't see, figuratively speaking: how could he possibly come from five shots behind with only nine holes to play? But he did. Then Matsuyama, noted for his economy of expression, explained through an interpreter: "I got on a roll." Henley, who won the 2013 Sony Open in his rookie debut and was on the verge of winning this one, was the unfortunate victim. "It stings," he said. "I played some great golf. I didn't have too many mental lapses like I have other tournaments where I've been close to the lead."

Matsuyama, the 2021 Masters champion, rallied down the final nine, erased that five-shot deficit and caught Henley, who had stalled out. Matsuyama shot the par-70 Waialae in 66-65-63-63 and Henley in 62-63-67-65. They tied at 23-under 257.

The first disappointment fell to Kevin Na in the first round, after his career-fifth 61. "I tell you, I had a chance for a 59," said Na. "My iron play was amazing. I'm a little disappointed." He led by one over Jim Furyk and Henley, but cooled and would tie for 20th. It became Henley's show after a two-eagle 63 in the second round. Matsuyama trailed by six, then needed just 25 putts in Saturday's 63 to close within two.

Henley raced into the turn in 29 with four birdies and an eagle at the par-five ninth from three feet. Matsuyama answered with three birdies in the seven-foot range and so Henley was leading by five with nine to play. Then Henley hit a wall. He bogeyed the par-three 11th out of a bunker and parred in. Matsuyama picked up a shot at 10 with a birdie from seven feet, two more with a birdie from 12 feet at the next, then made two more birdies, on an 18-footer at the 15th and a two-putt birdie at the 18th for his second 63.

Then came Matsuyama's eagle in the playoff. To commemorate it? "I'll have my share of sake tonight," Matsuyama said.

Waialae Country Club, Honolulu, Hawaii — January 13-16
Par 70 (35-35); 7,044 yards — Purse: $7,500,000

1	**Hideki Matsuyama**	66	65	63	63	257	$1,350,000
2	**Russell Henley**	62	63	67	65	257	817,500
	Matsuyama won playoff at first extra hole						
3	**Kevin Kisner**	68	64	65	64	261	442,500
	Seamus Power	63	68	65	65	261	442,500
5	Lucas Glover	67	66	64	65	262	289,688
	Michael Thompson	63	67	69	63	262	289,688
7	Russell Knox	67	67	64	65	263	227,813
	Matt Kuchar	64	65	67	67	263	227,813
	Keith Mitchell	67	68	65	63	263	227,813
	Adam Svensson	64	67	65	67	263	227,813
11	Corey Conners	64	67	69	64	264	189,375
12	Keegan Bradley	69	65	66	65	265	148,875
	Hayden Buckley	67	66	67	65	265	148,875
	Satoshi Kodaira	71	64	65	65	265	148,875
	Haotong Li	63	65	68	69	265	148,875
	Ryan Palmer	64	68	68	65	265	148,875
17	Christiaan Bezuidenhout	65	69	65	67	266	114,375
	Jason Kokrak	64	68	67	67	266	114,375
	Vince Whaley	66	67	69	64	266	114,375
20	Ryan Armour	71	63	68	65	267	79,018
	Joseph Bramlett	68	66	69	64	267	79,018
	Davis Riley	65	66	69	67	267	79,018
	Erik van Rooyen	66	68	69	64	267	79,018
	Dylan Wu	65	66	70	66	267	79,018
	Kramer Hickok	66	69	65	67	267	79,018
	Kevin Na	61	71	67	68	267	79,018
27	Wesley Bryan	67	65	69	67	268	49,250
	Cam Davis	66	66	66	70	268	49,250
	Luke Donald	68	65	67	68	268	49,250
	Talor Gooch	67	66	66	69	268	49,250
	Chris Kirk	66	65	71	66	268	49,250
	Ben Kohles	68	67	64	69	268	49,250
	Maverick McNealy	65	67	70	66	268	49,250
	Andrew Putnam	68	67	66	67	268	49,250
	Kyle Stanley	66	67	69	66	268	49,250
36	Stewart Cink	68	63	70	68	269	35,700
	Billy Horschel	65	67	70	67	269	35,700
	Charles Howell III	69	63	71	66	269	35,700
	Marc Leishman	67	68	68	66	269	35,700
	Brandt Snedeker	66	65	68	70	269	35,700
41	Keita Nakajima (A)	67	64	72	67	270	
42	Jim Furyk	62	72	72	65	271	27,375
	Patton Kizzire	63	68	72	68	271	27,375
	JT Poston	64	69	72	66	271	27,375
	Greyson Sigg	67	66	68	70	271	27,375
	Sepp Straka	66	67	73	65	271	27,375
	Vaughn Taylor	65	70	69	67	271	27,375
48	Paul Barjon	66	68	71	67	272	19,639
	Brian Harman	67	68	69	68	272	19,639
	Denny McCarthy	71	64	71	66	272	19,639
	Hudson Swafford	68	67	70	67	272	19,639
	Kyoung-Hoon Lee	69	66	69	68	272	19,639
	Sahith Theegala	65	69	69	69	272	19,639
	Brendon Todd	67	66	70	69	272	19,639
55	Kevin Chappell	63	72	70	68	273	17,400
	Brett Drewitt	68	67	69	69	273	17,400
	Harris English	66	67	69	71	273	17,400
	Si Woo Kim	68	66	69	70	273	17,400
	Jim Knous	68	67	68	70	273	17,400
	Henrik Norlander	68	67	70	68	273	17,400
61	Webb Simpson	67	68	71	69	275	16,800
	Kevin Tway	66	67	71	71	275	16,800
63	Sam Ryder	68	67	72	69	276	16,575
64	Justin Lower	67	67	74	69	277	16,425
65	Jimmy Walker	69	66	71	72	278	16,275

The American Express

Golfers often speak of inspiration and strength drawn from loved ones who had passed away. For Hudson Swafford, in The American Express, there seemed to be something even stronger. He spoke of a spiritual experience so intense, it perhaps could be described as almost a vision of his late father David Swafford, who had passed away just some six weeks earlier, at age 83. As he described it, it was especially powerful when he was coming down the final stretch.

"So I had a couple moments where I looked up and knew that he was following and knew that he was there," Swafford said, "and I could just hear his voice saying, 'Just be confident in what you're doing, you're playing great,' and he goes, 'Just play to win'."

Swafford, on a 70, trailed by a whopping eight strokes after the first round on the La Quinta course, and got to within five with a 65 at the Nicklaus course in the second. He played the last two rounds on the Stadium course, closing to within three with a 66 in the third, then fought his way into a logjam in the final round. And then running out of holes, he had to fight his way out. Which he did, with a fireworks finish — eagle-birdie-clutch par for a 64 and 23-under-par 265, beating Tom Hoge (68) by two for his second Amex win in five years and his third tour win overall.

If Swafford's finish was spiritual and poignant, what to make of his baffling start to the fourth round? Trailing rookies Lee Hodges and Paul Barjon by three, he opened the finale with a bogey, and was thrilled. "I had all the confidence in the world," he said. "And there was just something about bogeying the first hole here for me on Sunday that gets me in my comfort zone. But I just felt like I was going to win today. I didn't know how, I didn't know what I was going to do or how it was going to happen, but I just had a crazy good feeling."

How crazy? After his opening bogey, Swafford birdied seven of the next 11 holes, plunging deep into the chase. He bogeyed the par-three 13th, three-putting from 50 feet, birdied 14 from 10 feet, and bogeyed 15 after missing the green, and was tied with Brian Harman and Francesco Molinari at 20 under. He burst into the lead at the par-five 16th, firing his seven-iron approach to eight feet and getting the eagle. At the par-three 17th — "Alcatraz" with its island green ringed by rocks, not water — he rolled in a 20-footer for birdie. At the par-four 18th, he saved par with an eight-foot putt and saluted his dad. "One of the best people I know, and he taught me everything I know," Swafford said. "How to be a dad, how to be a friend, how to be a champion ..."

PGA West (Stadium), La Quinta, California — January 20-23
Par 72 (36-36); 7,158 yards — Purse: $7,600,000
PGA West (Nicklaus Tournament) (R1-3) par 72 (36-36); 7,147 yards
La Quinta Country Club (R1-3) par 72 (36-36); 7,060 yards

1	**Hudson Swafford**	70	65	66	64	265	$1,368,000
2	**Tom Hoge**	65	66	68	68	267	828,400
3	**Lanto Griffin**	67	65	69	67	268	402,800
	Brian Harman	67	70	67	64	268	402,800
	Lee Hodges	62	72	64	70	268	402,800
6	Denny McCarthy	67	67	68	67	269	256,500
	Francesco Molinari	67	67	67	68	269	256,500
	Will Zalatoris	71	61	70	67	269	256,500
9	Patrick Cantlay	62	68	72	68	270	222,300
10	Paul Barjon	66	67	65	73	271	207,100
11	Sungjae Im	69	67	70	66	272	184,300
	Si Woo Kim	68	68	69	67	272	184,300
13	Wyndham Clark	65	69	69	70	273	161,500
14	Russell Henley	67	70	70	67	274	119,700
	Zach Johnson	67	66	72	69	274	119,700
	David Lipsky	67	68	69	70	274	119,700
	Seamus Power	65	69	66	74	274	119,700
	Andrew Putnam	70	66	70	68	274	119,700
	Jon Rahm	66	70	67	71	274	119,700
	Roger Sloan	66	67	71	70	274	119,700
	Brandt Snedeker	65	69	71	69	274	119,700
22	Patton Kizzire	67	67	71	70	275	79,420
	Luke List	70	70	66	69	275	79,420
	Harold Varner III	68	66	67	74	275	79,420
25	Adam Hadwin	68	72	68	68	276	55,955
	Charles Howell III	69	68	68	71	276	55,955
	JT Poston	69	69	69	69	276	55,955
	Scottie Scheffler	69	70	70	67	276	55,955
	Greyson Sigg	65	67	73	71	276	55,955
	Alex Smalley	67	70	69	70	276	55,955
	JJ Spaun	75	67	67	67	276	55,955
	Stephen Stallings Jr	69	67	73	67	276	55,955
33	Joseph Bramlett	65	67	72	73	277	39,683
	Lucas Glover	66	69	69	73	277	39,683
	Justin Rose	68	73	67	69	277	39,683
	Camilo Villegas	69	68	70	70	277	39,683
	Jared Wolfe	70	65	72	70	277	39,683
	Nick Taylor	69	69	71	68	277	39,683
	Sahith Theegala	72	62	68	75	277	39,683
40	Abraham Ancer	67	71	70	70	278	27,014
	Christiaan Bezuidenhout	66	72	68	72	278	27,014
	Jason Dufner	70	67	71	70	278	27,014
	Tony Finau	72	70	67	69	278	27,014
	Graeme McDowell	66	69	73	70	278	27,014
	Patrick Rodgers	70	68	69	71	278	27,014
	Vince Whaley	70	64	74	70	278	27,014
	Harry Higgs	66	68	67	77	278	27,014
	Cameron Young	64	68	69	77	278	27,014
49	Sam Ryder	65	68	73	73	279	18,949
	Sepp Straka	67	69	72	71	279	18,949
	Bronson Burgoon	66	70	73	70	279	18,949
	Jason Day	67	75	67	70	279	18,949
	Hank Lebioda	68	69	71	71	279	18,949
	Adam Svensson	69	67	68	75	279	18,949
55	Kevin Chappell	67	69	72	72	280	17,632
	Michael Gligic	68	68	72	72	280	17,632
	Patrick Reed	71	70	68	71	280	17,632
	Martin Trainer	66	71	68	75	280	17,632
59	Doug Ghim	67	68	73	73	281	17,024
	Trey Mullinax	70	68	71	72	281	17,024
	Aaron Rai	67	67	72	75	281	17,024
	Davis Riley	66	69	68	78	281	17,024
63	Emiliano Grillo	71	65	73	73	282	16,492
	Kyoung-Hoon Lee	64	71	71	76	282	16,492
	Henrik Norlander	69	67	73	73	282	16,492
66	Anirban Lahiri	69	67	72	75	283	16,188
67	Nick Hardy	68	71	68	77	284	15,884
	Taylor Moore	66	70	72	76	284	15,884
	Seung-Yul Noh	68	71	70	75	284	15,884
70	Brice Garnett	68	71	69	77	285	15,580

Farmers Insurance Open

Luke List was under orders, more or less. Happily for him, his little girl didn't want the universe. Merely a bauble from where daddy worked. Even though where daddy worked, playing the PGA Tour, getting the universe might be easier. "She's been telling me for a long time, 'Daddy, I want a trophy'," List explained. He further explained that to his three-year-old, a trophy might not be so much a nice, shiny symbol of victory as a receptacle that could contain candy.

At any rate, Ryann List this time wanted the trophy at the Farmers Insurance Open, being played at Torrey Pines. Where, on this occasion, Bryson DeChambeau, Rickie Fowler, Brooks Koepka, Phil Mickelson and Jordan Spieth were among those who missed the cut.

And so List lifted that trophy, beating Will Zalatoris on the first hole of a playoff. And a historic moment it was, List's first win in his 206th start. "I really believed I could win on this course," he said. But his figures hardly suggested as much. He opened with 67 on Torrey South and trailed Billy Horschel by four strokes. He shot the North in 68 in the second and was four behind the trio of Adam Schenk (62), Jon Rahm (65) and Justin Thomas (63). Worse, back on the South, List shot 72 in the third and was five behind Jason Day (67) and Zalatoris (65).

Then Saturday's final round (avoiding a clash with the NFL on Sunday): List birdied four straight from the third, birdied 12, holing out from a bunker, and closed birdie-bogey-birdie, underlining his performance with a 13-footer at the 18th for a 66, a 15-under total of 273 and the nerve-racking clubhouse lead.

Well, List had waited long enough for that first win — since 2013. A little longer wouldn't hurt. So he settled in the dining room with his wife Chloe, and Ryann and seven-month-old Harrison to sweat out the last eight groups. And he did sweat. Zalatoris had a frustrating day. After a birdie at number six, he parred all the way home, barely missing a winning eight-foot birdie putt at the 18th. He shot 71 and tied List at 273. Three others fell a shot short of the tie. Jon Rahm (71) bogeyed the 15th out of a greenside bunker, Jason Day (72) bogeyed 16 and 17, and Cameron Tringale cooled off to a 70.

The playoff, at the par-five 18th, was brief and to the point. List and Zalatoris both hit their tee shots into a fairway bunker, both escaped. Then List lofted a 131-yard wedge shot to within a foot of the cup. Zalatoris missed his 13-foot birdie putt and List tapped in for that precious first victory. "I fought like hell all day," Zalatoris said.

And List lifted his first trophy. But it wasn't a shiny cup. It was a carving of the endangered Torrey pine he showed to his little daughter. "This doesn't look like you can fit any candy in here," List said. "But she was happy. She said, 'Oh, flowers!'"

Torrey Pines Golf Course (South), San Diego, California — January 26-29
Par 72 (36-36); 7,765 yards — Purse: $8,400,000
Torrey Pines North (R1&2) par 72 (36-36); 7,258 yards

1	**Luke List**	67	68	72	66	273	$1,512,000
2	**Will Zalatoris**	69	68	65	71	273	915,600
	List won playoff at first extra hole						
3	**Jason Day**	70	65	67	72	274	445,200
	Jon Rahm	66	65	72	71	274	445,200
	Cameron Tringale	67	65	72	70	274	445,200
6	Sungjae Im	70	66	68	71	275	265,020
	Joaquin Niemann	69	68	71	67	275	265,020
	Pat Perez	72	68	67	68	275	265,020
	Aaron Rai	67	68	68	72	275	265,020
	Justin Rose	67	71	69	68	275	265,020
11	Billy Horschel	63	73	69	71	276	180,180
	Si Woo Kim	71	64	70	71	276	180,180
	Taylor Montgomery	72	64	71	69	276	180,180
	Austin Smotherman	67	71	72	66	276	180,180
	Michael Thompson	64	73	70	69	276	180,180
16	Marc Leishman	71	67	69	70	277	132,300
	Ryan Palmer	67	69	69	72	277	132,300
	Taylor Pendrith	67	71	68	71	277	132,300
	Sepp Straka	73	66	67	71	277	132,300
20	Daniel Berger	67	72	68	71	278	95,508
	Talor Gooch	73	66	72	67	278	95,508
	Scottie Scheffler	70	67	70	71	278	95,508
	Justin Thomas	68	63	73	74	278	95,508
	Cameron Young	67	74	64	73	278	95,508
25	Dustin Johnson	68	69	69	73	279	65,940
	Peter Malnati	67	66	73	73	279	65,940
	Mito Pereira	69	69	70	71	279	65,940
	Doc Redman	74	63	72	70	279	65,940
	Sahith Theegala	67	68	73	71	279	65,940
30	Lanto Griffin	73	68	74	65	280	53,760
	Hideki Matsuyama	72	67	73	68	280	53,760
	Maverick McNealy	67	71	67	75	280	53,760
	Nick Taylor	73	65	71	71	280	53,760
34	Doug Ghim	66	73	71	71	281	43,764
	Matthew NeSmith	68	71	69	73	281	43,764
	Xander Schauffele	68	72	69	72	281	43,764
	Greyson Sigg	72	68	72	69	281	43,764
	JJ Spaun	73	66	71	71	281	43,764
39	Bill Haas	67	69	70	76	282	33,180

	Sebastian Munoz	74	65	70	73	282	33,180
	Alex Noren	70	69	71	72	282	33,180
	Chad Ramey	71	67	73	71	282	33,180
	Kevin Streelman	70	71	69	72	282	33,180
	Jhonattan Vegas	71	69	71	71	282	33,180
	Gary Woodland	72	68	69	73	282	33,180
46	Christiaan Bezuidenhout	69	69	72	73	283	22,008
	Cameron Champ	75	65	70	73	283	22,008
	Kevin Chappell	73	68	73	69	283	22,008
	Anirban Lahiri	71	70	72	70	283	22,008
	Martin Laird	67	74	70	72	283	22,008
	Hank Lebioda	74	67	72	70	283	22,008
	Patrick Reed	72	66	72	73	283	22,008
	Scott Stallings	69	72	76	66	283	22,008
	Kevin Tway	65	74	72	72	283	22,008
	Jimmy Walker	69	70	69	75	283	22,008
56	Wyndham Clark	69	72	72	71	284	19,152
	Cam Davis	68	72	71	73	284	19,152
	David Lipsky	68	73	74	69	284	19,152
	Adam Schenk	69	62	75	78	284	19,152
	Alex Smalley	73	62	76	73	284	19,152
	Robert Streb	67	73	68	76	284	19,152
62	Francesco Molinari	66	72	73	74	285	18,480
	Patrick Rodgers	71	69	71	74	285	18,480
64	Matthew Wolff	71	70	71	74	286	18,228
65	Keegan Bradley	70	70	71	76	287	17,976
	Adam Long	72	69	73	73	287	17,976
67	Joseph Bramlett	73	66	71	78	288	17,556
	Curtis Thompson	70	71	72	75	288	17,556
	Camilo Villegas	70	69	73	76	288	17,556
70	Andrew Novak	71	70	77	71	289	16,968
	Carlos Ortiz	72	69	75	73	289	16,968
	Chez Reavie	70	70	73	76	289	16,968
	Rory Sabbatini	71	68	73	77	289	16,968
74	Bronson Burgoon	70	70	74	76	290	16,464
	Seung-Yul Noh	73	68	74	75	290	16,464
76	Scott Piercy	72	66	76	78	292	16,212
77	Michael Gligic	67	74	75	77	293	16,044
78	CT Pan	67	72	77	79	295	15,876
79	Adam Svensson	72	69	79	78	298	15,708

AT&T Pebble Beach Pro-Am

"I'm almost a little in shock," Tom Hoge was saying, on winning the AT&T Pebble Beach Pro-Am. "It's been so long since I won anything that I forgot how to celebrate." Actually, this was his first victory on the PGA Tour. "I won a couple mini-tour events since 2011, when I turned professional," he said, "but nothing like this."

But Hoge had smelled victory. He was the runner-up twice in his previous 202 tour starts, the second time just two weeks earlier at The American Express. In the AT&T, played at three courses, he caught the sweet aroma again, first when he led the first round, and then, in the final round, when he broke out of a logjam and took the lead for the last two holes. When Beau Hossler couldn't catch him at the final hole, leaving him the winner, instead of high-fiving he quietly made his way to his wife and hugged her. "It was a tough grind out there," Hoge would say. "But I hung in there really well."

Hoge opened spectacularly, holing a 30-foot birdie putt at the 10th and added a 40-footer at the eighth, his 17th, for a one-stroke lead on a flawless nine-under 63 at Pebble Beach. He followed with a two-under 69 at Monterey Peninsula, a four-under 68 at Spyglass Hill and came from behind with a 68 in the finale at Pebble to win by two at 19-under 268.

Ireland's Seamus Power took the second-round lead with a second 64, this at Pebble, for a tournament-record 16-under 128, and led Hoge by five, in relation to par. The third round ended up in a traffic jam, but not before Jordan Spieth stole the show with a death-defying cliffhanger of a shot at Pebble's notorious seaside eighth. His drive ended up at the edge of the cliff overlooking the yawning chasm. Ignoring a safe penalty drop, his caddie's pleas and his own misgivings, he opted to hit from there, which meant his left foot was perched just scant inches from a 70-foot plunge to the rocks below. Spieth slashed a seven-iron, then recoiled and dashed back to safety. He carried the abyss, 162 yards, but missed the green, chipped on and holed a 12-foot putt for, if not the greatest par ever at number eight, certainly the most dramatic "Not worth it, to be honest," Spieth was to say.

Then Spieth dominated the last 10 holes for a 63 to lie a stroke out of the three-way tie for the lead at 15 under held by Hoge, and Hossler (65) and Andrew Putnam (68). Things got more complicated in the grand finale, with seven players taking at least a share of the lead. Hoge stumbled through the front nine on three birdies, a bogey and a double bogey. Then he surged to four birdies coming in, catching Spieth with a tap-in at the 16th after narrowly missing a hole-out eagle. The clincher came at the par-three 17th. Spieth bogeyed out of a bunker and would close with a 69, two back. Hoge birdied 17 from 22 feet for the win.

Pebble Beach Golf Links, Pebble Beach, California
Par 72 (36-36); 6,972 yards
Spyglass Hill Golf Club (R1-3) par 72 (36-36); 7,042 yards
Monterey Peninsula Country Club (Shore) (R1-3) par 71 (34-37); 6,957 yards

February 3-6
Purse: $8,700,000

1	**Tom Hoge**	63	69	68	68	268	$1,566,000
2	**Jordan Spieth**	68	70	63	69	270	948,300
3	**Beau Hossler**	70	65	65	71	271	600,300
4	Patrick Cantlay	65	68	68	71	272	391,500
	Troy Merritt	68	67	70	67	272	391,500
6	Joel Dahmen	71	64	66	72	273	293,625
	Matt Fitzpatrick	69	67	69	68	273	293,625
	Andrew Putnam	65	67	68	73	273	293,625
9	Jonathan Byrd	66	72	69	67	274	237,075
	Pat Perez	70	67	69	68	274	237,075
	Seamus Power	64	64	74	72	274	237,075
12	Denny McCarthy	68	70	66	71	275	193,575
	Keith Mitchell	69	68	68	70	275	193,575
14	Christiaan Bezuidenhout	71	70	66	69	276	163,125
	Nick Taylor	69	69	69	69	276	163,125
16	Robert Garrigus	74	65	70	68	277	119,843
	Lanto Griffin	69	73	65	70	277	119,843
	Adam Hadwin	72	68	68	69	277	119,843
	Mackenzie Hughes	71	69	67	70	277	119,843
	Taylor Moore	68	69	71	69	277	119,843
	Sean O'Hair	67	67	71	72	277	119,843
	JJ Spaun	72	70	64	71	277	119,843
	Brendon Todd	68	69	70	70	277	119,843
24	Jason Day	68	66	70	74	278	74,603
	Dylan Frittelli	69	68	68	73	278	74,603
	David Lipsky	67	67	72	72	278	74,603
	Bo Van Pelt	67	70	68	73	278	74,603
28	Ryan Armour	73	68	67	71	279	59,595
	Kelly Kraft	68	67	72	72	279	59,595
	Nate Lashley	68	69	71	71	279	59,595
	Trey Mullinax	70	71	68	70	279	59,595
	Vaughn Taylor	68	72	69	70	279	59,595
33	Mark Hubbard	72	70	65	73	280	43,548
	Russell Knox	70	69	70	71	280	43,548
	Austin Smotherman	65	68	75	72	280	43,548
	Satoshi Kodaira	68	67	71	74	280	43,548
	Maverick McNealy	69	72	68	71	280	43,548
	Doc Redman	66	71	73	70	280	43,548
	Seth Reeves	71	70	68	71	280	43,548
	Greyson Sigg	67	68	70	75	280	43,548
	Jimmy Walker	70	66	74	70	280	43,548
42	Jonas Blixt	64	72	73	72	281	29,195
	Peter Malnati	67	71	69	74	281	29,195
	Ryan Moore	66	73	69	73	281	29,195
	Austin Cook	70	66	74	71	281	29,195
	Luke Donald	71	68	70	72	281	29,195
	Sung Kang	70	71	68	72	281	29,195
	Seung-Yul Noh	71	72	66	72	281	29,195
49	Mark Baldwin	69	72	66	75	282	21,089
	Hayden Buckley	71	64	73	74	282	21,089
	Tyler Duncan	68	68	73	73	282	21,089
	Taylor Pendrith	70	69	69	74	282	21,089
	Davis Riley	69	70	68	75	282	21,089
	Matthias Schwab	72	62	75	73	282	21,089
	Chris Stroud	69	71	69	73	282	21,089
	Adam Svensson	69	63	77	73	282	21,089
	Curtis Thompson	69	67	73	73	282	21,089
	Camilo Villegas	67	72	70	73	282	21,089
59	Dylan Wu	69	69	72	73	283	19,749
60	Brian Stuard	72	70	68	74	284	19,488
	Johnson Wagner	75	70	65	74	284	19,488
62	Justin Rose	70	67	70	78	285	19,227
63	Ben Kohles	68	70	72	76	286	19,053

WM Phoenix Open

This WM Phoenix Open ended up having more twists than a villain's moustache. Scottie Scheffler, winless in his 70 previous PGA Tour starts, trailed for nearly the first 70 holes, and then beat Patrick Cantlay in a playoff, but he'd been chasing Sahith Theegala, unknown rookie and former college star in the tournament on a sponsor's exemption; who had stolen the show by sleeping on the lead for three consecutive nights; who had fans chanting "Thee-gala! Thee-gala!" ("It was awesome!" he said) and who entered the final round leading defending champion Brooks Koepka by one, but then with only two holes left, watered his tee shot, thus clearing the way for Scheffler's playoff victory.

Theegala, instant hero, was leading at seven under through 16 holes when darkness halted the first round. He resumed early Friday by bogeying his last two holes for a 66, surrendering the lead briefly to Kyoung-Hoon Lee (65). He opened the second round with three straight birdies, on his way to a 64, leading by two over Koepka (66) and Xander Schauffele (65). Scheffler, noted for beating top-ranked Jon Rahm in singles in the 2021 Ryder Cup, opened with 68-71 and trailed by nine strokes after 36 holes. For comparison, consider Rickie Fowler, Tony Finau and Viktor Hovland missing the cut and Rahm punching a trash can. "Just thankful," Theegala said. "No expectations at all, honestly."

Scheffler rebounded in the third round, torching his first nine for a 29, then posting a flawless 62, tying for third with Cantlay (68) at 12 under.

Theegala scraped out a 69 and at 14 under was clinging on by one over Koepka (68). "Really exhausted," Theegala said. The tournament came down to the home stretch for the final threesome. Koepka was in the hunt until a bogey at the 16th. He would tie for third, one behind. Through the 12th,

Theegala was 15 under after three birdies and two bogeys, and Scheffler was three behind after four birdies and four bogeys. Then Scheffler caught fire and birdied four of the last six.

But the pivotal moment was Theegala's tee shot at the par-four 17th. "It was cutting," he said. "Kick straight and it's good. Kicked left, into the water." He bogeyed, shot 70 and tied for third. "I just didn't hit the shots at the right time when it counted," Theegala said. "But definitely proud of the way I played this week."

Scheffler shot 67 for 16-under 268 to tie with Cantlay (67), who had finished in the group ahead. In their third trip at the par-four 18th, Scheffler dropped his 25-footer for a birdie, and had his first victory when Cantlay missed from 11. "I really don't know what to say," Scheffler said. "My head is kind of spinning right now. But that was nice, for sure."

The tournament was capped by two holes-in-one for the first time since 1997, both at the 17,000-seat stadium par-three 16th. Sam Ryder got his with a wedge from 124 yards, and Carlos Ortiz his with a nine-iron from 178, both triggering storms of beer cans from the fans.

TPC Scottsdale, Scottsdale, Arizona — February 10-13
Par 71 (35-36); 7,261 yards — Purse: $8,200,000

1	**Scottie Scheffler**	68	71	62	67	268	$1,476,000
2	**Patrick Cantlay**	67	66	68	67	268	893,800
	Scheffler won playoff at third extra hole						
3	**Brooks Koepka**	66	66	68	69	269	434,600
	Xander Schauffele	67	65	69	68	269	434,600
	Sahith Theegala	66	64	69	70	269	434,600
6	Billy Horschel	67	69	68	66	270	287,000
	Alex Noren	67	68	67	68	270	287,000
8	Hideki Matsuyama	68	68	66	69	271	248,050
	Justin Thomas	67	70	68	66	271	248,050
10	Matt Fitzpatrick	70	68	67	67	272	198,850
	Patton Kizzire	71	65	68	68	272	198,850
	Keith Mitchell	69	69	66	68	272	198,850
	Jon Rahm	67	70	68	67	272	198,850
14	Brian Harman	68	68	70	67	273	133,250
	Tom Hoge	69	66	67	71	273	133,250
	Max Homa	69	65	68	71	273	133,250
	Chris Kirk	70	66	69	68	273	133,250
	Martin Laird	70	67	69	67	273	133,250
	Louis Oosthuizen	67	70	67	69	273	133,250
	Bubba Watson	67	69	68	69	273	133,250
21	Garrick Higgo	70	69	64	71	274	96,350
	Scott Stallings	67	70	68	69	274	96,350
23	Sebastian Munoz	70	67	70	68	275	79,130
	JT Poston	69	66	70	70	275	79,130
	Sam Ryder	72	64	71	68	275	79,130
26	Keegan Bradley	68	68	74	66	276	58,630
	Talor Gooch	70	64	67	75	276	58,630
	Adam Hadwin	66	68	68	74	276	58,630
	Sung Kang	70	70	71	65	276	58,630
	Si Woo Kim	70	68	71	67	276	58,630
	Brendon Todd	68	69	67	72	276	58,630
	Cameron Young	68	69	72	67	276	58,630
33	Russell Henley	71	69	68	69	277	45,715
	Russell Knox	72	68	67	70	277	45,715
	Carlos Ortiz	69	67	74	67	277	45,715
	Rory Sabbatini	69	68	67	73	277	45,715
37	Lucas Glover	73	65	70	70	278	40,590
38	Corey Conners	72	66	69	72	279	35,670
	Kevin Kisner	67	69	74	69	279	35,670
	Kyoung-Hoon Lee	65	70	74	70	279	35,670
	Troy Merritt	72	67	68	72	279	35,670
	Adam Scott	68	70	69	72	279	35,670
43	Kevin Chappell	70	69	68	73	280	26,705
	Stewart Cink	67	71	70	72	280	26,705
	Zach Johnson	69	70	69	72	280	26,705
	Martin Trainer	71	69	68	72	280	26,705
	Abraham Ancer	68	67	71	74	280	26,705
	Francesco Molinari	70	69	73	68	280	26,705
49	Doug Ghim	69	71	72	69	281	20,869
	Branden Grace	68	69	72	72	281	20,869
	Harry Higgs	66	72	76	67	281	20,869
	Ryan Moore	69	71	68	73	281	20,869
53	Joseph Bramlett	73	66	71	72	282	19,303
	Brice Garnett	69	69	74	70	282	19,303
	Kramer Hickok	70	67	72	73	282	19,303
	Luke List	73	66	73	70	282	19,303
	Kevin Tway	68	70	75	69	282	19,303
58	Matt Jones	72	68	72	71	283	18,696
	Brian Stuard	71	69	68	75	283	18,696
60	Jordan Spieth	70	69	72	73	284	18,368
	Hudson Swafford	71	69	71	73	284	18,368
62	Joel Dahmen	71	69	74	71	285	18,040
	Stephan Jaeger	73	67	72	73	285	18,040
64	Austin Eckroat	70	69	69	78	286	17,794
65	Peter Malnati	69	71	75	72	287	17,630
66	Sepp Straka	72	68	73	78	291	17,466
67	Charley Hoffman	67	72	79	75	293	17,302

Genesis Invitational

The Spanish have a word for it. Well, two words: abrazo grupa. In English, that's "group hug", and so at the final putt, Spain's Sergio Garcia, Mexico's Carlos Ortiz and Chile's Mito Pereira swept onto Riviera's 18th to spring the joyful Latino assault on Chile's resolute Joaquin Niemann, who had just won the Genesis Invitational. "They're awesome, all the Latinos," Niemann said. "It makes our life easier, more fun, more entertainment."

Against a loaded field that included all 10 of the world's top 10, the 23-year-old had just shaken off a few anxious moments and completed a historic run in the Genesis, becoming the first wire-to-wire winner in 53 years, since the late Charlie Sifford won it as the Los Angeles Open, at Rancho Park in 1969. The crowning moment for Niemann in his second win was receiving the trophy from tournament host Tiger Woods, still recovering from the injuries he suffered in an SUV-rollover crash a year earlier, after the 2021 Genesis. "Being able to see him doing as well as he's doing is awesome," Niemann said. "He's one of my idols." The moment was also a tribute to the cigar-chomping Sifford, a pioneer — the first Black golfer to win on the PGA Tour. This year was the 100th anniversary of his birth.

From the start, Niemann was a kid having a blast, opening with a pair of eight-under 63s. The first matched the record first-round low at Riviera, and of his nine birdies, eight were from inside 10 feet. He led by three over Jordan Spieth, Cameron Young, Scottie Scheffler, who scored his first win the previous week in Phoenix, and defending champion Max Homa.

Niemann's second 63 was more putting magic. After he eagled the first from four feet, he holed four birdie putts from 15 feet or more, capped by a 40-footer at the 12th. He broke the tournament's 36-hole record with his 16-under 126 total, and in so doing dealt an amazingly short shrift to Young, a hopeful rookie. Young had just set the record 20 minutes earlier. He'd birdied his last four holes for a 62 and 128, breaking the previous record of 130, and now he trailed by two.

Niemann's closing 68-71 were more like the workaday golf Riviera usually demands of its suitors. Although three birdies and an eagle over six holes, as he did from the fifth in the third round, is hardly workaday stuff. In the fourth, a short birdie at the eighth and a 45-foot eagle at the 11th offset three bogeys to give him a 19-under-par total of 265 and a two-stroke win over Young (70) and Collin Morikawa (65).

Riviera Country Club, Pacific Palisades, California — February 17-20
Par 71 (35-36); 7,322 yards — Purse: $12,000,000

1	**Joaquin Niemann**	63	63	68	71	265	$2,160,000
2	**Collin Morikawa**	67	67	68	65	267	1,068,000
	Cameron Young	66	62	69	70	267	1,068,000
4	Viktor Hovland	71	64	65	70	270	540,000
	Adam Scott	68	65	71	66	270	540,000
6	Justin Thomas	67	64	70	70	271	435,000
7	Maverick McNealy	68	68	67	69	272	390,000
	Scottie Scheffler	66	72	65	69	272	390,000
9	CT Pan	67	70	69	67	273	351,000
10	Max Homa	66	70	67	71	274	303,000
	Rory McIlroy	69	70	67	68	274	303,000
	Chez Reavie	74	68	66	66	274	303,000
13	Xander Schauffele	69	70	66	70	275	243,000
	Cameron Tringale	69	68	69	69	275	243,000
15	Paul Casey	68	71	66	71	276	189,000
	Matt Jones	70	67	71	68	276	189,000
	Marc Leishman	70	66	67	73	276	189,000
	Robert MacIntyre	71	67	67	71	276	189,000
	Mito Pereira	70	68	68	70	276	189,000
	Sepp Straka	74	68	66	68	276	189,000
21	Emiliano Grillo	69	70	65	73	277	125,880
	Danny Lee	70	70	65	72	277	125,880
	Taylor Moore	69	69	69	70	277	125,880
	Sebastian Munoz	70	66	69	72	277	125,880
	Jon Rahm	69	73	70	65	277	125,880
26	Dylan Frittelli	68	73	68	69	278	85,800
	Jason Kokrak	67	72	66	73	278	85,800
	Kyoung-Hoon Lee	72	67	67	72	278	85,800
	Peter Malnati	69	68	69	72	278	85,800
	Sam Ryder	70	69	68	71	278	85,800
	Jordan Spieth	66	67	73	72	278	85,800
	Will Zalatoris	69	70	68	71	278	85,800
33	Patrick Cantlay	70	72	66	71	279	64,000
	Tony Finau	69	71	71	68	279	64,000
	Russell Henley	72	66	69	72	279	64,000
	Sungjae Im	71	66	75	67	279	64,000
	Russell Knox	68	67	74	70	279	64,000
	Cameron Smith	67	68	74	70	279	64,000
39	Abraham Ancer	69	72	68	71	280	45,000
	Sergio Garcia	71	68	69	72	280	45,000
	Lanto Griffin	74	66	68	72	280	45,000
	Lee Hodges	71	70	68	71	280	45,000
	Martin Laird	68	71	68	73	280	45,000
	Hideki Matsuyama	72	70	68	70	280	45,000
	Carlos Ortiz	68	71	68	73	280	45,000
	Pat Perez	70	68	70	72	280	45,000
	Erik van Rooyen	74	65	68	73	280	45,000
48	Keegan Bradley	69	68	71	73	281	30,429
	Cam Davis	71	71	70	69	281	30,429
	Beau Hossler	69	69	68	75	281	30,429
	Alex Noren	70	70	72	69	281	30,429
	Andrew Putnam	70	70	69	72	281	30,429
	Sahith Theegala	69	72	69	71	281	30,429
	Kevin Tway	68	69	74	70	281	30,429
55	Rickie Fowler	71	71	69	71	282	27,600
	Harry Higgs	75	67	69	71	282	27,600
	Francesco Molinari	70	70	74	68	282	27,600
	Matthew NeSmith	69	73	70	70	282	27,600
	Jhonattan Vegas	70	72	68	72	282	27,600
	Nick Watney	71	67	74	70	282	27,600
61	James Hahn	72	69	69	73	283	26,160
	Patton Kizzire	68	72	69	74	283	26,160
	Scott Piercy	70	67	72	74	283	26,160
	Aaron Rai	72	70	68	73	283	26,160
	Doc Redman	69	70	70	74	283	26,160
	Brian Stuard	73	68	71	71	283	26,160
67	Cameron Champ	72	70	70	72	284	24,960
	Matt Kuchar	69	73	71	71	284	24,960
	Hank Lebioda	69	73	70	72	284	24,960
	Aaron Wise	70	70	71	73	284	24,960
71	Charley Hoffman	67	75	72	71	285	24,360
72	Alex Smalley	69	72	72	73	286	24,120
73	Si Woo Kim	69	69	74	75	287	23,880
74	Joel Dahmen	70	72	73	73	288	23,640
75	Adam Long	68	73	74	75	290	23,400

Honda Classic

Sepp Straka was trying, but he just couldn't get it said, and it had nothing to do with being Austrian. His English was excellent. "The words," he apologised, through his happy turmoil, "aren't really coming to me now." This was Straka fresh from winning the Honda Classic at PGA National's tough Champion course, the first Austrian to win on the PGA Tour.

Straka, whose best previous finish was a tie for fifth, trailed by seven in the first round and five in the second and third. Then he came to a point in the final round where he told himself, "If I just kept my head down and just tried to score maybe the best score I could on every hole, just try to make the best swing I could, in the end there was a good chance of being there."

"There", to the aforementioned surprise, turned out to be the trophy presentation ceremony. Straka shot the grumpy Champion course in 71-64-69-66 — including three birdies over the last five holes — and won by a stroke on 10-under-par 270.

But first, as so often happens, the gods of golf had to have their fun. This time they singled out Daniel Berger, who entered the final round leading by five, the biggest 54-hole lead ever in the Honda. And it evaporated in just five holes. Shane Lowry, his playing partner, birdied the first and fourth. Berger double-bogeyed the par-five third out of a bunker, then bogeyed the par-three fifth on three putts from 50 feet, and shot 74 to drop to fourth. "Didn't play well, so I didn't win," he said.

Straka, in the pairing ahead, was at even par through eight on two birdies, from eight and three feet, and two three-putt bogeys. Then he birdied four of his last 10 holes, holing nine-footers at nine and 14, and a 19-footer at 16 to tie Lowry at nine under. Then came the wry twist at the par-five 18th. Straka and Kurt Kitayama hit their tee shots, and then the downpour hit, catching them in the fairway. Straka hit a six-iron across the water to 50 feet past the flag. His eagle try was inches short, and he tapped in for a birdie.

The storm caught Lowry on the 18th tee. "As bad a break as I've ever got," he said. After running all pars from the 12th, now he would need a birdie at 18 to tie Straka. He drove into the left rough, hit short of the water and put his third 43 feet past the flag. His birdie try was short and right, and he parred for a 67 and finished second at 271. "Feel like I've got the tournament stolen from me today," Lowry said.

Once Straka found the words, he was perfectly clear: "I just was in disbelief really. You try to believe that you can win, but until you actually get it done, it really is hard to believe."

PGA National (Champion), Palm Beach Gardens, Florida — February 24-27
Par 70 (35-35); 7,125 yards — Purse: $8,000,000

1	**Sepp Straka**	71	64	69	66	270	$1,440,000
2	**Shane Lowry**	70	67	67	67	271	872,000
3	**Kurt Kitayama**	64	69	71	68	272	552,000
4	Daniel Berger	65	65	69	74	273	392,000
5	Alex Noren	69	69	70	68	276	309,000
	Gary Woodland	69	69	71	67	276	309,000
7	Chris Kirk	65	68	71	73	277	260,000
	Matthias Schwab	67	72	70	68	277	260,000
9	Lee Hodges	71	66	71	70	278	194,000
	John Huh	72	65	71	70	278	194,000
	Keith Mitchell	71	70	69	68	278	194,000
	Sam Ryder	71	68	69	70	278	194,000
	Brian Stuard	70	70	69	69	278	194,000
	Adam Svensson	69	65	71	73	278	194,000
15	Mark Hubbard	70	64	75	70	279	146,000
16	CT Pan	70	70	71	69	280	106,533
	Nick Taylor	77	65	71	67	280	106,533
	Cameron Young	68	73	74	65	280	106,533
	Martin Contini	68	70	70	72	280	106,533
	Dylan Frittelli	68	70	70	72	280	106,533
	Billy Horschel	68	74	68	70	280	106,533
	Beau Hossler	69	69	71	71	280	106,533
	Brooks Koepka	68	72	71	69	280	106,533
	Kevin Streelman	71	71	68	70	280	106,533
25	Christiaan Bezuidenhout	69	71	75	66	281	62,800
	Bill Haas	70	72	71	68	281	62,800
	Matthew NeSmith	72	70	70	69	281	62,800
	Taylor Pendrith	69	69	74	69	281	62,800
	Chase Seiffert	69	66	75	71	281	62,800
30	Lucas Glover	69	72	74	67	282	43,133
	Denny McCarthy	71	71	71	69	282	43,133
	JJ Spaun	71	71	72	68	282	43,133
	Callum Tarren	68	73	75	66	282	43,133
	Andrew Kozan	67	75	68	72	282	43,133
	Rick Lamb	72	70	70	70	282	43,133
	Trey Mullinax	72	70	71	69	282	43,133
	Louis Oosthuizen	75	65	72	70	282	43,133
	Mito Pereira	68	71	72	71	282	43,133
	Ian Poulter	71	71	69	71	282	43,133
	Nick Watney	71	67	71	73	282	43,133
	Dylan Wu	68	73	69	72	282	43,133
42	Rickie Fowler	72	70	70	71	283	27,600
	Brian Gay	76	66	73	68	283	27,600
	JT Poston	70	70	73	70	283	27,600
	Davis Riley	70	72	71	70	283	27,600
	Jhonattan Vegas	69	71	72	71	283	27,600

	Lee Westwood	69	70	71	73	283	27,600
48	Stephan Jaeger	68	73	75	68	284	20,286
	Brendon Todd	74	67	74	69	284	20,286
	Danny Willett	67	72	77	68	284	20,286
	Mackenzie Hughes	70	70	70	74	284	20,286
	Kyoung-Hoon Lee	70	72	69	73	284	20,286
	Rory Sabbatini	65	74	72	73	284	20,286
	Martin Trainer	69	72	74	69	284	20,286
55	Brett Drewitt	74	68	75	68	285	18,160
	Russell Knox	69	69	75	72	285	18,160
	David Lipsky	68	71	74	72	285	18,160
	Roger Sloan	69	68	75	73	285	18,160
	Alex Smalley	71	70	72	72	285	18,160
	Samuel Stevens	70	68	73	74	285	18,160
	Vaughn Taylor	73	68	75	69	285	18,160
	Curtis Thompson	70	72	68	75	285	18,160
	Peter Uihlein	67	72	78	68	285	18,160
64	Justin Lower	73	69	74	70	286	17,280
	Patrick Rodgers	68	74	72	72	286	17,280
66	Bronson Burgoon	68	72	77	70	287	16,800
	Garrick Higgo	68	72	75	72	287	16,800
	William McGirt	68	70	75	74	287	16,800
	Aaron Rai	67	72	73	75	287	16,800
70	Joshua Creel	72	69	73	74	288	16,320
	Ryan Palmer	68	74	75	71	288	16,320
72	Austin Cook	72	70	80	70	292	16,000
	Robert Streb	72	69	81	70	292	16,000

Arnold Palmer Invitational

And Scottie Scheffler thought his first win was tough. That was merely coming from behind, then going through a three-hole playoff in the WM Phoenix Open two starts ago. Now came the Arnold Palmer Invitational early in March, at Arnie's Bay Hill Club, plenty demanding to begin with but becoming the kind of obstacle course the King could chuckle over.

"I'm exhausted," said Scheffler. Was he the winner or survivor? He had trailed all the way and finally got a grip on the tournament down the final nine — by not making bogeys. "This course," he said, "is a total beat-down."

"It's just on a knife's edge," said Rory McIlroy, with the wind, the rough and the wicked greens. "I feel punch-drunk, to be honest." McIlroy had had another good start in the Palmer, opening with a seven-under 65, then shot 72 with the winds and the greens quickening, and finished with 76-76. Said injury-plagued Gary Woodland, after taking the lead with an eagle at the 16th, then double-bogeying 17: "I'm glad I'm off that golf course."

Scheffler shot the first three rounds in 70-73-68, and trailed different leaders all the way on the slippery slope of Bay Hill — McIlroy by five in the first round, Viktor Hovland by eight in the second and Billy Horschel and Talor Gooch by two in the third. In the fourth, starting from two behind, Scheffler bogeyed three holes, catching bunker, water and rough, and he birdied two and made the turn in one over. But with the demolition derby going on around him, he was far from out of it.

Apart from winning, Scheffler's crowning achievement may have been going bogey-free down Bay Hill's back nine, and with a birdie, even. Gooch was the only other of the top 10 to go bogey-free, and he had two birdies. But he'd already shot 43 on the front.

The mere notion of par took on a new, heroic connotation. Scheffler made his birdie at the par-five 12th, but the slickness of the greens was evident from his two-putt. The first putt was from 20 feet, the birdie from five. Of his first four two-putt pars, only one was a true tap-in, a four-incher at the par-three 14th.

Two amazing saves followed. At the par-four 15th, his awkward second from behind a tree left him in heavy rough 149 yards from the hole and his third barely reached the green. But he saved his par on a 20-footer. At the par-five 16th, his drive skipped out of a bunker but into a lie that kept him from getting back to the fairway, and so he had to lay up short of the water, 67 yards from the green. He wedged to six feet and made his par. The last two pars were two-putt marvels, mere tap-ins after tries from 45 feet at 17 and 69 feet at 18.

Scheffler, with 72, shot five-under 283, had his second victory in three starts by a stroke over Tyrrell Hatton (69), Hovland (74) and Horschel (75), and moved up to number five in the world. "I'm very pleased," said Scheffler, one of only 10 in the field to finish under par, "I didn't have to play any extra holes today."

Bay Hill Club & Lodge, Orlando, Florida — March 3-6
Par 72 (36-36); 7,466 yards — Purse: £12,0000

1	**Scottie Scheffler**	70	73	68	72	283	$2,160,000
2	**Tyrrell Hatton**	69	68	78	69	284	908,000
	Billy Horschel	67	71	71	75	284	908,000
	Viktor Hovland	69	66	75	74	284	908,000
5	Chris Kirk	69	76	68	72	285	463,500
	Gary Woodland	70	72	70	73	285	463,500
7	Talor Gooch	69	68	72	77	286	390,000
	Lucas Herbert	73	71	74	68	286	390,000
9	Sam Burns	72	69	75	71	287	339,000
	Matt Fitzpatrick	73	71	70	73	287	339,000
11	Keegan Bradley	71	75	70	72	288	291,000
	Corey Conners	72	73	69	74	288	291,000
13	Russell Henley	70	72	72	75	289	228,000
	Graeme McDowell	68	76	69	76	289	228,000
	Rory McIlroy	65	72	76	76	289	228,000
	Cameron Young	70	71	76	72	289	228,000
17	Max Homa	69	74	73	74	290	183,000
	Jon Rahm	72	70	74	74	290	183,000
	Aaron Wise	69	73	74	74	290	183,000
20	Christiaan Bezuidenhout	73	74	69	75	291	131,400
	Tommy Fleetwood	74	73	70	74	291	131,400
	Beau Hossler	67	74	75	75	291	131,400
	Sungjae Im	68	77	70	76	291	131,400
	Hideki Matsuyama	73	72	76	70	291	131,400
	Nick Watney	74	72	69	76	291	131,400
26	Si Woo Kim	69	76	73	74	292	87,600
	Jason Kokrak	73	74	71	74	292	87,600
	David Lipsky	71	71	78	72	292	87,600
	Sebastian Munoz	72	74	71	75	292	87,600
	Adam Scott	68	76	74	74	292	87,600
	Brendan Steele	70	73	77	72	292	87,600
32	Tom Hoge	78	69	69	77	293	67,000
	Charles Howell III	68	73	74	78	293	67,000
	Patton Kizzire	69	72	76	76	293	67,000
	Adam Long	69	78	72	74	293	67,000
	Thomas Pieters	74	73	72	74	293	67,000
	Nick Taylor	70	77	72	74	293	67,000
38	Sergio Garcia	75	70	75	74	294	53,400
	Patrick Rodgers	72	75	74	73	294	53,400
	Alex Smalley	73	71	77	73	294	53,400
	Will Zalatoris	68	77	70	79	294	53,400
42	Dylan Frittelli	70	76	76	73	295	37,464
	Padraig Harrington	73	74	75	73	295	37,464
	Zach Johnson	72	75	75	73	295	37,464
	Kyoung-Hoon Lee	70	76	72	77	295	37,464
	Taylor Moore	71	75	72	77	295	37,464
	Taylor Pendrith	71	72	74	78	295	37,464
	Pat Perez	71	75	76	73	295	37,464
	Ian Poulter	68	75	75	77	295	37,464
	Adam Schenk	70	74	76	75	295	37,464
	Davis Thompson	73	71	75	76	295	37,464
52	Rickie Fowler	70	73	76	77	296	28,170
	Lanto Griffin	70	73	76	77	296	28,170
	Stephan Jaeger	70	73	75	78	296	28,170
	Matt Jones	70	75	76	75	296	28,170
	Martin Laird	72	69	75	80	296	28,170
	John Pak	74	73	75	74	296	28,170
	JJ Spaun	67	75	75	79	296	28,170
	Danny Willett	73	71	75	77	296	28,170
60	Brendon Todd	73	72	74	78	297	27,000
61	Cameron Champ	70	75	74	79	298	26,040
	Danny Lee	73	74	77	74	298	26,040
	Denny McCarthy	73	74	73	78	298	26,040
	Keith Mitchell	72	74	78	74	298	26,040
	Sam Ryder	73	72	77	76	298	26,040
	Vince Whaley	72	75	72	79	298	26,040
	Matthew Wolff	72	73	77	76	298	26,040
68	Hayden Buckley	69	73	84	73	299	24,720
	Marc Leishman	70	73	78	78	299	24,720
	Greyson Sigg	71	75	79	74	299	24,720
	Lee Westwood	70	74	76	79	299	24,720
72	Paul Casey	71	70	77	83	301	24,120
73	Maverick McNealy	73	74	76	79	302	23,880
74	Lucas Glover	74	72	77	81	304	23,400
	Anirban Lahiri	73	73	76	82	304	23,400
	Troy Merritt	71	72	74	87	304	23,400
77	Chez Reavie	72	75	77	83	307	22,920

Puerto Rico Open

For a golfer whose career was hanging by the slenderest of threads, Ryan Brehm had the most modest of goals. Brehm's situation, when he entered the Puerto Rico Open, would reasonably have called for full-blown desperation with a goodly dash of panic. He was about to lose his playing status on the PGA Tour. The Puerto Rico was his last chance. He had to win or finish a solo second or he was out. Instead, his goal was just "to improve every day, every shot, every round, every hole."

Brehm, 35, winless on the PGA Tour and ranked 773rd in the world, was in the final start of a minor medical exemption, this after he had tested positive for Covid in 2021. "It would be wrong to say you don't think about it," Brehm conceded. But, he said, his focus remained on improving day by day. So he kept his head down, round after round, and when he finally lifted it, he had a luxurious six-stroke victory — the fifth first-time winner in six tournaments. And his victory hug was right there. His wife Chelsey was his caddie. How about the nerves of a wife-caddie? "I have to check what I feel outside the ropes," she said, "and put one foot in front of the other, take a breath."

Brehm shot Grand Reserve in 66-67-68-67 for 268, 20 under, and in a reverse kind of way, his most notable hole was the par-four 14th in the third round, where he missed fairway, green and par putt, and made his only bogey of the tournament. A smash eagle-birdie finish to his second round had put him one ahead at halfway, then on Saturday he birdied 16 and 18 for a 68 to lead by three. "All Chelsey and I are trying to do," Brehm insisted, "is make one good swing after another."

Three consecutive birdies from the ninth sent him to a closing 67, the six-shot margin, his first win — and his playing rights. "I just need to put my head down," Brehm said again, "and hit good golf shot after good golf shot." But there was something else this time. "It was a special week," he added. "I don't know, there was just something special about it from the moment we landed."

Grand Reserve Golf Club, Rio Grande, Puerto Rico — March 3-6
Par 72 (36-36); 7,506 yards — Purse: $3,700,000

1	**Ryan Brehm**	66	67	68	67	268	$666,000
2	**Max McGreevy**	70	64	71	69	274	403,300
3	**Tommy Gainey**	69	67	69	70	275	218,300
	Brandon Wu	69	69	68	69	275	218,300
5	Chad Ramey	69	68	68	71	276	142,913
	Callum Tarren	70	65	71	70	276	142,913
7	Brice Garnett	70	68	69	70	277	97,356
	Mark Hensby	70	67	71	69	277	97,356
	Jim Herman	76	66	66	69	277	97,356
	Nate Lashley	69	72	69	67	277	97,356
	Cameron Percy	72	68	71	66	277	97,356
	Matthias Schwab	70	66	72	69	277	97,356
	Vaughn Taylor	68	72	69	68	277	97,356
	Chun-an Yu	73	66	70	68	277	97,356
	Christopher Gotterup (A)	68	68	70	71	277	
16	Chan Kim	70	70	69	69	278	58,275
	Michael Kim	65	69	70	74	278	58,275
	Ben Kohles	68	70	71	69	278	58,275
	David Lingmerth	72	69	70	67	278	58,275
	Spencer Ralston	71	68	68	71	278	58,275
	Kyle Stanley	71	69	69	69	278	58,275
22	Patrick Flavin	68	68	74	69	279	37,308
	Josh Teater	71	68	71	69	279	37,308
	Ricky Barnes	70	69	73	67	279	37,308
	Sung Kang	69	68	72	70	279	37,308
	Andrew Novak	69	67	69	74	279	37,308
	Brian Stuard	71	69	68	71	279	37,308
28	Kiradech Aphibarnrat	67	69	70	74	280	25,345
	Aaron Baddeley	67	72	69	72	280	25,345
	Joseph Bramlett	72	69	70	69	280	25,345
	Nick Hardy	68	75	71	66	280	25,345
	Kurt Kitayama	76	66	67	71	280	25,345
	Richy Werenski	69	71	69	71	280	25,345
	Jared Wolfe	70	71	69	70	280	25,345
35	Tyler Duncan	73	69	73	66	281	20,165
	Satoshi Kodaira	68	66	77	70	281	20,165
	Justin Lower	69	70	70	72	281	20,165
38	Rafa Cabrera Bello	69	71	71	71	282	17,575
	Mark Hubbard	73	69	73	67	282	17,575
	Peter Uihlein	68	72	71	71	282	17,575
41	Greg Chalmers	68	71	70	74	283	13,151
	Michael Gligic	70	72	71	70	283	13,151
	Bill Haas	72	66	70	75	283	13,151
	Jim Knous	71	65	77	70	283	13,151
	Scott Brown	71	69	67	76	283	13,151
	Scott Gutschewski	72	71	71	69	283	13,151
	Seth Reeves	71	71	72	69	283	13,151
	Chase Seiffert	65	72	71	75	283	13,151
	Dawie van der Walt	72	66	70	75	283	13,151
50	Sangmoon Bae	69	67	76	72	284	9,317
	Brett Drewitt	71	71	73	69	284	9,317
	Fabian Gomez	73	68	72	71	284	9,317
	Kelly Kraft	70	71	72	71	284	9,317
	Curtis Thompson	71	72	72	69	284	9,317
55	Seung-Yul Noh	71	70	73	71	285	8,658
	Victor Perez	73	69	74	69	285	8,658
	DA Points	69	72	75	69	285	8,658
	Austin Smotherman	73	67	74	71	285	8,658
59	Rafael Campos	70	68	73	75	286	8,436
	DJ Trahan	70	69	74	73	286	8,436
61	Austin Cook	71	72	71	73	287	8,177
	Brian Davis	69	72	72	74	287	8,177
	Derek Ernst	72	69	70	76	287	8,177
	Chesson Hadley	71	70	72	74	287	8,177
	Richard Johnson	75	68	69	75	287	8,177
66	Robert Garrigus	72	71	75	70	288	7,918
	Bo Hoag	73	70	74	71	288	7,918
68	Trevor Werbylo	72	71	74	72	289	7,807
69	Bryson Nimmer	73	70	74	73	290	7,733
70	Matt Every	71	70	74	79	294	7,659

The Players Championship

It was a week when Sawgrass appeared to be under the spell of that famous Scottish article of faith: "If it's nae rain and nae wind, it's nae golf." That being the case, the Players Championship was naething but golf from the start, when the first tee time had to be delayed Thursday morning to the drop of the final putt on Monday evening. In between was weather more suited for a spin around Cape Horn — rain, thunderstorms, lightning, whipping winds, near-freezing cold, with disorienting long gaps in start-and-stop golf. For the powerful field, capped by 48 of the top 50 in the world rankings, this was golf not as seen through Alice's Looking-Glass but trapped in it.

Who should emerge from five days of chaos but a personable, easy-talking Aussie, Cameron Smith, who just three months earlier, in January, made the lead-off Sentry Tournament of Champions his fourth tour win. After shooting the treacherous, storm-beaten TPC Sawgrass in 69-71-69-66, he had come from behind in the final round for 13-under 275, winning by a shot over India's Anirban Lahiri.

"It's unreal," Smith said. From the season-high $20 million purse, Smith won the top first prize, $3.6 million. "That's a lot of money," he noted. "I'm not sure what I'm going to do with it."

Only 66 completed the first round on Thursday, and 12 didn't even start. Harold Varner arrived at the nasty little par-three 17th at seven under and leading by two. He left trailing by one. His tee shot had hit safely, but backspin drew his ball some 40 feet all the way across the green and off into the water. A triple bogey. More delays on Friday due to an unplayable course meant 47 players still needed to complete the first rounds on Saturday. The whole thing took 54 hours and 16 minutes. Tommy Fleetwood and Tom Hoge tied at 66 and led by one with Smith three back.

The second round started at noon Saturday in sharp winds. Jason Day made three double bogeys. Justin Rose watered two shots at 17 and made a seven. Jordan Spieth made four straight bogeys from the 12th and double-bogeyed the 18th. Xander Schauffele triple-bogeyed 18 off a watered tee shot. Brooks Koepka double-bogeyed twice, then triple-bogeyed 17. They all missed the cut. Smith, on the other hand, had a ragged day of six birdies and five bogeys for a 71.

Sunday started in near-freezing temperatures, about 35 degrees fahrenheit. Hoge, for one, was shivering under three sweaters. Sam Burns wasn't sure what day it was. "It's strange going from Thursday and not playing again until Sunday," he said. Burns holed a 75-foot putt for an eagle at 16 and an 18-footer for par at 18 for a 69 to tie Hoge (71) for the halfway lead at seven-under 137. Hoge was atop the leaderboard for four straight days, but he played golf on only two of them.

Lahiri had won in his native India but never on the PGA Tour, had no top-25 finishes in 12 starts this year and was ranked 322nd in the world, and there he was, after finishing a third-round 67 on Monday, leading the Players Championship by a stroke going into the final round. "You grind away, you keep chipping away," he explained, "and when it clicks, it clicks." Smith, two back, shot a comparatively subdued 69 in the third round. He had one bogey, and of his four birdies, one was a heroic two-putt from 63 feet at the par-five second, another a 12-inch tap-in at the 17th.

The third round ended Monday morning and then 14 players immediately teed off within three of the lead. Smith's mullet hair-do, grown long in the back and flowing over the collar, is something like his version of Superman's cape. He had said that if he could just find the fairway, his irons and putter would do the rest, and this would be his Players. Prophet that he was.

He had possibly the wildest ride of his career — 10 birdies, four pars, four bogeys, 13 one-putt greens, 24 putts in all. He launched it with four straight birdies, beginning with a 38-foot putt at the first, and was leading. He added another at the sixth, then lurched to three consecutive bogeys — a missed green at seven, missed green at eight and a missed fairway and three putts from 70 feet at nine. They had him talking to himself. "Just keeping it simple, back to one shot at a time, just kind of knuckling down." He ran off four more birdies, from a tap-in at the 10th, then three pars, and then came the frightful little 17th.

"Heart was in the throat there for a second," he said. He'd fired right at the flag, to four feet. "I'd be lying," he offered, "if I said I was aiming there." Then he holed his 10th birdie and was leading by three. Lahiri, in the final group behind him, would close with a 69 and finish second by a shot, generally pleased but a bit miffed at himself. "I've been here seven years, haven't gotten over the line yet," he said. "That's definitely a monkey I want to get off my back. Today was as good an opportunity as any."

Smith, just ahead, nearly threw it all away at the par-four 18th. He drove under some trees, punched out, but into the water; took a penalty drop from 58 yards — and then stuck his approach to three feet. Smith holed that for his fourth bogey, wrapping up a 66 and the one-shot win. Paul Casey had a one-bogey 69 and finished third, and Kevin Kisner birdied three straight from the 15th for a 68 to finish fourth.

So ended what began as Smith's great family week. His mom, Susan, and sister, Melanie, whom he hadn't seen since 2019 because of Covid restrictions, had come from Australia to visit. "My main priority really was just to hang out with them, I hadn't seen them for so long," he said. "It's so cool to get a win for them." Then there was the other thing. "Sleep," Smith said. "I feel like I haven't slept in five or six days. I'm sure there will be a few beers around the fire tonight, but I can't wait for a good sleep."

TPC Sawgrass (Stadium), Ponte Vedra Beach, Florida
Par 72 (36-36); 7,256 yards

March 10-14
Purse: $20,000,000

1	**Cameron Smith**	69	71	69	66	275	$3,600,000
2	**Anirban Lahiri**	67	73	67	69	276	2,180,000
3	**Paul Casey**	70	69	69	69	277	1,380,000
4	Kevin Kisner	68	74	68	68	278	980,000
5	Keegan Bradley	72	71	68	68	279	820,000
6	Doug Ghim	70	70	68	72	280	675,000
	Russell Knox	71	71	68	70	280	675,000
	Harold Varner III	69	69	72	70	280	675,000
9	Adam Hadwin	72	72	70	67	281	525,000
	Viktor Hovland	71	73	68	69	281	525,000
	Dustin Johnson	69	73	76	63	281	525,000
	Sepp Straka	69	74	71	67	281	525,000
13	Russell Henley	69	73	72	68	282	327,222
	Taylor Pendrith	68	71	74	69	282	327,222
	Daniel Berger	67	75	70	70	282	327,222
	Tyrrell Hatton	70	73	69	70	282	327,222
	Max Homa	72	73	71	66	282	327,222
	Shane Lowry	73	70	67	72	282	327,222
	Keith Mitchell	67	72	74	69	282	327,222
	Brendan Steele	73	69	69	71	282	327,222
	Erik van Rooyen	71	67	74	70	282	327,222
22	Tommy Fleetwood	66	73	72	72	283	201,000
	Patton Kizzire	68	76	72	67	283	201,000
	Joaquin Niemann	67	73	73	70	283	201,000
	Kevin Streelman	73	71	66	73	283	201,000
26	Sam Burns	68	69	71	76	284	143,000
	Corey Conners	70	69	75	70	284	143,000
	Sergio Garcia	71	71	71	71	284	143,000
	Alex Noren	69	75	71	69	284	143,000
	Doc Redman	71	70	72	71	284	143,000
	Patrick Reed	73	70	68	73	284	143,000
	Will Zalatoris	69	71	70	74	284	143,000
33	Abraham Ancer	68	71	74	72	285	100,111
	Joel Dahmen	70	71	71	73	285	100,111
	Tom Hoge	66	71	72	76	285	100,111
	Rory McIlroy	73	73	73	66	285	100,111
	Sebastian Munoz	70	73	65	77	285	100,111
	Pat Perez	70	72	75	68	285	100,111
	Ian Poulter	73	70	71	71	285	100,111
	Seamus Power	71	71	73	70	285	100,111
	Justin Thomas	72	69	72	72	285	100,111
42	Kramer Hickok	67	75	71	73	286	73,000
	Francesco Molinari	70	73	69	74	286	73,000
	Louis Oosthuizen	69	72	69	76	286	73,000
	Scott Stallings	71	75	65	75	286	73,000
46	Adam Long	71	71	75	70	287	57,700
	Peter Malnati	70	75	72	70	287	57,700
	Maverick McNealy	70	76	70	71	287	57,700
	Troy Merritt	74	71	71	71	287	57,700
50	Dylan Frittelli	73	72	73	70	288	50,200
	Brice Garnett	67	76	74	71	288	50,200
	Aaron Wise	71	74	74	69	288	50,200
53	Branden Grace	71	72	73	73	289	47,800
	Jason Kokrak	72	72	71	74	289	47,800
55	Sungjae Im	72	72	70	76	290	46,200
	Kyoung-Hoon Lee	70	73	76	71	290	46,200
	Jon Rahm	69	72	72	77	290	46,200
	Scottie Scheffler	70	76	68	76	290	46,200
	Jimmy Walker	70	73	71	76	290	46,200
60	Denny McCarthy	70	76	73	72	291	44,600
	Sam Ryder	69	74	73	75	291	44,600
	Michael Thompson	72	73	74	72	291	44,600
63	Chesson Hadley	70	74	71	77	292	43,400
	Brian Harman	68	74	75	75	292	43,400
	Hank Lebioda	72	70	72	78	292	43,400
66	Hayden Buckley	72	71	76	74	293	42,400
	Nick Watney	75	71	75	72	293	42,400
68	Lucas Herbert	70	74	75	76	295	41,600
	Bubba Watson	73	68	78	76	295	41,600
70	Lee Hodges	72	74	75	76	297	41,000

Valspar Championship

As strategy goes, Sam Burns's game plan for the Valspar Championship, in which he was the defending champion, was a study in subdued moderation. Burns, one of the tour's rising young stars, reminded himself that golf is a game best served cool. "All through today," he said, of the final round, "just trying to make sure that I never got too high or too low and just tried to stay even-keeled." But when he dropped that 30-foot birdie putt on the second playoff hole, no more even keel. His arms stiffened and he erupted into fist pumps and shouts. "It felt like it looked," Burns said. "And to see that go in, I mean, that's just what I felt."

Davis Riley, tour rookie, Burns' good friend and playoff opponent, faced a 20-foot chip shot for a birdie to tie, but he missed and so ended his chance for that first win. "I can't hang my head about anything," said Riley, who took the lead with a nine-under 62 in the third round. "Unfortunately, I didn't have my best stuff today, and I stumbled on hole five. But it's a great week to build on."

Thus did Burns notch his third tour win, all in a one-year span, after the 2021 Valspar and the 2021 Sanderson Farms and now the '22 Valspar. He played Innisbrook's par-71 Copperhead in 64-67-67-69 – 267, tying at 17-under 267 with Riley (65-68-62-72).

Matthew NeSmith led the fireworks in the second round, tying the course record of 61 and with a 14-under 128 resetting the course 36-hole record by two shots to lead by two. "I'm done getting in my own way," he said. Riley then shot 62 in the third round, holing out from 70 feet on the fly from a bunker at nine. Said his playing partner and longtime pal Justin Thomas, "He made nine under look very, very easy." Riley also reset the 54-hole record by four strokes, to 18-under 195 and led NeSmith by two and Burns by three.

In the next-to-last pairing in the final round, Burns birdied the fifth from four feet, 11 from four and 12 from 15. He bogeyed the par-three 17th from a bunker and waited on 17 under. In the final pairing, Riley's stumble at the par-five fifth was a jagged triple bogey out of rough and trees. It was his first misstep after 34 holes without a bogey. Two birdies and a bogey later, he salvaged a tie with Burns on a six-foot birdie at 17. They tied at the first playoff hole, the 18th, and then at the par-four 16th, Burns made his energising 30-footer for a victory that shook up the world golf standings. The win lifted Burns to 10th in the world for the first time and knocked Dustin Johnson out of the top 10 for the first time in seven years.

Innisbrook Resort (Copperhead), Palm Harbor, Florida — March 17-20
Par 71 (36-35); 7,340 yards — Purse: $7,800,000

1	**Sam Burns**	64	67	67	69	267	$1,404,000
2	**Davis Riley**	65	68	62	72	267	850,200
	Burns won playoff at second extra hole						
3	**Matthew NeSmith**	67	61	69	71	268	460,200
	Justin Thomas	66	66	66	70	268	460,200
5	Matt Fitzpatrick	67	68	67	68	270	301,275
	Brian Harman	67	67	68	68	270	301,275
7	Stewart Cink	67	68	69	68	272	228,930
	Adam Hadwin	64	66	70	72	272	228,930
	Robert Streb	68	69	65	70	272	228,930
	Kevin Streelman	67	69	68	68	272	228,930
	Sahith Theegala	67	71	67	67	272	228,930
12	Brooks Koepka	67	70	71	65	273	159,900
	Shane Lowry	69	68	68	68	273	159,900
	Alex Noren	68	70	65	70	273	159,900
	Xander Schauffele	67	67	68	71	273	159,900
16	Luke Donald	68	71	67	68	274	118,950
	Tommy Fleetwood	67	68	68	71	274	118,950
	Matt Kuchar	67	72	66	69	274	118,950
	Scott Stallings	65	66	74	69	274	118,950
	Brian Stuard	68	69	69	68	274	118,950
21	Brandon Hagy	70	67	70	68	275	85,020
	Tyrrell Hatton	68	68	70	69	275	85,020
	Richy Werenski	65	70	72	68	275	85,020
	Gary Woodland	67	68	71	69	275	85,020
25	Tyler Duncan	69	69	65	73	276	65,910
	Austin Smotherman	68	71	70	67	276	65,910
27	Brice Garnett	67	71	68	71	277	54,600
	Nate Lashley	71	68	67	71	277	54,600
	Troy Merritt	68	67	67	75	277	54,600
	Mito Pereira	69	70	68	70	277	54,600
	JJ Spaun	67	71	69	70	277	54,600
	Jhonattan Vegas	64	71	72	70	277	54,600
33	Kramer Hickok	66	71	70	71	278	41,600
	Viktor Hovland	69	70	68	71	278	41,600
	Kevin Kisner	70	66	73	69	278	41,600
	Patton Kizzire	69	67	70	72	278	41,600
	Bernd Wiesberger	69	70	66	73	278	41,600
	Brandon Wu	72	65	69	72	278	41,600
39	Kiradech Aphibarnrat	69	68	71	71	279	29,250
	Joel Dahmen	68	69	70	72	279	29,250
	Harry Higgs	70	68	68	73	279	29,250
	Dustin Johnson	67	71	72	69	279	29,250
	Seung-Yul Noh	70	67	73	69	279	29,250
	Chez Reavie	67	72	69	71	279	29,250
	Doc Redman	66	72	71	70	279	29,250
	Adam Svensson	71	68	67	73	279	29,250
	Curtis Thompson	70	69	72	68	279	29,250
48	Martin Kaymer	69	66	74	71	280	19,439
	Max McGreevy	70	69	70	71	280	19,439
	Webb Simpson	67	67	76	70	280	19,439
	Joseph Bramlett	69	67	71	73	280	19,439
	Bill Haas	71	66	71	72	280	19,439
	Danny Lee	65	74	68	73	280	19,439
	Denny McCarthy	69	70	70	71	280	19,439
	CT Pan	71	66	69	74	280	19,439
	Greyson Sigg	67	72	67	74	280	19,439
57	Paul Barjon	68	71	70	72	281	17,706
	Russell Knox	71	68	67	75	281	17,706
	Henrik Stenson	70	69	70	72	281	17,706
	Michael Thompson	72	66	74	69	281	17,706
	Harold Varner III	72	67	70	72	281	17,706
62	Christiaan Bezuidenhout	70	69	73	70	282	17,004
	Wesley Bryan	68	71	70	73	282	17,004
	Louis Oosthuizen	67	68	74	73	282	17,004
	Cameron Tringale	68	71	70	73	282	17,004
66	Ryan Brehm	71	68	75	69	283	16,536
	John Huh	71	67	72	73	283	16,536
68	David Lipsky	64	71	74	76	285	16,224
	Collin Morikawa	68	70	74	73	285	16,224
70	Pat Perez	67	70	75	74	286	15,912
	Nick Taylor	69	70	68	79	286	15,912
72	Blake Kennedy	67	72	72	76	287	15,678

WGC Dell Technologies Match Play

Scottie Scheffler's problem was that he wasn't dreaming far enough. A quick check of his record showed that he won the WM Phoenix Open in mid-February, then won the Arnold Palmer Invitational early in March, and then on Sunday, March 27, he took the WGC Dell Technologies Match Play. Put into career context, this was his third PGA Tour win, also his third win in his last five starts and also his third win in 43 calendar days. The victory lifted him, at age 25, to number one in the world rankings. All of which was a bit much. "I never got that far in my dreams," Scheffler said after defeating Kevin Kisner in the final.

Scheffler began at Austin Country Club by beating Ian Poulter, a match play whizz, 2 and 1 and after getting tripped up by Tommy Fleetwood 2 and 1, rolled over Matt Fitzpatrick 5 and 4. To win his round-robin group, he then had to beat the same Fitzpatrick with a birdie at the sixth playoff hole. In the knockouts, Scheffler then defeated Billy Horschel, the man who beat him in the 2021 final, one up and Seamus Power 3 and 2.

Kisner, the runner-up in 2018 and champion a year later, raced past Marc Leishman 4 and 3 and strung out wins over Luke List one up, and Justin Thomas 4 and 3, before eliminating Adam Scott one up (after being three down with four to play, then won the next four holes; "I don't ever give up," he said), then Will Zalatoris 4 and 3.

In the semi-finals Sunday morning, while Kisner was scoring a tough two-up win over Corey Conners, match play aficionados had a mind-numbing feast in what looked like a comfortable win for Scheffler against a struggling Dustin Johnson. Actually, it was one for the books. Scheffler went three up through four. Johnson couldn't buy a break. Even his colossal 350-yard drive at the fifth ended up merely a matching par. Scheffler went a towering five up with seven to play through the 11th. Then in a wrenching reversal, Johnson won four straight holes from number 12 on three birdies and Scheffler's watery bogey. Thus Scheffler was hanging at one up with three to play. But he righted himself. He took the par-five 16th on a two-putt birdie, then at the par-three 17th, on an eight-footer, it was birdie, hole and match, 3 and 1.

Scheffler went into the final on 57 holes without trailing. This had to sting his opponent: at the first, Kisner stuck a wedge to only three feet, but Scheffler beat him in from eight. Then Scheffler took the lead on Kisner's bogey out of a bunker at the second, went two up on a birdie from 15 feet at four, then three up on a fine chip and birdie at the sixth, and they halved the next seven holes. At the par-five 12th, Scheffler flubbed his eagle chip into a bunker. Kisner, with a six-footer for birdie, was drawing a bead on winning his first hole. But Scheffler holed his bunker shot for a birdie. Kisner got his birdie, but it only served to delay the end, which came two holes later, 4 and 3.

"I don't feel like number one in the world," said Scheffler, at 25, the sixth-youngest to reach the top. "I feel like the same guy I was four months ago, and I hope that doesn't change."

Austin Country Club, Austin, Texas — March 23-27
Par 71 (35-36); 7,108 yards — Purse: $12,000,000

ROUND OF 16

Scottie Scheffler defeated Billy Horschel by one hole
Seamus Power defeated Tyrrell Hatton 4 and 3
Dustin Johnson defeated Richard Bland 3 and 2
Brooks Koepka defeated Jon Rahm at the 19th
Kevin Kisner defeated Adam Scott by one hole
Will Zalatoris defeated Kevin Na at the 22nd
Corey Conners defeated Takumi Kanaya 5 and 3
Abraham Ancer defeated Collin Morikawa 7 and 6
Defeated players received $220,000

QUARTER-FINALS

Scottie Scheffler defeated Seamus Power 3 and 2
Dustin Johnson defeated Brooks Koepka by two holes
Kevin Kisner defeated Will Zalatoris 4 and 3
Corey Conners defeated Abraham Ancer by two holes
Defeated players received $386,000

SEMI-FINALS

Scottie Scheffler defeated Dustin Johnson 3 and 1
Kevin Kisner defeated Corey Conners by two holes

THIRD-FOURTH PLAYOFF

Corey Conners ($852,000) defeated Dustin Johnson ($685,000) 3 and 1

FINAL

Scottie Scheffler ($2,100,000) defeated Kevin Kisner ($1,320,000) 4 and 3

Corales Puntacana Championship

The subject was winning and the wear and tear it inflicts on the golfer. "It was honestly like I always thought it would be," said Chad Ramey, 29-year-old rookie, upon winning the Corales Puntacana Championship, his first PGA Tour victory. "It was very stressful, very nerve-racking coming down the stretch, but I just ground it out, kind of stuck to my process, stayed within myself and pulled it out."

As breakthroughs go, this one was like going through a wall. Ramey had to come from behind not just in the final round, not just on the final nine, but over the last six holes, and with four straight birdies, taking the lead on the fourth of them, then holding on with two pars. "The nerves were there all day," Ramey said, "so I just stuck to my game plan. I got off to a slow start, but the putter kind of heated up on the back and it all worked out."

The Puntacana, in the Dominican Republic late in March, was played opposite the tour's WGC Dell Match Play. Ramey, trailing for the first 69 holes and chasing Ben Martin all the way, shot 70-65-69-67 and won by a stroke on 17-under 271. Martin double-bogeyed the first in the final round, shot 70 and tied at 272 with Alex Smalley, who charged to a 65.

After Martin, the leader for the first three days, got tangled up in the rough at the first, he made four birdies over five holes from the third, and was leading at 16 under at the turn. Ramey trailed him by two at the start, bogeyed the second, then after two birdies was three behind at the turn. Martin would cool to a bogey and a birdie coming in. But Ramey caught fire from the 13th, finally taking the lead on a 25-footer at the 16th.

Smalley, who had finished earlier, just shrugged at how close he'd come. His 20-foot birdie try at 18 stopped just a tad short, costing him a tie. "Whatever's meant to be is meant to be," he said, "so I take a lot of positives from this week." Martin said he'd never been this emotional about golf. "That's a good thing," he said. "Means I competed hard and it obviously stung." And said Ramey: "I've always had the self-belief that I've belonged out here, and to win, it just kind of validates that."

Puntacana Resort & Club (Corales), Punta Cana, Dominican Republic — March 24-27
Par 72 (36-36); 7,670 yards — Purse: $3,700,000

1	**Chad Ramey**	70	65	69	67	271	$666,000
2	**Ben Martin**	66	66	70	70	272	329,300
	Alex Smalley	69	65	73	65	272	329,300
4	Cameron Percy	71	68	67	67	273	166,500
	Jhonattan Vegas	70	70	65	68	273	166,500
6	Rasmus Hojgaard	73	67	67	67	274	134,125
7	David Lipsky	73	65	68	69	275	112,388
	Adam Schenk	67	68	74	66	275	112,388
	Brian Stuard	70	68	69	68	275	112,388
	Martin Trainer	69	70	67	69	275	112,388
11	Bryson Nimmer	70	72	69	65	276	89,725
	Andrew Novak	70	69	69	68	276	89,725
13	Hayden Buckley	68	74	68	67	277	74,925
	Kramer Hickok	73	68	70	66	277	74,925
15	Ryan Armour	69	71	69	69	278	56,425
	Wesley Bryan	70	72	67	69	278	56,425
	Kevin Chappell	73	67	72	66	278	56,425
	Thomas Detry	69	69	68	72	278	56,425
	Rick Lamb	72	70	68	68	278	56,425
	Nate Lashley	69	68	69	72	278	56,425
	Justin Lower	74	65	68	71	278	56,425
22	Wyndham Clark	70	68	70	71	279	38,665
	Chase Seiffert	70	70	75	64	279	38,665
	Sahith Theegala	71	68	71	69	279	38,665
25	Greyson Sigg	69	69	73	69	280	30,402
	Nick Taylor	72	68	69	71	280	30,402
	Vaughn Taylor	68	71	69	72	280	30,402
28	Greg Chalmers	73	69	69	70	281	23,749
	Jason Dufner	70	73	67	71	281	23,749
	Tyler Duncan	71	71	69	70	281	23,749
	Brandon Wu	69	72	72	68	281	23,749
	Scott Brown	71	71	67	72	281	23,749
	Rafael Campos	72	68	69	72	281	23,749
	Ben Kohles	72	67	69	73	281	23,749
	Vince Whaley	70	68	70	73	281	23,749
36	Robert Garrigus	70	72	71	69	282	16,488
	Hudson Swafford	74	67	72	69	282	16,488
	Peter Uihlein	75	68	72	67	282	16,488
	Danny Willett	71	69	75	67	282	16,488
	Jonathan Byrd	70	72	68	72	282	16,488
	Michael Gligic	72	70	70	70	282	16,488
	Hank Lebioda	71	71	70	70	282	16,488
	Seung-Yul Noh	71	71	71	69	282	16,488
44	Kiradech Aphibarnrat	68	73	73	69	283	11,371
	Curtis Thompson	72	69	72	70	283	11,371
	Bill Haas	72	67	73	71	283	11,371
	Brandon Hagy	70	70	71	72	283	11,371
	David Lingmerth	69	70	72	72	283	11,371
	Matthias Schwab	73	69	69	72	283	11,371
50	Graeme McDowell	68	68	73	75	284	9,195
	Trey Mullinax	73	70	70	71	284	9,195
	Sean O'Hair	71	71	70	72	284	9,195
	DJ Trahan	70	73	71	70	284	9,195
54	Patrick Flavin	72	71	71	71	285	8,732
	Bo Hoag	74	69	68	74	285	8,732
56	Dylan Wu	73	69	71	73	286	8,621
57	Scott Gutschewski	73	70	76	68	287	8,547
58	Austin Cook	73	70	74	71	288	8,362
	Brice Garnett	74	67	76	71	288	8,362
	Jim Knous	73	70	75	70	288	8,362
	Camilo Villegas	74	69	71	74	288	8,362
62	John Huh	73	70	75	71	289	8,103
	DA Points	72	71	75	71	289	8,103
	Seth Reeves	70	70	77	72	289	8,103
65	Kevin Stadler	72	70	77	74	293	7,955

Valero Texas Open

Must be something in the water. When JJ Spaun tapped in on the final hole and locked up the Valero Texas Open, he had — to his immense satisfaction and relief — scored his first PGA Tour victory. And anyone casually scanning the results of these first three months-and-change of 2022 would note that Spaun was the seventh first-time winner out of 12 tournaments. "Yeah, it's still unbelievable," Spaun said. "I knew I could win out here on tour. When I first got out here, I was playing really good and then had a setback two years ago. It's just perseverance, trying to push through and stay strong."

Spaun gave a first-class demonstration of same at San Antonio, trailing from the start, tying for the lead in the third round, then pressing ahead with 67-70-69-69 for 13-under 275 and a two-stroke win over Matt Jones and Matt Kuchar. It had taken patience, hard work and confidence. Spaun, 31, joined the tour in 2017, had a tie for second in 2018, then later had to play the Korn Ferry Tour in 2021 to regain his PGA Tour card. In October, he was ranked 396th in the world, and the Texas Open in March was his 147th start.

Spaun entered the final round tied for the lead with Brandt Snedeker, Beau Hossler and Dylan Frittelli at 10 under, and no matter how daunting the heavy traffic, he had the reasonable ambition of scoring his first win. Then came a brutal blow, at the very first hole: missed fairway, missed green, poor chip, three putts for a double bogey. "I was pretty upset," Spaun said. "The saving grace to that is it's the first hole."

He proceeded to produce a tight little five-birdie work of art as his chief challengers stalled out. Hossler doubled-bogeyed the 14th and tied for fourth; Frittelli took two late bogeys but a closing birdie lifted him to a tie for eighth, and Snedeker had 15 pars and three bogeys, shot 75 and tied for 18th. Jones sprinted to a 31 on the front nine and shot 66, and Kuchar posted three birdies coming home for a 69.

Against this backdrop, Spaun birdied the sixth and eighth holes on short putts and the ninth with a 50-foot hole-out from the rough. He took the lead at the 11th with a birdie from three feet. Jones birdied 17 up ahead, and Spaun answered with a nicely crafted birdie at the par-five 14th, coming out of a greenside bunker to nine feet and holing the putt. He parred in for his magical first tour win. "It's a great feeling to be in the winner's circle," Spaun said, "and now it's like a game-changer."

So much a game-changer that now he was heading to his first Masters. The top three things he was looking forward to at Augusta National? "Magnolia Drive, the par-three contest and a pimento cheese sandwich," Spaun said. "Not too many, though."

TPC San Antonio (Oaks), San Antonio, Texas — March 31-April 3
Par 72 (36-36); 7,438 yards — Purse: $8,600,000

1	**JJ Spaun**	67	70	69	69	275	$1,548,000
2	**Matt Jones**	68	75	68	66	277	765,400
	Matt Kuchar	67	69	72	69	277	765,400
4	Adam Hadwin	70	70	71	67	278	344,000
	Beau Hossler	73	66	67	72	278	344,000
	Charles Howell III	70	67	72	69	278	344,000
	Troy Merritt	69	71	69	69	278	344,000
8	Keegan Bradley	71	71	71	66	279	234,350
	Dylan Frittelli	70	66	70	73	279	234,350
	Matthias Schwab	69	72	70	68	279	234,350
	Brendon Todd	68	69	72	70	279	234,350
	Gary Woodland	70	67	72	70	279	234,350
13	Zach Johnson	72	71	70	67	280	158,670
	Si Woo Kim	69	72	68	71	280	158,670
	Anirban Lahiri	68	73	69	70	280	158,670
	Mito Pereira	71	70	69	70	280	158,670
	Scott Stallings	68	72	67	73	280	158,670
18	Scott Gutschewski	70	68	73	70	281	92,606
	Rasmus Hojgaard	66	73	74	68	281	92,606
	Nate Lashley	71	70	71	69	281	92,606
	Henrik Stenson	70	69	73	69	281	92,606
	Aaron Baddeley	69	74	68	70	281	92,606
	Kevin Chappell	71	65	73	72	281	92,606
	Lucas Glover	71	66	73	71	281	92,606
	Denny McCarthy	67	74	68	72	281	92,606
	Brandt Snedeker	73	66	67	75	281	92,606
	Kevin Streelman	70	71	69	71	281	92,606
	Jhonattan Vegas	71	68	72	70	281	92,606
29	Tony Finau	70	71	72	69	282	55,112
	Martin Laird	70	73	69	70	282	55,112
	Vince Whaley	70	72	71	69	282	55,112
	Jared Wolfe	72	68	74	68	282	55,112
	Richard Bland	70	71	69	72	282	55,112
	Aaron Rai	67	74	68	73	282	55,112
35	Corey Conners	70	71	75	67	283	41,925
	Chris Kirk	70	72	69	72	283	41,925
	Adam Long	72	70	70	71	283	41,925
	Robert MacIntyre	69	69	76	69	283	41,925
	Maverick McNealy	70	72	67	74	283	41,925
	Jordan Spieth	72	70	74	67	283	41,925
41	John Huh	69	73	72	70	284	30,530
	Peter Malnati	71	71	70	72	284	30,530

	CT Pan	69	74	72	69	284	30,530
	JT Poston	70	69	74	71	284	30,530
	Andrew Putnam	71	71	73	69	284	30,530
	Chad Ramey	74	68	70	72	284	30,530
	Greyson Sigg	73	70	71	70	284	30,530
48	William McGirt	71	70	73	71	285	22,308
	Ryan Palmer	68	66	77	74	285	22,308
	David Skinns	68	70	77	70	285	22,308
	Brendan Steele	68	74	71	72	285	22,308
	Richy Werenski	70	72	74	69	285	22,308
53	Lanto Griffin	75	66	73	72	286	20,244
	Chesson Hadley	71	70	76	69	286	20,244
	Luke List	68	74	71	73	286	20,244
	Henrik Norlander	68	71	76	71	286	20,244
	Roger Sloan	74	69	71	72	286	20,244
58	Luke Donald	71	70	71	75	287	19,522
	Patrick Rodgers	70	71	71	75	287	19,522
	Hudson Swafford	71	70	70	76	287	19,522
61	Russell Knox	65	76	71	76	288	19,092
	Austin Smotherman	68	75	74	71	288	19,092
63	Bill Haas	70	71	77	71	289	18,576
	Ben Martin	69	72	75	73	289	18,576
	Seung-Yul Noh	70	72	73	74	289	18,576
	Davis Riley	70	70	76	73	289	18,576
67	Doc Redman	69	70	73	78	290	18,060
	Sahith Theegala	77	66	71	76	290	18,060
69	James Hahn	69	74	72	76	291	17,716
	Peter Uihlein	68	71	76	76	291	17,716
71	Wyndham Clark	73	70	74	77	294	17,372
	Jim Herman	69	73	77	75	294	17,372

RBC Heritage

Jordan Spieth nibbled at the edges for the first three rounds of the RBC Heritage, then announced his arrival with two eagles and a birdie on the front nine of the fourth. Then he spent the finish demonstrating that golf is not really a spectator sport — at least not to a leader in the clubhouse, a guy clinging to a one-shot edge who can hardly bear to sneak a peek with an army riding a chance to beat him, taking shot after shot at him coming down the stretch. "Every single putt," said Spieth, breathing again, "looks like it's going it."

Well, maybe not an army. Actually, it was only the last five twosomes. But to a guy who hadn't won in a year and who was hanging by a thread, it seemed like an army and an eternity. And there was still the fresh pain of missing the cut in the Masters the previous week.

One golfer did catch him: Patrick Cantlay, with a birdie at the 17th, and then Spieth beat him on the first playoff hole, dropping a 56-foot bunker shot to tap-in range for a par. Cantlay had caught a fried-egg lie in the same bunker. "With it plugged like that," Cantlay said, "it's darned near impossible to get it close." He got the ball out and on but was 35 feet long and missed his par try. "What a great tournament to win," Spieth said. And what a great way to win it.

There was his grand entrance in the final round. He eagled both par-fives on the front nine — the second on a hole-out bunker shot from 57 feet and the fifth on a 23-foot putt. He birdied the eighth, then backslid. He bogeyed the ninth from a bunker and three-putted the 11th from 45 feet that put him back to 11 under. His closing stretch brought him back. He birdied 13 on a 12-footer, and then a 10-footer at the 18th for a 66, getting to 13 under.

Spieth shot Harbour Town in 69-68-68-66, trailing Cameron Young by six in the first round, then Cantlay by four, then Harold Varner by three. He would eventually be tied on 271 by Cantlay (66-67-70-68), but first came the scares. Shane Lowry (69) was leading until a double bogey at 18. Sepp Straka (68) tied Spieth with a birdie at 17, then bogeyed the 18th out of long grass in front of the green. Varner could only grind out pars for the entire back nine for a 70. They ended up in the crush of a seven-way tie for third at 272.

Cantlay's birdie at the 17th merely slowed Spieth in scoring the win he never expected. Sometimes, he said, you play well and expect to win and someone outplays you. And sometimes you feel you played well, but not well enough. "And I honestly felt like this was that week," he said. "I needed a lot of things to go right."

Harbour Town Golf Links, Hilton Head, South Carolina — April 14-17
Par 71 (36-35); 7,191 yards — Purse: $8,000,000

1	**Jordan Spieth**	69	68	68	66	271	$1,440,000
2	**Patrick Cantlay**	66	67	70	68	271	872,000
	Spieth won playoff at first extra hole						
3	**Cam Davis**	69	73	67	63	272	330,857
	JT Poston	68	72	68	64	272	330,857
	Matt Kuchar	68	69	67	68	272	330,857
	Shane Lowry	66	72	65	69	272	330,857
	Sepp Straka	66	71	67	68	272	330,857

	Harold Varner III	67	72	63	70	272	330,857			
	Cameron Young	63	73	70	66	272	330,857			
10	Tommy Fleetwood	71	70	64	68	273	210,000			
	Erik van Rooyen	69	67	67	70	273	210,000			
12	Tyler Duncan	68	73	69	65	275	140,667			
	Adam Long	69	73	67	66	275	140,667			
	Troy Merritt	69	70	68	68	275	140,667			
	Matthew NeSmith	70	68	69	68	275	140,667			
	Scott Piercy	67	72	69	67	275	140,667			
	Cameron Tringale	69	67	70	69	275	140,667			
	Corey Conners	66	72	68	69	275	140,667			
	Joel Dahmen	69	67	69	70	275	140,667			
	Joaquin Niemann	65	72	69	69	275	140,667			
21	Daniel Berger	71	70	68	67	276	83,920			
	Billy Horschel	69	69	67	71	276	83,920			
	Sungjae Im	70	70	67	69	276	83,920			
	Graeme McDowell	66	76	66	68	276	83,920			
	Aaron Wise	68	68	68	72	276	83,920			
26	Adam Hadwin	69	69	70	69	277	54,844			
	Tyrrell Hatton	67	72	71	67	277	54,844			
	Patton Kizzire	67	71	70	69	277	54,844			
	Collin Morikawa	70	70	69	68	277	54,844			
	Maverick McNealy	71	70	65	71	277	54,844			
	Kevin Na	70	69	68	70	277	54,844			
	Mito Pereira	66	71	69	71	277	54,844			
	Adam Svensson	66	73	67	71	277	54,844			
	Brendon Todd	72	68	68	69	277	54,844			
35	Wyndham Clark	68	73	66	71	278	38,171			
	Doug Ghim	70	72	67	69	278	38,171			
	Branden Grace	71	70	68	69	278	38,171			
	Brian Harman	72	70	68	68	278	38,171			
	Jason Kokrak	70	68	70	70	278	38,171			
	Justin Thomas	70	71	70	67	278	38,171			
	Hudson Swafford	69	69	66	74	278	38,171			
42	Si Woo Kim	69	70	71	69	279	27,600			
	Peter Malnati	69	73	65	72	279	27,600			
	Alex Noren	70	70	67	72	279	27,600			
	CT Pan	70	70	71	68	279	27,600			
	Ian Poulter	71	68	67	73	279	27,600			
	Robert Streb	68	67	71	73	279	27,600			
48	Joseph Bramlett	69	73	74	64	280	21,360			
	Lucas Glover	68	71	68	73	280	21,360			
	Doc Redman	69	71	70	70	280	21,360			
51	Pat Perez	68	73	69	71	281	19,653			
	Brian Gay	67	75	68	71	281	19,653			
	Danny Willett	70	72	67	72	281	19,653			
54	Charl Schwartzel	68	72	71	71	282	18,880			
	Henrik Stenson	71	71	72	68	282	18,880			
56	Luke Donald	70	69	76	68	283	18,480			
	Jim Herman	69	71	70	73	283	18,480			
	Denny McCarthy	67	75	70	71	283	18,480			
59	Bill Haas	67	74	68	75	284	17,680			
	Ben Martin	71	70	68	75	284	17,680			
	Chad Ramey	67	70	71	76	284	17,680			
	Matthias Schwab	67	74	71	72	284	17,680			
	Webb Simpson	69	73	69	73	284	17,680			
	Roger Sloan	68	71	72	73	284	17,680			
	Camilo Villegas	71	67	74	72	284	17,680			
66	Dylan Frittelli	70	71	68	76	285	16,960			
	Anirban Lahiri	69	73	69	74	285	16,960			
68	Stewart Cink	67	75	71	74	287	16,720			
69	Brian Stuard	73	69	75	71	288	16,560			
70	Jonathan Byrd	68	74	78	70	290	16,320			
	Sahith Theegala	71	70	70	79	290	16,320			

Zurich Classic

Maybe they just should hang up a sign — Cantlay & Schauffele: Winning Made Easy. More to the immediate point, the stoic Patrick Cantlay and the animated Xander Schauffele, who met in their college days, were the Dynamic Duo, going 4-0 as rookies in the US victories in both the 2019 Presidents Cup and the 2021 Ryder Cup. Next, looking for new worlds to conquer, they paired up for the 2022 Zurich Classic of New Orleans, and lifted the first wire-to-wire victory since the tournament became a team event in 2017. Setting a collection of records.

Why do they click so well? Said Cantlay: "We really always enjoy being with each other, and we both played exceptional this week and had a great time doing it. We definitely bring out the best in each other."

Said Schauffele: "We just play the way we play in normal stroke play. We just keep plodding along, and we just stayed very patient. Pat is really good at that. I obviously found a really good partner."

So much for dramatic insider stuff. The Zurich is played at stroke play, but in best ball in the first and third rounds and in alternate shot in the second and fourth. They led all the way. Further, it was a runaway until Sam Burns and Billy Horschel surged in the final round and held them to a merely comfortable two-shot win on a card of 59-68-60-72, with a record total of 29-under 259 at TPC Louisiana.

They set the first of their records with that first-round 13-under 59, in which Cantlay eagled the par-five second on a 25-foot putt, and added five birdies, and Schauffele made six birdies. The winds came up and so did the scores in alternate shot in the second round. Cantlay-Schauffele posted a 68 and they kept their one-stroke lead with a tournament-record 17 under. In the third, they sprinted to a best-ball 60 for a tournament 54-hole record of 29 under, stretching their lead to five over South Africa's Garrick Higgo and Branden Grace, and six over Horschel and Burns.

On the final day, Higgo and Grace birdied three straight from the 10th, then bogeyed three of the last five, shot 73 and tied for fourth. Burns and Horschel, meantime, pressed their case. They birdied the second, then Cantlay and Schauffele answered with an eagle at the par-five seventh on Cantlay's 254-yard approach to seven feet. "Unbelieveable shot," Schauffele said. Then Schauffele missed a three-foot birdie putt at eight, next missed the greens on nine and 10, leading to bogeys. "I feel like those bogeys were pretty much my fault," he said.

Horschel and Burns closed in, birdieing four of seven from the fifth, including the 10th from three feet and the 11th from four, and Schauffele set up a matching birdie at 11 with a pitch to two feet. Both sides settled into a tug of pars. But Horschel missed the green at the par-three 17th, which led to a bogey and that was that.

TPC Louisiana, Avondale, Louisiana — April 21-24
Par 72 (36-36); 7,425 yards — Purse: $8,300,000

1	**Patrick Cantlay/ Xander Schauffele**	59	68	60	72	259	$1,199,350
2	**Sam Burns/ Billy Horschel**	62	68	63	68	261	489,700
3	**Doc Redman/ Sam Ryder**	61	67	69	67	264	320,588
4	Keegan Bradley/ Brendan Steele	64	71	63	67	265	191,938
	Branden Grace/ Garrick Higgo	64	65	63	73	265	191,938
	David Lipsky/ Aaron Rai	61	67	65	72	265	191,938
	Taylor Moore/ Matthew NeSmith	60	73	64	68	265	191,938
	Davis Riley/ Will Zalatoris	64	71	64	66	265	191,938
	Harold Varner III/ Bubba Watson	62	71	64	68	265	191,938
10	Wyndham Clark/ Cameron Tringale	62	67	65	72	266	98,286
	Jason Day/ Jason Scrivener	65	65	63	73	266	98,286
	Justin Lower/ Dylan Wu	64	69	63	70	266	98,286
13	Shane Lowry/ Ian Poulter	64	69	64	70	267	69,803
14	Byeong Hun An/ Sungjae Im	65	69	64	70	268	55,247
	Ryan Brehm/ Mark Hubbard	65	69	62	72	268	55,247
	Tyler Duncan/ Adam Schenk	64	72	63	69	268	55,247
	Justin Rose/ Henrik Stenson	66	70	63	69	268	55,247
18	Sam Horsfield/ Matt Wallace	64	70	65	71	270	40,048
	Hank Lebioda/ Chase Seiffert	63	70	65	72	270	40,048
	Ryan Palmer/ Scottie Scheffler	64	72	63	71	270	40,048
21	Talor Gooch/ Max Homa	66	68	64	73	271	24,112
	Nick Hardy/ Curtis Thompson	66	69	65	71	271	24,112
	Tyrrell Hatton/ Danny Willett	63	72	64	72	271	24,112
	Chris Kirk/ Brendon Todd	64	70	66	71	271	24,112
	Russell Knox/ Brian Stuard	63	70	64	74	271	24,112
	Marc Leishman/ Cameron Smith	65	68	66	72	271	24,112
	Sean O'Hair/ Scott Piercy	66	70	63	72	271	24,112
	Patrick Rodgers/ Brandon Wu	65	68	65	73	271	24,112
29	Kevin Chappell/ James Hahn	64	71	66	71	272	18,343
	Joel Dahmen/ Stephan Jaeger	63	73	67	69	272	18,343
	Viktor Hovland/ Collin Morikawa	65	70	65	72	272	18,343
32	Christiaan Bezuidenhout/ Charl Schwartzel	67	68	65	73	273	17,513
	Doug Ghim/ Matthias Schwab	65	71	67	70	273	17,513
34	David Skinns/ Callum Tarren	64	72	63	75	274	17,015
35	Scott Brown/ Kevin Kisner	66	70	65	74	275	16,683
36	Ryan Armour/ Michael Gligic	65	69	67	75	276	16,185
	Jay Haas/ Bill Haas	65	71	68	72	276	16,185
38	Kiradech Aphibarnrat/ Kurt Kitayama	66	70	68	74	278	15,521
	Kyle Stanley/ Camilo Villegas	65	71	67	75	278	15,521

Mexico Open

"Fortunately, I got my seventh PGA Tour win," Jon Rahm was saying, exhaling in relief like a *norte* wind upon taking the Mexico Championship in his first wire-to-wire victory. "It was a pretty stressful weekend, all the way to the end."

Wire-to-wire? The expression ordinarily suggests comforting authority. But this one was closer to skin-of-my-teeth. In the first round, he was stuck in a six-way tie for the lead. In the second and third, what looked like the breathing room of two-stroke leads were illusions, and included having to regain the lead in the third, and in the finale, he had to break out of a four-way tie down the stretch. So after shooting Vidanta Vallarta, a par-71 beauty on Mexico's Pacific Coast, in 64-66-68-69 for 267, 17 under par, Rahm had his first victory in nearly a year, since the 2021 US Open. He won by a stroke in a frantic finish over Tony Finau (63), Kurt Kitayama (68) and tour rookie Brandon Wu (63).

The early keys for Rahm: he got his share of the opening tie with an eagle at the 311-yard seventh, driving the green and holing the 40-foot putt. In the second, he made three of his five bogeys of the tournament, but made eight birdies to take a two-stroke lead over Alex Smalley. In the third, big-hitting Cameron Champ took the lead, but three poor chip shots cost him. Rahm birdied 14 and 18 and led by two.

Down the final stretch it was a wild and volatile leaderboard. Rahm bogeyed the 10th, slipping to 16 under. Up ahead, Wu holed a 24-footer for birdie at 16 to tie. Kitayama, paired with Rahm, two-putted from 65 feet to birdie the par-five 12th and was also at 16 under. Then Finau, who'd gone on a birdie-eagle-birdie rampage from the 13th, closed with a five-foot birdie at 18 to match Wu's 63 and make it a four-way tie at 16 under.

The spell was soon broken. Rahm dropped an 11-footer for birdie at the 14th and led by one at 17 under. Kitayama bogeyed alongside him and fell two behind. The scorecard was another illusion. It showed Rahm coasting home on four safe pars. In truth, he had to scratch for them. At the 15th, he was short with his wedge and had to hole a five-footer. He two-putted 16, but the first was from 50 feet. He tapped in at 17 after just missing a 10-footer. At the par-five 18th, which he'd birdied three times, he drove into rough on a steep slope, whacked the next to the fairway, and knocked his approach just off the back, but got down in two. "You know, I'll take it," Rahm said. "My first wire-to-wire victory, and even though it was hard at the end, I'll take it."

Vidanta Vallarta (Norman), Nuevo Vallarta, Mexico — April 28-May 1
Par 71 (35-36); 7,456 yards — Purse: $7,300,000

1	**Jon Rahm**	64	66	68	69	267	$1,314,000
2	**Tony Finau**	71	68	66	63	268	552,367
	Brandon Wu	69	70	66	63	268	552,367
	Kurt Kitayama	64	70	66	68	268	552,367
5	Davis Riley	69	65	67	68	269	299,300
6	Cameron Champ	67	66	67	70	270	238,163
	David Lipsky	69	68	69	64	270	238,163
	Alex Smalley	66	66	70	68	270	238,163
	Aaron Wise	65	75	66	64	270	238,163
10	Patrick Rodgers	66	69	66	70	271	198,925
11	Nate Lashley	69	68	64	71	272	177,025
	Martin Trainer	72	65	71	64	272	177,025
13	Grayson Murray	73	67	66	67	273	147,825
	Chez Reavie	67	71	67	68	273	147,825
15	Lanto Griffin	71	69	69	65	274	104,187
	Anirban Lahiri	68	68	72	66	274	104,187
	Jonathan Byrd	64	70	71	69	274	104,187
	Stephan Jaeger	69	71	64	70	274	104,187
	Satoshi Kodaira	67	69	67	71	274	104,187
	Kelly Kraft	68	69	70	67	274	104,187
	Adam Long	67	66	71	70	274	104,187
	Peter Malnati	68	68	72	66	274	104,187
	Andrew Novak	66	67	70	71	274	104,187
24	Michael Gligic	67	70	71	67	275	60,955
	Trey Mullinax	64	69	73	69	275	60,955
	Aaron Rai	65	69	69	72	275	60,955
	Sahith Theegala	65	73	69	68	275	60,955
	Gary Woodland	67	72	69	67	275	60,955
29	Ryan Blaum	66	70	70	70	276	48,910
	Hank Lebioda	67	67	69	73	276	48,910
	Sebastian Munoz	66	69	71	70	276	48,910
	CT Pan	66	70	69	71	276	48,910
33	Brice Garnett	70	67	72	68	277	36,541
	Emiliano Grillo	72	65	71	69	277	36,541
	Graeme McDowell	70	70	69	68	277	36,541
	Scott Piercy	70	68	71	68	277	36,541
	Greyson Sigg	66	73	70	68	277	36,541
	Wesley Bryan	68	69	67	73	277	36,541
	Doug Ghim	72	65	71	69	277	36,541
	Charles Howell III	66	69	70	72	277	36,541
	Cameron Tringale	70	68	70	69	277	36,541
42	Abraham Ancer	71	69	68	70	278	23,287
	Robert Garrigus	68	72	69	69	278	23,287
	Brandon Hagy	66	67	71	74	278	23,287
	John Huh	67	70	73	68	278	23,287
	Ben Kohles	70	69	72	67	278	23,287
	Kevin Na	70	67	73	68	278	23,287
	Alvaro Ortiz	68	69	70	71	278	23,287
	Patrick Reed	67	66	70	75	278	23,287
	Brian Stuard	71	68	70	69	278	23,287
51	Scott Brown	65	69	73	72	279	17,356
	Tommy Gainey	69	71	72	67	279	17,356
	Lee Hodges	68	72	69	70	279	17,356
	Mark Hubbard	68	71	71	69	279	17,356
	Sung Kang	68	72	69	70	279	17,356
	Carlos Ortiz	70	69	71	69	279	17,356
	Turk Pettit	72	67	70	70	279	17,356
	David Skinns	69	69	74	67	279	17,356
59	Bill Haas	70	70	65	75	280	16,498
	Matt Jones	71	69	70	70	280	16,498
61	Kiradech Aphibarnrat	70	66	71	74	281	16,133
	Hayden Buckley	66	73	69	73	281	16,133
	Callum Tarren	73	67	72	69	281	16,133
64	Justin Lower	70	70	69	73	282	15,768
	Brendon Todd	64	74	71	73	282	15,768
66	Pat Perez	67	71	73	72	283	15,549
67	Wyndham Clark	68	72	72	72	284	15,111
	DA Points	69	71	74	70	284	15,111
	Austin Smotherman	74	66	76	68	284	15,111
	Kevin Streelman	71	68	70	75	284	15,111
	Matt Wallace	70	66	75	73	284	15,111
72	Bryson Nimmer	64	74	74	73	285	14,673
73	Brett Drewitt	68	70	76	74	288	14,527
74	Joshua Creel	68	70	77	74	289	14,381

Wells Fargo Championship

Things began looking up for popular podcaster Max Homa when he decided to quit talking a good game and stick to playing one, instead. It paid off again at the Wells Fargo Championship in May, in British Open rain and cold, where he trailed through the first three rounds then broke through in the fourth to win by two strokes. While it was his fourth victory overall, it was his second in eight months after dropping the microphone.

The podcast, "Get A Grip", had gotten popular in his 21 months on it. But it became a psychological drain for him. In constantly reviewing his latest play, he discovered a dark side. Revisiting hooks, slices and bogeys was grinding him down. "I love doing it," Homa had said, "but having to regurgitate all the bad things that happened wasn't healthy for me."

Homa's first tour win was in the 2019 Wells Fargo at its longtime home, Quail Hollow, and next he took the 2021 Genesis. Then he quit the podcast early in September 2021, and won the very next week at the Fortinet. And next came this Wells Fargo, his second win in eight months, post-podcast, played at the TPC Potomac in Maryland, with Quail Hollow preparing to host the Presidents Cup in September.

For two rounds, the tournament seemed like the return of Jason Day, hugely successful until back problems hurt his game. His last win was the 2018 Wells Fargo, and now in the 2022 edition, starting 63-67, he was leading by three strokes. But his remade swing folded to a third-round 79.

Heavy rain hit on Friday, and in a biting chill in the third round, Keegan Bradley shot 67, one of only four to shoot in the 60s. At eight-under 202, he had a two-stroke lead on Homa, who shot an economical 71 on two birdies and three bogeys. Bradley's two-shot lead evaporated in a double bogey at the second on Sunday, and he closed with a rocky two-over 72 that contained five birdies, three bogeys and two double bogeys. He tied for second with Cameron Young (66) and England's Matt Fitzpatrick (67), both seeking that first win. Young was encouraged. "I think I played really well knowing that I had to do something special to have a chance to win and almost did," he said. Fitzpatrick was pleased with his no-bogey finish. "I felt pretty stress-free," he said.

Homa kept his balance through a bumpy final round. He scattered three bogeys from stray tee shots, birdied the first and fifth, both from eight feet, as Bradley stumbled. After a bogey, Homa birdied the ninth from nine feet, then alternated birdies and bogeys at 10, 13, 15 and 16 for a 68 and the two-stroke win on eight-under 272. "I care about nothing more than making that Presidents Cup team," Homa said. "So I really hope captain Davis Love III was watching."

TPC Potomac at Avenel Farm, Potomac, Maryland — May 5-8
Par 70 (35-35); 7,160 yards — Purse: $9,000,000

1	**Max Homa**	67	66	71	68	272	$1,620,000
2	**Keegan Bradley**	70	65	67	72	274	681,000
	Matt Fitzpatrick	68	68	71	67	274	681,000
	Cameron Young	68	71	69	66	274	681,000
5	Rory McIlroy	67	73	68	68	276	369,000
6	Lanto Griffin	70	69	71	67	277	303,750
	Stephan Jaeger	67	71	73	66	277	303,750
	Anirban Lahiri	68	68	70	71	277	303,750
9	Stewart Cink	66	73	74	65	278	218,250
	James Hahn	66	68	72	72	278	218,250
	Brian Harman	69	66	73	70	278	218,250
	Mackenzie Hughes	66	73	72	67	278	218,250
	JT Poston	68	69	74	67	278	218,250
	Adam Schenk	69	68	73	68	278	218,250
15	Jason Day	63	67	79	70	279	141,750
	Kurt Kitayama	67	67	76	69	279	141,750
	CT Pan	68	71	70	70	279	141,750
	Chez Reavie	69	71	72	67	279	141,750
	Nick Taylor	67	73	69	70	279	141,750
	Jhonattan Vegas	68	69	72	70	279	141,750
21	Corey Conners	69	71	70	70	280	98,100
	Rickie Fowler	66	72	74	68	280	98,100
	Sergio Garcia	67	71	74	68	280	98,100
	Chad Ramey	69	66	73	72	280	98,100
25	Ryan Armour	72	67	76	66	281	69,150
	Luke Donald	71	68	75	67	281	69,150
	Kyoung-Hoon Lee	66	73	70	72	281	69,150
	Denny McCarthy	65	69	74	73	281	69,150
	Austin Smotherman	68	71	73	69	281	69,150
	Matthew Wolff	65	73	70	73	281	69,150
31	Luke List	68	66	74	74	282	55,013
	Justin Lower	68	70	76	68	282	55,013
	Matthew NeSmith	67	72	75	68	282	55,013
	Turk Pettit	67	72	71	72	282	55,013
35	Russell Knox	68	72	72	71	283	47,925
	Troy Merritt	71	69	71	72	283	47,925
37	Michael Gligic	71	69	71	73	284	41,850
	Tyrrell Hatton	70	66	76	72	284	41,850
	Si Woo Kim	67	72	70	75	284	41,850
	Scott Piercy	67	71	73	73	284	41,850
41	Tony Finau	69	69	74	73	285	33,750
	Russell Henley	68	72	74	71	285	33,750
	Hank Lebioda	68	70	73	74	285	33,750
	Rory Sabbatini	67	69	77	72	285	33,750

	Dawie van der Walt	69	70	76	70	285	33,750
46	Dylan Frittelli	71	69	74	72	286	26,670
	David Lingmerth	71	69	72	74	286	26,670
	Chase Seiffert	67	73	74	72	286	26,670
49	Kelly Kraft	70	70	74	73	287	23,490
	Matt Kuchar	67	73	73	74	287	23,490
51	Paul Barjon	65	74	76	73	288	21,762
	Joel Dahmen	64	75	76	73	288	21,762
	Peter Malnati	67	73	77	71	288	21,762
	Ben Martin	68	70	76	74	288	21,762
	Brendan Steele	68	70	78	72	288	21,762
56	Abraham Ancer	69	68	76	76	289	20,790
	Callum Tarren	65	74	77	73	289	20,790
	Camilo Villegas	69	69	75	76	289	20,790
59	Ben Kohles	67	72	75	76	290	20,340
	Henrik Norlander	70	69	75	76	290	20,340
61	Martin Laird	70	69	76	76	291	20,070
62	Kevin Chappell	70	69	79	75	293	19,800
	Dylan Wu	66	73	76	78	293	19,800
64	Taylor Moore	69	71	79	76	295	19,440
	Michael Thompson	71	69	82	73	295	19,440

AT&T Byron Nelson

It might be a bit threadbare, the cliché about a guy "being known by the company he keeps," but who's going to complain about keeping company with Sam Snead, Jack Nicklaus and Tom Watson? That was Korea's Kyoung-Hoon Lee, on the occasion of his joining that august group as the fourth to win back-to-back AT&T Bryon Nelsons.

And if there's also a cliché about having victory snatched away, Jordan Spieth would just as soon nobody brought it up. This Nelson was at TPC Craig Ranch, near Dallas, and Spieth is a Dallas native. He didn't want to be a prophet in his own hometown. He'd settle for being a Nelson winner. "I love playing at home," said Spieth. "I would like to win it someday."

It was 12 years earlier, in the 2010 Nelson, that Spieth, then a 16-year-old high school kid, awed the homefolks by contending in his debut. He was tied for seventh after the third round and eventually finished tied for 16th. This time he was duelling for the lead down the stretch when Lee, the defending champion, dashed from behind to edge him out for his second tour victory and that second straight Nelson. "It still feels like I'm dreaming," said Lee. "Last year and this year, to make a good memory."

More like a nightmare for Spieth, who had won the RBC Heritage five weeks earlier. "Shot five under, and a guy went out and shot eight under right in front of us," he said. "So, sometimes that happens."

When it came to nightmares, Sebastian Munoz, 29, a Colombian living in North Texas, had a beauty. He'd opened with a 12-under 60 and led for the first three rounds. Munoz, looking for his second win, added 69-66 and led Spieth by one entering the final round. Then at the first hole, he made what would be his only bogey of the round, and soon he was one of the chasers. He closed with a 69 and tied for third at 24 under with Hideki Matsuyama, who eagled the 18th for a 62.

In the final round, Spieth and Lee both posted five birdies through the front nine, but Spieth had made a couple of early bogeys and his one-stroke edge at the turn disappeared with another at the 10th on a three-putt from inside seven feet. The par-five 12th was the decisive point. Both reached in two. Spieth two-putted from 14 feet for a birdie, but Lee holed his five-footer for an eagle and a one-stroke lead that held up. Lee birdied the 13th, Spieth the 14th and both birdied 18.

Spieth closed with a 67 to be the runner-up, his best-ever Nelson finish, but a bittersweet one. "This one will sting just a little bit," he said. Lee shot 64-68-67-63, for 26-under 262, to join Snead, Nicklaus and Watson as a repeat winner. "I can't believe it," said Lee, often known as "KH". "Just hopefully people remember my name."

TPC Craig Ranch, McKinney, Texas — May 12-15
Par 72 (36-36); 7,468 yards — Purse: $9,100,000

1	**Kyoung-Hoon Lee**	64	68	67	63	262	$1,638,000
2	**Jordan Spieth**	67	65	64	67	263	991,900
3	**Hideki Matsuyama**	67	66	69	62	264	536,900
	Sebastian Munoz	60	69	66	69	264	536,900
5	Ryan Palmer	67	62	70	66	265	336,700
	Xander Schauffele	72	67	65	61	265	336,700
	Justin Thomas	68	66	64	67	265	336,700
8	Charl Schwartzel	66	65	68	67	266	284,375
9	James Hahn	69	68	61	69	267	247,975
	Peter Malnati	64	70	67	66	267	247,975
	Davis Riley	72	64	64	67	267	247,975
12	Christiaan Bezuidenhout	67	70	64	67	268	193,375
	Matt Kuchar	67	68	69	64	268	193,375
	Alex Noren	70	63	71	64	268	193,375
15	Brice Garnett	68	68	69	64	269	161,525
	Scottie Scheffler	67	68	65	69	269	161,525

17	Tom Hoge	68	68	67	67	270	116,708
	Beau Hossler	69	64	67	70	270	116,708
	Joohyung Kim	70	67	66	67	270	116,708
	Jason Kokrak	68	65	68	69	270	116,708
	Nate Lashley	72	67	67	64	270	116,708
	Francesco Molinari	69	70	67	64	270	116,708
	Mito Pereira	64	69	70	67	270	116,708
	Seamus Power	66	67	69	68	270	116,708
25	David Lipsky	69	66	66	70	271	68,445
	Joaquin Niemann	67	65	65	74	271	68,445
	Rory Sabbatini	69	67	68	67	271	68,445
	Austin Smotherman	68	69	66	68	271	68,445
	Scott Stallings	67	67	70	67	271	68,445
	Michael Thompson	70	67	67	67	271	68,445
	Vince Whaley	69	69	66	67	271	68,445
32	Mark Hubbard	70	65	69	68	272	50,808
	Patrick Rodgers	69	67	68	68	272	50,808
	Maverick McNealy	69	65	67	71	272	50,808
	Taylor Moore	72	66	65	69	272	50,808
	Trey Mullinax	68	69	66	69	272	50,808
	Adam Scott	67	69	71	65	272	50,808
38	Cameron Champ	70	68	70	65	273	36,855
	Branden Grace	70	69	67	67	273	36,855
	Stephan Jaeger	71	65	65	72	273	36,855
	Carlos Ortiz	66	69	68	70	273	36,855
	Pat Perez	73	65	67	68	273	36,855
	Conrad Shindler	67	72	67	67	273	36,855
	David Skinns	66	63	74	70	273	36,855
	JJ Spaun	66	68	68	71	273	36,855
46	Emiliano Grillo	71	64	72	67	274	25,680
	Justin Lower	64	66	74	70	274	25,680
	Andrew Novak	69	69	72	64	274	25,680
	Aaron Rai	68	68	68	70	274	25,680
	Callum Tarren	71	68	68	67	274	25,680
51	Joseph Bramlett	69	70	66	70	275	21,635
	Jason Day	68	68	73	66	275	21,635
	Lanto Griffin	71	64	72	68	275	21,635
	Marc Leishman	73	66	69	67	275	21,635
	Matthew NeSmith	71	68	66	70	275	21,635
	Aaron Wise	68	68	68	71	275	21,635
	Jared Wolfe	68	71	71	65	275	21,635
	Brandon Wu	73	66	66	70	275	21,635
59	Tyler Duncan	68	71	69	68	276	20,202
	Tommy Fleetwood	72	67	70	67	276	20,202
	Dustin Johnson	67	70	66	73	276	20,202
	Ian Poulter	69	68	71	68	276	20,202
	Matthias Schwab	67	68	73	68	276	20,202
	Jhonattan Vegas	71	68	71	66	276	20,202
65	Paul Barjon	69	68	69	71	277	19,292
	Wesley Bryan	70	68	73	66	277	19,292
	Bill Haas	71	67	69	70	277	19,292
	Peter Uihlein	69	70	69	69	277	19,292
69	Dylan Frittelli	69	68	70	71	278	18,564
	Chesson Hadley	69	70	68	71	278	18,564
	Seth Reeves	71	67	68	72	278	18,564
	Adam Svensson	69	69	71	69	278	18,564
73	Michael Gligic	72	67	70	70	279	17,927
	Sepp Straka	70	69	70	70	279	17,927
	Vaughn Taylor	70	68	70	71	279	17,927
76	Kiradech Aphibarnrat	69	70	74	67	280	17,381
	Keith Mitchell	69	70	69	72	280	17,381
	Martin Trainer	69	70	70	71	280	17,381
79	Adam Schenk	68	70	69	74	281	16,926
	Sahith Theegala	72	67	70	72	281	16,926
81	Dawie van der Walt	67	71	73	71	282	16,562
	Kyle Wilshire	65	73	71	73	282	16,562
83	Patton Kizzire	71	68	74	71	284	16,198
	Max McGreevy	69	70	71	74	284	16,198

Charles Schwab Challenge

Considering that Sam Burns trailed by a bunch day after day, he didn't seem to have all that much to play for in the Charles Schwab Challenge. Maybe the love of the game and a good payday. It sure didn't look like a shootout in the final round, not with Burns starting out seven huge shots behind Scottie Scheffler, his best friend. Also the world number one.

But a shootout it was, with Burns winning on a long-range birdie putt on the first playoff hole. "I can assure you," Burns said, "he wanted to beat me more than anybody else, and I wanted to beat him more than anybody else."

This after a brutally hot week in the 90s at Colonial Country Club — Hogan's Alley, Ben Hogan's old digs — with 20 mph winds, gusts in the 30s, carrying shots one way and another and moving even three-footers on the greens. "It's not just go up there and brush it in," Burns said. "It's going to have your full attention."

Scheffler was part of an eight-man jam at four-under 66 in the first round, and in a three-way tie with a 65 in the second round, with Scott Stallings (64) and Beau Hossler (65). Scheffler made his first bogey of the tournament in the third round, at the 17th, and took the solo lead with a 68 for 11-under 199, two ahead of Stallings (70) and Brendon Todd (65).

Burns, well astern for all three rounds with 71-68-67, got his game in order in a hurry in the final round. He birdied three of the first four holes, his longest putt a 10-footer. He bogeyed the fifth, then birdied four of the next six, with a 15-footer his longest. A stray drive cost him a bogey at the par-four 12th, and he parred in for a 65 and nine-under-par 271. "Hit some good shots that didn't end up in great spots," he said, "and I hit some bad shots that I got away with."

Then he watched the 16 challengers in front of him fall away, one by one. Harold Varner III was tied for the lead going to the 12th, then crashed painfully with two triple bogeys and two doubles. Rookie

Davis Riley, looking for his first win, was leading at 11 under through the 11th, then missed a three-foot par putt at 13 and double-bogeyed 14 when his tee shot sailed out of bounds. Stallings was 10 under but flew the green with his approach at the 12th and bogeyed. Scheffler had an uncharacteristic day. He had no birdies, made some outstanding pars, and bogeyed twice, missing a 40-inch par putt at the 12th, for a 72.

In the playoff at the 18th, Burns's second was just off the back edge, 38 feet away. Scheffler was on the green, 36 feet away. Burns's putt curled in for a birdie, and Scheffler's missed. "I just didn't have it today," Scheffler said. "Props to Sam. He played great."

Colonial Country Club, Fort Worth, Texas — May 26-29
Par 70 (35-35); 7,209 yards — Purse: $8,400,000

1	**Sam Burns**	71	68	67	65	271	$1,512,000
2	**Scottie Scheffler**	66	65	68	72	271	915,600
	Burns won playoff at first extra hole						
3	**Brendon Todd**	68	68	65	71	272	579,600
4	Tony Finau	71	68	67	67	273	353,500
	Davis Riley	67	67	70	69	273	353,500
	Scott Stallings	67	64	70	72	273	353,500
7	Cam Davis	66	68	69	72	275	246,540
	Kevin Na	67	71	68	69	275	246,540
	Mito Pereira	70	66	68	71	275	246,540
	Patrick Reed	66	66	71	72	275	246,540
	Jordan Spieth	69	66	70	70	275	246,540
12	John Huh	69	66	68	73	276	178,500
	Matt Jones	70	66	71	69	276	178,500
	Pat Perez	67	66	72	71	276	178,500
15	Christiaan Bezuidenhout	68	68	69	72	277	132,300
	Tyler Duncan	71	67	72	67	277	132,300
	Sungjae Im	70	70	67	70	277	132,300
	Chris Kirk	66	67	70	74	277	132,300
	Russell Knox	68	68	70	71	277	132,300
	Andrew Putnam	73	65	67	72	277	132,300
21	Beau Hossler	66	65	73	74	278	98,700
	Viktor Hovland	69	65	73	71	278	98,700
23	Daniel Berger	71	70	69	69	279	77,700
	Max Homa	69	69	73	68	279	77,700
	Zach Johnson	70	71	67	71	279	77,700
	Danny Lee	73	64	77	65	279	77,700
27	Talor Gooch	72	69	67	72	280	56,333
	Bill Haas	68	71	71	70	280	56,333
	Denny McCarthy	68	68	71	73	280	56,333
	Chad Ramey	70	66	69	75	280	56,333
	Chez Reavie	68	72	71	69	280	56,333
	Webb Simpson	66	69	73	72	280	56,333
	Alex Smalley	72	66	69	73	280	56,333
	Harold Varner III	66	68	68	78	280	56,333
35	Tommy Fleetwood	70	69	73	69	281	41,832
	Dylan Frittelli	67	70	70	74	281	41,832
	Lee Hodges	69	71	68	73	281	41,832
	Adam Long	68	71	73	69	281	41,832
	Patrick Rodgers	71	70	74	66	281	41,832
40	Luke Donald	69	69	71	73	282	30,660
	Lucas Glover	70	67	70	75	282	30,660
	Kurt Kitayama	71	65	70	76	282	30,660
	Collin Morikawa	70	71	70	71	282	30,660
	Ryan Palmer	69	69	71	73	282	30,660
	Ian Poulter	70	69	71	72	282	30,660
	Adam Svensson	69	68	69	76	282	30,660
	Michael Thompson	73	67	71	71	282	30,660
48	Lucas Herbert	71	70	70	72	283	22,092
	David Lipsky	71	68	73	71	283	22,092
	Sebastian Munoz	70	70	70	73	283	22,092
	Nick Taylor	66	71	72	74	283	22,092
52	Mark Hubbard	71	70	72	71	284	20,009
	Max McGreevy	68	66	74	76	284	20,009
	CT Pan	69	69	74	72	284	20,009
	Rory Sabbatini	71	69	71	73	284	20,009
	Martin Trainer	68	70	74	72	284	20,009
57	Rickie Fowler	69	70	71	75	285	18,984
	Troy Merritt	73	66	72	74	285	18,984
	Matthew NeSmith	69	71	72	73	285	18,984
	Matthias Schwab	69	71	70	75	285	18,984
	Brandt Snedeker	71	69	70	75	285	18,984
	Sahith Theegala	70	69	67	79	285	18,984
63	Joel Dahmen	71	70	70	75	286	18,228
	Emiliano Grillo	69	68	71	78	286	18,228
	Austin Smotherman	67	71	70	78	286	18,228
66	Charley Hoffman	68	70	71	78	287	17,892
67	Jason Kokrak	69	71	76	72	288	17,724
68	Aaron Rai	71	68	76	74	289	17,556
69	Harry Higgs	69	71	75	80	295	17,388

Memorial Tournament

As celebrations go, this one barely met the minimum qualifications. There was no whooping and hollering, no fist pumps, no high-fives, no hand slaps. Billy Horschel watched his long putt roll obediently across the green and when it slowed down and took that last little turn to the left, and dropped, he simply lifted his arms, in a kind of slow sign-off. It could be argued that the putt was worthy of a heartier reception. It was a 53-footer for eagle at the 15th in the final round, and with it, Horschel pretty much locked up the Memorial Tournament.

Horschel got a proper celebration a little while later at Muirfield Village's elevated amphitheatre 18th. He was still holding his putter when his wife and their three little children swarmed him on the green on the occasion of his seventh tour victory. Hugs 'n kisses all around. Horschel won by four, but it wasn't as comfy as it looked on the scoreboard. It came down to what might be called a "Tiger and Jack Moment".

Horschel had taken the lead with a flawless 65 in the third round, sparked at the first by chipping in from 44 feet. He led by five over Aaron Wise (69) and Cameron Smith (72). Smith stumbled early in the final round and was on his way to a 77. Wise chipped away and got within two when Horschel bogeyed the 12th. Then Wise bogeyed 13 and Horschel was three ahead again.

Horschel said he'd learned from Tiger Woods and Jack Nicklaus that a golfer leading by five didn't have to do anything special unless the moment called for it. And the moment certainly was calling at the par-five 15th when Wise slipped his wedge shot to within two feet, setting up an easy birdie. Horschel was on the green with his second, but nearly 55 feet away. "If I had to do something special, I was ready for it," he said. Then that cross-green putt took that final turn and dropped. "Making that," Horschel said, "was huge."

Wise got his birdie but Horschel was leading by four again. After an exchange of bogeys coming in, Horschel wrapped up his card of 70-68-65-72 to finish out at 13-under 275.

Horschel was spared some heat when two top challengers, Rory McIlroy and defending champion Patrick Cantlay, had strange third rounds. McIlroy started three off the lead then stalled out on nine pars and a bogey through the 10th and was nine back after a 73. Cantlay double-bogeyed the first off a watered tee shot, then had two eagles. He shot 69 and slipped from five to seven behind, then ended up third on Sunday with Joaquin Niemann.

Horschel, along the way, had a run of 58 holes without a bogey before catching the rough at the sixth in the fourth round. "Having a five-shot lead, knowing it was mine to win," Horschel said, "I really wanted to get the monkey off my back."

Muirfield Village Golf Club, Dublin, Ohio — June 2-5
Par 72 (36-36); 7,533 yards — Purse: $12,000,000

1	**Billy Horschel**	70	68	65	72	275	$2,160,000
2	**Aaron Wise**	70	69	69	71	279	1,308,000
3	**Patrick Cantlay**	72	69	69	71	281	708,000
	Joaquin Niemann	71	69	70	71	281	708,000
5	Daniel Berger	70	72	67	73	282	411,600
	Max Homa	69	74	70	69	282	411,600
	Denny McCarthy	68	69	73	72	282	411,600
	Sahith Theegala	68	75	68	71	282	411,600
	Will Zalatoris	68	73	71	70	282	411,600
10	Sungjae Im	70	70	75	69	284	303,000
	Jon Rahm	72	70	73	69	284	303,000
	Brendan Steele	69	76	68	71	284	303,000
13	Corey Conners	69	73	74	69	285	221,400
	Si Woo Kim	72	71	71	71	285	221,400
	Mito Pereira	73	72	70	70	285	221,400
	Davis Riley	67	71	72	75	285	221,400
	Cameron Smith	67	69	72	77	285	221,400
18	Adam Hadwin	76	68	70	72	286	142,800
	Brian Harman	73	70	71	72	286	142,800
	Garrick Higgo	75	71	70	70	286	142,800
	Charles Howell III	71	72	70	73	286	142,800
	Rory McIlroy	70	69	73	74	286	142,800
	Keith Mitchell	70	69	76	71	286	142,800
	Xander Schauffele	70	73	73	70	286	142,800
	Jordan Spieth	70	74	69	73	286	142,800
26	Luke List	67	71	72	77	287	89,400
	Francesco Molinari	71	68	70	78	287	89,400
	Pat Perez	72	72	73	70	287	89,400
	Aaron Rai	74	72	69	72	287	89,400
	Adam Schenk	74	72	69	72	287	89,400
31	Jason Day	71	74	68	75	288	78,600
32	Abraham Ancer	69	72	71	77	289	68,520
	Joel Dahmen	69	73	71	76	289	68,520
	Emiliano Grillo	71	73	70	75	289	68,520
	Beau Hossler	72	70	71	76	289	68,520
	Shane Lowry	69	72	72	76	289	68,520
37	Keegan Bradley	69	75	69	77	290	51,000
	Wyndham Clark	68	76	73	73	290	51,000
	Mackenzie Hughes	67	73	76	74	290	51,000
	Martin Laird	72	73	71	74	290	51,000
	David Lipsky	71	70	73	76	290	51,000
	Matthew NeSmith	69	72	70	79	290	51,000
	JT Poston	78	68	74	70	290	51,000
	Jhonattan Vegas	69	69	71	81	290	51,000
45	Matt Kuchar	70	75	72	74	291	37,800
	Sepp Straka	71	70	74	76	291	37,800
	Adam Svensson	72	71	76	72	291	37,800
48	Lucas Herbert	70	76	70	76	292	32,040
	David Lingmerth	74	72	73	73	292	32,040
	Cameron Tringale	73	70	71	78	292	32,040
51	Lanto Griffin	74	72	76	71	293	29,760
	Viktor Hovland	71	73	78	71	293	29,760
53	Cam Davis	71	75	78	70	294	27,994
	Chris Kirk	75	68	76	75	294	27,994
	CT Pan	76	68	76	74	294	27,994
	Camilo Villegas	73	72	78	71	294	27,994
	Kyoung-Hoon Lee	67	70	75	82	294	27,994
	Troy Merritt	73	72	69	80	294	27,994
	Patrick Reed	76	70	73	75	294	27,994
60	Doug Ghim	77	68	72	78	295	26,640
	Lucas Glover	75	70	77	73	295	26,640
	Brandt Snedeker	72	74	72	77	295	26,640
	Cameron Young	67	71	73	84	295	26,640
64	Rickie Fowler	70	74	75	77	296	25,800
	Kramer Hickok	75	71	76	74	296	25,800
	Carlos Ortiz	71	72	75	78	296	25,800
67	Chan Kim	73	73	70	83	299	25,200
	Adam Scott	70	76	73	80	299	25,200
69	Brandon Wu	71	69	80	80	300	24,840
70	Ryan Moore	74	72	78	79	303	24,600

RBC Canadian Open

Rory McIlroy, affable Irishman, is one of the best in the world at his profession, an artist with every club in the golf bag. On winning the RBC Canadian Open, however, one particular thought seemed uppermost in his mind. "Twenty-one PGA Tour wins," McIlroy said, "one more than somebody else."

To take the win first, oddly enough, McIlroy was the defending champion after the Canadian Open had been cancelled for two years because of the Covid-19 pandemic. The 2019 winner took control of a wild scramble in 2022 that went down to the last two holes, and shot St George's in 66-68-65-62 to win on 19-under-par 261, beating Tony Finau by two and Justin Thomas by four.

McIlroy was one behind Wyndham Clark (63-70) after 36 holes. Then the tournament heated up for a roaring finish, with Finau and McIlroy in the grip of varying inspirations. Finau was miffed at himself for two late second-round bogeys. "All it did was light a fire in my belly," he said. And so in the third, he rang up seven birdies and an eagle (on a 40-foot putt at the par-five ninth) for a 62, going to 11 under. McIlroy got charged up by Finau's surge. "I need to be super aggressive and make some birdies," he said. And he did – six of them against a bogey for a 65 to tie Finau.

In the fourth round, Justin Rose nearly stole the show, shooting a course and tournament-record 10-under 60. "I'm totally disappointed," he said. "I've never shot 59 before."

Finau rolled bogey-free through the final round and punctuated it with his sixth birdie at the 18th on a 42-foot putt for a 64 and 17 under par, second by two to McIlroy. "Hat's off to him," Finau said. "I played great – he just played a couple shots better."

McIlroy was a man consumed in the final round. He birdied eight of the first 12 holes, a string highlighted by a 26-foot putt at the first, a 32-footer at the sixth, and a 40-footer at 12. Bogeys at two par-threes, the 13th and 16th, tied him with Thomas, who was paired with him and Finau in the final group. McIlroy effectively won on a two-shot swing at the 17th, holing a two-foot birdie putt as Thomas bogeyed. Thomas, who made six of his eight birdies in a row from the sixth, also bogeyed the last for a 64 and finished four back. In front of the packed gallery, McIlroy birdied the last for his 10th of the day and that 21st PGA Tour win.

Among those on 20 tour wins is Greg Norman, now CEO of the LIV Golf Invitational Series, which had just concluded its inaugural event in London. McIlroy was not hiding his feelings on the matter. "I had extra motivation because of what's going on across the pond," he said. "This is a day I'll remember for a long, long time."

St George's Golf & Country Club, Toronto, Ontario, Canada — June 9-12
Par 70 (34-36); 7,014 yards — Purse: $8,700,000

1	**Rory McIlroy**	66	68	65	62	261	$1,566,000
2	**Tony Finau**	66	71	62	64	263	948,300
3	**Justin Thomas**	69	69	63	64	265	600,300
4	Sam Burns	67	69	65	65	266	391,500
	Justin Rose	69	70	67	60	266	391,500
6	Corey Conners	71	69	66	62	268	315,375
7	Wyndham Clark	63	70	68	69	270	273,325
	Chris Kirk	69	69	66	66	270	273,325
	Keith Mitchell	67	67	70	66	270	273,325
10	Matt Fitzpatrick	64	70	70	67	271	219,675
	Danny Lee	68	69	69	65	271	219,675
	Shane Lowry	67	69	69	66	271	219,675
13	Austin Cook	71	64	68	69	272	160,515
	Kelly Kraft	69	69	70	64	272	160,515
	Aaron Rai	69	70	67	66	272	160,515
	Brendon Todd	69	69	68	66	272	160,515
	Harold Varner III	65	72	68	67	272	160,515
18	Doug Ghim	65	71	68	69	273	123,975
	Patrick Rodgers	67	69	72	65	273	123,975
	Scottie Scheffler	69	67	71	66	273	123,975
21	Adam Long	70	67	67	70	274	94,830
	Scott Piercy	70	70	66	68	274	94,830
	Alex Smalley	67	67	67	73	274	94,830
	Adam Svensson	72	68	67	67	274	94,830
25	John Huh	69	69	72	65	275	71,485
	Jim Knous	67	67	69	72	275	71,485
	Sebastian Munoz	69	70	65	71	275	71,485
28	Emiliano Grillo	70	70	67	69	276	57,047
	Mackenzie Hughes	66	75	68	67	276	57,047
	Jonas Blixt	67	74	70	65	276	57,047
	Hank Lebioda	69	70	71	66	276	57,047
	Chase Seiffert	69	70	67	70	276	57,047
	Nick Taylor	70	68	67	71	276	57,047
	Danny Willett	71	68	72	65	276	57,047
35	Ryan Armour	72	66	68	71	277	39,730
	Adam Hadwin	69	70	69	69	277	39,730
	Nick Hardy	68	73	65	71	277	39,730
	Charley Hoffman	68	68	71	70	277	39,730
	Justin Lower	70	68	70	69	277	39,730
	Ryan Moore	69	69	69	70	277	39,730
	Seung-Yul Noh	69	70	68	70	277	39,730
	Matt Wallace	70	66	70	71	277	39,730
	Vince Whaley	72	69	67	69	277	39,730
44	Mark Hubbard	67	73	72	66	278	30,015
	Austin Smotherman	72	68	70	68	278	30,015
46	Paul Barjon	72	67	70	70	279	26,535

	Carlos Ortiz	67	73	69	70	279	26,535	59	JJ Henry	69	71	71	71	282	19,662
48	Aaron Cockerill	70	68	73	69	280	22,568		Cameron Percy	71	68	71	72	282	19,662
	Lee Hodges	66	70	77	67	280	22,568	61	Dylan Frittelli	74	67	70	72	283	19,314
	Cameron Smith	76	65	68	71	280	22,568		Kramer Hickok	68	73	71	71	283	19,314
	Brandt Snedeker	68	70	72	70	280	22,568	63	Ben Crane	72	67	74	71	284	19,053
	Vaughn Taylor	68	70	75	67	280	22,568	64	Rafa Cabrera Bello	71	70	72	72	285	18,531
53	Brett Drewitt	71	70	69	71	281	20,387		Brandon Hagy	73	68	74	70	285	18,531
	Ben Martin	71	66	73	71	281	20,387		Andrew Novak	72	68	73	72	285	18,531
	Robert Streb	69	70	71	71	281	20,387		Sean O'Hair	70	71	70	74	285	18,531
	Sahith Theegala	71	70	67	73	281	20,387		David Skinns	71	69	73	72	285	18,531
	Bo Van Pelt	71	69	65	76	281	20,387	69	Trey Mullinax	70	71	74	71	286	18,009
	Jhonattan Vegas	71	70	72	68	281	20,387	70	Dawie van der Walt	73	68	78	69	288	17,835

Travelers Championship

It was bound to happen. Xander Schauffele and Patrick Cantlay, the Dynamic Duo side-by-side in team play (see also Presidents Cup, Zurich Classic), finally met head-to-head. It came to pass in the final round of the Travelers Championship in June. And after Cantlay crumbled, Schauffele proceeded to his sixth PGA Tour title. Schauffele shot TPC River Highlands in 63-63-67-68, 19-under 261, to beat JT Poston and the broken-hearted Sahith Theegala by two for his first individual victory in three years. "Don't remind me," Schauffele cracked.

But it was possible only because the pitiless gods of golf snatched what would have been Theegala's first tour win off his fingertips at the final hole. A bladed bunker shot, a lipped-out putt, and that was it.

The Travelers opened with Rory McIlroy doing an iron man routine, playing in his fourth straight tournament and getting off to a sizzling start, tying Poston for the first-round lead at eight-under 62. In the second, he reached 13 under and was leading by a stroke until his incredible crash — a quadruple-bogey eight at the 12th and a double bogey at the par-four 15th. His race was run.

Not so Schauffele, who opened with the two 63s, then shot 67 in the third round, getting to 17 under. Cantlay shot 63, a stroke behind, setting up that showdown of pals in the final round. Schauffele grinned. "I've been looking forward to hashing it out with Pat," he said. Said Cantlay: "I'm going out there to try as hard as I can and let the chips fall where they may."

But the shootout never got off the ground. Cantlay got swept away by a frantic final round: three pars, five birdies, nine bogeys and a double bogey for a 76 and a tie for 13th. But the finish didn't lack for drama and suspense.

Poston, seeking his second tour victory, made a mad dash from nine behind, but his flawless 64 fell two shots short. He summed up a harmonious round: "I putted well, drove it well, hit my irons good."

Theegala started from three behind, holed an 11-footer for birdie at 17 to inch past Schauffele, then crashed at the par-four 18th. He drove into the front lip of a fairway bunker, and didn't get his first try out. "Somehow I just straight bladed it," he said. He got the second out to 12 feet, then lipped out the bogey putt. He dropped to his knees in anguish. He double-bogeyed for a 67 to tie with Poston.

"To watch what happened was a bit of a shock," Schauffele said. "I really had to try and focus on the task at hand." Which he did, hitting a wedge to three feet and holing for a three-shot swing and the long-awaited victory. "Subconsciously, I was getting a little impatient," he said. "And this week I was just trying to stay as patient as possible."

TPC River Highlands, Cromwell, Connecticut — June 23-26
Par 70 (35-35); 6,852 yards — Purse: $8,300,000

1	**Xander Schauffele**	63	63	67	68	261	$1,494,000		Brian Harman	68	69	66	66	269	243,605
2	**JT Poston**	62	70	67	64	263	738,700		William McGirt	66	70	66	67	269	243,605
	Sahith Theegala	67	65	64	67	263	738,700		Chez Reavie	67	69	66	67	269	243,605
4	Michael Thorbjornsen (A)	68	65	66	66	265			Scott Stallings	74	64	68	63	269	243,605
5	Chesson Hadley	68	67	67	64	266	406,700	13	Patrick Cantlay	64	67	63	76	270	159,775
6	Kevin Kisner	67	64	66	71	268	320,588		Tony Finau	68	68	65	69	270	159,775
	Keith Mitchell	66	68	67	67	268	320,588		John Huh	67	65	69	69	270	159,775
8	Nick Hardy	67	64	68	70	269	243,605		Martin Laird	63	69	66	72	270	159,775

	Scottie Scheffler	68 67 65 70	270	159,775
	Webb Simpson	64 69 66 71	270	159,775
19	Keegan Bradley	69 69 66 67	271	106,102
	Luke List	68 68 70 65	271	106,102
	Rory McIlroy	62 70 72 67	271	106,102
	Matthew NeSmith	65 67 68 71	271	106,102
	Harris English	66 65 69 71	271	106,102
	Kyoung-Hoon Lee	68 64 66 73	271	106,102
25	Ryan Armour	68 66 72 66	272	61,835
	Bill Haas	72 64 68 68	272	61,835
	Lee Hodges	68 65 67 72	272	61,835
	Mackenzie Hughes	70 66 68 68	272	61,835
	Nate Lashley	68 68 67 69	272	61,835
	Adam Long	68 65 70 69	272	61,835
	Seamus Power	67 65 70 70	272	61,835
	Brendan Steele	68 66 69 69	272	61,835
	Kevin Streelman	71 67 67 67	272	61,835
	Adam Svensson	71 64 66 71	272	61,835
35	Wyndham Clark	66 68 71 68	273	43,243
	Christopher Gotterup	68 68 70 67	273	43,243
	Charles Howell III	64 68 70 71	273	43,243
	Sam Ryder	68 68 71 66	273	43,243
	Robert Streb	69 69 68 67	273	43,243
40	Michael Gligic	70 68 68 68	274	36,105
	Aaron Rai	68 68 67 71	274	36,105
	Matthew Wolff	71 66 71 66	274	36,105
43	Hayden Buckley	67 68 69 71	275	31,125
	Conrad Shindler	70 66 67 72	275	31,125
	Harold Varner III	72 63 67 73	275	31,125
46	Tyler Duncan	69 67 71 69	276	23,679
	Ben Silverman	70 68 69 69	276	23,679
	Matt Wallace	67 71 72 66	276	23,679
	Tommy Fleetwood	69 66 70 71	276	23,679
	Mark Hubbard	71 64 71 70	276	23,679
	Andrew Novak	72 64 70 70	276	23,679
	Andrew Putnam	68 69 67 72	276	23,679
53	Paul Barjon	71 67 66 73	277	20,003
	Stewart Cink	71 66 71 69	277	20,003
	Matthias Schwab	69 68 71 69	277	20,003
56	Jonas Blixt	69 66 73 70	278	19,007
	Joseph Bramlett	67 71 70 70	278	19,007
	Cam Davis	65 66 73 74	278	19,007
	Luke Donald	70 67 70 71	278	19,007
	Kelly Kraft	68 70 70 70	278	19,007
	Hank Lebioda	66 70 74 68	278	19,007
	Taylor Moore	68 68 70 72	278	19,007
63	Austin Cook	72 65 69 73	279	18,343
64	Patton Kizzire	67 69 70 74	280	18,011
	Peter Malnati	69 68 69 74	280	18,011
	Davis Riley	68 69 69 74	280	18,011
67	Kevin Tway	71 67 69 74	281	17,679
68	Morgan Hoffmann	68 70 73 71	282	17,513
69	Joel Dahmen	67 69 73 75	284	17,347
70	Lucas Glover	70 68 75 72	285	17,098
	Harry Higgs	71 64 73 77	285	17,098

John Deere Classic

When JT Poston gets around to writing his book, he'll have two chapters ready-made. The first chapter, "Pressure golf made easy", would be from the 2019 Wyndham, his breakthrough win. In that one, he had the comfort of trailing through the first three rounds before closing with a 62. Of course, running all through the tournament, there was the matter of going all 72 holes without a bogey, the first PGA Tour winner to do so since Lee Trevino in 1974. Poston had played so well that he had to rise above modesty and concede that his performance was "pretty awesome".

The second chapter would be from winning the 2022 John Deere Classic: "The Art of Managing to Breathe While Going Wire-to-Wire". Poston entered the final round leading by three and erupted with birdies on the first three holes, on short putts at the first and second and a 23-footer at the third. Then came a shock, two quick bogeys. He three-putted the fifth and caught a bunker at the sixth, and his lead was down to one. "I don't want to say jarring," Poston said, "but it got my attention."

The jolt left Poston needing what he called a "reset". "The mental reset for me was saving par on seven and kind of settling the nerves a little bit," he said. He'd missed the green of the par three, but got up-and-down from 60 feet, holing a six-footer for his par. That led to a string of 10 pars capped by a chip-and-putt birdie from 90 feet at the par-five 17th. A tidy finishing par wrapped up a card of 62-65-67-69 and a wire-to-wire win on 21-under 263, three ahead of South Africa's Christiaan Bezuidenhout (66) and Argentina's Emiliano Grillo (69).

The win gave Poston a berth in The 150th Open in two weeks at the Old Course in St Andrews. "I've always wanted to play in one," Poston said. "I cant wait to get there and see what it's like." Bezuidenhout and Grillo also qualified. "I needed a good solid week, so I'm pleased to have done that and pleased to have secured my spot," Bezuidenhout said. Grillo was especially pleased. He noted that raising his ranking for next year was even more important than The Open. "Now I get both," he said, "so that's pretty special."

Poston could reflect on the pressure of knowing the entire pack is at your heels. "It's just tough to play with the lead," he said. "The truth is, it's hard not to think about the finish line and what comes with it. As much as you try and put that aside and not think about it, it's tough not to."

And then he reduced the entire experience to the most intense personal level. Said Poston: "I was just trying to breathe."

TPC Deere Run, Silvis, Illinois
Par 71 (35-36); 7,289 yards

June 30-July 1
Purse: $7,100,000

1	**JT Poston**	62	65	67	69	263	$1,278,000
2	**Christiaan Bezuidenhout**	69	65	66	66	266	631,900
	Emiliano Grillo	68	64	65	69	266	631,900
4	Christopher Gotterup	65	67	69	66	267	319,500
	Scott Stallings	67	66	64	70	267	319,500
6	Denny McCarthy	66	65	66	71	268	248,500
	Callum Tarren	68	65	65	70	268	248,500
8	Cam Davis	68	68	65	68	269	214,775
	Maverick McNealy	70	63	68	68	269	214,775
10	Patrick Flavin	70	66	68	66	270	179,275
	Michael Gligic	64	69	68	69	270	179,275
	Chesson Hadley	67	69	67	67	270	179,275
13	Charles Howell III	68	67	68	68	271	139,042
	Adam Long	70	67	66	68	271	139,042
	Mark Hubbard	67	67	68	69	271	139,042
16	Austin Cook	69	67	70	66	272	97,803
	Bo Hoag	67	69	63	73	272	97,803
	Patton Kizzire	69	65	68	70	272	97,803
	Chris Naegel	66	66	67	73	272	97,803
	Matthias Schwab	67	65	68	72	272	97,803
	Greyson Sigg	70	66	67	69	272	97,803
	Alex Smalley	71	67	68	66	272	97,803
	Sahith Theegala	74	65	65	68	272	97,803
24	Kelly Kraft	70	63	68	72	273	57,865
	David Lipsky	68	67	68	70	273	57,865
	Ryan Moore	72	64	69	68	273	57,865
	Taylor Moore	67	66	72	68	273	57,865
	CT Pan	69	64	69	71	273	57,865
	Adam Svensson	67	67	68	71	273	57,865
30	Nick Hardy	71	68	71	64	274	39,082
	Stephan Jaeger	69	70	69	66	274	39,082
	Brandon Wu	72	65	70	67	274	39,082
	Hayden Buckley	69	66	72	67	274	39,082
	Dylan Frittelli	66	70	70	68	274	39,082
	Satoshi Kodaira	71	68	64	71	274	39,082
	Martin Laird	69	68	70	67	274	39,082
	Peter Malnati	73	66	68	67	274	39,082
	Andrew Novak	70	67	70	67	274	39,082
	Patrick Rodgers	69	69	69	67	274	39,082
	Vaughn Taylor	65	68	73	68	274	39,082
41	Andrew Putnam	70	66	68	71	275	28,755
	Kevin Streelman	69	68	72	66	275	28,755
43	Jonathan Byrd	70	68	71	67	276	21,975
	Fabian Gomez	71	68	71	66	276	21,975
	Lee Hodges	68	71	68	69	276	21,975
	Hank Lebioda	69	65	67	75	276	21,975
	Seung-Yul Noh	70	66	67	73	276	21,975
	Brendon Todd	71	65	71	69	276	21,975
	Vince Whaley	70	69	68	69	276	21,975
	Dylan Wu	69	70	71	66	276	21,975
51	Aaron Baddeley	69	70	69	69	277	16,880
	Derek Ernst	71	68	72	66	277	16,880
	Tommy Gainey	68	69	66	74	277	16,880
	Morgan Hoffmann	72	64	73	68	277	16,880
	Anirban Lahiri	69	67	74	67	277	16,880
	Justin Lower	70	67	67	73	277	16,880
	Preston Stanley	72	67	65	73	277	16,880
	Curtis Thompson	67	67	68	75	277	16,880
59	Michael Thompson	70	68	65	75	278	16,117
60	Zach Johnson	69	69	67	74	279	15,904
	Sam Ryder	71	68	70	70	279	15,904
62	Kramer Hickok	71	68	68	74	281	15,691
63	Brandon Hagy	70	69	68	75	282	15,407
	Rory Sabbatini	70	68	72	72	282	15,407
	Martin Trainer	67	70	75	70	282	15,407
66	Seth Reeves	68	69	67	79	283	15,123
67	James Hahn	68	70	75	71	284	14,910
	Omar Uresti	72	67	73	72	284	14,910
69	Ricky Barnes	66	72	70	77	285	14,697

Barbasol Championship

Played in the same week as the Genesis Scottish Open, the Barbasol Championship, held at Keene Trace in Nicholasville, Kentucky, was the first of two events in America that were also co-sanctioned by the PGA Tour and the DP World Tour. Thus 50 players from the latter circuit were in the field of 156, and the first prize was unusually inspiring: $666,000 and the final berth in The 150th Open at the Old Course the following week. "What an incredible honour to be able to go over there and play," Trey Mullinax, Alabama native, was to say on Sunday. "What a dream come true to be able to go to St Andrews and be able to play."

The Europeans were getting the flavour of the American Upper South in July, with temperatures in the 90s and thunderstorms that delayed play, folding one round into the next. So Mullinax would have to play 33 holes on Sunday to score his first PGA Tour victory on his 106th start. He shot 25-under 263, on rounds of 65-65-67-66, for a one-stroke victory over playing partner and good friend Kevin Streelman. "Yeah, I knew me and him were battling it out," Mullinax said. "I didn't know what the guys behind us were doing. I know that after we birdied 15 there was a leaderboard there and I was trying not to look at all, so I kind of kept my mind away from it."

"I'm frustrated," Streelman said. "I hit two incredible shots there into the last two holes and hit two good putts. One of them went in, one of them didn't."

They were head-to-head down the final stretch. Streelman slipped behind with a bogey at the par-three 16th but snapped right back at the 17th, holing a nine-footer for birdie to tie again. At the 18th,

Mullinax rolled in a 15-footer for birdie, and Streelman's birdie try from nine feet slid by to the right, and he parred for a 67 and 264, a stroke behind. Mullinax had that precious first victory.

Germany's Hurly Long, who played at the University of Oregon and Texas Tech, was the low European, shooting 68-65-63-71 for 267, 21 under, finishing fourth, four behind. "You know, I definitely played well enough to win here," Long said. "Just kind of didn't get it going today."

"Yeah, what a week," Mullinax said, after his 33-hole finale. "Tired. It was a long day today, it was a grind. But we stayed sharp, we stayed focused pretty much all day. We knew it was going to be a grind, we knew we were going to get worn down, but we had to just keep at it, keep firing. And at the end of the day I walked away with the low score."

Keene Trace Golf Club, Nicholasville, Kentucky — July 7-10
Par 72 (36-36); 7,328 yards — Purse: $3,700,000

1	**Trey Mullinax**	65	65	67	66	263	$666,000
2	**Kevin Streelman**	66	64	67	67	264	403,300
3	**Mark Hubbard**	65	67	69	65	266	255,300
4	Hurly Long	68	65	63	71	267	181,300
5	Vince Whaley	70	64	67	67	268	151,700
6	Adam Svensson	62	67	69	71	269	134,125
7	Michael Kim	65	68	67	70	270	124,875
8	Ricardo Gouveia	64	65	72	70	271	100,825
	Marcus Helligkilde	70	69	66	66	271	100,825
	Justin Lower	69	70	66	66	271	100,825
	Sean O'Hair	68	65	65	73	271	100,825
	Matti Schmid	65	63	66	77	271	100,825
13	Espen Kofstad	69	66	70	67	272	64,354
	Tyler Duncan	67	64	69	72	272	64,354
	Kramer Hickok	67	66	69	70	272	64,354
	Ben Kohles	67	66	69	70	272	64,354
	Max McGreevy	65	63	74	70	272	64,354
	Taylor Pendrith	71	68	67	66	272	64,354
	Camilo Villegas	65	68	70	69	272	64,354
20	Yannik Paul	66	67	68	72	273	49,025
21	Patrick Flavin	71	67	67	69	274	37,308
	Doc Redman	66	70	70	68	274	37,308
	Kevin Chappell	69	70	69	66	274	37,308
	Michael Gligic	69	63	73	69	274	37,308
	Taylor Moore	66	72	68	68	274	37,308
	Dylan Wu	66	67	73	68	274	37,308
27	Lucas Bjerregaard	70	66	69	70	275	21,909
	Austin Cook	70	64	73	68	275	21,909
	Satoshi Kodaira	67	67	70	71	275	21,909
	Hugo Leon	67	68	69	71	275	21,909
	Niklas Norgaard Moller	68	67	68	72	275	21,909
	Seth Reeves	69	68	68	70	275	21,909
	Greyson Sigg	66	69	69	71	275	21,909
	Chris Stroud	69	66	70	70	275	21,909
	Julien Brun	67	67	70	71	275	21,909
	Jason Dufner	67	67	73	68	275	21,909
	Brandon Hagy	70	62	71	72	275	21,909
	James Hahn	70	69	68	68	275	21,909
	Robin Roussel	64	68	71	72	275	21,909
	Bo Van Pelt	65	69	72	69	275	21,909
41	Aaron Baddeley	69	70	65	72	276	13,505
	Jonathan Byrd	67	67	71	71	276	13,505
	Hank Lebioda	71	66	71	68	276	13,505
	Lukas Nemecz	71	68	66	71	276	13,505
	Seung-Yul Noh	68	70	70	68	276	13,505
	Cameron Percy	66	69	72	69	276	13,505
47	Greg Chalmers	70	69	68	70	277	10,348
	Alfredo Garcia-Heredia	71	68	71	67	277	10,348
	Gunner Wiebe	72	67	68	70	277	10,348
50	Josh Geary	71	67	70	70	278	9,195
	Tom Lewis	66	68	74	70	278	9,195
	William McGirt	69	66	71	72	278	9,195
	Kevin Tway	67	71	71	69	278	9,195
54	Paul Barjon	71	68	68	72	279	8,584
	Scott Brown	69	69	68	73	279	8,584
	Scott Jamieson	71	67	72	69	279	8,584
	Ryan Moore	68	68	73	70	279	8,584
	Carlos Pigem	68	70	71	70	279	8,584
	Austin Smotherman	69	68	69	73	279	8,584
60	Aaron Cockerill	71	66	71	72	280	8,251
	Conrad Shindler	68	70	70	72	280	8,251
	Santiago Tarrio	69	66	71	74	280	8,251
63	Arjun Atwal	70	69	70	72	281	7,955
	Hayden Buckley	69	70	72	70	281	7,955
	Ben Crane	69	69	73	70	281	7,955
	Josh Teater	68	68	74	71	281	7,955
	Justin Walters	66	71	69	75	281	7,955
68	Sebastian Garcia Rodriguez	71	67	72	72	282	7,548
	Chesson Hadley	71	68	71	72	282	7,548
	Chase Hanna	73	66	72	71	282	7,548
	David Hearn	67	67	75	73	282	7,548
	Richard Johnson	70	68	71	73	282	7,548
	David Skinns	65	70	71	76	282	7,548
74	JJ Henry	72	66	74	71	283	7,215
	Soren Kjeldsen	70	69	71	73	283	7,215
	Dawie van der Walt	69	68	75	71	283	7,215
77	Jim Knous	69	70	74	71	284	7,067
78	Jacob Bridgeman	68	69	75	73	285	6,919
	Jim Herman	72	65	73	75	285	6,919
	Stephen Stallings Jr	70	69	70	76	285	6,919
81	Ryan Brehm	68	69	75	76	288	6,697
	John Merrick	70	69	74	75	288	6,697
	Marcel Siem	69	70	73	76	288	6,697

Barracuda Championship

For Chez Reavie in the Barracuda Championship, the tale was in the bogeys. He made just three, the fewest in the entire tournament. Why is this a significant fact? Because the Barracuda, co-sanctioned by the DP World Tour, was played under the modified Stableford system, which awarded eight points for a double eagle, five for an eagle, two for a birdie, and deducted one for a bogey and three for a double or worse.

Reavie had two eagles and 18 birdies, and just the three bogeys, which totalled up to 43 points, edging Sweden's Alex Noren by one. Noren made 25 birdies and eight bogeys for 42 points. In stroke play Reavie would have shot the par-71 Tahoe Mountain in 67-62-67-69 for 265, 19 under, and Noren 71-65-66-65 for 17-under 267.

On Reavie's three bogeys — he made the first in the third round, on his 51st hole, out of a greenside bunker at the par-three 15th. He made the other two in the final round, with Noren on his heels. "I've been working hard," said Reavie. "I knew I could do it. I just kept grinding, and here we are." It was the third tour win for Reavie, 40, making him the first PGA Tour winner of age 40 or older since Lucas Glover in the 2021 John Deere Classic.

Reavie, who won the 2008 RBC Canadian Open and the 2019 Travelers, started slowly in the Barracuda, with nine points, only four points but a host of players behind the leaders, Charley Hoffman and Mark Hubbard, tied with 13. Taking a lead he would hold the rest of the way, Reavie chipped in for an eagle and made seven birdies for 19 points on Friday. On 28 he had a three-point lead on Hubbard, who had a 12-point round, and Henrik Norlander (14). Reavie doubled his lead to six points at 37 in the third round. Scotland's Martin Laird, based in Denver, birdied the last three holes for a 13-point round and was second at 31, and Noren and Cam Davis had 12-point rounds and were nine back.

In the windy final round, Reavie had four birdies against his two bogeys for six points and a one-point win over the charging Noren. The Sweden was an alternate for The Open and would have got to tee up at St Andrews if he had stayed in Scotland but instead he made the last-minute dash to America. He closed hard with a 14-point round. "Well, this is a great week anyway," he said. "I had a blast today."

Tahoe Mountain Club (Old Greenwood), Truckee, California — July 14-17
Par 71 (36-35); 7,480 yards — Purse: $3,700,000

1	**Chez Reavie**	9	19	9	6	43	$666,000
2	**Alex Noren**	4	12	12	14	42	403,300
3	**Martin Laird**	10	8	13	7	38	255,300
4	Mark Hubbard	13	12	0	12	37	181,300
5	Scott Gutschewski	6	8	11	10	35	151,700
6	Cam Davis	8	8	12	6	34	134,125
7	Hurly Long	6	5	10	12	33	124,875
8	Austin Smotherman	7	9	6	9	31	115,625
9	Maverick McNealy	11	8	7	4	30	104,525
	Michael Thompson	10	-2	18	4	30	104,525
11	Harry Higgs	4	11	11	2	28	89,725
	Taylor Pendrith	5	6	9	8	28	89,725
13	Sean Crocker	12	5	2	8	27	72,458
	Nick Hardy	5	8	10	4	27	72,458
	Marcus Helligkilde	8	7	9	3	27	72,458
16	Joshua Creel	10	5	11	0	26	58,275
	Brice Garnett	12	5	10	-1	26	58,275
	Espen Kofstad	5	7	6	8	26	58,275
	Justin Lower	6	9	6	5	26	58,275
20	Nino Bertasio	7	10	3	5	25	47,175
	Yannik Paul	8	8	4	5	25	47,175
22	Stephan Jaeger	3	5	4	12	24	37,185
	Scott Jamieson	8	7	3	6	24	37,185
	Callum Tarren	11	-4	12	5	24	37,185
	Kevin Tway	6	15	-2	5	24	37,185
26	Bill Haas	8	6	2	7	23	27,565
	James Hahn	-1	10	10	4	23	27,565
	James Morrison	9	6	3	5	23	27,565
	Greyson Sigg	4	12	4	3	23	27,565
	Julian Suri	3	4	3	13	23	27,565
31	Michael Gligic	11	5	-1	7	22	21,169
	Chesson Hadley	5	4	5	8	22	21,169
	Matthieu Pavon	7	5	6	4	22	21,169
	Vince Whaley	6	9	3	4	22	21,169
	Charley Hoffman	13	2	9	-2	22	21,169
	Kelly Kraft	8	8	3	3	22	21,169
	Henrik Norlander	11	14	2	-5	22	21,169
38	Matti Schmid	4	10	1	6	21	17,575
39	Joseph Bramlett	7	4	6	3	20	15,355
	Aaron Cockerill	12	0	6	2	20	15,355
	David Hearn	1	6	12	1	20	15,355
	Francesco Laporta	6	3	7	4	20	15,355
	Martin Trainer	8	11	5	-4	20	15,355
44	Rafa Cabrera Bello	4	5	8	2	19	12,025
	Sebastian Garcia Rodriguez	-2	9	9	3	19	12,025
	Richy Werenski	6	3	3	7	19	12,025
	Ashun Wu	4	3	5	7	19	12,025
48	Pep Angles	3	7	5	3	18	10,064
	Rasmus Hojgaard	6	2	0	10	18	10,064
50	Mark Baldwin	0	8	4	5	17	9,109
	Fabian Gomez	9	2	4	2	17	9,109
	Ben Kohles	4	5	4	4	17	9,109
	Michael Lorenzo-Vera	9	1	5	2	17	9,109
	Cameron Percy	8	3	2	4	17	9,109
55	Kevin Chappell	6	2	1	7	16	8,584
	John Huh	2	13	-2	3	16	8,584
	Jim Knous	11	-2	10	-3	16	8,584
	Seung-Yul Noh	5	4	3	4	16	8,584
59	Lucas Bjerregaard	3	5	5	2	15	8,399
60	Ricky Barnes	2	6	4	2	14	8,214
	Austin Cook	-1	11	8	-4	14	8,214
	Bo Hoag	7	3	4	0	14	8,214
	Chad Ramey	5	3	0	6	14	8,214
64	David Lingmerth	2	6	1	4	13	8,029
65	Taylor Moore	1	9	1	1	12	7,881
	Scott Piercy	8	0	5	-1	12	7,881
	Chase Seiffert	7	6	3	-4	12	7,881
68	Bo Van Pelt	2	5	0	3	10	7,733
69	Jason Dufner	5	2	7	-6	8	7,659
70	Sung Kang	3	7	-3	0	7	7,585
71	Preston Stanley	6	1	1	-3	5	7,511

3M Open

Some days, it's just your day. No explanation needed. No explanation possible. Things happen. Be happy. It's just your day. It was Tony Finau's day in the final round of the 3M Championship. At the 17th, especially. A par-three, all-water carry. Finau arrived at the tee leading by four — a lock. But the word "lock", in this context, is not in the vocabulary of any rational golfer. As Finau was to discover, in a routine heart-in-your-throat episode.

Sometimes the reverse is true. For another golfer, it's just not your day. This was the case for the unfortunate Scott Piercy, in the last group, just behind Finau. Piercy, 43, was rolling along quite nicely toward his fifth tour victory — for three rounds and six holes. Shooting 65-64-66, he tied for the lead in the first round and led by three after the second. Then came the soul-testing third. Piercy had developed a blister on his right foot from new shoes, and then he was walking wearing only one shoe and putting on the other only to hit. Then there was the grind of a six and a half-hour rain delay. And yet he shot 66 and finished the day at 18-under 195 and was leading Argentina's Emiliano Grillo by four. Finau was five behind on 67-68-65.

In the final round, two birdies got Piercy to 20 under, and then across the last 11 holes, practically everything he touched turned to bogey. He made two more birdies, but also six bogeys and a devastating triple bogey at the par-four 14th, going from bunker to bunker to water then rough. He shot 76 and finished in a tie for fourth.

As these things developed, Finau was one surprised golfer. "I was almost chasing 20 under all day, I felt like," he said. Playing in the group ahead of Piercy, he pecked away. He birdied two and four, bogeyed the ninth out of the rough, then birdied 11, 14, 15 and 16. "I didn't see a leaderboard until 16 green," Finau said. "My heart almost skipped a beat." His putt there was not to tie, as he thought, but to go four ahead.

Then at 17, his heart did skip a beat. His tee shot banged off the grandstand beyond the green and his ball ricocheted wickedly back across the green, heading back to the water it had just flown. Then it stopped just in time, caught up in the rough before it could plunge over the stone wall and fatally down into the water. In mock relief, Finau clutched at his chest. Thus spared, he chipped and putted for par. But at the tough par-five 18th, he did catch water off the tee, and finally holed a three-footer for bogey and a 67, finishing at 17-under 267 to beat Sungjae Im and Emiliano Grillo by three.

Finau explained the ricochet that saved him at the 17th. It was his day. "I called 'bank' in the air," he said, "so I think that cancels everything out."

TPC Twin Cities, Blaine, Minnesota — July 21-24
Par 71 (35-36); 7,431 yards — Purse: $7,500,000

1	**Tony Finau**	67	68	65	67	267	$1,350,000
2	**Emiliano Grillo**	67	65	67	71	270	667,500
	Sungjae Im	65	70	67	68	270	667,500
4	James Hahn	69	70	67	65	271	315,625
	Tom Hoge	67	68	66	70	271	315,625
	Scott Piercy	65	64	66	76	271	315,625
7	Greyson Sigg	70	68	64	72	274	235,625
	Callum Tarren	71	63	71	69	274	235,625
	Danny Willett	72	66	68	68	274	235,625
10	Chesson Hadley	68	69	66	72	275	204,375
11	Kelly Kraft	70	71	68	67	276	160,875
	Peter Malnati	68	69	69	70	276	160,875
	JT Poston	71	69	64	72	276	160,875
	Andrew Putnam	71	68	64	73	276	160,875
	Robert Streb	68	67	71	70	276	160,875
16	Scott Brown	69	74	64	70	277	103,313
	Cameron Champ	75	68	67	67	277	103,313
	Cam Davis	70	68	70	69	277	103,313
	Doug Ghim	67	68	65	77	277	103,313
	Michael Gligic	72	69	67	69	277	103,313
	Lee Hodges	70	67	67	73	277	103,313
	Hank Lebioda	68	74	67	68	277	103,313
	Adam Long	69	69	67	72	277	103,313
24	Stewart Cink	71	69	65	73	278	69,375
	Austin Smotherman	72	70	67	69	278	69,375
26	Hayden Buckley	72	70	68	69	279	55,875
	Joohyung Kim	73	68	67	71	279	55,875
	Cameron Percy	72	69	66	72	279	55,875
	Michael Thompson	72	69	68	70	279	55,875
	Matt Wallace	70	70	71	68	279	55,875
31	Chris Gotterup	75	67	69	69	280	42,911
	Ryan Palmer	75	67	68	70	280	42,911
	CT Pan	69	71	72	68	280	42,911
	Paul Barjon	72	67	69	72	280	42,911
	Ryan Brehm	71	71	68	70	280	42,911
	Brice Garnett	67	71	68	74	280	42,911
	Scott Gutschewski	72	67	70	71	280	42,911
38	Wyndham Clark	72	68	67	74	281	31,125
	Rickie Fowler	70	72	69	70	281	31,125
	Adam Hadwin	68	75	71	67	281	31,125
	Patton Kizzire	68	69	72	72	281	31,125
	Seung-Yul Noh	69	71	69	72	281	31,125

	Roger Sloan	70 69 70 72	281	31,125
	Dawie van der Walt	75 67 69 70	281	31,125
45	Ricky Barnes	68 71 71 72	282	22,950
	Tyler Duncan	73 70 66 73	282	22,950
	Bo Hoag	75 67 68 72	282	22,950
	Chase Seiffert	71 67 70 74	282	22,950
49	Aaron Baddeley	72 68 70 73	283	18,885
	Maverick McNealy	71 71 68 73	283	18,885
	Troy Merritt	72 69 70 72	283	18,885
	Chez Reavie	75 68 69 71	283	18,885
	Bo Van Pelt	75 68 70 70	283	18,885
54	Andrew Novak	70 69 72 73	284	17,550
	Adam Schenk	73 69 70 72	284	17,550
	David Skinns	72 71 68 73	284	17,550
	Jared Wolfe	68 69 66 81	284	17,550
58	Jonathan Byrd	72 71 67 75	285	16,800
	Paul Goydos	70 73 68 74	285	16,800
	Nick Hardy	71 71 71 72	285	16,800
	Rick Lamb	71 69 68 77	285	16,800
	George McNeill	72 71 66 76	285	16,800
	Camilo Villegas	72 69 69 75	285	16,800
64	Jason Day	70 72 72 72	286	15,975
	Jim Knous	73 70 67 76	286	15,975
	Satoshi Kodaira	73 68 70 75	286	15,975
	Grayson Murray	73 69 69 75	286	15,975
	Brendon Todd	70 72 71 73	286	15,975
69	Kevin Chappell	77 66 69 75	287	15,525
70	Greg Chalmers	70 71 75 72	288	15,300
	David Lingmerth	68 71 69 80	288	15,300
72	Jonas Blixt	69 73 76 71	289	14,850
	JJ Henry	72 70 72 75	289	14,850
	Matthew NeSmith	71 70 73 75	289	14,850
	Matthias Schwab	70 73 73 73	289	14,850

Rocket Mortgage Classic

As Cameron Young put it after finishing second for the fifth time in this, his rookie season, "I'd be lying if I said it was easy to just watch other people win." In this instance, he was speaking of Tony Finau, who had just won the Rocket Mortgage Classic, just the week after he'd taken the 3M Open. And Finau knew what Young meant. Finau's first tour win was in the 2016 Puerto Rico Open, his second five years later, the 2021 Northern Trust, and in between he had eight runner-up finishes and 39 top 10s. Even for all the frustration, he was famed for being a gracious non-winner. "It's all due in part to me just looking at myself square in the eyes and knowing I'm not as good as I can be," Finau said.

Finau shot the Detroit Golf Club in 64-66-65-67 for a tournament-record 26-under-par total of 262, a five-stroke victory that looked easy but was a heavyweight bout for the first three rounds. It was Finau versus Taylor Pendrith, 31, a winless rookie from Canada, just back after a rib injury and saying, "When I'm healthy, I can compete with the best." They led the first round. In the second, Pendrith (65) led by one and Finau caught him in the third. Then Pendrith slipped early in the fourth and Finau swept to his third win in 11 months, his fourth overall. Pendrith closed with a 72 and tied for second, with Patrick Cantlay and Young. "It wasn't that close," Young said. "Tony put on a show."

Finau had an elegant time in the first round, hitting all 18 greens in regulation for the first time in 728 stroke-play rounds on tour. "I think I'm just riding some great momentum off last week," he said the following day, when Young tied the club record with a 63. Young was four back of Finau and Pendrith after a Saturday 65. "I have to play a ridiculous round of golf to have any chance," he said. Cantlay was six back after a 66. "I have to get off to a hot start," he said.

In the final round, Pendrith bogeyed the second off a stray drive and was out of the lead for good. Finau, a big hitter, feasted on the par fives. Four of his six birdies were on two-putts at the four par-fives. In the tournament, he had 12 birdies in 16 trips. There was only one blotch on his entire card, a three-putt from 70 feet at the par-three 11th, his only bogey. He closed with a 67 and the record 26 under, and the five-shot win that wasn't as cushy as it looked. "Tony beat us all by a lot," said Young, who closed with a 68. Said Cantlay (66): "Just keep knocking on the door." And Pendrith, "Tony played great, so hats off to him."

Said Finau: "They say a winner is just a loser who kept trying — and that's me."

Detroit Golf Club, Detroit, Michigan — July 28-31
Par 72 (36-36); 7,370 yards — Purse: $8,400,000

1	**Tony Finau**	64 66 65 67	262	$1,512,000
2	**Patrick Cantlay**	70 65 66 66	267	635,600
	Taylor Pendrith	64 65 66 72	267	635,600
	Cameron Young	71 63 65 68	267	635,600
5	Stephan Jaeger	67 68 65 68	268	344,400
6	Taylor Moore	67 71 65 66	269	304,500
7	Joohyung Kim	69 72 66 63	270	283,500
8	Wyndham Clark	69 68 69 65	271	254,100
	JJ Spaun	69 71 66 65	271	254,100
10	Russell Henley	69 65 70 68	272	203,700

	Charley Hoffman	67	69	69	67	272	203,700
	Scott Stallings	70	65	67	70	272	203,700
	Matt Wallace	66	71	69	66	272	203,700
14	Cam Davis	68	73	65	67	273	153,300
	Si Woo Kim	67	68	68	70	273	153,300
	Troy Merritt	68	72	68	65	273	153,300
17	Jason Day	69	70	69	66	274	128,100
	Chris Kirk	68	69	67	70	274	128,100
	Vince Whaley	68	71	68	67	274	128,100
20	Cameron Champ	66	75	67	67	275	99,120
	Kurt Kitayama	67	72	67	69	275	99,120
	Callum Tarren	67	69	73	66	275	99,120
	Will Zalatoris	70	71	69	65	275	99,120
24	Hayden Buckley	72	68	69	67	276	68,460
	Max Homa	72	68	67	69	276	68,460
	Ben Martin	69	71	68	68	276	68,460
	Sam Ryder	67	69	72	68	276	68,460
	Adam Svensson	69	68	67	72	276	68,460
	Michael Thompson	66	71	69	70	276	68,460
30	Bo Hoag	71	68	71	67	277	50,340
	Justin Lower	67	69	73	68	277	50,340
	Henrik Norlander	67	74	66	70	277	50,340
	Brendan Steele	69	69	67	72	277	50,340
	Nick Watney	67	72	67	71	277	50,340
	Richy Werenski	70	66	72	69	277	50,340
	Brandon Wu	69	69	72	67	277	50,340
37	Adam Hadwin	70	69	72	67	278	36,540
	Sung Kang	69	69	70	70	278	36,540
	Russell Knox	71	70	69	68	278	36,540
	David Lipsky	67	74	70	67	278	36,540
	Trey Mullinax	71	70	69	68	278	36,540
	Seth Reeves	71	67	72	68	278	36,540
	Adam Scott	69	66	78	65	278	36,540
44	Keegan Bradley	72	69	68	70	279	26,527
	Tyler Duncan	70	70	65	74	279	26,527
	Lee Hodges	66	66	77	70	279	26,527
	KK Limbhasut	70	68	68	73	279	26,527
	Patrick Rodgers	69	71	68	71	279	26,527
49	Kiradech Aphibarnrat	67	71	74	68	280	20,622
	Luke Donald	70	70	74	66	280	20,622
	Chris Gotterup	70	71	67	72	280	20,622
	Zach Johnson	67	69	69	75	280	20,622
	Rory Sabbatini	69	72	72	67	280	20,622
	Roger Sloan	70	69	70	71	280	20,622
	Kevin Streelman	71	69	69	71	280	20,622
	Jhonattan Vegas	68	71	73	68	280	20,622
57	Ryan Brehm	69	70	72	70	281	18,648
	Wesley Bryan	70	70	69	72	281	18,648
	Stewart Cink	68	66	74	73	281	18,648
	Austin Cook	69	69	72	71	281	18,648
	John Huh	67	69	74	71	281	18,648
	Nate Lashley	68	73	69	71	281	18,648
	David Lingmerth	71	70	70	70	281	18,648
	Doc Redman	69	71	73	68	281	18,648
	Sahith Theegala	68	67	73	73	281	18,648
	Cameron Tringale	71	69	73	68	281	18,648
67	Bo Van Pelt	70	70	69	73	282	17,640
	Danny Willett	70	68	69	75	282	17,640
69	Beau Hossler	71	70	72	70	283	17,136
	Chris Naegel	68	73	72	70	283	17,136
	Webb Simpson	66	73	70	74	283	17,136
	Austin Smotherman	68	68	74	73	283	17,136
73	Peter Malnati	71	70	72	71	284	16,716
74	Patton Kizzire	71	69	74	72	286	16,548
75	William McGirt	71	70	74	72	287	16,380

Wyndham Championship

Joohyung Kim, promising and ambitious young Korean golfer, had a neat, orderly plan for reaching the PGA Tour. The problem was, success kept getting in the way and before he knew it he had won the Wyndham Championship, and in a performance that was one for the books. Kim started with a quadruple-bogey eight and closed with a 61 in the final round and won by five shots. There he was, a full-fledged member of the tour. And barely 20.

"It's been a crazy month," Kim said. Actually, it was five weeks. And call him Tom. Kim named himself after *Thomas the Tank Engine*, from the British kids' TV show. "I loved the show as a kid," Kim said.

As shows go, Kim was putting on a beauty of his own. Kim, who had turned pro at 15, had plotted his course to the PGA Tour through the Korn Ferry Tour Finals. But he kept playing too well. His play on the Asian Tour had earned him a rare start on the newly co-sanctioned Scottish Open. He finished third there, then made the cut in the Open Championship, which earned him a special temporary PGA Tour membership. Then in succession came a tie for 26th in the 3M Open, a seventh in the Rocket Mortgage Classic, which won him his tour card, and next he won the Wyndham. That made him a member of the PGA Tour and made him eligible for the FedEx Cup playoffs.

His win in the Wyndham was a marvel of serendipity. Just take the first hole. It took him four to get to the fairway, two to get to the fringe, and a chip and a putt makes a quad. "I was laughing," Kim said. "There was nothing I could do. It was one bad hole and I just told myself, you know what, I can still get this, I can still shoot under par today and somehow I did, yeah." Yeah, seven birdies, crowned by the 59-footer at the 14th, for a 67 at the par-70 Sedgefield Country Club. He was six behind John Huh, who took the lead on a flawless 61 fed by five straight birdies from the fourth. Sungjae Im was second on a two-eagle 63.

Kim, already up to 34th in the world, shot 64-68 across the middle rounds, tying for the lead in the second and slipping two behind in the storm-split third. Then he was gone. The front nine for his last round read: par-birdie-birdie-birdie-eagle-birdie-par-birdie-birdie for a 27. The 61 gave him a 20-under-par 260 total with Im and Huh trailing by five. Tom Kim's train had just left the station. "Last month, before the Scottish, I guess just Korn Ferry Finals for me, that was the plan. One month later I secured my PGA Tour card without even going to Korn Ferry Finals. Yeah, it's crazy, but I guess just happy and grateful, that's what it is."

Sedgefield Country Club, Greensboro, North Carolina — August 4-7
Par 70 (35-35); 7,131 yards — Purse: $7,300,000

1	**Joohyung Kim**	67	64	68	61	260	$1,314,000
2	**John Huh**	61	71	66	67	265	649,700
	Sungjae Im	63	69	65	68	265	649,700
4	Ben Griffin	69	69	64	64	266	357,700
5	Russell Henley	67	65	69	66	267	270,100
	Max McGreevy	68	67	67	65	267	270,100
	Taylor Moore	69	67	64	67	267	270,100
8	Chesson Hadley	69	66	70	64	269	198,925
	Tyrrell Hatton	68	67	70	64	269	198,925
	Anirban Lahiri	66	67	68	68	269	198,925
	Cameron Percy	65	70	68	66	269	198,925
	Brandon Wu	64	67	68	70	269	198,925
13	Kiradech Aphibarnrat	72	65	63	70	270	123,188
	Stephan Jaeger	69	70	69	62	270	123,188
	Taylor Pendrith	71	67	65	67	270	123,188
	Davis Riley	67	66	68	69	270	123,188
	Alex Smalley	65	70	71	64	270	123,188
	Scott Stallings	67	71	67	65	270	123,188
	Richy Werenski	70	65	67	68	270	123,188
	Aaron Wise	65	70	67	68	270	123,188
21	Corey Conners	70	69	66	66	271	73,608
	JT Poston	66	70	69	66	271	73,608
	Russell Knox	70	69	64	68	271	73,608
	Ryan Moore	65	66	72	68	271	73,608
	Doc Redman	68	71	68	64	271	73,608
	Will Zalatoris	71	66	66	68	271	73,608
27	Stewart Cink	68	70	70	64	272	47,937
	Billy Horschel	67	69	68	68	272	47,937
	David Lipsky	68	69	69	66	272	47,937
	Peter Malnati	64	72	69	67	272	47,937
	Scott Piercy	69	70	66	67	272	47,937
	Kevin Tway	67	69	68	68	272	47,937
	Andrew Putnam	70	64	69	69	272	47,937
	Brian Stuard	65	68	68	71	272	47,937
	Callum Tarren	70	69	69	64	272	47,937
36	Zach Johnson	67	68	70	68	273	30,328
	Vaughn Taylor	69	69	68	67	273	30,328
	Scott Brown	70	66	68	69	273	30,328
	Harry Higgs	68	69	72	64	273	30,328
	Satoshi Kodaira	68	66	70	69	273	30,328
	Justin Lower	72	66	66	69	273	30,328
	Matthew NeSmith	66	69	67	71	273	30,328
	Yannik Paul	71	66	67	69	273	30,328
	Patrick Rodgers	69	70	68	66	273	30,328
	Robert Streb	69	69	67	68	273	30,328
	Brendon Todd	68	71	67	67	273	30,328
47	Lee Hodges	66	71	70	67	274	19,116
	Christiaan Bezuidenhout	66	70	68	70	274	19,116
	James Hahn	70	68	65	71	274	19,116
	Bo Hoag	68	69	70	67	274	19,116
	Martin Laird	69	67	67	71	274	19,116
	Henrik Norlander	69	67	72	66	274	19,116
	Chez Reavie	68	71	69	66	274	19,116
54	Luke Donald	70	68	66	71	275	16,863
	Lucas Glover	70	66	71	68	275	16,863
	Chris Gotterup	70	69	69	67	275	16,863
	Ben Kohles	65	70	71	69	275	16,863
	Kelly Kraft	66	73	68	68	275	16,863
	Keith Mitchell	68	68	70	69	275	16,863
	Justin Rose	73	66	67	69	275	16,863
61	Brett Drewitt	67	67	71	71	276	15,841
	Michael Gligic	65	73	71	67	276	15,841
	Mark Hubbard	70	69	70	67	276	15,841
	Kyoung-Hoon Lee	67	71	66	72	276	15,841
	Sam Ryder	67	70	69	70	276	15,841
	Rory Sabbatini	68	71	72	65	276	15,841
	Chris Stroud	69	70	70	67	276	15,841
68	Joseph Bramlett	70	69	72	66	277	15,111
	Charley Hoffman	68	68	69	72	277	15,111
	Martin Trainer	67	67	72	71	277	15,111
71	Jonathan Byrd	70	69	73	66	278	14,600
	Brian Harman	67	69	73	69	278	14,600
	Kramer Hickok	66	70	70	72	278	14,600
	Aaron Rai	70	69	66	73	278	14,600
75	Jared Wolfe	68	70	70	71	279	14,235
76	Blake McShea	69	65	70	76	280	14,016
	Adam Scott	68	70	74	68	280	14,016
78	Rafa Cabrera Bello	65	72	72	72	281	13,724
	Adam Svensson	70	69	70	72	281	13,724
80	David Skinns	70	69	73	70	282	13,505
81	Joel Dahmen	69	68	76	70	283	13,286
	Nick Taylor	67	71	73	72	283	13,286
83	Jason Dufner	66	73	71	74	284	12,994
	Shane Lowry	71	68	74	71	284	12,994

FedEx St Jude Championship

Golfers have different ways of rejoicing over important putts, from gentle fist pumps to aerial putter stabs to certifiable histrionics, depending on the magnitude of the moment. But the display by Will Zalatoris on the 72nd hole of the FedEx St Jude Championship at TPC Southwind was far, far different. This wasn't even for a win, it was merely for a life-saving tie in regulation in this first event of the FedEx Cup Playoffs. A 10-footer, and when it obediently took that graceful break to the right at the end and dropped in, Zalatoris exploded. Still in his putting crouch, he gave three fierce chops with his right fist, and with his face contorted, screamed at the camera, "What are they gonna say now!"

Zalatoris wasn't asking, he was venting, in the style made famous by Seth Curry at the NBA Finals. For a non-winner, Zalatoris had a stunning record. He finished second by a stroke in the 2021 Masters, and now, in 2022, he was a playoff runner-up at the PGA Championship in May, and in June he tied for second in the US Open. But he still hadn't won, still hadn't lived up to the promise he'd shown.

Zalatoris was in the next-to-last pairing and tied with Sepp Straka, just behind him. At the par-four 18th, Zalatoris drove into a fairway bunker, hit his next into the rough and pitched to 10 feet. And he made that liberating clutch putt, completing a card of 71-63-65-66 for a total of 265, 15 under, then had to sweat out Straka's finish.

Straka parred 18, wrapping up a card of 64-66-68-67, tying Zalatoris and setting off a playoff for the books. It took three holes. They parred the par-four 18th on the first try. Then, as Straka explained later, things "can get a little crazy." Zalatoris drove wide right, to near a boundary fence. He had to chip out. Then he hit his third to the green. Straka, on the other hand, cleared the water on the left but was inside the hazard line and opted to take a penalty drop. Then he hit to the green. Zalatoris holed his 15-footer for a par and Straka matched him from seven feet.

The playoff moved to the 11th, a 151-yard par three over water. Zalatoris's tee shot hit the bank, then the rocks, bounced seven times and ended up next to the lip of grass. Straka's tee shot flew to the right, bounced off the slope and then off the rocks and into the water. Straka re-teed at the drop zone, hit into a back bunker, and blasted out to four feet. Zalatoris, on finding his ball on rocks, opted to drop, and wedged to seven feet. Playing first, he faced another clutch putt. He holed it, and this time just lifted his arms, welcoming his first PGA Tour win. "It's kind of hard to say 'about time' when it's your second year on tour," Zalatoris said, "but — about time."

TPC Southwind, Memphis, Tennessee — August 11-14
Par 70 (35-35); 7,243 yards — Purse: $15,000,000

1	**Will Zalatoris**	71	63	65	66	265	$2,700,000
2	**Sepp Straka**	64	66	68	67	265	1,635,000
	Zalatoris won playoff at third extra hole						
3	**Lucas Glover**	65	68	69	66	268	885,000
	Brian Harman	66	66	69	67	268	885,000
5	Tony Finau	64	68	69	68	269	480,000
	Matt Fitzpatrick	68	66	67	68	269	480,000
	Collin Morikawa	67	69	66	67	269	480,000
	Trey Mullinax	66	67	66	70	269	480,000
	Andrew Putnam	66	68	67	68	269	480,000
	Jon Rahm	67	69	67	66	269	480,000
	Adam Scott	66	67	70	66	269	480,000
12	Sungjae Im	70	68	63	69	270	348,750
13	Cam Davis	67	71	67	66	271	260,893
	Lee Hodges	65	69	72	65	271	260,893
	Joohyung Kim	66	70	66	69	271	260,893
	Sahith Theegala	63	70	69	69	271	260,893
	Justin Thomas	67	67	71	66	271	260,893
	Joaquin Niemann	71	66	65	69	271	260,893
	Cameron Smith	67	65	69	70	271	260,893
20	Sam Burns	65	69	67	71	272	152,813
	Dylan Frittelli	66	70	66	70	272	152,813
	Viktor Hovland	67	70	67	68	272	152,813
	Kevin Kisner	69	64	70	69	272	152,813
	Kyoung-Hoon Lee	64	69	69	70	272	152,813
	Denny McCarthy	66	65	71	70	272	152,813
	Ryan Palmer	65	67	69	71	272	152,813
	JT Poston	64	72	68	68	272	152,813
28	Wyndham Clark	67	67	67	72	273	107,250
	Corey Conners	67	71	67	68	273	107,250
	Troy Merritt	65	65	70	73	273	107,250
31	Maverick McNealy	67	67	75	65	274	78,886
	Taylor Moore	67	70	69	68	274	78,886
	Aaron Wise	66	71	70	67	274	78,886
	Cameron Young	67	71	70	66	274	78,886
	Tyler Duncan	70	63	67	74	274	78,886
	Emiliano Grillo	67	66	72	69	274	78,886
	Tyrrell Hatton	65	70	69	70	274	78,886
	Keith Mitchell	68	69	67	70	274	78,886
	Davis Riley	69	67	68	70	274	78,886
	Adam Schenk	71	66	66	71	274	78,886
	Michael Thompson	65	70	70	69	274	78,886
42	Max Homa	66	69	69	71	275	54,750
	Si Woo Kim	62	73	72	68	275	54,750
	Mito Pereira	67	71	68	69	275	54,750
	JJ Spaun	62	67	68	78	275	54,750
46	Mackenzie Hughes	67	70	71	68	276	42,330
	Stephan Jaeger	71	67	69	69	276	42,330
	David Lipsky	67	70	69	70	276	42,330
	Shane Lowry	68	68	71	69	276	42,330
	Sebastian Munoz	68	68	71	69	276	42,330
51	Aaron Rai	69	68	69	71	277	36,050
	Chez Reavie	67	71	67	72	277	36,050
	Sam Ryder	68	66	71	72	277	36,050
	Robert Streb	67	70	69	71	277	36,050
	Adam Svensson	66	71	67	73	277	36,050
	Gary Woodland	69	69	73	66	277	36,050
57	Patrick Cantlay	67	68	71	72	278	34,200
	Beau Hossler	68	69	72	69	278	34,200
	Martin Laird	66	71	68	73	278	34,200
	Xander Schauffele	68	68	73	69	278	34,200
61	Hayden Buckley	69	67	65	78	279	33,150
	James Hahn	65	69	72	73	279	33,150
	Greyson Sigg	70	68	72	69	279	33,150
64	Christiaan Bezuidenhout	69	66	76	70	281	32,250
	Rickie Fowler	65	71	72	73	281	32,250
	Marc Leishman	69	69	75	68	281	32,250
67	Brendon Todd	69	68	70	75	282	31,650
68	Taylor Pendrith	66	70	74	73	283	31,350
69	Adam Hadwin	69	67	76	77	289	31,050

BMW Championship

The PGA Tour had come to Delaware for the first time, and a princely debut it was at the BMW Championship, the second of the three-event FedEx Cup Playoffs. The field of 70 for the no-cut tournament found Wilmington Country Club a long, narrow test, a par 71 stretching over 7,500 yards. Patrick Cantlay, the defending champion, offered a pre-tournament thumbnail strategy for playing the course. "You've got to hit it as far as you can and hit a lot of fairways," he said. "I think most times, you see when guys win they just got hot with the putter, which I did last year."

Cantlay had just given a preview of his success. He took the lead in the third round and held it stubbornly for a one-stroke victory, becoming the first player to win the BMW back-to-back since the FedEx Cup began in 2007. It was also his second win of the year and lifted him to number three in the world.

Keegan Bradley led the first day on a 64, which Rory McIlroy looked likely to catch until a triple bogey at the 15th. Adam Scott, who couldn't remember the last time he led a tour event, did just that after the second round, with Cantlay two back with a pair of 68s, on the same mark as Xander Schauffele, who holed out a 75-yard wedge shot for an eagle at 17. Cantlay went ahead in the third round in a mini-shootout with his friend Schauffele, who had led by as much as two shots. Then Cantlay went on a birdie-birdie-eagle tear: a tap-in at 12, an eight-footer at 13 and a 104-yard hole-out at 14. He shot 65 and at 12 under led Schauffele (66) and Scott Stallings (66) by one.

It was Stallings rather than Schauffele who provided the opposition to Cantlay in the final round. Both bogeyed twice, but Stallings made four birdies to Cantlay's three and they were tied at 13 under with two holes to play. Stallings two-putted for a textbook par at 17. Cantlay, in the final pairing just behind, took the bold route. He tried to cut the dogleg, had too tight a line, but got away with it. His tee shot hit just short of the last bunker, bounced over and out into the fairway, just 64 yards from the hole. "I thought for sure it would be in the bunker," a relieved Cantlay said. "Maybe one of the best breaks I've gotten." He wedged to five feet, birdied, and nosed ahead by a stroke.

Stallings parred the 18th for a 69. Cantlay still had another scare to survive. Needing a par to win, this time he did catch a fairway bunker. "Ball was above my feet. I had about 160 to the hole and I tried to slice an eight-iron about as hard as I could. It was one of the best shots I hit all week." To 46 feet, in fact, and he two-putted for a par, a 69 and won by one on 14-under 270. "I think I'm very competitive," Cantlay said, stating the obvious. "It definitely grinds my gears if I don't win."

Wilmington Country Club (South), Wilmington, Delaware — August 18-21
Par 71 (35-36); 7,534 yards — Purse: $15,000,000

1	**Patrick Cantlay**	68	68	65	69	270	$2,700,000
2	**Scott Stallings**	68	68	66	69	271	1,620,000
3	**Xander Schauffele**	67	69	66	71	273	870,000
	Scottie Scheffler	68	67	68	70	273	870,000
5	Corey Conners	68	67	70	69	274	547,500
	Kyoung-Hoon Lee	68	70	71	65	274	547,500
	Adam Scott	65	69	69	71	274	547,500
8	Rory McIlroy	68	68	70	69	275	420,000
	Joaquin Niemann	69	68	68	70	275	420,000
	Taylor Pendrith	71	68	67	69	275	420,000
	Jon Rahm	73	70	65	67	275	420,000
12	Christiaan Bezuidenhout	67	73	67	69	276	315,000
	Shane Lowry	66	71	71	68	276	315,000
	Trey Mullinax	71	68	69	68	276	315,000
15	Lucas Herbert	70	70	68	69	277	247,500
	Sungjae Im	70	69	67	71	277	247,500
	Sahith Theegala	72	68	69	68	277	247,500
	Aaron Wise	69	68	67	73	277	247,500
19	Sam Burns	69	69	70	70	278	188,250
	Emiliano Grillo	68	71	70	69	278	188,250
	Kurt Kitayama	71	66	72	69	278	188,250
	Jordan Spieth	68	67	74	69	278	188,250
23	Tyrrell Hatton	67	71	69	72	279	133,500
	Max Homa	72	69	68	70	279	133,500
	Andrew Putnam	73	68	66	72	279	133,500
	JJ Spaun	68	74	67	70	279	133,500
	Cameron Young	67	68	72	72	279	133,500
28	Tony Finau	77	68	67	68	280	104,250
	Marc Leishman	68	71	71	70	280	104,250
	Denny McCarthy	68	72	66	74	280	104,250
	Sepp Straka	72	72	68	68	280	104,250
32	Maverick McNealy	70	71	72	68	281	88,750
	Keith Mitchell	74	66	70	71	281	88,750
	Brendan Steele	76	67	65	73	281	88,750
35	Cam Davis	69	67	75	71	282	67,750
	Brian Harman	72	71	68	71	282	67,750
	Russell Henley	67	71	72	72	282	67,750
	Billy Horschel	69	73	69	71	282	67,750
	Viktor Hovland	73	69	75	65	282	67,750
	Matt Kuchar	69	71	70	72	282	67,750
	Hideki Matsuyama	70	67	71	74	282	67,750
	Sebastian Munoz	70	74	69	69	282	67,750
	JT Poston	72	69	68	73	282	67,750
44	Adam Hadwin	69	70	72	72	283	48,000
	Taylor Moore	73	70	68	72	283	48,000
	Collin Morikawa	67	72	65	79	283	48,000

	Alex Smalley	69	76	69	69	283	48,000
48	Matt Fitzpatrick	69	73	71	71	284	38,700
	Tom Hoge	70	70	74	70	284	38,700
	Kevin Kisner	71	75	70	68	284	38,700
	Harold Varner III	66	71	71	76	284	38,700
52	Alex Noren	72	69	72	72	285	35,700
	Justin Thomas	66	73	75	71	285	35,700
54	Joohyung Kim	71	71	74	70	286	34,350
	Mito Pereira	74	73	70	69	286	34,350
	Chez Reavie	67	72	77	70	286	34,350
	Davis Riley	77	68	67	74	286	34,350
58	Keegan Bradley	64	74	73	76	287	33,300
	Mackenzie Hughes	75	68	72	72	287	33,300
	Troy Merritt	69	72	73	73	287	33,300
61	Chris Kirk	70	71	73	74	288	32,550
	Luke List	78	68	69	73	288	32,550
63	Cameron Tringale	72	69	76	72	289	32,100
64	Wyndham Clark	77	76	67	70	290	31,800
65	Seamus Power	71	68	77	75	291	31,500
66	Lucas Glover	75	70	71	76	292	31,200
67	Si Woo Kim	78	70	68	78	294	30,900

2021-22 MONEY LIST

1	Scottie Scheffler	$14,046,910
2	Cameron Smith	10,107,897
3	Will Zalatoris	9,405,082
4	Patrick Cantlay	9,369,605
5	Rory McIlroy	8,654,566
6	Xander Schauffele	7,427,299
7	Sam Burns	7,073,986
8	Matt Fitzpatrick	7,012,672
9	Justin Thomas	6,829,576
10	Cameron Young	6,520,598

Tour Championship

"Not the best way to start," Rory McIlroy was saying at the Tour Championship, again demonstrating his eloquence, this time as a grandmaster of the understatement. Under the starting strokes scoring system, he was already six behind Scottie Scheffler. Then after playing only two holes — a triple bogey at the first, a bogey at the second — he was fully 10 behind. Then three days later, demonstrating his artistry in bounce-back, McIlroy found himself trailing by six shots heading into the final round, and in due course was lifting his cap and was $18 million richer. "Six behind on the first tee on Thursday and I was 10 behind on the third tee, I guess it just shows you anything's possible," McIlroy said.

Heroic as McIlroy's rally was, he couldn't have won without the baffling collapse of Scheffler, number one in the world and top seed in the tournament, who led by two from the start, was leading by six strokes entering the final round, and then came undone. "I just didn't get off to a good start," a mystified Scheffler said. "But after that, I tried as hard as I could. For whatever reason, my swing wasn't where it had been."

McIlroy showed his eloquence in another way when he apologised to Scheffler's parents for beating their son. "I'm sorry," McIlroy said to Scott and Diane Scheffler. "He deserves it. He's had an unbelievable year." Said Scheffler's dad: "So did you. Good playing."

At stake for the 30 qualifiers in the third and final tournament of the FedEx Cup Playoffs was the $18 million bonus. Scheffler was two ahead of Patrick Cantlay at 10 under before even teeing off. He set out to grind his way through this finale, but drilled an uphill three-iron 230 yards to 15 feet for eagle at the par-five sixth, then birdied the last three for a five-under 65. At 15 under he was leading by five from Xander Schauffele, who scored 66. McIlroy hooked his opening tee shot out of bounds, but chipped in from 35 yards for an eagle at the sixth. It was a wild ride. He made an eagle, eight birdies, four bogeys, the triple bogey and only four pars in a 67 that left him eight back. "Proud of how I bounced back," McIlroy said.

The race tightened in the second round. Scheffler had a spotless four-birdie 66 to get to 19 under, but his lead was cut to two on Schauffele's 63. Schauffele made a five-footer at the last as he finished birdie-birdie-eagle. Paying attention to what others are doing, Scheffler said, "has never served me too well". Said Schauffele: "There's a lot of golf to be played on this property."

A heavy storm hit Saturday afternoon, forcing 10 players to finish the third round on Sunday morning. When they resumed, McIlroy birdied his final two holes for a 63, and Scheffler proceeded to birdie four of his last six, for a 66 and more to the point, a six-stroke lead going into the last round. It was gone in seven holes. His game misfiring, Scheffler bogeyed three of the first six holes, and McIlroy, after a bogey at the first, birdied three, five, six and seven. Scheffler got a birdie at the eighth. McIlroy holed a 32-foot putt for birdie at the par-three 15th to tie for the lead, and went ahead on a patchwork par at 16, while Scheffler missed fairway and green and bogeyed, falling behind for the first time in the tournament. They finished with two tense pars, Scheffler shooting 73 but tying for second at 20 under with Sungjae Im, while McIlroy shot 66 for the tournament-low 17-under 263, but totalling 21 under to win the $18 million.

"I put myself in position to win this tournament when I wasn't playing my best today," Scheffler said, "and so I'm proud of how I fought." Said McIlroy: "Incredible day, incredible week. Four-over through two holes, 10 shots out of the lead, to claw my way back and end up winning the tournament — incredible."

East Lake Golf Club, Atlanta, Georgia — August 25-28
Par 70 (35-35); 7,346 yards — FedEx Cup bonus pool: $75,000,000

		START						FINISH	
1	**Rory McIlroy**	-4	67	67	63	66	263	-21	$18,000,000
2	**Sungjae Im**	-4	67	65	66	66	264	-20	5,750,000
	Scottie Scheffler	-10	65	66	66	73	270	-20	5,750,000
4	Xander Schauffele	-6	66	63	70	69	268	-18	4,000,000
5	Max Homa	-2	71	62	66	66	265	-17	2,750,000
	Justin Thomas	-3	67	68	63	68	266	-17	2,750,000
7	Sepp Straka	-4	68	68	64	68	268	-16	1,750,000
	Patrick Cantlay	-8	70	66	66	70	272	-16	1,750,000
9	Tony Finau	-4	72	66	67	64	269	-15	1,250,000
10	Tom Hoge	-1	66	66	66	69	267	-14	1,000,000
11	Hideki Matsuyama	-2	70	66	63	70	269	-13	925,000
	Joaquin Niemann	-2	64	67	69	69	269	-13	925,000
13	Aaron Wise	E	65	67	66	70	268	-12	825,000
	Jordan Spieth	-2	68	68	69	65	270	-12	825,000
15	JT Poston	E	65	69	66	69	269	-11	715,000
	Viktor Hovland	-2	71	68	67	65	271	-11	715,000
	Matt Fitzpatrick	-3	64	71	67	70	272	-11	715,000
	Jon Rahm	-3	67	63	71	71	272	-11	715,000
19	Cameron Young	-3	67	67	70	69	273	-10	660,000
20	Cameron Smith	-4	67	71	68	69	275	-9	640,000
21	Brian Harman	-1	68	70	68	67	273	-8	600,000
	Billy Horschel	-1	68	70	66	69	273	-8	600,000
	Collin Morikawa	-1	66	69	65	73	273	-8	600,000
24	Sam Burns	-5	69	74	67	68	278	-7	565,000
25	Adam Scott	E	68	70	68	70	276	-4	550,000
26	Corey Conners	-1	74	66	71	67	278	-3	540,000
27	Kyoung-Hoon Lee	E	68	72	69	70	279	-1	530,000
28	Sahith Theegala	E	71	72	67	71	281	+1	520,000
29	Scott Stallings	-3	70	74	69	73	286	+3	510,000

Fortinet Championship

All set for the most predictable of routine finishes at the Fortinet Championship, the opening event of the 2022-23 season. The setting was Silverado's par-five 18th. There was Danny Willett, leading by a stroke, lying three and just a 43-inch putt from the birdie that would lock up the win. Actually, his situation was even riper than that, for Max Homa, the defending champion, was trailing by one, also lying three, but he wasn't even on the green yet. He was 33 feet from the hole, but down in a swale. In short, how could Willett lose?

Well, one way would be for Homa to flip that 33-foot chip shot up over the shoulder and rough, and into the hole for a birdie, and then for Willett to somehow three-putt from 43 inches for a bogey.

Which, golf being golf, is precisely what happened. "That was crazy," Homa said. "I still don't really know what happened. My coach told me this morning. He said just hang around as long as you can and see what happens."

Willett, trying for his first PGA Tour win since the 2016 Masters, knew what happened. "I hit it obviously far too hard," he said of his 43-inch birdie putt. It nicked the left edge and went nearly five feet past. He missed the par coming back and tapped in for an other-worldly bogey. "Just a shame how I finished," Willett said, "but that's golf. We're going to do it again another day."

Homa was something of a new man after winning the 2021 Fortinet. He'd admitted he found it hard to believe in himself. This time, on learning he was the tournament favourite, he said it felt good. "Oddly, it felt OK," he said. "It didn't feel like too much pressure." The new Homa came in handy in the battle down the stretch with Willett. Homa shot the par-72 Silverado in 65-67-72-68 for 272, 16 under, and Willett in 68-64-72-69. The pair shared the 36-hole lead, then each slipped a shot behind Justin Lower in the third round.

Willett went three ahead after eight in the fourth round, then Homa made three birdies in a row to tie at the 11th. A birdie at 14 returned Willett to the lead and set the stage for the stunning finish. Homa had about written himself off with Willett so close at the final hole. "I kind of had to assume he was going to make it," Homa said. But he soldiered on. He had put his second into a greenside bunker, 90 feet from the hole, and with Willett threatening, went for what he called "the hero bunker shot, and didn't quite catch it". But the chip for four went in and then he was lifting his cap, winning for the third time in just over a year. "I just kept hitting the right shot I felt like," Homa said, "and just kept doing what I could, and then magic kind of happened."

Silverado Resort and Spa (North), Napa, California — September 15-18
Par 72 (36-36); 7,123 yards — Purse: $8,000,000

1	**Max Homa**	65	67	72	68	272	$1,440,000
2	**Danny Willett**	68	64	72	69	273	872,000
3	**Taylor Montgomery**	68	71	72	64	275	552,000
4	Byeong Hun An	66	68	71	71	276	360,000
	Justin Lower	63	71	69	73	276	360,000
6	Rickie Fowler	67	72	69	69	277	270,000
	Nick Taylor	67	75	67	68	277	270,000
	Sahith Theegala	67	69	71	70	277	270,000
9	Harris English	71	70	71	66	278	218,000
	Davis Thompson	68	73	65	72	278	218,000
	Brendon Todd	71	71	68	68	278	218,000
12	Zac Blair	70	69	69	71	279	140,667
	Joseph Bramlett	68	71	70	70	279	140,667
	Thomas Detry	69	70	71	69	279	140,667
	Tom Hoge	69	70	70	70	279	140,667
	Brian Stuard	68	69	71	71	279	140,667
	Adam Svensson	68	71	67	73	279	140,667
	Harrison Endycott	72	70	65	72	279	140,667
	Paul Haley II	73	67	66	73	279	140,667
	Matt Kuchar	68	68	70	73	279	140,667
21	Zecheng Dou	71	67	70	72	280	87,200
	Mark Hubbard	70	70	67	73	280	87,200
	Robby Shelton	67	70	74	69	280	87,200
	Matt Wallace	70	71	72	67	280	87,200
25	Emiliano Grillo	67	72	73	69	281	55,273
	Kramer Hickok	71	70	68	72	281	55,273
	Beau Hossler	70	72	69	70	281	55,273
	Mackenzie Hughes	70	71	68	72	281	55,273
	Russell Knox	70	71	70	70	281	55,273
	Denny McCarthy	71	70	69	71	281	55,273
	Ben Taylor	69	69	72	71	281	55,273
	Jimmy Walker	70	71	69	71	281	55,273
	Hideki Matsuyama	69	72	75	65	281	55,273
	Cameron Percy	74	68	72	67	281	55,273
	Austin Smotherman	71	69	67	74	281	55,273
36	Aaron Baddeley	73	69	69	71	282	36,457
	Alex Noren	72	68	71	71	282	36,457
	Will Gordon	70	69	71	72	282	36,457
	Brandon Hagy	69	73	68	72	282	36,457
	Seonghyeon Kim	66	72	71	73	282	36,457
	Taylor Moore	68	68	73	73	282	36,457
	Vincent Norrman	70	69	71	72	282	36,457
43	Wyndham Clark	72	69	69	73	283	24,760
	Brice Garnett	67	75	71	70	283	24,760
	Scott Harrington	67	71	72	73	283	24,760
	Stephan Jaeger	69	70	73	71	283	24,760
	Chris Kirk	74	68	67	74	283	24,760
	Andrew Putnam	72	70	72	69	283	24,760
	Alex Smalley	70	70	71	72	283	24,760
	Chris Stroud	69	72	72	70	283	24,760
51	Chris Gotterup	73	67	71	73	284	19,480
	James Hahn	71	68	72	73	284	19,480
	Matthias Schwab	70	69	72	73	284	19,480
	Greyson Sigg	67	73	73	71	284	19,480
55	Jacob Bridgeman	70	72	72	71	285	18,560
	Andrew Landry	70	70	72	73	285	18,560
	Nate Lashley	72	70	71	72	285	18,560
	Adam Schenk	69	72	70	74	285	18,560
59	Troy Merritt	71	69	71	75	286	17,840
	Matti Schmid	67	71	75	73	286	17,840
	Brandt Snedeker	70	69	72	75	286	17,840
	JJ Spaun	66	73	73	74	286	17,840
	Kevin Streelman	68	71	72	75	286	17,840
64	Austin Eckroat	69	70	71	77	287	17,280
	Gary Woodland	70	71	73	73	287	17,280
66	Lucas Glover	74	68	75	71	288	17,040
67	Nick Hardy	71	70	71	77	289	16,720
	Ben Martin	69	68	73	79	289	16,720
	Taylor Pendrith	71	70	71	77	289	16,720
70	Michael Thompson	71	71	74	74	290	16,320
	Nick Watney	73	69	71	77	290	16,320
72	Doug Ghim	71	70	70	81	292	16,000
	CT Pan	70	71	77	74	292	16,000

Presidents Cup

Life was still good for the Americans in the Presidents Cup. For example, Jordan Spieth and Justin Thomas, a formidable pairing under any circumstances, were not exactly sitting pretty in their opening foursomes match against Canada's Corey Conners and South Korea's Sungjae Im. But they were as resourceful as ever. At the 15th, usually Quail Hollow's final hole, Spieth's tee shot ended up on the wrong side of the creek. Thomas somehow got the ball to the back of the green. Spieth then ran his downhill putt 25 feet past the hole. And their opponents were all set to pounce, having just a seven-footer for par to win the hole and square the match. But then Thomas drilled the long par putt, Conners missed, and the Americans went two up and were on their way to another point.

Spieth and Thomas were 4-2 in Ryder Cup play, but this week was the first time they'd been paired together in the Presidents Cup. Spieth would go a perfect 5-0 and Thomas went 4-1, leading the Americans to yet another pleasant week of golf in September. This was the first Presidents Cup since 2019, the schedule having been battered by the Covid-19 pandemic, but it was business as usual. This was the 14th playing of the match against the International Team, 12 players from around the world, minus Europe. The US led the series 11-1-1. South Africa's Trevor Immelman, International captain, found his talent pool further depleted when Cameron Smith, the brilliant Australian, and Chile's fast-rising Joaquin Niemann, both declared for LIV Golf just weeks before the match and thus were ineligible. So Immelman had only three top-25 golfers on his team and US captain Davis Love had 12. Immelman's strategy was clear — go full bore. "It's quite clear that we're the underdogs," he said. "We have nothing to lose." Said Love, on being the favourites: "That's on paper. The game's not played on paper."

The Spieth-Thomas two-headed monster wasn't the Internationals' only vexation. Taylor Pendrith and Mito Pereira were about to take the lead over Max Homa and Tony Finau at the 15th. Homa's bunker shot was heading for the water. But it bounced off the rocks and into the rough. Finau pitched to eight feet, and Homa made the putt to save a half. They got the win at the 18th. The Americans got another point when tour Rookie of the Year Cameron Young, partnering Collin Morikawa, holed a 25-foot birdie putt at the 17th for a 2 and 1 win over Kyoung-Hoon Lee and Joohyung Kim. And Patrick Cantlay and Xander Schauffele, a redoubtable pairing since the 2019 Presidents, ran their alternate-shot record to 5-0, thumping Hideki Matsuyama and Adam Scott 6 and 5. The Internationals at least salvaged a point, with Cam Davis and Si Woo Kim winning the last four holes for a two-hole victory over Sam Burns and world number one Scottie Scheffler, leaving the Americans 4-1 ahead. "I told the guys last night we need to set the tone, and we did," said Love. Said Immelman, "We'll keep going, man. We'll keep going till they ring the bell."

There was more of the same in Friday's fourballs. Spieth and Thomas struck again, leading off with a 2 and 1 win over Scott and Davis. Im and Sebastian Munoz posted a 63, only to be tied by Scheffler and Burns. The Internationals completed the point with Pereira and Christiaan Bezuidenhout tying Young and Kevin Kisner. It was Cantlay and Schauffele again with the day's heaviest win, 3 and 2 over Matsuyama and Joohyung Kim, who finally made a birdie at the seventh, only to lose to an eagle. And finally, Pendrith holed a long putt to give himself and Conners a birdie at the 18th only to have Homa match him with an 11-footer for a one-hole win with Billy Horschel. With another 4-1 day, the US was running away, 8-2.

Then came the uprising. The Internationals had their finest hour and gave Immelman his biggest smile of the week Saturday. In the split format, they tied the Americans 2-2 in the morning alternate shot, and beat them 3-1 in the afternoon fourballs. The spark was provided by 20-year-old Joohyung Kim, becoming known as Tom and the third youngest Presidents Cup player ever. He teamed in foursomes with KH Lee, two of a record four Koreans on the International team, to beat Scheffler and Burns 2 and 1 after Kim holed an eagle putt of 36 feet at the 11th. Then in the afternoon fourballs, Kim, who lost both his first two matches, won twice in the same day, this time with Si Woo Kim as they took down Cantlay and Schauffele when Tom hit his approach at the 18th to 10 feet and made the birdie. "I wanted it more than anything in the world," he said. "I'm just trying to bring positive vibes." Immelman said: "He has an ability to be a global superstar, this kid. We've seen he has the game. But what I've learned about his personality and his heart and what he stands for this week, man, I am a huge fan." The last match of the day also went to the 18th, with Davis finishing eagle-birdie-birdie for a one-hole win with Aussie compatriot Scott over Horschel and Burns. But Spieth and Thomas rolled along in a world of their own. They took both Saturday matches by 4 and 3, beating Matsuyama and Pendrith in the afternoon when Spieth chipped in for birdie at the 15th. "We have full trust and belief that we can beat whoever we play," Thomas said. Spieth said: "Seemed like when we needed something to go in, we found a way to do it."

The no-quit Internationals had some steam left over from Saturday, and their uprising carried over into the Sunday singles. The Spieth-Thomas juggernaut did sputter at the very end. Spieth kept his record perfect, becoming only the sixth player to do it, and winning his first singles ever in a 4 and 3 win over Davis. He had been a combined 0-6-1 in the Presidents Cup and the Ryder Cup. "I was more nervous than I probably should have been today," Spieth said, "just because I wanted to get that monkey off my back." But Thomas's bid to match his pal's perfect record was spiked by Si Woo Kim's birdie at the last for a one-hole win. Burns and Matsuyama finished birdie-par-par and tied. The Americans moved closer with Cantlay going three up through the fourth and beating Scott 3 and 2, and Finau won five of the final nine holes in a 3 and 1 win over Pendrith.

Schauffele scored the Americans' decisive point, but it did not come easy. Schauffele took the lead twice and Conners tied him both times. Schauffele ended it with a six-foot par putt at the 18th, giving the Americans a 17½-12½ victory, their ninth straight win and 12th in all. The Internationals were looking ahead to Royal Montreal in 2024. Said Immelman: "We love this event, and we love our team. And we cannot wait to run this back and have another shot." And said Scott: "A cup is coming our way soon." Love of his team: "They're unbelievably prepared and unbelievably confident. That's why these guys are the best players in the world."

Quail Hollow Club, Charlotte, North Carolina — September 22-25
Par 71 (35-36); 7,576 yards

Thursday Foursomes — USA 4, Internationals 1
Patrick Cantlay and Xander Schauffele defeated Adam Scott and Hideki Matsuyama 6 and 5
Jordan Spieth and Justin Thomas defeated Sungjae Im and Corey Conners 2 and 1
Cameron Young and Collin Morikawa defeated Joohyung Kim and Kyoung-Hoon Lee 2 and 1
Scottie Scheffler and Sam Burns lost to Si Woo Kim and Cam Davis by two holes
Tony Finau and Max Homa defeated Taylor Pendrith and Mito Pereira by one hole

Friday Fourballs — USA 4, Internationals 1
Jordan Spieth and Justin Thomas defeated Adam Scott and Cam Davis 2 and 1
Scottie Scheffler and Sam Burns tied with Sungjae Im and Sebastian Munoz
Kevin Kisner and Cameron Young tied with Mito Pereira and Christiaan Bezuidenhout
Patrick Cantlay and Xander Schauffele defeated Hideki Matsuyama and Joohyung Kim 3 and 2
Billy Horschel and Max Homa defeated Corey Conners and Taylor Pendrith by one hole

Saturday morning Foursomes — USA 2, Internationals 2
Jordan Spieth and Justin Thomas defeated Sungjae Im and Corey Conners 4 and 3
Cameron Young and Collin Morikawa lost to Adam Scott and Hideki Matsuyama 3 and 2
Scottie Scheffler and Sam Burns lost to Kyoung-Hoon Lee and Joohyung Kim 2 and 1
Tony Finau and Max Homa defeated Si Woo Kim and Cam Davis 4 and 3

Saturday afternoon Fourballs — USA 1, Internationals 3
Patrick Cantlay and Xander Schauffele lost to Si Woo Kim and Joohyung Kim by one hole
Justin Thomas and Jordan Spieth defeated Hideki Matsuyama and Taylor Pendrith 4 and 3
Tony Finau and Kevin Kisner lost to Sungjae Im and Sebastian Munoz 3 and 2
Billy Horschel and Sam Burns lost to Adam Scott and Cam Davis by one hole

Sunday Singles — USA 6½, Internationals 5½
Justin Thomas lost to Si Woo Kim by one hole
Jordan Spieth defeated Cam Davis 4 and 3
Sam Burns tied with Hideki Matsuyama
Patrick Cantlay defeated Adam Scott 3 and 2
Scottie Scheffler lost to Sebastian Munoz 2 and 1
Tony Finau defeated Taylor Pendrith 3 and 1
Xander Schauffele defeated Corey Conners by one hole
Cameron Young lost to Sungjae Im by one hole
Billy Horschel lost to Kyoung-Hoon Lee 3 and 1
Max Homa defeated Joohyung Kim by one hole
Collin Morikawa defeated Mito Pereira 3 and 2
Kevin Kisner lost to Christiaan Bezuidenhout 2 and 1

Final Result — USA 17½, Internationals 12½

Sanderson Farms Championship

The difference between Mackenzie Hughes and an escape artist is, well, it's not as though Hughes was hitting trick shots wearing boxing gloves, but it did seem he was developing a name as a guy who never met a do-or-die spot he didn't love. "I was tested and was able to pull through," he said after his win at the Sanderson Farms Championship. "It's kind of my MO a little bit is to scramble and save some pars."

It was a little like golf's version of Indiana Jones as Hughes made his way across the Country Club of Jackson, eluding one danger after another, especially the great par save at the 72nd hole in which he wrapped up a card of 71-63-68-69 to tie Sepp Straka (69-66-69-67) at 17-under 271. And then after yet another close call, beat him on the second playoff hole. "Mac played great," Straka said. "The 18th hole is no bargain, and he had a good up-and-down to force a playoff and then to birdie on that hole was great."

Hughes trailed by five in the first round and tied Tom Detry (67) at 10 under in the second with a flawless with that 63. In the third round, chasing Mark Hubbard, he had to escape the bushes to save par at 15. At 18, after a too-long approach and a free drop he holed an uphill 30-footer from off the green for a birdie to stay within one.

Straka set Hughes a tough pace in the fourth. He shot 32 going out in a one-bogey 67 to get to 17 under. Hughes bogeyed only once, never touching the fairway at the sixth, and made four birdies on putts of five, eight, eight and three feet, and parred the 14th on a 15-footer. Then came the 18th. Needing a par to tie Straka, he put his tee shot where it had bogey or worse written all over it, in the left rough, behind a tree. He had to punch out, low enough to stay under the tree but high enough to carry the rough. The ball raced across the green, to the grandstand. He received a free drop, about 12 feet off the green, then faced a transcontinental putt of 100 feet. ("You just don't practise putts that long," he noted.) He rapped it to about 40 inches, and holed that for the par. He needed another heroic save there on the first playoff hole. On a no-room bunker shot, he blasted to five feet. On the next playoff try, Straka missed his birdie from 18 feet, but Hughes holed his eight-footer for a second tour win. Of all the adventures, the big save at the 18th was the toughest. "Because," he said, "I just didn't want to lose by bogeying 18 in regulation."

The Country Club of Jackson, Jackson, Mississippi — September 29-October 2
Par 72 (36-36); 7,461 yards — Purse: $7,900,000

1	**Mackenzie Hughes**	71	63	68	69	271	$1,422,000
2	**Sepp Straka**	69	66	69	67	271	861,100
	Hughes won playoff at second extra hole						
3	**Garrick Higgo**	70	66	68	68	272	545,100
4	Dean Burmester	70	68	68	67	273	387,100
5	Keegan Bradley	70	71	64	70	275	280,944

	Emiliano Grillo	73	65	68	69	275	280,944
	Nick Hardy	70	67	68	70	275	280,944
	Mark Hubbard	67	69	65	74	275	280,944
9	Thomas Detry	67	67	74	68	276	207,375
	Taylor Montgomery	72	68	67	69	276	207,375
	Matthew NeSmith	72	69	71	64	276	207,375
	Greyson Sigg	69	71	69	67	276	207,375
13	Ryan Armour	71	68	69	69	277	141,542
	Joel Dahmen	71	68	68	70	277	141,542
	Dylan Frittelli	71	69	68	69	277	141,542
	Callum Tarren	72	68	68	69	277	141,542
	Seonghyeon Kim	68	72	66	71	277	141,542
	Scott Stallings	69	67	68	73	277	141,542
19	Hayden Buckley	71	70	72	65	278	97,091
	Scott Piercy	71	70	70	67	278	97,091
	Davis Riley	66	71	70	71	278	97,091
	Nick Taylor	68	70	70	70	278	97,091
	Chun-an Yu	67	73	68	70	278	97,091
24	Ben Griffin	72	66	73	68	279	64,385
	Russell Knox	68	71	72	68	279	64,385
	William McGirt	71	68	69	71	279	64,385
	Taylor Moore	71	70	69	69	279	64,385
	Henrik Norlander	71	69	68	71	279	64,385
	Kevin Streelman	71	67	71	70	279	64,385
30	Will Gordon	66	76	70	68	280	45,337
	Lee Hodges	70	72	71	67	280	45,337
	Sam Burns	70	69	71	70	280	45,337
	Cody Gribble	73	67	67	73	280	45,337
	Stephan Jaeger	69	68	72	71	280	45,337
	Chris Kirk	74	67	70	69	280	45,337
	Adam Long	70	70	70	70	280	45,337
	Seamus Power	71	71	67	71	280	45,337
	Andrew Putnam	67	72	69	72	280	45,337
39	Christiaan Bezuidenhout	67	72	69	73	281	31,995
	Brandon Matthews	67	75	71	68	281	31,995
	Denny McCarthy	71	68	71	71	281	31,995
	Ben Taylor	70	70	70	71	281	31,995
	Alejandro Tosti	72	68	69	72	281	31,995
	Brandon Wu	69	69	73	70	281	31,995
45	Michael Gligic	72	68	73	69	282	21,795
	Justin Lower	70	72	71	69	282	21,795
	Erik Barnes	70	69	72	71	282	21,795
	Joseph Bramlett	71	71	70	70	282	21,795
	Stewart Cink	70	72	71	69	282	21,795
	Trevor Cone	67	71	71	73	282	21,795
	Adam Hadwin	73	69	67	73	282	21,795
	Peter Malnati	73	69	70	70	282	21,795
	Sam Ryder	71	70	71	70	282	21,795
54	Zecheng Dou	69	72	68	74	283	18,249
	Austin Eckroat	71	71	70	71	283	18,249
	Brice Garnett	72	67	71	73	283	18,249
	Paul Haley II	72	70	70	71	283	18,249
	Patrick Rodgers	73	69	68	73	283	18,249
	Adam Svensson	69	70	74	70	283	18,249
	Kyle Westmoreland	71	67	75	70	283	18,249
61	MJ Daffue	70	70	70	74	284	17,222
	Nate Lashley	71	69	69	75	284	17,222
	Aaron Rai	73	69	70	72	284	17,222
	Robby Shelton	71	70	73	70	284	17,222
	Brian Stuard	69	73	70	72	284	17,222
	Vince Whaley	70	69	74	71	284	17,222
67	CT Pan	70	71	71	73	285	16,274
	Austin Smotherman	70	70	70	75	285	16,274
	Samuel Stevens	73	68	73	71	285	16,274
	Chris Stroud	71	70	72	72	285	16,274
	Davis Thompson	72	70	70	73	285	16,274
	Dylan Wu	73	69	69	74	285	16,274
73	John Huh	72	70	70	74	286	15,563
	Luke List	69	72	75	70	286	15,563
	Nick Watney	73	69	71	73	286	15,563
76	Kevin Roy	68	71	74	74	287	15,247
77	Carson Young	72	70	76	72	290	15,089
78	Tano Goya	70	71	75	77	293	14,931

Shriners Children's Open

As Joohyung Kim, 20, brand-new Korean whizz on the tour, was saying upon taking the Shriners Children's Open, "I'm a five-year-old at Disneyland, for sure." This was shortly after he'd also said, "When you have a guy like Patrick coming at you, no lead is safe." This being after he outlasted Patrick Cantlay, world number four, on the final hole. And made history in the process.

Kim, who took the nickname "Tom" from a TV cartoon character, was some three months on the tour and already had 'em talking and now he was in the conversation with Tiger Woods. In taking the Shriners, Kim became the first player since Woods in 1996 to win twice on the PGA Tour before turning 21. "It's really amazing," said Kim, whose first win was in the Wyndham Championship in August. "A few months ago, I didn't have any status in the US, and now being a two-time winner on tour, having that place with Tiger, it's an unbelievable feeling for me."

He won with excellent golf and incredible luck. In shooting the par-71 TPC Summerlin in 65-67-62-66 for 260, 24 under, Kim had gone bogey-free. The incredible luck, on the other hand, was Cantlay's, and all of it was bad.

In the third round, Cantlay's 60 tied him with Kim at 19 under. Kim birdied five of his last six holes, ending with a wedge to two feet at the 18th for a 62. Said Kim, facing Cantlay's rampage: "I just told myself, let's play my own game." Kim led by two at the turn on Sunday, and had Cantlay playing catch-up down the back nine. Cantlay tied Kim at 22 under with birdies at 11 and 12 from about 12 feet. Kim jumped ahead by two again, making birdies at 13 and 14 from four and 13 feet. Cantlay responded with two breathtaking birdies of his own, two-putting for near eagles from 30 feet at the driveable par-four 15th and the par-five 16th. They were tied at 24 under coming to the last.

This time, Cantlay hooked his drive into the Las Vegas desert landscape, into a wiry scrub brush. He took a hack. No luck. He took a penalty drop in the rocky sand, and his approach splashed down short in a pond. He took another penalty drop, then hit his approach to 35 feet. Kim had hit fairway and green. His first putt finished 15 inches away. Then Cantlay rolled in his 35-footer for a triple-bogey seven and a 69 to tie Matthew NeSmith (66) at 21 under. "All in all, it was a good week," Cantlay said. "Obviously the last hole makes the whole week kind of sour."

Kim tapped in for his par and won by three. "I just stayed really patient and I got really fortunate," Kim offered. And then he added: "I'm having fun playing on the PGA Tour. It's awesome."

TPC Summerlin, Las Vegas, Nevada — October 6-9
Par 71 (35-36); 7,255 yards — Purse: $8,000,000

1	**Joohyung Kim**	65	67	62	66	260	$1,440,000
2	**Patrick Cantlay**	67	67	60	69	263	712,000
	Matthew NeSmith	68	66	63	66	263	712,000
4	Tom Hoge	63	72	65	64	264	336,667
	Mito Pereira	67	63	67	67	264	336,667
	Seonghyeon Kim	65	69	64	66	264	336,667
7	Sungjae Im	65	70	63	67	265	270,000
8	Jason Day	66	71	66	63	266	242,000
	Si Woo Kim	64	68	67	67	266	242,000
10	Adam Hadwin	67	67	65	68	267	210,000
	Maverick McNealy	64	68	71	64	267	210,000
12	Andrew Putnam	68	69	64	67	268	170,000
	Adam Schenk	69	66	67	66	268	170,000
	Davis Thompson	66	69	66	67	268	170,000
15	Harry Hall	66	70	69	64	269	130,000
	Brian Harman	70	67	68	64	269	130,000
	Taylor Montgomery	70	66	66	67	269	130,000
	Robby Shelton	68	63	68	70	269	130,000
	JJ Spaun	66	71	68	64	269	130,000
20	Christiaan Bezuidenhout	68	67	67	68	270	81,500
	Hayden Buckley	68	69	68	65	270	81,500
	Lucas Herbert	67	70	65	68	270	81,500
	Max Homa	67	67	69	67	270	81,500
	Justin Lower	70	68	67	65	270	81,500
	JT Poston	67	69	63	71	270	81,500
	Aaron Rai	69	68	62	71	270	81,500
	Kevin Streelman	66	67	69	68	270	81,500
28	Harris English	69	69	68	65	271	51,350
	Mark Hubbard	69	66	70	66	271	51,350
	Ryan Moore	68	70	68	65	271	51,350
	Chad Ramey	67	66	69	69	271	51,350
	Patrick Rodgers	66	68	70	67	271	51,350
	Sam Ryder	65	69	70	67	271	51,350
	Brendon Todd	69	68	69	65	271	51,350
	Matt Wallace	69	68	67	67	271	51,350
	Patrick Welch	71	67	68	65	271	
37	Joel Dahmen	66	72	68	66	272	36,457
	Chesson Hadley	67	70	69	66	272	36,457
	Dean Burmester	71	65	69	67	272	36,457
	Cam Davis	67	66	68	71	272	36,457
	Martin Laird	66	69	68	69	272	36,457
	Kyoung-Hoon Lee	72	66	65	69	272	36,457
	Chun-an Yu	69	68	66	69	272	36,457
44	Byeong Hun An	69	68	73	63	273	23,000
	Stewart Cink	69	66	71	67	273	23,000
	Will Gordon	65	72	73	63	273	23,000
	Chris Gotterup	68	70	65	70	273	23,000
	Nick Hardy	67	69	69	68	273	23,000
	Jim Herman	69	67	71	66	273	23,000
	Stephan Jaeger	66	72	67	68	273	23,000
	Spencer Levin	71	65	69	68	273	23,000
	David Lipsky	69	68	71	65	273	23,000
	Alex Noren	68	69	68	68	273	23,000
	Taylor Pendrith	71	67	66	69	273	23,000
	Greyson Sigg	68	69	68	68	273	23,000
56	Doug Ghim	68	68	70	68	274	18,560
	Tano Goya	68	67	71	68	274	18,560
	Michael Thompson	68	68	68	70	274	18,560
	Brandon Wu	72	65	69	68	274	18,560
60	Austin Eckroat	71	66	68	70	275	17,920
	Ben Griffin	68	69	67	71	275	17,920
	Keith Mitchell	65	69	70	71	275	17,920
	Austin Smotherman	68	69	71	67	275	17,920
64	Tyson Alexander	72	65	73	66	276	17,200
	Beau Hossler	69	68	64	75	276	17,200
	Philip Knowles	70	68	67	71	276	17,200
	Ben Martin	70	68	72	66	276	17,200
	Aaron Wise	69	67	67	73	276	17,200
69	Thomas Detry	65	73	65	74	277	16,560
	Harrison Endycott	67	71	69	70	277	16,560
	Adam Svensson	67	70	67	73	277	16,560
72	Tyler Duncan	65	71	70	72	278	16,240
73	Emiliano Grillo	71	67	73	69	280	16,000
	Andrew Landry	72	66	71	71	280	16,000
75	Patton Kizzire	67	69	71	74	281	15,680
	Matthias Schwab	71	67	71	72	281	15,680
77	Trevor Werbylo	68	70	70	75	283	15,440

Zozo Championship

Keegan Bradley said he couldn't remember the last time he cried, but indications are that he won't soon forget this time. An absolutely glorious day in a golfer's life, this one at Narashino on the outskirts of Tokyo, it started almost the instant he tapped in at the 18th to win the Zozo Championship — his first PGA Tour victory in over four years. And he couldn't stop. "I've been crying since I finished," said Bradley. "I talked to my wife on the phone a second ago. I couldn't keep things together. I don't know what's wrong with me."

Well, one good guess might be that after that long drought and all the stress that went with it, a bit of joy might be involved, to say nothing of relief. "I knew it wasn't going to be easy," Bradley said. "Things aren't easy for me normally. I've never experienced emotions like this after a tournament."

The Zozo, the only PGA Tour event in Japan, drew a field of 78. In an odd coincidence, the leading contenders hadn't won in a while: Rickie Fowler, not since the 2019 WM Phoenix Open; Andrew Putnam, the 2018 Barracuda Championship, and Keegan Bradley, the 2018 BMW Championship.

The threesome had nothing to report on the bogey front through the second round. Putnam, after a 62, was asked what he liked about the day. "Pretty much everything," he said. "No bogeys through the first 36 holes, so that's obviously great." Said Fowler, after his 63, "I guess I wasn't aware yet that I was bogey-free." They were tied at 10-under 130. Bradley was a stroke behind after a 65, also bogey-free. "I just played perfect today," he said.

After matching 66s with Fowler in the third round and staying within one, Bradley moved into the lead in the fourth with birdies at five, six and 11, then bogeyed 14 and 16 and was clinging to a one-stroke lead and facing a 20-foot birdie putt at the 17th. "I realised if I made this putt, I'd have a two-shot lead," Bradley said. "I just buried it. The perfect putt. It was meant to be, and I'm proud of the way I handled that hole."

Bradley parred the 18th for a 68, a total of 265, 15 under, and a one-stroke win over Fowler (70) and Putnam (68), who both birdied the 18th. "I didn't feel like my irons were quite as sharp as they needed to be to win," Putnam said, "but it was close."

"Kind of bittersweet," Fowler said, saluting Bradley. "And I hit some darn good putts. It was like there was a cover over the hole." And for Bradley, famed for winning the PGA Championship as a rookie in 2011, the Zozo was more than just his fifth victory. "This is what I want to do," he said. "I want to win tournaments, I want to play in Ryder Cups, I want to be in the conversation, and this is a good start."

Accordia Golf Narashino Country Club, Inzi, Chiba, Japan — October 13-16
Par 70 (34-36); 7,079 yards — Purse: $1,000,000

1	**Keegan Bradley**	66	65	66	68	265	$1,980,000
2	**Rickie Fowler**	67	63	66	70	266	968,000
	Andrew Putnam	68	62	68	68	266	968,000
4	Emiliano Grillo	70	68	65	64	267	528,000
5	Hayden Buckley	68	68	64	68	268	401,500
	Viktor Hovland	69	66	64	69	268	401,500
	Sahith Theegala	71	67	63	67	268	401,500
8	Cameron Champ	69	67	64	69	269	341,000
9	Tom Hoge	70	66	65	69	270	297,000
	Matthew NeSmith	66	68	67	69	270	297,000
	Xander Schauffele	67	69	69	65	270	297,000
12	Ryo Hisatsune	69	67	65	70	271	222,310
	Maverick McNealy	67	69	64	71	271	222,310
	Taylor Moore	70	66	65	70	271	222,310
	Keita Nakajima	70	63	69	69	271	222,310
16	Wyndham Clark	71	66	68	67	272	151,674
	Mikumu Horikawa	73	68	66	65	272	151,674
	Satoshi Kodaira	70	66	69	67	272	151,674
	Patrick Rodgers	71	65	69	67	272	151,674
	Joel Dahmen	68	67	66	71	272	151,674
	Beau Hossler	68	68	66	70	272	151,674
	Adam Schenk	65	70	68	69	272	151,674
23	Lee Hodges	73	64	67	69	273	107,360
	Mackenzie Hughes	70	68	68	67	273	107,360
25	Corey Conners	73	67	67	67	274	85,085
	Joonhyung Kim	70	68	67	69	274	85,085
	Alex Smalley	68	69	67	70	274	85,085
	JJ Spaun	71	67	69	67	274	85,085
29	Christiaan Bezuidenhout	68	73	66	68	275	65,796
	Cam Davis	70	67	69	69	275	65,796
	Dylan Frittelli	71	68	68	68	275	65,796
	Sungjae Im	71	68	70	66	275	65,796
	Kurt Kitayama	69	71	70	65	275	65,796
	Luke List	69	66	68	72	275	65,796
	Brandon Wu	68	69	66	72	275	65,796
36	Kazuki Higa	67	70	70	69	276	50,298
	Sebastian Munoz	72	67	68	69	276	50,298
	Aaron Rai	71	66	70	69	276	50,298
	Sam Ryder	66	68	68	74	276	50,298
40	Stephan Jaeger	69	73	65	70	277	40,260
	David Lipsky	69	69	69	70	277	40,260
	Hideki Matsuyama	71	69	66	71	277	40,260
	Scott Stallings	73	66	69	69	277	40,260
	Brendan Steele	64	73	67	73	277	40,260
45	Tyrrell Hatton	70	70	70	68	278	27,638
	John Huh	71	61	72	74	278	27,638
	Si Woo Kim	71	66	69	72	278	27,638
	Martin Laird	75	66	66	71	278	27,638
	Collin Morikawa	71	64	73	70	278	27,638
	Mito Pereira	67	77	68	66	278	27,638
	Chez Reavie	74	69	68	67	278	27,638
	Sepp Straka	72	68	68	70	278	27,638
53	Takumi Kanaya	72	67	70	70	279	22,587
	Danny Lee	68	75	65	71	279	22,587
	Adam Long	68	68	68	75	279	22,587
	Cameron Young	70	67	72	70	279	22,587
	Tommy Fleetwood	70	71	69	69	279	22,587
	Yuto Katsuragawa	69	70	73	67	279	22,587
59	Lucas Herbert	74	72	71	63	280	21,340
	Rikuya Hoshino	73	70	69	68	280	21,340
	Kyoung-Hoon Lee	71	68	69	72	280	21,340
	CT Pan	71	67	69	73	280	21,340
	Adam Svensson	74	68	68	70	280	21,340
64	Naoyuki Kataoka	74	68	71	68	281	20,570
	Matt Wallace	72	70	69	70	281	20,570
66	Mark Hubbard	71	71	69	71	282	20,240
67	Aguri Iwasaki	76	70	69	68	283	19,910
	Davis Riley	75	73	67	68	283	19,910
69	Hiroshi Iwata	70	73	71	70	284	19,470
	Chad Ramey	74	67	69	74	284	19,470

71	Troy Merritt	68 71 71 75	285	19,140		Kevin Streelman	74 71 70 73	288	18,370
72	Riki Kawamoto	72 75 69 71	287	18,810	76	Kaito Onishi	72 73 72 72	289	18,040
	Peter Malnati	74 73 73 67	287	18,810	77	Tomoharu Otsuki	76 69 73 72	290	17,820
74	Russell Knox	74 73 74 67	288	18,370	78	Shugo Imahira	78 70 73 72	293	17,600

CJ Cup

Knowledgeable Rory McIlroy watchers say you can tell how he's playing by his walk. Strolling along, looking down — not so good. Swinging along, perky, looking around — doing fine. At the CJ Cup, then, his feet must have been barely touching the ground. He was on his way to a repeat CJ victory, his third win of the year, his 23rd career win, and a return to world number one. It was all about coming up out of that rabbit hole. "It's been a wild six months," the spirited Northern Irishman was saying, after holding off contenders and shaking off a few late bumps. "I figured a few things out with my game, and I've just been on a really good run."

It was a year earlier that McIlroy was having his woes, having suffered a 1-3 Ryder Cup. But something about the CJ Cup seemed to rejuvenate him. He was down by nine strokes after the second round, then caught fire, shot 62-66, and won by a stroke. "This tournament last year was the start of me trying to build myself back up to this point," he said. "I think I was outside the top 10 in the world. It's not a position that I'm used to being in."

Course knowledge didn't help him. A Korean event temporarily in the US because of Covid-19 travel restrictions, the 2021 CJ Cup was played at the Summit in Las Vegas. This one was at the Congaree Golf Club in South Carolina. It wasn't easy. He trailed Jon Rahm (69-62) and Kurt Kitayama (66-65) after 36 holes, but recovered, shooting Congaree in 66-67-67-67 for a one-stroke victory on 17-under 267.

McIlroy took the lead in the third round and noted, "It's nice when you get that question." The question: which eagle was his favourite? He hit the fourth with a drive and a six-iron to two feet, and at the 12th, he crushed a drive 376 yards and finished by holing a 30-foot putt from off the green. The rest of the round was, he said, "a little scrappy", a mix of three birdies and three bogeys. He would go into the final round with a one-shot lead on Rahm (70), Kitayama (70) and KH Lee (66). He also set a task for himself from the last time he was number one, in July 2020. "I went down a couple of rabbit holes since then, as well with my swing and my game," he said. "So being able to come back up out of those rabbit holes and find my way back, that's the real satisfying part."

There were twists and turns, but McIlroy found his way out of the rabbit hole in the final round. He was tied with Kitayama with five holes to play, then erupted into three straight birdies. At the par-three 14th, he hit a five-iron to 15 feet, got up-and-down out of a bunker at 15, and he essentially locked it up at the 16th with a wedge under the tree limbs to 20 feet. The bogeys at 17 and 18 only cut his winning margin to one.

Congaree Golf Club, Ridgeland, South Carolina — October 20-23
Par 71 (36-35); 7,655 yards — Purse: $10,500,000

1	**Rory McIlroy**	66 67 67 67	267	$1,890,000		Tyrrell Hatton	67 68 71 69	275	189,756
2	**Kurt Kitayama**	66 65 70 67	268	1,134,000		Tom Hoge	68 67 70 70	275	189,756
3	**Kyoung-Hoon Lee**	68 67 66 68	269	714,000		Taylor Montgomery	69 71 73 62	275	189,756
4	Tommy Fleetwood	73 66 66 65	270	462,000	18	Maverick McNealy	69 70 66 71	276	144,480
	Jon Rahm	69 62 70 69	270	462,000		Mito Pereira	71 67 69 69	276	144,480
6	Aaron Wise	66 66 71 69	272	378,000		Brendan Steele	68 70 69 69	276	144,480
7	Sam Burns	70 68 68 67	273	316,313	21	Keegan Bradley	71 69 67 70	277	119,280
	Lee Hodges	68 67 70 68	273	316,313		Viktor Hovland	67 71 68 71	277	119,280
	Billy Horschel	68 67 72 66	273	316,313	23	Corey Conners	70 68 69 71	278	88,305
	Brendon Todd	68 67 69 69	273	316,313		Brian Harman	68 69 70 71	278	88,305
11	Jason Day	69 69 69 67	274	252,000		Max Homa	72 65 72 69	278	88,305
	Tom Kim	66 69 69 70	274	252,000		Shane Lowry	68 67 71 72	278	88,305
13	Cam Davis	66 66 73 70	275	189,756		Taylor Moore	67 69 67 75	278	88,305
	Matt Fitzpatrick	70 69 68 68	275	189,756		Cameron Young	73 69 66 70	278	88,305

29	Wyndham Clark	66	70	71	72	279	65,730		Davis Riley	72	75	72	66	285	21,840
	Matt Kuchar	71	68	71	69	279	65,730		Webb Simpson	71	72	74	68	285	21,840
	Collin Morikawa	70	69	68	72	279	65,730		Alex Smalley	70	69	73	73	285	21,840
	Andrew Putnam	69	68	74	68	279	65,730		Jordan Spieth	75	69	72	69	285	21,840
	Justin Suh	74	67	69	69	279	65,730	58	Lucas Glover	69	73	73	71	286	20,685
34	Rickie Fowler	74	66	73	67	280	54,180		Luke List	73	69	71	73	286	20,685
	Sungjae Im	67	70	74	69	280	54,180		JJ Spaun	69	72	69	76	286	20,685
	Hideki Matsuyama	71	71	71	67	280	54,180		Scott Stallings	72	69	72	73	286	20,685
37	Bio Kim	72	69	68	72	281	46,830	62	Byeong Hun An	73	70	70	74	287	20,055
	Denny McCarthy	68	73	70	70	281	46,830		Sepp Straka	71	70	73	73	287	20,055
	Alex Noren	69	71	70	71	281	46,830	64	Seonghyeon Kim	73	71	73	71	288	19,740
40	Harris English	69	72	71	70	282	38,430	65	Christiaan Bezuidenhout	70	71	75	74	290	19,425
	Keith Mitchell	71	69	72	70	282	38,430		John Huh	70	75	72	73	290	19,425
	Sebastian Munoz	68	72	73	69	282	38,430	67	Troy Merritt	72	73	68	78	291	18,795
	Justin Thomas	68	73	72	69	282	38,430		JT Poston	74	72	71	74	291	18,795
	Danny Willett	69	67	74	72	282	38,430		Sahith Theegala	79	70	73	69	291	18,795
45	Emiliano Grillo	71	68	73	71	283	29,085		Gary Woodland	65	73	79	74	291	18,795
	Russell Henley	74	70	67	72	283	29,085	71	Trey Mullinax	65	72	77	78	292	18,270
	Ryan Palmer	76	71	68	68	283	29,085	72	Chanmin Jung	74	74	73	72	293	17,850
	Scottie Scheffler	71	68	74	70	283	29,085		Kevin Kisner	73	74	75	71	293	17,850
49	Adam Hadwin	71	67	74	72	284	24,010		Chez Reavie	75	69	76	73	293	17,850
	Sanghyun Park	69	72	72	71	284	24,010	75	Yongjun Bae	71	74	72	77	294	17,430
	Seamus Power	67	69	74	74	284	24,010	76	Sanghun Shin	78	73	77	73	301	17,220
52	Si Woo Kim	67	74	73	71	285	21,840	77	Yeongsu Kim	74	76	76	77	303	16,905
	Chris Kirk	71	68	71	75	285	21,840		Yoseop Seo	76	72	77	78	303	16,905

Butterfield Bermuda Championship

It's an article of faith in golf: timing is everything. But it was more urgent than that to Ireland's Seamus Power in the Butterfield Bermuda Championship. A different kind of timing. "You knew you had to make your score in the first 11 or 12," said Power, "and then kind of hold on for dear life."

The reference was to the Bermuda winds, evoking images of sails billowing and pennants streaming and perfectly struck golf balls flying hither and yon. In this setting in the third round, Power did make his score before the winds got up and went on to take his second PGA Tour win and rise in the world rankings. He had come to Port Royal 48th, the highest ranked player in the field, and left as number 32. "This course was always going to be a tale of two sides," said Power. "I knew it was going to be hard coming in and it was. I'm delighted to get it done." He shot 65-65-65-70 and, at 19-under 265, won by one over Belgium's Thomas Detry, after the collapse of the intriguing Ben Griffin.

Said Detry of the wind: "It was a challenge on every putt, every tee shot." Thus went the Bermuda Championship. Arjun Atwal, 49, who hadn't played in three months since the death of his father, and without a spot in the field, flew to Bermuda in hopes that one would open up. One did, as he was having breakfast. He had time for a few practice hits, then shot 63 and was one off the lead of Austin Smotherman and Australia's Harrison Endycott. Ben Crane, 46, on a sponsor's exemption, shot 62, led the second round by a stroke. "The best I've played in a long time," said Crane. Power surfaced in the third round, making four straight birdies from the second, adding two more, then at the par-three 13th taking a wind-blown double bogey. Birdies at 16 and 17 got him back to six under and into a tie with Griffin at 18 under.

Griffin, 26, was quietly famous as the pro who gave up competitive golf and became a mortgage officer and later was encouraged to return to golf. After four birdies and a bogey in the final round, he birdied 10 and 11 and was leading by two going to the 12th. As Power had said: "You knew once you got to 12 tee that the next hour and a half was going to be really tough going." Griffin got mauled. From the 12th, he made four straight bogeys, then double-bogeyed 16. He shot 72 and tied for third, two behind, and won $344,500. "I can't get mad at anything that I do," Griffin said, "because it's so cool to be able to play on the PGA Tour."

Power, on getting his second win, said: "I'm absolutely over the moon. The first one was amazing but to be able to win again, it's fantastic."

Port Royal Golf Course, Southampton, Bermuda — October 27-30
Par 71 (36-35) 6,828 yards — Purse: $6,500,000

1	**Seamus Power**	65	65	65	70	265	$1,170,000
2	**Thomas Detry**	64	67	68	67	266	708,500
3	**Ben Griffin**	65	64	66	72	267	344,500
	Patrick Rodgers	65	67	70	65	267	344,500
	Chun-an Yu	64	66	67	70	267	344,500
6	Aaron Baddeley	65	64	68	71	268	227,500
	Denny McCarthy	63	69	69	67	268	227,500
8	Justin Lower	64	68	69	68	269	196,625
	Max McGreevy	65	70	66	68	269	196,625
10	Harrison Endycott	62	70	70	68	270	177,125
11	Brian Gay	66	66	66	73	271	134,875
	David Lingmerth	68	68	68	67	271	134,875
	Sean O'Hair	64	68	70	69	271	134,875
	Greyson Sigg	64	69	66	72	271	134,875
	Alex Smalley	65	69	69	68	271	134,875
	Nick Watney	67	67	70	67	271	134,875
17	Byeong Hun An	65	70	70	67	272	89,375
	Akshay Bhatia	68	67	69	68	272	89,375
	Zecheng Dou	65	65	75	67	272	89,375
	Fabian Gomez	68	63	73	68	272	89,375
	Chesson Hadley	66	67	71	68	272	89,375
	Andrew Novak	68	68	70	66	272	89,375
23	Nico Echavarria	66	64	72	71	273	56,550
	Nick Hardy	65	71	71	66	273	56,550
	Robby Shelton	63	66	73	71	273	56,550
	Austin Smotherman	62	67	74	70	273	56,550
	Nick Taylor	66	68	71	68	273	56,550
	Richy Werenski	67	66	70	70	273	56,550
29	MJ Daffue	65	70	73	66	274	41,654
	Garrick Higgo	68	68	74	64	274	41,654
	Adam Schenk	63	66	76	69	274	41,654
	Robert Streb	66	69	73	66	274	41,654
	Scott Harrington	66	66	70	72	274	41,654
	Charley Hoffman	67	66	71	70	274	41,654
35	Jonathan Byrd	69	66	73	67	275	29,683
	Nate Lashley	66	70	70	69	275	29,683
	Seung-Yul Noh	68	67	71	69	275	29,683
	Will Gordon	68	66	66	75	275	29,683
	Brent Grant	66	67	69	73	275	29,683
	Cameron Percy	66	68	71	70	275	29,683
	Erik van Rooyen	66	66	72	71	275	29,683
	John VanDerLaan	69	67	67	72	275	29,683
	Brandon Wu	71	64	70	70	275	29,683
44	Tyson Alexander	68	67	68	73	276	20,527
	Austin Cook	68	67	67	74	276	20,527
	Tano Goya	68	68	73	67	276	20,527
	Adam Long	68	68	72	68	276	20,527
	CT Pan	66	67	69	74	276	20,527
49	Arjun Atwal	63	71	70	73	277	16,367
	Ben Crane	66	62	73	76	277	16,367
	Russell Knox	66	67	72	72	277	16,367
	Ben Martin	64	69	69	75	277	16,367
	Dylan Wu	64	66	76	71	277	16,367
54	Aaron Rai	69	67	71	71	278	15,275
	Brian Stuard	65	67	73	73	278	15,275
	Camilo Villegas	68	68	73	69	278	15,275
57	Philip Knowles	66	70	74	69	279	14,950
	Ben Taylor	70	65	77	67	279	14,950
59	Scott Gutschewski	65	70	70	75	280	14,690
	Trevor Werbylo	65	68	71	76	280	14,690
61	Matti Schmid	67	67	70	77	281	14,495
62	Scott Brown	63	68	81	70	282	14,365
63	Lucas Glover	66	67	78	72	283	14,170
	Harry Hall	66	69	77	71	283	14,170
65	Greg Chalmers	66	70	76	73	285	13,975
	Caleb Surratt (A)	71	64	85	65	285	
67	Augusto Nunez	67	69	73	77	286	13,845

World Wide Technology Championship

Russell Henley spent a delightful week at the Mexican Caribbean resort of Mayakoba, winning the World Wide Technology Championship early in November. Henley, it should be noted, won the event quite comfortably, despite the fact that, as he revealed, he has trouble sleeping on a lead, even a cushy one. And really cushy is six shots going into the fourth round, and he went on to win by four. But in the face of such success, perhaps his triumph would be best measured by its imperfections. His bogeys, that is.

There was the one at the par-five fifth, which included a visit to the rough and a penalty, and the one at the par-four 16th, involving rough and a bunker. And with that, the bogey discussion is over. Henley had made just two bogeys in the entire tournament. He had gone the first 58 holes before making his first, then another 11 until his second. He didn't merely win the tournament, he dominated it from the second round, shooting the par-71 El Camaleon in 63-63-65-70 for a tournament-record tying 261, 23 under par, and four better than Brian Harman, distancing himself from such as Scottie Scheffler, until recently world number one; Viktor Hovland, seeking his third straight Mayakoba win, and Collin Morikawa, who had cooled off since his fifth win, the 2021 Open Championship.

It was more than just the fourth career win for Henley. It was perhaps the breaking of the 54-hole curse. The last five times Henley had at least a share of the 54-hole lead, it got away from him. The most recent slip was in the Sony Open in January when Hideki Matsuyama erased his two-stroke lead and beat him in a playoff. To Henley, there was no mystery to the curse. "I've just choked, you know," Henley said. "The nerves have gotten to me and I've made bad mistakes, bad mental mistakes, and just haven't gotten it done on Sunday."

Was this getting the monkey off the back? "I just tried to learn from my past screw-ups," Henley said. "All those events I didn't close out, they hurt. You never know if you'll win another. To come down 18 with a four-shot lead was really cool."

Before that, Harman cut the big overnight lead to three with birdies at the third and fifth. Was the curse about to strike again? Not this time. Henley righted himself after the bogey at five and birdied three consecutively from the sixth, and nobody got closer than four from there.

El Camaleon Golf Course, Mayakoba, Riviera Maya, Mexico — November 3-6
Par 71 (36-35); 7,034 yards — Purse: $8,200,000

1	**Russell Henley**	63	63	65	70	261	$1,476,000
2	**Brian Harman**	66	66	67	66	265	893,800
3	**Joel Dahmen**	68	67	66	65	266	375,560
	Will Gordon	62	67	68	69	266	375,560
	Troy Merritt	65	69	65	67	266	375,560
	Seamus Power	67	68	63	68	266	375,560
	Scottie Scheffler	65	71	68	62	266	375,560
8	David Lingmerth	65	66	71	65	267	248,050
	Sam Ryder	64	65	73	65	267	248,050
10	Viktor Hovland	65	69	66	68	268	190,650
	Patton Kizzire	65	65	67	71	268	190,650
	David Lipsky	66	70	66	66	268	190,650
	Maverick McNealy	65	68	69	66	268	190,650
	Taylor Montgomery	65	70	67	66	268	190,650
15	Thomas Detry	70	66	64	69	269	129,150
	Martin Laird	65	67	69	68	269	129,150
	Collin Morikawa	71	63	68	67	269	129,150
	Henrik Norlander	67	70	65	67	269	129,150
	JJ Spaun	65	70	67	67	269	129,150
	Aaron Wise	67	71	67	64	269	129,150
21	Ryan Armour	67	69	70	64	270	82,683
	Nick Hardy	67	70	67	66	270	82,683
	Jason Day	73	64	67	66	270	82,683
	Davis Riley	67	67	68	68	270	82,683
	Matthias Schwab	66	68	66	70	270	82,683
	Danny Willett	65	71	67	67	270	82,683
27	Eric Cole	70	68	66	67	271	58,630
	Austin Cook	70	67	66	68	271	58,630
	John Huh	65	70	68	68	271	58,630
	Matt Kuchar	66	67	71	67	271	58,630
	Patrick Rodgers	66	67	70	68	271	58,630
32	Harris English	64	70	71	67	272	45,783
	Adam Hadwin	66	70	67	69	272	45,783
	Dean Burmester	68	70	64	70	272	45,783
	Harry Higgs	70	62	69	71	272	45,783
	Scott Piercy	64	69	68	71	272	45,783
	Brandon Wu	68	66	67	71	272	45,783
38	Austin Eckroat	69	68	67	69	273	36,490
	Lucas Glover	69	69	71	64	273	36,490
	Lee Hodges	67	71	64	71	273	36,490
	Beau Hossler	71	65	71	66	273	36,490
42	Emiliano Grillo	67	69	73	65	274	28,290
	Charley Hoffman	68	68	67	71	274	28,290
	Kyoung-Hoon Lee	69	68	70	67	274	28,290
	Alex Noren	67	69	67	71	274	28,290
	Greyson Sigg	66	67	67	74	274	28,290
	Robert Streb	68	67	70	69	274	28,290
48	Philip Knowles	68	70	70	67	275	21,271
	Russell Knox	71	67	71	66	275	21,271
	Ryan Moore	69	69	71	66	275	21,271
	Andrew Putnam	71	66	69	69	275	21,271
	Justin Suh	67	69	67	72	275	21,271
53	Nick Taylor	70	67	72	67	276	19,489
	Brendon Todd	67	68	74	67	276	19,489
	Carson Young	70	67	71	68	276	19,489
56	Billy Horschel	70	67	71	69	277	18,942
	Justin Lower	68	68	69	72	277	18,942
	Sebastian Munoz	70	68	69	70	277	18,942
59	Hayden Buckley	68	68	71	71	278	18,368
	Dylan Frittelli	72	66	68	72	278	18,368
	Ben Griffin	66	71	72	69	278	18,368
	Ben Taylor	68	70	67	73	278	18,368
63	Joseph Bramlett	65	72	68	74	279	17,958
64	Chris Kirk	71	67	71	72	281	17,712
	Danny Lee	71	67	72	71	281	17,712
66	MJ Daffue	69	69	72	72	282	17,384
	Rory Sabbatini	67	70	73	72	282	17,384
68	Francesco Molinari	64	70	77	75	286	17,138

Cadence Bank Houston Open

Tony Finau was doing so swimmingly in the Cadence Bank Houston Open that his wife and son decided to fly in and catch the finish. They arrived just after he made the final turn. Pity. They missed the best part. When Finau birdied the ninth, it gave him an eight-shot lead. It also gave him something of a headache. How do you play the last nine holes with an eight-shot lead? Do you get super-cautious, trying to avoid mistakes? Do you try to add to it, just as a means of not becoming complacent? "Yeah, it's a place I've never been before," Finau said. "It's an interesting mindset. A little bit of 'don't screw it up', or maybe 'if we hit some good shots we can extend this lead'. You kind of live in the middle."

Golf, in its own contrary way, answered Finau's question for him. Three bogeys over six holes, as many bogeys as he'd made through the first three and a half rounds. He responded to the sobering experience with three closing pars, wrapping up his Memorial Park card of 65-62-68-69, for 16-under 264. His final margin was trimmed to four when Tyson Alexander holed a 32-footer for birdie at the

18th. "It was one of those days I fought and fought, and I made a lot of nice putts," Finau said. "I've never been in this position. I had a lot of nerves. Overall, as the round went on, I felt better. I was happy to get the 'W' today."

This win marked a huge career reversal for Finau. He had won once in his first 185 tournaments. Now he had three in 2022, and four in the last 30 months. Finau acknowledged that he'd already had a good year, what with victories in the 3M Open and the Rocket Mortgage. "But I want to finish the year strong," he said. He made five birdies coming home to share the first-round lead with Alex Noren and Aaron Wise. Then Finau went on a 10-birdie rampage in the second round, interrupted by two bogeys. "It was a really nice round of golf," he said, now leading by four. And he stayed there with a compelling third round, in a cold November wind, of two birdies and 16 pars. "The score doesn't say that, but I think I played better than yesterday."

Then came his eight-shot lead — four birdies from 16, seven, 40 and 19 feet. And then what to do with an eight-shot lead? "Overall this was a special week," Finau said. "You know, I won this golf tournament from start to finish. To have played that well for four straight days, all the hard work is starting to pay off, which is fun."

There was also runner-up Alexander, 34, PGA Tour rookie, of celebrated lineage — father Buddy, grandfather Skip — falling short of a first win with a closing 66. "Great week for me," Alexander cracked. "I wish Tony would have taken the week off."

Memorial Park Golf Course, Houston, Texas — November 10-13
Par 70 (35-35); 7,412 yards — Purse: $8,400,000

1	**Tony Finau**	65	62	68	69	264	$1,512,000
2	**Tyson Alexander**	66	66	70	66	268	915,600
3	**Ben Taylor**	66	68	65	70	269	579,600
4	Trey Mullinax	67	66	72	67	272	353,500
	Alex Noren	65	66	73	68	272	353,500
	Alex Smalley	71	64	70	67	272	353,500
7	Adam Hadwin	70	65	70	68	273	273,000
	Aaron Rai	70	64	70	69	273	273,000
9	Joseph Bramlett	70	65	70	69	274	196,500
	Joel Dahmen	67	68	68	71	274	196,500
	Stephan Jaeger	70	67	70	67	274	196,500
	Keith Mitchell	66	70	70	68	274	196,500
	Justin Rose	67	69	66	72	274	196,500
	Scottie Scheffler	70	66	71	67	274	196,500
	Gary Woodland	69	67	67	71	274	196,500
16	Wyndham Clark	66	68	68	73	275	123,900
	Jason Day	69	69	69	68	275	123,900
	Ben Griffin	67	67	71	70	275	123,900
	Mackenzie Hughes	66	68	70	71	275	123,900
	Scott Piercy	67	70	67	71	275	123,900
	Patrick Rodgers	68	63	73	71	275	123,900
22	Martin Laird	68	69	73	66	276	84,420
	David Lipsky	66	73	70	67	276	84,420
	Sahith Theegala	71	68	73	64	276	84,420
	Aaron Wise	65	71	71	69	276	84,420
26	Callum Tarren	73	66	70	68	277	67,620
27	Ryan Armour	72	68	66	72	278	56,333
	Austin Cook	68	67	71	72	278	56,333
	James Hahn	68	65	71	74	278	56,333
	Cole Hammer	74	65	71	68	278	56,333
	Russell Knox	69	65	70	74	278	56,333
	Maverick McNealy	67	72	69	70	278	56,333
	Davis Riley	71	64	71	72	278	56,333
	Kyle Westmoreland	68	72	69	69	278	56,333
35	Eric Cole	71	68	69	71	279	42,735
	Si Woo Kim	68	69	69	73	279	42,735
	Andrew Putnam	68	70	71	70	279	42,735
	Carl Yuan	67	66	77	69	279	42,735
39	Harris English	69	69	69	73	280	36,540
	Harry Hall	69	70	72	69	280	36,540
	Adam Svensson	73	67	72	68	280	36,540
	Travis Vick (A)	68	69	71	72	280	
43	Erik Barnes	68	71	70	72	281	30,660
	Will Gordon	68	71	73	69	281	30,660
	Davis Thompson	68	71	74	68	281	30,660
	Kevin Tway	71	69	70	71	281	30,660
47	Zack Fischer	69	70	74	69	282	23,705
	Michael Kim	70	68	73	71	282	23,705
	Seonghyeon Kim	68	70	74	70	282	23,705
	Francesco Molinari	69	71	72	70	282	23,705
	Justin Suh	69	68	71	74	282	23,705
52	Robby Shelton	71	68	73	71	283	21,084
53	Byeong Hun An	70	67	75	72	284	20,118
	Denny McCarthy	67	72	70	75	284	20,118
	Matthew NeSmith	74	64	78	68	284	20,118
	Nick Watney	69	71	72	72	284	20,118
57	Stewart Cink	68	71	74	72	285	19,236
	Zach Johnson	69	70	72	74	285	19,236
	Luke List	69	70	69	77	285	19,236
	Taylor Montgomery	71	68	76	70	285	19,236
	Samuel Stevens	70	69	71	75	285	19,236
62	Paul Haley II	72	68	74	72	286	18,648
	Brandon Wu	71	69	71	75	286	18,648
64	Seung-Yul Noh	71	67	74	75	287	18,312
	Matthias Schwab	73	65	77	72	287	18,312
66	Taylor Pendrith	66	72	71	79	288	18,060
67	Max McGreevy	66	73	75	77	291	17,892
68	Zecheng Dou	67	72	76	78	293	17,724

RSM Classic

There was not a great deal to recommend Adam Svensson in the RSM Classic, the final tournament of 2022 on the PGA Tour. His start was shaky, a 73 that left him a distant 108th in the field. Next, his chances thin, he wanted very badly to make the cut, and he did, by a shot. Then at the start of the final round, 16 players were within three shots of the lead, and while he was one of them, he was hardly accustomed to that kind of traffic. He'd had one top-10 finish.

So in keeping with the best crafted golf tales, there was Svensson saying, "To be honest, it's not even real, right now", while cradling the trophy. "I'm so happy. I put so much work in. To win on the PGA Tour means everything to me. I just kept believing in myself, and here I am."

The toughest part of the job came with a four-man tie coming down the final stretch of Sea Island's Seaside course. Svensson, 28, from Canada, broke away at the 16th, dropping an 18-foot birdie putt, and then he rolled in a 10-footer for birdie at the 17th for a card of 73-64-62-64 and a 19-under 263 total, winning by two over Callum Tarren (64), Sahith Theegala (66) and Brian Harman (65). He trailed by nine in the first round, seven in the second and one in the third.

Svensson was to note that he'd been working hard on his putting, and it showed. It was either angelic or demonic, depending on the observer's viewpoint. In his one-bogey 62 in the third round, the longest of his seven birdies were from 12 and 14 feet, and the other five ranged from five to nine feet, and he capped them off with an eagle putt of 10 feet at 15. And in his flawless closing 64, he holed birdie putts of 30, 20, 36 and 16 feet before the two clinchers at the end. Overall, he ranked first in Strokes Gained: Putting at 9.160.

And in the post-tournament discussion, Svensson was reminded that not only did he win $1,458,000, but enchanting names such as Kapalua, the Masters and the Players, were in his immediate future. "I didn't even think about it until it was brought up to me 15 minutes ago," he said. "I'm more proud of what I've accomplished from the direction I was to the direction I've gone now, it's more fulfilling than money to me. I'm more just proud of myself for things I've been doing."

For Theegala it was a second runner-up finish of the year and his career, and he moved into the world's top 50 for the first time. "Yeah, a lot of it's positive, for sure," he said. "It's just awesome to be in this position. And I feel like I'm getting more and more comfortable and also don't necessarily have to play my A-plus or A-game to get there."

Sea Island Golf Club (Seaside), St Simons Island, Georgia — November 17-20
Par 70 (35-35); 7,005 yards — Purse: $8,100,000
Plantation course (R1&2) par 72 (36-36); 7,060 yards

1	**Adam Svensson**	73	64	62	64	263	$1,458,000
2	**Brian Harman**	67	69	64	65	265	612,900
	Callum Tarren	64	68	69	64	265	612,900
	Sahith Theegala	68	63	68	66	265	612,900
5	Joel Dahmen	67	64	72	64	267	277,830
	Cole Hammer	64	66	72	65	267	277,830
	Seamus Power	66	68	67	66	267	277,830
	Alex Smalley	67	66	67	67	267	277,830
	Chris Stroud	70	66	66	65	267	277,830
10	Erik Barnes	70	67	65	66	268	188,325
	Wyndham Clark	71	65	66	66	268	188,325
	David Lingmerth	67	65	70	66	268	188,325
	Patrick Rodgers	69	65	64	70	268	188,325
	Robby Shelton	68	70	65	65	268	188,325
15	Will Gordon	69	64	68	68	269	127,575
	Taylor Montgomery	69	66	65	69	269	127,575
	Seung-Yul Noh	68	64	70	67	269	127,575
	Taylor Pendrith	69	66	65	69	269	127,575
	Greyson Sigg	66	69	70	64	269	127,575
	JJ Spaun	67	68	69	65	269	127,575
21	Harry Higgs	67	63	70	70	270	76,646
	Beau Hossler	64	67	69	70	270	76,646
	Russell Knox	67	70	66	67	270	76,646
	Danny Lee	70	66	66	68	270	76,646
	Ben Martin	69	64	65	72	270	76,646
	JT Poston	70	67	66	67	270	76,646
	Andrew Putnam	65	65	69	71	270	76,646
	Ben Taylor	71	65	65	69	270	76,646
29	Zac Blair	67	69	68	67	271	51,908
	Harris English	68	68	70	65	271	51,908
	Ben Griffin	65	71	67	68	271	51,908
	Paul Haley II	68	67	67	69	271	51,908
	Kevin Kisner	70	67	67	67	271	51,908
	Justin Rose	68	67	67	69	271	51,908
35	Chris Gotterup	65	68	71	68	272	41,209
	Michael Kim	67	69	69	67	272	41,209
	Patton Kizzire	67	68	70	67	272	41,209
	Kevin Streelman	68	64	68	72	272	41,209
39	Aaron Baddeley	69	68	68	68	273	32,805
	Hayden Buckley	69	66	69	69	273	32,805
	Eric Cole	69	68	70	66	273	32,805
	Keith Mitchell	67	68	69	69	273	32,805
	Henrik Norlander	67	69	70	67	273	32,805
	Carl Yuan	70	68	69	66	273	32,805

45	Akshay Bhatia	73	63	69	69	274	27,135
46	Ryan Armour	70	67	73	65	275	21,749
	Brice Garnett	68	69	69	69	275	21,749
	Jim Herman	72	65	70	68	275	21,749
	Stephan Jaeger	67	70	71	67	275	21,749
	Denny McCarthy	66	70	68	71	275	21,749
	Davis Riley	68	69	69	69	275	21,749
	Kevin Roy	69	68	68	70	275	21,749
	Dylan Wu	70	68	70	67	275	21,749
54	Jacob Bridgeman	69	67	73	67	276	18,630
	Dean Burmester	66	68	71	71	276	18,630
	Trevor Cone	69	68	68	71	276	18,630
	Brent Grant	71	67	71	67	276	18,630
	Scott Stallings	70	66	67	73	276	18,630
	Martin Trainer	70	67	67	72	276	18,630
	Brandon Wu	70	68	67	71	276	18,630
	Chun-an Yu	72	66	69	69	276	18,630
62	Tyson Alexander	68	69	70	70	277	17,820
	Matthias Schwab	72	66	68	71	277	17,820
64	Joseph Bramlett	68	69	72	69	278	17,496
	Doc Redman	70	68	73	67	278	17,496
66	Justin Suh	66	68	70	75	279	17,253
67	Zecheng Dou	69	67	71	74	281	17,010
	Andrew Landry	75	63	72	71	281	17,010
69	MJ Daffue	70	68	70	75	283	16,767

TaylorMade Pebble Beach Invitational

Still in his first year as a professional, Parker Coody claimed his second win with a three-stroke victory over Lauren Stephenson at the TaylorMade Pebble Beach Invitational. The unofficial event, in its 51st edition, brings together players from the PGA Tour, the Champions Tour, the Korn Ferry Tour and the LPGA. Coody, 22, from Texas, is the grandson of 1971 Masters champion Charles Coody, while he joined twin Pierceson in helping the University of Texas win the 2022 NCAA Championship. Both twins then turned pro, with Pierceson winning on the Korn Ferry Tour and Parker claiming the Manitoba Open by eight strokes on his sixth start on the Canadian Tour. He later earned status for the Korn Ferry.

Coody was the only player in the field with four sub-70 rounds, opening with a 69 at The Links at Spanish Bay, then posting a 68 at Spyglass Hill, followed by 64-69 at Pebble Beach for a total of 18-under 270. Coody went out in 31 on Saturday in a round of nine birdies, including at the clifftop ninth and 10th holes. He led by three from Scott McCarron and Stephenson, who set a new women's course record at Spyglass Hill with her own 64 on Saturday.

While McCarron faded on Sunday, Coody and Stephenson both went three under in the final round with five birdies. Coody made three in the first six holes to give himself a cushion for a couple of bogeys before picking up shots at the 13th and the par-three 17th. "This was by far the best course conditions I've ever played and the most amazing time I've had playing in an event," said Coody.

Stephenson's only hiccup came with a double bogey at the ninth, but she responded with three birdies in four holes on the back nine to finish two ahead of Mac Meissner. She was the first woman to finish runner-up in the event since Mina Harigae in 2018, while Annika Sorenstam had previously done so in 1999. Juli Inkster won the tournament in 1990.

Pebble Beach Golf Links, Pebble Beach, California — November 17-20
Par 72 (36-36); 6,828 yards — Purse: $300,000
Spyglass Hill (R1-3) par 72 (36-36); 6,960 yards
Links at Spanish Bay (R1-3) par 72 (35-37); 6,821 yards

1	**Parker Coody**	69	68	64	69	270	$60,000
2	**Lauren Stephenson**	74	66	64	69	273	
3	**Mac Meissner**	70	68	68	69	275	
4	Isaiah Salinda	68	73	69	66	276	
5	Alex Cejka	72	71	66	68	277	
	Scott McCarron	71	66	67	73	277	
7	Kevin Velo	68	68	72	70	278	
	William McGirt	67	71	69	71	278	
9	Jeff Gove	70	71	70	68	279	
	Maria Fassi	66	74	69	70	279	
	Patrick Fishburn	72	71	64	72	279	
12	Paul Stankowski	71	72	68	69	280	
	Steve Marino	67	75	70	68	280	
	Matt Gogel	68	72	66	74	280	
15	Kevin Sutherland	72	72	72	66	282	
	Andrew Yun	73	66	74	69	282	
	Matt McCarty	74	67	71	70	282	
	Brandon Harkins	72	72	68	70	282	
	RJ Manke	72	72	68	70	282	
	Andrew Kozan	68	71	71	72	282	
	John Mallinger	68	68	69	77	282	

Hero World Challenge

It was the same one-two as in 2021 at the Hero World Challenge. But a very different story. Then Viktor Hovland came from six behind Collin Morikawa to win by one over Scottie Scheffler. Hovland won again from Scheffler in 2022 — by two strokes, but that was not what was different. This time it was a front-running effort from the Norwegian and all the pressure that builds over four days, even somewhere as agreeable as Albany.

Hovland survived a last-hole scare for a wire-to-wire win, sharing the lead on the first day with a 69, then going one in front of a string of US Presidents Cup players with a 70 in the second round. It was on Saturday, with a 64, the low round of the week, that Hovland put down the marker that he was serious about retaining his title. Now he led by three from Scheffler, with the best of the rest two further back. The Masters champion briefly tied for the lead when he chipped in for an eagle at the sixth, but Hovland then birdied the same hole to stay ahead. Hovland won the short-game battle at the next for a two-shot swing, before Scheffler had a double bogey at the ninth.

Scheffler had four birdies coming home, and Hovland a bogey and two birdies before arriving at the 18th two ahead. Comfortable, but suddenly not. From an awkward lie, his second shot found the water and he was faced with a 20-footer for bogey. Scheffler had missed the green, saw his chip roll over the hole and had a 10-footer for his par. It could still go either way. Until Hovland rolled in his putt for a 69 and 16-under-par 272. "I made it a little more exciting, I guess," Hovland smiled. "It's frigging nerve-racking. You're never that comfortable. I didn't play that great on the back nine, but it was good enough."

Hovland, who had not won anywhere since the Dubai Desert Classic at the start of the year, became the second player to defend the title. The first was Tiger Woods at Sherwood in 2007. Woods, the tournament host, had hoped to play for the first time since the Open Championship but plantar fasciitis meant his participation was limited to handing Hovland the trophy.

Scheffler had the chance to go back to world number one with a win, but instead closed with a 68 and finished two ahead of Cameron Young. As well as a repeat from Albany the year before, this was Scheffler's fourth runner-up finish since the last of his four 2022 victories at Augusta National. "I said earlier in the week that I don't like finishing second," he said. "It's not a good feeling right now. But I'm proud of the fight."

Albany Golf Course, New Providence, Bahamas — December 1-4
Par 72 (36-36); 7,449 yards — Purse: $3,500,000

1	**Viktor Hovland**	69	70	64	69	272	$1,000,000
2	**Scottie Scheffler**	72	68	66	68	274	375,000
3	**Cameron Young**	71	69	68	68	276	225,000
4	Xander Schauffele	72	68	69	68	277	150,000
5	Justin Thomas	72	70	66	70	278	135,000
6	Collin Morikawa	69	71	69	70	279	120,000
7	Tony Finau	72	72	70	68	282	115,000
8	Sungjae Im	74	71	70	68	283	112,500
	Jon Rahm	73	71	68	71	283	112,500
10	Joohyung Kim	69	72	74	69	284	109,500
	Sepp Straka	69	74	70	71	284	109,500
12	Sam Burns	70	75	69	72	286	108,000
13	Matt Fitzpatrick	74	70	76	67	287	106,500
	Billy Horschel	73	70	72	72	287	106,500
15	Jordan Spieth	76	72	72	69	289	105,000
16	Corey Conners	75	76	72	67	290	104,000
17	Max Homa	71	78	71	72	292	103,000
18	Shane Lowry	74	77	71	71	293	102,000
19	Kevin Kisner	74	72	77	71	294	101,000
20	Tommy Fleetwood	71	76	72	76	295	100,000

QBE Shootout

Sahith Theegala, who made it to the Tour Championship as a rookie, had come close to winning a few times. He was twice a runner-up, including just recently at the RSM Classic. And although the QBE Shootout is an unofficial team event, holing a winning putt is always special. Theegala stepped up on the 18th green at Tiburon and made the 15-footer that gave him and Tom Hoge the win when both Ryan Palmer and Charley Hoffman missed chances to force a playoff from shorter range.

Theegala and Hoge were the first pair of rookies to win the event since Keegan Bradley and Brendan

Steele 11 years previously. They started the final round two behind Palmer and Hoffman, who set a new 36-hole record with 56-62 for 26-under-par 118. The first day was played as a scramble and the second as greensomes, where both players tee off, pick a ball and alternate shots from there. Theegala and Hoge scored 60 both days. The final round was betterball and the winners matched the low round of the day with a 62 for a 34-under-par total of 182.

Hoge had won his maiden PGA Tour title at the AT&T Pebble Beach Pro-Am, but Theegala had yet to lift a trophy. "It's nice to get a taste of victory because it's so hard out here," he said. Theegala had been worried by a slight muscle pull in his ribs on the first hole, but said it eased up during the round. "I had to check later in the round if Tom's back was OK for carrying me all day."

Three-time winners Harris English and Matt Kuchar were third, while Nelly Korda, on her debut with Denny McCarthy, finished tied for fifth after they scored 62 in the final round. The previous day, the pair had scored seven under for the last six holes to post a 67 in greensomes. Korda chipped in twice, at the 16th and the 18th holes, while she put their second shot on the green at the par-five 17th and McCarthy holed from long range for an eagle.

Tiburon Golf Club (Gold), Ritz Carlton Resort, Naples, Florida — December 9-11
Par 72 (36-36); 7,382 yards — Purse: $3,800,000

1	**Tom Hoge/ Sahith Theegala**	60	60	62	182	$950,000
2	**Charley Hoffman/ Ryan Palmer**	56	62	65	183	590,000
3	**Harris English/ Matt Kuchar**	60	62	62	184	360,000
4	Max Homa/ Kevin Kisner	58	65	63	186	284,000
5	Nelly Korda/ Denny McCarthy	60	67	62	189	230,500
	Trey Mullinax/ Scott Stallings	61	66	62	189	230,500
7	Steve Stricker/ Cameron Young	62	63	65	190	205,000
8	Corey Conners/ Brian Harman	58	68	65	191	197,500
	Kyoung-Hoon Lee/ Sepp Straka	58	68	65	191	197,500
10	Jason Day/ Billy Horschel	61	61	70	192	187,500
	Maverick McNealy/ Lexi Thompson	60	67	65	192	187,500
12	Keith Mitchell/ JJ Spaun	60	69	64	193	180,000

PNC Championship

Tiger Woods celebrated his 47th birthday on 30 December 2022, which means that by the time of the 2026 PNC Championship he will be eligible for the PGA Tour Champions at which age, following Vijay Singh's win in the latest edition of this tournament contested by 20 major champions, he might feel the time is right to attach this title to his enviable CV. For not only did Singh at the age of 59, and alongside his son Qass, claim the Willie Park Trophy — a red leather belt named in honour of the inaugural winner of the Open Championship — but also defending champion John Daly, aged 56, finished tied runner-up and Padraig Harrington (51), Bernhard Langer and Mark O'Meara, both 65, were all in the top eight.

The two-day 36-hole scramble for two-ball family teams started in 1995 and while this was only Woods's third appearance it provided a landmark win for Singh with this being the 16th time he has participated. "This is a highlight of my career winning with Qass," said Singh. "He's played this so many times and I wanted to win so bad for him. We have always wanted to get it together. It got harder and harder. We'd talk about it a lot – about going back to win it. So this mean a lot."

Justin Thomas, partnered by his father Mike, exhibited his newly worked-on "all-out-lift-the-left-heel" drive as with 11 birdies and two eagles Team Thomas set the first-round pace with a 15-under-par 57. Thomas explained: "It gives me an extra three to five miles per hour club speed, six to seven miles an hour ball speed. It feels comfortable. If I hit it solid I can fly it 315 yards maybe 320."

Team Thomas, making their third appearance, edged two shots ahead of Team Woods — Tiger and his 13-year-old son Charlie — with whom they were partnered and Team Singh. Woods, limited to nine official rounds in 2022 and suffering from the foot ailment plantar fasciitis, said: "We had a blast slaying it today. I don't really care about the foot problem, being their alongside my son is far more important."

Team Woods wore Tiger's traditional Sunday red with their eyes on that red leather belt but with Charlie also struggling with a left ankle injury the 15-time major champion confessed "we were both like walking penguins out there" as they shot 65. Meanwhile, Team Singh carded a second successive 59 for a 26-under-par winning total of 118, two ahead of John Daly and John Daly II (61-59) and Team Thomas, who shot a second-round 63. Daly was scheduled for knee-replacement surgery so skipped a practice range warm-up, but Harrington with son Paddy posted their best finish in five attempts in fourth after following an opening 62 with a 60. Nelly Korda, on her debut with dad Petr, the 1998 Australian Open tennis champion, shared fifth place on 61-62.

Qass Singh, who first played at the age of 16 and now at 32 has a full-time job after giving up his professional golf career, summed-up what winning meant: "We wanted this all year so just to have it finally is like it's almost a dream come true. It's going to be a memory I'm going to have forever."

Ritz-Carlton Golf Club, Grande Lakes, Orlando, Florida — December 17-18
Par 72 (36-36); 7,106 yards — Purse: $1,085,000

1	**Vijay Singh/ Qass Singh**	59	59	118	$200,000
2	**John Daly/ John Daly II**	61	59	120	68,625
	Justin Thomas/ Mike Thomas	57	63	120	68,625
4	Padraig Harrington/ Paddy Harrington	62	60	122	50,000
5	Nelly Korda/ Petr Korda	62	61	123	48,000
	Matt Kuchar/ Carson Kuchar	61	62	123	48,000
	Bernhard Langer/ Jason Langer	60	63	123	48,000
8	Mark O'Meara/ Shaun O'Meara	61	63	124	45,167
	Jordan Spieth/ Shawn Spieth	61	63	124	45,167
	Tiger Woods/ Charlie Woods	59	65	124	45,167
11	Stewart Cink/ Connor Cink	61	64	125	44,000
12	David Duval/ Brady Duval	63	63	126	43,500
13	Tom Lehman/ Sean Lehman	61	66	127	42,750
	Lee Trevino/ Daniel Trevino	62	65	127	42,750
15	Nick Faldo/ Matthew Faldo	63	65	128	41,750
	Jim Furyk/ Tanner Furyk	64	64	128	41,750
17	Justin Leonard/ Luke Leonard	61	68	129	40,750
	Annika Sorenstam/ Will McGee	62	67	129	40,750
19	Gary Player/ Jordan Player	65	65	130	40,125
	Nick Price/ Greg Price	66	64	130	40,125

Korn Ferry Tour

This was Justin Suh's first season on the Korn Ferry Tour — the PGA Tour's developmental circuit — and once he got the hang of things, he was on his way to sweeping the honours and winning the Player of the Year Award. But off his start, he looked more like a guy headed for the nearest exit.

In the season opener, the Bahamas Great Exuma Classic, he shot a closing one-birdie 78 and tied for 55th. Next, he missed the cut at the Great Abaco Classic, then tied for 50th in the Panama Championship and then missed the cut in the Astara Championship. And this by the former world number one amateur (2018-19). Then something clicked. Suh made a stunning U-turn for the last 22 tournaments, peaking with victory in the season-ending Korn Ferry Tour Championship. Suh also topped the points race for both the regular season (the first 23 tournaments) and the last three (the finals) and so gained fully exempt status on the 2023 PGA Tour, a spot in the Players Championship and, for the first time, a berth in the US Open. He was only the third player, after Chesson Hadley (2017) and Scottie Scheffler (2019), to lead both lists.

"It feels great," Suh said. "It was a long day but it feels great to finish at number one, to win the last event. My game has progressed so much over the course of the year and it feels extremely gratifying that it paid off." Suh got a grip on the tour in a three-week stretch in mid-summer — a solo seventh in the Price Cutter, a tie for second in the Utah Championship and a tie for fifth in the Pinnacle Bank. He led the tour with 10 top-10 finishes in 24 starts, and five top-10s in his last six, including his win.

In the Tour Championship, at Victoria National in Indiana, he scored 66-69-64-68 for a 21-under 267 and a two-stroke win over Austin Eckroat. It was a perfect show-biz finish for the former standout in Hollywood country, the University of Southern California, not only scoring his first pro win but doing it in the championship finale. "I haven't won in a while," Suh said. "To take the next step and win out here, it's a big confidence boost."

Seonghyeon Kim was named Rookie of the Year after three top threes in his first seven starts and nine top-25s in 22 starts.

Among other 2022 highlights:

The season was going swimmingly, one victory per customer, until Robby Shelton, who won the BMW Charity Pro-Am in June, then won the Pinnacle Bank Championship in August, thus becoming the KFT's only multiple winner of 2022. Shelton took the BMW in a somewhat scary finish. He entered the final round leading by five after a 61 on day three, got caught by playing partner Ben Griffin's 66 and won the playoff on two pars. "I've been trending and trending and trending," Shelton said. In the Pinnacle Bank Championship, Shelton closed with a 65 for a one-shot victory, his seventh career win. "It feels awesome to finally put a Sunday round together," Shelton said.

Reedy (130-pound) Ashkay Bhatia launched a free-wheeling KFT season in the opening Bahamas Great Exuma Classic, coming from three behind in the final round with a 65 to become, just 12 days from his 20th birthday, the third youngest ever to win on the tour. "Golf," he announced, "is crazy."

In the Astara Golf Championship, Brandon Matthews took a different view of a clutch finish. He had birdied 16 and 17, and needed an eagle three at the 18th for his first KFT win in his 50th start. "And it was fun," he said, "going into that putt realising that this could be the one." And he got it with a five-under 66.

It was a kind of revelation for Byeong Hun An in the Lecom Suncoast Classic. He'd opened with 65-66, then finished with 67-69 for 17-under 267 to win by one over four players, and noted: "I finally realised I don't need to play four days of perfect golf. I had a mediocre day yesterday and today, and still got away with this."

Brandon Harkins finally found a tournament he could call his own, in the Bahamas Great Abaco Classic. In Canada's 2013 Great Waterway Classic, Harkins closed with a 62 and lost by a stroke. In the 2017 Bogota Country Club Championship, he missed a playoff by a stroke. In the 2017 Ellie May Classic, he closed with a 66 and lost by one. This time, he came from two behind over the last three holes, shot 68, tied Zecheng Dou (69) at 270, parred the second playoff hole and won on his 134th KFT start. "This is my first big win out here," Harkins said. "I'm starting to get a little bit emotional."

And in the NV5 Invitational, after making just one birdie through the first 11 holes, Harry Hall closed on a rampage, birdieing five of the last seven, then three straight in a playoff, the last beating Nick Hardy. Said Hall: "I think my best is good enough to beat anybody."

2022 SCHEDULE

Bahamas Great Exuma Classic	**Akshay Bhatia**
Bahamas Great Abaco Classic	**Brandon Harkins**
Panama Championship	**Carson Young**
Astara Golf Championship	**Brandon Matthews**
Lecom Suncoast Classic	**Byeong Hun An**
Chitimacha Louisiana Open	**Carl Yuan**
Lake Charles Championship	**Trevor Werbylo**
Club Car Championship	**TJ Vogel**
Veritex Bank Championship	**Tyson Alexander**
Huntsville Championship	**Harrison Endycott**
Simmons Bank Open	**Brent Grant**
Visit Knoxville Open	**Anders Albertson**
AdventHealth Championship	**Trevor Cone**
NV5 Invitational	**Harry Hall**
Rex Hospital Open	**Davis Thompson**
BMW Charity Pro-Am	**Robby Shelton**
Wichita Open	**Norman Xiong**
Live and Work in Maine Open	**Pierceson Coody**
The Ascendant	**Marty Dou Zecheng**
Memorial Health Championship	**Paul Haley II**
Price Cutter Charity Championship	**David Kocher**
Utah Championship	**Andrew Kozan**
Pinnacle Bank Championship	**Robby Shelton (2)**
Albertsons Boise Open	**Will Gordon**
Nationwide Children's Hospital Championship	**David Lingmerth**
Korn Ferry Tour Championship	**Justin Suh**

Bahamas Great Exuma Classic

Sandals Emerald Bay, Great Exuma, Bahamas — January 16-19
Par 72 (36-36); 7,001 yards — Purse: $750,000

1	**Akshay Bhatia**	69	72	68	65	274	$135,000
2	**Paul Haley II**	74	67	67	68	276	67,500
3	**Michael Gellerman**	75	69	68	66	278	35,750
	Corey Shaun	70	72	64	72	278	35,750
	Carl Yuan	71	70	66	71	278	35,750
6	AJ Crouch	73	70	71	65	279	24,938
	Marcelo Rozo	73	67	69	70	279	24,938
8	Scott Brown	73	68	68	71	280	20,625
	Clay Feagler	69	70	68	73	280	20,625
	Ben Griffin	72	74	67	67	280	20,625
11	Dan McCarthy	75	71	69	66	281	15,966
	Ryan McCormick	73	72	70	66	281	15,966
	Chris Baker	70	67	72	72	281	15,966
	Joey Garber	70	71	71	69	281	15,966
15	MJ Daffue	74	69	69	70	282	12,750
	Grant Hirschman	73	67	70	72	282	12,750
	Ben Taylor	73	73	66	70	282	12,750
18	Matt McCarty	71	71	68	73	283	11,250
19	Brandon Crick	70	72	72	70	284	8,036
	Harrison Endycott	72	70	72	70	284	8,036
	Seonghyeon Kim	75	71	70	68	284	8,036
	Tano Goya	70	70	72	72	284	8,036
	Jonathan Grey	75	67	72	70	284	8,036
	Harry Hall	68	69	72	75	284	8,036
	Kyle Reifers	72	68	69	75	284	8,036
	Charlie Saxon	71	69	73	71	284	8,036
	TJ Vogel	72	72	70	70	284	8,036

Bahamas Great Abaco Classic

The Abaco Club on Winding Bay, Great Abaco, Bahamas — January 23-26
Par 72 (36-36); 7,141 yards — Purse: $750,000

1	**Brandon Harkins**	69	65	68	68	270	$135,000
2	**Zecheng Dou**	69	66	66	69	270	67,500
	Harkins won playoff at second extra hole						
3	**Seonghyeon Kim**	71	65	70	66	272	45,000
4	Erik Barnes	72	67	64	72	275	29,375
	Tain Lee	71	66	68	70	275	29,375
	Kevin Roy	68	69	68	70	275	29,375
7	Dawson Armstrong	65	70	72	69	276	20,723
	Eric Cole	67	70	67	72	276	20,723
	Kevin Dougherty	69	71	67	69	276	20,723
	Julian Etulain	66	70	68	72	276	20,723
	Trevor Werbylo	69	69	70	68	276	20,723
12	Ben Griffin	68	75	67	67	277	14,063
	Vince India	72	67	70	68	277	14,063
	Vincent Norrman	66	69	71	71	277	14,063
	Davis Thompson	65	69	71	72	277	14,063
	Ashton Van Horne	67	70	73	67	277	14,063
	John VanDerLaan	70	67	67	73	277	14,063
18	Ryan Brehm	70	71	68	69	278	10,153
	Roberto Diaz	70	69	71	68	278	10,153
	Jeremy Paul	66	70	72	70	278	10,153
	Jose de Jesus Rodriguez	67	71	70	70	278	10,153
22	Byeong Hun An	72	66	69	72	279	7,160
	AJ Crouch	73	68	67	71	279	7,160
	Bo Hoag	70	70	71	68	279	7,160
	Brandon Matthews	72	67	71	69	279	7,160
	Alvaro Ortiz	65	67	71	76	279	7,160
	Shad Tuten	71	70	69	69	279	7,160

Panama Championship

Panama Golf Club, Panama City, Panama — February 3-6
Par 70 (35-35); 7,325 yards — Purse: $750,000

1	**Carson Young**	68	65	71	68	272	$135,000
2	**Brandon Matthews**	68	67	69	69	273	48,750
	Jimmy Stanger	64	69	70	70	273	48,750
	Carl Yuan	65	69	71	68	273	48,750
5	Erik Barnes	71	68	71	65	275	25,125
	Zecheng Dou	69	67	71	68	275	25,125
	Zack Fischer	65	70	68	72	275	25,125
	Ben Taylor	68	67	68	72	275	25,125
9	Martin Contini	68	69	72	67	276	20,625
10	Alex Chiarella	69	68	70	70	277	16,598
	Eric Cole	68	70	69	70	277	16,598
	Joey Garber	67	66	72	72	277	16,598
	Gregor Main	66	70	72	69	277	16,598
	TJ Vogel	67	67	71	72	277	16,598
15	Max Greyserman	68	70	71	69	278	10,922
	Michael Kim	68	70	70	70	278	10,922
	McClure Meissner	69	67	71	71	278	10,922
	Marcelo Rozo	70	69	74	65	278	10,922
	Quade Cummins	66	73	68	71	278	10,922
	Vince India	67	68	71	72	278	10,922
	Andrew Kozan	68	68	67	75	278	10,922
	Brett White	66	70	68	74	278	10,922
23	Julian Etulain	68	66	70	75	279	7,613
	Vincent Norrman	70	70	69	70	279	7,613
25	Andrew Yun	69	71	73	67	280	5,859
	Clay Feagler	66	72	72	70	280	5,859
	David Kocher	65	73	71	71	280	5,859
	Augusto Nunez	71	69	72	68	280	5,859
	Jeremy Paul	71	69	68	72	280	5,859
	Kyle Westmoreland	70	70	70	70	280	5,859
	Xinjun Zhang	68	68	77	67	280	5,859

Astara Golf Championship

Country Club de Bogota (Lagos), Bogota, Colombia — February 10-13
Par 71 (35-36); 7,237 yards — Purse: $750,000
Pacos course (R1&2) par Par 70 (35-35); 6,249 yards

1	**Brandon Matthews**	67	65	66	66	264	$135,000
2	**Ben Griffin**	68	61	68	68	265	56,250
	Ryan McCormick	61	69	69	66	265	56,250
4	Joey Garber	69	64	64	69	266	33,750
5	Marcos Montenegro	70	62	69	67	268	27,188
	Rob Oppenheim	67	64	70	67	268	27,188
7	Eric Cole	68	65	71	65	269	23,063
	Augusto Nunez	66	67	71	65	269	23,063
9	MJ Daffue	63	67	72	69	271	18,497
	Timothy Kelly	64	68	73	66	271	18,497
	Ryan Brehm	64	72	65	70	271	18,497
	Jay Card III	67	68	66	70	271	18,497
13	Erik Compton	66	66	72	68	272	12,422
	Brad Hopfinger	70	66	69	67	272	12,422
	Whee Kim	69	66	70	67	272	12,422
	Josh Teater	66	67	70	69	272	12,422
	Nicolas Echavarria	65	70	68	69	272	12,422
	David Hearn	70	65	67	70	272	12,422
	Taylor Montgomery	66	70	62	74	272	12,422
	Sam Saunders	67	67	66	72	272	12,422

21	Zack Fischer	68	67	70	68	273	7,044
	Steven Fisk	71	64	70	68	273	7,044
	Chip McDaniel	69	68	71	65	273	7,044
	Corey Pereira	70	66	71	66	273	7,044
	Jose de Jesus Rodriguez	65	71	70	67	273	7,044
	Shad Tuten	67	70	68	68	273	7,044
	Ben Taylor	68	67	65	73	273	7,044
	Alex Weiss	72	65	66	70	273	7,044
	Brett White	68	67	68	70	273	7,044

Lecom Suncoast Classic

Lakewood National Golf Club (Commander), Lakewood Ranch, Florida — February 17-20
Par 71 (36-35); 7,113 yards — Purse: $750,000

1	**Byeong Hun An**	65	66	67	69	267	$135,000
2	**MJ Daffue**	68	65	64	71	268	43,688
	Ben Griffin	69	64	65	70	268	43,688
	Scott Harrington	65	69	67	67	268	43,688
	Seonghyeon Kim	67	66	69	66	268	43,688
6	Will Gordon	65	68	70	66	269	20,170
	Nicholas Lindheim	68	65	69	67	269	20,170
	Jay Card III	66	67	67	69	269	20,170
	Albin Choi	64	67	70	68	269	20,170
	Michael Gellerman	65	66	65	73	269	20,170
	Mark Hubbard	69	62	70	68	269	20,170
	Justin Lower	69	66	66	68	269	20,170
	Sean O'Hair	67	66	68	68	269	20,170
14	Eric Cole	69	62	69	70	270	13,500
	Paul Haley II	69	67	69	65	270	13,500
	McClure Meissner	65	71	68	66	270	13,500
17	Nicolas Echavarria	66	70	67	68	271	10,523
	John Pak	67	66	71	67	271	10,523
	Justin Suh	70	66	69	66	271	10,523
	Callum Tarren	70	61	69	71	271	10,523
	Peter Uihlein	66	70	64	71	271	10,523
22	Dawson Armstrong	66	66	72	68	272	7,160
	Brad Brunner	68	65	70	69	272	7,160
	Zack Fischer	64	68	70	70	272	7,160
	Max Greyserman	65	66	71	70	272	7,160
	Philip Knowles	67	66	71	68	272	7,160
	Pontus Nyholm	65	70	70	67	272	7,160

Chitimacha Louisiana Open

Le Triomphe Golf & Country Club, Broussard, Louisiana — March 17-20
Par 71 (36-35); 6,961 yards — Purse: $750,000

1	**Carl Yuan**	68	66	71	65	270	$135,000
2	**Peter Uihlein**	65	68	67	70	270	67,500
	Yuan won playoff at first extra hole						
3	**Jose de Jesus Rodriguez**	66	68	69	68	271	39,375
	Trevor Werbylo	69	64	68	70	271	39,375
5	Curtis Luck	66	73	68	65	272	22,570
	Matt McCarty	68	70	69	65	272	22,570
	Erik Barnes	67	69	69	67	272	22,570
	Brad Brunner	67	66	73	66	272	22,570
	Mark Hubbard	65	68	70	69	272	22,570
	Justin Suh	67	67	71	67	272	22,570
	Ben Taylor	66	72	68	66	272	22,570
12	Mark Anderson	66	69	70	68	273	15,375
	Ben Kohles	71	66	69	67	273	15,375
	Augusto Nunez	65	72	72	64	273	15,375
15	Chris Baker	68	70	70	66	274	11,625
	Bo Hoag	66	69	72	67	274	11,625
	Taylor Montgomery	66	68	72	68	274	11,625
	Davis Thompson	71	69	67	67	274	11,625
	Kyle Westmoreland	67	72	67	68	274	11,625
	Tom Whitney	66	71	68	69	274	11,625
21	Byeong Hun An	71	68	67	69	275	7,439
	Scott Brown	70	70	67	68	275	7,439
	Michael Feagles	69	70	71	65	275	7,439
	Justin Lower	70	67	71	67	275	7,439
	Brandon Matthews	70	66	74	65	275	7,439
	David Skinns	68	70	68	69	275	7,439
	Garett Reband	67	69	69	70	275	7,439

Lake Charles Championship

The Country Club at Golden Nugget, Lake Charles, Louisiana — March 24-27
Par 71 (36-35); 6,940 yards — Purse: $750,000

1	**Trevor Werbylo**	70	69	64	63	266	$135,000
2	**Seonghyeon Kim**	68	66	64	68	266	67,500
	Werbylo won playoff at third extra hole						
3	**Eric Cole**	69	67	66	67	269	45,000
4	MJ Daffue	68	69	68	65	270	31,125
	Anders Albertson	70	67	65	68	270	31,125

6	Brent Grant	69	67 67 68	271	24,000
	Vince India	66 67 69 69		271	24,000
	Corey Pereira	67 67 66 71		271	24,000
9	Ben Griffin	70 68 68 66		272	16,233
	Justin Suh	67 69 69 67		272	16,233
	Stuart Macdonald	71 68 66 67		272	16,233
	Nicolas Echavarria	68 67 69 68		272	16,233
	Augusto Nunez	68 67 69 68		272	16,233
	Taylor Montgomery	70 69 65 68		272	16,233
	Jose de Jesus Rodriguez	68 70 65 69		272	16,233
	Tyson Alexander	71 68 64 69		272	16,233
17	Matt McCarty	70 67 68 68		273	10,875
	Chase Parker	69 70 66 68		273	10,875
	Kevin Dougherty	71 69 68 65		273	10,875
	George Cunningham	67 66 66 74		273	10,875
21	Chun-an Yu	73 67 66 68		274	6,312
	Erik Barnes	73 66 67 68		274	6,312
	Curtis Luck	66 70 69 69		274	6,312
	Tano Goya	71 67 67 69		274	6,312
	Matthew Picanso	70 68 69 67		274	6,312
	Ryan Ruffels	70 67 70 67		274	6,312
	Pontus Nyholm	72 68 68 66		274	6,312
	Thomas Rosenmueller	71 65 68 70		274	6,312
	David Kocher	69 66 69 70		274	6,312
	Zecheng Dou	77 61 66 70		274	6,312
	Rhein Gibson	66 71 71 66		274	6,312
	Samuel Stevens	71 68 70 65		274	6,312
	Luis Gagne	75 65 63 71		274	6,312
	Brandon Matthews	69 68 63 74		274	6,312

Club Car Championship

The Landings Club (Deer Creek), Savannah, Georgia — March 31-April 3
Par 72 (36-36); 7,165 yards — Purse: $750,000

1	**TJ Vogel**	69 67 68 67	271	$135,000
2	**Mark Anderson**	66 67 68 71	272	56,250
	Ryan Blaum	71 65 66 70	272	56,250
4	Jimmy Stanger	69 69 68 68	274	33,750
5	Martin Contini	69 69 70 67	275	27,188
	Nicolas Echavarria	72 66 67 70	275	27,188
7	Erik Barnes	66 65 73 72	276	23,063
	Carl Yuan	64 73 65 74	276	23,063
9	Grant Hirschman	70 66 67 74	277	19,875
	Mark Hubbard	64 70 71 72	277	19,875
11	Pontus Nyholm	71 68 68 71	278	17,738
12	Byeong Hun An	73 67 69 70	279	15,375
	Sean O'Hair	71 71 71 66	279	15,375
	Justin Suh	71 67 70 71	279	15,375
15	Rafael Campos	70 72 69 69	280	13,125
	Fabian Gomez	67 71 72 70	280	13,125
17	Tano Goya	71 68 74 68	281	11,250
	Michael Johnson	67 72 68 74	281	11,250
	Alex Weiss	70 69 70 72	281	11,250
20	Dawson Armstrong	71 70 71 70	282	8,225
	Eric Cole	75 63 72 72	282	8,225
	Brandon Crick	73 68 72 69	282	8,225
	Seonghyeon Kim	70 66 75 71	282	8,225
	Braden Thornberry	72 70 72 68	282	8,225
	John VanDerLaan	71 69 71 71	282	8,225

Veritex Bank Championship

Texas Rangers Golf Club, Arlington, Texas — April 13-16
Par 71 (35-36); 7,010 yards — Purse: $750,000

1	**Tyson Alexander**	65 66 66 65	262	$135,000
2	**Byeong Hun An**	68 62 68 66	264	56,250
	Pontus Nyholm	68 64 70 62	264	56,250
4	Martin Flores	65 68 69 63	265	29,375
	Taylor Montgomery	65 66 64 70	265	29,375
	Rob Oppenheim	69 63 66 67	265	29,375
7	Nicolas Echavarria	70 67 67 62	266	20,723
	Augusto Nunez	68 67 67 64	266	20,723
	Justin Suh	64 67 70 65	266	20,723
	Callum Tarren	68 67 66 65	266	20,723
	Alex Weiss	68 64 70 64	266	20,723
12	Anders Albertson	67 70 68 62	267	14,063
	Brett Drewitt	70 64 68 65	267	14,063
	Mark Hubbard	66 66 67 68	267	14,063
	Chase Parker	67 62 65 73	267	14,063
	Shawn Stefani	65 63 69 70	267	14,063
	Tom Whitney	67 64 72 64	267	14,063
18	Chris Baker	69 68 64 67	268	8,888
	Wilson Bateman	69 65 70 64	268	8,888
	Clay Feagler	67 67 69 65	268	8,888
	Patrick Fishburn	65 68 68 67	268	8,888
	Seonghyeon Kim	70 65 71 62	268	8,888
	Ryan Ruffels	69 66 71 62	268	8,888
	Robby Shelton	67 66 67 68	268	8,888
	Samuel Stevens	68 66 67 67	268	8,888

Huntsville Championship

The Ledges, Huntsville, Alabama — April 28-May1
Par 70 (35-35); 7,114 yards — Purse: $750,000

1	**Harrison Endycott**	63	67	64	70	264	$135,000
2	**Ben Taylor**	68	67	64	70	269	67,500
3	**Erik Barnes**	64	65	72	69	270	45,000
4	Quade Cummins	68	64	68	71	271	31,125
	Kris Ventura	68	66	71	66	271	31,125
6	Seonghyeon Kim	64	69	69	70	272	24,000
	Sam Saunders	70	70	67	65	272	24,000
	Davis Thompson	68	67	69	68	272	24,000
9	Taylor Dickson	70	68	65	70	273	18,497
	Kevin Dougherty	69	68	68	68	273	18,497
	Paul Haley II	71	67	65	70	273	18,497
	Spencer Ralston	70	68	64	71	273	18,497
13	Patrick Fishburn	68	70	71	65	274	12,804
	Zecheng Dou	64	70	70	70	274	12,804
	Chip McDaniel	66	70	69	69	274	12,804
	McClure Meissner	69	69	67	69	274	12,804
	Kyle Reifers	70	68	69	67	274	12,804
	Marcelo Rozo	69	71	71	63	274	12,804
	Justin Suh	70	69	69	66	274	12,804
20	Dawson Armstrong	69	70	71	65	275	8,225
	Brandon Crick	70	68	69	68	275	8,225
	MJ Daffue	71	66	73	65	275	8,225
	Theo Humphrey	66	71	66	72	275	8,225
	Josh Teater	69	70	69	67	275	8,225
	John VanDerLaan	70	68	70	67	275	8,225

Simmons Bank Open

The Grove, College Grove, Tennessee — May 5-8
Par 72 (36-36); 7,368 yards — Purse: $750,000

1	**Brent Grant**	69	65	69	69	272	$135,000
2	**Chun-an Yu**	67	68	67	71	273	67,500
3	**Zack Fischer**	66	69	72	67	274	39,375
	Vincent Norrman	68	70	69	67	274	39,375
5	Zecheng Dou	69	66	68	72	275	26,125
	Jeremy Paul	68	66	70	71	275	26,125
	Tom Whitney	65	70	69	71	275	26,125
8	Mark Anderson	70	68	72	66	276	20,625
	Sangmoon Bae	68	68	68	72	276	20,625
	Robby Shelton	66	69	70	71	276	20,625
11	John VanDerLaan	71	65	68	73	277	17,119
	Xinjun Zhang	67	69	70	71	277	17,119
13	Alex Chiarella	68	71	72	67	278	13,969
	Patrick Fishburn	67	68	70	73	278	13,969
	Will Gordon	66	71	70	71	278	13,969
	Taylor Montgomery	72	69	70	67	278	13,969
17	Tyson Alexander	70	69	72	68	279	10,523
	Fabian Gomez	66	74	72	67	279	10,523
	Ben Griffin	70	67	73	69	279	10,523
	Samuel Stevens	68	70	68	73	279	10,523
	Ben Taylor	70	69	69	71	279	10,523
22	Erik Barnes	70	70	70	70	280	7,377
	Kevin Dougherty	69	69	72	70	280	7,377
	Paul Haley II	69	69	70	72	280	7,377
	Vince India	70	69	71	70	280	7,377
	McClure Meissner	68	69	72	71	280	7,377

Visit Knoxville Open

Holston Hills Country Club, Knoxville, Tennessee — May 12-15
Par 70 (35-35); 7,163 yards — Purse: $750,000

1	**Anders Albertson**	62	67	65	66	260	$135,000
2	**Carl Yuan**	68	65	62	66	261	67,500
3	**MJ Daffue**	64	65	68	65	262	45,000
4	Taylor Montgomery	65	68	63	68	264	31,125
	Sean O'Hair	65	67	65	67	264	31,125
6	Tano Goya	68	67	67	64	266	24,938
	Rob Oppenheim	65	66	67	68	266	24,938
8	Taylor Dickson	69	66	67	65	267	22,125
9	Erik Barnes	67	67	68	66	268	18,497
	Julian Etulain	67	66	70	65	268	18,497
	Tain Lee	67	68	65	68	268	18,497
	Augusto Nunez	66	68	66	68	268	18,497
13	Scott Harrington	65	72	65	67	269	14,375
	Michael Johnson	70	68	67	64	269	14,375
	Ryan McCormick	67	68	70	64	269	14,375
16	George Cunningham	65	66	71	68	270	10,223
	Ben Griffin	66	67	71	66	270	10,223
	Jeremy Paul	66	69	68	67	270	10,223
	Robby Shelton	68	67	68	67	270	10,223
	Ashton Van Horne	68	65	69	68	270	10,223
	Carson Young	70	67	68	65	270	10,223
	Michael Kim	68	69	65	68	270	10,223
	Justin Suh	69	66	65	70	270	10,223
24	Samuel Stevens	67	67	70	67	271	6,040
	Xinjun Zhang	67	71	66	67	271	6,040
	Chris Baker	67	67	69	68	271	6,040
	Akshay Bhatia	73	63	67	68	271	6,040
	Scott Brown	68	65	67	71	271	6,040
	Patrick Fishburn	66	69	69	67	271	6,040
	Christopher Petefish	68	67	68	68	271	6,040
	Tom Whitney	68	67	66	70	271	6,040

AdventHealth Championship

Blue Hills Country Club, Kansas City, Missouri — May 19-22
Par 72 (36-36); 7,364 yards — Purse: $750,000

1	**Trevor Cone**	65	67	70	70	272	$135,000
2	**Taylor Montgomery**	66	70	67	70	273	67,500
3	**MJ Daffue**	65	71	66	72	274	45,000
4	Michael Feagles	65	69	69	72	275	31,125
	Grayson Murray	70	67	70	68	275	31,125
6	Kevin Roy	68	67	69	73	277	25,875
7	Jeremy Paul	71	69	70	68	278	21,469
	Samuel Stevens	69	67	65	77	278	21,469
	Josh Teater	68	70	72	68	278	21,469
	Kyle Westmoreland	68	67	70	73	278	21,469
11	Tain Lee	68	71	67	73	279	17,738
12	Chandler Blanchet	70	70	70	70	280	14,906
	Brandon Crick	69	68	70	73	280	14,906
	Brent Grant	69	74	68	69	280	14,906
	Michael Kim	68	70	74	68	280	14,906
16	Erik Barnes	69	72	70	70	281	11,250
	Akshay Bhatia	71	67	70	73	281	11,250
	Scott Gutschewski	69	69	73	70	281	11,250
	Alexandre Rocha	67	70	72	72	281	11,250
	Jose de Jesus Rodriguez	71	69	70	71	281	11,250
21	David Lingmerth	71	70	71	70	282	8,813
	Augusto Nunez	70	68	71	73	282	8,813
23	Will Gordon	75	67	71	70	283	6,387
	Philip Knowles	74	69	68	72	283	6,387
	David Kocher	68	71	72	72	283	6,387
	Chase Parker	71	71	71	70	283	6,387
	Garett Reband	73	69	70	71	283	6,387
	Tag Ridings	75	69	70	69	283	6,387
	Austin Eckroat	69	73	67	74	283	6,387
	Alvaro Ortiz	71	67	70	75	283	6,387

NV5 Invitational

The Glen Club, Glenview, Illinois — May 26-29
Par 71 (36-35); 7,257 yards — Purse: $750,000

1	**Harry Hall**	65	67	65	65	262	$135,000
2	**Nick Hardy**	64	68	65	65	262	67,500
	Hall won playoff at third extra hole						
3	**Christopher Petefish**	65	66	68	66	265	39,375
	Jimmy Stanger	66	67	67	65	265	39,375
5	McClure Meissner	65	67	68	66	266	26,125
	Spencer Ralston	70	66	68	62	266	26,125
	Davis Thompson	67	68	62	69	266	26,125
8	Taylor Montgomery	67	68	67	65	267	21,375
	Justin Suh	65	69	69	64	267	21,375
10	Ben Martin	66	68	67	67	268	19,125
11	Brandon Crick	67	68	66	68	269	17,119
	Paul Haley II	69	65	70	65	269	17,119
13	Aaron Baddeley	65	71	65	69	270	13,575
	Ben Griffin	66	70	67	67	270	13,575
	Nelson Ledesma	68	70	67	65	270	13,575
	Chun-an Yu	67	70	66	67	270	13,575
	Carl Yuan	66	70	67	67	270	13,575
18	Trace Crowe	68	68	65	70	271	10,500
	Tano Goya	66	69	68	68	271	10,500
	Samuel Stevens	68	69	67	67	271	10,500
21	Steven Fisk	67	67	71	67	272	8,813
	Nick Voke	65	70	73	64	272	8,813
23	Michael Kim	63	73	70	67	273	7,093
	Ryan Linton	65	70	71	67	273	7,093
	Austin Eckroat	66	69	69	69	273	7,093
	Dylan Meyer	69	69	65	70	273	7,093

Rex Hospital Open

The Country Club at Wakefield Plantation, Raleigh, North Carolina — June 2-5
Par 71 (36-35); 7,269 yards — Purse: $750,000

1	**Davis Thompson**	64	66	68	69	267	$135,000
2	**Vincent Norrman**	66	69	65	68	268	56,250
	Andrew Yun	68	64	68	68	268	56,250
4	Will Gordon	68	68	67	66	269	33,750
5	Harry Hall	70	65	68	67	270	28,500
6	Paul Haley II	68	65	67	71	271	25,875
7	Alexandre Rocha	66	69	71	66	272	22,250
	John VanDerLaan	66	69	69	68	272	22,250
	Carl Yuan	70	69	64	69	272	22,250
10	Nicholas Lindheim	69	69	66	69	273	17,184
	Shawn Stefani	69	68	68	68	273	17,184
	Tyson Alexander	68	67	68	70	273	17,184
	Spencer Ralston	66	68	67	72	273	17,184
14	Sangmoon Bae	66	68	68	72	274	12,750
	Brandon Harkins	67	69	67	71	274	12,750
	Brad Hopfinger	72	66	66	70	274	12,750
	Alvaro Ortiz	66	71	66	71	274	12,750
	Chase Parker	69	66	72	67	274	12,750
19	Chris Baker	67	67	72	69	275	8,850
	Erik Barnes	67	69	68	71	275	8,850
	Michael Johnson	66	66	70	73	275	8,850
	Rob Oppenheim	67	71	67	70	275	8,850
	Jeremy Paul	63	69	71	72	275	8,850
	Kris Ventura	71	65	67	72	275	8,850
25	Philip Knowles	69	66	72	69	276	6,249
	Gregor Main	70	68	70	68	276	6,249
	Austin Eckroat	68	68	70	70	276	6,249
	McClure Meissner	67	70	67	72	276	6,249

BMW Charity Pro-Am

Thornblade Club, Greer, South Carolina — June 9-12
Par 71 (35-36); 7,062 yards — Purse: $750,000
Carolina Country Club (R1&2) par 72 (36-36); 6,929 yards

1	**Robby Shelton**	66	65	61	71	263	$135,000
2	**Ben Griffin**	66	68	63	66	263	67,500
	Shelton won playoff at second extra hole						
3	**Ryan McCormick**	71	65	64	65	265	39,375
	Augusto Nunez	65	66	66	68	265	39,375
5	Jacob Bridgeman	68	68	65	65	266	27,188
	Nicolas Echavarria	64	67	68	67	266	27,188
7	Zack Fischer	63	71	64	69	267	22,250
	Paul Haley II	65	70	63	69	267	22,250
	Nelson Ledesma	63	66	70	68	267	22,250
10	Anders Albertson	66	65	67	70	268	18,431
	Charlie Saxon	67	66	68	67	268	18,431
12	John Augenstein	68	68	64	69	269	15,375
	Philip Knowles	68	66	64	71	269	15,375
	Rob Oppenheim	68	67	65	69	269	15,375
15	Vincent Norrman	68	70	68	64	270	11,266
	Blayne Barber	67	64	70	69	270	11,266
	Fabian Gomez	67	69	66	68	270	11,266
	Michael Kim	66	68	69	67	270	11,266
	Brandon Matthews	69	67	67	67	270	11,266
	Justin Suh	66	69	68	67	270	11,266
	Ben Taylor	69	67	66	68	270	11,266
22	Tano Goya	67	71	65	69	272	7,913
	Brent Grant	68	71	70	63	272	7,913
	Ryan Ruffels	64	69	71	68	272	7,913
25	Brandon Crick	67	68	68	70	273	5,979
	Austin Eckroat	67	70	71	65	273	5,979
	Julian Etulain	66	71	67	69	273	5,979
	Rhein Gibson	70	68	67	68	273	5,979
	Curtis Luck	73	62	68	70	273	5,979
	Patrick Newcomb	67	68	69	69	273	5,979

Wichita Open

Crestview Country Club, Wichita, Kansas — June 16-19
Par 70 (35-35); 6,910 yards — Purse: $750,000

1	**Norman Xiong**	66	61	64	63	254	$135,000
2	**Kevin Roy**	62	66	67	64	259	67,500
3	**Chun-an Yu**	67	63	62	68	260	45,000
4	Tyson Alexander	62	66	69	64	261	31,125
	Pierceson Coody	66	67	65	63	261	31,125
6	Augusto Nunez	63	71	61	67	262	25,875
7	Kyle Westmoreland	65	64	65	69	263	24,000
8	Roberto Diaz	70	66	66	62	264	20,625
	MJ Maguire	67	66	62	69	264	20,625
	Vincent Norrman	66	65	68	65	264	20,625
11	Dawson Armstrong	67	68	63	67	265	14,588
	Erik Compton	69	64	66	66	265	14,588
	Paul Haley II	71	63	64	67	265	14,588
	Jamie Lovemark	71	63	65	66	265	14,588
	Jimmy Stanger	65	65	66	69	265	14,588
	Justin Suh	68	68	69	60	265	14,588
	Josh Teater	66	65	67	67	265	14,588
18	Trevor Cone	69	64	66	67	266	9,825
	Harrison Endycott	68	64	67	67	266	9,825
	Whee Kim	69	65	67	65	266	9,825
	Garett Reband	67	66	67	66	266	9,825
	Trevor Werbylo	66	64	65	71	266	9,825
23	Jacob Bergeron	63	68	71	66	268	6,704
	Alex Chiarella	62	68	69	69	268	6,704
	Brandon Crick	66	69	65	68	268	6,704
	Alistair Docherty	68	66	68	66	268	6,704
	Aman Gupta	70	66	65	67	268	6,704
	Michael Kim	72	62	69	65	268	6,704

Live and Work in Maine Open

Falmouth Country Club, Falmouth, Maine — June 23-26
Par 71 (35-36); 7,299 yards — Purse: $750,000

1	**Pierceson Coody**	69	62	67	66	264	$135,000
2	**Jacob Bergeron**	66	70	67	66	269	67,500
3	**Nelson Ledesma**	68	66	70	66	270	35,750
	Will Gordon	68	69	67	66	270	35,750
	Fabian Gomez	68	66	66	70	270	35,750
	Cole Anderson (A)	67	67	64	72	270	
7	Zack Sucher	68	70	70	64	272	25,875
8	Ryan McCormick	71	68	68	66	273	23,063
	John VanDerLaan	65	67	70	71	273	23,063
10	Tom Whitney	70	70	66	68	274	19,163
	MJ Maguire	70	71	65	68	274	19,163
	Scott Brown	72	68	65	69	274	19,163
13	Braden Thornberry	70	68	70	67	275	15,938
	Brandon Harkins	71	63	71	70	275	15,938
15	Curtis Luck	75	66	70	65	276	10,623
	Brandon Matthews	71	67	71	67	276	10,623
	Rob Oppenheim	68	68	73	67	276	10,623
	Andrew Yun	69	70	70	67	276	10,623

	Clay Feagler	72	67	70	67	276	10,623
	Michael Johnson	69	69	70	68	276	10,623
	Patrick Cover	64	73	70	69	276	10,623
	AJ Crouch	70	69	68	69	276	10,623
	Xinjun Zhang	67	70	69	70	276	10,623
	Tee-K Kelly	68	68	69	71	276	10,623
	Austin Eckroat	68	68	69	71	276	10,623

The Ascendant

TPC Colorado, Berthoud, Colorado
Par 72 (36-36); 7,995 yards

June 30-July 3
Purse: $750,000

1	**Zecheng Dou**	69	67	68	67	271	$135,000
2	**Carl Yuan**	71	70	64	67	272	67,500
3	**Brandon Matthews**	70	67	68	68	273	35,750
	Augusto Nunez	66	70	69	68	273	35,750
	Jeremy Paul	67	71	69	66	273	35,750
6	MJ Daffue	71	70	68	65	274	24,000
	Davis Thompson	71	70	66	67	274	24,000
	Shad Tuten	70	69	68	67	274	24,000
9	Harrison Endycott	71	71	65	68	275	20,625
10	Conner Godsey	70	67	74	65	276	17,788
	Kevin Roy	71	67	70	68	276	17,788
	Justin Suh	75	65	68	68	276	17,788
13	Dawson Armstrong	69	65	70	73	277	13,575
	Jay Card III	69	69	71	68	277	13,575
	Ryan McCormick	67	67	70	73	277	13,575
	Samuel Stevens	72	70	68	67	277	13,575
	John VanDerLaan	73	68	66	70	277	13,575
18	Austin Eckroat	70	70	70	68	278	9,825
	Patrick Fishburn	71	71	68	68	278	9,825
	Steven Fisk	70	68	72	68	278	9,825
	Michael Kim	67	71	70	70	278	9,825
	Braden Thornberry	73	70	66	69	278	9,825
23	Zac Blair	70	73	67	69	279	6,539
	Martin Flores	70	70	70	69	279	6,539
	Luis Gagne	69	72	70	68	279	6,539
	Scott Harrington	67	76	67	69	279	6,539
	Brad Hopfinger	72	71	68	68	279	6,539
	Robby Shelton	74	69	70	66	279	6,539
	Kyle Westmoreland	73	68	67	71	279	6,539

Memorial Health Championship

Panther Creek Country Club, Springfield, Illinois
Par 71 (35-36); 7,228 yards

July 14-17
Purse: $750,000

1	**Paul Haley II**	65	67	61	64	257	$135,000
2	**Austin Eckroat**	65	63	64	68	260	67,500
3	**Michael Kim**	61	69	64	67	261	45,000
4	Patrick Newcomb	65	64	64	69	262	33,750
5	Stephen Franken	67	65	68	63	263	27,188
	Augusto Nunez	66	66	61	70	263	27,188
7	Nico Echavarria	69	65	63	67	264	23,063
	Cole Hammer	68	63	64	69	264	23,063
9	Blayne Barber	70	64	64	67	265	17,873
	Kevin Dougherty	65	67	66	67	265	17,873
	Cody Gribble	68	66	62	69	265	17,873
	Nelson Ledesma	67	67	66	65	265	17,873
	Samuel Stevens	68	67	65	65	265	17,873
14	Byeong Hun An	67	66	63	70	266	12,000
	Mark Anderson	67	66	67	66	266	12,000
	Quade Cummins	63	68	69	66	266	12,000
	Ryan Hall	68	67	64	67	266	12,000
	RJ Manke	69	67	65	65	266	12,000
	Rob Oppenheim	64	68	60	74	266	12,000
	Ben Taylor	67	67	66	66	266	12,000
21	Martin Flores	68	68	70	61	267	7,920
	Tripp Kinney	66	69	66	66	267	7,920
	Stuart Macdonald	69	65	67	66	267	7,920
	Marcelo Rozo	66	67	67	67	267	7,920
	Robby Shelton	66	67	68	66	267	7,920

Price Cutter Charity Championship

Highland Springs Country Club, Springfield, Missouri
Par 72 (36-36); 7,115 yards)

July 21-24
Purse: $750,000

1	**David Kocher**	63	66	65	66	260	$135,000
2	**Taylor Montgomery**	63	68	66	69	266	43,688
	Augusto Nunez	66	67	66	67	266	43,688
	Robby Shelton	66	66	64	70	266	43,688
	Chun-an Yu	65	67	68	66	266	43,688
6	Zack Fischer	69	66	69	64	268	25,875
7	Justin Suh	65	69	67	68	269	24,000
8	Harry Hall	65	68	69	68	270	19,903
	Sam Saunders	66	69	65	70	270	19,903
	Austin Eckroat	67	66	66	71	270	19,903
	Matt McCarty	65	70	66	69	270	19,903
12	Ben Silverman	67	68	70	66	271	16,500
13	Clay Feagler	68	70	67	67	272	12,804
	Zac Blair	69	67	68	68	272	12,804

	Trevor Cone	68	66	69	69	272	12,804
	Patrick Fishburn	73	65	67	67	272	12,804
	Michael Kim	68	70	67	67	272	12,804
	Philip Knowles	68	65	69	70	272	12,804
	Kevin Roy	66	65	66	75	272	12,804
20	Chris Baker	68	66	69	70	273	9,125
	Logan McAllister	69	70	67	67	273	9,125
	Shad Tuten	69	68	66	70	273	9,125
23	Joey Garber	65	70	70	69	274	7,613
	Christopher Petefish	67	67	70	70	274	7,613
25	Eric Cole	69	69	69	68	275	5,979
	Martin Contini	70	67	68	70	275	5,979
	AJ Crouch	66	69	73	67	275	5,979
	Brandon Harkins	66	67	72	70	275	5,979
	Jamie Lovemark	69	69	66	71	275	5,979
	Ashton Van Horne	67	68	68	72	275	5,979

Utah Championship

Oakridge Country Club, Farmington, Utah
Par 71 (36-35); 7,045 yards

August 4-7
Purse: $750,000

1	**Andrew Kozan**	63	70	67	63	263	$135,000
2	**Patrick Fishburn**	65	68	67	64	264	48,750
	Justin Suh	68	68	65	63	264	48,750
	Ashton Van Horne	68	66	66	64	264	48,750
5	Trevor Cone	69	66	64	66	265	24,225
	Harrison Endycott	67	68	63	67	265	24,225
	Will Gordon	66	66	67	66	265	24,225
	Michael Kim	67	64	69	65	265	24,225
	Peter Kuest	68	64	67	66	265	24,225
10	Zecheng Dou	68	66	69	63	266	17,184
	McClure Meissner	69	67	63	67	266	17,184
	Mark Anderson	67	66	64	69	266	17,184
	Pierceson Coody	68	67	63	68	266	17,184
14	Akshay Bhatia	64	69	70	64	267	12,000
	Alex Chiarella	68	67	66	66	267	12,000
	Roberto Diaz	67	67	65	68	267	12,000
	Jeremy Paul	63	68	68	68	267	12,000
	Kevin Roy	69	67	65	66	267	12,000
	Charlie Saxon	65	67	71	64	267	12,000
	Samuel Stevens	70	65	65	67	267	12,000
21	Michael Feagles	68	65	66	69	268	8,813
	Pontus Nyholm	65	64	69	70	268	8,813
23	Martin Flores	69	66	68	66	269	7,325
	Nicholas Lindheim	68	66	66	69	269	7,325
	Chun-an Yu	66	68	70	65	269	7,325

Pinnacle Bank Championship

The Club at Indian Creek, Omaha, Nebraska
Par 71 (36-35); 7,721 yards

August 11-14
Purse: $850,000

1	**Robby Shelton**	66	70	66	65	267	$153,000
2	**Ben Taylor**	67	71	62	68	268	76,500
3	**Kevin Dougherty**	70	66	67	66	269	44,625
	Taylor Montgomery	66	68	66	69	269	44,625
5	Will Gordon	70	66	66	68	270	27,455
	Michael Kim	68	67	71	64	270	27,455
	McClure Meissner	69	70	66	65	270	27,455
	Justin Suh	69	68	65	68	270	27,455
	Carl Yuan	67	73	62	68	270	27,455
10	Ryan Hall	72	68	64	67	271	20,889
	Philip Knowles	65	71	64	71	271	20,889
12	MJ Daffue	67	68	66	72	273	16,894
	Austin Eckroat	71	67	67	68	273	16,894
	Cody Gribble	68	68	67	70	273	16,894
	TJ Vogel	68	68	69	68	273	16,894
16	Joey Garber	70	70	66	68	274	13,600
	Andrew Yun	66	68	70	70	274	13,600
	Xinjun Zhang	69	70	67	68	274	13,600
19	Samuel Stevens	71	69	73	62	275	9,385
	Carson Young	68	71	71	65	275	9,385
	Roberto Diaz	70	68	71	66	275	9,385
	Zack Fischer	73	67	66	69	275	9,385
	Conner Godsey	69	66	70	70	275	9,385
	Cole Hammer	67	72	66	70	275	9,385
	Andrew Kozan	67	69	70	69	275	9,385
	Shad Tuten	70	71	66	68	275	9,385

2022 REGULAR SEASON POINTS LIST

		Points
1	Carl Yuan	1819
2	Robby Shelton	1603
3	Paul Haley II	1341
4	Zecheng Dou	1321
5	Taylor Montgomery	1216
6	Augusto Nunez	1157
7	Justin Suh	1145
8	Ben Griffin	1102
9	Ben Taylor	1095
10	Brandon Matthews	1094

Albertsons Boise Open

Hillcrest Country Club, Boise, Idaho
Par 71 (36-35); 6,880 yards

August 18-21
Purse: $1,000,000

1	**Will Gordon**	67	66	67	63	263	$180,000
2	**MJ Daffue**	69	66	63	65	263	75,000
	Philip Knowles	61	64	68	70	263	75,000
	Gordon won playoff at first extra hole						
4	Erik Barnes	73	63	65	63	264	34,417
	Dean Burmester	66	69	65	64	264	34,417
	Austin Cook	70	62	65	67	264	34,417
	Thomas Detry	67	66	65	66	264	34,417
	Scott Harrington	68	67	62	67	264	34,417
	Taylor Montgomery	67	65	63	69	264	34,417
10	Doc Redman	64	67	69	65	265	25,500
11	Brice Garnett	67	67	66	66	266	21,288
	Seonghyeon Kim	66	70	64	66	266	21,288
	Satoshi Kodaira	64	65	69	68	266	21,288
	Nicholas Lindheim	66	68	66	66	266	21,288
15	Nick Hardy	64	69	68	66	267	17,000
	Ben Martin	69	66	62	70	267	17,000
	Davis Thompson	67	67	64	69	267	17,000
18	Anders Albertson	70	67	66	65	268	11,850
	Byeong Hun An	67	68	66	67	268	11,850
	Joseph Bramlett	65	65	70	68	268	11,850
	Harrison Endycott	68	64	69	67	268	11,850
	Chris Gotterup	67	66	65	70	268	11,850
	Brandon Matthews	65	69	66	68	268	11,850
	Grayson Murray	71	63	66	68	268	11,850
	Carson Young	64	67	67	70	268	11,850
26	Min Woo Lee	63	69	70	67	269	7,613
	Justin Lower	67	70	66	66	269	7,613
	Michael Kim	65	67	68	69	269	7,613
	Vincent Norrman	68	69	65	67	269	7,613
	Jason Scrivener	70	66	64	69	269	7,613
	Brian Stuard	68	69	64	68	269	7,613

Nationwide Children's Hospital Championship

Ohio State University Golf Club (Scarlet), Columbus, Ohio
Par 71 (36-35); 6,880 yards

August 25-28
Purse: $1,000,000

1	**David Lingmerth**	62	66	71	68	267	$180,000
2	**Paul Haley II**	68	68	65	68	269	90,000
3	**Zecheng Dou**	67	67	67	70	271	60,000
4	Michael Gligic	67	67	69	69	272	45,000
5	Ben Taylor	70	67	70	66	273	38,000
6	Joseph Bramlett	66	68	72	68	274	32,000
	Seonghyeon Kim	69	70	67	68	274	32,000
	Henrik Norlander	69	70	68	67	274	32,000
9	Justin Lower	68	68	70	69	275	23,830
	Taylor Montgomery	71	70	63	71	275	23,830
	Matti Schmid	71	70	67	67	275	23,830
	Justin Suh	68	71	70	66	275	23,830
	Kyle Westmoreland	71	68	68	68	275	23,830
14	Hurly Long	70	71	68	67	276	15,519
	William McGirt	69	69	68	70	276	15,519
	Seung-Yul Noh	68	72	68	68	276	15,519
	Sean O'Hair	72	64	71	69	276	15,519
	Kevin Roy	67	68	71	70	276	15,519
	Brian Stuard	66	71	66	73	276	15,519
	Norman Xiong	66	71	67	72	276	15,519
	Carl Yuan	67	71	69	69	276	15,519
22	Byeong Hun An	72	67	68	70	277	9,547
	Patrick Fishburn	69	70	71	67	277	9,547
	David Kocher	68	70	69	70	277	9,547
	Kelly Kraft	68	67	73	69	277	9,547
	Ryan Armour	68	72	72	65	277	9,547
	Sung Kang	70	68	68	71	277	9,547
28	Aaron Baddeley	65	73	70	70	278	7,025
	Bill Haas	71	70	68	69	278	7,025
	Nick Hardy	72	64	65	77	278	7,025
	Ben Martin	71	63	69	75	278	7,025
	Robby Shelton	67	72	68	71	278	7,025
	Samuel Stevens	71	69	72	66	278	7,025

Korn Ferry Tour Championship

Victoria National Golf Club, Newburgh, Indiana — September 1-4
Par 72 (36-36); 7,265 yards — Purse: $1,000,000

1	**Justin Suh**	66	69	64	68	267	$180,000
2	**Austin Eckroat**	68	65	68	68	269	90,000
3	**Eric Cole**	66	68	68	68	270	52,500
	Harry Hall	69	65	71	65	270	52,500
5	Ryan Armour	71	68	67	65	271	31,167
	Dean Burmester	69	68	69	65	271	31,167
	Nico Echavarria	67	71	67	66	271	31,167
	Carl Yuan	66	70	66	69	271	31,167
	Michael Gligic	64	66	71	70	271	31,167
	Tano Goya	66	69	65	71	271	31,167
11	Brent Grant	66	70	68	68	272	23,650
12	Joey Garber	70	67	69	67	273	19,300
	Nick Hardy	71	67	67	68	273	19,300
	Samuel Stevens	70	70	62	71	273	19,300
	Vaughn Taylor	67	72	69	65	273	19,300
	Carson Young	68	67	68	70	273	19,300
17	Michael Kim	68	68	67	71	274	14,030
	Philip Knowles	73	68	66	67	274	14,030
	Nicholas Lindheim	68	68	65	73	274	14,030
	Ben Martin	75	62	68	69	274	14,030
	Yannik Paul	70	69	68	67	274	14,030
22	Camilo Villegas	71	62	73	69	275	11,350
23	Tain Lee	68	68	72	68	276	9,767
	Andrew Novak	70	71	67	68	276	9,767
	Joseph Bramlett	69	73	65	69	276	9,767
26	Tyson Alexander	68	73	66	70	277	7,108
	Paul Barjon	69	68	73	67	277	7,108
	Austin Cook	74	65	68	70	277	7,108
	Tommy Gainey	69	69	69	70	277	7,108
	Will Gordon	66	66	72	73	277	7,108
	Ben Kohles	75	64	68	70	277	7,108
	Henrik Norlander	73	69	67	68	277	7,108
	Robby Shelton	70	69	72	66	277	7,108
	Chris Stroud	68	69	67	73	277	7,108
	Martin Trainer	69	72	68	68	277	7,108

2022 ALL ROUND RANKING

		Points
1	Justin Suh	152
2	Taylor Montgomery	210
3	Carl Yuan	227
4	Philip Knowles	239
5	MJ Daffue	251
6	Seonghyeon Kim	253
7	Augusto Nunez	273
8	Brent Grant	285
9	Will Gordon	296
10	Samuel Stevens	298

PGA Tour Canada

In the spirit of heroic oversimplification, it can be said that Wil Bateman rode two miraculous chip shots to the peak of the 2022 PGA Tour Canada — two victories, the Player of the Year award, a berth on the 2023 Korn Ferry Tour, a spot in the next RBC Canadian Open, a tour-topping C$119,920 in winnings, and a $25,000 bonus for winning the inaugural Fortinet Cup.

"Some things," he said, "just go your way when you win."

Bateman's first-ever tour win came at the ATB Classic. He'd closed with a 65 and tied Jorge Villar and Joe Highsmith at 19-under-par 265, then chipped in for an eagle on the second playoff visit to the Edmonton Petroleum Club's par-five 18th.

The second chip, a par-saver and a tournament-saver, came in the final round of the season-ending Fortinet Cup Championship at Deer Ridge. Bateman, who started the round four behind, was lying three in thick rough 20 yards short of the green at the par-four 14th, hoping to get his ball within 50 feet. And he holed it. "And I blacked out for a minute or two," he said. He went on to take the lead, and shot a one-under 69 for an eight-under 272 and a two-stroke win over Jeffrey Kang. And he spoke of his improved play from four years ago.

"If someone would have told me that I would be here," he said, "I would say they were insane."

The next four in the Fortinet Cup points standings earned conditional Korn Ferry status. Jake Knapp, playing "conservatively aggressive", made five eagles (one an ace), only two bogeys in a 26-under total of 254 to beat Bateman by two in the CRMC Championship, the first tour event to be played in the US, this at Cragun's Resort in Minnesota. It was his third tour win.

Noah Goodwin, 22, a pro for only a month, missed the cut in three of his first four starts, then went on to become the tour's first double winner of the season. He raced off with a seven-stroke win in the Sotheby's International Realty Canada Ontario Open at Woodington Lake. "The stars aligned for me this week," he said. They lined up again a month later in the GolfBC Championship at Gallagher's Canyon. "You never get used to this feeling," he said.

In Scott Stevens's case, the fourth time was the charm in the season-opening Royal Beach Victoria Open at Uplands. He birdied the 18th to tie Knapp, then birdied it three more times in the playoff, the last for his first professional win. After all that hard work? "Pretty awesome," he said.

And Ryan Gerard, 23, former University of North Carolina star, learned fast as a pro. In only his fourth event, "I just tried to take it one shot at a time," he said. Result: a wire-to-wire one-stroke win in the Quebec Open at Blainviller. "And sometimes," he added, "it's your week and you win."

Elsewhere on the schedule: the Elk Ridge Open (June 23-26) barely got started but was washed out by heavy rains ... Danny Walker birdied the first playoff hole from five feet to beat Cooper Musselman in the Osprey Valley Open ... First wins: Parker Coody, 22, closing with a 67 for 27 under to win the CentrePort Canada Rail Park Manitoba Open by eight strokes, tying the tour's winning margin record; former Purdue University star Brian Carlson, with a closing 65 to finish at 19 under, by a stroke at the Prince Edward Island Open.

2022 SCHEDULE

Royal Beach Victoria Open	**Scott Stevens**	
ATB Classic	**Wil Bateman**	
Elk Ridge Open		*abandoned*
Prince Edward Island Open	**Brian Carlson**	
Osprey Valley Open	**Danny Walker**	
Sotheby's International Realty Canada Ontario Open	**Noah Goodwin**	
Quebec Open	**Ryan Gerard**	
CentrePort Canada Rail Park Manitoba Open	**Parker Coody**	
CRMC Championship	**Jake Knapp**	
GolfBC Championship	**Noah Goodwin (2)**	
Fortinet Cup Championship	**Wil Bateman (2)**	

Royal Beach Victoria Open

Uplands Golf Club, Victoria, British Columbia — June 2-5
Par 70 (35-35); 6,420 yards — Purse: C$200,000

1	**Scott Stevens**	67	65	65	67	264	C$36,000
2	**Jake Knapp**	66	67	68	63	264	21,600
	Stevens won playoff at third extra hole						
3	**Cooper Dossey**	67	66	64	68	265	13,600
4	Joey Savoie	65	66	69	66	266	9,600
5	Etienne Papineau	66	69	69	64	268	7,600
	Nolan Ray	66	67	68	67	268	7,600
7	Jeffrey Kang	65	69	71	64	269	6,233
	Brett Bennett	69	68	65	67	269	6,233
	Cooper Musselman	66	68	67	68	269	6,233
10	Michael Blair	63	69	69	69	270	5,000
	Chris Crisologo	69	67	64	70	270	5,000
	Ian Holt	68	66	69	67	270	5,000
13	Lee Detmer	65	70	69	67	271	3,325
	Briggs Duce	65	68	69	69	271	3,325
	Eric Lilleboe	70	62	68	71	271	3,325
	James Nicholas	66	67	68	70	271	3,325
	Jamie Sadlowski	70	64	71	66	271	3,325
	Jake Scott	69	66	66	70	271	3,325
	Davis Shore	66	66	68	71	271	3,325
	Zack Taylor	66	67	71	67	271	3,325

ATB Classic

Edmonton Petroleum Golf & Country Club, Spruce Grove, Alberta — June 16-19
Par 71 (36-35); 7,036 yards — Purse: C$225,000

1	**Wil Bateman**	65	67	68	65	265	C$40,500
2	**Joe Highsmith**	66	67	66	66	265	19,800
	Jorge Villar	67	66	66	66	265	19,800
	Bateman won playoff at second extra hole						
4	Trent Phillips	67	66	67	68	268	9,900
	Rhett Rasmussen	64	67	71	66	268	9,900
6	Dalton Ward	67	68	66	68	269	8,100
7	Chris Crisologo	70	66	66	68	270	6,548
	JT Griffin	70	66	68	66	270	6,548
	Jonathan Hardee	67	66	66	71	270	6,548
	Jake Scott	67	68	69	66	270	6,548
	Danny Walker	66	65	68	71	270	6,548
12	Eric Lilleboe	66	69	70	66	271	4,725
	Thomas Longbella	68	67	69	67	271	4,725
	Derek Oland	70	66	66	69	271	4,725
15	James Allenby	68	67	69	68	272	3,268
	Ian Holt	64	65	73	70	272	3,268
	Steven Setterstrom	67	69	68	68	272	3,268
	Cameron Sisk	71	67	66	68	272	3,268
	Parker Coody	66	69	67	70	272	3,268
	Jared du Toit	65	67	69	71	272	3,268
	Carter Jenkins	66	67	68	71	272	3,268
	Jeffrey Kang	69	64	67	72	272	3,268

Elk Ridge Open

Elk Ridge Resort (Tournament), Waskesiu Lake, Saskatchewan — June 23-26
Par (34-36); 6,781 yards — Purse: C$250,000

Abandoned due to a waterlogged course

Prince Edward Island Open

Dundarave Golf Course, Cardigan, Prince Edward Island — June 30-July 3
Par 72 (36-36); 7,089 yards — Purse: C$200,000

1	**Brian Carlson**	68	70	66	65	269	C$36,000
2	**Chris R Wilson**	71	64	66	69	270	21,600
3	**Austin Hitt**	68	67	69	67	271	13,600
4	Joe Highsmith	70	67	69	67	273	8,267
	Myles Creighton	70	67	69	67	273	8,267
	Trent Phillips	71	67	67	68	273	8,267
7	Joey Vrzich	67	73	66	68	274	6,450
	Parker Gillam	69	69	67	69	274	6,450
9	Charles Huntzinger	69	70	69	67	275	5,000
	Benjamin Shipp	67	70	70	68	275	5,000
	Harrison Ott	73	69	65	68	275	5,000
	Brad Reeves	70	69	68	68	275	5,000
	Cooper Dossey	66	71	68	70	275	5,000
14	Andrew Dorn	68	71	70	67	276	3,500
	Kieran Vincent	67	73	69	67	276	3,500
	Dalton Ward	70	68	70	68	276	3,500
	Blake Maum	70	69	68	69	276	3,500
18	Ryan Gerard	70	70	71	66	277	2,608
	Jacob Solomon	71	69	70	67	277	2,608
	John Duthie	71	69	69	68	277	2,608
	Joseph Harrison	69	69	68	71	277	2,608
	Brendan MacDougall	71	70	63	73	277	2,608

Osprey Valley Open

TPC Toronto at Osprey Valley (Heathlands), Caledon, Ontario — July 21-24
Par 71 (36-35); 6,810 yards — Purse: C$225,000

1	**Danny Walker**	69	62	69	68	268	C$40,500
2	**Cooper Musselman**	68	67	68	65	268	24,300
	Walker won playoff at first extra hole						
3	**Thomas Longbella**	71	71	64	64	270	13,050
	Harrison Ott	68	68	68	66	270	13,050
5	Parker Gillam	67	68	70	66	271	8,213
	JT Griffin	72	69	67	63	271	8,213
	Jacob Solomon	67	67	70	67	271	8,213
8	Cooper Dossey	71	68	64	69	272	6,300
	Gavin Hall	71	69	66	66	272	6,300
	Jeffrey Kang	73	67	64	68	272	6,300
	Kieran Vincent	70	65	72	65	272	6,300
12	Blake Maum	71	68	69	65	273	5,175
13	Wil Bateman	68	68	69	69	274	3,975
	Myles Creighton	73	68	68	65	274	3,975
	Andrew Harrison	71	71	67	65	274	3,975
	Eric Lilleboe	69	67	70	68	274	3,975
	Christian Salzer	71	65	70	68	274	3,975
	Maxwell Sear	69	73	63	69	274	3,975
19	Joey Vrzich	70	65	71	69	275	3,150
20	Chandler Eaton	71	70	68	67	276	2,529
	Joseph Harrison	70	63	72	71	276	2,529
	Brendan MacDougall	73	67	69	67	276	2,529
	Rhett Rasmussen	72	66	70	68	276	2,529
	Brian Richey	72	64	70	70	276	2,529

Sotheby's International Realty Canada Ontario Open

Woodington Lake Golf Club (Legend), Tottenham, Ontario — July 28-31
Par 71 (36-35); 6,863 yards — Purse: C$200,000

1	**Noah Goodwin**	64	68	68	67	267	C$36,000
2	**Thomas Walsh**	70	70	67	67	274	14,933
	Lee Detmer	71	67	68	68	274	14,933
	Cameron Sisk	71	68	65	70	274	14,933
5	Ian Holt	73	69	69	64	275	7,300
	Danny Walker	67	72	69	67	275	7,300
	Trent Phillips	72	71	64	68	275	7,300
8	Easton Paxton	70	71	67	68	276	5,800
	Blake Hathcoat	71	66	69	70	276	5,800
	Dylan Meyer	67	70	68	71	276	5,800
11	Brayden Garrison	70	67	73	67	277	3,971
	Austin Squires	73	70	66	68	277	3,971
	Derek Oland	72	67	68	70	277	3,971
	Brendan MacDougall	71	67	69	70	277	3,971
	Brian Carlson	75	66	66	70	277	3,971
	Alex Fitzpatrick	66	69	71	71	277	3,971
	Justin Doeden	70	66	69	72	277	3,971
18	Mike Van Sickle	75	67	70	66	278	2,700
	Jeffrey Kang	72	69	69	68	278	2,700
	Jared du Toit	67	71	67	73	278	2,700
	Jacob Solomon	71	71	63	73	278	2,700

Quebec Open

Club de Golf Le Blainviller (Heritage), Blainville, Quebec — August 4-7
Par 72 (36-36); 6,952 yards — Purse: C$200,000

1	**Ryan Gerard**	65	68	66	73	272	C$36,000
2	**Thomas Walsh**	68	66	72	67	273	21,600
3	**Jeffrey Kang**	70	65	71	69	275	10,400
	Jake Knapp	70	68	72	65	275	10,400
	Travis Trace	69	66	72	68	275	10,400
6	Sudarshan Yellamaraju	72	69	68	67	276	7,200
7	Wil Bateman	68	70	70	69	277	6,025
	Van Holmgren	66	73	68	70	277	6,025
	Thomas Longbella	69	71	68	69	277	6,025
	Blake Wagoner	68	69	69	71	277	6,025
11	Brett Bennett	71	69	72	66	278	4,800
	Bryce Hendrix	66	69	71	72	278	4,800
13	Cooper Dossey	70	72	70	67	279	3,533
	Davis Shore	68	71	72	68	279	3,533
	Justin Doeden	70	67	66	76	279	3,533
	Ian Holt	70	69	67	73	279	3,533
	Drew Nesbitt	70	69	67	73	279	3,533
	Joey Savoie	68	67	71	73	279	3,533
19	Brian Carlson	69	72	68	71	280	2,510
	Max Gilbert	71	67	73	69	280	2,510
	Harrison Ott	69	70	69	72	280	2,510
	Rhett Rasmussen	71	70	71	68	280	2,510
	Viraj Garewal (A)	68	70	69	73	280	

CentrePort Canada Rail Park Manitoba Open

Southwood Golf & Country Club, Winnipeg, Manitoba — August 18-21
Par 72 (36-36); 7,311 yards — Purse: C$200,000

1	**Parker Coody**	65	62	67	67	261	C$36,000
2	**Ian Holt**	67	69	67	66	269	21,600
3	**Gavin Hall**	66	68	70	66	270	11,600
	David Kim	68	69	69	64	270	11,600
5	Carter Jenkins	71	66	67	67	271	7,300
	Jeffrey Kang	70	67	65	69	271	7,300
	Sudarshan Yellamaraju	68	69	70	64	271	7,300
8	Lee Detmer	68	67	70	67	272	5,400
	Joe Highsmith	68	69	69	66	272	5,400
	Harrison Ott	69	68	68	67	272	5,400
	Noah Steele	69	67	67	69	272	5,400
	Scott Stevens	68	70	68	66	272	5,400
13	Josh Hart	69	68	69	67	273	4,200
14	Wil Bateman	67	69	70	68	274	3,300
	Rhett Rasmussen	68	68	67	71	274	3,300
	Isaiah Salinda	69	69	69	67	274	3,300
	Mitchell Schow	65	70	70	69	274	3,300
	Tyler Strafaci	67	70	66	71	274	3,300
	Travis Trace	72	64	68	70	274	3,300
20	Trent Phillips	69	69	64	73	275	2,600

CRMC Championship

Cragun's Resort, Brainerd, Minnesota, USA — August 25-28
Par 70 (35-35); 7,123 yards — Purse: C$200,000

1	**Jake Knapp**	64	65	61	64	254	C$36,000
2	**Wil Bateman**	63	65	66	62	256	21,600
3	**Thomas Walsh**	63	64	68	63	258	9,020
	Joe Highsmith	63	63	69	63	258	9,020
	Ryan Gerard	65	63	65	65	258	9,020
	Trent Phillips	68	61	62	67	258	9,020
	Conner Godsey	62	65	65	66	258	9,020
8	Guillaume Fanonnel	65	64	67	63	259	5,800
	Myles Creighton	65	68	62	64	259	5,800
	Alexander Herrmann	61	62	69	67	259	5,800
11	Gavin Hall	63	64	68	65	260	5,000
12	Yi Cao	66	62	69	64	261	4,400
	Brett White	63	68	65	65	261	4,400
14	Lee Detmer	66	68	64	64	262	3,700
	Isaiah Salinda	67	65	64	66	262	3,700
16	Eric Lilleboe	69	66	65	63	263	2,715
	Nolan Ray	68	67	65	63	263	2,715
	Derek Oland	69	66	64	64	263	2,715
	Stuart Macdonald	68	65	65	65	263	2,715
	Austin Hitt	70	65	63	65	263	2,715
	Scott Stevens	65	66	66	66	263	2,715
	Ian Holt	67	62	68	66	263	2,715
	Kieran Vincent	67	65	63	68	263	2,715

GolfBC Championship

Gallagher's Canyon Golf & Country Club, Kelowna, British Columbia — September 1-4
Par 71 (36-35); 6,786 yards — Purse: C$200,000

1	**Noah Goodwin**	67	61	69	64	261	C$36,000
2	**Scott Stevens**	66	65	66	65	262	21,600
3	**Cameron Sisk**	66	66	67	64	263	13,600
4	Ryan Gerard	68	64	67	66	265	8,800
	James Hervol	66	63	67	69	265	8,800
6	Luke Schniederjans	64	67	67	68	266	7,200
7	Dalton Ward	70	61	69	67	267	6,700
8	Jake Knapp	68	66	65	69	268	5,800
	Etienne Papineau	67	66	69	66	268	5,800
	Joey Savoie	67	68	68	65	268	5,800
11	Parker Coody	66	69	69	65	269	3,971
	Taylor Funk	67	69	66	67	269	3,971
	Joe Highsmith	68	68	68	65	269	3,971
	Derek Oland	66	67	68	68	269	3,971
	Tyler Strafaci	71	65	66	67	269	3,971
	Sudarshan Yellamaraju	69	68	69	63	269	3,971
	Gavin Hall	68	64	65	72	269	3,971
18	Myles Creighton	68	67	67	68	270	2,608
	Andrew Dorn	67	68	66	69	270	2,608
	Jared du Toit	68	68	66	68	270	2,608
	Stuart Macdonald	67	68	69	66	270	2,608
	Cole Madey	64	65	69	72	270	2,608

Fortinet Cup Championship

Deer Ridge Golf Club, Kitchener, Ontario — September 15-18
Par 70 (35-35); 7,172 yards — Purse: C$225,000

1	**Wil Bateman**	70	65	68	69	272	C$40,500
2	**Jeffrey Kang**	71	69	64	70	274	24,300
3	**Nolan Ray**	69	67	69	71	276	13,050
	Thomas Walsh	66	66	67	77	276	13,050
5	Etienne Papineau	69	65	76	67	277	8,213
	Jacob Solomon	67	73	67	70	277	8,213
	Trent Phillips	65	72	68	72	277	8,213
8	Joey Vrzich	66	70	70	72	278	6,075
	Rhett Rasmussen	69	68	69	72	278	6,075
	Guillaume Fanonnel	71	68	67	72	278	6,075
	Scott Stevens	66	67	71	74	278	6,075
	Joe Highsmith	67	68	69	74	278	6,075
13	Carter Jenkins	72	73	70	64	279	4,219
	Ian Holt	69	73	68	69	279	4,219
	Cooper Musselman	70	71	65	73	279	4,219
	Tyler Strafaci	69	67	69	74	279	4,219
17	Harrison Ott	67	72	70	71	280	3,263
	Ryan Gerard	68	71	70	71	280	3,263
	Myles Creighton	70	70	68	72	280	3,263
	Austin Hitt	68	70	69	73	280	3,263

2022 FORTINET CUP

		Points
1	Wil Bateman	1,654
2	Jake Knapp	1,117
3	Noah Goodwin	1,063
4	Scott Stevens	1,055
5	Ryan Gerard	899
6	Thomas Walsh	849
7	Jeffrey Kang	832
8	Danny Walker	762
9	Joe Highsmith	746
10	Ian Holt	729

PGA Tour Latinoamerica

When Mitchell Meissner gets around to writing his memoirs, he can title the chapter on 2022, "The Fine Art of Winning It All without Winning". This was an unprecedented performance on the PGA Tour Latinoamerica. Meissner, 26, former Rice University standout, didn't win any of the tour's 12 tournaments yet swept the top season honours — the inaugural Totalplay Cup, the Player of the Year award and a berth on the Korn Ferry Tour. He also topped the money list with $94,510 and earned a bonus of $20,000 for winning the Totalplay Cup, the rebranded points-based Order of Merit. The next four finishers won conditional status on the Korn Ferry.

"I'm happy," Meissner said, in what sounded like an exercise in understatement. "I really don't have words to express how happy I am." He made the cut in all 12 events, finished second three times, third twice and had nine top 10s in all. "It's not fun having your fate in everyone else's hands," he said, "but I played well enough this season to put myself in this position, where guys had to come get me."

The closest he came to winning was in the Volvo Golf Championship, at El Rincon in Colombia, citing his "worst" shot of the season. "Absolutely ... the two-footer I missed in the final round," he said. In fact, on the next-to-last hole. He was tied with Cristobal Del Solar coming to the 17th. "I guess I should have marked it and waited," he said, but he wanted to get out of the way of his playing partner, Adam Navigato. The putt broke off and he bogeyed, losing to Del Solar by a stroke.

Chile's Del Solar, second in the Totalplay standings after his hot-cold Volvo win, started the final round trailing by two, made eight birdies through the 15th, then double-bogeyed the 16th and won after Meissner bogeyed 17. "It was a tough round," Del Solar said.

Jorge Fernandez Valdes rode victory in his national championship at the Visa Open de Argentina — at the start of the season in December 2021 — to third place on the standings. Rookie Kevin Velo, 24, of the US, had the adventure of a lifetime in the Termas de Rio Hondo Invitational in Argentina. It was his fourth start, his first cut made and his first win. He led by four starting the final round, triple-bogeyed the par-five ninth, bogeyed 10, birdied three of the last five, including the 18th, shot a one-over 73, an 18-under 270 and won by one. "I was in the right mental headspace the entire week," he said.

Argentina's Alejandro Tosti took the fifth Korn Ferry spot in a breeze, by eight strokes in the Abierto del Centro Memorial Eduardo "Gato" Romero. For shaky moments, go to the final round, when he started with a five-shot lead, then missed a short birdie putt at the first and bogeyed the second. "I stayed very calm after that," he said. "It was an unbelievable day." He went on to handle the 30mph winds at Cordoba for a 69 and 10-under 274, and the second-largest tour victory margin.

When the new season began in December, Del Solar won the windy Neuquen Argentina Classic by three strokes for his fourth title on the circuit and second of the year. Matt Ryan, who won the Estrella del Mar Open in February, also won again at the last event of the year, the Scotia Wealth Management Chile Open, by one from fellow American left-hander Conner Godsey with an eagle at the last thanks to a two-iron to 12 feet. The season-opening Visa Open de Argentina went to Zack Fischer, with his first win as a professional in his first start on the Latinoamerica circuit, earning himself a trip to The 151st Open at Hoylake in 2023.

As to Meissner and his quest for that first victory: "I believe it's going to happen," he said, "when it's going to happen."

2022 SCHEDULE

Estrella del Mar Open	**Matt Ryan**
Termas de Rio Hondo Invitational	**Kevin Velo**
Abierto del Centro memorial Eduardo "Gato" Romero	**Alejandro Tosti**
JHSF Aberto do Brasil	**Jamie Lopez Rivarola**
Diners Club Peru Open	**Jose Toledo**
Quito Open	**Manav Shah**
Jalisco Open GDL	**Jose de Jesus Rodriguez**
Volvo Golf Championship	**Cristobal Del Solar**
Fortox Colombia Classic	**Tommy Cocha**

Bupa Tour Championship	**Jesus Montenegro**
Visa Open de Argentina	**Zack Fischer**
Neuquen Argentina Classic	**Cristobal Del Solar (2)**
Scotia Wealth Management Chile Open	**Matt Ryan (2)**

Estrella del Mar Open

Estrella del Mar Country Club, Mazatlan, Mexico — February 17-20
Par 72 (36-36); 7,015 yards — Purse: $175,000

1	**Matt Ryan**	63	70	66	66	265	$31,500
2	**Cristobal Del Solar**	66	67	68	67	268	15,400
	Mitchell Meissner	67	67	69	65	268	15,400
4	Joseph Winslow	65	68	70	66	269	8,400
5	Brian Ohr	70	67	66	67	270	7,000
6	Armando Favela	65	68	66	72	271	5,863
	Emilio Gonzalez	66	67	68	70	271	5,863
	Anthony Paolucci	67	65	67	72	271	5,863
9	Andreas Halvorsen	68	70	66	68	272	4,725
	Raul Pereda	70	69	65	68	272	4,725
	Andy Spencer	70	67	67	68	272	4,725
12	Rodolfo Cazaubon	69	69	68	67	273	3,325
	Linus Lilliedahl	66	71	69	67	273	3,325
	Velten Meyer	68	68	69	68	273	3,325
	David Pastore	69	71	67	66	273	3,325
	Stephen Stallings Jr	68	66	67	72	273	3,325
	Alejandro Tosti	67	70	65	71	273	3,325
18	Denzel Ieremia	71	69	69	65	274	2,211
	Jose Toledo	66	68	73	67	274	2,211
	Santiago Gomez	70	70	68	66	274	2,211
	Carson Roberts	66	70	69	69	274	2,211
	Jorge Villar	66	68	66	74	274	2,211
	Tim Widing	71	68	65	70	274	2,211

Termas de Rio Hondo Invitational

Termas de Rio Hondo Golf Club, Santiago del Estero, Argentina — March 24-27
Par 72 (36-36); 7,471 yards — Purse: $175,000

1	**Kevin Velo**	66	67	64	73	270	$31,500
2	**Tommy Cocha**	66	70	70	65	271	15,400
	Jorge Fernandez Valdes	67	67	67	70	271	15,400
4	David Pastore	69	69	68	66	272	8,400
5	Cristobal Del Solar	70	68	66	69	273	6,388
	Jeremy Gandon	69	66	67	71	273	6,388
	Austin Hitt	68	67	69	69	273	6,388
8	Nicolo Galletti	69	72	68	66	275	4,725
	Matt Gilchrest	68	71	70	66	275	4,725
	Roland Massimino	68	70	69	68	275	4,725
	James McCarthy	71	70	66	68	275	4,725
	Alex Scott	73	68	69	65	275	4,725
13	Camilo Aguado	70	66	72	68	276	3,092
	Rafael Becker	70	71	68	67	276	3,092
	John Hill	68	68	74	66	276	3,092
	Hayden Springer	68	69	71	68	276	3,092
	Cesar Costilla	70	70	67	69	276	3,092
	Andreas Halvorsen	71	68	67	70	276	3,092
19	Charlie Hillier	69	72	65	71	277	2,198
	Cole Madey	67	73	70	67	277	2,198
	Mitchell Meissner	67	73	69	68	277	2,198
	Josh Radcliff	70	70	66	71	277	2,198

Abierto del Centro Memorial Eduardo "Gato" Romero

Cordoba Golf Club, Villa Allende, Cordoba, Argentina — March 31-April 3
Par 71 (35-36); 6,878 yards — Purse: $175,000

1	**Alejandro Tosti**	71	66	68	69	274	$31,500
2	**Clodomiro Carranza**	72	70	72	68	282	18,900
3	**Rodolfo Cazaubon**	71	69	72	71	283	10,150
	Alan Wagner	72	69	72	70	283	10,150
5	Cristobal Del Solar	68	72	75	69	284	5,731
	Nicolo Galletti	67	68	75	74	284	5,731
	John Hill	71	72	68	73	284	5,731
	Leandro Marelli	67	72	71	74	284	5,731
	Mitchell Meissner	71	71	73	69	284	5,731
	Tim Widing	71	69	71	73	284	5,731
11	Tommy Cocha	72	73	71	69	285	4,025
	Jeremy Gandon	70	72	70	73	285	4,025
	Velten Meyer	70	75	68	72	285	4,025
14	Emilio Gonzalez	71	73	70	72	286	2,975
	Anthony Paolucci	73	67	72	74	286	2,975
	David Pastore	70	71	72	73	286	2,975
	Raul Pereda	72	73	72	69	286	2,975
	Gustavo Silva	73	69	72	72	286	2,975

19	Camilo Aguado	70	74	71	72	287	1,945
	Isidro Benitez	70	74	72	71	287	1,945
	Myles Creighton	72	71	73	71	287	1,945
	Rodrigo Lee	73	70	72	72	287	1,945
	Dalan Refioglu	66	72	76	73	287	1,945
	Juan Carlos Serrano	75	69	76	67	287	1,945
	Evan Katz	73	69	70	75	287	1,945
	Jose Narro	68	75	71	73	287	1,945

JHSF Aberto do Brasil

Fazenda Boa Vista, Porot Feliz, Brazil
Par 71 (35-36); 6,830 yards

April 21-24
Purse: $175,000

1	**Jaime Lopez Rivarola**	63	63	69	69	264	$31,500
2	**Rowin Caron**	67	67	64	67	265	18,900
3	**Cristobal Del Solar**	64	66	67	71	268	10,150
	Jose Toledo	67	66	64	71	268	10,150
5	Davis Shore	71	68	66	64	269	6,650
	Hayden Springer	65	69	67	68	269	6,650
7	Joel Thelen	70	67	66	67	270	5,863
8	Mitchell Meissner	66	65	69	71	271	5,425
9	Myles Creighton	69	68	70	65	272	4,375
	Andres Gallegos	63	65	73	71	272	4,375
	Santiago Gomez	68	65	69	70	272	4,375
	Austin Hitt	64	70	70	68	272	4,375
	Jose Narro	67	66	67	72	272	4,375
14	Emilio Gonzalez	71	67	69	66	273	3,150
	Raul Pereda	64	69	69	71	273	3,150
	Kevin Velo	67	69	70	67	273	3,150
17	Ryan Baca	69	68	70	67	274	2,713
	Linus Lilliedahl	63	70	72	69	274	2,713
19	Camilo Aguado	68	66	75	66	275	2,003
	Rak Cho	71	64	68	72	275	2,003
	Christopher Crawford	67	69	71	68	275	2,003
	Jorge Fernandez Valdes	70	68	72	65	275	2,003
	Corbin Mills	71	68	71	65	275	2,003
	Jesus Montenegro	70	65	69	71	275	2,003
	Andy Spencer	66	68	71	70	275	2,003

Diners Club Peru Open

Los Inkas Golf Club, Lima, Peru
Par 72 (36-36); 6,882 yards

April 28-May 1
Purse: $175,000

1	**Jose Toledo**	67	64	69	66	266	$31,500
2	**Raul Pereda**	70	66	66	70	272	18,900
3	**Rafael Becker**	66	69	64	74	273	10,150
	Mitchell Meissner	69	64	69	71	273	10,150
5	Denzel Ieremia	71	69	68	67	275	7,000
6	Cristobal Del Solar	68	68	66	74	276	6,300
7	Cole Madey	65	72	74	66	277	4,915
	Joseph Winslow	69	71	70	67	277	4,915
	Juan Carlos Benitez	71	71	65	70	277	4,915
	Paul Imondi	69	69	65	74	277	4,915
	Guillermo Pumarol	67	68	68	74	277	4,915
	Hayden Springer	71	69	66	71	277	4,915
13	Manav Shah	68	69	71	70	278	3,675
14	Camilo Aguado	70	71	69	69	279	2,975
	Derek Castillo	68	74	65	72	279	2,975
	Fred Meyer	68	67	73	71	279	2,975
	Anthony Paolucci	69	72	71	67	279	2,975
	Tim Widing	72	67	69	71	279	2,975
19	Myles Creighton	71	70	69	70	280	2,198
	Jeremy Gandon	72	70	72	66	280	2,198
	Stephen Stallings Jr	70	72	68	70	280	2,198
	Alejandro Tosti	70	71	67	72	280	2,198

Quito Open

Quito Tennis & Golf Club, Quito, Ecuador
Par 72 (36-36); 7,412 yards

May 5-8
Purse: $175,000

1	**Manav Shah**	63	69	68	66	266	$31,500
2	**Mitchell Meissner**	65	68	67	68	268	15,400
	Joel Thelen	69	67	64	68	268	15,400
4	Kevin Velo	69	62	70	69	270	8,400
5	Rowin Caron	69	66	70	66	271	7,000
6	Camilo Aguado	70	69	66	68	273	6,081
	Ricardo Celia	69	65	67	72	273	6,081
8	Jesus Montenegro	70	66	69	69	274	5,075
	Davis Shore	68	68	67	71	274	5,075
	Alejandro Tosti	66	70	68	70	274	5,075
11	Rodolfo Cazaubon	68	69	71	67	275	3,850
	Rak Cho	70	67	69	69	275	3,850
	Christopher Crawford	74	67	67	67	275	3,850
	Joseph Winslow	70	70	68	67	275	3,850
15	Anthony Paolucci	71	70	67	68	276	3,063
	Tim Widing	72	67	68	69	276	3,063
17	Isidro Benitez	68	71	67	71	277	2,538
	Will Cannon	70	66	70	71	277	2,538
	Alex Scott	70	68	69	70	277	2,538
	Jose Toledo	68	69	69	71	277	2,538

Jalisco Open GDL

Atlas Country Club, Guadalajara, Mexico — May 26-29
Par 71 (35-36); 7,169 yards — Purse: $175,000

1	**Jose de Jesus Rodriguez**	66	67	72	64	269	$31,500
2	**Austin Hitt**	69	71	66	66	272	18,900
3	**Myles Creighton**	68	67	69	69	273	9,100
	Mitchell Meissner	70	66	67	70	273	9,100
	Kevin Velo	70	64	69	70	273	9,100
6	Andrew Alligood	65	72	72	65	274	5,863
	Will Cannon	71	65	68	70	274	5,863
	Raul Pereda	68	69	69	68	274	5,863
9	Rafael Becker	69	71	69	66	275	4,550
	Cristobal Del Solar	72	69	67	67	275	4,550
	Leandro Marelli	67	71	67	70	275	4,550
	Andres Romero	66	70	70	69	275	4,550
13	Jeremy Gandon	72	68	67	69	276	3,383
	Rodolfo Cazaubon	72	66	69	69	276	3,383
	Alan Wagner	68	69	69	70	276	3,383
16	Rak Cho	70	66	74	67	277	2,456
	Christopher Crawford	68	69	70	70	277	2,456
	Brendon Doyle	68	66	73	70	277	2,456
	Jorge Fernandez Valdes	70	70	70	67	277	2,456
	Matt Ryan	69	71	73	64	277	2,456
	Gustavo Silva	71	68	68	70	277	2,456
	Aaron Terrazas	70	71	69	67	277	2,456

Volvo Golf Championship

Club El Rincon de Cajica, Bogota, Colombia — June 2-5
Par 72 (36-36); 7,464 yards — Purse: $175,000

1	**Cristobal Del Solar**	67	70	69	66	272	$31,500
2	**Mitchell Meissner**	75	65	65	68	273	18,900
3	**Adam Navigato**	70	67	67	70	274	11,900
4	Trevor Sluman	75	66	68	66	275	6,891
	Kevin Velo	71	71	69	64	275	6,891
	Matt Gilchrest	72	69	66	68	275	6,891
	Josh Goldenberg	72	67	67	69	275	6,891
8	Jose Toledo	73	70	67	66	276	5,425
9	Rak Cho	67	73	69	68	277	4,725
	Matias Dominguez	68	71	70	68	277	4,725
	Anthony Paolucci	69	70	69	69	277	4,725
12	Armando Favela	70	71	70	67	278	3,128
	Jeremy Gandon	69	68	72	69	278	3,128
	Hayden Springer	66	71	73	68	278	3,128
	Manuel Torres	71	72	72	63	278	3,128
	Brendon Doyle	72	69	66	71	278	3,128
	Barrett Kelpin	73	68	68	69	278	3,128
	Chris Nido	70	68	70	70	278	3,128
	Alan Wagner	69	68	71	70	278	3,128
20	Jorge Fernandez Valdes	74	69	66	70	279	2,188
	Alex Scott	71	70	71	67	279	2,188

Fortox Colombia Classic

Ruitoque Golf & Country Club, Floridablanca, Colombia — June 9-12
Par 70 (36-34); 6,592 yards — Purse: $175,000

1	**Tommy Cocha**	67	64	62	65	258	$31,500
2	**Isidro Benitez**	67	65	61	65	258	18,900
	Cocha won playoff at first extra hole						
3	**Alejandro Tosti**	63	65	65	66	259	10,150
	Kevin Velo	63	67	65	64	259	10,150
5	Samuel Anderson	68	68	62	62	260	6,388
	Rowin Caron	65	66	62	67	260	6,388
	Hayden Springer	68	64	63	65	260	6,388
8	Camilo Aguado	64	68	62	67	261	5,250
	Christopher Crawford	65	63	65	68	261	5,250
10	Roland Massimino	66	65	65	66	262	4,550
	Mitchell Meissner	64	68	66	64	262	4,550
12	Charlie Hillier	71	61	65	66	263	3,675
	Austin Hitt	68	64	62	69	263	3,675
	Cole Madey	66	64	67	66	263	3,675
15	Shintaro Ban	67	65	72	60	264	3,063
	James McCarthy	65	64	69	66	264	3,063
17	Dillon Board	66	67	66	66	265	2,450
	Rak Cho	66	68	64	67	265	2,450
	Ryan Cole	63	67	66	69	265	2,450
	Luis Gerardo Garza	68	65	67	65	265	2,450
	Chris Nido	65	68	66	66	265	2,450

Bupa Tour Championship

PGA Riviera Maya, Tulum, Mexico — June 23-26
Par-72 (36-36); 7,272 yards — Purse: $200,000

1	**Jesus Montenegro**	68	71	71	72	282	$36,000
2	**Andres Gallegos**	72	70	70	72	284	17,600
	Manav Shah	70	71	73	70	284	17,600
4	Samuel Anderson	68	76	73	68	285	8,800
	Jose de Jesus Rodriguez	74	67	76	68	285	8,800
6	Rafael Becker	73	72	71	70	286	6,475
	Andy Spencer	71	76	70	69	286	6,475
	Manuel Torres	67	78	70	71	286	6,475
	Joseph Winslow	72	70	73	71	286	6,475
10	Myles Creighton	70	72	69	76	287	5,000
	Michael Perras	75	68	74	70	287	5,000
	Alejandro Tosti	71	70	72	74	287	5,000
13	Anthony Paolucci	75	71	72	70	288	4,000
	Davis Shore	72	70	77	69	288	4,000
15	Rodolfo Cazaubon	72	70	73	74	289	3,300
	Armando Favela	75	71	71	72	289	3,300
	Jorge Fernandez Valdes	74	69	69	77	289	3,300
	Raul Pereda	73	74	69	73	289	3,300
19	Brendon Doyle	73	74	73	70	290	2,289
	Camilo Aguado	76	71	74	69	290	2,289
	Ryan Cole	72	74	70	74	290	2,289
	Emilio Gonzalez	71	72	73	74	290	2,289
	Austin Hitt	70	75	73	72	290	2,289
	Kevin Velo	75	72	75	68	290	2,289
	Alan Wagner	73	75	72	70	290	2,289

2021-2022 TOTALPLAY CUP

		Points
1	Mitchell Meissner	1,528
2	Cristobal Del Solar	1,377
3	Jorge Fernandez Valdes	1,262
4	Kevin Velo	1,169
5	Alejandro Tosti	1,034
6	Alan Wagner	960
7	Jose Toledo	922
8	Manav Shah	890
9	Tommy Cocha	869
10	Jesus Montenegro	776

Visa Open de Argentina

Nordelta Golf Club, Tigre, Buenos Aires, Argentina — December 1-4
Par 72 (36-36); 7,233 yards — Purse: $175,000

1	**Zack Fischer**	69	66	67	68	270	$31,500
2	**Linus Lilliedahl**	67	67	71	66	271	18,900
3	**Santiago Bauni**	69	69	69	69	276	10,150
	Myles Creighton	74	70	67	65	276	10,150
5	Chandler Blanchet	70	70	66	71	277	6,388
	Augusto Nunez	68	68	71	70	277	6,388
	Alejandro Tosti	70	71	68	68	277	6,388
8	Danny Ochoa	69	66	73	70	278	5,075
	Alan Wagner	70	70	70	68	278	5,075
	Alex Weiss	73	71	67	67	278	5,075
11	Charlie Hillier	75	69	68	69	281	3,588
	Evan Knight	69	71	68	73	281	3,588
	Nelson Ledesma	71	69	68	73	281	3,588
	Alvaro Ortiz	71	70	68	72	281	3,588
	Peyton Wilhoit	68	72	69	72	281	3,588
	Joseph Winslow	70	68	76	67	281	3,588
17	Rafael Becker	70	69	72	71	282	2,450
	Rodolfo Cazaubon	70	73	72	67	282	2,450
	Briggs Duce	69	70	70	73	282	2,450
	John Greco	72	72	69	69	282	2,450
	Charles Osborne	75	67	71	69	282	2,450

Neuquen Argentina Classic

Chapelco Golf & Resort, San Martin de los Andes, Argentina — December 8-11
Par 72 (36-36); 7,163 yards — Purse: $175,000

1	**Cristobal Del Solar**	69	66	69	68	272	$31,500
2	**Linus Lilliedahl**	71	66	70	68	275	18,900
3	**Tim Widing**	70	68	68	70	276	11,900
4	Raul Pereda	71	71	69	66	277	8,400
5	Sandy Scott	68	69	73	68	278	7,000
6	Joel Thelen	70	69	70	70	279	5,666
	Alejandro Tosti	72	67	70	70	279	5,666
	Dalan Refioglu	69	73	65	72	279	5,666
	Jorge Villar	69	68	71	71	279	5,666
10	Nelson Ledesma	68	71	70	71	280	4,550
	Davis Shore	71	69	68	72	280	4,550
12	Skyler Finnell	64	76	72	69	281	3,544
	Jeremy Gandon	69	71	72	69	281	3,544
	Walker Lee	73	68	70	70	281	3,544
	Alex Scott	72	70	68	71	281	3,544
16	Martin Contini	75	66	71	70	282	2,456
	Conner Godsey	71	69	69	73	282	2,456
	Andreas Halvorsen	70	70	71	71	282	2,456
	Austin Hitt	68	69	75	70	282	2,456
	Leandro Marelli	70	71	69	72	282	2,456
	David Pastore	68	74	69	71	282	2,456
	Gustavo Silva	76	68	66	72	282	2,456

Scotia Wealth Management Chile Open

Hacienda Chicureo Club, Santiago, Chile — December 15-18
Par 72 (36-36); 7,349 yards — Purse: $175,000

1	**Matt Ryan**	66	71	71	70	278	$31,500
2	**Conner Godsey**	68	70	70	71	279	18,900
3	**Cristobal Del Solar**	68	72	71	70	281	11,900
4	Christopher Crawford	70	73	72	67	282	7,700
	Toni Hakula	69	70	72	71	282	7,700
6	Jorge Fernandez Valdes	71	66	73	73	283	6,081
	Leandro Marelli	70	72	72	69	283	6,081
8	Griffin Barela	71	73	70	70	284	4,550
	Isidro Benitez	73	70	68	73	284	4,550
	Josh Goldenberg	68	75	73	68	284	4,550
	Rodrigo Lee	76	68	70	70	284	4,550
	Alexandre Rocha	74	68	71	71	284	4,550
	Matias Simaski	70	71	73	70	284	4,550
14	Carlos Bustos	70	73	70	72	285	2,975
	Julian Etulain	65	73	74	73	285	2,975
	Peter Gasperini	71	70	77	67	285	2,975
	Walker Lee	69	70	73	73	285	2,975
	Joel Thelen	75	69	73	68	285	2,975
19	Jeremy Gandon	75	69	70	72	286	2,198
	Adrien Pendaries	70	75	71	70	286	2,198
	Davis Shore	69	71	76	70	286	2,198
	Sandy Scott	69	69	72	76	286	2,198

DP World Tour

No single player dominated in terms of wins during 2022, which may have been one reason why Rory McIlroy was able to top the DP World Tour Rankings without having done so. That would only be one reason, however. Another was the Northern Irishman's brilliant level of consistency. His average finishing position in 10 starts on tour was fourth, compared to a previous best average of 12th in 2011.

After finishing 12th in the Abu Dhabi HSBC Championship to start the year, McIlroy was never again outside the top 10. He was second at the Masters and the BMW PGA Championship, third at the Dubai Desert Classic and the Open Championship, and was stuck in fourth to end the year at the DS Automobiles Italian Open, the Alfred Dunhill Links and the DP World Tour Championship. This was his fourth Harry Vardon Trophy, having also won it in 2012, 2014 and 2015. McIlroy was also the FedEx Cup champion for a third time, having also lifted that trophy in 2016 and 2019. This was the first time he had held both at the same time and he joined Henrik Stenson in 2013 as the only players to have achieved that. Along with all that, McIlroy was back as the world number one.

"It's an amazing achievement, an achievement I haven't been able to accomplish before," McIlroy said. "I've been able to win this Tour's Rankings and finish the year as world number one. But to do it in America as well, yeah, it's very cool. I keep saying that I've been a pro now for over 15 years, and to figure out ways to try to accomplish new things, that's what keeps me coming back. There are certain things that I can improve on, and the majors, that's the one thing that I haven't achieved the last few years that I would love to achieve again. I feel like I'm healthy. I'm 33 and I feel like my body is in as good shape as it's ever been, and hopefully I'll keep on moving on."

McIlroy was chased all the way to the European number one spot by Ryan Fox, hoping to be the first player from New Zealand to win the Vardon Trophy. Fox was not as consistent as McIlroy, that would be difficult, but week-to-week, it seemed he was the player all the others had to beat. He won twice, had four runner-up finishes and four other top 10s. Fox had only won once on tour previously but started the year nicely with victory at the Ras al Khaimah Classic, had a string of near misses in the summer, then claimed an emotional win at the Alfred Dunhill Links Championship, where he paid tribute to the late Shane Warne, a friend and previous amateur partner in the event. Finishing second to Tommy Fleetwood at the Nedbank Golf Challenge gave Fox the chance to overtake McIlroy in the season-ender at Jumeirah Golf Estates, but he finished 19th and the Northern Irishman held on.

Fox did win the Seve Ballesteros Award as the player of the year as voted by his peers. He had long since ticked off his goals for the year, finishing inside the top 30 in the world, let alone top 50 that get invited to the Masters, where he will make his debut in 2023. "That's one I've been wanting for a long time, since before I turned pro," said the 35-year-old Kiwi. "I guess a couple of years ago, I probably thought I was getting a bit old and it was going to be a little bit too hard. But to get it done this year is amazing and I have a few mates who are looking forward to a trip to Augusta, that's for sure.

"The big goal at the start of the year was to get a win and to get in that top 50, and I knocked those off pretty quickly this year. Probably felt like a year I may have let a couple of other chances to win slip. But it's pretty hard to win out here and to get a couple is pretty cool. It's just a great experience to be in contention all the time. I started to feel a lot more comfortable in that position than I had in previous years, so hopefully I can build on it a little bit more for next year."

Jon Rahm finished third on the points list after two late wins. At each of the Acciona Open de Espana and the DP World Tour Championship the Spaniard won for the third time in four attempts. Rahm had not played in the Dubai finale for the previous two years and it was his fifth Rolex Series title. The other Rolex Series events were won by Thomas Pieters in Abu Dhabi and Viktor Hovland at the Dubai Desert Classic at the start of the year, Xander Schauffele at the Genesis Scottish Open and Shane Lowry at the BMW PGA Championship.

Although Wentworth fell silent on the Friday as a mark of respect following the death of HM Queen Elizabeth II, there was a cacophonous climax when Rahm eagled the 18th, Lowry birdied it and McIlroy's eagle try to tie stopped on the edge of the hole. It was Lowry's first win since the 2019 Open. There was a new major winner to celebrate, too, with Matt Fitzpatrick taking over Rahm's crown as US Open champion with a one-stroke victory over Will Zalatoris and Scottie Scheffler at The Country

Club at Brookline, where he had won the US Amateur nine years earlier. The man from Sheffield showed his steel by hitting a superb fairway bunker shot on the 72nd hole and left his veteran caddie Billy Foster in tears after finally guiding a player to a major title. "Something I've learnt massively this year is to be more patient," Fitzpatrick reflected. "I wouldn't necessarily say I'm the best at it. I've got so much better, probably since being told off by Billy in April. So I think that's been a big thing that's come on for me is just being patient and knowing that I'm playing some good golf."

Perhaps the most historic moment of the season, however, arrived when Linn Grant became the first woman to win on the DP World Tour. Grant won the Volvo Car Scandinavian Mixed in the second year of the event with equal numbers of men and women, albeit playing from different tees, competing for one title and the same prize money. Swedish legends Stenson and Annika Sorenstam hosted the tournament and Stenson was among those trying to chase down the number one player on the Ladies European Tour. Grant started the final round with a two-shot lead and scored 64 to win by nine from Stenson and Marc Warren, with the next female player 14 shots back. The local Swedish crowd loved it.

As well as Fox and Rahm, six other players won twice during the year, including Scottie Scheffler at the WGC Dell Match Play and the Masters, and Cameron Smith at The 150th Open and the Fortinet Australian PGA. Thriston Lawrence, who won the Joburg Open late in 2021, also claimed the Omega European Masters and became the first South African to win the Sir Henry Cotton Rookie of the Year award. Then, early in the 2022-23 season, Lawrence returned home to win his national championship at the Investec South African Open. Poland's Adrian Meronk added to his list of "firsts" when he became the first from his country to win on the DP World Tour at the Horizon Irish Open, and late in the year he added the ISPS Handa Australian Open title. Scotland's Ewen Ferguson, another consistent contender, made his breakthrough with wins at the Commercial Bank Qatar Masters and the ISPS Handa World Invitational. Spain's Pablo Larrazabal also showed the global nature of the DP World Tour by winning the MyGolfLife Open in South Africa and then on home soil for the first time at the ISPS Handa Championship.

It was at the Catalunya Championship in April that Antonio Garrido hit an honorary opening tee shot to commemorate his victory in the 1972 Open de Espana and mark the 50th anniversary of the founding of the modern European Tour. "We've had one of the greatest years we have ever had," said chief executive Keith Pelley. Among recent changes, the Scottish Open was co-sanctioned with the PGA Tour for the first time which meant 14 of the top 15 players in the world teed up. There were also co-sanctioned events in America at the Barbasol Championship and the Barracuda Championship. In addition, the top-10 finishers on the 2023 DP World Tour Rankings would earn PGA Tour cards, if not already members, while the alliance allowed Pelley to state that purses were due to increase over the next five years, members would be guaranteed $150,000 from a new players' assurance programme, and the schedule evolve, with 2023 as a "transition year". "With the major changes happening in 2024, we will play less events in a smaller timescale for more purses," he said. "I think the relationship with the PGA Tour and the opportunities are really endless."

Pelley, along with the PGA Tour, also worked on a number of alliances from other tours, including the Sunshine Tour, the PGA Tour of Australasia and the Japan Tour among others, some building on long-standing relationships and others new. The fallout from the establishment of the LIV Golf Invitational Series included Europe replacing Stenson with Luke Donald as Ryder Cup captain for the 2023 match in Rome. Players who featured in LIV Golf events were initially handed a short suspension and were subject to an escalating series of fines, but a temporary injunction allowed those players to continue playing on the DP World Tour, with Adrian Otaegui winning the Andalucia Masters and Smith the Aussie PGA. A full arbitration hearing was due to be held early in 2023, when the players' eligibility for the Ryder Cup, being played in Italy for the first time and a highlight of the 2023 season, would become clearer.

2022 SCHEDULE		
Abu Dhabi HSBC Championship	**Thomas Pieters**	
Slync.io Dubai Desert Classic	**Viktor Hovland**	
Ras al Khaimah Championship	**Nicolai Hojgaard**	
Ras al Khaimah Classic	**Ryan Fox**	
Magical Kenya Open	**Ashun Wu**	
MyGolfLife Open	**Pablo Larrazabal**	*See chapter 16*
Steyn City Championship	**Shaun Norris**	*See chapter 16*
WGC Dell Technologies Match Play	**Scottie Scheffler (1,3)**	*See chapter 10*
Commercial Bank Qatar Masters	**Ewen Ferguson**	
Masters Tournament	**Scottie Scheffler (2,4)**	*See chapter 2*
ISPS Handa Championship Spain	**Pablo Larrazabal (2)**	
Catalunya Championship	**Adri Arnaus**	
Betfred British Masters	**Thorbjorn Olesen**	
Soudal Open	**Sam Horsfield**	
PGA Championship	**Justin Thomas**	*See chapter 3*
Dutch Open	**Victor Perez**	
Porsche European Open	**Kalle Samooja**	
Volvo Car Scandinavian Mixed	**Linn Grant (1,5)**	*See chapter 23*
US Open	**Matt Fitzpatrick**	*See chapter 5*
BMW International Open	**Haotong Li**	
Horizon Irish Open	**Adrian Meronk**	
Genesis Scottish Open	**Xander Schauffele (1,3)**	
Barbasol Championship	**Trey Mullinax**	*See chapter 10*
The 150th Open	**Cameron Smith (1,3)**	*See chapter 7*
Barracuda Championship	**Chez Reavie**	*See chapter 10*
Cazoo Classic	**Richie Ramsay**	
Hero Open	**Sean Crocker**	
Cazoo Open	**Callum Shinkwin**	
ISPS Handa World Invitational	**Ewen Ferguson (2)**	
D+D Real Czech Masters	**Maximilian Kieffer**	
Omega European Masters	**Thriston Lawrence**	
Made in HimmerLand	**Oliver Wilson**	
BMW PGA Championship	**Shane Lowry**	
DS Automobiles Italian Open	**Robert MacIntyre**	
Cazoo Open de France	**Guido Migliozzi**	
Alfred Dunhill Links Championship	**Ryan Fox (2)**	
Acciona Open de Espana	**Jon Rahm (1,2)**	
Estrella Damm Andalucia Masters	**Adrian Otaegui**	
Mallorca Golf Open	**Yannik Paul**	
Portugal Masters	**Jordan Smith**	
Nedbank Golf Challenge	**Tommy Fleetwood**	
DP World Tour Championship	**Jon Rahm (2,3)**	
Fortinet Australian PGA Championship	**Cameron Smith (2,5)**	*See chapter 19*
Joburg Open	**Dan Bradbury**	*See chapter 16*
ISPS Handa Australian Open	**Adrian Meronk (2)**	*See chapter 19*
Investec South African Open	**Thriston Lawrence (2)**	*See chapter 16*
Alfred Dunhill Championship	**Ockie Strydom**	*See chapter 16*
AfrAsia Bank Mauritius Open	**Antoine Rozner**	*See chapter 16*

Abu Dhabi HSBC Championship

A new venue for the Abu Dhabi HSBC Championship threw up new challenges for the first Rolex Series event of the DP World Tour era. After many years at Abu Dhabi Golf Club, the tournament moved to Yas Links, a waterfront layout next to the Yas Marina motor racing circuit. Once Thomas Pieters got his nose in front during the final round, no one was able to overtake the Belgian as he won by a stroke from Rafa Cabrera Bello and Shubhankar Sharma.

Four days before his 30th birthday, this was the biggest win of Pieters's career, his sixth DP World Tour title and his second in three starts dating back to the Portugal Masters late in 2021. "I kind of disappeared for a couple years I guess," Pieters said. "Now I'm happy to be back." Specifically, back in the world's top 50. "As a golfer, the top 50 is your striving point, and when I jumped out maybe three years ago, I took it badly, but I'm happy to be back again. I feel like I've turned the corner. I'm really in control of my ball flight and my putting has improved massively. That's the thing that really kept me going on the weekend."

It was a particularly impressive display of controlled golf on the exposed course where the wind can cause havoc. Scott Jamieson opened with a new course record of nine-under-par 63 and a 74 the next afternoon, in the midst of a gale, kept the Scot at the top of the leaderboard, tying with James Morrison. Jamieson birdied the 18th on Saturday to start the final round one ahead of Pieters and Shane Lowry, the 2019 champion. Jamieson bogeyed four of his first five holes on Sunday as both he and Lowry scored 77s.

Pieters, after scores of 65-74-67, produced a steady round of 72. He birdied the eighth to go three ahead and dropped his only shot at the 11th as he finished on 10-under 278. Cabrera Bello and Sharma scored 70 and 71 respectively to move into a share of second, one ahead of Viktor Hovland and Victor Dubuisson. Rory McIlroy holed his second shot at the ninth as he made a Sunday charge but fell back to 12th, while defending champion Tyrrell Hatton tied for sixth despite a double bogey at the 18th on Friday and a quadruple-bogey nine at the same hole on Saturday. He left no one in any doubt of his displeasure at the design of the finishing hole.

Yas Links, Abu Dhabi, United Arab Emirates — January 20-23
Par 72 (36-36); 7,425 yards — Purse: $8,000,000

1	**Thomas Pieters**	65	74	67	72	278	€1,200,291
2	**Rafa Cabrera Bello**	69	71	69	70	279	610,736
	Shubhankar Sharma	70	71	67	71	279	610,736
4	Victor Dubuisson	70	72	69	69	280	326,197
	Viktor Hovland	64	74	70	72	280	326,197
6	Tyrrell Hatton	66	77	71	67	281	198,401
	James Morrison	66	71	72	72	281	198,401
	Ian Poulter	66	72	71	72	281	198,401
	Jeff Winther	71	69	71	70	281	198,401
10	Scott Jamieson	63	74	68	77	282	135,562
	Adam Scott	70	72	68	72	282	135,562
12	Sam Horsfield	74	70	68	71	283	102,554
	Romain Langasque	72	73	67	71	283	102,554
	Shane Lowry	67	72	67	77	283	102,554
	Rory McIlroy	72	75	67	69	283	102,554
	Jordan Smith	71	72	71	69	283	102,554
	Erik van Rooyen	69	71	73	70	283	102,554
	Bernd Wiesberger	69	77	67	70	283	102,554
	Ashun Wu	69	77	70	67	283	102,554
20	Adri Arnaus	71	76	72	65	284	79,925
	Alexander Bjork	68	71	72	73	284	79,925
	Padraig Harrington	73	71	68	72	284	79,925
	Rasmus Hojgaard	70	72	73	69	284	79,925
	Lee Westwood	71	74	70	69	284	79,925
25	Julien Brun	69	69	77	70	285	63,898
	Dean Burmester	71	75	70	69	285	63,898
	Justin Harding	69	72	70	74	285	63,898
	Takumi Kanaya	66	73	75	71	285	63,898
	Mikko Korhonen	69	77	68	71	285	63,898
	Pablo Larrazábal	70	71	72	72	285	63,898
	Wade Ormsby	73	72	69	71	285	63,898
	Andrea Pavan	69	72	69	75	285	63,898
	Richie Ramsay	71	76	68	70	285	63,898
	Callum Shinkwin	71	75	72	67	285	63,898
35	Daniel Gavins	69	74	70	73	286	49,600
	Min Woo Lee	71	76	72	67	286	49,600
	Robert Rock	68	75	68	75	286	49,600
	Dale Whitnell	68	74	72	72	286	49,600
39	Ewen Ferguson	71	74	73	69	287	44,481
	Charl Schwartzel	67	76	68	76	287	44,481
	Henrik Stenson	72	75	75	65	287	44,481
42	Nacho Elvira	69	74	75	70	288	38,127
	Marcus Helligkilde	69	75	72	72	288	38,127
	Soren Kjeldsen	70	74	70	74	288	38,127
	Thorbjorn Olesen	71	74	74	69	288	38,127
	Jack Singh Brar	70	76	72	70	288	38,127
	Matthew Southgate	70	73	71	74	288	38,127
48	Kristoffer Broberg	69	74	69	77	289	30,360
	Jorge Campillo	74	72	71	72	289	30,360
	Jamie Donaldson	74	69	70	76	289	30,360
	Tommy Fleetwood	68	76	74	71	289	30,360
	Justin Walters	74	71	71	73	289	30,360
53	Thomas Detry	67	76	72	75	290	24,147
	Ricardo Gouveia	73	72	70	75	290	24,147

	David Horsey	70 75 73 72	290	24,147			
	Daan Huizing	71 76 72 71	290	24,147			
	Connor Syme	70 77 74 69	290	24,147			
58	Thomas Bjorn	70 72 73 76	291	21,535			
	Josh Hill (A)	71 76 69 75	291				
	Victor Perez	66 74 73 78	291	21,535			
61	Ryan Fox	72 74 70 76	292	20,476			
62	Joachim B Hansen	70 77 69 77	293	19,063			
	Matthew Jordan	70 74 74 75	293	19,063			
	Collin Morikawa	73 74 71 75	293	19,063			
65	Masahiro Kawamura	71 76 75 72	294	16,945			
	Maximilian Kieffer	75 72 74 73	294	16,945			
	David Law	69 75 72 78	294	16,945			
68	Santiago Tarrio	70 75 75 75	295	14,827			
	Daniel van Tonder	71 75 72 77	295	14,827			
	Matt Wallace	72 75 72 76	295	14,827			
71	Fabrizio Zanotti	71 76 70 79	296	13,415			
72	Chris Paisley	73 74 77 73	297	10,588			
	Brandon Stone	74 72 74 77	297	10,588			
	Sami Valimaki	69 75 76 77	297	10,588			
75	Marcus Kinhult	68 78 74 79	299	10,582			
	Adrian Meronk	69 73 70	WD	10,579			

Slync.io Dubai Desert Classic

All you need to know about Viktor Hovland is what he did in the moments immediately after he sealed a playoff victory over Richard Bland. The 24-year-old Norwegian saw a television interviewer coming towards him, realised it was the coach of the opponent he had just vanquished and apologised. "No need to apologise," Tim Barter replied, "you played quite beautifully." Winners' interviews do not often start that way but the new world number three is no ordinary golfer.

Hovland started the final round of the Slync.io Dubai Desert Classic six strokes behind Justin Harding and produced a brilliant finish before beating a man twice his age with a birdie four in the playoff. "This is pretty wild," Hovland said. "I didn't really think this was possible going in today. I knew I had to shoot a really low number but a lot of things had to go my way and I'm thankful that they did."

South African Harding led the way with 65-68-71 on an Emirates course that had seen all 18 greens relaid in the previous year. Hovland was in touch after going 68-69, but got ragged with a 73 on Saturday. Rory McIlroy, who was hoping to join Ernie Els as a three-time winner of the Dallah trophy, appeared well placed with birdies at the sixth and seventh holes but found the water at the 18th and finished third. Harding found bunker trouble at the 11th, took a triple-bogey six and tied for fourth.

Hovland picked up three shots going out but three-putted the 15th. "I was fuming after that and thought that was it," he said. It wasn't. He holed from 35 feet for a birdie at the 16th, drove the green at the 17th and holed from 33 feet for an eagle and then made a four at the last for a 66 and a 12-under-par total of 276.

Bland tied for the lead with a 68, having holed a bunker shot at the 11th for his third birdie in a row before birdieing the last two. The 48-year-old Englishman, who won his first title in a playoff at the 2021 British Masters, could not get up and down to match Hovland's two-putt four in the playoff. After his second tour title, first Rolex Series title and third win worldwide in five starts, Hovland said: "I'm pumped right now. It's a little bit surreal."

Emirates Golf Club (Majlis), Dubai, United Arab Emirates — January 27-30
Par 72 (35-37); 7,428 yards — Purse: $8,000,000

1	**Viktor Hovland**	68 69 73 66	276	€1,219,757
2	**Richard Bland**	69 68 71 68	276	789,254
	Hovland won playoff at first extra hole			
3	**Rory McIlroy**	71 66 69 71	277	452,028
4	Justin Harding	65 68 71 76	280	261,745
	Tyrrell Hatton	69 66 73 72	280	261,745
	Sam Horsfield	69 69 75 67	280	261,745
	Adrian Meronk	69 68 71 72	280	261,745
	Erik van Rooyen	69 67 71 73	280	261,745
9	Padraig Harrington	70 70 69 72	281	145,414
	Adam Scott	69 72 71 69	281	145,414
	Jordan Smith	72 69 69 71	281	145,414
12	Marcus Armitage	70 68 72 72	282	108,702
	Paul Casey	70 68 70 74	282	108,702
	Tommy Fleetwood	67 71 69 75	282	108,702
	Sergio Garcia	67 74 69 72	282	108,702
	Thomas Pieters	70 69 76 67	282	108,702
	Kalle Samooja	68 74 69 71	282	108,702
18	Lucas Herbert	70 73 70 70	283	85,144
	Joakim Lagergren	69 74 70 70	283	85,144
	Romain Langasque	70 70 72 71	283	85,144
	Collin Morikawa	68 73 71 71	283	85,144
	Andrea Pavan	67 73 73 70	283	85,144
	Fabrizio Zanotti	66 70 72 75	283	85,144
24	Shane Lowry	71 74 68 71	284	75,697
	Bernd Wiesberger	71 68 69 76	284	75,697
26	Ryan Fox	72 73 69 71	285	69,239
	Julien Guerrier	73 72 70 70	285	69,239
	Edoardo Molinari	70 72 71 72	285	69,239
	Brandon Stone	68 72 73 72	285	69,239
30	Nino Bertasio	70 70 76 70	286	62,782
	Ashun Wu	75 70 69 72	286	62,782

32	Haotong Li	73	70	73	71	287	57,400
	Richie Ramsay	74	69	72	72	287	57,400
	Lee Westwood	69	69	71	78	287	57,400
35	Nacho Elvira	70	74	70	74	288	47,445
	Scott Jamieson	69	71	73	75	288	47,445
	Pablo Larrazabal	67	75	76	70	288	47,445
	Thorbjorn Olesen	73	71	74	70	288	47,445
	Matti Schmid	73	68	69	78	288	47,445
	Johannes Veerman	71	74	72	71	288	47,445
	Matt Wallace	69	73	69	77	288	47,445
	Justin Walters	69	72	77	70	288	47,445
43	Thomas Bjorn	75	70	73	71	289	38,745
	Grant Forrest	70	74	72	73	289	38,745
	Soren Kjeldsen	69	73	74	73	289	38,745
	Daniel van Tonder	73	71	72	73	289	38,745
47	Rafa Cabrera Bello	72	73	69	76	290	30,135
	George Coetzee	70	72	71	77	290	30,135
	Ross Fisher	71	72	74	73	290	30,135
	Garrick Higgo	70	73	78	69	290	30,135
	Rasmus Hojgaard	73	71	70	76	290	30,135
	Adrian Otaegui	71	74	72	73	290	30,135
	Antoine Rozner	71	73	72	74	290	30,135
	Andy Sullivan	72	73	70	75	290	30,135
55	Dean Burmester	71	74	69	77	291	23,319
	Jorge Campillo	72	73	69	77	291	23,319
	Daniel Gavins	70	75	74	72	291	23,319
	Josh Hill (A)	70	74	69	78	291	
	David Law	70	74	77	70	291	23,319
60	Alexander Bjork	75	69	72	76	292	19,731
	John Catlin	72	69	76	75	292	19,731
	Jazz Janewattananond	71	72	76	73	292	19,731
	Victor Perez	73	72	73	74	292	19,731
	Henrik Stenson	73	72	73	74	292	19,731
	Nicolai von Dellingshausen	77	66	74	75	292	19,731
66	Maverick Antcliff	69	75	71	78	293	16,144
	Kiradech Aphibarnrat	68	72	76	77	293	16,144
	Ricardo Gouveia	71	72	75	75	293	16,144
	Joachim B Hansen	65	72	81	75	293	16,144
70	Sebastian Garcia Rodriguez	68	76	74	76	294	12,915
	Thongchai Jaidee	67	73	81	73	294	12,915
	Matthew Jordan	70	73	73	78	294	12,915
73	Laurie Canter	75	69	77	74	295	10,758
	Sebastian Soderberg	70	74	77	74	295	10,758
75	Shubhankar Sharma	72	72	76	76	296	10,754
76	David Drysdale	74	70	76	77	297	10,749
	Charl Schwartzel	74	69	76	78	297	10,749

Ras al Khaimah Championship

Asked what the Hojgaard brothers would like to take from the game of their twin, Rasmus suggested Nicolai's massive length, and Nicolai noted Rasmus's ability to keep making forward progress under pressure. Nicolai may be learning fast if the final round of the Ras al Khaimah Championship is any guide.

The 20-year-old Dane certainly put his big hitting to good effect on the Al Hamra course, finishing on a 24-under-par total of 264 with rounds of 67-65-64-68. Five birdies in the last six holes on Saturday put him into the lead by three strokes. He quickly went five clear when he hit an iron from a sandy waste area at the third to a few inches from the hole, making an eagle that was almost an albatross.

But then Hojgaard started going backwards. A wayward drive at the ninth cost a double bogey and in trying to cut off too much of the lake at the 12th, he cleared the water but found an unplayable lie in the penalty area. With a bogey there he suddenly fell two behind Jordan Smith. Winner of a Challenge Tour event on the same course in 2016, Smith had gone out in four under and then made a hat-trick of birdies from the 12th. He left the 14th green at 21 under, while Hojgaard was back to 19 under and in need of his twin's forward propulsion.

He got it with a birdie at the 13th, as Smith was bogeying the short 15th and settling for a 66, and then Hojgaard made an eagle at the 14th with a five-iron, again from a sandy area, to eight feet. Birdies at the last two holes gave him a four-shot win over Smith, with no one else closer than seven strokes. It was Hojgaard's second win after he took the Italian Open in 2021, and the twins had combined for five titles before their 21st birthdays.

"It's very sweet," Hojgaard said. "It's been such a tough grind today. Got off to a good start and then I struggled quite a bit. I had to dig deep. I was thinking that I was throwing the tournament away. When I saw on the green at 13 that Jordan had made a run, I stepped up with a clutch finish so I'm really happy."

Al Hamra Golf Club, Ras Al Khaimah, United Arab Emirates — February 3-6
Par 72 (36-36); 7,325 yards — Purse: $2,000,000

1	**Nicolai Hojgaard**	67	65	64	68	264	€296,729
2	**Jordan Smith**	71	64	67	66	268	192,001
3	**Haotong Li**	74	66	68	63	271	83,084
	Lukas Nemecz	70	66	69	66	271	83,084
	Adrian Otaegui	71	63	70	67	271	83,084
	Matthieu Pavon	68	69	68	66	271	83,084
7	David Law	66	64	69	73	272	48,000
	Tapio Pulkkanen	68	68	64	72	272	48,000
9	Oliver Bekker	70	65	66	72	273	35,375
	Thomas Detry	66	69	67	71	273	35,375

	Shaun Norris	68	68	68	69	273	35,375
12	Johannes Veerman	66	70	66	72	274	30,022
13	Julien Brun	71	66	71	67	275	25,728
	Julien Guerrier	71	69	66	69	275	25,728
	Matthew Jordan	69	69	68	69	275	25,728
	Robert MacIntyre	69	67	66	73	275	25,728
	Daniel van Tonder	73	68	69	65	275	25,728
18	Ross Fisher	70	67	72	67	276	21,702
	Hurly Long	68	71	73	64	276	21,702
	Matthew Southgate	67	72	67	70	276	21,702
21	David Horsey	71	70	67	69	277	18,938
	Craig Howie	69	69	69	70	277	18,938
	Scott Jamieson	65	73	71	68	277	18,938
	Francesco Laporta	70	67	70	70	277	18,938
	Callum Shinkwin	71	66	70	70	277	18,938
	Marcel Siem	71	67	68	71	277	18,938
27	Maverick Antcliff	69	70	69	70	278	15,273
	George Coetzee	68	69	70	71	278	15,273
	Alfredo Garcia-Heredia	69	68	69	72	278	15,273
	Padraig Harrington	69	70	72	67	278	15,273
	Masahiro Kawamura	68	72	68	70	278	15,273
	Edoardo Molinari	72	66	68	72	278	15,273
	Connor Syme	71	67	72	68	278	15,273
	Oliver Wilson	72	68	67	71	278	15,273
35	Marcus Armitage	69	67	73	70	279	11,720
	Wil Besseling	73	68	72	66	279	11,720
	Benjamin Hebert	69	71	71	68	279	11,720
	Richard Mansell	71	70	70	68	279	11,720
	Brandon Stone	66	69	76	68	279	11,720
	Danny Willett	69	71	70	69	279	11,720
	Fabrizio Zanotti	71	70	67	71	279	11,720
42	Kristoffer Broberg	73	68	68	71	280	9,600
	Steven Brown	71	67	72	70	280	9,600
	Joachim B Hansen	69	68	69	74	280	9,600
	Sebastian Heisele	65	71	73	71	280	9,600
	Rasmus Hojgaard	69	68	68	75	280	9,600
47	Ricardo Santos	72	69	72	68	281	8,553
48	Nacho Elvira	69	71	66	76	282	7,505
	Lorenzo Gagli	72	69	73	68	282	7,505
	Joakim Lagergren	70	71	72	69	282	7,505
	Richard McEvoy	74	66	69	73	282	7,505
	James Morrison	68	73	69	72	282	7,505
53	Frederic Lacroix	73	66	71	73	283	6,065
	Thriston Lawrence	69	72	75	67	283	6,065
	Yannik Paul	71	69	71	72	283	6,065
	Jason Scrivener	73	68	71	71	283	6,065
57	John Catlin	70	67	73	74	284	5,062
	Jamie Donaldson	72	69	73	70	284	5,062
	Zander Lombard	72	67	74	71	284	5,062
	Adrian Meronk	70	71	74	69	284	5,062
	Andrea Pavan	72	69	69	74	284	5,062
	Matti Schmid	73	67	72	72	284	5,062
	Jeff Winther	69	69	75	71	284	5,062
64	Grant Forrest	69	72	68	76	285	4,189
	Niklas Norgaard Moller	71	67	68	79	285	4,189
	Andrew Wilson	73	67	73	72	285	4,189
67	Ashley Chesters	74	67	71	74	286	3,665
	Guido Migliozzi	71	70	73	72	286	3,665
	Richard Sterne	69	72	71	74	286	3,665
70	Soren Kjeldsen	74	67	74	72	287	2,967
	Sami Valimaki	71	69	74	73	287	2,967
72	Alexander Levy	69	72	73	76	290	2,615

Ras al Khaimah Classic

The way Ryan Fox paced around the greens at Al Hamra, and especially at the 18th as he waited to putt out for his second victory on the DP World Tour, it was hard to see him settling into a 10-day hotel quarantine on his return home to New Zealand. But the Kiwi, who last won at the World Super 6 in Perth in 2019, is used to it, travelling from a country with strict Covid protocols and also having to stay away for long periods, during which he missed his 14-month-old daughter taking her first steps. A five-stroke victory at the Ras al Khaimah Classic made it all worthwhile.

"I've got nervous energy, my old man is the same — he paces around on the phone — and I think I probably walked 25 km today with how much I paced around the greens. That's just me and I was definitely thinking about the family coming down the last couple of holes. I'm a bit disappointed I missed Isabel walking for the first time." Of course, Fox's "old man" is rugby legend Grant Fox, a World Cup winner in 1987.

Fox had missed the cut on the same course the previous week as he suffered back trouble and the 35-year-old thanked the physiotherapists who got him into shape for a wire-to-wire win a few days later. He opened with a nine-under-par 63, thanks to 10 birdies and one bogey, to lead by two. He went three ahead with a 69 on Friday, when Oliver Bekker lowered the course record to 62, and then birdied his first four holes on Saturday on the way to a 65 and a six-shot advantage.

"I didn't sleep too well on a six-shot lead," Fox admitted. "I had that awful feeling in the pit of my stomach all day." He was still level par for the day, his lead was down to two strokes, when he holed a putt from 44 feet at 12 and at the next he got up and down from a bunker for two crucial birdies. He also birdied the last for a 69 and a 22-under-par total of 266. Ross Fisher grabbed second place with a 66, while Hurly Long scored 64 and Zander Lombard a 65 as they tied for third with Pablo Larrazabal, who put pressure on the leader but played the last seven holes in one over for a 69.

Al Hamra Golf Club, Ras Al Khaimah, United Arab Emirates
Par 72 (36-36); 7,325 yards

February 3-6
Purse: $2,000,000

1	**Ryan Fox**	63	69	65	69	266	€298,948
2	**Ross Fisher**	70	69	66	66	271	193,437
3	**Pablo Larrazabal**	68	67	68	69	272	91,091
	Zander Lombard	72	63	72	65	272	91,091
	Hurly Long	67	70	71	64	272	91,091
6	Masahiro Kawamura	68	68	68	69	273	52,755
	Adrian Meronk	71	68	64	70	273	52,755
	Connor Syme	69	67	69	68	273	52,755
9	Marcus Armitage	67	72	66	69	274	28,296
	Adri Arnaus	70	67	66	71	274	28,296
	Oliver Bekker	73	62	72	67	274	28,296
	George Coetzee	70	68	67	69	274	28,296
	Julien Guerrier	68	69	70	67	274	28,296
	Justin Harding	68	67	73	66	274	28,296
	Scott Jamieson	72	66	65	71	274	28,296
	Maximilian Kieffer	68	68	71	67	274	28,296
	Robert MacIntyre	66	70	68	70	274	28,296
	Jason Scrivener	66	69	70	69	274	28,296
	Marcel Siem	71	69	64	70	274	28,296
20	Jazz Janewattananond	67	70	68	70	275	19,906
	Thriston Lawrence	72	68	67	68	275	19,906
	Tapio Pulkkanen	70	67	72	66	275	19,906
	Brandon Stone	67	73	69	66	275	19,906
	Daniel van Tonder	70	68	71	66	275	19,906
25	Laurie Canter	69	68	70	69	276	17,233
	Frederic Lacroix	73	67	66	70	276	17,233
	David Law	69	69	68	70	276	17,233
	Callum Shinkwin	72	69	68	67	276	17,233
	Sebastian Soderberg	66	71	69	70	276	17,233
30	Rasmus Hojgaard	69	68	70	70	277	15,123
	Craig Howie	67	72	70	68	277	15,123
	Matthieu Pavon	68	70	67	72	277	15,123
33	Shergo Al Kurdi	68	68	74	68	278	12,251
	Nino Bertasio	72	69	71	66	278	12,251
	Alexander Bjork	67	69	70	72	278	12,251
	Haotong Li	69	71	68	70	278	12,251
	Joost Luiten	66	72	70	70	278	12,251
	Wade Ormsby	69	68	72	69	278	12,251
	Yannik Paul	66	71	72	69	278	12,251
	Richie Ramsay	69	70	70	69	278	12,251
	Andrew Wilson	66	72	72	68	278	12,251
42	Wil Besseling	70	70	70	69	279	8,441
	Kristoffer Broberg	69	71	69	70	279	8,441
	Jorge Campillo	71	69	71	68	279	8,441
	Sebastian Heisele	70	71	73	65	279	8,441
	Espen Kofstad	71	68	71	69	279	8,441
	Mike Lorenzo-Vera	69	68	72	70	279	8,441
	Niklas Norgaard Moller	69	71	70	69	279	8,441
	Shaun Norris	67	72	70	70	279	8,441
	Adrian Otaegui	69	68	74	68	279	8,441
	Justin Walters	68	71	70	70	279	8,441
	Ashun Wu	70	71	70	68	279	8,441
	Fabrizio Zanotti	72	67	69	71	279	8,441
54	Richard Bland	66	71	71	72	280	5,891
	Thomas Detry	70	70	71	69	280	5,891
	Marcus Helligkilde	72	66	67	75	280	5,891
	Sami Valimaki	73	65	71	71	280	5,891
58	Maverick Antcliff	67	70	72	72	281	5,100
	Oliver Farr	67	72	69	73	281	5,100
	Francesco Laporta	66	69	74	72	281	5,100
	Hugo Leon	69	71	73	68	281	5,100
	Lukas Nemecz	69	69	70	73	281	5,100
63	David Drysdale	66	71	72	73	282	4,220
	Matthew Jordan	69	72	70	71	282	4,220
	Edoardo Molinari	71	67	73	71	282	4,220
	James Morrison	69	72	67	74	282	4,220
	Robert Rock	69	72	70	71	282	4,220
68	Marcus Kinhult	70	71	71	71	283	3,693
69	Rikard Karlberg	71	68	71	74	284	3,165
	Richard Sterne	69	72	71	72	284	3,165
	Darius van Driel	71	69	71	73	284	3,165
72	Gaganjeet Bhullar	70	67	74	74	285	2,632
	Joakim Lagergren	71	68	75	71	285	2,632
	Jordan Smith	72	69	74	70	285	2,632
75	Daan Huizing	71	70	74	72	287	2,626
76	Oliver Fisher	72	69	75	72	288	2,623

Magical Kenya Open

Ashun Wu became the first Chinese player to win four times on the DP World Tour when he came from four behind to win by four at the Magical Kenya Open. Wu claimed the Volvo China Open in 2015, then added victories in Austria in 2016 and the Netherlands in 2018. His wife and three-month-old baby were present to help celebrate his latest triumph, achieved with a final round of 65 at Muthaiga as the 36-year-old became the first Asian winner in the 55-year history of the tournament.

After rounds of 69 and 68, Wu hoped a pair of five-under rounds on the weekend would get him into contention. He was spot on for Saturday with a 66 and then continued his ever lower progression with seven birdies following an early bogey on Sunday. Wu started the final round in a share of second place, but was helped by the overnight leader Ewen Ferguson closing with a 76, nine strokes higher than the young Scot's previous worst for the week.

South African Thriston Lawrence, winner of the Joburg Open at the end of 2021, claimed the lead with an eagle and four birdies but bogeyed the 14th and stalled at 12 under par, sharing runner-up honours with Germany's Hurly Long, who also scored 66, and Canada's Aaron Cockerill (67).

Wu recovered his dropped shot at the second with a birdie at the fourth before a tournament-stealing run of four birdies in a row from the seventh. The highlight of the streak was a 35-foot triple-breaking putt at the ninth. He played a sublime bunker shot at the 14th to save par and then finished in style with birdies at the last two holes, with a 10-footer at the 17th and a sandy four at the last. He was one better than his weekend target at 16-under-par 268.

"It's a big celebration, I'm so happy with my family here," Wu said. "It was very tough today, I played very well. After two rounds I told myself if I can make five under every day on the weekend and finish 15 under, I think I'll have a chance. Today I was four shots behind and still playing to my plan. After 10 holes I had a good feeling and I told myself I'll keep playing and make a couple of birdies and it's fine."

Muthaiga Golf Club, Nairobi, Kenya — March 3-6
Par 71 (36-35); 7,228 yards — Purse: €1,750,000

1	**Ashun Wu**	69 68 66 65	268	€297,500			
2	**Aaron Cockerill**	70 68 67 67	272	130,083			
	Thriston Lawrence	69 66 71 66	272	130,083			
	Hurly Long	68 68 70 66	272	130,083			
5	David Horsey	69 70 65 69	273	74,200			
6	Daniel Gavins	64 73 70 67	274	56,875			
	Matthieu Pavon	69 68 68 69	274	56,875			
8	Adri Arnaus	69 69 71 66	275	36,050			
	Oliver Bekker	71 70 71 63	275	36,050			
	Ewen Ferguson	66 67 66 76	275	36,050			
	Marcus Kinhult	71 68 64 72	275	36,050			
	Stuart Manley	70 71 67 67	275	36,050			
13	Julien Brun	68 71 69 68	276	26,338			
	Jorge Campillo	70 69 65 72	276	26,338			
	Garrick Porteous	68 70 69 69	276	26,338			
	Shubhankar Sharma	65 67 75 69	276	26,338			
17	Marcus Armitage	69 73 67 68	277	20,572			
	Sebastian Garcia Rodriguez	70 68 66 73	277	20,572			
	Alfredo Garcia-Heredia	73 69 66 69	277	20,572			
	Angel Hidalgo	68 68 72 69	277	20,572			
	Espen Kofstad	69 70 68 70	277	20,572			
	Niklas Lemke	70 68 71 68	277	20,572			
	Lukas Nemecz	68 70 69 70	277	20,572			
	Max Schmitt	70 69 69 69	277	20,572			
	Lee Slattery	66 73 69 69	277	20,572			
26	Dean Burmester	67 69 76 66	278	15,838			
	Thomas Detry	71 68 66 73	278	15,838			
	Ricardo Santos	72 70 72 64	278	15,838			
	Richard Sterne	71 68 67 72	278	15,838			
	Jesper Svensson	70 66 71 71	278	15,838			
	Connor Syme	69 71 66 72	278	15,838			
	Santiago Tarrio	70 69 70 69	278	15,838			
	Johannes Veerman	65 73 72 68	278	15,838			
34	David Drysdale	70 71 69 69	279	12,338			
	Lorenzo Gagli	70 68 70 71	279	12,338			
	Niall Kearney	70 71 69 69	279	12,338			
	Adrian Otaegui	69 70 74 66	279	12,338			
	Antoine Rozner	69 72 70 68	279	12,338			
	Jayden Schaper	70 67 71 71	279	12,338			
40	Wil Besseling	67 73 72 68	280	10,850			
	Renato Paratore	68 71 73 68	280	10,850			
42	Hennie du Plessis	70 67 73 71	281	9,450			
	Justin Harding	68 70 72 71	281	9,450			
	Craig Howie	70 69 68 74	281	9,450			
	Masahiro Kawamura	67 66 72 76	281	9,450			
	Yannik Paul	74 68 68 71	281	9,450			
	Matti Schmid	69 71 64 77	281	9,450			
48	Oliver Farr	70 71 69 72	282	7,875			
	Scott Jamieson	69 73 64 76	282	7,875			
	David Law	68 70 75 69	282	7,875			
51	Nino Bertasio	69 72 69 73	283	6,067			
	Paul Dunne	70 72 71 70	283	6,067			
	Joachim B Hansen	71 69 69 74	283	6,067			
	Marcus Helligkilde	69 70 72 72	283	6,067			
	Frederic Lacroix	70 72 70 71	283	6,067			
	Francesco Laporta	68 73 71 71	283	6,067			
	Niklas Norgaard Moller	72 67 69 75	283	6,067			
	Adrien Saddier	75 67 70 71	283	6,067			
	Daniel van Tonder	68 69 75 71	283	6,067			
60	Jacques Kruyswijk	68 73 69 74	284	5,075			
61	Jens Dantorp	69 72 69 75	285	4,725			
	Matt Ford	70 72 73 70	285	4,725			
	Adrian Meronk	71 68 81 65	285	4,725			
64	Njoroge Kibugu (A)	70 66 73 77	286				
65	Jonathan Caldwell	76 66 72 73	287	3,938			
	Ashley Chesters	68 71 75 73	287	3,938			
	Ben Evans	71 71 75 70	287	3,938			
	Alfie Plant	70 68 72 77	287	3,938			
	Henric Sturehed	72 70 73 72	287	3,938			
	Blake Windred	71 68 74 74	287	3,938			
71	Matthew Jordan	71 70 78 69	288	2,857			
	Chris Paisley	69 70 78 71	288	2,857			
	Bernd Ritthammer	72 67 75 74	288	2,857			
74	Sebastian Heisele	72 69 73 76	290	2,618			
	Cormac Sharvin	70 72 78 70	290	2,618			

Commercial Bank Qatar Masters

With the Commercial Bank Qatar Masters returning to its original home at Doha Golf Club, there was a familiar feeling as the windswept layout produced its third Scottish winner. Andrew Coltart won the inaugural title in 1998 and Paul Lawrie won the following year prior to claiming The Open at Carnoustie. Lawrie took the Qatar title again in 2012 and 10 years later it was Ewen Ferguson's turn. The 25-year-old former Walker Cup player claimed his first victory with a stunning finish to win by one stroke from American Chase Hanna.

Ferguson started three behind the overnight leaders Adrian Meronk and Matthew Jordan, but the wind played havoc again and it was Ferguson, despite an early double bogey, who suddenly jumped into pole position. Ferguson had spent his time pre-round practising his chipping on instruction from his coach Jamie Gough. That paid off when he chipped in for an eagle at the short par-four 16th hole. Then at the par-five 18th, Ferguson chipped from a tricky spot to 15 feet and rolled in the putt for what turned out to be an unassailable lead.

Rounds of 67-71-73-70 gave Ferguson a seven-under-par total of 281, while Hanna, playing alongside the Scot, closed with a 71. Poland's Meronk parred the last four holes for a 75 to tie for third with Marcus Kinhult (71), while Jordan finished a further shot back after a 76.

Ferguson, who was a runner-up three times on the Challenge Tour in 2021, let a 54-hole lead slip with a closing 76 at the Magical Kenya Open earlier in the month. "I can't believe it," Ferguson said. "It's years and years of hard work. My mum, dad, brother and sister and my whole family have given everything for me to have this moment and it's just an absolute dream come true.

"It was one of those days when you just kept fighting to the end. I'd been in contention a bit over the last couple of years and not managed to win, to the point where I thought I don't know if I'll ever manage to win. Just to get over the line is an absolute dream come true."

Doha Golf Club, Doha, Qatar — March 24-27
Par 72 (36-36); 7,466 yards — Purse: $2,000,000

1	**Ewen Ferguson**	67	71	73	70	281	€308,344
2	**Chase Hanna**	70	66	75	71	282	199,517
3	**Marcus Kinhult**	74	65	73	71	283	102,479
	Adrian Meronk	66	70	72	75	283	102,479
5	Marcus Armitage	71	73	71	69	284	50,061
	Gavin Green	77	67	69	71	284	50,061
	Justin Harding	76	68	70	70	284	50,061
	Matthew Jordan	69	69	70	76	284	50,061
	Pablo Larrazabal	64	71	75	74	284	50,061
	Adrian Otaegui	70	70	70	74	284	50,061
	Kalle Samooja	74	69	66	75	284	50,061
12	Laurie Canter	68	73	73	71	285	25,836
	Marcus Helligkilde	66	75	75	69	285	25,836
	Craig Howie	70	74	70	71	285	25,836
	Wilco Nienaber	68	68	74	75	285	25,836
	Thorbjorn Olesen	71	69	76	69	285	25,836
	Wade Ormsby	68	72	73	72	285	25,836
	Justin Walters	74	68	71	72	285	25,836
	Paul Waring	69	71	73	72	285	25,836
	Oliver Wilson	71	70	71	73	285	25,836
21	Nino Bertasio	69	75	71	71	286	19,680
	Wil Besseling	71	71	70	74	286	19,680
	Aaron Cockerill	72	72	69	73	286	19,680
	Romain Langasque	66	71	75	74	286	19,680
	Thriston Lawrence	70	69	76	71	286	19,680
	Nicolai von Dellingshausen	76	68	68	74	286	19,680
27	Louis de Jager	73	70	73	71	287	15,871
	Hennie du Plessis	72	70	73	72	287	15,871
	Jacques Kruyswijk	71	71	75	70	287	15,871
	Ross McGowan	69	71	73	74	287	15,871
	Lukas Nemecz	71	67	74	75	287	15,871
	Matthieu Pavon	72	71	71	73	287	15,871
	Robert Rock	67	76	71	73	287	15,871
	Jason Scrivener	72	72	69	74	287	15,871
35	Julien Brun	70	69	78	71	288	12,551
	George Coetzee	71	72	72	73	288	12,551
	Zander Lombard	68	72	72	76	288	12,551
	Andrea Pavan	69	73	71	75	288	12,551
	Bernd Ritthammer	71	70	72	75	288	12,551
40	Dean Burmester	70	72	76	71	289	9,976
	Jonathan Caldwell	71	70	71	77	289	9,976
	David Drysdale	72	68	78	71	289	9,976
	Nacho Elvira	73	71	73	72	289	9,976
	Maximilian Kieffer	71	71	72	75	289	9,976
	Edoardo Molinari	69	70	72	78	289	9,976
	Joel Sjoholm	70	73	73	73	289	9,976
	Brandon Stone	75	68	70	76	289	9,976
	Sami Valimaki	71	72	72	74	289	9,976
49	Darren Fichardt	72	70	74	74	290	6,376
	Ross Fisher	69	72	72	77	290	6,376
	Grant Forrest	76	67	72	75	290	6,376
	Lorenzo Gagli	71	70	75	74	290	6,376
	Niall Kearney	70	71	72	77	290	6,376
	Sihwan Kim	73	71	70	76	290	6,376
	Niklas Norgaard Moller	71	72	68	79	290	6,376
	Carlos Pigem	74	67	76	73	290	6,376
	Tapio Pulkkanen	71	73	70	76	290	6,376
	Ricardo Santos	75	68	70	77	290	6,376
	Shubhankar Sharma	66	73	76	75	290	6,376
	Chris Wood	72	71	76	71	290	6,376
	Ashun Wu	69	74	73	74	290	6,376
62	Jens Dantorp	68	71	76	76	291	4,716
	Daniel Gavins	71	67	76	77	291	4,716
	Julien Guerrier	70	73	74	74	291	4,716
65	Jorge Campillo	70	74	77	71	292	4,262
	Soren Kjeldsen	72	71	74	75	292	4,262
67	Mikko Korhonen	69	72	74	78	293	3,900
	Callum Shinkwin	72	72	75	74	293	3,900
69	Ondrej Lieser	74	70	75	75	294	3,265
	Yannik Paul	69	74	77	74	294	3,265
	Robin Roussel	71	69	76	78	294	3,265
72	Joakim Lagergren	68	76	75	77	296	2,718
73	Lucas Bjerregaard	73	70	78	76	297	2,713
	Antoine Rozner	68	76	73	80	297	2,713
75	Jack Senior	70	73	78	78	299	2,709

ISPS Handa Championship Spain

"As a professional golfer, you have to realise that you are an entertainer." Pablo Larrazabal lived up to his words by scoring a 62 on the final day of the ISPS Handa Championship Spain. The 38-year-old from Barcelona had been speaking prior to the first tournament of the year in Europe and after his first round ever on the Lakes course at Infinitum, although the resort in Tarragona is only an hour or so from his home. By Sunday he had delivered his seventh victory on the DP World Tour and his first on home soil. It was also a second win in just over a month after Larrazabal won the MyGolfLife Open in South Africa.

On that occasion he won in a playoff and he was waiting to see if extra holes might be required again but ended up with a one-stroke win over compatriot Adrian Otaegui. Larrazabal had started three strokes behind the three 54-hole leaders, Otaegui, Aaron Cockerill and Hennie du Plessis. Otaegui and Cockerill both had a chance to tie with an eagle at the last but Otaegui's putt missed and he could only make a birdie, while Cockerill parred.

Storms had delayed the third round and Larrazabal, along with the other leaders, had to complete nine holes on Sunday morning. He had posted 67-68-68 before his entertaining eight-under-par final round, which left him on 15-under-par 265. He had not made a birdie in finishing off his third round but made up for that soon enough. After two early birdies, he made five in a row from the ninth. He holed from long range at the 12th to get into a tie for the lead and hit a wedge to two feet at the 13th to go in front. There was a bogey at the 15th, but he responded with two more birdies at 16 and 18 to set a target no one could reach.

"What a day. I knew that my golf was there," he said. "I couldn't make any putts the first three days, but I told my girlfriend last night that she had to choose her clothing carefully for the pictures today! I knew that I had a low one in my bag and that's what I did. Today I holed putts and to shoot 62 in windy conditions with the flags out there, it was good."

Infinitum (Lakes), Tarragona, Spain — April 21-24
Par 70 (34-36); 6,963 yards — Purse: $2,000,000

1	**Pablo Larrazabal**	67	68	68	62	265	€313,467
2	**Adrian Otaegui**	66	66	68	66	266	202,832
3	**Aaron Cockerill**	69	69	62	67	267	104,182
	Hennie du Plessis	64	70	66	67	267	104,182
5	Antoine Rozner	67	68	66	67	268	78,182
6	Haotong Li	71	68	64	67	270	64,537
7	Andrew Wilson	68	69	65	69	271	55,318
8	Darren Fichardt	69	67	69	67	272	43,701
	Victor Perez	70	68	68	66	272	43,701
10	Oliver Bekker	68	71	67	67	273	32,084
	Scott Jamieson	66	63	74	70	273	32,084
	Tom Lewis	67	71	70	65	273	32,084
	Yannik Paul	67	71	65	70	273	32,084
	Jack Senior	65	70	68	70	273	32,084
15	Ross Fisher	68	67	68	71	274	23,625
	Ryan Fox	69	69	69	67	274	23,625
	Matthew Jordan	67	70	71	66	274	23,625
	Mikko Korhonen	69	67	69	69	274	23,625
	Lukas Nemecz	69	64	71	70	274	23,625
	Eddie Pepperell	71	68	70	65	274	23,625
	Adrien Saddier	69	67	70	68	274	23,625
	Jack Singh Brar	67	68	73	66	274	23,625
23	Ashley Chesters	66	68	71	70	275	18,624
	Sebastian Garcia Rodriguez	67	70	70	68	275	18,624
	Gavin Green	70	68	66	71	275	18,624
	Mike Lorenzo-Vera	68	70	65	72	275	18,624
	Thorbjorn Olesen	69	65	71	70	275	18,624
	Tapio Pulkkanen	64	67	73	71	275	18,624
	Justin Walters	72	67	68	68	275	18,624
30	Jorge Campillo	69	68	68	71	276	14,498
	Laurie Canter	70	65	74	67	276	14,498
	Lorenzo Gagli	68	69	68	71	276	14,498
	Angel Hidalgo	69	67	71	69	276	14,498
	Craig Howie	70	66	73	67	276	14,498
	Richard Mansell	69	64	73	70	276	14,498
	Matti Schmid	69	69	68	70	276	14,498
	Oliver Wilson	72	67	68	69	276	14,498
38	Louis de Jager	66	72	69	70	277	10,510
	Raphael Jacquelin	67	68	72	70	277	10,510
	Jazz Janewattananond	71	67	69	70	277	10,510
	Thriston Lawrence	68	68	73	68	277	10,510
	Jake McLeod	66	71	73	67	277	10,510
	Robert Rock	70	67	68	72	277	10,510
	Kalle Samooja	70	68	69	70	277	10,510
	Clement Sordet	66	70	70	71	277	10,510
	Jonathan Thomson	72	67	68	70	277	10,510
	Johannes Veerman	64	69	72	72	277	10,510
	Bernd Wiesberger	70	67	69	71	277	10,510
49	Pep Angles	66	73	69	70	278	7,560
	Jens Dantorp	70	68	71	69	278	7,560
	Julien Guerrier	70	67	71	70	278	7,560
	Joachim B Hansen	69	70	71	68	278	7,560
	Nicolai von Dellingshausen	70	69	69	70	278	7,560
54	Jean-Baptiste Gonnet	72	67	71	69	279	6,362
	David Law	65	68	73	73	279	6,362
56	Julien Brun	73	66	68	73	280	5,440
	SSP Chawrasia	70	69	71	70	280	5,440
	Emilio Cuartero Blanco	68	70	70	72	280	5,440
	Soren Kjeldsen	69	68	71	72	280	5,440
	Guido Migliozzi	65	72	71	72	280	5,440
	Wade Ormsby	68	70	71	71	280	5,440
	Benjamin Poke	71	67	72	70	280	5,440
	Jeff Winther	67	70	71	72	280	5,440
64	John Catlin	70	69	69	73	281	4,425
	Daniel van Tonder	69	70	70	72	281	4,425
	Marc Warren	68	70	72	71	281	4,425
67	Niall Kearney	68	71	71	72	282	3,964
	Matthew Southgate	68	69	71	74	282	3,964
69	Stephen Gallacher	74	65	68	76	283	3,596
	Rasmus Hojgaard	66	67	77	73	283	3,596
71	Ivan Cantero Gutierrez	72	67	71	74	284	2,764
	Nicolai Hojgaard	71	68	71	74	284	2,764
73	Ben Stow	71	68	70	77	286	2,760

Catalunya Championship

As the European, now DP World, Tour celebrated its 50th anniversary, 78-year-old Antonio Garrido, winner of the first official event in 1972, hit a ceremonial honorary tee shot ahead of the Catalunya Championship. Garrido won the Open de Espana at nearby Golf de Pals so it was fitting that the latest winner on the recently upgraded Stadium course at PGA Catalunya was also a home player. Adri Arnaus came from seven strokes behind in the final round to beat Oliver Bekker at the sixth extra hole for his maiden victory.

Arnaus, who has an apartment in Girona and practises at the host club, had been a runner-up five times, including in playoffs at the 2021 Open de Espana and the MyGolfLife Open in April. Pablo Larrazabal had won the South African event and Arnaus followed Larrazabal with back-to-back Spanish wins on home soil.

While Bekker, the 54-hole leader, and Laurie Canter, the 36-hole leader, were battling out for the title, Arnaus (68-76-68) was still recovering from a nightmare spell of three bogeys and a double in five holes on the back nine on Friday. He went out in two under on Sunday, still not a factor, but then came home in 31, with three birdies and an eagle at the 12th, where he holed from 35 feet. A 65, the second lowest score of the week, left him on 11-under-par 277, which was matched when Bekker closed with a 72 having been leading until three-putting the 16th. Canter had a double bogey at the 17th and dropped into a tie for third place, two shots outside the playoff, with Richard McEvoy and Adrian Meronk.

In five trips down the 18th in the playoff, both Arnaus and Bekker made pars, then they switched to the 17th, where Bekker missed the green and could not get up and down "It's a dream come true," said Arnaus, who was on the brink of breaking into the world's top 50 for the first time. "I've been looking for this one for a while. To be able to come through here, where I practise in the summers, they take care of me so well. I know the course quite well. I've been able to play some really good golf and to do it here is special."

PGA Catalunya Golf and Wellness (Stadium), Girona, Spain — April 28-May 1
Par 72 (36-36); 7,353 yards — Purse: $2,000,000

1	**Adri Arnaus**	68	76	68	65	277	€322,614
2	**Oliver Bekker**	66	72	67	72	277	208,751
	Arnaus won playoff at sixth extra hole						
3	**Laurie Canter**	70	67	70	72	279	98,303
	Richard McEvoy	69	72	69	69	279	98,303
	Adrian Meronk	71	71	67	70	279	98,303
6	Hennie du Plessis	68	74	74	64	280	61,676
	Edoardo Molinari	73	69	66	72	280	61,676
8	Bernd Wiesberger	73	70	67	71	281	47,443
9	Wil Besseling	73	70	69	70	282	37,006
	Ryan Fox	71	68	70	73	282	37,006
	Lorenzo Gagli	71	72	65	74	282	37,006
	Tapio Pulkkanen	72	71	71	68	282	37,006
13	Daniel Gavins	69	70	72	72	283	27,973
	Nicolai Hojgaard	69	72	72	70	283	27,973
	Pablo Larrazabal	72	69	69	73	283	27,973
	Marcel Schneider	71	69	74	69	283	27,973
	Nicolai von Dellingshausen	70	71	73	69	283	27,973
18	Thriston Lawrence	70	72	73	69	284	23,200
	Jason Scrivener	74	72	70	68	284	23,200
	Jordan Smith	71	73	71	69	284	23,200
	Sami Valimaki	73	70	69	72	284	23,200
22	Gavin Green	71	71	70	73	285	20,590
	Sebastian Heisele	67	73	73	72	285	20,590
	Espen Kofstad	72	73	70	70	285	20,590
	Niklas Lemke	73	71	72	69	285	20,590
26	Darren Fichardt	66	74	75	71	286	17,459
	Sebastian Garcia Rodriguez	72	71	71	72	286	17,459
	Ricardo Gouveia	69	71	75	71	286	17,459
	Haotong Li	67	76	71	72	286	17,459
	Richard Mansell	70	71	71	74	286	17,459
	Lukas Nemecz	68	74	71	73	286	17,459
	Ashun Wu	75	70	71	70	286	17,459
33	Alexander Bjork	73	72	71	71	287	13,221
	Thomas Bjorn	69	70	72	76	287	13,221
	Jorge Campillo	71	74	72	70	287	13,221
	Mikko Korhonen	70	70	72	75	287	13,221
	James Morrison	67	71	73	76	287	13,221
	Niklas Norgaard	71	70	75	71	287	13,221
	Thorbjorn Olesen	69	71	74	73	287	13,221
	Adrien Saddier	70	69	73	75	287	13,221
	Darius van Driel	73	71	72	71	287	13,221
42	Julien Brun	68	75	72	73	288	9,489
	Alejandro Canizares	72	74	74	68	288	9,489
	Ross Fisher	72	72	72	72	288	9,489
	Rasmus Hojgaard	72	74	72	70	288	9,489
	David Law	72	69	74	73	288	9,489
	Hurly Long	73	72	72	71	288	9,489
	Andrea Pavan	71	72	71	74	288	9,489
	Daniel van Tonder	75	70	72	71	288	9,489
	Justin Walters	69	74	75	70	288	9,489
	Oliver Wilson	73	73	73	69	288	9,489
52	David Drysdale	69	74	71	75	289	7,022
	Ewen Ferguson	71	70	70	78	289	7,022
	Yannik Paul	70	73	73	73	289	7,022
55	Ivan Cantero Gutierrez	71	68	71	80	290	6,073
	Grant Forrest	70	76	73	71	290	6,073
	Angel Hidalgo	71	74	68	77	290	6,073

	Raphael Jacquelin	71	70	74	75	290	6,073
	Lars van Meijel	72	74	71	73	290	6,073
60	Dave Coupland	73	69	70	79	291	5,314
	Alejandro Del Rey	72	72	73	74	291	5,314
	Marcus Helligkilde	70	75	74	72	291	5,314
63	Maverick Antcliff	72	68	77	75	292	4,744
	Jazz Janewattananond	76	70	74	72	292	4,744
	Matti Schmid	71	71	73	77	292	4,744
66	Richard Bland	73	71	71	78	293	3,985
	David Howell	73	72	76	72	293	3,985
	Guido Migliozzi	72	73	74	74	293	3,985
	Ricardo Santos	70	76	72	75	293	3,985
	Jeff Winther	66	75	69	83	293	3,985
71	Jonathan Caldwell	73	71	75	75	294	2,847
	Jean-Baptiste Gonnet	68	74	76		RT	2,844

Betfred British Masters

Just to prove it was no fluke, Thorbjorn Olesen did it again the next day. He finished the third round of the Betfred British Masters eagle-birdie to take a three-shot lead, then repeated the feat on Sunday to claim a one-shot victory. On a difficult day on the Brabazon course at The Belfry, the 32-year-old Dane was four over par for the day after dropping back-to-back shots at 14 and 15. He had fallen two behind Sebastian Soderberg, who came home in 32 for a 68 and had set the clubhouse target at nine under par. Olesen holed a putt from 28 feet for the eagle at 17 to draw level, then made a 35-footer at the last to win in front of a packed grandstand at the first event of the year on British soil. There had already been drama at the 18th when Scotland's Richie Ramsey made a double bogey to fall out of the lead and finish in a tie for third place with Conor Syme and Justin Walters.

Olesen scored 66-70-69-73 for his 10-under-par total of 278. This was his sixth win on the DP World Tour but his first since 2018, and since being cleared in a lengthy court case that took over two years to be resolved. The former Ryder Cup player joined compatriot Thomas Bjorn on the illustrious roll of honour for the British Masters.

"There's so much emotions, it's been a long time since I won and I knew how hard it was going to be," Olesen said. "I was really struggling out there and just didn't have it. Somehow just kept on fighting and scrambling some pars and saw I still had a chance there on 17. If I could make birdie-birdie, I thought I could force a playoff, so that was my thinking. But obviously when I got the chance on 17, I prefer to take that. The 18th is a tough hole, so par is a good score. I just gave it everything. It's a massive tournament won by so many great names so it's a privilege to have my name on the trophy."

The Belfry (Brabazon), Sutton Coldfield, England — May 5-8
Par 72 (36-36); 7,328 yards — Purse: £1,850,000

1	**Thorbjorn Olesen**	66	70	69	73	278	€369,214
2	**Sebastian Soderberg**	70	68	73	68	279	238,903
3	**Richie Ramsay**	67	69	73	71	280	112,502
	Connor Syme	74	68	68	70	280	112,502
	Justin Walters	68	70	71	71	280	112,502
6	Chase Hanna	70	73	66	72	281	70,585
	Hurly Long	67	68	73	73	281	70,585
8	Julien Brun	71	69	71	71	282	40,478
	Jamie Donaldson	69	74	69	70	282	40,478
	Ryan Fox	66	73	72	71	282	40,478
	Mikko Korhonen	70	69	73	70	282	40,478
	Romain Langasque	76	67	68	71	282	40,478
	Richard Mansell	71	70	73	68	282	40,478
	JC Ritchie	73	70	69	70	282	40,478
	Fabrizio Zanotti	70	70	69	73	282	40,478
16	Justin Harding	70	73	69	71	283	28,191
	Rasmus Hojgaard	68	69	72	74	283	28,191
	Yannik Paul	71	71	70	71	283	28,191
	Callum Shinkwin	73	69	70	71	283	28,191
	Danny Willett	73	65	74	71	283	28,191
21	Marcus Armitage	71	67	70	76	284	23,565
	Sam Horsfield	71	69	72	72	284	23,565
	Frederic Lacroix	72	71	73	68	284	23,565
	Victor Perez	71	72	69	72	284	23,565
	Jordan Smith	69	72	74	69	284	23,565
	Santiago Tarrio	72	71	70	71	284	23,565
27	Oliver Bekker	75	69	70	71	285	18,678
	Sebastian Garcia Rodriguez	73	71	70	71	285	18,678
	Jazz Janewattananond	73	68	71	73	285	18,678
	Marcus Kinhult	70	66	74	75	285	18,678
	James Morrison	71	73	72	69	285	18,678
	Adrian Otaegui	71	70	73	71	285	18,678
	Jack Singh Brar	72	71	69	73	285	18,678
	Daniel van Tonder	71	72	68	74	285	18,678
	Ashun Wu	67	72	73	73	285	18,678
36	John Catlin	71	73	74	68	286	14,117
	George Coetzee	71	70	73	72	286	14,117
	Espen Kofstad	71	71	74	70	286	14,117
	Thriston Lawrence	72	70	75	69	286	14,117
	Joost Luiten	71	71	73	71	286	14,117
	Robert MacIntyre	74	67	76	69	286	14,117
	Edoardo Molinari	68	74	72	72	286	14,117
43	Niklas Norgaard	72	72	71	72	287	12,162
	Brandon Stone	68	75	73	71	287	12,162
45	Benjamin Hebert	71	72	73	72	288	11,076
	Robin Roussel	71	71	72	74	288	11,076

	Jason Scrivener	70 74 73 71	288	11,076		Darius van Driel	74 69 75 74	292	6,841
48	Adri Arnaus	70 72 69 78	289	9,773	59	Pep Angles	75 69 76 73	293	6,298
	Gavin Green	71 70 74 74	289	9,773		Thomas Bjorn	70 74 74 75	293	6,298
	Eddie Pepperell	73 69 75 72	289	9,773		Mike Lorenzo-Vera	69 75 73 76	293	6,298
51	Dave Coupland	72 72 72 74	290	8,470	62	Hugo Leon	71 73 80 70	294	5,864
	Daan Huizing	69 71 74 76	290	8,470	63	Richard McEvoy	72 72 73 78	295	5,430
	Joel Stalter	74 69 71 76	290	8,470		Ben Schmidt	71 73 75 76	295	5,430
54	Thomas Detry	74 67 74 76	291	7,384		Paul Waring	70 69 80 76	295	5,430
	Raphael Jacquelin	69 71 78 73	291	7,384	66	Zander Lombard	72 72 77 75	296	4,995
	Richard Sterne	73 71 71 76	291	7,384	67	Rafa Cabrera Bello	74 70 75 78	297	4,778
57	Matthew Southgate	71 73 75 73	292	6,841	68	Gonzalo Fdez-Castano	72 72 84 75	303	4,561

Soudal Open

Just two weeks into a comeback after a back injury kept him out for three months, Sam Horsfield held off Ryan Fox in a classic final-round duel to win the Soudal Open as the DP World Tour returned to Belgium for the first time since 2019. Horsfield finished two in front of Fox, the 54-hole leader, and Germany's Yannik Paul for his third victory. The 25-year-old Englishman, originally from Manchester but who grew up in Orlando, Florida, had previously won twice in August 2020.

Horsfield shared the lead on the first two days with 65-69 at Rinkven International, then Fox went one in front thanks to a third-round 66. The Kiwi made three birdies in a row from the third hole and led by three strokes with 10 to play. He played a wonder recovery at the ninth but could not save his par, and three more bogeys followed on the back nine. Horsfield parred the first six holes and then got himself going with a long putt for birdie at the seventh. Two more birdies at 10 and 12 sandwiched his only dropped shot at the 11th. It was when Fox bogeyed the 16th that Horsfield went ahead for the first time. Both men then birdied the 17th and Horsfield made sure of his par at the last to close with a 68 to Fox's 71. Paul finished with a two-birdie 69 as the winner posted a 13-under-par total of 271.

"I was trying not to cry while I was over that little tap-in," Horsfield said of his winning putt. With regular caddie Mick Seaborn unable to make the trip to Antwerp, Horsfield had girlfriend Issi on the bag. "Mick is going through a little bit of a tough time right now. I wish he was here. I said yesterday I wanted to do it for him and I was able to do it for him. I definitely thought about Mick quite a lot. Especially on the back nine, I pulled a few clubs that he definitely would have wanted me to hit. Issi has been amazing. I've been so happy on the golf course. I asked her coming down 18, 'Are you nervous?' and she said, 'Yeah'. But we've had an amazing week and I'm just so happy that she was here to enjoy this."

Ukrainian-born Lev Grinberg, a member at Rinkven International, scored 70-69 on the first two days to become the second youngest player to make the cut on the DP World Tour at 14 years, six months and six days. He was a month older than Tianlang Guan at the 2013 Masters.

Rinkven International Golf Club, Antwerp, Belgium — May 12-15
Par 71 (36-35); 6,924 yards — Purse: $2,000,000

1	**Sam Horsfield**	65 69 69 68	271	€327,000		Hennie du Plessis	68 69 70 71	278	24,645
2	**Ryan Fox**	68 68 66 71	273	166,386		Angel Hidalgo	68 73 66 71	278	24,645
	Yannik Paul	66 70 68 69	273	166,386		Matthew Jordan	68 68 71 71	278	24,645
4	Oliver Bekker	67 69 69 69	274	88,867		Niall Kearney	69 67 69 73	278	24,645
	Chase Hanna	70 68 68 68	274	88,867		Francesco Laporta	68 70 71 69	278	24,645
6	Adrian Meronk	66 70 72 67	275	67,324		Adrian Otaegui	71 67 69 71	278	24,645
7	Sean Crocker	69 69 72 66	276	52,897		Richie Ramsay	71 70 68 69	278	24,645
	Marcel Schneider	70 67 68 71	276	52,897	23	Wil Besseling	69 69 71 70	279	18,562
9	Nacho Elvira	66 70 73 68	277	35,072		Alexander Bjork	66 70 73 70	279	18,562
	Grant Forrest	70 69 68 70	277	35,072		John Catlin	72 67 70 70	279	18,562
	Edoardo Molinari	69 70 71 67	277	35,072		Jens Dantorp	69 70 68 72	279	18,562
	Thomas Pieters	69 70 71 67	277	35,072		Oliver Farr	71 66 71 71	279	18,562
	Ricardo Santos	69 66 74 68	277	35,072		Julien Guerrier	73 68 69 69	279	18,562
	Andy Sullivan	71 66 69 71	277	35,072		David Horsey	75 66 73 65	279	18,562
15	Jorge Campillo	69 67 70 72	278	24,645		Masahiro Kawamura	70 70 69 70	279	18,562

	Richard Mansell	69	66	73	71	279	18,562
	Dale Whitnell	65	69	72	73	279	18,562
33	Daan Huizing	70	71	69	70	280	14,523
	Victor Perez	69	69	70	72	280	14,523
	Maximilian Schmitt	68	72	73	67	280	14,523
	Santiago Tarrio	71	69	69	71	280	14,523
37	Richard Mcevoy	68	71	73	69	281	12,118
	Robin Roussel	68	72	66	75	281	12,118
	Matti Schmid	70	64	72	75	281	12,118
	Callum Shinkwin	65	74	74	68	281	12,118
	Paul Waring	67	73	66	75	281	12,118
	Bernd Wiesberger	68	71	72	70	281	12,118
	Fabrizio Zanotti	70	70	65	76	281	12,118
44	Alejandro Canizares	71	70	69	72	282	10,002
	Ashley Chesters	69	70	73	70	282	10,002
	Gavin Green	67	74	73	68	282	10,002
	Ashun Wu	70	71	69	72	282	10,002
48	Victor Dubuisson	70	68	73	72	283	8,464
	Garrick Porteous	70	70	75	68	283	8,464
	Alvaro Quiros	66	74	71	72	283	8,464
	Joel Sjoholm	69	72	68	74	283	8,464
52	Raphael Jacquelin	68	72	74	70	284	7,117
	Guido Migliozzi	69	71	74	70	284	7,117
	Connor Syme	68	70	76	70	284	7,117
55	Joachim B Hansen	68	69	77	71	285	6,348
	Rikard Karlberg	71	70	71	73	285	6,348
	Jeff Winther	66	74	75	70	285	6,348
58	Ewen Ferguson	67	72	75	72	286	5,578
	Josh Geary	70	71	74	71	286	5,578
	Thriston Lawrence	71	70	69	76	286	5,578
	Hurly Long	70	71	73	72	286	5,578
	Lukas Nemecz	71	69	75	71	286	5,578
63	Marcel Siem	70	71	76	71	288	5,001
64	Lev Grinberg (A)	70	69	76	74	289	
	JC Ritchie	72	65	80	72	289	4,809
66	Ondrej Lieser	70	70	75	77	292	4,520
	Carlos Pigem	73	68	80	71	292	4,520

Dutch Open

Among a clutch of amazing shots and putts in the final round of the Dutch Open, Victor Perez delivered the killer blow when he holed from 40 feet for a birdie two at 17, the fourth playoff hole, to defeat Ryan Fox. Earlier at the same hole, Perez had been three behind the Kiwi before holing from 35 feet to start his run of incredible putts.

At the same time, Fox was taking a double-bogey seven at the 18th hole. His tee shot finished in the reeds by the creek and he had to take a penalty drop. Then his third went over the green and his first chip came up short in a bunker. The lie was such that the Ras al Khaimah Classic winner could only splash it out and his curling putt for a bogey slid by the edge of the hole.

That meant Perez could win with a birdie at the last but missed from eight feet. It was probably too short for the Frenchman to make it. At the first extra hole he matched Fox's birdie at 18 by making a 20-footer and, after the pair parred the second extra hole, he made another lengthy putt for a half in fours. When the playoff switched to the par-three 17th, Fox hit the better tee shot, with Perez having to come up over a ridge. But Perez holed and Fox missed from half the distance.

"There was a fair amount of fortune, I've got to be honest with myself, holing out those long putts in the playoff," said Perez after adding to his 2019 Alfred Dunhill Links victory. "I just tried to focus on me all day, that's all I can do, is try to keep a champion mindset and hit good shot after good shot."

Fox, the 54-hole leader at the Soudal Open two weeks earlier, had charged into the lead on the back nine with his own highlights reel — chipping in at the 11th, making a putt from 80 feet for an eagle at the 12th and holing from 45 feet at the 14th. His scores of 70-67-70-68 for a 13-under-par total of 275 were matched by Perez's 67-70-69-69. With wind making the links-style course at Bernardus a challenge over the four days, Adrian Meronk finished one behind with a bogey-free 68. By joining Perez and Fox in qualifying for The Open at St Andrews he became the first Pole to play in the championship.

Bernardus Golf, Cromvoirt, Netherlands — May 26-29
Par 72 (36-36); 7,445 yards — Purse: €1,750,000

1	**Victor Perez**	67	70	69	69	275	€297,500
2	**Ryan Fox**	70	67	70	68	275	192,500
	Perez won playoff at fourth extra hole						
3	**Adrian Meronk**	68	68	72	68	276	110,250
4	Marcel Schneider	67	71	71	68	277	87,500
5	Sebastian Soderberg	71	68	68	71	278	67,725
	Matt Wallace	69	67	70	72	278	67,725
7	Alexander Bjork	68	70	70	72	280	48,125
	Ricardo Gouveia	68	66	74	72	280	48,125
9	Richard Mansell	68	71	73	69	281	39,200
10	Rasmus Hojgaard	66	75	70	71	282	31,369
	Hurly Long	71	70	71	70	282	31,369
	Guido Migliozzi	69	68	70	75	282	31,369
	Thomas Pieters	69	71	73	69	282	31,369
14	Kristoffer Broberg	68	71	71	73	283	23,725
	Scott Hend	70	69	68	76	283	23,725

	Maximilian Kieffer	72	71	72	68	283	23,725
	Mikko Korhonen	67	70	73	73	283	23,725
	Eddie Pepperell	66	73	73	71	283	23,725
	Shubhankar Sharma	71	71	69	72	283	23,725
	Dale Whitnell	73	70	70	70	283	23,725
21	Jorge Campillo	72	71	71	70	284	19,775
	Ashley Chesters	70	71	74	69	284	19,775
	Antoine Rozner	70	72	70	72	284	19,775
24	Lorenzo Gagli	68	73	72	72	285	17,150
	Stephen Gallacher	68	73	71	73	285	17,150
	Alfredo Garcia-Heredia	73	70	70	72	285	17,150
	Frederic Lacroix	73	70	71	71	285	17,150
	JC Ritchie	69	73	71	72	285	17,150
	Jordan Smith	68	70	76	71	285	17,150
	Bernd Wiesberger	72	71	75	67	285	17,150
31	Marcus Armitage	74	69	73	70	286	13,738
	Jazz Janewattananond	70	70	77	69	286	13,738
	Sihwan Kim	70	70	75	71	286	13,738
	Romain Langasque	72	71	75	68	286	13,738
	Niklas Norgaard Moller	71	72	72	71	286	13,738
	Jack Senior	69	68	78	71	286	13,738
37	Ewen Ferguson	68	72	75	72	287	11,200
	Darren Fichardt	68	73	77	69	287	11,200
	David Law	68	75	68	76	287	11,200
	Haotong Li	72	63	77	75	287	11,200
	Edoardo Molinari	73	70	72	72	287	11,200
	Callum Shinkwin	70	70	73	74	287	11,200
43	Grant Forrest	70	73	71	74	288	9,450
	Raphael Jacquelin	68	73	73	74	288	9,450
	Joost Luiten	65	75	79	69	288	9,450
	Richie Ramsay	71	71	72	74	288	9,450
47	Masahiro Kawamura	72	71	74	72	289	8,050
	Daniel van Tonder	70	72	72	75	289	8,050
	Jeff Winther	72	70	78	69	289	8,050
	Ashun Wu	73	68	77	71	289	8,050
51	Thomas Bjorn	71	70	73	76	290	6,510
	Oliver Farr	71	72	73	74	290	6,510
	Ross Fisher	68	71	75	76	290	6,510
	Matthew Jordan	75	68	77	70	290	6,510
	Andrea Pavan	67	74	81	68	290	6,510
56	Hennie du Plessis	70	73	72	76	291	5,338
	Gonzalo Fdez-Castano	71	69	75	76	291	5,338
	Francesco Laporta	71	71	74	75	291	5,338
	Ross McGowan	69	73	76	73	291	5,338
	Joel Stalter	69	71	78	73	291	5,338
	Lars van Meijel	71	70	77	73	291	5,338
62	Sebastian Heisele	71	71	80	70	292	4,725
63	Alvaro Quiros	75	68	81	69	293	4,550
64	Oliver Wilson	71	69	80	74	294	4,375
65	Adrian Otaegui	71	72	78	76	297	4,200

Porsche European Open

Two hours Kalle Samooja had to wait but it was well worth it when the 34-year-old Finn won his first DP World Tour victory at the Porsche European Open. In contrast to his efforts earlier in the week, Samooja scored a course-record 64 in the final round at Green Eagle and set a clubhouse target at six-under-par 282 that no one could match. Wil Besseling took second place two strokes behind, with Victor Perez, hoping for back-to-back victories, finishing in a tie for third place with Richard Mansell.

For the first time since Jeev Milkha Singh at the 2006 Volvo Masters at Valderrama, the winner had only one round under par during the week. Samooja had scored 72-72-74 to be two over par and seven behind 54-hole leader Perez. In a week that saw different leaders every evening, Perez had a hole-in-one with a six-iron at the second hole on Saturday as the Frenchman tried to follow his Dutch Open win the previous week with another victory.

Scoring was difficult on the Porsche Nord course all week, particularly with the strong winds, but Samooja's eyes lit up when he saw the pin positions for the final round. He felt a low score was possible. His record 64 was the lowest score of the week by three strokes. He made his eight birdies in the last 13 holes. A fine tee shot at the short 17th, finding the small pocket of green at the back, set up a two to put him into the lead on his own. At the par-five 18th, his chip from beside the hospitality stand hit the flagstick and stopped right in front of the hole. He tapped in for his last birdie.

"It is truly special, I've been close a few times," Samooja said. "We had a number in mind today and we reached that. We thought it might be enough and it was a long two-hour wait at the clubhouse, seeing the guys battle it out. In the end, fortunately it was enough."

Perez birdied the 10th and 11th holes to draw level but then dropped three shots coming home for a 74, while Besseling finished with a double bogey, a bogey and two birdies in the last four holes. Samooja, along with Perez, Besseling and Mansell, were among 10 players who qualified for the US Open at Brookline from a qualifying series over four tournaments.

Green Eagle Golf Courses (Porsche Nord), Hamburg, Germany — June 2-5
Par 72 (34-38); 7,475 yards — Purse: €1,750,000

1	**Kalle Samooja**	72	72	74	64	282	€297,500
2	**Wil Besseling**	68	75	70	71	284	192,500
3	**Richard Mansell**	72	71	72	70	285	98,875
	Victor Perez	69	71	71	74	285	98,875
5	Masahiro Kawamura	74	69	74	69	286	54,180
	Joakim Lagergren	67	74	71	74	286	54,180
	Edoardo Molinari	74	72	70	70	286	54,180
	Marcel Schneider	73	73	73	67	286	54,180
	Brandon Stone	76	68	73	69	286	54,180
10	Tommy Fleetwood	75	72	69	71	287	29,663
	Julien Guerrier	69	73	76	69	287	29,663
	Daan Huizing	69	75	71	72	287	29,663
	Niklas Norgaard Moller	74	67	74	72	287	29,663
	Jordan Smith	70	68	77	72	287	29,663
	Johannes Veerman	72	71	74	70	287	29,663
16	Adri Arnaus	69	76	74	69	288	24,150
	Justin Walters	70	75	69	74	288	24,150
18	Thriston Lawrence	78	70	72	69	289	20,475
	Haotong Li	67	75	71	76	289	20,475
	Adrian Otaegui	72	71	75	71	289	20,475
	Yannik Paul	74	71	73	71	289	20,475
	Marcel Siem	71	72	75	71	289	20,475
	Nicolai von Dellingshausen	75	71	74	69	289	20,475
	Matt Wallace	74	74	70	71	289	20,475
25	Alexander Bjork	75	73	73	69	290	17,413
	John Catlin	71	73	72	74	290	17,413
	Alexander Knappe	73	70	73	74	290	17,413
	Jason Scrivener	70	73	73	74	290	17,413
29	Pep Angles	74	74	73	70	291	15,050
	Thomas Detry	72	75	72	72	291	15,050
	Ross Fisher	74	72	73	72	291	15,050
	Lukas Nemecz	73	73	70	75	291	15,050
	Alvaro Quiros	73	72	75	71	291	15,050
34	Kiradech Aphibarnrat	72	74	75	71	292	12,338
	Julien Brun	69	72	71	80	292	12,338
	Scott Jamieson	70	76	74	72	292	12,338
	Matti Schmid	70	75	72	75	292	12,338
	Matthew Southgate	73	72	73	74	292	12,338
	Henrik Stenson	77	70	74	71	292	12,338
40	Darren Fichardt	74	73	72	74	293	9,975
	Espen Kofstad	75	71	72	75	293	9,975
	Mikko Korhonen	71	77	72	73	293	9,975
	Romain Langasque	75	73	72	73	293	9,975
	Mike Lorenzo-Vera	75	71	76	71	293	9,975
	Wilco Nienaber	74	74	73	72	293	9,975
	Richard Sterne	70	74	73	76	293	9,975
47	Alfredo Garcia-Heredia	73	73	76	72	294	8,050
	Hurly Long	77	71	73	73	294	8,050
	Matthieu Pavon	75	73	73	73	294	8,050
	Ricardo Santos	76	72	73	73	294	8,050
51	Sean Crocker	77	70	73	75	295	6,169
	Rasmus Hojgaard	72	71	76	76	295	6,169
	Thorbjorn Olesen	72	71	84	68	295	6,169
	Antoine Rozner	74	73	77	71	295	6,169
	Freddy Schott	70	76	73	76	295	6,169
	Jack Senior	77	69	78	71	295	6,169
	Connor Syme	75	73	73	74	295	6,169
	Ashun Wu	74	70	74	77	295	6,169
59	Hugo Leon	74	73	73	76	296	4,988
	Zander Lombard	77	71	73	75	296	4,988
	Carlos Pigem	72	76	77	71	296	4,988
	Santiago Tarrio	74	72	77	73	296	4,988
63	Jeff Winther	75	68	78	76	297	4,550
64	Marcus Armitage	70	73	78	77	298	4,025
	Kristoffer Broberg	71	76	77	74	298	4,025
	Jesper Kennegard	76	71	75	76	298	4,025
	Andrea Pavan	69	76	74	79	298	4,025
	Joel Sjoholm	73	75	76	74	298	4,025
69	Oliver Farr	74	73	75	77	299	3,500
70	Aaron Cockerill	70	77	73	80	300	2,857
	Jamie Donaldson	72	76	73	79	300	2,857
	Ricardo Gouveia	75	73	80	72	300	2,857
73	Jack Singh Brar	74	73	81	79	307	2,619

BMW International Open

"It's golf. It's hard." Haotong Li reprised the eternal refrain except with added adjectival obscenity for emphasis, on live worldwide television moments after winning for the first time in four years. The 26-year-old from China had holed an unlikely putt from 40 feet in the playoff to beat Thomas Pieters and then enjoyed an extravagant, emotional celebration. He made the BMW International Open his first victory in Europe and third in all on the DP World Tour, the last having come against Rory McIlroy in the Dubai Desert Classic.

But the pandemic, when he was unable to return home, played havoc with Li's game. In 2021 he missed 14 cuts in 18 events and plummeted to 460th in the world. Victory at Munchen Eichenreid took him back to 134th, still over 100 places above his best ranking.

"No one knows how much I have gone through over the last couple of years," Li admitted. "Ten months ago I nearly decided to not play golf. I thought I couldn't play golf again. If someone told me then I would win again, I wouldn't believe that. I never thought that one day I would have a trophy in my hands again. I didn't realise I could be that emotional. Maybe just because I never thought golf could be that tough."

Li led all week after equalling the course record with a 62 on the opening day, with six birdies and then two eagles in his last four holes. He added two 67s to lead by three from Pieters, who scored 66 on Friday and came home in 31 for a 66 on Saturday. A poor run in the middle of the final round dropped

Li into a tie with Pieters and Ryan Fox, who closed with a 67 but could not birdie the par-five 18th.

After his drive at the short par-four 16th only just carried the stream, Li (70) got up and down for a three to match Pieters, went ahead with a two at 17 before Pieters (67) birdied the last as they tied on 22-under-par 266. In the playoff, at 18, Li twice skirted the water, then thinned a chip before his incredible putt. Pieters, having been in a greenside bunker, had a 10-footer to stay alive but it slipped past. "Somehow I thought that I would make that putt," Li said. "I don't know how. Sometimes things go your way, sometimes not."

Golfclub Munchen Eichenried, Munich, Germany — June 23-26
Par 72 (36-36); 7,284 yards — Purse: €2,000,000

1	**Haotong Li**	62	67	67	70	266	€340,000
2	**Thomas Pieters**	69	64	66	67	266	220,000
	Li won playoff at first extra hole						
3	**Ryan Fox**	66	64	71	67	268	126,000
4	Sami Valimaki	69	66	68	67	270	100,000
5	Romain Langasque	68	68	66	69	271	71,600
	Pablo Larrazabal	70	67	67	67	271	71,600
	Nicolai von Dellingshausen	64	73	66	68	271	71,600
8	Louis Oosthuizen	70	69	65	68	272	47,400
	Jordan Smith	67	66	67	72	272	47,400
10	Kazuki Higa	67	72	64	70	273	37,067
	Frederic Lacroix	70	67	70	66	273	37,067
	Darius van Driel	70	67	64	72	273	37,067
13	Lukas Nemecz	70	67	67	70	274	31,400
	Richie Ramsay	68	68	70	68	274	31,400
15	Jorge Campillo	69	70	68	68	275	26,533
	Thomas Detry	71	66	69	69	275	26,533
	Niall Kearney	72	68	66	69	275	26,533
	Antoine Rozner	68	67	71	69	275	26,533
	Marcel Schneider	71	69	69	66	275	26,533
	Brandon Stone	72	66	68	69	275	26,533
21	Dean Burmester	69	68	71	68	276	22,000
	Ewen Ferguson	68	72	67	69	276	22,000
	Edoardo Molinari	71	69	67	69	276	22,000
	Wilco Nienaber	66	70	69	71	276	22,000
	Kalle Samooja	72	66	67	71	276	22,000
26	Wil Besseling	69	70	67	71	277	18,700
	Alfredo Garcia-Heredia	70	70	66	71	277	18,700
	Billy Horschel	70	69	65	73	277	18,700
	Maximilian Kieffer	68	66	71	72	277	18,700
	Mikko Korhonen	72	68	67	70	277	18,700
	Paul Waring	70	70	69	68	277	18,700
32	Laurie Canter	71	66	72	69	278	15,700
	Mike Lorenzo-Vera	66	71	68	73	278	15,700
	Yannik Paul	69	69	69	71	278	15,700
	Fabrizio Zanotti	69	71	67	71	278	15,700
36	George Coetzee	68	71	69	71	279	12,000
	Sean Crocker	70	68	73	68	279	12,000
	Rasmus Hojgaard	66	69	73	71	279	12,000
	Daan Huizing	63	69	73	74	279	12,000
	Martin Kaymer	66	72	70	71	279	12,000
	Francesco Laporta	68	68	69	74	279	12,000
	Thriston Lawrence	67	72	71	69	279	12,000
	Zander Lombard	69	71	68	71	279	12,000
	Hurly Long	68	69	73	69	279	12,000
	Timo Vahlenkamp	69	69	72	69	279	12,000
	Daniel van Tonder	66	69	70	74	279	12,000
	Dale Whitnell	67	69	73	70	279	12,000
48	Kristoffer Broberg	67	73	69	71	280	8,600
	Sergio Garcia	73	66	70	71	280	8,600
	Espen Kofstad	70	70	72	68	280	8,600
	Jacques Kruyswijk	69	71	71	69	280	8,600
	Garrick Porteous	70	68	69	73	280	8,600
53	Louis de Jager	67	71	70	73	281	6,950
	Niklas Norgaard Moller	73	66	68	74	281	6,950
	Victor Perez	69	69	68	75	281	6,950
	Marcel Siem	69	69	72	71	281	6,950
57	Joakim Lagergren	72	68	71	71	282	6,400
58	Steven Brown	69	71	69	74	283	6,000
	Rikard Karlberg	70	69	70	74	283	6,000
	Adrian Otaegui	73	67	75	68	283	6,000
61	Nacho Elvira	71	68	72	74	285	5,500
	Bernd Wiesberger	72	68	72	73	285	5,500
63	Jamie Donaldson	67	72	73	74	286	5,100
	Richard Mansell	69	69	70	78	286	5,100
65	Rafa Echenique	68	72	76	71	287	4,800
66	James Morrison	69	71	75	73	288	4,600
67	Craig Howie	69	70	76	75	290	4,300
	Wade Ormsby	68	72	78	72	290	4,300

Horizon Irish Open

Adrian Meronk was positively battering on the door and he finally became the first Pole to win on the DP World Tour at the Horizon Irish Open. The 29-year-old, who was actually born in Hamburg, Germany, is a golfing pioneer for his country, becoming the first Pole to win on the Challenge Tour in 2019, gain his card for the main tour the following year and the first to play in a major championship at the 2021 US Open.

In the 2022 season Meronk had been in the top 10 six times and over the last three seasons had been a runner-up twice and finished third three times. A brilliant finish at Mount Juliet left him clear at the top of the leaderboard for the first time. Having been overtaken by a charging Ryan Fox, Meronk birdied the 15th and 16th holes, then eagled the 17th after a putt from 25 feet. A par at the last hole secured a three-stroke win over Fox on 20-under-par 268 after scores of 67-67-68-66.

Fox had led on the first day with a 64, but having fallen out of contention over the next two days, rallied on Sunday with another 64. He also eagled the 17th but then bogeyed the last and had to settle for a third runner-up finish of the summer.

Meronk had taken the lead on Saturday night, but it was the way he swept past Fox over the closing holes that was decisive. "It's such a relief to be honest. I've been coming quite close a couple of times this year, and to finally open the door, it's just a dream come true," Meronk said. "I'm excited I achieved it here in Ireland, such a great history, and I'm just super excited."

Big crowds returned to the Irish Open, with huge home support for Seamus Power, Padraig Harrington and Shane Lowry, who was the leading home player in ninth. Thriston Lawrence took third place, with Open qualifying places going to a trio in fourth: David Law, John Catlin and Fabrizio Zanotti.

But the week ended up being about Poland, with the former national goalkeeper Jerzy Dudek congratulating Meronk in a video that evening: "You were waiting for that moment so many years. That's a first Pole on the podium in this beautiful sport. You are a legend of this game. We're very proud of you. Enjoy every single moment. All the best, come on!"

Mount Juliet Estate, Thomastown, Co Kilkenny, Ireland — June 30-July 3
Par 72 (36-36); 7,264 yards — Purse: $6,000,000

1	**Adrian Meronk**	67	67	68	66	268	€974,606
2	**Ryan Fox**	64	73	70	64	271	630,627
3	**Thriston Lawrence**	66	72	67	67	272	361,177
4	John Catlin	67	72	65	69	273	243,460
	David Law	67	69	70	67	273	243,460
	Fabrizio Zanotti	65	69	69	70	273	243,460
7	Jorge Campillo	65	68	70	71	274	171,989
8	Thorbjorn Olesen	70	69	70	66	275	143,324
9	Lucas Herbert	69	68	68	71	276	111,793
	Espen Kofstad	67	72	65	72	276	111,793
	Shane Lowry	71	70	68	67	276	111,793
	Aaron Rai	66	70	70	70	276	111,793
13	Robert MacIntyre	68	73	67	69	277	88,097
	James Morrison	69	68	69	71	277	88,097
	Antoine Rozner	66	75	65	71	277	88,097
16	Oliver Bekker	68	71	72	67	278	75,819
	Matthew Southgate	71	68	67	72	278	75,819
	Santiago Tarrio	71	68	72	67	278	75,819
	Dale Whitnell	66	74	66	72	278	75,819
20	Alexander Bjork	67	72	70	70	279	65,786
	Jamie Donaldson	69	69	72	69	279	65,786
	Marcel Schneider	65	73	72	69	279	65,786
	Justin Walters	70	71	69	69	279	65,786
24	Alfredo Garcia-Heredia	71	71	69	69	280	57,043
	Matthew Jordan	71	71	68	70	280	57,043
	Edoardo Molinari	75	67	67	71	280	57,043
	Callum Shinkwin	68	74	68	70	280	57,043
	Jordan Smith	66	73	72	69	280	57,043
	Johannes Veerman	72	70	69	69	280	57,043
30	Julien Brun	72	68	70	71	281	45,864
	Padraig Harrington	70	71	71	69	281	45,864
	Maximilian Kieffer	67	74	71	69	281	45,864
	Romain Langasque	68	70	74	69	281	45,864
	Seamus Power	68	68	77	68	281	45,864
	Matti Schmid	70	68	69	74	281	45,864
	Sami Valimaki	68	73	74	66	281	45,864
37	Marcus Armitage	73	69	71	69	282	34,971
	Sebastian Garcia Rodriguez	69	71	70	72	282	34,971
	Mikko Korhonen	67	70	75	70	282	34,971
	Frederic Lacroix	65	71	73	73	282	34,971
	Hurly Long	73	69	70	70	282	34,971
	Thomas Pieters	73	67	69	73	282	34,971
	Richie Ramsay	69	72	70	71	282	34,971
	Jack Senior	69	67	67	79	282	34,971
	Marcel Siem	68	70	73	71	282	34,971
46	Nino Bertasio	68	68	73	74	283	23,219
	Sean Crocker	69	71	71	72	283	23,219
	Oliver Farr	67	73	72	71	283	23,219
	Lorenzo Gagli	75	67	75	66	283	23,219
	Julien Guerrier	71	70	73	69	283	23,219
	Marcus Helligkilde	68	71	76	68	283	23,219
	Soren Kjeldsen	73	67	70	73	283	23,219
	Joakim Lagergren	70	71	71	71	283	23,219
	Pablo Larrazabal	66	73	70	74	283	23,219
	Hugo Leon	73	68	68	74	283	23,219
	Sebastian Soderberg	70	66	73	74	283	23,219
	Brandon Stone	69	72	71	71	283	23,219
58	Wil Besseling	69	71	73	71	284	15,479
	Thomas Detry	72	69	73	70	284	15,479
	Stephen Gallacher	72	69	72	71	284	15,479
	Scott Hend	72	70	71	71	284	15,479
	Niall Kearney	68	74	72	70	284	15,479
	Min Woo Lee	72	70	71	71	284	15,479
	Niklas Norgaard Moller	69	72	72	71	284	15,479
	Renato Paratore	70	70	74	70	284	15,479
	Yannik Paul	71	71	71	71	284	15,479
67	Maverick Antcliff	71	69	75	70	285	12,039
	Matthieu Pavon	70	71	73	71	285	12,039
	Alvaro Quiros	69	70	73	73	285	12,039
70	Ricardo Gouveia	69	72	73	72	286	9,363
	Rikard Karlberg	69	69	70	78	286	9,363
	Oliver Wilson	68	74	74	70	286	9,363
73	Tapio Pulkkanen	72	70	74	72	288	8,593
74	Nicolai Hojgaard	70	72	70	77	289	8,589
	Marc Warren	69	70	76	74	289	8,589
76	Zander Lombard	67	73	76	74	290	8,583
	Andy Sullivan	67	72	73	78	290	8,583
78	Kazuki Higa	69	70	78	75	292	8,578

Genesis Scottish Open

Whatever the status of the event, Xander Schauffele was winning it. The 28-year-old Californian won for the first time on the DP World Tour and for the third time in the season on the PGA Tour. The Genesis Scottish Open was the first of three events co-sanctioned by the DP World Tour and the PGA Tour. But only one of them had 14 of the world's best 15 players in the field and that was at Renaissance. Seven of them missed the cut, however, including world number one Scottie Scheffler and Collin Morikawa.

There was no stopping Schauffele, though. This was his third win in a row, in one sense. He had won the Travelers Championship in his last full start and at the beginning of Scottish Open week he claimed the unofficial JP McManus Pro-Am in Ireland with scores of 64-70 by one from Sam Burns. Once in Scotland, Schauffele gave Cameron Tringale an 11-shot start and still came out on top. Tringale equalled the course record with a 61 in the calm morning conditions on Thursday, with nine birdies in 11 holes at one point, while Schauffele scored 72 on a blowy afternoon. But the following morning, which was not nearly as friendly as the previous day, Schauffele posted a 65. Tringale maintained his three-shot lead with a 72, but dropped back with a 74 on Saturday. That was the day Schauffele went ahead with a 66 for a two-shot advantage.

He birdied the first two holes on Sunday but then bogeyed three out of four holes to close the front nine. Kurt Kitayama went ahead before a bogey at the 17th to post four under par after a 66. Schauffele responded with birdies at the short 14th, where Jordan Spieth had a double bogey when one off the lead, and the par-five 16th, where he hit a fine second shot. Schauffele saved par at the 17th which meant a bogey at the last, the hardest hole on the course averaging 4.56, did not matter. He finished with a 70 for seven-under-par 273, to win by three from Kitayama, while young Korean Joohyung Kim was third. The Open qualifying spots went to Kitayama, Jamie Donaldson and Brandon Wu.

"It's special," said Schauffele after winning his first Rolex Series event. "It's different playing over here. You've got to play golf differently. The fans are incredible. They pushed me along all day and this is definitely a nice win. It was nice to hit a few better shots coming down the stretch and kind of calm the ship here. It was looking pretty bad for a bit but this one is extra special because of that."

Due to legal action on behalf of golfers who had played in LIV Golf events, four players were added to the field once the initial 156-man draw had been announced. Branden Grace, Justin Harding and Adrian Otaegui all made the cut but Ian Poulter failed to qualify after an opening 78.

The Renaissance Club, North Berwick, Scotland — July 7-10
Par 70 (35-35); 7,237 yards — Purse: $8,000,000

1	**Xander Schauffele**	72	65	66	70	273	€1,378,143
2	**Kurt Kitayama**	66	71	71	66	274	862,324
3	**Joohyung Kim**	68	71	69	67	275	517,001
4	Patrick Cantlay	70	70	69	67	276	356,348
	Tommy Fleetwood	73	69	67	67	276	356,348
6	Jamie Donaldson	70	71	69	67	277	239,895
	Matt Fitzpatrick	71	66	70	70	277	239,895
	Cameron Tringale	61	72	74	70	277	239,895
	Brandon Wu	67	72	71	67	277	239,895
10	Dean Burmester	68	72	70	68	278	155,336
	Thomas Detry	73	67	69	69	278	155,336
	Rasmus Hojgaard	66	72	70	70	278	155,336
	Alex Smalley	67	73	67	71	278	155,336
	Cameron Smith	68	75	68	67	278	155,336
	Jordan Spieth	68	72	66	72	278	155,336
16	Christiaan Bezuidenhout	73	70	70	66	279	103,262
	Wyndham Clark	71	71	70	67	279	103,262
	Doug Ghim	67	69	74	69	279	103,262
	Max Homa	71	71	66	71	279	103,262
	Maverick McNealy	73	70	69	67	279	103,262
	Joaquin Niemann	69	69	70	71	279	103,262
	Ryan Palmer	67	72	67	73	279	103,262
	Jason Scrivener	69	73	72	65	279	103,262
24	Stewart Cink	70	73	70	67	280	72,254
	Branden Grace	69	72	67	72	280	72,254
	Tyrrell Hatton	68	70	72	70	280	72,254
	Thriston Lawrence	69	71	71	69	280	72,254
	Jordan Smith	68	69	69	74	280	72,254
	Sami Valimaki	70	73	71	66	280	72,254
30	Maximilian Kieffer	71	68	72	70	281	57,193
	Mikko Korhonen	69	74	68	70	281	57,193
	Troy Merritt	74	69	71	67	281	57,193
	Alex Noren	73	68	71	69	281	57,193
	Thorbjorn Olesen	73	69	72	67	281	57,193
	Gary Woodland	64	72	72	73	281	57,193
36	Rafa Cabrera Bello	69	69	67	77	282	45,315
	Keith Mitchell	73	70	73	66	282	45,315
	James Morrison	75	68	69	70	282	45,315
	Matthieu Pavon	72	70	73	67	282	45,315
	Jhonattan Vegas	72	68	70	72	282	45,315
	Fabrizio Zanotti	70	72	69	71	282	45,315
42	Alexander Bjork	68	73	67	75	283	36,619
	Harris English	71	71	71	70	283	36,619
	Russell Knox	68	75	69	71	283	36,619
	Adrian Otaegui	71	72	68	72	283	36,619
	Connor Syme	70	69	74	70	283	36,619
47	Adri Arnaus	69	72	71	72	284	27,711
	Rickie Fowler	69	69	71	75	284	27,711

	Ryan Fox	74	68	73	69	284	27,711
	Dylan Frittelli	67	76	69	72	284	27,711
	Rikard Karlberg	73	70	69	72	284	27,711
	Matt Kuchar	73	68	69	74	284	27,711
	David Law	72	71	72	69	284	27,711
	Sebastian Soderberg	71	70	76	67	284	27,711
55	Haotong Li	70	73	70	72	285	22,917
	Jon Rahm	68	72	74	71	285	22,917
	Nick A Taylor	75	68	70	72	285	22,917
	Ashun Wu	71	68	72	74	285	22,917
59	Matthew Jordan	68	74	71	73	286	21,499
	JJ Spaun	70	71	71	74	286	21,499
61	Marcus Armitage	74	69	72	72	287	19,845
	Corey Conners	70	73	71	73	287	19,845
	Nacho Elvira	70	73	72	72	287	19,845
	Ewen Ferguson	67	76	71	73	287	19,845
	Marc Warren	71	72	70	74	287	19,845
66	Sam Burns	67	76	71	74	288	17,168
	Sean Crocker	68	75	73	72	288	17,168
	Justin Harding	65	74	77	72	288	17,168
69	Charley Hoffman	69	72	72	76	289	16,774
	Justin Rose	68	72	78	71	289	16,774
71	Chris Kirk	71	71	74	75	291	16,538
72	Guido Migliozzi	72	71	76	74	293	16,380

Cazoo Classic

Richie Ramsay's daughter is six years old. He had not won for seven years. The 39-year-old Scot was finally able to fulfil a promise to get her a trophy when he made an eight-foot putt for par on the 18th green at Hillside to win the Cazoo Classic. This was Ramsay's fourth victory, but his first since the 2015 Hassan Trophy. Always at home on a links, he came from one behind Julien Guerrier to finish one ahead of local Paul Waring. Only two months previously he had made a double bogey at the final hole to lose the chance of winning at the Betfred British Masters.

"The biggest thing for me was I made a promise to my daughter and I don't break promises to her," Ramsay said. "I got a bit emotional there at the end. I haven't won since my daughter was born and that's six years. That one's for Olivia. I've got the US Amateur trophy and the European Masters in the living room and she likes those trophies. We were playing one day and she's like 'Dad, I really like these.' And I said, 'Would you want one?' She said, 'Yeah, I want one.' I said, 'Every time I leave the house, my goal is to get you a trophy.' And that was a good two years ago.

"I've had some bad times over the last couple of years but I kept believing, I knew my game was good. There's nothing better than holing a putt under the gun, when it matters, when the tournament is on the line. It's just hours and hours of practice and it comes down to one shot and I managed to do it. It doesn't matter what happens now, I'll remember that for the rest of my life."

Ramsay scored 69-69-67-69 for a 14-under-par total of 274, making birdies at the 14th, 15th and, to take the lead for good, the 17th. Waring, who opened with a 63, closed with a 70 but could not get in front of Ramsay. Guerrier led for much of the day, but his advantage started dwindling as he bogeyed 13, 15 and 17 for a 72. He tied for third, two back, with Marcus Kinhult, Robin Petersson, Daan Huizing and Grant Forrest. Kinhult, who won the British Masters at Hillside in 2019, was four under for the back nine until a bogey at the last.

Hillside Golf Club, Southport, England — July 21-24
Par 72 (36-36); 7,109 — Purse: €1,750,000

1	**Richie Ramsay**	69	69	67	69	274	€297,500
2	**Paul Waring**	63	70	72	70	275	192,500
3	**Grant Forrest**	66	69	71	70	276	77,140
	Julien Guerrier	66	69	69	72	276	77,140
	Daan Huizing	68	68	71	69	276	77,140
	Marcus Kinhult	72	68	69	67	276	77,140
	Robin Petersson	68	70	70	68	276	77,140
8	Jens Dantorp	66	69	70	73	278	39,317
	Angel Hidalgo	69	70	69	70	278	39,317
	Andy Sullivan	73	71	65	69	278	39,317
11	Victor Dubuisson	70	70	70	69	279	28,595
	Thorbjorn Olesen	71	71	66	71	279	28,595
	Eddie Pepperell	68	74	68	69	279	28,595
	Lee Slattery	71	70	69	69	279	28,595
	Santiago Tarrio	68	71	73	67	279	28,595
16	Marcus Armitage	69	69	70	72	280	23,144
	Garrick Porteous	65	72	73	70	280	23,144
	Callum Shinkwin	69	68	75	68	280	23,144
	Sami Valimaki	71	66	69	74	280	23,144
20	Matthew Baldwin	71	72	71	67	281	19,542
	Alexander Bjork	72	70	64	75	281	19,542
	Darren Fichardt	68	71	72	70	281	19,542
	Robert MacIntyre	73	69	66	73	281	19,542
	Richard Sterne	70	68	69	74	281	19,542
	Jordan Wrisdale	69	72	69	71	281	19,542
26	Todd Clements	70	72	68	72	282	17,150
	David Drysdale	71	72	70	69	282	17,150
	Gavin Green	72	69	72	69	282	17,150
29	Craig Howie	67	77	71	68	283	15,050
	Richard Mansell	66	75	71	71	283	15,050
	Adrian Otaegui	72	70	70	71	283	15,050
	Alfie Plant	71	73	69	70	283	15,050

	Darius van Driel	71	71	71	70	283	15,050	52	Jorge Campillo	68	74	73	72	287	6,344
34	Ashley Chesters	70	72	69	73	284	12,150		Jarryd Felton	72	69	74	72	287	6,344
	Nacho Elvira	73	65	72	74	284	12,150		Zander Lombard	72	72	71	72	287	6,344
	Matthew Jordan	72	72	73	67	284	12,150		Stuart Manley	68	76	69	74	287	6,344
	Richard McEvoy	71	71	71	71	284	12,150	56	Ross Fisher	70	74	71	73	288	5,513
	Lukas Nemecz	71	73	67	73	284	12,150		David Horsey	69	69	78	72	288	5,513
	Antoine Rozner	74	70	70	70	284	12,150		Frederic Lacroix	74	70	73	71	288	5,513
	Andrew Wilson	69	71	74	70	284	12,150		Matthew Southgate	67	71	75	75	288	5,513
41	Gonzalo Fdez-Castano	72	71	70	72	285	9,975	60	Kristoffer Broberg	72	72	71	74	289	5,075
	Raphael Jacquelin	71	71	71	72	285	9,975	61	Pedro Figueiredo	71	73	72	74	290	4,725
	Ricardo Santos	71	72	73	69	285	9,975		Aman Gupta	68	76	74	72	290	4,725
	Jack Senior	67	72	74	72	285	9,975		Hugo Leon	72	72	74	72	290	4,725
	Ben Stow	68	73	71	73	285	9,975	64	Oliver Bekker	68	76	74	73	291	4,288
46	Oliver Farr	69	73	71	73	286	8,050		Damien Perrier	70	74	75	72	291	4,288
	Sihwan Kim	70	70	71	75	286	8,050	66	Anton Karlsson	71	73	71	77	292	3,938
	Romain Langasque	73	70	69	74	286	8,050		Dale Whitnell	71	72	76	73	292	3,938
	JC Ritchie	70	72	71	73	286	8,050	68	Daniel Hillier	70	74	73	76	293	3,675
	Robin Roussel	71	72	71	72	286	8,050	69	Wilco Nienaber	71	72	77	74	294	3,500
	Henric Sturehed	71	70	73	72	286	8,050	70	Oliver Fisher	68	76	79	72	295	3,325

Hero Open

"Winning a golf tournament is not easy," gasped Sean Crocker. "And Eddie did not make that easy for me either." That would be Eddie Pepperell, who closed with a 65 at Fairmont St Andrews, but Crocker held on for a wire-to-wire maiden victory. "I was nervous," he added. "I've felt pressure like that before but it's my first pro win. That door has been locked shut for me for almost five years. To go wire-to-wire I think I knocked the door clean off its hinges, which is nice."

Little about tournament golf is easy and Crocker started the 2022 season on the DP World Tour with eight missed cuts and a retirement in his first nine events. But in Scotland the 25-year-old, born in Zimbabwe but based in America, went ahead with an opening 63 with eight birdies, an eagle and one bogey. He stayed in front with 66-69, extending his lead to two shots with one round to play. On Sunday, Crocker made two birdies and a bogey going out, which kept his pursuers interested. Pepperell was chief among them, making seven birdies in the first 15 holes, only faltering at the ninth.

Crocker responded with three birdies in four holes to start the back nine, holing from 15 feet at the 13th to go two clear again. But Pepperell birdied the 18th to finish on 21 under par so Crocker was only one ahead. He drove the green at the short par-four 15th only to three-putt for a par, and was tested at the last two holes, holing from seven feet at 17 and four feet at the last, having left his approach on the lower tier, for vital pars. Crocker closed with a 68 for a 22-under-par total of 266. David Law, who was fourth in 2021, shared third place with Adrian Otaegui, two behind Pepperell.

"It just shows you that you just don't know what this game is going to bring you," Crocker said. "We go out there every day trying our hardest and we can play terrible for a long time and then all of a sudden you have a week like this where every bounce seemed to go my way, putts dropped, I hit the ball beautifully and it just makes me appreciate this game I play and what I get to do for a living."

Fairmont St Andrews (Torrance), St Andrews, Fife, Scotland — July 28-31
Par 72 (36-36); 7,230 yards — Purse: €1,750,000

1	**Sean Crocker**	63	66	69	68	266	€297,500	12	Daniel Young	68	69	67	69	273	29,138
2	**Eddie Pepperell**	67	66	69	65	267	192,500		Daniel Hillier	66	70	68	69	273	29,138
3	**David Law**	65	66	70	68	269	98,875	14	Romain Langasque	64	68	75	67	274	24,675
	Adrian Otaegui	64	67	70	68	269	98,875		Hurly Long	69	69	68	68	274	24,675
5	Oliver Hundeboll	67	67	69	67	270	67,725		Masahiro Kawamura	68	68	70	68	274	24,675
	Jens Dantorp	64	67	69	70	270	67,725		Joel Stalter	68	70	71	65	274	24,675
7	Callum Shinkwin	69	65	71	66	271	45,150		Louis de Jager	68	66	68	72	274	24,675
	Soren Kjeldsen	66	68	71	66	271	45,150	19	Jesper Svensson	70	68	68	69	275	21,000
	Wilco Nienaber	71	61	71	68	271	45,150		Jacques Kruyswijk	68	68	68	71	275	21,000
10	Alvaro Quiros	66	71	68	67	272	33,600		Victor Dubuisson	65	70	67	73	275	21,000
	Oliver Farr	65	67	70	70	272	33,600	22	Stuart Manley	70	67	70	69	276	17,938

	Henric Sturehed	70	68	69	69	276	17,938
	Niall Kearney	68	66	72	70	276	17,938
	Justin Walters	70	66	69	71	276	17,938
	Robert Rock	70	66	69	71	276	17,938
	Ryan Fox	68	70	71	67	276	17,938
	Ross Fisher	65	66	72	73	276	17,938
	Christoffer Bring	68	70	72	66	276	17,938
30	Garrick Porteous	68	70	69	70	277	13,109
	Chase Hanna	69	69	69	70	277	13,109
	Robin Roussel	71	66	70	70	277	13,109
	Matthew Southgate	69	66	73	69	277	13,109
	Ewen Ferguson	73	61	72	71	277	13,109
	Bryce Easton	67	70	71	69	277	13,109
	David Horsey	67	69	70	71	277	13,109
	Jorge Campillo	67	65	76	69	277	13,109
	JC Ritchie	66	69	70	72	277	13,109
	Ben Stow	64	69	76	68	277	13,109
	Paul Waring	72	65	67	73	277	13,109
41	Jeff Winther	68	67	72	71	278	9,450
	Francesco Laporta	67	70	70	71	278	9,450
	Grant Forrest	68	70	69	71	278	9,450
	Dimitrios Papadatos	66	71	71	70	278	9,450
	Connor Syme	65	70	73	70	278	9,450
	Darius van Driel	70	68	70	70	278	9,450
	Scott Jamieson	66	64	75	73	278	9,450
	Oliver Wilson	67	71	70	70	278	9,450
49	Raphael Jacquelin	70	68	69	72	279	6,850
	Jonathan Thomson	66	65	75	73	279	6,850
	Jack Senior	71	67	71	70	279	6,850
	Adam Keogh	67	67	70	75	279	6,850
	Aman Gupta	69	63	77	70	279	6,850
	Andy Sullivan	67	67	76	69	279	6,850
	Josh Geary	69	68	74	68	279	6,850
56	Matthew Baldwin	69	69	71	72	281	5,600
	Gavin Green	67	69	74	71	281	5,600
	Tom Gandy	65	69	76	71	281	5,600
59	Niklas Lemke	68	68	73	73	282	5,163
	Ashley Chesters	64	71	77	70	282	5,163
61	Graeme Storm	67	71	72	73	283	4,813
	David Carey	71	67	76	69	283	4,813
63	Brandon Stone	69	68	71	76	284	4,463
	Frank Kennedy (A)	70	68	71	75	284	
	Alfie Plant	68	70	77	69	284	4,463
66	Adilson Da Silva	66	71	74	74	285	4,025
	Lukas Nemecz	71	67	75	72	285	4,025
	Oliver Fisher	66	72	76	71	285	4,025
69	Albin Bergstrom	67	71	73	76	287	3,588
	Jean-Baptiste Gonnet	69	68	78	72	287	3,588

Cazoo Open

Callum Shinkwin secured a second win on the DP World Tour when he finished four strokes clear of the field at the Cazoo Open. The 29-year-old from Watford had been fourth and eighth on his last appearances on the Twenty Ten course at Celtic Manor and capitalised on his past experience during a week when scoring was not generally low. After opening 69-68, it was a 65 on Saturday, matching the low round for the tournament, that sent Shinkwin into the lead. A birdie at the 18th left him one ahead of Julian Guerrier, the leader for the first two days.

Guerrier, the 54-hole leader at Hillside two weeks earlier, drew level at the second hole on Sunday only then to make three bogeys in a row. The initial skirmishes went decisively to the Englishman as he made three birdies in a row from the fourth with putts of 17, seven and five feet. Six ahead at that point, Shinkwin mixed three birdies and four bogeys the rest of the way but Connor Syme still gave him something to think about. The Scot eagled the 11th, then birdied the 15th and the 16th, where Shinkwin bogeyed. Another birdie, his third in a row, at the 17th brought Syme within three going to the tricky par-five 18th but while Shinkwin made sure of his par, Syme bogeyed.

A closing 70 for 12-under-par 272 gave Shinkwin a four-shot win over Syme, who closed with a 68, while Guerrier's 76 dropped him into a large tie for third place. "I feel great, even though I had a few shots of a lead heading into the back nine it's still not easy, especially when Connor then made a charge," said Shinkwin, who took his maiden title at the Cyprus Open in 2020. "There was a lot of pressure still and even down the last, it's not an easy hole, a lot of people have made a high number there even if they've hit the fairway.

"The scores haven't been there before this but this week was my week. Winning anywhere is fantastic, it's a great feeling. There were no crowds in Cyprus so winning with family and friends here, it means so much more."

David Howell, at the age of 47, became the third player, and the youngest so far, to make 700 appearances on the DP World Tour after Sam Torrance and Miguel Angel Jimenez.

Celtic Manor Resort (Twenty Ten), City of Newport, Wales
Par 71 (36-35); 7,503

August 4-7
Purse: €1,750,000

1	**Callum Shinkwin**	69	68	65	70	272	€297,500
2	**Connor Syme**	67	73	68	68	276	192,500
3	**Renato Paratore**	70	71	72	66	279	77,140
	Andy Sullivan	74	67	71	67	279	77,140
	David Dixon	70	73	69	67	279	77,140
	Lucas Bjerregaard	71	72	68	68	279	77,140
	Julien Guerrier	67	68	68	76	279	77,140
8	Paul Waring	74	70	65	71	280	43,750
9	Marcus Armitage	68	70	76	67	281	35,467
	Jazz Janewattananond	70	70	72	69	281	35,467
	Matti Schmid	75	71	66	69	281	35,467
12	Thomas Detry	72	66	76	68	282	28,350
	Ewen Ferguson	68	71	72	71	282	28,350
	Nacho Elvira	70	70	71	71	282	28,350
15	Daan Huizing	70	73	72	68	283	24,675
	Matthew Baldwin	72	70	71	70	283	24,675
	Mikko Korhonen	68	71	70	74	283	24,675
18	Dale Whitnell	67	72	76	69	284	22,138
	Alfredo Garcia-Heredia	69	74	70	71	284	22,138
20	Robert Rock	70	74	71	70	285	19,810
	Richard Mansell	70	74	73	68	285	19,810
	Eddie Pepperell	68	74	70	73	285	19,810
	Paul Dunne	70	71	71	73	285	19,810
	Johannes Veerman	69	68	72	76	285	19,810
25	Frederic Lacroix	70	70	75	71	286	15,838
	Pep Angles	70	75	70	71	286	15,838
	Espen Kofstad	70	68	77	71	286	15,838
	Anton Karlsson	70	74	73	69	286	15,838
	Ivan Cantero Gutierrez	68	74	72	72	286	15,838
	Lee Slattery	70	72	72	72	286	15,838
	Henric Sturehed	72	73	69	72	286	15,838
	Ross McGowan	71	69	73	73	286	15,838
	David Howell	73	71	68	74	286	15,838
	Ashley Chesters	72	71	69	74	286	15,838
35	Oliver Farr	72	73	70	72	287	12,110
	Garrick Porteous	69	74	74	70	287	12,110
	Daniel Hillier	72	72	73	70	287	12,110
	Zhengkai Bai	75	70	72	70	287	12,110
	Bryce Easton	73	70	68	76	287	12,110
40	Louis de Jager	70	73	72	73	288	10,675
	Chase Hanna	75	71	70	72	288	10,675
	Jorge Campillo	70	75	72	71	288	10,675
43	Ricardo Santos	71	73	72	73	289	9,100
	Haydn Porteous	70	70	78	71	289	9,100
	Marcus Helligkilde	71	70	71	77	289	9,100
	David Law	72	74	72	71	289	9,100
	Rikard Karlberg	71	74	74	70	289	9,100
	Stephen Gallacher	74	72	75	68	289	9,100
49	Jack Senior	71	67	78	74	290	7,175
	Gregory Havret	71	69	74	76	290	7,175
	Darren Fichardt	69	77	72	72	290	7,175
	Ross Fisher	71	75	72	72	290	7,175
	Josh Geary	72	72	75	71	290	7,175
54	John Catlin	70	73	72	76	291	6,125
55	Francesco Laporta	70	74	73	75	292	5,863
	Lorenzo Gagli	72	71	76	73	292	5,863
57	Jeff Winther	72	72	73	76	293	5,513
	Maximilian Kieffer	68	76	77	72	293	5,513
59	Barclay Brown (A)	79	67	71	77	294	
	Jacques Blaauw	74	70	74	76	294	5,075
	Thorbjorn Olesen	72	69	71	82	294	5,075
	Niall Kearney	72	73	76	73	294	5,075
63	Stuart Manley	74	71	71	79	295	4,550
	Tom Gandy	73	70	77	75	295	4,550
	Dimitrios Papadatos	70	76	75	74	295	4,550
66	Chris Wood	71	71	75	79	296	4,200
67	Alfie Plant	71	74	75	78	298	3,938
	Jens Dantorp	71	74	79	74	298	3,938
69	Jonathan Thomson	73	71	78	78	300	3,675
70	Greig Hutcheon	71	74	77	82	304	3,500
71	Joachim B Hansen	71	73	77	84	305	3,325

ISPS Handa World Invitational

While Maja Stark made an incredible final-round charge to win the women's version of the ISPS Handa World Invitational, Ewen Ferguson started fast and claimed a three-shot wire-to-wire win on the men's side at Galgorm Castle. It was the 26-year-old Scot's second title after he won the Commercial Bank Qatar Masters earlier in the year.

The two tournaments were played alongside each other, utilising two courses for the first two days, with alternating groups of men and women. Ferguson opened at Galgorm with a course-record 61 thanks to five birdies and eagles at the 10th and 18th holes. He holed out from a bunker at the 10th and chipped in from 14 yards at the last. Two weeks earlier he had also made a course-record 61 at Fairmont St Andrews during the Hero Open. Four ahead after 18 holes, he added a 70 at Massereene, seeing his lead cut to one, but then returned to Galgorm and posted a 68 to go three clear.

A bogey at the ninth on Sunday meant Ferguson was out in level par and only two ahead of Richard Mansell, although he holed a nine-footer for a birdie at the 10th. Then Spain's Borja Virto made four birdies in five holes to get within one before dropping a shot at the short 14th, and also at the last. Virto closed with a 68 for nine under par, while Connor Syme, runner-up the previous week, birdied three of the last four holes for his own 68 to tie with Virto.

Ferguson, meanwhile, ground out the pars on the last eight holes and signed for a 69 and a 12-under-par total of 268. "It feels unbelievable," he said. "I just can't believe how calm I was out there. It couldn't have worked out any better playing with Connor. I felt although I played with him the first two days and he was playing so, so good, and I felt he was my main rival for the day, so managing to play with him and hold each other off and keep up with each other was so good. Just can't believe I'm a winner again."

Galgorm Castle Golf Club, Ballymena, Northern Ireland — August 11-14
Par 70 (34-36); 7,151 yards — Purse: $1,500,000
Massereene Golf Club (R1&2) par 70 (35-35); 6,817 yards

1	**Ewen Ferguson**	61	70	68	69	268	€247,186
2	**Connor Syme**	66	68	69	68	271	125,774
	Borja Virto	65	67	71	68	271	125,774
4	Marcus Helligkilde	67	72	64	69	272	61,748
	Richard Mansell	71	65	68	68	272	61,748
	Renato Paratore	67	68	73	64	272	61,748
7	Matthew Baldwin	68	69	68	68	273	39,986
	Filippo Celli (A)	66	67	72	68	273	
	Jordan Smith	68	67	74	64	273	39,986
10	Tom McKibbin	69	72	66	67	274	29,468
	Robin Petersson	66	70	70	68	274	29,468
	Jamie Rutherford	70	68	67	69	274	29,468
13	John Catlin	67	69	66	73	275	22,508
	Calum Fyfe	66	71	72	66	275	22,508
	Angel Hidalgo	67	71	72	65	275	22,508
	Craig Howie	69	68	70	68	275	22,508
	Jack Senior	69	69	65	72	275	22,508
18	Oliver Farr	70	68	68	70	276	19,193
	Guido Migliozzi	70	68	67	71	276	19,193
20	Thomas Aiken	66	74	69	68	277	17,448
	Ryan Evans	66	71	73	67	277	17,448
	Jens Fahrbring	68	70	68	71	277	17,448
23	Sebastian Garcia Rodriguez	66	73	70	69	278	15,994
	Jake McLeod	72	68	69	69	278	15,994
	Wilco Nienaber	66	72	71	69	278	15,994
26	Jens Dantorp	68	71	70	70	279	14,904
	Haraldur Magnus	71	69	69	70	279	14,904
28	David Borda	70	67	72	71	280	13,595
	Stephen Stallings Jr	69	68	73	70	280	13,595
	Dale Whitnell	66	69	75	70	280	13,595
	Jordan Wrisdale	71	69	69	71	280	13,595
32	Steven Brown	72	69	68	72	281	12,287
	Zach Murray	70	70	69	72	281	12,287
34	David Carey	67	73	68	74	282	11,196
	David Dixon	70	67	70	75	282	11,196
	Joakim Wikstrom	71	68	71	72	282	11,196
37	Felix Palson	65	68	75	78	286	10,324
38	Ryan Lumsden	68	70	72	78	288	10,033

D+D Real Czech Masters

In his rookie season in 2013, Maximilian Kieffer lost a nine-hole playoff. In 2021, he lost a five-hole playoff and was runner-up again, for the fourth time in total, the following week. But at the 249th attempt, Kieffer secured a victory on the DP World Tour at the D+D Real Czech Masters. The 32-year-old German won by a single stroke from Gavin Green at Albatross.

Green took the 36-hole lead with rounds of 67-63 for a three-stroke lead, with Kieffer a further shot behind. Heavy rain on Friday night and throughout Saturday led to the third round being suspended long before the leaders got on the course. Play resumed on Sunday with the event reduced to 54 holes. Malaysian Green led by two strokes with five holes to play before finding the water at the 14th and making a double-bogey six. Kieffer had made six birdies in the first 11 holes and, despite dropping a shot on the 15th, he hit a fine approach at the 17th for another birdie. After an opening 68, Kieffer had twin rounds of 66 to finish on a 16-under-par total of 200.

Green gave himself a chance of forcing a playoff at the last but his birdie putt horseshoed back at him. His 71 left Green one ahead of Tapio Pulkkanen, the runner-up in 2021 whose only bogey in a 67 came at the 18th, and Louis de Jager.

Kieffer was waiting to see if he would face extra holes again when he was informed the victory was his. "I wanted to be ready in case he made birdie," Kieffer said. "When the guy from the TV said 'you've won it' the feeling was ridiculous.

"I just love to play golf. Even if I had not won I still have a great life, I still enjoy playing golf. So now to win it's even better. You've just got to keep trying. I had a few difficult years where I didn't play well and then this year I feel like I'm playing very well."

Albatross Golf Resort, Prague, Czech Republic — August 18-21
Par 72 (36-36); 7,468 yards — Purse: €1,750,000

1	**Maximilian Kieffer**	68	66	66	200	€297,500
2	**Gavin Green**	67	63	71	201	192,500
3	**Louis de Jager**	64	70	68	202	98,875
	Tapio Pulkkanen	66	69	67	202	98,875
5	Zander Lombard	70	69	64	203	74,200
6	Jake McLeod	67	68	69	204	56,875
	Marcel Schneider	66	67	71	204	56,875
8	Thriston Lawrence	68	69	68	205	36,050

	Wilco Nienaber	71	67	67	205	36,050
	Eddie Pepperell	69	68	68	205	36,050
	Thomas Pieters	65	68	72	205	36,050
	Carlos Pigem	68	69	68	205	36,050
13	Pep Angles	68	67	71	206	23,433
	Zhengkai Bai	71	64	71	206	23,433
	Alfredo Garcia-Heredia	69	69	68	206	23,433
	Tom Lewis	69	69	68	206	23,433
	Renato Paratore	67	68	71	206	23,433
	Antoine Rozner	67	70	69	206	23,433
	Rory Sabbatini	68	69	69	206	23,433
	Jack Senior	68	68	70	206	23,433
	Cormac Sharvin	71	69	66	206	23,433
	Lee Slattery	69	69	68	206	23,433
23	Laurie Canter	72	68	67	207	17,675
	Jannik De Bruyn	71	69	67	207	17,675
	Grant Forrest	67	68	72	207	17,675
	Marcus Kinhult	68	70	69	207	17,675
	Richard Mansell	67	66	74	207	17,675
	Victor Perez	70	71	66	207	17,675
	Ian Poulter	70	71	66	207	17,675
30	Oliver Farr	69	70	69	208	15,050
	Stephen Gallacher	71	69	68	208	15,050
	Kalle Samooja	71	68	69	208	15,050
33	Julien Brun	73	68	68	209	12,381
	Jens Dantorp	70	71	68	209	12,381
	Ross Fisher	70	69	70	209	12,381
	Gregory Havret	70	70	69	209	12,381
	Daan Huizing	70	70	69	209	12,381
	Scott Jamieson	68	69	72	209	12,381
	Frederic Lacroix	69	71	69	209	12,381
	Oliver Wilson	70	69	70	209	12,381
41	Nino Bertasio	69	70	71	210	9,800
	Sean Crocker	71	71	68	210	9,800
	Joakim Lagergren	68	72	70	210	9,800
	Joost Luiten	71	70	69	210	9,800
	Zach Murray	71	68	71	210	9,800
	Ricardo Santos	69	71	70	210	9,800
47	Alejandro Canizares	69	72	70	211	8,225
	John Catlin	71	68	72	211	8,225
	Benjamin Hebert	70	66	75	211	8,225
50	Hugo Leon	67	73	72	212	7,525
51	Gregory Bourdy	71	70	72	213	6,510
	Sebastian Garcia Rodriguez	70	71	72	213	6,510
	Jordan Gumberg	66	74	73	213	6,510
	Soren Kjeldsen	70	70	73	213	6,510
	David Tomi (A)	69	71	73	213	
	Johannes Veerman	66	72	75	213	6,510
57	Hennie du Plessis	75	67	72	214	5,600
	Andrea Pavan	70	71	73	214	5,600
	Borja Virto	71	71	72	214	5,600
60	Maverick Antcliff	70	72	73	215	5,075
	Angel Hidalgo	67	75	73	215	5,075
	Ales Korinek	68	73	74	215	5,075
63	Thomas Aiken	70	72	75	217	4,550
	Matej Baca (A)	71	71	75	217	
	Gonzalo Fdez-Castano	73	69	75	217	4,550
	Uli Weinhandl	72	69	76	217	4,550
67	Jordan Zunic	68	74	77	219	4,200
68	David Carey	71	70	80	221	4,025
	Victor Dubuisson	72	70		WD	3,850

Omega European Masters

When Thriston Lawrence won the Joburg Open, the first event of the 2022 season late in 2021, the tournament was curtailed to 36 holes. Winning over the full 72 holes meant a lot to the 25-year-old South African but, in fact, it took a 73rd before he could lift the trophy at the Omega European Masters, one of the circuit's most historic events.

One thing that was the same for the big-hitting Lawrence was his ability to take advantage of the altitude, whether at home in Johannesburg or up the mountain in Crans-sur-Sierre. He opened with a 62 to share the lead with Alejandro Canizares, then fell a stroke behind the Spaniard when he completed a 64 on Saturday morning after storms interrupted play on Friday. By Saturday night he was ahead on his own, with a 67 moving him three clear of Matt Wallace.

Sunday produced a fine duel, Lawrence chipping in at the ninth after a mixed front nine, which also saw him take a double bogey at the fifth. He holed from 20 feet at the 12th to go two ahead but Wallace made his fourth birdie of the day at the 14th before Lawrence dropped a shot at the 16th. For the first time during the round he was back to sharing the lead and the pair parred home, Lawrence for a 69, Wallace for a bogey-free 66, as they tied on 18-under-par 262.

Wallace had not dropped a shot until the playoff at the 18th, three-putting from the back of the green as Lawrence made a par to take his second DP World Tour title. For the first time he broke into the world's top 100. "It's a privilege to be able to take this victory," he said. "There's so much history around this event, all the past champions, so I can't wait to get my hands on that trophy. Looking at Seve Ballesteros winning back-to-back, 1977-78, I wasn't even born yet. It's my first week here but definitely it's one of my favourites.

"There was a lot of talk after the Joburg Open, only winning a tournament over 36 holes. I think I've proved myself even before this win, having six top 10s. Not a lot of missed cuts. It's a little extra having a four-round victory, hopefully many more to come."

Crans-sur-Sierre Golf Club, Crans Montana, Switzerland
Par 70 (35-35); 6,824 yards

August 25-28
Purse: $2,000,000

1	**Thriston Lawrence**	62	64	67	69	262	€340,000
2	**Matt Wallace**	64	64	68	66	262	220,000
	Lawrence won playoff at first extra hole						
3	**Richard Mansell**	67	64	66	67	264	126,000
4	Jorge Campillo	66	65	68	66	265	84,933
	Scott Jamieson	64	67	66	68	265	84,933
	Antoine Rozner	70	65	64	66	265	84,933
7	Alejandro Canizares	62	63	73	68	266	55,000
	Marcel Schneider	67	66	67	66	266	55,000
9	Adri Arnaus	69	63	66	69	267	37,640
	Louis de Jager	64	64	72	67	267	37,640
	Nacho Elvira	65	65	69	68	267	37,640
	Masahiro Kawamura	68	65	65	69	267	37,640
	Danny Willett	70	67	64	66	267	37,640
14	Joachim B Hansen	71	65	68	64	268	30,000
	Sebastian Soderberg	67	67	70	64	268	30,000
16	Alexander Bjork	68	67	67	67	269	25,086
	Julien Brun	70	64	69	66	269	25,086
	George Coetzee	65	66	70	68	269	25,086
	Hennie du Plessis	70	66	64	69	269	25,086
	Francesco Laporta	71	66	68	64	269	25,086
	Marcel Siem	65	65	70	69	269	25,086
	Fabrizio Zanotti	68	68	65	68	269	25,086
23	Daan Huizing	68	66	71	65	270	20,500
	Marcus Kinhult	68	68	66	68	270	20,500
	Joost Luiten	65	70	65	70	270	20,500
	Benjamin Rusch	69	67	64	70	270	20,500
	Matthew Southgate	65	70	69	66	270	20,500
	Darius van Driel	66	66	68	70	270	20,500
29	David Drysdale	67	68	68	68	271	16,022
	Marcus Helligkilde	71	65	66	69	271	16,022
	Nicolai Hojgaard	68	68	64	71	271	16,022
	Mikko Korhonen	71	66	66	68	271	16,022
	Edoardo Molinari	69	67	67	68	271	16,022
	Niklas Norgaard	75	61	69	66	271	16,022
	Renato Paratore	67	70	66	68	271	16,022
	Daniel van Tonder	69	68	64	70	271	16,022
	Jeff Winther	67	69	66	69	271	16,022
38	Eduardo De La Riva	64	64	71	73	272	12,400
	Gavin Green	71	66	71	64	272	12,400
	Adrian Meronk	68	69	68	67	272	12,400
	Guido Migliozzi	68	66	72	66	272	12,400
	Carlos Pigem	68	65	72	67	272	12,400
	Santiago Tarrio	65	70	68	69	272	12,400
44	Darren Fichardt	65	69	71	68	273	9,800
	Matthew Jordan	70	67	70	66	273	9,800
	James Morrison	70	64	69	70	273	9,800
	Wilco Nienaber	69	68	65	71	273	9,800
	Richie Ramsay	67	68	68	70	273	9,800
	Lee Slattery	69	67	65	72	273	9,800
	Oliver Wilson	71	64	70	68	273	9,800
51	Aaron Cockerill	70	65	68	71	274	7,600
	Calum Fyfe	70	65	67	72	274	7,600
	Scott Hend	69	66	68	71	274	7,600
	Joel Sjoholm	69	68	71	66	274	7,600
55	Marcus Armitage	70	66	67	72	275	6,200
	Zhengkai Bai	70	65	69	71	275	6,200
	Wil Besseling	67	69	70	69	275	6,200
	Dimitrios Papadatos	68	69	68	70	275	6,200
	Matthieu Pavon	67	69	71	68	275	6,200
	Alvaro Quiros	68	66	74	67	275	6,200
	Robin Roussel	69	66	67	73	275	6,200
62	Oliver Bekker	66	70	67	73	276	5,200
	Jean-Baptiste Gonnet	69	68	69	70	276	5,200
	Lukas Nemecz	67	65	72	72	276	5,200
65	Sebastian Garcia Rodriguez	70	67	66	74	277	4,600
	Mike Lorenzo-Vera	71	66	69	71	277	4,600
	Andy Sullivan	69	67	70	71	277	4,600
68	Joel Girrbach	67	69	67	75	278	4,000
	Benjamin Hebert	71	66	70	71	278	4,000
	Ricardo Santos	70	66	70	72	278	4,000
71	Thomas Aiken	71	65	71	72	279	2,999
	Tom Lewis	70	67	71	71	279	2,999
73	Ashley Chesters	70	67	70	75	282	2,993
	Hugo Leon	71	66	71	74	282	2,993
	Maximilien Sturdza (A)	69	67	70	76	282	
76	Gonzalo Fdez-Castano	67	67	74	75	283	2,988

Made in HimmerLand

Newly appointed as Europe's Ryder Cup captain for 2023, Luke Donald teed up for the first of three successive events on the DP World Tour keen to assess the young talent to be found on the circuit. Players such as Scotland's Ewen Ferguson, who appeared to be heading for a third win of the season when he set the clubhouse target at 20 under par. He had started two shots behind the four 54-hole leaders, eagled the eighth and went two clear when he birdied the 14th, closing with a 66.

Yet Ferguson was not to be the winner of the Made in HimmerLand event, thanks to an inspired burst by a player who had played in the Ryder Cup as long ago as 2008. It was Oliver Wilson's only appearance and it took him six more years to win for the first time on the DP World Tour, and another eight to win again, 10 days short of his 42nd birthday.

Scores of 66-65-65 put Wilson, ranked 745th in the world, into a share of the lead with Ross McGowan, who had the advantage on the first day with a 62, Francesco Laporta and Matthew Southgate. In common with the others in the final groups, Wilson was treading water at first, birdieing the eighth and otherwise notching up the pars. Then the fireworks started. He holed a putt of 66 feet at the 13th, saw a chip lip out on 14, and made a 14-footer at the short 16th to draw level with Ferguson. At the next, he holed another bomb, from 64 feet, to go in front and signed off with a 67 for the winning total of 21-under-par 263.

An emotional Wilson said: "I was so confident. I knew I could get the job done. Everything I've done to this point to rebuild my game, I knew I could do it. And I was so in control, and I said I wasn't going to cry! I was so calm there. I almost enjoyed the last hole. It's pretty special. I'm so proud of myself. I feel like there's a lot ahead of me and I'm so pleased to get win number two.

"I love this place. I've done well here before. I holed two bombs on the back nine and I guess it was my day, but I feel like I deserved it. I guess 18 years' experience gets you to hang in there. And to get over the line, it feels good. It feels so good."

HimmerLand Golf & Spa Resort, Farso, Denmark — September 1-4
Par 71 (36-35); 6,651 yards — Purse: €3,000,000

1	**Oliver Wilson**	66	65	65	67	263	€510,000
2	**Ewen Ferguson**	63	67	68	66	264	330,000
3	**Kristian Krogh Johannessen**	67	65	69	65	266	189,000
4	Matthew Jordan	68	67	62	70	267	118,050
	Ross McGowan	62	65	69	71	267	118,050
	Francesco Laporta	64	64	68	71	267	118,050
	Matthew Southgate	63	68	65	71	267	118,050
8	Daan Huizing	68	68	70	62	268	64,350
	Marcus Helligkilde	63	67	70	68	268	64,350
	Nicolai von Dellingshausen	64	68	69	67	268	64,350
	Justin Walters	63	69	66	70	268	64,350
12	Fabrizio Zanotti	66	69	67	68	270	48,600
	Robert MacIntyre	65	66	69	70	270	48,600
	Tom Lewis	66	64	68	72	270	48,600
15	Angel Hidalgo	66	66	72	67	271	42,300
	Jeff Winther	66	67	70	68	271	42,300
	Rikard Karlberg	64	71	68	68	271	42,300
18	Zander Lombard	65	72	69	66	272	36,675
	Eddie Pepperell	67	67	71	67	272	36,675
	Alexander Bjork	66	69	67	70	272	36,675
	Jack Senior	68	66	68	70	272	36,675
22	Tapio Pulkkanen	69	65	72	67	273	28,500
	James Morrison	71	62	72	68	273	28,500
	George Coetzee	70	65	70	68	273	28,500
	Benjamin Hebert	71	67	67	68	273	28,500
	Masahiro Kawamura	68	67	69	69	273	28,500
	Andy Sullivan	68	66	70	69	273	28,500
	Anton Karlsson	66	69	69	69	273	28,500
	Richard McEvoy	70	67	67	69	273	28,500
	Rasmus Hojgaard	63	70	70	70	273	28,500
	Craig Howie	64	68	71	70	273	28,500
	Niklas Lemke	67	68	68	70	273	28,500
	Thorbjorn Olesen	71	66	66	70	273	28,500
	John Catlin	66	65	69	73	273	28,500
35	Ashun Wu	72	66	72	65	275	20,450
	Ricardo Gouveia	68	68	71	68	275	20,450
	Guido Migliozzi	70	67	68	70	275	20,450
	Marcel Siem	67	70	68	70	275	20,450
	Richard Mansell	64	64	76	71	275	20,450
	Darren Fichardt	71	64	69	71	275	20,450
41	Rory Sabbatini	67	67	72	70	276	16,800
	Richie Ramsay	66	69	71	70	276	16,800
	Lucas Bjerregaard	65	71	70	70	276	16,800
	Nacho Elvira	66	72	67	71	276	16,800
	Soren Kjeldsen	64	66	73	73	276	16,800
	Matthieu Pavon	67	67	69	73	276	16,800
47	Julian Suri	70	67	71	69	277	13,500
	Jamie Lovemark	67	67	73	70	277	13,500
	David Drysdale	68	68	70	71	277	13,500
	Gregory Havret	68	67	70	72	277	13,500
	Gavin Green	67	69	67	74	277	13,500
52	Jonathan Caldwell	65	71	73	69	278	10,000
	Shubhankar Sharma	68	70	71	69	278	10,000
	Kristoffer Broberg	69	68	71	70	278	10,000
	Gonzalo Fdez-Castano	69	68	71	70	278	10,000
	Renato Paratore	68	70	70	70	278	10,000
	Thomas Aiken	70	68	70	70	278	10,000
	Matt Ford	69	68	70	71	278	10,000
	Edoardo Molinari	67	70	70	71	278	10,000
	Stephen Gallacher	66	70	69	73	278	10,000
61	Garrick Porteous	65	68	71	75	279	8,400
62	Grant Forrest	66	72	73	69	280	7,800
	Frederic Lacroix	68	70	71	71	280	7,800
	Ricardo Santos	70	68	71	71	280	7,800
65	Santiago Tarrio	70	67	74	70	281	7,200
66	Aman Gupta	70	68	73	71	282	6,600
	David Law	68	69	73	72	282	6,600
	Justin Harding	67	71	70	74	282	6,600
69	Christian Jacobsen	71	65	76	72	284	5,400
	Paul Waring	68	67	75	74	284	5,400
	Jamie Donaldson	66	68	74	76	284	5,400
72	Oliver Hundeboll	72	66	77	70	285	4,497
73	Paul Dunne	67	71	75	73	286	4,494

BMW PGA Championship

A week that at times was both surreal and sombre ended in suitably celebratory fashion with Shane Lowry winning the BMW PGA Championship by one stroke from Rory McIlroy and Jon Rahm, with drama aplenty at the famous 18th hole of the West course at Wentworth. It was a fitting conclusion to the DP World Tour's biggest event staged at their headquarters. For some time, however, it was doubtful if the event could be concluded after the news of the death of Queen Elizabeth II was announced on Thursday evening.

Play in the first round was immediately suspended. Sensitive to the death of a head of state in any of the countries the tour visits around the world, now officials had a delicate decision to make as the United Kingdom entered a period of official mourning. In line with other sports, Friday's play was cancelled and it was only confirmed that afternoon that the tournament would resume on Saturday and be concluded over 54 holes. For the first time sell-out crowds were expected on each of Friday, Saturday and Sunday, but evening concerts and other activities at the venue, including some marking the centenary of the Wentworth Estate, were curtailed.

Keith Pelley, the Canadian chief executive of the European Tour Group, talked movingly of how much the Queen meant to the citizens of his own country, a member of the Commonwealth. Both home players and those from overseas felt it had been right to both halt play, and then resume, as a mark of respect. At 9.50am on Saturday, shortly before the official proclamation of His Majesty King Charles III, play stopped again for an impeccably observed two-minute silence.

A sombre air early in the day mellowed into a more joyful atmosphere as McIlroy returned a 65 in the second round to lie one shot off the 36-hole lead. "She was dignity, dedication and grace personified," was the Northern Irishman's tribute to the Queen. Australian Min Woo Lee scored a 62, perhaps inspired by heading into central London on Friday and joining the thousands paying their respects at the gates of Buckingham Palace. Other players, including American defending champion Billy Horschel, made the short journey to Windsor Castle on their enforced day off. Rahm said he was grateful for the two-minute silence on Saturday morning adding perspective even as he faced a three-foot putt for a double bogey. Sergio Garcia, after an opening 76, withdrew from the second round without providing a reason, attending a college football game in Austin, Texas on Saturday.

On a course saturated by rain earlier in the week, Patrick Reed scored an early 63 on Sunday to finish at 14 under par, eventually tying for fifth place alongside Thomas Detry and the joint 36-hole leaders, Soren Kjeldsen and Viktor Hovland. Talor Gooch had a tap-in eagle at the last to finish in fourth at 15 under. Due to a temporary injunction gained in the week of the Genesis Scottish Open, players who had appeared in LIV Golf events could participate and 15 did just that.

Lowry, who had not won since the 2019 Open at Royal Portrush, said it was "a win for one of the good guys". Starting the final round two off the lead after scores of 66-68, he eagled the fourth from 10 feet, while McIlroy hit an even better approach at the same hole to seven feet for the same result. But it was Rahm who set the tournament alight with a run of six under for five holes from the ninth. He holed from 20 feet for his second eagle of the day at the 18th and a 62 to post 16 under par. "Everything clicked," Rahm said. "Starting on nine, everything was firing on all cylinders. Not too often where I get to shoot a 29 with a bogey. It was definitely a fun round of golf. I've had a long year of having good rounds going and just not finishing them off."

Lowry birdied the seventh, eighth and 10th holes to get to within one with three par fives to come. He drew level with a four at the 12th and then had a run of pars, including a five at the 17th. But a fine drive and a superb five-iron to 20 feet set up a two-putt birdie for a 65 and a 17-under-par total of 199. He had not dropped a shot for 54 holes.

But there was still McIlroy to come. The FedEx Cup winner a fortnight earlier holed a long putt at the 15th to get to 15 under, drove poorly at 17 and only made a par, then hit a four-iron to 23 feet at the last. His eagle try to force a playoff looked in all the way — he was convinced, Lowry was convinced — but stopped on the edge of the hole.

In 2014, Lowry had been pipped by McIlroy's birdie-birdie finish. Now the tables had been turned and the pair embraced outside the recorder's hut. "Shane winning softens the blow," McIlroy said. "Seeing a friend win is always great. I'm really happy for him."

"Before I teed off I felt that if I went out and beat Rory I'd be in with a great chance," Lowry said. In his 13th appearance in the event, this was his fifth top 10 and 10th top-20 finish. "I'm just so happy that I've won this tournament. I'm not sure how that putt of Rory's missed on the last, which is not to say I wasn't hoping he was going to miss. I wouldn't have fancied a playoff with him.

"Since the first day I came here back in 2010, I've absolutely loved it. I love this tournament and I love this course. I love coming here, the area, I just love everything about it. I'm so happy that I can come here and win the tournament this year. I feel like I've had a great year. But it's not a great year unless you win. This is just the glaze on the cake for me."

Wentworth Club (West), Virginia Water, Surrey, England — September 8-11
Par 72 (35-37); 7,267 yards — Purse: $8,000,000

1	**Shane Lowry**	66	68	65	199	€1,351,106
2	**Rory McIlroy**	68	65	67	200	687,474
	Jon Rahm	70	68	62	200	687,474
4	Talor Gooch	70	64	67	201	397,384
5	Thomas Detry	68	65	69	202	263,068
	Viktor Hovland	64	68	70	202	263,068
	Soren Kjeldsen	68	64	70	202	263,068
	Patrick Reed	70	69	63	202	263,068
9	Rafa Cabrera Bello	68	65	70	203	154,980
	Billy Horschel	68	68	67	203	154,980
	Francesco Molinari	69	65	69	203	154,980
	Matthieu Pavon	68	70	65	203	154,980
13	Guido Migliozzi	68	68	68	204	117,149
	Adrian Otaegui	69	65	70	204	117,149
	Matthew Southgate	70	67	67	204	117,149
	Lee Westwood	68	71	65	204	117,149
	Fabrizio Zanotti	66	69	69	204	117,149
18	Abraham Ancer	68	70	67	205	95,690
	Rasmus Hojgaard	67	69	69	205	95,690
	David Horsey	72	66	67	205	95,690
	Sam Horsfield	70	68	67	205	95,690
	Masahiro Kawamura	68	67	70	205	95,690
23	Richard Bland	74	65	67	206	77,887
	Grant Forrest	69	67	70	206	77,887
	Justin Harding	69	67	70	206	77,887
	Matthew Jordan	65	69	72	206	77,887
	Joost Luiten	70	68	68	206	77,887
	Thomas Pieters	69	71	66	206	77,887
	Johannes Veerman	68	70	68	206	77,887
	Bernd Wiesberger	68	72	66	206	77,887
	Oliver Wilson	70	67	69	206	77,887
32	Jorge Campillo	70	66	71	207	56,429
	George Coetzee	67	69	71	207	56,429
	Scott Hend	70	70	67	207	56,429
	Kristian Krogh Johannessen	69	67	71	207	56,429
	Kurt Kitayama	68	71	68	207	56,429
	Pablo Larrazabal	69	67	71	207	56,429
	Adrian Meronk	70	68	69	207	56,429
	Eddie Pepperell	69	67	71	207	56,429
	Ian Poulter	69	71	67	207	56,429
	Andy Sullivan	64	72	71	207	56,429
42	Maverick Antcliff	69	69	70	208	41,328
	Oliver Bekker	69	70	69	208	41,328
	Wil Besseling	71	68	69	208	41,328
	Matt Fitzpatrick	69	67	72	208	41,328
	Daniel Gavins	69	70	69	208	41,328
	Min Woo Lee	76	62	70	208	41,328
	Adam Scott	69	70	69	208	41,328
	Jason Scrivener	66	69	73	208	41,328
50	Scott Jamieson	69	69	71	209	29,747
	Joakim Lagergren	71	69	69	209	29,747
	David Law	67	70	72	209	29,747
	Robert MacIntyre	71	69	69	209	29,747
	Graeme McDowell	71	69	69	209	29,747
	Victor Perez	69	71	69	209	29,747
	Antoine Rozner	69	68	72	209	29,747
57	Marcus Armitage	66	69	75	210	22,651
	Tommy Fleetwood	64	73	73	210	22,651
	Tyrrell Hatton	69	69	72	210	22,651
	Romain Langasque	69	68	73	210	22,651
	James Morrison	68	67	75	210	22,651
	Richie Ramsay	71	67	72	210	22,651
	Jack Senior	72	66	72	210	22,651
	Justin Walters	73	67	70	210	22,651
65	Maximilian Kieffer	71	69	71	211	18,280
	Frederic Lacroix	73	67	71	211	18,280
	Edoardo Molinari	72	68	71	211	18,280
68	Callum Shinkwin	69	71	72	212	15,895
	Connor Syme	69	70	73	212	15,895
	Daniel van Tonder	66	74	72	212	15,895
71	Julien Brun	69	69	75	213	11,922
72	Shaun Norris	71	69	74	214	11,919

DS Automobiles Italian Open

All roads lead to Rome and Marco Simone for the 2023 Ryder Cup and the DS Automobiles Italian Open featured a number of the most recent European team members, including Rory McIlroy, Matt Fitzpatrick, Tyrrell Hatton and Viktor Hovland, as well as current captain Luke Donald. US Open champion Fitzpatrick held the lead on Thursday and Saturday, FedEx Cup winner McIlroy on Friday.

But it was a player hoping to make his debut for Europe 12 months later who stole the title on Sunday with Robert MacIntyre scoring the best round of the week, a seven-under-par 64, and then beating Fitzpatrick at the first extra hole. It was a second win for the 26-year-old Scot, whose first came in the Cyprus Showdown in 2020, when the scores were wiped for a final-round shootout. It was almost similar in Rome with MacIntyre, after scores of 70-69-67, going out in 29 with six birdies, including three tap-ins in a row from the fifth.

The back nine was more mixed with three bogeys and four birdies. He led by three after back-to-back birdies at 12 and 13, then bogeyed the next two. He also got some help from his rivals. McIlroy started with a double bogey at the first, got himself back into contention before finding the water at the 16th. A week after being pipped at Wentworth, he finished fourth. Victor Perez scored 66 but missed a birdie chance at the last so finished at 13 under, one back of the playoff.

Fitzpatrick parred the first 10 holes, then drove the green at the short par-four 11th to make a birdie and hit the flagstick at the par-five 12th, settling for an eagle but oh-so-close to an albatross. He birdied the 16th to lead, then bogeyed the 17th as MacIntyre birdied the last. The Englishman got up and down for a four at 18 and a 67 to tie on 14-under-par 270.

Fitzpatrick drove into rough at the 18th in the playoff and could not match MacIntyre's birdie four. "I didn't think it was going to come again," said MacIntyre, who had slipped out of the world's top 100. "I've struggled the last year and made a lot of changes the last three months in my iron play. This week it has been absolutely brilliant." As for the 2023 Ryder Cup, the left-hander from Oban added: "Might as well say it: it's my number one priority. I was close last time. I think I've made a good start."

Fitzpatrick was among three sets of brothers who played in the event, all making the cut. He played in a tournament with his younger brother Alex, newly turned professional, for the first time, while Francesco Molinari was joined by his brother Edoardo, a vice-captain for 2023, and defending champion Nicolai Hojgaard was alongside twin Rasmus in 27th place.

Marco Simone Golf & Country Club, Rome, Italy — September 15-18
Par 71 (35-36); 7,268 yards — Purse: $3,000,000

1	**Robert MacIntyre**	70	69	67	64	270	€510,000
2	**Matt Fitzpatrick**	65	69	69	67	270	330,000
	MacIntyre won playoff at first extra hole						
3	**Victor Perez**	70	66	69	66	271	189,000
4	Rory McIlroy	67	66	71	68	272	150,000
5	Lucas Herbert	70	67	68	68	273	116,100
	Aaron Rai	69	70	65	69	273	116,100
7	Kurt Kitayama	71	67	67	69	274	90,000
8	Tyrrell Hatton	72	65	70	68	275	75,000
9	Oliver Bekker	68	70	68	70	276	63,600
	Jorge Campillo	70	71	68	67	276	63,600
11	Mikko Korhonen	73	67	68	69	277	55,200
12	Kiradech Aphibarnrat	70	73	68	67	278	47,475
	Eddie Pepperell	67	73	70	68	278	47,475
	Jordan Smith	69	68	71	70	278	47,475
	Dale Whitnell	69	73	69	67	278	47,475
16	Scott Jamieson	67	71	73	68	279	37,629
	Tom Lewis	70	65	73	71	279	37,629
	Thorbjorn Olesen	72	70	68	69	279	37,629
	Antoine Rozner	67	71	71	70	279	37,629
	Marcel Schneider	70	68	73	68	279	37,629
	Santiago Tarrio	72	70	69	68	279	37,629
	Andrew Wilson	74	69	68	68	279	37,629
23	Jesper Kennegard	74	68	68	70	280	32,550
	Tapio Pulkkanen	69	69	72	70	280	32,550
25	Thomas Bjorn	66	76	68	71	281	30,750
	Adrian Otaegui	74	69	69	69	281	30,750
27	Alex Fitzpatrick	70	69	72	71	282	26,700
	Nicolai Hojgaard	68	70	74	70	282	26,700
	Rasmus Hojgaard	70	73	73	66	282	26,700
	Ross McGowan	70	73	70	69	282	26,700
	Edoardo Molinari	70	72	72	68	282	26,700
	Yannik Paul	68	75	73	66	282	26,700
	Matthew Southgate	70	69	73	70	282	26,700
34	Alexander Bjork	74	69	68	72	283	20,829
	Luke Donald	69	68	76	70	283	20,829
	Gonzalo Fdez-Castano	69	74	69	71	283	20,829
	Gavin Green	67	75	70	71	283	20,829
	Viktor Hovland	71	68	73	71	283	20,829
	Guido Migliozzi	70	71	71	71	283	20,829
	Francesco Molinari	73	68	68	74	283	20,829
41	Louis de Jager	69	71	72	72	284	15,900
	Darren Fichardt	69	71	72	72	284	15,900
	Matt Ford	70	71	71	72	284	15,900
	Gregory Havret	72	69	73	70	284	15,900
	Romain Langasque	69	74	70	71	284	15,900
	Mike Lorenzo-Vera	71	70	70	73	284	15,900
	Alvaro Quiros	67	71	75	71	284	15,900
	Kalle Samooja	71	69	72	72	284	15,900
	Andy Sullivan	71	71	72	70	284	15,900
50	Niklas Norgaard Moller	76	65	71	73	285	11,700
	Robert Rock	72	71	72	70	285	11,700
	Robin Roussel	69	70	73	73	285	11,700
	Nicolai von Dellingshausen	69	73	73	70	285	11,700
	Ashun Wu	70	68	73	74	285	11,700
55	Maverick Antcliff	72	69	72	73	286	9,450
	Julien Brun	74	68	72	72	286	9,450
	Sebastian Garcia Rodriguez	71	66	77	72	286	9,450
	Lukas Nemecz	72	71	73	70	286	9,450
	Jason Scrivener	70	70	74	72	286	9,450
	Brandon Stone	71	72	74	69	286	9,450
61	Rafa Cabrera Bello	67	75	71	74	287	7,650
	Filippo Celli	69	72	72	74	287	7,650
	Rikard Karlberg	71	70	70	76	287	7,650
	Soren Kjeldsen	72	70	73	72	287	7,650
	Callum Shinkwin	72	70	72	73	287	7,650
	Justin Walters	71	69	75	72	287	7,650
67	Joost Luiten	66	71	77	74	288	6,450
	Stefano Mazzoli	71	72	71	74	288	6,450
69	David Howell	71	70	76	72	289	6,000
	Flavio Michetti (A)	70	69	73	77	289	
71	Niall Kearney	75	67	74	74	290	5,100
	Marc Warren	71	71	73	75	290	5,100
73	Ricardo Santos	71	71	74	75	291	4,497
74	Marco Florioli (A)	73	70	79	70	292	
	Espen Kofstad	72	67	78	75	292	4,494
76	Marcus Armitage	72	70	78	73	293	4,491
77	Chris Wood	74	69	78	73	294	4,488
	Julien Quesne	72	71	82		WD	4,485

Cazoo Open de France

Rasmus Hojgaard opened the Cazoo Open de France by equalling the course record of 62 at Le Golf National. He led for most of the way, but it was another 62, by Guido Migliozzi in the final round that brought victory. Migliozzi was 13 strokes behind at the halfway stage and still five behind with a round to play before posting nine birdies. The last of them was the winning blow, with a faded approach from 192 yards, over the water, that pitched 15 feet from the edge of the green, almost went in for a two and pulled up six feet behind the hole. It was the first birdie, and one of only two, on the final day at the dangerous finishing hole of the 2018 Ryder Cup venue.

"The shot was something incredible," said the 25-year-old Italian. "I went for it and it paid off. My caddie was not happy: it was not the real strategy but I felt I could try."

Migliozzi had not won since his first two wins on tour in 2019 at the Kenya Open and the Belgium Knockout. He added: "It was one of those days that I love to play golf. I love to battle on the golf course and today I received something back from golf. It was a beautiful day of golf."

Hojgaard, still looking for his first win of the year, led by two shots after his opening 62, then added a 65 to be six ahead of the field. But on the par-three second hole on Saturday the Dane found the water three times, holing a 14-footer for a quintuple-bogey eight. A 74 kept him one ahead of George Coetzee. The next day Hojgaard not only birdied the second but chipped in for an eagle at the third to go three clear.

However, bogeys at eight and nine let Coetzee and Thomas Pieters back into the mix, but they were all left trailing by Migliozzi, who ran off five birdies in a row from the sixth, then made three in a row from the 13th before the coup de grace at the last. He won by one from Hojgaard, who could not find a birdie at either of the last two holes to tie. Migliozzi scored 69-71-66-62 for a 16-under-par total of 268, while Hojgaard closed with a 68. Four strokes further back were Coetzee, Pieters and France's Paul Barjon.

Le Golf National (Albatross), Saint-Quentin-en-Yvelines, France — September 22-25
Par 71 (36-35); 7,247 yards — Purse: €3,000,000

1	**Guido Migliozzi**	69	71	66	62	268	€510,000
2	**Rasmus Hojgaard**	62	65	74	68	269	330,000
3	**Paul Barjon**	65	68	70	70	273	155,400
	George Coetzee	68	66	68	71	273	155,400
	Thomas Pieters	67	70	66	70	273	155,400
6	Jamie Donaldson	66	72	67	69	274	105,000
7	Jordan Smith	68	70	67	70	275	90,000
8	Robert MacIntyre	67	70	71	68	276	67,400
	Yannik Paul	68	69	67	72	276	67,400
	Jeff Winther	72	67	70	67	276	67,400
11	Adrian Meronk	72	67	70	69	278	53,400
	Antoine Rozner	69	66	69	74	278	53,400
13	Julien Brun	66	73	70	70	279	42,429
	Alex Fitzpatrick	68	70	70	71	279	42,429
	Joachim B Hansen	70	69	74	66	279	42,429
	Jazz Janewattananond	68	70	72	69	279	42,429
	Adrian Otaegui	70	70	67	72	279	42,429
	Marcel Schneider	69	72	69	69	279	42,429
	Julian Suri	70	69	69	71	279	42,429
20	Lucas Bjerregaard	72	68	68	72	280	33,500
	Alexander Bjork	64	71	76	69	280	33,500
	Thriston Lawrence	70	67	73	70	280	33,500
	Thorbjorn Olesen	71	69	71	69	280	33,500
	Sami Valimaki	70	71	70	69	280	33,500
	Nicolai von Dellingshausen	69	69	70	72	280	33,500
26	Nicolas Colsaerts	73	67	72	69	281	29,400
	Julien Sale (A)	72	69	68	72	281	
	Dale Whitnell	73	65	73	70	281	29,400
	Andrew Wilson	69	71	66	75	281	29,400
30	Grant Forrest	71	66	75	70	282	24,033
	Alfredo Garcia-Heredia	71	71	70	70	282	24,033
	Ricardo Gouveia	74	66	69	73	282	24,033
	Craig Howie	68	73	73	68	282	24,033
	Scott Jamieson	69	70	68	75	282	24,033
	Lukas Nemecz	72	69	70	71	282	24,033
	Matthieu Pavon	68	70	73	71	282	24,033
	Victor Perez	69	69	68	76	282	24,033
	Tapio Pulkkanen	66	73	75	68	282	24,033
39	Jonathan Caldwell	69	71	68	75	283	18,600
	David Horsey	69	72	69	73	283	18,600
	Niklas Lemke	72	69	74	68	283	18,600
	Zander Lombard	69	72	71	71	283	18,600
	Johannes Veerman	71	68	72	72	283	18,600
	Marc Warren	71	69	75	68	283	18,600
45	Kiradech Aphibarnrat	69	71	71	73	284	16,200
	Martin Couvra (A)	66	76	68	74	284	
	Oihan Guillamoundeguy (A)	69	69	72	74	284	
	Tom Vaillant (A)	68	71	68	77	284	
	Darius van Driel	73	68	70	73	284	16,200
50	Kristoffer Broberg	70	72	70	73	285	12,630
	Sean Crocker	72	69	69	75	285	12,630
	Gavin Green	72	70	74	69	285	12,630
	Tom Lewis	71	69	67	78	285	12,630
	Pierre Pineau	72	69	73	71	285	12,630
	Alvaro Quiros	68	74	73	70	285	12,630
	Ricardo Santos	70	69	71	75	285	12,630
	Marcel Siem	71	70	71	73	285	12,630
	Matthew Southgate	70	70	69	76	285	12,630
	Santiago Tarrio	71	71	71	72	285	12,630
60	Hennie du Plessis	73	67	72	74	286	9,300
	Sebastian Garcia Rodriguez	72	67	72	75	286	9,300
	Scott Hend	71	70	74	71	286	9,300
	Nicolai Hojgaard	69	69	73	75	286	9,300
	Hurly Long	70	71	74	71	286	9,300
65	Mathieu Decottignies-Lafon	68	68	74	77	287	8,100
	Angel Hidalgo	70	71	73	73	287	8,100
	Maximilian Kieffer	71	71	69	76	287	8,100
68	Francesco Laporta	73	69	76	70	288	7,350
	Adrien Saddier	69	72	72	75	288	7,350
70	Soren Kjeldsen	70	72	71	76	289	6,750
	James Morrison	66	73	79	71	289	6,750
72	Niall Kearney	70	72	76	72	290	6,000
	Carlos Pigem	70	72	72	76	290	6,000
	Huilin Zhang	73	69	75	73	290	6,000
75	Jean-Baptiste Gonnet	69	72	80	72	293	4,500
76	Joakim Lagergren	71	71	74	79	295	4,497

Alfred Dunhill Links Championship

Shane Warne was an Australian cricket superstar who died suddenly in March 2022. Warne regularly played as a celebrity amateur at the Alfred Dunhill Links Championship and often partnered his friend Ryan Fox, the Kiwi golfer and son of All Black rugby legend Grant Fox. The pair finished as runners-up in the team event in 2021. A year on Fox won the individual title, the biggest of his career to date, and immediately recalled his friend in an emotional interview.

"To be honest the only person I can really think of at the moment is Warne," Fox said. "He meant a lot to me and this event and was a great mate. It's a terrible shame he's not here. But he was definitely helping me out. Obviously, I was pretty nervy the last three holes. I didn't hit very good shots, to be honest, down the 16th, 17th and 18th. There was definitely some luck out there."

Fox, who also won the Ras al Khaimah Classic earlier in the year, opened with a 66 at St Andrews but was five behind Romain Langasque, who equalled the Old Course record with 61. Fox had a 74 at Carnoustie the next day, and then a 65 at Kingsbarns to lie in second place, four behind Richard Mansell. The Englishman's large lead soon dwindled and he closed with a 76 at St Andrews on Sunday. Fox, on the other hand, made six birdies in the first 12 holes to lead by three.

One shot went at the 13th, which he recovered at the 15th, then came the Road Hole, where he drove into thick rough and ended up two-putting from long range for a bogey. He could not birdie the last but it was fine, the 35-year-old New Zealander still finished one ahead of Alex Noren (69) and Callum Shinkwin (67). Fox closed with a 68 to be 15 under par on 273. Rory McIlroy finished off with a 66 to share fourth place with Antoine Rozner. Shinkwin and amateur partner Alex Acquavella won the team event by three shots on 37 under par.

Fox added: "I don't think it gets any better as a golfer to be honest. Obviously, winning The Open would be the next level up, but to say I've won a tournament on the Old Course coming down the last few holes on Sunday, which so many great champions have done, not only in this event but in Opens gone past, to add my name on that list is very, very cool."

St Andrews Links (Old Course), Fife, Scotland — September 29-October 2
Par 72 (36-36); 7,318 yards — Purse: $5,000,000
Carnoustie Golf Links (Championship) (R1-3) par 72 (36-36); 7,394 yards
Kingsbarns Golf Links (R1-3) par 72 (36-36); 7,227 yards

1	**Ryan Fox**	66	74	65	68	273	€830,609
2	**Alex Noren**	67	69	69	69	274	422,633
	Callum Shinkwin	68	71	68	67	274	422,633
4	Rory McIlroy	68	75	66	66	275	225,730
	Antoine Rozner	63	74	69	69	275	225,730
6	Daniel Gavins	65	73	67	71	276	171,008
7	Tyrrell Hatton	68	76	66	67	277	126,057
	Richard Mansell	66	68	67	76	277	126,057
	Niklas Norgaard	63	74	69	71	277	126,057
10	Grant Forrest	70	74	67	67	278	80,827
	Billy Horschel	71	71	67	69	278	80,827
	Louis Oosthuizen	72	73	65	68	278	80,827
	Tapio Pulkkanen	66	73	69	70	278	80,827
	Connor Syme	68	76	65	69	278	80,827
	Peter Uihlein	65	77	68	68	278	80,827
	Dale Whitnell	66	77	67	68	278	80,827
17	George Coetzee	67	75	72	65	279	63,191
	Padraig Harrington	69	71	69	70	279	63,191
	Rasmus Hojgaard	67	74	67	71	279	63,191
20	Robert MacIntyre	68	70	71	71	280	57,654
	Daniel van Tonder	70	73	68	69	280	57,654
22	Adri Arnaus	67	80	66	68	281	51,547
	Louis de Jager	68	75	70	68	281	51,547
	Matt Fitzpatrick	71	71	69	70	281	51,547
	Tommy Fleetwood	70	72	72	67	281	51,547
	Adrian Meronk	71	70	72	68	281	51,547
	Sami Valimaki	70	73	70	68	281	51,547
28	Alejandro Canizares	67	74	70	71	282	41,286
	Alex Fitzpatrick	73	69	69	71	282	41,286
	Francesco Molinari	68	73	73	68	282	41,286
	Eddie Pepperell	68	74	70	70	282	41,286
	Thomas Pieters	65	83	64	70	282	41,286
	Marcel Schneider	71	74	68	69	282	41,286
	Marcel Siem	66	74	73	69	282	41,286
	Matthew Southgate	67	73	69	73	282	41,286
36	Sebastian Garcia Rodriguez	68	73	68	74	283	32,247
	Matthew Jordan	67	76	71	69	283	32,247
	Romain Langasque	61	80	72	70	283	32,247
	Hurly Long	70	71	69	73	283	32,247
	David Micheluzzi	69	73	70	71	283	32,247
	Victor Perez	69	74	72	68	283	32,247
42	Jaco Ahlers	67	78	70	69	284	26,384
	Maximilian Kieffer	66	74	70	74	284	26,384
	Frederic Lacroix	62	78	72	72	284	26,384
	David Law	68	78	67	71	284	26,384
	Richie Ramsay	70	79	66	69	284	26,384
	Laird Shepherd	67	74	71	72	284	26,384
48	Christiaan Burke	66	77	65	77	285	21,498
	Stephen Gallacher	69	76	68	72	285	21,498
	Benjamin Hebert	68	76	70	71	285	21,498
	Richard Sterne	69	72	74	70	285	21,498
52	Julien Brun	66	73	74	73	286	17,712
	Nacho Elvira	64	76	75	71	286	17,712
	Daan Huizing	68	74	73	71	286	17,712

	Johannes Veerman	69	73	73	71	286	17,712
56	Oliver Bekker	66	74	69	78	287	15,635
	Richard Bland	70	78	67	72	287	15,635
	Joakim Lagergren	70	75	68	74	287	15,635
59	Thorbjorn Olesen	69	76	69	74	288	14,414
	Sebastian Soderberg	70	75	68	75	288	14,414
61	Maverick Antcliff	68	74	72	75	289	13,436
	Casey Jarvis	67	76	72	74	289	13,436
63	Jorge Campillo	70	79	66	76	291	12,703

Acciona Open de Espana

A split second before the packed gallery around the 18th green at Club de Campo burst into excited celebrations at Jon Rahm's victory in the Acciona Open de Espana, a lone voice shouted: "Viva Seve". Rahm was less than a year old when Seve Ballesteros won his third Open de Espana at Club de Campo in 1995 — his 50th and last European Tour victory. Although Angel de la Torre won five of the first seven Spanish Opens a century earlier, no one had won it more in modern times and now Rahm, having also won in 2018 and 2019, tied Seve in only his fourth appearance.

This latest victory, his eighth on the DP World Tour, was a barnstorming effort, Rahm finishing with eight birdies, an eagle and one bogey for the lowest round of the week. With 64-68-65-62 for a 25-under-par total of 259, the 27-year-old world number six won by six strokes and hugged his parents and grandmother with the cheers of the crowd still ringing in their ears.

"It was the goal coming in," Rahm said. "Seve is a great hero of mine and to do something he took his whole career to do in just a few years is quite humbling. It's emotional. Going up the 18th hole I knew what was about to happen and to get it done like that, I can't describe it."

France's Matthieu Pavon took second place with a birdie at the last for a 65. But for most of the day the last man between Rahm and his destiny was Min Woo Lee. The young Australian played with the Spanish star all four days and when Rahm took over the lead on Saturday, Lee was just one behind.

He just could not get his claws into Rahm on Sunday. He hit close at the sixth and made a birdie but not before Rahm had holed from 50 feet for a three of his own. At the next, a par five, Lee rolled in an eagle putt from just off the front of the green, but Rahm got up and down for a four to stay one in front. The Spaniard holed a 35-footer at the 11th to go three ahead, dropped his only shot of the weekend at the 12th after driving into the trees, then recovered with a birdie at the next, before hitting the flagstick from over 200 yards at the 14th and making an eagle. Finally, Lee cracked, taking a bogey and falling into third place with a 68.

Club de Campo Villa de Madrid (Black), Madrid, Spain — October 6-9
Par 71 (36-35); 7,112 yards — Purse: €1,750,000

1	**Jon Rahm**	64	68	65	62	259	€297,500
2	**Matthieu Pavon**	64	68	68	65	265	192,500
3	**Min Woo Lee**	67	65	66	68	266	110,250
4	Zander Lombard	69	66	66	67	268	80,850
	Edoardo Molinari	68	70	63	67	268	80,850
6	Louis de Jager	71	64	65	69	269	56,875
	Alfredo Garcia-Heredia	69	65	71	64	269	56,875
8	Kiradech Aphibarnrat	63	69	68	70	270	36,050
	Hennie du Plessis	65	66	72	67	270	36,050
	Yannik Paul	70	66	68	66	270	36,050
	Darius van Driel	63	69	72	66	270	36,050
	Marc Warren	70	65	65	70	270	36,050
13	Dan Bradbury	69	64	73	65	271	26,338
	Renato Paratore	67	69	66	69	271	26,338
	Eddie Pepperell	67	66	67	71	271	26,338
	Ashun Wu	63	72	68	68	271	26,338
17	Rikard Karlberg	71	69	66	66	272	23,625
18	Stephen Gallacher	65	65	70	73	273	22,138
	Jeremy Paul	70	70	67	66	273	22,138
20	Alejandro Canizares	66	71	68	69	274	20,358
	Niklas Norgaard Moller	66	69	71	68	274	20,358
	Marcel Siem	69	70	67	68	274	20,358
23	Lucas Bjerregaard	71	69	67	68	275	18,463
	Joakim Lagergren	64	69	69	73	275	18,463
	Joel Stalter	71	69	68	67	275	18,463
	Oliver Wilson	69	69	68	69	275	18,463
27	Jorge Campillo	68	68	69	71	276	15,575
	Joachim B Hansen	71	67	68	70	276	15,575
	Marcus Helligkilde	71	67	69	69	276	15,575
	Niklas Lemke	70	65	72	69	276	15,575
	Alvaro Quiros	66	71	66	73	276	15,575
	Santiago Tarrio	70	67	70	69	276	15,575
	Paul Waring	67	63	74	72	276	15,575
34	Ashley Chesters	72	67	70	68	277	12,731
	Dave Coupland	70	68	67	72	277	12,731
	Sebastian Garcia Rodriguez	70	64	69	74	277	12,731
	Angel Hidalgo	69	68	69	71	277	12,731
	Luis Masaveu (A)	66	68	70	73	277	
39	Steven Brown	71	66	69	72	278	10,675
	Victor Dubuisson	67	69	70	72	278	10,675
	Tommy Fleetwood	70	69	69	70	278	10,675
	Daniel Gavins	71	69	68	70	278	10,675
	Joost Luiten	71	68	68	71	278	10,675
	Daniel van Tonder	68	68	72	70	278	10,675
	Quim Vidal (A)	68	71	70	69	278	
	Chris Wood	70	69	69	70	278	10,675

47	Wil Besseling	69	71	70	69	279	8,925
	Paul Dunne	71	69	69	70	279	8,925
	Raphael Jacquelin	67	68	73	71	279	8,925
50	David Drysdale	65	66	72	77	280	7,175
	Grant Forrest	70	70	70	70	280	7,175
	Craig Howie	69	70	71	70	280	7,175
	Daan Huizing	70	70	70	70	280	7,175
	Espen Kofstad	71	69	69	71	280	7,175
	Frederic Lacroix	73	67	72	68	280	7,175
	Pablo Larrazabal	68	67	77	68	280	7,175
57	Jonathan Caldwell	69	71	74	67	281	5,775
	Mike Lorenzo-Vera	68	70	78	65	281	5,775
	James Morrison	69	71	72	69	281	5,775
60	Jazz Janewattananond	70	68	72	72	282	5,338
	Wilco Nienaber	72	68	72	70	282	5,338
62	Maverick Antcliff	69	69	75	70	283	5,075
63	Juan Salama	70	67	74	73	284	4,813
	Tristen Strydom	69	68	74	73	284	4,813
65	Ben Evans	70	69	76	71	286	4,463
	Niall Kearney	69	69	73	75	286	4,463
67	David Law	70	70	75	72	287	4,200
68	Jack Singh Brar	73	67	78	70	288	3,938
	Sami Valimaki	68	70	77	73	288	3,938
70	Tyler Koivisto	70	70	82	69	291	3,675

Estrella Damm Andalucia Masters

Adrian Otaegui showed few nerves as he converted a six-shot lead after 54 holes into a six-stroke victory at the Estrella Damm Andalucia Masters. On the relentlessly daunting Valderrama course, where disaster lurks at every turn, it was no mean feat. The 29-year-old Spaniard made three birdies going out, dropped his only shot at the 11th and finished in style with a three at the 18th in front of a large gallery for his first win on home soil.

This was also the first victory on the DP World Tour by a player who had appeared on the LIV Golf Invitational Series. Otaegui played three times and, along with other DP World Tour members, was initially suspended before the ruling was stayed ahead of a full arbitration hearing in 2023.

Otaegui scored 67-66-64-68 for a 19-under-par total of 265, a new record for the tournament. He was one off the five-way tie for the lead on the first day, but it was his third round which was the core of his victory. Dropping only one shot on the day, he made five birdies in the first eight holes, then at the last three holes to jump half-a-dozen shots ahead. His plan for Sunday was to imagine he was square with the field.

"I feel so happy to have my first win in Spain, in front of these crowds, on my favourite golf course in Spain," Otaegui said of his fourth title and first since the Scottish Championship in 2020. "It's just unbelievable. I'm very happy with everything, the week went perfect. I'm very happy with the way I managed today because it was my first time with such a big shot difference. The plan was just to start strong, forget the shot difference I had and try to beat the others today. I played very well until the end. I tried to follow the plan and think I did well."

Joakim Lagergren closed with a 68 to finish second and jump from 127th on the DP World Tour points list into the top 50, while Angel Hidalgo's fourth place moved him up from 130th to 88th. Min Woo Lee was third for the second week running after he was a runner-up at Valderrama in 2021.

Real Club Valderrama, Sotogrande, Spain — October 13-16
Par 71 (35-36); 7,028 yards — Purse: €3,000,000

1	**Adrian Otaegui**	67	66	64	68	265	€510,000
2	**Joakim Lagergren**	69	67	67	68	271	330,000
3	**Min Woo Lee**	66	67	71	70	274	189,000
4	Angel Hidalgo	70	63	70	73	276	150,000
5	Rasmus Hojgaard	69	71	68	70	278	127,200
6	Marcus Kinhult	76	67	68	68	279	90,000
	Thriston Lawrence	69	69	72	69	279	90,000
	Jordan Smith	69	69	69	72	279	90,000
9	Robert MacIntyre	67	70	69	74	280	63,600
	Lukas Nemecz	70	69	73	68	280	63,600
11	John Catlin	70	68	71	72	281	51,700
	Andy Sullivan	72	69	72	68	281	51,700
	Andrew Wilson	75	70	67	69	281	51,700
14	Ross Fisher	73	66	69	74	282	42,300
	Sebastian Garcia Rodriguez	68	69	76	69	282	42,300
	Jazz Janewattananond	66	72	74	70	282	42,300
	Zander Lombard	72	72	72	66	282	42,300
	Antoine Rozner	72	69	69	72	282	42,300
19	Ricardo Gouveia	69	74	70	70	283	36,600
	Darius van Driel	69	71	71	72	283	36,600
21	Pep Angles	66	75	71	72	284	32,100
	Maverick Antcliff	73	68	74	69	284	32,100
	Marcus Armitage	72	67	74	71	284	32,100
	Nacho Elvira	72	70	71	71	284	32,100
	Masahiro Kawamura	71	71	72	70	284	32,100
	Thorbjorn Olesen	75	69	71	69	284	32,100
	Yannik Paul	71	68	74	71	284	32,100
28	Jamie Donaldson	74	70	67	74	285	27,150
	Benjamin Hebert	69	74	71	71	285	27,150
	Joost Luiten	68	74	68	75	285	27,150
	Richie Ramsay	70	74	74	67	285	27,150
32	Alexander Bjork	73	71	74	68	286	23,100
	Romain Langasque	73	71	69	73	286	23,100
	Vincent Norrman	72	71	71	72	286	23,100

	Renato Paratore	73	70	71	72	286	23,100
	Connor Syme	73	72	70	71	286	23,100
37	Nicolas Colsaerts	70	73	69	75	287	18,600
	Alex Fitzpatrick	70	72	74	71	287	18,600
	Stephen Gallacher	74	71	71	71	287	18,600
	Nicolai Hojgaard	73	71	72	71	287	18,600
	Richard Mansell	73	67	76	71	287	18,600
	Callum Shinkwin	71	73	69	74	287	18,600
	Marcel Siem	70	74	70	73	287	18,600
	Jeff Winther	74	69	72	72	287	18,600
45	Oliver Bekker	77	66	75	70	288	14,700
	Wil Besseling	72	72	72	72	288	14,700
	Thomas Detry	75	69	75	69	288	14,700
	Adrian Meronk	75	69	70	74	288	14,700
	Ashun Wu	72	69	69	78	288	14,700
50	Jorge Campillo	69	74	73	73	289	11,700
	Soren Kjeldsen	66	74	78	71	289	11,700
	Espen Kofstad	71	72	75	71	289	11,700
	Johannes Veerman	70	74	70	75	289	11,700
	Marc Warren	68	73	72	76	289	11,700
55	Angel Ayora (A)	73	72	74	71	290	
	Gonzalo Fdez-Castano	71	72	74	73	290	9,900
	Francesco Laporta	73	71	74	72	290	9,900
	Santiago Tarrio	75	70	71	74	290	9,900
59	Louis de Jager	68	77	73	73	291	9,300
60	Kristoffer Broberg	73	71	72	76	292	9,000
61	Chase Hanna	72	73	73	75	293	8,400
	Pedro Oriol	73	72	73	75	293	8,400
	Erik van Rooyen	74	71	72	76	293	8,400
64	Jack Singh Brar	72	72	73	77	294	7,800
65	Pablo Larrazabal	68	75	73	80	296	7,500
66	David Horsey	66	75	80	77	298	7,200

Mallorca Golf Open

Yannik Paul made three eagles in his third round but as remarkable as that was, it paled by comparison with the putt he made on the final hole to win the Mallorca Golf Open for his maiden title. The 28-year-old rookie from Germany was playing in just his 26th event on the DP World Tour, but at the end of a difficult final day at Son Muntaner Paul made his 15-footer from the fringe to avoid a playoff. He won by one stroke from Nicolai von Dellingshausen and Paul Waring.

Paul shot into the 54-hole lead with Ryan Fox (68-64-65) when he followed an opening 71, leaving him eight shots off the lead, with a 64 on day two and then a 62 on Saturday. The eagles came at the fifth, where he drove the green and holed from 11 feet, the eighth, where he chipped in from short of the green, and more conventionally at the par-five 11th.

Fox had not dropped a shot for 53 holes when he took a double bogey at the first hole on Sunday. The Kiwi could not add to his two wins already for the season as he finished with a 74 but he still overtook Matt Fitzpatrick in second place on the DP World Tour points list. Paul also dropped a couple of early shots, but birdies at the eighth and 11th settled him down before bogeys at the 14th and the 15th. Marcus Armitage, the first-round leader on 63, birdied for the fourth time in six holes at 15 to suddenly take a two-shot lead but the Englishman then dropped four shots over the last three holes to drop into a tie for sixth. Paul still needed a birdie and it came at the last to pip von Dellingshausen (69) and Waring (66).

"I'm speechless, just so happy," said Paul, whose twin brother Jeremy is also a professional golfer. "My girlfriend and I, we worked a lot on my mental side and we were dreaming that she would be here for my first win, and she's here now. I saw after nine holes that I was in the lead and then Marcus obviously hit a great shot on 15 and holed a great putt so I was two shots away and I thought, 'OK, now it's going to get close'. I couldn't have dreamt of a better ending so I'm over the moon."

Son Muntaner Golf Club, Palma, Mallorca, Spain — October 20-23
Par 71 (35-36); 6,952 yards — Purse: $2,000,000

1	**Yannik Paul**	71	64	62	72	269	€347,826
2	**Nicolai von Dellingshausen**	71	66	64	69	270	176,982
	Paul Waring	70	66	68	66	270	176,982
4	Ryan Fox	68	64	65	74	271	94,527
	Dale Whitnell	68	63	68	72	271	94,527
6	Marcus Armitage	63	73	63	73	272	61,381
	Jazz Janewattananond	66	69	66	71	272	61,381
	Jeff Winther	67	69	68	68	272	61,381
9	Ewen Ferguson	69	70	65	69	273	43,376
	Hurly Long	67	69	66	71	273	43,376
11	Gavin Green	66	69	70	69	274	33,432
	Scott Hend	70	69	68	67	274	33,432
	Richard Mansell	69	70	61	74	274	33,432
	Lukas Nemecz	65	70	67	72	274	33,432
	Johannes Veerman	69	69	68	68	274	33,432
16	Ricardo Gouveia	67	74	67	67	275	25,663
	Nicolai Hojgaard	68	69	64	74	275	25,663
	Mike Lorenzo-Vera	67	70	70	68	275	25,663
	Richie Ramsay	68	69	67	71	275	25,663
	Andy Sullivan	69	68	66	72	275	25,663
	Ashun Wu	70	68	70	67	275	25,663
	Fabrizio Zanotti	68	72	66	69	275	25,663
23	Jonathan Caldwell	73	67	67	69	276	20,665
	Chase Hanna	72	66	69	69	276	20,665
	Daan Huizing	64	73	67	72	276	20,665
	Renato Paratore	70	69	63	74	276	20,665

	Marcel Schneider	69	68	69	70	276	20,665
	Jack Senior	70	69	69	68	276	20,665
	Connor Syme	67	72	63	74	276	20,665
30	Rasmus Hojgaard	65	69	68	75	277	16,368
	Scott Jamieson	69	71	70	67	277	16,368
	Joost Luiten	67	70	70	70	277	16,368
	Eddie Pepperell	73	65	69	70	277	16,368
	Alvaro Quiros	69	70	70	68	277	16,368
	Matthew Southgate	68	70	69	70	277	16,368
	Marc Warren	67	70	67	73	277	16,368
37	Kiradech Aphibarnrat	69	71	69	69	278	13,095
	Julien Brun	68	73	68	69	278	13,095
	Rafa Cabrera Bello	71	69	67	71	278	13,095
	Alejandro Canizares	65	70	70	73	278	13,095
	Tom Lewis	71	69	67	71	278	13,095
	Darius van Driel	71	66	65	76	278	13,095
43	Louis de Jager	71	68	68	72	279	11,049
	Lorenzo Gagli	68	69	71	71	279	11,049
	Matthew Jordan	70	70	72	67	279	11,049
	Justin Walters	68	70	69	72	279	11,049
47	Ashley Chesters	71	68	67	74	280	9,207
	Sebastian Garcia Rodriguez	70	71	71	68	280	9,207
	Hugo Leon	70	64	70	76	280	9,207
	Adrian Otaegui	70	71	69	70	280	9,207
	Santiago Tarrio	74	66	72	68	280	9,207
52	David Drysdale	69	69	71	72	281	7,161
	Grant Forrest	70	69	69	73	281	7,161
	Masahiro Kawamura	70	70	70	71	281	7,161
	Shubhankar Sharma	69	69	73	70	281	7,161
	Sebastian Soderberg	71	70	69	71	281	7,161
	Daniel van Tonder	69	71	68	73	281	7,161
58	Pep Angles	70	71	69	72	282	5,627
	Steven Brown	68	70	69	75	282	5,627
	Aaron Cockerill	68	70	70	74	282	5,627
	Maximilian Kieffer	68	66	72	76	282	5,627
	Espen Kofstad	68	72	70	72	282	5,627
	Robin Roussel	70	70	72	70	282	5,627
	Richard Sterne	74	66	70	72	282	5,627
	Chris Wood	70	71	67	74	282	5,627
66	Gregory Bourdy	69	71	71	73	284	4,399
	Darren Fichardt	66	74	73	71	284	4,399
	Alfredo Garcia-Heredia	69	71	68	76	284	4,399
	Ricardo Santos	70	71	70	73	284	4,399
70	Maverick Antcliff	71	70	70	74	285	3,478
	Angel Hidalgo	72	69	72	72	285	3,478
72	Niklas Lemke	71	68	71	76	286	3,066
73	David Howell	71	70	75	71	287	3,063
74	Brandon Stone	69	71	67	82	289	3,060

Portugal Masters

Going on a stag weekend and ending up with flu was one way to help break Jordan Smith's winless drought. So, too, was bringing forward a planned winter overhaul of his putting by using a new putter and grip combination. It added up to a three-stroke victory for Smith at the Portugal Masters, his second win on the DP World Tour.

The first came in his rookie season of 2017 at the Porsche European Open. Five years later the 29-year-old from Wiltshire was having a fine season. All that was missing was a win, two runner-up finishes having arrived early in the year. At Dom Pedro Victoria, always a low-scoring venue in favourable conditions, Smith put his well-honed ball-striking together with new-found putting magic. He made 27 birdies and three eagles to finish at 30 under par on a total of 254. He was one better than Ernie Els' record of 29 under par at the 2003 Johnnie Walker Classic but this was not official as preferred lies were in operation throughout the event.

Spare a thought for Gavin Green as the Malaysian finished runner-up for the second time in the season. Green was at 27 under, five strokes ahead of Tapio Pulkkanen, after three 64s and a 65. Smith went in front with an opening 62, added a 67 on Friday to share the lead with Green, then was on pace for a 59 on Saturday before settling for another 62. He closed with a 63 made up of six birdies and an eagle at the fifth from 27 feet. He led by two overnight and was pushed all the way by Green, with both out in 31. Smith went five ahead with three to play but Green finished eagle-birdie to Smith's birdie-par.

"It's been a long grind for those five seasons," said Smith, who emotionally dedicated the win to the family of a close friend who had died recently. "I knew there would be a lot guys trying to catch me. Gavin was getting closer and closer but I managed to hold him off. It's great knowing you can do it again."

At the last full-field event of the season, there were no changes to the top 117 on the points list who retained their cards, with Sebastian Garcia Rodriguez holding on to the last spot despite missing the cut. Italy's Renato Paratore holed a birdie putt of 58 feet at the last but agonisingly missed out in 118th place. Sebastian Heisele played in the final group on Sunday and finished fifth as the 34-year-old German announced it was his last ever event as he was about to become a coach.

Dom Pedro Victoria Golf Course, Vilamoura, Portugal — October 27-30
Par 71 (35-36); 7,191 yards — Purse: $2,000,000

1	**Jordan Smith**	62	67	62	63	254	€340,813
2	**Gavin Green**	64	65	64	64	257	220,526
3	**Tapio Pulkkanen**	66	64	68	64	262	126,301
4	Eddie Pepperell	67	64	67	65	263	100,239
5	Sebastian Heisele	67	64	65	69	265	77,585
	Hurly Long	65	67	66	67	265	77,585
7	Joost Luiten	63	69	68	66	266	60,143
8	David Drysdale	66	68	65	68	267	43,003
	Mikko Korhonen	66	70	67	64	267	43,003
	Antoine Rozner	67	66	68	66	267	43,003
	Marcel Schneider	68	67	65	67	267	43,003
12	Daniel Hillier	65	68	68	67	268	32,477
	Frederic Lacroix	67	66	71	64	268	32,477
	Joel Stalter	65	67	68	68	268	32,477
15	Alex Fitzpatrick	71	66	67	65	269	28,267
	Edoardo Molinari	70	68	66	65	269	28,267
	Sebastian Soderberg	67	68	66	68	269	28,267
18	Ross Fisher	66	67	67	70	270	22,810
	Benjamin Hebert	66	64	69	71	270	22,810
	Rikard Karlberg	66	65	70	69	270	22,810
	Mike Lorenzo-Vera	67	69	64	70	270	22,810
	Robert MacIntyre	68	69	66	67	270	22,810
	Renato Paratore	68	66	70	66	270	22,810
	Garrick Porteous	70	68	68	64	270	22,810
	Jason Scrivener	66	67	66	71	270	22,810
	Darius van Driel	66	68	70	66	270	22,810
27	Kiradech Aphibarnrat	65	70	63	73	271	17,843
	Filippo Celli	70	67	68	66	271	17,843
	Aaron Cockerill	68	65	70	68	271	17,843
	Taehee Lee	67	67	69	68	271	17,843
	Richard Sterne	68	69	68	66	271	17,843
	Sami Valimaki	66	69	67	69	271	17,843
	Jeff Winther	63	70	70	68	271	17,843
34	Maverick Antcliff	70	66	67	69	272	13,499
	Lucas Bjerregaard	70	67	67	68	272	13,499
	Julien Brun	66	69	68	69	272	13,499
	Matthew Jordan	67	67	69	69	272	13,499
	Marcus Kinhult	66	67	68	71	272	13,499
	David Law	65	70	68	69	272	13,499
	Lukas Nemecz	69	67	68	68	272	13,499
	Daniel van Tonder	69	69	68	66	272	13,499
	Nicolai von Dellingshausen	65	66	71	70	272	13,499
43	Alfredo Garcia-Heredia	67	68	70	68	273	10,024
	Espen Kofstad	71	65	73	64	273	10,024
	Joakim Lagergren	64	71	70	68	273	10,024
	Wilco Nienaber	68	66	72	67	273	10,024
	Marcel Siem	68	70	68	67	273	10,024
	Matt Wallace	67	67	69	70	273	10,024
	Dale Whitnell	69	69	65	70	273	10,024
	Andrew Wilson	68	65	72	68	273	10,024
51	Wil Besseling	68	67	70	69	274	7,317
	Ashley Chesters	67	68	69	70	274	7,317
	Niklas Lemke	65	70	68	71	274	7,317
	Robin Roussel	64	68	70	72	274	7,317
	Kalle Samooja	70	64	72	68	274	7,317
	Oliver Wilson	69	66	70	69	274	7,317
57	Marcus Helligkilde	71	65	67	72	275	6,315
	Matthew Southgate	69	66	72	68	275	6,315
59	Ricardo Santos	69	69	69	69	276	5,914
	Andy Sullivan	69	69	72	66	276	5,914
61	David Horsey	73	64	71	69	277	5,513
	Jazz Janewattananond	70	68	69	70	277	5,513
63	Daniel Gavins	67	71	70	70	278	5,012
	David Howell	69	69	73	67	278	5,012
	Yannik Paul	66	69	70	73	278	5,012
66	Ross McGowan	68	70	71	70	279	4,511
	Marc Warren	66	71	72	70	279	4,511
68	Kristoffer Broberg	67	70	71	72	280	4,110
	Scott Hend	67	67	71	75	280	4,110
70	Tomas Bessa	67	71	69	74	281	3,809
71	Masahiro Kawamura	69	67	70	78	284	3,007
72	Gregory Havret	70	68	69	79	286	3,003
	Chris Wood	66	71	73	76	286	3,003

Nedbank Golf Challenge

No wonder the emotions got the better of Tommy Fleetwood while he watched Ryan Fox putt out for a bogey at the 18th hole of the Nedbank Golf Challenge. Fleetwood had just hit a superb lag putt that stopped on the edge of the cup and tapped in for a par while his co-leader going to the 72nd hole failed to get up and down.

This was the 31-year-old Englishman's sixth win on the DP World Tour but his first since winning the same title in 2019. Due to the Covid pandemic, this 40th edition of "Africa's major" had twice been postponed so this was a successful defence by Fleetwood as he joined the likes of Seve Ballesteros, David Frost, Nick Price and Lee Westwood as back-to-back winners.

It was also his first win since the death of his mother in the summer and almost completed a goal of winning in front of his wife and children, though due to a weather delay earlier in the day, they were actually heading to the airport when his one-stroke win over Fox was confirmed. Instead, Fleetwood handed the winning ball to the son of the Sun City doctor who enabled him to tee up in the first place. Ailed by a stomach bug, Fleetwood almost did not tee off on Thursday and after storms wiped out most of Friday's play, he was struggling with the prospect of a long day's golf on Saturday.

"It was touch and go on Thursday morning," Fleetwood said. "The doctor here has been amazing. Without him there was not a chance I'd have played. Then Saturday when we were up early, I felt like I had nothing in me. Felt really poorly again. I just had in my mind to keep going ... and you never know what happens."

What happened is that 54-hole leaders Rasmus Hojgaard and Thomas Detry fell back in the final round as Fleetwood went to the turn in four under. He dropped a shot at the 12th but the moment of the day came at the par-five 14th. In the bunker to the left of the green, Fleetwood holed out for an eagle. "It wasn't the best lie but it came out lovely and went in. That spark, those kind of things happen." Fleetwood parred home as the wind got up with another storm approaching and added a 67 to three earlier 70s for 11-under 277.

Fox had led on Thursday with a 64, then shot 74 in the second round, when 2023 Ryder Cup captain Luke Donald shared the lead with Richard Bland. A closing 68 featured four birdies in a row from the seventh with his only dropped shot at the last. "I didn't miss a shot until 18," he said.

Gary Player Country Club, Sun City, North West Province, South Africa — November 10-13
Par 72 (36-36); 7,891 yards — Purse: $6,000,000

1	**Tommy Fleetwood**	70	70	70	67	277	€1,003,227
2	**Ryan Fox**	64	74	72	68	278	650,874
3	**Shubhankar Sharma**	72	69	69	69	279	372,907
4	Richie Ramsay	69	71	71	69	280	295,585
5	Christiaan Bezuidenhout	73	68	68	72	281	229,029
	Sebastian Soderberg	71	71	72	67	281	229,029
7	Gavin Green	72	65	75	70	282	178,134
8	Richard Bland	68	68	75	72	283	122,149
	Branden Grace	70	67	71	75	283	122,149
	Rasmus Hojgaard	69	69	69	76	283	122,149
	Maximilian Kieffer	70	72	69	72	283	122,149
	Min Woo Lee	68	76	70	69	283	122,149
13	Thomas Detry	73	67	67	77	284	85,641
	Luke Donald	65	71	73	75	284	85,641
	Ewen Ferguson	71	73	69	71	284	85,641
	Scott Jamieson	71	71	70	72	284	85,641
	Thriston Lawrence	74	69	65	76	284	85,641
	Jordan Smith	75	70	69	70	284	85,641
19	Ross Fisher	71	69	72	73	285	68,513
	Sam Horsfield	72	68	73	72	285	68,513
	David Law	70	69	74	72	285	68,513
	Adrian Otaegui	69	70	72	74	285	68,513
	Richard Sterne	71	69	71	74	285	68,513
	Paul Waring	70	70	71	74	285	68,513
25	Lucas Herbert	69	72	74	71	286	58,872
	Yannik Paul	73	72	74	67	286	58,872
	Marcel Schneider	71	68	76	71	286	58,872
	Ashun Wu	74	71	72	69	286	58,872
29	Joakim Lagergren	72	71	74	70	287	52,657
	Romain Langasque	70	72	73	72	287	52,657
	Fabrizio Zanotti	68	73	70	76	287	52,657
32	Jorge Campillo	72	75	74	67	288	46,491
	Robert MacIntyre	73	72	73	70	288	46,491
	Edoardo Molinari	69	71	72	76	288	46,491
	Antoine Rozner	71	77	69	71	288	46,491
36	Oliver Bekker	72	72	75	70	289	39,601
	Sean Crocker	71	74	73	71	289	39,601
	Adrian Meronk	76	73	72	68	289	39,601
	Dale Whitnell	70	75	70	74	289	39,601
	Oliver Wilson	72	74	71	72	289	39,601
41	Marcus Armitage	74	75	68	73	290	34,844
	Rafa Cabrera Bello	72	74	73	71	290	34,844
	Matthieu Pavon	75	72	72	71	290	34,844
44	George Coetzee	72	77	73	69	291	30,146
	Matthew Jordan	70	73	72	76	291	30,146
	Guido Migliozzi	67	76	72	76	291	30,146
	Thorbjorn Olesen	72	73	71	75	291	30,146
	Victor Perez	74	74	70	73	291	30,146
49	Shaun Norris	71	75	72	74	292	25,448
	Eddie Pepperell	75	74	70	73	292	25,448
	Connor Syme	71	74	73	74	292	25,448
52	Hurly Long	75	73	72	73	293	21,924
	JC Ritchie	72	74	76	71	293	21,924
	Justin Walters	70	77	74	72	293	21,924
55	Nicolai Hojgaard	75	74	71	74	294	20,162
56	Richard Mansell	74	74	72	75	295	19,282
	Tapio Pulkkanen	78	72	77	68	295	19,282
58	Wil Besseling	74	73	77	72	296	17,813
	Kalle Samooja	75	73	71	77	296	17,813
	Matthew Southgate	77	70	78	71	296	17,813
61	Adri Arnaus	75	75	71	76	297	16,345
	Haotong Li	72	74	74	77	297	16,345
63	Pablo Larrazabal	80	72	73	73	298	15,464
64	Zander Lombard	76	70	73	80	299	14,322
	Callum Shinkwin	71	77	73	78	299	14,322
	Nicolai von Dellingshausen	74	73	73	79	299	14,322

DP World Tour Championship

In a battle that included no fewer than three two-time winners of the DP World Tour Championship, it was Jon Rahm who became the first to lift the famous mace trophy for a third time at Jumeirah Golf Estates in Dubai. This was the 28-year-old Spaniard's fourth appearance in the season-ending event, with a tie for fourth on the only occasion he did not win. Rahm won by two strokes from Alex Noren and Tyrrell Hatton on a 20-under-par total of 268, a stroke better than his tally for both the wins in 2017 and 2019. Matt Fitzpatrick (2016 and 2020) played alongside Rahm in Sunday's final pairing but ended up in a tie for fifth with Tommy Fleetwood, while Rory McIlroy (2012 and 2015) was fourth to secure a fourth Harry Vardon Trophy for topping the DP World Tour Rankings.

While Fitzpatrick and Hatton shared the lead on each of the first two days, scoring 65-67 a piece,

Rahm went 70-66-65 to move one ahead of his successor as US Open champion, Fitzpatrick (70), on Saturday in the week that they were both presented with honorary life membership of the DP World Tour. Rahm started brilliantly on Sunday, with birdies at the first three holes. He holed from 13 feet at the first, ran his approach shot through a bunker onto the green at the par-five second and two-putted, then made a 10-footer at the third. A shot went at the fourth but he was now in command, making an 18-footer at the seventh and a 30-footer at the 13th. A number of fine saves were mixed through the day, a sixth birdie arriving at the 15th. Hatton rallied from a 72 on Saturday to score a 66 and get to 18 under par, the same mark as Noren after a 67. Rahm flirted with the trees and the stream at the last but maintained his two-shot advantage.

"Because of Covid I never got the chance to defend my 2019 title," Rahm said. "Even though I decided not to come last year, I came here with the mentality of 'Well, nobody beat me in the last two years so they're going to have to beat me again'. I came in with that confidence."

Fitzpatrick needed to win to have any chance of dethroning McIlroy at the top of the Race to Dubai but his challenge stalled with a double bogey at the eighth. Ryan Fox, lying second to McIlroy on the points list, finished 19th as the Northern Irishman added to his titles in 2012, 2014 and 2015.

Rahm, who won the Open de Espana on his last start on the DP World Tour, had said it was "laughable" that the season-ending tournament had fewer OWGR points on offer than the full-field RSM Classic in America."Hopefully, people can stop telling me that it was a bad year," he said. "Three wins worldwide, three wins in three different continents. Yeah, there wasn't a major win, but it's still a really, really good season."

Jumeirah Golf Estates (Earth), Dubai, UAE — November 17-20
Par 72 (36-36); 7,706 yards — Purse: $10,000,000

1	**Jon Rahm**	70	66	65	67	268	€2,891,271
2	**Tyrrell Hatton**	65	67	72	66	270	1,007,126
	Alex Noren	66	69	68	67	270	1,007,126
4	Rory McIlroy	71	68	65	68	272	452,966
5	Matt Fitzpatrick	65	67	70	73	275	332,014
	Tommy Fleetwood	68	70	68	69	275	332,014
7	Rasmus Hojgaard	68	70	72	67	277	233,711
	Adrian Meronk	70	71	65	71	277	233,711
9	Adri Arnaus	67	68	75	68	278	170,344
	Jorge Campillo	71	65	71	71	278	170,344
11	Maximilian Kieffer	69	70	70	71	280	143,600
12	Joakim Lagergren	73	71	71	66	281	120,229
	Min Woo Lee	71	67	74	69	281	120,229
	Victor Perez	69	73	73	66	281	120,229
	Connor Syme	73	71	70	67	281	120,229
16	Sam Horsfield	71	70	70	71	282	101,435
	Adrian Otaegui	71	68	72	71	282	101,435
	Richie Ramsay	69	70	73	70	282	101,435
19	Ryan Fox	73	72	70	68	283	92,762
20	Gavin Green	70	73	68	73	284	86,337
	Romain Langasque	71	69	72	72	284	86,337
	David Law	70	74	74	66	284	86,337
23	Viktor Hovland	74	70	71	70	285	77,101
	Shane Lowry	73	70	71	71	285	77,101
	Guido Migliozzi	71	69	73	72	285	77,101
	Yannik Paul	68	71	74	72	285	77,101
	Callum Shinkwin	68	76	71	70	285	77,101
28	Richard Mansell	73	71	70	72	286	69,511
	Ashun Wu	78	64	72	72	286	69,511
30	Haotong Li	75	75	69	68	287	63,006
	Thorbjorn Olesen	75	71	72	69	287	63,006
	Jordan Smith	76	72	71	68	287	63,006
	Paul Waring	70	72	74	71	287	63,006
34	Oliver Bekker	72	74	74	68	288	51,699
	Rafa Cabrera Bello	75	71	70	72	288	51,699
	Robert MacIntyre	70	73	71	74	288	51,699
	Eddie Pepperell	76	73	69	70	288	51,699
	Antoine Rozner	72	72	73	71	288	51,699
	Marcel Schneider	72	71	74	71	288	51,699
	Fabrizio Zanotti	73	70	73	72	288	51,699
41	Thriston Lawrence	72	76	71	70	289	45,297
42	Ewen Ferguson	76	72	70	72	290	43,128
	Kurt Kitayama	68	69	72	81	290	43,128
44	Richard Bland	77	72	70	72	291	40,237
	Shubhankar Sharma	73	71	74	73	291	40,237
46	Sebastian Soderberg	70	76	74	72	292	38,068
47	Pablo Larrazabal	69	79	78	69	295	35,900
	Oliver Wilson	70	72	75	78	295	35,900
49	Matthieu Pavon	75	76	72	73	296	33,732
50	Hurly Long	76	73	73	75	297	32,286

2021-22 DP WORLD TOUR RANKINGS

		Points
1	Rory McIlroy	4,754.1
2	Ryan Fox	4,173.6
3	Jon Rahm	3,703.0
4	Matt Fitzpatrick	3,620.0
5	Tommy Fleetwood	3,301.4
6	Viktor Hovland	2,837.4
7	Will Zalatoris	2,661.5
8	Adrian Meronk	2,648.1
9	Shane Lowry	2,597.4
10	Thomas Pieters	2,575.5

Challenge Tour

It does not matter the level, the sentiment is the same. "Winning golf tournaments isn't easy," said Nathan Kimsey. He should know. The 29-year-old Englishman looked like a veteran as he closed out a one-shot victory at the Rolex Challenge Tour Grand Final. But it took a putt from over 50 feet for an eagle at the 13th hole in the final round and then a solid finish to pip Bryce Easton and John Parry by a single shot at Club de Golf Alcanada in Mallorca. This was a double victory for Kimsey as he jumped from sixth to first on the Race to Mallorca Rankings and claimed the Challenge Tour's number one crown for 2022.

This was a first appearance at the Grand Final for a player who turned professional in 2013 after appearing in the Walker Cup and England's victorious European Championship team. He had not ranked higher than 58th on the Challenge Tour in previous years, but did win the Qualifying School in 2016 by becoming only the second player to do so after making it through from the first stage, a total of 14 rounds. He did not retain his card on the European Tour in 2017.

But a maiden win on the Challenge Tour arrived in July 2022 when he defeated Robin Sciot-Siegrist on the fourth extra hole at the Le Vaudreuil Golf Challenge. He also had five other top-10 finishes before heading to Mallorca with promotion to the European Tour assured. After opening with a 70, a 73 in the high winds of Friday was no disaster. A 66 on Saturday put Kimsey in a tie for the lead with South Africa's Easton. A closing 70 gave the winner a nine-under-par total of 279. After an early bogey, birdies at the sixth and eighth holes put him in front and the eagle at 13 meant he could afford another dropped shot coming home.

Easton and Parry moved up 20 and 17 places on the rankings respectively to get into the top 20 and get their cards, as did Matthew Baldwin, who finished the Grand Final tied for fourth. Easton's compatriot Deon Germishuys hung on to 20th spot.

"That was a battle out there," Kimsey said. "I didn't have my best stuff but I hit some good shots and holed some putts when it mattered. It's a whole mix of stuff. Relief, happiness, just everything. Coming into the week, knowing I had it in my own hands, if I won to then finish as number one, it just feels great.

"I just tried to keep grinding. Nerves were a part of it so it was about trying to battle that and hit solid shots. I wanted to keep myself in with a chance coming up the last few holes and I did that. The eagle was massive. I've three-putted that green the last two days from not very long distances either so I just thought, walking up, if I can just lay it dead and make four, I'd be happy. It was tracking the whole way and it was nice to see it go in.

"The start of the year we all have it as a goal to be number one, but top 20, to get your card, is the main thing. To come here and win this tournament and become number one, it's just awesome. The card was wrapped up but you just want to finish as high as possible to secure as many starts as possible next year, so I knew it was tight at the top."

Kimsey was the 11th Englishman to finish as the Challenge Tour number one and the first since Jordan Smith in 2016. Jeremy Freiburghaus, 26, missed out on becoming the first player from Switzerland to top the rankings after entering the week in first place following his maiden win in the penultimate event, the English Trophy, in a playoff over Max Schmitt. Alexander Knappe was third after winning twice, at the season-opening Dimension Data Pro-Am in South Africa and the B-NL Challenge Trophy in Belgium, the 33-year-old German's fourth Challenge Tour title.

Two wins in his homeland at the start of the season helped South Africa's JC Ritchie into fourth place on the rankings, with Swede Mikael Lindberg, winner at the Indoor Golf Group Challenge, completing the top five who will benefit from receiving John Jacobs Bursary Awards in 2023.

The others to receive cards were Jens Dantorp, Daniel Hillier, Oliver Hundeboll, Freddy Schott, Tom McKibbin, Robin Sciot-Siegrist, Kristian Krogh Johannessen, Clement Sordet, Martin Simonsen, Jeong Weon Ko and Todd Clements. McKibbin, a 19-year-old from Northern Ireland, was the youngest player at the Grand Final and finished tied for sixth to move up from 15th to 10th on the final rankings. He was the highest placed not to have recorded a victory over the season, having been runner-up at the Irish Challenge at the K Club but six behind commanding winner Clements.

Poland's Mateusz Gradecki missed out in 21st place on the Road to Mallorca after losing a playoff at the Big Green Egg German Challenge to Alejandro Del Rey. The Spaniard ended up 22nd on the rankings, but a week later closed with a 63 in the sixth round of the Final Stage of the Qualifying School to secure his card via that route. Four-time DP World Tour winners Kiradech Aphibarnrat, David Horsey and Marcel Siem all regained their cards, while Sweden's Simon Forsstrom won by two strokes from France's David Ravetto at Infinitum Golf Club in Tarragona, Spain.

	2022 SCHEDULE	
Dimension Data Pro-Am	**Alexander Knappe**	*See chapter 16*
Bain's Whisky Cape Town Open	**JC Ritchie**	*See chapter 16*
Jonsson Workwear Open	**JC Ritchie (2)**	*See chapter 16*
Mangaung Open	**Oliver Hundeboll**	*See chapter 16*
SDC Open	**Clement Sordet**	*See chapter 16*
Limpopo Championship	**Mateusz Gradecki**	*See chapter 16*
Challenge de Espana	**Jens Dantorp**	
Farmfoods Scottish Challenge	**Javier Sainz**	
D+D Real Czech Challenge	**Nicolai B Kristensen**	
Emporda Challenge	**Liam Johnston**	
Kaskada Golf Challenge	**Martin Simonsen**	
Blot Open de Bretagne	**Alfie Plant**	
Italian Challenge Open	**Kristian Krogh Johannessen**	
Le Vaudreuil Golf Challenge	**Nathan Kimsey**	
Euram Bank Open	**Marc Hammer**	
Big Green Egg German Challenge	**Alejandro Del Rey**	
Irish Challenge	**Todd Clements**	
Vierumaki Finnish Challenge	**Velten Meyer**	
Frederikshavn Challenge	**Freddy Schott**	
Dormy Open	**Emilio Cuartero Blanco**	
Indoor Golf Group Challenge	**Mikael Lindberg**	
B-NL Challenge Trophy	**Alexander Knappe (2)**	
Open de Portugal	**Pierre Pineau**	
Swiss Challenge	**Daniel Hillier**	
Hopps Open de Provence	**Joel Sjoholm**	
British Challenge	**Euan Walker**	
English Trophy	**Jeremy Freiburghaus**	
Rolex Challenge Tour Grand Final	**Nathan Kimsey (2)**	

Challenge de Espana

Iberostar Real Club de Golf Novo Sancti Petri, Cadiz, Spain — May 19-22
Par 72 (36-36); 7,064 yards — Purse: €250,000

1	**Jens Dantorp**	74	71	67	66	278	€40,000
2	**Victor Pastor**	70	74	67	70	281	27,500
3	**Mikael Lindberg**	69	73	71	70	283	17,500
4	Jeremy Freiburghaus	67	82	70	65	284	15,000
5	Edgar Catherine	70	75	72	68	285	11,250
	Eduardo de la Riva	69	76	70	70	285	11,250
7	Ivan Cantero Gutierrez	71	77	69	69	286	6,625
	John Parry	74	71	75	66	286	6,625
	Benjamin Rusch	70	74	73	69	286	6,625
	Jonathan Thomson	73	71	73	69	286	6,625
11	Nick Bachem	72	74	70	71	287	4,875
	Matteo Manassero	73	74	73	67	287	4,875
13	Tomas Bessa	72	76	71	69	288	3,514
	Todd Clements	74	75	69	70	288	3,514
	Pedro Figueiredo	74	70	71	73	288	3,514
	Alfredo Garcia-Heredia	78	72	67	71	288	3,514
	Jesper Kennegard	72	77	68	71	288	3,514
	Stan Kraai	76	69	71	72	288	3,514
	Oliver Lindell	72	77	67	72	288	3,514
	JC Ritchie	74	75	70	69	288	3,514
	Mitch Waite	69	75	74	70	288	3,514
22	Kristian Krogh Johannessen	71	74	69	75	289	2,425
	Bernd Ritthammer	76	68	69	76	289	2,425
24	Enrico Di Nitto	74	73	69	74	290	2,200
	Scott Fernandez	73	78	70	69	290	2,200
	Bjorn Hellgren	72	76	68	74	290	2,200
	Conor Purcell	72	72	68	78	290	2,200
	Eduard Rousaud	72	75	73	70	290	2,200
	Gary Stal	75	75	74	66	290	2,200
	Lars van Meijel	70	80	68	72	290	2,200

Farmfoods Scottish Challenge

Newmachar Golf Club, Aberdeenshire, Scotland — May 26-29
Par 71 (35-36); 6,740 yards — Purse: £230,000

1	**Javier Sainz**	72	65	71	65	273	€43,271
2	**Jeremy Freiburghaus**	67	71	64	71	273	29,749
	Sainz won playoff at second extra hole						
3	**Tom Sloman**	70	68	68	68	274	18,931
4	Martin Simonsen	67	70	71	68	276	16,227
5	Nick Bachem	70	70	69	68	277	9,412
	Jens Dantorp	72	68	69	68	277	9,412
	Nathan Kimsey	64	71	71	71	277	9,412
	Conor Purcell	69	73	67	68	277	9,412
	Benjamin Rusch	68	71	72	66	277	9,412
10	Adam Blomme	71	70	70	67	278	5,341
	Alejandro Del Rey	68	71	73	66	278	5,341
	Scott Fernandez	70	73	71	64	278	5,341
	Josh Geary	71	71	67	69	278	5,341
14	Todd Clements	67	69	75	68	279	4,192
	Mikael Lindberg	74	69	68	68	279	4,192
	Marco Penge	65	74	69	71	279	4,192
	Adrien Saddier	68	71	69	71	279	4,192
18	David Boote	70	67	71	72	280	3,381
	Oliver Lindell	69	70	70	71	280	3,381
20	Calum Fyfe	69	70	70	72	281	2,822
	Bernd Ritthammer	69	68	74	70	281	2,822
	Daniel Young	72	69	70	70	281	2,822
23	Christofer Blomstrand	69	69	73	71	282	2,380
	Emilio Cuartero Blanco	69	74	68	71	282	2,380
	Mateusz Gradecki	70	71	69	72	282	2,380
	Marc Hammer	69	71	71	71	282	2,380
	Marco Iten	68	68	73	73	282	2,380
	Jonas Kolbing	72	69	70	71	282	2,380
	Pedro Oriol	67	70	73	72	282	2,380
	Henric Sturehed	73	69	72	68	282	2,380
	Aron Zemmer	72	68	72	70	282	2,380

D+D Real Czech Challenge

Golf & Spa Kuneticka Hora, Dritec, Czech Republic — June 2-5
Par 70 (35-35); 7,195 yards — Purse: €260,000

1	**Nicolai Kristensen**	66	71	63	66	266	€41,600
2	**Ugo Coussaud**	69	65	64	68	266	28,600
	Kristensen won playoff at first extra hole						
3	**Oscar Lengden**	70	69	65	65	269	18,200
4	Clement Berardo	70	68	66	66	270	15,600
5	David Boote	70	64	69	68	271	9,750
	Alejandro Del Rey	68	68	67	68	271	9,750
	John Parry	71	68	67	65	271	9,750
	Lars van Meijel	72	64	68	67	271	9,750
9	Jeremy Freiburghaus	68	69	69	66	272	5,720
	Matias Honkala	70	67	70	65	272	5,720
	Lorenzo Scalise	68	66	69	69	272	5,720
12	Jack McDonald	70	69	65	69	273	4,680
	Eduard Rousaud	67	72	68	66	273	4,680
	Martin Simonsen	64	74	64	71	273	4,680
15	Gary Boyd	69	68	68	69	274	3,640
	Ivan Cantero Gutierrez	67	70	70	67	274	3,640
	Manuel Elvira	72	68	68	66	274	3,640
	Ben Stow	68	67	68	71	274	3,640
	Tristen Strydom	69	69	67	69	274	3,640
20	Elias Bertheussen	67	71	67	70	275	2,578
	Harry Ellis	69	69	69	68	275	2,578
	Joel Girrbach	69	69	68	69	275	2,578
	Mikael Lundberg	69	68	70	68	275	2,578
	Philipp Mejow	70	69	71	65	275	2,578
	Benjamin Rusch	72	67	69	67	275	2,578

Emporda Challenge

Emporda Golf, Girona, Spain — June 9-12
Par 70 (35-35); 6,943 yards — Purse: €250,000

1	**Liam Johnston**	71	65	64	67	267	€40,000
2	**Todd Clements**	67	68	69	65	269	27,500
3	**Jens Dantorp**	70	62	67	71	270	17,500
4	Gary Stal	67	67	69	68	271	15,000
5	Daniel Hillier	69	68	69	66	272	10,167
	Kristian Krogh Johannessen	70	69	67	66	272	10,167
	Clement Sordet	67	70	70	65	272	10,167
8	Clement Berardo	71	68	67	67	273	5,125
	Daniel Brown	68	69	66	70	273	5,125
	Alejandro Del Rey	66	69	72	66	273	5,125
	Matteo Manassero	69	70	69	65	273	5,125
	Marco Penge	71	64	72	66	273	5,125
	Hannes Ronneblad	70	68	70	65	273	5,125
	Borja Virto	68	71	66	68	273	5,125
	Joakim Wikstrom	69	67	69	68	273	5,125
16	Adam Blomme	69	70	67	68	274	3,375
	David Borda	67	68	71	68	274	3,375
	Matias Honkala	66	74	64	70	274	3,375
	Euan Walker	71	63	71	69	274	3,375
20	Scott Fernandez	73	67	69	66	275	2,515
	Roope Kakko	69	71	68	67	275	2,515
	Ruaidhri McGee	76	62	66	71	275	2,515
	Robin Petersson	70	69	64	72	275	2,515
	Tristen Strydom	68	68	68	71	275	2,515
25	Christofer Blomstrand	70	70	68	68	276	2,225
	Emilio Cuartero Blanco	69	68	74	65	276	2,225
	Niklas Regner	72	66	67	71	276	2,225
	Henric Sturehed	67	69	70	70	276	2,225

Kaskada Golf Challenge

Kaskada Golf Resort, Brno, Czech Republic — June 16-19
Par 71 (36-35); 7,053 yards — Purse: €260,000

1	**Martin Simonsen**	64	65	68	67	264	€41,600
2	**Marco Penge**	66	69	65	68	268	28,600
3	**Jens Dantorp**	69	70	64	68	271	18,200
4	Jeremy Freiburghaus	64	68	67	73	272	11,830
	Oliver Hundeboll	70	66	63	73	272	11,830
	Victor Riu	67	65	65	75	272	11,830
	Freddy Schott	66	64	67	75	272	11,830
8	Jannik de Bruyn	70	67	72	64	273	6,413
	Niklas Regner	66	70	69	68	273	6,413
	Borja Virto	65	68	70	70	273	6,413
11	David Boote	73	67	71	63	274	5,070
	Deon Germishuys	70	71	64	69	274	5,070
13	Nick Bachem	74	64	68	69	275	4,160
	Matthew Baldwin	67	72	66	70	275	4,160
	Nathan Kimsey	68	67	68	72	275	4,160
	Lorenzo Scalise	66	70	69	70	275	4,160
	Clement Sordet	68	68	69	70	275	4,160
18	Robert Foley	68	70	68	70	276	3,120
	Kristian Krogh Johannessen	67	70	70	69	276	3,120
	Ben Stow	71	69	66	70	276	3,120
21	Philip Eriksson	68	73	69	67	277	2,639
	Tadeas Tetak	70	67	73	67	277	2,639
23	Christopher Feldborg Nielsen	70	65	72	71	278	2,366
	Scott Fernandez	70	70	69	69	278	2,366
	Alex Hietala	66	71	67	74	278	2,366
	Vitor Lopes	67	69	71	71	278	2,366
	Mikael Lundberg	67	72	70	69	278	2,366
	Robin Petersson	65	70	69	74	278	2,366

Blot Open de Bretagne

Golf Blue Green de Pleneuf Val Andre, Pleneuf, France — June 23-26
Par 70 (35-35); 6,453 yards — Purse: €250,000

1	**Alfie Plant**	65	67	69	68	269	€40,000
2	**Ruaidhri McGee**	61	73	67	69	270	27,500
3	**Borja Virto**	64	69	71	67	271	17,500
4	Freddy Schott	66	71	68	67	272	15,000
5	David Dixon	67	73	65	69	274	12,500
6	Ugo Coussaud	69	68	68	70	275	10,000
7	Todd Clements	70	71	68	67	276	6,625
	Emilio Cuartero Blanco	74	68	70	64	276	6,625
	Pelle Edberg	72	66	71	67	276	6,625
	Mikael Lindberg	68	69	73	66	276	6,625
11	Jordi Garcia	71	71	67	68	277	4,625
	Deon Germishuys	70	71	72	64	277	4,625
	Dermot McElroy	70	65	72	70	277	4,625
	Robin Sciot-Siegrist	64	67	72	74	277	4,625
15	Cyril Bouniol	69	72	66	71	278	3,750
	Ivan Cantero Gutierrez	67	68	76	67	278	3,750
	Max Orrin	68	70	68	72	278	3,750
18	Stuart Manley	70	67	72	70	279	3,125
	Adrien Saddier	67	71	73	68	279	3,125
20	Ben Evans	66	72	69	73	280	2,556
	Jens Fahrbring	70	65	73	72	280	2,556
	Sebastian Petersen	66	72	74	68	280	2,556
	Jaco Prinsloo	67	68	75	70	280	2,556
24	Zheng-Kai Bai	67	71	76	67	281	2,225
	Gregory Bourdy	72	69	72	68	281	2,225
	Ryan Evans	71	67	75	68	281	2,225
	Dominic Foos	68	71	74	68	281	2,225
	Sebastien Gros	69	73	66	73	281	2,225
	Steven Tiley	69	70	75	67	281	2,225

Italian Challenge Open

Golf Nazionale, Viterbo, Italy — June 30-July 1
Par 71 (36-35); 6,994 yards — Purse: €350,000

1	**Kristian Krogh Johannessen**	66	69	71	67	273	€56,000
2	**Oliver Hundeboll**	68	67	71	67	273	38,500
	Johannessen won playoff at first extra hole						
3	**Benjamin Rusch**	69	69	66	70	274	22,750
	Lorenzo Scalise	70	66	74	64	274	22,750
5	Christopher Feldborg Nielsen	67	68	71	69	275	12,180
	Tom McKibbin	71	69	65	70	275	12,180
	Jamie Rutherford	71	66	69	69	275	12,180
	Freddy Schott	66	67	71	71	275	12,180
	Joakim Wikstrom	66	76	65	68	275	12,180
10	Anton Karlsson	73	68	67	68	276	7,117
	Nathan Kimsey	73	68	69	66	276	7,117
	Pedro Oriol	70	71	67	68	276	7,117
13	Bryce Easton	71	68	69	69	277	5,775
	Jens Fahrbring	69	67	71	70	277	5,775
	Angel Hidalgo	71	66	71	69	277	5,775
	Damien Perrier	69	65	72	71	277	5,775
17	Adam Blomme	68	71	74	65	278	4,375
	Jordi Garcia	70	68	72	68	278	4,375
	Victor Riu	71	70	68	69	278	4,375
	Robin Sciot-Siegrist	73	68	66	71	278	4,375
21	David Boote	74	68	67	70	279	3,395
	Kieran Cantley	70	67	71	71	279	3,395
	Luca Cianchetti	74	68	70	67	279	3,395
	Deon Germishuys	67	70	71	71	279	3,395
	Filip Mruzek	68	74	66	71	279	3,395

Le Vaudreuil Golf Challenge

Golf PGA France du Vaudreuil, Le Vaudreuil, France
Par 72 (35-37); 6,966 yards

July 7-10
Purse: €260,000

1	**Nathan Kimsey**	68	66	69	71	274	€41,600
2	**Robin Sciot-Siegrist**	68	69	67	70	274	28,600
	Kimsey won playoff at fourth extra hole						
3	**Mathieu Decottignies-Lafon**	67	75	70	64	276	15,600
	Mikael Lundberg	68	70	66	72	276	15,600
	Clement Sordet	71	68	66	71	276	15,600
6	Deon Germishuys	74	67	68	68	277	8,060
	Ruaidhri McGee	69	68	72	68	277	8,060
	Philipp Mejow	69	73	66	69	277	8,060
	Jesper Svensson	69	70	71	67	277	8,060
10	Matthew Baldwin	66	73	66	73	278	5,287
	Jens Dantorp	71	69	73	65	278	5,287
	Christopher Feldborg Nielsen	70	69	71	68	278	5,287
13	Ugo Coussaud	70	67	72	70	279	4,420
	Anton Karlsson	69	74	68	68	279	4,420
	Joakim Wikstrom	73	68	70	68	279	4,420
16	Stuart Manley	75	67	68	70	280	3,770
	Freddy Schott	72	69	66	73	280	3,770
18	Peter Launer Baek	68	68	76	69	281	3,120
	Jeong Weon Ko	69	67	73	72	281	3,120
	Eduard Rousaud	71	68	73	69	281	3,120
21	Adam Blomme	76	67	68	71	282	2,492
	Angel Hidalgo	69	70	70	73	282	2,492
	Sam Locke	69	68	71	74	282	2,492
	David Ravetto	70	71	71	70	282	2,492
	Jonathan Thomson	70	73	67	72	282	2,492
	Steven Tiley	71	69	70	72	282	2,492

Euram Bank Open

Golf Club Adamstal, Ramsau, Austria
Par 70 (36-34); 6,475 yards

July 14-17
Purse: 250,000

1	**Marc Hammer**	68	70	66	66	270	€40,000
2	**Pierre Pineau**	67	66	71	68	272	27,500
3	**Emilio Cuartero Blanco**	65	67	71	70	273	13,750
	Oliver Lindell	70	68	69	66	273	13,750
	Freddy Schott	68	68	64	73	273	13,750
	Euan Walker	69	70	68	66	273	13,750
7	Manuel Elvira	67	69	70	68	274	7,500
	Daniel Hillier	74	66	63	71	274	7,500
9	Josh Geary	66	68	69	72	275	5,500
	Jacopo Vecchi Fossa	70	66	72	67	275	5,500
	Martin Wiegele	69	70	64	72	275	5,500
12	Robin Dawson	70	66	68	72	276	4,000
	Scott Fernandez	67	71	68	70	276	4,000
	Pedro Figueiredo	71	69	66	70	276	4,000
	Robert Foley	71	68	70	67	276	4,000
	Sebastien Gros	69	68	68	71	276	4,000
	Tom McKibbin	70	68	71	67	276	4,000
	Craig Ross	65	69	76	66	276	4,000
19	Christoph Bleier (A)	69	64	72	72	277	
	David Borda	73	66	68	70	277	2,706
	Gregory Bourdy	68	68	71	70	277	2,706
	Velten Meyer	70	68	69	70	277	2,706
	Javier Sainz	73	65	65	74	277	2,706
24	Gordan Brixi	69	70	67	72	278	2,325
	Bjarki Petursson	69	70	72	67	278	2,325
	Conor Purcell	70	66	75	67	278	2,325
	Felix Schulz	66	70	71	71	278	2,325

Big Green Egg German Challenge

Wittelsbacher Golfclub, Neuburg an der Donau, Germany
Par 72 (36-36); 7,463 yards

July 21-24
Purse: €250,000

1	**Alejandro Del Rey**	68	66	68	69	271	€40,000
2	**Mateusz Gradecki**	66	68	69	68	271	27,500
	Del Rey won playoff at second extra hole						
3	**Manuel Elvira**	65	69	69	69	272	17,500
4	Felix Mory	70	67	70	69	276	12,500
	Maximilian Schmitt	67	71	71	67	276	12,500
	Robin Sciot-Siegrist	68	68	70	70	276	12,500
7	Daniel Young	71	68	68	70	277	8,000
8	Jens Fahrbring	69	69	71	69	278	6,500
	Borja Virto	68	71	72	67	278	6,500
10	Timon Baltl	73	69	71	66	279	4,938
	Albin Bergstrom	69	70	70	70	279	4,938
	Kristian Krogh Johannessen	70	71	69	69	279	4,938
	Roope Kakko	71	71	71	66	279	4,938
14	Adam Blomme	73	67	74	66	280	3,500
	Joel Girrbach	68	74	71	67	280	3,500
	Tom McKibbin	67	73	72	68	280	3,500
	Velten Meyer	70	71	69	70	280	3,500
	Christopher Mivis	69	69	71	71	280	3,500
	Freddy Schott	69	71	71	69	280	3,500
	Steven Tiley	70	70	72	68	280	3,500
21	Nick Bachem	71	70	70	70	281	2,368
	Christofer Blomstrand	73	68	71	69	281	2,368
	Ivan Cantero Gutierrez	67	75	70	69	281	2,368
	Allen John	70	69	74	68	281	2,368
	Jeong Weon Ko	72	69	69	71	281	2,368
	Ruaidhri McGee	70	71	72	68	281	2,368
	Lauri Ruuska	70	72	69	70	281	2,368

Irish Challenge

The K Club (Palmer South), Straffan, County Kildare, Ireland
Par 72 (36-36); 7,319 yards

July 28-31
Purse: €250,000

1	**Todd Clements**	66	65	70	68	269	€40,000
2	**Tom McKibbin**	67	70	72	66	275	27,500
3	**John Murphy**	66	67	74	70	277	17,500
4	Harry Ellis	67	67	74	70	278	15,000
5	Alejandro Del Rey	71	69	69	70	279	7,714
	Deon Germishuys	66	72	73	68	279	7,714
	Joel Girrbach	64	74	73	68	279	7,714
	Gary Hurley	68	69	69	73	279	7,714
	Jeong Weon Ko	66	73	70	70	279	7,714
	Matteo Manassero	69	69	72	69	279	7,714
	Conor Purcell	65	68	76	70	279	7,714
12	OJ Farrell	68	71	73	68	280	4,250
	Victor Garcia Broto	68	71	75	66	280	4,250
	Robin Petersson	69	71	72	68	280	4,250
	Jamie Rutherford	69	67	74	70	280	4,250
	Adrien Saddier	67	74	70	69	280	4,250
17	Ryan Evans	69	70	74	68	281	3,125
	Sebastien Gros	70	66	75	70	281	3,125
	David Ravetto	69	72	68	72	281	3,125
	Robin Sciot-Siegrist	71	72	71	67	281	3,125
21	Kristian Krogh Johannessen	74	65	71	72	282	2,456
	Stefano Mazzoli	65	70	73	74	282	2,456
	Pierre Pineau	73	70	68	71	282	2,456
	Gary Stal	65	70	73	74	282	2,456
25	Alexander Knappe	70	72	75	66	283	2,300

Vierumaki Finnish Challenge

Vierumaki Resort, Vierumaki, Finland
Par 72 (36-36); 7,010 yards

August 4-7
Purse: €250,000

1	**Velten Meyer**	70	62	65	65	262	€40,000
2	**Marc Hammer**	68	62	67	70	267	27,500
3	**Gudmundur Kristjansson**	69	67	67	65	268	16,250
	John Murphy	67	69	62	70	268	16,250
5	Niklas Regner	67	69	67	66	269	12,500
6	Nathan Kimsey	69	65	68	68	270	9,000
	Jeong Weon Ko	70	64	67	69	270	9,000
8	Martin Simonsen	67	65	69	70	271	7,000
9	Jeremy Freiburghaus	69	68	65	70	272	5,313
	Alexander Knappe	68	68	67	69	272	5,313
	Victor Riu	68	63	69	72	272	5,313
	Freddy Schott	67	63	72	70	272	5,313
13	Bjorn Akesson	68	62	71	72	273	4,250
	Manuel Elvira	67	66	69	71	273	4,250
	Ben Stow	67	70	70	66	273	4,250
16	Timon Baltl	70	68	67	69	274	3,250
	Christopher Feldborg Nielsen	68	72	67	67	274	3,250
	Simon Forsstrom	71	66	67	70	274	3,250
	Joel Girrbach	70	68	67	69	274	3,250
	Kristof Ulenaers	69	71	67	67	274	3,250
21	David Borda	68	68	72	67	275	2,396
	Edgar Catherine	67	69	67	72	275	2,396
	Ugo Coussaud	68	66	70	71	275	2,396
	Juuso Kahlos	69	67	71	68	275	2,396
	Mikael Lindberg	70	69	68	68	275	2,396
	Felix Mory	70	67	68	70	275	2,396

Frederikshavn Challenge

Frederikshavn Golfklub, Frederikshavn, Denmark
Par 72 (36-36); 7,113 yards

August 11-14
Purse: €250,000

1	**Freddy Schott**	65	67	66	73	271	€40,000
2	**Nick Bachem**	68	69	68	69	274	22,500
	Simon Forsstrom	75	65	68	66	274	22,500
4	Martin Eriksson	68	69	69	69	275	13,750
	Nathan Kimsey	72	70	68	65	275	13,750
6	Jarand Ekeland Arnoy	73	70	65	68	276	9,000
	Sam Hutsby	71	71	65	69	276	9,000
8	Frederik Kjettrup (A)	69	68	67	73	277	
	Alexander Knappe	72	69	68	68	277	6,167
	Vitor Lopes	67	67	68	75	277	6,167
	Niklas Regner	70	72	69	66	277	6,167
12	Axel Boasson	72	72	67	67	278	4,750
	Manuel Elvira	66	69	71	72	278	4,750
	Clement Sordet	69	70	70	69	278	4,750
15	Daniel Brown	71	68	69	71	279	4,125
	Kristian Krogh Johannessen	74	69	66	70	279	4,125
17	Dan Bradbury	68	70	71	71	280	3,375
	Linus Lilliedahl	68	73	69	70	280	3,375
	John Parry	69	72	71	68	280	3,375
	Harley Smith (A)	71	68	74	67	280	
	Tim Widing	70	70	73	67	280	3,375
22	Marc Hammer	70	69	73	69	281	2,750
23	Maximilian Schmitt	68	73	73	68	282	2,625
24	Luca Cianchetti	72	70	71	70	283	2,300
	Pedro Figueiredo	66	76	71	70	283	2,300
	August Thor Host	77	66	72	68	283	2,300
	Olly Huggins	68	75	69	71	283	2,300
	Jack McDonald	69	75	67	72	283	2,300
	Timo Vahlenkamp	72	72	67	72	283	2,300
	Lars van Meijel	69	70	69	75	283	2,300

Dormy Open

Osterakers Golfklubb, Stockholm, Sweden — August 18-21
Par 72 (36-36); 7,252 yards — Purse: €250,000

1	**Emilio Cuartero Blanco**	67	72	67	67	273	€40,000
2	**Jeremy Freiburghaus**	69	70	70	65	274	27,500
3	**Koen Kouwenaar**	67	72	71	65	275	15,000
	Lauri Ruuska	64	69	71	71	275	15,000
	Maximilian Schmitt	67	69	74	65	275	15,000
6	Daniel Brown	68	68	73	67	276	8,333
	Sam Locke	71	71	69	65	276	8,333
	Stefano Mazzoli	70	68	70	68	276	8,333
9	Kristian Krogh Johannessen	71	68	70	68	277	5,500
	Mikael Lindberg	69	68	70	70	277	5,500
	Stuart Manley	67	68	74	68	277	5,500
12	Jarand Ekeland Arnoy	71	67	67	73	278	4,250
	Matthew Baldwin	69	71	70	68	278	4,250
	Tobias Eden	69	69	68	72	278	4,250
	Nathan Kimsey	71	70	68	69	278	4,250
	Maximilian Rottluff	72	67	68	71	278	4,250
17	Nick Bachem	70	72	69	68	279	3,025
	Elias Bertheussen	71	72	67	69	279	3,025
	Todd Clements	72	71	69	67	279	3,025
	Robin Petersson	67	72	74	66	279	3,025
	Niklas Regner	69	69	71	70	279	3,025
22	Christopher Feldborg Nielsen	69	72	72	67	280	2,350
	Jeong Weon Ko	70	71	74	65	280	2,350
	Oscar Lengden	73	69	71	67	280	2,350
	John Murphy	72	68	72	68	280	2,350
	Euan Walker	70	70	73	67	280	2,350

Indoor Golf Group Challenge

Allerum Golf Club, Helsingborg, Sweden — August 25-28
Par 71 (35-36); 6,889 yards — Purse: €250,000

1	**Mikael Lindberg**	68	62	66	196	€40,000
2	**Robin Sciot-Siegrist**	67	66	66	199	20,000
	Steven Tiley	66	68	65	199	20,000
	Nicolai Tinning	68	64	67	199	20,000
5	Christopher Feldborg Nielsen	69	66	65	200	10,167
	Jakob Hansson	73	63	64	200	10,167
	Kristian Krogh Johannessen	67	67	66	200	10,167
8	Simon Forsstrom	65	69	67	201	7,000
9	Alexander Knappe	71	65	66	202	5,313
	Velten Meyer	68	64	70	202	5,313
	Gary Stal	70	64	68	202	5,313
	Jordan Wrisdale	68	66	68	202	5,313
13	Ben Evans	71	66	66	203	3,625
	Dominic Foos	68	68	67	203	3,625
	Oliver Hundeboll	65	70	68	203	3,625
	Paul McBride	68	65	70	203	3,625
	David Ravetto	67	67	69	203	3,625
	Lorenzo Scalise	68	70	65	203	3,625
	Clement Sordet	64	67	72	203	3,625
	Jonathan Thomson	66	65	72	203	3,625
21	Jesper Hagborg Asp	66	67	71	204	2,396
	Per Langfors	70	65	69	204	2,396
	Max Orrin	64	73	67	204	2,396
	Maximilian Schmitt	69	64	71	204	2,396
	Ben Stow	69	67	68	204	2,396
	Tim Widing	68	68	68	204	2,396

B-NL Challenge Trophy

Hulencourt, Genappe, Belgium — September 1-4
Par 72 (36-36); 7,209 yards — Purse: €250,000

1	**Alexander Knappe**	68	66	66	68	268	€40,000
2	**Mikael Lindberg**	66	69	68	66	269	27,500
3	**Nathan Kimsey**	68	67	67	68	270	17,500
4	Jeong Weon Ko	65	67	67	72	271	12,500
	Tom McKibbin	68	69	66	68	271	12,500
	Robin Sciot-Siegrist	68	65	69	69	271	12,500
7	Bryce Easton	70	65	66	71	272	7,500
	Henric Sturehed	70	68	66	68	272	7,500
9	Christopher Feldborg Nielsen	67	68	68	70	273	5,150
	Dominic Foos	69	65	69	70	273	5,150
	Oscar Lengden	68	68	68	69	273	5,150
	David Ravetto	68	70	66	69	273	5,150
	Maximilian Rottluff	71	65	66	71	273	5,150
14	Christofer Blomstrand	66	71	69	68	274	3,750
	Simon Forsstrom	65	69	69	71	274	3,750
	Joel Girrbach	65	70	71	68	274	3,750
	Nicolai Kristensen	70	68	67	69	274	3,750
	Tim Widing	68	71	66	69	274	3,750
19	Jens Fahrbring	67	70	68	70	275	2,645
	Federico Maccario	67	67	69	72	275	2,645
	Davey Porsius	71	64	67	73	275	2,645
	Clement Sordet	63	72	70	70	275	2,645
	Euan Walker	67	72	69	67	275	2,645
24	Elias Bertheussen	68	69	68	71	276	2,225
	Deon Germishuys	70	67	69	70	276	2,225
	Allen John	68	68	65	75	276	2,225
	Filip Mruzek	66	70	71	69	276	2,225
	John Murphy	66	72	68	70	276	2,225
	Adrien Saddier	65	71	70	70	276	2,225

Open de Portugal

Royal Obidos Spa & Golf Resort, Vau Obidos, Portugal
Par 72 (36-36); 7,283 yards

September 15-18
Purse: €250,000

1	**Pierre Pineau**	74	66	66	67	273	€40,000
2	**Felix Mory**	70	71	66	66	273	22,500
	David Ravetto	70	71	64	68	273	22,500
	Pineau won playoff at first extra hole						
4	Oscar Lengden	72	69	65	69	275	13,750
	Oliver Lindell	72	68	66	69	275	13,750
6	Tomas Bessa	71	71	66	68	276	9,000
	Euan Walker	69	72	67	68	276	9,000
8	Jeremy Freiburghaus	70	68	69	70	277	5,875
	Jeong Weon Ko	71	66	67	73	277	5,875
	Jerome Lando-Casanova	70	69	68	70	277	5,875
	Ben Stow	71	73	66	67	277	5,875
12	Todd Clements	67	69	68	74	278	4,250
	Tom McKibbin	74	67	69	68	278	4,250
	Max Rottluff	71	69	72	66	278	4,250
	Gary Stal	70	73	71	64	278	4,250
	Jesper Svensson	70	68	72	68	278	4,250
17	Christofer Blomstrand	69	72	70	68	279	3,025
	Alejandro Del Rey	74	66	67	72	279	3,025
	Anton Karlsson	68	72	70	69	279	3,025
	Clement Sordet	70	70	73	66	279	3,025
	Borja Virto	69	71	70	69	279	3,025
22	Pedro Figueiredo	70	70	68	72	280	2,350
	Haraldur Magnus	69	70	71	70	280	2,350
	Robin Sciot-Siegrist	75	69	66	70	280	2,350
	Kristof Ulenaers	71	69	70	70	280	2,350
	Lars van Meijel	71	72	69	68	280	2,350

Swiss Challenge

Golf Saint Apollinaire, Folgensbourg, France
Par 72 (36-36); 7,434 yards

September 22-25
Purse: €250,000

1	**Daniel Hillier**	68	70	72	64	274	€40,000
2	**Jeong Weon Ko**	66	68	72	70	276	27,500
3	**Oscar Lengden**	70	71	69	68	278	17,500
4	Matthew Baldwin	74	69	67	69	279	12,500
	Ben Stow	70	66	72	71	279	12,500
	Steven Tiley	70	70	69	70	279	12,500
7	Martin Simonsen	68	67	72	73	280	8,000
8	Daniel Brown	68	74	71	68	281	5,650
	Bryce Easton	66	72	71	72	281	5,650
	Alexander Knappe	70	72	68	71	281	5,650
	Maximilian Schmitt	76	66	69	70	281	5,650
	Jonathan Thomson	71	69	71	70	281	5,650
13	Alejandro Del Rey	71	70	72	69	282	3,875
	Felix Mory	69	73	70	70	282	3,875
	Joel Moscatel Nachshon	71	68	73	70	282	3,875
	David Ravetto	72	72	70	68	282	3,875
	Clement Sordet	72	70	67	73	282	3,875
	Jesper Svensson	69	68	75	70	282	3,875
19	Manuel Elvira	70	68	71	74	283	2,645
	Deon Germishuys	69	73	73	68	283	2,645
	Bradley Neil	67	73	74	69	283	2,645
	JC Ritchie	73	69	74	67	283	2,645
	Euan Walker	71	69	74	69	283	2,645
24	Christopher Feldborg Nielsen	70	70	73	71	284	2,300
	Gary Hurley	70	74	69	71	284	2,300
	John Parry	73	72	66	73	284	2,300

Hopps Open de Provence

Golf International de Pont Royal, Mallemort, France
Par 72 (36-36); 6,920 yards

September 29-October 2
Purse: €250,000

1	**Joel Sjoholm**	68	71	65	67	271	€40,000
2	**Daniel Brown**	70	69	68	67	274	22,500
	Deon Germishuys	68	71	67	68	274	22,500
4	Daniel Hillier	70	66	70	69	275	15,000
5	Martin Simonsen	71	72	69	64	276	12,500
6	Bryce Easton	69	69	68	71	277	8,333
	Sebastien Gros	71	73	67	66	277	8,333
	Mikael Lindberg	71	71	69	66	277	8,333
9	Ruaidhri McGee	72	68	69	69	278	5,750
	Adrien Saddier	69	74	68	67	278	5,750
11	Nathan Kimsey	68	72	67	72	279	4,750
	Maximilian Schmitt	75	68	68	68	279	4,750
	Robin Sciot-Siegrist	68	71	69	71	279	4,750
14	Matt Ford	70	71	74	65	280	4,000
	Jonathan Thomson	68	74	67	71	280	4,000
	Robbie van West	68	70	73	69	280	4,000
17	Benjamin Poke	72	71	66	72	281	3,125
	David Ravetto	74	69	69	69	281	3,125
	Javier Sainz	72	70	67	72	281	3,125
	Borja Virto	76	69	68	68	281	3,125
21	Franck Daux	73	71	70	68	282	2,368
	Bailey Gill	67	69	71	75	282	2,368
	Oscar Lengden	70	68	75	69	282	2,368
	Stuart Manley	71	73	68	70	282	2,368
	Christopher Mivis	71	75	67	69	282	2,368
	Felix Mory	72	72	66	72	282	2,368
	Maximilian Rottluff	72	67	74	69	282	2,368

British Challenge

St Mellion Estate (Nicklaus Signature), Cornwall, England — October 6-9
Par 72 (36-36); 7,010 yards — Purse: £230,000

1	**Euan Walker**	71	66	72	71	280	€41,953
2	**JC Ritchie**	70	72	70	69	281	28,843
3	**Matthew Baldwin**	68	69	69	76	282	18,355
4	Simon Forsstrom	67	72	73	71	283	13,110
	John Parry	71	71	70	71	283	13,110
	Adrien Saddier	73	65	76	69	283	13,110
7	Nick Bachem	72	75	69	68	284	7,866
	Mateusz Gradecki	72	73	70	69	284	7,866
9	Oscar Lengden	72	74	71	68	285	6,031
	Conor Purcell	69	73	69	74	285	6,031
11	Daniel Brown	73	72	71	70	286	4,064
	Daniel Hillier	69	72	66	79	286	4,064
	Jeong Weon Ko	71	71	72	72	286	4,064
	Haraldur Magnus	68	71	74	73	286	4,064
	Stuart Manley	71	74	71	70	286	4,064
	Javier Sainz	72	70	69	75	286	4,064
	Ben Schmidt	68	72	75	71	286	4,064
	Maximilian Schmitt	68	75	69	74	286	4,064
	Martin Simonsen	70	72	71	73	286	4,064
	Aron Zemmer	75	73	70	68	286	4,064
21	Jannik de Bruyn	71	70	69	77	287	2,576
	Eduard Rousaud	70	76	70	71	287	2,576
	Jamie Rutherford	71	71	69	76	287	2,576
	Clement Sordet	73	75	69	70	287	2,576
25	Mathieu Decottignies-Lafon	74	71	71	72	288	2,307
	Paul Maddy	69	73	74	72	288	2,307
	Velten Meyer	71	70	72	75	288	2,307
	Niklas Regner	72	73	74	69	288	2,307
	Ben Stow	72	72	70	74	288	2,307

English Trophy

Frilford Heath Golf Club, Abingdon, England — October 13-16
Par 72 (36-36); 7,045 yards — Purse: £230,000

1	**Jeremy Freiburghaus**	68	65	67	66	266	€42,592
2	**Maximilian Schmitt**	69	65	64	68	266	29,282
	Freiburghaus won playoff at first extra hole						
3	**Ben Schmidt**	68	66	69	65	268	18,634
4	Ugo Coussaud	66	65	68	71	270	9,735
	Jens Dantorp	66	70	69	65	270	9,735
	OJ Farrell	69	66	68	67	270	9,735
	Sam Hutsby	69	64	73	64	270	9,735
	Mikael Lindberg	67	68	70	65	270	9,735
	Tom McKibbin	69	66	70	65	270	9,735
	Henric Sturehed	65	68	69	68	270	9,735
11	John Parry	67	68	68	68	271	5,058
	Adrien Saddier	64	69	73	65	271	5,058
	Joel Sjoholm	66	69	68	68	271	5,058
14	Adam Blomme	69	66	70	67	272	4,392
	Maximilian Rottluff	68	70	70	64	272	4,392
16	Daniel Brown	67	67	68	71	273	3,085
	Alejandro Del Rey	69	65	72	67	273	3,085
	Jens Fahrbring	70	67	70	66	273	3,085
	Jeong Weon Ko	66	71	68	68	273	3,085
	Velten Meyer	68	67	71	67	273	3,085
	Bradley Neil	66	70	68	69	273	3,085
	Marco Penge	67	65	70	71	273	3,085
	Lee Slattery	66	70	73	64	273	3,085
	Ben Stow	67	67	74	65	273	3,085
25	David Ravetto	68	68	69	69	274	2,422
	Jesper Svensson	70	67	68	69	274	2,422

Rolex Challenge Tour Grand Final

Club de Golf Alcanada, Port d'Alcudia, Mallorca, Spain — November 3-6
Par 72 (36-36); 7,174 yards — Purse: €500,000

1	**Nathan Kimsey**	70	73	66	70	279	€87,000
2	**Bryce Easton**	71	72	66	71	280	45,650
	John Parry	70	72	70	68	280	45,650
4	Matthew Baldwin	70	69	71	71	281	24,455
	Jeong Weon Ko	69	72	72	68	281	24,455
6	Oscar Lengden	70	75	66	71	282	18,143
	Tom McKibbin	73	73	70	66	282	18,143
	Adrien Saddier	74	65	72	71	282	18,143
9	Velten Meyer	72	72	71	68	283	15,550
10	Nick Bachem	70	70	75	69	284	11,665
	Daniel Brown	78	77	65	64	284	11,665
	Alexander Knappe	69	74	69	72	284	11,665
	Alfie Plant	73	72	69	70	284	11,665
	Javier Sainz	68	76	71	69	284	11,665
	Euan Walker	68	75	70	71	284	11,665
16	Kristian Krogh Johannessen	72	73	70	71	286	7,453
	Benjamin Rusch	73	76	68	69	286	7,453
18	Mateusz Gradecki	75	70	69	73	287	6,425
	Oliver Hundeboll	76	69	73	69	287	6,425
	Mikael Lindberg	72	74	71	70	287	6,425
	JC Ritchie	72	76	76	63	287	6,425
22	Maximilian Schmitt	70	75	70	73	288	5,725
23	Jens Dantorp	75	74	71	69	289	5,165
	Deon Germishuys	72	75	71	71	289	5,165
	Daniel Hillier	74	71	71	73	289	5,165

2022 ROAD TO MALLORCA RANKINGS

		Points
1	Nathan Kimsey	208,918.1
2	Jeremy Freiburghaus	160,024.6
3	Alexander Knappe	146,051.5
4	JC Ritchie	141,285.7
5	Mikael Lindberg	139,847.6
6	Jens Dantorp	133,771.9
7	Daniel Hillier	123,473.3
8	Oliver Hundeboll	123,082.3
9	Freddy Schott	122,455.8
10	Tom McKibbin	120,719.1

ALPS TOUR

Ein Bay Open	**Stefano Mazzoli**
Red Sea Little Venice Open	**Oihan Guillamoundeguy** (A)
New Giza Open	**Tomas Guimaraes Bessa**
Winter Series Terre dei Consoli	**Adrien Pendaries**
Winter Series Golf Nazionale	**Mathias Eggenberger**
Abruzzo Alps Open	**Manuel Morugan**
Molinetto Alps Open	**Koen Kouwenaar**
Goesser Open	**Markus Brier**
Memorial Giorgio Bordoni	**Gregorio De Leo**
Open de la Mirabelle d'Or	**Tom Vaillant** (A)
Aravell Golf Open	**Tom Vaillant** (A) **(2)**
Alps de Andalucia	**Gary Hurley**
Hauts de France-Pas de Calais Golf Open	**Davey Porsius**
Alps de Las Castillas	**Gregorio De Leo (2)**
Fred Olsen Alps de La Gomera	**Vince van Veen**
Roma Alps Open	**Gregorio De Leo (3)**
Castelconturbia Alps Open	**Ben Schmidt**
Emilia Romagna Alps Tour Grand Final	**Jonathan Yates**

EUROPRO TOUR

Cubefunder Shootout	**James Allan**
Ignis Management Championship	**Josh Hilleard**
World Snooker & Jessie May Championship	**Nick Cunningham**
IFX Payments Championship	**Jake Ayres**
Bendac Championship	**Ryan Brooks**
PDC Golf Championship	**Pavan Sagoo**
CPG Classic	**Dermot McElroy**
Glal.uk Worcestershire Masters	**Brandon Robinson-Thompson**
Q Hotels Collection Championship	**Nicholas Poppleton**
Dell Technologies Championship	**James Allan (2)**
Lancer Scott Open	**Jack Davidson**
Northern Ireland Masters	**Sam Broadhurst**
Spey Valley Golf Resort	**Stuart Grehan**
Eagle Orchid Scottish Masters	**Michael Stewart**
Wright-Morgan Championship	**Josh Hilleard (2)**
Matchroom Tour Championship	**James Allan (3)**

NORDIC GOLF LEAGUE	
GolfStar Winter Series I	**John Axelsen**
GolfStar Winter Series II	**Marcus Kinhult**
Ecco Tour Spanish Masters	**Sebastian Friedrichsen**
PGA Catalunya Resort Championship	**Jeppe Kristian Andersen**
Bravo Tours Open	**Frederik Birkelund (A)**
Barncancerfonden Open	**Nicolai Tinning**
Rewell Elisefarm Challenge	**Axel Boasson**
Stora Hotellet Fjallbacka Open	**Simon Forsstrom**
Moss & Rygge Open	**August Thor Host**
Thisted Forsikring Championship	**Nicolai Nohr Madsen**
Thomas Bjorn Samso Classic	**Mathias Gladbjerg**
Junet Open	**Jesper Hagborg Asp**
UNICEF Championship	**Christian Jacobsen**
PGA Championship Landeryd Masters	**Rasmus Holmberg**
Big Green Egg Swedish Matchplay Championship	**Mathias Gladbjerg**
Holtsmark Open	**Tobias Ruth**
Goteborg Open	**Jeppe Kristian Andersen**
Timberwise Finnish Open	**Viktor Edin**
Esbjerg Open	**Christian Jacobsen**
Greatdays Trophy	**Rasmus Holmberg (2)**
BMW Onsjo Open	**Frederik Severin Tottenborg**
Trust Forsikring Championship	**August Thor Host**
Great Northern Challenge	**Frederik Birkelund (A) (2)**
Gumbalde Open	**Adam Andersson**
Race to Himmerland	**John Axelsen (2)**
MoreGolf Mastercard Tour Final	**John Axelsen (3)**
Sydbank Road to Europe Final	**Jeppe Kristian Andersen (2)**

PRO GOLF TOUR	
Dreamland Pyramids Classic	**Alan De Bondt**
Allegria Open	**Victor Veyret**
New Giza Pyramids Challenge	**Maximilian Herrmann**
Red Sea Ain Sokhna Classic	**Jan Cafourek**
Red Sea Egyptian Classic	**Yente Van Doren**
Haugschlag NO Open	**Dario Antonisse**
Gradi Polish Open	**Michael Hirmer**
Raiffeisen Pro Golf Tour St Polten	**Jean Bekirian**
Weihenstephan Open	**Marc Hammer**
Richter+Frenzel Open	**Alexandre Liu**
Altepro Trophy	**Jean Bekirian**
FaberExposize Gelpenberg Open	**Floris de Haas**
Castanea Resort Championship	**Jannik de Bruyn**

Top: A three-wood to two feet for eagle handed Hideki Matsuyama a playoff win at the Sony Open in Hawaii.
Bottom: Harold Varner III holes a 90-foot eagle putt at the 18th to win the PIF Saudi International.

Julio Aguilar/Getty Images

Clockwise from top left: Danielle Kang claimed the LPGA's Tournament of Champions; Jin Young Ko won on her first start of the year at the HSBC WWC; Hannah Green and Dimitrios Papadatos triumphed at the Vic Open.

Matthew Lewis/R&A

Clockwise from top: Scottie Scheffler, the world number one at the WGC Dell Match Play; Ratchanon Chantananuwat, 15-year-old amateur, the Asian Tour's youngest winner; Cameron Smith, The Players champion.

Sean M. Haffey/Getty Images

Clockwise from top left: Hyo Joo Kim wins the Lotte in Hawaii; Jordan Spieth, champion in the RBC Heritage at Harbour Town; Xander Schauffele and Patrick Cantlay combine at the Zurich Classic in New Orleans.

Atsushi Tomura/Getty Images

Clockwise from top: A second Wells Fargo win for Max Homa; a fifth victory in 10 starts for Mao Saigo at the Bridgestone Open; a first major title for New Zealand's Steven Alker at the KitchenAid Senior PGA.

Top: A prized picture for Billy Horschel with Memorial host Jack Nicklaus after a four-shot win. Bottom: Lin Grant becomes the first woman to win on the DP World Tour by nine strokes at the Scandinavian Mixed.

Stuart Franklin/Getty Images

Sam Greenwood/Getty Images

Clockwise from top left: Bronte Law, winner of the Aramco London event; Haotong Li, BMW International victor; Padraig Harrington, US Senior Open champion; Rory McIlroy, a 21st PGA Tour win at the Canadian Open.

Richard Heathcote/Getty Images

Clockwise from top left: Adrian Meronk, Poland's first DP World Tour winner at the Irish Open; Darren Clarke with another jug at The Senior Open; Jennifer Kupcho and Lizette Salas teamed up at Great Lakes Bay.

African Sunshine Tour

Thriston Lawrence achieved something no other South African golfer had done before when he claimed the Sir Henry Cotton Rookie of the Year award on the 2021-22 DP World Tour. Lawrence had won the Joburg Open at the end of 2021 and then added the Omega European Masters at Crans-sur-Sierre, as well as posting a string of consistently high finishes. "It's a dream come true," Lawrence said. "If you look at the names on the trophy, it's incredible. A year ago I didn't even have a category, so when I started off with a victory, it came to mind straight away to go for this award. To have accomplished it is an incredible feeling — I'm very grateful and honoured."

Lawrence was determined not to let the winning stop and he started the new season on the DP World Tour by winning one of the crown jewels of the domestic circuit at the Investec South African Open. It was a wire-to-wire win at Blair Atholl but, five ahead with five to play, he suddenly found himself tied with Clement Sordet on the 17th tee before winning by one. It was his third win on both the Sunshine and DP World Tours. "This is the one you want to win, your national Open," said Lawrence, who celebrated his 26th birthday on the Saturday of the event. "It was so special to have Gary Player watching as well. He's won 13 of these, and now I've got one. It's what you dream of. This is by far my best victory ever."

Lawrence finished the year at 63rd in the world, his highest ranking ever, with only Louis Oosthuizen and Dean Burmester as compatriots ahead of him. A seventh place finish at the Alfred Dunhill Championship was key to Oosthuizen staying in the world's top 50 at the end of the year after the former Open champion moved to play on the LIV Golf Invitational Series, where there were wins for Charl Schwartzel and Branden Grace.

The link up between the Sunshine Tour and the DP World and Challenge Tours expanded in 2022 with six events co-sanctioned by each of the European circuits during the year. The Challenge Tour events all took place early on, with JC Ritchie retaining his title at the Bain's Whisky Cape Town Open and then winning again the following week at the Jonsson Workwear Open. The two early DP World Tour events included Shaun Norris winning the Steyn City Championship after a tight duel with Burmester. It was his first win in South Africa for 11 years and allowed Norris, who won the 2021 Japan Open, to win the 2021-22 Sunshine Tour Order of Merit ahead of Burmester and Lawrence. Jayden Schaper was the Rookie of the Year.

The new season started with three first-time winners, with Albert Venter, who won the FBC Zim Open, adding another title at the SunBet Challenge — Time Square. Martin Rohwer won twice during the year, having taken the Vodacom Origins of Golf Final at the start of the year and then combining with Merrick Bremner to win the Bain's Whisky Ubunye Championship. George Coetzee also won twice, following his fifth VOG win at De Zalze by taking the PGA Championship for a second time in November.

There were four DP World Tour events to close out the year, with Lawrence's SA Open win followed by Ockie Strydom's at the Alfred Dunhill Championship, his second Sunshine Tour title but a major breakthrough in a co-sanctioned event. At year's end he was leading Lawrence at the top of the Luno Order of Merit, with the winner at the end of the 2022-23 season earning R500,000 worth of Bitcoin. The Sunshine Tour switched to a points-based ranking system for the new season rather than one based on prize money. Casey Jarvis, who won as an amateur on the Big Easy Tour earlier in the year, turned professional in August and was leading the Rookie of the Year race.

Another of South African golf's great occasions returned for the first time in three years when the Nedbank Golf Challenge was contested at Sun City. The event only counted on the DP World Tour and was won by an emotional Tommy Fleetwood, the defending champion.

Sun City also played host to the Gary and Vivienne Player Invitational, an unofficial 36-hole event won by the team of Sunshine Tour professional Brooklin Bailey, former South African football star Mark Fish and businessmen Anthony Phillips and Ashok Pundit. "It's been a dream of mine to get trophies handed to me from the greats in the game so this is a special experience," Bailey said. "Gary Player is an absolute legend and he's done so much for golf and through his philanthropy."

Player, 87, said of the fundraising event for the Gary and Vivienne Foundation: "When people ask me, 'What is your legacy?' they all think it's golf. My legacy is not golf. It's that through golf and through our foundation, we've raised over $100 million for underprivileged people. That is my legacy."

2022 SCHEDULE

Vodacom Origins of Golf Final	**Martin Rohwer**	
Kit Kat Group Pro-Am		*abandoned*
Dimension Data Pro-Am	**Alexander Knappe**	
Bain's Whisky Cape Town Open	**JC Ritchie**	
Jonsson Workwear Open	**JC Ritchie (2)**	
Mangaung Open	**Oliver Hundeboll**	
MyGolfLife Open	**Pablo Larrazabal**	
Steyn City Championship	**Shaun Norris**	
SDC Open	**Clement Sordet**	
Limpopo Championship	**Mateusz Gradecki**	
Stella Artois Players Championship	**Jaco Ahlers**	
Sunshine Tour Championship	**Tristen Strydom**	
Lombard Insurance Classic	**Herman Loubser**	
FBC Zim Open	**Albert Venter**	
Sishen Classic	**Deon Germishuys**	
SunBet Challenge	**Rourke van der Spuy**	
Kit Kat Group Pro-Am	**Dylan Mostert**	
FNB Eswatini Nkonyeni Challenge	**Jaco Prinsloo**	
Vodacom Origins of Golf — De Zalze	**George Coetzee**	
Bain's Whisky Ubunye Championship	**Merrick Bremner/Martin Rohwer (2)**	
SunBet Challenge — Time Square	**Albert Venter (2)**	
Vodacom Origins of Golf — Highland Gate	**Anthony Michael**	
Gary & Vivienne Player Challenge	**Jaco Van Zyl**	
Vodacom Origins of Golf — San Lameer	**Wynand Dingle**	
SunBet Challenge — Wild Coast Sun	**MJ Viljoen**	
Vodacom Origins of Golf — St Francis Links	**Ruan Korb**	
Fortress Invitational	**Pieter Moolman**	
Blue Label Challenge	**Stephen Ferreira**	
SunBet Challenge — Sun Sibaya	**Dylan Naidoo**	
Vodacom Origins of Golf Final	**Combrinck Smit**	
PGA Championship	**George Coetzee (2)**	
Nedbank Golf Challenge*	**Tommy Fleetwood**	*See chapter 14*
Joburg Open	**Dan Bradbury**	
Investec South African Open	**Thriston Lawrence (1,2)**	
Alfred Dunhill Championship	**Ockie Strydom**	
AfrAsia Bank Mauritius Open	**Antoine Rozner**	

**non-Order of Merit event*

Vodacom Origins of Golf Final

Martin Rohwer took time off in December to analyse his game following a 2021 season in which his only top-10 finish came with a runner-up finish at the Gauteng Championship in March. It was time well used for the 28-year-old South African as he started 2022 with a two-stroke victory at the Vodacom Origins of Golf Final at the Gary Player Country Club at Sun City.

Rohwer built his second Sunshine Tour victory, after winning the 2019 Royal Swazi Open, on rounds of 66-67 to go four in front with a round to play. On the first day he chipped in twice and took only 21 putts. The following day Rohwer felt he played better, hitting more greens in regulation and not dropping a shot. On the final day, he had an early bogey at the second but responded with a birdie at the next and then made two more in a 70 for a 13-under-par total of 203. Alex Haindl, his nearest challenger overnight, dropped to sixth with a 72, while Tristen Strydom rallied with a 64, with six birdies and an eagle at the last, to take second place on 11 under, three ahead of Wilco Nienaber, Luca Filippi and Germany's Freddy Schott.

Rohwer said: "My strategy helped even more today in terms of staying focused on each shot. I knew if I just played steady golf it would force the others to be aggressive." Winning on the Player at Sun City was also a boost. "It's one of the iconic courses in South Africa and I've always loved it. I feel that if your game can hold up under pressure on the Gary Player Country Club course, then it can hold up anywhere."

Gary Player Country Club, Sun City, North West Province — January 28-29
Par 72 (36-36); 7,832 yards — Purse: R1,000,000

1	**Martin Rohwer**	66	67	70	203	R158,500
2	**Tristen Strydom**	71	70	64	205	115,000
3	**Freddy Schott**	70	72	66	208	63,333
	Wilco Nienaber	73	67	68	208	63,333
	Luca Filippi	68	71	69	208	63,333
6	Pieter Moolman	68	70	71	209	34,750
	Alex Haindl	67	70	72	209	34,750
8	Hennie du Plessis	68	73	70	211	26,000
	Dylan Mostert	66	72	73	211	26,000
10	Jake Redman	71	72	69	212	21,167
	Trevor Fisher Jr	71	70	71	212	21,167
	Louis de Jager	70	68	74	212	21,167
13	Jared Harvey	71	73	69	213	18,000
	Christiaan Basson	69	71	73	213	18,000
	Kyle Barker	69	71	73	213	18,000
16	Michael Hollick	69	76	69	214	15,367
	Ockie Strydom	73	70	71	214	15,367
	Hennie O'Kennedy	74	68	72	214	15,367
19	Malcolm Mitchell	75	70	70	215	13,700
	Jayden Schaper	74	70	71	215	13,700
	Jason Roets	68	72	75	215	13,700
22	Jaco Van Zyl	75	70	71	216	11,100
	Jacques Blaauw	73	72	71	216	11,100
	Hennie Otto	69	75	72	216	11,100
	JJ Senekal	72	72	72	216	11,100
	Dylan Naidoo	77	66	73	216	11,100
	Rhys West	74	69	73	216	11,100
	Stefan Wears-Taylor	72	71	73	216	11,100
	MJ Viljoen	69	71	76	216	11,100
30	Anton Haig	69	76	72	217	9,050
	Keagan Thomas	73	71	73	217	9,050
	Lyle Rowe	74	69	74	217	9,050
	Byron Coetzee	71	72	74	217	9,050

Kit Kat Group Pro-Am

Only a few hours of play were possible at the Kit Kat Group Pro-Am before flooding from the Hennops River damaged several holes at the Irene Country Club in Centurion. Friday's opening round was delayed by three hours due to the wet conditions, with Dylan Naidoo seven under par after 13 holes when new thunderstorms arrived. Only 12 players completed their first rounds, with Rupert Kaminski leading in the clubhouse on 67.

But the following morning the course was unplayable and the 54-hole event was abandoned and rescheduled for later in the year. Said Ludwick Manyama, tournament director: "Waterlogged is really an understatement of what we are dealing with here. The river is all over the golf course. We have four holes that are heavily underwater, and others that are severely damaged."

Irene Country Club, Centurion, Gauteng — February 4-6
Par 71 (35-36); 7,093 yards — Purse: R1,000,000

Dimension Data Pro-Am

It turns out Germany's Alexander Knappe was more of a home player at the first event of the year co-sanctioned with the Challenge Tour. Knappe has had a winter base at Fancourt for many years, was there at the end of 2021 and arrived for the Dimension Data Pro-Am three weeks early.

"Fancourt is like a home for me," Knappe said. "I live here on the estate. The three courses here are so good to practise on and get ready for tournaments. I've always wanted to win this tournament." The 32-year-old finished third in 2016, the year he won twice on the Challenge Tour, but six years later he defeated Dean Burmester with a birdie at the last.

An emotional Knappe said: "I've spent so many hours on these courses, in the rain, when there's been a threat of lightning, when nobody has been out here, I've been working on these greens, and when it happened now all that hard work just came out in tears."

Knappe opened with a 65 on the Outeniqua course, then had a 67 on The Links, followed by weekend scores on the Montagu of 66-68 for a 23-under-par total of 266. Playing the same rotation of the courses, SA PGA champion Burmester started the first round with a triple bogey as he twice went out of bounds trying to drive the Outeniqua's first green. But he rallied for a 71, then scored a 65 on The Links and a 63 on the Montagu to trail Knappe by one after 54 holes. It was a fine duel on the last day, Burmester birdieing the 16th to draw level but just missing for a birdie at the last. Knappe, who holed a long putt at the 11th that rattled the flagstick, almost holed for eagle from long range at the last before tapping in for the win.

The German had not dropped a shot to par during the entire tournament. "I felt a little bit of pressure sometimes because I knew that," he said. "I played a little bit safe over those last few holes. I was left with long putts but it's incredible, four rounds bogey-free, I never thought that was possible. It's unbelievable."

Fancourt Golf Estate (Montagu), George, Western Cape — February 10-13
Par 72 (36-36); 7,342 yards — Purse: $375,000
Outeniqua (R1-3) par 72 (36-36); 6,891 yards
The Links (R1-3) par 73 (36-37); 7,388 yards

1	**Alexander Knappe**	65	67	66	68	266	R951,000
2	**Dean Burmester**	71	65	63	68	267	663,000
3	**Daniel Hillier**	64	72	63	71	270	419,400
4	JC Ritchie	68	72	66	67	273	199,000
	Nicolai Kristensen	72	64	68	69	273	199,000
	Neil Schietekat	69	65	71	68	273	199,000
7	Adrien Saddier	63	66	77	68	274	135,000
	Deon Germishuys	67	69	70	68	274	135,000
	Jaco Ahlers	65	69	73	67	274	135,000
10	Angel Hidalgo	67	68	71	69	275	94,800
	Haydn Porteous	68	66	74	67	275	94,800
	Wilco Nienaber	72	65	68	70	275	94,800
13	MJ Viljoen	70	67	69	70	276	83,400
	Garrick Porteous	67	70	69	70	276	83,400
	Tristen Strydom	69	66	71	70	276	83,400
	David Ravetto	69	68	69	70	276	83,400
	Rupert Kaminski	70	69	66	71	276	83,400
18	Pieter Moolman	67	71	68	71	277	78,000
19	Jacques Blaauw	66	68	69	75	278	72,600
	Hennie O'Kennedy	70	67	71	70	278	72,600
	Hennie du Plessis	70	72	66	70	278	72,600
	Richard Mansell	66	69	68	75	278	72,600
	Ivan Cantero Gutierrez	68	66	69	75	278	72,600
24	Jayden Schaper	67	74	67	71	279	66,000
	David Dixon	71	71	65	72	279	66,000
	Matthew Baldwin	67	71	69	72	279	66,000
27	Scott Vincent	70	69	74	67	280	59,400
	Jaco Prinsloo	71	69	70	70	280	59,400
	Peter Karmis	71	70	69	70	280	59,400
	Wynand Dingle	67	72	70	71	280	59,400
	Ruan Korb	76	67	67	70	280	59,400
	Liam Johnston	70	74	66	70	280	59,400
	Max Schmitt	66	70	71	73	280	59,400
	Louis de Jager	71	70	70	69	280	59,400

Bain's Whisky Cape Town Open

Making a habit of successfully defending a title, JC Ritchie did it for the third time at the Bain's Whisky Cape Town Open. After needing a playoff to win in 2021, thanks to birdies at the 18th both in regulation and at the extra hole, it took another three at Royal Cape's final hole to win by a single stroke — achieved with a putt from almost 30 feet. The 27-year-old clenched his fists and immediately embraced his caddie.

"I didn't have the energy for a playoff," Ritchie admitted. "I haven't made a long putt all week so I said to myself on the 18th, 'It's time to make a long one now'. I've hit that same putt on 18 a couple of times in the past. When I walked onto the green I knew the line already and felt like I had a good chance of making it. Luckily it went in. It feels amazing. It means everything to me."

Ritchie's ninth Sunshine Tour title arrived with scores of 69-66-67-68 for an 18-under-par total of 270. Tom McKibbin, who scored a 62 at Royal Cape in the second round after starting with seven birdies in a row, had led after 36 and 54 holes, but the 19-year-old from Northern Ireland closed with a

73 to tie for third place with Zander Lombard and Bryce Easton. Belgium's Christopher Mivis charged through the field on the final day with a bogey-free 66 to set the clubhouse target at 17 under and ended up with second place.

Ritchie, starting the last day two behind McKibbin, went out in four under but suffered a couple of hiccups at 13 and 14 before birdieing the 16th and the last. He had previously defended his titles at the Gauteng Team Championship, with Jaco Prinsloo, and the Limpopo Championship, both in 2020. "It's special to have that under your belt — to say you've been able to defend titles," he said. "Especially multiple times."

Royal Cape Golf Club, Wynberg, Cape Town — February 17-20
Par 72 (36-36); 6,633 yards — Purse: $250,000
Rondebosch Golf Club (R1&2) par 72 (36-36); 6,567 yards

1	**JC Ritchie**	69	66	67	68	270	R598,338
2	**Christopher Mivis**	72	66	67	66	271	417,138
3	**Zander Lombard**	68	65	70	70	273	178,558
	Bryce Easton	71	65	67	70	273	178,558
	Tom McKibbin	68	62	70	73	273	178,558
6	Neil Schietekat	68	68	67	71	274	99,094
	Ivan Cantero Gutierrez	65	68	69	72	274	99,094
8	Jamie Rutherford	71	68	71	65	275	67,875
	Daniel Hillier	67	68	71	69	275	67,875
	Clement Sordet	70	68	68	69	275	67,875
	Matteo Manassero	66	72	67	70	275	67,875
	Gary Stal	69	65	69	72	275	67,875
13	Felix Mory	72	62	70	72	276	54,171
	Niklas Lemke	67	69	68	72	276	54,171
15	Alex Haindl	69	70	73	65	277	49,641
	Benjamin Rusch	72	67	71	67	277	49,641
	Dylan Naidoo	68	71	70	68	277	49,641
	Alfie Plant	70	65	72	70	277	49,641
	Blake Windred	72	64	70	71	277	49,641
	Pieter Moolman	73	62	68	74	277	49,641
21	Jbe' Kruger	69	70	70	69	278	44,545
	Jaco Ahlers	69	69	70	70	278	44,545
	Wilco Nienaber	69	70	69	70	278	44,545
24	Michael Palmer	70	68	72	69	279	40,770
	Yubin Jung	69	70	71	69	279	40,770
	Byron Coetzee	71	66	72	70	279	40,770
	Luca Filippi	70	69	70	70	279	40,770
	Christofer Blomstrand	65	70	73	71	279	40,770
29	Todd Clements	71	68	74	67	280	36,240
	Keenan Davidse	68	67	77	68	280	36,240
	Trevor Fisher Jr	69	68	73	70	280	36,240
	Hennie du Plessis	70	67	72	71	280	36,240
	Toto Thimba Jr	70	67	72	71	280	36,240
	Niall Kearney	67	71	71	71	280	36,240
	Tristen Strydom	71	68	69	72	280	36,240

Jonsson Workwear Open

After his victory the previous week in Cape Town, things got even better for JC Ritchie at the Jonsson Workwear Open. The opening day was his 28th birthday and he celebrated with a new course record nine-under-par 61 at The Woods at Mount Edgecombe. His two eagles included a hole-in-one at the 213-yard second hole with a five-iron. "Today was pretty strange," Ritchie said. "It was probably the best ball-striking day I've had in my life. I don't remember ever having that control on a golf course. And to have a hole-in-one on my birthday was pretty awesome."

Ritchie went on to win the tournament wire-to-wire. His two-shot lead after day one turned into a six-shot advantage with a 63 at Durban Country Club, which also included two eagles. He was one shot away from John Bland's 1993 course record and sat at 18 under par for 36 holes. A 65 the next day took him to 25 under par breaking the Challenge Tour record for 54 holes of 23 under set by Kristoffer Broberg in the 2012 Rolex Trophy. He led by 10 strokes from Tom McKibbin. "It was another brilliant day," Ritchie said. "This golf course has been very generous to me. I keep trying to respect this golf course as much as I can and it keeps giving."

A windy Sunday meant Mark McNulty's Sunshine Tour record of 29 under par at the 1987 Royal Swazi Sun Open proved out of reach for Ritchie, who closed with a 71 for a 26-under-par total of 260. He suffered his only two bogeys of the week but made three birdies, including at the last two holes. Belgium's Christopher Mivis made it a repeat one-two from the previous week, getting within two after going birdie-eagle-birdie from the 13th, playing the first 15 holes in eight under, but then bogeyed the last two holes for a 66. Ritchie won by six strokes, with Haraldur Magnus one further back in third.

"I don't have the words for this," Ritchie said after his 10th Sunshine Tour win, and fourth on the Challenge Tour. "This week has been unbelievable."

Durban Country Club, Durban, KwaZulu-Natal — February 20-24
Par 72 (36-36); 6,691 yards — Purse: $250,000
Mount Edgecombe Country Club (The Woods) (R1&2) par 70 (35-35); 6,459 yards

1	**JC Ritchie**	61	63	65	71	260	R598,338
2	**Christopher Mivis**	66	65	69	66	266	417,138
3	**Haraldur Magnus**	68	66	67	66	267	263,873
4	Keenan Davidse	67	70	68	65	270	125,204
	Jaco Prinsloo	70	64	70	66	270	125,204
	Ross McGowan	67	68	67	68	270	125,204
7	David Ravetto	71	65	70	65	271	89,656
	Tom McKibbin	65	68	66	72	271	89,656
9	Mikael Lindberg	69	69	67	67	272	66,188
	Steven Tiley	67	68	69	68	272	66,188
	Hennie Otto	73	63	68	68	272	66,188
12	Trevor Fisher Jr	64	73	72	64	273	53,039
	Emilio Cuartero Blanco	70	65	73	65	273	53,039
	Daniel Brown	69	64	70	70	273	53,039
	Philipp Mejow	69	66	68	70	273	53,039
	Jbe' Kruger	64	66	71	72	273	53,039
	Adam Blomme	67	64	69	73	273	53,039
18	Tristen Strydom	67	70	72	65	274	45,678
	John Parry	72	66	71	65	274	45,678
	Robin Sciot-Siegrist	69	69	68	68	274	45,678
	Damien Perrier	72	65	68	69	274	45,678
	John Murphy	71	67	67	69	274	45,678
	MJ Viljoen	66	71	67	70	274	45,678
	Nicolai Kristensen	71	65	64	74	274	45,678
25	Romain Wattel	71	67	71	66	275	39,638
	David Boote	71	66	71	67	275	39,638
	Kristian Krogh Johannessen	68	70	67	70	275	39,638
	Ruan Korb	71	66	67	71	275	39,638
	Ruan Conradie	71	66	67	71	275	39,638
	Richard Joubert	71	67	65	72	275	39,638

Mangaung Open

A week of delays due to dangerous weather in Bloemfontein and a Sunday that was merely wet — like "good weather in Denmark," said the winner — Oliver Hundeboll posted a target at the Mangaung Open that no one else was able to match. The 22-year-old Dane was five behind with a round to play and only one under par for the day after a bogey at the ninth but came home in 31 to take his first title on either the Challenge or Sunshine Tours.

A birdie at the last from a greenside bunker gave Hundeboll a 66, after earlier scores of 68-67-66, for a 21-under-par total of 267. Then he had to wait and see if it was good enough. "It feels amazing," he said. "I still don't quite believe it to be honest, especially after the front nine. I managed to put together a strong back nine and the conditions felt like I was playing in Denmark. The key moment was making a birdie at the 10th hole after my bogey at nine. The putts started to roll in after that."

Scotland's Craig Ross, the leader after 54 holes, bogeyed the 16th and doubled the 17th before a birdie at the last to tie Spain's Scott Fernandez for fourth place. Luke Jerling had a bogey six at the 18th for a 70 to tie for second place, one behind, with Tristen Strydom, who finished bogey-birdie-par for a 68. Jbe' Kruger, who scored a course-record 61 at Bloemfontein in his home city on Saturday, closed with a 72 to tie for sixth.

Bloemfontein Golf Club, Bloemfontein, Free State — March 3-6
Par 72 (36-36); 7,302 yards — Purse: $250,000
Schoeman Park Golf Club (R1&2) par 72 (36-36); 6,993 yards

1	**Oliver Hundeboll**	68	67	66	66	267	R610,225
2	**Tristen Strydom**	71	65	64	68	268	347,270
	Luke Jerling	63	68	67	70	268	347,270
4	Scott Fernandez	63	72	63	71	269	138,600
	Craig Ross	65	69	62	73	269	138,600
6	John Parry	68	65	70	67	270	91,438
	Jamie Rutherford	67	69	67	67	270	91,438
	Keenan Davidse	67	65	70	68	270	91,438
	Jbe' Kruger	68	69	61	72	270	91,438
10	Lars van Meijel	66	66	73	66	271	62,755
	Mitch Waite	69	67	67	68	271	62,755
12	Daniel Hillier	69	69	62	72	272	56,403
	Alejandro Del Rey	63	71	66	72	272	56,403
14	Mikael Lindberg	70	68	68	67	273	52,938
	Mathieu Decottignies-Lafon	68	69	68	68	273	52,938
	JC Ritchie	67	67	70	69	273	52,938
	Lorenzo Scalise	72	65	65	71	273	52,938
18	Peter Karmis	71	66	69	68	274	46,585
	Clement Sordet	69	69	68	68	274	46,585
	Jeremy Freiburghaus	67	67	70	70	274	46,585
	Eduard Rousaud	69	69	70	66	274	46,585
	Benjamin Rusch	65	69	68	72	274	46,585
	Deon Germishuys	67	68	66	73	274	46,585
	John Murphy	69	68	64	73	274	46,585
25	Matthew Baldwin	71	67	68	69	275	39,655
	Ugo Coussaud	69	69	68	69	275	39,655
	Justin Walters	65	66	74	70	275	39,655
	Bjorn Akesson	68	68	71	68	275	39,655
	Brooklin Bailey	70	65	70	70	275	39,655
	MJ Viljoen	66	63	74	72	275	39,655
	Wilco Nienaber	67	69	67	72	275	39,655
	Louis Albertse	69	68	63	75	275	39,655

MyGolfLife Open

It wasn't to be for the man with a one-minute commute at the MyGolfLife Open. Hennie du Plessis lives on the Pecanwood estate, on the southern banks of the Hartbeespoort Dam Reservoir and led all the way after an opening 62. But home advantage did not help on the final day as three Europeans swept past the local man in the first of two events co-sanctioned with the DP World Tour. In the end Spain's Pablo Larrazabal defeated Jordan Smith at the second extra hole, having twice birdied the 18th, while Adri Arnaus had dropped out on the first playoff hole.

It was Larrazabal's sixth DP World Tour victory and his second in a row in South Africa after the 38-year-old won the Alfred Dunhill Championship in 2019. "This win means a lot," Larrazabal said. "I've been working so hard and I'm very happy to get it done. I love this place. I love good golf courses and nature, and South Africa has it all. The crowds here have been so special to me all these years."

While du Plessis stalled to a final-round 72, winding up in a tie for sixth place, Larrazabal and Arnaus came from two behind with a pair of 67s and Smith scored a bogey-free 65 to tie on 22-under-par 266. George Coetzee was the leading South African in fourth place, one behind, after a 64, with Richard Sterne fifth.

Larrazabal went out in three under and then parred only two holes on a rollercoaster back nine. He eagled the 10th with a 40-footer and made a 25-footer at the 15th but bogeyed the 17th to fall back into a tie. He eventually won with a five-footer. "What a day," said the Spaniard. "It was one of those days where you just feel great and you know you're going to have a chance. I started fast to get into the lead very quick. I had that bogey on 17 which I wasn't expecting. But then in the playoff, I knew we had to attack."

Pecanwood Golf & Country Club, Hartbeespoort, North West Province — March 10-13
Par 72 (36-36); 7,697 yards — Purse: $1,500,000

1	**Pablo Larrazabal**	63	65	71	67	266	R3,932,100
2	**Jordan Smith**	68	65	68	65	266	2,000,745
	Adri Arnaus	70	65	64	67	266	2,000,745
	Larrazabal won playoff at second extra hole						
4	George Coetzee	68	66	69	64	267	1,156,500
5	Richard Sterne	64	65	70	69	268	980,712
6	Ross Fisher	62	70	69	68	269	693,900
	Nacho Elvira	62	66	71	70	269	693,900
	Hennie du Plessis	62	65	70	72	269	693,900
9	Thriston Lawrence	66	67	71	66	270	490,356
	Romain Langasque	70	65	67	68	270	490,356
11	Oliver Bekker	66	69	69	67	271	387,428
	Trevor Fisher Jr	65	67	71	68	271	387,428
	Tristen Strydom	62	66	74	69	271	387,428
	Marcus Armitage	66	67	69	69	271	387,428
15	Matthieu Pavon	67	68	73	64	272	326,133
	Keenan Davidse	65	69	69	69	272	326,133
	Julien Brun	66	68	67	71	272	326,133
18	Francesco Laporta	67	67	73	66	273	278,485
	Scott Jamieson	68	70	68	67	273	278,485
	Dean Burmester	65	68	72	68	273	278,485
	Louis de Jager	68	70	67	68	273	278,485
	Brandon Stone	66	66	71	70	273	278,485
23	Laurie Canter	65	67	74	68	274	240,552
	Steven Brown	67	71	68	68	274	240,552
	Justin Harding	66	69	70	69	274	240,552
	JC Ritchie	64	70	70	70	274	240,552
	Ashun Wu	67	68	67	72	274	240,552
28	Jorge Campillo	65	72	69	69	275	198,918
	Antoine Rozner	68	70	68	69	275	198,918
	Aaron Cockerill	65	66	74	70	275	198,918
	Adrian Meronk	68	67	70	70	275	198,918
	Richard Bland	69	66	70	70	275	198,918
	Grant Forrest	69	68	68	70	275	198,918
	Jbe' Kruger	67	69	65	74	275	198,918
35	Daniel Gavins	70	66	73	67	276	143,599
	Jacques Kruyswijk	70	65	72	69	276	143,599
	Martin Rohwer	68	68	71	69	276	143,599
	Fabrizio Zanotti	65	71	70	70	276	143,599
	Santiago Tarrio	69	68	69	70	276	143,599
	Stephen Ferreira	70	68	68	70	276	143,599
	David Law	68	70	68	70	276	143,599
	Joost Luiten	66	69	70	71	276	143,599
	Luke Brown	70	66	69	71	276	143,599
	Masahiro Kawamura	66	69	69	72	276	143,599
	Connor Syme	67	69	68	72	276	143,599
	Darren Fichardt	66	67	68	75	276	143,599
47	Jake Redman	68	69	73	67	277	93,214
	Shaun Norris	65	69	74	69	277	93,214
	JJ Senekal	65	67	75	70	277	93,214
	Maximilian Kieffer	68	69	70	70	277	93,214
	Richie Ramsay	66	68	72	71	277	93,214
	Neil Schietekat	65	72	69	71	277	93,214
	Jayden Schaper	69	66	70	72	277	93,214
	Sebastian Soderberg	67	69	69	72	277	93,214
	Matti Schmid	69	67	69	72	277	93,214
	Jazz Janewattananond	66	66	71	74	277	93,214
57	Thomas Detry	68	70	71	69	278	70,547
	Bernd Wiesberger	69	69	70	70	278	70,547
	Alejandro Canizares	66	72	67	73	278	70,547
	Hurly Long	69	66	69	74	278	70,547
61	Andy Sullivan	67	69	74	69	279	61,295
	Michael Palmer	73	65	71	70	279	61,295
	Nicolai von Dellingshausen	64	71	70	74	279	61,295
	Ewen Ferguson	68	67	67	77	279	61,295
65	Lucas Bjerregaard	68	68	76	68	280	47,582
	Jaco Van Zyl	69	68	74	69	280	47,582
	Rourke van der Spuy	70	68	72	70	280	47,582
	Ruan Conradie	70	65	74	71	280	47,582
	Joachim B Hansen	70	67	71	72	280	47,582

	MJ Viljoen	68	70	70	72	280	47,582
	Zander Lombard	71	66	69	74	280	47,582
72	Jason Scrivener	66	72	72	71	281	34,619
	Louis Albertse	67	67	74	73	281	34,619
74	Kalle Samooja	68	70	71	73	282	34,517
	James Hart du Preez	67	71	68	76	282	34,517
76	Wil Besseling	71	66	75	71	283	34,364
	Maverick Antcliff	70	67	74	72	283	34,364
	Dylan Naidoo	69	68	73	73	283	34,364
	James Morrison	69	67	73	74	283	34,364
80	CJ du Plessis	68	70	75		213	34,237

Steyn City Championship

There would be a chunk of the tale missing to say Shaun Norris led after 54 holes by four strokes and won the Steyn City Championship by three. That would be the part where he went out in two over and a hole later found himself two strokes behind Dean Burmester, who was in the middle of a run of five under for six holes thanks to a pitch-in eagle at the seventh and three other birdies.

There was more. Norris came home in four under but the turnaround was really sparked at the 13th hole when he saw his wife Candice and three-week-old daughter Riley-Grace appear in the crowd. Norris explained: "As we walked onto the 13th tee box my brother Kyle" — also his caddie — "said to me, 'Look up there'. It was my wife and baby daughter. I didn't think they would be able to come. When I saw them I said to myself, 'Ok, now you do this'."

Birdies at the 14th and 16th holes got Norris back level with Burmester, who did not make a birdie after the 11th. Then came a three-shot swing at the 17th, where Norris birdied but Burmester took a double bogey after finding a bunker and going over the green with his escape shot.

With both men finding the green at Steyn City's 18th, Burmester slapped Norris on the back and led the applause as the champion-in-waiting approached the green. Norris had opened with a 64 and then added a 62 with an eagle and eight birdies to lead by three after 36 holes. His weekend scores of 67-70 gave the 39-year-old a 25-under-par total of 263. Burmester kept a hold on second place after a 69, with Oliver Bekker and Germany's Matti Schmid sharing third place.

This was Norris's first European Tour win after two decades as a professional, his third on the Sunshine Tour — but first for 11 years — and his 10th worldwide, including six in Japan where he won the Japan Open in 2021. "Dean came out of the blocks strong and definitely made me think about it," Norris said. "It's so special to have finally done this. This has been 11 years since I won in South Africa. I don't often get the chance for my family to be with me, and for me to win in front of them is an absolute blessing." Norris dedicated the victory to his late father Patrick, who died from cancer in 2019.

The Club at Steyn City, Johannesburg, Gauteng — March 17-20
Par 72 (36-36); 7,716 yards — Purse: $1,500,000

1	**Shaun Norris**	64	62	67	70	263	R3,845,400
2	**Dean Burmester**	66	65	66	69	266	2,488,200
3	**Oliver Bekker**	69	63	70	67	269	1,278,030
	Matti Schmid	69	65	64	71	269	1,278,030
5	Tapio Pulkkanen	68	67	68	67	270	809,796
	James Hart du Preez	63	66	73	68	270	809,796
	Joachim B Hansen	68	64	67	71	270	809,796
8	Thriston Lawrence	69	68	68	66	271	536,094
	Romain Langasque	65	68	67	71	271	536,094
10	Jacques Kruyswijk	71	67	68	66	272	383,409
	Dale Whitnell	69	69	67	67	272	383,409
	Wilco Nienaber	66	72	67	67	272	383,409
	Joost Luiten	68	66	69	69	272	383,409
	Mikko Korhonen	68	65	68	71	272	383,409
	Sebastian Soderberg	65	67	67	73	272	383,409
16	Jaco Ahlers	64	70	71	68	273	293,608
	Daniel van Tonder	66	70	69	68	273	293,608
	Jordan Smith	71	67	67	68	273	293,608
	Sami Valimaki	67	68	69	69	273	293,608
	Jazz Janewattananond	70	68	65	70	273	293,608
21	Niklas Norgaard Moller	66	67	75	66	274	252,213
	Connor Syme	67	71	70	66	274	252,213
	Hurly Long	70	67	69	68	274	252,213
	Ross McGowan	67	68	70	69	274	252,213
25	Jorge Campillo	68	68	71	68	275	211,497
	Ashun Wu	70	67	69	69	275	211,497
	Antoine Rozner	71	67	68	69	275	211,497
	George Coetzee	65	69	71	70	275	211,497
	Ockie Strydom	70	66	69	70	275	211,497
	Nino Bertasio	64	69	71	71	275	211,497
	Pieter Moolman	67	68	69	71	275	211,497
	Hennie du Plessis	66	67	70	72	275	211,497
33	Rourke van der Spuy	70	67	72	67	276	170,781
	Michael Palmer	67	69	69	71	276	170,781
	Oliver Wilson	68	70	67	71	276	170,781
	Estiaan Conradie	68	68	68	72	276	170,781
37	Craig Howie	69	69	71	68	277	151,554
	Yannik Paul	69	69	69	70	277	151,554
	Jacques Blaauw	67	72	68	70	277	151,554
40	Marcus Armitage	73	66	71	68	278	126,672
	Daniel Gavins	68	67	74	69	278	126,672
	Espen Kofstad	70	69	70	69	278	126,672

	Ewen Ferguson	67	69	72	70	278	126,672		CJ du Plessis	66	73	71	70	280	70,122
	Andrea Pavan	71	67	70	70	278	126,672	60	Marcus Helligkilde	68	71	74	68	281	62,205
	Combrinck Smit	70	69	68	71	278	126,672		Richard Sterne	70	69	73	69	281	62,205
	Jamie Donaldson	67	69	70	72	278	126,672		Alejandro Canizares	71	65	72	73	281	62,205
	Haydn Porteous	70	68	67	73	278	126,672		Kalle Samooja	70	68	70	73	281	62,205
48	Matthieu Pavon	68	68	74	69	279	88,972	64	Kristoffer Broberg	69	69	73	71	282	53,157
	Jaco Prinsloo	69	68	73	69	279	88,972		Darius van Driel	65	74	72	71	282	53,157
	Nacho Elvira	69	68	73	69	279	88,972		Maverick Antcliff	71	68	71	72	282	53,157
	Lukas Nemecz	68	69	73	69	279	88,972		Jason Scrivener	67	72	70	73	282	53,157
	Jake Redman	68	71	71	69	279	88,972	68	Dylan Naidoo	71	68	73	71	283	45,240
	Rhys Enoch	69	69	70	71	279	88,972		Adilson Da Silva	69	68	73	73	283	45,240
	Keenan Davidse	72	66	68	73	279	88,972		Ruan de Smidt	65	73	70	75	283	45,240
	Alfredo Garcia-Heredia	69	69	68	73	279	88,972	71	Edoardo Molinari	69	69	72	74	284	33,930
	Fabrizio Zanotti	71	68	67	73	279	88,972	72	Andy Sullivan	68	68	76	73	285	33,880
57	Hugo Leon	70	68	72	70	280	70,122	73	Justin Walters	68	68	73	77	286	33,805
	Laurie Canter	68	71	71	70	280	70,122		MJ Viljoen	66	71	70	79	286	33,805

SDC Open

In the first of two Challenge Tour co-sanctioned events in Limpopo, Clement Sordet won for the first time in almost five years at the SDC Open. The 29-year-old Frenchman defeated Ruan Conradie at the first extra hole after both overtook third-round leader Dean Germishuys, whose bogey at the 17th hole dropped him a stroke outside the playoff.

Sordet won four times in three seasons on the Challenge Tour between 2015-17 but had struggled on the European Tour in recent seasons. At Zebula he rediscovered the winning touch, dominating the par-five 18th in the playoff by hitting a three-iron onto the green and two-putting for a birdie that Conradie could not match.

"I've played amazing all week and it is nice to finish with a birdie in the playoff to get that fifth win on the Challenge Tour," Sordet said. "The only thing I could control out there was my game. The leaderboard was packed up the top, but I just had to focus on my score because I knew I was playing well. I was focused on creating birdie chances and I managed to do that pretty well today, so I am very happy."

Sordet had scores of 64-66-70-67 for a 21-under-par total of 267. Conradie closed with a 68 and Germishuys a 71, with Marco Penge taking fourth place.

Zebula Golf Estate, Bela Bela, Limpopo — March 24-27
Par 72 (36-36); 7,469 yards — Purse: $250,000
Elements Private Golf Reserve (R1&2) par 72 (36-36); 7,427 yards

1	**Clement Sordet**	64	66	70	67	267	R576,544		Jamie Rutherford	69	66	71	69	275	48,379
2	**Ruan Conradie**	66	68	65	68	267	401,944		John Parry	70	69	67	69	275	48,379
	Sordet won playoff at first extra hole								Stephen Ferreira	71	68	66	70	275	48,379
3	**Deon Germishuys**	66	68	63	71	268	254,261		MJ Viljoen	68	66	69	72	275	48,379
4	Marco Penge	65	71	63	70	269	152,775	20	Nick Bachem	68	69	73	66	276	42,438
5	CJ du Plessis	67	68	67	69	271	104,578		David Borda	68	71	71	66	276	42,438
	Freddy Schott	68	64	68	71	271	104,578		Nicolai Kristensen	66	72	69	69	276	42,438
7	Jacopo Vecchi Fossa	69	70	67	66	272	72,823		Dylan Mostert	68	67	71	70	276	42,438
	Todd Clements	68	72	65	67	272	72,823		Pedro Figueiredo	70	69	67	70	276	42,438
	JJ Senekal	66	65	73	68	272	72,823		Anthony Michael	72	67	64	73	276	42,438
	JC Ritchie	67	70	67	68	272	72,823	26	Jens Fahrbring	71	69	69	68	277	37,830
	Matteo Manassero	69	66	65	72	272	72,823		Robbie van West	68	71	69	69	277	37,830
12	Pieter Moolman	69	67	68	69	273	52,744		Oliver Hundeboll	72	68	66	71	277	37,830
	Lorenzo Scalise	68	69	65	71	273	52,744		Jake Redman	66	67	72	72	277	37,830
	Stefan Wears-Taylor	71	67	64	71	273	52,744		Daniel van Tonder	67	67	70	73	277	37,830
15	Ockie Strydom	69	71	68	67	275	48,379								

Limpopo Championship

Mateusz Gradecki became the first international winner of the Limpopo Championship and only the second winner from Poland on the Challenge Tour with a brilliant final round at Euphoria. Gradecki came from five behind to win by three strokes from South Africa's Hennie du Plessis. His bogey-free 66 was the best round of the final day, which was twice interrupted by dangerous weather, the second suspension coming as he stood over a five-foot putt for par at the final hole. When he was allowed to return to the green, he holed the putt.

Gradecki, who had missed three of his four cuts so far on the South African swing of the Challenge Tour season, had earlier posted rounds of 68-68-67 and finished with a 19-under-par total of 269. "I just wanted to keep doing the same things I'd been doing over the previous three rounds," he said. "I knew I was playing well and I just needed to keep calm and stay in the moment. I knew my game was good enough to do it. I'm really pleased with the way I played. I can't believe I've finally got my first win on the Challenge Tour."

Du Plessis was a runner-up at the event for the second year running after contesting the playoff won by Brandon Stone in 2021. One of the joint first-round leaders, du Plessis was in second place four behind Oliver Hundeboll after 54 holes and closed with a 70 to finish one ahead of Germany's Nick Bachem. Hundeboll, aiming for a second win in three starts after he took the Mangaung Open, had taken the lead with a 63 in the second round but closed with a 76.

Euphoria Golf & Lifestyle Estate, Modimolle, Limpopo — March 31-April 3
Par 72 (36-36); 7,699 yards — Purse: $250,000
Koro Creek Golf Club par 72 (36-36); 7,436 yards

1	**Mateusz Gradecki**	68	68	67	66	269	R578,525
2	**Hennie du Plessis**	65	70	67	70	272	403,325
3	**Nick Bachem**	68	63	73	69	273	255,135
4	Lars van Meijel	71	64	70	69	274	121,058
	Bryce Easton	66	67	71	70	274	121,058
	Oliver Hundeboll	67	63	68	76	274	121,058
7	Luke Jerling	68	67	68	73	276	86,688
	Pieter Moolman	66	70	67	73	276	86,688
9	Clement Sordet	71	67	69	70	277	68,438
	MJ Viljoen	69	69	69	70	277	68,438
11	Nordin van Tilburg	70	69	70	69	278	52,925
	Victor Garcia Broto	70	68	70	70	278	52,925
	Dylan Mostert	66	71	71	70	278	52,925
	Gudmundur Kristjansson	68	69	70	71	278	52,925
	Rourke van der Spuy	75	62	68	73	278	52,925
16	Alexander Knappe	69	70	72	68	279	47,450
	Jake Redman	70	69	68	72	279	47,450
	Rupert Kaminski	68	70	69	72	279	47,450
	Max Rottluff	71	63	72	73	279	47,450
	Robin Sciot-Siegrist	67	67	70	75	279	47,450
21	Jamie Rutherford	69	69	72	70	280	42,048
	Allen John	72	66	71	71	280	42,048
	Dylan Naidoo	71	66	74	69	280	42,048
	Ockie Strydom	67	68	72	73	280	42,048
	Kristian Krogh Johannessen	69	67	71	73	280	42,048
26	Gary Stal	72	67	70	72	281	38,325
	JC Ritchie	70	66	73	72	281	38,325
	Jeong Weon Ko	71	67	71	72	281	38,325
	Dominic Foos	69	69	70	73	281	38,325
30	Niklas Regner	67	69	73	73	282	35,040
	Marco Penge	73	65	72	72	282	35,040
	Quintin Wilsnach	71	65	74	72	282	35,040
	Peter Launer Baek	71	68	69	74	282	35,040
	Hennie Otto	67	69	72	74	282	35,040

Stella Artois Players Championship

Jaco Ahlers showed he was the man for a playoff once again when he defeated Ockie Strydom in overtime to win the Stella Artois Players Championship. It was a 10th win on the Sunshine Tour for the 39-year-old from Centurion, the first also having come in a playoff in 2009. In fact, half his wins required extra holes, with a playoff record of five out of seven.

Ahlers (64-67-69) and Strydom (66-63-71) were in a three-way tie for the lead after 54 holes at Dainfern and both closed with 66 to finish on 18-under-par 266. With both men going out in 32, it was Strydom who edged ahead with birdies at the 10th and 11th, while Ahlers bogeyed the latter, only his second bogey of the week. He then made up the three shots with three birdies over the last seven holes, including with a long putt at the 17th to draw level.

Both missed birdie chances at the par-five 18th in regulation before claiming a four apiece at the first extra hole. On the second extra hole, Ahlers reached the green in two and two-putted for another four, but Strydom was just short and could not get up and down. Ahlers had not won since 2019 and his exemption was about to run out but he also enjoyed receiving the new sponsor's trophy.

"I actually asked the Stella Artois people whether it was a working beer tap because this trophy is going to look great in my bar," Ahlers said. "It's just so good to win. My win exemption was going to end in the final tournament of the season next week so the timing couldn't be more perfect. I've had a bit of experience with playoffs. It's really nice to get this win."

JJ Senekal, who shared the 54-hole lead with Ahlers and Strydom, closed with a 67 to finish one behind in third place, alongside Tristen Strydom (65) and Estiaan Conradie (66).

Dainfern Golf Estate, Dainfern, Johannesburg, Gauteng — April 21-24
Par 71 (35-36); 7,308 yards — R2,000,000

1	**Jaco Ahlers**	64	67	69	66	266	R317,000
2	**Ockie Strydom**	66	63	71	66	266	
	Ahlers won playoff at second extra hole						
3	**Estiaan Conradie**	67	68	66	66	267	
	JJ Senekal	69	64	67	67	267	
	Tristen Strydom	64	72	66	65	267	
6	Jared Harvey	66	67	71	64	268	
	Jaco Prinsloo	67	65	71	65	268	
8	Hennie O'Kennedy	68	66	70	65	269	
9	Keenan Davidse	72	66	65	67	270	
	Malcolm Mitchell	72	66	67	65	270	
	Dylan Mostert	72	67	66	65	270	
	Neil Schietekat	67	69	71	63	270	
13	Louis Albertse	68	71	66	66	271	
	Madalitso Muthiya	63	70	69	69	271	
	Martin Rohwer	70	66	69	66	271	
	Rourke van der Spuy	69	65	67	70	271	
17	George Coetzee	73	68	66	65	272	
	Stefan Wears-Taylor	69	66	69	68	272	
19	Jacques Blaauw	68	68	68	69	273	
	Luca Filippi	65	71	69	68	273	
	Luke Jerling	70	71	62	70	273	
	Dylan Naidoo	64	71	71	67	273	
	Martin Vorster	68	67	73	65	273	
24	Merrick Bremner	69	69	68	68	274	
	Michael Palmer	67	68	71	68	274	
	Freddy Schott	69	67	70	68	274	
	CJ du Plessis	68	69	67	70	274	
28	Christiaan Basson	66	73	68	68	275	
	Hayden Griffiths	71	70	67	67	275	
	Keagan Thomas	68	69	70	68	275	

Sunshine Tour Championship

A week relaxing in Zanzibar prior to the Players Championship, where he was third, may have been the key for Tristen Strydom claiming his maiden victory at the Sunshine Tour Championship. Learning when to take breaks was vital for a player who had been a top amateur but had yet to find his feet in the professional ranks. The 25-year-old from Pretoria, who went to the Qualifying School three times before winning it in 2000, had been a runner-up five times, four of them in the previous nine months.

Yet at his home club of Serengeti, Strydom looked like a veteran winner as he took over the lead on day two and never surrendered his status. After scores of 69-64-68, to be two ahead of Pieter Moolman, he closed with a 66 to finish on a 21-under-par total of 267. That was a record tally for the tournament, as was his six-shot winning margin over Moolman, who closed with a 70. George Coetzee took third place, 10 strokes behind the winner.

Three birdies in a row on the front nine propelled Strydom clear of his challengers and the icing on the cake was a final birdie at the 18th. "I can't describe how it feels," Strydom said. "I've worked extremely hard to get where I am today. It makes it so special to get that first victory for everybody who believes in me. I came out with an attacking mindset. I didn't want to give anybody a chance. I had a good game plan and I felt really comfortable with the golf course. I've had so many second-place finishes and it does get to you after a while. But my caddie just kept telling me to stay patient and it will happen at the right place and right time. And it's great to have finally done it."

As this was the last tournament of the 2021-22 season, Shaun Norris was confirmed as the Order of Merit winner with R4,890,994 following his victory in the Steyn City Championship.

Serengeti Golf & Wildlife Estate (Nicklaus Signature), Kempton Park, Gauteng — April 28-May 1
Par 72 (36-36); 7,761 yards — R1,500,000

1	**Tristen Strydom**	69	64	68	66	267	R240,000
2	**Pieter Moolman**	66	68	69	70	273	
3	**George Coetzee**	69	68	70	70	277	
4	Jayden Schaper	70	69	70	70	279	
5	Luca Filippi	72	69	71	68	280	
	Deon Germishuys	70	69	72	69	280	
7	Justin Harding	72	70	70	69	281	
8	Luke Jerling	69	73	70	70	282	
9	Ockie Strydom	71	73	71	69	284	
10	Trevor Fisher Jr	68	77	74	67	286	
	Jacques Blaauw	71	75	72	68	286	
	Neil Schietekat	74	75	69	68	286	
	Estiaan Conradie	70	70	76	70	286	
14	Hennie Otto	71	70	74	72	287	
15	Wilco Nienaber	72	76	69	71	288	
	Louis Albertse	70	73	72	73	288	
	Jaco Ahlers	75	69	69	75	288	
18	Lyle Rowe	76	70	71	72	289	
	Martin Rohwer	71	72	73	73	289	
	James Hart du Preez	71	75	70	73	289	
21	JC Ritchie	78	75	70	67	290	
	Jaco Prinsloo	70	75	72	73	290	
23	Rupert Kaminski	75	76	72	69	292	
24	Ruan Conradie	73	76	71	73	293	
25	Louis de Jager	78	70	76	70	294	
	Rourke van der Spuy	70	76	73	75	294	
27	Alex Haindl	75	74	72	74	295	
28	Keenan Davidse	71	78	75	72	296	
	Jean Hugo	76	77	71	72	296	
30	Stephen Ferreira	75	75	73	74	297	
	CJ du Plessis	76	71	73	77	297	
	Jake Redman	71	73	74	79	297	

2020-22 ORDER OF MERIT

1	Shaun Norris	R4,890,994
2	Dean Burmester	4,196,182
3	Thriston Lawrence	3,854,950
4	Oliver Bekker	3,359,398
5	Hennie du Plessis	2,779,485
6	JC Ritchie	2,691,199
7	Zander Lombard	1,949,393
8	Daniel van Tonder	1,943,891
9	Tristen Strydom	1,843,480
10	George Coetzee	1,816,637

Lombard Insurance Classic

Herman Loubser required extra holes both before and after the regulation 54 at Arabella to win the Lombard Insurance Classic, the opening event of the 2022-23 season. Loubser survived a qualifying round to get into the tournament, then needed two extra holes to defeat Ockie Strydom in a playoff. Four behind Keith Horne after scoring 67-73, Loubser closed with a 68, birdieing the 16th to tie Strydom, who made four birdies in five holes from the ninth for a 68, on seven-under-par 209. Horne finished with a 74 to be third.

Loubser and Strydom, who lost a playoff to Jaco Ahlers at the Stella Artois Players Championship in April, both parred the 18th in the playoff and then playing the par five again, Loubser chipped in for a birdie and his maiden victory on the Sunshine Tour. The 23-year-old from Modderfontein turned professional on winning the Qualifying School in 2017 but lost his card just before the Covid-19 pandemic hit, although he did win on the Big Easy Tour in 2020.

"I had a drink from the trophy, and it tasted so sweet," said Loubser. "I sat out for two years watching my friends do well on tour and knowing I had the game to be there as well, so that was tough. I worked hard last year and felt like I came into this event ready. Ockie's such a great ball-striker and it was intimidating. I also haven't had a great record in playoffs before this. But I got it done."

Arabella Country Estate, Kleinmond, Western Cape — May 13-15
Par 72 (36-36); 6,805 yards — Purse: R1,200,000

1	**Herman Loubser**	67	73	69	209	R190,200
2	**Ockie Strydom**	70	71	68	209	138,000
	Loubser won playoff at second extra hole					
3	**Keith Horne**	68	68	74	210	96,000
4	Hennie Otto	68	73	70	211	59,200
	Hennie O'Kennedy	69	71	71	211	59,200
	Rupert Kaminski	70	69	72	211	59,200
7	Pieter Moolman	69	73	70	212	35,400
	Luca Filippi	75	66	71	212	35,400
9	MJ Viljoen	71	71	72	214	28,200
	Louis Albertse	66	73	75	214	28,200
11	JJ Senekal	73	72	70	215	23,400
	Tristen Strydom	75	69	71	215	23,400
	Trevor Fisher Jr	74	70	71	215	23,400
	Keagan Thomas	74	68	73	215	23,400
15	Wynand Dingle	70	74	72	216	19,360
	Luke Jerling	73	70	73	216	19,360
	Luke Brown	72	68	76	216	19,360
18	Merrick Bremner	78	68	71	217	17,040
	Dean O'Riley	68	76	73	217	17,040
	Jacques P de Villiers	70	72	75	217	17,040
21	Jake Roos	71	76	71	218	14,940
	Bradley Bawden	73	72	73	218	14,940
	Christiaan Basson	77	67	74	218	14,940
	Jacques Blaauw	73	69	76	218	14,940
25	Chris Cannon	75	72	72	219	12,720
	Combrinck Smit	73	72	74	219	12,720
	Kyle Barker	69	75	75	219	12,720
	Deon Germishuys	73	70	76	219	12,720
29	Keelan van Wyk	75	72	73	220	11,580
	Clancy Waugh	71	73	76	220	11,580

FBC Zim Open

Albert Venter spent more than an hour on the putting green at Royal Harare after taking 31 putts in the third round of the FBC Zim Open and the extra effort paid off the next day with his maiden victory on the Sunshine Tour. The 26-year-old Venter, who had one win on the Big Easy Tour, made a birdie from 16 feet on the second extra hole to win a playoff against Stefan Wears-Taylor and Louis Albertse.

Even before that winning moment, Venter's putter had been on fire earlier in the day as he made eight birdies in 10 holes, with two bogeys, from the seventh hole. Venter scored 68-71-73-66 for a 10-under-par total of 278 to tie with Wears-Taylor, who finished birdie-birdie-bogey for a 66, and Albertse, who birdied the 16th and the 18th holes in a 67. Luca Filippi, the 54-hole leader, closed with a 75 to fall into seventh place, while American Dan Erickson had the lead until bogeying the last two holes as he finished in a share of fourth place with Louis de Jager and Jaco Ahlers.

After Venter, who started the final round five off the lead, sank his putt at the second playoff hole, neither of his opponents could convert from shorter range. "I knew I needed to just keep grinding today, follow my processes, my goal just to get in contention on the back nine," said Venter. "I caught fire and the putter paid off today. To get to this professional level is hard enough, but then to win is a whole other level. At the moment, it's still kind of surreal."

Royal Harare Golf Club, Harare, Zimbabwe — May 19-22
Par 72 (36-36); 7,241 yards — Purse: R2,000,000
Chapman Golf Club (R1&2) par 72 (36-36); 7,198 yards

1	**Albert Venter**	68	71	73	66	278	R317,000
2	**Stefan Wears-Taylor**	74	68	70	66	278	180,400
	Louis Albertse	65	74	72	67	278	180,400
	Venter won playoff at second extra hole						
4	Dan Erickson	70	69	73	68	280	66,333
	Louis de Jager	69	69	72	70	280	66,333
	Jaco Ahlers	70	69	71	70	280	66,333
7	Luca Filippi	68	65	74	75	282	50,000
8	Madalitso Muthiya	67	72	72	72	283	45,000
9	Hennie O'Kennedy	71	70	75	68	284	35,067
	Neil Schietekat	72	69	71	72	284	35,067
	Wynand Dingle	70	70	68	76	284	35,067
12	Dylan Naidoo	75	72	71	67	285	29,300
	Ryan Van Velzen	68	76	70	71	285	29,300
14	Ryan Cairns	71	70	76	69	286	28,100
	Ricky Hendler	71	75	69	71	286	28,100
16	Herman Loubser	66	81	70	70	287	26,600
	Keagan Thomas	67	74	75	71	287	26,600
	Nikhil Rama	70	70	73	74	287	26,600
19	Hayden Griffiths	72	72	77	67	288	24,200
	Therion Nel	69	76	75	68	288	24,200
	Kyle Barker	71	72	76	69	288	24,200
	Slade Pickering	70	72	75	71	288	24,200
	JJ Senekal	69	75	73	71	288	24,200
24	Lyle Rowe	74	73	73	69	289	22,200
	Deon Germishuys	72	72	73	72	289	22,200
26	Erhard Lambrechts	71	78	76	65	290	20,200
	Michael Kok	72	72	78	68	290	20,200
	Joe Long	77	70	74	69	290	20,200
	Clancy Waugh	71	72	77	70	290	20,200
	Stephen Ferreira	73	74	72	71	290	20,200
	Michael Palmer	72	76	71	71	290	20,200
	Rupert Kaminski	73	73	71	73	290	20,200
	Martin Vorster	71	71	70	78	290	20,200

Sishen Classic

Deon Germishuys made it three first-time winners in a row to start the new season as the 22-year-old won the Sishen Classic with a super performance on the final day. One behind Trevor Fisher Jr going into Sunday, Germishuys rolled off eight birdies, capped by the last of them from 75 feet at the 16th hole, to win by six strokes from Louis de Jager.

Germishuys scored 66-71-70-64 for a 17-under-par total of 271, while de Jager closed with a 67 and Fisher a 74 to fall into a tie for sixth place. His eventful week in the Camelthorn forest on the edge of the Kalahari Desert included having to smash his car window prior to the third round to retrieve his golf clubs after losing his car keys. On Sunday he did a smash-and-grab on the field by making five birdies going out and then three more coming back to distance himself from the rest.

"It's an emotional first win for me because I've worked so hard for everyone who has supported me. I'm really glad that I got it over the line," said Germishuys. "I thought if I could just go three or four under I would be happy. And I managed to go eight under. When I could attack the flags I did so, and when I had to go for the middle of the green I did that, too, and luckily I holed a couple of big putts."

In the mining town, Germishuys won the unique iron ore trophy as well as his weight in braai meat. Asked how much he weighed, he said: "If it's for the braai meat, then I weigh 200kg."

Sishen Golf & Country Club, Kathu, Northern Cape — May 26-29
Par 72 (36-36); 7,171 yards — Purse: R3,000,000

1	**Deon Germishuys**	66	71	70	64	271	R475,500
2	**Louis de Jager**	72	71	67	67	277	331,500
3	**Jacques Blaauw**	68	68	73	69	278	167,850
	Hennie O'Kennedy	71	69	67	71	278	167,850
5	CJ du Plessis	69	68	73	69	279	90,000
6	Rupert Kaminski	69	70	73	68	280	75,000
	Lyle Rowe	70	70	72	68	280	75,000
	Trevor Fisher Jr	70	66	70	74	280	75,000
9	Jean Hugo	70	69	74	68	281	49,140
	MJ Viljoen	70	69	73	69	281	49,140
	Jaco Van Zyl	68	72	71	70	281	49,140
	Erhard Lambrechts	71	71	68	71	281	49,140
	Jaco Ahlers	69	68	70	74	281	49,140
14	Riekus Nortje	69	69	74	70	282	42,600
15	Combrinck Smit	74	66	76	67	283	39,450
	Keith Horne	74	71	72	66	283	39,450
	Danie Van Niekerk	67	72	74	70	283	39,450
	Hayden Griffiths	68	69	74	72	283	39,450
	Bradley Bawden	66	71	73	73	283	39,450
	Louis Albertse	67	67	75	74	283	39,450
21	Jaco Prinsloo	72	67	75	70	284	35,850
	Dan Erickson	68	72	73	71	284	35,850
23	Dylan Naidoo	71	69	74	71	285	33,700
	Alex Haindl	69	69	75	72	285	33,700
	Byron Coetzee	69	72	71	73	285	33,700
26	Keagan Thomas	70	73	74	69	286	31,500
	Matias Calderon	71	72	74	69	286	31,500
	Herman Loubser	75	70	68	73	286	31,500
	Dylan Mostert	71	68	73	74	286	31,500
30	Ockie Strydom	66	72	74	75	287	29,700
	Ryan Van Velzen	69	70	71	77	287	29,700

SunBet Challenge

Playing alongside proven winners Hennie Otto and Louis de Jager, Rourke van der Spuy collected his third title on the Sunshine Tour at the SunBet Challenge. The 32-year-old from Durban converted a one-stroke overnight lead into a three-shot victory on the famed Gary Player Country Club layout at Sun City.

Van der Spuy was one behind after an opening 68 but then went ahead with a 71 on a cool second morning. In the final round he produced two early birdies followed by two bogeys, but took charge with gains at the eighth, 10th and 11th. Although he dropped a shot at the 14th, at the 17th he holed from 25 feet for a three which left him unreachable at the final hole. A closing 69 gave van der Spuy an eight-under-par total of 208. De Jager finished second on five under with a 71, while Otto had a 72 to tie with Jaco Prinsloo for a third place.

Having won in his rookie season in 2015, van der Spuy had only won once more in 2018. "Today I realised some childhood dreams," he said. "Playing with Hennie was a wonderful feeling because growing up, and when I started at the bottom of the Sunshine Tour, I looked up to him as a mentor. He is such an accomplished and successful golfer, and Louis as well. Something under par was our target today and I'm very proud to have broken 70 on a tough course like this. That birdie on 17 was my most clutch putt of the day."

Gary Player Country Club, Sun City, North West Province — June 1-3
Par 72 (36-36); 7,847 yards — Purse: R1,000,000

1	**Rourke van der Spuy**	68	71	69	208	R158,500
2	**Louis de Jager**	72	68	71	211	115,000
3	**Jaco Prinsloo**	70	71	71	212	71,500
	Hennie Otto	71	69	72	212	71,500
5	Ockie Strydom	74	71	68	213	38,833
	JJ Senekal	73	69	71	213	38,833
	Louis Albertse	71	70	72	213	38,833
8	Jaco Van Zyl	74	70	70	214	27,500
9	Jacques P de Villiers	70	73	72	215	22,667
	Alex Haindl	71	71	73	215	22,667
	Kyle Barker	70	70	75	215	22,667
12	Dylan Mostert	75	68	73	216	19,000
	Lyle Rowe	70	73	73	216	19,000
	Stefan Wears-Taylor	72	69	75	216	19,000
15	Martin Rohwer	73	72	72	217	15,167
	Ryan Van Velzen	73	74	70	217	15,167
	Joe Long	75	72	70	217	15,167
	Dan Erickson	71	71	75	217	15,167
	Harry Konig	69	72	76	217	15,167
	Dylan Naidoo	74	74	69	217	15,167
21	Keagan Thomas	73	71	74	218	12,950
	Hennie O'Kennedy	75	73	70	218	12,950
23	MJ Viljoen	69	77	73	219	11,700
	Heinrich Bruiners	75	70	74	219	11,700
	Herman Loubser	75	73	71	219	11,700
26	Kyle McClatchie	74	72	74	220	10,250
	Matias Calderon	72	75	73	220	10,250
	Matthew Spacey	73	74	73	220	10,250
	Christiaan Basson	72	72	76	220	10,250
30	Michael Kok	72	73	76	221	8,900
	James Pennington	73	73	75	221	8,900
	Nikhil Rama	73	74	74	221	8,900
	Madalitso Muthiya	75	69	77	221	8,900
	Divan van den Heever	76	72	73	221	8,900

Kit Kat Group Pro-Am

Rescheduled from February after the tournament was abandoned due to Irene Country Club being under water at the time, the Kit Kat Group Pro-Am was not only completed at the second attempt but provided a first Sunshine Tour victory for Dylan Mostert. The 23-year-old from Modderfontein won by three strokes from MJ Viljoen after playing the last 10 holes of the final round in four under par.

The big-hitting left-hander found the quick, sloping greens at Irene to his liking. Scores of 65-66 took Mostert from one behind Ryan Van Velzen to two in front of Keagan Thomas. A chip-in at the third hole on Sunday made up for an early bogey but he was still level par for the day after a bogey at the eighth. Then he birdied the ninth and blasted a hybrid from under the trees at the 10th onto the green and holed the putt to pick up another shot. He also birdied the 12th and 17th for a 68 and a 17-under-par total of 199.

Thomas slipped back with a 73, while Malcolm Mitchell charged into contention by going out in 33 before a double bogey at the 14th and bogeys at the next two holes. Viljoen's 67 secured second place ahead of Louis Albertse and victory in the team event with amateur partner Japie Holtzhausen.

Irene Country Club, Centurion, Gauteng — June 10-12
Par 72 (36-36); 7,093 yards — Purse: R1,000,000

1	**Dylan Mostert**	65	66	68	199	R158,500
2	**MJ Viljoen**	69	66	67	202	115,000
3	**Louis Albertse**	66	68	70	204	80,000
4	Kyle Barker	70	68	67	205	55,000
	Ryan Van Velzen	64	70	71	205	55,000
6	Jovan Rebula	69	68	69	206	32,333
	Madalitso Muthiya	69	66	71	206	32,333
	Keagan Thomas	66	67	73	206	32,333
9	Jaco Prinsloo	70	69	68	207	23,500
	Malcolm Mitchell	66	69	72	207	23,500
11	Pieter Moolman	74	67	67	208	20,000
	Dean O'Riley	69	68	71	208	20,000
	Ockie Strydom	67	68	73	208	20,000
14	Jaco Van Zyl	71	70	68	209	17,500
	Jean Hugo	70	72	67	209	17,500
16	Albert Venter	76	65	69	210	14,533
	Combrinck Smit	70	71	69	210	14,533
	Dayne Moore	70	70	70	210	14,533
	JJ Senekal	67	72	71	210	14,533
	Jason Smith	70	69	71	210	14,533
	Herman Loubser	69	69	72	210	14,533
22	Merrick Bremner	67	72	72	211	12,450
	Michael Hollick	70	72	69	211	12,450
24	Michael Palmer	73	69	70	212	11,450
	Richard Joubert	73	70	69	212	11,450
26	Rupert Kaminski	69	72	72	213	10,400
	Riekus Nortje	72	71	70	213	10,400
	Wynand Dingle	71	72	70	213	10,400
29	Stephen Ferreira	70	72	72	214	9,650
	Trevor Fisher Jr	73	69	72	214	9,650

FNB Eswatini Nkonyeni Challenge

Jaco Prinsloo went wire-to-wire to win for the fourth time as an individual on the Sunshine Tour at the FNB Eswatini Nkonyeni Challenge. The 32-year-old from Centurion opened with a 65, which contained two eagles, for a two-shot lead and never looked back. A 70 the next day kept his advantage intact, but Prinsloo had to keep his nerve as things tightened up in the last round at Nkonyeni Lodge & Golf Estate, a spectacular bushveld course by the Usuthu River.

Three birdies in a row from the seventh put him three ahead, yet a bogey at the 14th meant Jean Hugo was back within one as he birdied the same hole. Two holes later, there was another two-shot swing, this time in favour of Prinsloo and he parred the last two holes to secure a three-shot victory. A 69 gave him a 12-under-par total of 204. Hugo closed with a 68 to finish one ahead of Wynand Dingle, Keagan Thomas and Martin Rohwer. Prinsloo had won twice in 2021, at the Players Championship and the Serengeti Pro-Am Invitational.

Nkonyeni Lodge & Golf Estate, Manzini, Eswatini — July 28-30
Par 72 (36-36); 7,215 yards — Purse: R1,000000

1	**Jaco Prinsloo**	65	70	69	204	221.90
2	**Jean Hugo**	71	68	68	207	161.00
3	**Wynand Dingle**	70	70	68	208	87.27
	Keagan Thomas	71	69	68	208	87.27
	Martin Rohwer	71	68	69	208	87.27
6	Combrinck Smit	72	70	67	209	51.10
	Doug McGuigan	72	69	68	209	51.10
8	Danie Van Niekerk	72	71	67	210	35.47
	Ruan Korb	72	71	67	210	35.47
	Dylan Naidoo	72	70	68	210	35.47
11	Kyle McClatchie	68	73	70	211	28.00
	MJ Viljoen	71	74	66	211	28.00
	CJ du Plessis	69	68	74	211	28.00
14	Lyle Rowe	69	73	70	212	22.54
	Therion Nel	71	71	70	212	22.54
	Heinrich Bruiners	70	71	71	212	22.54
	Madalitso Muthiya	72	69	71	212	22.54
	Ricky Hendler	68	71	73	212	22.54
19	Herman Loubser	67	72	74	213	19.60
20	Teaghan Gauche	71	73	70	214	17.85
	Merrick Bremner	71	73	70	214	17.85
	Michael Kok	73	72	69	214	17.85
	Rhys West	70	69	75	214	17.85
24	Sean Bradley	74	69	72	215	15.28
	Harry Konig	71	71	73	215	15.28
	Thanda Mavundla	74	70	71	215	15.28
	Ryan Van Velzen	71	70	74	215	15.28
28	Dylan Mostert	74	71	71	216	14.10
29	Hennie O'Kennedy	70	73	74	217	13.10
	Jovan Rebula	69	75	73	217	13.10
	Rourke van der Spuy	71	73	73	217	13.10
	Keelan van Wyk	74	71	72	217	13.10

Vodacom Origins of Golf — De Zalze

Clearly, George Coetzee enjoys himself in the winelands of Stellenbosch. Just as he did in 2021, Coetzee won the opening event of the Vodacom Origins of Golf series at De Zalze. It was his fifth victory on the series, which gave him his first Sunshine Tour title in 2007, and put him second only behind Jean Hugo's 11 VOG wins. It was his 13th Sunshine Tour victory in all.

In defending his title, the 36-year-old from Pretoria led from the start with an opening 61 with nine birdies and an eagle two at the 18th. He led by five strokes after the first round, but England's Joe Long closed to within two by returning a 62 in the second round, with eight birdies, two eagles and two bogeys. The pair duelled on the final day, with Coetzee making five birdies in an outward 31 to go four clear. Long hit back with birdies at 13, 14 and 16 and was one behind playing the last, but then bogeyed and finished with a 67, four ahead of Kyle Barker in third. Coetzee's 67-67 for the last two rounds gave him a 21-under-par total of 195 and a two-shot winning margin.

De Zalze Winelands Golf Estate, Stellenbosch, Western Cape — August 4-6
Par 72 (36-36); 6,920 yards — Purse: R1,150,000

1	**George Coetzee**	61	67	67	195	221.90
2	**Joe Long**	68	62	67	197	161.00
3	**Kyle Barker**	67	68	66	201	112.00
4	Albert Venter	66	68	69	203	82.60
5	Louis Albertse	70	69	66	205	67.20
6	Jaco Prinsloo	66	73	67	206	56.00
7	Ockie Strydom	70	70	67	207	42.70
	Christiaan Basson	73	65	69	207	42.70

9	Estiaan Conradie	68	71	69	208	33.60		Wynand Dingle	67	72	72	211	18.90
	Bradley Bawden	71	67	70	208	33.60	23	Jean Hugo	72	69	71	212	15.58
11	CJ du Plessis	70	70	70	210	25.20		Rupert Kaminski	69	70	73	212	15.58
	Peter Karmis	70	70	70	210	25.20		Luke Brown	70	72	70	212	15.58
	Dayne Moore	70	69	71	210	25.20		Jacquin Hess	67	72	73	212	15.58
	Michael Kok	70	72	68	210	25.20		Michael Palmer	73	69	70	212	15.58
	Luca Filippi	71	67	72	210	25.20	28	Keenan Davidse	72	68	73	213	13.08
	Adam Breen	66	72	72	210	25.20		Madalitso Muthiya	73	69	71	213	13.08
	Wallie Coetsee	69	68	73	210	25.20		Merrick Bremner	68	71	74	213	13.08
18	Ryan Van Velzen	69	71	71	211	18.90		JJ Senekal	72	71	70	213	13.08
	Fredrik From	69	71	71	211	18.90		Jared Harvey	72	71	70	213	13.08
	Zander Lombard	70	71	70	211	18.90		Riekus Nortje	70	73	70	213	13.08
	James Hart du Preez	70	69	72	211	18.90							

Bain's Whisky Ubunye Championship

Merrick Bremner and Martin Rohwer combined for a six-stroke victory at the Bain's Whisky Ubunye Championship at Blue Valley. But the volatile nature of the team format was in evidence all week as they resisted an incredible charge at the start of the final round from Combrinck Smit and Erhard Lambrechts. While Bremner and Rohwer were four ahead after 36 holes, Smit and Lambrechts started seven back, but picked up six shots in the first three holes. They birdied the first hole, then Smit made a hole-in-one at the 190-yard second and, not to be outdone, Lambrechts made an albatross at the par-five third. The pair ended up with a 61 as they tied for second place with Hennie du Plessis and Jean Hugo, who also closed with a 61. Yet they still ended up half-a-dozen shots short of the winners.

Bremner and Rohwer opened with a betterball of 60 and were in second place, three behind Estiaan Conradie and Fredrik From, who made 13 birdies and an eagle for a 15-under-par 57. The next day in foursomes, Conradie and From had a 75, while Bremner and Rohwer produced the best score of the day, a 66, containing their only bogey of the week, to go four clear. If that was the round that looked to give the pair from Durban the title, there was still work to do on a blustery final day when play reverted to betterball. They made five birdies going out but their advantage was down to two before Rohwer, winner of the Vodacom Final at the start of the year, chipped in for an eagle at the 10th. Bremner, 36, who had not won since 2020, then played a superb chip at the 13th to set up a birdie and then they cruised to a 62 and a 28-under-par total of 188.

"The wind was up today so it made it tough," Rohwer said. "But we hung in there and stayed pretty aggressive. Those three shots gained at 10 and 13 made it much easier for us down the stretch. It's always special teaming up with a mate. And I absolutely loved the format, from start to finish."

Blue Valley Golf & Country Estate, Centurion, Gauteng — August 11-13
Par 72 (36-36); 7,386 yards — Purse: R1,200,000

1	**Merrick Bremner/ Martin Rohwer**	60	66	62	188	98.00	10	Ruan Korb/ Albert Venter	65	69	66	200	28.84
2	**Erhard Lambrechts/ Combrinck Smit**	65	68	61	194	79.03		Rupert Kaminski/ Michael Palmer	63	70	67	200	28.84
	Hennie du Plessis/ Jean Hugo	63	70	61	194	79.03		Luca Filippi/ Ryan Van Velzen	61	70	69	200	28.84
4	Kyle Barker/ Dylan Mostert	65	68	62	195	58.92	13	Sean Bradley/ Danie Van Niekerk	66	71	64	201	23.57
	George Coetzee/ Darren Fichardt	62	70	63	195	58.92		Kyle McClatchie/ James Pennington	64	71	66	201	23.57
6	Clinton Grobler/ Jaco Prinsloo	61	69	66	196	49.04		Jake Redman/ Lyle Rowe	62	71	68	201	23.57
7	Daniel van Tonder/ MJ Viljoen	63	67	68	198	40.95	16	Riekus Nortje/ Quintin Wilsnach	63	73	66	202	20.32
8	Estiaan Conradie/ Fredrik From	57	75	67	199	35.51		Louis Albertse/ Hennie O'Kennedy	66	69	67	202	20.32
	Luke Brown/ Hayden Griffiths	64	67	68	199	35.51		Jared Harvey/ Michael Hollick	64	69	69	202	20.32

SunBet Challenge — Time Square

Testing conditions that became increasingly blustery and cool over the final two days of the SunBet Challenge — Time Square did not prevent Albert Venter securing a wire-to-wire victory and his second title of the season. Venter opened with a 63 at Wingate Park to lead by four strokes. A 69 the next day put him five in front and a closing 71 confirmed a six-stroke win on a 13-under-par total of 203.

With Wingate playing firm and fast in the Pretoria winter, the 26-year-old Silver Lakes golfer birdied his first three holes in the opening round and had a run of birdie-eagle-birdie from the 12th. He did not drop a shot in his nine-under-par effort, while in the final round he mixed five birdies with four bogeys but never lost his sizeable cushion. Ruan Korb took second place with a closing 71, with Estiaan Conradie, winner on the course 12 months earlier, third after a 73.

Venter won the Zim Open in May for his maiden title and here played like a veteran. "Even with a five-shot cushion I knew I could take nothing for granted because there have been a lot of cases where someone has a big lead and they don't get over the line," Venter said. "So my mindset was that I was tied for the lead and just needed to play as solidly as I could. Starting off the tournament with a 63 put me in a really good position, so the last two rounds were just about maintaining that and trying to increase my lead."

Wingate Park Country Club, Pretoria, Gauteng — August 17-19
Par 72 (35-37); 7,373 yards — Purse: R1,000,000

1	**Albert Venter**	63	69	71	203	221.90
2	**Ruan Korb**	68	70	71	209	161.00
3	**Estiaan Conradie**	68	69	73	210	112.00
4	Michael Palmer	73	69	69	211	82.60
5	Jean Hugo	69	68	75	212	67.20
6	Hennie Otto	74	69	70	213	41.72
	Siyanda Mwandla	75	68	70	213	41.72
	Keagan Thomas	68	73	72	213	41.72
	Richard Joubert	67	72	74	213	41.72
	Luke Brown	72	66	75	213	41.72
11	Lyle Rowe	73	68	73	214	28.70
	Heinrich Bruiners	69	71	74	214	28.70
13	Jacques Blaauw	75	68	72	215	25.20
	Luca Filippi	72	70	73	215	25.20
	Rourke van der Spuy	73	68	74	215	25.20
16	Ruan de Smidt	71	72	73	216	19.70
	Dylan Mostert	75	68	73	216	19.70
	Wallie Coetsee	72	71	73	216	19.70
	JJ Senekal	69	73	74	216	19.70
	Jared Harvey	73	69	74	216	19.70
	Matthew Spacey	73	69	74	216	19.70
	Martin Rohwer	67	73	76	216	19.70
23	Madalitso Muthiya	70	74	73	217	15.33
	Hennie O'Kennedy	67	77	73	217	15.33
	Herman Loubser	73	71	73	217	15.33
	Daniel van Tonder	72	71	74	217	15.33
	Dylan Naidoo	70	70	77	217	15.33
	Dayne Moore	69	70	78	217	15.33
29	Pieter Moolman	75	69	74	218	13.30
	Malcolm Mitchell	70	73	75	218	13.30
	Clayton Mansfield	73	70	75	218	13.30

Vodacom Origins of Golf — Highland Gate

When Wynand Dingle missed from four feet on the 18th green to force a playoff, a tidal wave of relief flooded through Anthony Michael. What might have been another near-miss after his bogey at the 17th, had become a maiden victory for the 37-year-old from Randpark. Michael had been a runner-up three times, including at the 2010 Alfred Dunhill Championship, and had nine other top-five finishes before claiming the Vodacom Origins of Golf event at Highland Gate, the Ernie Els-designed course high up in the Drakensberg Mountains.

Michael scored 68-69-69 for 10 under par on a total of 206 and finished one clear of Herman Loubser (67) and Dingle (70). Michael had shared the 36-hole lead with Dingle and Combrinck Smit. "I'm over the moon," Michael, who had been out for four months with a painful elbow injury, said. "After so many years and so many runner-up finishes, I felt like I wasn't carrying just a monkey on my back anymore. It felt like a gorilla. When Wynand missed, there was just massive relief. I was preparing myself for the playoff. I'm just so relieved. I've seen all my friends on the Sunshine Tour win, and after 12 years of being on tour you wonder if it will ever happen."

Highland Gate Golf & Trout Estate, Dullstroom, Mpumalanga — August 25-27
Par 72 (36-36); 7,338 yards — Purse: R1,150,000

1	**Anthony Michael**	68	69	69	206	221.90
2	**Herman Loubser**	71	69	67	207	136.50
	Wynand Dingle	68	69	70	207	136.50
4	Combrinck Smit	67	70	71	208	82.60
5	Jared Harvey	73	71	65	209	67.20
6	Ockie Strydom	69	72	69	210	47.13
	Matthew Spacey	73	68	69	210	47.13
	Stephen Ferreira	70	70	70	210	47.13
9	MJ Viljoen	74	71	66	211	30.24
	Stefan Wears-Taylor	69	74	68	211	30.24
	Jayden Schaper	71	71	69	211	30.24
	Brooklin Bailey	71	68	72	211	30.24
	Jacques Blaauw	69	70	72	211	30.24
14	Jaco Prinsloo	69	70	73	212	25.20
15	JJ Senekal	70	70	73	213	23.80
16	Michael Palmer	73	72	69	214	20.83
	Martin Rohwer	73	72	69	214	20.83
	Kyle McClatchie	72	72	70	214	20.83
	James Hart du Preez	69	70	75	214	20.83
20	Heinrich Bruiners	72	74	69	215	17.50
	Kyle Barker	69	76	70	215	17.50
	Keelan van Wyk	69	76	70	215	17.50
	Dylan Mostert	73	71	71	215	17.50
	Adam Breen	75	69	71	215	17.50
25	Martin Vorster	71	74	71	216	14.78
	Jordan Duminy	72	73	71	216	14.78
	Casey Jarvis	68	74	74	216	14.78
	Luke Brown	71	70	75	216	14.78

Gary & Vivienne Player Challenge

After six and a half years of battling injuries and personal issues since his last win, Jaco Van Zyl added his 15th Sunshine Tour victory at the Gary & Vivienne Player Challenge at Selborne Park. That the win came here was appropriate for two reasons. Earlier in his career the Pretoria-born Van Zyl, 43, lived for five years just down the KwaZulu-Natal coast at Port Shepstone and he knows the short but tricky Selborne layout well, while winning the tournament named for South Africa's greatest ever player and his late wife meant much to him. "Gary was our team captain at the Rio Olympics in 2016, which was very special for me," Van Zyl said. "I spent quite a bit of time talking with him in Rio and it's really nice to now win his tournament."

An opening 68 left Van Zyl four behind American Brooklin Bailey, but he took the lead with a 65 the next day. He led by one from Hennie Otto at that stage, yet after 10 holes of the final round Otto had gone one ahead. Van Zyl responded with a birdie at the 12th, while Otto bogeyed the 13th. Van Zyl also dropped a shot at the 14th but holing from seven feet for a bogey, he said, gave him momentum for the closing stretch. He made a 15-footer at the short 15th and then hit a wedge to two feet at the 17th to win by two shots at 14-under-par 202. He closed with a 69, to Otto's 70, while Sean Bradley was third after a double bogey at the 17th.

"I'm over the moon with the win, it's been a rocky road and I've been fighting a lot of demons," said Van Zyl, who last won at the 2016 Eye of Africa PGA Championship. "So it's a real sense of accomplishment. In golf, it's a case of how well you are doing both on and off the course, and I can sense I am on the right track."

Selborne Park Golf Club, Pennington, KwaZulu-Natal — September 8-10
Par 72 (36-36); 6,481 yards — Purse: R1,200,000

1	**Jaco Van Zyl**	68	65	69	202	221.90
2	**Hennie Otto**	66	68	70	204	161.00
3	**Sean Bradley**	65	71	69	205	112.00
4	Jaco Ahlers	67	71	68	206	74.90
	Pieter Moolman	66	69	71	206	74.90
6	Kyle McClatchie	71	70	66	207	47.13
	Louis Albertse	71	69	67	207	47.13
	Brooklin Bailey	64	72	71	207	47.13
9	Stefan Wears-Taylor	68	73	67	208	31.15
	Neil Schietekat	70	68	70	208	31.15
	Jared Harvey	67	70	71	208	31.15
	Albert Venter	65	70	73	208	31.15
13	Martin Vorster	71	70	68	209	25.20
	Wynand Dingle	68	72	69	209	25.20
	Nikhil Rama	69	70	70	209	25.20
	Daniel Bennett (A)	73	64	72	209	
17	Rourke van der Spuy	70	72	68	210	20.44
	Ryan Van Velzen	69	73	68	210	20.44
	Lyle Rowe	72	70	68	210	20.44
	Herman Loubser	74	67	69	210	20.44
	Fredrik From	68	72	70	210	20.44
	Kyle De Beer (A)	66	72	72	210	
23	Keagan Thomas	72	70	70	212	16.50
	Sean Cronje	66	76	70	212	16.50
	Combrinck Smit	67	75	70	212	16.50
	Anthony Michael	68	74	70	212	16.50
	Casey Jarvis	69	72	71	212	16.50
	Luca Filippi	71	67	74	212	16.50

Vodacom Origins of Golf — San Lameer

Wynand Dingle already had been third on the Sunshine Tour in 2022 when he improved his best result on the circuit to second at the Vodacom Origins of Golf event at Highland Gate in August. There was only one place Dingle still had to reach and three weeks later as the VOG series moved to San Lameer on the south coast of KwaZulu-Natal, the 38-year-old golfer from Silver Lakes Country Club secured his maiden victory.

Dingle won by a single shot from Jaco Prinsloo with scores of 66-68-66 for a 16-under-par total of 200. He started the final round one behind Danie Van Niekerk, who came home in 40 to drop into a tie for seventh place. Sean Bradley made a fast start to the final round to take the lead before a triple-bogey six at the 14th and the Royal Cape golfer finished in third for the second week running. Prinsloo, who matched Dingle's closing 66, entered the picture with three birdies in a row from the 13th, but could only par the last three holes.

Like Prinsloo, Dingle's only dropped shot came at the seventh hole. He birdied five of the first 10 holes, then got a three at the 15th to stay level with Prinsloo before claiming a four at the par-five 17th to seal a first win in his 192nd appearance on the Sunshine Tour.

San Lameer Country Club, Southbroom, KwaZulu-Natal — September 15-17
Par 72 (36-36); 6,678 yards — Purse: R1,150,000

1	**Wynand Dingle**	66	68	66	200	221.90
2	**Jaco Prinsloo**	68	67	66	201	161.00
3	**Sean Bradley**	66	69	69	204	112.00
4	Rupert Kaminski	68	69	69	206	82.60
5	Malcolm Mitchell	69	71	67	207	61.60
	Luca Filippi	69	70	68	207	61.60
7	Harry Konig	73	68	67	208	36.40
	Luke Jerling	70	69	69	208	36.40
	Herman Loubser	66	73	69	208	36.40
	Rourke van der Spuy	69	68	71	208	36.40
	Danie Van Niekerk	67	66	75	208	36.40
12	MJ Viljoen	72	69	68	209	25.20
	Lyle Rowe	69	70	70	209	25.20
	Pieter Moolman	71	68	70	209	25.20
	Merrick Bremner	66	71	72	209	25.20
	Joe Long	71	66	72	209	25.20
17	Adam Breen	70	72	68	210	19.60
	Combrinck Smit	68	72	70	210	19.60
	Neil Schietekat	70	70	70	210	19.60
	Albert Venter	67	72	71	210	19.60
	Stefan Wears-Taylor	67	70	73	210	19.60
22	Jacques P de Villiers	70	70	71	211	16.80
	Christiaan Basson	68	71	72	211	16.80
	Jaco Ahlers	71	68	72	211	16.80
25	Martin Vorster	69	73	70	212	14.14
	Richard Joubert	72	69	71	212	14.14
	Heinrich Bruiners	69	72	71	212	14.14
	Ockie Strydom	66	73	73	212	14.14
	Wallie Coetsee	68	71	73	212	14.14
	Doug McGuigan	66	73	73	212	14.14
	Jason Smith	72	66	74	212	14.14

SunBet Challenge — Wild Coast Sun

It had been five long years for MJ Viljoen since his maiden victory at the Sun Fish River Challenge in 2017. There had been some near misses since then, with his third runner-up finish arriving at the Kit Kat Group Pro-Am. After working hard for so long, a change of coach to Dougie Wood the week before the SunBet Challenge at Wild Coast Sun seemed to do the trick. The 27-year-old from Bloemfontein, who represents Serengeti Golf Estate, won by three strokes despite a bogey at the final hole.

"It's been a long time and I've just been so focused on winning again that I now don't really know what it means," Viljoen said. "I've been struggling for a long time, but I kept feeling that I was so close. I made some changes in the last week and they just sparked the feeling on the course that I have been looking for for so long. It sounds almost magical and I think it is quite magical. It feels like the start of a new chapter."

Jacques Blaauw had dominated the opening day, needing a birdie at the last for a 59, but taking a double bogey instead for an eight-under-par 62 and a two-stroke lead. While Blaauw slipped back the next day, Viljoen added to his 65 on Wednesday with a 64 and went into Friday's final round with a one-shot advantage over Keenan Davidse. With a tricky wind blowing, Viljoen grabbed birdies at the second and third holes and, while Davidse came home in 39 for a 74, was then able to play par golf the rest of the day. He closed with a 68 for a total of 197, 13 under par, while Stephen Ferreira, with a 64, and Pieter Moolman, who had three bogeys, two birdies, an eagle and no pars in his last six holes for a 67, shared second place on 10 under.

Wild Coast Sun Country Club, Alfred Nzo, Eastern Cape — September 21-23
Par 70 (35-35); 6,351 yards — Purse: R1,000,000

1	**MJ Viljoen**	65	64	68	197	221.90
2	**Stephen Ferreira**	68	68	64	200	136.50
	Pieter Moolman	65	68	67	200	136.50
4	Martin Vorster	66	65	70	201	82.60
5	Christiaan Burke	67	65	70	202	61.60
	Madalitso Muthiya	64	68	70	202	61.60
7	Neil Schietekat	64	72	67	203	40.13
	Jordan Duminy	64	69	70	203	40.13
	Heinrich Bruiners	65	67	71	203	40.13
10	Ryan Van Velzen	66	70	68	204	29.87
	Jaco Ahlers	66	65	73	204	29.87
	Keenan Davidse	64	66	74	204	29.87
13	Wynand Dingle	67	69	69	205	24.50
	Merrick Bremner	68	67	70	205	24.50
	Joe Long	67	67	71	205	24.50
	Casey Jarvis	66	66	73	205	24.50
17	Clancy Waugh	71	65	70	206	19.60
	Ockie Strydom	68	68	70	206	19.60
	Herman Loubser	69	67	70	206	19.60
	Kyle Barker	65	70	71	206	19.60
	Anthony Michael	68	67	71	206	19.60
22	Luca Filippi	68	68	71	207	16.45
	Michael Kok	66	69	72	207	16.45
	Fredrik From	67	67	73	207	16.45
	Luke Jerling	66	67	74	207	16.45
26	Jean-Paul Strydom	69	68	71	208	15.00
27	Andre De Decker	71	67	71	209	13.72
	Franklin Manchest	66	71	72	209	13.72
	Adam Breen	69	68	72	209	13.72
	Jacques Blaauw	62	72	75	209	13.72
	Jaco Van Zyl	65	68	76	209	13.72

Vodacom Origins of Golf — St Francis Links

It was a day of days for Ruan Korb, who started the final round of the Vodacom Origins of Golf event at St Francis Links seven strokes behind Ockie Strydom. Korb went out early and played superb golf, holing putt after putt. He made only one par in the first 10 holes, along with three bogeys, five birdies and an eagle at the sixth. A delay while a player in the group in front searched for a ball led to Korb bogeying the ninth and 10th holes. But he was soon back into the zone, birdieing the 12th and 13th holes and then the final three. After earlier scores of 71-69, Korb signed for a final round of 63 and posted a total of 13-under-par 203.

If all that was not good enough, he was even more fortunate in the misfortune of Strydom. Having gone 66-67, Strydom went out in four under with an eagle at the sixth to reach 15 under par but then, just as Korb was finishing at the 18th, he took a quadruple-bogey eight at the 11th. Shocked at what had just happened, Strydom parred in over the last seven holes and finished in second place on 11 under after a 72. Veteran Doug McGuigan took third place after bogeying the last two holes in pursuit of birdies to catch Korb.

"I enjoyed myself out there today, the weather was better and my putting was the main reason for my win, every putt just seemed to find the bottom of the cup," Korb said. The 27-year-old Silver Lakes golfer had won once before, at the 2020 Time Square Casino Challenge. "It's a big confidence-booster to win at this time of year, with the big summer events coming up."

St Francis Links, St Francis Bay, Eastern Cape — September 29-October 1
Par 72 (36-36); 7,192 yards — Purse: R1,150,000

1	**Ruan Korb**	71	69	63	203	221.90
2	**Ockie Strydom**	66	67	72	205	161.00
3	**Doug McGuigan**	69	67	71	207	112.00
4	Hennie O'Kennedy	69	68	71	208	82.60
5	Dylan Naidoo	67	67	75	209	67.20
6	Bradley Bawden	72	68	70	210	41.72
	Jayden Schaper	72	67	71	210	41.72
	Brooklin Bailey	67	72	71	210	41.72
	Heinrich Bruiners	65	74	71	210	41.72
	Keenan Davidse	70	67	73	210	41.72
11	Dan Erickson	69	72	71	212	28.00
	Christiaan Basson	73	68	71	212	28.00
	Jaco Prinsloo	67	72	73	212	28.00
14	Luca Filippi	71	75	67	213	22.54
	Wynand Dingle	72	73	68	213	22.54
	Adam Breen	70	73	70	213	22.54
	Hennie Otto	70	70	73	213	22.54
	Riekus Nortje	72	67	74	213	22.54
19	Jacques P de Villiers	72	73	69	214	18.55
	Estiaan Conradie	71	71	72	214	18.55

	MJ Viljoen	73	69	72	214	18.55		Pieter Moolman	70	74	73	217	13.93
	Herman Loubser	75	67	72	214	18.55		Kyle Barker	73	71	73	217	13.93
23	James Kamte	71	69	75	215	16.45		Matthew Spacey	70	72	75	217	13.93
	Peter Karmis	69	70	76	215	16.45		Steve Surry	69	73	75	217	13.93
25	Therion Nel	72	74	70	216	15.40		Dean O'Riley	69	70	78	217	13.93
26	Lyle Rowe	69	77	71	217	13.93							

Fortress Invitational

Pieter Moolman came from three behind a player on his home course to win the Fortress Invitational in a playoff and claim his first title. The 31-year-old, who turned professional in 2011, caught Jayden Schaper with an eagle at the final hole and then won with a birdie when playing the 18th again.

Schaper, a former star amateur who was second at the 2020 Alfred Dunhill Championship just after turning professional, led by two shots on his home course after 36 holes, although he had been three ahead when the second round was suspended on Saturday. The 21-year-old had shared the first-round lead on 65, then added a 67 but could only close with a 70 to join Moolman on 14-under-par 202. Moolman, another local from Benoni, scored 68-67-67 after his second shot at the par-five 18th finished 10 feet away and he holed the putt for an eagle. Schaper then bogeyed the 17th to fall one behind before birdieing the 18th to reach the playoff. At the 18th in extra time, Moolman reached the edge of the green in two, chipped to four feet and made his four having seen Schaper miss a 10-footer for birdie.

"I've lost a few times in these situations, but I've played better golf a few times than I did today," said Moolman, who had been a runner-up three times, including at the Tour Championship and just a few weeks earlier at Wild Coast. "So to get over the line is really special and it shows that it does not take a perfect performance to win. It's more mental, about believing you can still put a score on the board. Finishing second at the Wild Coast a few weeks back, I made some mistakes down the back nine, but I learnt from that and how to stay strong."

With the final round starting after the completion of the second round on Sunday morning, Sean Bradley almost missed his tee-time, arriving with minutes to spare, had a double bogey at the first hole, made a hole-in-one at the 127-yard eighth and eagled the last with a putt from off the green for a 63 to tie for fourth.

Ebotse Links, Rynfield, Benoni, Gauteng — October 7-9
Par 72 (36-36); 7,522 yards — Purse: R1,500,000

1	**Pieter Moolman**	68	67	67	202	253.60		Clancy Waugh	69	71	69	209	24.57
2	**Jayden Schaper**	65	67	70	202	176.00		Steve Surry	70	69	70	209	24.57
	Moolman won playoff at first extra hole							Kyle Barker	70	68	71	209	24.57
3	**Dan Erickson**	66	70	67	203	118.20	19	MJ Viljoen	72	69	69	210	19.83
4	Sean Bradley	70	71	63	204	76.40		Jean Hugo	70	70	70	210	19.83
	Richard Joubert	66	69	69	204	76.40		Kyle De Beer (A)	66	74	70	210	
6	Ruan Korb	71	67	67	205	56.80		Heinrich Bruiners	72	70	68	210	19.83
7	Bradley Bawden	69	68	69	206	46.40	23	Jonathan Broomhead (A)	69	72	70	211	
8	Ryan Van Velzen	70	71	66	207	40.00		Neil Schietekat	70	70	71	211	17.26
9	Martin Rohwer	70	71	67	208	32.70		Peter Karmis	70	72	69	211	17.26
	Hennie Otto	66	72	70	208	32.70		Dylan Mostert	71	71	69	211	17.26
	Makhetha Mazibuko	66	68	74	208	32.70		Jbe' Kruger	71	71	69	211	17.26
12	Andre Van Dyk	75	65	69	209	24.57		Clinton Grobler	65	74	72	211	17.26
	Fredrik From	69	73	67	209	24.57		Quintin Wilsnach	68	70	73	211	17.26
	Doug McGuigan	71	69	69	209	24.57		Joe Long	69	68	74	211	17.26
	Keelan van Wyk	71	71	67	209	24.57							

Blue Label Challenge

In a volatile format such as the modified Stableford scoring system — eight points for an albatross, five for an eagle, two for a birdie, zero for a par, minus-one for a bogey, minus-three for a double bogey or worse — to hold the lead after 36 and 54 holes, and hang on for victory is impressive. Stephen Ferreira did just that at the Blue Label Challenge to win for the first time on the Sunshine Tour thanks to a birdie at the last at Gary Player Country Club. The 30-year-old who lives in Harare, Zimbabwe, but plays under the flag of Portugal, dropped three points at the 14th hole in the final round, then birdied the 15th and the 18th to win by one point from Luca Filippi. Fortress Invitational winner Pieter Moolman continued his good form to finish in third place, two points behind, and Jayden Schaper was fourth.

Ferreira scored 11-13-6-8 for a total of 38 points. Filippi, who started seven points behind in the final round, opened with an eagle and birdied the last three holes to make Ferreira work for the title. Ferreira, who turned professional in 2011, had been second on his previous start at Wild Coast after a putting tip from his friend Madalitso Muthiya.

"I'm glad to finally get the win," Ferreira said. "I love the Gary Player Country Club. I come here a lot and have finally managed to tame the beast. I've been on the Sunshine Tour for a while and have come close a few times. You know, you doubt yourself, but I finally got the win and I'm ecstatic. I knew I had to go low and make a lot of birdies. Luca fought hard today and pushed me to the last hole. It was nice to hole that big putt for the victory."

Gary Player Country Club, Sun City, North West Province — October 12-15
Par 72 (36-36); 7,831 yards — Purse: R2,500,000

1	**Stephen Ferreira**	11	13	6	8	38	317.00
2	**Luca Filippi**	7	10	6	14	37	221.00
3	**Pieter Moolman**	6	9	13	8	36	139.80
4	Jayden Schaper	7	8	8	12	35	86.80
5	Jbe' Kruger	9	13	2	6	30	70.00
6	JJ Senekal	6	5	9	8	28	58.80
7	Jaco Prinsloo	6	5	15	1	27	48.40
8	Madalitso Muthiya	0	4	10	12	26	42.00
9	Brooklin Bailey	15	-9	10	8	24	35.10
	Wynand Dingle	7	1	4	12	24	35.10
11	Keith Horne	4	6	5	8	23	29.00
	Jaco Ahlers	2	9	5	7	23	29.00
	Steve Surry	6	2	5	10	23	29.00
	Dylan Naidoo	2	11	5	5	23	29.00
15	Lyle Rowe	6	4	9	3	22	27.00
16	Rupert Kaminski	-1	3	8	11	21	26.10
	Ockie Strydom	10	-2	8	5	21	26.10
18	Hennie Otto	-3	5	8	10	20	24.90
	Louis Albertse	8	2	2	8	20	24.90
20	Heinrich Bruiners	-5	9	5	10	19	23.60
	Jared Harvey	5	2	5	7	19	23.60
	Peter Karmis	6	4	10	-1	19	23.60
23	Dan Erickson	3	7	-1	9	18	22.80
24	Herman Loubser	1	0	7	9	17	22.20
	Anthony Michael	5	12	4	-4	17	22.20
26	Michael Kok	2	7	-3	9	15	21.00
	Ruan Korb	-5	7	4	9	15	21.00
	Martin Vorster	2	6	8	-1	15	21.00
	Stefan Wears-Taylor	8	0	9	-2	15	21.00
30	Neil Schietekat	3	7	2	2	14	19.80
	MJ Viljoen	9	7	5	-7	14	19.80

SunBet Challenge — Sun Sibaya

Finishing fifth, his best ever result, a month earlier at St Francis Links helped Dylan Naidoo to believe his maiden victory was not far away and it duly arrived at the SunBet Challenge hosted by Sun Sibaya at Umhlali Country Club on the Dolphin Coast. The 24-year-old from Johannesburg is a member of the Sunshine Tour's Papwa Sewgolum Class for historically disadvantaged professionals.

Naidoo scored 66-74-67 to go from the first-round leader, to two behind Richard Joubert with a round to go, before surging back to win by two from Jaco Prinsloo, Luke Brown, Iain Snyman and amateur Jonathan Broomhead. Naidoo finished on a six-under-par total of 207. While Joubert fell back with two double bogeys on the front nine, Naidoo made two birdies going out but still trailed Brown, who then bogeyed twice early in the back nine.

An eagle at the 10th hole, where he hit a seven-iron to eight feet, set Naidoo on his way and birdies at the 16th and 17th holes, holing a 25-footer at the latter, sealed the win despite a dropped shot at the last. "The most important thing is that I felt I had the win coming," Naidoo said. "I've been playing very well for the last few weeks. It's the culmination of having really good processes and discipline out on the course. The best part is that it does not feel like a lightning bolt came down from the sky and I got lucky and won. I feel like I can replicate this."

Umhlali Country Club, Ballito, KwaZulu-Natal — October 19-21
Par 71 (35-36); 6,499 yards — Purse: R1,000,000

1	**Dylan Naidoo**	66	74	67	207	221.90
2	**Jaco Prinsloo**	67	74	68	209	118.53
	Jonathan Broomhead (A)	69	71	69	209	
	Luke Brown	69	70	70	209	118.53
	Ian Snyman	71	68	70	209	118.53
6	Brooklin Bailey	75	69	66	210	61.60
	JJ Senekal	71	68	71	210	61.60
8	Keelan van Wyk	70	72	69	211	46.20
9	Jean Hugo	69	75	68	212	35.47
	Jared Harvey	72	67	73	212	35.47
	Richard Joubert	67	71	74	212	35.47
12	Ockie Strydom	77	68	69	214	25.20
	Ruan Korb	72	71	71	214	25.20
	Clayton Mansfield	73	70	71	214	25.20
	Benjamin Follett-Smith	69	74	71	214	25.20
	Kyle McClatchie	67	73	74	214	25.20
	Matthew Spacey	72	68	74	214	25.20
	Peter Karmis	71	68	75	214	25.20
19	Keenan Davidse	73	72	70	215	18.90
	Thanda Mavundla	72	73	70	215	18.90
	Adam Breen	71	73	71	215	18.90
	Clinton Grobler	70	71	74	215	18.90
	Kevin Rhoderick	71	70	74	215	18.90
24	Callum Mowat	73	73	70	216	15.83
	Rhys West	67	77	72	216	15.83
	Louis Albertse	71	71	74	216	15.83
	Makhetha Mazibuko	71	70	75	216	15.83
28	Clancy Waugh	74	72	71	217	13.52
	Christiaan Burke	70	76	71	217	13.52
	Quintin Wilsnach	72	72	73	217	13.52
	Michael Hollick	68	75	74	217	13.52
	Rourke van der Spuy	73	70	74	217	13.52
	Lindani Ndwandwe	67	74	76	217	13.52

Vodacom Origins of Golf Final

Pinnacle Point, on the cliffs above the Indian Ocean at Mossel Bay, is one of the most spectacular courses in the world and one of the most exposed to the vagaries of the coastal winds. No wonder local resident Louis Oosthuizen became an Open champion in 2010 at St Andrews. "If the wind blows like it blew on Friday, then this is probably one of the hardest golf courses I've ever played," said Combrinck Smit, the eventual winner of the Vodacom Origins of Golf Final.

Smit scored a 76 in the second round on Friday, 11 shots worse than the 65 that gave the 28-year-old from KwaZulu-Natal the first-round lead. Only one player broke 70 and a 71 from Martin Rohwer put him in the lead, with Smit only dropping to third place, two behind. A calmer Saturday enabled Smit to post a 67 and take back the lead by one from Malcolm Mitchell and Albert Venter.

His march to a maiden victory on the Sunshine Tour was not straightforward, however. A bogey at the first was followed by birdies at the third and the eighth before a double bogey at the par-five 16th. That dropped him one behind Jake Redman, who closed with a 68. Smit rallied to birdie the 18th for a 72 to tie on eight-under-par 280. Mitchell (73) and Oliver Bekker (68) tied for third, two behind.

At the par-five 18th in the playoff, both secured pars first time but on the second extra hole Redman drove into the heather-like fynbos plants that are found only on the southern tip of Africa. He could only make a seven and Smit won with a par for his maiden title.

"It's never a great thing playing against a good friend, but somebody has to win and thank goodness it could be me," said Smit. "I don't really know what happened today. There were some surprising shots out there. I've clipped the fynbos quite a bit this week and I was a bit shocked after the 16th. But I just told myself to keep going and that I still had a great chance to win the tournament. I got it done in the end."

Pinnacle Point Estate, Mossel Bay, Western Cape — October 27-30
Par 72 (36-36); 7,063 yards — Purse: R1,500,000

1	**Combrinck Smit**	65	76	67	72	280	253.60
2	**Jake Redman**	72	73	67	68	280	176.00
	Smit won playoff at second extra hole						
3	**Oliver Bekker**	69	74	71	68	282	101.50
	Malcolm Mitchell	71	71	67	73	282	101.50
5	Albert Venter	68	72	69	75	284	68.00

6	Martin Vorster	74	72	68	71	285	51.60		Jayden Schaper	70	76	69	74	289	20.90
	Ockie Strydom	72	69	70	74	285	51.60	20	Keelan van Wyk	77	73	70	70	290	18.88
8	Hennie Otto	68	75	74	69	286	33.38		Andre De Decker	70	78	73	69	290	18.88
	Ruan Korb	75	71	70	70	286	33.38		Divan van den Heever	76	76	69	69	290	18.88
	Jacques P de Villiers	69	72	72	73	286	33.38		Bradley Bawden	73	76	69	72	290	18.88
	Jake Roos	68	76	69	73	286	33.38		Doug McGuigan	75	75	67	73	290	18.88
	Jared Harvey	72	70	70	74	286	33.38	25	Callum Mowat	72	72	76	71	291	16.40
13	Stephen Ferreira	66	77	72	72	287	26.40		Matias Calderon	70	82	68	71	291	16.40
	Martin Rohwer	68	71	72	76	287	26.40		Jovan Rebula	72	78	69	72	291	16.40
15	Hennie O'Kennedy	69	73	76	70	288	24.00		Riekus Nortje	72	77	70	72	291	16.40
	Jean Hugo	73	71	74	70	288	24.00	29	Stefan Wears-Taylor	71	81	67	73	292	15.03
17	Christiaan Burke	73	75	71	70	289	20.90		Chris Cannon	75	77	68	72	292	15.03
	Neil Schietekat	72	78	71	68	289	20.90		James Pennington	69	77	70	76	292	15.03

PGA Championship

There is no secret to winning golf tournaments, George Coetzee advised after taking the 54-hole lead in the PGA Championship with a bogey-free 67 at St Francis Links. "I think only Tiger Woods really knew how to win, the rest of us are all learning as we go along," Coetzee said. "I've won a few tournaments, but there's no pattern to it, no magic recipe."

How right he was as the 36-year-old veteran chalked up his 14th Sunshine Tour victory, and second of the season, the following day with an eclectic mix of golf. He made two eagles, at the third and the par-four 10th, where he holed out with a sand-wedge approach, and almost another at the short par-four fifth where he drove the green but the putt just missed. All his scoring was contained in two spurts. From the second he went: bogey-eagle-bogey-birdie, and from the 10th he went eagle-bogey-birdie-birdie.

It was those last two birdies at 12 and 13 that gave Coetzee a relatively comfortable run to the clubhouse, eventually winning by three strokes from rookie Casey Jarvis. Coetzee scored 67-71-67-68 for a 15-under-par total of 273. Jarvis, the 36-hole leader, collected his best result as a professional with a closing 69, one ahead of Hennie Otto and Jake Redman.

"I was pretty much under pressure all day, I didn't really feel comfortable and my swing wasn't 100 per cent," said Coetzee, who also won the PGA title in 2011. "But golf is one of those games, you can have one swing on one day and then the next day another swing. I was really happy with my two eagles but then it was a bit hard to calm down and get back into my rhythm, get my head back into a good space. But I stuck to the game plan, made good choices and luckily it was enough in the end."

St Francis Links, St Francis Bay, Eastern Cape — November 3-6
Par 72 (36-36); 7,192 yards — Purse: 1,200,000

1	**George Coetzee**	67	71	67	68	273	221.90	17	Matias Calderon	73	70	72	68	283	19.95
2	**Casey Jarvis**	68	68	71	69	276	161.00		Albert Venter	73	70	70	70	283	19.95
3	**Hennie Otto**	69	69	69	70	277	97.30		Danie Van Niekerk	67	73	71	72	283	19.95
	Jake Redman	72	67	68	70	277	97.30		Jean Hugo	70	73	68	72	283	19.95
5	Martin Vorster	71	67	71	69	278	61.60	21	Stephen Ferreira	73	70	73	68	284	17.15
	Peter Karmis	72	70	67	69	278	61.60		Jacques Blaauw	73	71	69	71	284	17.15
7	Jean-Paul Strydom	72	72	68	67	279	42.70		Samuel Simpson	69	72	71	72	284	17.15
	Rhys West	68	70	68	73	279	42.70		Combrinck Smit	71	72	66	75	284	17.15
9	Dylan Mostert	72	68	72	68	280	35.00	25	Hennie O'Kennedy	68	70	74	73	285	15.40
10	Jayden Schaper	71	71	73	66	281	30.80	26	Robin Williams	72	70	72	72	286	14.35
	Luke Jerling	74	68	67	72	281	30.80		Bradley Bawden	72	72	70	72	286	14.35
12	Malcolm Mitchell	70	68	75	69	282	25.20		Sean Bradley	72	72	69	73	286	14.35
	Jake Roos	68	74	71	69	282	25.20		Erhard Lambrechts	71	70	71	74	286	14.35
	Heinrich Bruiners	74	70	69	69	282	25.20	30	CJ du Plessis	73	69	76	69	287	12.90
	Doug McGuigan	72	72	68	70	282	25.20		Richard Joubert	74	69	74	70	287	12.90
	Stefan Wears-Taylor	69	71	67	75	282	25.20		JJ Senekal	68	76	71	72	287	12.90

Joburg Open

Dan Bradbury had no status on any tour in the world, nowhere to play. He turned professional in the summer after five years at college in America, where he won multiple times, playing his last year at Florida State. He missed the cut on his professional debut at the Cazoo Open, improved during a run of three outings on the Challenge Tour, but then three-putted the final hole, his 11th three-putt of the week, to miss out by one shot on getting through the first stage of the DP World Tour Qualifying School. A last-minute invitation to the Open de Espana yielded a 13th place finish, on the back of which the 23-year-old Englishman from Yorkshire applied for other invitations. The only one to come through was from the Joburg Open, the first week on the new 2022-23 DP World Tour season, and arrived on the Friday before the event, allowing enough time for mum Sandra to get the week off work and accompany her son on a life-changing journey.

For a start, he only packed for one week, but victory in his sixth professional start, his third on the DP World Tour and first on the Sunshine Tour meant an extended stay. As well as the winner's exemption which would allow him to tee it up at the following week's SA Open and the Alfred Dunhill Championship, Bradbury also earned a qualification to The 151st Open at Hoylake in 2023.

"I can't tell you how it feels because it hasn't sunk in yet. It means the world to me," said Bradbury. "I wouldn't have anywhere to play in the world without this. It's been life changing. I'm going to play everything. I love playing. I was meant to be on a flight out this evening but happily that's changed, though I didn't even pack enough clothes for more than one week."

In a stunning performance, Bradbury led wire-to-wire and won by three strokes from Finland's Sami Valimaki, with home favourites Christiaan Bezuidenhout and Danie van Tonder tying for third and Louis de Jager in fifth. Bradbury tied the Houghton course record of 63 in the opening round, including eagles at the third and fifth holes, and stayed in front with 66-67 as storms disrupted the first half of the event.

Bradbury almost holed his second shot at the first on Sunday and also birdied the second, but had tree trouble at the sixth before chipping in for a par. "That was a big momentum changer," he said. "If I hadn't made that I might have been tied for the lead, or even behind. To come out of that hole still leading was a bonus."

Bezuidenhout made an early charge, going birdie-birdie-eagle-birdie from the third and closed with a 66. Bradbury birdied the ninth, with a long putt, the 13th and 16th holes, holding a four-shot lead at one point. Valimaki kept up dogged pursuit with a 69, but Bradbury could laugh off a three-putt bogey at the last as a 67 gave him the winning total of 21-under-par 263. There was a big hug from mum, while dad Richard was watching in a packed clubhouse at Wakefield Golf Club.

Houghton Golf Club, Johannesburg, Gauteng — November 24-27
Par 71 (36-35); 7,241 yards — Purse: R17,500,000

1	**Dan Bradbury**	63	66	67	67	263	R2,975,000
2	**Sami Valimaki**	66	65	66	69	266	1,925,000
3	**Christiaan Bezuidenhout**	68	64	69	66	267	988,750
	Daniel van Tonder	69	63	67	68	267	988,750
5	Louis de Jager	67	65	70	67	269	742,000
6	Dale Whitnell	68	68	70	65	271	525,000
	Heinrich Bruiners	71	67	67	66	271	525,000
	JJ Senekal	68	71	66	66	271	525,000
9	Simon Forsstrom	67	69	71	65	272	341,250
	Tom Murray	70	69	66	67	272	341,250
	Romain Langasque	65	67	70	70	272	341,250
	Casey Jarvis	67	63	71	71	272	341,250
13	Nathan Kimsey	66	66	74	67	273	268,917
	Francesco Laporta	67	69	68	69	273	268,917
	Oliver Bekker	71	67	65	70	273	268,917
16	Rhys Enoch	72	67	70	65	274	241,500
	Marcel Siem	70	72	65	67	274	241,500
18	Tom McKibbin	68	67	74	66	275	207,667
	Jayden Schaper	71	67	72	65	275	207,667
	Neil Schietekat	70	69	69	67	275	207,667
	Ricardo Gouveia	71	69	67	68	275	207,667
	Dylan Mostert	67	71	67	70	275	207,667
	Shaun Norris	70	68	67	70	275	207,667
24	Kyle Barker	70	67	72	67	276	174,125
	Ross McGowan	67	72	70	67	276	174,125
	Matthew Southgate	69	67	72	68	276	174,125
	Jacques Kruyswijk	68	72	68	68	276	174,125
	Wilco Nienaber	67	67	72	70	276	174,125
	Jbe' Kruger	65	67	72	72	276	174,125
30	Thomas Aiken	71	70	68	68	277	150,500
	Alejandro Del Rey	72	70	68	67	277	150,500
	Daniel Gavins	70	70	68	69	277	150,500
33	Renato Paratore	68	68	73	69	278	127,750
	Keith Horne	69	70	71	68	278	127,750
	Hennie du Plessis	70	68	73	67	278	127,750
	Thriston Lawrence	66	73	73	66	278	127,750

	Nikhil Rama	73	68	71	66	278	127,750
	Todd Clements	67	71	66	74	278	127,750
39	Jeremy Freiburghaus	68	72	70	69	279	106,750
	Kristian Krogh Johannessen	70	69	70	70	279	106,750
	Aman Gupta	72	70	69	68	279	106,750
	Nick Bachem	64	73	71	71	279	106,750
	Wynand Dingle	68	70	76	65	279	106,750
44	Louis Albertse	71	68	70	71	280	91,000
	Craig Howie	70	67	69	74	280	91,000
	Chase Hanna	70	70	74	66	280	91,000
	Brandon Stone	71	71	73	65	280	91,000
48	Clement Berardo	69	70	71	71	281	73,500
	Julien Guerrier	69	71	69	72	281	73,500
	Luke Jerling	70	72	69	70	281	73,500
	Daniel Brown	70	71	71	69	281	73,500
	Jean Hugo	72	70	70	69	281	73,500
	Luca Filippi	73	69	71	68	281	73,500
54	Elias Bertheussen	70	71	70	71	282	57,750
	Keagan Thomas	71	70	71	70	282	57,750
	Zander Lombard	69	72	72	69	282	57,750
	Lorenzo Scalise	73	68	72	69	282	57,750
	Robin Sciot-Siegrist	71	69	74	68	282	57,750
59	Sean Bradley	69	68	74	72	283	52,500
60	Anton Karlsson	69	69	71	75	284	48,125
	MJ Viljoen	70	69	72	73	284	48,125
	Darius van Driel	75	66	73	70	284	48,125
	Hennie O'Kennedy	70	71	73	70	284	48,125
64	Jens Dantorp	75	65	74	71	285	42,875
	Toby Tree	72	70	72	71	285	42,875
66	Jaco Ahlers	72	69	71	74	286	36,750
	Estiaan Conradie	73	69	70	74	286	36,750
	Deon Germishuys	71	70	73	72	286	36,750
	Jeong Weon Ko	70	70	75	71	286	36,750
	Adilson Da Silva	72	70	75	69	286	36,750
71	Jake Redman	72	67	75	73	287	26,250
72	Ruan Conradie	69	68	74	78	289	26,144
	Pieter Moolman	72	69	74	74	289	26,144
	Jacquin Hess	68	74	75	72	289	26,144
75	Jordan Duminy	72	70	77	77	296	26,037

Investec South African Open

It got a little too close for comfort but Thriston Lawrence did eventually win his national championship in wire-to-wire fashion. Five ahead with five to play at Blair Atholl, Lawrence found himself tied with Clement Sordet three holes later. "It felt all easy going through the round and then golf happened at the end," said the new Investec South African Open champion. "Clement was playing really well, I was playing well then made a few mistakes, missed them on the wrong sides. I managed to get it done and I'm really pleased. It was unfortunate for Clement on 17 to miss that short one — it's just golf. I want to cry, I've got no words."

It was a third win on both the Sunshine and DP World Tours for a player who had just become the first South African to win the Sir Henry Cotton Rookie of the Year Award on the latter circuit for 2021-22. At 8,161 yards — the longest ever on the DP World Tour — the Gary Player-designed course played long even allowing for the high altitude but that just played into Lawrence's hands. He opened with a 64 to match the course record he set in the final round of the Blair Atholl Championship in 2021. He explained: "It's a very long golf course, but I like to play full shots into the greens. I think my mid to high irons are the key to my game. It is a long golf course but it suits me."

A putting lesson from his dad after the Joburg Open also helped and although he lost his course record to Ockie Strydom's nine-under 63 the next day, Lawrence went on his way, pushing two ahead with a 67 and adding another in the third round on his 26th birthday.

Sordet, who won in South Africa at the SDC Open earlier in the year to help graduate from the Challenge Tour, immediately drew level at the first with a birdie to Lawrence's bogey. But the Frenchman then had a double bogey at the fourth for a three-shot swing to the home favourite. Another two-shot swing went in Lawrence's favour at the ninth and he also birdied the 10th to go five ahead. Then he started giving back shots. Both players bogeyed the 12th but Sordet's birdie at the 14th set up the first of two successive two-shot swings. At the 15th, Lawrence misjudged the wind and found the river to the left of the green, ending up with a double bogey. He then failed to get up and down from off the 16th green so the pair were level before Sordet bunkered his tee shot at the 17th and dropped one back.

Eventually, Lawrence signed for a 74 and a 16-under-par total of 272, while Sordet's 73 kept him one ahead of Jens Fahrbring. Christiaan Maas, the 19-year-old amateur, won the Freddie Tait Cup. "This is the one you want to win, your national Open," Lawrence said. "It was so special to have Gary Player watching as well. He's won 13 of these, and now I've got one. It's what you dream of. This is by far my best victory ever."

Blair Atholl Golf & Equestrian Estate, Lanseria, Gauteng — December 1-4
Par 72 (25-37); 8,161 yards — Purse: $1,500,000

1	**Thriston Lawrence**	64	67	67	74	272	R4,477,290
2	**Clement Sordet**	68	66	66	73	273	2,897,070
3	**Jens Fahrbring**	65	70	69	70	274	1,659,231
4	Matti Schmid	66	73	69	69	277	1,316,850
5	Chase Hanna	69	73	69	67	278	871,755
	Daniel Brown	71	70	69	68	278	871,755
	Marcel Siem	69	68	70	71	278	871,755
	Dean Burmester	70	71	66	71	278	871,755
9	Charl Schwartzel	68	74	69	68	279	480,211
	Jayden Schaper	68	72	70	69	279	480,211
	Hennie du Plessis	70	72	67	70	279	480,211
	Jaco Prinsloo	70	71	68	70	279	480,211
	Edoardo Molinari	67	70	70	72	279	480,211
	Ashun Wu	71	67	67	74	279	480,211
15	Tom McKibbin	67	71	73	69	280	337,443
	Scott Jamieson	66	71	72	71	280	337,443
	Renato Paratore	70	70	69	71	280	337,443
	Richard Sterne	69	71	74	66	280	337,443
	Ockie Strydom	70	63	75	72	280	337,443
	MJ Daffue	71	64	73	72	280	337,443
	Wilco Nienaber	67	69	70	74	280	337,443
	Martin Simonsen	73	68	65	74	280	337,443
23	Luke Brown	67	72	72	70	281	266,004
	Joost Luiten	72	69	68	72	281	266,004
	Alejandro Del Rey	72	67	70	72	281	266,004
	James Hart du Preez	70	68	70	73	281	266,004
	Ross Fisher	65	71	71	74	281	266,004
	Adrian Otaegui	70	66	71	74	281	266,004
	Deon Germishuys	69	69	69	74	281	266,004
30	Christoffer Bring	68	71	72	71	282	218,597
	Zander Lombard	69	71	71	71	282	218,597
	Jeong Weon Ko	69	66	75	72	282	218,597
	Wynand Dingle	71	68	71	72	282	218,597
	David Ravetto	71	69	70	72	282	218,597
35	JJ Senekal	66	75	70	72	283	185,017
	Jorge Campillo	73	67	72	71	283	185,017
	Gary Hurley	69	70	71	73	283	185,017
	Aaron Cockerill	68	74	72	69	283	185,017
	Christiaan Maas (A)	69	65	72	77	283	
40	Romain Langasque	71	71	69	73	284	165,923
	Albert Venter	71	70	69	74	284	165,923
	Francesco Laporta	71	69	70	74	284	165,923
43	Nathan Kimsey	69	69	73	74	285	142,220
	Santiago Tarrio	67	72	73	73	285	142,220
	Yurav Premlall (A)	72	67	71	75	285	
	Freddy Schott	70	71	71	73	285	142,220
	Kristian Krogh Johannessen	68	74	71	72	285	142,220
	Todd Clements	72	70	72	71	285	142,220
	Pieter Moolman	70	71	74	70	285	142,220
50	Jens Dantorp	68	73	70	75	286	110,615
	Louis Albertse	73	66	73	74	286	110,615
	Dylan Frittelli	70	71	71	74	286	110,615
	Jacques Kruyswijk	70	69	74	73	286	110,615
	Simon Forsstrom	71	70	67	78	286	110,615
	JC Ritchie	73	69	73	71	286	110,615
56	Sami Valimaki	72	70	71	74	287	89,546
	Dan Bradbury	68	71	75	73	287	89,546
	Adrien Saddier	73	69	73	72	287	89,546
59	Brandon Stone	72	69	70	77	288	82,962
	Tapio Pulkkanen	70	67	74	77	288	82,962
	Aldrich Potgieter (A)	71	71	71	75	288	
62	Thomas Aiken	68	73	71	77	289	77,694
	Marc Warren	68	69	76	76	289	77,694
64	Daniel van Tonder	74	68	73	75	290	71,110
	Tristen Strydom	70	71	75	74	290	71,110
	Jean Hugo	70	69	79	72	290	71,110
67	Rourke van der Spuy	71	68	73	79	291	63,209
	Darren Fichardt	68	70	75	78	291	63,209
	Oliver Bekker	71	68	75	77	291	63,209
70	Kyle De Beer (A)	69	72	77	74	292	
71	Alex Haindl	70	71	75	77	293	56,625
	MJ Viljoen	71	70	77	75	293	56,625
73	Merrick Bremner	71	69	74	80	294	52,674
74	Matthew Spacey	70	69	81	75	295	50,040
75	Jonathan Broomhead (A)	71	70	77	78	296	
	Lukas Nemecz	73	68	79	76	296	39,506
77	Malcolm Mitchell	71	70	75	81	297	39,450

Alfred Dunhill Championship

Ockie Strydom had won once before. It came at the Vodacom Origins of Golf event at Sishen in 2019. He had also had 16 second places, including two earlier in the season, and not including three on the Big Easy Tour before he made it to the full Sunshine Tour. But the numbers might have been the other way round for all the poise the 37-year-old from Kempton Park, in Gauteng, showed on the way to a two-stroke victory in the Alfred Dunhill Championship. As well as his second Sunshine victory, it was his first on the DP World Tour as the tournament resumed after being cancelled in 2021.

Strydom, the co-leader overnight with Scott Jamieson, had a rollercoaster end of the front nine, following five pars with birdie-bogey-birdie-double bogey. After finding the water at the ninth, Strydom rallied by birdieing four of the first five holes on the way home. He then went back to a run of pars, holing out impressively at the 16th and 17th holes before enjoying a stress-free run down to Leopard Creek's famous island-green 18th. "To sink the winning putt on such a prestigious green as this 18th is amazing for me," Strydom said. "Walking onto this island green is always special. It's something I always wanted to achieve. I've finally done it. To do it on Leopard Creek as well is something special."

Strydom equalled the course record on Saturday as he scored 68-70-63-69 for an 18-under-par total of 270. Spain's Adrian Otaegui birdied the last for a 68 to take second place, one ahead of Laurie

Canter, who set the early target with a closing 64. Jamieson, who like Strydom had a double bogey at the ninth, bogeyed the last three holes for a 76 to fall out of the top 10. Former winner Branden Grace tied for fourth, as Louis Oosthuizen would have done but for a bogey at the last.

In a stifling week on the edge of the Kruger National Park, players were allowed to wear shorts. The setting as well as help from his caddie Jaris Kruger, his brother-in-law, played a part in Strydom's life-changing victory. "It's my favourite place, this. I'm calm in the bush. My first win was in the bush and now we're back in the bush. Jaris kept me in the game out there. This changes my life. It's two years on the DP World Tour now. It will be tough with the wife at home and the kids, but in the long run it will be better for them as well."

Leopard Creek Country Club, Malelane, Mpumalanga — December 8-11
Par 72 (35-37); 7,249 yards — Purse: €1,500,000

1	**Ockie Strydom**	68	70	63	69	270	R4,616,520
2	**Adrian Otaegui**	70	69	65	68	272	2,987,160
3	**Laurie Canter**	68	69	72	64	273	1,710,828
4	Aaron Cockerill	70	65	70	69	274	1,153,225
	Branden Grace	67	70	67	70	274	1,153,225
	Oliver Bekker	69	66	68	71	274	1,153,225
7	Louis Oosthuizen	70	66	71	68	275	746,790
	Dean Burmester	65	70	68	72	275	746,790
9	David Ravetto	67	67	73	69	276	575,707
	MJ Daffue	69	66	72	69	276	575,707
11	Nathan Kimsey	70	64	74	69	277	483,377
	Scott Jamieson	68	63	70	76	277	483,377
13	Tom McKibbin	68	73	71	66	278	408,698
	George Coetzee	73	68	67	70	278	408,698
	Joost Luiten	69	70	69	70	278	408,698
	Dylan Frittelli	70	66	68	74	278	408,698
17	Christiaan Maas (A)	71	70	70	68	279	
	JC Ritchie	72	66	72	69	279	344,881
	Joshua Lee	71	69	69	70	279	344,881
	Eddie Pepperell	69	65	73	72	279	344,881
	Ross Fisher	71	65	71	72	279	344,881
22	Darren Fichardt	67	70	74	69	280	302,789
	Kristian Krogh Johannessen	68	72	71	69	280	302,789
	Alexander Knappe	68	68	72	72	280	302,789
	Bryce Easton	69	69	70	72	280	302,789
26	Matthew Southgate	71	71	70	69	281	262,055
	Jayden Schaper	69	68	72	72	281	262,055
	Christiaan Bezuidenhout	70	72	67	72	281	262,055
	Daniel Brown	71	70	73	67	281	262,055
	Ryo Hisatsune	71	72	71	67	281	262,055
	Dale Whitnell	69	68	66	78	281	262,055
32	Matthew Baldwin	72	70	69	71	282	221,321
	Niklas Norgaard Moller	70	71	70	71	282	221,321
	Gary Hurley	73	68	71	70	282	221,321
	Ernie Els	70	69	71	72	282	221,321
36	Thriston Lawrence	69	71	72	71	283	187,920
	Jaco Ahlers	67	73	71	72	283	187,920
	Lukas Nemecz	66	70	74	73	283	187,920
	Daniel van Tonder	72	67	71	73	283	187,920
	Chase Hanna	74	69	71	69	283	187,920
41	Jean Hugo	70	72	70	72	284	162,936
	Scott Vincent	70	72	71	71	284	162,936
	Santiago Tarrio	69	69	76	70	284	162,936
	Jaco Prinsloo	70	68	70	76	284	162,936
45	Wynand Dingle	70	67	74	74	285	146,642
	Jacques Blaauw	73	68	69	75	285	146,642
47	Joachim B Hansen	73	68	72	73	286	133,064
	Dylan Mostert	70	65	79	72	286	133,064
	Marcel Siem	71	72	71	72	286	133,064
50	Grant Forrest	72	70	74	71	287	119,486
	Wilco Nienaber	68	73	67	79	287	119,486
52	Shaun Norris	71	70	72	75	288	99,119
	JJ Senekal	70	70	74	74	288	99,119
	Jorge Campillo	69	69	71	79	288	99,119
	CJ du Plessis	72	70	73	73	288	99,119
	Merrick Bremner	78	65	72	73	288	99,119
	Jbe' Kruger	71	72	74	71	288	99,119
58	James Hart du Preez	70	69	73	77	289	81,468
	John Axelsen	75	66	72	76	289	81,468
	Martin Simonsen	72	70	72	75	289	81,468
	Sami Valimaki	74	69	71	75	289	81,468
	Adam Breen	71	72	74	72	289	81,468
63	Neil Schietekat	70	72	74	74	290	71,963
	Dan Bradbury	74	68	75	73	290	71,963
65	Jovan Rebula	70	72	75	74	291	65,174
	Luke Jerling	70	72	76	73	291	65,174
	Combrinck Smit	72	71	76	72	291	65,174
68	Alejandro Canizares	69	69	73	81	292	58,385
	Kyle De Beer (A)	72	70	75	75	292	
	Jens Fahrbring	70	72	77	73	292	58,385
71	Tobias Eden	68	74	76	75	293	48,881
	Erik van Rooyen	69	72	78	74	293	48,881
	Justin Walters	72	70	79	72	293	48,881
74	Nick Bachem	72	71	75	76	294	40,680
75	Wil Besseling	71	72	76	79	298	40,625
76	Deon Germishuys	67	72	80	85	304	40,571

AfrAsia Bank Mauritius Open

Three years is a long time to wait for the chance to make amends for a painful loss. The last time the AfrAsia Bank Mauritius Open was held it was in 2019 and Antoine Rozner lost out in a playoff to Rasmus Hojgaard. In 2022 at Mont Choisy, Rozner did not let it get to extra time. The 29-year-old from Paris won by five strokes from Spain's Alfredo Garcia-Heredia.

In 2019 Rozner was still seeking his first win on the DP World Tour. That came a year later and in 2021 he won the Qatar Masters. This week in Mauritius represented the last chance to keep extending his run of annual victories. In an emotional interview afterwards, he said: "Unbelievable. It's so hard to win. It's a tough game. It tests your mind and your game. We practise so hard all year long and a win is a win, and I'm so glad I got this done. I couldn't dream of a better way to finish the year."

On day one on the windy layout, Rozner's 70 put him eight behind Sami Valimaki's new course record of 62. The Finn scored 10 shots higher on Friday but Rozner fired up his challenge with a 64 which put him in a share of the lead. A 68 on Saturday put him two strokes ahead of fellow Frenchman Julien Brun, who closed with a 72 to take third place.

It was Garcia-Heredia, on his 41st birthday, who made a charge by going out in 31, then parring the back nine for a 67. But Rozner was not to be outdone. He also went out in 31. Initially, he needed to extricate himself from a patch of thick rough beside the third green to save par. Then he birdied the fifth, eagled the seventh after an approach to 10 feet, added a two at the eighth and holed a long putt for another birdie at the ninth. After the turn he parred the next seven holes, finishing bogey-birdie for a 67 and 19-under-par 269.

"I played solid all week," Rozner said. "My first nine holes was one of my best nines ever. To play that front nine, the harder nine, in five under made a massive difference. I didn't know the scores and I just tried to stay focused in the moment. I started missing a few shots here and there, but I had a big enough lead to get it done."

Mont Choisy Le Golf, Grand Baie, Mauritius — December 15-18
Par 72 (36-36); 7,051 yards — Purse: €1,000,000

1	**Antoine Rozner**	70	64	68	67	269	R3,163,020
2	**Alfredo Garcia-Heredia**	68	66	73	67	274	2,046,660
3	**Julien Brun**	69	68	67	72	276	1,172,178
4	Jeong Weon Ko	67	71	70	69	277	790,135
	Dylan Mostert	69	71	68	69	277	790,135
	Simon Forsstrom	71	69	67	70	277	790,135
7	Ricardo Gouveia	69	69	71	69	278	511,665
	Oliver Bekker	64	71	70	73	278	511,665
9	Niklas Norgaard Moller	72	67	71	69	279	394,447
	Jayden Schaper	68	72	67	72	279	394,447
11	Brandon Stone	71	72	67	70	280	320,643
	Sami Valimaki	62	72	72	74	280	320,643
	Pierre Pineau	65	71	70	74	280	320,643
14	Matthew Southgate	69	70	75	67	281	273,508
	Gary Hurley	72	68	71	70	281	273,508
	Julien Guerrier	69	75	67	70	281	273,508
17	Alejandro Canizares	71	71	75	65	282	245,599
	Pedro Figueiredo	71	72	70	69	282	245,599
19	Marcel Siem	73	69	73	68	283	230,714
20	Ross McGowan	74	68	73	69	284	213,504
	Louis de Jager	71	71	73	69	284	213,504
	Marco Penge	73	70	68	73	284	213,504
	Christoffer Bring	67	69	73	75	284	213,504
24	Jens Fahrbring	69	75	73	68	285	193,502
	Jens Dantorp	71	71	74	69	285	193,502
	Bryce Easton	72	69	70	74	285	193,502
27	Craig Howie	70	71	76	69	286	171,175
	Alexander Knappe	70	72	73	71	286	171,175
	Anthony Michael	75	69	69	73	286	171,175
	Nathan Kimsey	75	69	69	73	286	171,175
	Oihan Guillamoundeguy	72	66	73	75	286	171,175
32	Dan Erickson	68	75	74	70	287	138,482
	Ian Snyman	71	73	72	71	287	138,482
	Matthieu Pavon	73	69	73	72	287	138,482
	Jeremy Freiburghaus	71	72	71	73	287	138,482
	Stephen Ferreira	70	68	75	74	287	138,482
	JC Ritchie	66	72	75	74	287	138,482
	Sean Bradley	73	69	70	75	287	138,482
39	Todd Clements	70	73	73	72	288	120,939
40	Tom McKibbin	70	71	76	72	289	109,775
	Henric Sturehed	73	71	72	73	289	109,775
	Casey Jarvis	69	67	77	76	289	109,775
	Jaco Prinsloo	74	68	70	77	289	109,775
	Ugo Coussaud	70	73	69	77	289	109,775
45	David Ravetto	70	73	75	72	290	93,030
	Keenan Davidse	72	72	74	72	290	93,030
	Gary Stal	71	70	76	73	290	93,030
	Christiaan Burke	73	69	74	74	290	93,030
49	Thomas Bjorn	70	74	78	69	291	72,829
	Keagan Thomas	72	69	79	71	291	72,829
	Santiago Tarrio	70	72	76	73	291	72,829
	Manuel Elvira	71	73	74	73	291	72,829
	Niklas Lemke	67	75	75	74	291	72,829
	Joel Stalter	73	70	72	76	291	72,829
	Danie Van Niekerk	74	69	72	76	291	72,829
56	Nikhil Rama	72	71	73	76	292	60,469
	Albert Venter	69	75	72	76	292	60,469
58	Martin Vorster	72	72	76	73	293	53,027
	Lyle Rowe	69	73	75	76	293	53,027
	Richard Sterne	71	71	75	76	293	53,027
	Dylan Naidoo	74	69	74	76	293	53,027
	Bradley Bawden	68	74	73	78	293	53,027
	Thomas Aiken	71	70	71	81	293	53,027
64	Neil Schietekat	72	70	80	72	294	45,585
	Pieter Moolman	74	68	77	75	294	45,585
66	Laurie Canter	70	72	73	80	295	41,863
	Ruan Korb	71	72	71	81	295	41,863
68	Thomas Detry	68	74	74	80	296	39,073
69	Martin Rohwer	69	75	75	78	297	37,212
70	Ockie Strydom	69	73	81		WD	35,351

ALTRON BIG EASY TOUR	
Blue Valley	**Christiaan Maas** (A)
Huddle Park	**Dongkwan Kim**
Reading	**Gregory Mckay**
Randpark	**Adam Breen**
Houghton	**Ricky Hendler**
Kyalami	**Casey Jarvis** (A)
Soweto	**Gerhard Pepler**
ERPM	**Ruan de Smidt**
Tour Playoff	**Gerhard Pepler (2)**
Tour Final	**Gerhard Pepler (3)**

Asian Tour

He started the year as one of Korea's bright young things and ended it as Asia's best and one of the game's most exciting players. As a 19-year-old, Joohyung Kim claimed the Order of Merit title for the elongated 2020-22 season. Later, having turned 20 and now often known by his nickname of "Tom", Kim won twice on the PGA Tour in America — at a younger age than Tiger Woods was after his first two wins — and starred for the International team at the Presidents Cup. Having started out 131st on the world ranking, he finished it at 15th, having eclipsed his compatriot Sungjae Im and Japan's Hideki Matsuyama. It was quite the star-is-born year. "It's crazy," said Kim. "Beating Tiger is, it's amazing for me. I've just got to keep playing well and hopefully I'll have a lot more in the bag. I mean, I'm playing on the PGA Tour as a 20-year-old. I'm a five-year-old at Disneyland, for sure."

Kim, whose father was also a professional golfer, lived in Australia, the Philippines and Thailand growing up and earned his family nickname due to his love of Thomas the Tank Engine as a child, "Thomas" becoming "Tom" over time. He progressed through the Asian Development Tour with three quick victories and then won on his third start on the Asian Tour as a 17-year-old at the Panasonic Open in India in 2019. He had two fourth places before the Asian Tour was curtailed in 2020 due to the Covid pandemic, and was second at the first event when it resumed 18 months later at the end of 2021.

There were two tournaments at the start of 2022 to finish off the season, with Kim winning a playoff against Thailand's Rattanon Wannasrichan at the Singapore International. The following week he was a runner-up to Sadom Kaewkanjana at the SMBC Singapore Open, which secured his Order of Merit title. Although the Asian Tour number one did not qualify for a place in The 150th Open, as previously had been the case, the leading finishers at the Singapore Open did earn a spot at St Andrews. Kim took advantage with a top-50 finish which, added to his third place the previous week at the Genesis Scottish Open, gave him temporary status on the PGA Tour.

Kim opened the Wyndham Championship with a quadruple bogey, but on Sunday went out in 27 and posted a 61 to become the first player born in the 2000s to win on the PGA Tour. Only Jordan Spieth had been a younger winner on the PGA Tour in modern times. He went on to win the Shriners Children's Open and this time went bogey-free the entire way. In between, Kim brought youthful exuberance to Trevor Immelman's team at the Presidents Cup, playing all five times. Although the team ended up on the losing side, and Kim had three defeats, the two wins on Saturday were memorable, especially the 18th hole defeat of Patrick Cantlay and Xander Schauffele with partner Si Woo Kim.

"He has an ability to be a global superstar, this kid," said Immelman. "We've seen he has the game. But what I've learned about his personality and his heart, I am a huge fan. I thought something that was so cool on the final hole ... he's about 240 yards out, probably 60 yards behind his opponents. I see a who's who of American golf in golf carts behind him. And this kid pures a two-iron to 10 feet and makes the putt. To me, that's impressive stuff."

Another young star who may not be far behind, although he still has to go to college and turn professional, is Thailand's Ratchanon Chantananuwat. Also known as "TK", he led early in the final round of the Singapore International after going out in 31 and, at 14 years and 10 months, just missed out on the playoff won by Kim when he had a double bogey at the 17th hole.

But Chantananuwat turned the tables on Kim a few months later at the Trust Golf Asian Mixed Cup, birdieing five of the last eight holes to win by two strokes at Siam Country Club. At the age of 15 years and 37 days, Chantananuwat became the youngest male player to win on a major tour — Ryo Ishikawa was 15 years and eight months when he won the Japan Tour's 2007 Munsingwear Open KSB Cup, while the youngest previous winner on the Asian Tour was Thailand's Chinnarat Phadungil who claimed the 2005 Double A International Open when he was 17 years and five days.

"I am very excited, but I felt a lot of pressure," said the young Thai, who had spent the previous few weeks concentrating on his schoolwork. He insisted: "Nothing's going to change. I'm going to stay in school, go to college, practise more. That's been my plan all along."

The tournament was the first of two co-sanctioned with the Ladies European Tour and played as mixed events. In the following week's Stableford Challenge, American Sihwan Kim went to the final hole seven points ahead but a wild drive meant he lost three for a double bogey and he finished only two ahead of Maja Stark, one of Sweden's emerging talents.

It was Sihwan Kim's second win of the year, the first having also arrived in Thailand at the inaugural International Series event, his maiden victory after 11 years as a professional. He had finished second or third 11 times on the Asian Tour or the Challenge Tour in Europe. "To get that monkey off your back is more of a relief, and happiness, I guess," said Kim. "I know I had it in me, but I guess I just stayed diligent throughout my career, and here I am."

Kim, who was born in Seoul but grew up in California and attended Stanford, went on to top the 2022 Order of Merit, recovering from a mid-year drop in form to finish third at the International Series event in Egypt and reclaim the number one spot. Then, on his 34th birthday, he held on at the season-ending BNI Indonesian Masters despite pressure from Korea's Bio Kim, who won the GS Caltex Maekyung Open, Zimbabwe's Scott Vincent, who claimed the International Series — England event, and Chan Shih-chang, who joined Sihwan Kim as the only other two-time winner, with titles at the Royal's Cup and, on home soil, at the Mercuries Taiwan Masters. Eight players in all had the chance to be the new number one at the final event.

"It feels good, finally the season's done and I can't wait to get some rest," said Sihwan Kim. "Right at the start of the year, I was playing badly, and then suddenly just upped my game. Then it went really cold again and I struggled for about two or three months, and then I just found something the last month and a half, and I kind of rolled with it."

The 2022 season proper started at the PIF Saudi International, an event that had previously been played on the DP World Tour but was now billed as the Asian Tour's flagship event. The circuit also featured the newly created International Series, with seven events including visits to England, Morocco and Egypt as well as stops in Thailand, Singapore, Korea and at the season-ending BNI Indonesian Masters. Vincent, winner at the Slaley Hall event in June, where the leading finishers earned invitations to the inaugural LIV Golf event, topped the standings for the International Series and secured a place on the LIV circuit for 2023.

An increase in the International Series to 10 events was promised for 2023, with purses of $2 million as a minimum and one of the new ones to be held in Oman in February. "The 2022 campaign was a highly successful one for us and it is great to see the profile of the Asian Tour being raised," said Cho Minn Thant, the tour's commissioner. "Next year promises more of the same, with our 2023 schedule the biggest and best in the history of the tour."

2022 SCHEDULE

Singapore International	**Joohyung Kim**	
SMBC Singapore Open	**Sadom Kaewkanjana**	
PIF Saudi International	**Harold Varner III**	
Royal's Cup	**Chan Shih-chang**	
International Series — Thailand	**Sihwan Kim**	
DGC Open	**Nitithorn Thippong**	
Trust Golf Asian Mixed Cup	**Ratchanon Chantananuwat (A)**	
Trust Golf Asian Stableford Challenge	**Sihwan Kim (2)**	
GS Caltex Maekyung Open	**Bio Kim**	
Asia Pacific Open Diamond Cup	**Shugo Imahira**	*See chapter 18*
International Series — England	**Scott Vincent (1,2)**	
Kolon Korea Open	**Minkyu Kim**	
Mandiri Indonesia Open	**Gaganjeet Bhullar**	
International Series — Singapore	**Nitithorn Thippong (2)**	
International Series — Korea	**Taehoon Ok**	
Shinhan Donghae Open	**Kazuki Higa (1,3)**	*See chapter 18*
Yeangder TPC	**Travis Smyth**	
Mercuries Taiwan Masters	**Chan Shih-chang (2)**	
International Series — Morocco	**Jazz Janewattananond**	
International Series — Egypt	**Andy Ogletree**	
Bangabandhu Cup Bangladesh Open	**Danthai Boonma**	
BNI Indonesian Masters	**Sarit Suwannarut**	

Singapore International

There was a teenage winner at the Singapore International but, at 19, Joohyung Kim was a positive veteran compared to one of his rivals at Tanah Merah. Thai amateur Ratchanon Chantananuwat led early in the final round as he went out in 31 and at 14 years and 10 months would have been the youngest winner on any of the men's major tours.

Chantananuwat picked up his sixth birdie of the day at the 10th, then had two bogeys and a double at the 17th before birdieing the last for a 69 and third place. "People will look at those scores online, see those dropped shots, and think I played badly but I didn't. I was trying so hard and playing well," said Chantananuwat, who finished two strokes outside of the playoff won by Kim.

Coming from two strokes behind with a 70, the Korean tied Thailand's Rattanon Wannasrichan on four-under-par 284 after four windy days on the Tampines course. Kim was two ahead with two to play but found the lake at the 17th and took a bogey. At the par-five 18th, he took two in a greenside bunker and parred after Wannasrichan, the leader after the second and third rounds, got up and down for a birdie with a brilliant chip.

But in the playoff at the 18th, Kim birdied from 14 feet to win his second Asian Tour title. The first came as a 17-year-old in his third start on tour in 2019. Asked which was the harder earned, Kim, who went to the top of the 2020-22 Order of Merit, said: "Has to be this one. Just because it's a tough golf course, all the players played their heart out. I'm very lucky to be on top. It was a grind today. I think it was a lot harder than the first one but definitely glad I finished on top."

Tanah Merah Country Club (Tampines), Singapore — January 13-16
Par 72 (36-36); 7,535 yards — Purse: $1,000,000

1	**Joohyung Kim**	72	73	69	70	284	$180,000
2	**Rattanon Wannasrichan**	73	66	73	72	284	110,000
	Kim won playoff at first extra hole						
3	**Ratchanon Chantananuwat** (A)	75	66	76	69	286	
4	Pavit Tangkamolprasert	71	75	74	68	288	63,000
5	Paul Peterson	70	73	76	70	289	45,500
	Kosuke Hamamoto	74	75	69	71	289	45,500
7	Bio Kim	72	77	72	70	291	33,300
8	Wade Ormsby	72	74	76	70	292	19,600
	William Harrold	69	78	75	70	292	19,600
	Shahriffuddin Ariffin	73	75	74	70	292	19,600
	Steve Lewton	73	75	73	71	292	19,600
	Jazz Janewattananond	71	73	76	72	292	19,600
	Chan Shih-chang	71	77	71	73	292	19,600
	Donlaphatchai Niyomchon	75	73	69	75	292	19,600
	Khalin Joshi	67	74	75	76	292	19,600
16	Angelo Que	72	71	80	70	293	12,670
	Phachara Khongwatmai	73	74	76	70	293	12,670
	Rory Hie	73	74	75	71	293	12,670
	Doyeob Mun	73	75	74	71	293	12,670
	Richard T Lee	77	74	75	67	293	12,670
21	Masanori Kobayashi	72	76	76	70	294	10,883
	Viraj Madappa	77	71	76	70	294	10,883
	Siddikur Rahman	75	76	71	72	294	10,883
24	Sadom Kaewkanjana	75	73	76	71	295	9,122
	Danny Chia	73	75	75	72	295	9,122
	Atiruj Winaicharoenchai	74	77	71	73	295	9,122
	Panuphol Pittayarat	78	73	73	71	295	9,122
	Jack Harrison	74	74	74	73	295	9,122
	Rashid Khan	75	76	70	74	295	9,122
	Koh Deng Shan	74	76	71	74	295	9,122
	Berry Henson	72	75	73	75	295	9,122
	Abhijit Chadha	72	79	75	69	295	9,122

SMBC Singapore Open

An impressive piece of front-running on a sweltering day at Sentosa saw Sadom Kaewkanjana win the SMBC Singapore Open at the conclusion of the drawn-out 2020-22 season. It was a second Asian Tour victory for the 23-year-old Thai who won the Bangabandhu Cup in 2019 on his very first start on the circuit. Kaewkanjana did not drop a shot over the weekend and drew ahead of his co-leader after 54 holes when Sihwan Kim bogeyed the first hole. Kaewkanjana had birdies at the sixth and seventh holes to go three ahead and stayed in front for the rest of the round.

Scores of 67-70-65-69 on the Serapong course gave Kaewkanjana a 13-under-par total of 271. He finished three in front of Japan's Yuto Katsuragawa (68) and Joohyung Kim (69), of Korea. The 19-year-old Kim secured the Order of Merit title, with Kaewkanjana taking second place.

"This is amazing, it wasn't easy," said Kaewkanjana, who ended 2021 with a string of wins on the

Thai circuit. "It has taken a lot of hard work to get here, especially over the last two years. This is a great way to start the year. I hope it's the start of a great year."

Part of that great year would be a spot in The 150th Open at St Andrews. "I am very excited to be playing my first major at the home of golf," he said. "It is very special to me." Each of the top-four finishers earned invitations to St Andrews through the Open Qualifying Series, including Sihwan Kim, despite closing with a 73. Joohyung Kim had earned a place in The 149th Open but was unable to take part due to pandemic travel restrictions.

Sentosa Golf Club (Serapong), Singapore — January 20-23
Par 71 (36-35); 7,403 yards — Purse: $1,250,000

1	**Sadom Kaewkanjana**	67	70	65	69	271	$225,000
2	**Yuto Katsuragawa**	68	70	68	68	274	108,125
	Joohyung Kim	68	68	69	69	274	108,125
4	Sihwan Kim	67	66	69	73	275	62,500
5	Doyeob Mun	70	70	71	66	277	42,833
	Jarin Todd	71	72	68	66	277	42,833
	Veer Ahlawat	68	70	70	69	277	42,833
8	Ben Campbell	70	70	69	69	278	30,625
9	Shintaro Kobayashi	69	70	73	67	279	22,338
	Kosuke Hamamoto	68	71	71	69	279	22,338
	Shiv Kapur	71	69	70	69	279	22,338
	Bio Kim	71	70	66	72	279	22,338
	Zach Murray	68	73	65	73	279	22,338
14	Ben Leong	71	73	67	69	280	17,688
	Justin De Los Santos	67	71	68	74	280	17,688
16	Paul Casey	76	68	71	66	281	14,670
	Dongkyu Jang	68	69	73	71	281	14,670
	Matthew Griffin	71	69	70	71	281	14,670
	Suradit Yongcharoenchai	66	73	70	72	281	14,670
	Richard T Lee	73	66	70	72	281	14,670
	Travis Smyth	72	70	67	72	281	14,670
	Steve Lewton	68	74	65	74	281	14,670
23	Panuphol Pittayarat	71	72	71	68	282	11,403
	Prom Meesawat	73	71	69	69	282	11,403
	Siddikur Rahman	70	71	71	70	282	11,403
	Shunya Takeyasu	69	73	69	71	282	11,403
	Guxin Chen	72	70	69	71	282	11,403
	Jake Higginbottom	71	71	68	72	282	11,403
	Taehoon Ok	66	72	71	73	282	11,403
	Phachara Khongwatmai	70	71	68	73	282	11,403
	Genki Okada	70	69	69	74	282	11,403

2020-22 ORDER OF MERIT

1	Joohyung Kim	$507,553
2	Sadom Kaewkanjana	378,972
3	Wade Ormsby	270,154
4	Phachara Khongwatmai	264,723
5	Chan Shih-chang	231,375
6	Trevor Simsby	197,107
7	Bio Kim	181,611
8	Jarin Todd	170,063
9	Kosuke Hamamoto	151,363
10	Jazz Janewattananond	132,600

PIF Saudi International

Harold Varner provided a stunning finish to the new flagship event of the Asian Tour as it opened its 2022 season. Varner jumped for joy after his putt from off the front of the 18th green ran up onto the top tier and, after more than 90 feet of travel, curled into the hole. With the eagle, Varner won by one stroke from Bubba Watson, who had earlier made a three from 15 feet to look a likely winner at 12 under par. Varner matched his compatriot's birdie-eagle finish to come from two behind with two to play.

Watson ran back through the hospitality area behind the 18th green to congratulate the champion. "I'm not mad at him for beating me. I'm happy for him. He's a dear friend of mine, and I applaud him," said the two-time Masters winner. "This is a guy that's just starting to play better and better each year."

Varner won the Australian PGA Championship in 2016 but although he had established himself on the PGA Tour since then, the 31-year-old from North Carolina had not picked up a second victory until he played Royal Greens in 64-66-68-69 for a 13-under-par total of 267. Watson closed with a 64, matching his opening effort. Spain's Adri Arnaus, playing alongside Varner in the final group, had gone ahead at 14 under with an eagle at the seventh but then had five bogeys and a birdie at the last for a 71 to finish in third place.

Varner and Arnaus were two behind Italy's Matteo Manassero on the opening day, then shared the 36-hole lead before Varner went one in front with a round to play. He birdied the fifth going out on Sunday, but then had a double bogey at the 14th and bogeyed the 16th. Not to worry, his miracle finish brought home the title.

"Awesome," Varner said. "It's been pretty crazy since it happened and I'm just trying to take it in. Winning never gets old. I know there's been times where it just didn't go my way and today it did. I'm pumped."

After three years on the European Tour schedule, the tournament was now the premier event on the Asian Tour, featuring the strongest field ever for a regular event with over 30 players obtaining releases from the PGA Tour and the DP World Tour to play. Dustin Johnson, winner for two of the first three years, finished tied for eighth, Phil Mickelson tied for 18th and Bryson DeChambeau withdrew after an opening 73 due to injuries suffered when he slipped and fell a few days earlier.

Royal Greens Golf & Country Club, King Abdullah Economic City, Saudi Arabia — February 3-6
Par 70 (35-35); 7,048 yards — Purse: $5,000,000

1	**Harold Varner III**	64	66	68	69	267	$1,000,000
2	**Bubba Watson**	64	70	70	64	268	525,000
3	**Adri Arnaus**	64	66	69	71	270	300,000
4	Steve Lewton	68	67	69	67	271	217,500
	Cameron Smith	66	66	70	69	271	217,500
6	Matthew Wolff	65	67	73	67	272	150,500
	Pablo Larrazabal	68	68	68	68	272	150,500
8	Abraham Ancer	68	70	69	66	273	93,125
	Jhonattan Vegas	68	74	65	66	273	93,125
	Joaquin Niemann	65	72	68	68	273	93,125
	Ryosuke Kinoshita	64	70	69	70	273	93,125
	Dustin Johnson	65	71	67	70	273	93,125
	Tommy Fleetwood	66	67	67	73	273	93,125
14	Shane Lowry	68	70	70	66	274	68,500
	Takumi Kanaya	67	70	70	67	274	68,500
	Brad Kennedy	67	72	67	68	274	68,500
17	Henrik Stenson	66	72	70	67	275	62,500
18	Phil Mickelson	67	69	71	69	276	57,167
	Xander Schauffele	67	68	69	72	276	57,167
	Wade Ormsby	68	67	68	73	276	57,167
21	Berry Henson	67	73	71	66	277	52,250
	Lee Westwood	71	69	71	66	277	52,250
	Lucas Herbert	66	73	71	67	277	52,250
24	Sergio Garcia	70	70	71	67	278	47,000
	Thomas Pieters	73	67	71	67	278	47,000
	Justin Harding	71	73	66	68	278	47,000
	Paul Casey	68	74	64	72	278	47,000
28	Marc Leishman	74	69	72	64	279	38,100
	Thongchai Jaidee	69	72	71	67	279	38,100
	Sebastian Crampton	73	70	69	67	279	38,100
	Tyrrell Hatton	67	69	75	68	279	38,100
	Tony Finau	68	72	70	69	279	38,100
	Rikuya Hoshino	70	71	69	69	279	38,100
	Matteo Manassero	62	73	74	70	279	38,100
	Bio Kim	66	72	71	70	279	38,100
	Kevin Na	70	68	70	71	279	38,100
	Phachara Khongwatmai	65	76	66	72	279	38,100

Royal's Cup

Returning to Thailand did the world of good for Chan Shih-chang as the 35-year-old from Chinese Taipei claimed his fourth victory on the Asian Tour at the Royal's Cup. Chan won his first title in the country at the King's Cup in 2016, as well as the tour's first event after a 20-month shutdown late in 2021 at the Blue Canyon Phuket Championship. Since then he had missed the cut in three of his four events but at Grand Prix Golf Club in Kanchanaburi, Chan got to the top of the grid with an opening 64 and never looked back, taking the chequered flag for a three-stroke victory over Sihwan Kim and Singapore Open winner Sadom Kaewkanjana.

Chan won wire-to-wire with scores of 64-66-67-68 for a 23-under-par total of 265. A crucial stretch came on Friday afternoon when he went out in one over par. Chan then came home in 29 with eagles at two of the last three holes. He almost holed in one at the 12th, finishing a foot away, and then aced the 16th with a seven-iron from 173 yards. It was his second in competition, seventh in all, and won him a Toyota car. Two holes later he finished the round with an eagle after hitting his approach to eight feet at the par-five 18th.

With Chan going four ahead halfway through Saturday's round, Kim rallied to draw level at the turn on Sunday. At that point the American had not dropped a shot all tournament but he promptly started the back nine with four in a row. Although Chan bogeyed the 11th, three birdies in a row put him five clear before Kim (70) and Kaewkanjana (68) both birdied the last two holes.

"It has been a great week, claiming the hole-in-one prize and winning again in Thailand," said Chan. "To be honest, I wasn't expecting much this week. I didn't play well in Singapore and Saudi. But I got off to a good start and just kept riding that good form. That ace kept me going as well."

Grand Prix Golf Club, Kanchanaburi, Thailand — February 24-27
Par 72 (36-36); 7,215 yards — Purse: $400,000

1	**Chan Shih-chang**	64	66	67	68	265	$72,000
2	**Sadom Kaewkanjana**	66	67	67	68	268	34,600
	Sihwan Kim	67	65	66	70	268	34,600
4	Nitithorn Thippong	69	69	67	66	271	18,200
	Bio Kim	69	66	68	68	271	18,200
6	Jazz Janewattananond	69	70	69	65	273	9,617
	Chaiphat Koonmark	68	73	66	66	273	9,617
	Rashid Khan	72	69	70	62	273	9,617
	Atiruj Winaicharoenchai	67	69	70	67	273	9,617
	Jakraphan Premsirigorn	70	62	72	69	273	9,617
	Steve Lewton	70	68	66	69	273	9,617
12	Bjorn Hellgren	66	69	71	68	274	5,836
	Itthipat Buranatanyarat	71	70	70	63	274	5,836
	John Catlin	67	72	66	69	274	5,836
	Chikkarangappa S	67	67	70	70	274	5,836
	Kosuke Hamamoto	74	66	64	70	274	5,836
17	Joohyung Kim	67	72	71	65	275	5,060
18	Seungsu Han	71	68	70	67	276	4,500
	Miguel Carballo	73	68	68	67	276	4,500
	Pavit Tangkamolprasert	68	70	69	69	276	4,500
	Prom Meesawat	70	70	67	69	276	4,500
	Berry Henson	69	70	66	71	276	4,500
23	Andrew Dodt	73	66	70	68	277	3,649
	Tanapat Pichaikool	70	66	72	69	277	3,649
	Chapchai Nirat	72	69	67	69	277	3,649
	Kwanchai Tannin	70	70	68	69	277	3,649
	Doyeob Mun	73	67	68	69	277	3,649
	Phachara Khongwatmai	69	69	72	67	277	3,649
	Bongsub Kim	70	68	70	69	277	3,649
	Sungyeol Kwon	70	66	69	72	277	3,649
	Ben Leong	70	68	66	73	277	3,649

International Series — Thailand

A win was coming for Sihwan Kim and it finally arrived at Black Mountain in the International Series — Thailand, the first of the new events promoted by Greg Norman's LIV Golf. Kim had been fourth twice since the Asian Tour restarted late in 2021, and was runner-up in the Royal's Cup, but it had taken 11 years for a first victory to arrive since the 33-year-old American turned professional after playing college golf at Stanford.

"To get that monkey off your back is more of a relief, and happiness, I guess," said Kim, who had finished second or third 11 times on the Challenge Tour or Asian Tour in his career. "I know I had it in me, but I guess I just stayed diligent throughout my career, and here I am."

Kim opened at Black Mountain with a course-record 62, 10 under par, but fell out of the lead with a 72 the next day. A 65 on Saturday brought Kim into a share of second place, three behind young Thai star Phachara Khongwatmai. Although Khongwatmai made an eagle at the second hole on Sunday, Kim swept in front with an astonishing run of seven birdies in a row between the second and the eighth. Having gone out in 29, Kim birdied the 10th and the 13th before finishing with two bogeys and two more birdies for a 63 and a 26-under-par total of 262.

"When you get off to a hot start and when the leaders see your name going up the leaderboard it kind of puts pressure on," Kim said. "I was swinging it really freely and it felt like I was going to make everything today." Holing a bunker shot at the 15th was the highlight of Kim's round, giving him a three-shot cushion over Khongwatmai, who birdied the 16th moments after Kim had bogeyed it. But Kim responded with a final birdie at the 17th for a two-shot victory, while Khongwatmai closed with a 68 to finish two ahead of compatriot Itthipat Buranatanyarat and South Africa's Ian Snyman.

Black Mountain Golf Club, Hua Hin, Thailand — March 3-6
Par 72 (36-36); 7,507 yards — Purse: $1,500,000

1	**Sihwan Kim**	62	72	65	63	262	$270,000
2	**Phachara Khongwatmai**	63	70	63	68	264	165,000
3	**Ian Snyman**	67	68	67	64	266	84,750
	Itthipat Buranatanyarat	64	70	65	67	266	84,750
5	Gaganjeet Bhullar	67	69	69	64	269	41,950
	Paul Peterson	69	67	67	66	269	41,950
	Steve Lewton	68	68	66	67	269	41,950
	Bio Kim	64	69	68	68	269	41,950
	Ryosuke Kinoshita	68	69	64	68	269	41,950
	Rattanon Wannasrichan	68	66	66	69	269	41,950
11	Mathiam Keyser	67	71	66	66	270	23,738
	Scott Vincent	65	68	69	68	270	23,738

	Jazz Janewattananond	68	70	64	68	270	23,738	23	Kwanchai Tannin	68	65	75	64	272	14,325
	Ratchanon Chantananuwat (A)	70	68	63	69	270			Prom Meesawat	65	69	71	67	272	14,325
	Poosit Supupramai	72	65	62	71	270	23,738		Joohyung Kim	64	68	71	69	272	14,325
16	Sungyeol Kwon	65	66	72	68	271	18,300		Jaco Ahlers	69	63	71	69	272	14,325
	Todd Baek	66	66	71	68	271	18,300		Sirapob Yapala (A)	67	68	68	69	272	
	Angelo Que	68	68	67	68	271	18,300		Jack Harrison	69	68	65	70	272	14,325
	Todd Sinnott	66	68	68	69	271	18,300		Atiruj Winaicharoenchai	70	65	66	71	272	14,325
	Taehee Lee	68	64	69	70	271	18,300		Nicholas Fung	68	69	64	71	272	14,325
	Sebastian Soderberg	67	66	68	70	271	18,300		Doyeob Mun	65	66	68	73	272	14,325
	Karandeep Kochhar	65	68	66	72	271	18,300								

DGC Open

Nitithorn Thippong goes by the nickname of "Fever". The 25-year-old Thai certainly got hot at Delhi Golf Club to win the DGC Open for his first title on the Asian Tour. Having turned professional in 2015, Thippong won on the Asian Development Tour in 2018 but had to wait four years to win on the main circuit. He defeated India's Ajeetesh Sandhu at the first extra hole after holing from 10 feet for a birdie at the last hole of regulation.

It was a battle between the two all day with Thippong leading Sandhu by two at the start of the final round and the gap remained the same at the turn. Thippong then bogeyed 10, 14 and 16 to allow Sandhu to go two ahead. But at the short 17th, Sandhu's tee shot went right of the green and was lost, leading to a double bogey. "In hindsight, I would say on the 17th I tried to hit a shot which was not a high percentage one," Sandhu said. "I tried to move it with the wind to go into the flag but just didn't make a good swing."

Sandhu (71) did hole from four feet to match Thippong's birdie at the last and set up the playoff on seven-under 281. But then the home player drove near the trees on the right of the 18th in the playoff. He could only make the par-five green in three and made a par, while Thippong hit a fine approach to 12 feet and two-putted for his maiden title.

"I can't describe my feeling right now," Thippong said. "To win on the Asian Tour, I have been waiting for this for a long time. It's amazing. I didn't putt so good today. I just tried to hit it on the green and make the putts, but I couldn't make them. On the 14th, where I made bogey, I was so nervous there, but I did not lose my mind. In the playoff I wasn't as nervous as in normal time. I felt more free and so comfortable."

Delhi Golf Club (Lodhi), New Delhi, India — March 24-27
Par 72 (36-36); 6,912 yards — Purse: $500,000

1	**Nitithorn Thippong**	68	70	70	73	281	$90,000		Aman Raj	71	73	73	71	288	6,208
2	**Ajeetesh Sandhu**	69	68	73	71	281	55,000		Shankar Das	67	74	74	73	288	6,208
	Thippong won playoff at first extra hole								Sachin Baisoya	71	75	69	73	288	6,208
3	**Settee Prakongvech**	71	70	70	71	282	31,500		Bjorn Hellgren	71	70	73	74	288	6,208
4	Gaganjeet Bhullar	73	66	73	72	284	25,000	21	Om Prakash Chouhan	72	73	71	73	289	5,450
5	Justin Quiban	74	72	69	70	285	20,500	22	SSP Chawrasia	77	71	69	73	290	5,300
6	Yuvraj Singh Sandhu	75	70	74	67	286	13,463	23	Rashid Khan	72	69	79	72	292	5,000
	Shiv Kapur	71	73	74	68	286	13,463		Sunit Chowrasia	74	74	73	71	292	5,000
	Mithun Perera	73	70	74	69	286	13,463		Chanat Sakulpolphaisan	72	67	79	74	292	5,000
	Veer Ahlawat	68	67	78	73	286	13,463	26	William Harrold	73	73	75	72	293	4,625
10	Travis Smyth	67	73	79	68	287	8,240		Manu Gandas	71	69	75	78	293	4,625
	Danthai Boonma	76	73	74	64	287	8,240	28	Paul Peterson	76	68	76	74	294	4,083
	Shamim Khan	71	75	71	70	287	8,240		Dhruv Sheoran	72	72	74	76	294	4,083
	Yashas Chandra	73	73	70	71	287	8,240		Mathiam Keyser	72	72	74	76	294	4,083
	M Dharma	71	69	73	74	287	8,240		Ian Snyman	71	73	78	72	294	4,083
15	Karandeep Kochhar	69	71	78	70	288	6,208		Cory Crawford	72	74	72	76	294	4,083
	Kevin Yuan	71	75	72	70	288	6,208		Kasidit Lepkurte	71	68	77	78	294	4,083

Trust Golf Asian Mixed Cup

In what was already an historic week with the Ladies European Tour combining with the Asian Tour for the first time to stage the Trust Golf Asian Mixed Cup, Ratchanon "TK" Chantananuwat completed a remarkable victory at Siam Country Club. At the age of 15 years and 37 days, Chantananuwat became the youngest male player to win on a major tour — Ryo Ishikawa was 15 years and eight months when he won the Japan Tour's 2007 Munsingwear Open KSB Cup, while the youngest previous winner on the Asian Tour was Thailand's Chinnarat Phadungil, who claimed the 2005 Double A International Open when he was 17 years and five days.

On a congested leaderboard that included Americans Paul Peterson and John Catlin, who have won on both the Asian and European Tours, as well as 2020-22 Asian Tour number one Joohyung Kim, Chantananuwat birdied five of the last eight holes to win by two strokes from Kim.

Chantananuwat scored 63-70-70-65 for a 20-under-par total of 268. He did not drop a shot on the opening day and he shared the lead for the first two rounds with Sanna Nuutinen. While the Finn dropped away over the weekend, Chantananuwat only fell one behind on Saturday before a stunning final round. Although he missed a short putt at the 10th for his only dropped shot of the day, advice from his mentor Thongchai Jaidee overnight paid off as he raced for home. He played a superb approach from the rough at the 15th for his fourth birdie in five holes. Korea's Kim, 19, was one of seven leaders on the final day before finding the water at the 17th, but he eagled the last from 15 feet for a 64 to seal second place. Leading by one at the last, Chantananuwat finished with a birdie.

"I am very excited, but I felt a lot of pressure," said the 15-year-old Thai. "I have got to be honest, I got pretty lucky, I had hit two or three terrible drives. I actually had no confidence coming into this week. I wasn't striking the ball well. But now that I've won an Asian Tour event my confidence will grow."

Peterson, who holed a bunker shot at the 16th, said: "I got my ass kicked by a kid! But it was fun out there — fun to watch him. He plays with so much maturity. You could see him getting the adrenalin going. He handled himself really well."

Chantananuwat had made the cut in all his previous six Asian Tour events, finishing third at the Singapore International while still only 14. He had spent the past few weeks concentrating on his schoolwork and said he was not thinking of turning professional. "Nothing's going to change," he insisted. "I'm going to stay in school, go to college, practise more. That's been my plan all along."

After Nuutinen ran out of steam with 76-73 on the weekend, Thailand's Chanoknan Angurasaranee finished as the leading female player in a tie for sixth place on 15 under par, with locals Chanette Wannasaen, Arpichaya Yubol, Jaravee Boonchant and Scotland's Michele Thomson all among those a stroke behind.

Siam Country Club (Waterside), Pattaya, Thailand — April 7-10
Par 72 (36-36); men 7,439 yards, women 6,276 yards — Purse: $750,000

1	**Ratchanon Chantananuwat** (A)	63	70	70	65	268	
2	**Joohyung Kim**	72	65	69	64	270	$135,000
3	**Paul Peterson**	69	66	68	68	271	64,875
	Bio Kim	67	67	68	69	271	64,875
5	John Catlin	68	71	66	67	272	37,500
6	Taehee Lee	69	67	70	67	273	23,869
	Ian Snyman	67	67	71	68	273	23,869
	Chanoknan Angurasaranee	67	70	67	69	273	23,869
	Phachara Khongwatmai	65	69	68	71	273	23,869
10	Sihwan Kim	68	68	71	68	275	12,975
	Rashid Khan	71	66	69	69	275	12,975
	Chanettee Wannasaen	66	73	67	69	275	12,975
	Michele Thomson	70	69	67	69	275	12,975
	Arpichaya Yubol	67	68	70	70	275	12,975
	Jaravee Boonchant	71	66	66	72	275	12,975
16	Danthai Boonma	70	70	70	66	276	9,938
	Andrew Dodt	71	67	68	70	276	9,938
	Kyongjun Moon	67	70	68	71	276	9,938
19	Travis Smyth	71	70	67	69	277	8,688
	Nitithorn Thippong	69	71	68	69	277	8,688
	Tiia Koivisto	68	71	68	70	277	8,688
22	Eila Galitsky (A)	67	73	70	68	278	
	Meghan MacLaren	66	72	71	69	278	7,500
	Nobuhle Dlamini	72	66	71	69	278	7,500
	Ben Leong	69	70	72	67	278	7,500
	Suradit Yongcharoenchai	71	71	70	66	278	7,500
	Rory Hie	72	64	71	71	278	7,500
	Karolin Lampert	69	70	68	71	278	7,500
	Jazz Janewattananond	72	69	73	64	278	7,500
30	Tanapat Pichaikool	68	70	72	69	279	5,883
	Kosuke Hamamoto	71	70	68	70	279	5,883
	Hung Chien-yao	65	73	72	69	279	5,883
	Pavit Tangkamolprasert	71	69	69	70	279	5,883
	Sadom Kaewkanjana	70	70	69	70	279	5,883
	Chang Wei-lun	71	66	71	71	279	5,883
	Nicole Garcia	70	68	70	71	279	5,883
	Maja Stark	72	70	69	68	279	5,883
	Ajeetesh Sandhu	72	67	68	72	279	5,883

Trust Golf Asian Stableford Challenge

Sihwan Kim illustrated the dramatic swings of the Modified Stableford system perfectly in winning for the second time in little more than a month at the Trust Golf Asian Stableford Challenge. With the event again co-sanctioned by the Asian and Ladies European Tours, and played on the Waterside course at Siam Country Club, the difference in week two was the scoring system: eight points for an albatross, five for an eagle, two for a birdie, minus-one for a bogey and minus-three for a double bogey or worse.

It was a thrilling finish, even though Kim went to the par-five 18th with a seven-point lead. In the end he could have picked up, tapping in for a double bogey after losing his first tee shot, but still won by two points. Maja Stark would have stolen the win by chipping in from behind the green for an eagle.

Kim twice posted the tournament's best score of 22 points, in the first and third rounds. In Wednesday's first round, he had nine birdies and an eagle, plus a bogey, while on Friday he had 11 birdies. But on Thursday the 33-year-old American had posted minus-two points, with two birdies and four bogeys, while in Saturday's final round he had six birdies, two bogeys and the double for seven points and a total of 49. In old money, he had 62-76-61-70 for 19-under-par 269.

The Asian Tour Order of Merit leader had only won for the first time at the International Series event in Thailand in March. An interruption for dangerous weather on Saturday proved beneficial as he returned to birdie the 14th, 15th and 16th holes, though it was still interesting at the last. "Obviously any win is hard," Kim said. "My putting has just been phenomenal, that's pretty much what got me through it. Those putts on 14 and 16 were pretty lengthy ones, I am really confident in my putting now."

Stark said: "There was a bit of pressure when he made those birdies after the break. It was also more fun because I knew I had seven points to catch up and wanted to make an eagle on 18. I was very surprised when Sihwan was driven back to the tee, and it made me think 'Ooh, it could happen'." Stark had 253 yards into the wind for her second at the 18th and admitted the adrenalin led her to go long.

Stark was looking at missing the cut until she played the second nine of the second round in 17 points with six birdies and an eagle. The two-time LET winner did not drop a shot over the last 35 holes and finished with 13 points for a total of 47, five better than Budsabakorn Sukapan in third. Chanettee Wannasaen, who turned 18 on the final day of the event as she tied for eighth, was the halfway leader having already won two mixed events in Thailand in 2022.

Siam Country Club (Waterside), Pattaya, Thailand — April 13-16
Par 72 (36-36); men 7,439 yards, women 6,276 yards — Purse: $750,000

1	**Sihwan Kim**	22	-2	22	7	49	$135,000
2	**Maja Stark**	5	17	12	13	47	82,500
3	**Budsabakorn Sukapan**	7	10	16	9	42	47,250
4	Phachara Khongwatmai	13	3	14	11	41	37,500
5	Sadom Kaewkanjana	8	6	14	12	40	30,750
6	Joohyung Kim	15	9	8	7	39	23,175
	Natipong Srithong	5	20	9	5	39	23,175
8	Andrew Dodt	9	7	9	13	38	16,250
	Jazz Janewattananond	12	6	9	11	38	16,250
	Chanettee Wannasaen	13	15	6	4	38	16,250
11	Manon De Roey	6	11	10	10	37	12,213
	Pavit Tangkamolprasert	5	14	10	8	37	12,213
	Travis Smyth	3	18	11	5	37	12,213
14	Mim Sangkapong	12	6	3	15	36	10,613
	Kyongjun Moon	10	15	6	5	36	10,613
16	Todd Sinnott	6	9	8	12	35	9,938
17	Jaravee Boonchant	9	13	3	9	34	9,263
	Natthakritta Vongtaveelap (A)	11	9	7	7	34	
	Miguel Carballo	8	13	9	4	34	9,263
20	Yikeun Chang	7	7	11	8	33	8,663
21	Veer Ahlawat	6	5	10	11	32	8,269
	Hung Chien-yao	15	5	4	8	32	8,269
23	Arpichaya Yubol	13	3	5	10	31	7,613
	Chloe Williams	1	19	1	10	31	7,613
	Dodge Kemmer	12	7	3	9	31	7,613
	Kultida Pramphun	11	7	5	8	31	7,613
27	Suteepat Prateeptienchai	10	10	0	10	30	6,825
	Jarin Todd	7	6	9	8	30	6,825
	Danthai Boonma	4	14	8	4	30	6,825
30	Berry Henson	11	4	7	7	29	6,200
	Gabriella Cowley	7	9	2	11	29	6,200
	Paul Peterson	6	9	7	7	29	6,200

GS Caltex Maekyung Open

Korea's Bio Kim made his debut on the Asian Tour in 2007 at the GS Caltex Maekyung Open. Playing as an amateur he finished fourth. The following year, still an amateur, he was third. He then won the tournament in 2012 but that year it was not an Asian Tour event. A decade later he won it again — and this time had his first victory on the Asian Tour.

There was a huge crowd at Namseoul to cheer on the popular Kim at what is one of Korea's most important tournaments alongside the Korea Open. Kim went four shots ahead after three days with scores of 67-68-68 but on Sunday was soon tied by Mingyu Cho, who made three birdies in a row. But Cho bogeyed the eighth and was then handed a two-shot penalty at the ninth for playing from the green at the second hole instead of taking a drop. Kim cruised home for a 72, a nine-under-par total of 275 and a two-shot victory, while Cho's 70 included a birdie at the last from 25 feet to secure second place by one from Kyongjun Moon.

"Today was very tough, I lost my concentration a few times, but I am happy to make it through," said Kim after the 31-year-old collected his seventh Korean title. "It took all of me to win today. Namseoul Country Club is very difficult, and a lot of good players were chasing me. As I have been doing all week, and all year, I tried to stay in the present, clear my mind and not think about things too much, like my four-shot lead on the back nine."

Namseoul Country Club, Seongnam, Korea — May 5-8
Par 71 (36-35); 7,039 yards — Purse: ₩1,200,000,000

1	**Bio Kim**	67	68	68	72	275	$255,537
2	**Mingyu Cho**	69	70	68	70	277	102,215
3	**Kyongjun Moon**	69	71	71	67	278	63,884
4	Jiho Yang	69	67	71	72	279	44,293
5	Jaeho Kim	72	71	69	68	280	32,084
	Taehoon Ok	69	73	69	69	280	32,084
	Joohyung Kim	70	68	72	70	280	32,084
8	Jinho Choi	70	72	70	69	281	24,489
	Minjun Kim	69	70	68	74	281	24,489
10	Hyungjoon Lee	66	72	75	69	282	14,126
	Junggon Hwang	67	74	70	71	282	14,126
	Sanghyun Park	69	69	73	71	282	14,126
	Junsub Park	71	67	72	72	282	14,126
	Rattanon Wannasrichan	72	72	66	72	282	14,126
	Viraj Madappa	71	65	72	74	282	14,126
16	Daihan Lee	71	72	73	67	283	8,731
	Jaco Ahlers	74	67	71	71	283	8,731
	Minhyuk Song (A)	69	66	75	73	283	
19	Nitithorn Thippong	73	71	70	70	284	7,922
	Minchel Choi	70	67	76	71	284	7,922
	Yoon Chung	68	74	70	72	284	7,922
	Richard T Lee	68	75	68	73	284	7,922
	Jeongwoo Ham	69	71	71	73	284	7,922
	Honey Baisoya	72	71	66	75	284	7,922
	Settee Prakongvech	72	70	68	74	284	7,922
26	Yeongsu Kim	72	71	71	71	285	7,070
	Sungmin Cho	71	68	75	71	285	7,070
	Kyungnam Kang	70	73	72	70	285	7,070
	IJ Jang	70	70	73	72	285	7,070
	Neil Schietekat	68	72	73	72	285	7,070
	Dongmin Lee	65	70	77	73	285	7,070
	Natipong Srithong	68	73	70	74	285	7,070

International Series — England

A week after winning for the third time on the Japan Tour at the Mizuno Open, Scott Vincent claimed his maiden title on the Asian Tour. It came as the circuit staged its first standalone event in Europe with the second of the International Series events at Slaley Hall, a regular European Tour venue near Newcastle in the north-east of England.

Vincent's long trip from Japan was not without incident as his golf clubs did not arrive on the same flight, although they did turn up prior to the start of the tournament itself. The 30-year-old Zimbabwean continued his fine form with rounds of 69-68-69-66 for a 12-under-par total of 272. He defeated Australia's Travis Smyth, the 54-hole leader, by one after a dramatic duel over the closing holes.

One behind starting the final day under cloudy skies on a cool Platinum Jubilee weekend, Vincent birdied the first two holes only to take a double bogey at the third. Joohyung Kim briefly shared the lead before a triple-bogey six at the sixth as the Korean ended up in fifth place. South Africa's Justin Harding made his third birdie in a row at the 12th to lead by three before a bogey at the 13th and a double at the 15th dropped him to fourth place. Thailand's Sadom Kaewkanjana finished a stroke better in third place but Vincent and Smyth emerged at the top of the leaderboard.

Four birdies in six holes from the 11th got Vincent to 12 under par, while Smyth birdied the 16th from long range and the short 17th from 10 feet to draw level. At the last, Vincent found the rough off the tee but was able to reach the green, while Smyth, from a downslope on the fairway, blocked his seven-iron approach into a bunker on the right. His recovery went 20 feet past the hole and the Australian bogeyed, while Vincent two-putted from long range, holing a six-footer for the victory.

"It's amazing," Vincent said. "This is the tour I started on, so obviously it's nice to get the first win out here. It has felt like a long time but my game is trending in a good direction. It got very close there at the end, but it fell in my favour and I'm very thankful."

Smyth was one of five players to join Vincent in earning exemptions for the inaugural LIV Golf Invitational the following week at Centurion.

Slaley Hall Hotel Spa & Golf Resort, Hexham, Northumberland, England — June 2-5
Par 71 (35-36); 7,069 yards — Purse: $2,000,000

1	**Scott Vincent**	69	68	69	66	272	$360,000
2	**Travis Smyth**	69	70	66	68	273	220,000
3	**Sadom Kaewkanjana**	69	72	65	69	275	126,000
4	Justin Harding	70	66	71	69	276	100,000
5	Joohyung Kim	67	69	70	72	278	82,000
6	Sihwan Kim	70	68	74	67	279	57,533
	Turk Pettit	74	68	67	70	279	57,533
	Viraj Madappa	68	70	70	71	279	57,533
9	Wade Ormsby	72	70	70	68	280	34,600
	Kevin Yuan	74	68	70	68	280	34,600
	Jarin Todd	69	71	70	70	280	34,600
	Kosuke Hamamoto	72	65	71	72	280	34,600
	Neil Schietekat	69	68	70	73	280	34,600
	Ian Snyman	70	68	69	73	280	34,600
15	Itthipat Buranatanyarat	69	74	72	66	281	25,340
	Chang Wei-lun	65	72	75	69	281	25,340
	Richard T Lee	71	69	72	69	281	25,340
	Jazz Janewattananond	67	74	70	70	281	25,340
	Graeme McDowell	70	69	70	72	281	25,340
20	Todd Sinnott	70	69	73	70	282	22,050
	Hayden Hopewell (A)	72	72	68	70	282	
	Gonzalo Fdez-Castano	72	70	67	73	282	22,050
23	Dodge Kemmer	72	72	70	69	283	20,900
	Gaganjeet Bhullar	72	70	69	72	283	20,900
25	Jack Davidson	71	71	72	70	284	19,100
	Stuart Manley	69	71	73	71	284	19,100
	Adilson Da Silva	70	71	71	72	284	19,100
	Taichi Kho (A)	72	67	71	74	284	
	Jaco Ahlers	68	72	70	74	284	19,100
30	Bjorn Hellgren	70	73	71	71	285	16,333
	Jack Harrison	74	70	70	71	285	16,333
	Tanapat Pichaikool	67	71	76	71	285	16,333
	SSP Chawrasia	67	74	74	70	285	16,333
	Ren Yonezawa	70	74	68	73	285	16,333
	Pawin Ingkhapradit	69	72	76	68	285	16,333

Kolon Korea Open

Minkyu Kim had won on minor tours in Europe, and in 2018 in the Czech Republic became the youngest ever winner on the Challenge Tour when he was 17. But Kim had to wait until he turned 21 for his first win in Korea, and on the Asian Tour. It came at his national championship, the Kolon Korea Open, and only after a three-hole aggregate playoff that had plenty of twists.

After scores of 72-71-68, Kim had started the final round at Woo Jeong Hills three off the lead but posted a 69 for a four-under-par total of 280. He might have rued a bogey at the last hole but Hyungjoon Lee had a double-bogey seven at the last to fall into a tie for third with American Jarin Todd. Mingyu Cho, who had recovered from a nightmare start of two bogeys and a double in the first four holes, missed from 20 feet for a birdie at 18 and tied Kim after a 72.

Both Kim and Cho parred the short 16th, then Kim missed the green at the 17th and dropped a shot to fall one behind. But Cho pulled his drive into the trees at 18 and had to chip out, while Kim was beside the green in two and chipped close. Cho's third shot from near the green, came up a long way short and he took a bogey six, while Kim secured the win with a birdie.

"I can't believe I have actually won," said Kim, who had posted seven top 10s in his last 10 starts. "I have come close to winning before and I wondered if I would ever win. I felt good on the back nine and started to feel I had a chance. Straight after I won, I thought of my father; I have to thank him for this. My golf is just beginning." In a consolation for Cho, both players qualified for The 150th Open at St Andrews.

Woo Jeong Hills Country Club, Cheonan, Korea — June 23-26
Par 71 (36-35); 7,326 yards — Purse: ₩1,350,000,000

1	**Minkyu Kim**	72	71	68	69	280	$383,305
2	**Mingyu Cho**	71	70	67	72	280	102,215
	Kim won three-hole playoff						
3	**Jarin Todd**	69	69	73	70	281	54,089
	Hyungjoon Lee	71	68	71	71	281	54,089
5	Junseok Lee	72	72	66	72	282	35,775
6	Kyongjun Moon	69	70	74	70	283	26,014
	Taeho Kim	72	72	70	69	283	26,014
	Taehee Lee	72	66	73	72	283	26,014
	Taehoon Ok	69	69	70	75	283	26,014
	Sarit Suwannarut	71	72	67	73	283	26,014
11	Yoseop Seo	77	67	70	70	284	17,100
	Junghwan Lee	68	71	71	74	284	17,100
13	Soonsang Hong	69	73	73	70	285	11,863
	Junsung Kim	72	69	72	72	285	11,863
	Jaemin Hwang	68	74	71	72	285	11,863
	Sanghee Lee	69	68	75	73	285	11,863
17	Bio Kim	72	69	74	71	286	9,016
	Chan Shih-chang	73	72	70	71	286	9,016
	Junggon Hwang	71	73	71	71	286	9,016
	Yongjun Bae	74	71	69	72	286	9,016
21	Kyungnam Kang	74	71	68	74	287	8,313
22	Bjorn Hellgren	73	73	72	70	288	7,604
	Pavit Tangkamolprasert	73	73	72	70	288	7,604
	Hanbyeol Kim	71	73	73	71	288	7,604
	Rattanon Wannasrichan	73	70	72	73	288	7,604
	Doyeon Hwang	71	68	73	76	288	7,604
	Nitithorn Thippong	69	74	68	77	288	7,604
28	Taehoon Kim	72	72	75	70	289	6,555
	Sanghyun Park	73	67	77	72	289	6,555
	Neil Schietekat	74	72	71	72	289	6,555
	Prom Meesawat	76	69	71	73	289	6,555
	Dongkyu Jang	74	68	73	74	289	6,555
	Jeongwoo Ham	70	73	71	75	289	6,555
	Guntaek Koh	75	70	69	75	289	6,555

Mandiri Indonesia Open

Indonesia has been good to Gaganjeet Bhullar. His first Asian Tour win came in the country in 2009 and his 10th arrived with the Mandiri Indonesia Open. It was the 34-year-old Indian's third victory in the tournament after his wins in 2013 and 2016, but his first title since the 2018 Fuji International. "I love this course," he said of Pondok Indah.

With rounds of 68-67-68, Bhullar was one behind compatriot Rashid Khan and Thailand's Atiruj Winaicharoenchai going into the final round when the man from Amritsar made seven birdies for a 65 to finish on 268, 20 under par. He won by two strokes from Khan, who closed with a 68, and England's Steve Lewton, who had set the clubhouse target with a 64.

Khan parred the entire front nine before making four birdies coming home. By then it was too late. Bhullar, who dedicated the victory to his 11-month-old daughter, went out in 33, picked up another shot at the 10th and then made three birdies in a row from the 13th. "I played like a champion tee to green and gave myself so many birdie opportunities," Bhullar said.

"I was riding high on confidence, hit the ball really good. It is a great week, I had a lot of positive memories having won this tournament two times before, that was definitely on my subconscious mind. The goal was just to go out there and give 100 per cent." He was the first player to win the title three times and joined a fabled list of those who have won a national championship in Asia at least three times, which includes Peter Thomson, Jumbo Ozaki, Miguel Angel Jimenez and Adam Scott, among others.

Pondok Indah Golf Course, Jakarta, Indonesia — August 4-7
Par 72 (36-36); 7,243 yards — Purse: $500,000

1	**Gaganjeet Bhullar**	68	67	68	65	268	$90,000
2	**Steve Lewton**	68	71	67	64	270	43,250
	Rashid Khan	*68*	*70*	*64*	*68*	270	43,250
4	Yoseop Seo	69	72	65	66	272	22,750
	Chang Wei-lun	67	64	72	69	272	22,750
6	Minkyu Kim	66	67	74	66	273	14,383
	Doyeob Mun	71	68	67	67	273	14,383
	Atiruj Winaicharoenchai	71	63	68	71	273	14,383
9	Poom Saksansin	73	68	63	70	274	10,125
	Itthipat Buranatanyarat	64	67	72	71	274	10,125
11	Kyongjun Moon	70	69	70	66	275	7,913
	Natipong Srithong	67	70	70	68	275	7,913
	Pavit Tangkamolprasert	68	72	67	68	275	7,913
	Taichi Kho (A)	64	70	70	71	275	
	Adilson Da Silva	68	70	66	71	275	7,913
16	Keith Horne	66	69	72	69	276	6,625
	Trevor Simsby	69	70	68	69	276	6,625
	Chapchai Nirat	65	69	69	73	276	6,625
19	Ajeetesh Sandhu	71	71	67	68	277	5,625
	Kevin Yuan	71	64	73	69	277	5,625
	Jbe' Kruger	69	72	66	70	277	5,625
	Kwanchai Tannin	68	68	70	71	277	5,625
	Nitithorn Thippong	67	68	70	72	277	5,625
24	Paul Peterson	72	67	71	68	278	5,000

	Ben Campbell	68 68 72 70	278	5,000	30	Thaworn Wiratchant	72 68 69 71	280	4,075
	Prayad Marksaeng	65 69 71 73	278	5,000		Donlaphatchai Niyomchon	70 72 68 70	280	4,075
27	Shiv Kapur	70 68 71 70	279	4,550		Udayan Mane	72 69 67 72	280	4,075
	Danny Masrin	70 70 69 70	279	4,550		Chan Shih-chang	69 72 71 68	280	4,075
	Suradit Yongcharoenchai	67 70 69 73	279	4,550					

International Series — Singapore

Without knowing it at the time, when Nitithorn Thippong holed a putt for par from 18 feet at the 18th hole of the Tampines course at Tanah Merah it proved to be the winning moment. Thippong had to wait to find out that he had won his second Asian Tour victory of the season. The 25-year-old Thai, whose maiden win came at the DGC Open in India in March, watched as the final group played the 18th. Taiwan's Chan Shih-chang held the lead on the tee but a double-bogey seven knocked him down to a tie for fifth with Todd Sinnott, whose closing 64 included nine birdies in the last 13 holes.

Thailand's Phachara Khongwatmai needed an eagle at the last to tie his countryman and his wedge shot finished inches from the hole as he joined Canada's Richard T Lee (67) one behind Thippong. That left Malaysia's Gavin Green, the halfway leader and joint 54-hole leader with Khongwatmai. Green faced a 15-footer on the final green to force a playoff and saw it roll over the edge of the hole. "I don't think the last putt could have gone any closer. I thought I had made it. But it stopped breaking right at the end," said Green (71) after making it a trio of runners-up at the Singapore leg of the International Series, which saw American Patrick Reed finish in a tie for 31st place.

Thippong, whose nickname is "Fever", had sweated out the victory with scores of 68-67-68-69 for a 16-under-par total of 272. He did not drop a shot on the final day and claimed all three of his birdies at par threes, including the 14th and 16th holes on the back nine.

"I'm really lost for words with this victory," he said. "It's my biggest win so far and I cannot describe my feeling. I was fully focused on the process and playing my own game the entire week. I kept believing in myself and did not allow myself to be distracted by other pressures. I'm so happy I managed to win this week."

Tanah Merah Country Club (Tampines), Singapore — August 11-14
Par 72 (36-36); 7,535 yards — Purse: $1,500,000

1	**Nitithorn Thippong**	68 67 68 69	272	$270,000		Trevor Simsby	72 67 70 68	277	20,058
2	**Richard T Lee**	70 69 67 67	273	111,500		Turk Pettit	68 74 71 64	277	20,058
	Gavin Green	65 65 72 71	273	111,500		Sadom Kaewkanjana	67 70 70 70	277	20,058
	Phachara Khongwatmai	67 66 69 71	273	111,500		Shubhankar Sharma	70 69 68 70	277	20,058
5	Todd Sinnott	68 70 72 64	274	55,725		Veer Ahlawat	69 65 72 71	277	20,058
	Chan Shih-chang	69 68 66 71	274	55,725	21	Yuki Inamori	73 70 68 67	278	16,350
7	Jarin Todd	74 67 68 67	276	33,285	22	Chapchai Nirat	71 66 74 68	279	14,100
	Ryo Hisatsune	70 69 68 69	276	33,285		Sungyeol Kwon	73 70 68 68	279	14,100
	Ryosuke Kinoshita	70 70 67 69	276	33,285		Jazz Janewattananond	70 67 73 69	279	14,100
	Jaco Ahlers	70 66 69 71	276	33,285		Lee Chieh-po	72 65 72 70	279	14,100
	Peter Uihlein	68 70 67 71	276	33,285		Juvic Pagunsan	67 71 71 70	279	14,100
12	Pavit Tangkamolprasert	71 72 67 67	277	20,058		Kieran Vincent	68 70 71 70	279	14,100
	Kevin Yuan	71 71 68 67	277	20,058		Yoseop Seo	69 65 72 73	279	14,100
	Tirawat Kaewsiribandit	67 75 70 65	277	20,058		Jeunghun Wang	70 67 69 73	279	14,100
	Ben Leong	71 69 70 67	277	20,058		Steve Lewton	67 68 69 75	279	14,100

International Series — Korea

It was going to work out alright for Taehoon Ok sooner or later. The 23-year-old Korean had what he described as a "heart-breaking" finish at the Kolon Korea Open when he tied for the lead after 54 holes but slipped to sixth on the final day. Earlier in the season Ok had his best Asian Tour result of fifth at the GS Caltex Maekyung Open, where countryman Bio Kim earned his first Asian Tour victory.

After 36 holes in the latest International Series event in Korea, at Lotte Skyhill Country Club on Jeju Island, the pair were tied after Kim had a 63 and Ok a 64 on Friday. Ok said: "I really want to win on the Asian Tour and take my game forward and help my dream of getting onto the PGA Tour. I'm not good enough yet. Plan is to make a success in Korea first and really challenge myself."

Despite bogeys at the last two holes for a 69 on Saturday, Ok took a one-shot lead over Kim, Yoseop Seo and 20-year-old Korean amateur Wooyoung Cho, who birdied five of last six holes for a stunning 61, although preferred lies were in operation. Cho eventually finished seventh as the final day developed into a battle between Ok and Kim. Ok briefly dropped behind before three birdies in a row from the 11th put him two ahead. But as he bogeyed the 17th, Kim birdied the par-five 18th for a 68.

Ok responded at the last by hitting his third shot to five feet and holing the putt for his own 68 and a winning total of 15-under-par 269. American Trevor Simsby took third place with a 67 and Yunseok Gang was fourth after weekend rounds of 66-66.

This was Ok's first win as a professional and he dedicated it to his father, who died when Ok was 10. "I asked my caddie on 17 if he really thought I can birdie 18 and he said, 'Go for it'," said Ok. "I have learned a lot by playing in the final pairings recently so that really helped."

Lotte Skyhill Country Club, Jeju Island, Korea — August 18-21
Par 71 (35-36); 7,079 yards — Purse: $1,500,000

1	**Taehoon Ok**	68 64 69 68	269	$270,000
2	**Bio Kim**	69 63 70 68	270	165,000
3	**Trevor Simsby**	67 69 68 67	271	94,500
4	Yunseok Gang	67 73 66 66	272	75,000
5	Gaganjeet Bhullar	72 65 69 67	273	55,725
	Jeunghun Wang	68 71 67 67	273	55,725
7	Woohyun Kim	68 71 69 66	274	39,750
	Pavit Tangkamolprasert	63 73 67 71	274	39,750
	Wooyoung Cho (A)	72 69 61 72	274	
10	Natipong Srithong	69 70 68 68	275	26,805
	Junghwan Lee	70 70 67 68	275	26,805
	Sadom Kaewkanjana	70 70 67 68	275	26,805
	Justin Harding	66 70 69 70	275	26,805
	Phachara Khongwatmai	71 69 63 72	275	26,805
15	Scott Vincent	71 69 69 67	276	18,113
	Todd Sinnott	69 73 67 67	276	18,113
	Taeho Kim	70 66 72 68	276	18,113
	Zach Bauchou	70 70 71 65	276	18,113
	Jeongwoo Ham	70 70 68 68	276	18,113
	Seung Park	70 68 69 69	276	18,113
	Andy Ogletree	67 75 64 70	276	18,113
	Ian Snyman	66 70 70 70	276	18,113
	Eric Chun	65 72 68 71	276	18,113
	Yoseop Seo	69 66 67 74	276	18,113
25	Travis Smyth	70 72 66 69	277	14,325
	Berry Henson	68 69 70 70	277	14,325
	Chase Koepka	70 68 69 70	277	14,325
	Seungtaek Lee	70 68 68 71	277	14,325
29	Kyongjun Moon	70 71 68 69	278	11,767
	Sanghun Shin	69 71 69 69	278	11,767
	Kyungnam Kang	71 70 68 69	278	11,767
	Hanbyeol Kim	68 66 74 70	278	11,767
	Seonghyeon Jeon	69 68 71 70	278	11,767
	Veer Ahlawat	70 66 74 68	278	11,767
	Jarin Todd	68 73 70 67	278	11,767
	Sam Brazel	68 71 69 70	278	11,767
	Jazz Janewattananond	66 72 69 71	278	11,767

Yeangder TPC

Australia's Travis Smyth made up for his narrow defeat at the International Series event in England earlier in the year by winning his first title on the Asian Tour at the Yeangder TPC. The 27-year-old from Sydney won by two strokes from local favourite Lee Chieh-po, who won the event in 2021 when it was played as a domestic event.

Smyth, who won the Northern Territory PGA on the Australasian Tour shortly after turning professional in 2017, held the 54-hole lead at Slaley Hall and duelled with Scott Vincent on the last day all the way to the 18th, where his bogey was decisive. At Linkou International, Smyth scored 68-69 and then posted twin 66s on the weekend to win at 19-under-par 269. He took the lead after the third round, by one over Lee, and this time made sure he kept in front on the final day by making four birdies in the first six holes.

He then added three birdies in a row to start the back nine, yet Lee was not to be dismissed easily as he made five birdies in the first 12 holes. At the 15th, Smyth found himself plugged in a bunker and, after escaping, he then three-putted for a double bogey. That tightened things up but Lee bogeyed the same hole so Smyth was still two ahead and the Aussie birdied the next for good measure. Lee birdied the last for a 67 to finish three ahead of the quartet in third place.

"I got so close in England, I felt like I let it go," Smyth said. "I want to be the player that I believe I can be, and winning this week is one step along the journey. Lee played amazing. He kept applying pressure, so it wasn't easy that's for sure."

Linkou International Golf & Country Club, Linkou, Chinese Taipei — September 22-25
Par 72 (36-36); 7,108 yards — Purse: $700,000

1	**Travis Smyth**	68	69	66	66	269	$126,000
2	**Lee Chieh-po**	67	68	69	67	271	77,000
3	**Wang Wei-hsuan**	70	68	69	67	274	32,778
	Nicholas Fung	72	68	67	67	274	32,778
	Berry Henson	68	67	71	68	274	32,778
	Bjorn Hellgren	68	68	69	69	274	32,778
7	Liu Yen-Hung	69	68	69	69	275	19,950
8	Honey Baisoya	71	69	69	67	276	15,167
	Ajeetesh Sandhu	67	68	73	68	276	15,167
	Rashid Khan	68	70	70	68	276	15,167
11	Chan Shih-chang	66	71	74	66	277	11,398
	Ben Leong	66	73	68	70	277	11,398
	Settee Prakongvech	69	66	70	72	277	11,398
14	Pawin Ingkhapradit	71	73	67	67	278	9,485
	Daniel Fox	69	70	71	68	278	9,485
	Justin Quiban	73	66	69	70	278	9,485
	Chapchai Nirat	69	64	71	74	278	9,485
18	Lin Keng-wei	67	71	72	69	279	7,989
	Kevin Yuan	70	70	70	69	279	7,989
	Chikkarangappa S	69	68	72	70	279	7,989
	Wang Tsung-chieh	68	70	70	71	279	7,989
22	Suradit Yongcharoenchai	70	72	71	67	280	7,105
	Huang Yi-tseng	69	70	73	68	280	7,105
	Prom Meesawat	67	72	71	70	280	7,105
	Sarit Suwannarut	71	69	69	71	280	7,105
26	Mathiam Keyser	69	70	74	68	281	6,370
	Lu Wei-chih	71	70	71	69	281	6,370
	Rattanon Wannasrichan	68	69	73	71	281	6,370
29	Shiv Kapur	64	74	74	70	282	5,553
	Nitithorn Thippong	67	71	75	69	282	5,553
	Lu Sun-yi (A)	67	74	71	70	282	
	Rahil Gangjee	70	70	72	70	282	5,553
	Sung Mao-chang	70	69	72	71	282	5,553
	Yeh Yu-chen	69	73	69	71	282	5,553
	Tirawat Kaewsiribandit	68	68	72	74	282	5,553

Mercuries Taiwan Masters

A first Asian Tour title on home soil was the prize for Chan Shih-chang, a first win for eight years was the aim for Rashid Khan. The pair produced a thrilling finale to the Mercuries Taiwan Masters with the local star winning at the second extra hole having birdied the 18th hole three times in a row.

India's Khan led by four shots at halfway after scores of 67-65, then a 73 on Saturday allowed Chan to tie for the 54-hole lead with 68-68-69. Each produced 68s on the final day at Taiwan Golf and Country Club to set a new tournament record of 15-under-par 273. Chan made two early birdies but Rashid produced his fifth of the day at the 13th to go ahead by three shots. "It was going really well, just that I knew the last four holes are crucial," said Khan.

Chan, who was second and third in the event over the previous two years when it was only a local tournament due to pandemic travel restrictions, was not finished. He birdied the par-five 15th, where Khan three-putted for a par. Khan then bogeyed the 17th and missed from six feet for the win at the last, having seen Chan hole from nine feet for the tying birdie. At the same hole in the playoff, Khan hit to two feet for a birdie but Chan holed from 21 feet to stay alive. Next time around, Khan two-putted from 20 feet but Chan holed another nine-footer for the win.

"Really happy to win my first Asian Tour title at home. I have always wanted to do this. To be honest, it's really pressurising. My friends, sponsors and family were out there supporting me today," said Chan. It was the 36-year-old's second win of the year and third since the Asian Tour resumed after the pandemic late in 2021.

Taiwan Golf & Country Club, Tamsui, Chinese Taipei — September 29-October 2
Par 72 (36-36); 6,923 yards — Purse: $1,000,000

1	**Chan Shih-chang**	68	68	69	68	273	$200,000
2	**Rashid Khan**	67	65	73	68	273	120,000
	Chan won playoff at second extra hole						
3	**Siddikur Rahman**	70	69	69	71	279	60,000
	Sarit Suwannarut	67	73	68	71	279	60,000
5	Danthai Boonma	72	66	75	68	281	35,000
	Nitithorn Thippong	67	69	73	72	281	35,000
	Pavit Tangkamolprasert	69	69	71	72	281	35,000
8	Veer Ahlawat	69	72	69	72	282	22,500
	Yeh Yu-chen	70	70	69	73	282	22,500

10	Shiv Kapur	68	73	71	71	283	17,000		Chang Wei-lun	72	72	72	71	287	9,840
	Suradit Yongcharoenchai	68	71	72	72	283	17,000		Nicholas Fung	72	73	70	72	287	9,840
	Wang Wei-hsiang	66	70	74	73	283	17,000		Berry Henson	71	73	70	73	287	9,840
13	Huang Chi	74	67	72	71	284	14,500		Ajeetesh Sandhu	73	68	72	74	287	9,840
	Scott Strange	68	72	71	73	284	14,500	27	Lu Chien-soon	74	72	70	72	288	9,100
15	SSP Chawrasia	71	71	73	70	285	12,500		Adilson Da Silva	73	71	71	73	288	9,100
	Tirawat Kaewsiribandit	73	67	72	73	285	12,500	29	Viraj Madappa	73	72	73	71	289	8,300
	Aman Raj	73	72	67	73	285	12,500		Honey Baisoya	71	69	76	73	289	8,300
18	Hung Chien-yao	67	75	74	70	286	11,000		Khalin Joshi	73	69	74	73	289	8,300
	Ian Snyman	73	71	71	71	286	11,000		Chikkarangappa S	70	74	72	73	289	8,300
	Kevin Yuan	71	70	73	72	286	11,000		Donlaphatchai Niyomchon	67	71	77	74	289	8,300
21	Jack Harrison	73	73	73	68	287	9,840		Poom Pattaropong	74	71	70	74	289	8,300
	Ratchanon Chantananuwat (A)	70	73	74	70	287									

International Series — Morocco

Timing his run for him to perfection, Jazz Janewattananond came from three behind with two to play and won for the first time in three years. The 26-year-old Thai won four times in 2019 to top the Order of Merit but had struggled playing constantly during the pandemic without being able to go home.

With the Asian Tour's International Series moving to Morocco, Janewattananond enjoyed his first visit to Rabat and the famous Red course at Royal Golf Dar Es Salam. He came home in five under par, with the main action taking place at the driveable par-four 17th. Janewattananond found the green and holed an eagle putt from 20 feet to move one behind Canada's Richard T Lee. Then the Thai got up and down from a bunker at the par-five 18th for a birdie and a closing six-under-par 67. With earlier scores of 71-70-72, that left him on 12-under-par 280.

"It's been a long time since my last trophy, since before Covid. Now everything's changed, I've found my way through and we're here," said the Thai, whose seventh Asian Tour win came with girlfriend Sarina Schmidt, also a professional golfer, as his caddie. "I had three holes left and I wasn't even nearly at the top. I just had a really good finish. I just feel so relieved. I've been out nine weeks in a row and I'm tired and my back's hurting. But I came in with an open mind to exploring Morocco and Rabat, and I think that helped me win."

As Janewattananond closed out on the 18th, Lee found trouble at the previous hole. His drive finished behind a tree on the left. He had no shot and could only chip back to the fairway backhanded. He ended up with a bogey and now trailed by one. His attempt to make a four at the last was stymied by a poor chip which left him with a 20-footer from the fringe.

Lee, seeking his first Asian Tour win since 2017, had taken a two-shot lead on Friday with a 65 and though he trailed overnight, four birdies in a row to close out the front nine looked to have put him in command but he could only replicate his second place at the International Series Singapore event after a 70.

Royal Golf Dar Es Salam (Red), Rabat, Morocco — November 3-6
Par 73 (36-37); 7,633 yards — Purse: $1,500,000

1	**Jazz Janewattananond**	71	70	72	67	280	$270,000		Berry Henson	71	73	70	76	290	19,875
2	**Richard T Lee**	72	65	74	70	281	165,000		Scott Hend	71	69	72	78	290	19,875
3	**David Puig**	70	70	69	73	282	94,500	19	Sam Brazel	74	74	71	72	291	16,575
4	Scott Vincent	70	71	71	71	283	75,000		Rattanon Wannasrichan	70	71	75	75	291	16,575
5	Jinichiro Kozuma	72	73	75	66	286	47,738		Jaco Ahlers	72	73	70	76	291	16,575
	Taehoon Ok	71	73	75	67	286	47,738		Turk Pettit	73	73	68	77	291	16,575
	Kiradech Aphibarnrat	70	74	72	70	286	47,738	23	Doyeob Mun	75	75	72	70	292	14,550
	Kieran Vincent	73	75	64	74	286	47,738		Sarit Suwannarut	69	76	74	73	292	14,550
9	Sadom Kaewkanjana	70	73	71	73	287	30,375		Jeunghun Wang	70	74	74	74	292	14,550
	Erik Compton	72	70	71	74	287	30,375		Nitithorn Thippong	67	72	76	77	292	14,550
11	Chase Koepka	71	71	75	71	288	26,175		Cole Madey	67	76	72	77	292	14,550
12	Ryo Hisatsune	75	72	75	67	289	23,550	28	Ayoub Lguirati	74	73	74	72	293	12,600
	Kosuke Hamamoto	73	69	76	71	289	23,550		Sihwan Kim	74	75	71	73	293	12,600
14	Ian Snyman	72	77	74	67	290	19,875		Poom Pattaropong	74	74	71	74	293	12,600
	Todd Sinnott	70	72	73	75	290	19,875		Kevin Yuan	70	76	72	75	293	12,600
	Steve Lewton	68	73	73	76	290	19,875								

International Series — Egypt

Visit the Pyramids. Tick. Stay at a great hotel. Tick. Love the golf course. Tick. Win your maiden professional title. Tick. "My first trip to Egypt is one that I will never forget," said Andy Ogletree.

In only his 12th event as a professional, Ogletree won the International Series — Egypt event at Madinaty by four strokes from Austrian veteran Bernd Wiesberger. The 24-year-old from Mississippi won the US Amateur in 2019 and turned professional in 2020 after playing in the November Masters. But surgery for a hip problem in 2021 put him out for six months and left him with minimal status in the US for 2022. He played in the first LIV Golf event in London, finished last of the 48 players and dropped out of Invitational league.

Instead he had status for the Asian Tour's International Series, finishing 15th in Korea, his best result before arriving in Egypt. Rounds of 66-64-65, finishing birdie-eagle on Saturday, put Ogletree three ahead of Wiesberger. With the eight-time DP World Tour winner, now a LIV Golf player, doing his best to put pressure on the youngster with a closing 63, Ogletree was not daunted. His final-round 62 was the lowest of the day and matched the low score of the week. He dropped only one shot and posted seven birdies in the first 14 holes. Wiesberger, who holed his second shot for an eagle two at the 10th, got within two before a two-shot swing at the 16th put the American comfortably in front again. Wiesberger birdied the 17th, but Ogletree responded with his ninth birdie of the day at the last.

"I have always been a huge fan of matchplay and that is kind of what it came to in the end, it was basically a two-man race," Ogletree said. "I just tried to keep matching what he was doing, I kept making a lot of putts. Bernd's a great player and it was really awesome to come out on top."

Jeunghun Wang enjoyed his best result since returning to golf following his 18-month national service in Korea, tying for third place with Sihwan Kim, who returned to the top of the Asian Tour Order of Merit ahead of Bio Kim.

Madinaty Golf Club, Cairo, Egypt — November 10-13
Par 70 (36-34); 6,936 yards — Purse: $1,500,000

1	**Andy Ogletree**	66	64	65	62	257	$270,000
2	**Bernd Wiesberger**	66	67	65	63	261	165,000
3	**Jeunghun Wang**	65	68	67	64	264	84,750
	Sihwan Kim	65	66	68	65	264	84,750
5	James Piot	65	70	64	66	265	61,500
6	Jarin Todd	66	66	67	67	266	43,150
	Prom Meesawat	67	66	66	67	266	43,150
	Richard T Lee	64	65	69	68	266	43,150
9	Sadom Kaewkanjana	70	66	68	63	267	28,975
	Kieran Vincent	66	69	67	65	267	28,975
	Jinichiro Kozuma	67	64	68	68	267	28,975
12	Travis Smyth	65	67	69	67	268	24,375
13	Gunn Charoenkul	68	71	66	64	269	19,519
	Seungtaek Lee	63	70	71	65	269	19,519
	Todd Sinnott	68	69	67	65	269	19,519
	Kevin Yuan	71	67	66	65	269	19,519
	David Puig	68	71	64	66	269	19,519
	Nitithorn Thippong	66	70	66	67	269	19,519
	Sarit Suwannarut	68	68	66	67	269	19,519
	Scott Hend	62	74	64	69	269	19,519
21	Kosuke Hamamoto	69	70	66	65	270	15,675
	Brett Rumford	65	71	69	65	270	15,675
	Jakraphan Premsirigorn	67	69	66	68	270	15,675
	Jaco Ahlers	64	68	69	69	270	15,675
25	Berry Henson	68	67	68	68	271	14,325
	Trevor Simsby	65	67	69	70	271	14,325
27	Turk Pettit	67	68	71	67	273	12,625
	Shergo Al Kurdi	69	70	67	67	273	12,625
	Pawin Ingkhapradit	63	70	73	67	273	12,625
	Cole Madey	70	69	67	67	273	12,625
	Ajeetesh Sandhu	70	69	65	69	273	12,625
	Ian Snyman	67	69	68	69	273	12,625

Bangabandhu Cup Bangladesh Open

As part of a Thai one-two-three at the Bangabandhu Cup Bangladesh Open, dinner companions Danthai Boonma and Kosuke Hamamoto fought out the title at Kurmitola. Boonma had waited seven years for his second Asian Tour victory and edged it by one stroke.

A fine amateur, Boonma won the World Classic Championship at Laguna National in his rookie season in 2015. A title on the Asian Development Tour followed in 2016 but nothing on the main circuit until now despite three runner-up finishes. The 26-year-old Thai scored 68-70-65-68 for a 13-under-par total of 271, while 54-hole leader Hamamoto, still seeking a first win, closed with a 70.

Compatriot Rattanon Wannasrichan finished in third place, two behind Hamamoto, after a 67, while local favourite Siddikur Rahman was supported strongly by the crowd as he tied for fourth. He was attempting to win his national championship for a second time (and a first as an Asian Tour event).

Boonma, one behind at the start of play on Sunday, took the lead with three birdies in a row to finish the front nine. After both he and Hamamoto bogeyed the 16th, a birdie at the 17th gave him a two-shot cushion that the runner-up could only halve with a birdie at the last. "I'm so excited about my second win on the Asian Tour," said Boonma.

"It's been tough in the past two years, I didn't really play very good, I struggled with my mind and my short game. I can't believe it about this week. Actually, Kosuke and I ate dinner together every day, we're close friends and we practise together. It was a bit tight you know, I tried to keep fighting and just keep focus, just relax and focus."

Kurmitola Golf Club, Dhaka, Bangladesh — November 24-27
Par 71 (35-36); 6,642 yards — Purse: $400,000

1	**Danthai Boonma**	68	70	65	68	271	$72,000
2	**Kosuke Hamamoto**	66	69	67	70	272	44,000
3	**Rattanon Wannasrichan**	71	66	70	67	274	25,200
4	Karandeep Kochhar	73	71	68	65	277	15,280
	Poom Saksansin	70	69	69	69	277	15,280
	Siddikur Rahman	69	66	72	70	277	15,280
	Atiruj Winaicharoenchai	71	66	69	71	277	15,280
8	Hung Chien-yao	71	71	70	66	278	8,245
	David Puig	70	68	69	71	278	8,245
	Jamal Hossain	68	69	69	72	278	8,245
	Veer Ahlawat	69	69	68	72	278	8,245
12	Yoseop Seo	72	68	72	67	279	6,280
	Pavit Tangkamolprasert	68	71	70	70	279	6,280
14	Chan Shih-chang	68	76	68	68	280	5,300
	Pawin Ingkhapradit	68	70	70	72	280	5,300
	Cole Madey	70	70	68	72	280	5,300
	Itthipat Buranatanyarat	65	68	74	73	280	5,300
	Badal Hossain	68	70	69	73	280	5,300
19	Justin Quiban	72	69	73	67	281	4,480
	Miguel Tabuena	70	70	71	70	281	4,480
	Kevin Yuan	73	72	70	66	281	4,480
22	Thitipan Pachuayprakong	72	70	72	68	282	3,880
	Aman Raj	70	69	73	70	282	3,880
	Ben Jones	68	72	72	70	282	3,880
	SSP Chawrasia	71	68	76	67	282	3,880
	Khalin Joshi	70	70	71	71	282	3,880
	Natipong Srithong	74	68	69	71	282	3,880
	Miguel Carballo	71	74	65	72	282	3,880
29	Chikkarangappa S	71	74	69	69	283	3,340
	Sungyeol Kwon	71	69	70	73	283	3,340
	Ratchanon Chantananuwat (A)	71	70	68	74	283	

BNI Indonesian Masters

Against a strong field in the last event of the season, Sarit Suwannarut impressively eased away to his maiden victory on the Asian Tour at the BNI Indonesian Masters. The 24-year-old from Thailand had won once on his home circuit in 2019, but 2022 had not been plain sailing by any means. You would not have known as he coped with the many weather delays at Royale Jakarta to post a four-stroke victory over India's Anirban Lahiri, with Graeme McDowell and Chan Shih-chang sharing third place a further stoke back.

Scores of 66-67 put Suwannarut into a share of the halfway lead with South Africa's Mathiam Keyser, the first-round leader on 65. Suwannarut started to pull away on Saturday but still needed to complete the last four holes of his third round on Sunday morning. Another 67 put him three clear of compatriot Kosuke Hamamoto, the previous week's runner-up.

Although three-time winner Lee Westwood was in contention, along with former Ryder Cup colleague McDowell, Chan, a two-time winner on the season, and Lahiri, who opened and closed the week with 66s, the leader was barely perturbed. He birdied the sixth and eagled the ninth, adding two more birdies at 12 and 15 before missing a small putt at the 16th for his only dropped shot of the final round. He was on the 17th with a five-stroke lead when another thunderstorm caused an 80-minute delay and although Lahiri returned to birdie the 18th, Suwannarut was home and dry and thanking his coach for a tweak to his stance earlier in the week.

"I think I almost cried coming down the 18th," said Sarit. "I just can't put into words how I feel. I am just happy. I didn't feel the pressure that much, I was just enjoying my game. It's been a really tough year. I had Covid at the start of the year, later I couldn't get a visa for Korea, and I was battling to keep my card at one point. I worked with my coach and we discovered something with the setup. We looked at the video and decided to squat more and get my chin up a little bit, just small things that made a really big impact."

American Sihwan Kim, a two-time winner during the season, finished in 28th to secure the Order of Merit title on his 34th birthday, while Zimbabwe's Scott Vincent finished 10th to top the standings for the International Series events, of which this was the seventh of the season.

Royale Jakarta Golf Club, Jakarta, Indonesia — December 1-4
Par 72 (36-36); 7,368 yards — Purse: 1,500,000

1	**Sarit Suwannarut**	66	67	67	68	268	$270,000
2	**Anirban Lahiri**	66	70	70	66	272	165,000
3	**Chan Shih-chang**	69	68	67	69	273	84,750
	Graeme McDowell	70	67	67	69	273	84,750
5	Gaganjeet Bhullar	69	70	70	66	275	61,500
6	Sadom Kaewkanjana	68	69	72	67	276	43,150
	Kosuke Hamamoto	66	70	67	73	276	43,150
	Jazz Janewattananond	71	65	69	71	276	43,150
9	Lee Westwood	74	66	66	71	277	32,100
10	Scott Vincent	71	70	67	70	278	24,720
	Eunshin Park	69	72	67	70	278	24,720
	Scott Hend	69	72	70	67	278	24,720
	Tirawat Kaewsiribandit	70	69	72	67	278	24,720
	Veer Ahlawat	67	68	70	73	278	24,720
15	Richard T Lee	68	70	67	74	279	20,325
	Itthipat Buranatanyarat	70	68	70	71	279	20,325
17	Travis Smyth	72	69	73	66	280	18,125
	Ben Jones	70	70	70	70	280	18,125
	Miguel Tabuena	68	69	73	70	280	18,125
20	Bjorn Hellgren	69	73	71	68	281	15,216
	Steve Lewton	70	72	69	70	281	15,216
	Kevin Phelan	70	72	68	71	281	15,216
	Karandeep Kochhar	69	70	67	75	281	15,216
	Kiradech Aphibarnrat	75	68	69	69	281	15,216
	Chapchai Nirat	70	73	69	69	281	15,216
	Lee Chieh-po	68	69	70	74	281	15,216
	Taehoon Ok	71	72	69	69	281	15,216
28	Jarin Todd	72	70	72	68	282	12,250
	Chikkarangappa S	72	70	72	68	282	12,250
	Honey Baisoya	70	70	72	70	282	12,250
	Settee Prakongvech	72	71	69	70	282	12,250
	Phachara Khongwatmai	69	69	70	74	282	12,250
	Sihwan Kim	73	70	69	70	282	12,250

2022 ORDER OF MERIT

1	Sihwan Kim	$627,458
2	Bio Kim	599,609
3	Scott Vincent	517,845
4	Nitithorn Thippong	506,390
5	Sadom Kaewkanjana	487,909
6	Chan Shih-chang	461,041
7	Travis Smyth	453,490
8	Jazz Janewattananond	436,354
9	Phachara Khongwatmai	430,523
10	Sarit Suwannarut	415,499

ASIAN DEVELOPMENT TOUR

Gurugram Challenge	**Dodge Kemmer**
Laguna Phuket Challenge	**Thomas Sloman**
Laguna Phuket Cup	**Sarun Sirithon**
Blue Canyon Classic	**Chen Guxin**
Blue Canyon Open	**Settee Prakongvech (1,2)**
OB Golf Invitational	**Naraajie E Ramadhanputra**
Indo Masters	**Harrison Gilbert**
Gunung Geulis Golf Invitational	**Chonlatit Chuenboonngam**
BNI Ciputra Golfpreneur Tournament	**Suteepat Prateeptienchai**
BRG Open	**Chen Guxin (2)**
OB Golf Invitational Jababeka	**Suteepat Prateeptienchai (2)**
Combiphar Players Championship	**Suteepat Prateeptienchai (3)**
PKNS Selangor Masters	**Shahriffudin Ariffin**
PIF Saudi Open	**Naraajie E Ramadhanputra (2)**
Aramco Invitational	**Varanyu Rattanaphiboonkij (1,2)**
Taifong Open	**Hung Chien-Yao**

ALL THAILAND GOLF TOUR

Boonchu Ruangkit Championship	**Settee Prakongvech**	
Singha E-San Open	**Atiruj Winaicharoenchai**	
Singha All Thailand Memorial	**Atiruj Winaicharoenchai (2)**	
Singha Classic	**Varanyu Rattanaphiboonkij**	
Singha Laguna Phuket Open	**Witchayanon Chothirunrungrueng**	
Singha All Thailand Premier Championship	**Denwit David Boriboonsub**	
Singha Pattaya Open	**Settee Prakongvech (2,3)**	
Singha Championship	**Gunn Charoenkul**	
Singha Chiang Mai Open	**Warun Ieamgaew**	
Thailand Open	**Kwanchai Tannin**	
Singha Bangkok Open	**Nitithorn Thippong (1,3)**	
Singha Thailand Masters	**Poom Saksansin**	

CHINA TOUR

Hangzhou International Championship	**An Tong** (A)	
Shenyang International Open	**She Zihan**	
Hengdian Championship	**Ma Chengyao**	
Mitsubishi Electric Open	**Xiao Bowen**	
Hainan Golf Open	**Bai Bobby Zhengkai**	
CGA Championship	**Zhou Ziqin** (A)	
Chongqing Open	**Zhou Yanhan** (A)	

KPGA KOREAN TOUR

DB Damage Insurance Promy Open	**Sanghyun Park**	
GS Caltex Maekyung Open	**Bio Kim**	*See chapter 17*
Woori Financial Group Championship	**Heemin Chang**	
Descente Korea Munsingwear Match Play	**Eunshin Park**	
KB Finance LIIV Championship	**Jiho Yang**	
SK Telecom Open	**Bio Kim (2)**	
KPGA Championship	**Sanghun Shin**	
Hana Bank Invitational	**Junseok Lee**	
Kolon Korea Open	**Minkyu Kim**	*See chapter 17*
Asiad CC Busan Open	**Junggon Hwang**	
Honors K Sollago Han Jangsang Invitational	**Yongjun Bae**	
Woosung Construction Open	**Yonggu Shin**	
Bodyfriend Phantom Rovo Gunsan Open	**Yoseop Seo**	
LX Championship	**Yoseop Seo (2)**	
Shinhan Donghae Open	**Kazuki Higa (1,3)**	*See chapter 18*
Bizplay-Electronic Times Open	**Jinho Choi**	
DGB Financial Group Open	**Doyeob Mun**	
Hyundai Insurance KJ Choi Invitational	**Hyungjoon Lee**	
Genesis Championship	**Yeongsu Kim**	
Golfzone-Toray Open	**Eunshin Park (2)**	
LG Signature Players Championship	**Yeongsu Kim (2)**	

MENA TOUR

Bangkok Invitational	**Eugenio Lopez-Chacarra**	*See chapter 20*
Jeddah Invitational	**Brooks Koepka**	*See chapter 20*
Tournament 3	**Bailey Gill**	
Tournament 4	**Aron Zemmer**	

PROFESSIONAL GOLF TOUR OF INDIA

Gujarat Open	**Karandeep Kochhar**	
Glade One Masters	**Manu Gandas**	
Mujib Borsho Chattogram Open	**Kshitij Naveed Kaul**	
Tata Steel PGTI Players — Tollygunge	**Yuvraj Singh Sandhu**	
DGC Open	**Nitithorn Thippong**	*See chapter 17*
Gurugram Challenge	**Dodge Kemmer**	
Tata Steel PGTI Players — Chandigarh	**Yuvraj Singh Sandhu (2)**	
Delhi-NCR Open	**Manu Gandas (2)**	
Tata Steel PGTI Players — KGISL	**Khalin H Joshi**	
Impiger Technologies Chennai Open	**Manu Gandas (3)**	
J&K Open	**Yuvraj Singh Sandhu (3)**	
Rajasthan Tourism Jaipur Open	**Om Prakash Chouhan**	
Kapil Dev Grant Thornton Invitational	**Varun Parikh**	
Tata Steel PGTI Players — American Express	**Yuvraj Singh Sandhu (4)**	
Jeev Milkha Singh Invitational	**Gaganjeet Bhullar (1,2)**	
Pune Open	**Veer Ahlawat**	
Telangana Golconda Masters	**Manu Gandas (4)**	
Indianoil Servo Masters	**Yuvraj Singh Sandhu (5)**	
Dream Valley Vooty Masters	**Manu Gandas (5)**	
SSP Chawrasia Invitational	**Manu Gandas (6)**	
Tata Steel Tour Championship	**Chikkarangappa S**	

Japan Tour

A famous American author who used the pen name O Henry wrote an abundance of short stories that were acclaimed for their surprise endings. That same element applied to the "short story" that was the best seller on the 2022 Japan Tour.

Even though he had had some success during his first five seasons, Kazuki Higa, all five-feet-two of him, didn't seem likely to suddenly burst into stardom as he did as the number one player of the 2022 season. As he was racking up four victories and seriously contending in a half dozen other tournaments, Higa noted that "my height appeared in the headlines more than my name". Regardless, the accomplishments of the 27-year-old Higa overshadowed the rest of the players when it was all said and done. No other player won more than twice and he ran away with the money-winning title, clinching it three weeks before the end of the season. His ¥181,598,825 was over ¥67 million more than the earnings of runner-up Rikuya Hoshino.

His victories included the major Tour Championship and he finished second to another unexpected winner in the Japan Open Championship. That title was claimed by then 21-year-old amateur Taiga Semikawa, who had earlier won the Panasonic Open. Semikawa turned pro after winning the Open and had further flashes of contention before season's end.

Three other players were double winners. Yuki Inamori bagged the Japan Players Championship along with the long-standing Crowns. Shugo Imahira, the two-time season champion in 2018 and 2019, won back-to-back tournaments early in the year and Riki Kawamoto, the only rookie winner beside Semikawa, snared a pair of one-stroke victories. Three other players — Yuto Katsuragawa, Kaito Onishi and Shintaro Kobayashi — won for the first time. Mikumu Horikawa landed the Japan PGA Championship. Zimbabwe's Scott Vincent and American Chan Kim, along with Thai Sadom Kaewkanjana, who won the season-opening SMBC Singapore Open, co-sanctioned with the Asian Tour, were the only overseas winners during the 27-tournament season, while Keegan Bradley won the PGA Tour's Zozo Championship.

As one provision of a joint agreement of the Japan Tour with the DP World Tour and the PGA Tour announced late in the year, the leading three players on the money list — Higa, Hoshino and Aguri Iwasaki — were to be tendered memberships on the DP World Tour for the 2023 season.

2022 SCHEDULE

SMBC Singapore Open	**Sadom Kaewkanjana**	*See chapter 17*
Token Homemate Cup	**Jinichiro Kozuma**	
Kansai Open	**Kazuki Higa**	
ISPS Handa Championship Japan	**Yuto Katsuragawa**	
The Crowns	**Yuki Inamori**	
Asia Pacific Diamond Cup	**Shugo Imahira**	
Golf Partner Pro-Am	**Shugo Imahira (2)**	
Gateway to The Open Mizuno Open	**Scott Vincent**	
BMW Japan Tour Championship	**Kazuki Higa (2)**	
Aso Iizuka Challenge	**Tomoyo Ikemura**	
Japan Players Championship	**Yuki Inamori (2)**	
Japan PGA Championship	**Mikumu Horikawa**	
Shigeo Nagashima Invitational Sega Sammy Cup	**Hiroshi Iwata**	
Sansan KBC Augusta	**Riki Kawamoto**	
Fujisankei Classic	**Kaito Onishi**	
Shinhan Donghae Open	**Kazuki Higa (3)**	
ANA Open	**Tomoharu Otsuki**	
Panasonic Open	**Taiga Semikawa (A) (1,2)**	
Vantelin Tokai Classic	**Riki Kawamoto (2)**	
For The Players By The Players	**Shintaro Kobayashi**	
Japan Open Championship	**Taiga Semikawa (A) (2,3)**	

Heiwa PGM Championship	**Rikuya Hoshino**
Mynavi ABC Championship	**Mikumu Horikawa (2)**
Mitsui Sumitomo Visa Taiheiyo Masters	**Ryo Ishikawa**
Dunlop Phoenix	**Kazuki Higa (4)**
Casio World Open	**Chan Kim**
Golf Nippon Series JT Cup	**Hideto Tanihara**

Token Homemate Cup

Wins were a long time in coming for Jinichiro Kozuma and when they did, they didn't come easily. Kozuma nearly holed a 230-yard fairway shot and eagled the final hole of the Taiheiyo Masters near the end of his eighth year on the Japan Tour to nail his first victory by a single stroke in 2020. Eighteen months later in the Token Homemate Cup, the first regular event of the season, he birdied the 72nd hole to force a playoff and birdied again on the first extra hole for his second victory.

"It's definitely an amazing feeling to have won this tournament under such tough conditions. I just didn't feel right today," remarked the 27-year-old veteran, who was unhappy with his swing despite his dominating play all week. He took a one-stroke lead after two rounds at the par-71 Token Tado Country Club with 66-69, supplanting Tomoyasu Sugiyama, who opened with a 65. A six-birdie, one-bogey 66 on Saturday moved Kozuma three shots in front of chasers Rikuya Hoshino and Aguri Iwasaki on 12 under par.

Instead of from that duo, the challenge Sunday came from Yuto Katsuragawa, winless in his first two years on the tour, who started the day five shots back and was seven off the pace after Kozuma eagled the par-four fifth hole and he bogeyed the sixth. Katsuragawa's charge began with a birdie at the eighth and he then made six in eight holes for a 30 coming home. A 64 left him on 14-under-par 270, while Kozuma bogeyed the 13th and the 16th. But he made his only two birdies of the day at 17 and 18 to tie with a 69, then followed up by birdieing the 18th again with a 20-footer for the playoff win. "I did not give up until the very end and I'm just so pleased with my win today," summed up Kozuma, while Katsuragawa said that "while I did not win today, I'm proud of the effort I made".

Token Tado Country Club, Nagoya, Wie — March 31-April 3
Par 71 (35-36); 7,062 yards — Purse: ¥130,000,000

1	**Jinichiro Kozuma**	66	69	66	69	270	¥26,000,000
2	**Yuto Katsuragawa**	69	70	67	64	270	13,000,000
	Kozuma won playoff at first extra hole						
3	**Rikuya Hoshino**	68	68	68	67	271	8,840,000
4	Naoyuki Kataoka	66	73	68	65	272	6,240,000
5	Aguri Iwasaki	66	72	67	68	273	5,200,000
6	Taichi Nabetani	68	70	68	68	274	4,680,000
7	Riki Kawamoto	67	74	67	67	275	4,290,000
8	Tomoyasu Sugiyama	65	72	71	68	276	3,965,000
9	Yuki Shino	69	72	69	67	277	2,904,571
	Konosuke Nakazato	76	67	66	68	277	2,904,571
	Shaun Norris	68	74	67	68	277	2,904,571
	Han Lee	68	74	66	69	277	2,904,571
	Kodai Aoyama	72	67	68	70	277	2,904,571
	Ryuko Tokimatsu	69	67	70	71	277	2,904,571
	Shugo Imahira	73	71	69	64	277	2,904,571
16	Yuki Takeuchi	70	71	70	67	278	1,976,000
	Yuta Uetake	70	73	67	68	278	1,976,000
	Chan Kim	69	70	70	69	278	1,976,000
19	Mikiya Akutsu	73	67	71	68	279	1,586,000
	Seungsu Han	66	74	71	68	279	1,586,000
	Mitsumasa Tamura	73	69	65	72	279	1,586,000
	Kazuki Higa	71	71	72	65	279	1,586,000
23	Yuta Ikeda	71	69	71	69	280	1,098,500
	Eric Sugimoto	71	72	68	69	280	1,098,500
	Kunihiro Kamii	65	73	72	70	280	1,098,500
	Mikumu Horikawa	74	69	67	70	280	1,098,500
	Tomoki Mitsuda	71	72	69	68	280	1,098,500
	Yuki Furukawa	69	72	72	67	280	1,098,500
	Shingo Katayama	71	73	71	65	280	1,098,500
	Ryutaro Nagano	73	70	73	64	280	1,098,500

Kansai Open

Kazuki Higa's solid finish and victory in the venerable Kansai Open negated what would have been a historic achievement. Higa ran off nine successive pars on the back nine of Yomiuri Country Club to finish one stroke ahead of Rikuya Hoshino, who was trying to become the first player in 48 years to successfully defend a victory in the long-existing tournament.

Hoshino, who had made the Kansai Open his third Japan Tour victory in 2021, was trying to do what the legendary Teruo Sugihara did in the mid-1970s when he was the last player to win back-to-back in the tournament. (Sugihara won the Kansai Open seven times, including three in a row 1973-75.)

The diminutive Higa had taken a two-stroke lead over Hoshino into the final day after rounds of 65-67-68, the Saturday round a wild scramble that included an eagle, six birdies and five bogeys. Hoshino, with 65-67-70, was the only serious challenger to Higa on Sunday, two strokes back and two ahead of third-place amateur Taiga Semikawa, who faded to 77 the last day.

Higa never trailed Sunday, matching Hoshino with two birdies and a bogey on the front nine before running off nine back-nine pars for a 70 and the winning total of 270, 14 under par. Hoshino closed with 69, while Korean-American Han Lee shot 64 to grab third place. "It feels great to be back to winning ways again," Higa remarked. "I would like to win two or three more from here."

Yomiuri Country Club, Hyogo — April 14-17
Par 71 (35-36); 7,180 yards — Purse: ¥80,000,000

1	**Kazuki Higa**	65	67	68	70	270	¥16,000,000
2	**Rikuya Hoshino**	65	67	70	69	271	8,000,000
3	**Han Lee**	67	72	72	64	275	5,440,000
4	Genki Okada	67	72	68	69	276	3,840,000
5	Ryosuke Kinoshita	65	70	74	68	277	3,040,000
	Hiroshi Iwata	65	72	70	70	277	3,040,000
7	Takanori Konishi	66	72	73	67	278	2,445,333
	Tsubasa Ukita (A)	66	73	71	68	278	
	Mikiya Akutsu	63	70	75	70	278	2,445,333
	Yuta Ikeda	66	69	72	71	278	2,445,333
11	Todd Baek	72	69	70	68	279	1,936,000
	Shingo Katayama	67	72	72	68	279	1,936,000
	Kensei Hirata	66	70	73	70	279	1,936,000
14	Toshinori Muto	70	69	73	68	280	1,536,000
	Akio Sadakata	68	71	72	69	280	1,536,000
	Kohei Tsuda (A)	69	71	70	70	280	
17	Tomoyasu Sugiyama	71	69	75	66	281	1,376,000
	Taiga Semikawa (A)	64	67	73	77	281	
19	Takashi Ogiso	67	68	77	70	282	1,145,600
	Andrew Evans	67	72	73	70	282	1,145,600
	Kunihiro Kamii	70	71	74	67	282	1,145,600
	Brad Kennedy	70	70	71	71	282	1,145,600
	Yosuke Tsukada	66	73	72	71	282	1,145,600
24	Hideto Kobukuro	66	71	76	70	283	800,000
	Mikumu Horikawa	69	72	71	71	283	800,000
	Mitsumasa Tamura	64	72	75	72	283	800,000
	Yuto Katsuragawa	70	69	72	72	283	800,000
	Takahiro Hataji	64	70	82	67	283	800,000
	Hirotaka Ashizawa	64	70	75	74	283	800,000
30	Tomohiro Ishizaka	72	69	73	70	284	608,000
	Kodai Aoyama	70	70	75	69	284	608,000
	Ryo Ishikawa	68	73	70	73	284	608,000
	Taihei Sato	68	70	72	74	284	608,000

ISPS Handa Championship Japan

For a player ranked 1,036th in the world, Yuto Katsuragawa was off to a start on the 2022 season that questioned its validity. Just weeks after finishing second in the Singapore Open and then losing in a playoff at the Token Homemate Cup, the unheralded 23-year-old picked up his first win in the ISPS Handa Championship Japan at PGM Ishioka Golf Club in Ibaraki Prefecture. The event was meant to be co-sanctioned with the DP World Tour but that was not possible due to travel restrictions.

Katsuragawa prevailed against Rikuya Hoshino, a five-time winner coming off third and second-place finishes in the two previous tournaments. Katsuragawa's final-round 65 for 24-under-par 260 was just enough to edge Hoshino with his closing 64 by one stroke. "It feels great to have finally won my first tournament after several runner-up finishes," Katsuragawa enthused. "I'm looking forward to challenging for more honours either in Japan or overseas."

Katsuragawa started the week five strokes behind first-round leader Yuki Furukawa and his dazzling 62, but jumped into a share of first place with 67-63 with five others, including Furukawa (62-68) and Hoshino (66-64). His third-round 65 kept him in first place, now with little-known Justin De Los Santos (64), with five players within two strokes of them.

Hoshino gave the winner all he could handle in the late going Sunday. A bogey-birdie swap at the 16th hole pulled Hoshino within a shot, but Katsuragawa matched his birdie-par finish to secure the maiden victory. All-time star Shingo Katayama made his best showing in years, the 49-year-old winner of 31 tournaments finishing fifth, four strokes behind.

PGM Ishioka Golf Club, Ibaraki — April 21-24
Par 71 (36-35); 7,071 yards — Purse: ¥103,000,000

1	**Yuto Katsuragawa**	67	63	65	65	260	¥20,000,000
2	**Rikuya Hoshino**	66	64	67	64	261	10,000,000
3	**Yuta Uetake**	65	67	64	66	262	6,800,000
4	Kaito Onishi	64	70	62	67	263	4,800,000
5	Shingo Katayama	65	67	65	67	264	4,000,000
6	Anthony Quayle	67	69	64	65	265	3,192,500
	Yuki Inamori	66	68	64	67	265	3,192,500
	Kazuki Higa	63	67	66	69	265	3,192,500
	Justin De Los Santos	65	66	64	70	265	3,192,500
10	Michael Hendry	66	66	69	65	266	2,420,000
	Shaun Norris	67	70	64	65	266	2,420,000
	Naoto Nakanishi	66	67	65	68	266	2,420,000
13	Hyunwoo Ryu	69	68	65	65	267	1,853,333
	Katsumasa Miyamoto	63	67	70	67	267	1,853,333
	Koumei Oda	64	68	66	69	267	1,853,333
16	Yusaku Hosono	70	62	69	67	268	1,432,000
	Brad Kennedy	66	67	68	67	268	1,432,000
	Eric Sugimoto	63	69	68	68	268	1,432,000
	Yoshikazu Haku	69	65	64	70	268	1,432,000
	Toshinori Muto	68	66	64	70	268	1,432,000
21	Thanyakon Khrongpha	70	62	70	67	269	1,100,000
	Yuki Furukawa	62	68	71	68	269	1,100,000
	Ryutaro Nagano	65	69	67	68	269	1,100,000
24	Shugo Imahira	66	71	66	67	270	900,000
	Riki Kawamoto	68	67	65	70	270	900,000
	Mitsumasa Tamura	64	67	68	71	270	900,000
27	Shintaro Kobayashi	66	68	69	68	271	740,000
	Keisuke Ozaki	66	68	70	67	271	740,000
	Tatsuya Kodai	66	70	68	67	271	740,000
	Daijiro Izumida	64	66	70	71	271	740,000
	Taihei Sato	67	68	63	73	271	740,000

The Crowns

Stormy weather made things unpleasant for the first galleries on hand for a Japan Tour event in three years, but it didn't deter Yuki Inamori from scoring his third victory in the venerable The Crowns on May Day. "The course conditions were challenging due to the heavy rains," said the 27-year-old Inamori, whose two previous wins were in the 2018 and 2020 Japan Opens. "Thank you very much for visiting us in such heavy rains," he remarked to the soggy spectators.

Hiroshi Iwata, who won the 2021 Crowns that also encountered wet weather, didn't handle the rain as well this time after taking the lead into the final round. At 11 under par the 41-year-old veteran was a shot in front of Junggon Hwang and two ahead of Inamori, Daiki Imano and Jinichiro Kozuma after 54 holes.

Hwang, who had been in a four-way tie for the halfway lead, was the only player who stayed within sight of Inamori on Sunday. The 29-year-old South Korean, a four-time tour winner making just his second start since 2019 after completing mandatory military service, was no match for the winner despite a closing 67. Inamori birdied the first two holes and punched out four more over five holes starting at the eighth, widening his lead to three, his ultimate winning margin. He matched birdies with Hwang at the 16th and 17th holes and closed with a 63 and a 16-under-par 264 total.

Of note, 27-year-old Australian Anthony Quayle led the first day with 61, the low round of the young season, but wound up 15 strokes behind Inamori.

Nagoya Golf Club (Wago), Aichi — April 28-May1
Par 70 (35-35); 6,557 yards — Purse: ¥100,000,000

1	**Yuki Inamori**	64	71	66	63	264	¥20,000,000
2	**Junggon Hwang**	65	67	68	67	267	10,000,000
3	**Hiroshi Iwata**	70	64	65	70	269	6,800,000
4	Ryuko Tokimatsu	69	67	68	66	270	4,800,000
5	Ryosuke Kinoshita	66	72	68	65	271	3,800,000
	Daiki Imano	63	73	65	70	271	3,800,000
7	Rikuya Hoshino	69	71	69	63	272	2,947,500
	Ryo Ishikawa	70	70	64	68	272	2,947,500
	Naoyuki Kataoka	72	64	67	69	272	2,947,500
	Keita Nakajima (A)	69	66	68	69	272	
	Jinichiro Kozuma	69	68	64	71	272	2,947,500
12	Kunihiro Kamii	69	72	65	67	273	2,120,000
	Chan Kim	69	65	72	67	273	2,120,000
	Shugo Imahira	70	68	67	68	273	2,120,000
	Todd Baek	66	70	67	70	273	2,120,000
16	Kazuki Higa	68	67	71	68	274	1,570,000
	Tomohiro Ishizaka	68	69	68	69	274	1,570,000
	Shunsuke Sonoda	68	70	67	69	274	1,570,000
	Andrew Evans	66	68	70	70	274	1,570,000
20	Koumei Oda	64	71	72	68	275	1,220,000
	Hirotaro Naito	66	70	71	68	275	1,220,000
	Tomohiro Kondo	68	67	71	69	275	1,220,000
	Kota Kaneko	65	67	72	71	275	1,220,000
24	Matthew Griffin	68	68	71	69	276	908,000
	Dongkyu Jang	65	71	72	68	276	908,000
	Daijiro Izumida	70	67	69	70	276	908,000
	Yuto Katsuragawa	65	69	69	73	276	908,000
	Mikumu Horikawa	70	68	65	73	276	908,000
29	Tomoharu Otsuki	71	65	71	70	277	702,000
	Ryuichi Oiwa	66	71	71	69	277	702,000
	Yuta Ikeda	67	69	73	68	277	702,000
	Kyung-Tae Kim	70	70	69	68	277	702,000
	Yuta Uetake	67	68	70	72	277	702,000

Asia Pacific Diamond Cup

Shugo Imahira picked a fine time to re-establish his position as a dominant star on the Japan Tour when he won the Asia Pacific Diamond Cup. Not only did the two-time leading money winner (2018-19) score his first victory of the season, but also the win gave him an entry into The 150th Open at coveted St Andrews later in the season.

The triumph, his sixth on the Japan Tour, did not come easily. A stroke off the lead after 54 holes, the 29-year-old player, who had mediocre showings earlier in the year, had to fend off challenges from a handful of contenders to prevail at Oarai Golf Club in Ibaraki. "I am very happy with this victory," said the eight-season veteran, who has won at least once each season since 2017. "I didn't get any good results so far this year, so I'm very glad to be able to win here."

Imahira entered the final round tied with Yuki Inamori, the previous week's Crowns winner, and a shot off the pace, set at seven-under-par 203 by four players — money-leader Yuto Katsuragawa, Ryuko Tokimatsu, New Zealand's Ben Campbell and Kaito Onishi, who had led the first two days.

Katsuragawa, shooting for his second win in 2022, seized the lead on Sunday with an outgoing 33, two ahead of Imahira and Onishi, and stayed in front until he double-bogeyed the par-five 15th. Imahira jumped in front with a birdie there and parred in for 68 and eight-under 272 for a one-stroke victory over Katsuragawa (70), Onishi (70), Hiroshi Iwata (68) and amateur Kosuke Suzuki, who pieced together a 63 with an eagle, six birdies and a bogey the last day.

Oarai Golf Club, Ibaraki — May 12-15
Par 70 (35-35); 7,163 yards — Purse: ¥100,000,000

1	**Shugo Imahira**	66	69	69	68	272	¥20,000,000
2	**Kosuke Suzuki** (A)	70	70	70	63	273	
	Hiroshi Iwata	65	74	66	68	273	7,900,000
	Kaito Onishi	65	67	71	70	273	7,900,000
	Yuto Katsuragawa	67	69	67	70	273	7,900,000
6	Kazuma Kobori (A)	67	70	68	69	274	
	Rikuya Hoshino	67	67	72	68	274	4,200,000
8	Jinichiro Kozuma	71	67	69	68	275	3,033,333
	Yuki Inamori	70	64	70	71	275	3,033,333
	Ben Campbell	67	70	66	72	275	3,033,333
11	Itthipat Buranatanyarat	71	70	69	66	276	2,050,000
	Ryuko Tokimatsu	71	66	66	73	276	2,050,000
13	Yosuke Tsukada	70	69	72	66	277	1,490,000
	Steve Lewton	70	69	73	65	277	1,490,000
	Daijiro Izumida	70	71	69	67	277	1,490,000
	Ryo Hisatsune	69	70	71	67	277	1,490,000
17	Ajeetesh Sandhu	70	69	69	70	278	1,180,000
18	Todd Sinnott	66	68	77	68	279	978,333
	Ryuichi Oiwa	72	69	70	68	279	978,333
	Gunn Charoenkul	72	66	72	69	279	978,333
	Ryo Noro	71	67	72	69	279	978,333
	Berry Henson	66	71	72	70	279	978,333
	Yuta Ikeda	67	72	70	70	279	978,333
24	Mikumu Horikawa	71	71	67	71	280	840,000
	Taichiro Ideriha (A)	70	73	71	66	280	
26	Ryo Ishikawa	70	67	73	71	281	770,000
	Yusaku Hosono	73	69	68	71	281	770,000
	Azuma Yano	71	71	70	69	281	770,000
	Yosuke Asaji	69	72	72	68	281	770,000
	Hiroki Abe	68	72	73	68	281	770,000
	Shingo Katayama	70	72	67	72	281	770,000

Golf Partner Pro-Am

Shugo Imahira emerged with a playoff victory on the East course at Toride Kokusai Golf Club that was a virtual shooting gallery. The 2018 leading money winner and the two players he defeated in overtime — Tomohiro Kondo and Tomoharu Otsuki — shot 22-under-par 258s. Two players, first-round leader Yuta Ikeda and Kondo shot 59s. Scores of 61-62-63 abounded. Even last-placed (61st) Kensei Hirata finished two strokes under Toride Kokusai's par 70.

When all of that par-slaughtering was over, Imahira, who won the Asia-Pacific the previous Sunday, exclaimed: "I'm so happy to win for two consecutive weeks. I really wanted to try to achieve it as I had never won back-to-back before in my career."

The 59 of Ikeda, 36, a former number one (2016) with 21 wins on his record, set the pace for the week in the first round, a new putter riding him to 11 birdies and a two-stroke lead. Australia's Brad Kennedy, 47, a three-time winner on the Japan Tour, moved two shots in front of Ikeda (67) and Otsuki (62-64) Friday scoring 61-63 for 16 under.

Imahira entered contention on Saturday with a 61, which tied him in second place with Kennedy (69) and Kazuki Higa (62), two strokes behind Otsuki (65) on 19 under. He matched front-nine 33s with Otsuki Sunday and racked up three birdies coming home for a 65 to tie Otsuki (69). Meanwhile, Kondo had been burning up the course. He birdied eight of the last 10 holes for the 59 that thrust him into the playoff.

Otsuki lost out with a bogey on the first extra hole and Imahira took the title, his seventh, with a birdie the second time playing the par-four 18th.

Toride Kokusai Golf Club (East), Ibaraki — May 19-22
Par 70 (35-35); 6,804 yards — Purse: ¥50,000,000

1	**Shugo Imahira**	65	67	61	65	258	¥10,000,000
2	**Tomohiro Kondo**	66	67	66	59	258	4,200,000
	Tomoharu Otsuki	62	64	65	67	258	4,200,000
	Imahira won playoff at second extra hole						
4	Brad Kennedy	61	63	69	66	259	2,200,000
	Kazuki Higa	65	66	62	66	259	2,200,000
6	Kaito Onishi	67	65	64	64	260	1,800,000
7	Yuta Ikeda	59	67	72	63	261	1,650,000
8	Taisei Shimizu	65	67	64	66	262	1,467,500
	Gunn Charoenkul	65	65	65	67	262	1,467,500
10	Shotaro Wada	66	68	64	65	263	1,210,000
	Mitsumasa Tamura	68	68	61	66	263	1,210,000
	Scott Vincent	65	64	66	68	263	1,210,000
13	Akio Sadakata	64	67	70	63	264	926,666
	Daisuke Yasumoto	65	68	66	65	264	926,666
	Sho Nagasawa	67	62	66	69	264	926,666
16	Anthony Quayle	66	68	67	64	265	737,500
	Yuto Katsuragawa	68	66	64	67	265	737,500
	Jbe' Kruger	67	67	64	67	265	737,500
	Koumei Oda	65	65	67	68	265	737,500
20	Kodai Ichihara	66	65	67	68	266	610,000
	Taihei Sato	69	66	67	64	266	610,000
22	Younghan Song	64	70	66	67	267	447,500
	Tomohiro Ishizaka	69	66	66	66	267	447,500
	Justin De Los Santos	66	67	66	68	267	447,500
	Tomoyasu Sugiyama	67	68	66	66	267	447,500
	Naoki Sekito	66	67	66	68	267	447,500
	Brendan Jones	70	63	69	65	267	447,500
	Konosuke Nakazato	65	65	67	70	267	447,500
	Shintaro Kobayashi	68	67	68	64	267	447,500
30	Ryuko Tokimatsu	67	69	64	68	268	310,833
	Mikiya Akutsu	67	66	68	67	268	310,833
	Taichi Nabetani	66	68	67	67	268	310,833
	Yushi Ito	68	66	65	69	268	310,833
	Takashi Ogiso	63	70	67	68	268	310,833
	Yosuke Tsukada	68	65	69	66	268	310,833

Gateway to The Open Mizuno Open

The home country players on the Japan Tour took a back seat to a quintet of internationals — two from Australia and the other three from Zimbabwe, Thailand and the Philippines — who took the top-five places at the finish of the Gateway to The Open Mizuno Open at the end of May.

The Zimbabwean, Scott Vincent, led the way, coming from seven strokes off the pace the last day to overtake Australian Anthony Quayle and defeating him in the subsequent two-hole playoff at JFE Setonaikai Golf Club just days after his 30th birthday and a month after Kelsey, his wife and caddie, gave birth to their first child. "I had no idea where I was standing when I walked up to the 18th," recalled Vincent, who won twice in 2021 with Kelsey on the bag. "To make the playoff and then win it, that was pretty amazing and unbelievable."

He had started the final round at five under par, tied for 11th place and seven behind Quayle. The 27-year-old Aussie pro, seeking his first win in Japan after coming close in the 2019 Casio World Open, had taken a four-stroke lead with a third-round 69 in demanding conditions, breaking from a Friday tie with Ryuichi Oiwa after Todd Baek opened the tournament a shot ahead of Quayle with a two-eagle 64, the week's low round.

Vincent played a flawless round Sunday with an eagle and five birdies for 65, then waited as Quayle struggled to a 72, a third bogey at the 17th hole bringing about the tie and playoff at 12-under 276. They both parred the par-five 18th to begin the playoff and Vincent won when Qualyle drove into a pond and bogeyed the hole the second time around.

Besides Vincent and Quayle, Australian Brad Kennedy and American-born Filipino Justin De Los Santos, who finished third and fourth, earned invitations to The Open later in the season at famed St Andrews. Thailand's Thanyakon Khrongpha finished fifth, completing the overseas sweep of the first five spots.

JFE Setonaikai Golf Club, Okayama — May 26-29
Par 72 (36-36); 7,461 yards — Purse: ¥80,000,000

1	**Scott Vincent**	69	72	70	65	276	¥16,000,000
2	**Anthony Quayle**	65	70	69	72	276	8,000,000
	Vincent won playoff at second extra hole						
3	**Brad Kennedy**	67	70	71	70	278	5,440,000
4	Justin De Los Santos	71	69	71	68	279	3,840,000
5	Thanyakon Khrongpha	73	68	70	69	280	3,200,000
6	Taisei Shimizu	68	72	70	71	281	2,554,000
	Michael Hendry	70	69	71	71	281	2,554,000
	Shingo Katayama	67	71	70	73	281	2,554,000
	Shintaro Kobayashi	67	73	68	73	281	2,554,000
10	Kaito Onishi	71	71	73	67	282	1,453,090
	Koumei Oda	67	74	73	68	282	1,453,090
	Han Lee	68	73	74	67	282	1,453,090
	Yoshitaka Takeya	71	72	70	69	282	1,453,090
	Aguri Iwasaki	70	70	72	70	282	1,453,090
	Takumi Murakami	66	73	73	70	282	1,453,090
	Takanori Konishi	72	65	74	71	282	1,453,090
	Hideto Tanihara	69	70	72	71	282	1,453,090
	Tomoyo Ikemura	67	72	72	71	282	1,453,090
	Jbe' Kruger	69	72	70	71	282	1,453,090
	Ryuichi Oiwa	70	65	73	74	282	1,453,090
21	Tatsuya Kodai	70	71	71	71	283	822,400
	Takahiro Hataji	70	69	72	72	283	822,400
	Ryo Ishikawa	66	72	72	73	283	822,400
	Ryo Hisatsune	71	68	71	73	283	822,400
	Todd Baek	64	75	70	74	283	822,400
26	Kazuki Higa	68	70	76	70	284	656,000
	Daijiro Izumida	68	74	72	70	284	656,000
	Ryutaro Nagano	69	69	73	73	284	656,000
29	Taichi Kimura	69	69	75	72	285	560,000
	Jay Choi	70	67	75	73	285	560,000
	Kazuki Yasumori	69	72	72	72	285	560,000

BMW Japan Tour Championship

When Kazuki Higa, a small man with big ambitions, won the Kansai Open in April, he proclaimed that: "I would like to win two or three more from here". Higa took a big step in that direction in early June when he won the BMW Japan Tour Championship, the year's first major. Besides becoming the second double winner of the 2022 season and earning invitations to The 150th Open, the BMW International Open on the DP World Tour and the big Zozo Championship later in the season, he moved into first place on the money list with the ¥30 million prize.

Higa's fourth career victory was decided on the 72nd hole of Shishido Hills Country Club's West course as he came from three strokes back on the final day in a tournament he never led until he won it. The 27-year-old was six strokes behind Aguri Iwasaki (70-64) and Taichi Kimura (67-67) with his 69-71 after 36 holes, then cut the gap in half Saturday as both he and Rikuya Hoshino fired six-under-par 65s, Hoshino taking a two-stroke lead over Iwasaki.

Higa made his first of two eagles on the second hole Sunday to move into serious contention, but, despite the second eagle at the 15th, he was still two behind hot-playing veteran Tomoharu Otsuki, who was then eight under par for the day. But Otsuki double-bogeyed the 17th hole, setting up the drama at the 18th hole. Higa had a 15-footer for the winning birdie and said: "I was really feeling very nervous when I lined up for my putt on the last hole, but I told myself to calm down." That birdie and his 67 for 12-under 272 gave him the win by a shot over Otsuki (par for 65) and two over Iwasaki (bogey for 70). "I'm really happy as one of my goals this year was to win the JGTO's flagship event," summed up the winner.

Shishido Hills Country Club (West), Ibaraki — June 2-5
Par 71 (36-35); 7,387 yards — Purse: ¥150,000,000

1	**Kazuki Higa**	69	71	65	67	272	¥30,000,000
2	**Tomoharu Otsuki**	71	70	67	65	273	15,000,000
3	**Aguri Iwasaki**	70	64	70	70	274	10,200,000
4	Anthony Quayle	70	66	70	69	275	7,200,000
5	Todd Baek	70	70	69	67	276	6,000,000
6	Eunshin Park	67	73	68	69	277	5,400,000
7	Kensei Hirata	66	70	70	72	278	4,762,500
	Rikuya Hoshino	68	69	65	76	278	4,762,500
9	Ryo Hisatsune	71	70	72	66	279	4,080,000
	Brad Kennedy	69	70	70	70	279	4,080,000
11	Daijiro Izumida	68	72	71	69	280	2,683,333
	Takumi Kanaya	73	67	71	69	280	2,683,333
	Yoshikazu Haku	73	69	69	69	280	2,683,333
	Tomohiro Kondo	72	69	70	69	280	2,683,333
	Yuki Inamori	69	67	73	71	280	2,683,333
	Akio Sadakata	70	67	72	71	280	2,683,333
	Takahiro Hataji	69	69	70	72	280	2,683,333
	Keita Nakajima (A)	72	70	66	72	280	
	Shugo Imahira	70	70	68	72	280	2,683,333
	Yusuke Sakamoto	67	72	68	73	280	2,683,333
21	Brendan Jones	76	67	70	68	281	1,650,000
	Tomoyo Ikemura	72	68	73	68	281	1,650,000
	Ryosuke Kinoshita	70	68	72	71	281	1,650,000
	Mitsumasa Tamura	71	70	69	71	281	1,650,000
	Taichi Kimura	67	67	72	75	281	1,650,000
26	Hiroki Abe	73	70	70	69	282	1,320,000

	Eric Sugimoto	69	71	72	70	282	1,320,000	Ryo Ishikawa	71	72	71	69	283	1,056,428
28	Ryuichi Oiwa	69	75	72	67	283	1,056,428	Yuki Shino	71	72	70	70	283	1,056,428
	Tomoyasu Sugiyama	77	67	71	68	283	1,056,428	Jay Choi	65	75	74	69	283	1,056,428
	Mikumu Horikawa	71	72	72	68	283	1,056,428	Koumei Oda	71	68	69	75	283	1,056,428

Aso Iizuka Challenge

It was quite a contrast. Tomoyo Ikemura came from five strokes back the last day when he won his first title in 2021 at the ISPS Handa Gatsu-n To tobase Tour event. He never trailed on his way to his second win less than a year later in the Aso Iizuka Challenge. Still he had to survive a shaky finish at the Aso Iizuka Golf Club in a new addition to the tour schedule.

That tight squeeze was set up by his earlier exploits. He and veteran Yusaku Miyazato, the 2017 money leader, shared the opening-round lead on nine-under-par 63 before the 26-year-old Ikemura took sole possession of first place the second day with a 68 for 13 under, a shot in front of Taiga Nagano (68-64) and 47-year-old Australian Brad Kennedy (66-66).

Ikemura widened the gap to three over Ryuko Tokimatsu on a rain-delayed Saturday with a 66 to move to 19 under. He maintained control over the first 12 holes on Sunday, working up an eagle and four birdies against a single bogey. Two bogeys on the next four holes gave his closest pursuers hope, but he finished birdie-par for 68 and 23-under-par 265 to edge Kennedy (65) and 19-year-old Ryo Hisatsune by a stroke, Hisatsune coming out of nowhere with a 61 that included two eagles and seven birdies. It was the fourth straight top-10 finish for Kennedy, a three-time winner in Japan.

Relishing the celebration with his fiancée/caddie by his side, Ikemura termed the victory "especially special as I had to manage the pressure I was facing on the last few holes. It feels so good."

Aso Iizuka Golf Club, Fukuoka — June 9-12
Par 72 (36-36); 6,809 yards — Purse: ¥100,000,000

1	**Tomoyo Ikemura**	63	68	66	68	265	¥20,000,000		Taichi Nabetani	68	69	69	66	272	1,720,000
2	**Ryo Hisatsune**	69	67	69	61	266	8,400,000	17	Mikiya Akutsu	68	68	70	67	273	1,426,666
	Brad Kennedy	66	66	69	65	266	8,400,000		Hyunwoo Ryu	66	70	69	68	273	1,426,666
4	Yusaku Miyazato	63	70	70	64	267	4,400,000		Katsumasa Miyamoto	68	71	65	69	273	1,426,666
	Ryuko Tokimatsu	66	67	67	67	267	4,400,000	20	Takumi Kanaya	71	67	68	68	274	1,220,000
6	Jbe' Kruger	69	66	70	63	268	3,316,666		Juvic Pagunsan	69	69	67	69	274	1,220,000
	Taiga Nagano	68	64	69	67	268	3,316,666	22	Shintaro Kobayashi	70	67	71	67	275	873,333
	Kaito Onishi	69	65	67	67	268	3,316,666		Aguri Iwasaki	71	69	67	68	275	873,333
9	Yuto Katsuragawa	71	68	66	64	269	2,820,000		Tatsuya Kodai	68	71	69	67	275	873,333
10	Tomoharu Otsuki	65	71	69	65	270	2,520,000		Takahiro Hataji	68	69	70	68	275	873,333
	Tomohiro Ishizaka	70	68	66	66	270	2,520,000		Todd Baek	69	68	70	68	275	873,333
12	Shugo Imahira	70	68	69	64	271	2,120,000		Hiroshi Iwata	69	69	72	65	275	873,333
	Toshinori Muto	69	67	66	69	271	2,120,000		Kazuki Higa	67	72	72	64	275	873,333
14	Hirotaro Naito	70	65	73	64	272	1,720,000		Younghan Song	70	68	68	69	275	873,333
	Ryutaro Nagano	72	68	67	65	272	1,720,000		Mikumu Horikawa	69	69	68	69	275	873,333

Japan Players Championship

Yuki Inamori doesn't win often on the Japan Tour, but when he does he seems to specialise in acquiring major titles. As the circuit staged its last tournament before entering a five-week summer hiatus, Inamori added the Japan Players Championship to the Japan Opens of 2018 and 2020 on his career record. His only other win came earlier in the 2022 season in the The Crowns in April. He became the third double winner of the year, joining Kazuki Higa and Shugo Imahira, the two-time season number one.

The 27-year-old Inamori needed a birdie-birdie finish to nail the Players title at Nishi Nasuno Country Club and nose out Kaito Onishi, the runner-up for a second time in 2022, who finished second in the Asia Pacific in May after leading for three rounds.

Disappointment, too, came to 49-year-old Katsumasa Miyamoto, who had assumed a one-stroke lead Saturday, shooting a six-under-par 66 for 17 under par as he sought his 13th career victory and first in three years. He had moved ahead of unheralded Taihei Sato, who led for two days with his 64-67 postings. With 69, Sato slipped a stroke behind at 16 under, joined there by Inamori, who sported rounds of 68-66-66.

Inamori roared in front early in the final round with four birdies on the first seven holes. He commanded the lead until Onishi rattled off four birdies in a row (13 through 16) and edged a shot in front. Onishi parred in for a 65 and watched as Inamori scored his seventh and eighth birdies of the day on those last two holes for his own 65 and 23-under-par 265. Two back-nine bogeys and 68 knocked Miyamoto back into a third-place tie with 21-tournament winner Yuta Ikeda and young Yuto Katsuragawa, who strengthened his hold on second place on the season money list. Ikeda, the 2016 money king, shot 63 and Katsuragawa 64.

"It's a great end to the first half of the season. I'm so relieved. I had a chance to win it outright at the final hole and I didn't want to miss that," said Inamori, who then headed for America and was one of four Japanese players to compete in the following week's tournament in Oregon on the rebel LIV Golf Series.

Nishi Nasuno Country Club, Tochigi — June 23-26
Par 72 (36-36); 7,036 yards — Purse: ¥50,000,000

1	**Yuki Inamori**	68	66	66	65	265	¥10,000,000
2	**Kaito Onishi**	67	71	63	65	266	5,000,000
3	**Yuta Ikeda**	69	67	68	63	267	2,600,000
	Yuto Katsuragawa	66	69	68	64	267	2,600,000
	Katsumasa Miyamoto	65	68	66	68	267	2,600,000
6	Kodai Ichihara	72	66	66	65	269	1,800,000
7	Takanori Konishi	71	69	67	63	270	1,650,000
8	Taihei Sato	64	67	69	71	271	1,525,000
9	Mikiya Akutsu	69	71	68	64	272	1,410,000
10	Mao Ishizaki	67	71	70	65	273	1,210,000
	Taisei Shimizu	68	71	67	67	273	1,210,000
	Ren Kurosaki	66	68	69	70	273	1,210,000
13	Aguri Iwasaki	70	67	71	66	274	772,222
	Yuto Katsumata	67	69	72	66	274	772,222
	Taichi Nabetani	70	70	68	66	274	772,222
	Mitsumasa Tamura	69	71	66	68	274	772,222
	Nobuaki Oda	67	67	71	69	274	772,222
	Rikuya Hoshino	73	65	67	69	274	772,222
	Yuta Uetake	73	65	67	69	274	772,222
	Tomohiro Ishizaka	68	69	67	70	274	772,222
	Ryo Hisatsune	69	66	68	71	274	772,222
22	Tomoharu Otsuki	71	67	72	65	275	510,000
	Ryutaro Nagano	73	67	70	65	275	510,000
	Shintaro Kobayashi	67	68	69	71	275	510,000
25	Tatsuya Kodai	70	70	68	68	276	420,000
	Eric Sugimoto	72	66	70	68	276	420,000
	Shunya Takeyasu	70	67	68	71	276	420,000
	Daiki Imano	69	66	69	72	276	420,000
29	Sho Nagasawa	67	71	71	68	277	341,250
	Taichi Kimura	68	70	70	69	277	341,250
	Justin De Los Santos	71	66	69	71	277	341,250
	Kensei Hirata	71	68	66	72	277	341,250

Japan PGA Championship

Like Yuki Inamori in the previous tournament, Mikumu Horikawa's wins have been few and far between, but when he does win, he bags the big ones. On the circuit since 2015, Horikawa had several near misses in his early seasons before breaking the ice with victory in the major Japan Tour Championship in 2019 and winning the rich Casio World Open in 2020. His third win came the first week of August in another major, the Japan PGA Championship, as the schedule resumed after the mid-summer break.

The 29-year-old carried an unusual season record into the PGA Championship at Grand Fields Country Club in Shizuoka Prefecture. Before missing the cut in the Players Championship, he had finished between 22nd and 32nd in each of his eight prior starts. He made another such showing unlikely when he opened the PGA with a five-under-par 66 in a four-way tie for second, a stroke behind leader Taiki Yoshida. Another four-player deadlock followed Friday. Horikawa and Daijiro Izumida shot 69s and were joined at the top on seven under by Daisuke Yasumoto (66) and Terumichi Kakazu (67) before Horikawa took command Saturday with 64 for 14 under par. He racked up eight birdies, four on the last six holes, against a lone bogey, taking a three-stroke lead over Kakazu (67) and at least five over the rest of the field.

He finished off the victory with a run-of-the-mill 70 Sunday, matching four birdies against a bogey and a double bogey, the 15-under 269 three better than the seven-birdie 65 posted by runner-up Naoyuki Kataoka. "I was not feeling nervous," Horikawa remarked. "I just want to win every tournament where I tee up. So, I'm glad I managed to do it again today."

Grand Fields Country Club, Shizuoka — August 4-7
Par 71 (36-35); 7,219 yards — Purse: ¥150,000,000

1	**Mikumu Horikawa**	66	69	64	70	269	¥30,000,000
2	**Naoyuki Kataoka**	68	72	67	65	272	15,000,000
3	**Taiki Yoshida**	65	71	68	69	273	10,200,000
4	Yuki Usami	70	72	65	68	275	6,200,000
	Tomoyo Ikemura	66	74	64	71	275	6,200,000
	Terumichi Kakazu	68	67	67	73	275	6,200,000
7	Kaito Onishi	71	66	71	69	277	4,421,250
	Ryo Hisatsune	67	70	71	69	277	4,421,250
	Ryosuke Kinoshita	68	72	68	69	277	4,421,250
	Scott Vincent	70	70	68	69	277	4,421,250
11	Yuki Inamori	69	71	73	65	278	3,630,000
12	Yosuke Asaji	72	69	69	69	279	3,330,000
13	Ryo Katsumata	71	72	71	66	280	2,455,714
	Yusuke Sakamoto	71	72	70	67	280	2,455,714
	Taisei Yamada	70	69	70	71	280	2,455,714
	Koichi Kitamura	68	74	67	71	280	2,455,714
	Hiroki Tanaka	68	72	69	71	280	2,455,714
	Daijiro Izumida	66	69	72	73	280	2,455,714
	Daisuke Yasumoto	69	66	69	76	280	2,455,714
20	Rikuya Hoshino	68	75	71	67	281	1,600,000
	Tomohiro Ishizaka	71	71	71	68	281	1,600,000
	Ryo Ishikawa	67	72	71	71	281	1,600,000
	Kenshiro Ikegami	70	70	70	71	281	1,600,000
	Taichi Teshima	70	71	68	72	281	1,600,000
	Juvic Pagunsan	66	72	70	73	281	1,600,000
26	Shintaro Kobayashi	71	72	74	65	282	1,140,000
	Yuta Kinoshita	70	68	75	69	282	1,140,000
	Ryuko Tokimatsu	67	75	70	70	282	1,140,000
	Kazuki Higa	67	74	71	70	282	1,140,000
	Hiroshi Iwata	71	72	67	72	282	1,140,000
	Hiroyuki Fujita	70	69	69	74	282	1,140,000

Shigeo Nagashima Invitational Sega Sammy Cup

Hiroshi Iwata, at 41, is old school, so he resisted a present-day celebration when he landed the Shigeo Nagashima Invitational Sega Sammy Cup after holding off the all-day challenge of Tomoharu Otsuki, another Japan Tour veteran, to win the tournament for a second time. "I wanted to do a flashy fist pose," he admitted. "But I couldn't do it."

Iwata matched birdies with Otsuki, 32, on the par-five final hole for a two-stroke win, closing with a five-under-par 67 and a 269 total. "It's been seven years since I last won here," he noted after scoring his fourth tour victory after near-misses earlier in the season at the Crowns and Asia Pacific Diamond Cup. "The first one was a come-from-behind victory, so I'm happy I started in the lead this time and won."

For the first two days at The North Country Club in Hokkaido, though, Takumi Kanaya, the 24-year-old former world number one amateur with three tour victories to his credit, had the upper hand. A hole-in-one at the 16th hole led him to a leading 66 the first day and his 69 on Friday gave him a one-stroke lead over Iwata, who started with a pair of 68s.

Iwata birdied three of the last four holes on a rain-swept Saturday for 66 and edged a shot in front of Kanaya (68) and four ahead of Otsuki and Kaito Onishi. He never trailed on a pleasant Sunday as things developed into a duel between Iwata and Otsuki on the front nine, Kanaya slipping back with 35 as Iwata went out in 32 and Otsuki 30. The eventual outcome became likely when Otsuki double-bogeyed the 14th hole, giving Iwata a three-stroke lead.

It was another disappointment for Otsuki, who lost in a playoff and by a stroke in two events earlier in the season as he sought a second win in his 14 years on tour to go with his Kansai Open victory in 2019. Kanaya shot 69, finishing third.

The North Country Golf Club, Hokkaido — August 18-21
Par 72 (36-36); 7,178 yards — Purse: ¥120,000,000

1	**Hiroshi Iwata**	68	68	66	67	269	¥24,000,000
2	**Tomoharu Otsuki**	70	68	68	65	271	12,000,000
3	**Takumi Kanaya**	66	69	68	69	272	8,160,000
4	Ryuko Tokimatsu	70	70	72	65	277	4,710,000
	Ryutaro Nagano	72	71	69	65	277	4,710,000
	Ryo Ishikawa	71	68	70	68	277	4,710,000
	Junya Kameshiro	71	70	67	69	277	4,710,000
8	Shunya Takeyasu	71	68	72	67	278	3,522,000

	Aguri Iwasaki	71	68	70	69	278	3,522,000
10	Mikumu Horikawa	70	73	70	66	279	2,784,000
	Tomohiro Kondo	72	66	73	68	279	2,784,000
	Mitsumasa Tamura	71	72	68	68	279	2,784,000
	Takahiro Hataji	72	70	69	68	279	2,784,000
14	Jinichiro Kozuma	72	69	72	67	280	1,944,000
	Taihei Sato	68	69	75	68	280	1,944,000
	Tomoyasu Sugiyama	72	71	70	67	280	1,944,000
	Mikiya Akutsu	70	69	72	69	280	1,944,000
	Brad Kennedy	69	70	71	70	280	1,944,000
19	Shugo Imahira	68	73	72	68	281	1,512,000
	Yoshitaka Takeya	70	67	73	71	281	1,512,000
	Rikuya Hoshino	70	71	67	73	281	1,512,000
22	Daijiro Izumida	68	75	70	69	282	1,188,000
	Naoyuki Kataoka	72	70	71	69	282	1,188,000
	Taisei Shimizu	67	72	70	73	282	1,188,000
	Kaito Onishi	71	67	68	76	282	1,188,000
26	Taichi Nabetani	71	69	74	69	283	912,000
	Yosuke Tsukada	71	71	70	71	283	912,000
	Takanori Konishi	69	69	72	73	283	912,000
	Shintaro Kobayashi	71	67	72	73	283	912,000
	Dongkyu Jang	71	67	71	74	283	912,000
	Takumi Murakami	72	68	70	73	283	912,000

Sansan KBC Augusta

It had been a struggle in his rookie year for 22-year-old Riki Kawamoto. Although he had failed to win a card at the qualifying tournament for the 2022 Japan Tour, he got into and played decently in the first three events in the spring. After that, though, he made the field in only three of the next nine tournaments and missed the cut every time.

Next up was the Sansan KBC Augusta, Kawamoto was invited to play and, lo and behold, he came through with a last-minute victory, becoming the youngest winner in the long history of the tournament, supplanting Yuta Ikeda, who was 23 when he won in 2009. "It was my first time playing in the last group on the final day and I didn't know it would be such a tough battle," observed the ebullient Kawamoto as he dedicated the win to his LPGA pro sister, Yui, who won the AXA Ladies tournament in 2019, on the day before her 24th birthday. "I think this is a good present for her."

Kawamoto achieved the victory when he birdied the final hole for a 70, and a 16-under-par total of 272, to win by a shot at the expense of Korea's Sanghee Lee, who led or shared the lead the previous two days at Keya Golf Club in his bid for his first win since joining the tour in 2013. He, Kawamoto, Taiga Nagano and Zimbabwe's Scott Vincent were tied atop the standings at 133 after 36 holes.

Lee, who missed the last two seasons due to the Covid pandemic and mandatory national service in his country, where he won four times earlier on the Korean Tour, inched a stroke in front of Kawamoto Saturday with a six-birdie, two-bogey 68 to Kawamoto's five-birdie, two-bogey 69. Neither player started auspiciously on Sunday, both bogeying the fourth and fifth holes, before Kawamoto went four strokes ahead with birdies on four of the next seven holes. Lee fought back with four back-nine birdies that brought him into a tie when Kawamoto bogeyed the 16th hole. Kawamoto holed the deciding putt on the 18th green to become just the tour's second first-time winner in 2022.

Keya Golf Club, Itoshima, Fukuoka — August 25-28
Par 72 (36-36); 7,191 yards — Purse: ¥100,000,000

1	**Riki Kawamoto**	66	67	69	70	272	¥20,000,000
2	**Sanghee Lee**	68	65	68	72	273	10,000,000
3	**Taisei Shimizu**	65	72	69	69	275	6,800,000
4	Hyunwoo Ryu	67	73	67	69	276	4,133,333
	Takanori Konishi	67	70	68	71	276	4,133,333
	Tomoyo Ikemura	67	68	68	73	276	4,133,333
7	Naoyuki Kataoka	67	71	70	69	277	3,175,000
	Taichi Nabetani	70	67	66	74	277	3,175,000
9	Ryo Hisatsune	72	65	70	71	278	2,620,000
	Kazuki Higa	68	68	69	73	278	2,620,000
	Shugo Imahira	68	68	68	74	278	2,620,000
12	Nobuaki Oda	68	70	71	70	279	1,945,000
	Daijiro Izumida	69	72	70	68	279	1,945,000
	Mikiya Akutsu	70	69	69	71	279	1,945,000
	Scott Vincent	67	66	70	76	279	1,945,000
16	Ryo Ishikawa	70	69	71	70	280	1,432,000
	Taiko Nishiyama	68	71	69	72	280	1,432,000
	Ryosuke Kinoshita	69	68	70	73	280	1,432,000
	Ryuko Tokimatsu	67	73	67	73	280	1,432,000
	Yuki Inamori	67	69	69	75	280	1,432,000
21	Tomohiro Umeyama	69	69	71	72	281	974,285
	Mitsumasa Tamura	69	72	69	71	281	974,285
	Yusaku Miyazato	68	70	71	72	281	974,285
	Brad Kennedy	68	66	74	73	281	974,285
	Kensei Hirata	70	69	69	73	281	974,285
	Yuki Furukawa	66	73	69	73	281	974,285
	Kaito Onishi	68	72	67	74	281	974,285
28	Kodai Ichihara	67	72	70	73	282	740,000
	Tadahiro Takayama	67	71	69	75	282	740,000
	Jbe' Kruger	67	71	67	77	282	740,000

Fujisankei Classic

Confident that success would come quickly, Kaito Onishi filed an entry for the Qualifying School of Europe's DP World Tour before he even had a victory to his credit on the Japan Tour. The 23-year-old, who honed his skills in college golf in America at the University of Southern California and benefited from the guidance of Japanese star Shigeki Maruyama during that time, justified the bold move when he pulled out a playoff victory in the Fujisankei Classic in early September. "I'm going to the PGA Tour and I want to be number one in the world," enthused Onishi, who has been playing golf since he was five years old and went to the United States when he was just nine.

He had good reason to come to Fujizakura Country Club in Yamanashi Prefecture with that confidence, having piled up a pair of runner-up finishes and seven top-10s in the 12 starts of his second season on the Japan Tour. He stayed within easy reach of the lead for three days with rounds of 67-70-68, sitting in a tie for third place Saturday, three behind leader Sanghyun Park, the 39-year-old veteran who won the Fujisankei the only previous time he entered it in 2019.

Seeking his third win in Japan, Park maintained the lead all day Sunday. Playing ahead of him, Onishi ran off his second string of three birdies on holes 14-16, but when he bogeyed the 18th, his 68 leaving him a stroke behind Park, he lamented: "I'm second again this week." However, the Korean also bogeyed the last hole minutes later for 71, dropping into a tie with Onishi at 11-under-par 273. Hiroshi Iwata, the 2014 Fuji champion, missed the playoff by a stroke after a 70.

Onishi settled things quickly, holing a birdie putt on the first playoff hole, to become the third first-time winner of 2022 a week after 22-year-old Riki Kawamoto nailed his initial title in the KBC Augusta. The ¥22 million first prize lifted Onishi into third place on the money list, only ¥6 million behind number one Kazuki Higa.

Fujizakura Country Club, Yamanashi — September 1-4
Par 71 (35-36); 7,541 yards — Purse: ¥110,000,000

1	**Kaito Onishi**	67	70	68	68	273	¥22,000,000
2	**Sanghyun Park**	68	67	67	71	273	11,000,000
	Onishi won playoff at first extra hole						
3	**Hiroshi Iwata**	68	69	67	70	274	7,480,000
4	Mikumu Horikawa	65	76	68	66	275	5,280,000
5	Ryo Ishikawa	72	68	69	67	276	3,996,666
	Aguri Iwasaki	65	69	72	70	276	3,996,666
	Ryosuke Kinoshita	68	70	67	71	276	3,996,666
8	Hideto Tanihara	68	72	72	65	277	3,228,500
	Takumi Kanaya	72	70	67	68	277	3,228,500
10	Gunn Charoenkul	67	75	70	66	278	2,662,000
	Kodai Ichihara	67	73	68	70	278	2,662,000
	Taihei Sato	68	71	68	71	278	2,662,000
13	Shugo Imahira	69	71	71	68	279	2,222,000
14	Kensei Hirata	74	69	69	68	280	1,947,000
	Yuta Uetake	68	71	72	69	280	1,947,000
16	Tomoyo Ikemura	68	75	70	68	281	1,622,500
	Shingo Katayama	70	71	72	68	281	1,622,500
	Tomohiro Ishizaka	66	73	75	67	281	1,622,500
	Daijiro Izumida	71	70	71	69	281	1,622,500
20	Jbe' Kruger	69	72	72	69	282	1,140,857
	Yusuke Sakamoto	68	75	69	70	282	1,140,857
	Yuto Katsuragawa	69	73	70	70	282	1,140,857
	Ryuko Tokimatsu	71	70	71	70	282	1,140,857
	Genki Okada	69	69	72	72	282	1,140,857
	Koumei Oda	68	71	70	73	282	1,140,857
	Fumihiro Ebine	67	71	70	74	282	1,140,857
27	Nobuaki Oda	69	74	71	69	283	858,000
	Dongkyu Jang	70	73	69	71	283	858,000
	Rikuya Hoshino	67	75	68	73	283	858,000
30	Sejung Hiramoto	66	73	74	71	284	658,625
	Shunya Takeyasu	71	71	71	71	284	658,625
	Adam Bland	70	74	70	70	284	658,625
	Konosuke Nakazato	73	70	69	72	284	658,625
	Junya Kameshiro	69	76	69	70	284	658,625
	Tomoharu Otsuki	69	73	70	72	284	658,625
	Todd Baek	66	76	70	72	284	658,625
	Naoyuki Kataoka	64	75	71	74	284	658,625

Shinhan Donghae Open

Back in April when he won the Kansai Open, Kazuki Higa remarked: "I would like to win two or three more from here." Make that mission partially accomplished. In June Higa won the Tour Championship and in early September he added the Shinhan Donghae Open, normally an important tournament on the Korean Tour that is tri-sanctioned by the Asian, Korean and Japan Tours. It was played in Japan for the first time at Koma Country Club, outside Osaka.

"As long as it is held in Japan, I want to win as a Japan Golf Tour player," said Higa, who birdied the final two holes to defeat Thailand's Tirawat Kaewsiribandit, the second- and third-round leader, Korea's Mingyu Cho and Canada's Yonggu Shin. He closed with a 65, winning by two strokes on 20-under 264, becoming the season's first three-time victor.

As for his aspirations to win the money list, Higa went on: "Being the prize king is one of my dreams." He was well on the way. The ¥23 million-plus he won at Koma opened his number one lead to nearly ¥30 million.

After Canadian Richard T Lee shot a course-record 62 the first day, Kaewsiribandit took charge with a 64 Friday and 66 Saturday. He surged three strokes ahead of Korea's Si Woo Kim, a triple winner on the US PGA Tour and member of the International team in the upcoming Presidents Cup in America. At that point, Higa was five shots off the pace, following an eight-birdie 63 Friday with a one-under-par 70 Saturday.

Kaewsiribandit was all over the place Sunday, his wild card showing two birdies, four bogeys, a double bogey and an albatross two on the par-five third hole, it all amounting to a 72. Cho shot 66 and Shin 68 for their matching 266s. Meanwhile, Higa got off to a fast start with birdies on the first three holes and the sixth, then bounced back from his lone bogey at the 10th with another birdie before closing with the final pair, holing a 15-footer on the 18th green to establish the final two-stroke margin. Kim, too, had a zany round, finishing double bogey-bogey-par-birdie-eagle for 70 and a share of fifth place.

Koma Country Club, Nara — September 8-11
Par 71 (35-36); 7,065 yards — Purse: ¥132,580,000

1	**Kazuki Higa**	66	63	70	65	264	¥23,864,400
2	**Mingyu Cho**	68	65	67	66	266	9,855,113
	Tirawat Kaewsiribandit	64	64	66	72	266	9,855,113
	Yonggu Shin	68	64	66	68	266	9,855,113
5	Jbe' Kruger	66	69	69	63	267	4,219,358
	Riki Kawamoto	66	65	71	65	267	4,219,358
	Taehoon Kim	69	67	65	66	267	4,219,358
	Si Woo Kim	65	65	67	70	267	4,219,358
9	Eunshin Park	69	68	67	64	268	2,373,182
	Tomoharu Otsuki	70	66	66	66	268	2,373,182
	Hideto Tanihara	66	69	67	66	268	2,373,182
	Sanghee Lee	66	66	66	70	268	2,373,182
	Ryosuke Kinoshita	68	65	66	69	268	2,373,182
14	Dongkyu Jang	67	68	68	66	269	1,725,749
	Ryuko Tokimatsu	69	68	66	66	269	1,725,749
	Danthai Boonma	68	68	67	66	269	1,725,749
	Yoseop Seo	69	68	65	67	269	1,725,749
	Yosuke Asaji	67	68	67	67	269	1,725,749
	Todd Baek	65	68	66	70	269	1,725,749
20	Toshinori Muto	67	68	69	66	270	1,365,574
	Hanbyeol Kim	67	67	69	67	270	1,365,574
	Seungsu Han	65	72	66	67	270	1,365,574
	Kyongjun Moon	68	69	68	65	270	1,365,574
	Rikuya Hoshino	71	65	67	67	270	1,365,574
	Tomohiro Kondo	66	67	68	69	270	1,365,574
	Bongsub Kim	68	68	65	69	270	1,365,574
27	Nicholas Fung	73	64	67	67	271	1,132,233
	Yuto Katsuragawa	67	69	68	67	271	1,132,233
	Juvic Pagunsan	65	69	69	68	271	1,132,233
	Yosuke Tsukada	68	69	66	68	271	1,132,233
	Yuki Inamori	70	62	68	71	271	1,132,233

ANA Open

Tomoharu Otsuki was in his 12th season on the Japan Tour and his record showed a lone victory in the 2019 Kansai Open as he teed it up in the ANA Open. Twice in the last year he had yielded third-round leads and twice he had lost in playoffs in the Golf Partner Pro-Am. He had finished second two other times in the current season. Furthermore, he had blown a three-stroke lead and finished second to Scott Vincent a year earlier in the 2021 ANA Open. No wonder he exclaimed: "Every week I've been worrying about it. Why can't I win?"

The answer proved to be: go into the final round five strokes off the lead, shoot 66 and win a playoff in sensational fashion by holing his approach shot.

Until Otsuki authored that exciting finish, the ANA Open seemed to be safely in the hands of Yuta Ikeda, the long-time Japan Tour star with 21 wins on his record but none since the 2019. The 36-year-old blistered Sapporo Golf Club's Wattsu course with an eight-birdie 64 start and repeated it with an eagle and six birdies Friday. Still, he only led by a shot over Shugo Imahira (65-64).

A 70 on Saturday was enough to move him three strokes ahead of Imahira (72) and five in front of Otsuki, who shot 68 after a 68-67 start. While Otsuki was running off a flawless, six-birdie 66 Sunday for 19-under-par 269, Ikeda stumbled to a 72, his fourth bogey on the back nine at the 18th hole depriving him of a playoff spot with Otsuki and the ever-popular Ryo Ishikawa, shooting for an 18th Japan Tour win, who climbed into a tie with Otsuki with an eight birdie 65. The subsequent playoff ended quickly when Otsuki's 131-yard pitch shot sucked back into the hole for an eagle deuce on the first extra hole.

Sapporo Golf Club (Wattsu), Hokkaido — September 15-18
Par 72 (36-36); 7,063 yards — Purse: ¥100,000,000

1	**Tomoharu Otsuki**	68	67	68	66	269	¥20,000,000
2	**Ryo Ishikawa**	66	70	68	65	269	10,000,000
	Otsuki won playoff at first extra hole						
3	**Yuta Ikeda**	64	64	70	72	270	6,800,000
4	Ryuko Tokimatsu	65	70	69	68	272	4,400,000
	Ryo Hisatsune	69	66	69	68	272	4,400,000
6	Taichi Kimura	67	69	70	67	273	3,450,000
	Justin De Los Santos	69	68	68	68	273	3,450,000
8	Adam Bland	70	68	70	66	274	2,727,500
	Dongkyu Jang	69	66	71	68	274	2,727,500
	Shunya Takeyasu	66	72	68	68	274	2,727,500
	Tomoyasu Sugiyama	65	70	69	70	274	2,727,500
12	Hideto Tanihara	70	69	70	66	275	1,880,000
	Tomoyo Ikemura	65	70	73	67	275	1,880,000
	Ryosuke Kinoshita	69	65	77	64	275	1,880,000
	Mikumu Horikawa	68	65	70	72	275	1,880,000
	Shugo Imahira	65	64	72	74	275	1,880,000
17	Yuki Inamori	70	69	70	67	276	1,426,666
	Naoyuki Kataoka	68	69	71	68	276	1,426,666
	Matthew Griffin	71	68	68	69	276	1,426,666
20	Mitsumasa Tamura	67	69	71	70	277	1,100,000
	Gunn Charoenkul	68	68	71	70	277	1,100,000
	Koumei Oda	66	72	69	70	277	1,100,000
	Kazuki Higa	67	71	68	71	277	1,100,000
	Tatsuya Kodai	68	68	69	72	277	1,100,000
25	Younghan Song	74	65	71	68	278	860,000
	Kaito Onishi	69	69	69	71	278	860,000
	Junya Kameshiro	64	69	72	73	278	860,000
28	Ryuichi Oiwa	67	72	74	66	279	760,000
	Anthony Quayle	69	72	71	67	279	760,000
30	Aguri Iwasaki	69	71	69	71	280	621,666
	Todd Baek	69	67	73	71	280	621,666
	Sanghee Lee	69	69	71	71	280	621,666
	Taihei Sato	66	74	70	70	280	621,666
	Rikuya Hoshino	70	67	75	68	280	621,666
	Kodai Ichihara	68	68	70	74	280	621,666

Panasonic Open

Victories by amateurs on professional golf tours are few and far between, which made Taiga Semikawa's brilliant win in the Panasonic Open exceptional in itself. It was even more so, since it came a year after Keita Nakajima, then the number one amateur in the world, won the same tournament. Like Nakajima, Semikawa was a 21-year-old college student when he ran off a string of five birdies on the back nine of Onotoyo Golf Club to land a one-stroke victory and become just the sixth amateur winner in Japan Tour history. Besides Nakajima, he joined a distinguished group — Ryo Ishikawa, Masahiro Kuramoto, Hideki Matsuyama and, in 2019, Takumi Kanaya. The win jumped Semikawa to second in the World Amateur Golf Rankings.

"I have never experienced anything like this before," Semikawa remarked. "I really never imagined that I could win a JGTO championship as a student," he added, although pointing out that "it was really frustrating to lose the Kansai Open in April". He finished third that week.

At Onotoyo, Semikawa was nowhere in sight the first two days as Yuto Katsuragawa and Shugo Imahira opened with 65s, and 50-year-old Katsumasa Miyamoto, owner of 12 tour titles, squeezed into a one-stroke lead over five other players the second day with his 67-66. Semikawa entered the fray in spectacular fashion Saturday, racking up an eagle and nine birdies. The 11-under-par 61 elevated him into a first-place tie with Miyamoto (67) and Tomoharu Otsuki (66), coming off his victory the previous Sunday in the ANA Open.

Semikawa started fast Sunday with two early birdies before wrapping things up with the five consecutive birdies starting at the 13th hole. With a two-shot cushion, he bogeyed the last hole for a 66, a 22-under-par total of 266 and the one-shot triumph over Aguri Iwasaki, who jumped into second place with a bogey-free 66. Miyamoto and Otsuki fell back, shooting 71 and 73 respectively, as Katsuragawa posted another strong showing, finishing third.

Onotoyo Golf Club, Ono, Hyogo
Par 72 (36-36); 7,113 yards

September 22-25
Purse: ¥100,000,000

1	**Taiga Semikawa** [(A)]	71	68	61	66	266	
2	**Aguri Iwasaki**	70	65	66	66	267	¥20,000,000
3	**Yuto Katsuragawa**	65	69	67	68	269	10,000,000
4	Ryo Hisatsune	71	66	65	68	270	6,800,000
5	Juvic Pagunsan	71	66	66	68	271	4,400,000
	Katsumasa Miyamoto	67	66	67	71	271	4,400,000
7	Yuki Inamori	67	67	68	70	272	3,316,666
	Brad Kennedy	69	68	65	70	272	3,316,666
	Koumei Oda	69	68	65	70	272	3,316,666
10	Jinichiro Kozuma	74	67	65	67	273	2,620,000
	Satoshi Kodaira	68	70	66	69	273	2,620,000
	Tomoharu Otsuki	68	66	66	73	273	2,620,000
13	Mitsumasa Tamura	67	70	71	66	274	2,020,000
	Tomoyo Ikemura	69	65	73	67	274	2,020,000
	Hyunwoo Ryu	69	68	69	68	274	2,020,000
16	Shugo Imahira	65	69	73	68	275	1,437,142
	Riki Kawamoto	73	66	69	67	275	1,437,142
	Kaito Onishi	69	68	70	68	275	1,437,142
	Shunya Takeyasu	68	70	69	68	275	1,437,142
	Michael Hendry	68	70	68	69	275	1,437,142
	Mikiya Akutsu	70	68	67	70	275	1,437,142
	Taihei Sato	70	70	65	70	275	1,437,142
23	Yusaku Miyazato	69	67	74	66	276	1,020,000
	Yuta Kinoshita	69	66	69	72	276	1,020,000
	Taisei Shimizu	72	65	67	72	276	1,020,000
26	Anthony Quayle	69	70	70	68	277	761,250
	Kensei Hirata	71	69	68	69	277	761,250
	Ryuichi Oiwa	68	67	72	70	277	761,250
	Hirotaro Naito	70	67	70	70	277	761,250
	Justin De Los Santos	69	70	68	70	277	761,250
	Shingo Katayama	73	68	65	71	277	761,250
	Rikuya Hoshino	70	69	67	71	277	761,250
	Andrew Evans	69	69	74	65	277	761,250

Vantelin Tokai Classic

Riki Kawamoto exhibited a pleasant form of greed after eking out his second win of the season in the Vantelin Tokai Classic. "Now that I have won twice, I want to ride on the confidence to bring in more victories. I didn't expect to get a second win so quickly," remarked the 22-year-old rookie, who joined Kazuki Higa, Shugo Imahira and Yuki Inamori as a 2022 multiple winner a month after bagging the Sansan KBC Augusta title. "I hope to end the season with three or four wins."

Kawamoto overcame the four-stroke lead Yuto Katsuragawa carried into the final round on Miyoshi Country Club's West course in Aichi Prefecture. Katsuragawa, who won the ISPS Handa Championship in April and sat in second place on the Japan Tour money list, had taken the lead Friday with a blazing, eight-under-par 63 after Genki Okada opened on top with 65. With his 11-under 131, he had a three-stroke lead over unheralded Okada and was five shots ahead of his later challengers Kawamoto and veteran Yuta Ikeda, who was looking for his 22nd tour win and first in more than three years.

Despite a double bogey, Katsuragawa played out a 67 Saturday, widening his lead to four over Kawamoto (66) and five on Ikeda (67). It was a different story on the front nine Sunday as Katsuragawa, with another double bogey, shot 38, falling back into a tie with Kawamoto, who put up a 34. In an erratic back nine, Kawamoto went eagle-bogey-bogey starting at the 15th to go to the final hole in a 12-under-par tie with Katsuragawa. Then he won when he holed a 13-foot birdie putt on the last green for a 69 and 13-under 271.

Miyoshi Country Club (West), Aichi
Par 71 (35-36); 7,300 yards

September 29-October 2
Purse: ¥110,000,000

1	**Riki Kawamoto**	69	67	66	69	271	¥22,000,000
2	**Yuto Katsuragawa**	68	63	67	74	272	11,000,000
3	**Kazuki Higa**	70	69	67	69	275	6,380,000
	Yuta Ikeda	70	66	67	72	275	6,380,000
5	Satoshi Kodaira	69	68	71	69	277	4,400,000
6	Ryutaro Nagano	68	72	70	68	278	3,648,333
	Yuki Inamori	68	68	73	69	278	3,648,333
	Ryuko Tokimatsu	68	69	69	72	278	3,648,333
9	Aguri Iwasaki	73	70	70	66	279	2,772,000
	Adam Bland	69	68	73	69	279	2,772,000
	Tomoharu Otsuki	68	70	71	70	279	2,772,000
	Yuta Kinoshita	67	73	69	70	279	2,772,000
13	Ryo Hisatsune	70	72	71	67	280	1,974,500
	Ryuichi Oiwa	70	71	69	70	280	1,974,500
	Yusuke Sakamoto	70	70	69	71	280	1,974,500
	Anthony Quayle	69	66	72	73	280	1,974,500
17	Michael Hendry	72	72	65	72	281	1,617,000
	Kota Kaneko	70	71	68	72	281	1,617,000
19	Koumei Oda	68	70	75	69	282	1,216,285
	Yosuke Tsukada	71	71	71	69	282	1,216,285
	Yuta Uetake	71	72	69	70	282	1,216,285
	Todd Baek	68	70	72	72	282	1,216,285
	Kodai Ichihara	69	71	70	72	282	1,216,285
	Brad Kennedy	67	73	70	72	282	1,216,285
	Chan Kim	71	72	65	74	282	1,216,285
26	Keita Nakajima	67	71	73	72	283	924,000

	Kohei Okada (A)	68	70	73	72	283			Gunn Charoenkul	68	75	71	70	284	737,000
	Kaito Onishi	69	66	73	75	283	924,000		Shunya Takeyasu	71	72	72	69	284	737,000
29	Takahiro Hataji	70	72	72	70	284	737,000		Yusaku Miyazato	70	69	72	73	284	737,000
	Shugo Imahira	70	70	74	70	284	737,000		Daiki Imano	66	76	76	66	284	737,000
	Matthew Griffin	71	71	71	71	284	737,000								

For The Players By The Players

Talk about dark horses. Who would have thought Shintaro Kobayashi would win the uniquely-named For The Players By The Players tournament, a new event on the Japan Tour. After all, he was well into his 14th season without a win and in his previous five starts he had tied for 55th and 54th places, missed two cuts and tied for 53rd the most recent Sunday. Perhaps it happened because the 36-year-old was comfortable with the tournament and its modified Stableford format being played at The Raysum golf course in his hometown area of Gunma Prefecture.

"It took me 14 years to get my first win. Can you imagine how happy I am," gushed a soaked Kobayashi after being saluted by his local friends with a traditional water shower. "It's not flashy, but I don't hit bogeys."

Actually, he had two of them in the final round, but he offset them with five birdies, his eight points and 41 total putting him five points ahead of Ryuichi Oiwa and nine ahead of Justin De Los Santos. He had taken the lead the third day with seven birdies and one bogey for 13 points, moving six points ahead of Oiwa, and eased to the long-sought victory Sunday in the tour's first use of the Stableford system in 24 years.

The Raysum Golf & Spa Resort, Gunma — October 6-9
Par 71 (35-36); 7,137 yards — Purse: ¥50,000,000

1	**Shintaro Kobayashi**	9	11	13	8	41	¥10,000,000		Han Lee	14	3	6	2	25	835,000
2	**Ryuichi Oiwa**	13	1	13	9	36	5,000,000	17	Yosuke Tsukada	4	2	10	8	24	735,000
3	**Justin De Los Santos**	6	6	11	9	32	3,400,000		Michael Hendry	7	-2	8	11	24	735,000
4	Tatsuya Kodai	2	12	6	11	31	2,200,000	19	Kenya Nakayama	8	2	4	9	23	570,000
	Shunya Takeyasu	6	6	8	11	31	2,200,000		Yuki Inamori	9	3	3	8	23	570,000
6	Chan Kim	3	3	14	10	30	1,800,000		Junya Kameshiro	4	2	10	7	23	570,000
7	Naoyuki Kataoka	7	5	14	3	29	1,650,000		Toru Nakajima	3	8	8	4	23	570,000
8	Nobuaki Oda	12	4	10	2	28	1,525,000		Masashi Nakamura	3	2	7	11	23	570,000
9	Daiki Imano	8	13	5	1	27	1,360,000		Hyunwoo Ryu	7	5	6	5	23	570,000
	Taisei Shimizu	9	7	9	2	27	1,360,000	25	Koki Ishihara	7	6	0	9	22	400,000
11	Satoshi Kodaira	1	5	11	9	26	1,060,000		Taihei Sato	3	8	4	7	22	400,000
	Jinichiro Kozuma	4	6	9	7	26	1,060,000		Sushi Ishigaki	3	7	9	3	22	400,000
	Keisuke Otawa	6	2	12	6	26	1,060,000		Yushi Ito	10	0	9	3	22	400,000
	Taiki Yoshida	0	9	12	5	26	1,060,000		Takahiro Hataji	5	6	-3	14	22	400,000
15	Tomoyasu Sugiyama	8	3	12	2	25	835,000		Taiga Mishima	5	4	11	2	22	400,000

Japan Open Championship

Twenty-one years after Taiga Semikawa's parents named their newborn son in tribute to the great Tiger Woods, this talented young amateur was flashing a season chock full of Tiger-esque performances, the climax coming in late October with his resounding victory in the Japan Open Championship.

Semikawa became the first amateur to win the season's most prestigious championship in 95 years. Rokuro Akahoshi did it in 1927, the tour's inaugural season. He was the first amateur to win twice in a single Japan Tour season. He was just the sixth amateur in modern history to win on the Japan Tour. The impressive others: Ryo Ishikawa, Masahiro (Massy) Kuramoto, Hideki Matsuyama, Keita Nakajima and Takumi Kanaya. He became the number one on the world amateur rankings. His rounds of 63 and 64 were the two low scores of the week when only 41 sub-par 70 scores were shot on Sanko Golf Club's Japan course in Miki, Hyogo, Taiga's home prefecture. His wire-to-wire hold on first place was the first in the Japan Open since Shingo Katayama did it 2008 and by an amateur since Kuramoto in 1980.

"I'm delighted to win this tournament, which only one amateur had won in the past," said the Tohoku Fukushi University senior. "I feel it's a historic accomplishment. I learned I have to be aggressive to win a tournament. Now I can imagine winning every tournament, not lose against any golfer."

Semikawa got off to a fast start with the 64 the first day, two ahead the aforementioned Kanaya, then shot 70, sharing the top spot Friday on six under with Kanaya (68) and Kazuki Higa (66), the leading money-winner. He raced away from the field Saturday, capping a front-nine 32 with an eagle at the ninth hole and following up with a three-birdie back nine for the 63. At 13 under par he was six strokes ahead of Higa (69) in second place and nine in front of the rest of the field.

It took on the appearance of a runaway when he birdied the first two holes on a windy Sunday with tough pin positions. (Only two players broke par.) However, Semikawa bogeyed the fifth hole, and at the ninth, where he eagled Saturday, he absorbed a triple bogey. Game on. After seven consecutive pars, he bogeyed the 17th, his lead over charging Higa down to two strokes. He bunkered his approach and hit a poor sand shot at the home hole, but sank the daunting 18-footer for a 73 and the winning total of 10-under-par 270. Higa, with his 69 to be two back, fattened his money-list lead to nearly ¥55 million. Another Taiga, Taiga Nagano, tied for third with another amateur, Yuta Sugiura, a distant six shots behind Semikawa.

Sanko Golf Club (Japan), Miki, Hyogo — October 20-23
Par 70 (35-35); 7,178 yards — Purse: ¥210,000,000

1	**Taiga Semikawa** (A)	64	70	63	73	270	
2	**Kazuki Higa**	68	66	69	69	272	¥42,000,000
3	**Taiga Nagano**	70	69	70	67	276	23,100,000
	Yuta Sugiura (A)	71	66	69	70	276	
5	Takumi Kanaya	66	68	74	71	279	16,170,000
6	Terumichi Kakazu	71	66	75	70	282	8,890,000
	Adam Scott	71	72	68	71	282	8,890,000
	Chan Kim	67	70	72	73	282	8,890,000
9	Shunya Takeyasu	71	71	70	71	283	5,460,000
	Yuta Ikeda	68	73	69	73	283	5,460,000
	Tomoyasu Sugiyama	70	71	69	73	283	5,460,000
12	Tomoyo Ikemura	69	70	73	72	284	3,661,000
	Tatsunori Shogenji	72	71	69	72	284	3,661,000
	Satoshi Kodaira	67	75	67	75	284	3,661,000
15	Aguri Iwasaki	72	67	71	75	285	2,667,000
	Sadom Kaewkanjana	69	69	72	75	285	2,667,000
	Yuki Inamori	70	72	68	75	285	2,667,000
18	Scott Vincent	68	73	71	74	286	2,310,000
19	Tomohiro Kondo	70	75	72	70	287	2,205,000
	Kosuke Suzuki (A)	72	72	71	72	287	
21	Brad Kennedy	73	72	68	75	288	2,047,500
	Yuto Katsuragawa	71	72	68	77	288	2,047,500
23	Kenshiro Ikegami	70	73	75	71	289	1,827,000
	Adam Bland	73	71	73	72	289	1,827,000
	Takahiro Hataji	73	68	75	73	289	1,827,000
26	Ryuko Tokimatsu	71	74	71	74	290	1,701,000
	Daijiro Izumida	74	69	70	77	290	1,701,000
28	Jinichiro Kozuma	75	71	73	72	291	1,512,000
	Kohei Okada (A)	71	74	73	73	291	
	Younghan Song	72	74	72	73	291	1,512,000
	Keita Nakajima	71	74	71	75	291	1,512,000
	Ryuichi Oiwa	73	71	71	76	291	1,512,000
	Akira Endo	73	73	69	76	291	1,512,000
	Shaun Norris	71	72	71	77	291	1,512,000
	Mikumu Horikawa	71	68	73	79	291	1,512,000

Heiwa PGM Championship

It took a little longer and the emotional lift of hometown support, but Rikuya Hoshino kept alive his streak of winning at least once every year since the first of six victories in 2018 with his decisive five-stroke triumph in the Heiwa PGM Championship. Despite a strong early season that started with two seconds and a third-place finish and followed with three more top-sevens, the 26-year-old Hoshino couldn't muster a victory until he arrived at the familiar par-70 PGM Ishioka Golf Club back home in Ibaraki Prefecture in late October.

He was so choked up as he played the final hole assured of victory that he was leaking tears. "It's the first time I've ever experienced tears even before I hit the winning putt," he said. "After becoming a professional, one of the things I wanted to do the most was to win a championship in my hometown. I'm really happy to have won in front of everyone who supports me."

No wonder he won in the first Heiwa PGM Championship since 2019. He started and finished with seven-under-par 63s to go with a 64 Saturday that still only gave him a one-stroke lead over 48-year-old Australian Brad Kennedy, a three-time winner in Japan, most recently the Shigeo Nagashima Invitational in 2018. Five others were within four shots of Hoshino, but he gave them no chance on Sunday. For instance, Chan Kim, the 2020-21 leading money winner, shot 64 but all it did was raise him into the runner-up position with Aguri Iwasaki five back, as Hoshino carved out his second 63 of the week with five birdies and an exclamation-point eagle on the 16th hole. His 22-under-par 258 total matched the season's low winning score shot by Shugo Imahira in the Golf Partner Pro-Am in May.

PGM Ishioka Golf Club, Ibaraki — October 27-30
Par 70 (35-35); 7,039 yards — Purse: ¥150,000,000

1	**Rikuya Hoshino**	63	68	64	63	258	¥30,000,000
2	**Chan Kim**	65	67	67	64	263	12,600,000
	Aguri Iwasaki	69	65	63	66	263	12,600,000
4	Eric Sugimoto	67	68	65	64	264	7,200,000
5	Keita Nakajima	66	64	68	67	265	5,700,000
	Brad Kennedy	65	67	64	69	265	5,700,000
7	Kaito Onishi	67	65	70	64	266	4,421,250
	Naoyuki Kataoka	66	70	64	66	266	4,421,250
	Ryuichi Oiwa	64	68	67	67	266	4,421,250
	Yuta Kinoshita	65	68	65	68	266	4,421,250
11	Mikumu Horikawa	69	66	67	65	267	3,180,000
	Terumichi Kakazu	67	67	65	68	267	3,180,000
	Ryuko Tokimatsu	66	68	65	68	267	3,180,000
	Ryosuke Kinoshita	69	63	65	70	267	3,180,000
15	Tomoyasu Sugiyama	67	68	69	64	268	2,355,000
	Hiroshi Iwata	66	70	67	65	268	2,355,000
	Yuta Ikeda	69	70	67	62	268	2,355,000
	Juvic Pagunsan	69	65	68	66	268	2,355,000
19	Yuki Inamori	69	65	68	67	269	1,950,000
	Shugo Imahira	68	68	66	67	269	1,950,000
21	Azuma Yano	67	67	70	66	270	1,590,000
	Tomoyo Ikemura	69	68	67	66	270	1,590,000
	Sanghee Lee	65	69	67	69	270	1,590,000
	Kazuki Higa	68	68	65	69	270	1,590,000
25	Matthew Griffin	68	68	68	67	271	1,260,000
	Hyunwoo Ryu	69	68	66	68	271	1,260,000
	Shota Akiyoshi	68	69	66	68	271	1,260,000
	Koumei Oda	66	70	67	68	271	1,260,000
29	Hiroki Abe	68	70	68	66	272	1,023,750
	Ryo Ishikawa	67	69	67	69	272	1,023,750
	Brendan Jones	67	63	72	70	272	1,023,750
	Daijiro Izumida	68	67	64	73	272	1,023,750

Mynavi ABC Championship

Mikumu Horikawa avenged a near-miss with a carefully planned victory in the Mynavi ABC Championship as the Japan Tour swung into its usual November stretch run. "Last year was a disappointment, so I wanted to win no matter what," reflected the 29-year-old Horikawa, who had won his third Japan Tour title in style in August at the Japan PGA Championship. He was nosed out by Yosuke Asaji on the final holes in the 2021 Mynavi ABC. "I think my game fits very well with this course. It's a highly strategic course with the fastest greens in Japan, something I'm very comfortable with," he said, pointing out that he teed off with a "specialty" three-wood on most of the holes, hitting "stingers" into the narrow fairways.

Horikawa got off to a slow start at the ABC Golf Club, Hyogo Prefecture. He trailed leader Riki Kawamoto by four strokes the first day and seven after the second round as the two-time 2022 winner fired rounds of 65 and 68 compared to his own 69-71. Horikawa then surged into the picture on Saturday with a flawless, eight-birdie 64. His 204 elevated him into a three-way tie for second place, a shot behind Yuki Inamori, who posted 69 for 13 under as he sought his third win of the season.

Horikawa bypassed Inamori early Sunday with a four-birdie front nine, countered a bogey with two more birdies coming in for a 67 and a 17-under-par total of 271, finishing two shots in front of Kawamoto, Hiroshi Iwata and Daijiro Izumida. "It was a tough battle and I'm really grateful to my caddie for providing me with sound advice throughout the day," Horikawa said. He climbed to fourth place on the money list and became the sixth multiple winner of the season, joining Inamori, Kawamoto, Kazuki Higa, Shugo Imahira and Taiga Semikawa, who was playing his first event as a professional after winning the Japan Open as an amateur.

ABC Golf Club, Hyogo
Par 72 (36-36); 7,217 yards

November 3-6
Purse: ¥120,000,000

1	**Mikumu Horikawa**	69	71	64	67	271	¥24,000,000
2	**Hiroshi Iwata**	69	67	70	67	273	8,640,000
	Daijiro Izumida	67	69	68	69	273	8,640,000
	Riki Kawamoto	65	68	72	68	273	8,640,000
5	Tomoyo Ikemura	68	69	67	70	274	4,800,000
6	Yuki Inamori	69	65	69	72	275	4,320,000
7	Sanghee Lee	68	71	69	68	276	3,810,000
	Ryutaro Nagano	69	72	67	68	276	3,810,000
9	Ryuichi Oiwa	71	69	70	67	277	3,264,000
	Hyunwoo Ryu	69	71	69	68	277	3,264,000
11	Brad Kennedy	69	71	70	68	278	2,448,000
	Justin De Los Santos	72	68	70	68	278	2,448,000
	Tomohiro Ishizaka	69	69	69	71	278	2,448,000
	Gunn Charoenkul	67	69	71	71	278	2,448,000
	Takahiro Hataji	69	71	67	71	278	2,448,000
16	Yoshikazu Haku	70	72	70	67	279	1,569,000
	Ryosuke Kinoshita	68	70	72	69	279	1,569,000
	Sanghyun Park	69	72	70	68	279	1,569,000
	Shugo Imahira	66	69	74	70	279	1,569,000
	Tomoyasu Sugiyama	67	71	71	70	279	1,569,000
	Kensei Hirata	70	70	69	70	279	1,569,000
	Todd Baek	69	72	68	70	279	1,569,000
	Kodai Ichihara	71	68	67	73	279	1,569,000
24	Satoshi Kodaira	69	71	71	69	280	1,056,000
	Hirotaro Naito	74	69	69	68	280	1,056,000
	Kazuki Higa	66	70	71	73	280	1,056,000
	Brendan Jones	68	69	69	74	280	1,056,000
28	Taiga Semikawa	74	68	70	69	281	822,000
	Naoto Nakanishi	72	70	69	70	281	822,000
	Taichi Nabetani	70	72	69	70	281	822,000
	Andrew Evans	72	70	71	68	281	822,000
	Taihei Sato	71	71	71	68	281	822,000
	Yuta Uetake	70	71	69	71	281	822,000

Mitsui Sumitomo Visa Taiheiyo Masters

Nearly three winless years had elapsed since gallery-favourite Ryo Ishikawa had re-established his status as a top star in Japan with three victories, including two majors — the Japan PGA and the Golf Nippon Series — during the 2019 season. Denied victory in September of 2022 in one playoff when Tomoharu Otsuki holed out for an eagle on the first extra hole, Ishikawa prevailed in another overtime clash in November, this time against Rikuya Hoshino, to notch the 18th Japan Tour win of a spangled career that began when he won the Munsingwear Open in 2007 when he was just a 15-year-old high school amateur. It was his third victory in the prestigious Mitsui Sumitomo Visa Taiheiyo Masters, a rich tournament which he also won in 2010 and 2012 early in his pro career.

"It's unbelievable," gushed Ishikawa. "It still hasn't sunk in. I'm 31 now and so glad to win this wonderful tournament."

After moderate starts, Ishikawa and Hoshino moved into strong contention on Saturday behind 21-year-old Taiga Semikawa, playing in just his second pro tournament after winning the Panasonic Open and Japan Open as an amateur earlier in the season. Semikawa had taken the third-round lead with 67-67-66 on Taiheiyo Club's Gotemba course in Shizuoka Prefecture, three strokes ahead of Ishikawa and Hoshino, his closest pursuers. Semikawa's game came apart Sunday, though. His 76 opened the door for Ishikawa and Hoshino.

Hoshino had the upper hand until Ishikawa rebounded from a double bogey with a birdie against Hoshino's bogey at the 15th hole. Both players then parred in for 69s and the eight-under-par 272 tie that forced the playoff. It went two holes, Ishikawa holing a 13-foot birdie putt for the win. "I wanted to win so badly," he said. "I'll continue to aim higher."

Despite only winning half of Ishikawa's ¥40 million first-place money, Hoshino moved into second place on the money list, within reach of, but still well behind, leader Kazuki Higa.

Taiheiyo Club (Gotemba), Shizuoka
Par 70 (35-35); 7,262 yards

November 10-13
Purse: ¥200,000,000

1	**Ryo Ishikawa**	68	66	69	69	272	¥40,000,000
2	**Rikuya Hoshino**	72	65	66	69	272	20,000,000
	Ishikawa won playoff at second extra hole						
3	**Ryo Katsumata**	67	67	70	69	273	11,600,000
	Hiroshi Iwata	66	66	72	69	273	11,600,000
5	Riki Kawamoto	76	66	63	69	274	8,000,000
6	Mikumu Horikawa	70	70	69	66	275	6,900,000
	Chan Kim	67	70	69	69	275	6,900,000
8	Taiga Semikawa	67	67	66	76	276	6,100,000
9	Yujiro Ohori	65	74	68	70	277	5,240,000
	Todd Baek	68	71	68	70	277	5,240,000
	Aguri Iwasaki	70	70	66	71	277	5,240,000
12	Ryuichi Oiwa	70	71	68	69	278	3,760,000
	Younghan Song	72	67	69	70	278	3,760,000
	Sanghee Lee	69	70	69	70	278	3,760,000
	Jbe' Kruger	73	69	65	71	278	3,760,000

	Naoto Nakanishi	64	71	69	74	278	3,760,000
17	Brendan Jones	69	72	70	68	279	2,940,000
	Yuki Inamori	73	68	71	67	279	2,940,000
19	Shugo Imahira	70	72	69	69	280	2,280,000
	Taihei Sato	68	72	70	70	280	2,280,000
	Taichiro Ideriha (A)	71	71	67	71	280	
	Akio Sadakata	67	72	70	71	280	2,280,000
	Kazuki Higa	69	70	69	72	280	2,280,000
	Ryosuke Kinoshita	68	69	69	74	280	2,280,000
	Yuto Katsumata	69	70	65	76	280	2,280,000
26	Daijiro Izumida	69	69	70	73	281	1,760,000
	Tomoyo Ikemura	69	68	70	74	281	1,760,000
28	Ryutaro Nagano	73	70	68	71	282	1,408,571
	Taisei Shimizu	70	71	70	71	282	1,408,571
	Yoshikazu Haku	72	69	69	72	282	1,408,571
	Hideto Tanihara	71	69	69	73	282	1,408,571
	Ryuko Tokimatsu	74	68	67	73	282	1,408,571
	Tomoharu Otsuki	73	69	67	73	282	1,408,571
	Brad Kennedy	71	66	69	76	282	1,408,571

Dunlop Phoenix

Undaunted by the presence of a handful of strong players from the US PGA Tour, Kazuki Higa continued along the path to the money title on the Japan Tour with an impressive victory in the highly regarded Dunlop Phoenix tournament. "I was aiming for 20 under or lower this week," the pint-sized dynamo commented after securing his fourth win of the season and all but clinched the final number one spot. "I'm so glad I did just that and was rewarded with a victory." The ¥40 million first prize moved him ¥75 million ahead of runner-up Rikuya Hoshino with just two events remaining on the schedule.

The five-foot-two player finished three strokes in front of Chile's Mito Pereira, who complimented Higa after he closed out the victory with a bogey-free 64 and a 21-under-par total of 263. "He's a really good player. He's hitting so straight and accurately," Pereira opined. "He deserved to win the championship."

Higa began his victory run in the 50-year-old tournament at Phoenix Country Club, Miyazaki Prefecture, with a routine 69, four off the pace of Taihei Sato and Pereira, then moved within a stroke of co-leaders Sato and Tomoharu Otsuki with 65 Friday, sharing second place with Pereira and Joohyung Kim, the new young star from Korea. A bogey-free 65 Saturday carried Higa two shots ahead of Pereira (67), Sato and Otsuki (68s) and he breezed to victory Sunday. He followed four front-nine birdies with an eagle at the 13th and a final birdie at the home hole for his sixth career victory. "Winning the money rankings has been a dream of mine since I was young," enthused Higa. "Achieving this feat is a big thing for me."

Phoenix Country Club, Miyazaki — November 17-20
Par 71 (36-35); 7,042 yards — Purse: ¥200,000,000

1	**Kazuki Higa**	69	65	65	64	263	¥40,000,000
2	**Mito Pereira**	65	69	67	65	266	20,000,000
3	**Tomoharu Otsuki**	70	63	68	66	267	13,600,000
4	Satoshi Kodaira	68	68	68	64	268	8,266,666
	Joohyung Kim	68	66	70	64	268	8,266,666
	Taisei Shimizu	67	74	62	65	268	8,266,666
7	Scott Vincent	69	67	69	65	270	6,600,000
8	Mikumu Horikawa	69	67	69	66	271	5,660,000
	Rikuya Hoshino	66	70	69	66	271	5,660,000
	Taihei Sato	65	68	68	70	271	5,660,000
11	Corey Conners	67	69	70	66	272	4,640,000
	Yuto Katsuragawa	71	67	66	68	272	4,640,000
13	Ryosuke Kinoshita	67	69	70	67	273	4,040,000
14	Jinichiro Kozuma	69	69	71	65	274	3,540,000
	Aguri Iwasaki	66	71	69	68	274	3,540,000
16	Seungsu Han	71	69	70	65	275	3,140,000
	Sanghyun Park	69	70	72	64	275	3,140,000
18	Tomohiro Ishizaka	71	69	69	67	276	2,600,000
	Eric Sugimoto	69	71	68	68	276	2,600,000
	Ryutaro Nagano	69	67	71	69	276	2,600,000
	Jay Choi	69	68	70	69	276	2,600,000
22	Shingo Katayama	68	71	71	67	277	1,790,000
	Junggon Hwang	68	70	72	67	277	1,790,000
	Tomoyasu Sugiyama	69	72	69	67	277	1,790,000
	Mikiya Akutsu	69	72	67	69	277	1,790,000
	Tatsuya Kodai	68	69	71	69	277	1,790,000
	Juvic Pagunsan	68	71	69	69	277	1,790,000
	Ryuichi Oiwa	67	73	68	69	277	1,790,000
	Shugo Imahira	67	71	68	71	277	1,790,000
30	Yuta Ikeda	71	67	72	68	278	1,268,000
	Yuki Inamori	69	71	70	68	278	1,268,000
	Yoshitaka Takeya	68	68	73	69	278	1,268,000
	Kaito Onishi	67	71	73	67	278	1,268,000
	Hirotaro Naito	68	71	68	71	278	1,268,000

Casio World Open

It made an interesting picture. Six-feet-two Chan Kim standing beside five-feet-two Kazuki Higa at the ceremony at the end of the Casio World Open. Kim, the 2021 money-winning king, had just won his eighth tournament on the Japan Tour in record fashion while Higa was clinching that number one money title for the 2022 season in a much more subdued way.

The Kochi Kuroshio Country Club course in Kochi Prefecture was a bit of a shooting gallery all week as Kim piled up a 32-under-par total of 256. Kim's par attack shattered the existing record of 28 under and was, by two shots, the lowest score of the season. The 32-year-old pro, a native Korean who grew up as an American in Hawaii, led from start to finish, pursued closely until the final holes by winless 24-year-old tour rookie Aguri Iwasaki, who had to settle for his third runner-up finish of the year.

Kim, who spent much of the season playing elsewhere in the world, led Iwasaki by two strokes with his opening, eight-under-par 64, matched 66s with him Friday. Despite shooting another 64 Saturday for 194, he carried only a one-stroke lead into the final round when Iwasaki dazzled with a 63. Veteran winners Yuta Ikeda and Satoshi Kodaira were four shots back. Any hopes Iwasaki had of catching Kim on Sunday dissolved when he had a two-bogey 35 going out to Kim's 32 on his way to a three-birdie finish, 62 and the record.

Acknowledging that achievement, Kim remarked: "It's hard to come up with 32 under. I'm the most surprised. I hope it will remain as a record of our Japan Tour for as long as possible."

Higa finished in a distant tie for 37th place, but still wrapped up the money title as second-placed Rikuya Hoshino tied for eighth when needing to win the tournament and having Higa miss the cut to stay barely alive in the money race. "I feel a little relieved ... a weight has been lifted from my shoulders," Higa said. "I think my height appears in the headlines more than my name," remarked the man who became the shortest money king in Japan Tour history.

Kochi Kuroshio Country Club, Kochi — November 24-27
Par 72 (36-36); 7,335 yards — Purse: ¥200,000,000

1	**Chan Kim**	64	66	64	62	256	¥40,000,000
2	**Aguri Iwasaki**	66	66	63	67	262	20,000,000
3	**Yuta Ikeda**	68	66	64	66	264	13,600,000
4	Sanghyun Park	68	67	66	64	265	9,600,000
5	Satoshi Kodaira	67	67	64	68	266	8,000,000
6	Shugo Imahira	70	66	66	65	267	6,900,000
	Younghan Song	67	66	66	68	267	6,900,000
8	Taisei Shimizu	72	66	66	65	269	5,252,000
	Rikuya Hoshino	67	68	67	67	269	5,252,000
	Justin De Los Santos	67	69	66	67	269	5,252,000
	Keita Nakajima	67	68	66	68	269	5,252,000
	Mikumu Horikawa	69	67	64	69	269	5,252,000
13	Dongkyu Jang	67	69	63	71	270	4,040,000
14	Yuta Uetake	69	71	66	65	271	3,540,000
	Ryosuke Kinoshita	68	68	68	67	271	3,540,000
16	Riki Kawamoto	72	69	64	67	272	3,140,000
	Kaito Onishi	68	65	70	69	272	3,140,000
	Kaito Sato (A)	67	71	64	70	272	
19	Brendan Jones	68	65	72	68	273	2,520,000
	Ryutaro Nagano	67	71	68	67	273	2,520,000
	Hideto Tanihara	69	71	68	65	273	2,520,000
	Konosuke Nakazato	67	69	68	69	273	2,520,000
	Yuwa Kosaihira	67	69	67	70	273	2,520,000
24	Tadahiro Takayama	71	68	68	67	274	1,690,000
	Genki Okada	70	67	70	67	274	1,690,000
	Hiroki Abe	72	67	69	66	274	1,690,000
	Shunya Takeyasu	70	71	66	67	274	1,690,000
	Ryo Ishikawa	69	69	67	69	274	1,690,000
	Daisuke Kataoka	68	70	66	70	274	1,690,000
	Junggon Hwang	67	70	67	70	274	1,690,000
	Yusaku Miyazato	71	70	69	64	274	1,690,000

Golf Nippon Series JT Cup

It hadn't been a very productive season for Hideto Tanihara, a Japan Tour stalwart with 16 victories on his excellent record. He hadn't finished any better than eighth place in his 18 starts in Japan in 2022 as he defended his most recent win in the 2021 Golf Nippon Series. "I didn't expect to win, so I'm really happy," said the 44-year-old after coming from four strokes off the lead in the final round and waiting out three challengers to post a one-stroke victory.

Tanihara, who only made 18 starts in Japan among his sojourns overseas during the year, lingered just off the lead during the early rounds at Tokyo Yomiuri Country Club. He was just a shot back as Chan Kim, coming off his dazzling victory the previous Sunday in the Casio World Open, shared the first-round lead on 65 with Yuki Inamori and Casio runner-up Aguri Iwasaki, and as Brad Kennedy, the 48-year-old Australian playing on a bad knee, and Satoshi Kodaira, the 2018 Nippon Series winner, took over first place Friday with their back-to-back 66s for eight-under-par 132.

Tanihara fell four back with a 70 Saturday as Kodaira strengthened his bid for his eighth tour victory. He shot 67 to lead Kennedy and Daijiro Izumida by a shot and carried the lead into the back nine Sunday before two back-nine bogeys derailed his hopes. Tanihara made his move with three front-side birdies and added two coming in for a five-under-par 65 and a 12-under-par total of 268, as Kim and Hiroshi Iwata, also with 65s, and Izumida, with 68, all came up a stroke short.

Kazuki Higa, who had already clinched the money-winning title, finished in 20th place and later learned that, as one provision of a just-announced joint agreement of the Japan Tour with the DP World Tour and the PGA Tour, he and the two players who finished in second and third place on the money list — Rikuya Hoshino and Aguri Iwasaki — were to be tendered memberships on the DP World Tour for the 2023 season.

Tokyo Yomiuri Country Club, Tokyo — December 1-4
Par 70 (35-35); 7,023 yards — Purse: ¥130,000,000

1	**Hideto Tanihara**	66	67	70	65	268	¥40,000,000
2	**Hiroshi Iwata**	68	66	70	65	269	10,403,864
	Chan Kim	65	72	67	65	269	10,403,864
	Daijiro Izumida	66	70	65	68	269	10,403,864
5	Ryo Ishikawa	68	68	69	65	270	4,911,593
	Satoshi Kodaira	66	66	67	71	270	4,911,593
7	Rikuya Hoshino	67	69	67	68	271	4,261,593
8	Yuto Katsuragawa	67	69	70	66	272	3,517,343
	Taiga Semikawa	70	67	69	66	272	3,517,343
	Yuki Inamori	65	69	70	68	272	3,517,343
	Brad Kennedy	66	66	69	71	272	3,517,343
12	Ryosuke Kinoshita	69	70	67	67	273	2,597,593
	Aguri Iwasaki	65	68	69	71	273	2,597,593
	Riki Kawamoto	68	67	68	70	273	2,597,593
15	Taiga Nagano	67	70	72	65	274	2,207,593
16	Kaito Onishi	72	70	65	68	275	2,077,593
17	Yuta Ikeda	71	67	70	68	276	1,947,593
18	Anthony Quayle	71	72	68	66	277	1,765,593
	Tomoharu Otsuki	70	72	66	69	277	1,765,593
20	Ryuko Tokimatsu	69	71	69	69	278	1,557,592
	Kazuki Higa	69	69	70	70	278	1,557,592
22	Shugo Imahira	71	72	70	66	279	1,349,592
	Ryuichi Oiwa	67	70	71	71	279	1,349,592
24	Jinichiro Kozuma	72	70	68	70	280	1,167,592
	Tomoyo Ikemura	73	67	69	71	280	1,167,592
26	Mikumu Horikawa	68	72	71	71	282	1,089,592
27	Taisei Shimizu	78	69	67	69	283	985,592
	Todd Baek	76	70	66	71	283	985,592
	Shintaro Kobayashi	71	68	71	73	283	985,592
30	Naoyuki Kataoka	72	71	70	73	286	881,592

2022 MONEY LIST

1	Kazuki Higa	¥181,598,825
2	Rikuya Hoshino	111,414,305
3	Aguri Iwasaki	96,670,570
4	Mikumu Horikawa	95,594,744
5	Hiroshi Iwata	87,317,389
6	Chan Kim	86,805,149
7	Tomoharu Otsuki	84,902,380
8	Yuto Katsuragawa	83,324,433
9	Riki Kawamoto	77,766,121
10	Ryo Ishikawa	76,949,337

ABEMA TV TOUR

Novil Cup	**Yuto Soeda**
iGolf Shaper Challenge	**Hiroki Tanaka**
Taiheiyo Club Challenge	**Taisei Yamada**
Landic Challenge 9	**Taiko Nishiyama**
Japan Create Challenge	**Taiga Semikawa** (A)
Daisendori Cup	**Shota Matsumoto**
Japan Players Championship Challenge	**Chisato Takamiya** (A)

Minami Akita Michinoku Challenge	**Takashi Ogiso**
Dunlop Phoenix Challenge	**Masayuki Yamashita** (A)
PGM Challenge	**Yujiro Ohori**
ISPS Handa Hero ni Nare Challenge	**Masanori Kobayashi**
Elite Grips Challenge	**Takashi Ogiso (2)**
Ryo Ishikawa Everyone Project Challenge	**Takuya Higa**
Delight Works JGTO Final	**Yujiro Ohori (2)**

ISPS Handa PGA Tour of Australasia

Cameron Smith received a rock-star reception when he arrived at Brisbane Airport after the year of his life. His homecoming gave the 29-year-old Queenslander a chance to fathom what he had achieved in 2022 — with no doubt what the highlight was. In July he joined Peter Thomson and Kel Nagle as Aussies to win the Claret Jug at St Andrews and the fact that it was The 150th Open made it all the more special. His performance lived up to the historic occasion, closing with a 64 to beat Cameron Young by one and Rory McIlroy, the fan favourite, by two — thanks to that amazing spurt of five birdies in a row to start the back nine and then the two putts around the Road Hole bunker for a vital par at the dangerous 17th.

"I still can't believe it's here. I still can't believe I won it," Smith said of the precious Claret Jug as he prepared for the Fortinet Australian PGA Championship at Royal Queensland. "I didn't realise how much joy and emotion that that trophy brings out of people. It's insane. It's like they've seen a ghost the first time they've seen it. It's awesome to have it and I don't want to give it back. I want to keep hanging onto it."

At a reception at Wantima Country Club, his home course as a child, members drank XXXX Gold beer from the Claret Jug. He became the 52nd person, and first golfer, to be given the keys to the city of Brisbane, was made an honorary member of Royal Queensland and won the Greg Norman Medal for the second time in three years. "I've got to thank my family first and foremost," said Smith. "Mum and Dad gave up a lot for me to play golf." Then he won the Joe Kirkwood Cup for the third time as he took his victory tally for 2022 to five.

To beat Minjee Lee, the 2021 winner and US Women's Open champion, to the Norman Medal, Australia's highest golfing accolade, required an extraordinary season. He started it by winning the Sentry Tournament of Champions with a record PGA Tour score of 34 under par. Then the Queenslander single-putted eight of the last nine greens at TPC Sawgrass to win the Players Championship. After his Open triumph, and the end of the FedEx Cup season, Smith then joined the LIV Golf Invitational Series, winning on his second appearance.

One of his reasons for joining the new circuit was the desire to have more time to return Down Under. Ironically, it was the travel restrictions over the previous couple of years that led to Smith creating a greater work ethic and which led to his stellar 2022 season. "I didn't really have much to do other than go fishing and drink a few beers with the boys," he explained. "Obviously, not being able to come home, I had a lot of spare time. It could have been one of those times where I just laid on the couch and not done anything, but I made a really big effort to get in the gym and do all those little one per-centers that were going to make me a better golfer. I didn't really expect it to come together so quickly, but I'm happy it did, and I'm really excited by what I can keep doing. I really want to keep pushing myself and really want to keep making myself a better golfer."

Back at the start of the year, it was also the Fortinet PGA Championship that got the Australian golf scene going again after two difficult years. And the winner was another local Queenslander. Jediah Morgan, in his fourth start as a professional, won by the little matter of 11 strokes, a new record for the historic tournament, while alongside Su Oh claimed the inaugural Women's PGA title. Morgan went on to clinch the Norman Von Nida Medal for winning the 2021-22 Order of Merit. He got to tee up in the US Open and The 150th Open and, along with Blake Windred and Andrew Dodt, earned an exemption for the DP World Tour for 2022-23. The affiliation with the DP World Tour included the Australian PGA and Open tournaments being co-sanctioned at the end of the year.

"This is something that I'm going to treasure forever," said Morgan, 22. "Obviously as a young player I'm heading away to follow my dreams and I'm focused on what is ahead of me, but to win an Order Of Merit is something special, I know, and the opportunities that it provides for me are priceless."

No player won more than once on the circuit in 2022, but there was no shortage of interest as the Webex Players Series expanded to four events and Hannah Green created history by becoming the first female player to win a mix gendered event at TPS Murray River. One of those left in the major champion's wake was her boyfriend Jarryd Felton, who won the next outing in Sydney, while at Hunter Valley Momoka Kobori lost in a playoff to Aaron Pike.

There were still obstacles to be overcome, with the Covid restrictions in New Zealand forcing the late cancellation of both the country's Open and PGA Championships. Meanwhile, heavy rain in New South Wales led to some events being reduced to 54 holes.

But there was a rousing finale with the ISPS Handa Australian Open returning for the first time since pre-Covid times and featuring the men's, women's and All Abilities events being conducted alongside each other at Victoria Golf Club — a world first for national championships — with Adrian Meronk, Ashleigh Buhai and Kipp Popert claiming an overseas clean sweep. Looking to the next few years, the PGA Tour of Australasia and the WPGA Tour agreed to align their tournament operations more closely in order to offer greater playing opportunities for both male and female players.

2022 SCHEDULE

Fortinet Australian PGA Championship	**Jediah Morgan**	
Queensland PGA Championship	**Anthony Qualye**	
TPS Victoria	**Todd Sinnott**	
Vic Open	**Dimitrios Papadatos**	
TPS Murray River	**Hannah Green**	*See chapter 26*
TPS Sydney	**Jarryd Felton**	
TPS Hunter Valley	**Aaron Pike**	
Golf Challenge NSW Open	**Harrison Crowe** (A)	
The National PGA Classic	**Derek Ackerman**	
CKB WA PGA Championship	**Jay Mackenzie**	
Nexus Advisernet WA Open	**Braden Becker**	
Tailor-Made Building Services NT PGA Championship	**Austin Bautista**	
CKB WA PGA Championship	**David Micheluzzi**	
Nexus Advisernet WA Open	**Deyen Lawson**	
Victorian PGA Championship	**Andrew Martin**	
Queensland PGA Championship	**Aaron Wilkin**	
Fortinet Australian PGA Championship	**Cameron Smith (1,5)**	
ISPS Handa Australian Open	**Adrian Meronk (1,2)**	
Cathedral Invitational*	**Nick Flanagan**	
Gippsland Super6	**Tom Power Horan**	
Sandbelt Invitational*	**Cam Davis**	

**unofficial event*

Fortinet Australian PGA Championship

A blond, charismatic Queenslander. Once there was Greg Norman, now here was Jed Morgan — or Jediah as he insisted went on the famous Joe Kirkwood Cup. Morgan, in his fourth start as a professional, made his share of history at the Fortinet Australian PGA Championship. At the age of 22 he was the youngest winner for 61 years. His score to par of 22 under matched the championship record and his total of 262 was a new record by four. His 11-stroke victory overshadowed the previous record winning margin of eight set by Hale Irwin in 1978 and equalled twice by Norman in 1984 and 1985.

Alongside the Norman looks and big hitting, Morgan added a dash of Aussie tennis ace Lleyton Hewitt with his fist-pumps and "Come ons". He is mentored by former Australian cricket captain Ricky Ponting and shares a coach with Cameron Smith. In short, a star was born at Royal Queensland, his home club for the previous five years, where his brother is on the greenkeeping staff and Jed won the Australian Amateur in 2020.

"I was thinking on Wednesday I'd hate to miss the cut at my home track and not put on a show," Morgan said. "To have done what I've done is so sick." Almost literally. Leading by nine going into the final round, he was not treating it like a normal club outing. "I'm pretty sure before a Sunday game at Royal Queensland I don't want to vomit," he admitted. "I've been feeling sick for the last three days, especially last night. I thought, 'There's no way back from here'. I tried to press as hard as I could and tried to keep pushing. It's been amazing what's happened."

Morgan's opening 65 left him one behind Louis Dobbelaar before a 63 on Friday put him six ahead of the field. A 65 the next day extended his lead to nine. A closing 69 meant he pulled even further in front as runner-up Andrew Dodt closed with a 71. The moment of the day came when Morgan holed from over 20 feet at the 15th for a par five after his approach ended on the edge of a lake and he took a drop. All the way he was roared on by his supporters from the host club, tapping in for victory at the 18th moments after Su Oh had secured her victory in the inaugural WPGA Championship.

Royal Queensland Golf Club, Brisbane, Queensland — January 13-16
Par 71 (36-35); 7,153 yards — Purse: A$1,000,000

1	**Jediah Morgan**	65	63	65	69	262	A$180,000
2	**Andrew Dodt**	68	66	68	71	273	102,000
3	**Louis Dobbelaar**	64	71	70	69	274	67,500
4	Min Woo Lee	68	70	69	68	275	44,000
	Brad Kennedy	67	73	67	68	275	44,000
6	Aaron Pike	65	70	74	67	276	32,333
	Anthony Quayle	72	67	68	69	276	32,333
	Jake McLeod	70	67	67	72	276	32,333
9	Brett Rankin	71	71	70	65	277	24,667
	Cameron John	70	69	67	71	277	24,667
	David Micheluzzi	68	69	66	74	277	24,667
12	Haydn Barron	71	72	69	66	278	17,080
	Elvis Smylie	68	73	70	67	278	17,080
	Jack Thompson	68	70	72	68	278	17,080
	Chang Gi Lee	70	67	70	71	278	17,080
	Daniel Gale	68	70	68	72	278	17,080
17	Josh Armstrong	72	71	71	65	279	11,490
	Gavin Fairfax	72	68	72	67	279	11,490
	Samuel Eaves	70	70	70	69	279	11,490
	Andrew Evans	71	71	66	71	279	11,490
	Lawry Flynn	75	68	65	71	279	11,490
22	Ben Campbell	68	73	71	68	280	9,183
	Peter Wilson	69	71	71	69	280	9,183
	Dylan Perry	66	75	70	69	280	9,183
	Jordan Zunic	75	68	68	69	280	9,183
	Richard Green	69	73	68	70	280	9,183
	Blake Windred	69	70	70	71	280	9,183
28	Christopher Wood	73	71	70	67	281	7,100
	Todd Sinnott	71	70	70	70	281	7,100
	Michael Wright	66	72	72	71	281	7,100

Queensland PGA Championship

Anthony Quayle added to winning his home state's Open title in 2020 by taking the Queensland PGA Championship for his second victory on the PGA Tour of Australasia. The 27-year-old from the Gold Coast saw a handsome 54-hole lead disappear before he recovered to win by two strokes from Daniel Gale on the Kurrai course at Nudgee Golf Club in Brisbane.

In both the first and third rounds, Quayle went bogey-free, a six-under-par 66 on Thursday putting him into a tie for the lead with Gale and Cameron John. Winds of up to 30mph swept across the course on Friday and Quayle's one-birdie, one-bogey 72 put him in front by two strokes. Gale had got to seven under before he came home in 42 for a 77 to drop down the leaderboard.

On Saturday Quayle added a 65 to set a new course record for the Kurrai, named in honour of the Aboriginal term for "sunset" in the Turrbal language. Quayle led by six strokes from Justin Warren but certainly the sun had not set on a victory yet. Quayle had a double bogey at the first hole on Sunday, while Warren birdied the next four holes. Quayle had to take off his shoes and socks to play from the edge of a pond at the fifth but when he could not match Warren's birdie four, the pair were tied. At the sixth, however, the New South Welshman had his own double bogey, while Quayle hit a five-iron to two feet for the first of two birdies in three holes.

Warren finished tied for fourth after a 73, while Louis Dobbelaar was third and Gale rallied with a 66 for second place. Quayle dropped a shot at the 12th but a 73, for 12-under-par 276, was good enough for the win. "It was more stressful than I thought it would be but it was a lot of fun," Quayle said. "I was a little bit surprised my lead had gone that quickly. I got off to a terrible start and Justin was pushing really hard. He didn't miss a shot for the first five holes and then I hit that five-iron at six and that settled me down. To start the year like this and to get a win is a little bit of validation that I can still compete and play well."

Nudgee Golf Club (The Kurrai), Brisbane, Queensland — January 20-23
Par 72 (36-36); 7,058 yards — Purse: A$200,000

1	**Anthony Quayle**	66	72	65	73	276	A$36,000
2	**Daniel Gale**	66	77	69	66	278	20,000
3	**Louis Dobbelaar**	69	72	69	71	281	14,000
4	Josh Armstrong	73	69	70	70	282	9,100
	Justin Warren	69	74	66	73	282	9,100
6	John Lyras	69	75	67	73	284	6,910
7	Daniel Beckmann	72	77	69	68	286	5,840
	Jordan Mullaney	70	72	75	69	286	5,840
9	Joshua Greer (A)	69	74	75	69	287	
	Jarryd Felton	73	72	71	71	287	4,100
	Brad Kennedy	72	74	70	71	287	4,100
	David Micheluzzi	68	72	73	74	287	4,100
	Cameron John	66	77	70	74	287	4,100
14	Bryden Macpherson	70	73	73	72	288	2,960
	Kade McBride	74	71	70	73	288	2,960
16	Deyen Lawson	73	71	76	69	289	2,560
	Braden Becker	74	75	69	71	289	2,560
18	Elvis Smylie	76	68	75	71	290	2,185
	William Bruyeres	76	68	74	72	290	2,185
	Jordan Zunic	71	72	73	74	290	2,185
	Damien Jordan	72	73	71	74	290	2,185
22	Shae Wools-Cobb	69	79	75	68	291	1,960
	Michael Sim	74	73	73	71	291	1,960
	Brett Rankin	73	74	72	72	291	1,960
	Matthew Millar	69	72	75	75	291	1,960
26	Matias Sanchez	73	73	77	69	292	1,800
	Ben A Campbell	72	74	75	71	292	1,800
	Aaron Pike	71	72	77	72	292	1,800
	Kai Komulainen (A)	73	75	72	72	292	
	Jack Murdoch	73	76	71	72	292	1,800

TPS Victoria

Todd Sinnott was so focused on what he was doing, and nothing else, that he did not know he had won the Webex Players Series Victoria event until he saw his mother's fist pump in the alley beside the 18th green at Rosebud. The 29-year-old from Melbourne won by a stroke from Anthony Quayle and Daniel Gale, the winner and runner-up from the Queensland PGA.

A winner on the Asian Tour in 2017, Sinnott later suffered a stress fracture in his back before he was unable to resume his Japan Tour career in 2020 due to the Covid pandemic. "I'm not going to lie, it was really, really hard," Sinnott said of regaining his fitness and form. "But I have a belief and I practise my butt off."

Sinnott, who scored 68-65-65-66 for a 20-under-par total of 264, went bogey-free on the final day with five birdies, three of them crucially on the back nine, at the 13th and then the back-to-back par-fives 15 and 16. "I said to my caddie, 'I don't care what anyone else does. I just want to shoot the lowest score that I can shoot, and see where we end up.' I think that's a good mentality."

Quayle's bid for a second successive win looked strong when he made four birdies and an eagle in the first 10 holes but a couple of late bogeys at 15 and 17 meant a closing 66, the same as Gale. The pair were part of a seven-way tie for third after 54 holes, behind Sinnott and Richard Green, that included Lydia Hall, who finished as the leading female competitor in a tie for sixth place, and Momoka Kobori, a winner of a mixed event in New Zealand in 2021 that included Ryan Fox in the field. Kobori was the halfway leader at Rosebud after starting 65-66 before the Kiwi slipped down to finish in ninth.

Rosebud Country Club (Composite), Rosebud, Victoria — February 3-6
Par 71 (35-36); men 6,308 yards, women 5,960 yards — Purse: A$200,000

1	**Todd Sinnott**	68	65	65	66	264	A$36,000
2	**Daniel Gale**	66	66	67	66	265	17,000
	Anthony Quayle	64	70	65	66	265	17,000
4	Blake Collyer	65	67	69	65	266	10,000
5	Cameron John	67	67	65	68	267	8,200
6	Bryden Macpherson	72	67	68	61	268	6,197
	Jake McLeod	66	69	69	64	268	6,197
	Lydia Hall	68	64	67	69	268	6,197
9	Austin Bautista	71	64	70	64	269	4,313
	Momoka Kobori	65	66	68	70	269	4,313
	Ben Campbell	71	63	65	70	269	4,313
12	Grace Kim	67	71	68	64	270	3,010
	Whitney Hillier	69	66	70	65	270	3,010
	James Marchesani	66	66	70	68	270	3,010
	Richard Green	70	65	63	72	270	3,010
16	Peter Wilson	68	65	70	68	271	2,380
	Joshua Greer (A)	68	69	66	68	271	
	Kelsey Bennett (A)	68	64	69	70	271	
	Aaron Pike	69	65	67	70	271	2,380
20	John Lyras	70	66	70	66	272	2,180
	Belinda Ji (A)	70	66	69	67	272	
	Aaron Townsend	68	64	71	69	272	2,180
23	Scott Arnold	63	69	73	68	273	2,027
	David Micheluzzi	72	66	67	68	273	2,027
	Cassie Porter	67	69	68	69	273	2,027
26	Jordan Zunic	69	68	70	67	274	1,920
	Andre Stolz	67	65	67	75	274	1,920
28	Hanee Song	69	68	70	68	275	1,840
	Julienne Soo	66	68	72	69	275	1,840
	Jeneath Wong (A)	65	71	66	73	275	

Vic Open

For a player who had not won in almost four years, Dimitrios Papadatos kept his cool in the scorching temperatures to birdie the final hole at 13th Beach Links. The 30-year-old from Sydney was rewarded not just with the trophy and first-place cheque but a place in The 150th Open at St Andrews and he joined the likes of Aussie legends Peter Thomson and Kel Nagle as a two-time winner of the Vic Open. Papadatos first claimed the title in 2017, one of three previous wins on the PGA Tour of Australasia, while his last victory anywhere came at the Open de Portugal on the Challenge Tour the following year.

"I wasn't sure if I still had it in me," Papadatos said after beating Ben Campbell by a stroke. "It goes to show I didn't fluke it the first time. Winning in the final group, I did it once before at the NZ Open, it is definitely a different feeling. There's a lot more pressure, expectation, the crowds are there. You know exactly what you've got to do so I'll take a lot from that."

John Lyras led for the first three days, while Papadatos was lying second each day with scores of 65-68-68. But while Lyras faded on Sunday, going out in 39 on the way to a 74 on the Beach course, Papadatos and Campbell got into a stirring duel, both posting bogey-free 66s, with the winner finishing at 21 under par on 267.

Kiwi Campbell drew level with Papadatos with a birdie at the 11th, but the Sydneysider edged ahead again at the 15th. Both birdied the last, with Papadatos putting from off the green to five feet for his third and then sinking that for the victory. "I've made a few today so I felt pretty comfortable over it, surprisingly," Papadatos said. "It was a bit of a nightmare putt. Left-to-right, downhill with the wind off the left but it went straight in." Papadatos, Campbell and Matthew Griffin, who finished in third place, all qualified for The 150th Open at St Andrews.

13th Beach Golf Links (Beach), Barwon Heads, Victoria — February 10-13
Par 72 (36-36); 6,818 yards — Purse: A$410,000
Creek (R1&2) par 72 (36-36); 6,980 yards

1	**Dimitrios Papadatos**	65	68	68	66	267	A$73,800
2	**Ben Campbell**	70	66	66	66	268	41,820
3	**Matthew Griffin**	68	67	67	70	272	27,675
4	Josh Younger	70	65	68	70	273	19,680
5	David Micheluzzi	70	68	69	67	274	15,580
	John Lyras	64	66	70	74	274	15,580
7	Brad Kennedy	71	69	70	65	275	13,120
8	Peter Wilson	70	71	65	70	276	11,070
	Aaron Pike	69	66	67	74	276	11,070
	Zach Murray	66	69	67	74	276	11,070
11	Richard Green	67	72	69	69	277	7,893
	James Marchesani	66	73	69	69	277	7,893
	Cameron John	66	68	73	70	277	7,893
	Matthew Millar	69	71	67	70	277	7,893
15	Hayden Hopewell (A)	68	68	74	69	279	
	Deyen Lawson	68	71	71	69	279	5,465
	Jordan Zunic	67	71	70	71	279	5,465
	Douglas Klein	67	71	70	71	279	5,465
	Austin Bautista	72	70	65	72	279	5,465
	Braden Becker	73	69	62	75	279	5,465
21	Elvis Smylie	69	71	69	71	280	4,291
	Ashley Hall	71	69	68	72	280	4,291
	Jake McLeod	67	67	71	75	280	4,291
24	Christopher Fan (A)	70	71	70	70	281	
	Nathan Barbieri	69	72	70	70	281	3,479
	Sam Brazel	70	73	68	70	281	3,479
	Marcus Fraser	67	71	72	71	281	3,479
	Brett Rumford	68	71	71	71	281	3,479
	Kade McBride	69	70	70	72	281	3,479
	Haydn Barron	70	69	70	72	281	3,479
	Scott Arnold	71	69	68	73	281	3,479

TPS Sydney

Jarryd Felton finished 18th at the TPS Murray River while his girlfriend Hannah Green took the title. A fortnight later, with Green having returned to the LPGA Tour, Felton joined her in the winner's circle at the TPS Sydney event at Boonie Doon. The 26-year-old from Perth defeated veteran Brendan Jones in a playoff at the 18th hole after the final round was abandoned due to torrential rain that over the previous week had caused life-threatening floods in northern New South Wales and southern Queensland.

The tournament had proceeded with minimal delays until play was halted on Sunday with the leaders having only played three holes. When time ran out to complete the round, 54-hole leaders

Felton and Jones played an extra hole with Felton winning thanks to a 15-foot birdie putt. Felton's drive just ran into the left rough, which turned out not to be a bad thing when Jones, playing from the fairway, hit his approach to the back of the green.

"When I hit it in the rough I kind of thought to myself, 'That's probably a good result'," said Felton. "Jonesy hit that wedge in there and had to fly it to the back edge and it didn't come back as far as he would have thought. It was definitely an advantage hitting it in the rough ... accidentally."

Felton scored 69-64-65 for a 15-under-par total of 198 as he tied with Jones (68-66-64). A late bogey in the third round turned out not to matter once Felton had collected his fourth tour title, and his first since the 2020 WA PGA. The pair finished three in front of Brady Watt, Austin Bautista and Lucas Higgins, the leader on days one and two. Grace Kim was the leading female competitor in a tie for sixth place after a third-round 65, while Cassie Porter finished a stroke further back.

Boonie Doon Golf Club, Pagewood, New South Wales — March 3-6
Par 71 (37-34); men 6,597 yards, women 5,584 yards — Purse: A$200,000

1	**Jarryd Felton**	69	64	65	198	A$36,000
2	**Brendan Jones**	68	66	64	198	20,000
	Felton won playoff at first extra hole					
3	**Brady Watt**	69	68	64	201	10,733
	Austin Bautista	70	66	65	201	10,733
	Lucas Higgins	66	65	70	201	10,733
6	David Micheluzzi	66	72	64	202	6,550
	Grace Kim	70	67	65	202	6,550
8	Cassie Porter	71	67	65	203	4,857
	Braden Becker	69	68	66	203	4,857
	Ben Wharton	69	66	68	203	4,857
11	Josh Armstrong	71	69	64	204	3,660
	Momoka Kobori	71	67	66	204	3,660
	Hayden Hopewell (A)	69	68	67	204	
14	Cameron John	68	73	64	205	3,060
15	David Bransdon	69	73	64	206	2,660
	Charlotte Thomas	71	70	65	206	2,660
	Michael Sim	70	68	68	206	2,660
18	William Bruyeres	70	72	65	207	2,073
	Matthew Millar	69	73	65	207	2,073
	Rohan Blizard	74	68	65	207	2,073
	Aaron Pike	70	71	66	207	2,073
	Peter Wilson	68	72	67	207	2,073
	Christopher Wood	69	71	67	207	2,073
	Dimitrios Papadatos	70	69	68	207	2,073
	Jason Norris	69	68	70	207	2,073
26	Harrison Crowe (A)	69	74	65	208	
	Kirsten Rudgeley (A)	71	68	69	208	
28	Darren Beck	73	70	66	209	1,720
	Jordan Mullaney	73	69	67	209	1,720
	Whitney Hillier	73	69	67	209	1,720
	Neven Basic	71	70	68	209	1,720
	Anthony Quayle	70	71	68	209	1,720
	Shae Wools-Cobb	74	67	68	209	1,720
	Tom Power Horan	71	69	69	209	1,720
	Matthew Stieger	72	68	69	209	1,720

TPS Hunter Valley

Heavy rainfall that led to flooding in much of New South Wales forced the TPS Hunter Valley to be reduced from 72 to 54 holes starting on Friday with players unable to play practice rounds. For the first two rounds the 12th hole at Cypress Lakes was reduced to a par three and the overall par to 69 but it was back to the full par of 70 for a thrilling final round in which Aaron Pike finally prevailed over Momoka Kobori.

Pike, thanks to a seven-under 62 on Saturday, held a three-shot lead after 36 holes but the 36-year-old found himself three behind at the turn on Sunday. Pike dropped a couple of shots and could not capitalise on his chances as well as Kobori did. The New Zealander, a perennial contender in the TPS mixed events, shared the first-round lead with Bryden Macpherson on 64 — Pike had a 68 — and was tied for second after a second-round 69. But she birdied four holes in a row from the sixth in the final round to surge in front.

Four holes later Pike, with two birdies and a Kobori bogey at 11, was level, only for Kobori to birdie the 15th. The pair exchanged birdies on the next two holes but Kobori (67) missed from three feet for a par at the last while Pike got up and down for a 70 as the pair tied on eight-under-par 200. They finished three shots clear of a four-way tie for third place that included Cassie Porter.

Both Pike and Kobori parred the 18th in the playoff but on the third time of playing it in extra time, Pike hit his approach to two feet for the winning birdie. Pike was generous with his praise for the Kiwi. "I couldn't believe she was four under through nine," he said. "She's obviously playing like a gun at the moment. It's a matter of time until she wins, not if." His third tour victory came with a dose of maturity following his two-over 37 going out. "I didn't feel like I was doing much wrong to be honest," Pike said. "The old me probably would have got headless and started blowing up, but I just kept plugging away. That's the key with me. If I can stay patient and stay in the moment, good things can happen."

Cypress Lakes Golf & Country Club, Pokolbin, New South Wales — March 11-13
Par 70 (35-35); men 7,098 yards, women 5,843 yards — Purse: A$200,000

1	**Aaron Pike**	68	62	70	200	A$36,000
2	**Momoka Kobori**	64	69	67	200	20,000
	Pike won playoff at third extra hole					
3	**Lawry Flynn**	68	68	67	203	9,778
	Brad Kennedy	66	69	68	203	9,778
	Ben Wharton	71	64	68	203	9,778
	Cassie Porter	66	68	69	203	9,778
7	Louis Dobbelaar	68	69	67	204	6,190
8	Denzel Ieremia	67	70	68	205	5,140
	Peter Wilson	68	67	70	205	5,140
10	Dimitrios Papadatos	69	69	68	206	3,365
	Deyen Lawson	70	67	69	206	3,365
	Jediah Morgan	67	70	69	206	3,365
	Bryden Macpherson	64	72	70	206	3,365
	Kelsey Bennett (A)	67	68	71	206	
	Michael Sim	68	66	72	206	3,365
	Josh Armstrong	66	67	73	206	3,365
17	Sam Brazel	70	70	67	207	2,240
	Kade McBride	70	69	68	207	2,240
	Brendan Smith	68	70	69	207	2,240
	Jordan Zunic	67	70	70	207	2,240
	Jay Mackenzie	68	66	73	207	2,240
22	Daniel Gale	70	69	69	208	1,900
	David Bransdon	70	69	69	208	1,900
	Nathan Barbieri	71	67	70	208	1,900
	James Marchesani	69	69	70	208	1,900
	Max McCardle	71	67	70	208	1,900
	Jake McLeod	68	69	71	208	1,900
	Ben Campbell	66	69	73	208	1,900
29	Jeremy Fuchs	71	69	69	209	1,660
	David Micheluzzi	68	71	70	209	1,660
	Jack Munro	71	68	70	209	1,660
	Harrison Crowe (A)	66	72	71	209	
	Lachlan Armour	68	69	72	209	1,660
	Jason Norris	68	68	73	209	1,660

Golf Challenge NSW Open

Not since Jim Ferrier in the 1930s had someone held the state Amateur and Open titles. Harrison Crowe became only the second to do so with a one-stroke victory in the Golf Challenge NSW Open at Concord secured with a string of pars by the 20-year-old Sydney amateur from St Michael's Golf Club.

Crowe added to his victories in the NSW and Victorian Amateurs, as well as the Australian Masters of the Amateurs, during a prolific summer with scores of 64-64-67 for an 18-under-par total of 195. Crowe was one of nine players to share the lead on the opening day, then tied with Blake Collyer for the 36-hole lead. Saturday's play was washed out due to the return of Sydney's recent rain which left puddles on the course.

With the tournament reduced to 54 holes, Crowe greeted the Sunday's sunshine with birdies at the first three holes and then the eighth and ninth to be out in five under. His only bogey of the week came at the 10th, and he lipped out for birdies at the two back-nine par fives, the 11th and 15th, as he parred the last eight holes. Up ahead Blake Windred posted five birdies and an eagle in a 64 to set the clubhouse target at 17 under.

Crowe had no margin for error as he played the last two holes. "I've never been so nervous in my life," he admitted. His drive at the last was pulled towards the trees but he had a full swing for his approach, and then got down in two putts from 30 feet. "I don't know if I kept the putter still," he said. "I can't describe it. So good."

Windred pocketed the first-prize cheque of A$72,000, while Jordan Zunic and Jarryd Felton shared third place. Dimitrios Papadatos was sharing third place on Friday lunchtime when he made a rapid departure to carry out best-man duties for fellow professional Lincoln Tighe in Wollongong that afternoon, returning for the weekend and finishing tied for ninth.

Concord Golf Club, Sydney, New South Wales — March 17-20
Par 71 (35-36); 7,267 yards — Purse: A$400,000

1	**Harrison Crowe (A)**	64	64	67	195	
2	**Blake Windred**	68	64	64	196	A$72,000
3	**Jordan Zunic**	64	66	67	197	33,900
	Jarryd Felton	64	66	67	197	33,900
5	Jake Higginbottom	67	67	64	198	15,600
	John Lyras	66	68	64	198	15,600
	Adam Blyth	68	63	67	198	15,600
	Blake Collyer	66	62	70	198	15,600

	Adam Blyth	68	63	67	198	15,600		Brett Rankin	67	66	69	202	5,065
	Blake Collyer	66	62	70	198	15,600		Kade McBride	67	64	71	202	5,065
9	Christopher Wood	66	67	66	199	9,840	21	Andrew Richards (A)	66	70	67	203	
	Jackson Bugdalski	66	66	67	199	9,840		Alex Edge	69	68	66	203	4,080
	Josh Armstrong	67	65	67	199	9,840		Michael Sim	70	67	66	203	4,080
	Deyen Lawson	64	66	69	199	9,840		Michael Wright	68	66	69	203	4,080
	Dimitrios Papadatos	64	66	69	199	9,840		Peter Wilson	68	66	69	203	4,080
14	Brady Watt	68	67	65	200	6,800		Anthony Quayle	64	68	71	203	4,080
	Cameron John	66	69	65	200	6,800	27	Nick Flanagan	70	65	69	204	3,373
	Daniel Gale	71	67	62	200	6,800		Jye Pickin (A)	69	66	69	204	
17	Austin Bautista	66	70	66	202	5,065		Dale S Williamson	68	67	69	204	3,373
	Todd Sinnott	67	67	68	202	5,065		Tim Hart	70	69	65	204	3,373

The National PGA Classic

Derek Ackerman thanked his coach for suggesting he tried his luck overseas as the 25-year-old from San Francisco claimed his maiden victory after three years as a professional in The National PGA Classic. It was a family trip on which he played Royal Melbourne and New South Wales Golf Club that brought Ackerman to Australia when he first turned professional, and now he won on a course that reminded him of home — at least he compared the Tom Doak-designed Gunnamatta course at The National with Doak's Pacific Dunes in Portland, Oregon.

Ackerman birdied seven of his first 10 holes in the opening round to take the lead on 65. He was only pipped the next day when Blake Windred had a hole-in-one albatross at the par-four 12th hole, with a driver from 405 yards. The green was blind from the tee so he did not see it go in and thought the rules official who told him it was in was joking. "Then I thought, 'Why would he be joking?'" Windred said. "It was a pretty incredible moment. It was weird though. It's the best feeling ever but because I didn't see it go in my heart wasn't racing as much which was good."

Windred led by one on 66-67 but the wind increased so much on day three, up to 50mph, that play was suspended and it was Ackerman, after going 69-71, who shared the 54-hole lead with DJ Loypur. The American then closed out the title with a 68 for a 15-under-par total of 273 to win by two strokes from Windred (67), Nathan Barbieri (66), and Sydney amateur Harrison Crowe, who followed up his win at the NSW Open by finishing with a 65 thanks to seven birdies and an eagle.

Ackerman did not know how he stood coming down the stretch but after a bogey at the 16th he parred the last two calmly enough. "It hasn't hit me yet," he admitted. "My coach wanted me to play internationally, play different conditions, different courses. I had some connections out here to make it feel like home. I came here for a family trip three years ago. I love links golf, especially courses like this, because you have so many shots that you can hit. It's not just a stock shot like some American golf courses."

The National Golf Club (Gunnamatta), Cape Schanck, Victoria — April 5-8
Par 72 (37-35); 7,097 yards — Purse: A$200,000

1	**Derek Ackerman**	65	69	71	68	273	A$36,000	17	Matthew Stieger	68	69	75	70	282	2,327
2	**Nathan Barbieri**	70	68	71	66	275	17,000		Shae Wools-Cobb	70	70	72	70	282	2,327
	Harrison Crowe (A)	67	68	75	65	275			Kade McBride	68	67	75	72	282	2,327
	Blake Windred	66	67	75	67	275	17,000	20	Tom Power Horan	68	71	71	73	283	2,055
5	Jordan Mullaney	67	71	71	67	276	9,100		Zach Murray	67	72	76	68	283	2,055
	DJ Loypur	68	67	70	71	276	9,100		Peter Cooke	69	69	74	71	283	2,055
7	Cameron John	69	69	73	67	278	6,910		Peter Wilson	68	71	74	70	283	2,055
8	Matthew Millar	70	68	74	67	279	5,190	24	Daniel Gale	70	69	75	70	284	1,880
	Brady Watt	66	71	72	70	279	5,190		Jason Norris	66	73	74	71	284	1,880
	Jack Thompson	70	67	75	67	279	5,190		Jordan Zunic	70	70	73	71	284	1,880
	Kyle Michel	66	70	71	72	279	5,190		Douglas Klein	71	69	74	70	284	1,880
12	Michael Choi	66	71	72	71	280	3,460	28	Matt Jager	71	68	73	73	285	1,760
	Jediah Morgan	66	70	73	71	280	3,460		Max McCardle	67	71	76	71	285	1,760
	Jay Mackenzie	68	72	72	68	280	3,460	30	David Bransdon	69	70	79	68	286	1,660
15	David Micheluzzi	70	69	73	69	281	2,760		Elvis Smylie	68	71	77	70	286	1,660
	Aaron Wilkin	68	68	74	71	281	2,760		James Marchesani	68	72	76	70	286	1,660

CKB WA PGA Championship

They are the "unmentionables", unless you have overcome them to win your first tour title. Jay Mackenzie had missed a string of cuts early in the season when his ball was heading sideways. "I was hitting shanks every third shot, hozzling it constantly, and I didn't know what to do," he said. Making it through the halfway cut at the TPS Murray River proved a turning point. "Since then I've just felt like my game's slowly getting out of having serious swing problems. I can't even explain it. This week I hit everything pretty good. I don't even know how."

Mackenzie won the CKB WA PGA Championship, delayed from 2021 due to Western Australia's border restrictions, by two shots over Austin Bautista after the pair had a final-round duel at Kalgoorlie. They were both hunting their maiden titles with Mackenzie scoring 68-66-67 and Bautista 64-68-69 to tie after 54 holes. A birdie to a bogey at the second put Bautista up by two but after three birdies in the first four holes, Bautista bogeyed the fifth and eighth holes, then parred home for a 70, finishing one ahead of Ryan Chisnall.

Mackenzie went ahead with birdies at the sixth and seventh holes, then stretched his lead to three by the 14th. But at the short 17th, he chipped over the green, eventually taking a double bogey. "I was fine," said the 22-year-old from Lennox Head on the north coast of New South Wales. "I still had a one-shot lead. I just had to play a good last hole and I was able to do that." He played a chip-and-run from 45 yards to six feet to make his seventh birdie of the day and close with a 68 for a 19-under-par total of 269.

As well as job security with a two-year exemption on tour, Mackenzie could also contemplate retiring his grandfather's old van he uses for tournaments in the eastern states. "I might not have to sleep in my car as much!" he said. "I've got a job for another two years so it means a lot."

Kalgoorlie Golf Course, Kalgoorlie-Boulder, Western Australia — April 21-24
Par 72 (36-36); 7,444 yards — Purse: A$200,000

1	**Jay Mackenzie**	68	66	67	68	269	A$36,000
2	**Austin Bautista**	64	68	69	70	271	20,000
3	**Ryan Chisnall**	67	69	68	68	272	14,000
4	Sam Lee	71	66	70	67	274	10,000
5	Peter Wilson	67	72	69	67	275	7,100
	Connor McKinney (A)	70	69	68	68	275	
	Tom Power Horan	71	68	66	70	275	7,100
	Michael Wright	67	72	66	70	275	7,100
9	Louis Dobbelaar	66	69	76	65	276	4,378
	Braden Becker	70	66	73	67	276	4,378
	David Micheluzzi	67	69	70	70	276	4,378
	Douglas Klein	71	70	65	70	276	4,378
	Josh Armstrong	65	65	75	71	276	4,378
14	Aaron Wilkin	72	71	68	66	277	2,860
	Kade McBride	70	70	70	67	277	2,860
	Elvis Smylie	69	69	70	69	277	2,860
17	Damien Jordan	71	69	69	69	278	2,380
	Chang Gi Lee	70	67	68	73	278	2,380
19	Daniel Gale	70	70	68	71	279	2,180
	John Lyras	68	71	68	72	279	2,180
21	Jediah Morgan	71	71	68	70	280	2,005
	Jason Norris	71	72	70	67	280	2,005
	Josh Clarke	69	69	70	72	280	2,005
	Jack Munro	68	74	66	72	280	2,005
	Connor Fewkes (A)	69	70	68	73	280	
26	Jye Pickin (A)	72	71	67	72	282	
	Haydn Barron	71	67	72	72	282	1,840
	Jarryd Felton	70	70	72	70	282	1,840
	Jake Higginbottom	68	71	70	73	282	1,840
	George Worrall	73	71	69	69	282	1,840

Nexus Advisernet WA Open

It took an incredible bounce at the final hole but Braden Becker only cared that his maiden tour victory arrived at the Nexus Advisernet WA Open, his home state title. It came at the expense of defending champion Hayden Hopewell, the amateur finishing runner-up for the second time in three attempts. The event had been deferred from October 2021 when Western Australia remained in isolation from the rest of the country.

Becker, 29, won from wire-to-wire, sharing the lead on the first day, then building a four-stroke advantage after 54 holes with scores of 66-66-65. But it was not straightforward on the final day. Hopewell, who opened with a 72, set the Royal Fremantle course record with nine birdies in a 63 on Saturday to trail by five and made up the deficit with five birdies in the first 13 holes on Sunday. Becker three-putted for a two-shot swing at the 13th, birdied the 15th to edge ahead again, then three-putted the 17th to leave the pair level heading to the par-five last.

That's when things got spooky. Becker's third shot with a wedge appeared to have gone over the green but hit playing partner Nathan Barbieri's ball and spun back to within a foot of the hole. "I've never seen that happen to anyone," said Becker. "Normally it hits that ball and goes off the green. To help me out like that I think it was a bit of payback for a couple of things that happened earlier."

He tapped in for a par, while a startled Hopewell three-putted from long range for his only bogey of the day. Becker's 72 left him on 19-under-par 269, while Hopewell was one back after his 68. Barbieri was third with a 70 and Josh Armstrong tied for fourth by tying Hopewell's record 63.

Royal Fremantle Golf Club, Fremantle, Western Australia — April 28-May 1
Par 72 (36-36); 6,792 yards — Purse: A$150,000

1	**Braden Becker**	66	66	65	72	269	A$27,000
2	**Hayden Hopewell** (A)	72	67	63	68	270	
3	**Nathan Barbieri**	66	69	66	70	271	15,000
4	Josh Armstrong	72	71	67	63	273	9,000
	Oliver Goss	71	72	64	66	273	9,000
6	Kevin Yuan	68	69	73	64	274	5,666
	Daniel Gale	68	74	67	65	274	5,666
	Jeffrey Guan (A)	66	67	73	68	274	
9	Connor McKinney (A)	71	70	68	67	276	
	Dimitrios Papadatos	66	71	70	69	276	4,643
11	Brett Rankin	72	67	73	65	277	3,855
	Aaron Pike	69	68	71	69	277	3,855
13	Jackson Bugdalski	71	71	69	67	278	2,751
	Lucas Higgins	69	68	73	68	278	2,751
	Ryan Chisnall	71	68	70	69	278	2,751
	Rohan Blizard	68	74	67	69	278	2,751
17	Tom Power Horan	70	70	72	67	279	1,928
	Brett Rumford	69	71	70	69	279	1,928
	Peter Wilson	73	70	67	69	279	1,928
	Elvis Smylie	70	68	69	72	279	1,928
21	David Micheluzzi	68	70	74	68	280	1,566
	Jye Pickin (A)	70	75	66	69	280	
	James Marchesani	70	71	70	69	280	1,566
	Edward Donoghue	71	71	73	65	280	1,566
	James Grierson	68	68	73	71	280	1,566
	Austin Bautista	66	70	71	73	280	1,566
27	Daniel Fox	72	69	71	69	281	1,425
	Jack Thompson	73	72	66	70	281	1,425
	Jack Munro	73	68	70	70	281	1,425
30	Tim Hart	69	68	74	71	282	1,320
	Kade McBride	70	72	71	69	282	1,320
	Jay Mackenzie	70	73	67	72	282	1,320
	Derek Ackerman	68	70	68	76	282	1,320

Tailor-Made Building Services NT PGA Championship

Austin Bautista took possession of the famous crocodile trophy with a massive seven-stroke victory at the Tailor-Made Building Services NT PGA Championship. The 25-year-old from Sydney, runner-up at the WA PGA a fortnight earlier, took control of the tournament when he set a new course record at Palmerston with a 10-under-par 61 on Friday. He holed a 10-footer for eagle at the ninth to turn in seven-under 29 and thoughts of a 59 entered his head. "As soon as you get to seven under, you start thinking, 'What do I have to do to get that magic number?'" said Bautista. He had twice scored 11-under 61s on mini tours in the United States but had forgotten about Palmerston's par of 71. Five birdies and two bogeys coming home meant an inward 32.

Nevertheless, Bautista led by four at halfway and by six after 54 holes. His nearest challenger at that stage was Aaron Pike, the local player who was the defending champion from the last time the event was held in 2020. On a blustery final day, Bautista birdied the first two holes to go ahead by eight but a few bogeys later his lead was down to four. Three birdies in a row from the 15th sealed the runaway victory in style with scores of 66-61-68-69 to match the tournament record total of 20-under-par 264. Tim Hart, with a 67, and Ben Wharton, who got closest to the leader with three early birdies in a 68, shared second place, with Pike finishing fourth.

"This is my first major win so I'm ecstatic and I'll remember that croc forever," Bautista said, pointing at the trophy. "Today was definitely the harder round of the last three, just because I didn't make any putts for what felt like 13 holes. When I made one on 15, that one felt really good. It's hard because you're like, I'm six-up, I'm five-up, now I'm six-up. You just want to get to the finish line. I knew I could get it done. I've played really good golf this year, I've just played my own game and been really consistent."

Jediah Morgan was confirmed as the winner of the Order of Merit even though he was not playing in the final event of the 2021-22 season. Blake Windred also remained in second place, while Andrew

Dodt finished 21st to claim the third exemption on offer for the 2022-23 DP World Tour season.

Palmerston Golf & Country Club, Palmerston City, Northern Territory — May 5-8
Par 71 (36-35); 6,601 yards — Purse: A$150,000

1	**Austin Bautista**	66	61	68	69	264	A$27,000
2	**Tim Hart**	68	72	64	67	271	12,750
	Ben Wharton	67	67	69	68	271	12,750
4	Aaron Pike	67	66	68	71	272	7,500
5	Deyen Lawson	69	65	74	65	273	5,666
	Sam Brazel	67	67	70	69	273	5,666
7	Brett Rankin	67	70	71	66	274	4,117
	Tom Power Horan	70	68	68	68	274	4,117
	Adam Blyth	69	63	71	71	274	4,117
10	Ryan Chisnall	68	67	71	69	275	2,750
	Jackson Bugdalski	69	71	66	69	275	2,750
	Kade McBride	65	66	73	71	275	2,750
	David Micheluzzi	64	69	70	72	275	2,750
14	Jay Mackenzie	69	73	67	67	276	2,070
	Jordan Zunic	71	65	73	67	276	2,070
16	Matt Dowling	66	73	71	67	277	1,680
	TJ King	66	75	69	67	277	1,680
	Lawry Flynn	69	65	76	67	277	1,680
	Haydn Barron	67	70	70	70	277	1,680
	Daniel Gale	64	69	73	71	277	1,680
21	Connor Fewkes (A)	68	71	71	68	278	
	Andrew Dodt	68	70	68	72	278	1,500
	Michael Wright	68	65	71	74	278	1,500
24	Nathan Barbieri	70	68	70	71	279	1,410
	Josh Armstrong	68	72	72	67	279	1,410
	Jack Thompson	68	71	68	72	279	1,410
	Kyle Michel	68	67	70	74	279	1,410
28	Dimitrios Papadatos	67	69	73	71	280	1,230
	Rohan Blizard	67	72	71	70	280	1,230
	Louis Dobbelaar	70	71	69	70	280	1,230
	Brendan Smith	71	71	68	70	280	1,230
	Jack Munro	73	68	67	72	280	1,230
	Damien Jordan	71	68	69	72	280	1,230
	James Marchesani	70	69	73	68	280	1,230
	George Worrall	70	69	69	72	280	1,230

2021-22 ORDER OF MERIT

1	Jediah Morgan	A$190,409
2	Blake Windred	125,286
3	Andrew Dodt	112,731
4	Dimitrios Papadatos	111,491
5	Aaron Pike	100,981
6	Louis Dobbelaar	97,921
7	Anthony Quayle	97,217
8	Brad Kennedy	85,985
9	Austin Bautista	81,209
10	Daniel Gale	79,582

CKB WA PGA Championship

Desert winds that gusted to over 25mph on the final day of the CKB WA PGA Championship produced a thrilling duel between 54-hole leader Jarryd Felton and eventual champion David Micheluzzi. The opening event of the 2022-23 season saw the second staging of the tournament in six months. Felton was a runner-up at Kalgoorlie in 2019, and won in 2020 but it was not an official victory as the field was restricted to local state players due to the Covid pandemic.

Micheluzzi, a star amateur whose best result on tour came with a second place at the 2018 WA Open before he turned professional, had only just joined the paid ranks before Covid hit. It took a while for him to find his feet as a professional. After opening 71-67 here, it was a 65 in the third round that spurted him into contention, one behind Felton (69-66-67). Twice on the front nine Felton led by three strokes and when Micheluzzi bogeyed the 11th and 12th holes it looked like the challenge from the 26-year-old from Melbourne was stalling. But he rallied with four birdies in the last six holes for a 70, a 15-under-par total of 273 and a three-stroke victory over Western Australian Ben Ferguson, whose only bogey in a closing 69 came at the last. Felton bogeyed four of the last six holes to finish third, four back, alongside Andrew Martin.

"I knew I had to play good golf from 13 onwards because 'Felts' was three in front," Micheluzzi said. "It's weird winning a tournament. I haven't won one in five years, and I think I've only won about five tournaments ever. I didn't want it to be another sob story. I didn't think it would be like this but I'm so happy. I really got to see what I was like as a person."

Kalgoorlie Golf Course, Kalgoorlie Boulder, Western Australian — October 13-16
Par 72 (36-36); 7,444 yards — Purse: A$250,000

1	**David Micheluzzi**	71	67	65	70	273	A$45,000
2	**Ben Ferguson**	70	70	67	69	276	25,000
3	**Andrew Martin**	72	68	67	70	277	15,000
	Jarryd Felton	69	66	67	75	277	15,000
5	Brett Coletta	67	72	68	71	278	9,438
	Jack Murdoch	67	68	69	74	278	9,438
7	Matias Sanchez	66	69	71	73	279	7,300
	Brett Rankin	73	66	67	73	279	7,300
9	Cameron John	74	72	63	71	280	5,675
	Jeffrey Guan (A)	67	71	69	73	280	
	James Marchesani	69	70	67	74	280	5,675
12	Tim Hart	67	70	72	72	281	4,825
13	Peter Wilson	71	71	70	70	282	4,325
14	Christopher Wood	75	70	67	71	283	3,450
	Michael Sim	73	70	69	71	283	3,450
	Jack Thompson	71	69	70	73	283	3,450
	Connor McKinney (A)	74	67	69	73	283	
	Lucas Higgins	71	68	70	74	283	3,450
19	Haydn Barron	72	69	72	71	284	2,731
	Deyen Lawson	70	70	73	71	284	2,731
	Lincoln Tighe	72	72	67	73	284	2,731
	Lawry Flynn	67	73	70	74	284	2,731
23	Jak Carter	71	71	70	73	285	2,475
	George Worrall	73	72	68	72	285	2,475
	Kit Bittle	75	67	72	71	285	2,475
	Hayden Hopewell (A)	71	75	69	70	285	
27	Tom Power Horan	69	73	73	71	286	2,350
	Douglas Klein	74	69	68	75	286	2,350
29	Blake Collyer	69	72	72	74	287	2,250
	Jordan Garner	72	71	72	72	287	2,250

Nexus Advisernet WA Open

Fellow players were pretty amazed by Deyen Lawson's performance in the early rounds at the Western Australian Golf Club. Lawson equalled the course record of eight-under 62 in the opening round, which Lincoln Tighe called "insane". On Friday Lawson holed his wedge shot at the 10th for an opening eagle, then had two more at the par-five sixth and eighth holes, both with three-wood approaches, to close up a 63 and extend his lead from two to six at 15 under par. "Are you serious?" asked Michael Sim. Lawson's playing partner Jack Murdoch described the performance as: "Very good. With as many 'verys' as you want to put in front of it."

Lawson went eight ahead on Saturday with a 64 and led by nine after seven holes of the final round. He won the Nexus Advisernet WA Open all right, but not before a twitchy back nine meant the winning margin was knocked down to only two strokes. Lawson closed with a 71 for a 20-under-par total of 260, while Sim matched the best of the day with a 64 to be second. Christopher Wood was third and young amateur Jeffrey Guan, winner of the Junior Players at TPC Sawgrass, took fourth after a third-round 64 of his own.

It was a first tour victory for the 31-year-old Victorian, who is now based on the Gold Coast in Queensland and has spent time on the DP World and Challenge Tours in Europe. Three under through the first seven holes of the final round, Lawson, a four-time runner-up on his home circuit, came under pressure from Sim, who made his sixth birdie in 12 holes at the 14th. Lawson's struggles began with bogeys at 12 and 14, then he birdied 15, but three-putted the 16th for a double. Another bogey at the 17th meant he was only two ahead playing the last, where he made a four-footer for a par.

"It's not easy, it never is," said Lawson. "I've won some smaller events and it's never easy. Sometimes if you're that far in front ... you try not to have thoughts creep in. Nine ahead, I thought, 'Now just hang on'. Which was not the right thing to do. In future I know that if I've ever got a good lead I need to just keep pushing until I finish. Really keep firing. I've seen too many times everywhere in the world, guys let big leads slip. Until it's in, anything can happen."

Western Australian Golf Club, Perth, Western Australia — October 20-23
Par 70 (35-35); 6,380 yards — Purse: A$162,500

1	**Deyen Lawson**	62	63	64	71	260	A$29,250
2	**Michael Sim**	67	64	67	64	262	16,250
3	**Christopher Wood**	67	66	65	66	264	11,375
4	Jeffrey Guan (A)	67	67	64	68	266	
5	Denzel Ieremia	69	65	66	67	267	7,394
	Lawry Flynn	72	63	62	70	267	7,394
7	David Micheluzzi	70	67	66	65	268	4,747
	Jordan Zunic	69	65	68	66	268	4,747
	Michael Wright	71	66	65	66	268	4,747
	Aaron Wilkin	73	65	64	66	268	4,747
	Connor Fewkes (A)	70	68	62	68	268	
12	Josh Armstrong	68	71	66	64	269	3,486
13	James Marchesani	73	66	66	65	270	2,974
	James Conran	72	67	65	66	270	2,974
15	Daniel Fox	68	69	70	64	271	2,243
	Tom Power Horan	66	66	72	67	271	2,243

	Hayden Hopewell (A)	66	70	67	68	271	
	Douglas Klein	70	66	66	69	271	2,243
	Scott Strange	69	66	66	70	271	2,243
20	Haydn Barron	66	70	68	68	272	1,869
21	Ben Wharton	72	68	64	69	273	1,771
	Lincoln Tighe	66	67	69	71	273	1,771
23	Ben A Campbell	67	69	69	69	274	1,629
	Cameron John	70	70	67	67	274	1,629
	Jack Thompson	65	74	69	66	274	1,629
	Andrew Martin	71	68	70	65	274	1,629
	Adam Brady (A)	68	63	70	73	274	
28	Simon Hawkes	70	67	69	69	275	1,495
	DJ Loypur	68	70	68	69	275	1,495
	Blake Proverbs	67	71	68	69	275	1,495
	Aldrich Potgieter (A)	66	70	73	66	275	

Victorian PGA Championship

After surviving a four-way playoff over five trips down the par-five 18th hole of the Open course at Moonah Links, Andrew Martin claimed: "That hole doesn't get any easier every time you play it. It actually really doesn't suit me. I don't have links length." Yet the 38-year-old from Bendigo won his second tour title by producing five birdies in a row and eventually seeing off the challenge of the big-hitting New South Welshman Lincoln Tighe.

"I don't think I've seen five drives off 18 like that since I've been coming down here to play. That was pretty impressive by Lincoln and he definitely had a good week," Martin said. Time after time Tighe was able to reach the green in two but his undoing came in the bunker front left.

Tighe (72) came to the 18th in regulation one ahead but shanked his recovery shot from the sand and ended up with a bogey six. That left Adam Bland (73), whose overnight lead disappeared when he started bogey-double bogey, with a chance to win but his putt slipped by. Martin also had a chance in regulation at the last but posted the clubhouse target at nine-under-par 279 after a bogey-free 68. Brett Coletta also finished on that mark with a 70.

Bland and Coletta exited the playoff with pars at the first extra hole. Tighe kept on two-putting for birdies, but Martin had to work harder, getting up and down three times in a row, including, on the fourth extra hole, by following a very wayward second with a 50-yard wedge to 15 feet and making the putt. On the fifth occasion, it was Martin who found the green in two and two-putted, while Tighe was in the same bunker as in regulation and could not get up and down.

"It's amazing to get the win," said Martin, who won the TPS Sydney event in 2021 for his maiden title. "On the fourth extra hole, missing it right, I did get a little bit lucky as it was a good angle for me. I certainly wasn't as calm as I appeared on the outside over the putt. I just tried to take a deep breath and compose myself."

Moonah Links Resort (Open), Fingal, Victoria — November 10-13
Par 72 (36-36); 7,468 yards — Purse: A$250,000
Legends (R1&2) par 72 (37-35); 6,906 yards

1	**Andrew Martin**	75	65	71	68	279	A$45,000
2	**Brett Coletta**	73	68	68	70	279	18,333
	Lincoln Tighe	67	71	69	72	279	18,333
	Adam Bland	70	66	70	73	279	18,333
	Martin won playoff at fifth extra hole						
5	Douglas Klein	74	67	72	67	280	9,438
	Jack Thompson	75	66	68	71	280	9,438
7	Daniel Beckmann	77	65	72	67	281	5,561
	Harrison Gilbert	66	73	74	68	281	5,561
	Simon Hawkes	71	70	74	66	281	5,561
	Lucas Higgins	72	69	71	69	281	5,561
	Zach Murray	67	70	72	72	281	5,561
	Denzel Ieremia	71	67	71	72	281	5,561
	Marcus Fraser	70	67	70	74	281	5,561
14	Justin Warren	70	71	73	68	282	3,450
	Luke Toomey	68	71	74	69	282	3,450
16	Deyen Lawson	68	71	74	70	283	2,850
	Cameron John	73	67	72	71	283	2,850
	Josh Armstrong	67	72	72	72	283	2,850
	Christopher Wood	66	71	71	75	283	2,850
20	Mark Hutson	71	68	75	70	284	2,454
	Jamie Arnold	70	73	70	71	284	2,454
	Andre Lautee	69	74	70	71	284	2,454
	Lachlan Aylen	69	71	72	72	284	2,454
	Peter Wilson	75	69	71	69	284	2,454
	David Micheluzzi	73	71	72	68	284	2,454
26	Aaron Wilkin	74	68	74	69	285	2,225
	Devon Bling	71	70	70	74	285	2,225
	Blake Windred	71	72	74	68	285	2,225
29	Anthony Choat	74	70	70	72	286	2,025
	Scott Strange	70	70	75	71	286	2,025
	Matias Sanchez	72	69	71	74	286	2,025
	Tom Power Horan	71	73	74	68	286	2,025
	Matthew Millar	71	72	75	68	286	2,025

Queensland PGA Championship

When Justin Warren's accommodation for the Queensland PGA Championship fell through at the start of the week, he called Aaron Wilkin and asked to crash at his place in Brisbane. The pair drove to the course together each morning, talking about one of them winning. And indeed there was a party at Wilkin's place for the 29-year-old Queenslander's maiden victory, which Warren took in good heart — despite having lost out in a playoff to his host.

Wilkin won at the second extra hole on The Kurrai course at Nudgee having been the only player in the field not to have a round over par during the windy week. Wilkin had three 72s and then a 68 on Sunday, holing from 20 feet at the last, to tie Warren on four-under-par 284. Warren had posted the clubhouse target after a 67, which included a bogey on the final hole.

Yet both trailed Jak Carter, the first year PGA Associate from South Australia playing in only his fourth tournament. Carter (67-71-73) shared the lead on the first two days and was alone after 54 holes when the third-round scoring average was 3.73 strokes over par. Carter was at six under par before a bogey at the 16th and came to the par-three 18th one ahead. Alas, his seven-iron did not carry the water and he failed to get up and down from the drop zone. A double bogey meant a 74 and third place, one shot outside the playoff.

On the first playoff hole at the tricky 18th, Warren missed a chance for a winning par from four feet before he found a bunker on the second extra hole. He came out to 20 feet and missed the putt after Wilkin's birdie effort from 30 feet had rolled over the edge of the hole and finished an inch away, giving him a winning par.

"It's just the monkey off the back," said Wilkin, who worked as a welder in his father's factory during the tour's Covid shutdown. His previous best result was a tie for third at the TPS Murray River in February. "I'm definitely good enough, I just needed to do something like this maybe. It lets me know that I can do it. I've been in that position before, coming down the last with the lead and I've screwed it up so I knew it wasn't going to be easy for Jak. I wouldn't say I've been knocking at the door but I've just been wanting to win for a while. It's good to do it in front of my family and friends."

Nudgee Golf Club (The Kurrai), Brisbane, Queensland — November 17-20
Par 72 (36-36); 7,058 yards — Purse: A$250,000

1	**Aaron Wilkin**	72	72	72	68	284	A$45,000
2	**Justin Warren**	70	74	73	67	284	25,000
	Wilkin won playoff at second extra hole						
3	**Jak Carter**	67	71	73	74	285	17,500
4	Daniel Gale	71	73	71	71	286	11,375
	Lachlan Barker	73	70	70	73	286	11,375
6	Tyler Duncan (A)	71	72	76	68	287	
	Braden Becker	72	69	75	71	287	8,625
8	Michael Wright	75	71	76	66	288	6,488
	Stephen Allan	72	68	75	73	288	6,488
	David Micheluzzi	72	73	70	73	288	6,488
	Ben Wharton	71	73	70	74	288	6,488
12	Nick Voke	67	71	82	69	289	3,309
	Haydn Barron	77	65	78	69	289	3,309
	Lincoln Tighe	67	73	79	70	289	3,309
	Andrew Evans	68	72	78	71	289	3,309
	Jason Norris	72	74	72	71	289	3,309
	Denzel Ieremia	71	68	78	72	289	3,309
	Zinyo Garcia	68	75	74	72	289	3,309
	Jack Thompson	73	72	71	73	289	3,309
	James Marchesani	71	72	72	74	289	3,309
	John Lyras	70	69	74	76	289	3,309
	Douglas Klein	71	70	72	76	289	3,309
23	Adam Bland	72	74	76	69	291	2,375
	DJ Loypur	69	75	77	70	291	2,375
	Cooper Eccleston	70	71	77	73	291	2,375
	Scott Hend	71	71	75	74	291	2,375
	Blake Proverbs	70	70	76	75	291	2,375
28	Lucas Higgins	71	72	80	69	292	2,125
	Cameron John	73	70	79	70	292	2,125
	Sam Brazel	71	73	78	70	292	2,125
	Shae Wools-Cobb	71	70	78	73	292	2,125
	Kade McBride	70	68	77	77	292	2,125

Fortinet Australian PGA Championship

It was the perfect homecoming for Cameron Smith, who arrived in Brisbane to find posters of him everywhere promoting the Fortinet Australian PGA Championship. But before that, there was a reception at Wantima Country Club, the Open champion's childhood course, where members drank his favourite beer, XXXX Gold, out of the Claret Jug. Then Smith received honorary membership at Royal Queensland, where he had been a fee-paying member since joining as a teenager, and became the 52nd person, though first golfer, to be given the keys to Brisbane. Only after the 29-year-old was presented with the Greg Norman Medal as Australia's outstanding golfer of the year could he get down to business and that ended nicely, too, with fans around the 18th green at Royal Queensland chanting his name as Smith secured a three-stroke victory to win the Joe Kirkwood Cup for the third time.

It was Smith's fifth win of a stellar year and one of the more emotional as he played in front of family and friends for the first time since before the Covid pandemic. With the final day twice interrupted by thunderstorms, Smith was inspired by his father Des's birthday and his grandmother Carol walking all 72 holes following a couple of bouts of chemotherapy treatment. "I can't believe she did it," said Smith. "Everyone at the start of the week was telling her to pace herself. It was also my dad's birthday as well. After I got back to the tie for the lead there after 11, I really wanted to do it for those two.

"When we went in for that second time, I think I was just really tired. I had a coffee, tried to get some energy back in me and went out there and played really solid the last seven or eight holes. It was kind of nice to know that I can do that with not much in the tank."

Smith, the winner in 2017 and 2018, admitted his game was a "bit scratchy" at the start of the week as he opened with a 68, but a 65 on Friday afternoon got the crowd going, although the biggest roar came at the par-three 17th, ringed by crowded hospitality tents, when playing partner Adam Scott holed a monster putt. Smith was one behind Jason Scrivener (65-67) at halfway but a 69 on a windy Saturday was good enough for him to take a three-stroke lead.

Scrivener followed his 74 on Saturday with a closing 67, going five under through 15 holes. Ryo Hisatsune, the 20-year-old from Japan, started birdie-eagle on the way to a 65 and when Smith, after one birdie going out, bogeyed the 11th there was briefly a three-way tie for the lead. Smith responded with a brilliant high flop shot over a tree at the short par-four 12th for the first of two birdies in a row, and then also birdied the 16th on the way to a 68 and a 14-under-par total of 270. Scrivener was still in touch before putting off the green at the 17th and taking a double bogey, though he secured a tie for second with a birdie at the last. In the first DP World Tour event of the 2022-23 season, England's John Parry tied for fourth with Min Woo Lee.

Royal Queensland Golf Club, Brisbane, Queensland — November 24-27
Par 71 (36-35); 7,134 yards — Purse: A$2,000,000

1	**Cameron Smith**	68	65	69	68	270	A$323,000
2	**Ryo Hisatsune**	67	70	71	65	273	164,350
	Jason Scrivener	65	67	74	67	273	164,350
4	John Parry	71	70	69	65	275	87,780
	Min Woo Lee	65	73	68	69	275	87,780
6	David Micheluzzi	68	68	71	69	276	66,500
7	Greg Chalmers	71	69	71	66	277	44,004
	Cam Davis	70	73	66	68	277	44,004
	Takumi Kanaya	72	67	69	69	277	44,004
	Sam Brazel	69	73	66	69	277	44,004
	Masahiro Kawamura	68	66	71	72	277	44,004
12	Marc Leishman	69	72	70	67	278	28,785
	Alejandro Canizares	69	66	75	68	278	28,785
	Elvis Smylie	70	71	69	68	278	28,785
	Chang Gi Lee	68	70	71	69	278	28,785
	Tom Power Horan	68	71	70	69	278	28,785
	Brad Kennedy	66	70	70	72	278	28,785
18	Geoff Ogilvy	68	72	74	65	279	21,318
	Nick Voke	71	68	74	66	279	21,318
	Gunner Wiebe	69	72	70	68	279	21,318
	Nick Flanagan	71	70	70	68	279	21,318
	Harrison Endycott	73	69	69	68	279	21,318
	Denzel Ieremia	67	68	75	69	279	21,318
	Samuel Eaves	71	67	72	69	279	21,318
	Scott Hend	70	68	69	72	279	21,318
	Jake McLeod	70	66	70	73	279	21,318
	Yan Wei Liu	67	68	70	74	279	21,318
28	Maverick Antcliff	67	69	76	68	280	16,625
	Adam Scott	66	72	74	68	280	16,625
	Todd Sinnott	68	70	72	70	280	16,625
	Jarryd Felton	69	70	71	70	280	16,625
	Cameron John	69	65	74	72	280	16,625
	Alfredo Garcia-Heredia	68	72	67	73	280	16,625
34	Cory Crawford	69	71	72	69	281	13,191
	Tom Lewis	71	71	70	69	281	13,191
	Wade Ormsby	72	71	69	69	281	13,191
	Kade McBride	71	71	69	70	281	13,191
	John Lyras	65	72	73	71	281	13,191
	Derek Ackerman	70	69	71	71	281	13,191
	Adrian Meronk	68	67	74	72	281	13,191
41	Harrison Crowe (A)	71	72	73	66	282	
	Connor McKinney	71	67	77	67	282	10,640
	Michael Sim	70	71	71	70	282	10,640
	Deyen Lawson	69	74	68	71	282	10,640
	Nathan Barbieri	68	71	71	72	282	10,640
	Douglas Klein	70	71	69	72	282	10,640
	Scott Strange	69	74	66	73	282	10,640
48	Aaron Pike	70	73	73	67	283	8,550
	Jamie Arnold	71	69	75	68	283	8,550
	Jeunghun Wang	66	76	73	68	283	8,550
	Jack Thompson	72	70	70	71	283	8,550
	Pierre Pineau	67	75	68	73	283	8,550
53	Josh Geary	74	68	73	69	284	7,030
	Aaron Wilkin	71	72	72	69	284	7,030

	Andrew Martin	71 72 71 70	284	7,030		Adam Bland	69 70 74 74	287	4,750
56	Hayden Hopewell	71 69 74 71	285	6,460		Stephen Allan	69 72 72 74	287	4,750
57	Matthew Griffin	70 73 76 67	286	5,890	69	Marcus Fraser	72 70 74 72	288	3,990
	Christopher Wood	68 71 77 70	286	5,890	70	Scott Arnold	75 68 76 70	289	3,420
	Peter Wilson	71 72 72 71	286	5,890		Daniel Hillier	69 67 79 74	289	3,420
	Nicolai Hojgaard	68 71 74 73	286	5,890		Justin Warren	70 72 73 74	289	3,420
	Anthony Quayle	66 69 77 74	286	5,890	73	David Bransdon	75 68 75 72	290	2,843
62	Blake Collyer	71 70 77 69	287	4,750		Peter Cooke	66 76 73 75	290	2,843
	Travis Smyth	70 73 75 69	287	4,750	75	Lucas Higgins	70 72 75 74	291	2,837
	Jordan Zunic	70 71 74 72	287	4,750	76	Rohan Blizard	70 73 78 72	293	2,830
	Jack Munro	70 70 74 73	287	4,750		Charlie Dann	73 70 73 77	293	2,830
	Liam Johnston	69 74 71 73	287	4,750					

ISPS Handa Australian Open

Poland's Adrian Meronk completed a clean sweep of international champions at an historic ISPS Handa Australian Open which saw the men's, women's and All Abilities titles decided on the same course at Victoria Golf Club. South African Ashleigh Buhai and England's Kipp Popert won their respective crowns as the championship adopted a "Vic Open" style format for the first time.

Meronk had opened with a three-over-par 73 at Victoria, but then found his form by adding a 66 at Kingston Heath, the tournament's second venue. On Saturday he grabbed a share of the course record at Victoria with a 63 — a score posted by David Micheluzzi on the first day and Adam Scott on Friday. Scott eagled his final hole on both Friday and Saturday, which kept the 2013 Masters winner one ahead of the charging Meronk after 54 holes.

Sunday's rousing finale was lacking only Cameron Smith. The Open champion and winner of the previous week's Australian PGA, thought he had missed the cut and headed to the races on Friday afternoon, admitting he was a few beers in before discovering he had an early tee time on Saturday. However, with a 54-hole cut in operation, he still did not make it to Sunday.

A two-shot swing at the first hole put Meronk in the lead and it was a fine duel with Scott, who was attempting to win the Stonehaven Cup for a second time after his 2009 victory. The 29-year-old Pole, who created history by becoming the first player from his country to win on the DP World Tour at the Irish Open earlier in the year, birdied the 15th to go two ahead and then at the 17th, despite hitting an iron off the tee, Scott went out of bounds and took a double bogey. Meronk also dropped a shot but at the last he took a leaf out of his rival's playbook and finished with an eagle, rolling in a putt from off the back of the green for his second DP World Tour victory.

A closing 66 left Meronk at 14-under 268 and five shots in front of Scott (72), with Min Woo Lee (69) in third place. Lee secured a spot in The 151st Open at Hoylake along with Haydn Barron, thanks to an eagle at the last, and Alejandro Canizares. "I'm super excited and to finish like that on the 18th hole is just unreal," said Meronk. "I felt really good again today. I kept doing what I've done the last two days and it worked pretty well. I'm super proud of myself, proud of my team and super happy right now."

Victoria Golf Club, Melbourne, Victoria — December 1-4
Par 70 (35-35); 6,811 yards — Purse: A$1,700,000
Kingston Heath Golf Club (R1&2) par 72 (36-36); 7,269 yards

1	**Adrian Meronk**	73 66 63 66	268	A$289,000		Jason Norris	71 68 71 68	278	28,123
2	**Adam Scott**	71 63 67 72	273	187,000		Hayden Hopewell	73 68 68 69	278	28,123
3	**Min Woo Lee**	70 70 65 69	274	107,100		Lucas Herbert	70 72 67 69	278	28,123
4	Alejandro Canizares	70 73 68 64	275	78,540		David Micheluzzi	63 71 73 71	278	28,123
	Haydn Barron	69 68 68 70	275	78,540		Pierre Pineau	67 71 69 71	278	28,123
6	Josh Geary	68 69 69 70	276	59,500		Nicolai Hojgaard	67 71 69 71	278	28,123
7	Andrew Martin	73 69 68 67	277	43,860	17	Gunner Wiebe	69 68 70 72	279	22,950
	Matthew Millar	72 72 66 67	277	43,860	18	David Bransdon	73 69 69 69	280	20,173
	Conor Purcell	68 72 66 71	277	43,860		Michael Sim	73 69 69 69	280	20,173
10	Tom Lewis	68 71 72 67	278	28,123		Jack Thompson	73 70 67 70	280	20,173

	John Lyras	72	71	66	71	280	20,173
	Luke Toomey	71	70	67	72	280	20,173
	Jason Scrivener	72	70	66	72	280	20,173
24	David Horsey	71	71	69	70	281	17,425
	Takumi Kanaya	69	72	69	71	281	17,425
	Liam Johnston	69	73	67	72	281	17,425
	Jarryd Felton	73	67	68	73	281	17,425
28	Maverick Antcliff	74	69	66	73	282	15,640
	Velten Meyer	68	70	70	74	282	15,640
	Dimitrios Papadatos	73	67	68	74	282	15,640
31	Jack Munro	72	70	69	72	283	14,110
	Deyen Lawson	69	70	70	74	283	14,110
	Ryo Hisatsune	70	70	67	76	283	14,110
34	Justin Warren	73	70	68	74	285	12,835
	Connor McKinney	67	75	68	75	285	12,835
36	Blake Collyer	72	72	67	75	286	11,900
	Matt Jones	70	69	70	77	286	11,900

Cathedral Invitational

What might have been a swansong for Nick Flanagan may have booked his return to the Australasian Tour in 2023. It was only an unofficial event, but the A$100,000 first prize for winning the Cathedral Invitational was a boost for the 38-year-old from New South Wales who now lives in Texas. The 2003 US Amateur champion had not won since 2012 on the Korn Ferry Tour before defeating Scott Arnold with a par at the first playoff hole.

Both players scored 69-69 for six-under 138 in the two-day event at Cathedral Lodge, an exclusive club with a Greg Norman-designed course two hours north of Melbourne. The venue was opened to the public for the first time on the second day of action. The spectators got to see Australian legend Karrie Webb, winner of the 2022 Senior LPGA Championship, lead by two with two to play before she finished with a double bogey and a bogey. She shared third place, one shot behind, with Grace Kim, who bogeyed the 18th following her near miss at the Australian Open the previous weekend.

Flanagan, who only once finished better than 30th in 2022, said: "I pretty much just said we'll see what happens and if it goes great, great, and if it doesn't then we'll sit down over Christmas and decide what's next. It's not the first time I've done that — the last time I did it, I finished third two weeks in a row. Maybe there's something to that attitude of knowing it's not that big a deal if I'm not going to play golf as a career. It really just lets you go out and free-wheel it. With two kids now every cent counts. This will definitely give me a little bit of breathing room to be able to come back and play a little bit next year."

Cathedral Lodge & Golf Club, Thornton, Victoria — December 5-6
Par 72 (35-37); 6,991 yards — Purse: A$300,000

1	**Nick Flanagan**	69	69	138	A$100,000
2	**Scott Arnold**	69	69	138	50,000
	Flanagan won playoff at first extra hole				
3	**Grace Kim**	69	70	139	18,750
	Karrie Webb	69	70	139	18,750
5	Marc Leishman	71	69	140	10,000
6	Jarryd Felton	73	68	141	6,100
	Zach Murray	73	68	141	6,100
	Gabriela Ruffels	73	68	141	6,100
	Jordan Zunic	70	71	141	6,100
	Matt Jager	69	72	141	6,100
11	Adam Scott	72	71	143	2,750
	Michael Sim	72	71	143	2,750
	Denzel Ieremia	69	74	143	2,750
	Louis Dobbelaar	68	75	143	2,750
15	Deyen Lawson	74	70	144	2,000
	Wade Ormsby	74	70	144	2,000
17	Todd Sinnott	74	71	145	2,000
	Maverick Antcliff	70	75	145	2,000
19	Jason Scrivener	75	71	146	2,000
20	Elvis Smylie	75	72	147	1,750
	Justin Warren	75	72	147	1,750

Gippsland Super6

Tom Power Horan claimed his second tour victory at the same tournament where he won his first. The 29-year-old from Melbourne won the inaugural Gippsland Super6 in 2019 when the matchplay portion was washed out and the result decided on the 54-hole strokeplay qualifying. This time Power Horan (68-63-65) was one of three players to top the qualifying section at Warragul, along with Hayden Hopewell and Haydn Barron on 14-under-par 196. The trio were among the top-eight seeds to be given a bye into the second round of six-hole medal matches.

Power Horan still had to win four matches, culminating with a stunning performance in the final when he defeated Kyle Michel by three strokes, making birdies at five of the six holes. On the other hole, the second, he did well to make a bogey after playing a shot left-handed from behind a tree. That meant he was only two shots behind and the player now coached by Bradley Hughes roared back to seal the victory with a four-under-par score of 19. He made another fine recovery from under a tree at the third as conditions turned wet and windy, and finished in style by making a 20-footer on the final green.

"I'd been pretty happy with my start to the season and hopefully I'll move a bit higher up the rankings now," Power Horan said. "I feel like I'm playing well and this week shows that. At the second, I didn't want to take a drop for an unplayable. As left-handed shots go, it probably wasn't the hardest one, but I thought, I'm in the final, I might as well go for it."

Warragul Country Club, Warragul, Victoria — December 8-11
Par 70 (35-35); 6,087 yards — Purse: A$200,000

FIRST ROUND
Kyle Michel defeated Ben Ferguson
Kevin Yuan defeated Blake Proverbs
Daniel Beckmann defeated Jamie Arnold
David Micheluzzi defeated Ben Eccles
Christopher Wood defeated Devon Bling
Andre Lautee defeated David Bransdon
Shae Wools-Cobb defeated Andrew Martin
Blake Collyer defeated Quinnton Croker (A)

SECOND ROUND
Michel defeated Hayden Hopewell (1)
Yuan defeated Zach Murray (8)
Alex Edge (5) defeated Beckmann
Justin Warren (4) defeated Micheluzzi
Wood defeated Haydn Barron (3)
Lautee defeated Nick Voke (6)
Josh Armstrong (7) defeated Wools-Cobb
Tom Power Horan (2) defeated Collyer
(Number in brackets is the strokeplay qualifying seeding)

QUARTER-FINALS
Michel defeated Yuan
Edge defeated Warren
Lautee defeated Wood
Power Horan defeated Armstrong

SEMI-FINALS
Michel defeated Edge
Power Horan defeated Lautee

THIRD-FOURTH MATCH
Lautee defeated Edge

FINAL
Power Horan (A$36,000) defeated Michel (A$20,000)

Sandbelt Invitational

It may only have been an unofficial event, but victory at the Sandbelt Invitational was a positive way for Cam Davis to end the year. Having not finished better than sixth on the PGA Tour, where he won the Rocket Mortgage Classic in 2021, the 27-year-old from Sydney claimed a wire-to-wire win after a stirring duel with Momoka Kobori on the final day at Peninsula Kingswood. After emerging with a one-shot win, Davis said: "That was a hard-fought battle over the last couple of days. I'm very pleased that I was able to play good enough golf to get on top. It was such a good week playing these courses, I'd love to do this as many times as I can."

The tournament, which began in 2021, was created by Geoff Ogilvy and Mike Clayton. "It's the best courses that we have, set up as well as they can be set up, with the best players we can find. What else do you need, that's a pretty good formula," said Ogilvy in describing the philosophy of the event that utilises four courses over four days on the Melbourne sandbelt.

Davis led by two with a 65 at Kingston Heath, then added a 66 on the West course at Royal Melbourne, a 69 at Yarra Yarra and closed with a 67 at PK for a 16-under-par total of 267. He birdied the first three holes of the final round and was bogey-free for his closing effort, the winning birdie coming at the 17th, where the Presidents Cup player hit a driver off the deck for this second shot, from 291 yards, to 12 feet and two-putted.

Kobori, the New Zealander who won a card for the Ladies European Tour in 2023 with two wins on the Access Series, set two new women's course records with her 67 on Royal Melbourne's West track and a 68 at Yarra Yarra. After Davis led by three at halfway, Kobori drew level by birdieing her last three holes of the third round. She was five under for the day at PK before back-to-back bogeys at 12 and 13 in her closing 70. With the women playing a different par to the men across the four days, Kobori's total of 276 was 15 under par, just one behind. In the women's professional division, Cassie Porter finished next, fully 20 strokes behind Kobori.

David Micheluzzi, a member at Peninsula Kingswood, closed with a 66 a day after his course-record 64 at Yarra Yarra and finished two shots behind Davis in third place. The men's amateur title went to Connor McDade after he made four birdies in the last six holes, while the women's amateur prize was taken by 14-year-old Amelia Harris. In the team competition, Kobori, Jediah Morgan and amateur Niall Shields Donegan won by three strokes.

Kingston Heath, Royal Melbourne (West), Yarra Yarra,
Peninsula Kingswood (North), Melbourne, Victoria — December 19-22

1	**Cam Davis**	65 66 69 67	267	-16
2	**Momoka Kobori**	71 67 68 70	276	-15
3	**David Micheluzzi**	70 69 64 66	269	-14
4	Louis Dobbelaar	71 71 65 65	272	-11
5	Jake Hughes	71 70 68 69	278	-5
6	Jediah Morgan	71 71 66 72	280	-3
7	Tom Power Horan	67 71 70 73	281	-2
8	Matthew Griffin	73 71 68 70	282	-1
	Justin Warren	70 70 70 72	282	-1
	Connor McDade (A)	73 70 69 70	282	-1
11	Jack Buchanan (A)	70 67 75 71	283	E
	Jye Pickin (A)	68 71 74 70	283	E
	Brett Coletta	69 71 71 72	283	E
14	Zach Murray	69 72 72 71	284	+1
	Blake Windred	71 72 69 72	284	+1
	Matias Sanchez	74 66 69 75	284	+1
17	Todd Sinnott	70 73 74 68	285	+2
	Matt Millar	74 71 70 70	285	+2
	Tim Walker	72 66 75 72	285	+2
	Cameron John	70 71 71 73	285	+2

LIV Golf Invitational Series

The LIV Golf Invitational Series debuted at the Centurion Club, north of London, a week ahead of the US Open in June with Dustin Johnson and Phil Mickelson heading the field. The new circuit, backed by the Public Investment Fund of Saudi Arabia, comprised a schedule of eight events, seven with individual and team portions, and a final team championship, with total prize money of $225 million over the series. Each of the individual events was played over 54 holes, with no cut and shotgun starts to each round, and featured 48 players.

Bryson DeChambeau and Brooks Koepka joined the roster for the first event on US soil in Portland while Cameron Smith, then the world number two and the reigning Open and Players champion, was the highest ranked player to feature, joining for the final five events of the schedule.

Johnson, who won once and finished in the top eight on all but one occasion, led the individual LIV points list to win an $18 million bonus, while he captained the Four Aces to the title at the Team Championship.

2022 SCHEDULE

London Invitational	**Charl Schwartzel**
Portland Invitational	**Branden Grace**
Bedminster Invitational	**Henrik Stenson**
Boston Invitational	**Dustin Johnson**
Chicago Invitational	**Cameron Smith (1,4)**
Bangkok Invitational	**Eugenio Lopez-Chacarra**
Jeddah Invitational	**Brooks Koepka**
Miami Team Championship	**Four Aces**

London Invitational

Headline acts Dustin Johnson and Phil Mickelson, who was playing for the first time in four months, finished six and 17 shots, respectively, behind winner Charl Schwartzel at the opening event of the LIV Golf Invitational Series at Centurion. The 37-year-old South African had not won for six years but led by three after scoring 65-66 and then held on despite a double bogey at the 12th hole in the final round. He closed with a 72 for a seven-under-par total of 203 to win from compatriots Hennie du Plessis, by one in second, and Branden Grace, by two, his closing 65 meaning he took third place on countback.

All three were part of the Stinger team, captained by Louis Oosthuizen, which shared the $3 million team prize after finishing 14 shots ahead of Peter Uihlein's Crushers team, also containing Richard Bland, Phachara Khongwatmai and Travis Smyth. Two scores counted for the team score on the first two days, and three on the third.

"I really wanted to win again," said Schwartzel, who collected $4,750,000 for his individual and team prizes. "I worked very hard the last few years and there were signs of good golf and just haven't really been able to be in contention. I hit a wayward shot on 12 and it sort of derailed me. From there on, I was just trying to hang in."

Centurion Club, Hemel Hempstead, St Albans, Hertfordshire, England — June 9-11
Par 70 (34-36); 7,047 yards — Purse: $25,000,000

1	**Charl Schwartzel**	65	66	72	203	$4,000,000
2	**Hennie du Plessis**	66	68	70	204	2,125,000
3	**Branden Grace**	68	72	65	205	1,275,000
4	Peter Uihlein	70	66	69	205	1,275,000
5	Sam Horsfield	69	70	68	207	975,000
6	Adrian Otaegui	70	70	68	208	737,500
	Oliver Bekker	70	67	71	208	737,500
8	Dustin Johnson	69	70	70	209	625,000
9	Talor Gooch	71	70	69	210	580,000
10	Graeme McDowell	74	71	66	211	516,667
	Justin Harding	68	74	69	211	516,667
	Louis Oosthuizen	72	69	70	211	516,667

13	Pablo Larrazabal	72 69 71	212	315,000			
	Ryosuke Kinoshita	73 67 72	212	315,000			
15	Martin Kaymer	74 70 69	213	245,000			
	Jinichiro Kozuma	73 70 70	213	245,000			
17	Richard Bland	73 74 67	214	226,000			
	JC Ritchie	73 70 71	214	226,000			
	Laurie Canter	69 74 71	214	226,000			
20	Ian Poulter	75 66 74	215	190,000			
	Scott Vincent	67 72 76	215	190,000			
22	Shaun Norris	73 72 71	216	170,000			
	Wade Ormsby	71 72 73	216	170,000			
24	Sergio Garcia	71 70 75	216	170,000			
25	James Piot	71 73 73	217	163,000			
	Matt Jones	74 70 73	217	163,000			
	Ian Snyman	71 71 75	217	163,000			
	Phachara Khongwatmai	67 72 78	217	163,000			

Portland Invitational

After a third-placed finish at Centurion, Branden Grace followed his compatriot Charl Schwartzel into the winner's circle in the first US-based LIV event at Pumpkin Ridge. Grace won the Portland Invitational by two strokes from Carlos Ortiz with a final round of 65 for a 13-under-par total of 203. The 34-year-old South African, whose second PGA Tour win came at the Puerto Rico Open in 2021, was two behind Ortiz and Dustin Johnson at the start of the final round, but came home in five-under 30. A three at the 13th hole, after a three-iron to 20 feet, sparked a run of four birdies in five holes, with his chip-in at the 16th putting him two ahead.

"I just found a groove," said Grace, who previously had 14 official victories worldwide. "From the first hole I hit the ball great and made a couple of nice putts when it mattered. The birdie on 13 was huge."

Ortiz, who at one point led by five strokes, closed with a 69 to finish two ahead of Johnson and Patrick Reed, whose closing 67 secured third place. Johnson led his team, including Reed, Pat Perez and Talor Gooch, to victory at 23 under par. "I haven't played a Ryder Cup or a Presidents Cup," said Gooch, "but can't imagine there's a whole hell of a lot of a difference." The event saw the debuts on the circuit of Brooks Koepka and Bryson DeChambeau.

Pumpkin Ridge Golf Club, Portland, Oregon — June 30-July 2
Par 72 (37-35); 7,641 yards — Purse: $25,000,000

1	**Branden Grace**	69 69 65	203	$4,000,000
2	**Carlos Ortiz**	67 69 69	205	2,125,000
3	**Patrick Reed**	72 68 67	207	1,275,000
4	Dustin Johnson	68 68 71	207	1,275,000
5	Louis Oosthuizen	71 69 69	209	975,000
6	Jinichiro Kozuma	71 69 70	210	800,000
7	Talor Gooch	72 70 70	212	675,000
8	Matthew Wolff	72 71 70	213	602,500
	Justin Harding	72 67 74	213	602,500
10	Bryson DeChambeau	72 69 73	214	560,000
11	Abraham Ancer	73 71 71	215	374,000
	Yuki Inamori	71 73 71	215	374,000
	Kevin Na	75 68 72	215	374,000
	Sam Horsfield	73 68 74	215	374,000
	Sihwan Kim	72 68 75	215	374,000
16	Lee Westwood	76 71 69	216	223,600
	Hideto Tanihara	69 75 72	216	223,600
	Matt Jones	72 72 72	216	223,600
	Martin Kaymer	71 72 73	216	223,600
	Brooks Koepka	70 70 76	216	223,600
21	Adrian Otaegui	74 72 71	217	180,000
22	James Piot	73 76 69	218	172,000
23	Chase Koepka	73 74 72	219	168,000
	Ryosuke Kinoshita	75 71 73	219	168,000
	Scott Vincent	71 74 74	219	168,000

Bedminster Invitational

Henrik Stenson got back to winning ways on his LIV debut in the Bedminster event at Trump National. The 46-year-old Swede had not won since the 2019 Hero World Challenge and dropped out of the world's top 100 in March 2021 but made his mark immediately with an opening 64 and then added two 69s for an 11-under-par total of 202 to finish two strokes ahead of Matthew Wolff (64) and Dustin Johnson (68).

Suggesting he felt he had something to prove, Stenson said: "When we as players have that, I think we can bring out the good stuff. I certainly did that this week. I'm super-proud of the focus I managed to have. I've been working really hard to get my game back in shape, and it's certainly going in the right direction as we know now."

Johnson's Four Aces team won again, this time beating the Majesticks, who included newcomer Stenson, by seven strokes. Former president Donald Trump was an avid spectator at his family-owned course which was due to stage the 2022 PGA Championship before it was moved to Southern Hills following the attack on the Capitol Building in Washington on January 6, 2021.

Trump National Golf Club, Bedminster, New Jersey — July 29-31
Par 71 (35-36); 7,591 yards — Purse: $25,000,000

1	**Henrik Stenson**	64	69	69	202	$4,000,000
2	**Matthew Wolff**	70	70	64	204	1,812,500
3	**Dustin Johnson**	67	69	68	204	1,812,500
4	Carlos Ortiz	67	70	68	205	1,050,000
5	Patrick Reed	64	73	69	206	975,000
6	Paul Casey	72	71	66	209	648,000
	Sergio Garcia	70	70	69	209	648,000
	Turk Pettit	71	67	71	209	648,000
	Lee Westwood	69	69	71	209	648,000
	Talor Gooch	73	64	72	209	648,000
11	Brooks Koepka	68	76	66	210	495,000
	Martin Kaymer	68	71	71	210	495,000
13	Branden Grace	70	73	68	211	293,333
	Ian Poulter	68	72	71	211	293,333
	Phachara Khongwatmai	66	72	73	211	293,333
16	Sam Horsfield	70	72	70	212	240,000
17	Chase Koepka	69	73	71	213	229,000
	Charl Schwartzel	70	69	74	213	229,000
19	Matt Jones	72	73	69	214	200,000
	Louis Oosthuizen	73	71	70	214	200,000
	Justin Harding	70	74	70	214	200,000
22	Travis Smyth	69	73	73	215	172,000
23	Shaun Norris	72	74	70	216	168,000
	Eugenio Lopez-Chacarra	73	72	71	216	168,000
	Peter Uihlein	70	74	72	216	168,000

Boston Invitational

Dustin Johnson scored his first LIV Golf victory with a dramatic playoff win at The International, at Bolton, near Boston. After finishing in the top eight in each of the previous three events, the former world number one defeated Anirban Lahiri and Joaquin Niemann by sinking a 60-foot eagle putt at the first extra hole — the ball had plenty of speed but hit the hole and bounced up and then in. Johnson scored 67-63-65 for a 15-under-par total of 195.

"I felt we had a really good read on it," Johnson said. "I might have hit it a little harder than I wanted to, but as soon as I hit it, I'm like, whoa, and then it was on a good line, and I'm like, hit the hole, hit the hole, hit the hole, and it went in somehow. I wanted to finally get my first victory out here. I feel like I've had a really good chance to win every single week, just haven't played as well on Sunday as I'd like to."

Lahiri, who closed with a 64, had a birdie chance still to come, while Niemann (66) was already in for a par. Johnson led the Four Aces team to their third consecutive win, by two strokes from the Crushers, who included Lahiri. The Indian was one of six players making their debuts on the new circuit, including Niemann and Open champion Cameron Smith, who tied for fourth.

The International Golf Club, Bolton, Massachusetts — September 2-4
Par 70 (35-35); 6,944 yards — Purse: $25,000,000

1	**Dustin Johnson**	67	63	65	195	$4,000,000
2	**Anirban Lahiri**	66	65	64	195	1,812,500
3	**Joaquin Niemann**	64	65	66	195	1,812,500
	Johnson won playoff at first extra hole					
4	Lee Westwood	67	67	62	196	1,012,500
	Cameron Smith	64	69	63	196	1,012,500
6	Talor Gooch	63	65	69	197	800,000
7	Jason Kokrak	67	65	66	198	675,000
8	Abraham Ancer	69	65	65	199	625,000
9	Sergio Garcia	70	64	66	200	560,000
	Louis Oosthuizen	66	67	67	200	560,000
	Kevin Na	66	67	67	200	560,000
12	Branden Grace	67	66	68	201	450,000
13	Sadom Kaewkanjana	67	66	69	202	315,000
	Matthew Wolff	63	69	70	202	315,000
15	Charles Howell III	67	70	66	203	245,000
	Pat Perez	67	66	70	203	245,000
17	Bryson Dechambeau	69	69	66	204	219,500
	Richard Bland	68	70	66	204	219,500
	Ian Poulter	69	67	68	204	219,500
	Bernd Wiesberger	66	66	72	204	219,500
21	Paul Casey	66	75	64	205	171,200
	Laurie Canter	69	71	65	205	171,200
	Cameron Tringale	71	66	68	205	171,200
	Scott Vincent	70	66	69	205	171,200
	Martin Kaymer	68	67	70	205	171,200

Chicago Invitational

On his debut in Boston, the Open and Players champion Cameron Smith said: "Because I've changed tours, doesn't mean I'm a worse player for it." The 29-year-old Australian finished one stroke outside of the playoff in his first event but in Chicago he won by three strokes from Peter Uihlein and Dustin Johnson.

Smith, now the world number three having become the highest ranked player to join LIV Golf, scored 66-68-69 for a 13-under-par total of 203 at Rich Harvest Farms. His fourth win of the year was briefly in doubt when Johnson birdied the seventh to draw level, but Smith followed the American in and then birdied the next to extend his lead. "I think I had to prove to probably myself and some other people that I am still a great player, you know, I am still out here to win golf tournaments," Smith said.

Smith's birdie putt at the last hole did not change the result of the individual contest but earned his Punch team a tie for third place. "It was nice to get that done for the boys," Smith said. Johnson's Four Aces team, including Patrick Reed, Pat Perez and Talor Gooch, won for the fourth event in a row.

Rich Harvest Farms, Sugar Grove, Illinois — September 16-18
Par 72 (36-36); 7,408 yards — Purse: $25,000,000

1	**Cameron Smith**	66	68	69	203	$4,000,000
2	**Peter Uihlein**	71	66	69	206	1,812,500
3	**Dustin Johnson**	63	73	70	206	1,812,500
4	Sergio Garcia	72	69	67	208	1,012,500
	Joaquin Niemann	71	69	68	208	1,012,500
6	Louis Oosthuizen	69	71	69	209	737,500
	Charl Schwartzel	69	69	71	209	737,500
8	Phil Mickelson	70	74	66	210	576,250
	Chase Koepka	73	70	67	210	576,250
	Bryson Dechambeau	69	70	71	210	576,250
	Laurie Canter	70	68	72	210	576,250
12	Cameron Tringale	71	72	68	211	332,500
	Patrick Reed	74	69	68	211	332,500
	Scott Vincent	70	71	70	211	332,500
	Lee Westwood	68	71	72	211	332,500
16	Matt Jones	68	72	72	212	236,000
	Matthew Wolff	67	73	72	212	236,000
18	Branden Grace	70	72	71	213	215,333
	Richard Bland	72	70	71	213	215,333
	Charles Howell Iii	68	71	74	213	215,333
21	Paul Casey	73	72	69	214	170,000
	Brooks Koepka	70	74	70	214	170,000
	Anirban Lahiri	72	71	71	214	170,000
	Jason Kokrak	75	68	71	214	170,000
	Eugenio Lopez-Chacarra	71	72	71	214	170,000
	Harold Varner III	70	72	72	214	170,000

Bangkok Invitational

In June, Eugenio Lopez-Chacarra left Oklahoma State University prior to his senior year and turned professional with LIV Golf. In October, the 22-year-old Spaniard from Madrid won the Bangkok Invitational by three strokes from former Masters champion Patrick Reed. Lopez-Chacarra had built a large cushion of five shots on the first two days and two bogeys early in the final round, his only dropped shots of the tournament, did not dent his progress to a maiden victory and the $4,000,000 first prize. In four previous starts, his best finish had been a tie for 21st place.

At brand new Stonehill, which only opened for play in Bangkok in July, Lopez-Chacarra scored 65-63-69 for a 19-under-par total of 197. Reed closed with a 67 to finish at 16 under and Paul Casey took third place on countback after a 65. In the team event, the winner joined Sergio Garcia, Abraham Ancer and Carlos Ortiz in topping the leaderboard by seven strokes. "It means a lot," said Lopez-Chacarra. "There's no secret. It's trusting yourself, putting in the hard work. I knew it was going to be hard today and I'm very pleased."

Although Dustin Johnson finished outside the top eight for the first time in six events, the American secured the individual title and its $18 million bonus with one individual event remaining. "It's an honour to be LIV's first individual season champion," Johnson said.

Stonehill Golf Club, Bangkok, Thailand — October 7-9
Par 72 (36-36); 7,815 yards — Purse: $25,000,000

1	**Eugenio Lopez-Chacarra**	65	63	69	197	$4,000,000
2	**Patrick Reed**	68	65	67	200	2,125,000
3	**Paul Casey**	71	65	65	201	1,175,000
	Richard Bland	65	68	68	201	1,175,000
	Sihwan Kim	67	66	68	201	1,175,000
6	James Piot	69	65	68	202	737,500

	Harold Varner III	67 66 69	202	737,500			Phil Mickelson	69 69 69	207	233,600
8	Charles Howell III	69 67 67	203	602,500			Carlos Ortiz	72 65 70	207	233,600
	Brooks Koepka	67 67 69	203	602,500			Lee Westwood	69 66 72	207	233,600
10	Abraham Ancer	69 68 68	205	477,500		20	Joaquin Niemann	72 71 65	208	174,286
	Laurie Canter	70 66 69	205	477,500			Sergio Garcia	68 72 68	208	174,286
	Ian Poulter	66 70 69	205	477,500			Sadom Kaewkanjana	71 69 68	208	174,286
	Marc Leishman	66 69 70	205	477,500			Peter Uihlein	70 68 70	208	174,286
14	Bryson DeChambeau	69 68 69	206	270,000			Talor Gooch	70 67 71	208	174,286
15	Matt Jones	71 70 66	207	233,600			Jediah Morgan	67 69 72	208	174,286
	Dustin Johnson	70 70 67	207	233,600			Kevin Na	67 68 73	208	174,286

Jeddah Invitational

Brooks Koepka had not won since the 2021 Phoenix Open but finally showed a return to form by winning the Jeddah Invitational at the third extra hole of a playoff against Peter Uihlein. Both players had birdied the 18th hole at Royal Greens to get to 12-under-par 198 and eliminate Joaquin Niemann and Sergio Garcia in regulation, and each kept birdieing the par-five finisher in the playoff until Uihlein hit his bunker shot into the water the third time around.

"The last two years, they haven't been fun," Koepka said of battling knee, hip and wrist injuries. "It's been a long road. I didn't know if my career was over. I wasn't sure I was going to play. It's nice to be able to come back and win."

The four-time major winner, who scored 62-67-69 for the week, led his Smash team, that included brother Chase and one-time room-mate Uihlein, to a six-stroke victory over Bangkok winners, the Fireballs. With a win, Uihlein (65-63-70) would have picked up the $8 million bonus for finishing second on the points list, which instead went to Portland winner Branden Grace, while Uihlein pocketed a $4 million bonus for coming third.

Royal Greens Golf & Country Club, King Abdullah Economic City, Saudi Arabia — October 14-16
Par 70 (35-35); 7,048 yards — Purse: $25,000,000

1	**Brooks Koepka**	62 67 69	198	$4,000,000		Chase Koepka	68 67 68	203	289,714
2	**Peter Uihlein**	65 63 70	198	2,125,000		Lee Westwood	67 68 68	203	289,714
	Koepka won playoff at third extra hole					Graeme McDowell	70 65 68	203	289,714
3	**Joaquin Niemann**	68 66 65	199	1,275,000		Patrick Reed	65 69 69	203	289,714
	Sergio Garcia	67 64 68	199	1,275,000		Carlos Ortiz	66 68 69	203	289,714
5	Matthew Wolff	68 66 66	200	816,667	19	Charles Howell III	70 68 66	204	210,000
	Dustin Johnson	68 65 67	200	816,667		Sihwan Kim	68 65 71	204	210,000
	Paul Casey	68 64 68	200	816,667	21	Bryson Dechambeau	70 67 68	205	172,500
8	Bernd Wiesberger	68 68 65	201	602,500		Cameron Smith	68 69 68	205	172,500
	Charl Schwartzel	64 67 70	201	602,500		Jason Kokrak	70 65 70	205	172,500
10	Anirban Lahiri	67 66 69	202	550,000		James Piot	66 67 72	205	172,500
	Abraham Ancer	67 65 70	202	550,000	25	Phachara Khongwatmai	68 71 67	206	164,000
12	Talor Gooch	69 67 67	203	289,714		Richard Bland	71 67 68	206	164,000
	Jediah Morgan	67 68 68	203	289,714		Eugenio Lopez-Chacarra	69 67 70	206	164,000

2022 POINTS LIST

		Points
1	Dustin Johnson	135
2	Branden Grace	79
3	Peter Uihlein	79
4	Patrick Reed	79
5	Charl Schwartzel	66
6	Matthew Wolff	66
7	Joaquin Niemann	66
8	Brooks Koepka	62
9	Sergio Garcia	62
10	Cameron Smith	57

Miami Team Championship

Dustin Johnson's Four Aces team completed a clean sweep of LIV titles on US soil by adding to their four regular season victories by winning the Miami Team Championship, where a $50 million purse was on offer. Each member of the winning team earned $4 million. Johnson's par at the last, thanks to a nervy three-footer, meant a one-stroke victory over Cameron Smith's Punch team. Smith, playing in the final pairing with Johnson, birdied five of the last eight holes to post a 65, the best score of the day by three strokes at Trump National Doral.

Jason Kokrak, of Smash, was the only other player to break 70 on the Blue Monster, formerly a longtime venue on the PGA Tour. The key to the Four Aces's victory was their consistency on the final day. Johnson, Pat Perez, after two birdies over the last three holes, and Patrick Reed, with a birdie at the 18th, all scored 70. Along with Talor Gooch's 71, they finished the final-day shootout on a seven-under-par total of 281. Matt Jones, with 70, was the only player alongside Smith to break par for the Punch team, who finished on six under par. Smash finished at four over par and Stinger at 10 over.

"It was a team effort, but it ended up coming down to me and Cam playing the 18th," Johnson said. "You couldn't have drawn it up any better. I do not like stress, so that was a little more stress than I was looking for."

Trump National Doral Golf Club (Blue Monster), Miami, Florida — October 28-30
Par 72 (36-36); 7,702 yards — Purse: $50,000,000

FRIDAY

Smash (5) defeated Niblicks (12) 2-1
Brooks Koepka lost to Harold Varner III 4 and 3
Peter Uihlein defeated James Piot 5 and 3
Jason Kokrak and Chase Koepka defeated Turk Pettit and Hudson Swafford

Cleeks (10) defeated Torque (7) 2-1
Shergo Al Kurdi lost to Joaquin Niemann 5 and 3
Laurie Canter defeated Jediah Morgan by one hole
Graeme McDowell and Richard Bland defeated Scott Vincent and Adrian Otaegui by two holes

Punch (11) defeated Hy Flyers (8) 2-1
Cameron Smith defeated Phil Mickelson by one hole
Marc Leishman defeated Matthew Wolff 4 and 2
Matt Jones and Wade Ormsby lost to Bernd Wiesberger and Cameron Tringale 3 and 2

Majesticks (6) defeated Iron Heads (9) 3-0
Ian Poulter defeated Kevin Na 4 and 2
Lee Westwood defeated Sihwan Kim 4 and 3
Sam Horsfield and Henrik Stenson defeated Phachara Khongwatmai and Sadom Kaewkanjana 4 and 2
Losing teams earned $1,000,000 ($250,000 each)

SATURDAY

Four Aces (1) defeated Cleeks 2-1
Dustin Johnson defeated Al Kurdi 5 and 3
Patrick Reed lost to Canter 2 and 1
Pat Perez and Talor Gooch defeated McDowell and Bland by one hole

Punch defeated Fireballs (3) 2-1
Smith lost to Sergio Garcia 2 and 1
Leishman defeated Carlos Ortiz by one hole
Jones and Ormsby defeated Eugenio Lopez-Chacarra and Abraham Ancer by one hole

Smash defeated Majesticks 3-0
Brooks Koepka defeated Poulter 3 and 1
Uihlein defeated Westwood 4 and 2
Kokrak and Chase Koepka defeated Horsfield and Stenson by one hole

Stinger (4) defeated Crushers (2) 2-1
Louis Oosthuizen defeated Bryson DeChambeau at the 23rd
Branden Grace lost to Paul Casey at the 20th
Charl Schwartzel and Hennie du Plessis defeated Charles Howell III and Anirban Lahiri by two holes
Losing teams earned $3,000,000 ($750,000 each)

SUNDAY

Four Aces	281 (Johnson 70, Reed 70, Gooch 71, Perez 70)	$16,000,000
Punch	282 (Smith 65, Leishman 74, Jones 70, Ormsby 73)	8,000,000
Smash	292 (B Koepka 74, Kokrak 68, Uihlein 75, C Koepka 75)	6,000,000
Stinger	298 (Oosthuizen 71, Schwartzel 71, Grace 80, du Plessis 76)	4,000,000

CME GROUP
CME Group

LPGA Tour

A summation of Lydia Ko's season that points to a strong start and an even stronger finish does not do it justice. In 2022 Ko was strong from beginning to end. She won the second event of the year, at the Gainbridge, and two of the last three. When she won the BMW Ladies Championship in October, the 25-year-old Kiwi said: "I think this is probably the best I've played, the most consistently I've played. I wanted to finish my season off strong." She certainly did that, claiming the biggest single prize in the history of women's golf when she won the CME Group Tour Championship and its $2 million first-place cheque. As well as the CME Globe, Ko won the money list, the Rolex LPGA Player of the Year award and the Vare Trophy.

This was Ko 2.0. First there was the young prodigy who could not stop winning and became the world number one at the age of 17. Then the winning stopped. Women's golf has seen young phenomenons come and go. Few return to the heights as Ko did when she reached the top spot on the Rolex Rankings after a gap of five and a half years at the end of 2022. This was Ko the mature golfer and mature person. Her win in Korea was meaningful because it came in the land of her birth and in front of many of her extended family. The CME win was meaningful for more than just the financial aspect as her fiancé was alongside for the first time. The couple married in Seoul at the end of the year.

"This year has been an incredible year. I really could never ask for more to win so early in the season and then to have won in Korea and then win the last event of the year," said Ko after her 19th LPGA win, six more than anyone else currently under 30. "I couldn't have drawn it up any better. There have been so many exciting things in my life that's been going on. It will be my last win as a single lady. So I wanted to do this for my family. This has been one of the most consistent and solid years I've had."

Ko intimated that in her earlier incarnation as a winning machine there were not so many top-10 finishes to go alongside the victories. The figures do not entirely bear that out. She got into contention a lot, but at other times finished well down the field. In 22 events in 2022, however, Ko did not miss a cut and only once, with 46th place at the KPMG Women's PGA, finished outside the top 26. She had 18 top 20s, 14 of them top 10s, and 12 of those were top fives. In winning the Vare Trophy for the second year running, Ko's stroke average of 68.988 was the second lowest ever on the LPGA, behind only Annika Sorenstam's 68.79 in 2002. According to the KPMG performance insights, in operation for a full season for the first time, Ko led strokes gained putting and total strokes gained, and in the latter category over her last 10 events gained more than three strokes a round on the field.

The point Ko made several times at the end of the season was that the depth of competition was now so deep she needed to keep on improving. Her second Player of the Year title was only secured at the final event after a close duel with Minjee Lee, who won the Founders Cup and then the US Women's Open at Pine Needles, where previous champions include compatriot Karrie Webb, as well as Sorenstam and Cristie Kerr. Lee won the Aon Risk Reward title, earning $1 million just as Scottie Scheffler did on the PGA Tour, and the Rolex Annika Major Award as the Australian followed her dominant win at the US Open with a runner-up finish at the KPMG Women's PGA and fourth at the AIG Women's Open.

The strength of Lee's game was her approach play, as she led the LPGA in strokes gained ball-striking and approaches, and in proximity to the hole on approach shots from each distance range. In fact, the numbers put Lee ahead not just of the women but the men as well for strokes gained on approach shots.

Jennifer Kupcho, on the same weekend as three years earlier she had made her name by winning the inaugural Augusta National Women's Amateur, made her professional breakthrough by winning the Chevron Championship on its last playing at Mission Hills in Rancho Mirage. Kupcho won twice more, at the Meijer LPGA Classic and the Dow Great Lakes Bay Invitational alongside Lizette Salas, to match Ko for most wins. Korea's In Gee Chun, on the back of a brilliant first round, won the KPMG WPGA, her third major but first for six years, while Canada's Brooke Henderson had also waited six years to win her second major at the Amundi Evian Championship. Henderson won twice during the season, and Chun almost won a second major before losing at the fourth playoff hole at the AIG Women's Open to South Africa's Ashleigh Buhai. Chun received the 2022 Founders Award for exemplifying the spirit and values of the LPGA.

For the second year in a row Thailand's Atthaya Thitikul landed a rookie award, having done so on the Ladies European Tour in 2021, when she was also the LET number one. Thitikul won twice in playoffs and the 19-year-old spent two weeks as the world number one in November. Receiving the Louise Suggs Rookie of the Year award, Thitikul said: "I am just a little girl who always had a dream to compete on the LPGA Tour. But to be on this stage here, in front of you guys, is a dream come true."

Injury and health concerns were not far away during 2022. Nelly Korda missed much of the early season after surgery on a life-threatening blood clot in her left arm. The 2021 Olympic champion returned to win on the LET in the summer and retained her Pelican title in November. The player she duelled with for top honours so memorably in 2021, Jin Young Ko, won on her first appearance at the HSBC Women's World Championship, extended her record run of rounds under 70 to 16 and rounds under par to 34, but later in the year her form dipped as her lingering wrist injury deteriorated. And Danielle Kang, after winning the first event of the year and finishing runner-up to Ko in the second, was absent in the summer due to treatment for a tumour on her spine. Kang returned to the tour and was only beaten in a playoff by Thitikul at the Walmart tournament.

Following record increases in prize money at many of the major championships in 2022, the LPGA announced a 33-event schedule for 2023 with total prize money in excess of $100 million for the first time. As well as the Solheim Cup being played in Spain, the International Crown event was due to return for the first time since 2018. "It will be a banner year for the LPGA Tour," said commissioner Mollie Marcoux Samaan. "We have never had better or more committed partners who see the commercial value in investing in women's sports and who understand how their partnerships elevate women and girls on and off the golf course. As the home to the world's best female golfers, the LPGA provides a platform to inspire young girls and women to dream big."

2022 SCHEDULE

Hilton Grand Vacations Tournament of Champions	**Danielle Kang**	
Gainbridge LPGA	**Lydia Ko**	
LPGA Drive On Championship	**Leona Maguire**	
HSBC Women's World Championship	**Jin Young Ko**	
Honda LPGA Thailand	**Nanna Koerstz Madsen**	
JBTC Classic	**Atthaya Thitikul**	
Chevron Championship	**Jennifer Kupcho**	*See chapter 1*
Lotte Championship	**Hyo Joo Kim**	
Dio Implant LA Open	**Nasa Hataoka**	
Palos Verdes Championship	**Marina Alex**	
Cognizant Founders Cup	**Minjee Lee**	
Bank of Hope LPGA Match Play	**Eun-Hee Ji**	
US Women's Open	**Minjee Lee (2)**	*See chapter 4*
ShopRite LPGA Classic	**Brooke M Henderson**	
Meijer LPGA Classic	**Jennifer Kupcho (2)**	
KPMG Women's PGA Championship	**In Gee Chun**	*See chapter 6*
Dow Great Lakes Bay Invitational	**Jennifer Kupcho (3)/Lizette Salas**	
Amundi Evian Championship	**Brooke M Henderson (2)**	*See chapter 8*
Trust Golf Women's Scottish Open	**Ayaka Furue**	*See chapter 23*
AIG Women's Open	**Ashleigh Buhai**	*See chapter 9*
ISPS Handa World Invitational	**Maja Stark (1,3)**	*See chapter 23*
CP Women's Open	**Paula Reto (1,2)**	
Dana Open	**Gaby Lopez**	
Kroger Queen City Championship	**Ally Ewing**	
AmazingCre Portland Classic	**Andrea Lee (1,2)**	
Walmart NW Arkansas Championship	**Atthaya Thitikul (2)**	
The Ascendant LPGA	**Charley Hull**	
LPGA Mediheal Championship	**Jodi Ewart Shadoff**	

BMW Ladies Championship	**Lydia Ko (2)**	
Toto Japan Classic	**Gemma Dryburgh**	*See chapter 25*
Pelican Women's Championship	**Nelly Korda (1,2)**	
CME Group Tour Championship	**Lydia Ko (3)**	

Hilton Grand Vacations Tournament of Champions

Danielle Kang worked hard in the off-season. She worked on her fitness and nutrition, added weight and got stronger, aimed for a more consistent swing speed with coach Butch Harmon and went out on the worst of Las Vegas's winter days. All part of a plan. "If it's cold my body tightens up; if it's hot I'm ready to go," she explained. "I play really well in heat. I do not play well in the cold. We can all look at my stats. I miss the cut almost every year in the British Open."

Playing well in the UK major is something she would like for her English caddie, Olly Brett. But her preparations had immediate results when on a freezing Florida weekend Kang won the Hilton Grand Vacations Tournament of Champions. She had lost in a playoff to Jessica Korda in 2021 but now came from one behind the other Korda, world number one Nelly, for a three-stroke victory at Lake Nona.

The younger sister was not the defending champion but had won at the same venue in 2021 and appeared to be picking up where she left off. Korda led through the second and third rounds before closing with a 75 to fall into a tie for fourth. Canada's Brooke Henderson went bogey-free over the weekend to take second place, while 2020 winner Gaby Lopez was third.

Kang, with rounds of 68-67-69, was only a stroke away from the lead on the first three days before closing with a 68 for a 16-under-par total of 272. She charged clear with birdies at the ninth and 11th holes, and then three in a row from the 13th. At the short 16th, where her tee shot ended awkwardly in a bunker, she took her medicine and two-putted from 100 feet for the bogey. She had to hole a comebacker for the four but it was a sign of new-found maturity that it did not turn into a disaster. "Instead of freaking out or panicking about the results, what if I don't make a bogey, what If I don't make a double, I was more focused on what I needed to do to hit the next shot with 100 per cent commitment," she said. "That was to watch my putt, and I trusted that line and I made that bogey, so I was really proud of myself." It was Kang's sixth win and her first since she won back-to-back when the tour resumed in the summer of 2020.

In the celebrity division, Annika Sorenstam, the 2021 US Senior Open champion playing on her home course, was defeated at the first playoff hole when former baseball pitcher Derek Lowe made a 15-foot par putt. The pair had tied on 138 Stableford points.

Lake Nona Golf and Country Club, Orlando, Florida — January 20-23
Par 72 (36-36); 6,617 yards — Purse: $1,500,000

1	**Danielle Kang**	68	67	69	68	272	$225,000
2	**Brooke M Henderson**	69	68	68	70	275	177,229
3	**Gaby Lopez**	67	68	69	72	276	128,567
4	Celine Boutier	70	67	70	71	278	89,754
	Nelly Korda	68	66	69	75	278	89,754
6	Yuka Saso	68	70	68	73	279	65,497
7	Jessica Korda	69	67	72	72	280	54,823
8	Pajaree Anannarukarn	69	72	68	72	281	45,606
	Inbee Park	71	67	70	73	281	45,606
10	Matilda Castren	73	66	71	74	284	37,842
	Lydia Ko	71	68	71	74	284	37,842
12	Georgia Hall	70	72	75	69	286	33,960
13	Ryann O'Toole	68	72	75	72	287	30,856
	Patty Tavatanakit	70	71	70	76	287	30,856
15	A Lim Kim	74	70	73	71	288	27,362
	Moriya Jutanugarn	75	70	69	74	288	27,362
17	Madelene Sagstrom	70	71	79	69	289	25,229
18	Nasa Hataoka	71	71	76	72	290	23,158
	Sophia Popov	72	70	72	76	290	23,158
	Stacy Lewis	70	69	75	76	290	23,158
21	Ally Ewing	71	69	74	77	291	21,542
22	Ariya Jutanugarn	74	72	73	73	292	20,765
23	Angela Stanford	72	73	73	75	293	19,989
24	Mel Reid	73	72	75	75	295	19,212
25	Austin Ernst	74	76	78	71	299	18,533
26	Hee Young Park	76	75	73	79	303	17,855
27	Anna Nordqvist	76	73	75	80	304	17,174
28	Mirim Lee	77	77	81	73	308	16,156
	Michelle Wie West	71	78	78	81	308	16,156

Gainbridge LPGA

It is always worth learning from a current world number one, even if you have occupied an equivalent position in the past. So Lydia Ko took note of something Jon Rahm said on social media: "He said it's not about how many times you hit the fairway, in golf you have to try and get the best score you can in the circumstances."

Ko had the best score at the Gainbridge LPGA, beating the previous week's winner, Danielle Kang, by a stroke at Boca Rio. There was a little bit of everything from the one-time prodigy who won on the LPGA for the first time in three years in 2021. Ko opened with a nine-under 63 to lead by two but was caught by Kang the next day. On a cold, windy Saturday, Ko's battling 72 gave her a two-shot lead as Kang briefly lost her newly acquired grit on the back nine.

On Sunday, however, Kang was back on top form, drawing level after three holes and briefly taking the lead at the 12th. She dropped a shot at the 13th and that was enough for Ko to pounce. An exquisitely paced, curling putt at the 15th — the greens had sped up over the weekend — provided the decisive birdie. Both birdied the 16th but it was Ko's sand recoveries that ultimately brought her victory. Three times she got up and down from a bunker on the back nine, including at the last to avoid a playoff. Ko closed with a 69 for a 14-under-par total of 274, with Kang finishing with a 68. Yuka Saso was a further stroke behind with Celine Boutier and Charley Hull tying for fourth place.

This was Ko's 17th LPGA win and third worldwide in less than a year after she won the 2021 Saudi International on the LET. And the two-time Olympic medallist was still only 24.

As for Rahm's motivational post, Ko said: "I think his quote really helped me to realise that, you know what? It's golf. Sometimes I'm going to hit great shots; sometimes I'm going to hit not-so-pretty ones. I have to manage my way around and try and shoot the best score I can. Today I don't feel I had my 'A' game, but I was able to get up and down when I was out of position and not get too down when I did make mistakes."

Boca Rio Golf Club, Boca Raton, Florida — January 27-30
Par 72 (36-36); 6,701 yards — Purse: $2,000,000

1	**Lydia Ko**	63	70	72	69	274	$300,000
2	**Danielle Kang**	65	68	74	68	275	184,255
3	**Yuka Saso**	67	70	72	67	276	133,664
4	Charley Hull	67	71	71	68	277	93,312
	Celine Boutier	72	67	69	69	277	93,312
6	Lexi Thompson	70	70	73	68	281	62,545
	Brooke M Henderson	68	71	74	68	281	62,545
8	Maude-Aimee Leblanc	67	72	74	69	282	45,227
	Stacy Lewis	68	72	72	70	282	45,227
	Hye-Jin Choi	67	72	73	70	282	45,227
11	Georgia Hall	70	70	76	67	283	36,567
	Ally Ewing	68	73	72	70	283	36,567
13	Bronte Law	68	70	78	68	284	29,456
	Amy Yang	68	74	73	69	284	29,456
	Aditi Ashok	66	72	76	70	284	29,456
	Patty Tavatanakit	71	68	74	71	284	29,456
	Jodi Ewart Shadoff	68	69	76	71	284	29,456
18	Pauline Roussin	73	70	74	68	285	24,514
	Ayaka Furue	69	72	71	73	285	24,514
20	Pornanong Phatlum	72	71	74	69	286	20,824
	Megan Khang	70	74	72	70	286	20,824
	Carlota Ciganda	68	72	76	70	286	20,824
	Nelly Korda	68	72	76	70	286	20,824
	Jessica Korda	72	68	75	71	286	20,824
	In Gee Chun	68	72	73	73	286	20,824
	Nasa Hataoka	67	71	73	75	286	20,824
27	Ryann O'Toole	70	70	78	69	287	15,881
	Sarah Schmelzel	71	73	73	70	287	15,881
	Su Oh	69	70	78	70	287	15,881
	Anna Nordqvist	71	74	71	71	287	15,881
	Leona Maguire	73	70	71	73	287	15,881
	Sophia Schubert	70	72	72	73	287	15,881
	Morgane Metraux	72	66	76	73	287	15,881
34	Xiyu Lin	72	72	75	69	288	12,156
	Dana Finkelstein	68	75	76	69	288	12,156
	Gaby Lopez	68	73	78	69	288	12,156
	Narin An	71	70	75	72	288	12,156
	Perrine Delacour	69	72	75	72	288	12,156
	Marina Alex	68	71	77	72	288	12,156
40	Jennifer Kupcho	68	75	79	67	289	9,684
	Madelene Sagstrom	70	72	78	69	289	9,684
	Jasmine Suwannapura	71	73	75	70	289	9,684
	A Lim Kim	70	71	78	70	289	9,684
	Yaeeun Hong	70	73	74	72	289	9,684
45	Lilia Vu	70	73	77	70	290	8,120
	Jeongeun Lee[5]	70	75	74	71	290	8,120
	Hee Young Park	72	72	75	71	290	8,120
	Atthaya Thitikul	72	71	73	74	290	8,120
49	Brittany Lincicome	72	73	78	68	291	7,095
	Kelly Tan	75	69	74	73	291	7,095
	Rachel Rohanna	70	74	72	75	291	7,095
52	Emma Talley	76	68	76	72	292	6,254
	Albane Valenzuela	71	73	76	72	292	6,254
	Wichanee Meechai	72	72	75	73	292	6,254
	Pajaree Anannarukarn	70	72	77	73	292	6,254
	Karrie Webb	71	72	75	74	292	6,254
57	Cydney Clanton	74	71	76	72	293	5,195
	Stephanie Meadow	75	69	77	72	293	5,195
	Amanda Doherty	68	74	78	73	293	5,195
	Jenny Shin	72	73	74	74	293	5,195

	Christina Kim	70 75 74 74	293	5,195	68 Muni He	70 74 79 72	295	4,186
	Jeongeun Lee[6]	67 73 77 76	293	5,195	Linnea Johansson	72 71 77 75	295	4,186
63	Dewi Weber	71 71 82 70	294	4,540	70 Brittany Lang	72 73 76 75	296	4,011
	Lauren Stephenson	70 74 79 71	294	4,540	Lindsey Weaver-Wright	74 71 74 77	296	4,011
	Amy Olson	69 75 78 72	294	4,540	72 Jaye Marie Green	70 75 78 74	297	3,933
	Laura Restrepo	71 74 75 74	294	4,540	73 Allison Emrey	72 73 81 75	301	3,858
	Mel Reid	71 72 76 75	294	4,540	Gerina Mendoza	67 77 75 82	301	3,858

LPGA Drive On Championship

If the honour of becoming the first Irish player to win on the LPGA had been decided by a birdie contest in a Tuesday practice round, then Stephanie Meadow would be the answer to a future quiz question. Meadow did receive $20 from compatriot Leona Maguire and went on to have a hole-in-one, the first of the season, in the opening round, but it was Maguire who triumphed at the LPGA Drive On Championship. The 27-year-old from County Cavan defeated Lexi Thompson by three strokes at Crown Colony in Fort Myers.

This had long been expected for a longtime world number one amateur who starred for Duke University in college golf. She graduated from the Epson Tour at the first time of asking in 2019 before settling into LPGA life for the next two years. "It's been a meticulous journey," Maguire said. "I've worked my way up the levels."

Engaging Dermot Byrne, who spent many years alongside Shane Lowry, as her caddie in the middle of 2021 helped everything fall into place. She had a few near-misses, pushing Nelly Korda close at the Meijer Classic, and then producing a superb rookie performance at the Solheim Cup with four and a half points out of five. She received a hero's reception in her hometown a few days later but in the off-season she knew everyone was thinking the same thing. "I suppose people have always had expectations, and I feel like even at Christmas people were, 'When you going to win?' That was on the tip of everybody's tongue."

Maguire, who is managed by pop star Niall Horan, produced consistent rounds of 66-65-67 for an 18-under-par total of 198. She had 22 birdies and four bogeys, one at the last when it did not matter. She was one off the lead after day one, then shared the 36-hole lead with Marina Alex, who faded to a share of fourth place with a closing 72. Brittany Altomare also finished fourth after briefly holding the lead with her fifth birdie in a row at the sixth. Maguire responded with five birdies in the next seven holes. Thompson tried to get close with five birdies between the fifth and the 13th, plus an eagle at the 10th, but clutched her back after her drive at the 16th and bogeyed the hole. Sarah Schmelzel birdied six of the last seven holes to take third place.

Maguire revealed it was her mother's birthday the next day, making for a double celebration when she got home a week later. "I guess this is a pretty good present for her."

Crown Colony Golf & Country Club, Fort Myers, Florida — February 3-5
Par 72 (36-36); 6,592 yards — Purse: $1,500,000

1	**Leona Maguire**	66 65 67	198	$225,000		Nelly Korda	72 70 64	206	19,871
2	**Lexi Thompson**	69 67 65	201	138,527		Hye-Jin Choi	71 69 66	206	19,871
3	**Sarah Schmelzel**	69 69 64	202	100,492		Madelene Sagstrom	67 71 68	206	19,871
4	Xiyu Lin	68 72 63	203	54,379		Nanna Koerstz Madsen	68 69 69	206	19,871
	Patty Tavatanakit	66 70 67	203	54,379	20	Jenny Shin	74 68 65	207	15,940
	Brittany Altomare	68 67 68	203	54,379		Perrine Delacour	73 67 67	207	15,940
	Stacy Lewis	68 67 68	203	54,379		Kelly Tan	71 69 67	207	15,940
	Marina Alex	65 66 72	203	54,379		Caroline Masson	67 72 68	207	15,940
9	Pauline Roussin	70 67 67	204	32,233		Celine Boutier	70 67 70	207	15,940
	Jeongeun Lee[6]	67 69 68	204	32,233		Yaeeun Hong	68 69 70	207	15,940
11	Cheyenne Knight	70 69 66	205	25,805	26	Georgia Hall	70 71 67	208	13,159
	Brooke M Henderson	71 67 67	205	25,805		Megan Khang	68 72 68	208	13,159
	Atthaya Thitikul	71 66 68	205	25,805		In Gee Chun	70 68 70	208	13,159
	Charley Hull	67 70 68	205	25,805		Lauren Stephenson	72 65 71	208	13,159
15	Aditi Ashok	72 71 63	206	19,871	30	Yealimi Noh	74 69 66	209	10,574

	Ayaka Furue	70	72	67	209	10,574
	Amy Yang	70	72	67	209	10,574
	Allisen Corpuz	70	69	70	209	10,574
	Inbee Park	70	69	70	209	10,574
	Jasmine Suwannapura	69	70	70	209	10,574
	Linnea Johansson	66	69	74	209	10,574
37	Lilia Vu	71	72	67	210	8,400
	Isi Gabsa	71	71	68	210	8,400
	Narin An	71	70	69	210	8,400
	Jennifer Chang	70	68	72	210	8,400
41	Ruixin Liu	71	72	68	211	6,162
	Paula Reto	71	72	68	211	6,162
	Pajaree Anannarukarn	70	73	68	211	6,162
	Alison Lee	69	74	68	211	6,162
	Brittany Lincicome	73	69	69	211	6,162
	Anna Nordqvist	69	73	69	211	6,162
	A Lim Kim	72	69	70	211	6,162
	Bianca Pagdanganan	70	71	70	211	6,162
	Marissa Steen	69	72	70	211	6,162
	Cydney Clanton	70	70	71	211	6,162
	Nasa Hataoka	65	75	71	211	6,162
	Su Oh	68	71	72	211	6,162
53	Wichanee Meechai	72	70	70	212	4,475
	Lindsey Weaver-Wright	71	71	70	212	4,475
	Pernilla Lindberg	69	73	70	212	4,475
	Janie Jackson	72	69	71	212	4,475
	Ryann O'Toole	68	72	72	212	4,475
	Bronte Law	67	72	73	212	4,475
59	Dana Finkelstein	72	71	70	213	3,651
	Annie Park	69	74	70	213	3,651
	Pornanong Phatlum	73	69	71	213	3,651
	Moriya Jutanugarn	72	70	71	213	3,651
	Gemma Dryburgh	72	69	72	213	3,651
	Amy Olson	70	71	72	213	3,651
	Austin Ernst	70	71	72	213	3,651
66	Fatima Fernandez Cano	74	69	71	214	3,185
	Jodi Ewart Shadoff	72	71	71	214	3,185
	Ariya Jutanugarn	72	70	72	214	3,185
	Katherine Perry-Hamski	72	70	72	214	3,185
	Giulia Molinaro	68	74	72	214	3,185
71	Carlota Ciganda	72	71	72	215	2,977
	Angela Stanford	77	65	73	215	2,977
73	Rachel Rohanna	70	73	74	217	2,920

HSBC Women's World Championship

After ending 2021 with victory in the CME Group Tour Championship, Jin Young Ko promised to take some time off. She did just that. "I spent time with my family and friends, and my dog as well. And I watched Netflix in my bed with potato chips," Ko related. The 26-year-old Korean also rehabbed her wrist injury that plagued her last season and continued her quest to improve her game, missing the first three events of the 2022 LPGA season before arriving at the HSBC Women's World Championship in Singapore having already regained the Rolex Rankings number one spot from Nelly Korda.

An early double bogey on the first morning suggested there was a little rust to work off but by the end of her first tournament of the year on Sunday she was back to her best. Ko birdied five of the last six holes to win for the sixth time in her last 10 events. She also took her streak of rounds in the 60s to 15, breaking the record she matched in 2021 — in fact, her new streak started after just one score in the 70s and here Ko also set a new LPGA record of 30 consecutive scores under par. "I feel amazing right now," Ko said. "It's a great honour to have the new record."

Ko scored 69-67-69-66 for a 17-under-par total of 271 at Sentosa. She won by two strokes from Minjee Lee, who came home in 30 for a 63 to set the clubhouse target and In Gee Chun, the 54-hole leader. Chun had played through neck pain on Thursday and Friday before feeling much better with a 66 on Saturday. But a 69 was no defence against her compatriot. Jeongeun Lee[6], with five birdies in the first 14 holes, held the lead for much of Sunday, although she was joined at the top by Thai rookie Atthaya Thitikul, the LET number one in 2021. Thitikul had six birdies in the first 14 holes but failed to get a four at the par-five 16th and then three-putted the 17th to tie for fourth with Lee[6].

Ko birdied the eighth and ninth holes but then bogeyed the 12th. "I was angry," she said, "but I thought I still had six holes so I could get a lot of birdies." Four came at the next four holes, including a long curling effort from the fringe at the 15th. She arrived at the 18th tied with Lee[6], who missed the fairway and found a bunker behind the green. The former US Open champion took four to get down to finish with a double bogey. Ko, however, finished in style, finding the fairway and then hitting her approach over the flagstick to 18 feet. One putt was all the world number one needed.

Sentosa Golf Club (New Tanjong), Singapore — March 3-6
Par 72 (36-36); 6,749 yards — Purse: $1,700,000

1	**Jin Young Ko**	69	67	69	66	271	$255,000
2	**Minjee Lee**	71	69	70	63	273	138,747
	In Gee Chun	70	68	66	69	273	138,747
4	Atthaya Thitikul	69	68	70	67	274	81,447
	Jeongeun Lee6	70	70	65	69	274	81,447
6	Hannah Green	74	69	66	66	275	50,923
	Brooke M Henderson	69	68	71	67	275	50,923
	Amy Yang	69	67	71	68	275	50,923
9	A Lim Kim	68	70	73	66	277	37,422
	Danielle Kang	68	71	68	70	277	37,422
11	Xiyu Lin	69	72	71	66	278	31,918
	Nasa Hataoka	72	71	67	68	278	31,918
13	Momoko Ueda	71	71	73	64	279	26,415
	Sarah Schmelzel	69	71	73	66	279	26,415
	Perrine Delacour	70	72	69	68	279	26,415
	Leona Maguire	70	72	69	68	279	26,415
17	Nanna Koerstz Madsen	69	73	71	67	280	20,722
	Inbee Park	68	71	73	68	280	20,722
	Ariya Jutanugarn	72	68	71	69	280	20,722
	Yealimi Noh	75	64	71	70	280	20,722
	Megan Khang	69	68	73	70	280	20,722
	Pajaree Anannarukarn	69	69	71	71	280	20,722
23	Lydia Ko	69	73	72	67	281	17,464
	Ayaka Furue	72	70	71	68	281	17,464
	Gaby Lopez	70	70	71	70	281	17,464
26	Wei-Ling Hsu	70	71	74	67	282	14,428
	Hyo Joo Kim	72	70	72	68	282	14,428
	Jeongeun Lee5	71	73	69	69	282	14,428
	Carlota Ciganda	70	72	71	69	282	14,428
	Patty Tavatanakit	67	74	71	70	282	14,428
	Madelene Sagstrom	71	69	71	71	282	14,428
	Su Oh	69	70	71	72	282	14,428
33	Stacy Lewis	73	72	71	68	284	11,974
	Jenny Shin	70	71	70	73	284	11,974
35	Marina Alex	74	74	70	67	285	9,796
	Chella Choi	74	69	74	68	285	9,796
	Moriya Jutanugarn	74	72	70	69	285	9,796
	Alison Lee	72	70	74	69	285	9,796
	So Yeon Ryu	72	71	71	71	285	9,796
	Celine Boutier	72	72	69	72	285	9,796
	Jennifer Kupcho	69	71	71	74	285	9,796
	Angel Yin	69	69	73	74	285	9,796
43	Yuka Saso	71	73	73	69	286	7,638
	Emily Kristine Pedersen	71	70	75	70	286	7,638
	Min Lee	71	72	72	71	286	7,638
	Emma Talley	72	70	72	72	286	7,638
47	Hinako Shibuno	76	70	73	68	287	6,956
48	Sei Young Kim	74	74	67	73	288	6,692
49	Esther Henseleit	71	72	75	71	289	6,427
50	Lizette Salas	70	75	74	71	290	6,163
51	Jasmine Suwannapura	72	77	73	69	291	5,635
	Brittany Altomare	74	74	74	69	291	5,635
	Ashleigh Buhai	69	74	77	71	291	5,635
	Mina Harigae	74	74	71	72	291	5,635
	Caroline Masson	70	74	73	74	291	5,635
56	Wichanee Meechai	73	76	76	67	292	5,019
	Sarah Kemp	75	71	73	73	292	5,019
58	Matilda Castren	74	75	74	71	294	4,667
	Yu Liu	72	74	77	71	294	4,667
60	Mel Reid	78	72	76	69	295	4,403
61	Jenny Coleman	79	68	77	72	296	4,315
	Xiaowen Yin (A)	81	70	72	73	296	
63	Sung Hyun Park	75	76	72	76	299	4,226
64	Sock Hwee Koh	80	79	71	73	303	4,138
	Charley Hull	76				WD	4,051

Honda LPGA Thailand

"It was a crazy day," said Nanna Koerstz Madsen after becoming the first Dane to win on the LPGA but only after a dramatic conclusion to the Honda LPGA Thailand. The storm that delayed play for two and a half hours in the middle of the final round was far from the end of the drama. Koerstz Madsen, who holed out a pitch from rough on the first for an eagle and birdied the second to go four ahead, saw Xiyu Lin get back within one before going four ahead again with three to play.

But she three-putted the 16th and Lin, also seeking her first LPGA win, birdied the last two holes. Madsen was in the left rough at 18 and got a flier with an eight-iron that finished in the hospitality suites beside the green. Her first chip after the free drop failed to make the green and she ended with a bogey six. Madsen, with 65-64-66-67, and Lin's 64-66-66-66 tied on a new tournament record total of 26-under-par 262. Celine Boutier finished one behind after chipping in for an eagle at the last. Three-time winner Amy Yang tied for fourth with Brooke Henderson, while young Thai star Atthaya Thitikul, who narrowly missed out on the title in 2021, was eight under for the first 11 holes before fading to a tie for eighth.

On the first extra hole at the par-five 18th, Madsen was over 50 feet away but two-putted after Lin's chip from the front of the green for a winning eagle finished on the lip of the hole. The second extra hole at the 18th saw Madsen in a similar spot in the rough off the tee and this time she hit a nine-iron to 10 feet over the flag. Lin was all set for a birdie so Madsen had to hole for the eagle to win.

"It's amazing. It's a dream come true," said Koerstz Madsen, whose only LET win came in 2016 and who double-bogeyed the final hole at the 2021 AIG Women's Open. "It was a crazy day; a lot of good things. It was actually fun playing the playoff with Xiyu at the end. She really fought, finished up birdie-birdie, so she played amazing, too. I'm not going to lie, I was a little nervous there. I'm really excited to be standing with the trophy right now."

Siam Country Club (Old), Pattaya, Thailand — March 10-13
Par 72 (36-36); 6,576 yards — Purse: $1,600,000

1	**Nanna Koerstz Madsen**	65	64	66	67	262	$240,000
2	**Xiyu Lin**	64	66	66	66	262	150,488
	Koerstz Madsen won playoff at second extra hole						
3	**Celine Boutier**	65	64	67	67	263	109,168
4	Amy Yang	66	69	66	64	265	76,212
	Brooke M Henderson	65	67	66	67	265	76,212
6	Hyo Joo Kim	69	65	67	65	266	51,083
	Jennifer Kupcho	65	67	67	67	266	51,083
8	Jeongeun Lee[6]	66	68	70	64	268	35,428
	Atthaya Thitikul	70	67	66	65	268	35,428
	Danielle Kang	66	69	67	66	268	35,428
	Hinako Shibuno	67	68	66	67	268	35,428
12	Yuka Saso	68	70	69	62	269	24,223
	Leona Maguire	70	66	69	64	269	24,223
	Esther Henseleit	63	71	70	65	269	24,223
	Lucy Li	67	69	64	69	269	24,223
	Minjee Lee	69	64	67	69	269	24,223
	Alison Lee	65	68	66	70	269	24,223
	Nasa Hataoka	63	65	70	71	269	24,223
19	Patty Tavatanakit	71	66	68	65	270	19,279
	Gaby Lopez	68	66	64	72	270	19,279
21	Emma Talley	69	69	67	66	271	16,684
	Perrine Delacour	67	73	64	67	271	16,684
	A Lim Kim	67	69	68	67	271	16,684
	So Yeon Ryu	69	66	68	68	271	16,684
	Sarah Schmelzel	68	69	65	69	271	16,684
	Su Oh	63	65	73	70	271	16,684
27	Megan Khang	69	67	69	67	272	14,294
	Hannah Green	70	65	67	70	272	14,294
29	Lizette Salas	66	70	73	64	273	13,430
30	Pajaree Anannarukarn	68	71	69	66	274	12,441
	Matilda Castren	70	68	68	68	274	12,441
	Lindsey Weaver-Wright	65	71	67	71	274	12,441
33	Jennifer Song	69	71	70	65	275	10,146
	Madelene Sagstrom	68	69	73	65	275	10,146
	Jeongeun Lee[5]	68	68	73	66	275	10,146
	Jasmine Suwannapura	73	69	66	67	275	10,146
	Stacy Lewis	67	70	71	67	275	10,146
	Yu Liu	66	70	72	67	275	10,146
	Jaravee Boonchant	70	65	71	69	275	10,146
40	Ariya Jutanugarn	74	66	70	66	276	8,074
	Giulia Molinaro	71	72	66	67	276	8,074
	Wei-Ling Hsu	69	70	68	69	276	8,074
	Carlota Ciganda	66	67	71	72	276	8,074
44	Aditi Ashok	70	72	68	67	277	7,003
	Moriya Jutanugarn	70	68	72	67	277	7,003
	Kaitlyn Papp	68	70	71	68	277	7,003
47	Caroline Masson	68	74	70	66	278	6,138
	Angel Yin	71	68	71	68	278	6,138
	Chanettee Wannasaen	73	70	66	69	278	6,138
	Min Lee	67	68	71	72	278	6,138
51	Mina Harigae	68	76	69	66	279	5,191
	Chella Choi	71	71	70	67	279	5,191
	In Gee Chun	68	69	74	68	279	5,191
	Mel Reid	71	71	67	70	279	5,191
	Brittany Altomare	68	71	68	72	279	5,191
	Emily Kristine Pedersen	70	67	69	73	279	5,191
57	Jaye Marie Green	74	70	67	69	280	4,614
58	Yealimi Noh	71	69	70	71	281	4,449
59	Albane Valenzuela	71	75	70	67	283	4,202
	Marina Alex	71	67	74	71	283	4,202
61	Wichanee Meechai	75	74	68	70	287	4,038
	Rina Tatematsu (A)	69	70	74	74	287	
63	Na Yeon Choi	73	69	77	71	290	3,913
	Prima Thammaraks	71	75	71	73	290	3,913
65	Jenny Coleman	73	73	73	72	291	3,791
66	Ashleigh Buhai	77	70	69	76	292	3,707
	Sarah Kemp	80				WD	3,625

JBTC Classic

Streaks end in mysterious ways. Jin Young Ko, in only her second appearance of the season after winning the HSBC in Singapore, continued to cruise along at her supreme best with a 65 in the first round of the JBTC Classic at Aviara. But the next day, the world number one fell out of the lead with a 71, ending her record run of rounds in the 60s at 16. She just didn't have it that day. "I want to be at the beach," Ko told her caddie. By the end of the tournament, she was able to head to the first major of the year, the Chevron Championship, with the chance to start a new streak with a final round 68 and having gone 34 consecutive rounds under par. And she finished just two shots outside a playoff.

That playoff came about when Nanna Koerstz Madsen, in the attempt to win back-to-back after her maiden title in Thailand, suffered her only three-putt of the week at the 72nd green. Madsen, one behind Ko on the first day, had led after the second and third rounds but at the last gasp dropped into a tie with Atthaya Thitikul. Madsen went 66-67-69-70 for a 16-under-par total of 272, while Thitikul was six behind after going 69-70-69 before a 64 on the final day with nine birdies to set the target. Korea's Narin An, who won the 2021 Q-Series, finished one behind after a 68 in which her only dropped shot came at the par-five 17th. Pajaree Anannarukarn tied for fourth with Ko and Canada's Maude-Aimee Leblanc and then stayed around to watch her friend Thitikul win her maiden LPGA title.

Madsen got up and down at the 18th on the first extra hole to match Thitikul's par, then drove into the left rough at the same hole second time around. With her feet on a cart path, Madsen pushed her approach into the water and lipped out for a bogey. Thitikul, on the green but a long way from the hole, three-putted for a bogey but claimed the win in only her fifth start as an LPGA member.

The 19-year-old Thai was the youngest winner of the Race to the Costa del Sol in 2021 and this victory took her to fifth in the Rolex Rankings. "I would say it's a lot of things going through my head, but one thing that I really wanted to focus on is just do your best every single shot," Thitikul said. "If you lose, if you win, this is another chance to learn. I want to win but didn't expect that it was going to come really fast. It's crazy in my mind right now. I cannot believe that I became an LPGA winner. It feels amazing."

Aviara Golf Club, Carlsbad, California — March 24-27
Par 72 (36-36); 6,609 yards — Purse: $1,500,000

1	**Atthaya Thitikul**	69	70	69	64	272	$225,000
2	**Nanna Koerstz Madsen**	66	67	69	70	272	135,995
	Thitikul won playoff at second extra hole						
3	**Narin An**	69	67	69	68	273	98,654
4	Pajaree Anannarukarn	68	69	69	68	274	62,667
	Maude-Aimee Leblanc	68	68	70	68	274	62,667
	Jin Young Ko	65	71	70	68	274	62,667
7	Charley Hull	69	70	68	69	276	42,068
8	Inbee Park	71	68	70	68	277	34,995
	Lilia Vu	71	71	65	70	277	34,995
10	Amy Yang	72	69	69	68	278	29,038
	Stephanie Meadow	69	72	67	70	278	29,038
12	Chella Choi	72	70	70	67	279	23,751
	Ryann O'Toole	68	75	67	69	279	23,751
	Lydia Ko	68	67	74	70	279	23,751
	In Gee Chun	69	72	67	71	279	23,751
16	Lizette Salas	72	72	71	65	280	17,933
	Allison Emrey	72	71	69	68	280	17,933
	Xiyu Lin	70	71	71	68	280	17,933
	Alana Uriell	69	73	68	70	280	17,933
	Moriya Jutanugarn	69	72	68	71	280	17,933
	Nasa Hataoka	70	69	68	73	280	17,933
	Janie Jackson	70	68	69	73	280	17,933
23	Annie Park	72	70	71	68	281	13,212
	Mina Harigae	73	70	69	69	281	13,212
	Alison Lee	69	72	71	69	281	13,212
	Cheyenne Knight	67	73	72	69	281	13,212
	Paula Reto	72	71	68	70	281	13,212
	Austin Ernst	72	71	68	70	281	13,212
	Hyo Joo Kim	73	67	71	70	281	13,212
	Minjee Lee	69	71	70	71	281	13,212
	Brittany Altomare	71	68	69	73	281	13,212
32	Hee Jeong Lim	73	70	70	69	282	9,754
	Mo Martin	68	74	70	70	282	9,754
	Ayaka Furue	72	71	68	71	282	9,754
	Yealimi Noh	71	69	71	71	282	9,754
	Lauren Coughlin	71	70	69	72	282	9,754
	Hye-Jin Choi	67	68	72	75	282	9,754
38	Lexi Thompson	73	70	70	70	283	7,911
	Jeongeun Lee[5]	71	72	70	70	283	7,911
	Gemma Dryburgh	67	76	68	72	283	7,911
	Anna Nordqvist	71	71	69	72	283	7,911
42	Jenny Shin	76	68	71	69	284	6,130
	Marina Alex	73	71	71	69	284	6,130
	Sanna Nuutinen	73	70	71	70	284	6,130
	Danielle Kang	69	74	70	71	284	6,130
	A Lim Kim	75	69	68	72	284	6,130
	Emma Talley	69	74	69	72	284	6,130
	Kelly Tan	72	70	70	72	284	6,130
	Leona Maguire	69	70	71	74	284	6,130
	Pernilla Lindberg	73	68	68	75	284	6,130
51	Frida Kinhult	71	73	72	69	285	4,542
	Yaeeun Hong	71	73	69	72	285	4,542
	Haylee Rae Harford	71	70	72	72	285	4,542
	Emily Kristine Pedersen	71	70	72	72	285	4,542
	Jessica Korda	69	70	73	73	285	4,542
	Kaitlyn Papp	77	67	67	74	285	4,542
	Jasmine Suwannapura	71	70	70	74	285	4,542
	In-Kyung Kim	69	73	67	76	285	4,542
59	Sophia Popov	73	70	74	69	286	3,624
	Jaye Marie Green	71	72	73	70	286	3,624
	Hannah Green	73	69	74	70	286	3,624
	Jenny Coleman	72	70	73	71	286	3,624
	Jeongeun Lee[6]	70	74	66	76	286	3,624
	Muni He	70	71	69	76	286	3,624
65	Madelene Sagstrom	71	70	74	72	287	3,276
	Isi Gabsa	72	72	70	73	287	3,276
	Eun-Hee Ji	70	73	71	73	287	3,276
68	Katherine Kirk	71	73	72	72	288	3,053
	Ariya Jutanugarn	69	75	72	72	288	3,053
	Morgane Metraux	71	72	72	73	288	3,053
71	Stacy Lewis	70	73	74	73	290	2,942
72	Katherine Perry-Hamski	71	73	76	71	291	2,795
	Cristie Kerr	72	72	74	73	291	2,795
	Gerina Mendoza	70	72	76	73	291	2,795
	Pornanong Phatlum	72	72	73	74	291	2,795
	Sarah Schmelzel	70	72	73	76	291	2,795
	Stephanie Kyriacou	73	69	71	78	291	2,795
	Hinako Shibuno	71	72	68	80	291	2,795
79	Jiwon Jeon	76	68	73	75	292	2,656
80	Dewi Weber	71	73	75	74	293	2,622
81	Jennifer Song	72	72	75	76	295	2,588

Lotte Championship

In the winds of Hawaii, on the exposed Ernie Els-designed Hoakalei course less than a mile from the Pacific Ocean, scoring was never easy. That Hyo Joo Kim did not drop a shot until the seventh hole in the third round was remarkable. The 26-year-old Korean deservedly went on to win the Lotte Championship but she needed all her supreme scrambling skills to do so. Especially at the par-five 18th hole. On Friday, in the third round, she almost holed out of a bunker for an eagle. The birdie restored a three-shot lead from the previous night.

In Saturday's final round, Kim dropped a shot at the 17th and her lead was down to one shot, the lowest it had been during the round. Her drive finished in the rough near the bunkers and water, and her second pulled up short of the green. From there, Kim pitched to 18 inches. Hinako Shibuno, her nearest challenger, applauded the shot from the Korean knowing that she now had to hole her bunker shot to force a playoff. In fact, the Japanese star could only par and finished two behind having not dropped a shot in her closing 70. It was her best result on the LPGA since winning the 2019 AIG Women's Open.

Kim, who won the 2014 Evian Championship as a 19-year-old, scored 67-67-72-71 for an 11-under-par total of 277. She had been one behind Hannah Green's 66 on the first day, leading from then on. Two early birdies in the final round left her comfortably placed, but a bogey at the ninth was followed by seven pars before the bogey-birdie finish. "I'm proud of that shot," Kim said of her pitch at the last. "Maybe I made a lot of people sit on the edge of their chairs, so I felt great about it." Her fifth LPGA win came after playing in every previous Lotte Championship, an event with which she shares a sponsor. "I have been playing since the inaugural championship, and then because of this being my sponsor I always wanted to win and do well," she said.

Korean rookie Hye-Jin Choi took third place with a 69, while South Africa's Ashleigh Buhai was fourth. Brianna Do, who started the week by qualifying and was sharing second place with Shibuno after 54 holes thanks to Friday's 67, closed with a 77 to miss out on a top-10 finish and a place in the following week's tournament.

Hoakalei Country Club, Ewa Beach, Oahu, Hawaii — April 13-16
Par 72 (36-36); 6,603 yards — Purse: $2,000,000

1	**Hyo Joo Kim**	67	67	72	71	277	$300,000
2	**Hinako Shibuno**	71	70	68	70	279	182,956
3	**Hye-Jin Choi**	70	70	72	69	281	132,721
4	Ashleigh Buhai	71	71	70	70	282	102,670
5	So Mi Lee	71	70	69	73	283	82,638
6	Atthaya Thitikul	71	74	72	67	284	54,591
	Gerina Mendoza	74	72	69	69	284	54,591
	Ryann O'Toole	72	69	72	71	284	54,591
	Narin An	71	68	73	72	284	54,591
10	Brittany Altomare	70	77	72	66	285	39,065
	Celine Boutier	71	74	70	70	285	39,065
12	Charlotte Thomas	72	75	70	69	286	30,217
	Sophia Schubert	75	71	69	71	286	30,217
	Andrea Lee	71	70	73	72	286	30,217
	In Gee Chun	72	70	71	73	286	30,217
	Ariya Jutanugarn	70	68	73	75	286	30,217
	Brianna Do	72	70	67	77	286	30,217
18	Jodi Ewart Shadoff	67	77	76	67	287	21,874
	Lauren Stephenson	75	72	70	70	287	21,874
	Jennifer Kupcho	74	72	71	70	287	21,874
	Lydia Ko	69	75	73	70	287	21,874
	Emily Kristine Pedersen	74	69	71	73	287	21,874
	Allisen Corpuz	70	72	72	73	287	21,874
	Ruixin Liu	71	74	67	75	287	21,874
	Stephanie Meadow	71	70	69	77	287	21,874
26	Emma Talley	75	71	71	71	288	15,793
	Esther Henseleit	75	70	72	71	288	15,793
	Gaby Lopez	68	77	72	71	288	15,793
	Anna Nordqvist	70	77	69	72	288	15,793
	Perrine Delacour	71	72	73	72	288	15,793
	Stephanie Kyriacou	71	71	73	73	288	15,793
	Sarah Kemp	68	69	78	73	288	15,793
	Chella Choi	70	73	71	74	288	15,793
	Gemma Dryburgh	67	73	74	74	288	15,793
35	Georgia Hall	70	75	76	68	289	11,586
	Cheyenne Knight	70	71	77	71	289	11,586
	Wichanee Meechai	74	72	71	72	289	11,586
	Min Lee	69	73	75	72	289	11,586
	Kelly Tan	71	72	72	74	289	11,586
	Megan Khang	72	72	67	78	289	11,586
41	Amy Olson	76	71	74	69	290	8,901
	Yu Liu	74	72	74	70	290	8,901
	Lindsey Weaver-Wright	71	74	72	73	290	8,901
	Janie Jackson	68	72	77	73	290	8,901
	Aditi Ashok	67	73	76	74	290	8,901
	Haeji Kang	68	70	78	74	290	8,901
	Annie Park	73	73	69	75	290	8,901
48	Su Oh	74	73	77	67	291	6,749
	Haru Nomura	74	73	75	69	291	6,749
	Leona Maguire	71	75	76	69	291	6,749
	Ana Belac	75	71	73	72	291	6,749
	Jeongeun Lee[5]	71	71	77	72	291	6,749
	Alison Lee	67	76	75	73	291	6,749
	Hannah Green	66	76	75	74	291	6,749
	A Lim Kim	72	67	76	76	291	6,749
56	Yealimi Noh	77	70	74	71	292	5,184
	Matilda Castren	74	72	75	71	292	5,184
	Yuka Saso	73	74	73	72	292	5,184
	Giulia Molinaro	74	73	72	73	292	5,184
	Maria Fassi	70	76	72	74	292	5,184
	Albane Valenzuela	70	75	72	75	292	5,184
	Pernilla Lindberg	71	72	71	78	292	5,184
	Dewi Weber	70	74	69	79	292	5,184
64	Paula Reto	71	73	83	66	293	4,508
	Linnea Johansson	70	77	73	73	293	4,508
	Dottie Ardina	72	75	71	75	293	4,508
67	Bianca Pagdanganan	70	77	78	69	294	4,117
	Ayaka Furue	71	73	78	72	294	4,117
	Lilia Vu	73	73	75	73	294	4,117
	Isi Gabsa	71	72	77	74	294	4,117
	Dana Finkelstein	72	71	75	76	294	4,117
72	Frida Kinhult	74	72	75	75	296	3,906
73	Jenny Coleman	72	75	75	75	297	3,856
74	Yu-Sang Hou	71	76	78	73	298	3,783
	Ssu-Chia Cheng	71	75	76	76	298	3,783
76	Anne van Dam	71	76	75	77	299	3,713
77	Mi Hyang Lee	72	73	76	81	302	3,666

Dio Implant LA Open

Nasa Hataoka provided the perfect demonstration of playing with a big lead as the 23-year-old from Japan won the Dio Implant LA Open by five strokes at Wilshire. But the most significant moment of the week came at the end of the third round when Hataoka opened up a four-shot advantage.

Hataoka (67-68) was tied after 36 holes with Jin Young Ko (71-64) and they played together on Saturday. They were still level at the 16th, where Hataoka's birdie was part of a two-shot swing. After Ko bogeyed, the world number one compounded the error by taking a quadruple-bogey eight at the 17th. Twice Ko attempted to play from the mud bank of a stream at the bottom of a concrete wall in front of the green. Twice her ball hit the wall and rebounded at her feet before she took a penalty drop.

It was the first quad of Ko's LPGA career and she responded with a birdie two at the last but was now five behind Hataoka, who was four ahead of Hannah Green. "I played not bad; just 17 was big mistake," said Ko. "But this is golf. I don't have regret. Especially the birdie at the last hole is huge for next round."

But after her 72, Ko finished with a 75 to fall into a tie for 21st place. Meanwhile, Hataoka went serenely on her way, weekend rounds of 67-67 giving her a 15-under-par total of 269. She birdied three of the first five holes and made an eagle at the 15th to be six ahead before a bogey at the last. Green closed with a 68 to take second place ahead of Inbee Park, Madelene Sagstrom and Minjee Lee.

Hataoka's sixth LPGA victory came after she missed the cut in Hawaii the previous week. "I don't know if I can compare this, but on the PGA Tour, Jordan Spieth missed the cut at the Masters and then won Heritage," said Hataoka. "So you never know what's going to happen in golf. I did have a lead, but obviously this challenging course, you never know what's going to happen, so I was able to focus until the last putt. My goal set for today was 15 under, and my plan was to birdie as much as possible on the first nine holes, and that eagle really helped me relax a little bit."

Wilshire Country Club, Los Angeles, California — April 21-24
Par 71 (35-36); 6,447 yards — Purse: $1,500,000

1	**Nasa Hataoka**	67	68	67	67	269	$225,000
2	**Hannah Green**	70	67	69	68	274	138,191
3	**Madelene Sagstrom**	69	72	70	66	277	80,072
	Minjee Lee	70	68	71	68	277	80,072
	Inbee Park	72	67	68	70	277	80,072
6	Hye-Jin Choi	71	74	67	66	278	41,234
	Sei Young Kim	68	72	70	68	278	41,234
	Chella Choi	71	71	67	69	278	41,234
	Haeji Kang	69	69	69	71	278	41,234
10	Marina Alex	71	71	69	68	279	27,577
	Yealimi Noh	73	71	66	69	279	27,577
	Yu Liu	71	68	71	69	279	27,577
	Lilia Vu	74	69	66	70	279	27,577
14	Jenny Coleman	73	67	71	69	280	21,991
	Amanda Doherty	70	70	70	70	280	21,991
	Celine Boutier	69	71	70	70	280	21,991
17	Brittany Altomare	71	71	73	66	281	18,461
	Yuka Saso	75	66	74	66	281	18,461
	Eun-Hee Ji	73	70	68	70	281	18,461
	Allisen Corpuz	72	71	68	70	281	18,461
21	Georgia Hall	71	69	74	68	282	15,321
	Stacy Lewis	71	72	69	70	282	15,321
	Lauren Stephenson	69	73	70	70	282	15,321
	Dewi Weber	68	73	71	70	282	15,321
	Lizette Salas	69	70	72	71	282	15,321
	Jin Young Ko	71	64	72	75	282	15,321
27	Xiyu Lin	74	71	72	66	283	12,143
	Isi Gabsa	75	68	72	68	283	12,143
	Jodi Ewart Shadoff	70	73	69	71	283	12,143
	Ryann O'Toole	70	70	72	71	283	12,143
	Angel Yin	74	68	69	72	283	12,143
	Sanna Nuutinen	71	70	70	72	283	12,143
33	Carlota Ciganda	72	68	73	71	284	10,289
	Ruoning Yin	71	69	72	72	284	10,289
35	Christina Kim	72	73	73	67	285	8,417
	Patty Tavatanakit	73	69	73	70	285	8,417
	Danielle Kang	72	71	71	71	285	8,417
	Alison Lee	66	74	73	72	285	8,417
	Ana Belac	73	71	68	73	285	8,417
	Gemma Dryburgh	71	71	70	73	285	8,417
	Pajaree Anannarukarn	70	71	71	73	285	8,417
	Pauline Roussin	69	72	70	74	285	8,417
43	Ariya Jutanugarn	75	70	71	70	286	6,446
	Ashleigh Buhai	72	72	72	70	286	6,446
	Ayaka Furue	70	73	72	71	286	6,446
	Maude-Aimee Leblanc	74	71	69	72	286	6,446
	Rachel Rohanna	69	73	72	72	286	6,446
48	Hee Young Park	71	71	76	69	287	5,097
	Charlotte Thomas	73	72	72	70	287	5,097
	Peiyun Chien	69	75	73	70	287	5,097
	Atthaya Thitikul	70	74	70	73	287	5,097
	Paula Reto	73	69	72	73	287	5,097
	Katherine Perry-Hamski	70	74	69	74	287	5,097
	Nanna Koerstz Madsen	72	71	70	74	287	5,097
	Emma Talley	67	74	72	74	287	5,097
56	Frida Kinhult	71	74	71	72	288	4,237
	Sarah Schmelzel	72	72	72	72	288	4,237
	Matilda Castren	74	71	68	75	288	4,237
59	Bronte Law	70	73	75	71	289	3,764
	So Yeon Ryu	68	74	73	74	289	3,764
	Emily Kristine Pedersen	67	72	76	74	289	3,764
	Janie Jackson	68	75	69	77	289	3,764

63 Jennifer Song	68	77	73	72	290	3,405	Sung Hyun Park	73	69	72	77	291	3,102
Jennifer Kupcho	75	69	73	73	290	3,405	Gaby Lopez	73	69	72	77	291	3,102
Hinako Shibuno	71	74	71	74	290	3,405	71 Brooke Matthews	74	71	75	72	292	2,932
Min Lee	75	70	70	75	290	3,405	Pernilla Lindberg	73	72	72	75	292	2,932
Giulia Molinaro	72	73	67	78	290	3,405	Cheyenne Knight	72	73	72	75	292	2,932
68 Kelly Tan	75	70	73	73	291	3,102	Jenny Shin	73	71	73	75	292	2,932

Palos Verdes Championship

For the second week in the City of Stars, across La La Land at Palos Verdes, it was a member of the chorus line who emerged as the victor in a heart-warming win for Marina Alex. The 31-year-old from New Jersey had struggled with a back injury during the Covid pandemic and was not sure whether she could continue her LPGA career. But she came from three behind Hannah Green to charge to the top of a crowded leaderboard and beat Jin Young Ko by one stroke.

"I'm not going to lie, if you had talked to me last year, or even the beginning of this year, I didn't think there was a remote possibility that I was going to win ever again," Alex said. "I didn't know how much longer I really wanted to be golfing ever again. I'm getting older. My back has been a struggle. I went into this year and I was, like, I don't know how many more years I'm going to play if I'm being perfectly honest. I just want to give it my absolute best this year and try putting myself in contention and try to win tournaments. It's amazing that it's happened."

Green scored 67-66 to lead by three at halfway, but returned a pair of 72s on the weekend. The Australian still led after 54 holes before falling into a share of fifth place on Sunday. Jin Young Ko, rebounding from her disappointment at the LA Open, opened with a 64 to be one behind Minjee Lee and showed what was possible on the final day with a 66 to get to nine under par.

Megan Khang, with a 68, got to eight under, while Lydia Ko, who was lying second overnight, joined her with a 70 despite having frequent physiotherapy on her back during the round. Candidly, she explained: "It's that time of the month. I know the ladies watching are probably, like, yeah, I got you."

Alex, after 70-68-70, had a bogey at the third hole on Sunday, which "got all that anxious anxiety, whatever kind of nervous energy out of my system". She made six birdies from there, including at the 16th to edge in front on her own. A closing 66 left her on a winning total of 274, 10 under par.

Palos Verdes Club, Palos Verdes Estates, California — April 28-May 1
Par 71 (36-35); 6,258 yards — Purse: $1,500,000

1 **Marina Alex**	70	68	70	66	274	$225,000	Gemma Dryburgh	66	74	68	73	281	15,717
2 **Jin Young Ko**	64	72	73	66	275	139,217	26 Ruoning Yin	74	68	72	68	282	12,489
3 **Megan Khang**	67	69	72	68	276	89,559	Patty Tavatanakit	69	73	71	69	282	12,489
Lydia Ko	69	67	70	70	276	89,559	Emma Talley	70	70	73	69	282	12,489
5 Ryann O'Toole	68	71	70	68	277	48,781	Ally Ewing	69	70	73	70	282	12,489
Andrea Lee	70	68	70	69	277	48,781	Nanna Koerstz Madsen	69	69	72	72	282	12,489
Annie Park	68	69	71	69	277	48,781	Sarah Kemp	71	72	66	73	282	12,489
Hannah Green	67	66	72	72	277	48,781	Stephanie Meadow	73	68	68	73	282	12,489
9 Ashleigh Buhai	70	74	67	67	278	30,012	33 Amanda Doherty	69	74	73	67	283	9,578
Madelene Sagstrom	72	68	70	68	278	30,012	Celine Boutier	73	69	73	68	283	9,578
Jasmine Suwannapura	69	71	70	68	278	30,012	Sarah Jane Smith	69	74	71	69	283	9,578
Albane Valenzuela	66	74	69	69	278	30,012	Cheyenne Knight	72	70	71	70	283	9,578
13 Atthaya Thitikul	71	70	73	65	279	23,526	Mina Harigae	71	72	68	72	283	9,578
Lexi Thompson	69	73	66	71	279	23,526	Maude-Aimee Leblanc	69	68	72	74	283	9,578
Minjee Lee	63	73	72	71	279	23,526	39 So Yeon Ryu	73	70	72	69	284	6,936
16 Xiyu Lin	72	71	67	70	280	19,055	Wei-Ling Hsu	71	72	72	69	284	6,936
Jennifer Kupcho	71	71	68	70	280	19,055	Katherine Kirk	69	73	73	69	284	6,936
Agathe Laisne	68	74	68	70	280	19,055	Sarah Schmelzel	70	72	72	70	284	6,936
Allisen Corpuz	68	72	68	72	280	19,055	Ruixin Liu	67	75	72	70	284	6,936
Inbee Park	71	67	70	72	280	19,055	Robynn Ree	70	68	75	71	284	6,936
21 Yaeeun Hong	75	69	70	67	281	15,717	Ana Belac	68	73	71	72	284	6,936
Chella Choi	72	72	70	67	281	15,717	Sophia Schubert	69	71	72	72	284	6,936
Alana Uriell	69	70	71	71	281	15,717	Bronte Law	75	69	66	74	284	6,936
Hye-Jin Choi	69	71	69	72	281	15,717	Jennifer Chang	65	72	72	75	284	6,936

49	Jodi Ewart Shadoff	71 73 73 68	285	4,809			Wichanee Meechai	71 71 69 75	286	3,837
	Ayaka Furue	67 73 75 70	285	4,809		62	Yu Liu	71 73 72 71	287	3,582
	Amy Olson	69 75 70 71	285	4,809			Eun-Hee Ji	70 74 72 71	287	3,582
	Liz Nagel	70 73 71 71	285	4,809			Kaitlyn Papp	71 70 75 71	287	3,582
	Paula Reto	71 71 71 72	285	4,809		65	Charley Hull	65 75 77 71	288	3,392
	Min Lee	68 74 71 72	285	4,809			Pernilla Lindberg	75 68 70 75	288	3,392
	Pauline Roussin	67 75 70 73	285	4,809		67	Sanna Nuutinen	73 71 75 70	289	3,201
	Haeji Kang	71 72 68 74	285	4,809			Frida Kinhult	70 71 75 73	289	3,201
	Maria Fassi	72 71 67 75	285	4,809			Moriya Jutanugarn	65 74 73 77	289	3,201
	Kelly Tan	68 72 70 75	285	4,809		70	Anna Davis (A)	71 72 72 76	291	
59	Charlotte Thomas	72 68 76 70	286	3,837		71	Casey Danielson	71 70 75 76	292	3,049
	Hee Young Park	71 71 72 72	286	3,837		72	Katherine Perry-Hamski	70 71 77 75	293	3,011

Cognizant Founders Cup

"Hard work," Minjee Lee said. Winning is never easy, even after the Australian had led on Friday and Saturday at the Cognizant Founders Cup. A seventh LPGA victory, and a first since claiming her first major title at the Evian Championship in 2021, was sealed by two strokes over Lexi Thompson but was only confirmed with a fine approach at the last which finished three feet from the hole.

A 67 on the opening day left Lee four behind Madelene Sagstrom, but the 25-year-old from Perth produced her own 63 the following day to go in front by three. Lee's approach play was "dialled in" as she left herself with many short putts. She birdied four of the first six holes and started the back nine birdie-birdie-eagle.

Lee stayed in front with a 69 on Saturday, although Sagstrom rebounded from a 70 on Friday for a 67 to be one behind. The Swede went out in 39 on Sunday and finished in a tie for third with Angel Yin, who played the first nine in 32 on the way to a 67. Lee was finding it harder to make the putts drop in the final round, with eight pars and a bogey going out.

Thompson, who started three behind, birdied the second and then the 10th to tie for the lead. Both Lee and Thompson birdied the 12th, but it was Lee who went back in front with her second of the day at the 14th. Thompson parred in for a 69 to become the only player to score four rounds in the 60s at Upper Montclair. She finished as a runner-up for the second time in the season as she sought a first victory since 2019.

Lee, who finished with a 70 for 19-under-par 269, said: "I fought really hard this whole day, and to finish with a couple of birdies and to come out with a win is just really special. Situationally, it was in the final round and in the final group, so there was a little bit more pressure that I probably put on myself. Maybe that's what made it a little bit harder. But I don't remember the last time I worked this hard for a win. This is probably the first time. New experience. But I got the job done."

Upper Montclair Country Club, Clifton, New Jersey — May 12-15
Par 72 (36-36); 6,536 yards — Purse: $3,000,000

1	**Minjee Lee**	67 63 69 70	269	$450,000			Xiyu Lin	69 70 73 68	280	35,837
2	**Lexi Thompson**	67 66 69 69	271	273,190			Jin Young Ko	69 70 72 69	280	35,837
3	**Angel Yin**	70 67 68 67	272	175,744			Jennifer Kupcho	70 70 68 72	280	35,837
	Madelene Sagstrom	63 70 67 72	272	175,744			Paula Reto	69 67 71 73	280	35,837
5	Carlota Ciganda	67 69 73 64	273	123,396		22	Albane Valenzuela	72 71 71 67	281	27,587
6	Nasa Hataoka	65 73 70 66	274	92,733			Ryann O'Toole	67 72 73 69	281	27,587
	Megan Khang	64 72 71 67	274	92,733			Kelly Tan	71 70 70 70	281	27,587
8	Atthaya Thitikul	71 68 73 63	275	70,299			Bianca Pagdanganan	66 73 72 70	281	27,587
	Hye-Jin Choi	69 70 70 66	275	70,299			Alison Lee	72 69 69 71	281	27,587
10	Jenny Shin	75 64 70 67	276	60,576			Pajaree Anannarukarn	68 72 70 71	281	27,587
11	Sarah Schmelzel	72 67 71 68	278	56,087			Cheyenne Knight	69 69 71 72	281	27,587
12	Lydia Ko	69 74 69 67	279	46,366			Frida Kinhult	67 70 72 72	281	27,587
	Yuka Saso	73 68 70 68	279	46,366			In Gee Chun	74 65 69 73	281	27,587
	Lauren Stephenson	72 66 71 70	279	46,366		31	Jaye Marie Green	69 73 72 68	282	21,238
	Mina Harigae	70 68 71 70	279	46,366			Chella Choi	68 70 74 70	282	21,238
	Sanna Nuutinen	67 68 73 71	279	46,366			Anna Nordqvist	71 70 70 71	282	21,238
17	Ayaka Furue	72 71 69 68	280	35,837			Ally Ewing	67 66 74 75	282	21,238

35	Amy Yang	66	74	77	66	283	16,004
	Min Lee	73	69	72	69	283	16,004
	Ruixin Liu	70	72	72	69	283	16,004
	Celine Boutier	73	68	73	69	283	16,004
	Lauren Coughlin	74	69	70	70	283	16,004
	A Lim Kim	69	69	75	70	283	16,004
	Katherine Perry-Hamski	72	69	71	71	283	16,004
	Maria Fassi	71	69	72	71	283	16,004
	Sophia Popov	68	69	74	72	283	16,004
	Lilia Vu	70	69	71	73	283	16,004
45	Sung Hyun Park	68	70	77	69	284	11,816
	Eun-Hee Ji	72	71	70	71	284	11,816
	Amanda Doherty	71	72	70	71	284	11,816
	Jennifer Song	69	72	71	72	284	11,816
	Caroline Inglis	72	71	68	73	284	11,816
50	Jodi Ewart Shadoff	72	69	74	70	285	9,423
	Gerina Mendoza	72	69	73	71	285	9,423
	Brittany Lang	72	71	70	72	285	9,423
	Gemma Dryburgh	75	67	71	72	285	9,423
	Dana Finkelstein	74	68	71	72	285	9,423
	Annie Park	69	73	71	72	285	9,423
	Anna Davis (A)	70	70	72	73	285	
	Lindsey Weaver-Wright	74	68	68	75	285	9,423
	Brittany Altomare	70	68	71	76	285	9,423
59	Peiyun Chien	72	69	75	70	286	7,666
	Na Yeon Choi	69	74	72	71	286	7,666
	Isi Gabsa	71	70	74	71	286	7,666
	Jeongeun Lee[5]	74	68	70	74	286	7,666
63	Sarah Kemp	72	69	71	75	287	7,178
64	Gina Kim	68	69	79	72	288	6,805
	Dottie Ardina	73	70	71	74	288	6,805
	Matilda Castren	73	70	71	74	288	6,805
	Brittany Lincicome	71	72	71	74	288	6,805
68	Sei Young Kim	68	75	75	71	289	6,207
	Stephanie Meadow	71	72	73	73	289	6,207
	Jiwon Jeon	68	70	77	74	289	6,207
	Giulia Molinaro	66	75	72	76	289	6,207
72	Georgia Hall	69	73	75	73	290	5,871
	Charlotte Thomas	73	70	73	74	290	5,871
74	Weiwei Zhang	69	74	78	70	291	5,685
	Aditi Ashok	71	72	76	72	291	5,685
	Liz Nagel	74	69	72	76	291	5,685
77	Savannah Vilaubi	70	71	80	71	292	5,509
	Lauren Hartlage	71	72	72	77	292	5,509
79	Ana Belac	73	70	76	75	294	5,404
80	Hee Young Park	72	69	76	78	295	5,335

Bank of Hope LPGA Match Play

Eun-Hee Ji had played in the US Women's Open ever since 2008. She won it in 2009 but the 36-year-old Korean was no longer exempt and had one option left to play at Pine Needles the following week — she had to win the Bank of Hope LPGA Match Play. This was doing it the hard way, playing 111 holes over seven rounds and five days in high temperatures, and strong winds on the final day, at hilly Shadow Creek in Las Vegas. Somehow the odds worked out in favour of the 36th seed. "I really didn't think I'd be able to make it," Ji said of winning her sixth LPGA title and booking her place in the second major of the year. "It's still surreal and hasn't sunk in. Hopefully I can continue this week's momentum into next week."

First Ji had to win her group. She beat Pajaree Anannarukarn 4 and 2 on day one, then Danielle Kang, the local resident returning after time off for a back injury, 2 and 1 on Thursday. A tie with Kelly Tan on Friday put Ji through to the first round of the knockout section, where she defeated Hye-Jin Choi 2 and 1. Probably the key to her week came on Saturday afternoon as Ji, who had lost in the quarter-finals in 2021, made five birdies in 12 holes to slay Madelene Sagstrom, who had won all her previous four matches, 7 and 6. All the other semi-finalists had to go into extra holes to make it to Sunday. Andrea Lee defeated Gemma Dryburgh, who only got into the event on the night before when Anna Nordqvist withdrew, at the 20th, and Lilia Vu also went two extra holes before eliminating Jenny Shin. Ayaka Furue, who celebrated her 22nd birthday on Friday by beating Carlota Ciganda, came from four down to outlast Jodi Ewart Shadoff, who beat defending champion Ally Ewing on the first day, at the 22nd hole having not made a bogey.

The two young Americans lost in the semi-finals, with Vu taking the third-fourth playoff, to leave a Korea-Japan final. The wind was gusting up to 45mph but one shot not affected was Ji's wedge from 92 yards that went in for an eagle at the ninth. Furue, one down at the turn, was perhaps affected by her exertions earlier in the week as her normally reliable putting faltered on the back nine, with Ji winning 3 and 2.

Shadow Creek, Las Vegas, Nevada — May 25-29
Par 72 (37-35); 6,777 yards — Purse: $1,500,000

ROUND OF 16

Madelene Sagstrom defeated Emma Talley 4 and 2
Eun-Hee Ji defeated Hye-Jin Choi 2 and 1

Gemma Dryburgh defeated Moriya Jutanugarn at the 22nd
Andrea Lee defeated Caroline Masson 2 and 1
Jenny Shin defeated Annie Park 2 and 1
Lilia Vu defeated Allisen Corpuz 4 and 3
Ayaka Furue defeated Paula Reto 2 and 1
Jodi Ewart Shadoff defeated Tiffany Chan 4 and 3
Defeated players received $26,949

QUARTER-FINALS

Ji defeated Sagstrom 7 and 6
Lee defeated Dryburgh at the 20th
Vu defeated Shin at the 20th
Furue defeated Ewart Shadoff at the 22nd
Defeated players received $49,723

SEMI-FINALS

Ji defeated Lee 4 and 3
Furue defeated Vu 2 and 1

THIRD-FOURTH PLAYOFF

Lilia Vu ($102,942) defeated Andrea Lee ($79,634) 3 and 2

FINAL

Eun-Hee Ji ($225,000) defeated Ayaka Furue ($141,906) 3 and 2

ShopRite LPGA Classic

When Brooke Henderson scored a 64 in the final round of the ShopRite LPGA Classic in 2021, she finished second to Celine Boutier. At the 2022 version of the tournament on the Bay course at Seaview, across the water from Atlantic City, the 24-year-old Canadian again closed with a 64 and this time got into a playoff against Lindsey Weaver-Wright. It took just one extra hole for Henderson to claim her 11th LPGA victory, hitting a three-wood to five feet short of the hole on the 18th green and then holing the putt for an eagle after the American, still looking for her maiden victory, took five.

Henderson, after scoring 67-70, started the final round four behind Sweden's Frida Kinhult, who slipped down the leaderboard with a 75. Henderson forged ahead with three early birdies followed by an eagle at the ninth. She added birdies at the 12th and the 18th, where she two-putted from long range. Weaver-Wright birdied the last two holes for a 65 to join Henderson on 12-under-par 201, with England's Jodi Ewart Shadoff eagling the last to take third place, one shot outside the playoff.

"I actually thought I was too far back coming into today," said Henderson, who celebrated with her sister/caddie Brittany and her parents. "I just tried to go as low as I could and see what happened and here we are. I love when I can win with my parents and sister. She's on the bag always, but just makes the win a little bit extra special."

Since her last win at the 2021 LA Open, Henderson had had to adapt to using a 46-inch driver after her 48-incher was banned under the Rules of Golf at the start of the year. She was also working on her putting, having switched to left-hand-low the previous week. She hit every fairway on Sunday and holed her share of putts, including in the playoff. "I obviously only really had one opportunity, so I just tried to go at it and hit really solid shots in the playoff. To walk up the fairway and see that I was pretty close was a big relief. Just needing two putts to win was awesome."

Dolce Seaview Hotel (Bay), Galloway, New Jersey — June 10-12
Par 71 (37-34); 6,190 yards — Purse: $1,750,000

1	**Brooke M Henderson**	67	70	64	201	$262,500
2	**Lindsey Weaver-Wright**	68	68	65	201	161,223
	Henderson won playoff at first extra hole					
3	**Jodi Ewart Shadoff**	68	67	67	202	116,956
4	Lydia Ko	71	65	67	203	81,648
	Albane Valenzuela	70	66	67	203	81,648
6	Brittany Lincicome	69	68	67	204	51,049
	Marina Alex	67	70	67	204	51,049
	Nasa Hataoka	68	68	68	204	51,049
9	Celine Boutier	70	72	63	205	36,043
	Jenny Shin	69	70	66	205	36,043
	Brittany Lang	69	69	67	205	36,043
12	Jennifer Song	71	69	66	206	29,010
	Morgane Metraux	68	67	71	206	29,010
	Lauren Coughlin	69	65	72	206	29,010
15	Inbee Park	71	69	67	207	24,891
	Sung Hyun Park	68	69	70	207	24,891
17	Kelly Tan	74	67	67	208	20,037
	Hinako Shibuno	71	70	67	208	20,037
	Chella Choi	71	69	68	208	20,037
	Wichanee Meechai	70	69	69	208	20,037
	Hye-Jin Choi	69	70	69	208	20,037
	Jeongeun Lee[6]	68	71	69	208	20,037
	Jin Young Ko	67	71	70	208	20,037
	Frida Kinhult	66	67	75	208	20,037
25	Jasmine Suwannapura	70	70	69	209	15,932
	Caroline Masson	68	71	70	209	15,932
	Stephanie Kyriacou	65	73	71	209	15,932
	Su Oh	69	68	72	209	15,932
29	Emma Talley	69	73	68	210	11,420
	Pornanong Phatlum	74	67	69	210	11,420
	Jennifer Chang	73	68	69	210	11,420
	Gina Kim	71	70	69	210	11,420
	Nuria Iturrioz	70	71	69	210	11,420
	Yu Liu	69	72	69	210	11,420
	Peiyun Chien	72	68	70	210	11,420
	Stacy Lewis	72	68	70	210	11,420
	Jenny Coleman	72	68	70	210	11,420
	Robynn Ree	70	70	70	210	11,420
	Jeongeun Lee[5]	68	71	71	210	11,420
	Isi Gabsa	74	64	72	210	11,420
	Dottie Ardina	67	71	72	210	11,420
42	Anna Nordqvist	72	70	69	211	7,021
	Aditi Ashok	71	71	69	211	7,021
	Cydney Clanton	71	71	69	211	7,021
	Kaitlyn Papp	71	71	69	211	7,021
	Bailey Shoemaker (A)	73	68	70	211	
	Karis Davidson	73	68	70	211	7,021
	Bronte Law	73	68	70	211	7,021
	Perrine Delacour	70	71	70	211	7,021
	Ayaka Furue	69	72	70	211	7,021
	Lauren Stephenson	72	68	71	211	7,021
	Dewi Weber	69	70	72	211	7,021
	Ruixin Liu	69	69	73	211	7,021
54	A Lim Kim	73	69	70	212	4,881
	Giulia Molinaro	72	70	70	212	4,881
	Sarah Kemp	71	70	71	212	4,881
	Paula Reto	71	70	71	212	4,881
	Sarah Jane Smith	70	71	71	212	4,881
	Klara Spilkova	72	68	72	212	4,881
	Muni He	71	69	72	212	4,881
	Maisie Ventres Filler (A)	70	70	72	212	
	Cristie Kerr	68	72	72	212	4,881
	Caroline Inglis	69	70	73	212	4,881
	Alana Uriell	71	67	74	212	4,881
65	Anne van Dam	73	69	71	213	4,105
	Haru Nomura	70	70	73	213	4,105
67	Dani Holmqvist	73	69	72	214	3,795
	Kristen Gillman	69	73	72	214	3,795
	Jessica Peng	71	70	73	214	3,795
	Mel Reid	70	71	73	214	3,795
	Ssu-Chia Cheng	70	70	74	214	3,795
72	In Gee Chun	72	70	73	215	3,487
	Luna Sobron Galmes	70	72	73	215	3,487
	Pernilla Lindberg	68	70	77	215	3,487
75	Savannah Vilaubi	72	69	75	216	3,398
76	Dana Finkelstein	73	69	75	217	3,354

Meijer LPGA Classic

Jennifer Kupcho felt she could "birdie every hole" at Blythefield and in the first round almost did. She birdied the first two, six on the front nine, and added another plus an eagle coming home for a 63. The Chevron champion carried her lead through two days before slipping a shot behind Nelly Korda. But although it went to a playoff at the end of Sunday, Kupcho notched up her second career victory thanks to two more birdies on the par-five 18th. She should have won the playoff at the first attempt after hitting an eight-iron to three feet but she missed the putt. Korda three-putted to drop out of the three-way playoff and then Leona Maguire missed a short putt at the second extra hole. The win took Kupcho inside the top 10 in the world for the first time.

Her first title had come at the first major of the year and the leaderboard at the Meijer LPGA Classic was of the same quality. Lydia Ko, after a bogey-free 68, missed out on the playoff by one, and a further shot back were Lexi Thompson, Jessica Korda, Atthaya Thitikul and Carlota Ciganda.

Kupcho, who followed her opening round with 67-69-71 for 18-under-par 270, mixed a double bogey, a bogey, an eagle and a birdie on her front nine on Sunday, leading the way until a bogey at the 16th. Nelly Korda, in her second event back from surgery for a blood clot in her left arm, took the third-round lead with 67-65-66. But the defence of her title stuttered with three bogeys and three birdies in a 72 on Sunday. "If you told me three, four months ago when I was in the ER that I would be here, I would be extremely happy," Korda said. It was Maguire who came racing through the field with a 65 that included an inward 32.

"I thought she was going to make it," Kupcho said of the Irishwoman's putt to stay alive in the playoff. "When she hit it by the hole and I still had to putt from the fringe I thought to myself, that's not a gimme. But she doesn't miss putts, I was really just shocked."

Although her first win was a major, this Father's Day victory prompted Kupcho to say: "I think this one is even better than the first, personally. I had such a big lead going into the final round at Chevron, so to come out of this one with top-ranked players all over the place, I feel very proud of myself. I thought this morning that I should call my dad, but I kept telling myself, 'No, like we'll call him after the round with the trophy in our hand,' and I'm excited I can do that now."

Blythefield Country Club, Belmont, Michigan — June 16-19
Par 72 (36-36); 6,556 yards — Purse: $2,500,000

1	**Jennifer Kupcho**	63	67	69	71	270	$375,000
2	**Leona Maguire**	69	68	68	65	270	196,847
	Nelly Korda	67	65	66	72	270	196,847
	Kupcho won playoff at second extra hole						
4	Lydia Ko	70	68	65	68	271	128,045
5	Jessica Korda	68	68	69	67	272	79,951
	Carlota Ciganda	68	65	72	67	272	79,951
	Atthaya Thitikul	68	69	67	68	272	79,951
	Lexi Thompson	65	69	68	70	272	79,951
9	Wei-Ling Hsu	70	69	68	66	273	53,092
	Brooke M Henderson	68	66	67	72	273	53,092
11	Allisen Corpuz	69	70	70	65	274	46,845
12	Lilia Vu	68	71	71	65	275	39,849
	Cristie Kerr	69	72	65	69	275	39,849
	Hannah Green	70	68	68	69	275	39,849
	Caroline Masson	67	68	70	70	275	39,849
16	Sarah Schmelzel	71	68	69	68	276	33,354
	Gerina Mendoza	64	72	72	68	276	33,354
18	Dana Finkelstein	71	69	69	68	277	28,274
	Na Yeon Choi	69	71	68	69	277	28,274
	Gina Kim	71	68	69	69	277	28,274
	Chella Choi	68	74	65	70	277	28,274
	Anna Nordqvist	65	70	70	72	277	28,274
	Minjee Lee	68	69	66	74	277	28,274
24	Ayaka Furue	72	70	72	64	278	21,721
	Narin An	67	73	70	68	278	21,721
	Megan Khang	67	72	71	68	278	21,721
	Amy Olson	69	70	69	70	278	21,721
	Brittany Lincicome	69	69	69	71	278	21,721
	Haru Nomura	71	70	65	72	278	21,721
	Xiyu Lin	70	67	69	72	278	21,721
	Madelene Sagstrom	65	69	70	74	278	21,721
32	Jasmine Suwannapura	68	73	72	66	279	15,724
	Pornanong Phatlum	71	71	70	67	279	15,724
	Ryann O'Toole	67	72	72	68	279	15,724
	Stacy Lewis	67	71	73	68	279	15,724
	Alison Lee	70	71	68	70	279	15,724
	Paula Reto	71	65	73	70	279	15,724
	Su Oh	73	67	67	72	279	15,724
	Peiyun Chien	72	68	67	72	279	15,724
40	Albane Valenzuela	70	72	70	68	280	11,132
	Hyo Joo Kim	72	70	69	69	280	11,132
	Isi Gabsa	68	72	71	69	280	11,132
	Brittany Altomare	72	67	72	69	280	11,132
	Lindsey Weaver-Wright	69	70	72	69	280	11,132
	Maude-Aimee Leblanc	70	72	68	70	280	11,132
	Wichanee Meechai	68	71	71	70	280	11,132
	Hye-Jin Choi	70	72	67	71	280	11,132
	Celine Boutier	70	69	70	71	280	11,132
49	Jodi Ewart Shadoff	73	69	69	70	281	8,263
	Eun-Hee Ji	73	69	69	70	281	8,263
	Yu Liu	71	70	70	70	281	8,263
	Kaitlyn Papp	69	71	71	70	281	8,263
	Bianca Pagdanganan	67	72	72	70	281	8,263
	Nasa Hataoka	71	67	73	70	281	8,263
	Robynn Ree	71	67	73	70	281	8,263
56	Pajaree Anannarukarn	69	72	72	69	282	6,550
	Angel Yin	74	67	71	70	282	6,550
	Andrea Lee	66	71	75	70	282	6,550
	Alena Sharp	72	70	69	71	282	6,550
	Frida Kinhult	71	70	70	71	282	6,550
	Ruixin Liu	67	71	73	71	282	6,550
	Yealimi Noh	70	70	70	72	282	6,550
63	Jaye Marie Green	71	70	71	71	283	5,871
64	Pernilla Lindberg	69	73	73	69	284	5,622
	Katherine Kirk	68	71	73	72	284	5,622
	So Yeon Ryu	68	71	71	74	284	5,622
67	Brittany Lang	69	72	73	71	285	5,135
	A Lim Kim	70	70	72	73	285	5,135
	In Gee Chun	68	72	72	73	285	5,135
	Tiffany Chan	70	69	73	73	285	5,135
	Mirim Lee	69	70	72	74	285	5,135
72	Morgane Metraux	68	72	76	70	286	4,779
	Cydney Clanton	69	71	74	72	286	4,779
	Jeongeun Lee[5]	70	69	75	72	286	4,779
	Gemma Dryburgh	73	68	72	73	286	4,779
76	Sophia Schubert	71	70	78	68	287	4,630
77	Charlotte Thomas	70	70	77	72	289	4,571
78	Allison Emrey	70	72	73	77	292	4,513

Dow Great Lakes Bay Invitational

Jennifer Kupcho continued her hot form with a third win of the season at the Dow Great Lakes Bay Invitational, and in the process helped her Solheim Cup partner to a first win for eight years. The pair scored two fourball efforts of 61, including in Saturday's final round, to win by five strokes from Matilda Castren and Kelly Tan.

Kupcho followed up her Chevron Championship victory with her second title at the Meijer LPGA Classic a month previously. But Salas's second LPGA win took rather longer to appear as her first was the Kingsmill Championship in 2014. Salas added six of their birdies on the last day, the eve of her 33rd birthday. "It's been a long time. I couldn't have done it without her. You know, she's a great competitor, a great friend and an amazing partner on the golf course. We played some amazing golf this week. My goal was to play well for her. We showcased how our games can complement each other."

Salas and Kupcho, 25, teamed up to win two and a half points out of three at the Solheim Cup at Inverness in 2021. Kupcho has not looked back since. "I think after I got my first win, I felt a lot more confident in my game. It's so hard to win out here, so to know that I could do it, I think that kind of helped my confidence. And then to get the second win against a really stacked leaderboard and a playoff at Meijer, it made me all that more comfortable."

In a rare LPGA appearance, Annika Sorenstam teamed up with compatriot Madelene Sagstrom to share the first round lead on five under par with Pauline Roussin and Dewi Weber. It was the first time Sorenstam had led, or shared the lead, after 18 holes since the 2008 Lorena Ochoa Invitational. The Swedes fell back as Roussin and Weber took the halfway lead but it was the 64 as a foursome that put Kupcho and Salas into a four-shot lead after 54 holes. Castren and Tan closed with a 62, while Stacy Lewis and Maria Fassi posted the second betterball 59 of the week to take third place.

Midland Country Club, Midland, Michigan — July 13-16
Par 70 (35-35); 6,277 yards — Purse: $2,500,000

1	**Jennifer Kupcho/ Lizette Salas**	68	61	64	61	254	$603,172
2	**Matilda Castren/ Kelly Tan**	69	61	67	62	259	293,567
3	**Stacy Lewis/ Maria Fassi**	69	65	67	59	260	187,385
4	Elizabeth Szokol/ Cheyenne Knight	72	62	66	61	261	119,302
	Haeji Kang/ Tiffany Chan	68	62	69	62	261	119,302
6	Hye-Jin Choi/ Narin An	69	65	67	61	262	85,008
	Pauline Roussin/ Dewi Weber	65	61	73	63	262	85,008
8	Nelly Korda/ Jessica Korda	69	63	71	60	263	66,958
	Karis Davidson/ Daniela Darquea	71	63	67	62	263	66,958
10	Brooke Matthews/ Lauren Hartlage	71	62	71	60	264	50,719
	Wichanee Meechai/ Ruixin Liu	70	64	68	62	264	50,719
	Sarah Kemp/ Alena Sharp	69	61	72	62	264	50,719
	Sophia Popov/ Anne van Dam	70	61	70	63	264	50,719
	Yealimi Noh/ A Lim Kim	69	62	69	64	264	50,719
15	Xiyu Lin/ Perrine Delacour	69	66	69	61	265	34,228
	Paula Reto/ Amelia Lewis	69	63	70	63	265	34,228
	Lauren Stephenson/ Jillian Hollis	66	66	69	64	265	34,228
	Pornanong Phatlum/ Pavarisa Yoktuan	66	64	71	64	265	34,228
	Marina Alex/ Karrie Webb	69	62	69	65	265	34,228
20	Lauren Coughlin/ Savannah Vilaubi	70	64	70	62	266	26,482
21	Amy Olson/ Katherine Kirk	68	67	71	61	267	22,611
	Rachel Rohanna/ Haylee Rae Harford	71	64	69	63	267	22,611
	Sarah Schmelzel/ Maude-Aimee Leblanc	71	62	71	63	267	22,611
24	Casey Danielson/ Lauren Kim	71	64	71	62	268	17,426
	Frida Kinhult/ Linnea Johansson	68	66	70	64	268	17,426
	Pajaree Anannarukarn/ Aditi Ashok	72	62	69	65	268	17,426
	Yu Liu/ Peiyun Chien	68	65	70	65	268	17,426
28	Morgan Metraux/ Celine Herbin	70	62	76	61	269	13,335
	Cristie Kerr/ Stephanie Meadow	69	65	71	64	269	13,335
	Madelene Sagstrom/ Annika Sorenstam	65	66	72	66	269	13,335
	Mariajo Uribe/ Sarah Jane Smith	74	59	69	67	269	13,335
32	Angel Yin/ Yaeeun Hong	71	64	72	63	270	11,368
	Emma Talley/ Jodi Ewart Shadoff	66	64	76	64	270	11,368
34	Robynn Ree/ Jennifer Chang	73	62	72	64	271	10,618
35	Sophia Schubert/ Amanda Doherty	72	61	74	66	273	10,119
36	Sadena Parks/ Anita Uwadia	69	65	73	67	274	9,681
	Maddie Szeryk/ Kristy McPherson	69	64	74	67	274	9,681
38	Mo Martin/ Vicky Hurst	69	66	76	65	276	9,320
39	Mariah Stackhouse/ Sydnee Michaels	72	62	76	68	278	9,085

CP Women's Open

A big lead on the back nine when some of the game's best players are charging into contention is not a comfortable scenario. "I started putting on the brakes, and that's probably not what you want to do," said Paula Reto. "I haven't really much been in this position, and I was just trying to control myself and be in the moment."

Reto, the 32-year-old South African in her ninth season on the LPGA, set a new course record at Ottawa Hunt and Golf Club with a 62 on Thursday. She kept in contention with scores of 69-67 to be one behind Korean rookies Hye-Jin Choi and Narin An. Then five birdies on the front nine on Sunday put Reto four in front. But the CP Women's Open, being staged for the first time since 2019, was far from over. Lydia Ko posted a bogey-free 63 to get to 17 under par. Reto dropped a shot at 14 and was back to 19 under. Suddenly Nelly Korda was the big threat after holing out for an eagle two at the 12th. The American got within one with birdies at 15 and 16, barely missed another at 17, then was bunkered at the last and could only make a par. Korda closed with a 67 to finish second for the second time in the season, tying with Choi, who closed with a 69.

Reto parred home for a 67 to finish on 19-under-par 265 and win by one. She was the fourth South African to win on tour after Sally Little, Lee-Anne Pace and AIG Women's Open champion Ashleigh Buhai. She was also the fourth first-time winner in a row, which had not happened on the LPGA since 2005. "I'm really excited and just proud of myself for being able to stick through the shots and the routines," Reto said. "I was really nervous, especially as I started pulling a few shots, and I told myself, okay, just stay in the moment and breathe. You go through all those things that you think will help."

Danielle Kang finished 17th on her first appearance since announcing she had been diagnosed with a tumour on her spine at the US Women's Open. Jin Young Ko, the defending champion after her 2019 victory, missed the cut, the first time she had missed consecutive cuts on the LPGA having done so at the AIG Women's Open. Canada's Lori Kane, a four-time winner, was cheered up the 18th hole on Friday in her last appearance at the Canadian Open.

Ottawa Hunt & Golf Club, Ottawa, Ontario, Canada — August 25-28
Par 71 (36-35); 6,546 yards — Purse: $2,350,000

1	**Paula Reto**	62	69	67	67	265	$352,500
2	**Nelly Korda**	67	64	68	67	266	185,891
	Hye-Jin Choi	68	63	66	69	266	185,891
4	Lydia Ko	69	68	67	63	267	120,918
5	A Lim Kim	66	69	66	67	268	97,326
6	Sarah Schmelzel	69	64	66	70	269	73,141
	Narin An	64	65	68	72	269	73,141
8	Emma Talley	65	70	68	68	271	58,396
9	Alison Lee	68	71	70	63	272	46,450
	Sei Young Kim	70	68	71	63	272	46,450
	Lucy Li	66	70	69	67	272	46,450
	Lindy Duncan	69	62	70	71	272	46,450
13	Carlota Ciganda	68	68	70	67	273	35,390
	Megan Khang	70	66	69	68	273	35,390
	Ariya Jutanugarn	67	68	69	69	273	35,390
	Nasa Hataoka	66	67	69	71	273	35,390
17	Alena Sharp	67	72	68	67	274	26,308
	Haylee Rae Harford	68	70	68	68	274	26,308
	Lilia Vu	65	69	72	68	274	26,308
	Amy Yang	67	69	69	69	274	26,308
	Yealimi Noh	67	69	68	70	274	26,308
	Jessica Korda	67	68	69	70	274	26,308
	Stephanie Kyriacou	71	63	70	70	274	26,308
	Lizette Salas	68	64	72	70	274	26,308
	Danielle Kang	67	66	68	73	274	26,308
26	Allison Emrey	68	70	69	68	275	19,701
	Wichanee Meechai	71	66	70	68	275	19,701
	Allisen Corpuz	71	68	66	70	275	19,701
	Hannah Green	68	66	71	70	275	19,701
	Mo Martin	66	70	68	71	275	19,701
	Maddie Szeryk	67	68	69	71	275	19,701
32	Caroline Masson	68	70	70	68	276	16,073
	In Gee Chun	68	70	68	70	276	16,073
	Peiyun Chien	66	71	69	70	276	16,073
	Ashleigh Buhai	71	65	68	72	276	16,073
36	Lexi Thompson	70	68	73	66	277	12,348
	Xiyu Lin	72	65	72	68	277	12,348
	Elizabeth Szokol	66	69	74	68	277	12,348
	Sarah Kemp	68	70	70	69	277	12,348
	Sophia Schubert	69	68	71	69	277	12,348
	Cheyenne Knight	68	69	71	69	277	12,348
	Charlotte Thomas	68	70	69	70	277	12,348
	Frida Kinhult	72	65	70	70	277	12,348
	Ally Ewing	67	67	72	71	277	12,348
45	Pauline Roussin	66	71	72	69	278	9,496
	Matilda Castren	67	71	69	71	278	9,496
	Ruixin Liu	68	68	71	71	278	9,496
	Ayaka Furue	71	68	67	72	278	9,496
49	Mi Hyang Lee	68	72	70	69	279	7,803
	Brittany Altomare	68	71	71	69	279	7,803
	Brooke M Henderson	69	68	73	69	279	7,803
	Esther Henseleit	69	70	70	70	279	7,803
	Stacy Lewis	68	67	74	70	279	7,803
	Jeongeun Lee[6]	70	70	68	71	279	7,803
	Emily Kristine Pedersen	69	71	68	71	279	7,803
56	Albane Valenzuela	71	69	72	68	280	6,488
	Anna Davis (A)	70	68	71	71	280	
	Karis Davidson	69	67	72	72	280	6,488

	Jennifer Kupcho	67 68 73 72	280	6,488		Jennifer Song	69 70 73 72	284	4,769
	Atthaya Thitikul	66 70 70 74	280	6,488		Kaitlyn Papp	70 70 71 73	284	4,769
61	Jeongeun Lee[5]	68 72 72 69	281	5,663		Amanda Doherty	69 71 71 73	284	4,769
	Jodi Ewart Shadoff	67 70 74 70	281	5,663		Cristie Kerr	67 73 71 73	284	4,769
	Wei-Ling Hsu	66 71 73 71	281	5,663		So Yeon Ryu	70 68 72 74	284	4,769
	Dewi Weber	68 70 70 73	281	5,663		Perrine Delacour	66 74 68 76	284	4,769
	Andrea Lee	70 69 68 74	281	5,663	75	Lauren Zaretsky (A)	68 71 73 73	285	
66	Yu Liu	70 68 71 73	282	5,308	76	Yu-Sang Hou	73 66 76 71	286	4,428
67	Lauren Hartlage	71 68 74 70	283	5,191		Rebecca Lee-Bentham	70 70 74 72	286	4,428
68	Giulia Molinaro	69 71 72 72	284	4,769		Robynn Ree	65 72 73 76	286	4,428

Dana Open

Lucy Li had not expected this. The 19-year-old American was leading the Dana Open on the LPGA Tour after both the second and third rounds at Highland Meadows. Li had secured her card for 2023 by winning twice on the Epson Tour but played at the CP Women's Open on an invitation and finished in the top 10 to earn a start in rainy Toledo. "It's been a whirlwind couple of months," Li said. Unfortunately for her, the whirlwind on Sunday came from Gaby Lopez.

Lopez birdied the last three holes for the second day running for a one-shot win over Megan Khang. The 28-year-old Mexican claimed her third LPGA win, and first since the 2020 Tournament of Champions, with a bogey-free 63, coming from four behind Li and outside the top 10 after 54 holes. Lopez scored 67-70-66 for the first three days, going 13 under on the weekend for an 18-under-par total of 266. Li finished with a 70 to tie for fourth, while her playing partners Caroline Masson and Lexi Thompson scored 68 and 73 respectively.

It turned into a duel between Lopez and playing partner Khang, who scored 64. Lopez, whose season had been interrupted by a torn ligament in her neck and then tendonitis in her left wrist, made three birdies going out, then added two more at the 10th and the 13th. "I did a fist pump because I do a lot of fist pumps, but I stayed calm because I knew that we had a chance. That's all I wanted. I just wanted a chance." At the 16th she hit her approach to two feet on the soft greens, then almost holed her bunker shot at the 17th. The birdie put her one ahead as Khang's putt lipped out. Both were bunkered at the last and while Khang came out close, Lopez barely got hers to the green. But she holed the 15-footer with a shout of "Vamos!"

"Standing over the last putt I told myself, this is exactly what I trained for," said Lopez. "I knew I had to make it. I tried to be calm all day long, but sometimes excitement gets me and I couldn't hold it for the last putt."

She added: "I just felt like nothing was really clicking for me over the year. I was struggling physically, struggling mentally, and that's where the doubts and fears come from. You've just got to keep it real, accept where you are and surround yourself with great people."

Highland Meadows Golf Club, Sylvania, Ohio — September 1-4
Par 71 (34-37); 6,598 yards — Purse:$1,750,000

1	**Gaby Lopez**	67 70 66 63	266	$262,500	16	Jodi Ewart Shadoff	71 70 66 66	273	20,826
2	**Megan Khang**	71 65 67 64	267	160,837		Ashleigh Buhai	71 67 69 66	273	20,826
3	**Caroline Masson**	68 67 65 68	268	116,676		Lilia Vu	68 69 69 67	273	20,826
4	Sarah Schmelzel	67 71 65 66	269	74,115		Ariya Jutanugarn	69 68 68 68	273	20,826
	Ruoning Yin	65 69 68 67	269	74,115		Wei-Ling Hsu	69 66 70 68	273	20,826
	Lucy Li	68 64 67 70	269	74,115		Madelene Sagstrom	68 70 66 69	273	20,826
7	Frida Kinhult	69 68 67 66	270	44,176		Lydia Ko	66 72 64 71	273	20,826
	Xiyu Lin	67 69 66 68	270	44,176		Lexi Thompson	66 69 65 73	273	20,826
	Nasa Hataoka	69 66 67 68	270	44,176	24	Wichanee Meechai	68 68 73 65	274	16,203
10	Carlota Ciganda	65 69 69 68	271	33,168		Celine Herbin	68 73 65 68	274	16,203
	Hannah Green	74 62 66 69	271	33,168		Hye-Jin Choi	65 70 71 68	274	16,203
	Leona Maguire	66 70 66 69	271	33,168		Mina Harigae	70 67 68 69	274	16,203
13	Hyo Joo Kim	66 71 70 65	272	27,180		Moriya Jutanugarn	70 67 68 69	274	16,203
	Brooke M Henderson	72 66 65 69	272	27,180	29	Atthaya Thitikul	70 70 69 66	275	12,299
	Sei Young Kim	70 67 65 70	272	27,180		Amy Yang	70 68 70 67	275	12,299

	Amanda Doherty	70	68	69	68	275	12,299
	A Lim Kim	67	71	69	68	275	12,299
	So Yeon Ryu	67	70	70	68	275	12,299
	Lauren Stephenson	66	70	71	68	275	12,299
	Mi Hyang Lee	72	65	68	70	275	12,299
	Ayaka Furue	68	69	68	70	275	12,299
	Aline Krauter	66	71	68	70	275	12,299
38	Andrea Lee	70	71	69	66	276	8,818
	Azahara Munoz	72	69	68	67	276	8,818
	Yuka Saso	68	69	72	67	276	8,818
	Pajaree Anannarukarn	71	66	71	68	276	8,818
	Emma Talley	71	69	66	70	276	8,818
	Jennifer Chang	70	70	66	70	276	8,818
	Peiyun Chien	70	66	70	70	276	8,818
45	Elizabeth Szokol	72	68	70	67	277	7,088
	Stephanie Kyriacou	71	69	67	70	277	7,088
	Morgane Metraux	70	69	68	70	277	7,088
	Marina Alex	70	69	66	72	277	7,088
49	Danielle Kang	72	67	72	67	278	5,914
	Yu Liu	70	71	69	68	278	5,914
	Albane Valenzuela	72	67	71	68	278	5,914
	Natasha Andrea Oon	70	70	69	69	278	5,914
	Minjee Lee	67	72	70	69	278	5,914
	Brittany Altomare	68	69	68	73	278	5,914
55	Gerina Mendoza	70	71	70	68	279	4,931
	Cydney Clanton	71	68	71	69	279	4,931
	Yu-Sang Hou	71	70	68	70	279	4,931
	Chella Choi	70	69	68	72	279	4,931
	Jeongeun Lee[5]	70	67	70	72	279	4,931
60	Pornanong Phatlum	70	70	72	68	280	4,227
	Jeongeun Lee[6]	70	71	70	69	280	4,227
	Emily Kristine Pedersen	66	73	72	69	280	4,227
	Lauren Coughlin	70	70	70	70	280	4,227
	Haeji Kang	71	70	68	71	280	4,227
65	Maude-Aimee Leblanc	70	71	72	69	282	3,875
	Ana Belac	72	68	71	71	282	3,875
	Mariah Stackhouse	68	70	71	73	282	3,875
68	Angel Yin	71	70	73	69	283	3,577
	Christina Kim	70	69	74	70	283	3,577
	Bronte Law	71	69	70	73	283	3,577
	Amy Olson	66	71	73	73	283	3,577
72	Maddie Szeryk	72	69	74	70	285	3,434
73	In-Kyung Kim	69	71	78	68	286	3,368
	Maria Fassi	68	72	72	74	286	3,368
75	Jennifer Song	72	67	74	75	288	3,306

Kroger Queen City Championship

A second week in Ohio meant the LPGA returned to Cincinnati for the first time in over three decades, and to the Kendale course at Kenwood Country Club for the first time since Mary Mills won the US Women's Open in 1963. One player has proved highly successful at conquering courses unknown to the modern generation and for the third year in a row Ally Ewing did just that. The 29-year-old from Mississippi won the Kroger Queen City Championship by one stroke from China's Xiyu Lin, having taken the 2020 Drive On Championship at Reynolds Lake Oconee and the Bank of Hope Match Play at Shadow Creek.

Yet in 2022, Ewing had yet to notch a top 10 before posting rounds of 69-64-67-66 for a 22-under-par total of 266. A chip-in at the second on Friday sparked a run of six birdies in a row and although she took the 54-hole lead, it was a run of five birdies in a row on the back nine on Sunday that secured the title. Lin, the first-round leader on 64, rallied with three birdies going out to take the lead before Ewing, after eight pars, birdied the ninth.

Both birdied the 12th and 13th holes, and Ewing kept the run going while Lin had to birdie the 16th to stay two back. The Chinese player then claimed her third birdie of the week at the monster par-four 18th, where there were only 20 birdies for the entire tournament. Ewing had come up just short, the only green she missed on Sunday, but got down in two putts, holing from two feet for her third victory. Ewing came home in 31 and needed to as Lin scored a bogey-free 65 to finish as a runner-up for the second time in the season. Maria Fassi, the nearest challenger after 54 holes, had a slow start on Sunday but secured third place, two ahead of Jeongeun Lee[6], who scored a 63 on Friday to hold the 36-hole lead.

Ewing's husband Charlie, the head women's golf coach at their alma mater Mississippi State University, surprised her by appearing during the celebrations on the 18th green. "He has been a rock for me this year when I have fallen into a lot of doubt in my ability to get back into solid form," Ewing said. "He's poured so much into it, has helped me get right here back in the winner's circle, for sure."

For the third week in a row, 14-year-old Gianna Clemente, a runner-up in both the 2022 US Junior Girls' Championship and the 2022 Rolex Girls Junior Championship, Monday qualified, although missing the cut each time.

Kenwood Country Club (Kendale), Cincinnati, Ohio — September 8-11
Par 72 (36-36); 6,515 yards — Purse: $1,750,000

1	**Ally Ewing**	69	64	67	66	266	$262,500
2	**Xiyu Lin**	64	68	70	65	267	160,837
3	**Maria Fassi**	68	66	67	71	272	116,676
4	Jeongeun Lee[6]	68	63	73	70	274	90,258
5	Marina Alex	70	68	70	67	275	60,613
	Andrea Lee	69	66	71	69	275	60,613
	A Lim Kim	66	69	70	70	275	60,613
8	Sarah Kemp	66	68	70	72	276	43,589
9	Atthaya Thitikul	67	74	67	69	277	39,186
10	Jessica Korda	73	67	72	66	278	32,096
	Morgane Metraux	69	73	66	70	278	32,096
	Megan Khang	69	66	69	74	278	32,096
	Ariya Jutanugarn	68	67	69	74	278	32,096
14	Yealimi Noh	70	69	73	67	279	24,920
	Caroline Inglis	70	71	70	68	279	24,920
	Wei-Ling Hsu	73	68	69	69	279	24,920
	Hye-Jin Choi	67	71	71	70	279	24,920
18	Jodi Ewart Shadoff	71	69	71	69	280	21,398
	Brooke M Henderson	71	67	69	73	280	21,398
20	Nasa Hataoka	65	70	77	69	281	19,197
	Elizabeth Szokol	71	71	68	71	281	19,197
	Narin An	70	68	69	74	281	19,197
	Anna Nordqvist	71	66	70	74	281	19,197
24	Moriya Jutanugarn	67	71	75	69	282	15,028
	Yu Liu	72	68	72	70	282	15,028
	Hannah Green	70	70	72	70	282	15,028
	Maude-Aimee Leblanc	69	74	68	71	282	15,028
	Alena Sharp	70	72	69	71	282	15,028
	Haeji Kang	69	71	71	71	282	15,028
	Gaby Lopez	68	71	72	71	282	15,028
	Leona Maguire	70	67	73	72	282	15,028
	Angel Yin	69	67	73	73	282	15,028
33	Yuka Saso	73	70	71	69	283	11,741
	Sei Young Kim	67	73	72	71	283	11,741
	Lauren Stephenson	69	68	74	72	283	11,741
36	Sarah Schmelzel	71	71	72	70	284	9,774
	Ruixin Liu	73	70	70	71	284	9,774
	Alison Lee	73	70	70	71	284	9,774
	Mi Hyang Lee	72	69	72	71	284	9,774
	Pernilla Lindberg	71	70	71	72	284	9,774
	Emma Talley	69	69	74	72	284	9,774
42	Katherine Perry-Hamski	67	76	74	68	285	7,802
	Ayako Uehara	71	72	71	71	285	7,802
	Dottie Ardina	75	67	72	71	285	7,802
	Casey Danielson	73	70	69	73	285	7,802
	Paula Reto	74	68	70	73	285	7,802
47	Azahara Munoz	73	67	77	69	286	6,560
	Dana Finkelstein	72	69	73	72	286	6,560
	Jasmine Suwannapura	67	72	74	73	286	6,560
	Sung Hyun Park	71	70	69	76	286	6,560
51	Brooke Matthews	69	72	76	70	287	5,460
	Jennifer Chang	72	70	74	71	287	5,460
	Rachel Rohanna	73	70	72	72	287	5,460
	Lizette Salas	71	72	71	73	287	5,460
	Jenny Shin	70	73	71	73	287	5,460
	Mina Harigae	70	72	72	73	287	5,460
	Chella Choi	73	70	70	74	287	5,460
58	Wichanee Meechai	73	70	74	71	288	4,456
	Muni He	72	70	75	71	288	4,456
	Gemma Dryburgh	70	69	75	74	288	4,456
	Aditi Ashok	68	70	76	74	288	4,456
	Ayaka Furue	69	71	72	76	288	4,456
63	Pornanong Phatlum	68	74	73	74	289	3,963
	Gina Kim	68	73	73	75	289	3,963
	Sophia Schubert	72	71	70	76	289	3,963
	Charlotte Thomas	71	71	71	76	289	3,963
	Stephanie Meadow	71	71	69	78	289	3,963
68	Alana Uriell	71	70	77	72	290	3,577
	Maddie Szeryk	72	70	75	73	290	3,577
	Min Lee	68	74	74	74	290	3,577
	Anna Davis (A)	74	66	76	74	290	
	Luna Sobron Galmes	73	70	71	76	290	3,577
73	Lauren Coughlin	74	69	70	78	291	3,434
74	Paula Creamer	72	70	75	75	292	3,390
75	Jillian Hollis	70	72	76	75	293	3,346

AmazingCre Portland Classic

As many as nine players had a chance to win the AmazingCre Portland Classic in the closing stages. Maja Stark, in her first appearance on the circuit as an LPGA member following her victory in Northern Ireland, birdied five holes in a row on the front nine to take the lead only to finish in eighth place. Korea's Narin An went out in 30 at Columbia Edgewater, where the tournament returned after a one year absence, and scored 64 to join a large tie for third place that also included 2019 winner Hannah Green and Germany's Esther Henseleit, who was only knocked out of contention with a bogey at the 17th. Daniela Darquea, the only player from Ecuador on the circuit, birdied the last three holes to get to 18 under par with a 66 to finish second, her best ever result.

But the winner was Andrea Lee, who started the year on the Epson Tour, where she won at the Casino del Sol Golf Classic, before playing her way back on the LPGA for a third season. The Stanford star and former world number one amateur, now 24, turned professional in 2019 but had not found life on tour as smooth sailing as her college career. She opened quietly in Portland with a 72 to be seven off the lead but responded with a 64 the next day and took the lead with a 67 on Saturday.

Her closing 66, to get to 19-under-par 269, began with two early bogeys before three birdies in a row from the fifth. She birdied the 10th, then had three more in a row from the 12th and also the 16th. The sand save at the 17th was crucial as Darquea cut the lead to one playing the last.

"All the hard work has paid off," Lee said. "It's been my dream to win on the LPGA Tour, and the fact that I accomplished that today is just pretty surreal. I expected a lot out of myself coming into the LPGA and turning professional. Put a lot of pressure on myself to do really well off the bat. That wasn't the case at all — 2020 was a decent year, but then 2021 was a struggle. I have really grown as a golfer and am proud of the way that I managed to use all those experiences to get that win today."

Columbia Edgewater Country Club, Portland, Oregon — September 15-18
Par 72 (36-36); 6,478 yards — Purse: $1,500,000

1	**Andrea Lee**	72	64	67	66	269	$225,000
2	**Daniela Darquea**	69	67	68	66	270	139,217
3	**Narin An**	71	69	67	64	271	67,303
	Esther Henseleit	70	64	71	66	271	67,303
	Hannah Green	66	70	68	67	271	67,303
	Ayaka Furue	67	69	67	68	271	67,303
	Lilia Vu	68	66	69	68	271	67,303
8	Maja Stark	69	67	70	66	272	37,730
9	Ryann O'Toole	70	68	67	68	273	33,919
10	Weiwei Zhang	69	67	72	66	274	27,782
	Brooke M Henderson	68	70	69	67	274	27,782
	Frida Kinhult	73	68	65	68	274	27,782
	Paula Reto	71	66	67	70	274	27,782
14	Chella Choi	70	69	70	67	276	23,476
15	Amy Olson	70	71	70	66	277	20,427
	Georgia Hall	70	69	71	67	277	20,427
	Ruoning Yin	70	67	71	69	277	20,427
	Caroline Inglis	67	70	69	71	277	20,427
19	Bianca Pagdanganan	73	71	71	63	278	16,921
	Rachel Rohanna	69	74	67	68	278	16,921
	Pornanong Phatlum	70	70	70	68	278	16,921
	Hye-Jin Choi	70	70	68	70	278	16,921
	Carlota Ciganda	69	66	71	72	278	16,921
24	A Lim Kim	71	70	70	68	279	14,291
	Min Lee	70	71	70	68	279	14,291
	Ruixin Liu	72	68	71	68	279	14,291
	Marina Alex	71	71	68	69	279	14,291
28	Katie Yoo	71	72	70	67	280	12,449
	Mi Hyang Lee	71	68	70	71	280	12,449
	Hinako Shibuno	67	71	66	76	280	12,449
31	Isi Gabsa	70	70	72	69	281	10,823
	Gemma Dryburgh	72	70	69	70	281	10,823
	Jenny Shin	68	70	73	70	281	10,823
	Nelly Korda	67	73	69	72	281	10,823
35	So Yeon Ryu	70	69	71	72	282	9,757
36	Aditi Ashok	69	71	76	67	283	8,137
	Lauren Hartlage	69	73	73	68	283	8,137
	Angel Yin	69	73	72	69	283	8,137
	Lauren Stephenson	72	72	69	70	283	8,137
	Sarah Kemp	69	72	72	70	283	8,137
	Yealimi Noh	72	68	72	71	283	8,137
	Dana Finkelstein	71	69	71	72	283	8,137
	Cheyenne Knight	71	69	70	73	283	8,137
44	Maria Fassi	72	72	71	69	284	6,479
	Ayako Uehara	65	73	74	72	284	6,479
	Mo Martin	70	72	68	74	284	6,479
47	Albane Valenzuela	73	71	73	68	285	5,579
	Karis Davidson	73	68	73	71	285	5,579
	Ana Belac	69	71	74	71	285	5,579
	Anne van Dam	68	72	72	73	285	5,579
	Tiffany Chan	68	71	72	74	285	5,579
52	Charlotte Thomas	72	70	72	72	286	4,878
	Alena Sharp	68	72	72	74	286	4,878
	Mina Harigae	69	69	71	77	286	4,878
55	Jessica Peng	71	70	77	69	287	4,573
56	Cydney Clanton	71	72	77	68	288	4,192
	Morgane Metraux	74	70	71	73	288	4,192
	Na Yeon Choi	69	70	75	74	288	4,192
	Sung Hyun Park	70	73	70	75	288	4,192
60	Lindy Duncan	70	74	73	72	289	3,735
	Peiyun Chien	71	71	75	72	289	3,735
	Sarah Rhee	73	71	72	73	289	3,735
63	Haylee Harford	71	71	71	77	290	3,582
64	Jenny Coleman	69	74	72	76	291	3,468
	Savannah Vilaubi	71	68	74	78	291	3,468
66	Mariah Stackhouse	72	72	72	76	292	3,354
67	Maria McBride	73	70	77	73	293	3,239
	Linnea Johansson	74	70	73	76	293	3,239
69	Annie Park	72	71	77	74	294	3,062
	Cindy LaCrosse	76	67	75	76	294	3,062
	Sydnee Michaels	71	72	75	76	294	3,062

Walmart NW Arkansas Championship

Danielle Kang had not made a bogey over 55 holes at Pinnacle. At the second extra hole of a playoff against Atthaya Thitikul, Kang raced her first putt from the back of the 16th green past the hole and faced a tricky putt for par. But she did not have to see if she could keep her streak alive. Thitikul holed her 15-footer for birdie to win for the second time in the 19-year-old Thai's rookie season.

Thitikul, who also won her maiden LPGA title in extra time at the JBTC Classic, was the 36-hole leader after following an opening 67 with a 10-under 61 on Saturday. She finished the round eagle-birdie-birdie at seven, eight and nine to lead by one from Yuka Saso, with Kang four adrift after rounds of 67-65.

Kang closed her Sunday 64 in dramatic fashion by chipping in at the 18th for an eagle. "I kept telling my caddie that I just wanted to finish at 17 under," Kang said. "As we walked up to the ball on 18 I said, 'I really want to make an eagle. I'll chip that in'. He was like, 'You can chip that in easy'. We chipped it in." A huge roar greeted Kang taking the lead before Thitikul holed a long putt at the 17th to draw level and then parred the last for a 68 to tie on 17-under 196, the pair one ahead of Chella Choi (65).

Both Kang and Thitikul parred the short 15th in the playoff, then the young Thai won with a three at the next. Of the putt, she said: "In my mind I tell myself just do your best, even if it's not going in or whatever. Just do the best you can. Actually, I didn't think about anything at all. Just look at the line, get the speed right, and pretty much that's it."

Thitikul added: "I have to say that I really wanted to win. It means a lot to me to get my second win, because it seems like you prove that you can do it, even if you're in the final group and you have pressure on yourself."

Kang was runner-up at the Walmart for the second time and recorded her best result since opening the season with a win and a second, and since having treatment for a tumour on her spine during the summer. "I'm just so happy for my team that somehow got me back playing this year. There was part of me that I didn't think I would ever play again or contend, but here I am. I'm not that far off and I'm happy about that."

Pinnacle Country Club, Rogers, Arkansas — September 23-25
Par 71 (36-35); 6,438 yards — Purse: $2,300,000

1	**Atthaya Thitikul**	67	61	68	196	$345,000
2	**Danielle Kang**	67	65	64	196	214,011
	Thitikul won playoff at second extra hole					
3	**Chella Choi**	69	63	65	197	155,249
4	Pornanong Phatlum	68	65	66	199	120,098
5	Celine Boutier	68	67	65	200	63,355
	Lizette Salas	68	67	65	200	63,355
	Lydia Ko	67	66	67	200	63,355
	Muni He	66	66	68	200	63,355
	Charley Hull	66	66	68	200	63,355
	Megan Khang	64	68	68	200	63,355
	Ryann O'Toole	64	68	68	200	63,355
12	Lee-Anne Pace	68	68	65	201	37,376
	Cheyenne Knight	68	66	67	201	37,376
	Jenny Shin	66	68	67	201	37,376
	Hye-Jin Choi	67	65	69	201	37,376
16	Dewi Weber	70	66	66	202	29,292
	Jessica Korda	69	66	67	202	29,292
	Ayaka Furue	68	67	67	202	29,292
	Sei Young Kim	64	70	68	202	29,292
	Lilia Vu	65	65	72	202	29,292
21	Xiyu Lin	69	67	67	203	22,877
	Alison Lee	69	66	68	203	22,877
	Mina Harigae	67	67	69	203	22,877
	Frida Kinhult	67	67	69	203	22,877
	Andrea Lee	67	67	69	203	22,877
	Lauren Coughlin	64	70	69	203	22,877
	Isi Gabsa	67	66	70	203	22,877
	A Lim Kim	66	67	70	203	22,877
29	Anna Nordqvist	68	67	69	204	18,396
	Jasmine Suwannapura	67	68	69	204	18,396
	Yu Liu	69	64	71	204	18,396
32	Lindsey Weaver-Wright	69	69	67	205	15,048
	Ruixin Liu	67	71	67	205	15,048
	Eun-Hee Ji	67	71	67	205	15,048
	Charlotte Thomas	68	67	70	205	15,048
	Azahara Munoz	67	68	70	205	15,048
	Georgia Hall	66	68	71	205	15,048
	Yuka Saso	64	65	76	205	15,048
39	Stephanie Kyriacou	68	70	68	206	11,265
	Caroline Masson	70	66	70	206	11,265
	Tiffany Chan	68	68	70	206	11,265
	Karis Davidson	69	66	71	206	11,265
	Stephanie Meadow	69	66	71	206	11,265
	Jennifer Kupcho	67	65	74	206	11,265
	Jeongeun Lee[5]	64	68	74	206	11,265
46	Lauren Stephenson	70	68	69	207	9,080
	Agathe Laisne	68	70	69	207	9,080
	Caroline Inglis	70	65	72	207	9,080
	Narin An	68	67	72	207	9,080
50	Christina Kim	69	69	70	208	7,382
	Jennifer Song	70	67	71	208	7,382
	Angela Stanford	68	69	71	208	7,382
	Na Yeon Choi	71	65	72	208	7,382
	Jeongeun Lee[6]	67	69	72	208	7,382
	Sophia Schubert	66	70	72	208	7,382
	Annie Park	69	66	73	208	7,382
	Vivian Hou	65	69	74	208	7,382
58	Haeji Kang	70	68	71	209	5,859
	Emma Talley	69	69	71	209	5,859
	Kaitlyn Papp	67	71	71	209	5,859
	Brittany Lang	69	68	72	209	5,859
	Nasa Hataoka	68	69	72	209	5,859
	Pauline Roussin	68	68	73	209	5,859
64	Gaby Lopez	67	71	72	210	5,331
	Dana Finkelstein	70	67	73	210	5,331
66	Linnea Johansson	71	67	73	211	5,155
67	Robynn Ree	73	65	74	212	4,980
	Allisen Corpuz	71	67	74	212	4,980
69	Alana Uriell	72	66	75	213	4,746
	Nuria Iturrioz	67	69	77	213	4,746

The Ascendant LPGA

Charley Hull unashamedly says, "I'll do me". In 2022 that included having a plan to win for the first time on the LPGA since the 2016 CME Group Tour Championship. That plan included working on her putting and at The Ascendant LPGA at Old American the 26-year-old Englishwoman needed only 103 putts for the week as she claimed a trophy shaped like the state of Texas and the cowboy boots that went with it.

Hull is often at her best in match play competition and that was the case in the final round as Lydia Ko contended for her second title of the year. The Kiwi closed with a 65 to take third place, but Xiyu Lin, known by "Janet", kept the pressure on all the way to the 18th green. The golfer from China made an 18-footer for a birdie at the 16th, then holed from 25 feet for an eagle at the 17th, where Hull had to nudge in her three-footer for a birdie to keep a one-shot lead going to the last.

"When Xiyu made eagle on 17, I kind of enjoyed that," Hull said. "It made me want to birdie the last. I hit a good putt, it missed, but it was great fun. I find stuff like that fun because it puts the pressure on me, and then I've got to commit and do it."

While Hull parred the last to finish on 18-under-par 266, tying the tournament record, after rounds of 67-64-71-64, Lin still had a putt to force a playoff that just missed. She closed with a 65 to finish one back and runner-up for the third time in the season and for the second time in three starts. "Actually, at the beginning of the week, if you're telling me I'm going to shoot 17 under and finish second I will take this any time, because I always found this course is very challenging," Lin said.

Hull said: "I love a challenge, and this golf course is challenging. At home, I play off the back tees with the boys, and I always try and push myself on tricky courses." Perennial Hull associate "my mate James" also got a mention since he had won his club championship in 2016 and did so again in 2022. "He said, 'This is your year, because you win every year I win'. So I knew it was coming. Hopefully he wins the club champs next year."

Old American Golf Club, The Colony, Texas — September 29-October 2
Par 71 (35-36); 6,517 yards — Purse: $1,700,000

1	**Charley Hull**	67	64	71	64	266	$255,000
2	**Xiyu Lin**	65	68	69	65	267	154,808
3	**Lydia Ko**	70	66	67	65	268	112,302
4	Atthaya Thitikul	66	67	72	67	272	86,874
5	Cheyenne Knight	71	68	71	63	273	63,567
	Moriya Jutanugarn	67	68	70	68	273	63,567
7	Lizette Salas	66	72	69	67	274	44,921
	So Yeon Ryu	69	68	68	69	274	44,921
9	Celine Boutier	68	69	66	72	275	37,717
10	Lexi Thompson	67	70	69	70	276	34,326
11	Lilia Vu	72	73	69	63	277	27,986
	Wichanee Meechai	73	70	68	66	277	27,986
	Nasa Hataoka	70	73	67	67	277	27,986
	Albane Valenzuela	69	71	69	68	277	27,986
	A Lim Kim	71	68	67	71	277	27,986
16	Ruoning Yin	76	68	65	69	278	21,613
	Madelene Sagstrom	69	68	70	71	278	21,613
	Pornanong Phatlum	71	68	67	72	278	21,613
	Lindy Duncan	69	65	72	72	278	21,613
20	Yealimi Noh	73	70	70	66	279	18,477
	Ally Ewing	74	70	68	67	279	18,477
	Ayaka Furue	69	70	73	67	279	18,477
	Emily Kristine Pedersen	68	67	72	72	279	18,477
24	Allison Emrey	74	71	67	68	280	15,595
	Jennifer Kupcho	71	70	70	69	280	15,595
	Jessica Korda	69	66	76	69	280	15,595
	Frida Kinhult	72	68	68	72	280	15,595
	Maddie Szeryk	67	70	67	76	280	15,595
29	Daniela Darquea	71	71	70	69	281	12,798
	Brooke M Henderson	76	66	69	70	281	12,798
	Jodi Ewart Shadoff	72	69	70	70	281	12,798
	Yaeeun Hong	71	70	69	71	281	12,798
	Gaby Lopez	70	68	72	71	281	12,798
34	Linnea Johansson	74	69	70	69	282	10,425
	Georgia Hall	70	69	74	69	282	10,425
	Karis Davidson	70	70	71	71	282	10,425
	Ariya Jutanugarn	68	69	71	74	282	10,425
	Narin An	71	67	69	75	282	10,425
39	Emma Talley	73	71	69	70	283	8,814
	Danielle Kang	71	72	70	70	283	8,814
	Nanna Koerstz Madsen	70	69	73	71	283	8,814
42	Pauline Roussin	73	71	74	66	284	7,967
	Yuka Saso	73	70	70	71	284	7,967
44	Gerina Mendoza	72	73	68	72	285	6,950
	Brittany Altomare	71	72	70	72	285	6,950
	Matilda Castren	71	71	70	73	285	6,950
	Stephanie Meadow	71	71	70	73	285	6,950
	Jeongeun Lee[5]	72	71	68	74	285	6,950
49	Ashleigh Buhai	73	72	71	70	286	5,606
	Amanda Doherty	74	71	70	71	286	5,606
	Haeji Kang	72	72	70	72	286	5,606
	Ruixin Liu	71	73	70	72	286	5,606
	Caroline Masson	73	70	69	74	286	5,606
	Brittany Lang	72	69	70	75	286	5,606
	Sarah Schmelzel	69	71	71	75	286	5,606
56	Alana Uriell	74	71	71	71	287	4,746
	Lindsey Weaver-Wright	71	73	72	71	287	4,746
	Caroline Inglis	75	70	70	72	287	4,746
59	Anna Nordqvist	75	70	73	70	288	4,125
	Jasmine Suwannapura	73	70	75	70	288	4,125
	Lauren Coughlin	72	71	75	70	288	4,125
	Celine Herbin	74	69	71	74	288	4,125
	Jeongeun Lee[6]	73	68	73	74	288	4,125
	Stacy Lewis	69	72	72	75	288	4,125
65	Lauren Hartlage	71	73	77	68	289	3,644
	Katherine Perry-Hamski	72	72	76	69	289	3,644
	Aditi Ashok	74	71	74	70	289	3,644
	Tiffany Chan	71	72	76	70	289	3,644
	Bailey Shoemaker (A)	72	72	73	72	289	
	Megan Khang	73	69	73	74	289	3,644
71	Allisen Corpuz	75	69	73	73	290	3,370
	Gemma Dryburgh	72	73	70	75	290	3,370
73	Sophia Schubert	74	71	75	71	291	3,284
	Kelly Tan	73	72	72	74	291	3,284
75	Jennifer Song	70	71	76	75	292	3,221
76	Min Lee	76	69	73	75	293	3,182
77	Ryann O'Toole	73	72	72	77	294	3,141
78	Ayako Uehara	73	72	77	73	295	3,082
	Christina Kim	74	71	73	77	295	3,082
80	Cydney Clanton	71	74	75	76	296	3,023

LPGA Mediheal Championship

Something got her going in her 246th start in her 11th year on the LPGA. Maybe it was compatriot Charley Hull winning the previous week. Or maybe it was just hitting a three-wood to 10 feet on the 14th, her fifth hole, in the opening round of the LPGA Mediheal Championship. "I just got hot from there," said Jodi Ewart Shadoff. There has never been much wrong with her ball-striking, but hard work on the practice putting green was beginning to pay off. The 34-year-old Englishwoman from Yorkshire went on to post an eight-under 64 on Thursday and on Sunday wrapped up a wire-to-wire victory by one stroke from Yuka Saso.

Ewart Shadoff, married to a television news sports anchor in Orlando, led by two strokes after the first round and went ahead by four from Paula Reto after two 69s on Friday and Saturday. Sunday was not straightforward, however. A bogey at the ninth meant she had fallen one behind Reto, who went out in 32. Ewart Shadoff, an Olympic and Solheim Cup competitor, responded impressively with birdies at the 13th and 14th holes and then a string of pars. Reto also birdied the 14th before dropping back with bogeys at 16 and 17.

It was not just a two-way battle. Another Englishwoman, Georgia Hall, closed with a bogey-free 65 to get to 13 under par. Danielle Kang scored a 66 to tie with Hall and Reto (69) for third. The Saticoy Club in Somis, California, a new venue for the event, was founded in 1921 and rewarded the best strikers; Kang, watched by her family, grew up nearby and was an honorary member earlier in her career. Saso birdied the last three holes for a 66 to finish on 14 under and record her best finish since winning the US Women's Open in 2021.

An emotional Ewart Shadoff, who closed with a 71 for a 15-under-par total of 273, said: "I've waited a long time for this. It's been many times in my career that I didn't think this was ever going to happen, so just really grateful in this moment. I learned that I could fight through adversity. I can play under the nerves, which has been a problem for me in the past. I proved I can win."

The Saticoy Club, Somis, California — October 6-9
Par 72 (36-36); 6,635 yards — Purse: $1,800,000

1	**Jodi Ewart Shadoff**	64	69	69	71	273	$270,000
2	**Yuka Saso**	70	70	68	66	274	166,232
3	**Georgia Hall**	71	68	71	65	275	96,320
	Danielle Kang	67	73	68	67	275	96,320
	Paula Reto	67	70	69	69	275	96,320
6	Andrea Lee	71	70	66	69	276	61,433
7	Sei Young Kim	70	70	70	67	277	51,421
8	Atthaya Thitikul	67	72	71	68	278	37,679
	Lauren Coughlin	70	71	68	69	278	37,679
	Xiyu Lin	69	69	70	70	278	37,679
	Celine Boutier	69	72	66	71	278	37,679
	Hinako Shibuno	73	66	68	71	278	37,679
13	Caroline Inglis	75	67	68	69	279	28,941
	Amanda Doherty	73	69	68	69	279	28,941
15	Kelly Tan	74	69	71	66	280	23,845
	Lilia Vu	71	73	68	68	280	23,845
	Allisen Corpuz	69	72	70	69	280	23,845
	Jennifer Chang	68	74	68	70	280	23,845
	Gaby Lopez	68	70	71	71	280	23,845
20	Mina Harigae	71	68	72	70	281	20,569
	Daniela Darquea	71	69	69	72	281	20,569
22	Narin An	72	71	72	67	282	17,422
	Lucy Li	68	71	74	69	282	17,422
	Ruixin Liu	66	72	75	69	282	17,422
	Jenny Coleman	68	72	71	71	282	17,422
	Chella Choi	69	70	72	71	282	17,422
	Pauline Roussin	70	68	72	72	282	17,422
	Haeji Kang	69	69	72	72	282	17,422
29	Paula Creamer	74	68	75	66	283	14,289
	Hye-Jin Choi	75	66	72	70	283	14,289
	Eun-Hee Ji	70	68	73	72	283	14,289
32	Dewi Weber	70	72	74	68	284	10,219
	Karis Davidson	72	73	69	70	284	10,219
	A Lim Kim	69	76	69	70	284	10,219
	Linnea Johansson	68	74	72	70	284	10,219
	Angel Yin	72	68	74	70	284	10,219
	Jennifer Song	68	71	75	70	284	10,219
	Mi Hyang Lee	71	74	68	71	284	10,219
	Sarah Kemp	72	72	69	71	284	10,219
	Ayako Uehara	70	71	72	71	284	10,219
	Lindy Duncan	68	72	73	71	284	10,219
	Haylee Rae Harford	70	72	70	72	284	10,219
	Annie Park	68	72	72	72	284	10,219
	Dana Finkelstein	68	77	66	73	284	10,219
	Stephanie Meadow	68	70	71	75	284	10,219
46	Maja Stark	73	72	70	70	285	6,795
	Jeongeun Lee[6]	71	74	70	70	285	6,795
	Pernilla Lindberg	70	73	72	70	285	6,795
	Ruoning Yin	71	72	71	71	285	6,795
	Brittany Altomare	72	67	75	71	285	6,795
	Ana Belac	70	73	69	73	285	6,795
52	Emily Kristine Pedersen	73	72	72	69	286	5,460
	Amelia Lewis	72	73	70	71	286	5,460
	Alison Lee	66	73	76	71	286	5,460
	Yu Liu	69	75	70	72	286	5,460
	Ayaka Furue	72	71	70	73	286	5,460
	Stacy Lewis	72	71	69	74	286	5,460
	Pornanong Phatlum	69	71	72	74	286	5,460
59	Casey Danielson	71	73	74	69	287	4,430
	Brooke Matthews	70	74	72	71	287	4,430
	Pajaree Anannarukarn	73	70	72	72	287	4,430
	Giulia Molinaro	75	70	69	73	287	4,430
	Gemma Dryburgh	73	69	72	73	287	4,430
	Moriya Jutanugarn	70	72	71	74	287	4,430

65	Min Lee	71	71	75	71	288	4,095		Sophia Schubert	75	70	71	75	291	3,686
66	Aditi Ashok	71	74	73	72	290	3,913	71	Wei-Ling Hsu	72	73	74	74	293	3,596
	Mo Martin	70	72	74	74	290	3,913	72	Janie Jackson	77	67	78	72	294	3,549
	Stephanie Kyriacou	72	70	71	77	290	3,913	73	Alena Sharp	72	71	77	76	296	3,503
69	Rachel Rohanna	73	72	73	73	291	3,686								

BMW Ladies Championship

Lydia Ko had a dream to win in the land of her birth and, thronged by her relatives, the 25-year-old who grew up in New Zealand achieved that dream at the BMW Ladies Championship. It was a dominant performance on Sunday by the former world number one, surging to a four-stroke victory for her 18th LPGA victory. The 17th came in the second tournament of the season but another one had been coming — in her previous 11 events she had recorded eight top fives. No wonder Ko said it was the most consistent golf she had ever played.

Ko opened with a pair of 68s, lying five behind Atthaya Thitikul's first-round 63, then four behind Andrea Lee's halfway lead. Thitikul took the lead back on Saturday but Ko compiled a bogey-free 66 to move one behind the young Thai. Ko's run on Sunday started after her only dropped shot of the day at the seventh. She hit her approach stiff at the eighth, then holed a putt from the fringe at the 10th before adding another tap-in birdie at the 11th. She led by three before Hye-Jin Choi briefly cut that advantage to one. Ko responded in the perfect manner with three birdies in a row from the 15th. She closed with a 65 for a 21-under-par total of 267. "For me, the big turnaround was my birdie on 10," Ko said. "To be honest, if it didn't go in, I had a pretty hefty par putt coming back. I was able to feed off that. I normally don't do first pumps, and I did a couple of fist pumps on my back nine because I knew how much every single putt would count."

Ko added: "I feel so proud to be born in Korea. Because of that I really wanted to win here. It's not only just a place that I'm born, but a lot of my family is still here. This week my relatives are here, my direct family is here and I wanted to win it for them as well. To be able to do that this year in front of a lot of them, it means a lot."

Portland winner Lee birdied the last to claim second place with a 69, while Choi had a 68 to tie for third with local favourite Hyo Joo Kim and Lilia Vu. Thitikul finished with a 74 to be sixth and had the consolation of getting closer to becoming the world number one. Jin Young Ko just clung on to top spot after withdrawing after two rounds of 80-79. It was her first tournament in two months due to a long-term wrist injury and she suffered a quintuple-bogey 10 at the 18th on Thursday.

Oak Valley Country Club, Wonju, Korea — October 20-23
Par 72 (36-36); 6,647 yards — Purse: $2,000,000

1	**Lydia Ko**	68	68	66	65	267	$300,000		Lizette Salas	70	70	70	71	281	21,925
2	**Andrea Lee**	66	66	70	69	271	183,381		A Lim Kim	66	73	71	71	281	21,925
3	**Hye-Jin Choi**	69	69	66	68	272	106,256		Wichanee Meechai	71	70	68	72	281	21,925
	Hyo Joo Kim	69	69	66	68	272	106,256		Jasmine Suwannapura	74	66	69	72	281	21,925
	Lilia Vu	68	66	69	69	272	106,256		Stephanie Kyriacou	69	70	68	74	281	21,925
6	Atthaya Thitikul	63	71	67	74	275	67,770	27	Narin An	70	73	71	68	282	17,771
7	Ariya Jutanugarn	73	68	65	70	276	56,726		Gemma Dryburgh	70	70	72	70	282	17,771
8	Yuka Saso	70	73	65	69	277	47,189		Matilda Castren	72	73	66	71	282	17,771
	Linn Grant	70	69	68	70	277	47,189	30	Maria Fassi	73	72	70	68	283	14,859
10	Danielle Kang	70	70	70	68	278	36,595		Sarah Schmelzel	74	69	72	68	283	14,859
	Hannah Green	70	67	72	69	278	36,595		Jodi Ewart Shadoff	73	72	68	70	283	14,859
	Alison Lee	68	72	67	71	278	36,595		Carlota Ciganda	71	73	69	70	283	14,859
	Yaeeun Hong	66	70	71	71	278	36,595		Lauren Coughlin	73	70	70	70	283	14,859
	Minsol Kim (A)	64	70	71	73	278			Chella Choi	70	69	69	75	283	14,859
15	Paula Reto	72	70	70	67	279	30,019	36	Pajaree Anannarukarn	75	71	67	71	284	12,098
	Cheyenne Knight	71	68	70	70	279	30,019		Jennifer Kupcho	69	72	72	71	284	12,098
17	Sei Young Kim	71	70	70	69	280	26,807		Emily Kristine Pedersen	69	69	74	72	284	12,098
	Allisen Corpuz	70	69	71	70	280	26,807		Annie Park	71	70	70	73	284	12,098
19	Hinako Shibuno	72	70	72	67	281	21,925	40	Nanna Koerstz Madsen	71	75	70	69	285	9,653
	Eun-Hee Ji	72	68	71	70	281	21,925		Frida Kinhult	72	72	72	69	285	9,653
	Pauline Roussin	71	69	70	71	281	21,925		Anna Nordqvist	74	70	71	70	285	9,653

	Celine Boutier	73	70	72	70	285	9,653
	Moriya Jutanugarn	72	70	73	70	285	9,653
	Su Oh	70	72	73	70	285	9,653
	Albane Valenzuela	73	71	69	72	285	9,653
47	Na Yeon Choi	75	74	69	68	286	7,781
	Haeji Kang	70	75	71	70	286	7,781
	Wei-Ling Hsu	75	71	69	71	286	7,781
	Nasa Hataoka	69	72	70	75	286	7,781
51	Yealimi Noh	73	74	71	69	287	6,727
	Minjee Lee	70	73	73	71	287	6,727
	Leona Maguire	72	72	71	72	287	6,727
	Brittany Altomare	69	75	70	73	287	6,727
55	Daniela Darquea	71	73	71	73	288	6,225
56	Lindsey Weaver-Wright	71	72	77	69	289	5,823
	Emma Talley	74	73	72	70	289	5,823
	Sung Hyun Park	69	73	74	73	289	5,823
59	Ashleigh Buhai	78	73	70	69	290	5,020
	Angel Yin	81	68	71	70	290	5,020
	Peiyun Chien	75	72	72	71	290	5,020
	Amy Yang	76	73	69	72	290	5,020
	Pornanong Phatlum	69	74	75	72	290	5,020
	Bronte Law	69	73	72	76	290	5,020
65	Esther Henseleit	72	76	70	73	291	4,619
66	Kelly Tan	73	71	74	74	292	4,467
	So Yeon Ryu	71	72	73	76	292	4,467
68	Jenny Shin	74	72	72	75	293	4,318
	Hyunjo Yoo [A]	76	68	72	77	293	
70	Jeongeun Lee[6]	76	73	72	73	294	4,216
71	Jennifer Song	72	74	76	73	295	4,116
72	Stephanie Meadow	74	71	76	76	297	4,017
73	Patty Tavatanakit	77	78	72	72	299	3,967
74	Sophia Schubert	73	76	75	76	300	3,915
75	Mi Hyang Lee	77	77	75	74	303	3,865
76	In-Kyung Kim	73	78	74	79	304	3,815
77	Maude-Aimee Leblanc	80	77	72	79	308	3,769
	Jin Young Ko	80	79			WD	3,721

Pelican Women's Championship

In the time since the BMW Championship, Atthaya Thitikul had become the world number one for two weeks, but Nelly Korda reclaimed top spot on the Rolex Rankings by retaining her title at the Pelican Women's Championship. It was her first win on the LPGA since winning at Pelican, just down the road from her west Florida home, in 2021. The 24-year-old Olympic champion did win on the LET in August, but had missed the cut in her last two LPGA starts before finishing fourth in the LET's Aramco Team Series event in New York, where Lexi Thompson won.

Korda and Thompson duelled for the title here as they had a year before. Then Korda had taken a triple bogey at the 17th before twice birdieing the 18th to get into and then win a four-way playoff. Thompson had bogeyed the last in regulation.

This time Korda birdied the 16th and 17th holes to go two ahead before going long at the 18th and taking a bogey, her only dropped shot in a seven-birdie 64. After two opening 66s, she finished at 14-under-par 196. Thompson was just off the front of the 18th green and played a fine chip shot to a foot but came up one shot short after a 66.

Korda, who missed much of the early season due to a blood clot in her left arm, said: "It's just been such a rollercoaster season. I guess that's life. There have been more downs than ups this year, and I think that that's what makes this so much sweeter to me. With the way my game was in the last two LPGA starts I had, I didn't think that I had the confidence that I was going to win. But I had good memories on this golf course. I was home. I had the comfort level of my parents being in the crowd, too, which plays a part."

Hurricane Nicole, which deposited almost five inches of rain on Thursday, meant the event was delayed until Friday and reduced to 54 holes. Maria Fassi matched the tournament record with an opening 62 but bogeys at the last two holes on Sunday meant she missed out on qualifying for the CME Group Tour Championship by one shot. Rookie Allisen Corpuz took the lead into the last round and scored a 69 to take third place. Carlota Ciganda had birdied the first four holes to take the lead but ended with a 72, while Maja Stark was a longtime contender before a triple bogey at the last. Thompson swept into the lead with four birdies in a row of her own from the fifth, then dropped shots at 11 and 12 but birdied the next two.

Yet Korda was not to be stopped and jumped from fourth to first in the world rankings, having been deposed in January. "Obviously going through what I've been through this year and regaining that world number one ranking is really special," she said. "I just appreciate it a lot more."

Pelican Golf Club, Belleair, Florida — November 11-13
Par 70 (35-35); 6,341 yards — Purse: $2,000,000

1	**Nelly Korda**	66	66	64	196	$300,000
2	**Lexi Thompson**	64	67	66	197	186,096
3	**Allisen Corpuz**	65	65	69	199	135,000
4	Morgane Metraux	66	71	64	201	85,754
	Hannah Green	67	69	65	201	85,754
	Gaby Lopez	65	69	67	201	85,754
7	Lizette Salas	65	70	67	202	51,113
	Ally Ewing	68	65	69	202	51,113
	Maria Fassi	62	69	71	202	51,113
10	Matilda Castren	70	69	64	203	38,377
	Leona Maguire	71	64	68	203	38,377
	Maja Stark	68	63	72	203	38,377
13	Gemma Dryburgh	69	67	68	204	30,565
	Yuka Saso	68	68	68	204	30,565
	Yu Liu	69	65	70	204	30,565
	Carlota Ciganda	64	68	72	204	30,565
17	Sei Young Kim	70	70	65	205	24,412
	Pauline Roussin	65	71	69	205	24,412
	Ruoning Yin	69	66	70	205	24,412
	Emily Kristine Pedersen	68	67	70	205	24,412
	Hyo Joo Kim	64	69	72	205	24,412
22	Pernilla Lindberg	67	71	68	206	20,607
	Muni He	68	69	69	206	20,607
	Jodi Ewart Shadoff	68	68	70	206	20,607
	In Gee Chun	66	70	70	206	20,607
26	Lydia Ko	68	69	70	207	17,341
	Lauren Stephenson	66	71	70	207	17,341
	Gerina Mendoza	68	68	71	207	17,341
	Jennifer Song	69	66	72	207	17,341
	Brittany Lang	69	65	73	207	17,341
31	Linnea Johansson	69	70	69	208	13,907
	Alena Sharp	68	71	69	208	13,907
	Jennifer Kupcho	69	69	70	208	13,907
	Bianca Pagdanganan	69	69	70	208	13,907
	Pornanong Phatlum	69	68	71	208	13,907
	Anna Nordqvist	68	67	73	208	13,907
37	Haeji Kang	71	69	69	209	9,864
	Jenny Shin	71	69	69	209	9,864
	Lauren Coughlin	70	70	69	209	9,864
	Dana Finkelstein	72	67	70	209	9,864
	Dewi Weber	71	68	70	209	9,864
	Albane Valenzuela	70	69	70	209	9,864
	Angel Yin	67	70	72	209	9,864
	Jasmine Suwannapura	65	72	72	209	9,864
	Isi Gabsa	64	73	72	209	9,864
	Stephanie Meadow	67	68	74	209	9,864
	Ashleigh Buhai	69	65	75	209	9,864
48	Marina Alex	70	69	71	210	6,972
	Megan Khang	69	70	71	210	6,972
	Kristen Gillman	68	71	71	210	6,972
	Amy Olson	68	71	71	210	6,972
	Ayaka Furue	71	67	72	210	6,972
	Sophia Schubert	67	71	72	210	6,972
	Amy Yang	69	68	73	210	6,972
55	Eun-Hee Ji	72	68	71	211	5,517
	Aline Krauter	71	69	71	211	5,517
	Charlotte Thomas	70	70	71	211	5,517
	Azahara Munoz	69	71	71	211	5,517
	Ruixin Liu	69	70	72	211	5,517
	Ryann O'Toole	68	70	73	211	5,517
	Esther Henseleit	66	72	73	211	5,517
62	Stacy Lewis	71	69	72	212	4,738
	Celine Boutier	70	70	72	212	4,738
	Maude-Aimee Leblanc	69	71	72	212	4,738
	Frida Kinhult	71	68	73	212	4,738
66	Moriya Jutanugarn	72	67	74	213	4,432
	Min Lee	71	68	74	213	4,432
68	Brittany Altomare	68	72	74	214	4,228
	Yaeeun Hong	65	75	74	214	4,228
70	Sanna Nuutinen	71	68	76	215	4,076

CME Group Tour Championship

When Lydia Ko won the CME Group Tour Championship in 2014 she was a rookie teenage phenomenon with glasses to match. Eight years later the 25-year-old New Zealander, whose form had dipped after becoming the youngest world number one in golf, completed a resurgent season as a mature young woman on the brink of married life — having won the first ever $2 million first prize in women's golf but without the glasses. "I'm excited that my photo from winning here in 2014 with the glasses could get updated," Ko joked. "Better photo this year."

About the only thing Ko did not achieve at Tiburon was regaining the top spot on the Rolex Rankings as Nelly Korda held on by the barest of margins. That would come a week later. Otherwise, Ko swept the lot. She won the biggest financial prize in LPGA history with her 19th LPGA victory and third win of the season, following the Gainbridge win early in the year, also a wire-to-wire effort, and her recent victory at the BMW Ladies Championship in Korea, the land of her birth. It was her first multi-win LPGA season since 2016.

Ko won the Rolex LPGA Player of the Year Award for the second time (2015), after entering the final tournament one point ahead of US Open champion Minjee Lee, who finished down the leaderboard. Ko went ahead of Lee on the official money list and also won the Vare Trophy for the second year running. "This year has been an incredible year. I really could never ask for more to win so early in the season and then to have won in Korea and then win the last event of the year," said Ko, whose fiancé was present to see her win for the first time. "I couldn't have drawn it up any better. There has been so many exciting things in my life that's been going on. It will be my last win as a single lady.

So I wanted to do this for my family. This has been one of the most consistent and solid years I've had."

Ko led from the front with an opening 65 and then added a 66 the next day to take a five-stroke lead. It was only Leona Maguire's brilliant 63 on Saturday that kept the Kiwi in check, with Ko adding a 70 to leave the pair tied at 15 under par, five ahead of the rest. Ko bogeyed the first hole on Sunday but picked up two birdies on the front nine to lead by one and was never headed again. Maguire, not quite finding the magic of the previous day, appeared to have made a fatal error by topping her second into the water at the par-five 14th, only for Ko to follow her into the hazard.

Both bogeyed which allowed Anna Nordqvist to get within reach with a finish that included only one par on the back nine, two bogeys more than compensated for by six birdies, including at the last two holes, as the Swede closed with a 67 to be third, one behind Maguire's 72. It was a cold, wet and windy final day in Naples but Ko was ready to pounce. The pace of her putts had been spot on all day and a crucial one fell at the 16th for a birdie to go two clear. She then found the green in two at the 17th and matched Maguire's birdie. Ko's 70 gave her a 17-under-par total of 271.

"It would have been nice to play a little bit better today, but it was really tough out there," Maguire said. "The wind was strong. It was cold. Pins were tricky. Had some really key up-and-downs to keep me in it and keep a little pressure on Lydia, but she played really solid all day and she's a deserving winner."

Tiburon Golf Club (Gold), Ritz Carlton Resort, Naples, Florida — November 17-20
Par 72 (36-36); 6,556 yards — Purse: $7,000,000

1	**Lydia Ko**	65	66	70	70	271	$2,000,000
2	**Leona Maguire**	69	69	63	72	273	550,000
3	**Anna Nordqvist**	68	69	70	67	274	340,000
4	Georgia Hall	71	69	69	67	276	222,500
	Jeongeun Lee[6]	70	68	68	70	276	222,500
6	Pajaree Anannarukarn	66	73	69	70	278	150,000
7	Hyo Joo Kim	67	69	72	71	279	105,667
	Brooke M Henderson	68	74	65	72	279	105,667
	Gemma Dryburgh	67	70	69	73	279	105,667
10	Celine Boutier	71	71	69	69	280	83,500
	Atthaya Thitikul	73	67	71	69	280	83,500
	Nelly Korda	68	69	73	70	280	83,500
13	Moriya Jutanugarn	71	70	69	71	281	76,000
	Madelene Sagstrom	71	70	69	71	281	76,000
15	Jodi Ewart Shadoff	72	67	71	72	282	72,000
	Danielle Kang	66	74	68	74	282	72,000
17	Allisen Corpuz	71	71	72	69	283	67,250
	Chella Choi	73	71	69	70	283	67,250
	Andrea Lee	70	73	69	71	283	67,250
	Lizette Salas	70	69	72	72	283	67,250
21	Lexi Thompson	74	74	68	68	284	62,500
	Megan Khang	68	72	74	70	284	62,500
	Amy Yang	68	70	75	71	284	62,500
	Xiyu Lin	73	69	70	72	284	62,500
25	Marina Alex	73	69	71	72	285	58,000
	Sei Young Kim	68	74	71	72	285	58,000
	Ayaka Furue	72	69	72	72	285	58,000
	Caroline Masson	72	70	70	73	285	58,000
	Stacy Lewis	69	70	71	75	285	58,000
30	Charley Hull	71	78	67	70	286	54,250
	Lilia Vu	70	73	70	73	286	54,250
	Sophia Schubert	68	71	71	76	286	54,250
33	Nanna Koerstz Madsen	73	72	72	70	287	50,125
	Ashleigh Buhai	77	71	68	71	287	50,125
	Jin Young Ko	72	75	69	71	287	50,125
	Hannah Green	74	71	71	71	287	50,125
	Narin An	70	72	72	73	287	50,125
	Jennifer Kupcho	73	71	68	75	287	50,125
	In Gee Chun	74	68	70	75	287	50,125
	Minjee Lee	71	68	71	77	287	50,125
41	Eun-Hee Ji	72	76	71	69	288	46,250
	Sarah Schmelzel	70	72	74	72	288	46,250
	Alison Lee	71	72	69	76	288	46,250
	Nasa Hataoka	70	67	71	80	288	46,250
45	Ryann O'Toole	78	70	70	71	289	44,250
	Cheyenne Knight	73	71	74	71	289	44,250
	Maja Stark	74	68	75	72	289	44,250
	Ally Ewing	71	71	72	75	289	44,250
49	Pornanong Phatlum	76	73	69	72	290	42,750
	Hinako Shibuno	74	71	69	76	290	42,750
51	A Lim Kim	72	67	77	75	291	42,250
52	Matilda Castren	70	69	75	78	292	42,000
53	Mina Harigae	71	74	74	74	293	41,750
54	Hye-Jin Choi	75	73	74	72	294	41,125
	Ariya Jutanugarn	74	73	73	74	294	41,125
	Paula Reto	71	72	77	74	294	41,125
	Carlota Ciganda	75	73	71	75	294	41,125
58	Gaby Lopez	71	70	75	79	295	40,500
59	Yuka Saso	75	77	74	70	296	40,125
	Patty Tavatanakit	78	74	73	71	296	40,125

2022 ROLEX LPGA PLAYER OF THE YEAR

		Points
1	Lydia Ko	180
2	Minjee Lee	149
3	Brooke M Henderson	134
4	Atthaya Thitikul	131
5	In Gee Chun	96
6	Jennifer Kupcho	95
7	Hyo Joo Kim	93
8	Lexi Thompson	86
9	Leona Maguire	77
10	Nelly Korda	74

Epson Tour

When Andrea Lee defeated Lucy Li at the third extra hole of a playoff at the Casino del Sol Golf Classic in April, neither player could know what was in store for them for the rest of the year. Lee, the Stanford star who joined the LPGA in 2020, had struggled in her second season, so started 2022 on the renamed Epson Tour, the new sponsor bringing 21 events and record prize money of $4.41 million, plus a minimum purse for each event of $200,000.

Lee's first professional victory in the fourth tournament of the season brought a boost in confidence that on her return to the LPGA saw her finish 12th at the Lotte Championship and fifth at the Palos Verdes Championship, which allowed her to regain temporary membership of the main circuit. There was a fourth place at the Bank of Hope Match Play and then the ultimate, a win at the AmazingCre Portland Classic. Having started the season with no status, the 24-year-old Lee ended up 15th on the Race to the CME Globe.

But what of Li? She also ended up playing on the LPGA at the end of the year — with a best finish of fourth at the Dana Open — having become the first player to secure her elevation from the Epson Tour. The youngest player to qualify for the US Women's Open at the age of 11, Li was still only 19 when she won the Carolina Golf Classic in dramatic circumstances. Benefitting from a late collapse from Alexa Pano, Li birdied the final hole and then holed a long putt for eagle to win at the first extra hole. "Being four down with four holes to play, I definitely didn't expect to be here, but I never gave up," said Li. "It just feels so surreal to finally get my first professional win. I feel like it's been a long time coming, and it's a relief to finally get it done."

Three starts later at the Twin Bridges Championship, Li went wire-to-wire to win by four strokes from Linnea Strom. She ended up third on the Ascensus Race for the Card after switching her focus to getting as much experience in LPGA events. "It's definitely been a big goal of mine for a long time," Li said of earning her LPGA card. "To finally be able to be out there and compete with the best in the world is very exciting. There's a pretty big transition from amateur into professional golf and being on the Epson Tour was that pathway for me to make that transition. I think it's huge for people turning pro."

Strom, the 25-year-old from Sweden, graduated from the Epson Tour in 2018, but a poor 2021 saw her drop back down. A second win on the circuit at the IOA Championship helped her to top spot on the money list, but she also achieved a more personal goal. Strom explained: "After really struggling last season, my main goal for this year was to earn my card back, but it was also to find happiness again and enjoy playing golf. I'm extremely proud that I achieved that goal this season."

Xiaowen Yin, a 17-year-old rookie from Tianjin, China, finished second on the Race, winning back-to-back at the FireKeepers Casino Hotel Championship, where she won in a playoff, and the French Lick Charity Classic, the richest event on the circuit. Yin turned professional after finishing 24th at the Augusta National Women's Amateur and then posted five other top 10s on the Epson Tour as she collected the Rookie of the Year award.

In fourth place was Kiira Riihijarvi, the 2020 Finnish Amateur champion, who won the inaugural event in Ann Arbor, while 21-year-old Australian Grace Kim was fifth after winning the IOA Golf Classic with a closing seven-under-par 64. Norway's Celine Borge found form at the right moment, following a runner-up finish at the Guardian Championship two events later with her first win at the Tuscaloosa Toyota Classic, the penultimate tournament of the season, thanks to a closing 63.

Winning the Ladies European Tour's Qualifying School in December 2021 was the springboard for American Gabriella Then gaining her maiden Epson Tour win at the Garden City Charity Classic. The 26-year-old from California had been on the circuit since 2017 but had recorded only two top-20 finishes before adding six more in 2022 to be seventh on the standings.

Gina Kim, the Duke alumna and American Curtis Cup player in 2021, won on her fifth start at the Inova Mission Inn Resort & Club Championship, while China's Yan Liu, who won the Four Winds Invitational, and Korea's Hyo Joon Jang, who had five top-10 results, completed the 10 players who earned their cards for the LPGA. Pano, who was in 10th place going into the Epson Tour Championship, dropped down to 13th after the final event. Jaravee Boonchant, of Korea, won the championship with 21 birdies, an eagle and no bogeys over four rounds to move up to 12th, while Bailey Tardy finished third to end up 11th on the standings.

2022 SCHEDULE	
Florida's Natural Charity Classic	**Kum-Kang Park**
Carlisle Arizona Women's Golf Classic	**Fatima Fernandez Cano**
IOA Championship	**Linnea Strom**
Casino del Sol Golf Classic	**Andrea Lee**
Copper Rock Championship	**Dottie Ardina**
Garden City Charity Classic	**Gabriella Then**
IOA Golf Classic	**Grace Kim**
Inova Mission Inn Championship	**Gina Kim**
Carolina Golf Classic	**Lucy Li**
Ann Arbor's Road to the LPGA	**Kiira Riihijarvi**
Island Resort Championship	**Ssu-Chia Cheng**
Twin Bridges Championship	**Lucy Li (2)**
FireKeepers Casino Hotel Championship	**Xiaowen Yin**
French Lick Charity Classic	**Xiaowen Yin (2)**
Four Winds Invitational	**Yan Liu**
Circling Raven Championship	**Jillian Hollis**
Wildhorse Ladies Golf Classic	**Daniela Iacobelli**
Guardian Championship	**Maria Torres**
Murphy USA El Dorado Shootout	**Britney Yada**
Tuscaloosa Toyota Classic	**Celine Borge**
Epson Tour Championship	**Jaravee Boonchant**

Florida's Natural Charity Classic

Country Club of Winter Haven, Winter Haven, Florida — March 4-6
Par 72 (36-36); 6,151 yards — Purse: $200,000

1	**Kum-Kang Park**	70	67	70	207	$30,000
2	**Alana Uriell**	71	71	67	209	16,733
	Frida Kinhult	68	70	71	209	16,733
4	Maria Fernanda Torres	70	69	71	210	10,955
5	Haylee Rae Harford	75	70	67	212	6,508
	Pauline Roussin Bouchard	70	73	69	212	6,508
	Sierra L Brooks	71	71	70	212	6,508
	Weiwei Zhang	69	70	73	212	6,508
	Min-G Kim	67	71	74	212	6,508
10	Daniela Iacobelli	72	75	66	213	4,027
	Alexa Pano (A)	70	75	68	213	
	Dani Holmqvist	71	71	71	213	4,027
	Lindy Duncan	70	72	71	213	4,027
	Natalie Srinivasan	70	71	72	213	4,027
15	Daniela Darquea	76	70	68	214	3,172
	Rachel Rohanna	73	73	68	214	3,172
	Ana Belac	73	70	71	214	3,172
	Hyo Joon Jang	70	73	71	214	3,172
19	Tiffany Chan	69	76	70	215	2,663
	Beth Wu	73	71	71	215	2,663
	Celine Borge	71	72	72	215	2,663
	Sarah Elizabeth White	74	68	73	215	2,663
23	Katherine Smith	76	70	70	216	2,406
	Nishtha Madan	68	74	74	216	2,406

Carlisle Arizona Women's Golf Classic

Longbow Golf Club, Mesa, Arizona — March 17-20
Par 72 (36-36); 6,487 yards — Purse: $250,000

1	**Fatima Fernandez Cano**	70	70	61	70	271	$37,500
2	**Dani Holmqvist**	68	67	73	66	274	18,047
	Sofia Garcia	71	68	67	68	274	18,047
	Laura Restrepo	69	66	67	72	274	18,047
5	Kum-Kang Park	70	70	71	64	275	8,418
	Lucy Li	70	71	67	67	275	8,418
	Weiwei Zhang	71	67	67	70	275	8,418
	Sophie Hausmann	65	69	70	71	275	8,418
9	Lauren Coughlin	71	71	66	68	276	5,452
	Hira Naveed	70	68	69	69	276	5,452
	Alana Uriell	67	70	67	72	276	5,452
12	Gabriela Ruffels	72	68	70	67	277	4,432
	Natalie Srinivasan	67	70	70	70	277	4,432
	Jaclyn Lee	69	67	70	71	277	4,432
15	Maja Stark	68	72	70	68	278	3,655
	Daniela Iacobelli	71	70	68	69	278	3,655
	Casey Danielson	70	71	68	69	278	3,655
	Fernanda Lira	69	70	68	71	278	3,655
19	Alyaa Abdulghany	70	69	71	69	279	3,015
	Andrea Lee	76	66	67	70	279	3,015
	Laura Wearn	69	71	69	70	279	3,015
	Nishtha Madan	70	68	70	71	279	3,015
	Ruixin Liu	69	66	72	72	279	3,015
	Haylee Harford	68	68	67	76	279	3,015

IOA Championship

Morongo Golf Club at Tukwet Canyon, Beaumont, California — March 25-27
Par 72 (36-36); 6,527 yards — Purse: $200,000

1	**Linnea Strom**	71	67	67	205	$30,000
2	**Sarah Jane Smith**	69	70	69	208	14,438
	Milagros Chaves	68	69	71	208	14,438
	Sophie Hausmann	69	67	72	208	14,438
5	Celine Borge	76	69	64	209	6,000
	Emma Broze	71	69	69	209	6,000
	Andrea Lee	70	69	70	209	6,000
	Lucy Li	70	68	71	209	6,000
	Natalie Srinivasan	68	70	71	209	6,000
	Nishtha Madan	67	69	73	209	6,000
11	Ingrid Gutierrez Nunez	69	72	69	210	3,774
	Allie White	68	70	72	210	3,774
	Roberta Liti	68	68	74	210	3,774
14	Lindy Duncan	68	77	66	211	3,006
	Kum-Kang Park	72	71	68	211	3,006
	Brianna Do	73	68	70	211	3,006
	Katherine Smith	69	72	70	211	3,006
	Dani Holmqvist	69	67	75	211	3,006
19	Kendra Dalton	70	74	68	212	2,372
	Louise Ridderstrom	71	72	69	212	2,372
	Laura Restrepo	71	72	69	212	2,372
	Prima Thammaraks	72	70	70	212	2,372
	Elin Arvidsson	72	69	71	212	2,372
	Brittany Fan	73	67	72	212	2,372
	Ssu-Chia Cheng	66	73	73	212	2,372

Casino del Sol Golf Classic

Sewailo Golf Club, Tucson, Arizona — March 31-April 3
Par 72 (36-36); 6,385 yards — Purse: $200,000

1	**Andrea Lee**	69	65	67	69	270	$30,000
2	**Lucy Li**	70	65	67	68	270	18,834
	Lee won playoff at third extra hole						
3	**Daniela Darquea**	67	70	66	69	272	13,711
4	Brianna Do	67	72	69	65	273	9,625
	Emma Broze	69	67	70	67	273	9,625
6	Katelyn Sisk	69	68	68	69	274	6,510
	Jessica Porvasnik	65	65	74	70	274	6,510
8	Hira Naveed	67	68	73	67	275	5,233
9	Jessica Peng	72	65	72	67	276	4,064
	Miranda Wang	68	70	69	69	276	4,064
	Yan Liu	70	71	65	70	276	4,064
	Samantha Wagner	70	65	70	71	276	4,064
	Yue Ren	71	65	68	72	276	4,064
14	Sophie Hausmann	67	69	73	68	277	3,146
	Clariss Guce	70	69	69	69	277	3,146
	Becca Huffer	70	67	68	72	277	3,146
17	Pannarat Thanapolboonyaras	68	69	72	69	278	2,717
	Sarah Jane Smith	67	68	72	71	278	2,717
	Dottie Ardina	68	65	69	76	278	2,717
20	Kim Kaufman	72	70	70	67	279	2,210
	Linnea Strom	70	70	72	67	279	2,210
	Daniela Iacobelli	69	71	70	69	279	2,210
	Amelia Garvey	71	72	66	70	279	2,210
	Selena Costabile	70	73	66	70	279	2,210
	Beth Wu	71	71	67	70	279	2,210
	Kennedy Swann	70	69	70	70	279	2,210
	Alena Sharp	71	67	70	71	279	2,210
	Jillian Hollis	71	66	70	72	279	2,210

Copper Rock Championship

Copper Rock Golf Course, Hurricane, Utah — April 21-23
Par 72 (37-35); 6,552 yards — Purse: $200,000

1	**Dottie Ardina**	73	73	65	211	$30,000
2	**Marta Sanz Barrio**	75	71	67	213	16,733
	Laetitia Beck	72	73	68	213	16,733
4	Jaravee Boonchant	77	69	68	214	9,032
	Anita Uwadia	73	73	68	214	9,032
	Amelia Garvey	71	72	71	214	9,032
7	Sophie Hausmann	81	69	66	216	4,997
	Becca Huffer	75	73	68	216	4,997
	Sierra Brooks	74	73	69	216	4,997
	Kathleen Scavo	73	74	69	216	4,997
	Emma Broze	73	68	75	216	4,997
12	Kiira Riihijarvi	71	72	74	217	3,759
	Kim Kaufman	70	73	74	217	3,759
14	Clariss Guce	76	73	69	218	3,252
	Rachel Stous	76	72	70	218	3,252
	Gigi Stoll	73	75	70	218	3,252
17	Katherine Smith	79	73	67	219	2,462
	Grace Kim	78	73	68	219	2,462
	Lucy Li	74	77	68	219	2,462
	Julie Aime	74	77	68	219	2,462
	Soo Jin Lee	74	76	69	219	2,462
	Hira Naveed	77	72	70	219	2,462
	Linnea Strom	77	72	70	219	2,462
	Daniela Iacobelli	77	71	71	219	2,462
	Siyun Liu	75	73	71	219	2,462
	Gabriela Ruffels	81	66	72	219	2,462
	Robyn Choi	74	72	73	219	2,462

Garden City Charity Classic

Buffalo Dunes Golf Course, Garden City, Kansas — April 29-May 1
Par 72 (36-36); 6,481 yards — Purse: $200,000

1	**Gabriella Then**	67	70	67	204	$30,000
2	**Alexa Pano**	69	70	67	206	19,234
3	**Yan Liu**	69	69	70	208	14,007
4	Teresa Toscano	73	68	68	209	9,838
	Jillian Hollis	66	73	70	209	9,838
6	Sofia Garcia	69	72	69	210	7,232
7	Xiaowen Yin	69	73	69	211	5,721
	Maddi Caldwell-Young	71	68	72	211	5,721
9	Robyn Choi	73	72	67	212	4,301
	Haley Moore	72	72	68	212	4,301
	Emma Broze	74	69	69	212	4,301
	Kiira Riihijarvi	71	72	69	212	4,301
13	Julienne Soo	71	73	69	213	3,511
	Karis Davidson	72	70	71	213	3,511
15	Emilee Hoffman	74	71	69	214	2,820
	Amelia Lewis	70	75	69	214	2,820
	Riley Rennell	72	72	70	214	2,820
	Laetitia Beck	70	74	70	214	2,820
	Natalie Srinivasan	72	71	71	214	2,820
	Lindsey McCurdy	70	73	71	214	2,820
	Kristen Gillman	74	68	72	214	2,820

IOA Golf Classic

Alaqua Country Club, Longwood, Florida — May 20-22
Par 71 (35-36); 6,208 yards — Purse: $200,000

1	**Grace Kim**	66	65	64	195	$30,000
2	**Hyo Joon Jang**	69	67	64	200	16,514
	Sarah Jane Smith	66	66	68	200	16,514
4	Robyn Choi	68	66	67	201	9,773
	Katelyn Sisk	62	72	67	201	9,773
6	Weiwei Zhang	70	67	65	202	6,613
	Sophie Hausmann	67	69	66	202	6,613
8	Sofia Garcia	70	68	65	203	4,645
	Marissa Steen	67	68	68	203	4,645
	Gina Kim	67	68	68	203	4,645
	Kum-Kang Park	65	66	72	203	4,645
12	Gigi Stoll	69	68	67	204	3,702
	Daniela Darquea	67	70	67	204	3,702
14	Karen Chung	66	70	69	205	3,381
15	Klara Spilkova	67	73	66	206	2,967
	Pauline Del Rosario	66	72	68	206	2,967
	Hira Naveed	66	71	69	206	2,967
	Emma Broze	66	69	71	206	2,967
19	Lucy Li	70	69	68	207	2,490
	Pannarat Thanapolboonyaras	70	68	69	207	2,490
	Ingrid Gutierrez Nunez	69	69	69	207	2,490
	Lindy Duncan	69	65	73	207	2,490
	Jillian Hollis	67	66	74	207	2,490

Inova Mission Inn Championship

Mission Inn Resort & Club, Howey-in-the-Hills, Florida — May 27-29
Par 73 (36-37); 6,485 yards — Purse: $200,000

1	**Gina Kim**	66	69	73	208	$30,000
2	**Caroline Inglis**	73	67	70	210	16,566
	Maria Fassi	71	66	73	210	16,566
4	Dani Holmqvist	70	72	69	211	9,805
	Amy Lee	69	69	73	211	9,805
6	Gigi Stoll	68	71	73	212	7,207
7	Yu-Sang Hou	73	72	69	214	5,700
	Robyn Choi	70	70	74	214	5,700
9	Samantha Wagner	71	74	70	215	4,609
	Karen Chung	71	69	75	215	4,609
11	Maddi Caldwell-Young	75	69	72	216	3,960
	Jaravee Boonchant	72	71	73	216	3,960
13	Amelia Lewis	72	75	70	217	3,020
	Jessica Peng	74	72	71	217	3,020
	Gabriela Ruffels	74	70	73	217	3,020
	Alexa Pano	74	70	73	217	3,020
	Michaela Finn	70	74	73	217	3,020
	Hyo Joon Jang	73	70	74	217	3,020
	Sarah Jane Smith	72	70	75	217	3,020
	Gabby Lemieux	73	68	76	217	3,020

Carolina Golf Classic

Kinston Country Club, Kinston, North Carolina — June 9-12
Par 71(36-35); 6,367 yards — Purse: $200,000

1	**Lucy Li**	66	68	62	69	265	$30,000
2	**Alexa Pano**	66	63	65	71	265	19,297
	Li won playoff at first extra hole						
3	**Gabriela Ruffels**	67	68	63	68	266	14,054
4	Bailey Tardy	68	69	65	66	268	10,917
5	Louise Ridderstrom	69	69	66	66	270	7,397
	Robyn Choi	67	68	68	67	270	7,397
	Xiaowen Yin	68	65	66	71	270	7,397
8	Auston Kim	65	68	70	68	271	5,376
9	Lori Beth Adams	65	71	68	68	272	4,644
	Britney Yada	71	66	66	69	272	4,644
11	Pannarat Thanapolboonyaras	71	68	69	65	273	3,870
	Lindy Duncan	74	67	65	67	273	3,870
	Gabriella Then	62	69	74	68	273	3,870
14	Clariss Guce	66	70	71	67	274	3,159
	Grace Kim	67	68	70	69	274	3,159
	Marta Sanz Barrio	66	69	69	70	274	3,159
	Daniela Darquea	70	66	66	72	274	3,159
18	Katelyn Sisk	69	70	68	68	275	2,741
	Selena Costabile	68	70	69	68	275	2,741
20	Amy Lee	70	70	68	68	276	2,563
	Fernanda Lira	65	72	65	74	276	2,563

Ann Arbor's Road to the LPGA

Travis Pointe Country Club, Ann Arbor, Michigan — June 16-18
Par 72 (36-36); 6,494 yards — Purse: $200,000

1	**Kiira Riihijarvi**	68	69	69	206	$30,000
2	**Pavarisa Yoktuan**	66	69	73	208	18,886
3	**Ashley Lau** (A)	71	71	68	210	
4	Klara Spilkova	69	74	68	211	11,019
	Linnea Strom	71	69	71	211	11,019
	Grace Kim	68	71	72	211	11,019
7	Pannarat Thanapolboonyaras	69	74	69	212	7,093
8	Gabriela Ruffels	74	71	68	213	5,317
	Hyo Joon Jang	71	74	68	213	5,317
	Sarah Hoffman	69	74	70	213	5,317
11	Siyun Liu	70	75	69	214	3,797
	Weiwei Zhang	70	74	70	214	3,797
	Mariah Stackhouse	72	70	72	214	3,797
	Moeka Nishihata	69	71	74	214	3,797
	Karen Chung	68	72	74	214	3,797
16	Polly Mack	72	72	71	215	2,924
	Emma Broze	73	70	72	215	2,924
	Alexa Pano	73	70	72	215	2,924
	Kim Kaufman	73	68	74	215	2,924
20	Emilee Hoffman	74	74	68	216	2,412
	Karis Davidson	72	74	70	216	2,412
	Britney Yada	71	73	72	216	2,412
	Laura Wearn	71	73	72	216	2,412
	Malene Krolboll Hansen	70	74	72	216	2,412
	Dani Holmqvist	72	70	74	216	2,412

Island Resort Championship

Sweetgrass Golf Club, Harris, Michigan — June 24-26
Par 72 (36-36); 6,414 yards — Purse: $212,500

1	**Ssu-Chia Cheng**	68	64	67	199	$31,875
2	**Jiwon Jeon**	67	68	70	205	19,853
3	**Haylee Harford**	69	71	66	206	10,547
	Michaela Finn	68	69	69	206	10,547
	Clariss Guce	71	64	71	206	10,547
	Emilee Hoffman	67	68	71	206	10,547
7	Lucy Li	70	66	71	207	5,888
	Sofia Garcia	68	68	71	207	5,888
9	Kaitlin Milligan	69	67	72	208	4,973
10	Maddi Caldwell-Young	72	69	68	209	3,667
	Yue Ren	70	71	68	209	3,667
	Xiaowen Yin	71	69	69	209	3,667
	Gabriela Ruffels	70	70	69	209	3,667
	Karen Chung	71	67	71	209	3,667
	Celine Borge	68	70	71	209	3,667
	Jaravee Boonchant	69	67	73	209	3,667
	Samantha Wagner	66	67	76	209	3,667
18	Fernanda Lira	69	70	71	210	2,797
	Vivian Hou	69	68	73	210	2,797
20	Selena Costabile	67	72	72	211	2,443
	Alyaa Abdulghany	71	67	73	211	2,443
	Malene Krolboll Hansen	69	69	73	211	2,443
	Lauren Cox	68	69	74	211	2,443
	Kenzie Wright	66	70	75	211	2,443
	Moeka Nishihata	67	68	76	211	2,443

Twin Bridges Championship

Pinehaven Country Club, Albany, New York — July 8-10
Par 71 (35-36); 6,241 yards — Purse: $200,000

1	**Lucy Li**	66	68	69	203	$30,000
2	**Linnea Strom**	71	66	70	207	19,297
3	**Allie White**	70	71	68	209	14,054
4	Hira Naveed	70	72	68	210	9,871
	Chanoknan Angurasaranee	69	71	70	210	9,871
6	Gina Kim	75	69	67	211	6,247
	Jillian Hollis	71	71	69	211	6,247
	Xiaowen Yin	70	72	69	211	6,247
9	Britney Yada	70	75	67	212	4,644
	Alexa Pano	72	68	72	212	4,644
11	Carley Cox	72	74	67	213	3,554
	Amelia Garvey	74	69	70	213	3,554
	Gabriella Then	73	69	71	213	3,554
	Pannarat Thanapolboonyaras	72	70	71	213	3,554
	Anita Uwadia	71	71	71	213	3,554
	Nishtha Madan	69	69	75	213	3,554
17	Louise Ridderstrom	74	73	67	214	2,751
	Jaravee Boonchant	74	71	69	214	2,751
	Lindy Duncan	73	72	69	214	2,751
	Grace Kim	69	70	75	214	2,751

FireKeepers Casino Hotel Championship

Battle Creek Country Club, Battle Creek, Michigan — July 29-31
Par 72 (36-36); 6,474 yards — Purse: $200,000

1	**Xiaowen Yin**	67	68	68	203	$30,000
2	**Gina Kim**	68	67	68	203	18,685
	Yin won playoff at first extra hole					
3	**Laura Wearn**	69	70	66	205	10,898
	Grace Kim	69	68	68	205	10,898
	Rachel Rohanna	70	65	70	205	10,898
6	Celine Borge	70	71	65	206	6,032
	Vicky Hurst	71	68	67	206	6,032
	Kristin Coleman	70	69	67	206	6,032
9	Karen Chung	71	69	67	207	4,161
	Selena Costabile	69	69	69	207	4,161
	Maddie Szeryk	69	68	70	207	4,161
	Louise Ridderstrom	70	66	71	207	4,161
13	Katelyn Sisk	76	68	64	208	2,870
	Savannah Vilaubi	75	69	64	208	2,870
	Lucy Li	73	69	66	208	2,870
	Daniela Iacobelli	74	67	67	208	2,870
	Regina Plasencia	70	71	67	208	2,870
	Maria Parra	71	69	68	208	2,870
	Mi Hyang Lee	71	68	69	208	2,870
	Yu-Sang Hou	71	68	69	208	2,870
	Jaravee Boonchant	68	71	69	208	2,870

French Lick Charity Classic

French Lick Resort (Pete Dye), French Lick, Indiana — August 4-7
Par 72 (36-36); 6,505 yards — Purse: $335,000

1	**Xiaowen Yin**	70	72	70	69	281	$50,250
2	**Gabriella Then**	68	69	71	74	282	32,433
3	**Polly Mack**	74	74	67	68	283	23,621
4	Daniela Darquea	68	71	73	72	284	18,350
5	Linnea Strom	66	71	75	73	285	14,836
6	Dani Holmqvist	72	71	74	69	286	11,234
	Mi Hyang Lee	72	71	70	73	286	11,234
8	Jillian Hollis	71	76	70	70	287	7,896
	Laura Restrepo	71	74	71	71	287	7,896
	Laura Wearn	72	75	68	72	287	7,896
	Karen Kim	71	72	72	72	287	7,896
12	Gina Kim	74	71	70	73	288	6,490
13	Alena Sharp	71	74	72	72	289	5,928
	Ruoning Yin	73	73	68	75	289	5,928
15	Roberta Liti	70	73	73	74	290	5,295
	Maddi Caldwell-Young	72	67	71	80	290	5,295
17	Lindy Duncan	72	76	72	71	291	4,551
	Celine Borge	74	74	71	72	291	4,551
	Bailey Tardy	70	74	73	74	291	4,551
	Karen Fredgaard	71	72	73	75	291	4,551
	Pavarisa Yoktuan	70	71	75	75	291	4,551

Four Winds Invitational

South Bend Country Club, South Bend, Indiana — August 12-14
Par 72 (37-35); 6,266 yards — Purse: $200,000

1	**Yan Liu**	64	71	74	209	$30,000
2	**Kiira Riihijarvi**	72	69	68	209	16,413
	Gabby Lemieux	71	66	72	209	16,413
	Liu won playoff at first extra hole					
4	Weiwei Zhang	72	69	69	210	8,141
	Klara Spilkova	72	69	69	210	8,141
	Pinyada Kuvanun	69	71	70	210	8,141
	Selena Costabile	68	70	72	210	8,141
8	Milagros Chaves	71	72	68	211	4,613
	Cassie Porter	73	69	69	211	4,613
	Celine Borge	71	70	70	211	4,613
	Kim Kaufman	71	69	71	211	4,613
12	Alexa Pano	77	69	66	212	3,075
	Katelyn Sisk	72	74	66	212	3,075
	Kristin Coleman	71	75	66	212	3,075
	Julie Aime	74	69	69	212	3,075
	Regina Plasencia	69	74	69	212	3,075
	Amelia Garvey	72	70	70	212	3,075
	Gabriela Ruffels	70	72	70	212	3,075
	Pauline Del Rosario	70	72	70	212	3,075
	Polly Mack	70	72	70	212	3,075

Circling Raven Championship

Circling Raven Golf Club, Worley, Idaho — August 26-28
Par 72 (36-36); 6,690 yards — Purse: $200,000

1	**Jillian Hollis**	68	66	64	198	$30,000
2	**Robyn Choi**	68	66	66	200	18,940
3	**Alexa Pano**	67	70	65	202	13,790
4	Polly Mack	*65*	*71*	67	203	8,826
	Gabriela Ruffels	66	69	68	203	8,826
	Hyo Joon Jang	67	67	69	203	8,826
7	Grace Kim	67	68	70	205	5,625
	Jessica Welch	69	65	71	205	5,625
9	Kristin Coleman	70	70	66	206	4,752
10	Riley Rennell	69	71	67	207	3,925
	Dani Holmqvist	69	70	68	207	3,925
	Dottie Ardina	68	70	69	207	3,925
	Amelia Garvey	70	67	70	207	3,925
14	Laura Wearn	71	72	65	208	2,788
	Yue Ren	68	74	66	208	2,788
	Lauren Cox	71	69	68	208	2,788
	Sofia Garcia	68	72	68	208	2,788
	Jaravee Boonchant	68	71	69	208	2,788
	Pavarisa Yoktuan	65	74	69	208	2,788
	Lindsey McCurdy	68	70	70	208	2,788
	Breanne Jones	68	70	70	208	2,788
	Fernanda Lira	69	68	71	208	2,788

Wildhorse Ladies Golf Classic

Wildhorse Golf Course, Pendleton, Oregon — September 2-4
Par 72 (36-36); 6,617 yards — Purse: $200,000

1	**Daniela Iacobelli**	65	67	66	198	$30,000
2	**Pavarisa Yoktuan**	69	70	62	201	19,234
3	**Laura Wearn**	68	66	68	202	11,227
	Grace Kim	*64*	*69*	69	202	11,227
	Xiaowen Yin	63	70	69	202	11,227
6	Klara Spilkova	68	70	66	204	6,224
	Milagros Chaves	71	66	67	204	6,224
	Samantha Wagner	69	68	67	204	6,224
9	Sofia Garcia	71	67	67	205	4,453
	Gabriella Then	69	69	67	205	4,453
	Amelia Garvey	69	69	67	205	4,453
12	Jessica Peng	69	70	67	206	3,341
	Gabriela Ruffels	68	71	67	206	3,341
	Amy Lee	67	72	67	206	3,341
	Kum-Kang Park	69	69	68	206	3,341
	Gina Kim	67	70	69	206	3,341
	Anna Redding	67	68	71	206	3,341
18	Selena Costabile	66	73	68	207	2,684
	Yue Ren	69	69	69	207	2,684
	Bailey Tardy	66	72	69	207	2,684

Guardian Championship

Robert Trent Jones Golf Trail at Capitol Hill (Senator), Prattville, Alabama — September 16-18
Par 72 (36-36); 6,502 yards — Purse: $200,000

1	**Maria Torres**	68	66	68	202	$30,000
2	**Celine Borge**	68	70	66	204	16,413
	Clariss Guce	71	65	68	204	16,413
4	Hyo Joon Jang	*72*	*68*	65	205	7,102
	Abegail Arevalo	72	67	66	205	7,102
	Natalie Srinivasan	69	69	67	205	7,102
	Ssu-Chia Cheng	71	66	68	205	7,102
	Yan Liu	67	70	68	205	7,102
	Dani Holmqvist	70	66	69	205	7,102
10	Maggie Ashmore	72	69	65	206	4,201
	Jillian Hollis	67	71	68	206	4,201
12	Sierra Brooks	71	65	71	207	3,789
13	Amy Lee	71	70	67	208	3,274
	Yue Ren	70	69	69	208	3,274
	Milagros Chaves	67	71	70	208	3,274
	Grace Kim	70	66	72	208	3,274
17	Maria Fernanda Escauriza	73	70	66	209	2,441
	Min A Yoon	72	70	67	209	2,441
	Gina Kim	68	74	67	209	2,441
	Katelyn Sisk	72	68	69	209	2,441
	Maddi Caldwell-Young	68	72	69	209	2,441
	Sarah Elizabeth White	71	68	70	209	2,441
	Julie Aime	70	68	71	209	2,441
	Gabriela Ruffels	70	68	71	209	2,441
	Karen Chung	67	71	71	209	2,441
	Samantha Wagner	69	68	72	209	2,441

Murphy USA El Dorado Shootout

Mystic Creek Golf Club, El Dorado, Arkansas — September 23-25
Par 72 (36-36); 6,558 yards — Purse: $225,000

1	**Britney Yada**	69	71	65	205	$33,750
2	**Bailey Tardy**	65	71	71	207	21,500
3	**Kristen Gillman**	70	68	71	209	13,908
	Jiwon Jeon	*69*	*67*	73	209	13,908
5	Clariss Guce	72	69	69	210	8,236
	Daniela Iacobelli	71	69	70	210	8,236
	Kiira Riihijarvi	69	66	75	210	8,236
8	Linnea Strom	73	71	67	211	5,439
	Gabriela Ruffels	70	74	67	211	5,439
	Jaravee Boonchant	75	67	69	211	5,439
11	Karen Chung	72	69	71	212	4,305
	Jessica Peng	70	70	72	212	4,305
	Milagros Chaves	70	68	74	212	4,305
14	Ho-yu An	69	75	69	213	3,602
	Louise Ridderstrom	75	68	70	213	3,602
	Yan Liu	71	70	72	213	3,602
17	Hyo Joon Jang	75	70	69	214	3,112
	Pavarisa Yoktuan	72	71	71	214	3,112
	Dottie Ardina	70	73	71	214	3,112
20	Kum-Kang Park	77	68	70	215	2,848
	Grace Kim	68	74	73	215	2,848

Tuscaloosa Toyota Classic

Ol' Colony Golf Course, Tuscaloosa, Alabama
Par 72 (36-36); 6,563 yards

September 30-October 2
Purse: $200,000

1	**Celine Borge**	67	71	63	201	$30,000
2	**Hyo Joon Jang**	70	65	67	202	19,172
3	**Linnea Strom**	67	67	69	203	13,961
4	Bailey Tardy	*64*	*65*	75	204	10,844
5	Kiira Riihijarvi	70	69	66	205	8,766
6	Samantha Wagner	69	72	65	206	5,856
	Dani Holmqvist	68	72	66	206	5,856
	Gabriella Then	70	69	67	206	5,856
	Robyn Choi	62	75	69	206	5,856
10	Roberta Liti	73	66	68	207	4,107
	Pannarat Thanapolboonyaras	72	67	68	207	4,107
	Laura Wearn	65	71	71	207	4,107
13	Gina Kim	71	68	69	208	3,601
14	Daniela Iacobelli	70	73	66	209	3,214
	Becca Huffer	70	72	67	209	3,214
	Milagros Chaves	67	71	71	209	3,214
17	Gabriela Ruffels	68	74	68	210	2,639
	Moeka Nishihata	70	71	69	210	2,639
	Maria Torres	69	71	70	210	2,639
	Yan Liu	69	71	70	210	2,639
	Selena Costabile	68	72	70	210	2,639
	Kristin Coleman	68	68	74	210	2,639

Epson Tour Championship

LPGA International (Jones), Daytona Beach, Florida
Par 72 (36-36); 6,495 yards

October 6-9
Purse: $250,000

1	**Jaravee Boonchant**	67	64	68	66	265	$37,500
2	**Riley Rennell**	69	68	64	65	266	23,964
3	**Bailey Tardy**	66	66	68	68	268	17,451
4	Anita Uwadia	71	68	68	62	269	10,275
	Dottie Ardina	66	72	66	65	269	10,275
	Kiira Riihijarvi	68	67	67	67	269	10,275
	Linnea Strom	66	67	68	68	269	10,275
8	Laura Wearn	68	68	69	65	270	6,065
	Daniela Iacobelli	67	69	66	68	270	6,065
	Dorsey Addicks	68	70	63	69	270	6,065
11	Ssu-Chia Cheng	66	69	69	67	271	4,409
	Gabriela Ruffels	67	68	67	69	271	4,409
	Amelia Garvey	67	66	69	69	271	4,409
	Karen Chung	69	66	66	70	271	4,409
	Sophie Hausmann	68	65	68	70	271	4,409
	Hyo Joon Jang	66	66	67	72	271	4,409
17	Kendra Dalton	70	69	66	67	272	3,472
	Yan Liu	67	69	68	68	272	3,472
	Milagros Chaves	72	65	62	73	272	3,472
20	Teresa Toscano	71	68	70	64	273	3,073
	Kum-Kang Park	70	69	68	66	273	3,073
	Amy Lee	68	69	69	67	273	3,073
	Robyn Choi	68	69	66	70	273	3,073

2022 ASCENSUS RACE FOR THE CARD

1	Linnea Strom	$119,190
2	Xiaowen Yin	118,860
3	Lucy Li	110,111
4	Kiira Riihijarvi	90,483
5	Grace Kim	89,720
6	Celine Borge	89,710
7	Gabriella Then	86,578
8	Gina Kim	82,133
9	Yan Liu	80,139
10	Hyo Joon Jang	78,611

adidas
adidas

Ladies European Tour

How Swede it was on the Ladies European Tour in 2022. Linn Grant, Maja Stark and Johanna Gustavsson took the top three places on the Race to Costa del Sol Rankings and it was fitting in the closing event at the Open de Espana that Caroline Hedwall, a player the trio all look up to as a role model, claimed a long-awaited first win in four years.

Gustavsson, 30, had her best season yet, but had the misfortune to finish as a runner-up three times without winning. Part of the reason was that Stark and Grant were greedily hoarding victories to themselves. Both turned professional in August 2021 and became immediate success stories. The battle between the two friends for the season's number one spot was enthralling. Stark, who won twice at the end of 2021, led the standings for much of the year thanks to three victories. With a flair for the dramatic, Stark won two of them by five strokes, at the NSW Open and the ISPS Handa World Invitational, where she closed with a 10-under-par 63 at Galgorm Castle. In the Amundi German Masters, she came from three behind on the 71st tee with two birdies, while compatriot Jessica Karlsson bogeyed twice.

The win at Galgorm came in a co-sanctioned event with the LPGA, enabling Stark to take up membership of the LPGA without having to go back to Q-Series. "I hate qualifying," she said, "it's great that I don't have to do that again." Despite ending the season mostly in America, the 22-year-old from Abbekas still gave Grant a run for the Race title.

But Grant was relentless. Coming off two runner-up finishes in her first two LET starts as a professional and then a win on the Access Series in 2021, Grant started the new year in South Africa, winning three times on the Sunshine Tour. The third of those, the Joburg Open, was co-sanctioned so gave her a first LET title in her first event as a member of the tour. "That set the standard for the season," she said. She won wire-to-wire at the Mithra Belgian Open and then twice in Sweden, the second of them at the Skafto Open in August when she birdied the last two holes to pip another compatriot, Lisa Pettersson.

The undisputed highlight of the year came when Grant, just short of her 23rd birthday, made history by becoming the first woman to win on the DP World Tour in the Volvo Car Scandinavian Mixed. In a stunning performance that brought gasps of appreciation from the huge local gallery at Halmstad, as well as from tournament hosts Annika Sorenstam and Henrik Stenson, one of the runners-up fully nine strokes adrift. Grant started the final round with a two-stroke lead, all the attention on her, and scored a 64 to finish on 24 under par. The new star from Helsingborg finished 14 strokes ahead of the second woman, Gabriella Cowley, in a tie for 15th place. Though, as ever, the difference in yardage played by the men and women was highlighted, so too was an analysis of average hitting distances showing that the women should have been further forward than they actually were. "I hope this victory is big," Grant said. "I hope it brings women more forward and it gets people's eyes on us a little bit more. It is always nice to say that you beat the guys for a week!"

Before the season-ending event on the Costa del Sol, Stark explained the relationship between her and Grant. "When I look back on the year, it's not the results that come up it's more the fact it's been so fun to hang out with a friend for the whole year. All the competitions that we have done together, one of my favourite moments was at the German Masters. We were just so tired. We were sharing a room and talking and something silly came up and we were dying of laughter. That has been the best part about doing this together. It's fun that one of us is going to win it, too."

Grant said: "I feel like we've had a battle on and off throughout the year and it would be sad to have it be over already. I'm glad we've made it to the final event, and we'll give it a good go this week. I feel like it was supposed to be this way, it feels good."

In the end, Stark was seventh and Grant was third and took the title by 209.77 points. Stark rushed into the recorder's hut to give Grant a huge hug. "I'm very relieved to have beaten Maja, she stressed me out this week and she's been stressing me out the whole season," Grant said. She had already taken the Rookie of the Year award, becoming the fifth player to do the double after Dame Laura Davies, Carlota Ciganda, Esther Henseleit and Atthaya Thitikul. "It feels so nice to get both titles. They're all great players who have won both, I hope I can follow in their path. Of course, the Scandinavian Mixed was my standout moment. It was a big event and at home and everything that came with that."

Grant's only missed cut in her professional career to date came at the Trust Golf Scottish Open, otherwise her worst result was 19th at the AIG Women's Open and the KPMG Irish Open. On the LET, she played 17 events and finished in the top 10 an amazing 13 times, including eighth at the Evian Championship. On the LPGA — some of the events overlapping — she played six times and had four top 10s. She qualified for the CME Group Tour Championship but did not play, citing US travel restrictions. All the LPGA events she played were outside the US. In a statement, she said: "I understand some people want to know why I am not playing in the US. I respect that. The simple reason is that I am not vaccinated. Regarding why, I ask the same respect back." She concluded: "At the end of the day, no matter how I look at it, and despite all joggling, I have had a great year."

It was also a great year for the LET bouncing back from the Covid pandemic, with 33 tournaments in 23 countries and record prize money of €31 million. As well as the Scandinavian Mixed, there were two non-gendered events co-sanctioned with the Asian Tour and the Aramco Team Series expanded to five events, with winners including Nelly Korda and Lexi Thompson. Fellow major champions Georgia Hall and Anna Nordqvist won regular LET events for the first time, while the roll of honour also included 39-year-old mother Liz Young, who beat Grant by a stroke at the VP Bank Swiss Open, and 16-year-old German professional Chiara Noja, who defeated her hero Charley Hull at the second playoff hole at the Aramco Jeddah event and thought she would treat herself to a burger in celebration.

2022 SCHEDULE

Magical Kenya Ladies Open	**Esther Henseleit**	
Aramco Saudi Ladies International	**Georgia Hall**	
Joburg Ladies Open	**Linn Grant (1,3)**	
Investec SA Women's Open	**Lee-Anne Pace**	
Trust Golf Asian Mixed Cup	**Ratchanon Chantananuwat** (A)	*See chapter 17*
Trust Golf Asian Stableford Challenge	**Sihwan Kim (1,2)**	*See chapter 17*
Australian Women's Classic	**Meghan MacLaren**	*See chapter 26*
Women's NSW Open	**Maja Stark**	*See chapter 26*
Madrid Ladies Open	**Ana Pelaez Trivino**	
Aramco Team Series — Bangkok	**Manon De Roey**	
Jabra Ladies Classic	**Tiia Koivisto**	
Mithra Belgian Ladies Open	**Linn Grant (2,4)**	
Ladies Italian Open	**Morgane Metraux**	
Volvo Car Scandinavian Mixed	**Linn Grant (3,5)**	
Aramco Team Series — London	**Bronte Law**	
Tipsport Czech Ladies Open	**Jana Melichova** (A)	
Amundi German Masters	**Maja Stark (2)**	
Estrella Damm Ladies Open	**Carlota Ciganda**	
Big Green Egg Open	**Anna Nordqvist**	
Amundi Evian Championship	**Brooke Henderson (1,2)**	*See chapter 8*
Trust Golf Women's Scottish Open	**Ayaka Furue**	
AIG Women's Open	**Ashleigh Buhai**	*See chapter 9*
ISPS Handa World Invitational	**Maja Stark (3)**	
Aramco Team Series — Sotogrande	**Nelly Korda**	
Skafto Open	**Linn Grant (4,6)**	
Aland 100 Ladies Open	**Anne-Charlotte Mora**	
VP Bank Swiss Ladies Open	**Liz Young**	
Lacoste Ladies Open de France	**Ines Laklalech**	
KPMG Women's Irish Open	**Klara Spilkova**	
Aramco Team Series — New York	**Lexi Thompson**	
Hero Women's Indian Open	**Olivia Cowan**	
Aramco Team Series — Jeddah	**Chiara Noja (1,2)**	
Andalucia Costa del Sol Open de Espana	**Caroline Hedwall**	

Magical Kenya Ladies Open

When Esther Henseleit won the inaugural Magical Kenya Ladies Open late in 2019 it was the German's first victory and sealed her order of merit crown. A lot had happened since then. At the second staging of the tournament on the Baobab course at Vipingo Ridge in February, the curtain-raiser for the 2022 season, Henseleit won again on the long-awaited defence of her title.

Two gritty putts at the final two holes sealed a one-stroke victory for the 23-year-old from Hamburg over Spain's Marta Sanz Barrio. They were the only two players to break par for the tournament with the wind whipping through the trees on a firm layout which made scoring tricky all week.

Sweden's Linnea Strom led for the first three days thanks to an opening 68 and middle rounds of 73-72. Henseleit was six behind after each of the first two days after going 74-73, but rallied on the weekend with 69-70 for a two-under-par total of 286. Three behind starting out on Sunday, she bogeyed the first but then surged ahead with five birdies in the next 10 holes. Strom faded with a 77 to finish third, while Sanz Barrio posted the best score of the day with a 69 built on four birdies in five holes at the start of the back nine.

After a bogey at the 13th, Henseleit was two ahead with two to play but found the pond short of the 17th green. She dropped, then pitched to 10 feet and made the putt for a bogey four. At the last, she missed the green again but chipped to six feet, again sinking the putt, this time for a par four and the victory. "In the end, it was a bit of a struggle, but I made it and I'm pretty proud of my last few holes," Henseleit said. "I was shaking over the putt on 17 and I was shaking down 18 and especially that putt. I have been struggling with the putter over the last one and a half years so it is pretty cool that I holed that one."

Vipingo Ridge (Baobab), Kilifi, Kenya — February 10-13
Par 72 (36-36); 6,487 yards — Purse: €300,000

1	**Esther Henseleit**	74	73	69	70	286	€45,000
2	**Marta Sanz Barrio**	72	76	70	69	287	27,000
3	**Linnea Strom**	68	73	72	77	290	18,000
4	Sophie Hausmann	74	71	71	75	291	13,500
5	Lee-Anne Pace	74	73	73	73	293	9,500
	Jenny Haglund	74	77	69	73	293	9,500
	Emma Grechi	70	76	71	76	293	9,500
8	Nobuhle Dlamini	73	75	75	71	294	7,050
	Johanna Gustavsson	78	73	71	72	294	7,050
	Michele Thomson	79	66	75	74	294	7,050
	Luna Sobron Galmes	75	72	68	79	294	7,050
12	Elin Arvidsson	78	75	72	70	295	5,850
	Manon De Roey	72	80	71	72	295	5,850
	Smilla Tarning Soenderby	75	70	76	74	295	5,850
	Becky Morgan	73	72	74	76	295	5,850
16	Marta Martin	77	75	73	71	296	4,950
	Christine Wolf	74	81	69	72	296	4,950
	Karoline Lund	75	72	76	73	296	4,950
	Lina Boqvist	77	73	72	74	296	4,950
	Charlotte Liautier	78	74	70	74	296	4,950
21	Olivia Cowan	77	76	73	71	297	4,170
	Diksha Dagar	75	76	72	74	297	4,170
	Rachael Goodall	75	76	71	75	297	4,170
	Tiia Koivisto	73	73	75	76	297	4,170
	Nuria Iturrioz	74	70	76	77	297	4,170
26	Laura Beveridge	79	76	73	70	298	3,350
	Stacy Lee Bregman	76	77	72	73	298	3,350
	Virginia Elena Carta	79	75	71	73	298	3,350
	Lisa Pettersson	74	72	77	75	298	3,350
	Elina Nummenpaa	72	75	76	75	298	3,350
	Lucrezia Colombotto Rosso	77	77	69	75	298	3,350

Aramco Saudi Ladies International

"I was fine," Georgia Hall was saying, "until Emily started crying and that made me cry." The first person to congratulate the winner of the third Aramco Saudi Ladies International was Emily Kristine Pedersen, who beat Hall in a playoff in 2020 to win the first edition at Royal Greens. Pedersen did not bother with the usual water spray, but both were soon shedding happy tears as they embraced on the 18th green.

There was no need for a playoff this time with Hall winning by five strokes from Sweden's Johanna Gustavsson and Czech rookie Kristyna Napoleaova, both with their best results on tour. Hall scored 69-69-68-71 for an 11-under-par total of 277. Pedersen was fourth and Carlota Ciganda fifth. American Kelly Whaley, daughter of former PGA of America president Suzy Whaley, tied for sixth in her first overseas start with a closing 63 that equalled the LET record of eight birdies in a row.

Hall's victory was remarkable for her first round effort. Out in the worst of the wind in the afternoon, with gusts up to 40mph on the banks of the Red Sea, Hall was the only player to break par from her half of the draw. She had been five under par until a double-bogey seven at the last. The 25-year-old from Bournemouth shared the lead for the first two days but went five clear on Saturday and even reigning AIG Women's Open champion Anna Nordqvist, her nearest challenger overnight, had no response when Hall birdied three of the first four holes on Sunday. Her first regular LET win followed to add to her Women's Open title in 2018, while she also won the Portland Open on the LPGA in 2020.

Hall said: "To lead all week is very special. I think the first round really was very important for me. I played incredible that round. It set me up for the rest of the week. Sometimes it's not always easy with a five-shot lead into the last day, it's a little bit more pressure on you, but I was really happy with the way I conducted myself today."

Royal Greens Golf & Country Club, King Abdullah Economic City, Saudi Arabia — March 17-20
Par 72 (36-36); 6,321 yards — Purse: $1,000,000

1	**Georgia Hall**	69	69	68	71	277	€135,547
2	**Kristyna Napoleaova**	72	66	74	70	282	67,774
	Johanna Gustavsson	71	74	67	70	282	67,774
4	Emily Kristine Pedersen	77	67	72	67	283	40,664
5	Carlota Ciganda	73	71	70	70	284	32,531
6	Kelly Whaley	79	69	74	63	285	25,302
	Stephanie Kyriacou	75	66	72	72	285	25,302
	Anna Nordqvist	70	72	69	74	285	25,302
9	Anne van Dam	71	69	73	73	286	21,688
10	Sophie Witt	69	75	75	69	288	19,880
	Angel Yin	70	75	72	71	288	19,880
	Nicole Garcia	73	71	70	74	288	19,880
13	Sofie Bringner	76	74	70	69	289	16,830
	Elia Folch	73	72	74	70	289	16,830
	Hannah Burke	73	75	70	71	289	16,830
	Chiara Noja	71	74	69	75	289	16,830
17	Gabriella Then	74	76	73	67	290	13,929
	Sanna Nuutinen	79	66	76	69	290	13,929
	Manon De Roey	76	75	69	70	290	13,929
	Olivia Cowan	78	70	71	71	290	13,929
	Whitney Hillier	74	71	72	73	290	13,929
	Elin Arvidsson	74	74	69	73	290	13,929
	Cloe Frankish	74	69	71	76	290	13,929
24	Linda Wessberg	79	69	71	72	291	11,567
	Becky Brewerton	72	72	74	73	291	11,567
	Madelene Stavnar	80	68	70	73	291	11,567
27	Rachael Goodall	77	70	76	69	292	9,895
	Hazel MacGarvie	81	68	74	69	292	9,895
	Linda Henriksson	74	71	74	73	292	9,895
	Lee-Anne Pace	76	67	75	74	292	9,895

Joburg Ladies Open

Linn Grant capitalised on her fine form on the Sunshine Ladies Tour to win on her first start as a member of the Ladies European Tour at the Joburg Ladies Open, an event co-sanctioned by both circuits for the first time. The 22-year-old Swede produced the best score of the final day to sprint to a five-stroke victory at Modderfontein.

Following two runner-up finishes in her homeland when she turned professional in the summer of 2021, Grant got her full playing rights at the Qualifying School and then headed to South Africa to prepare for the season. In her three previous events Grant had won twice, at the Dimension Data Ladies Pro-Am and the Jabra Ladies Classic and finished third in the other.

After opening with a 72, Grant scored a 69 in the second round to draw level with first-round leader Maria Hernandez. The Spaniard faded with a 73 in the final round to tie for third place with local favourite Nicole Garcia and 2020 SA Open champion Alice Hewson. Swiss left-hander Kim Metraux scored a 71 to take second place on her own but Grant, having birdied the first three holes, established a four-shot lead when she went out in 33, four under par. Grant then holed from off the green at the 13th and finished with a seventh birdie of the day at the last for a 67. There was only one other score under 70 in the final round.

"It's always nice to get a win, it feels amazing," said Grant, who finished on 11-under-par 208. "It was great to come to the Sunshine Ladies Tour before the LET season to make the most of the good weather and get some practice in. There's some scary holes here, especially on the back nine, you have to keep your shots together and there's a couple of holes you have to look out for on the front nine as well, so I tried not to do anything stupid really."

Modderfontein Golf Club, Johannesburg, South Africa
Par 73 (37-36); 6,630 yards

March 24-26
Purse: €250,000

1	**Linn Grant**	72	69	67	208	€37,500
2	**Kim Metraux**	74	68	71	213	22,500
3	**Nicole Garcia**	72	71	71	214	11,750
	Alice Hewson	72	70	72	214	11,750
	Maria Hernandez	69	72	73	214	11,750
6	Kelly Whaley	74	69	72	215	7,750
7	Stacy Lee Bregman	75	72	70	217	6,625
	Alexandra Swayne	71	72	74	217	6,625
9	Becky Brewerton	73	75	70	218	5,875
	Kristyna Napoleaova	74	74	70	218	5,875
11	Anne-Lise Caudal	77	73	69	219	4,896
	Agathe Sauzon	77	71	71	219	4,896
	Smilla Tarning Soenderby	71	75	73	219	4,896
	Liz Young	73	73	73	219	4,896
	Michele Thomson	73	72	74	219	4,896
	Isabella van Rooyen (A)	74	71	74	219	
	Noora Komulainen	72	73	74	219	4,896
18	Felicity Johnson	78	72	70	220	4,063
	Virginia Elena Carta	71	78	71	220	4,063
	Luisa Dittrich	71	77	72	220	4,063
	Emma Grechi	72	71	77	220	4,063
22	Magdalena Simmermacher	76	73	72	221	3,533
	Isabella Deilert	74	72	75	221	3,533
	Becky Morgan	74	70	77	221	3,533
25	Nobuhle Dlamini	74	75	73	222	3,031
	Manon De Roey	72	77	73	222	3,031
	Lee-Anne Pace	77	74	71	222	3,031
	Marianne Skarpnord	79	68	75	222	3,031
29	Tereza Melecka	76	73	74	223	2,329
	Charlotte Liautier	79	71	73	223	2,329
	Ivanna Samu	72	76	75	223	2,329
	Leticia Ras-Anderica	76	71	76	223	2,329
	Linda Wessberg	77	75	71	223	2,329
	Lina Boqvist	73	79	71	223	2,329

Investec SA Women's Open

Lee-Anne Pace did it again, winning the Investec SA Women's Open for a record fifth time. But Pace's 11th LET title took a while to be confirmed as she defeated Magdalena Simmermacher at the sixth playoff hole at Steenberg with the sun rapidly disappearing behind Table Mountain. Playing the par-five 18th hole at its full length produced three pars each for the two contenders so the tee was moved up by 75 yards. On the fourth extra hole Simmermacher got up and down from a bunker to match Pace's birdie, while next time around both hit superb approaches to 12 feet and both holed for eagles. But on the sixth attempt, the Argentinian, looking for her maiden LET title, found the pond in front of the green and Pace two-putted for the winning birdie.

"I can't believe it, I honestly can't believe it, I'm in shock," said Pace, the 41-year-old from the Western Cape who was able to celebrate in front of her home crowd. "I've been struggling on the greens all week. I've been hitting so many greens, and everything came together except the putter, and nothing wanted to drop, but when it really counted it did on the last hole."

Pace (71-73-74-70) and Simmermacher (68-73-77-70) tied on level par, 288, as a strong, cold wind made scoring tricky over the weekend. Simmermacher led on the first day but Becky Brewerton produced the round of the week with a bogey-free 66 on day two to lead by four strokes. With only one player breaking par in the third round, Brewerton's 74 put her four in front, while both Pace and Simmermacher languished seven strokes adrift.

The last of Brewerton's two LET wins came in 2009, the year she topped the order of merit but she had struggled with her game so much in recent years that the Welsh player had contemplated giving up. She claimed her tour card for 2022 via the Qualifying School and was the emotional favourite in the final round but a 78 meant she missed the playoff by one stroke. Pace's birdie at the 16th, and Simmermacher's at the long par-three 17th, were crucial. "Nobody likes to see what happened to Becky, it's very disappointing for her, but it's so great to see her back at the top and back playing up there where she belongs," Pace said.

Steenberg Golf Club, Cape Town, South Africa
Par 72 (36-36); 6,521 yards

March 30-April 2
Purse: €300,000

1	**Lee-Anne Pace**	71	73	74	70	288	€45,000
2	**Magdalena Simmermacher**	68	73	77	70	288	27,000
	Pace won playoff at sixth extra hole						
3	**Becky Brewerton**	71	66	74	78	289	18,000
4	Casandra Alexander	72	72	75	72	291	12,150
	Felicity Johnson	71	71	75	74	291	12,150
6	Agathe Sauzon	74	70	77	72	293	9,300
7	Linn Grant	72	72	76	74	294	7,500
	Madelene Stavnar	72	76	72	74	294	7,500
	Tiia Koivisto	73	72	74	75	294	7,500

	Emma Grechi	71	74	72	77	294	7,500
11	Becky Morgan	74	73	77	71	295	5,875
	Rosie Davies	76	70	77	72	295	5,875
	Alice Hewson	69	77	77	72	295	5,875
	Hayley Davis	77	73	73	72	295	5,875
	Leonie Harm	72	71	75	77	295	5,875
	Maiken Bing Paulsen	73	70	73	79	295	5,875
17	Paz Marfa Sans	73	76	70	77	296	5,100
18	Nobuhle Dlamini	73	77	77	70	297	4,388
	Johanna Gustavsson	70	77	78	72	297	4,388
	Olivia Mehaffey	74	75	75	73	297	4,388
	Karolin Lampert	77	71	74	75	297	4,388
	Manon De Roey	74	74	74	75	297	4,388
	Celine Herbin	72	74	75	76	297	4,388
	Cloe Frankish	74	72	75	76	297	4,388
	Rachael Taylor	74	74	73	76	297	4,388
26	Charlotte Liautier	77	73	75	73	298	3,443
	Kelly Whaley	73	72	79	74	298	3,443
	Michele Thomson	74	74	75	75	298	3,443
	Kiera Floyd (A)	73	75	72	78	298	
	Lucie Malchirand	71	74	73	80	298	3,443

Madrid Ladies Open

Playing in her first event as an LET member, but having to rely on an invitation in order to compete at the Madrid Ladies Open, Ana Pelaez Trivino put the disappointment of missing her card at the Qualifying School behind her in the best way possible — winning by six strokes in the Spanish capital at Jarama-RACE Golf Club. "I've been dreaming about this moment my entire life and now I get to live it, so I'm very happy," said the 24-year-old from Malaga.

Pelaez was third at the Open de Espana as an amateur in 2020 and 11th in the same event a year later as a professional. Now she had her status on tour confirmed in the most emphatic manner. She scored 69-67 to be two behind Tiia Koivisto's halfway lead and kept the downward trend going with a course-record 63 on Saturday, a day after Linn Grant had lowered it to 65. Pelaez rattled in nine birdies and said: "It was a great day out there. It was also my mother's birthday and I didn't have a present for her, so I guess this round works for her."

Three ahead of the field going into final round, Pelaez added a 66 for a 23-under-par total of 265. She did not drop a shot over the last three days. Two birdies in the first three holes put her six ahead and she cruised along to the delight of the local gallery, especially when she chipped in for an eagle at the 14th. "That was a moment I'll never forget," she said. "The entire crowd went crazy and I love it. I love the energy. It was unreal." While Pelaez was endeavouring to stay calm, her brother Carlos, her caddie, was fist-pumping every great shot.

Sweden's Linnea Strom, who won on the Epson Tour in America in March, took second place, half-a-dozen shots behind, with a 64, while sharing third place were amateur Cayetana Fernandez, a 17-year-old from Madrid, Slovenia's Pia Babnik, Manon De Roey, of Belgium, and American Gabriella Then, winner of the Qualifying School.

Jarama-RACE Golf Club, Madrid, Spain — May 5-8
Par 72 (36-36); 6,439 yards — Purse: €300,000

1	**Ana Pelaez Trivino**	69	67	63	66	265	€45,000
2	**Linnea Strom**	72	68	67	64	271	27,000
3	**Pia Babnik**	71	66	69	67	273	14,100
	Manon De Roey	71	69	66	67	273	14,100
	Gabriella Then	73	68	64	68	273	14,100
	Cayetana Fernandez (A)	68	67	68	70	273	
7	Linn Grant	70	65	69	70	274	9,300
8	Ines Laklalech	70	68	73	64	275	8,400
9	Olivia Mehaffey	69	71	69	67	276	7,500
10	Elin Arvidsson	70	68	70	69	277	6,900
	Maja Stark	67	73	67	70	277	6,900
	Tiia Koivisto	68	66	72	71	277	6,900
13	Carmen Alonso	68	69	71	70	278	6,150
	Lottie Woad (A)	69	70	69	70	278	
	Agathe Sauzon	67	70	65	76	278	6,150
16	Paula Martin (A)	69	69	71	70	279	
	Leonie Harm	71	67	69	72	279	5,700
18	Karolin Lampert	70	74	68	68	280	5,325
	Gabriella Cowley	70	69	69	72	280	5,325
20	Lee-Anne Pace	74	68	69	70	281	5,025
	Pasqualle Coffa	69	70	69	73	281	5,025
22	Hayley Davis	69	69	74	70	282	4,650
	Anne van Dam	71	70	71	70	282	4,650
	Lauren Taylor	69	74	67	72	282	4,650
25	Maylis Lamoure (A)	74	68	71	70	283	
	Rosie Davies	69	72	71	71	283	4,350
27	Helen Tamy Kreuzer	71	70	72	71	284	3,750
	Linda Wessberg	73	69	71	71	284	3,750
	Linette Littau Durr Holmslykke	68	73	73	70	284	3,750
	Georgina Blackman	73	71	71	69	284	3,750
	Marianne Skarpnord	73	69	70	72	284	3,750
	Marta Sanz Barrio	70	69	71	74	284	3,750
	Ursula Wikstrom	72	70	67	75	284	3,750

Aramco Team Series — Bangkok

Manon De Roey admitted she was concentrating on the team side of things in the first Aramco Team Series event of the year at Thai Country Club in Bangkok. A change for 2022 was the team event concluding after 36 holes — with Whitney Hillier, Chonlada Chayanun, a member of the host club, Krista Bakker and amateur Pattanan Amatanon winning by three shots on 31 under par — but De Roey kept the positive attitude into the final round and equalled the course record to win the individual title by three strokes. It was a maiden victory for the 30-year-old from Belgium and on the weekend that the country staged a DP World Tour event, it was a first Belgian winner on the LET for a quarter of a century that took the headlines.

"I was waiting for this for a long time, so I'm very happy," said De Roey. "I fought really hard. I have been working hard on my game and I was just trying to stay patient for the win. I was really hoping to get this win last year, so I'm really happy I have got it now."

De Roey had to come from two behind Patty Tavatanakit on the final day. The home star, winner of the Chevron Championship in 2021, led for the first two days with a 66, setting the course record, and a 69. But on the last day, in sweltering heat again, Tavatanakit struggled with four bogeys before her first birdie of the day at the 12th. She finished with a 73 to tie for third with Kylie Henry, who had four months off after fracturing her elbow in October 2021.

Rounds of 70-67 put De Roey in the final group on the last day and, after going out in 34, she took control of the title by making four birdies in six holes after the turn. The 66, the low round of the day, gave her a 13-under-par total of 203. Felicity Johnson, who was vying with De Roey for the lead earlier in the round, finished with two late bogeys to be fifth, alongside Ariya Jutanugarn and Ana Pelaez Trivino, who was fresh from winning in Madrid the previous week. Sweden's Johanna Gustavsson closed with a 68 to be second just a fortnight after finishing runner-up at the NSW Open in Australia.

Thai Country Club, Bangkok, Thailand — May 12-14
Par 72 (36-36); 6,358 yards — Purse: $1,000,000

1	**Manon De Roey**	70	67	66	203	€71,857
2	**Johanna Gustavsson**	70	68	68	206	43,114
3	**Kylie Henry**	69	70	69	208	25,150
	Patty Tavatanakit	66	69	73	208	25,150
5	Ana Pelaez Trivino	67	73	69	209	15,170
	Ariya Jutanugarn	68	70	71	209	15,170
	Felicity Johnson	69	68	72	209	15,170
8	Charley Hull	71	71	68	210	11,737
	Whitney Hillier	71	70	69	210	11,737
10	Casandra Alexander	73	70	68	211	10,539
	Magdalena Simmermacher	71	71	69	211	10,539
	Paz Marfa Sans	73	69	69	211	10,539
13	Nicole Garcia	73	71	68	212	8,922
	Lee-Anne Pace	75	68	69	212	8,922
	Moriya Jutanugarn	68	72	72	212	8,922
	Tiia Koivisto	70	69	73	212	8,922
17	Maha Haddioui	68	73	72	213	7,665
	Marianne Skarpnord	68	73	72	213	7,665
	Chonlada Chayanun	73	67	73	213	7,665
	Anne van Dam	68	71	74	213	7,665
	Catriona Matthew	73	66	74	213	7,665
22	Hannah Burke	71	73	70	214	6,587
	Liz Young	72	72	70	214	6,587
	Chiara Noja	71	71	72	214	6,587
	Sophie Witt	74	68	72	214	6,587
26	Tvesa Malik	75	72	68	215	5,868
	Virginia Elena Carta	72	71	72	215	5,868
28	Nobuhle Dlamini	75	72	69	216	5,389
	Kelly Whaley	70	69	77	216	5,389
30	Michele Thomson	77	71	69	217	4,719
	Karolin Lampert	71	76	70	217	4,719
	Noora Komulainen	75	71	71	217	4,719
	Agathe Sauzon	71	72	74	217	4,719

Jabra Ladies Classic

A playoff birdie on Evian's famous 18th hole, where Minjee Lee defeated Jeongeun Lee6 in extra time to win the 2021 Amundi Evian Championship, gave Finland's Tiia Koivisto a maiden LET victory at the Jabra Ladies Classic. The 28-year-old from Mantsala, who had friend Sanna Nuutinen caddieing for her in the playoff, had already got a four at the 18th in regulation to close with a 66 and, after earlier scores of 72 and 69, finish on six-under-par 207.

Australia's Witney Hillier, also seeking her first individual victory but having scored team success the previous week in Bangkok, had been the 36-hole leader and closed with a 69 to tie. Hillier could not birdie the par-five finishing hole in either regulation or the playoff, but on the extra hole Koivisto hit her approach into the rough on the left of the green and then chipped to six feet and holed the putt for victory.

"Sanna's one of my best friends so it was great to have her on the bag to make me more relaxed," said Koivisto, who won on the Access Series in 2020. "We talked through all the shots. I knew that if I made a good stroke on the last putt I could do it, and when it went in, it felt so good. I actually made one of my first LET starts here in Evian and now I've won it, so I just can't believe it."

Johanna Gustavsson, runner-up the previous week in Bangkok, was third alongside Leonie Harm, both three shots behind. Hillier's 71 on day two was her highest round of the week but contained a hole-in-one at the eighth hole with an eight-iron from 140 yards. It was one of three aces at the hole in the second round, with Felicity Johnson and Aditi Ashok also holing out, as had Amy Boulden on the opening day.

Evian Resort Golf Club, Evian-Les-Bains, France — May 19-21
Par 71 (35-36); 6,481 yards — Purse: €250,000

1	**Tiia Koivisto**	72	69	66	207	€37,500
2	**Whitney Hillier**	67	71	69	207	22,500
	Koivisto won playoff at first extra hole					
3	**Leonie Harm**	68	75	67	210	13,125
	Johanna Gustavsson	68	73	69	210	13,125
5	Pia Babnik	73	72	66	211	8,375
	Carmen Alonso	66	73	72	211	8,375
7	Maja Stark	72	72	68	212	6,417
	Manon De Roey	74	69	69	212	6,417
	Magdalena Simmermacher	75	66	71	212	6,417
10	Rosie Davies	69	75	69	213	5,500
	Casandra Alexander	71	71	71	213	5,500
	Lee-Anne Pace	70	69	74	213	5,500
13	Constance Fouillet (A)	74	73	67	214	
	Meghan MacLaren	72	75	67	214	4,500
	Anne-Charlotte Mora	73	73	68	214	4,500
	Maha Haddioui	72	74	68	214	4,500
	Agathe Sauzon	73	73	68	214	4,500
	Linn Grant	74	72	68	214	4,500
	Anne-Lise Caudal	73	70	71	214	4,500
20	Lydia Hall	72	75	68	215	3,607
	Aditi Ashok	71	75	69	215	3,607
	Tereza Melecka	71	74	70	215	3,607
	Caroline Hedwall	70	74	71	215	3,607
	Lily May Humphreys	73	71	71	215	3,607
	Madelene Stavnar	70	74	71	215	3,607
	Helen Tamy Kreuzer	70	72	73	215	3,607
27	Lucrezia Colombotto Rosso	76	73	67	216	2,675
	Gabriella Cowley	73	75	68	216	2,675
	Agathe Laisne	77	71	68	216	2,675
	Nicole Garcia	73	73	70	216	2,675
	Emma Grechi	72	74	70	216	2,675
	Kylie Henry	73	72	71	216	2,675
	Sophie Witt	75	69	72	216	2,675
	Billie-Jo Smith	68	74	74	216	2,675

Mithra Belgian Ladies Open

"In my practice round," Linn Grant explained, "I had one word which I thought of, which was 'attack', because you can pretty much go on every pin." Grant lived up to her word by winning the Mithra Belgian Ladies Open at Naxhelet Golf Club wire-to-wire, although in the end the 22-year-old Swede still had to hole her par putt at the last to win by one from England's Cara Gainer.

Grant went in front on the first day with a 66 to lead the field by three strokes and maintained the advantage with a 68 the next day. And she was doing little wrong in the final round, with a couple of birdies going out, before Gainer, who started four behind, began to put on intense pressure. Gainer, in her best round on tour, scored a 64 with five birdies on the front nine and then, to fully capture Grant's attention, four in the first five holes coming home.

Grant responded with birdies at the 10th and 12th holes before the lifesaver of an eagle at the 14th for the second time in the week. She dropped a shot at the 16th, only her second bogey of the week, but Gainer bogeyed the last to give Grant the one-stroke advantage. The Swede, with her second LET victory and fourth of the year worldwide, closed with a 67 for a 15-under-par total of 201. Two behind Gainer in third at 12 under were Morgane Metraux, with a 67 after being in joint-second overnight, and Maja Stark, who matched Gainer's 64.

Grant said: "I knew Cara was playing so well. I was a little scared, but I managed to hole that eagle putt and make my way back in for the win. I was checking the leaderboard all the time just making sure everything was under control, which it wasn't! It wasn't under control, but I tried my best to keep up with her. On the last hole, I knew I just had to do my own thing."

Naxhelet Golf Club, Wanze, Belgium
Par 72 (36-36); 6,304 yards

May 27-29
Purse: €200,000

1	**Linn Grant**	66	68	67	201	€30,000
2	**Cara Gainer**	71	67	64	202	18,000
3	**Maja Stark**	71	69	64	204	10,500
	Morgane Metraux	72	65	67	204	10,500
5	Moa Folke	71	70	66	207	6,700
	Luna Sobron Galmes	70	67	70	207	6,700
7	Manon De Roey	73	69	67	209	5,133
	Ines Laklalech	70	71	68	209	5,133
	Magdalena Simmermacher	71	69	69	209	5,133
10	Karoline Lund	73	71	66	210	4,500
	Gabriella Cowley	72	69	69	210	4,500
12	Emma Grechi	73	71	67	211	4,100
	Virginia Elena Carta	72	69	70	211	4,100
14	Savannah De Bock (A)	71	73	68	212	
	Becky Brewerton	73	70	69	212	3,358
	Anne-Lise Caudal	71	71	70	212	3,358
	Nuria Iturrioz	71	70	71	212	3,358
	Hayley Davis	70	71	71	212	3,358
	My Leander	71	70	71	212	3,358
	Laura Gonzalez Escallon	71	70	71	212	3,358
	Lee-Anne Pace	70	69	73	212	3,358
	Elina Nummenpaa	70	68	74	212	3,358
23	Rachael Goodall	75	71	67	213	2,590
	Alexandra Swayne	73	72	68	213	2,590
	Elia Folch	73	71	69	213	2,590
	Hazel MacGarvie	74	70	69	213	2,590
	Noemi Jimenez Martin	72	71	70	213	2,590
	Ursula Wikstrom	71	72	70	213	2,590
29	Katja Pogacar	74	72	68	214	1,968
	Lauren Taylor	72	73	69	214	1,968
	Lejan Lewthwaite	70	73	71	214	1,968
	Stacy Lee Bregman	70	71	73	214	1,968
	Whitney Hillier	69	72	73	214	1,968

Ladies Italian Open

After Swiss sisters Kim and Morgane Metraux tied for the lead on the first day of the Ladies Italian Open at Margara, they joked about ending up in a playoff two days later. Morgane, at 25 the younger of the pair by two years, did make it to overtime, while left-handed Kim finished in seventh so she was watching on with mum Valerie as Morgane holed from 20 feet for an eagle at the 18th and embraced dad Oliver, her caddie.

It was Morgane's first win on the Ladies European Tour and followed her victory on what is now the Epson Tour in America in 2021 to earn her card for the LPGA. In a break from the tour in the US, Metraux finished third in Belgium before compiling rounds of 67-70-69 here for a 10-under-par total of 206. She birdied the 15th, 16th and 17th, where her approach finished a foot away, and then saw her six-footer for a winning birdie in regulation at the 18th lip out.

But she hit a superb long approach at the same hole in the playoff. "I had a bit of adrenalin on the second shot, because I wasn't planning to hit it all the way up to the top tier," Metraux said. "As soon as it came off the face, I knew it was somewhere on the green. I had a good read from my first putt in regulation, put a good stroke on it and it went in. I couldn't have dreamt it better, to be in Italy, a country that I love. My mum's Italian, so I have a bit of a link. It couldn't be better."

Meghan MacLaren, who birdied the last three holes in regulation, and Italian amateur Alessandra Fanali both scored 67s to make the playoff and both had tap-ins for birdie in the playoff before Metraux holed for her eagle. Fanali, having just finished her college career in America, was wearing the Italian national colours, as was Carolina Melgrati, who was also in contention to be the first home winner of the title until a bogey at the 17th. She tied for fourth with South Africa's Casandra Alexander, while Lee-Anne Pace, who led by three after after holing out for an eagle at the fourth, faded to sixth place.

La Margara Golf Club, Fubine Monferrato, Alessandria, Italy
Par 72 (36-36); 6,185 yards

June 2-4
Purse: €200,000

1	**Morgane Metraux**	67	70	69	206	€30,000
2	**Alessandra Fanali (A)**	70	69	67	206	
	Meghan MacLaren	69	70	67	206	18,000
	Metraux won playoff at first extra hole					
4	Casandra Alexander	71	67	69	207	12,000
	Carolina Melgrati (A)	69	68	70	207	
6	Lee-Anne Pace	69	67	72	208	9,000
7	Kim Metraux	67	72	70	209	6,333
	Nuria Iturrioz	69	70	70	209	6,333
	Roberta Liti	70	67	72	209	6,333
10	Linnea Strom	70	75	65	210	5,000
11	Ana Pelaez Trivino	72	71	68	211	4,700
	Tiia Koivisto	71	71	69	211	4,700
13	Liz Young	71	71	70	212	4,300
	Gabriella Cowley	70	72	70	212	4,300
15	Luna Sobron Galmes	71	72	70	213	3,900
	Verena Gimmy	70	70	73	213	3,900
17	Tereza Melecka	69	76	69	214	3,500

	Carmen Alonso	70	74	70	214	3,500	25 Noora Komulainen	71	74	71	216	2,530
	Sofie Bringner	67	76	71	214	3,500	Stacy Lee Bregman	74	72	70	216	2,530
20	Anne-Charlotte Mora	70	73	72	215	3,092	Camille Chevalier	72	71	73	216	2,530
	Sarah Schober	74	72	69	215	3,092	Becky Brewerton	71	72	73	216	2,530
	Cara Gainer	74	72	69	215	3,092	Virginia Elena Carta	70	70	76	216	2,530
	Emma Cabrera Bello	74	68	73	215	3,092	Nicole Broch Estrup	73	66	77	216	2,530
	Rosie Davies	70	72	73	215	3,092						

Volvo Car Scandinavian Mixed

Linn Grant did not just make history by becoming the first woman to win on the DP World Tour, but she produced an incredible display of golf on one of the biggest stages for the Ladies European Tour. In the second year of the Volvo Car Scandinavian Mixed, following Jonathan Caldwell's victory in 2021 with Alice Hewson as the leading female competitor in third place, Grant won at Halmstad by nine strokes from 2016 Open champion Henrik Stenson and Marc Warren. The 22-year-old from Helsingborg also finished 14 strokes ahead of the second woman, Gabriella Cowley, in a tie for 15th place.

A home winner, and a rising female star to boot, delighted the huge gallery and the tournament co-hosts, Swedish legends Stenson and Annika Sorenstam. Stenson said: "There was just one player out there today and she played amazing. Every time I looked back, she was in prime position and just gave herself birdie chance one after another. There wasn't much I could do against a player like that, so very well played and congratulations to Linn."

Sorenstam played alongside Grant for the first two rounds and, after missing the cut, was watching at the 18th green as history was made. "What a performance," Sorenstam said. "This shows that we can play against each other in a fair competition. I hope people see the quality of women's golf."

Grant admitted she was more nervous playing alongside 10-time major winner Sorenstam than when she teed up for the final round already leading by two strokes from Australia's Jason Scrivener. She started with five birdies in the first six holes to burst clear of the competition. After the turn she birdied the 10th, 11th and 14th holes, with none of her eight birdie putts coming from outside 10 feet. Her precision approach play included almost holing in one at the short fourth.

A closing 64, following scores of 66-68-66, left Grant on a total of 264, 24 under par. She was the only player not to have a bogey over the weekend. "I'm speechless and I'm so happy that I'm at home just to see all the kids, my family is here and everyone that I care about is watching, so it's really nice," Grant said. "I was actually surprisingly calm on the first tee. My first day with Annika was my most scary and stressful one, so today I was able to get in the zone and just enjoy the golf." She did not know about her huge lead until she saw the leaderboard at the 13th. "I saw it was eight shots and it was very relaxing not to have to change gears, I could just continue doing what I was doing."

Grant finished tied for 18th as an amateur at the same event in 2021. She won three times in South Africa to start the year, one of them her maiden LET title, before winning in Belgium and then here for her third LET victory in six events. "I hope this victory is big. I hope it brings women more forward and it gets people's eyes on us a little bit more. It is always nice to say that you beat the guys for a week! To be Swedish and hear everyone out there cheering for you, it was amazing."

Halmstad Golf Club, Tylosand, Sweden — June 9-12
Par 72 (36-36); men 7,001 yards, women 5,929 yards — Purse: $2,000,000

1	**Linn Grant**	66	68	66	64	264	€319,717		Matthieu Pavon	65	73	68	69	275	48,522
2	**Marc Warren**	69	68	71	65	273	162,679	10 Paul Waring	72	69	68	67	276	34,855
	Henrik Stenson	70	66	67	70	273	162,679	Niklas Norgaard Moller	67	70	69	70	276	34,855
4	Santiago Tarrio	65	71	71	67	274	79,866	Sebastian Garcia Rodriguez	68	69	67	72	276	34,855
	Darius van Driel	71	69	66	68	274	79,866	13 Jacques Kruyswijk	69	70	68	70	277	29,527
	Jason Scrivener	68	64	70	72	274	79,866	Mike Lorenzo-Vera	68	66	72	71	277	29,527
7	Maximilian Kieffer	71	66	70	68	275	48,522	15 Matthew Southgate	72	69	70	67	278	25,427
	Romain Langasque	68	70	69	68	275	48,522	Alex Noren	73	67	70	68	278	25,427

	Gabriella Cowley	69	69	71	69	278	25,427
	Craig Howie	65	70	72	71	278	25,427
	Daniel Gavins	68	67	72	71	278	25,427
20	Nacho Elvira	68	68	73	70	279	21,581
	Carolina Melgrati (A)	65	69	74	71	279	
	Justin Walters	70	69	69	71	279	21,581
	Johannes Veerman	69	71	68	71	279	21,581
	Jazz Janewattananond	66	70	71	72	279	21,581
25	John Catlin	70	72	70	68	280	19,277
	Edoardo Molinari	69	70	72	69	280	19,277
	Andrew Wilson	70	71	68	71	280	19,277
	Kristoffer Broberg	66	70	70	74	280	19,277
29	Caroline Hedwall	74	68	73	66	281	17,020
	Joakim Lagergren	74	66	71	70	281	17,020
	Becky Brewerton	70	69	70	72	281	17,020
	Whitney Hillier	71	69	69	72	281	17,020
33	Dale Whitnell	72	70	70	70	282	15,328
	Ingrid Lindblad (A)	69	71	71	71	282	
	Marianne Skarpnord	73	68	70	71	282	15,328
36	Manon De Roey	67	72	73	71	283	14,481
37	Jonathan Caldwell	71	71	72	70	284	11,298
	Leonie Harm	68	74	72	70	284	11,298
	David Horsey	68	70	74	72	284	11,298
	Ricardo Gouveia	72	69	71	72	284	11,298
	Noora Komulainen	69	73	70	72	284	11,298
	Zach Murray	73	69	70	72	284	11,298
	Jack Senior	68	71	72	73	284	11,298
	Ashley Chesters	70	71	70	73	284	11,298
	Joel Sjoholm	69	73	69	73	284	11,298
	Liz Young	66	73	71	74	284	11,298
	Zander Lombard	69	69	71	75	284	11,298
	Richard McEvoy	72	68	69	75	284	11,298
	Darren Fichardt	71	70	68	75	284	11,298
	Elin Arvidsson	73	69	67	75	284	11,298
51	Marcus Kinhult	72	70	71	72	285	8,087
	Niklas Lemke	72	68	72	73	285	8,087
	Lydia Hall	71	66	72	76	285	8,087
54	Felicity Johnson	71	67	76	72	286	6,695
	Julian Suri	68	71	72	75	286	6,695
	Johanna Gustavsson	69	71	71	75	286	6,695
	Casandra Alexander	70	69	71	76	286	6,695
	Virginia Elena Carta	68	69	71	78	286	6,695
59	Karoline Lund	71	71	73	72	287	5,924
	Karolin Lampert	68	72	73	74	287	5,924
61	Julia Engstrom	68	72	76	72	288	5,454
	Charlotte Liautier	70	71	74	73	288	5,454
	Stacy Lee Bregman	72	69	73	74	288	5,454
64	Espen Kofstad	71	68	74	76	289	4,984
	Linnea Strom	71	70	71	77	289	4,984
66	Magdalena Simmermacher	70	72	68	80	290	4,702
67	Paz Marfa Sans	73	69	75	77	294	4,514
68	Leo Johansson (A)	72	69	78	76	295	
69	Rosie Davies	68	74	75	84	301	4,326

Aramco Team Series — London

From 55 feet, up the length of the 18th green at Centurion, Bronte Law faced a testing two-putt for a birdie to tie Georgia Hall. In most everyone's mind, a playoff for the individual title at the Aramco Team Series — London was the likely outcome. Except for perhaps two people, one was Law herself and the other was an alert television commentator who noted that, "however unlikely", the 27-year-old Englishwoman from Stockport had a putt to win. And in it went for the only eagle of the final round at the 18th but a second LET victory for Law.

"That's why we play this game, for moments like that, and in front of a home crowd, it doesn't really get any better," Law said. "Coming down the stretch and holing a putt like that to win — that's the epitome of the sport that we play and why we do it; why we go through all the heartache, the pain and everything is for moments like that. I had a good read on the putt but you never really say, 'Oh yeah, I knew that was going in'. I hit it, saw it tracking towards the end and it went in — so a sigh of relief at that point."

Law, who won in Dubai in 2021, came from one behind 36-hole leader Hayley Davis, who suffered a double bogey at the 12th hole as she slid out of contention. Law then had a double-bogey seven at the next hole, tangling with the long rough, but responded magnificently with birdies at the 15th and 16th, a par at the short 17th and then the closing eagle. She scored 68-71-71 for a nine-under-par total of 210.

After two days of high temperatures, the final round was played in distinctly chilly conditions, with Scandinavian Mixed winner Linn Grant birdieing six of the last seven holes to get to seven under with a 69, before Hall birdied the last for a 71 and eight under. The major champion could only laugh when Law's putt went in and give the winner a long congratulatory hug.

Nicole Garcia won a playoff for the 36-hole team title as she defeated opposing captain Ursula Wikstrom at the first extra hole to share the win with Kelly Whaley, Madelene Stavnar and amateur Mia Baker.

Centurion Club, Hemel Hempstead, St Albans, Hertfordshire, England — June16-18
Par 73 (37-36); 6,372 yards — Purse: $1,000,000

1	**Bronte Law**	68	71	71	210	€71,588
2	**Georgia Hall**	67	73	71	211	42,953
3	**Linn Grant**	72	71	69	212	28,635
4	Charley Hull	69	75	69	213	21,476
5	Whitney Hillier	70	73	72	215	17,181
6	Johanna Gustavsson	69	78	69	216	13,363
	Becky Brewerton	74	70	72	216	13,363
	Nicole Garcia	70	71	75	216	13,363
9	Sophie Witt	74	72	71	217	10,738
	Anne van Dam	69	73	75	217	10,738
	Caroline Hedwall	70	70	77	217	10,738
	Hayley Davis	69	68	80	217	10,738
13	Ana Pelaez Trivino	70	74	74	218	9,068
	Pia Babnik	74	68	76	218	9,068
	Maria Hernandez	75	66	77	218	9,068
16	Tereza Melecka	75	70	74	219	8,352
17	Emma Grechi	75	75	70	220	7,617
	Virginia Elena Carta	74	76	70	220	7,617
	Madelene Stavnar	72	73	75	220	7,617
	Manon De Roey	74	71	75	220	7,617
	Sofie Bringner	66	79	75	220	7,617
22	Leonie Harm	73	75	73	221	6,586
	Thalia Martin	71	76	74	221	6,586
	Michele Thomson	69	75	77	221	6,586
25	Jessica Karlsson	72	78	72	222	5,400
	Gabriella Cowley	70	76	76	222	5,400
	Nuria Iturrioz	74	72	76	222	5,400
	Chloe Williams	72	74	76	222	5,400
	Celine Herbin	71	74	77	222	5,400
	Ursula Wikstrom	72	73	77	222	5,400
	Harang Lee	71	73	78	222	5,400

Tipsport Czech Ladies Open

Having just graduated from college in America, Jana Melichova was intending to go to the LET Qualifying School at the end of the year. Winning the Tipsport Czech Ladies Open as an amateur gave her a short cut and the 24-year-old turned professional in time to join the tour and play in Germany the following week.

Melichova became only the second Czech player to win on the circuit and by co-incidence she was playing in the final round at Royal Beroun with the first, Klara Spilkova, who won in Morocco in 2017. The pair, both scoring 68-65, started one behind the joint leaders, Nicole Broch Estrup (65-67), whose one LET title came in 2015, and another amateur, Austrian amateur Emma Spitz (66-66). It was Melichova who got off to the best start, with five birdies in the first 10 holes. Each was celebrated with a strawberry from her father's garden. Three bogeys in a row from the 12th might have derailed her title hopes but the support of the home crowd kept her going.

The decisive birdie came at the 17th and although Spilkova birdied the last two holes, Melichova finished one ahead after a 69 for a 14-under-par total of 202. Spilkova closed with a 70, while Broch Estrup had a 71 to tie for second and Spitz dropped into a tie for sixth place.

"It's a dream come true," Melichova said. "I always planned to play LET and I always wanted to win a title and I succeeded today, I'm incredibly happy. I was nervous, but I think I handled that stress really well. I was really happy with my game and everything was perfect. Even the three bogeys in a row didn't get me down because I had people here and they were cheering for me, so I just wanted to make more birdies."

Spilkova said: "It's an amazing thing Jana has done today, she should enjoy the moment because this doesn't happen very often. For her to be in a situation like this is very magical."

Royal Beroun Golf Club, Beroun, Czech Republic — June 24-26
Par 72 (36-36); 6,225 yards — Purse: €200,000

1	**Jana Melichova** (A)	68	65	69	202	
2	**Klara Spilkova**	68	65	70	203	€24,000
	Nicole Broch Estrup	65	67	71	203	24,000
4	Johanna Gustavsson	68	70	66	204	12,000
5	Laura Gomez Ruiz	71	69	65	205	9,000
6	Luna Sobron Galmes	68	69	69	206	7,200
	Emma Spitz (A)	66	66	74	206	
8	Chloe Williams	73	70	64	207	6,200
9	Elena Hualde	71	69	68	208	5,000
	Ursula Wikstrom	72	68	68	208	5,000
	Kim Metraux	70	70	68	208	5,000
	Lydia Hall	71	69	68	208	5,000
13	Georgia Iziemgbe Oboh	71	70	68	209	4,300
	Sara Kouskova	68	71	70	209	4,300
	Patricie Mackova (A)	72	66	71	209	
16	Lauren Taylor	72	70	68	210	3,488
	Denisa Vodickova (A)	71	71	68	210	
	Maria Hernandez	75	66	69	210	3,488
	Katja Pogacar	72	70	68	210	3,488
	Magdalena Simmermacher	72	69	69	210	3,488

	Ines Laklalech	72	71	67	210	3,488		Celine Herbin	71 73 67	211	2,810
	Laura Beveridge	69	71	70	210	3,488	30	Sophie Witt	72 70 70	212	2,310
	Tereza Melecka	71	69	70	210	3,488		Gabriella Cowley	71 72 69	212	2,310
	Anna Backman (A)	70	74	66	210			Becky Brewerton	70 71 71	212	2,310
	Paz Marfa Sans	68	69	73	210	3,488		Thalia Martin	70 73 69	212	2,310
26	Meghan MacLaren	69	73	69	211	2,810		Krista Bakker	69 71 72	212	2,310
	Casandra Alexander	72	70	69	211	2,810		Madelene Stavnar	72 68 72	212	2,310
	Harang Lee	72	69	70	211	2,810					

Amundi German Masters

After two weeks off, Maja Stark was back to her ruthless best, striking at the death to snatch the Amundi German Masters from compatriot Jessica Karlsson over the final two holes. Three behind on the 71st tee, Stark finished with two birdies, while Karlsson bogeyed each time. Their fellow Swedes both congratulated the winner and commiserated with a tearful Karlsson, who had led ever since a 63 on the first day. There was a big hug for Stark from her friend Linn Grant, even though Stark had displaced her at the top of the Race to Costa del Sol.

Stark and Grant played together on the first two days and both scored 68-68 to lie in third place, five behind Karlsson. The 29-year-old leader had been three ahead after round one, then four in front of Hayley Davis when the second round was completed on Saturday morning. Stark made a move in the third round with a 67 to lie one behind Karlsson (71).

Still looking for her first win, Karlsson, who missed the first part of the season suffering from prolonged fatigue following a bout of Covid in January, birdied the first hole on Sunday and stayed ahead until the denouement. She missed the green at the short 17th and could not get up and down while Stark, who had just three-putted the 16th, made a 12-footer for a two.

At the last, Karlsson leaked her drive into the trees on the right and could only chip out sideways, setting up another bogey when she missed from 15 feet. By then Stark had hit a brilliant second shot that landed two feet behind the hole and spun back to the lip of the cup. A 70 gave her a 15-under-par total of 273 at Seddiner See, while Karlsson's 72 left her in a tie for second with the leading German, Leonie Harm, who posted a bogey-free 68.

"I was so nervous on 18 because I thought I had no chance of winning it after I messed up on 16. I thought, 'What am I doing?' Finally, I made a putt on 17," said Stark after her second win of the season and fourth in all. "I could barely feel my hands on the 18th tee box, but I thought there was nothing to lose, really. I'm happy it's over."

Golf & Country Club Seddiner See, Berlin, Germany — June 30-July 3
Par 72 (36-36); 6,537 yards — Purse: €300,000

1	**Maja Stark**	68	68	67	70	273	€45,000		Lina Boqvist	72	71	69	71	283	4,865
2	**Leonie Harm**	66	71	69	68	274	22,500		Cara Gainer	68	76	67	72	283	4,865
	Jessica Karlsson	63	68	71	72	274	22,500		Karoline Lund	69	74	68	72	283	4,865
4	Polly Mack	69	69	70	67	275	10,500		Diksha Dagar	72	73	65	73	283	4,865
	Linn Grant	68	68	71	68	275	10,500		Carmen Alonso	71	68	67	77	283	4,865
	Olivia Cowan	68	71	68	68	275	10,500	22	Sarah Schober	71	74	68	71	284	3,573
	Laura Beveridge	69	71	67	68	275	10,500		Alice Hewson	69	69	75	71	284	3,573
8	Esther Henseleit	66	73	70	67	276	7,350		Isi Gabsa	68	73	71	72	284	3,573
	Ines Laklalech	68	74	66	68	276	7,350		Sara Kouskova	69	75	70	70	284	3,573
10	Klara Spilkova	66	74	67	72	279	6,900		Liz Young	70	72	69	73	284	3,573
11	Johanna Gustavsson	71	73	66	71	281	6,450		Mireia Prat	68	72	70	74	284	3,573
	Julia Engstrom	72	71	67	71	281	6,450		Hannah Burke	70	71	69	74	284	3,573
13	Lee-Anne Pace	70	73	70	69	282	5,700		Tereza Melecka	74	71	71	68	284	3,573
	Hayley Davis	68	67	74	73	282	5,700		Meghan MacLaren	74	72	71	67	284	3,573
	Linda Wessberg	70	67	72	73	282	5,700		Marta Perez	72	70	67	75	284	3,573
16	Lydia Hall	71	70	71	71	283	4,865								

Estrella Damm Ladies Open

It was a wire-to-wire victory but not without drama on the back nine of the final round. Carlota Ciganda led by four overnight but was trailing with eight holes to play. Level par for the day through 15 holes, the Spaniard responded to the calls of "vamos" that echoed around Terramar with a spell of the highest quality. She eagled the 16th with a long iron to 15 feet and then almost holed her tee shot at the par-three 17th. A bogey at the last did not matter as Ciganda won the Estrella Damm Ladies Open for the second time. She won it for the first time in 2019, with the 32-year-old from Pamplona also winning the Open de Espana in 2021.

"I love playing here in Spain and winning here is always special," Ciganda said. "My family is here and I have lots of support. There is always extra motivation to win here. Winning is never easy. It was a little shaky, I just hit a bad tee shot on nine and that cost me a double. But I'm very happy with how I handled myself. That eagle on 16 was amazing and then a birdie on the next one. I looked at the leaderboard on 11 and I just thought, 'If you do what you need to do, you are going to be fine'."

Ciganda shared the first-round lead on 65 with Jessica Karlsson, who had agonisingly missed out the previous week in Germany. But while the Swede then fell away, Ciganda went on to lead by five at halfway and then four after 54 holes with scores of 67-68. She closed with a 70 for an 18-under-par total of 270. Scotland's Laura Beveridge, following her fourth place at the German Masters, closed with a bogey-free 66 to take second place, two behind, while Elin Arvidsson, with a 64, and Magdalena Simmermacher (68) tied for third. It was Simmermacher who took the lead with six birdies in the first 11 holes, including four in a row from the eighth, but the player from Argentina then three-putted the 12th and bogeyed the 14th as Ciganda took control again.

Club de Golf Terramar, Sitges, Spain — July 7-10
Par 72 (37-35); 6,399 yards — Purse: €300,000

1	**Carlota Ciganda**	65	67	68	70	270	€45,000
2	**Laura Beveridge**	69	71	66	66	272	27,000
3	**Elin Arvidsson**	68	70	71	64	273	15,750
	Magdalena Simmermacher	69	68	68	68	273	15,750
5	Maja Stark	70	67	67	71	275	10,800
6	Manon De Roey	71	69	69	68	277	9,300
7	Anne-Lise Caudal	68	71	70	69	278	7,500
	Lydia Hall	70	70	69	69	278	7,500
	Ana Pelaez Trivino	70	70	69	69	278	7,500
	Nuria Iturrioz	73	66	69	70	278	7,500
11	Jessica Karlsson	65	74	69	71	279	6,600
12	Hazel MacGarvie	76	69	68	67	280	6,000
	Michele Thomson	68	69	75	68	280	6,000
	Pia Babnik	69	74	69	68	280	6,000
15	Sarah Kemp	69	75	71	67	282	5,100
	Hannah Burke	72	68	73	69	282	5,100
	Emma Grechi	69	72	71	70	282	5,100
	Liz Young	72	73	66	71	282	5,100
	Alice Hewson	68	73	69	72	282	5,100
20	Camille Chevalier	72	73	68	70	283	4,560
	Sofie Bringner	71	69	64	79	283	4,560
22	Emily Kristine Pedersen	73	73	68	70	284	4,170
	Agathe Laisne	71	72	73	68	284	4,170
	Miriam Ayora [(A)]	69	73	72	70	284	
	Rosie Davies	72	71	69	72	284	4,170
26	Caroline Hedwall	71	70	73	71	285	3,795
	Teresa Toscano	70	72	71	72	285	3,795
28	Linda Henriksson	69	71	72	74	286	3,495
	Lee-Anne Pace	74	68	70	74	286	3,495
30	Alexandra Swayne	71	74	69	73	287	2,880
	Agathe Sauzon	73	69	74	71	287	2,880
	Marta Martin	72	69	75	71	287	2,880
	Marianne Skarpnord	73	71	69	74	287	2,880
	Carmen Alonso	70	72	71	74	287	2,880
	Moa Folke	68	75	74	70	287	2,880
	Lauren Taylor	71	71	70	75	287	2,880

Big Green Egg Open

After taking a two-week break at home in Sweden to catch up with family and friends, Anna Nordqvist started a four-tournament run that included two major championships in the perfect manner. The 35-year-old from Eskilstuna won the Big Green Egg Open at Rosendaelsche by a stroke over Sarah Schober.

Understandably, Nordqvist started the week in the Netherlands slowly with 72-70 to be six strokes off the halfway lead of Whitney Hillier. But on a windy Saturday, the three-time major champion was back to her best, posting a 67 with birdies at each of the last three holes to go into the lead by one stroke from Austria's Schober and Indian Vani Kapoor. The only other score under 70 in the third round was a 69 from New Zealand's Momoka Kobori.

Sunday was another difficult day and Nordqvist, exchanging birdies and bogeys, was twice caught on the back nine but a fine pitch shot for a birdie at the 17th was the difference. Both Nordqvist, for a seven-under-par total of 281, and Schober scored 72s, level par. Kapoor, playing in the final group for the first time, had a 73 to fall into a tie for third place with Germany's Sophie Witt, who returned a best-of-the-day 67, and Spain's Nuria Iturrioz.

"It was a bit of a battle out there today," Nordqvist, the world number 22, said. "I played really well in the beginning then lost focus and rhythm around the turn. But I'm proud of myself for fighting through. The beginning of this week was a bit of a struggle, then I played so well yesterday in a bit of a breeze. I've done a lot of good things this week and it's nice to be back competing again."

This victory was Nordqvist's first at a regular LET event. The 2009 Rookie of the Year had previously twice won the European Nations Cup partnering Sophie Gustafson, followed by two majors, the 2017 Evian and the 2021 AIG Women's Open.

Rosendaelsche Golf Club, Arnhem, Netherlands — July 14-17
Par 72 (36-36); 6,556 yards — Purse: €250,000

1	**Anna Nordqvist**	72	70	67	72	281	€37,500
2	**Sarah Schober**	67	70	73	72	282	22,500
3	**Sophie Witt**	74	71	71	67	283	11,750
	Nuria Iturrioz	71	69	71	72	283	11,750
	Vani Kapoor	69	70	71	73	283	11,750
6	Momoka Kobori	73	70	69	72	284	7,750
7	Whitney Hillier	68	68	76	73	285	7,000
8	Zhen Bontan	77	71	70	68	286	5,750
	Anais Meyssonnier	69	72	76	69	286	5,750
	Virginia Elena Carta	76	71	70	69	286	5,750
	Lily May Humphreys	70	74	70	72	286	5,750
	Liz Young	67	74	71	74	286	5,750
13	Alice Hewson	70	77	70	70	287	4,875
	Anne-Charlotte Mora	70	74	71	72	287	4,875
15	Helen Tamy Kreuzer	74	69	73	72	288	4,438
	Hazel MacGarvie	69	76	71	72	288	4,438
17	Verena Gimmy	73	75	73	68	289	3,990
	Hayley Davis	72	71	75	71	289	3,990
	Hannah Burke	71	73	73	72	289	3,990
	Agathe Laisne	74	70	72	73	289	3,990
	Diksha Dagar	68	71	73	77	289	3,990
	Alexandra Forsterling (A)	71	69	72	77	289	
23	Rachael Goodall	72	71	76	71	290	3,325
	Elia Folch	74	71	74	71	290	3,325
	Jane Turner	74	74	71	71	290	3,325
	Ines Laklalech	79	69	71	71	290	3,325
	Mayka Hoogeboom (A)	72	68	77	73	290	
	Lejan Lewthwaite	71	73	73	73	290	3,325
29	Olafia Kristinsdottir	70	78	71	72	291	2,888
	Kristyna Napoleaova	73	75	70	73	291	2,888

Trust Golf Women's Scottish Open

Ayaka Furue had a secret weapon when she made her debut in the Trust Golf Women's Scottish Open. Glaswegian caddie Michael Scott helped guide the 22-year-old from Japan around the testing Dundonald Links. "He gave me a lot of good advice," Furue said. "He was very helpful with how much the ball would roll after it landed, and with the wind direction and how the wind affects play. Right after I was notified that I was the winner, I was very grateful that Mike got to experience it in his home country."

If the navigator was good, the pilot was even better. Furue came from four strokes behind Lydia Ko and Celine Boutier with a course-record 62 to set a new tournament record of 21 under par with a total of 267. She won by three shots from Boutier, with Ko dropping into a share of fifth place. The New Zealander, one behind Hye-Jin Choi on the first day, took the halfway lead with twin 65s, then played the weekend in 71-71. Boutier, who also opened with a 65, went 69-67-69 the rest of the way. The Frenchwoman went out in 33 on Sunday but came home in level par as Furue roared past her. "When someone just has their day, you can't do anything about it really," said Boutier.

Following scores of 68-69-69, the diminutive Furue, a rookie on the LPGA after seven wins in Japan, birdied her first hole on Sunday, then went on a roll with six in a row from the sixth. There were twos at the sixth and the 11th, where she hit her tee shot at the 113-yarder to a foot, and she also hit her approach stiff at the eighth. Her approaches from around 100 yards were pin-point accurate and her putting was remorseless. There was a par saved at the 13th, then she holed a pair of 20-footers at the 15th and 17th holes, before hitting her approach at the last to five feet for her 10th birdie of the day.

"I was four shots back," Furue said. "I thought it would be difficult to catch the top players. But I'm very happy I played good golf and I was able to come out as a winner. I had the right mindset. I thought I had to go low. I hit good shots. All around my game was good, and the birdie putts I wanted to make and had to make, I was able to make. My best part was I was very straight this week. I putted well today and all week."

Dundonald Links, Gailes, Ayrshire, Scotland — July 28-31
Par 72 (36-36); 6,494 yards — Purse: $200,000

1	**Ayaka Furue**	69	68	68	62	267	€294,188
2	**Celine Boutier**	65	69	67	69	270	176,513
3	**Hyo Joo Kim**	67	68	70	66	271	102,966
	Cheyenne Knight	69	68	67	67	271	102,966
5	Alison Lee	67	68	71	66	272	65,702
	Lydia Ko	65	65	71	71	272	65,702
7	Nasa Hataoka	68	69	68	68	273	54,915
8	Wichanee Meechai	69	65	70	70	274	47,070
	Lilia Vu	65	67	71	71	274	47,070
	Maude-Aimee Leblanc	67	69	66	72	274	47,070
11	Hye-Jin Choi	64	71	71	69	275	41,186
	In Gee Chun	70	67	69	69	275	41,186
	Narin An	66	70	69	70	275	41,186
14	Madelene Sagstrom	70	69	73	64	276	37,264
15	Ryann O'Toole	68	71	73	65	277	34,322
	Xiyu Lin	69	72	66	70	277	34,322
	Leonie Harm	67	68	67	75	277	34,322
18	Minjee Lee	67	72	71	68	278	29,190
	Bronte Law	68	71	70	69	278	29,190
	Charley Hull	70	71	68	69	278	29,190
	Gaby Lopez	69	71	69	69	278	29,190
	Georgia Hall	66	70	71	71	278	29,190
	Eun-Hee Ji	69	64	70	75	278	29,190
24	Yuka Saso	70	71	72	66	279	22,162
	Moriya Jutanugarn	69	74	69	67	279	22,162
	Megan Khang	72	68	70	69	279	22,162
	Sei Young Kim	69	71	70	69	279	22,162
	Chanettee Wannasaen	71	67	70	71	279	22,162
29	Chella Choi	71	70	70	69	280	18,044
	Patty Tavatanakit	76	66	67	71	280	18,044
31	Ally Ewing	69	70	74	68	281	15,494
	Amy Yang	70	68	72	71	281	15,494
	Jasmine Suwannapura	68	68	72	73	281	15,494
34	Jennifer Kupcho	72	68	74	68	282	12,748
	Perrine Delacour	73	69	69	71	282	12,748
	Hannah Green	72	67	72	71	282	12,748
	Gemma Dryburgh	69	73	66	74	282	12,748
38	Stephanie Meadow	72	71	70	70	283	10,787
	Anna Nordqvist	70	73	69	71	283	10,787
	Lauren Stephenson	70	72	70	71	283	10,787
41	Lindsey Weaver-Wright	69	69	77	69	284	9,778
	Carmen Alonso	74	67	72	71	284	9,778
	Mina Harigae	72	67	74	71	284	9,778
	Esther Henseleit	72	69	72	71	284	9,778
	Andrea Lee	67	69	74	74	284	9,778
	Sanna Nuutinen	71	71	68	74	284	9,778
	A Lim Kim	70	71	68	75	284	9,778
48	Pia Babnik	71	71	73	70	285	8,139
	Johanna Gustavsson	77	64	73	71	285	8,139
	Tiia Koivisto	72	68	74	71	285	8,139
	Sarah Schober	74	69	69	73	285	8,139
	Pannarat Thanapolboonyaras	70	73	69	73	285	8,139
	Haeji Kang	72	68	71	74	285	8,139
	Jeongeun Lee6	70	68	72	75	285	8,139
	Pauline Roussin	67	69	73	76	285	8,139
56	Sophia Popov	70	71	74	71	286	6,766
	Allisen Corpuz	71	71	72	72	286	6,766
	Marina Alex	72	70	72	72	286	6,766
	Emma Grechi	73	69	69	75	286	6,766
	Jennifer Chang	74	68	69	75	286	6,766
	Anne van Dam	70	69	72	75	286	6,766
62	Ariya Jutanugarn	74	69	74	70	287	5,884
	Becky Brewerton	71	72	73	71	287	5,884
	Wei Ling Hsu	72	67	75	73	287	5,884
65	Emily Kristine Pedersen	69	68	81	70	288	5,197
	Pornanong Phatlum	69	72	76	71	288	5,197
	Ana Pelaez Trivino	74	67	75	72	288	5,197
	Jessica Karlsson	71	70	72	75	288	5,197
69	Kylie Henry	71	71	75	72	289	4,609
	Kelly Tan	72	69	75	73	289	4,609
71	Morgane Metraux	74	67	77	73	291	4,217
	Jin Young Ko	70	71	74	76	291	4,217
73	Maria Hernandez	71	71	78	74	294	3,923
74	Arpichaya Yubol	72	71	75	77	295	3,628
	Chloe Williams	76	66	76	77	295	3,628

ISPS Handa World Invitational

For three days Amanda Doherty led the ISPS Handa World Invitational, but while Ewen Ferguson held on to win wire-to-wire in the concurrent men's event, Doherty could not. That was not down to her so much as another astonishing final-round charge two weeks after Ayaka Furue's at the Scottish Open. This time it was Maja Stark, who returned a course-record 63 at Galgorm Castle to win by five strokes. It was Stark's fifth LET win and third of the season after taking the titles at the NSW Open and the German Masters. The co-sanctioned event also gave the 22-year-old Swede her first LPGA victory and she immediately accepted membership, grateful at being able to bypass Q-Series. "I hate qualifying and going to Q-Series, it's great that I don't have to do that again," Stark said after posting the 100th win by a Swedish player on the LPGA.

Doherty opened with twin 67s, a six-under effort at Galgorm, followed by a five-under round at

Massereene, the second venue. She had also scored a 67 in her last round at Evian. In between she had narrowly missed getting into the Scottish Open and failed to Monday qualify for the AIG Women's Open, so she played Gullane and took a non-playing trip with her mother to St Andrews. On Saturday at Galgorm, the 24-year-old American, a rookie graduate of the Epson Tour, scored 72 but still led by one from Georgia Hall and Peiyun Chien. A closing 74 dropped her into eighth place.

Stark, with former Swedish star Sophie Gustafson as her caddie, was going in the opposite direction. After opening 69-70-69, the Swede quickly made up her two-shot overnight deficit with birdies at the first and third, and went out in six under. Three birdies in a row from the 12th put her well clear of everyone else and a 10th birdie arrived at the 17th. At the last she found the water but still saved par for the 63 and a 20-under-par total of 271. America's Allisen Corpuz took second place with a 68, followed by Hall and then Stark's friend, and rival, Linn Grant in fourth.

Explaining she played the course in three-hole chunks, Stark said: "I tried to not watch the leaderboards. I usually do, but just thought it's not going to help me. Then I caught a glimpse of one on 13 and saw I was leading, but it was still pretty tight at the top, so I tried to not look. Then I walked up on 17 green, and I saw that I was leading by five and thought, whoa, this is nice."

Galgorm Castle Golf Club, Ballymena, Northern Ireland — August 11-14
Par 73 (37-36); 6,621 yards — Purse: $1,500,000
Massereene Golf Club (R1&2) par 72 (36-36); 6,641 yards

1	**Maja Stark**	69	70	69	63	271	€218,105
2	**Allisen Corpuz**	71	67	70	68	276	148,912
3	**Georgia Hall**	68	69	70	70	277	108,025
4	Linn Grant	70	69	70	69	278	68,620
	Emily Kristine Pedersen	67	68	73	70	278	68,620
	Peiyun Chien	70	67	70	71	278	68,620
7	Liz Young	70	73	67	69	279	46,064
8	Lauren Stephenson	70	69	75	66	280	38,319
	Amanda Doherty	67	67	72	74	280	38,319
10	Leona Maguire	68	69	76	68	281	33,019
11	Pornanong Phatlum	73	68	73	68	282	26,920
	Jennifer Chang	74	72	67	69	282	26,920
	Daniela Darquea	70	72	70	70	282	26,920
	Olivia Cowan	75	67	73	67	282	26,920
	Gemma Dryburgh	70	69	72	71	282	26,920
16	Lauren Coughlin	67	68	76	72	283	21,768
	Lee-Anne Pace	68	72	70	73	283	21,768
18	A Lim Kim	72	71	70	71	284	19,119
	Meghan MacLaren	70	72	72	70	284	19,119
	Cara Gainer	69	67	75	73	284	19,119
	Karis Davidson	71	71	69	73	284	19,119
22	Mi Hyang Lee	72	69	72	72	285	17,121
	Pauline Roussin	75	71	67	72	285	17,121
24	Wichanee Meechai	74	70	71	71	286	15,572
	Haylee Harford	72	69	74	71	286	15,572
	Alice Hewson	71	71	69	75	286	15,572
27	Allison Emrey	71	69	74	73	287	13,595
	Stephanie Kyriacou	71	75	69	72	287	13,595
	Janie Jackson	68	73	75	71	287	13,595
	Lucy Li	72	72	73	70	287	13,595
31	Aditi Ashok	73	73	71	71	288	12,066
	Nicole Broch Estrup	71	73	73	71	288	12,066
33	Linnea Johansson	71	74	72	72	289	11,332
34	Becky Morgan	73	70	72	75	290	10,639
	Kylie Henry	72	73	71	74	290	10,639
36	Manon De Roey	69	73	73	76	291	9,824
	Nuria Iturrioz	72	72	72	75	291	9,824
38	Kristen Gillman	70	75	72	75	292	9,009
	Kaitlyn Papp	69	75	73	75	292	9,009

Aramco Team Series — Sotogrande

It took until August for Nelly Korda, who won five times in 2021 including her Olympic gold medal, to hoist her first trophy of 2022 and it came in fairly unlikely circumstances given the former world number one was 10 strokes behind her sister Jessica following a bogey at the second hole of the final round. Elder sister Jess, with birdies at the first two holes, led by seven at that stage — at one point in the week she had been eight ahead of the field — yet by the end of the round Nelly won by three strokes from Jess, as well as Ana Pelaez Trivino and Pauline Roussin.

It was a crazy turnaround. For two days, Jess Korda had held sway. She equalled the lowest round ever on the LET with a 61 on the first day that contained three eagles, something she had never achieved before. "For the last month and change, I think I haven't really been converting any putts and the floodgates opened today and, hopefully, they can continue tomorrow and that's the beauty of golf." She led by five strokes and her form did continue the next day as she added a 68 — the best of the day was a 67 — to lead by six in the individual and help her team, including Czech Tereza Melecka, Finland's Noora Komulainen and amateur Malcolm Borwick, to victory in the team event at 33 under par. It was Korda's second team win in the series after New York in 2021.

But on the final day it all started to unravel with back-to-back bogeys at the fourth and fifth holes. Her putting faltered and then so did her long game. At the short 17th, she turned her back as her tee shot headed for the water. A double bogey led to a 77. Meanwhile, playing partner Nelly only started to make birdies from the seventh but then could not stop, with seven in 10 holes. She even bogeyed the last but was then too far ahead as scores of 67-69-67 gave her a 13-under-par total of 203. It was her second LET title after winning the Open de France in 2019 and came in her seventh start since missing much of the early season due to a blood clot in her left arm.

There were mixed emotions, however. "I'm super excited to win," Nelly said. "I haven't won this year, so it feels nice to get a win under my belt, but I'm also very sad as it wasn't the day Jess was expecting. I guess we were hoping for a bit more of a battle going down the stretch, but it's golf and that sometimes happens."

La Reserva Club de Sotogrande, Sotogrande, Andalucia, Spain — August 18-20
Par 72 (36-36); 6,291 yards — Purse: $1,000,000

1	**Nelly Korda**	67	69	67	203	€73,955
2	**Ana Pelaez Trivino**	68	69	69	206	32,047
	Pauline Roussin	67	68	71	206	32,047
	Jessica Korda	61	68	77	206	32,047
5	Emma Grechi	73	67	67	207	16,517
	Pia Babnik	66	73	68	207	16,517
7	Alison Lee	72	68	68	208	12,326
	Anne van Dam	69	71	68	208	12,326
	Manon De Roey	66	72	70	208	12,326
	Linn Grant	69	69	70	208	12,326
11	Matilda Castren	75	71	63	209	10,847
12	Bronte Law	70	72	68	210	10,354
13	Lydia Hall	72	71	68	211	9,183
	Lee-Anne Pace	72	70	69	211	9,183
	Carmen Alonso	69	72	70	211	9,183
	Alice Hewson	71	70	70	211	9,183
17	Becky Morgan	73	69	70	212	8,258
	Marianne Skarpnord	68	73	71	212	8,258
19	Lina Boqvist	75	71	67	213	7,609
	Nanna Koerstz Madsen	70	73	70	213	7,609
	Maria Fassi	69	71	73	213	7,609
22	Anna Nordqvist	73	74	67	214	6,132
	Sophie Witt	72	75	67	214	6,132
	Leonie Harm	68	78	68	214	6,132
	Maria Hernandez	72	73	69	214	6,132
	Chloe Williams	72	73	69	214	6,132
	Lindsey Weaver-Wright	72	71	71	214	6,132
	Anne-Lise Caudal	70	70	74	214	6,132
	Johanna Gustavsson	72	67	75	214	6,132
30	Nicole Garcia	73	75	67	215	4,429
	Tiia Koivisto	72	74	69	215	4,429
	Kim Metraux	71	74	70	215	4,429
	Chiara Noja	72	71	72	215	4,429
	Ursula Wikstrom	73	69	73	215	4,429
	Virginia Elena Carta	71	69	75	215	4,429

Skafto Open

Returning to the Skafto Open on the west coast of Sweden, where they made their LET debuts a year earlier, Maja Stark and Linn Grant had collected a combined eight titles. By the end of the week, Grant had claimed her fourth victory of the season but Stark still led the Race to Costa del Sol. It was also Grant's second win in her homeland after her historic Scandinavian Mixed triumph against the men's DP World Tour.

Grant, a runner-up for the last two years (it was a local tour event in 2020), showed her class by turning an up-and-down Sunday into a ruthless finish with birdies at the last two holes to win by one from compatriot Lisa Pettersson. After an opening 67 at the par-69 layout, Grant posted a bogey-free 62 on Saturday to share the lead with Spain's Ana Pelaez Trivino. By the turn in the final round, she was ahead by two strokes, but three putts at the 11th, for a double bogey, and at the 15th, for her second bogey of the day, meant the 23-year-old from Helsingborg arrived at the 17th one behind the clubhouse lead.

No matter, she hit her tee shot at the par three to a couple of feet and then nearly drove the green at the par-four 18th, getting up and down from a bunker for a 68 and a 10-under-par total of 197. Pettersson, who had recently decided to concentrate solely on the LET rather than splitting her time with the Epson Tour in America, had opened with a 63 and closed with a 66, setting the target Grant needed to vault over. Stark, meanwhile, closed with a 65 to join a five-way tie for third place.

"It was exhausting, it was a rollercoaster today," said Grant. "I felt I started off a bit shaky. I missed some birdies on the par fives, but then got myself on a good setup after nine. My short game was both really good and really bad today, I managed to hit the bad ones first, then saved the good ones for the end."

Skafto Golf Club, Skafto, Sweden
Par 69 (37-32); 5,226 yards

August 26-28
Purse: €250,000

1	**Linn Grant**	67	62	68	197	€37,500
2	**Lisa Pettersson**	63	69	66	198	22,500
3	**Maja Stark**	65	69	65	199	10,000
	Becky Morgan	66	68	65	199	10,000
	Alice Hewson	65	67	67	199	10,000
	Jessica Karlsson	68	64	67	199	10,000
	Elina Nummenpaa	63	67	69	199	10,000
8	Ines Laklalech	65	67	68	200	6,125
	Caroline Hedwall	68	63	69	200	6,125
10	Lee-Anne Pace	66	69	66	201	5,625
	Emma Spitz	64	69	68	201	5,625
12	Tereza Melecka	66	69	68	203	5,000
	Carmen Alonso	65	70	68	203	5,000
	Rachael Taylor	67	67	69	203	5,000
15	Elin Arvidsson	66	71	67	204	4,313
	Whitney Hillier	70	66	68	204	4,313
	Emma Grechi	70	64	70	204	4,313
	Maiken Bing Paulsen	64	67	73	204	4,313
19	Vani Kapoor	72	66	67	205	3,858
	Linda Osala	66	69	70	205	3,858
	Ana Pelaez Trivino	64	65	76	205	3,858
22	Anais Meyssonnier	74	65	67	206	3,450
	Lydia Hall	66	72	68	206	3,450
	Nora Sundberg (A)	69	68	69	206	
	Florentyna Parker	69	67	70	206	3,450
26	Magdalena Simmermacher	71	70	66	207	2,647
	Thalia Martin	71	69	67	207	2,647
	Amandeep Drall	70	70	67	207	2,647
	Sofie Bringner	74	65	68	207	2,647
	Linda Wessberg	69	70	68	207	2,647
	Havanna Torstensson (A)	65	70	72	207	
	Anne-Charlotte Mora	66	69	72	207	2,647
	Elia Folch	67	67	73	207	2,647
	Genevieve Ling	66	68	73	207	2,647

Aland 100 Ladies Open

On the renovated course at Alands Golf Club in the grounds of Kastelholma Castle on the beautiful Aland archipelago, the scenery was spectacular but the view from the top of the leaderboard not appealing enough for anyone to stay there for long. Not until France's Anne-Charlotte Mora seized the Aland 100 Ladies Open with four birdies in the last five holes. The 25-year-old from Nantes won by one stroke from Sweden's Lisa Pettersson, with Ana Pelaez Trivino another shot back and Emma Spitz in fourth.

Pettersson and Pelaez were the joint leaders overnight, but it was Spitz, from Austria, who took over at the top of the leaderboard during the final round before Mora charged through to win. In only her second appearance on tour as a professional, Spitz three-putted the 17th and finished fourth after her 10th place the previous week. Pelaez closed with a 71 and Pettersson a 70, birdieing the 16th and 18th holes to finish as runner-up for the second week in a row. Finland's home hope, the 42-year-old Ursula Wikstrom, finished in a tie for fifth and enjoyed loud support for her back-to-back-birdies at 15 and 16.

It was at the 14th that Mora started her run. Her effort at the 17th for four birdies in a row only just missed but she buried the one from 10 feet at the last for the win. Rounds of 70-70-68 gave her an eight-under-par total of 208. "I tried to play my own game and not focus on the scores," said Mora, whose best result in three seasons on tour previously was eighth. "I was really nervous on 18 and we had to wait on the tee box, so I was getting more and more stressed, but it worked out. It means a lot. I actually can't believe it. I really liked the course. When I arrived, I thought, this is going to be a good week, no matter what."

Alands Golf Club (Castle), Kastelholma, Finland
Par 72 (37-35); 6,382 yards

September 1-3
Purse: €250,000

1	**Anne-Charlotte Mora**	70	70	68	208	€37,500
2	**Lisa Pettersson**	73	66	70	209	22,500
3	**Ana Pelaez Trivino**	71	68	71	210	15,000
4	Emma Spitz	68	72	71	211	11,250
5	Ursula Wikstrom	68	75	69	212	8,375
	Sofie Bringner	69	71	72	212	8,375
7	Chloe Williams	71	74	68	213	7,000
8	Linda Osala	76	71	68	215	6,000
	Sara Kjellker	74	71	70	215	6,000
	Caroline Hedwall	75	70	70	215	6,000
11	Sideri Vanova	75	70	71	216	5,500
12	Emie Peronnin	74	72	71	217	5,000
	Diksha Dagar	72	73	72	217	5,000
	Christine Wolf	76	69	72	217	5,000
15	Alexandra Swayne	75	72	71	218	4,250
	Emily Price	76	70	72	218	4,250
	Cara Gainer	72	74	72	218	4,250
	Marianne Skarpnord	73	71	74	218	4,250
	Anais Maggetti	74	68	76	218	4,250
20	Noora Komulainen	71	76	72	219	3,585
	Madelene Stavnar	74	75	70	219	3,585
	Smilla Tarning Soenderby	72	74	73	219	3,585

	Sarah Gee	70 75 74	219	3,585		28	Charlotte Liautier	71 77 73	221	2,485
	Isabella Deilert	70 72 77	219	3,585			Fie Olsen	73 75 73	221	2,485
25	Florentyna Parker	76 73 71	220	3,042			Elena Hualde	71 76 74	221	2,485
	Maiken Bing Paulsen	75 70 75	220	3,042			Tiia Koivisto	74 75 72	221	2,485
	Maha Haddioui	75 77 68	220	3,042			Luna Sobron Galmes	76 74 71	221	2,485

VP Bank Swiss Ladies Open

In 2020, Liz Young was one of the founders of the Rose Ladies Series, which grew out of her attempt to set up a one-day event at Brokenhurst Manor while the LET was paused due to the pandemic. In 2021, Young won twice during the Series, her first wins as a professional. In 2022, she claimed a maiden LET title at the VP Bank Swiss Ladies Open, defeating Linn Grant by one stroke at Holzhausern.

On a course saturated by heavy rain and occasional storms, Grant shared the lead in the first round with a 65 having not even had a practice round at the venue. Young opened with a 68, but added a bogey-free 67 on day two to go ahead by one. The 39-year-old mother dropped a shot at the opening hole in the final round before responding with birdies at the third, seventh, 11th and 14th holes. A scare came at the 10th, where she was millimetres from going out of bounds but managed to save her par.

Grant admitted to being grumpy on a final day when she could not initially get close to the pins. Level par for the day through 14, she then birdied the next three holes, though another at the last just escaped her. "Going out the first day with no preparation, I went out with a very chilled feeling, and I think I tried too hard the second day and I tried too hard today," said the Swede, who nevertheless overtook Maja Stark at the top of the Race to Costa del Sol. Grant's closing rounds of 71-69 put her one ahead of England's Rosie Davies, who finished with a 70.

Young said: "In Sotogrande I didn't play well, and I was burnt out. I took two weeks off which I needed and got my game back in shape. I knew it was coming together, I was getting better and better — that's why I'm still out here. I said I'd keep playing as long as I enjoy it and as long as I keep getting better — 14 years later we're here. I hope my daughter is watching. I have been out here a while and never really been close to the win, but I've had some good results in strong field events. To finally get across the line is ... yeah." The smile on her face meant no more words were necessary.

Golfpark Holzhausern, Ennetsee, Switzerland — September 8-10
Par 72 (35-37); 6,305 yards — Purse: €200,000

1	**Liz Young**	68 67 69	204	30,000			Mireia Prat	69 70 72	211	3,134
2	**Linn Grant**	65 71 69	205	18,000			Moa Folke	69 70 72	211	3,134
3	**Rosie Davies**	67 69 70	206	12,000			Pia Babnik	70 75 66	211	3,134
4	Ursula Wikstrom	68 71 68	207	7,467			Virginia Elena Carta	70 75 66	211	3,134
	Alexandra Forsterling	68 69 70	207	7,467			Christine Wolf	65 71 75	211	3,134
	Manon De Roey	69 68 70	207	7,467		25	Smilla Tarning Soenderby	69 73 70	212	2,390
7	Annabel Dimmock	69 70 69	208	5,133			Vani Kapoor	70 71 71	212	2,390
	Amandeep Drall	67 71 70	208	5,133			Diksha Dagar	70 71 71	212	2,390
	Charlotte Liautier	68 68 72	208	5,133			Karina Kukkonen	67 71 74	212	2,390
10	Emma Spitz	72 69 68	209	4,600		29	Georgina Blackman	71 71 71	213	2,120
11	Kylie Henry	68 74 68	210	4,100		30	Anais Meyssonnier	73 70 72	215	1,750
	Tiia Koivisto	72 68 70	210	4,100			Chanettee Wannasaen	70 72 73	215	1,750
	Linda Osala	71 69 70	210	4,100			Felicity Johnson	71 72 72	215	1,750
	Anne-Lise Caudal	68 69 73	210	4,100			Nastasia Nadaud (A)	71 70 74	215	
15	Marta Perez	72 70 69	211	3,134			Gabriella Cowley	72 69 74	215	1,750
	My Leander	70 72 69	211	3,134			Josefine Nyqvist	72 72 71	215	1,750
	Maha Haddioui	69 74 68	211	3,134			Tereza Melecka	71 73 71	215	1,750
	Elin Arvidsson	71 70 70	211	3,134			Sophie Witt	75 70 70	215	1,750
	Noora Komulainen	71 70 70	211	3,134			Verena Gimmy	70 75 70	215	1,750

Lacoste Ladies Open de France

What a place to create your own little bit of history. Deauville is one of France's most fashionable seaside resorts, on the Normandy coast close to Paris, and famous for its film festival, casino, racetrack and chic hotels. At Golf Barriere works of art were placed throughout the course to attract not just a golfing audience to the Lacoste Ladies Open de France. Those who attended did not just see an exciting finish but Ines Laklalech becoming the first Moroccan and the first North African to win on the LET.

Laklalech, a 24-year-old from Casablanca, defeated England's Meghan MacLaren at the first extra hole after the pair tied at 14-under-par 199. They had both scored 65s to join a share of the lead on day one. Laklalech edged ahead with a 66 to a 67 on Friday, but it was MacLaren, with two early birdies, who led for much of the final round. When the Moroccan bogeyed the 14th, she was two behind. She birdied the 16th, then MacLaren bogeyed the 17th, her first dropped shot since her first hole of the event. They both parred the last, meaning a 67 for MacLaren and a 68 for Laklalech, but MacLaren pulled her drive into long rough at the par-four 18th in the playoff. After one unsuccessful hack, she had to take a penalty drop and ended up with a six. Laklalech, who had reached the front of the green in two, won with a five.

It was a second playoff defeat of the season for Australian Classic winner MacLaren, who also lost out in extra time in Italy. The top two finished three ahead of Diksha Dagar, who closed with a 64, with Anais Meyssonnier in fourth and her compatriot Celine Boutier, the defending champion, in sixth.

Having taken up the game aged 12, Laklalech played for one year at Wake Forest in the US before stepping back from competitive golf and finishing her studies at UCL in London. After graduating, she got the bug again after attending the Lalla Meryem Cup in her home country and she turned professional in 2022 after earning her LET card at the Qualifying School. She had previously notched four top-10 finishes in her rookie season, including eighth in Sweden.

"I'm surprised because the last time I was in contention was in Sweden and I lost it over the last few holes," Laklalech said. "I was just too tense physically and that past experience helped me today. I'm just so happy. Of course going to the tee box in the playoff I felt very nervous but I hit a good shot and it was unfortunate how it ended, because Meghan didn't have a good lie. This is definitely something that I will remember for the rest of my life."

A big fan of Tunisian tennis star Ons Jabeur, Laklalech added: "Morocco is doing a great job in promoting golf and I think having a Moroccan winning on a major tour will be huge for the country and for the Arab world in general."

Golf Barriere, Deauville, France — September 15-17
Par 71 (35-36); 6,176 yards — Purse: €325,000

1	**Ines Laklalech**	65	66	68	199	48,750
2	**Meghan MacLaren**	65	67	67	199	29,250
	Laklalech won playoff at first extra hole					
3	**Diksha Dagar**	72	66	64	202	19,500
4	Anais Meyssonnier	67	70	66	203	14,625
5	Caroline Hedwall	68	69	67	204	11,700
6	Christine Wolf	71	68	66	205	9,588
	Celine Boutier	67	67	71	205	9,588
8	Leonie Harm	67	71	68	206	7,963
	Klara Spilkova	67	69	70	206	7,963
10	Kylie Henry	68	71	69	208	7,150
	Marianne Skarpnord	72	66	70	208	7,150
	Magdalena Simmermacher	68	68	72	208	7,150
13	Anais Maggetti	71	71	67	209	6,175
	Pia Babnik	68	71	70	209	6,175
	Smilla Tarning Soenderby	67	69	73	209	6,175
16	Hayley Davis	70	70	70	210	5,606
	Felicity Johnson	68	71	71	210	5,606
18	Alice Hewson	68	74	69	211	4,794
	Chloe Williams	69	74	68	211	4,794
	Cara Gainer	69	71	71	211	4,794
	Noora Komulainen	68	76	67	211	4,794
	Johanna Gustavsson	72	72	67	211	4,794
	Ursula Wikstrom	70	70	71	211	4,794
	Emie Peronnin	68	68	75	211	4,794
	Nicole Broch Estrup	68	67	76	211	4,794
26	Lydia Hall	70	71	71	212	3,900
	Mireia Prat	72	71	69	212	3,900
	Elena Hualde	73	71	68	212	3,900
	Chloe Salort (A)	71	74	67	212	
30	Lily May Humphreys	70	72	71	213	3,096
	Carmen Alonso	69	73	71	213	3,096
	Sophie Witt	73	70	70	213	3,096
	Lisa Pettersson	72	69	72	213	3,096
	Vairana Heck (A)	70	71	72	213	
	Karoline Lund	72	71	70	213	3,096
	Sofie Bringner	70	71	72	213	3,096
	Savannah De Bock (A)	69	70	74	213	
	Alexandra Swayne	68	68	77	213	3,096
	Liz Young	74	71	68	213	3,096

KPMG Women's Irish Open

A crowd of over 10,000 descended on Dromoland Castle in County Clare on the final day to cheer on Ireland's Solheim Cup star Leona Maguire in the first KPMG Women's Irish Open for 10 years. Maguire, who first played in the event aged 14, had seemingly scuppered her chances with a 75 on Friday. She responded with a 65 on Saturday and, remarkably, ended up in a tie for fourth place on Sunday, just one stroke outside the playoff in which Klara Spilkova defeated Finland's Ursula Wikstrom and Denmark's Nicole Broch Estrup.

It was a rousing return to the schedule for the tournament and Spilkova's birdie on the first extra hole earned the 27-year-old Czech her second LET title, five years after she won the Lalla Meryem Cup in Morocco. Spilkova closed with a 67 and, after rounds of 66-68-73, finished on 14-under-par 274. Although neither of the runners-up could match the four of Spilkova in the playoff, both had closed with 68s, Wikstrom finishing with four birdies in the last five holes and Broch Estrup with three in a row from the 15th.

Spilkova birdied both of the closing par fives at 16 and 18 in regulation but the shot of the tournament was her recovery from the edge of the pond on the short 17th. Shoes and socks came off as she waded into the water and hit an extraordinary shot to four feet, saving her par when the putt dropped. "It is definitely the best up-and-down I have made in my whole life, and I have been playing golf for 24 years," Spilkova exclaimed.

"I got there and it was lying really nicely. I thought it wasn't too bad even though my legs were in there. It felt like I had no idea what was under the mud! I just thought I'll try and get it somewhere on the green and two-putt for a bogey. It ended up being almost a metre from the flag. It was really fortunate. I couldn't control that shot, it was luck and I'm really grateful because it saved my whole day."

Dromoland Castle Golf & Country Club, Newmarket-On-Fergus, County Clare, Ireland — September 22-25
Par 72 (35-37); 6,335 yards — Purse: $400,000

1	**Klara Spilkova**	66	68	73	67	274	€60,000
2	**Ursula Wikstrom**	69	66	71	68	274	30,000
	Nicole Broch Estrup	70	66	70	68	274	30,000
	Spilkova won playoff at first extra hole						
4	Smilla Tarning Soenderby	69	65	73	68	275	14,000
	Christine Wolf	67	69	71	68	275	14,000
	Leona Maguire	67	75	65	68	275	14,000
	Annabel Dimmock	66	72	68	69	275	14,000
8	Laura Beveridge	69	71	71	65	276	9,600
	Gabriella Cowley	67	73	68	68	276	9,600
	Carmen Alonso	69	65	72	70	276	9,600
11	Helen Tamy Kreuzer	72	70	71	65	278	8,400
	Nobuhle Dlamini	73	67	70	68	278	8,400
	Sarah Schober	70	67	70	71	278	8,400
14	Casandra Alexander	70	69	73	67	279	7,040
	Leonie Harm	70	69	71	69	279	7,040
	Felicity Johnson	71	66	70	72	279	7,040
	Moa Folke	70	62	74	73	279	7,040
	Jessica Karlsson	71	68	67	73	279	7,040
19	Becky Brewerton	71	69	71	69	280	5,743
	Linn Grant	71	67	72	70	280	5,743
	Johanna Gustavsson	68	71	71	70	280	5,743
	Meghan MacLaren	70	72	68	70	280	5,743
	Pia Babnik	70	72	68	70	280	5,743
	Chloe Williams	67	71	70	72	280	5,743
	Anne van Dam	67	68	70	75	280	5,743
26	Liz Young	71	70	71	69	281	4,693
	Elin Arvidsson	67	70	74	70	281	4,693
	Lisa Pettersson	71	67	72	71	281	4,693
29	Lina Boqvist	65	72	76	69	282	3,833
	Mim Sangkapong	68	72	73	69	282	3,833
	Magdalena Simmermacher	71	72	70	69	282	3,833
	Sophie Witt	72	71	70	69	282	3,833
	Nicole Garcia	68	72	72	70	282	3,833
	Vani Kapoor	72	70	70	70	282	3,833

Aramco Team Series — New York

"I've been working extremely hard on my game," said Lexi Thompson. "I felt like it was a matter of time. I just wanted to play golf, put myself in contention in the final rounds and learn from the losses that I had and what I needed to work on, and I brought that into today."

Thompson had not won since the ShopRite LPGA Classic in 2019. And the losses had been tough, especially at the US Women's Open in 2021 and the KPMG Women's PGA earlier in the season. Finally, Thompson kept putting herself into contention and wound up with the win at the Aramco

Team Series event in New York on the Trump course at Ferry Point. After an opening 71, Thompson scored 65 on day two to take a one-shot lead over Nelly Korda, whose only win so far in 2022 had come at the Sotogrande Aramco tournament.

It promised a fascinating duel between the pair on the final day but Korda bogeyed the first, while Thompson birdied after hitting the flagstick with her approach. Korda's putter misfired on her three-over outward half and although others mustered a challenge, Thompson kept in front. Back-to-back birdies at the 10th and 11th were crucial, two more came at 15 and 17 and a bogey at the last still meant a three-stroke victory over Evian champion Brooke Henderson (68) and Madelene Sagstrom (69). Korda went three under on the way home for a 72 and fourth place, while Thompson closed with a 69 for 11-under-par 205.

"Today, I played the way I did yesterday with aggressive golf, kind of fiery. I hit a great shot on number one to six or seven feet and made it. I wanted to play fearless golf and not play away from pins by any means. I hit some really good shots and I hit some iffy ones, but with this wind, you have to take the bad ones as best you can. I turned it on on the back and really made the putts when I needed to."

In the team event that ended after 36 holes, Korda, with Noora Komulainen, Celine Herbin and amateur James Rawson, ended up in second place, one behind winners Johanna Gustavsson, Jessica Karlsson, Karolin Lampert and amateur Jennifer Rosenberg.

Trump Golf Links at Ferry Point, New York, USA — October 13-15
Par 72 (36-36); 6,418 yards — Purse: $1,000,000

1	**Lexi Thompson**	71	65	69	205	€77,055
2	**Brooke Henderson**	72	68	68	208	38,528
	Madelene Sagstrom	70	69	69	208	38,528
4	Nelly Korda	70	67	72	209	23,117
5	Kylie Henry	72	71	67	210	17,209
	Maja Stark	75	67	68	210	17,209
7	Linnea Strom	73	71	68	212	12,843
	Jessica Karlsson	73	70	69	212	12,843
	Annabel Dimmock	72	70	70	212	12,843
	Anne van Dam	74	68	70	212	12,843
11	Pernilla Lindberg	76	69	68	213	10,531
	Chiara Noja	75	68	70	213	10,531
	Daniela Holmqvist	74	69	70	213	10,531
	Pia Babnik	71	71	71	213	10,531
15	Anna Nordqvist	73	72	69	214	8,990
	Pauline Roussin	73	72	69	214	8,990
	Liz Young	73	72	69	214	8,990
18	Annie Park	74	73	68	215	7,380
	Jessica Korda	74	73	68	215	7,380
	Leona Maguire	74	72	69	215	7,380
	Bronte Law	75	70	70	215	7,380
	Stephanie Kyriacou	72	73	70	215	7,380
	Alice Hewson	74	71	70	215	7,380
	Agathe Sauzon	76	68	71	215	7,380
	Olivia Cowan	75	69	71	215	7,380
	Carlota Ciganda	73	70	72	215	7,380
27	Jillian Hollis	73	73	70	216	5,959
28	Magdalena Simmermacher	75	72	70	217	5,330
	Smilla Tarning Soenderby	76	71	70	217	5,330
	Lucie Malchirand	73	73	71	217	5,330
	Manon De Roey	68	76	73	217	5,330

Hero Women's Indian Open

Olivia Cowan was taking nothing for granted. "I was aware of what can happen even on the last hole," she said with a smile. She knew from personal experience. Cowan had suffered a double-bogey seven at Royal Greens in the Jeddah Aramco event in 2021 to lose by one. She also knew the history at DFL, where in 2018 Christine Wolf found water twice on 18 in the third round and had a quad, then had a double in the final round and still finished second — fortunately returning the following year to win.

At this edition of the Hero Women's Indian Open, after birdies at the 15th and 17th holes had put her two ahead, Cowan safely parred the 18th and saw Caroline Hedwall bogey to give the 26-year-old German her maiden LET victory by three strokes. It was the third time Hedwall had been second in the tournament since winning it in her rookie year in 2011. Cowan and Hedwall started the final round one stroke behind Amandeep Drall, who finished as runner-up with Hedwall, missing out on matching Aditi Ashok as a home winner in 2016. Ashok was fourth this time.

Cowan, the daughter of an English-born teaching professional who started her playing aged three, scored 71-71-65-68 for a 13-under-par total of 275. Five birdies in a row from the seventh on day three ignited her challenge. "I have come close a few times, but I am so happy to get over the line," Cowan said. "I love coming here and this is going to be one of my most memorable moments. I will come back again to try and win this trophy again. I was quite relaxed, to be honest, the whole weekend. I wasn't really thinking of winning this time. I just wanted to go out there and have a good mindset and just play good golf. I just decided to trust that, come out today and just see what happens."

DLF Golf and Country Club, Gurugram, India — October 20-23
Par 72 (36-36); 6,189 yards — Purse: $400,000

1	**Olivia Cowan**	71	71	65	68	275	€61,201
2	**Caroline Hedwall**	68	71	68	71	278	30,600
	Amandeep Drall	67	72	67	72	278	30,600
4	Aditi Ashok	70	71	69	71	281	18,360
5	Ana Pelaez Trivino	69	76	67	70	282	14,688
6	Anais Meyssonnier	66	78	68	72	284	12,036
	Gaurika Bishnoi	71	68	72	73	284	12,036
8	Vani Kapoor	72	71	73	69	285	9,996
	Elina Nummenpaa	70	75	69	71	285	9,996
10	Moa Folke	71	76	70	69	286	9,180
	Camille Chevalier	72	71	70	73	286	9,180
12	Avani Prashanth (A)	75	76	69	67	287	
	Alice Hewson	70	73	75	69	287	7,650
	Linda Wessberg	65	77	74	71	287	7,650
	Agathe Sauzon	72	73	71	71	287	7,650
	Elin Arvidsson	68	72	74	73	287	7,650
	Noora Komulainen	67	72	74	74	287	7,650
	Meghan MacLaren	72	69	72	74	287	7,650
19	Christine Wolf	74	71	70	73	288	6,732
20	Gabriella Then	73	75	74	67	289	6,310
	Hitaashee Bakshi	73	74	71	71	289	6,310
	Nishtha Madan	72	73	71	73	289	6,310
23	Marianne Skarpnord	73	75	71	71	290	5,875
24	Marta Sanz Barrio	70	76	72	73	291	5,467
	Nicole Garcia	69	72	76	74	291	5,467
	Helen Tamy Kreuzer	71	77	69	74	291	5,467
27	Neha Tripathi	74	72	74	72	292	4,753
	Johanna Gustavsson	71	78	72	71	292	4,753
	Thalia Martin	72	73	74	73	292	4,753
	Ursula Wikstrom	73	74	72	73	292	4,753

Aramco Team Series — Jeddah

In 2016 at Woburn, Chiara Noja got a treasured photo with her hero Charley Hull. Six years on and Noja claimed her first LET title by defeating Hull in a playoff at the Aramco Team Series — Jeddah event at the age of 16. It was a stunning upset by the young star-in-the-making from Germany. Noja won on the second extra hole with a birdie at the 18th hole at Royal Greens that Hull could not match. The Solheim Cupper had had to hole a 10-footer for a birdie at the first extra hole to stay alive.

"I can't even begin to fathom what I've just done," Noja said. "I'm just going to try and relax tonight. Maybe have a burger, I don't know, treat myself! Sleep. I think it'll be the best night of sleep I'm probably ever going to get, and see how I feel tomorrow."

Noja was born in Berlin and represents Germany but moved to the UK aged seven, reached a scratch handicap at 12 and at 14 joined the England National squad. After moving to Dubai, and after the amateur circuits were disrupted by the pandemic, she turned professional aged 15 late in 2021. She earned her LET card for 2023 by finishing second on the Access Series, where she won the Amundi Czech Ladies Challenge by nine strokes.

Playing her ninth LET event on a sponsor's invitation, Noja's 68-70 opening put her three behind Hull, who rallied from playing her first four holes in three over par to lead on 70-65. But Hull, whose own maiden LET win came at the age of 17, made a slow start to the final round. Caroline Hedwall was tied for the lead until a quadruple bogey at the 15th, while Noja had sprinted to the top of the leaderboard with an eagle at the fourth and seven birdies. Her second bogey of the day came at the 17th and a 65 put her on 13-under-par 203. Hull, level par for the first 12 holes, sparked into action with four birdies in the last six for a 68. But her effort to win on the 18th green in regulation just missed and at the second extra hole she could not get up and down.

Twice Noja found the heart of the 18th green in the playoff and two-putted for birdies. "This course, when you can go into par fives in two, it is a massive advantage. I tried to take advantage of that this week, and it paid off," Noja said. "It is hard work over a lot of years, a lot of commitment, just trying not to back out of shots and commit to everything that I do, and not be afraid to fail."

Nicole Garcia, who eagled the 18th to take third place in the individual competition, also captained the winning team although she elected for Cassandra Hall to play the playoff at the 18th and the South African delivered the win over Christine Wolf with a birdie. Also in the winning team were Czech Tereza Melecka and Moroccan amateur Sonia Bayahya.

Royal Greens Golf & Country Club, King Abdullah Economic City, Saudi Arabia — November 10-12
Par 72 (36-36); 6,295 yards — Purse: $1,000,000

1	**Chiara Noja**	68	70	65	203	€74,438
2	**Charley Hull**	70	65	68	203	44,663
	Noja won playoff at second extra hole					
3	**Nicole Garcia**	67	70	67	204	29,775
4	Virginia Elena Carta	67	69	69	205	22,331
5	Bronte Law	70	69	67	206	16,625
	Lee-Anne Pace	71	68	67	206	16,625
7	Caroline Hedwall	69	67	71	207	13,895
8	Laura Beveridge	72	67	69	208	11,910
	Vani Kapoor	69	70	69	208	11,910
	Pia Babnik	71	65	72	208	11,910
11	Georgia Hall	72	67	70	209	10,421
	Lucie Malchirand	68	70	71	209	10,421
	Sofie Bringner	69	69	71	209	10,421
14	Christine Wolf	71	72	67	210	9,015
	Cara Gainer	70	71	69	210	9,015
	Linda Wessberg	69	72	69	210	9,015
17	Gabriella Cowley	70	72	69	211	8,064
	Emma Grechi	70	71	70	211	8,064
	Alice Hewson	70	71	70	211	8,064
	Ana Pelaez Trivino	67	70	74	211	8,064
21	Stacy Lee Bregman	70	73	69	212	6,536
	Casandra Alexander	71	72	69	212	6,536
	Linnea Strom	69	74	69	212	6,536
	Agathe Laisne	70	71	71	212	6,536
	Nicole Broch Estrup	71	70	71	212	6,536
	Ursula Wikstrom	67	73	72	212	6,536
	Chloe Williams	70	68	74	212	6,536
28	Daniela Holmqvist	72	73	68	213	4,834
	Sarah Schober	74	70	69	213	4,834
	Helen Tamy Kreuzer	71	72	70	213	4,834
	Magdalena Simmermacher	74	68	71	213	4,834
	Kelly Whaley	71	70	72	213	4,834

Andalucia Costa del Sol Open de Espana

It was all about Sweden at the Andalucia Costa del Sol Open de Espana with Linn Grant securing top spot on the season-long standings ahead of Maja Stark and Johanna Gustavsson, and Caroline Hedwall claiming a morale-boosting victory in the tournament itself.

Hedwall won four times in her rookie season in 2011, and once the next year, but while remaining a Solheim Cup star, the 33-year-old Swede had only won once since, at the Open de France in 2018. At Alferini, Hedwall was back to driving the ball superbly as she dominated the par fives, ultimately winning a playoff against Morgane Metraux at the fourth extra hole. After each player had par threes at the short 18th three times in a row, the playoff moved to the par-five 17th which Hedwall had played in five under par for the week before claiming another birdie after reaching the green in two, while Metraux could not get up and down from short of the green.

"It just feels awesome, it feels forever that I have waited for that win," Hedwall said. "I wasn't sure I still had it in me. It's so nice to get it together and get this win. It has been a rollercoaster to be honest, I had an injury in 2014 that was really tough on me and my self-confidence."

Hedwall scored 70-68-69-67 for an 18-under-par total of 274 after starting the final round two behind Italian Open winner Metraux, who closed with a 69 to tie. The pair both birdied the back-to-back par-fives 16 and 17 to hold off the challenge of new European number one Grant, who eagled 17 to briefly take the lead with a 65. Ireland's Leona Maguire was also in the hunt, finishing fourth a week after being pipped by Lydia Ko at the CME Group Tour Championship in America.

Spain's 17-year-old amateur Cayetana Fernandez, who led after 36 holes following a second-round 65, shared fifth place with Alice Hewson, while Maja Stark, who needed to finish ahead of Grant to claim the Race to Costa del Sol title, tied for seventh.

Alferini Golf, Benahavis, Malaga, Spain — November 24-27
Par 73 (36-37); 6,367 yards — Purse: €650,000

1	**Caroline Hedwall**	70	68	69	67	274	€97,500
2	**Morgane Metraux**	68	70	67	69	274	58,500
	Hedwall won playoff at fourth extra hole						
3	**Linn Grant**	68	68	74	65	275	39,000
4	Leona Maguire	68	69	70	69	276	29,250
5	Alice Hewson	69	74	69	65	277	23,400
	Cayetana Fernandez (A)	70	65	72	70	277	
7	Maja Stark	69	69	73	68	279	19,175
	Carla Tejedo Mulet (A)	70	74	66	69	279	
	Carlota Ciganda	67	73	68	71	279	19,175
10	Olivia Cowan	73	69	70	68	280	15,535
	Anne van Dam	69	71	71	69	280	15,535
	Sofie Bringner	70	73	68	69	280	15,535
13	Pia Babnik	73	72	69	67	281	14,105
14	Chloe Williams	71	70	72	69	282	12,740
	Klara Spilkova	71	69	71	71	282	12,740
	Cara Gainer	66	72	72	72	282	12,740
17	Kim Metraux	75	69	69	71	284	11,473

19	Manon De Roey	75	73	70	67	285	10,286
	Ana Pelaez Trivino	72	73	73	67	285	10,286
	Emily Kristine Pedersen	72	70	75	68	285	10,286
	Azahara Munoz	69	72	75	69	285	10,286
	Paula Martin (A)	71	69	75	70	285	
24	Jessica Karlsson	69	71	72	74	286	9,555
25	Gabriella Cowley	73	72	73	69	287	9,003
	Lee-Anne Pace	69	72	74	72	287	9,003
27	Carmen Alonso	73	70	74	71	288	8,320
	Nuria Iturrioz	69	75	69	75	288	8,320
29	Linnea Strom	73	70	74	72	289	7,053
	Laura Beveridge	75	75	70	69	289	7,053
	Liz Young	70	72	72	75	289	7,053
	Marianne Skarpnord	70	74	69	76	289	7,053

2022 RACE TO COSTA DEL SOL

		Points
1	Linn Grant	3,624.91
2	Maja Stark	3,415.14
3	Johanna Gustavsson	1,946.08
4	Manon De Roey	1,816.46
5	Ana Pelaez Trivino	1,657.21
6	Magdalena Simmermacher	1,569.73
7	Meghan MacLaren	1,560.30
8	Caroline Hedwall	1,539.90
9	Lee-Anne Pace	1,488.55
10	Georgia Hall	1,371.95

LET ACCESS SERIES

Terre Blanche Ladies Open	**Lucrezia Colombotto Rosso**
Flumserberg Ladies Open	**Lauren Holmey**
PGA Championship Trelleborg	**Meja Ortengren**
Amundi Czech Ladies Challenge	**Chiara Noja**
Montauban Ladies Open	**Momoka Kobori**
Smorum Ladies Open	**Cecilie Leth-Nissen** (A)
Golf Vlaanderen LETAS Trophy	**Kristalle Blum**
Hauts de France – Pas de Calais Golf Open	**Momoka Kobori (2)**
Trust Golf Links Series — Ramside Hall	**Chanettee Wannasaen**
Trust Golf Links Series — Musselburgh	**Arpichaya Yubol**
Santander Golf Tour Malaga	**Sara Kouskova**
Vasteras Open	**Sara Ericsson** (A)
Big Green Egg Swedish Match Play Championship	**Patricia Schmidt**
Goteborg Open	**Nastasia Nadaud**
Elite Hotels Open	**Sara Kouskova (2)**
ASGI Lavaux Ladies Open	**Sara Kouskova (3)**
Rose Ladies Open	**My Leander**
Santander Golf Tour — Burgos	**Verena Gimmy**
Calatayud Ladies Open	**Amy Taylor**

SUNSHINE LADIES TOUR

Vodacom Origins of Golf Final Pro-Am	**Lejan Lewthwaite**	
SunBet Cape Town Ladies Open	**Nadia van der Westhuizen**	
Dimension Data Ladies Challenge	**Linn Grant**	
SuperSport Ladies Challenge	**Paula Reto**	
Jabra Ladies Classic — Sunshine	**Linn Grant (2)**	
Joburg Ladies Open	**Linn Grant (3)**	*See chapter 23*
Investec SA Women's Open	**Lee-Anne Pace**	*See chapter 23*

Korea LPGA Tour

While internationally there were mixed fortunes for the leading Koreans, with In Gee Chun winning her first major championship for six years at the KPMG Women's PGA and Jin Young Ko losing her world number one title after a recurrence of her long-term wrist injury, on the domestic Korea LPGA Tour one player again dominated. For the second year in a row, Min Ji Park won six times. Those 12 wins came in 47 tournaments meaning a success rate of better than one in four.

Park, 23, whose mother was an Olympic handball silver medallist in 1984, actually had to miss the opening event of the season with Covid and struggled on her first couple of starts. While she collected all her wins up to July in 2021, this time Park maintained her winning form across the season. She retained her titles at the NH Ladies Championship and the Celltrion Queens Masters, before adding the BC Card Hankyung Ladies Cup, the last two majors of the season, the KB Financial Group Star Championship and the Hite Jinro Championship, as well as the final event of the season at the SK Shieldus SK Telecom Championship.

That took her career tally of victories to 16, the most of any current player on the circuit, and four behind Jiyai Shin, now based mainly in Japan, and the late Ok Hee Ku. Park finished 2022 placed 14th on the Rolex Rankings, behind only compatriots Ko, Chun and Hyo Joo Kim. Although reluctant to look too far ahead earlier in the season, she revealed late in the year that she wanted to start to play in America and was heading there over the winter to practise. "My next goal is to go on to a bigger stage," said Park. "I want to build my body during the winter. I also want to improve my shots and techniques. I think I'm in my prime but I can't believe why I'm winning so many championships. It's amazing even when I see it."

Park topped the money list for the second year running, earning ₩1,477,921,143, but did not sweep the awards as she did in 2021. Instead, Su Ji Kim led the points list for Player of the Year with 17 top-10 finishes. She won twice, as she did in 2021, with back-to-back victories in September at the OK Financial Group Se Ri Pak Invitational and the Hana Financial Group Championship. Kim also won the stroke average award with 70.47. "I've been fortunate to have had a great year," Kim said. "I just took on the approach that I want to learn and gain the experience. It's been a fun season, it's been a rewarding year."

Hae Ran Ryu enjoyed another consistent year, although she did not add to her early win at the Nexen Saint Nine Masters. She finished second to Kim on both the points list and the stroke average table, and then went to America and won Q-Series to earn her LPGA card. Hee Jeong Lim also only won once but made it an important one, winning the DB Group Korea Women's Open by six strokes on a record total of 19 under par. Former US Open champion A Lim Kim won the CreaS F&C KLPGA Championship with a strong showing in the wind as Hyo Joo Kim faltered.

Yewon Lee, 19, was the Rookie of the Year and came close to winning on a number of occasions, including runner-up finishes at the Doosan Match Play, the OK Financial Group Se Ri Pak Invitational and the Hana Financial Group Championship. She finished third on the money list behind Park and Su Ji Kim. Lim was awarded the Most Popular Player of the Year accolade for the second year in a row and Yunji Jeong, who won the E1 Charity Open, took the Most Improved Player Award.

There were two events at the end of the year to start the 2023 season, beginning with the inaugural Hana Financial Group Singapore Women's Open, which had been delayed since 2020 due to the Covid pandemic. Beginning early in the 2022 season, crowds were allowed back to KLPGA events for the first time in three years, with A Yean Cho enjoying the support of her fans as she won twice early in the year, having not won since her rookie season of 2019. So Mi Lee, always strong in the wind, also won twice, taking the late-season double-header on Jeju Island.

2022 SCHEDULE

Lotte Rent a Car Ladies Open	**Su Yeon Jang**
Mediheal Hankook Ilbo Championship	**Ji Young Park**
Nexen Saint Nine Masters	**Hae Ran Ryu**
CreaS F&C KLPGA Championship	**A Lim Kim**
Kyochon Honey Ladies Open	**A Yean Cho**

NH Ladies Championship	**Min Ji Park**
Doosan Match Play Championship	**Jung Min Hong**
E1 Charity Open	**Yunji Jeong**
Lotte Open	**Yu Jin Sung**
Celltrion Queens Masters	**Min Ji Park (2)**
DB Group Korea Women's Open	**Hee Jeong Lim**
BC Card Hankyung Ladies Cup	**Min Ji Park (3)**
McCol Mona Park Open	**Jin Hee Im**
Daebo hausD Open	**Ga Run Song**
Ever Collagen Queens Crown	**Ina Yoon**
Hoban Seoul Shinmun Women's Classic	**A Yean Cho (2)**
Jeju Samdasoo Masters	**Han Sol Ji**
Dayouwinia MBN Ladies Open	**So Young Lee**
HighOne Resort Ladies Open	**Jin Seon Han**
Hanwha Classic	**Ji Won Hong**
KG Edaily Ladies Open	**Jeong Mee Hwang**
KB Financial Group Star Championship	**Min Ji Park (4)**
OK Financial Group Se Ri Pak Invitational	**Su Ji Kim**
Hana Financial Group Championship	**Su Ji Kim (2)**
Hite Jinro Championship	**Min Ji Park (5)**
Dongbu Koreit Championship	**Ga Young Lee**
Wemix Championship	**Hyo Ju You**
SK Networks Seoul Economics Ladies Classic	**So Mi Lee**
S-Oil Championship	**So Mi Lee (2)**
SK Shieldus SK Telecom Championship	**Min Ji Park (6)**
Hana Financial Group Singapore Women's Open	**Ji Young Park (2)**
PLK Pacific Links Championship	**Jung Min Lee**

Lotte Rent a Car Ladies Open

At a tournament that had been going since 2008, and won by the likes of Sei Young Kim, Hyo Joo Kim and Jeongeun Lee6, two players came to the last hole at Lotte Skyhill Jeju with a chance to become the first player to win the title twice. The first was Su Yeon Jang, the 2016 champion, who had eagled the 18th on Saturday, and now made her birdie four by holing a short putt. "Thanks to that eagle yesterday, I think I could just trust myself today," Jang said.

That put Jang at nine under par on a total of 279. In the final group was So Mi Lee, the defending champion, who needed a birdie to tie and force a playoff but her putt for a four from long range came up short. Lee's 71 meant she was one shot back and could not add to her three KLPGA titles.

In 2016 Jang claimed her maiden victory in the tournament and won again a few weeks later, and at the KLPGA Championship in 2017, but she had not won since. The 27-year-old scored 72-68-71-68 in coming from three strokes off the lead on the final day, when Hae Ran Ryu scored a 67 to share third place with Jin Hee Im.

"I am bewildered right now actually," Jang said after her first win in five years. "It's been a long time since I won, and it reminds me of the tough times and the hardships I had on the way. I really needed a win this season, and I am happy to start my season with a win."

Lotte Skyhill Jeju Country Club, Jeju Island — April 7-10
Par 72 (36-36); 6,395 yards — Purse: ₩700,000,000

1	**Su Yeon Jang**	72	68	71	68	279	₩126,000,000
2	**So Mi Lee**	72	69	68	71	280	77,000,000
3	**Hae Ran Ryu**	74	71	69	67	281	45,500,000
	Jin Hee Im	74	65	74	68	281	45,500,000
5	Yeun Jung Seo	71	71	70	70	282	22,750,000
	Min Song Ha	70	70	71	71	282	22,750,000

	Ju Yeon In	73	69	71	69	282	22,750,000
	Gyeol Park	75	69	68	70	282	22,750,000
9	Ji Hyun Oh	75	68	70	70	283	12,250,000
	Ha Na Jang	72	68	72	71	283	12,250,000
11	Min Kyung Choi	71	71	71	71	284	9,240,000
	Hee Won Na	69	71	68	76	284	9,240,000
13	Jae Hee Kim	74	67	75	69	285	8,400,000
	Hae Rym Kim	67	68	76	74	285	8,400,000
15	A Yean Cho	70	75	71	70	286	7,700,000
	Jin Seon Han	73	70	73	70	286	7,700,000
	Han Sol Ji	75	71	69	71	286	7,700,000
18	Sun Ju Ahn	69	72	73	73	287	7,070,000
	Se Lin Hyun	72	72	73	70	287	7,070,000
	Ji Won Hong	73	66	72	76	287	7,070,000
21	Ga Eun Song	74	70	73	71	288	6,282,500
	Seul Gi Jeong	70	72	73	73	288	6,282,500
	Bo Ah Kim	73	73	71	71	288	6,282,500
	Ye Rim Choi	71	70	73	74	288	6,282,500
	So Hye Park	75	71	67	75	288	6,282,500
	Seung Yeon Lee	72	70	74	72	288	6,282,500
	Hye Lim Jo	73	71	70	74	288	6,282,500
	Ye Sung Jun	74	69	71	74	288	6,282,500
29	Hee Won Jung	72	73	74	70	289	5,705,000
	So Young Lee	73	72	71	73	289	5,705,000
	Jeongmin Moon	72	71	72	74	289	5,705,000
	Yunji Jeong	75	65	76	73	289	5,705,000
	Ji Su Kim	74	71	72	72	289	5,705,000
	Ji Young Park	74	66	70	79	289	5,705,000

Mediheal Hankook Ilbo Championship

With crowds returning to the KLPGA for the first time since prior to the Covid pandemic, Ji Young Park punched the air and celebrated in style with a six-stroke victory in the inaugural Mediheal Hankook Ilbo Championship. Park went wire-to-wire and her prize included a place in the LPGA Mediheal Championship in California in October.

This was a fourth KLPGA title for the 26-year-old Park, who had not won for three years when she claimed the penultimate event of the 2021 season at the S-Oil Championship. The 2015 Rookie of the Year started the second tournament of the 2022 season by equalling the course record of 64 at Ferrum Club, with nine birdies and one bogey. Park's three-shot lead was cut to one by Da Yeon Lee, who also scored a 64 on Friday, while Park had a 68. Twin rounds of 69 on the weekend meant Park pulled away to an 18-under-par total of 270.

Six-time winner Lee closed with 72-73 and although she was only two behind early on Sunday, she dropped to third place. Park, four ahead on Saturday night, had a bogey and a birdie going out in the final round and although her nearest challenger fell away, Chae Eun Lee² got within two shots after birdies at the sixth and then the 11th and 12th holes. Park upped her game and dazzled on the greens, holing a par-saver at the 11th and then a 15-footer at the 13th to go three ahead. While Lee² bogeyed the 17th to finish with a 70, Park holed 18-footers at the last two holes for the handsome margin of victory. "I practised the most I ever have during the winter without a day off so it feels good to win so quickly," Park said.

Hae Ran Ryu and Hyun Kyung Park were fourth and fifth respectively, while the strong field included So Yeon Ryu, in 13th, and Sei Young Kim, who missed the cut with scores of 64-73. There were a KLPGA record five holes-in-one during the tournament — Jae Hee Kim won a Maserati, Ree An Kim ₩20 million worth of jewellery, Jin Seon Han a set of golf clubs, while Yea Lin Kang and Seo Yeon Kwon nothing as the prizes on their holes had already been claimed.

Ferrum Club, Yeoju, Gyeonggi — April 14-17
Par 72 (36-36); 6,628 yards — Purse: ₩1,000,000,000

1	**Ji Young Park**	64	68	69	69	270	₩180,000,000
2	**Chae Eun Lee²**	67	67	72	70	276	110,000,000
3	**Da Yeon Lee**	69	64	72	73	278	80,000,000
4	Hae Ran Ryu	69	70	70	70	279	50,000,000
5	Hyun Kyung Park	73	70	68	69	280	40,000,000
6	A Yean Cho	69	67	77	68	281	30,000,000
	Han Sol Ji	69	70	71	71	281	30,000,000
	Su Ji Kim	69	72	69	71	281	30,000,000
9	Bo Ah Kim	72	69	70	71	282	20,000,000
10	Gi Ppuem Lee	69	75	71	68	283	13,800,000
	Dasom Ma	69	71	72	71	283	13,800,000
	Joo Mi Lee	70	69	73	71	283	13,800,000
13	So Yeon Ryu	71	73	70	71	285	11,116,667
	Ina Yoon	70	72	70	73	285	11,116,667
	Bo Kyeom Park	71	69	72	73	285	11,116,667
	Jeong Mee Hwang	71	71	71	72	285	11,116,667
	Carrie Park	71	68	74	72	285	11,116,667
	Yeon Ju Jung	74	67	72	72	285	11,116,667
19	Yewon Lee	71	68	76	71	286	9,450,000
	Ga Young Lee	74	69	73	70	286	9,450,000
	U Ree Jun	71	70	71	74	286	9,450,000
	Ga Eun Song	72	72	71	71	286	9,450,000
23	Dan Yu Park	73	72	73	69	287	8,560,000
	Su Yeon Jang	68	69	78	72	287	8,560,000
	Jae Hee Kim	70	70	73	74	287	8,560,000
	Jee Hyun Ahn	72	70	74	71	287	8,560,000

	Ree An Kim	72	70	75	70	287	8,560,000	Seul Gi Jeong	71	72	71	74	288	7,950,000
28	Sae Ro Mi Kim	71	71	75	71	288	7,950,000	Seo Yeon Kwon	72	73	72	71	288	7,950,000
	Ye Sung Jun	68	74	76	70	288	7,950,000	Ju Young Pak	67	73	72	76	288	7,950,000
	Min Ji Park	73	71	71	73	288	7,950,000							

Nexen Saint Nine Masters

Winning the last tournament of 2021 gave Hae Ran Ryu a second victory of the season and she kept up that momentum with an early win in 2022 at the Nexen Saint Nine Masters at Gaya. It was a fifth title for the former Rookie of the Year and arrived by one stroke over a new rookie, Seo Yeon Kwon.

Ryu, 21, only dropped two shots during the tournament, the second of them on the 72nd hole when she left her downhill par putt short of the hole. "I didn't think that I would be nervous in the last hole, but I was extremely nervous and I missed my putt," said Ryu. With spectators allowed back into tournaments this season after two years of Covid restrictions, this was the first time Ryu had won in front of a crowd since her maiden victory in 2019. "My win feels even better because I had an audience around for all 18 holes," she said.

Scores of 67-68-67-70 gave Ryu a 16-under-par total of 272. Like the runner-up, she birdied the first, seventh and 11th holes. Kwon, who finished second on the Dream Tour in 2021, closed with a bogey-free 69 but could only make up one of her two-shot deficit, while Ha Na Jang and Gyeol Park both had 67s to finish in third place. Hyo Min Jeon, who led for the first two days with 66-69, started the final round one behind Ryu and closed with a 75 after bogeying the first two holes.

Gaya Country Club, Gimhae, Gyeongnam — April 21-24
Par 72 (36-36); 6,813 yards — Purse: ₩800,000,000

1	**Hae Ran Ryu**	67	68	67	70	272	₩144,000,000		Hyo Min Jeon	66	69	68	75	278	8,860,000
2	**Seo Yeon Kwon**	68	68	68	69	273	88,000,000		Ye Sung Jun	71	70	65	72	278	8,860,000
3	**Ha Na Jang**	70	70	67	67	274	52,000,000	18	Sebeen Jung	70	72	68	69	279	7,780,000
	Gyeol Park	68	72	67	67	274	52,000,000		Ji Min Jung[2]	73	70	68	68	279	7,780,000
5	Yewon Lee	69	71	69	66	275	30,000,000		Geena Yoo	69	70	70	70	279	7,780,000
	Ye Rim Choi	73	69	65	68	275	30,000,000		Seul Gi Jeong	71	70	67	71	279	7,780,000
7	Ji Young Park	69	70	69	68	276	22,000,000	22	Hyun Kyung Park	68	71	68	73	280	7,160,000
	Seung Yeon Lee	71	68	69	68	276	22,000,000		Da Som Ma	71	69	70	70	280	7,160,000
9	Ga Young Lee	72	69	71	65	277	11,776,000	24	Jee Hyun Ahn	69	72	69	71	281	6,700,000
	Yu Jin Sung	67	70	71	69	277	11,776,000		So Mi Lee	66	72	74	69	281	6,700,000
	Han Sol Ji	74	65	68	70	277	11,776,000		Yebeen Sohn	66	73	72	70	281	6,700,000
	Da Been Heo	71	68	68	70	277	11,776,000		Jeongmin Moon	70	74	67	70	281	6,700,000
	Hee Jeong Lim	68	70	71	68	277	11,776,000	28	So Hyun Bae	71	68	72	71	282	6,400,000
14	Su Yeon Jang	70	66	73	69	278	8,860,000		Min Ju Kim	73	68	71	70	282	6,400,000
	Sae Ro Mi Kim	68	70	71	69	278	8,860,000		Seung Hui Ro	68	72	70	72	282	6,400,000

CreaS F&C KLPGA Championship

A Lim Kim, then unknown outside Korea, famously won the 2020 US Women's Open during a cold December week that ended up with a Monday finish. Conditions were also cold and tough when Kim won the CreaS F&C KLPGA Championship, her first KLPGA major and her third local title in all after earlier victories in 2018 and 2019. The 26-year-old came from three behind another former global major winner, Hyo Joo Kim, to win by three at Ildong Lakes.

Hyo Joo Kim led for the first three days after an opening seven-birdie 65. She added two 69s to be one ahead of Seung Yeon Lee, who posted a 69 in the third round. A Lim Kim scored 68-70-68 to be in fourth position, three off the lead before matching the best round of a windy Sunday with a 70 for a 12-under-par total of 276.

A Lim went out in 35 and made up one shot on Hyo Joo, but as the wind strengthened it was her play coming home that was decisive. She made eight pars and a birdie at the 16th and was the only one of the leading contenders to post an under-par inward nine. In contrast, Hyo Joo was knocked off her game with a bogey at the 10th, a double bogey at the 11th, a triple at the 14th and another bogey at the 16th. She came home in 43 for a closing 79, finishing in a tie for fourth with Min Ji Park. Ga Young Lee scored a 72 to take second place, three behind the winner, while Seung Yeon Lee had a 76 to be third.

Ildong Lakes Golf Club, Pocheon, Gyeonggi — April 28-May 1
Par 72 (36-36); 6,689 yards — Purse: ₩1,200,000,000

1	**A Lim Kim**	68	70	68	70	276	₩216,000,000
2	**Ga Young Lee**	70	68	69	72	279	132,000,000
3	**Seung Yeon Lee**	69	68	67	76	280	96,000,000
4	Min Ji Park	69	68	74	71	282	54,000,000
	Hyo Joo Kim	65	69	69	79	282	54,000,000
6	Yewon Lee	68	69	70	76	283	33,000,000
	Min Kyung Choi	70	71	72	70	283	33,000,000
	Chae Eun Lee[2]	73	69	69	72	283	33,000,000
	Su Ji Kim	67	68	70	78	283	33,000,000
10	Hae Ran Ryu	70	70	74	70	284	14,413,333
	Hyun Kyung Park	71	69	70	74	284	14,413,333
	Han Sol Ji	71	73	69	71	284	14,413,333
	So Mi Lee	69	69	71	75	284	14,413,333
	Ji Young Park	71	68	71	74	284	14,413,333
	Ina Yoon	73	68	71	72	284	14,413,333
	Hyejun Park	67	71	71	75	284	14,413,333
	Ye Sung Jun	72	69	69	74	284	14,413,333
	Hee Ji Kim	66	73	67	78	284	14,413,333
19	Eun Soo Jang	70	73	71	71	285	11,340,000
	Min Song Ha	68	69	78	70	285	11,340,000
	So Young Lee	71	69	71	74	285	11,340,000
	Da Yeon Lee	71	69	71	74	285	11,340,000
23	Joo Mi Lee	69	74	69	74	286	10,560,000
24	Su Yeon Bae	69	72	73	73	287	10,200,000
	Hee Jun Kim	69	71	73	74	287	10,200,000
26	Ji Su Kim	72	70	73	73	288	9,394,286
	Seul Gi Jeong	70	74	70	74	288	9,394,286
	Yebeen Sohn	71	71	72	74	288	9,394,286
	Da Som Ma	75	69	70	74	288	9,394,286
	Yeun Jung Seo	71	70	72	75	288	9,394,286
	Woo Jeong Kim	70	69	73	76	288	9,394,286
	U Ree Jun	69	70	72	77	288	9,394,286

Kyochon Honey Ladies Open

It had been three years since A Yean Cho won twice in her rookie season. "I haven't had a chance for so long, I think I was very thirsty for a win," Cho said. Her chance came at Kingsdale as the 21-year-old won the Kyochon Honey Ladies Open. It was a wire-to-wire win with an eventual four-stroke margin over Ga Young Lee, the runner-up for the second week running, but it had been close for much of the final round.

Cho went two clear of the field with a six-birdie 66 on Friday, before a 69 the next day allowed both Ga Young Lee and Da Yeon Lee to grab a share of the lead. Da Yeon's chance went with a triple bogey at the fifth in the final round, while Ga Young fell two behind with a bogey at the fourth as Cho birdied. But Ga Young birdied the ninth to draw within one and extended her run to four in a row. From the 10th Cho matched her opponent with three consecutive birdies to stay in front by one and it was Ga Young who blinked with bogeys at the 13th and 16th holes. Cho birdied the 17th for a 67, matching the best of the day and her second bogey-free effort of the week. She ended on 14-under-par 202, with Ga Young Lee closing with a 71 and Da Yeon Lee a 74. Hae Ran Ryu, already a winner in the season, birdied the last to take third place.

"After getting good results in 2019, I didn't play well in 2020 and I felt like I wanted to give up on golf, but I was able to keep on playing because of other people's encouragement," Cho said. "I think the timing is a funny thing because I started to play badly when Covid struck and we had to compete without an audience, but now that the spectators are back, I won. I think I won thanks to my fans and how they cheered me on throughout the event."

Kingsdale Golf Club, Chungju, North Chungcheong — May 6-8
Par 72 (36-36); 6,709 yards — Purse: ₩800,000,000

1	**A Yean Cho**	66	69	67	202	₩144,000,000
2	**Ga Young Lee**	68	67	71	206	88,000,000
3	**Hae Ran Ryu**	69	69	69	207	64,000,000
4	Ji Young Park	71	70	67	208	40,000,000
5	Da Yeon Lee	68	67	74	209	32,000,000
6	Ju Young Pak	68	71	71	210	26,000,000
	Chae Yoon Park	70	70	70	210	26,000,000
8	Min Ji Park	69	73	69	211	16,000,000

	Hye Lim Jo	69	69	73	211	16,000,000		So Mi Lee	70	72	72	214	7,400,000
	Da Som Ma	71	69	71	211	16,000,000		Ji Su Kim	75	69	70	214	7,400,000
11	Gi Ppuem Lee	71	73	68	212	10,560,000		Bo Ah Kim	72	73	69	214	7,400,000
	Yewon Lee	71	69	72	212	10,560,000		Ha Na Jang	71	70	73	214	7,400,000
13	Hyo Min Jeon	72	71	70	213	9,200,000		Ye Sung Jun	69	72	73	214	7,400,000
	Eun Woo Choi	73	70	70	213	9,200,000		Bo Mi Kwak	74	65	75	214	7,400,000
	Hee Won Jung	71	72	70	213	9,200,000	27	Jeong Mee Hwang	75	69	71	215	6,272,000
	Jin Seon Han	72	69	72	213	9,200,000		Joo Mi Lee	75	70	70	215	6,272,000
17	Gyeol Park	70	71	73	214	7,400,000		Hee Won Na	70	72	73	215	6,272,000
	Jee Hyun Ahn	69	72	73	214	7,400,000		Ju Yeon In	72	70	73	215	6,272,000
	Hyejun Park	69	72	73	214	7,400,000		Su Yeon Bae	72	69	74	215	6,272,000
	Dan Yu Park	68	74	72	214	7,400,000							

NH Ladies Championship

When Min Ji Park won the NH Ladies Championship in 2021 it was the first time she had won more than once in a season. She did not stop there, ending up with six victories to be the KLPGA number one. But her last win of 2021 had come in July and her start to the 2022 was disrupted when she missed the opening event after testing positive for Covid. She then struggled in her early outings, missing the cut on the defence of the Nexen Saint Nine Masters.

Retaining her title at Suwon gave the 23-year-old Park her 11th career win by one stroke from three players, including amateur You Min Hwang, who led with eight holes to play. Hwang had impressed on the first day, lying second after a 65, and then added a 70 to tie Park's 67-68, though the defending champion would have been well clear but for a triple bogey at the fourth hole in the second round.

Hwang, who finished seventh at the 2021 OK Savings Se Ri Pak Invitational, made four birdies on the front nine on Sunday to go one clear, but Park then birdied the 11th and there was a two-shot swing in her favour at the 13th. Park then found a bunker at the 15th to drop the first of two shots in three holes so the pair came to the last tied. This time it was Hwang who found bunker trouble, finishing with a 71 to tie for second with Jeong Mee Hwang, who came home in 31 for a 67, and Yunji Jeong (69). Park closed with a 70 for an 11-under-par total of 205.

Suwon Country Club (New), Yongin, Gyeonggi — May 13-15
Par 72 (36-36); 6,581 yards — Purse: ₩800,000,000

1	**Min Ji Park**	67	68	70	205	₩144,000,000	16	Hae Rym Kim	70	69	74	213	8,171,429
2	**Jeong Mee Hwang**	69	70	67	206	76,000,000		Min Song Ha	70	71	72	213	8,171,429
	Yunji Jeong	67	70	69	206	76,000,000		Da Som Ma	69	71	73	213	8,171,429
	You Min Hwang (A)	65	70	71	206			Ye Rim Choi	72	72	69	213	8,171,429
5	Yewon Lee	71	67	70	208	40,000,000		Jae Hee Kim	69	73	71	213	8,171,429
6	Ji Hyun Oh	68	71	71	210	32,000,000		Su Ji Kim	71	70	72	213	8,171,429
7	Ga Eun Song	64	73	74	211	20,000,000		Bo Ah Kim	70	69	74	213	8,171,429
	Eun Woo Choi	65	75	71	211	20,000,000	23	Ina Yoon	69	73	72	214	6,765,714
	Jin Hee Im	69	72	70	211	20,000,000		Min Ju Kim	68	73	73	214	6,765,714
	So Mi Lee	66	70	75	211	20,000,000		Chae Yoon Park	72	68	74	214	6,765,714
	Ye Sung Jun	70	66	75	211	20,000,000		Jeongmin Moon	71	71	72	214	6,765,714
12	Hyo Ju You	69	75	68	212	10,060,000		Kum Kang Park	71	69	74	214	6,765,714
	Seul Gi Jeong	68	71	73	212	10,060,000		Seung Hui Ro	70	70	74	214	6,765,714
	Yebeen Sohn	69	69	74	212	10,060,000		Ji Su Kim	67	72	75	214	6,765,714
	Bo Kyeom Park	66	71	75	212	10,060,000							

Doosan Match Play Championship

Jung Min Hong did it the hard way to win her maiden title at the Doosan Match Play. After a tie in her first group match, the 20-year-old won her next two matches to reach the knockout stage. There it got more difficult. In the round of 16 she faced defending champion, and tour number one, Min Ji Park and only won after going to an extra hole. In the quarter-finals she defeated the player who had pipped her for 2021 Rookie of the Year honours, Ga Eun Song, by one hole, then in the semi-finals she went all the way to the 20th before seeing off regular tour winner Hee Jeong Lim. Lim went on to take third place by beating Song Yi Ahn 2 and 1.

The final was between Hong and a 2022 rookie, Yewon Lee, in only her ninth event and who won three of the first four holes. Hong won the next three to level the match, but Lee twice edged a hole ahead so Hong was one down with two to play. But she rallied to win the last two holes with birdies, sealing her victory with a fine approach close to the hole at the last.

Hong was a runner-up twice in her rookie season but in 2022 had missed the cut in three of her six events and not finished better than 30th. Yet she was not found wanting against the tour's best at Ladena. "Because I met so many competitive players on the way to the final, I didn't even imagine that I could win," said Hong. "But I did my best and I think that's what got me here."

Ladena Golf Club, Chuncheon, Gangwon
Par 72 (36-36); 6,350 yards

May 18-22
Purse: ₩800,000,000

ROUND OF 16
Chae Eun Lee[2] defeated So Hyun Bae 4 and 3
Hee Jeong Lim defeated Ju Young Pak 2 and 1
Jung Min Hong defeated Min Ji Park at the 19th
Song Yi Ahn defeated Jin Hee Im 2 and 1
Ji Su Kim defeated A Yean Cho by two holes
Ga Eun Song defeated Su Ji Kim 4 and 3
Yu Jin Sung defeated Ye Rim Choi 4 and 3
Yewon Lee defeated Jin Seon Han 3 and 2
Defeated players received ₩10,320,000

QUARTER-FINALS
Hee Jeong Lim defeated Yu Jin Sung 5 and 4
Jung Min Hong defeated Ga Eun Song by one hole
Yewon Lee defeated Chae Eun Lee[2] 5 and 4
Song Yi Ahn defeated Ji Su Kim by one hole
Defeated players received ₩24,560,000

SEMI-FINALS
Jung Min Hong defeated Hee Jeong Lim at the 20th
Yewon Lee defeated Song Yi Ahn 2 and 1

THIRD-FOURTH PLAYOFF
Hee Jeong Lim (₩68,000000) defeated Song Yi Ahn (₩48,000,000) by one hole

FINAL
Jung Min Hong (₩200,000,000) defeated Yewon Lee (₩92,000,000) by one hole

E1 Charity Open

To win her maiden title at the E1 Charity Open, Yunji Jeong had to win a five-hole, four-way playoff that included the last two winners of the tournament. Eventually, she defeated defending champion Han Sol Ji with a birdie to lift the title at South Springs two weeks after finishing runner-up at the NH Ladies Championship.

Ji had led on the first day on 66, while Min Song Ha took over after 36 holes thanks to a 65, the best of the week, on Saturday. Jeong, 21, opened 69-71 before adding a 68, with birdies coming home at 13, 16 and 18 to set the clubhouse target at eight-under-par 208. So Young Lee, who won the title in 2020, also birdied the last hole for a 69, a score also returned by Ji as they joined Jeong at eight under.

Ha, playing in the final group, had four birdies but also a double bogey at the seventh and a bogey at the eighth on the last day. She came to the last needing a birdie to win. Then came a sudden interruption when the sprinkler system for the green accidentally came on. The water was soon stopped but the unsettling delay meant Ha missed her putt and tied with a 71.

In the playoff, Ha hit the longest drive on the 18th but was the only one of the four not to make a birdie. The three remaining players parred the 18th twice more before Lee departed with another par, as Jeong and Ji birdied. At the fifth time of asking, Jeong made another birdie and Ji's title defence ended with a par.

South Springs Country Club, Icheon, Gyeonggi — May 27-29
Par 72 (36-36); 6,546 yards — Purse: ₩800,000,000

1	**Yunji Jeong**	69	71	68	208	₩144,000,000
2	**So Young Lee**	72	67	69	208	64,000,000
	Min Song Ha	72	65	71	208	64,000,000
	Han Sol Ji	66	73	69	208	64,000,000
	Jeong won playoff at fifth extra hole					
5	So Mi Lee	69	71	69	209	28,000,000
	Hee Ji Kim	69	71	69	209	28,000,000
	Ye Sung Jun	69	69	71	209	28,000,000
8	Hae Rym Kim	69	74	67	210	14,740,000
	Yeun Jung Seo	70	68	72	210	14,740,000
	Da Som Ma	69	70	71	210	14,740,000
	Yebeen Sohn	70	68	72	210	14,740,000
12	Ji Hyun Lee[3]	72	73	66	211	9,960,000
	Da Yeon Lee	74	68	69	211	9,960,000
14	Ga Eun Song	73	72	67	212	8,320,000
	Su Ji Kim	70	73	69	212	8,320,000
	So Hyun Bae	76	70	66	212	8,320,000
	Ji U Ko	72	69	71	212	8,320,000
	Yewon Lee	70	72	70	212	8,320,000
	Rae Hyeon Ku	70	71	71	212	8,320,000
	Hee Jeong Lim	72	69	71	212	8,320,000
	Woo Jeong Kim	71	70	71	212	8,320,000
22	Ha Na Jang	73	71	69	213	6,896,000
	Seung Yeon Lee	69	77	67	213	6,896,000
	Bo Kyeom Park	70	73	70	213	6,896,000
	Carrie Park	69	73	71	213	6,896,000
	Uh Jin Seo	67	71	75	213	6,896,000
27	Hye Lim Jo	72	71	71	214	6,182,857
	Ka Ram Choi	70	71	73	214	6,182,857
	Jung Min Lee	71	73	70	214	6,182,857
	Se Eun Kim	77	69	68	214	6,182,857
	Ree An Kim	68	73	73	214	6,182,857
	Eun Hye Jo	73	70	71	214	6,182,857
	Sae Ro Mi Kim	73	71	70	214	6,182,857

Lotte Open

In her fourth season on the KLPGA, Yu Jin Sung claimed her maiden victory at the Lotte Open at Bear's Best Cheongna. Sung won wire-to-wire, finishing four strokes ahead of Su Ji Kim with scores of 64-70-69-70 and a 15-under-par total of 273. The 22-year-old Sung, who had been twice a runner-up previously and reached the quarter-finals of the Doosan Match Play, opened the tournament with five birdies in her first six holes and shared the first-round lead with 19-year-old Yewon Lee, who played her second nine, the front side of the course, in 30.

Sung edged ahead by a stroke on Friday, then by three on Saturday and quickly established an even bigger advantage when she chipped in for an eagle at the second hole on Sunday. Three holes later, Sung's bunker shot ran over the green and stopped on the bank of the lake. She took three to get down for a double bogey, but birdied two of the next three holes to calm any nerves. She celebrated the win with a punch of the air on the 18th green.

Kim, who won twice in 2021, secured second place by holing a full wedge shot for her third at the 14th for an eagle. A bogey-free 67 put Kim one ahead of Lee, who followed her low opening effort with 71-72-71. Hee Jeong Lim, who shared second place with Lee following a 65 in the second round, faded over the weekend with 71-78.

Bear's Best Cheongna Golf Club, Incheon — June 2-5
Par 72 (36-36); 6,725 yards — Purse: ₩800,000,000

1	**Yu Jin Sung**	64	70	69	70	273	₩144,000,000
2	**Su Ji Kim**	66	71	73	67	277	88,000,000
3	**Yewon Lee**	64	71	72	71	278	64,000,000
4	Ji U Ko	69	73	69	68	279	36,000,000
	Han Sol Ji	68	69	72	70	279	36,000,000
6	Ina Yoon	72	67	72	69	280	24,000,000
	Jin Seon Han	71	70	71	68	280	24,000,000
	Da Yeon Lee	67	70	70	73	280	24,000,000
9	Seo Yeon Kwon	69	69	72	71	281	16,000,000
10	Hyejun Park	70	73	69	70	282	11,200,000
	Yunji Jeong	71	70	69	72	282	11,200,000
	Yeun Jung Seo	67	70	69	76	282	11,200,000
13	Seul Gi Jeong	66	74	74	69	283	9,600,000
	Jae Hee Kim	70	75	68	70	283	9,600,000
	Seo Yeon Yoo[2]	67	72	70	74	283	9,600,000
16	Ji Hyun Kim	71	73	71	69	284	8,600,000
	Kayoung Kim	69	72	72	71	284	8,600,000
	Ree An Kim	70	73	71	70	284	8,600,000
	Hee Jeong Lim	70	65	71	78	284	8,600,000
20	Yebeen Sohn	73	68	76	68	285	7,531,429
	Seung Hui Ro	71	71	73	70	285	7,531,429
	A Yean Cho	71	73	73	68	285	7,531,429
	Ji Su Kim	68	70	73	74	285	7,531,429
	Bo Ah Kim	75	70	69	71	285	7,531,429
	Ga Eun Song	70	66	76	73	285	7,531,429
	Ji Young Park	70	71	69	75	285	7,531,429
27	Yea Lin Kang	69	74	71	72	286	7,040,000
28	Min Ji Park	74	71	72	70	287	6,760,000
	Woo Jeong Kim	72	72	72	71	287	6,760,000
	So Hyun Bae	69	73	72	73	287	6,760,000
	Hyun Kyung Park	73	68	71	75	287	6,760,000
	Min Song Ha	72	70	73	72	287	6,760,000
	Eun Woo Choi	72	69	70	76	287	6,760,000

Celltrion Queens Masters

When it came to defending the multiple titles she won in 2021, Min Ji Park made her strike rate two out of four by retaining the Celltrion Queens Masters at Seolhaeone Country Club. It was a wire-to-wire win, the 12th in her career, with her three-stroke winning margin achieved by holing her eagle putt on the 18th green. Up to that point, she had a Faldo-esque run of 17 pars on her card.

It was in contrast to earlier in the tournament as Park posted 17 birdies over the first two rounds, seven of them in a back-nine 29 on the opening day. The first-round 65 gave her a one-stroke lead, which she maintained with a 67 the next day. The pin positions were much more difficult on Sunday and there was only one score better than her closing 70 for a 14-under-par total of 202.

Her nearest challenger was rookie Min Ju Kim, who opened the tournament by birdieing her first seven holes in a 66. Kim added scores of 68-71 to take second place and was still within one of Park until the KLPGA number one finished in dramatic fashion with the eagle at 18. "I did feel like I was being chased by Kim, especially because her driving distance is long," said Park. "When I found out that the pins had been moved to difficult locations, I felt nervous about that. But I told myself that I was doing well because I didn't bogey despite the difficult pin locations.

Park, 23, would also be the defending champion at the DB Group Korea Women's Open the following week. "I don't feel much of a burden to defend my title," she said. "Even though I don't think about being defending champion much, the Celltrion Queens Masters was very respectful about it, and I think that was why I could play comfortably, so I'm grateful towards Celltrion. I have decided not to think too far ahead. I play each and every event to win, and only to win. I won't think about other things and I promise to be that kind of player."

Seolhaeone Country Club, Yangyang, Gangwon — June 10-12
Par 72 (36-36); 6,633 yards — Purse: ₩1,000,000,000

1	**Min Ji Park**	65	67	70	202	₩180,000,000
2	**Min Ju Kim**	66	68	71	205	110,000,000
3	**Se Lin Hyun**	71	67	69	207	80,000,000
4	Ga Eun Song	67	66	75	208	50,000,000
5	Seo Yeon Kwon	68	68	73	209	37,500,000
	Ji U Ko	67	70	72	209	37,500,000
7	Han Sol Ji	69	69	72	210	27,500,000
	Chae Eun Lee[2]	68	70	72	210	27,500,000
9	Joo Mi Lee	72	69	70	211	16,233,333
	So Young Lee	71	70	70	211	16,233,333
	Hae Ran Ryu	71	67	73	211	16,233,333
12	Jeong Mee Hwang	69	73	70	212	12,450,000
	Jin Hee Im	69	69	74	212	12,450,000
14	Hyun Kyung Park	71	70	72	213	10,883,333
	Ji Hyun Kim	71	71	71	213	10,883,333
	Da Yeon Lee	70	71	72	213	10,883,333
	Bo Mi Kwak	66	74	73	213	10,883,333
	Seo Jin Park	67	71	75	213	10,883,333
	Jeongmin Moon	72	69	72	213	10,883,333
20	Jin Seon Han	69	74	71	214	9,500,000
	Hee Jeong Lim	71	72	71	214	9,500,000
	Ree An Kim	70	71	73	214	9,500,000
	Ye Bon Choi	70	72	72	214	9,500,000
24	So Yi Kim	71	71	73	215	8,307,692
	Hyo Jin Park	73	70	72	215	8,307,692
	Su Ji Kim	71	73	71	215	8,307,692
	Ga Young Lee	69	73	73	215	8,307,692
	Yea Lin Kang	70	73	72	215	8,307,692
	Yebeen Sohn	74	69	72	215	8,307,692
	Eun Woo Choi	67	72	76	215	8,307,692
	Joori Jeong	71	71	73	215	8,307,692
	Hee Ji Kim	72	69	74	215	8,307,692
	A Yean Cho	67	74	74	215	8,307,692
	Seung Yeon Lee	73	70	72	215	8,307,692
	Ka Ram Choi	70	72	73	215	8,307,692
	So Hye Park	69	69	77	215	8,307,692

DB Group Korea Women's Open

A record-breaking performance brought victory at the 36th DB Group Korea Women's Open for Hee Jeong Lim. The 21-year-old lowered the best score for 54 holes at the tournament to 16 under par with rounds of 68-66-66 at Rainbow Hills, and then added a 69 for a 19-under-par total of 269, two strokes better than the previous record, which was tied by Min Ji Park in 2021.

Having defended two titles already in 2022, including the previous week, Park opened with a 66 but then fell off Lim's pace as she added 71-69-70. Park dropped three shots in the last two holes to fall to third place, while Seo Yeon Kwon took second place by coming home in 32 for a 68 and 13 under par.

Lim's six-shot victory was her first of the season and the fifth of her career. She won only once in

2021 but also had three runner-up finishes, including to Jin Young Ko in a playoff at the BMW Ladies Championship, which was co-sanctioned with the US LPGA.

It was a difficult start to the season when Lim was involved in a car accident in April, hitting her head on the windscreen, and she struggled for health and fitness in subsequent weeks. A third place at the Doosan Match Play indicated she was on her way back but she revealed she was still dealing with the after effects of the accident. "I'm not in very good shape, but let's just endure this tournament," she said. "I am happy to win the championship by setting the record for 54 and 72 holes." Her six-shot overnight lead was soon extended with birdies at the first two holes on Sunday and she cruised to victory with two more birdies and only one dropped shot.

Rainbow Hills Golf Club, Eumseong, North Chungcheong — June 16-19
Par 72 (36-36); 6,699 yards — Purse: ₩1,200,000,000

1	**Hee Jeong Lim**	68	66	66	69	269	₩300,000,000
2	**Seo Yeon Kwon**	67	70	70	68	275	120,000,000
3	**Min Ji Park**	66	71	69	70	276	75,000,000
4	Hee Jun Kim	68	67	71	71	277	43,666,666
	Su Ji Kim	72	68	69	68	277	43,666,666
	Ga Young Lee	67	70	69	71	277	43,666,666
7	Seung Hui Ro	67	72	67	72	278	32,000,000
	Ji Yeo Lim (A)	70	71	68	69	278	
	Ju Yeon In	69	71	69	69	278	32,000,000
10	Ji Hyun Oh	70	73	71	65	279	27,500,000
11	Jin Hee Im	69	72	67	72	280	20,925,000
	Yu Jin Sung	69	70	70	71	280	20,925,000
	He Yong Choi	67	69	70	74	280	20,925,000
	Ji Young Park	69	72	67	72	280	20,925,000
15	Hee Ji Kim	69	70	71	71	281	15,666,666
	Ji Min Jung	68	71	70	72	281	15,666,666
	Jung Min Hong	67	69	71	74	281	15,666,666
18	Yewon Lee	69	73	69	71	282	12,650,000
	Yea Lin Kang	67	70	73	72	282	12,650,000
	Seung Yeon Lee	69	74	70	69	282	12,650,000
	Ye Sung Jun	68	74	71	69	282	12,650,000
	Hae Ran Ryu	69	72	71	70	282	12,650,000
	Min Ju Kim	69	74	67	72	282	12,650,000
24	Chae Yoon Park	70	74	69	70	283	11,300,000
25	Ji Su Kim	73	68	74	69	284	10,300,000
	Ga Eun Song	71	70	72	71	284	10,300,000
	Yunji Jeong	72	73	65	74	284	10,300,000
	Ree An Kim	70	72	70	72	284	10,300,000
29	Julie Kim	73	69	75	68	285	8,820,000
	Dasom Ma	67	73	72	73	285	8,820,000
	Eun Woo Choi	70	72	73	70	285	8,820,000
	Vongtaveelap Natthakritta (A)	71	73	70	71	285	
	Jinyeong Lim	67	72	72	74	285	8,820,000
	You Min Hwang (A)	72	70	71	72	285	
	Yeon Ju Jung	67	75	72	71	285	8,820,000

BC Card Hankyung Ladies Cup

A week after failing to defend her title at the Korea Open, Min Ji Park won for the second time in three weeks, and for the third time in just nine starts in 2022, with a playoff victory at the BC Card Hankyung Ladies Cup. Unlike in her first two wins of the season, the 2021 number one had not won the tournament in 2021, when she took six titles, but it counted among her 13 KLPGA victories no less.

Park, who shared the first-round lead with Ina Yoon on 64, started the final round two behind Uh Jin Seo, but was immediately on the charge with four birdies in the first five holes, plus a bogey at the third. She almost holed her third at the par-five first, tapping in from two inches, then hit to a couple of feet at the second and fourth holes and made an 18-footer at the fifth.

But there the birdies dried up in regulation play. While Seo went out in 40 on the way to a 75, and Yoon closed with a 70 for third place, Ji Young Park made up four strokes in the last 11 holes to tie on 12-under-par 204 with a 69 to Min Ji's 70. Ji Young birdied the eighth, ninth and 15th holes, before Min Ji dropped a shot at the 16th.

Both players had missed 10-footers at the par-five 18th in regulation before Min Ji holed from 12 feet in the playoff, only to see Ji Young, seeking her second win of the season, lip out from nine feet to extend the playoff.

Fortune Hills Golf Club, Pocheon, Gyeonggi — June 24-26
Par 72 (36-36); 6,610 yards — Purse: ₩800,000,000

1	**Min Ji Park**	64	70	70	204	₩144,000,000
2	**Ji Young Park**	66	69	69	204	88,000,000
	Min Ji Park won playoff at first extra hole					
3	**Ina Yoon**	64	71	70	205	64,000,000
4	Ji Hyun Oh	69	67	70	206	36,000,000
	So Mi Lee	69	69	68	206	36,000,000

6	Uh Jin Seo	66	66	75	207	26,000,000
	Jin Hee Im	69	68	70	207	26,000,000
8	So Young Lee	68	72	68	208	14,740,000
	Hae Ran Ryu	70	72	66	208	14,740,000
	Ye Sung Jun	68	72	68	208	14,740,000
	Ga Young Lee	69	69	70	208	14,740,000
12	Sebeen Jung	69	74	66	209	9,392,000
	Ye Rim Choi	73	70	66	209	9,392,000
	Han Sol Ji	71	68	70	209	9,392,000
	Eun Woo Choi	70	71	68	209	9,392,000
	Yeon Ju Jung	66	71	72	209	9,392,000
17	Ji Su Kim	69	74	67	210	7,904,000
	A Yean Cho	71	71	68	210	7,904,000
	Hyun Kyung Park	70	70	70	210	7,904,000
	Yunji Jeong	72	68	70	210	7,904,000
	He Yong Choi	66	72	72	210	7,904,000
22	Yewon Lee	73	71	67	211	6,980,000
	Dan Yu Park	71	72	68	211	6,980,000
	Ji U Ko	69	75	67	211	6,980,000
	Hee Jeong Lim	71	68	72	211	6,980,000
26	So Yi Kim	70	73	69	212	6,320,000
	Ga Eun Song	71	73	68	212	6,320,000
	Seul Gi Jeong	71	72	69	212	6,320,000
	Yea Lin Kang	71	73	68	212	6,320,000
	Ji Yoo Lim (A)	71	70	71	212	
	Ga Yun Kim	74	66	72	212	6,320,000
	Min Ju Kim	68	72	72	212	6,320,000

McCol Mona Park Open

A week after finishing sixth at the BC Hankyung Open in her first experience of being a defending champion, something she put down to "greed", Jin Hee Im secured her second KLPGA victory with a wire-to-wire effort at the McCol Mona Park Open at Birch Hill. While Im had burst out of the pack for her first win a year and a month earlier, the 24-year-old was involved at the top of the leaderboard throughout this time.

She opened with a 67 to share the lead with rookie Ina Yoon, who was third the week before. A 69 on Saturday put Im two ahead and the pair both finished with 69s to give Im a two-stroke win on 11-under-par 205. Im led by as many as four strokes in the final round, but Yoon hit back with four birdies in a row from the ninth, while Im faltered with bogeys at the 15th and 16th holes. Yoon birdied the 17th to get within two going to the par-five 18th and hit the green in two at the last.

Im had laid up but then played a delightful approach, finishing two feet from the hole. After Yoon missed for an eagle from 20 feet, Im tapped in for the win. "I am so happy that I was able to pull off a wire-to-wire victory," Im said. "I wasn't happy with my performance last week, and I think it was because of my greed. So I thought that I should focus on what I can do well this week.

"This week's victory feels very different from my first win. That was more unexpected, and I think I was lucky then. But now, I think I have worked hard to earn my win, so that will build my confidence."

Birch Hill Golf Club, Pyeongchang, Gangwon — July 1-3
Par 72 (36-36); 6,434 yards — Purse: ₩800,000,000

1	**Jin Hee Im**	67	69	69	205	₩144,000,000
2	**Ina Yoon**	67	71	69	207	88,000,000
3	**Eun Woo Choi**	71	70	69	210	52,000,000
	Min Kyung Choi	71	69	70	210	52,000,000
5	Yewon Lee	70	69	72	211	32,000,000
6	Ye Rim Choi	68	71	73	212	28,000,000
7	Bo Kyeom Park	69	73	71	213	22,000,000
	Hyun Kyung Park	73	68	72	213	22,000,000
9	Gi Ppuem Lee	69	70	75	214	12,986,667
	Su Yeon Bae	72	69	73	214	12,986,667
	So Hyun Bae	72	71	71	214	12,986,667
12	He Yong Choi	72	74	69	215	9,960,000
	Han Sol Ji	72	73	70	215	9,960,000
14	Min Song Ha	75	71	70	216	8,320,000
	A Yean Cho	73	69	74	216	8,320,000
	Seul Gi Jeong	73	71	72	216	8,320,000
	Bo Mi Kwak	76	70	70	216	8,320,000
	Dan Yu Park	71	73	72	216	8,320,000
	Su Jin Lee[3]	71	71	74	216	8,320,000
	So Hye Park	70	70	76	216	8,320,000
	So Mi Lee	70	71	75	216	8,320,000
22	Ye Sung Jun	71	74	72	217	6,980,000
	Jeong Mee Hwang	70	71	76	217	6,980,000
	Ga Young Lee	70	73	74	217	6,980,000
	Gyeol Park	69	70	78	217	6,980,000
26	Ree An Kim	73	71	74	218	6,440,000
	Hee Won Na	72	76	70	218	6,440,000
	Seo Yeon Kwon	73	73	72	218	6,440,000
	Hee Ji Kim	71	72	75	218	6,440,000
	Jee Hyun Ahn	71	74	73	218	6,440,000
	Seung Yeon Lee	73	69	76	218	6,440,000

Daebo hausD Open

Immaculate greens at Seowon Valley helped create low-scoring conditions which Ga Eun Song revelled in as the 2021 Rookie of the Year won the Daebo hausD Open wire-to-wire. Song started with 10 birdies in a 62 on Friday, dropped her only shot for the week during a second round of 68 and added another 68 to win by three strokes from Ji Hyun Oh. Hae Ran Ryu scored a 64 on the final day to share third place with Bo Mi Kwak (68), one behind Oh.

Song had led the field by four strokes after the first day and although she saw her advantage cut in half by Oh's 67-65, the runner-up's closing 69 could not maintain the pressure on the champion, albeit Song was far from complacent in the final round. "To tell the truth, I was nervous this morning," said Song. "I stayed nervous until the second-to-last hole. I felt that I could win only in the last hole. The second shot in the last hole I think was the most important shot of the day. I was glad I was able to land it near the hole."

A par left Song on 18-under-par 198, two shots better than Min Ji Park's winning total in the inaugural event in 2021. This was Song's second win on the KLPGA after she defeated Evian champion Minjee Lee at the Hana Financial Group Championship during her first season on tour in 2021. "My goal is to win two titles this season," Song added. "For events that I don't get to win, I want to at least stay in the top 10."

Seowon Valley Country Club, Paju, Gyeonggi — July 8-10
Par 72 (36-36); 6,741 yards — Purse: ₩1,000,000,000

1	**Ga Eun Song**	62	68	68	198	₩180,000,000
2	**Ji Hyun Oh**	67	65	69	201	110,000,000
3	**Hae Ran Ryu**	69	69	64	202	65,000,000
	Bo Mi Kwak	66	68	68	202	65,000,000
5	Ji Young Park	68	67	68	203	35,000,000
	Hee Jeong Lim	67	67	69	203	35,000,000
	Yu Jin Sung	66	67	70	203	35,000,000
8	Dana Kang[2]	66	69	69	204	22,500,000
	Su Ji Kim	67	68	69	204	22,500,000
10	Su Jin Lee[3]	71	67	67	205	12,485,714
	Jung Min Hong	71	68	66	205	12,485,714
	Ji Min Jung	70	69	66	205	12,485,714
	So Young Lee	68	68	69	205	12,485,714
	Ji Won Hong	71	67	67	205	12,485,714
	Min Ji Park	68	67	70	205	12,485,714
	Min Kyung Choi	66	70	69	205	12,485,714
17	Jee Hyun Ahn	69	71	66	206	10,025,000
	Ye Rim Choi	68	69	69	206	10,025,000
	Uh Jin Seo	69	67	70	206	10,025,000
	Eun Hye Jo	69	68	69	206	10,025,000
21	Ji Su Kim	71	69	67	207	8,950,000
	Han Sol Ji	69	68	70	207	8,950,000
	Jin Hee Im	69	69	69	207	8,950,000
	Sun Ju Ahn	69	66	72	207	8,950,000
25	Ji U Ko	71	70	67	208	8,300,000
	Hee Jun Kim	70	67	71	208	8,300,000
	Chae Eun Lee[2]	67	68	73	208	8,300,000
28	Seul Gi Jeong	71	70	68	209	7,800,000
	He Yong Choi	69	69	71	209	7,800,000
	Jung Min Lee	69	72	68	209	7,800,000
	Ree An Kim	70	68	71	209	7,800,000
	Hwayeong Yun	71	68	70	209	7,800,000
	Jo Yoo Hyeon (A)	69	70	70	209	
	Jin Seon Han	71	66	72	209	7,800,000
	Eun Woo Choi	68	69	72	209	7,800,000

Ever Collagen Queens Crown

Two weeks after finishing as a runner-up, Ina Yoon converted her first victory on the KLPGA in her 14th event of her rookie season. The big hitting 19-year-old went wire-to-wire although there was a wobble midway through the final round with the youngster holing from 18 feet at the last to beat Ji Young Park by one stroke.

Yoon opened with a bogey-free 65, added a 68 in which she dropped her only shot of the first three days, and then another 65 to be two ahead. For the last three days it was Park who was doing the chasing and she went out in three under in the final round to draw level at the turn after Yoon followed three early bogeys with bogeys at the seventh and ninth holes.

Another bogey at the 14th, when she went into the water for the second time in the day, meant Yoon slipped one behind Park, before she made a 10-footer at the 15th to get back on level terms. They came to the last tied and it was there that Yoon made the winning birdie, while Park, who parred all the way home on the back nine in her pursuit of a second win of the season, missed from 15 feet to force a playoff.

"I feel bewildered because I am so happy," Yoon said. "Honestly, I was very nervous before the last putt, but I thought that I should focus not on the results but on what I can actually do at that moment. I tried to do my best and have no regrets."

Lakewood Country Club, Yangju, Gyeonggi, Par (36-36); 6,539 yards

July 14-17
Purse: ₩800,000,000

1	**Ina Yoon**	65	68	65	70	268	₩144,000,000		Hee Jeong Lim	68	69	71	68	276	8,782,222
2	**Ji Young Park**	69	65	66	69	269	88,000,000		So Young Lee	69	68	68	71	276	8,782,222
3	**Min Song Ha**	69	68	68	66	271	52,000,000		Su Jin Lee[3]	68	69	69	70	276	8,782,222
	Bo Mi Kwak	70	69	66	66	271	52,000,000	21	Hee Jun Kim	71	71	69	66	277	7,280,000
5	Han Sol Ji	71	66	68	67	272	32,000,000		Seung Yeon Lee	70	67	71	69	277	7,280,000
6	Bo Kyeom Park	71	67	69	66	273	26,000,000		Joo Mi Lee	71	67	69	70	277	7,280,000
	Yunji Jeong	67	70	66	70	273	26,000,000	24	Jung Min Lee	68	73	70	67	278	6,880,000
8	Hae Ran Ryu	74	65	71	64	274	16,000,000		Jin Hee Im	73	67	69	69	278	6,880,000
	So Mi Lee	71	69	68	66	274	16,000,000	26	Da Yeon Lee	73	68	70	68	279	6,400,000
	Ga Eun Song	71	69	69	65	274	16,000,000		Gyeol Park	70	68	71	70	279	6,400,000
11	Su Ji Kim	67	68	72	68	275	10,960,000		Jin Seon Han	70	69	70	70	279	6,400,000
12	Ga Young Lee	72	68	70	66	276	8,782,222		Ye Bon Choi	71	68	68	72	279	6,400,000
	Jung Min Hong	71	70	69	66	276	8,782,222		Hyejun Park	68	71	71	69	279	6,400,000
	Ye Rim Choi	71	68	69	68	276	8,782,222		Uh Jin Seo	68	70	72	69	279	6,400,000
	So Hyun Bae	68	74	67	67	276	8,782,222		Seung Hui Ro	66	70	71	72	279	6,400,000
	Jee Hyun Ahn	72	68	67	69	276	8,782,222		Yeun Jung Seo	68	67	69	75	279	6,400,000
	Hee Won Na	72	68	66	70	276	8,782,222		Ji U Ko	70	68	70	71	279	6,400,000

Hoban Seoul Shinmun Women's Classic

After winning twice in her rookie season in 2019, A Yean Cho missed out for the next two years but victory at the Hoban Seoul Shinmun Women's Classic gave the now 22-year-old another two-win season. Cho won by two strokes at the H1 Club in Icheon from Min Song Ha and Jeong Mee Hwang, who both finished runner-up for the second time in the season.

Cho scored 67-69-68 for a 12-under-par total of 204 and came from two behind Je Yeong Lee, the leader for the first two days with 63-71. Lee faltered with three bogeys on the back nine on Sunday to fall into a tie for fourth place. Cho made her move with three birdies in a row from the eighth. She added another at the 14th, dropped a shot at the 16th, but recovered it at the penultimate hole. Ha had a 67 and Hwang a 68 to share second place.

"I think I had more fun than I felt nervous today," said Cho. "My caddie really helped me keep a level head. I also didn't really feel the pressure that I needed to win this title and I think that mindset helped, too. I think I am a player who can only win with the presence of my fans. I think 90 per cent of my wins are thanks to my fans and I want to thank them for coming out every time to cheer for me and applaud every shot."

H1 Club, Icheon, Gyeonggi
Par 72 (36-36); 6,654 yards

July 22-24
Purse: ₩1,000,000,000

1	**A Yean Cho**	67	69	68	204	₩180,000,000		Jung Min Lee	72	66	70	208	13,160,000
2	**Min Song Ha**	72	67	67	206	95,000,000		Jee Hyun Ahn	67	69	72	208	13,160,000
	Jeong Mee Hwang	71	67	68	206	95,000,000		Yewon Lee	71	70	67	208	13,160,000
4	Hae Ran Ryu	70	69	68	207	33,333,333		Ga Young Lee	72	69	67	208	13,160,000
	Ka Ram Choi	66	72	69	207	33,333,333	15	Hee Jeong Lim	69	71	69	209	10,950,000
	Ji Young Park	68	70	69	207	33,333,333		Ina Yoon	69	70	70	209	10,950,000
	Jin Seon Han	68	68	71	207	33,333,333		Ye Rim Choi	69	68	72	209	10,950,000
	Han Sol Ji	69	68	70	207	33,333,333		Hyejun Park	69	70	70	209	10,950,000
	Je Yeong Lee	63	71	73	207	33,333,333	19	Se Lin Hyun	72	67	71	210	9,825,000
10	Su Ji Kim	69	70	69	208	13,160,000		Seo Yeon Yoo[2]	72	67	71	210	9,825,000

	Min Ju Kim	69	70	71	210	9,825,000
	So Mi Lee	69	69	72	210	9,825,000
23	Jung Min Hong	70	70	71	211	8,627,273
	Seul Gi Jeong	73	69	69	211	8,627,273
	Hee Jun Kim	70	71	70	211	8,627,273
	Da Yeon Lee	70	71	70	211	8,627,273
	Ye Sung Jun	72	69	70	211	8,627,273
	Seoyoon Kim	72	72	67	211	8,627,273
	Hyun Kyung Park	69	72	70	211	8,627,273
	Eun Woo Choi	73	70	68	211	8,627,273
	Seo Jin Park	71	68	72	211	8,627,273
	Jin Hee Im	68	68	75	211	8,627,273
	Dan Yu Park	69	69	73	211	8,627,273

Jeju Samdasoo Masters

Three strokes behind with four holes to play, Han Sol Ji produced a stunning finish by birdieing each and every one of them to win the Jeju Samdasoo Masters by one shot from Ye Rim Choi. Looking for her maiden victory, Choi had led for the first three days following an opening 65. With a round to play, she was two ahead of two-time KLPGA champion Hyun Kyung Park and three ahead of Ji.

On the final day, Ji made three early birdies, hitting the flagstick for a tap-in birdie at the par-three seventh, before bogeying the eighth and 12th holes. With Park, winless so far in 2022, scoring a 72 to drop to third place, Choi had looked in a strong position with birdies at the fourth and eighth holes, and even after a bogey at the 11th. From there she parred in for a 71 and was not able to respond to Ji's incredible finish.

It started at the 15th, where Ji got up and down from a bunker for the first of her four birdies. She holed from 15 feet at the 16th and then from double that length at the 17th. At the last her approach again hit the flagstick and she tapped in for the victory on 14-under-par 274 after a closing 67.

It was Ji's third victory and made up for losing in a playoff when attempting to defend her title at the E1 Charity Open. "The mistake at 12, I just forgot about it right away because I thought I would have more chances," Ji said. "After 15 and 16, I felt that the tide had turned in my favour. I was confident with my putter and even though that putt on 17 was long, I could see the line on the green clearly, and I putted with confidence. Regarding my iron shot in the last hole, the distance left to reach the green was about 125 meters. That's my favourite distance to play using my nine-iron. I am so grateful for my fans who came all the way here to Jeju to cheer for me, and I am glad that I could win for them."

Elysian Jeju Country Club, Jeju Island — August 4-7
Par 72 (36-36); 6,654 yards — Purse: ₩900,000,000

1	**Han Sol Ji**	67	69	71	67	274	₩162,000,000
2	**Ye Rim Choi**	65	69	70	71	275	99,000,000
3	**Hyun Kyung Park**	68	69	69	72	278	72,000,000
4	Hae Ran Ryu	69	68	73	70	280	45,000,000
5	A Yean Cho	68	72	70	71	281	31,500,000
	Yewon Lee	69	70	70	72	281	31,500,000
	Ji Hyun Oh	68	68	73	72	281	31,500,000
8	Yu Jin Sung	69	72	71	70	282	16,582,500
	Seung Yeon Lee	72	70	69	71	282	16,582,500
	So Mi Lee	70	70	70	72	282	16,582,500
	Ji U Ko	67	70	72	73	282	16,582,500
12	Hee Jun Kim	70	66	74	73	283	11,205,000
	Sebeen Jung	72	68	71	72	283	11,205,000
14	Jung Min Lee	75	69	68	72	284	10,305,000
	Seul Gi Jeong	69	76	68	71	284	10,305,000
16	Bo Mi Kwak	71	72	72	70	285	9,180,000
	Seo Yeon Yoo[2]	67	72	72	74	285	9,180,000
	Seo Jin Park	68	72	72	73	285	9,180,000
	Su Ji Kim	72	72	69	72	285	9,180,000
	Uh Jin Seo	67	71	73	74	285	9,180,000
21	Hee Ji Kim	72	73	72	69	286	8,055,000
	Rae Hyeon Ku	66	75	75	70	286	8,055,000
	Min Song Ha	73	73	67	73	286	8,055,000
	Julie Kim	71	71	73	71	286	8,055,000
25	Ye Sung Jun	68	73	73	73	287	7,110,000
	Ji Won Hong	69	76	71	71	287	7,110,000
	Dan Yu Park	68	74	73	72	287	7,110,000
	Yunji Jeong	71	73	70	73	287	7,110,000
	Min Ju Kim	68	73	72	74	287	7,110,000
	Ji Young Park	71	70	72	74	287	7,110,000
	Min Ji Park	73	72	69	73	287	7,110,000
	Gyeol Park	68	68	74	77	287	7,110,000

Dayouwinia MBN Ladies Open

So Young Lee, the former Youth Olympics gold medallist, collected her sixth KLPGA title at the Dayouwinia MBN Ladies Open at Dayou Montvert Country Club. The 25-year-old defeated Hyun

Kyung Park with a long putt at the second extra hole of a sudden-death playoff. Lee, who won three times in 2018, had won only once since, at the 2020 E1 Charity Open, the event where she lost out in a playoff in 2022.

Lee scored 68-66-69 for a 13-under-par total of 203 to match Park's 72-64-67. Lee had been five behind first-round leader Eun Hye Jo, who led by four with a 63, and kept her lead after 36 holes. Jo's 70-71 in the last two rounds dropped her into a share of third place with defending champion So Mi Lee. The pair finished one shot outside the playoff, with So Mi regretting a poor chip at the 16th which cost her a bogey.

So Young Lee struggled with her game early in the final round, but dropped only one shot, at the first hole, before claiming three birdies going out, including via a long putt at the ninth, and another at the 14th. Park, who finished third the previous week and was still looking for her first win since the KLPGA Championship in May 2021, went bogey-free on Sunday and birdied the 14th and 16th holes to force the playoff.

Dayou Montvert Country Club, Pocheon, Gyeonggi — August 12-14
Par 72 (36-36); 6,590 yards — Purse: ₩900,000,000

1	**So Young Lee**	68	66	69	203	₩162,000,000
2	**Hyun Kyung Park**	72	64	67	203	99,000,000
	Lee won playoff at second extra hole					
3	**Eun Hye Jo**	63	70	71	204	58,500,000
	So Mi Lee	67	68	69	204	58,500,000
5	Ju Yeon In	71	67	68	206	36,000,000
6	Chae Yoon Park	69	69	69	207	19,465,714
	Jeongmin Moon	68	70	69	207	19,465,714
	Ji Young Park	71	67	69	207	19,465,714
	Ye Sung Jun	69	69	69	207	19,465,714
	Jinyeong Lim	71	66	70	207	19,465,714
	Su Yeon Jang	70	68	69	207	19,465,714
	Ji U Ko	71	64	72	207	19,465,714
13	Hae Ran Ryu	70	69	69	208	10,350,000
	Jin Seon Han	71	69	68	208	10,350,000
	U Ree Jun	71	69	68	208	10,350,000
	Hee Won Na	73	66	69	208	10,350,000
17	Hee Ji Kim	69	73	67	209	9,022,500
	Da Been Heo	69	68	72	209	9,022,500
	Sun Ju Ahn	67	70	72	209	9,022,500
	Hyejun Park	70	70	69	209	9,022,500
21	Yeon Ju Jung	72	68	70	210	7,956,000
	Min Byeol Kim (A)	70	68	72	210	
	Geena Yoo	73	69	68	210	7,956,000
	Hee Won Jung	70	68	72	210	7,956,000
	Ji Hyun Kim	70	70	70	210	7,956,000
	Da Som Ma	71	67	72	210	7,956,000
27	Jin Hee Im	73	70	68	211	7,164,000
	Ye Rim Choi	68	73	70	211	7,164,000
	Hee Jeong Lim	69	71	71	211	7,164,000
	Yunji Jeong	73	68	70	211	7,164,000
	Min Ji Park	73	67	71	211	7,164,000

HighOne Resort Ladies Open

By winter it is one of South Korea's largest ski resorts, by summer it hosts the HighOne Resort Ladies Open on the KLPGA. Jin Seon Han had climbed quite a mountain to gain her first victory on the top tour, finally winning in her 131st start over five seasons, the circuit's fourth longest streak prior to claiming a title. "I think I let many opportunities to win slide by until now, and so I am very happy to win," said Han, who had twice been a runner-up. "There were many opportunities in my rookie season. I even got into playoffs, but it never ended very well. People around me also awaited this win for so long. I grew up in Sokcho, Gangwon, and so it feels special to win here in my hometown. It took me a very long time to win my first title."

Han, 24, opened with rounds of 70-72 and had a double bogey on her first hole on Saturday before roaring back to post a 67 to lie three behind Sun Ju Ahn. An eighth KLPGA title in 13 years beckoned for Ahn but the veteran did not make a birdie in her closing 77. Han stumbled with an early bogey at the par-five fourth, but rallied with five birdies, three of them twos, including from a foot at the eighth and from 30 feet at the 14th.

She then holed from 10 feet at the 17th to get to 11 under par and, with a 68 for a total of 277, Han won by two strokes from Hae Ran Ryu, who like Han matched the lowest score of the day with a 68, and Ye Rim Choi, who bogeyed the 18th for a 70. Choi was a runner-up for the second time in three weeks following her second place at the Jeju Samdasoo Masters.

HighOne Resort, Jeongseon, Gangwon — August 18-21
Par 72 (36-36); 6,517 yards — Purse: ₩800,000,000

1	**Jin Seon Han**	70	72	67	68	277	144,000,000
2	**Hae Ran Ryu**	67	72	72	68	279	76,000,000
	Ye Rim Choi	69	72	68	70	279	76,000,000
4	Su Ji Kim	70	68	71	71	280	40,000,000
5	Yunji Jeong	71	71	68	71	281	32,000,000
6	Yeun Jung Seo	68	70	76	68	282	26,120,000
	Ye Sung Jun	68	75	69	70	282	26,120,000
8	Da Been Heo	67	72	73	71	283	16,080,000
	He Yong Choi	68	72	74	69	283	16,080,000
	Sun Ju Ahn	67	72	67	77	283	16,080,000
11	Ji Young Park	73	71	72	68	284	10,380,000
	Seo Yeon Yoo[2]	70	73	71	70	284	10,380,000
	Yewon Lee	70	73	71	70	284	10,380,000
	Ji U Ko	67	74	72	71	284	10,380,000
15	Ye Nah Hwang	70	76	70	69	285	8,920,000
	Do Eun Park	73	69	72	71	285	8,920,000
	Ju Yeon In	70	70	76	69	285	8,920,000
	So Mi Lee	71	71	72	71	285	8,920,000
19	Ji Hyun Kim	68	73	74	71	286	8,200,000
	Seul Gi Jeong	71	71	69	75	286	8,200,000
21	Jin Hee Im	73	73	70	71	287	7,474,286
	Gyeol Park	71	73	71	72	287	7,474,286
	Yebeen Sohn	72	74	72	69	287	7,474,286
	Su Yeon Bae	70	73	74	70	287	7,474,286
	Min Kyung Choi	72	67	73	75	287	7,474,286
	Se Lin Hyun	71	70	72	74	287	7,474,286
	So Hyun Bae	68	73	72	74	287	7,474,286
28	Seo Hyeon Park	72	73	74	69	288	6,880,000
	Eun Woo Choi	75	71	71	71	288	6,880,000
	Min Ju Kim	71	74	72	71	288	6,880,000
	So Hye Park	72	74	67	75	288	6,880,000
	Min Ji Park	70	76	70	72	288	6,880,000

Hanwha Classic

For the first time in seven years on the KLPGA Tour, the winning score was over par as Jade Palace provided a fearsome test for the circuit's third major of the season. Already one of the toughest courses on tour, the greens were running hard and fast, while the rough was exceptionally deep, plus conditions were foggy. Minimising mistakes was the key and Ji Won Hong managed to do that with 14 birdies and only 15 bogeys as the 22-year-old second-year player finished on one-over-par 289 with scores of 71-72-74-72 for a sensational maiden victory.

Hong was virtually unknown prior to surviving the brutal test at the Hanwah Classic and finishing four strokes ahead of tour number one Min Ji Park. Hong had finished third at Jade Palace as a rookie in 2021, but so far in 2022 she had recorded only one top 10 and she missed the cut on her previous two starts. She was struggling to retain her card but the win gave her an exemption on tour until 2025 and the first prize of ₩252 million virtually doubled her career earnings.

Finding the fairways was key throughout the week, yet Hong's success at hitting the greens in regulation 79 per cent of the time was actually an improvement on her season's average. She tied for the lead after 36 holes and then her two-over-par effort on Saturday, when she bogeyed the last two holes, matched the best of the day and put her three strokes in front. Hong made the turn in two under on Sunday and she was leading by six before another couple of late bogeys at 16 and 17. Park, looking for her fourth win of the season, attempted to put pressure on with three birdies in a row from the eighth but parred in from there for a 71. Su Ji Kim (73), Yunji Jeong (75) and Min Song Ha (75) all shared third place, with Jeong having posted the lowest score of the week with a 67 on Friday.

Jade Palace Golf Club, Chuncheon, Gangwon — August 25-28
Par 72 (36-36); 6,777 yards — Purse: ₩1,400,000,000

1	**Ji Won Hong**	71	72	74	72	289	₩252,000,000
2	**Min Ji Park**	70	76	76	71	293	154,000,000
3	**Yunji Jeong**	76	67	77	75	295	79,333,333
	Su Ji Kim	74	73	75	73	295	79,333,333
	Min Song Ha	71	73	76	75	295	79,333,333
6	Ji Young Park	74	73	81	68	296	45,500,000
	Jenny Shin	77	71	78	70	296	45,500,000
8	Ji Yeong Kim[2]	72	71	80	74	297	31,500,000
	Jin Hee Im	73	75	74	75	297	31,500,000
10	Ji Hyun Oh	73	77	79	70	299	18,312,000
	So Hyun Bae	74	75	74	76	299	18,312,000
	Hee Won Jung	74	71	80	74	299	18,312,000
	Hae Ran Ryu	74	73	79	73	299	18,312,000
	Seo Yeon Yoo[2]	69	82	76	72	299	18,312,000
15	So Young Lee	74	76	76	74	300	15,190,000
	Seung Hui Ro	79	70	76	75	300	15,190,000
	Joo Mi Lee	71	77	80	72	300	15,190,000
	A Yean Cho	79	70	75	76	300	15,190,000
19	Se Lin Hyun	76	74	78	73	301	13,930,000
	Ji Hyun Kim	71	72	80	78	301	13,930,000
21	Seul Gi Jeong	78	71	78	75	302	12,880,000
	Song Yi Ahn	73	78	76	75	302	12,880,000
	Gyeol Park	73	75	78	76	302	12,880,000
	Han Sol Ji	78	71	78	75	302	12,880,000
	Hee Jeong Lim	78	71	77	76	302	12,880,000
26	Ji U Ko	77	75	81	71	304	11,620,000
	Eun Hye Jo	77	74	80	73	304	11,620,000
	Hyun Kyung Park	72	78	76	78	304	11,620,000

Se Eun Kim	76 75 80 73	304	11,620,000	Da Som Ma	72 77 79 76	304	11,620,000
Yeon Ju Jung	74 75 78 77	304	11,620,000	Ye Sung Jun	77 73 80 74	304	11,620,000
Eun Woo Choi	77 74 77 76	304	11,620,000	So Mi Lee	77 74 78 75	304	11,620,000

KG Edaily Ladies Open

A year after winning her maiden victory at the KG Edaily Ladies Open, Su Ji Kim was back to retain her title and was only prevented in doing so when Jeong Mee Hwang won at the first extra hole. This was the 23-year-old Hwang's first victory on tour in a season when she had twice been a runner-up.

Kim started the defence of her title in good fashion by taking the lead on the first day with a 66. She slipped into second place on Saturday only because Hwang, following an opening 71, carded a 62 with 10 birdies and no bogeys. Hwang started the final round nervously, with three bogeys in the first seven holes to turn in one over par, but then came home in 32 with four birdies, including from 15 feet at the short 16th and from eight feet on the final green.

Hwang's closing 69 meant she tied with Kim on 14-under-par 202 as Kim posted twin weekend rounds of 68. Kim's liking of Sunning Point was obvious as she made only two bogeys for the tournament, and none on the final day, taking the lead when she holed out from the fairway from 84 yards for an eagle three at the 14th. In the playoff at the 18th, Hwang won with a birdie four to a five. Rookie Yewon Lee took third place with a 68.

Sunning Point Country Club, Yongin, Gyeonggi — September 2-4
Par 72 (36-36); 6,748 yards — Purse: ₩700,000,000

1	**Jeong Mee Hwang**	71 62 69	202	₩126,000,000
2	**Su Ji Kim**	66 68 68	202	77,000,000
	Hwang won playoff at first extra hole			
3	**Yewon Lee**	68 68 68	204	56,000,000
4	Jin Seon Han	71 66 68	205	31,500,000
	Ji U Ko	70 67 68	205	31,500,000
6	So Yi Kim	69 69 68	206	22,750,000
	Han Sol Ji	72 65 69	206	22,750,000
8	So Hyun Bae	67 69 71	207	15,750,000
	Se Eun Kim	70 67 70	207	15,750,000
10	Jung Min Hong	72 67 69	208	9,706,667
	Hyun Kyung Park	70 70 68	208	9,706,667
	Ji Young Park	69 69 70	208	9,706,667
13	Yebeen Sohn	67 72 70	209	8,172,500
	Ji Min Jung[2]	68 72 69	209	8,172,500
	Dan Yu Park	69 70 70	209	8,172,500
	Ga Eun Song	68 70 71	209	8,172,500
17	Yu Jin Sung	72 71 67	210	7,154,000
	Yeun Jung Seo	71 69 70	210	7,154,000
	So Young Lee	70 72 68	210	7,154,000
	Hee Ji Kim	69 71 70	210	7,154,000
	Kyo Rim Seo (A)	72 70 68	210	
	Bo Ah Kim	73 67 70	210	7,154,000
23	Hae Rym Kim	71 71 69	211	6,440,000
	Yeon Ju Jung	69 71 71	211	6,440,000
	Da Been Heo	69 70 72	211	6,440,000
	Jeongmin Moon	70 69 72	211	6,440,000
27	Hae Ran Ryu	71 71 70	212	5,915,000
	Ji Yeong Kim[2]	69 71 72	212	5,915,000
	Jin Young Hong[2]	72 69 71	212	5,915,000
	Joo Mi Lee	68 73 71	212	5,915,000
	Hyo Ju You	71 70 71	212	5,915,000
	Ji Hyun Lee[3]	72 71 69	212	5,915,000
	Hee Jeong Lim	69 72 71	212	5,915,000
	Jee Hyun Ahn	69 72 71	212	5,915,000

KB Financial Group Star Championship

Scoring was never easy at the KB Financial Group Star Championship. The Black Stone course in Icheon was playing long, with narrow fairways and thick rough. On the first two days, no player broke 70. In Gee Chun, the KPMG Women's PGA champion, did not break par on any day. The best scores on the weekend were a pair of 68s, by Hae Ran Ryu on Saturday and by Min Ji Park on Sunday.

In fact, the only time scoring looked remotely easy was when Park made four birdies on the final six holes. It was an inspired sprint to victory that brought the 24-year-old star a four-stroke victory over So Young Lee. Park was the joint first-round leader on 70, then went 73-72 to lie one behind Yunji Jeong, who scored a 69 on Saturday but closed with a 75 to fall into a tie for fourth place. Hee Jeong Lim, the 2019 winner, was the only player to score two rounds under 70, going 69-69 on the weekend to finish in third place, having been six over par at the halfway point.

Park was level par on Sunday when she holed a putt from 35 feet at the 13th to spark her run to the title. She holed from five feet at the next and although Lee birdied the 15th to get back within one, the challenger bogeyed the 17th, while Park hit a long approach at the same hole to within three feet. Park then wedged just as close at the par-five 18th for a four to complete a superb sequence that left her on a five-under-par total of 283. Lee, who closed with a 72, was the only other player to finish under par for the week.

This was Park's fourth win of the season and made her the first player to have consecutive seasons winning over ₩1 billion. She won six times in 2021, including her first major title at the Korea Open, so this was her second KLPGA major. Chun finished in a tie for 23rd place, while defending champion Ha Na Jang withdrew on the first day and Hyun Kyung Park missed the tournament having contracted Covid-19.

Black Stone Golf Club, Icheon, Gyeonggi — September 15-18
Par 72 (36-36); 6,689 yards — Purse: ₩1,200,000,000

1	**Min Ji Park**	70	73	72	68	283	216,000,000
2	**So Young Lee**	71	71	73	72	287	132,000,000
3	**Hee Jeong Lim**	74	76	69	69	288	96,000,000
4	Min Ju Kim	71	78	71	69	289	54,000,000
	Yunji Jeong	73	72	69	75	289	54,000,000
6	U Ree Jun	79	70	72	69	290	39,000,000
	Jung Min Hong	70	79	70	71	290	39,000,000
8	Yeun Jung Seo	71	76	72	72	291	24,000,000
	Jin Seon Han	76	72	72	71	291	24,000,000
	Eun Hye Jo	72	77	72	70	291	24,000,000
11	Su Ji Kim	78	74	70	70	292	15,440,000
	Ji Young Park	72	74	71	75	292	15,440,000
	Dasom Ma	76	74	71	71	292	15,440,000
14	Han Sol Ji	72	75	73	73	293	14,040,000
15	Ye Sung Jun	77	76	72	69	294	12,900,000
	Ji Hyun Kim	72	80	72	70	294	12,900,000
	A Yean Cho	78	70	73	73	294	12,900,000
	Hae Ran Ryu	77	74	68	75	294	12,900,000
19	Min Song Ha	78	76	71	70	295	11,680,000
	Ji Hyun Lee[3]	74	72	74	75	295	11,680,000
	Ye Rim Choi	79	74	72	70	295	11,680,000
	Shin Sil Bang[(A)]	79	72	73	71	295	
23	So Mi Lee	77	73	70	76	296	11,040,000
	In Gee Chun	73	76	73	74	296	11,040,000
25	Ji Min Jung	79	72	74	72	297	10,344,000
	Ji Won Hong	74	80	72	71	297	10,344,000
	Bo Mi Kwak	72	81	70	74	297	10,344,000
	Eun Woo Choi	77	76	72	72	297	10,344,000
	Yewon Lee	76	75	73	73	297	10,344,000
30	Dan Yu Park	76	74	74	74	298	9,780,000
	Seung Hui Ro	79	75	72	72	298	9,780,000
	Geena Yoo	77	76	69	76	298	9,780,000
	Jinyeong Lim	76	74	70	78	298	9,780,000

OK Financial Group Se Ri Pak Invitational

A season of consistent returns took a step up when Su Ji Kim claimed her first win of the year at the OK Financial Group Se Ri Pak Invitational, the event honouring Korea's greatest ever golfer. Kim, who lost in a playoff when attempting to defend her title at the KG Edaily Ladies Open, won by one stroke at Serenity Country Club after a tight contest with 19-year-old rookie Yewon Lee, who was also runner-up at the Doosan Match Play.

Kim, a two-time winner in 2021, produced the best round of the week on the second day when the 25-year-old followed a bogey at the opening hole with 10 birdies, five on each half, for a 63. It was nine strokes better than her first-round effort and put her into the lead by one from Lee (70-66). Kim again bogeyed the first hole on Sunday, and Lee birdied the second to go in front. Kim responded with gains at the sixth, ninth and 11th holes, while Lee birdied the 11th.

However, the youngster twice three-putted in the last five holes, including at the 17th where she raced her first putt six feet past the hole. She did respond to birdie the 18th but Kim was able to two-putt for her third victory. Both players closed with 70s, as Kim won on 11-under-par 205. Hae Ran Ryu birdied the last two holes for a 68 to take third place.

Serenity Country Club, Cheongju, Chungcheongbuk — September 23-25
Par 72 (36-36); 6,739 yards — Purse: ₩800,000,000

1	**Su Ji Kim**	72	63	70	205	₩144,000,000
2	**Yewon Lee**	70	66	70	206	88,000,000
3	**Hae Ran Ryu**	68	71	68	207	64,000,000
4	Woo Jeong Kim	74	69	65	208	36,000,000
	Su Yeon Jang	69	70	69	208	36,000,000
6	Seo Yeon Kwon	70	72	67	209	20,000,000
	Hee Jeong Lim	70	68	71	209	20,000,000
	Yeon Ju Jung	71	68	70	209	20,000,000

	Hee Ji Kim	69	68	72	209	20,000,000		Julie Kim	72 69 71	212	8,040,000
	Ji Hyun Lee[3]	68	71	70	209	20,000,000	23	Min Ji Park	72 71 70	213	6,920,000
11	Seung Hui Ro	75	66	69	210	10,293,333		You Min Hwang	73 71 69	213	6,920,000
	Hyo Joo Kim	69	69	72	210	10,293,333		Ji Min Jung[2]	71 69 73	213	6,920,000
	Jin Hee Im	72	67	71	210	10,293,333		Ye Bon Choi	70 73 70	213	6,920,000
14	So Young Lee	70	70	71	211	9,160,000		Eun Soo Jang	68 71 74	213	6,920,000
	Min Ju Kim	72	68	71	211	9,160,000		Ji Young Park	70 70 73	213	6,920,000
16	Eun Woo Choi	73	71	68	212	8,040,000	29	Jeongmin Moon	74 69 71	214	6,360,000
	Ji Sun Kang	74	68	70	212	8,040,000		Da Som Ma	72 73 69	214	6,360,000
	Ye Rim Choi	71	70	71	212	8,040,000		Yunji Jeong	67 75 72	214	6,360,000
	Su Yeon Bae	71	71	70	212	8,040,000		Se Lin Hyun	74 70 70	214	6,360,000
	So Hyun Bae	71	71	70	212	8,040,000		Yu Jin Sung	70 73 71	214	6,360,000
	Minsol Kim (A)	70	72	70	212			Hee Won Jung	69 73 72	214	6,360,000

Hana Financial Group Championship

For the second year running Su Ji Kim claimed a second win, this time winning for the second week running. Following her victory at the OK Se Ri Pak event, Kim also collected the Hana Financial Group Championship with a one-stroke win over Jung Min Hong and Yewon Lee. The 19-year-old Lee, leading the race for rookie honours, was runner-up for the second week running after holing her second shot at the 18th from 116 yards for an eagle.

Lee closed with a 68 but the main contest was between Hong, who led for the first three rounds, and Kim, who followed scores of 71-67 with a 65 to match the best score of the week in the third round. Starting two behind in second place on Sunday, Kim birdied three of the first four holes. She holed from 15 feet at the first, 20 feet at the third and eight feet at the fourth before three-putting the fifth.

But with Hong going out in three-over-par 39, Kim was in a comfortable position until another three-putt meant a bogey at the 17th, where Hong holed across the green for a birdie. With the margin down to one shot, both players parred the last, Hong signing for a 74, while Kim's 71 gave her a 14-under-par total of 274. "I think there was less pressure on me this week because I won last week," Kim said after her fourth victory. "I wasn't expecting to win two weeks in a row. I still have many important trophies left this season and I will do my best there."

Minjee Lee, the US Women's Open champion, and fellow major winner Hyo Joo Kim both missed the cut. Lee had lost a playoff to Ga Eun Song in the event in 2021. This year the tournament featured a record purse of ₩1,500,000,000.

Bear's Best Cheongna Golf Club, Cheongna, Incheon — September 29-October 2
Par 72 (36-36); 6,745 yards — Purse: ₩1,500,000,000

1	**Su Ji Kim**	71	67	65	71	274	270,000,000		Su Yeon Jang	70	70	71	70	281	15,825,000
2	**Yewon Lee**	68	68	71	68	275	142,500,000		Uh Jin Seo	72	69	69	71	281	15,825,000
	Jung Min Hong	66	67	68	74	275	142,500,000		Su Yeon Bae	67	72	70	72	281	15,825,000
4	Yu Jin Sung	74	68	68	67	277	67,500,000		Yunji Jeong	71	69	68	73	281	15,825,000
	So Mi Lee	70	68	72	67	277	67,500,000	21	Hyejun Park	72	70	72	68	282	14,100,000
6	Jaravee Boonchant	68	69	70	71	278	45,000,000		Ji Hyun Kim	70	70	70	72	282	14,100,000
	Han Sol Ji	73	67	67	71	278	45,000,000		Ree An Kim	70	74	68	70	282	14,100,000
	Jin Seon Han	68	68	73	69	278	45,000,000	24	Seung Yeon Lee	73	68	74	68	283	13,162,500
9	Si Woo Chung	72	71	67	69	279	26,250,000		Seo Yeon Yoo[2]	71	72	71	69	283	13,162,500
	U Ree Jun	68	69	71	71	279	26,250,000		Eun Hye Jo	71	68	71	73	283	13,162,500
11	Ji Yeong Kim[2]	70	70	71	69	280	18,900,000		Sun Ju Ahn	69	70	70	74	283	13,162,500
	Ji Young Park	71	68	70	71	280	18,900,000	28	Bo Kyeom Park	72	71	71	70	284	12,450,000
	Hee Jeong Lim	68	67	72	73	280	18,900,000		Min Ju Kim	77	67	70	70	284	12,450,000
	Min Kyung Choi	69	68	69	74	280	18,900,000		Seung Hui Ro	71	70	70	73	284	12,450,000
15	Ji Hyun Oh	71	73	68	69	281	15,825,000		Je Yeong Lee	73	70	71	70	284	12,450,000
	Hyun Kyung Park	71	70	73	67	281	15,825,000		Hae Ran Ryu	67	68	76	73	284	12,450,000

Hite Jinro Championship

Min Ji Park rose to the occasion of the last KLPGA major of the year by winning her second in a row at the Hite Jinro Championship. The long-running event in its 22nd year has been at Blue Heron since 2002 and the course was playing tough in the cool weather even before Sunday's cold and rain. Park's precision game proved successful as she won for the fifth time in the season and the 15th time in all. She had won the KB Financial Group Star Championship the previous month, while her six-victory season in 2021 included claiming the Korea Women's Open.

Park was four shots off the lead after the first day but her steadiness prevailed as scores of 73-71-70-72, for two-under-par 286, tied her with Yunji Jeong (69-71-75-71). Jeong, hoping to add to her E1 Charity Open win in May, shared the lead on the first two days, though it was on the tricky Sunday that the pair shone while others faltered. Jin Seon Han, the 54-hole leader, dropped to 15th with an 82 and Su Ji Kim, second overnight, fell to fifth with a 76, extinguishing hopes of not just a successful defence of her title but a third victory in three weeks. Hee Jeong Lim closed with a 75 and Hae Ran Ryu a 77, while there was a 74 for Sung Hyun Park, thrilling the gallery on her first appearance in Korea for a year, especially with a chip-in at the 16th. She tied for third, her best result anywhere since winning the Walmart NW Arkansas Championship in 2019.

Min Ji Park had two birdies and two bogeys in her final round. Holing from 18 feet at the 13th gave her a three-shot lead, but she missed a short putt at the 15th, while Jeong birdied the 16th and 18th holes. Park missed a 10-footer at the 18th to win and saw a four-footer lip out at the 18th on the first playoff hole. Back at the par-five 18th again, Park hit her third with a wedge to 12 feet and made it after Jeong failed to get up and down from between the rocks at the front of the green.

Blue Heron Golf Club, Yeoju, Gyeonggi — October 6-9
Par 72 (36-36); 6,763 yards — Purse: ₩1,200,000,000

1	**Min Ji Park**	73	71	70	72	286	₩216,000,000
2	**Yunji Jeong**	69	71	75	71	286	132,000,000
	Park won playoff at second extra hole						
3	**Jae Hee Kim**	72	74	72	70	288	78,000,000
	Sung Hyun Park	72	71	71	74	288	78,000,000
5	Eun Woo Choi	72	74	72	71	289	39,000,000
	Seul Gi Jeong	69	75	75	70	289	39,000,000
	Ji Hyun Oh	76	70	73	70	289	39,000,000
	Su Ji Kim	72	70	71	76	289	39,000,000
9	Hee Jeong Lim	73	72	70	75	290	24,000,000
10	Ji U Ko	75	77	71	68	291	17,220,000
	So Hyun Bae	72	68	75	76	291	17,220,000
12	Ye Rim Choi	74	73	74	72	293	14,640,000
	Ji Yeong Kim[2]	72	75	72	74	293	14,640,000
	Han Sol Ji	75	71	73	74	293	14,640,000
15	Hae Ran Ryu	71	75	71	77	294	13,260,000
	Jin Seon Han	72	71	69	82	294	13,260,000
17	Ji Young Park	70	74	75	76	295	12,030,000
	Seung Hui Ro	72	75	72	76	295	12,030,000
	So Young Lee	71	75	73	76	295	12,030,000
	Su Yeon Jang	73	75	68	79	295	12,030,000
21	Chae Yoon Park	72	77	74	73	296	11,160,000
22	Sun Ju Ahn	73	73	77	74	297	10,740,000
	Sae Ro Mi Kim	70	73	77	77	297	10,740,000
24	Ye Bon Choi	73	77	73	75	298	10,200,000
	Hyun Kyung Park	73	76	71	78	298	10,200,000
26	Hyo Ju You	81	69	74	75	299	9,720,000
	Yewon Lee	74	74	74	77	299	9,720,000
	Jinyeong Lim	79	71	74	75	299	9,720,000

Dongbu Koreit Championship

Ga Young Lee was one of the top juniors in Korea, alongside her great friend Hye-Jin Choi. But while Choi became a prolific winner at home and then moved to the LPGA in 2022, and while other contemporaries who debuted on the KLPGA in 2019 like Hee Jeong Lim and Hyun Kyung Park have become regular winners, Lee was still waiting for her first title. It finally came at the 98th attempt at the Dongbu Koreit Championship at Iksan.

There was little doubt the 23-year-old's game was up to it but there were suggestions she was just too nice to win. She had been a runner-up four times in her four seasons on tour, including back-to-back early in 2022 before she suffered from Covid-19. It took over two months to recover her form but it was worth it. There were tears when the win was confirmed and she could fulfil her promise of buying beef for her fans in celebration.

"Everyone talked about winning," Lee said. "I've always dreamed of winning. I thought I'd win someday, but this moment took too long. The win is still unbelievable. It was honestly difficult to see my friends win one by one. Now I hope I will become a player who is not satisfied with winning and continues to grow."

Her victory came in the second year of this modified Stableford event with eight points for an albatross, five for an eagle, two for a birdie, zero for a par, minus-one for a bogey and minus-three for a double bogey or worse. Lee set out to make birdies and was the only player to return four scores in double figures. Rounds of 11-11-12 put her one behind Jin Hee Im, who had 14 points on Saturday and started Sunday with birdies at the first two holes.

But Lee produced three birdies in a row from the second, eight in all and her only bogey was at the last. She looked set for victory when she holed a 30-footer at the 16th but the rest of her birdies came from 10 feet or less such was the precision of her approach play. In fact, at the seventh she lipped out for an eagle with her second shot of 132 yards. Her 15 point tally was the best of the day and she finished with 49, five ahead of Im, who closed with a round of nine points. Yewon Lee was third on 41 points, with Lim and Park sharing fourth place on 39.

Iksan Country Club, Iksan, Jeollabuk — October 13-16
Par 72 (36-36); 6,641 yards — Purse: ₩1,000,000,000

1	**Ga Young Lee**	11	11	12	15	49	₩180,000,000
2	**Jin Hee Im**	13	8	14	9	44	110,000,000
3	**Yewon Lee**	12	15	3	11	41	80,000,000
4	Hee Jeong Lim	10	10	9	10	39	45,000,000
	Hyun Kyung Park	15	9	6	9	39	45,000,000
6	Ji Yeong Kim[2]	2	8	15	12	37	35,000,000
7	Jinyeong Lim	7	7	10	12	36	27,500,000
	Yunji Jeong	15	3	13	5	36	27,500,000
9	Jung Min Hong	8	8	7	12	35	20,000,000
10	Hye Lim Jo	4	4	12	12	32	14,350,000
	Su Ji Kim	3	14	14	1	32	14,350,000
12	Hae Ran Ryu	7	6	8	10	31	12,700,000
13	Ka Ram Choi	7	6	10	7	30	12,200,000
14	Ji U Ko	11	2	6	10	29	11,075,000
	Julie Kim	9	10	6	4	29	11,075,000
	Jae Hee Kim	2	14	8	5	29	11,075,000
	So Hyun Bae	2	15	9	3	29	11,075,000
18	Su Yeon Bae	7	7	5	9	28	9,775,000
	Yu Jin Sung	11	5	2	10	28	9,775,000
	Sae Ro Mi Kim	6	6	4	12	28	9,775,000
	So Mi Lee	8	9	5	6	28	9,775,000
22	Seung Hui Ro	7	9	4	7	27	8,900,000
	Yeon Ju Jung	8	1	9	9	27	8,900,000
	Joo Mi Lee	9	7	5	6	27	8,900,000
	Hee Ji Kim	16	3	3	5	27	8,900,000
26	Hae Rym Kim	6	4	8	8	26	8,450,000
	Song Yi Ahn	2	8	13	3	26	8,450,000
28	Je Yeong Lee	7	3	10	5	25	8,150,000
	Hee Won Na	6	5	9	5	25	8,150,000
	Ji Won Hong	3	5	13	4	25	8,150,000
	Bo Mi Kwak	4	8	9	4	25	8,150,000

Wemix Championship

With the BMW Ladies Championship not being co-sanctioned by the KLPGA in 2022, the Wemix Championship at Alpensia was the local tour's offering the same week and allowed Hyo Ju You to claim her maiden victory. The 25-year-old You, who posted a third-place finish as long ago as 2017, had not finished better than 12th to date in 2022 but calmly got up and down from beside the final green for a birdie four to win by one stroke from Jung Min Hong and Carrie Park.

You scored 70-69-67 for a 10-under-par total of 206. Park made four birdies in the first seven holes but could not go better than nine under par. Hong, who won the Doosan Match Play earlier in the season, made five birdies in the first seven holes of the back nine and also finished at nine under. You, after an early birdie-bogey exchange, steadily picked up gains at the fifth, eighth and 11th holes, before reaching nine under with a birdie four at the 16th and then claiming the win at the final green. Among those sharing fourth place were Su Ji Kim and Yewon Lee.

Alpensia Country Club, Pyeongchang, Gangwon — October 21-23
Par 72 (36-36); 6,492 yards — Purse: ₩1,000,000,000

1	**Hyo Ju You**	70	69	67	206	₩180,000,000
2	**Jung Min Hong**	70	71	66	207	95,000,000
	Carrie Park	69	70	68	207	95,000,000
4	Han Sol Ji	73	68	67	208	36,000,000
	Yewon Lee	72	68	68	208	36,000,000
	Hee Won Na	72	67	69	208	36,000,000

	Su Ji Kim	72	68	68	208	36,000,000
	Woo Jeong Kim	73	66	69	208	36,000,000
9	Ji Hyun Lee[3]	75	64	70	209	17,500,000
	Da Som Ma	69	69	71	209	17,500,000
11	Ji Min Jung[2]	77	65	68	210	12,300,000
	Ji Young Park	68	72	70	210	12,300,000
	Jin Seon Han	68	69	73	210	12,300,000
	Ga Eun Song	69	70	71	210	12,300,000
	Hyun Kyung Park	71	68	71	210	12,300,000
16	Min Ju Kim	73	72	66	211	10,200,000
	So Young Lee	70	72	69	211	10,200,000
	Hee Ji Kim	74	72	65	211	10,200,000
	Uh Jin Seo	72	70	69	211	10,200,000
	Ye Rim Choi	70	71	70	211	10,200,000
21	Ji U Ko	72	71	69	212	8,816,667
	Eun Woo Choi	72	72	68	212	8,816,667
	So Mi Lee	72	70	70	212	8,816,667
	Ga Young Lee	72	67	73	212	8,816,667
	Seung Yeon Lee	72	70	70	212	8,816,667
	Gi Ppuem Lee	69	73	70	212	8,816,667
27	Jeongmin Moon	74	72	67	213	7,950,000
	Yunji Jeong	73	72	68	213	7,950,000
	Yeon Ju Jung	72	73	68	213	7,950,000
	Seo Yeon Yoo[2]	73	70	70	213	7,950,000
	Ji Hyun Kim	69	73	71	213	7,950,000
	Jae Hee Kim	72	71	70	213	7,950,000
	Min Song Ha	69	73	71	213	7,950,000
	Ye Sung Jun	71	72	70	213	7,950,000

SK Networks Seoul Economics Ladies Classic

The closest So Mi Lee had come to winning in 2022 had been at the two events where she was the defending champion — second at the Lotte Rent a Car Ladies Open to start the season and then third at the Dayouwinia MBN Ladies Open. It was a return to Jeju Island, where the she won the Lotte, that may have helped the 23-year-old over the line at the SK Networks Seoul Economics Ladies Classic for her fourth KLPGA title in two years.

Lee won by five strokes against a strong list of contenders, although defending champion Hyo Joo Kim was forced to withdraw on Saturday due to a sore back. With scores of 68-67-67 Lee took a one-stroke lead into the final round at Pinx but Jeongeun Lee[6] and Hae Ran Ryu were only a stroke behind and there was a fast Sunday start for Ga Young Lee.

So Mi Lee also began well with a tap-in birdie at the first before suffering three bogeys in the next five holes. She responded magnificently with five birdies in the next six, hit a wedge to tap-in range at the 12th to get two in front. She then parred the next five holes before holing a 10-footer at the last for a 68 and a tournament record 18-under-par total of 270.

Her spurt around the turn had seen off the quality opposition. Hyun Kyung Park took second place with a 71, while Ga Young Lee, after a double bogey at the 16th, shared third place with another recent winner, Su Ji Kim, as well as Yunji Jeong. Ryu bogeyed three of the last seven holes for a 74, a score matched by Lee6 as the pair shared sixth place. Lee6 finished with a bogey at the 17th and a double at the last after a shanked second shot into the water.

Pinx Golf Club, Seogwipo, Jeju — October 27-30
Par 72 (36-36); 6,727 yards — Purse: ₩800,000,000

1	**So Mi Lee**	68	67	67	68	270	₩144,000,000
2	**Hyun Kyung Park**	70	67	67	71	275	88,000,000
3	**Yunji Jeong**	67	70	69	70	276	45,333,333
	Su Ji Kim	70	66	69	71	276	45,333,333
	Ga Young Lee	70	68	68	70	276	45,333,333
6	Hae Ran Ryu	67	69	67	74	277	26,000,000
	Jeongeun Lee[6]	68	68	67	74	277	26,000,000
8	Ye Nah Hwang	72	70	69	67	278	20,000,000
9	So Young Lee	69	70	72	69	280	13,013,333
	Min Ju Kim	67	74	66	73	280	13,013,333
	Seul Gi Jeong	69	72	70	69	280	13,013,333
12	Yewon Lee	72	70	68	71	281	10,040,000
	So Hyun Bae	66	69	74	72	281	10,040,000
14	Hee Jeong Lim	71	71	72	68	282	9,520,000
	Hyojin Yang (A)	72	71	72	67	282	
16	Ji Young Park	72	66	72	73	283	9,000,000
	Ji U Ko	68	74	70	71	283	9,000,000
18	Ji Won Hong	71	69	73	71	284	8,280,000
	Yebeen Sohn	69	71	73	71	284	8,280,000
	Ye Sung Jun	68	74	69	73	284	8,280,000
	Ree An Kim	70	69	73	72	284	8,280,000
22	Ye Rim Choi	70	69	76	70	285	7,600,000
	Chae Yoon Park	70	70	69	76	285	7,600,000
	Jin Seon Han	74	68	69	74	285	7,600,000
25	Su Yeon Jang	69	71	73	73	286	6,971,429
	Se Lin Hyun	65	75	75	71	286	6,971,429
	Hee Jun Kim	68	72	72	74	286	6,971,429
	Hee Won Na	71	74	69	72	286	6,971,429
	Hyejun Park	71	71	69	75	286	6,971,429
	Min Ji Park	70	70	74	72	286	6,971,429
	Eun Hye Jo	74	71	68	73	286	6,971,429

S-Oil Championship

"I love Jeju Island so much," said So Mi Lee after winning at Pinx and a week later she swept the Jeju doubleheader with victory in the S-Oil Championship at Elysian Jeju. It was her third win on the island out of five KLPGA victories.

This time the 23-year-old needed a playoff and a wonderful shot to get into it. At the event where she finished third in 2021 due to three bogeys in a row late in the final round, Lee holed out from 90 yards for an eagle two at the 13th hole. Following two opening rounds of 72, she completed the weekend with twin 67s for a 10-under-par total of 278.

There was only one score better over the weekend than the two 67s of noted wind player Lee, who started the final round three behind Ji Hyun Oh and Hee Won Na. Oh came home in 38 on Sunday to finish fourth, one behind Hee Ji Kim, while Na's bogey at the 17th dropped her into a tie with Lee after a 70. At the par-five 18th in the playoff, Na saw her third shot spin back down to the lower tier, while Lee stuck her approach to six inches. In attempting to hole out from long range, Na ended up three-putting, while Lee tapped in for her second win in a row.

Na, 28, still looking for her first win, shared the 36-hole lead with Jeon Ju Jung, who scored 64-73 but then retired after six holes of the third round complaining of a sore throat on a chilly weekend in Jeju.

Although Min Ji Park fell to 35th place with weekend scores of 75-76, she still secured the money list title for the second consecutive year after Su Ji Kim finished 26th and left Park in an unassailable position with one tournament of the season remaining. Park was the first to win back-to-back titles since Jeongeun Lee[6] in 2017 and '18.

Elysian Jeju Country Club, Jeju — November 3-6
Par 72 (36-36); 6,711 yards — Purse: ₩800,000,000

1	**So Mi Lee**	72	72	67	67	278	₩144,000,000
2	**Hee Won Na**	68	69	71	70	278	88,000,000
	Lee won playoff on first extra hole						
3	**Hee Ji Kim**	67	74	71	67	279	64,000,000
4	Ji Hyun Oh	69	69	70	72	280	40,000,000
5	Jung Min Hong	70	71	70	70	281	30,000,000
	Hee Jeong Lim	70	71	68	72	281	30,000,000
7	Hae Ran Ryu	70	72	70	70	282	24,000,000
8	Jin Seon Han	72	72	69	70	283	20,000,000
9	Julie Kim	69	73	72	70	284	14,000,000
	Jin Hee Im	67	76	71	70	284	14,000,000
11	Se Eun Kim	71	71	76	67	285	10,080,000
	Hyun Kyung Park	71	73	71	70	285	10,080,000
	Geena Yoo	67	74	71	73	285	10,080,000
	Sun Ju Ahn	69	73	70	73	285	10,080,000
	Ye Sung Jun	71	74	69	71	285	10,080,000
16	Ji Yeong Kim[2]	71	74	75	66	286	8,480,000
	Ye Rim Choi	68	73	75	70	286	8,480,000
	Chae Yoon Park	70	77	68	71	286	8,480,000
	Jung Min Lee	73	72	71	70	286	8,480,000
	Min Ju Kim	70	71	74	71	286	8,480,000
21	Ree An Kim	70	76	68	73	287	7,600,000
	Ji Young Park	71	71	74	71	287	7,600,000
	Seo Yeon Yoo[2]	71	74	73	69	287	7,600,000
	Woo Jeong Kim	68	76	71	72	287	7,600,000
25	Eun Woo Choi	68	73	75	72	288	7,200,000
26	Dasom Ma	71	73	75	70	289	6,920,000
	Jae Hee Kim	72	74	72	71	289	6,920,000
	Dan Yu Park	66	78	75	70	289	6,920,000
	Bo Ah Kim	72	72	71	74	289	6,920,000
	Yewon Lee	70	75	70	74	289	6,920,000
	Su Ji Kim	72	74	70	73	289	6,920,000

SK Shieldus SK Telecom Championship

With victory in the season-ending SK Shieldus SK Telecom Championship at La Vie Est Belle, Min Ji Park matched her incredible performance from 2021 of winning six times. The 24-year-old KLPGA number one had already retained her money list title a week earlier and then secured a two-stroke victory over Song Yi Ahn at the event she also won in 2018. It was her 16th victory on the KLPGA, the most of any active player, one ahead of Ha Na Jang.

Park was four behind after the first day but posted the round of the tournament with a bogey-free 65 thanks to seven birdies on Saturday. It was the lowest score of the week, and the lowest of the day by three strokes from Ahn's 68. She was two strokes ahead of Ahn and extended her lead with three birdies in the first 11 holes on Sunday. In the cold, difficult conditions, Park played the last seven holes in three over for a 72 and a nine-under-par total of 207. Only two players beat par on Sunday, with Ahn, the 2019 winner, also closing with a 72 to take second place, only her second top 10 of the season, by one from So Hyun Bae.

Su Ji Kim finished in a tie for seventh place which was good enough to secure the Player of the Year honours on the points list, depriving Park of the clean sweep of honours she achieved in 2021. "Like any other event, I really wanted to win this one and came prepared," said Park after her 12th win in the last two seasons. "I think I'm in my prime. I can't believe why I'm winning so many championships. It's amazing even when I see it. My next goal is to go on to a bigger stage. I want to build my body during the winter. I also want to improve my shots and techniques."

La Vie Est Belle Country Club, Chuncheon, Gangwon — November 11-13
Par 72 (36-36); 6,794 yards — Purse: ₩1,000,000,000

1	**Min Ji Park**	70	65	72	207	₩200,000,000
2	**Song Yi Ahn**	69	68	72	209	115,000,000
3	**So Hyun Bae**	66	71	73	210	80,000,000
4	Jeong Mee Hwang	69	70	72	211	50,000,000
5	Min Song Ha	70	68	74	212	37,500,000
	So Young Lee	70	70	72	212	37,500,000
7	Ji Won Hong	69	72	72	213	18,271,429
	Hae Ran Ryu	71	69	73	213	18,271,429
	Yunji Jeong	69	69	75	213	18,271,429
	Su Ji Kim	68	70	75	213	18,271,429
	Dasom Ma	69	68	76	213	18,271,429
	Seung Yeon Lee	70	71	72	213	18,271,429
	Sun Ju Ahn	70	68	75	213	18,271,429
14	Su Yeon Bae	71	71	72	214	10,933,333
	Bo Mee Lee	71	68	75	214	10,933,333
	Seul Gi Jeong	69	73	72	214	10,933,333
17	Ji Min Jung	73	73	69	215	9,416,667
	Chae Eun Lee[2]	73	70	72	215	9,416,667
	Woo Jeong Kim	69	71	75	215	9,416,667
	Jae Hee Kim	70	68	77	215	9,416,667
	Seung Hui Ro	71	71	73	215	9,416,667
	Hyo Ju You	69	72	74	215	9,416,667
23	Yu Jin Sung	70	71	75	216	8,400,000
	Hee Ji Kim	68	71	77	216	8,400,000
25	Jin Hee Im	76	70	71	217	7,700,000
	So Mi Lee	71	73	73	217	7,700,000
	Jung Min Lee	70	73	74	217	7,700,000
	Ji Hyun Lee[3]	74	71	72	217	7,700,000
	Ji Yeong Kim[2]	70	72	75	217	7,700,000
	Ga Young Lee	72	69	76	217	7,700,000

2022 MONEY LIST

1	Min Ji Park	₩1,477,921,143
2	Su Ji Kim	1,082,580,549
3	Yewon Lee	849,784,000
4	Hae Ran Ryu	829,968,428
5	Hee Jeong Lim	750,137,222
6	Yunji Jeong	739,016,095
7	So Mi Lee	736,202,500
8	Ji Young Park	725,090,476
9	Ga Young Lee	636,742,580
10	Jung Min Hong	625,237,113

Hana Financial Group Singapore Women's Open

Rain washed out the final round of the Hana Financial Group Singapore Women's Open at Tanah Merah, leaving Ji Young Park holding the trophy at the opening event of the 2023 KLPGA season. The 26-year-old Korean had edged a stroke in front on Saturday with three birdies in a row from the third (her 12th) hole. She finished on 133, 11 under par for the 36 holes, with Hyun Kyung Park, So Young Lee and Jung Min Hong all finishing on 10 under.

The new event was first scheduled for 2020 but had been postponed for two years by the Covid pandemic. On Friday Ji Young matched the seven birdies of Hyun Kyung and Yunji Jeong, who shared the first-round lead on 65, but had one dropped shot. She went bogey-free the next day, relying on her putting to tidy up the odd wayward shot, while Hyun Kyung had a 69 and Jeong slipped to fifth with a 70. KLPGA number one Min Ji Park and world number three Atthaya Thitikul were among those four adrift in ninth place hoping for a big charge on Sunday but frustrated by the weather.

This was Ji Young Park's fifth victory and her second of the year after she won the second event of the 2022 season, the Mediheal Hankook Ilbo Championship in April. She had also won the opening event of the 2019 season, which was played in December 2018.

"A win is always fulfilling regardless of how it's attained," Park said. "I'm really happy and proud to be the inaugural winner. I've put in a lot of effort to improve my game and I'm so glad that it paid off this week. I've never had multiple wins in a season so hopefully that's something for me to experience next year."

Tanah Merah Country Club (Tampines), Singapore — December 9-11
Par 72 (36-36); 6,490 yards — Purse: S$1,100,000

1	**Ji Young Park**	66	67	133	₩191,184,840
2	**So Young Lee**	68	66	134	84,971,040
	Hyun Kyung Park	65	69	134	84,971,040
	Jung Min Hong	68	66	134	84,971,040
5	Yunji Jeong	65	70	135	42,485,520
6	So Mi Lee	67	69	136	31,864,140
	Hee Jeong Lim	67	69	136	31,864,140
	Hae Rym Kim	68	68	136	31,864,140
9	Min Ju Kim	68	69	137	14,642,335
	Su Yeon Jang	70	67	137	14,642,335
	Sun Ju Ahn	66	71	137	14,642,335
	Atthaya Thitikul	69	68	137	14,642,335
	Min Ji Park	68	69	137	14,642,335
	Se Lin Hyun	70	67	137	14,642,335
	Ga Eun Song	67	70	137	14,642,335
16	Chae Eun Lee[2]	69	69	138	11,364,877
	Yu Jin Sung	68	70	138	11,364,877
18	Da Som Ma	72	67	139	9,798,223
	Ga Young Lee	69	70	139	9,798,223
	Jin Hee Im	71	68	139	9,798,223
	Seo Yoon Kim[2]	69	70	139	9,798,223
	Seo Yeon Kwon	69	70	139	9,798,223
	Ka Bin Choi	69	70	139	9,798,223
	Yewon Lee	69	70	139	9,798,223
	Hye Jin Choi	68	71	139	9,798,223
26	Han Sol Ji	73	67	140	8,178,463
	Song Yi Ahn	73	67	140	8,178,463
	Yuting Shi	69	71	140	8,178,463
	Tiffany Chan	68	72	140	8,178,463
	Ji Su Kim	70	70	140	8,178,463
	You Min Hwang	69	71	140	8,178,463
	Min Kyung Choi	72	68	140	8,178,463
	Jeong Mee Hwang	72	68	140	8,178,463
	Sock Hwee Koh	68	72	140	8,178,463
	Eun Hye Jo	70	70	140	8,178,463
	Seung Hui Bong	67	73	140	8,178,463
	Jin Seon Han	69	71	140	8,178,463
	Eun Woo Choi	70	70	140	8,178,463

PLK Pacific Links Championship

On the KLPGA's return to Vietnam for the first time since 2019, a windy final round brought experience to the fore with Jung Min Lee claiming her 10th victory. The 30-year-old was the 14th player to reach that mark on tour. Lee won by three strokes from overnight leader Ye Rim Choi, who was a runner-up for a fifth time and third in 2022.

Lee had not won for five years before claiming the Dongbu Koreit Championship in 2021. But in 2022 she struggled for form, missing the cut 13 times and only posting one top-10 finish. A bogey-free 66 in the second round, equalling the best of the week, put Lee one behind Choi, who birdied the second hole on Sunday but then ended up with a 75. Lee sailed to the top of the leaderboard with four birdies, holing 25-footers at the fifth and the 11th and hitting her approach at the 12th to six feet.

But Lee dropped three shots in a row from the 14th, while Ji U Ko, who was second on the rookie standings in the 2022 season, birdied the 16th and 17th holes to draw within two shots. But disaster awaited the 20-year-old Ko at the par-five 18th. Twice she found the water and then she three-putted for a quadruple-bogey nine. A 77 dropped Ko to a share of seventh place at three under par. Lee's second shot just cleared the water in front of the green and she parred for a 71 and a nine-under-par total of 207. Uh Jin Seo's 70 was the best score of the day as she took a career-best third place, with So Young Lee, the runner-up in Singapore, tying for fourth.

Lee mused afterwards: "All the golfers here are already very skilled, and I don't think I have anything that I can tell them that would help. But if I have to say something, it would be that winners don't win because they are perfect. I think that golfers who have never won a trophy before have as much of a chance of winning as anyone else."

Twin Doves Golf Club, Ho Chi Minh City, Vietnam
Par 72 (36-36); 6,549 yards

December 16-18
Purse: ₩700,000,000

1	**Jung Min Lee**	70	66	71	207	₩126,000,000
2	**Ye Rim Choi**	68	67	75	210	77,000,000
3	**Uh Jin Seo**	71	70	70	211	56,000,000
4	Jung Min Hong	70	68	74	212	29,166,667
	Da Been Heo	73	68	71	212	29,166,667
	So Young Lee	67	71	74	212	29,166,667
7	Su Yeon Jang	74	67	72	213	15,750,000
	Jae Hee Kim	72	68	73	213	15,750,000
	Yeji Park (A)	69	71	73	213	
	Eun Hye Jo	69	70	74	213	15,750,000
	Ji U Ko	66	70	77	213	15,750,000
12	Hee Won Na	70	72	72	214	8,820,000
	Seung Yeon Lee	68	72	74	214	8,820,000
	Hyun Kyung Park	67	73	74	214	8,820,000
	Min Ju Kim	71	68	75	214	8,820,000
	So Mi Lee	68	69	77	214	8,820,000
17	Yealimi Noh	69	73	73	215	7,630,000
	Ji Su Kim	72	72	71	215	7,630,000
	So Hyun Bae	70	70	75	215	7,630,000
20	Ye Sung Jun	74	70	72	216	6,611,111
	Joo Mi Lee	73	70	73	216	6,611,111
	Cherry Lim (A)	71	70	75	216	
	Jin Hee Im	70	73	73	216	6,611,111
	Se Lin Hyun	70	71	75	216	6,611,111
	A Yean Cho	70	69	77	216	6,611,111
	Seung Hui Ro	71	68	77	216	6,611,111
	Ji Min Jung[2]	70	72	74	216	6,611,111
	Ji Hyun Lee[3]	71	67	78	216	6,611,111
	Seo Yoon Kim[2]	71	70	75	216	6,611,111
30	Min Byeol Kim	68	73	76	217	5,950,000
	Chae Yoon Park	71	73	73	217	5,950,000
	Carrie Park	74	71	72	217	5,950,000
	So Yi Jeong	71	68	78	217	5,950,000
	Woo Jeong Kim	69	68	80	217	5,950,000

KOREAN DREAM TOUR

Torbist Phoenix 3	**Seoyoon Kim[2]**
MC2 Gunsan 6	**Ka Bin Choi**
QCapital Partners Norangtongdak Challenge 1	**Hani Kim**
Muan-All For You 8	**Ka Bin Choi (2)**
Muan-All For You 10	**Yeonseo Hwang**
Qcapital Partners Norangtondak Challenge 2	**Hye Lim Jo**
Torbist Phoenix 12	**Hye Lim Jo (2)**
Qcapital Partners Dream Tour Grand Final	**Seoyoon Kim[2] (2)**

LPGA OF TAIWAN TOUR

Hitachi Ladies Classic	**Pei-Ying Tsai**	
WPG Ladies Open	**Hsin Lee**	
Jing Mao Ladies Open	**Hsin Lee (2)**	
Grin Cup Charity Open	**Juliana Hung**	
BGC Thailand Ladies Masters	**Patcharajutar Kongkraphan**	
Da Da Digital Ladies Open	**Yu-Ju Chen**	
Udon-Ken Ladies	**Kokona Sakurai (1,5)**	*See chapter 25*
Sampo Ladies Open	**Tsai-Ching Tseng**	
Party Golfers Ladies Open	**Peng-Shan Liu**	
Wistron Ladies Open	**Ya-Chun Chang**	
Taiwan Mobile Ladies Open	**Chia Yen Wu**	
CTBC Invitational	**Peiyun Chien**	

CHINA LPGA TOUR

Hangzhou International Championship	**Tong An (A)**
Golf Liquor Challenge	**Zixin Ni (A)**
CTBC Ladies Classic	**Jiaze Sun**
Beijing Ladies Open	**Jiaze Sun (2)**
Zhangjiagang Shuangshan Challenge	**Liqi Zeng**
CGA Ladies Championship	**Liqi Zeng (2)**
Guowie Centre Plaza Zhuhai Challenge	**Xiang Sui**

David Berding/Getty Images

Clockwise from top left: A last-day charge for Ayaka Furue at the Trust Golf Scottish Open; Tony Finau with the first of back-to-back wins at the 3M Open; Joohyung Kim with a 61 for his maiden US win at the Wyndham.

Top: After many close calls, Will Zalatoris finally gets his first PGA Tour win at the FedEx St Jude. Bottom: Oliver Wilson, 41, made up in Himmerland with second DP World Tour title, eight years after the first.

Top: Shane Lowry beat Rory McIlroy and Jon Rahm with a birdie at the 18th to win the BMW PGA at Wentworth.
Bottom: Robert MacIntyre defeated Matt Fitzpatrick in a playoff at Marco Simone, the 2023 Ryder Cup venue.

Top: The USA team, captained by Davis Love III, celebrate a 12th victory in the Presidents Cup at Quail Hollow.
Bottom: Rookie Joohyung "Tom" Kim starred for the International team with two wins in Saturday's play.

Tom Pennington/Getty Images

Clockwise from top: Ryan Fox celebrates his Alfred Dunhill Links victory at St Andrews; new cowboy boots for Charley Hull with her LPGA win in Texas; Nelly Korda back to world number one after defending the Pelican.

Japan's number ones: Miyuu Yamashita (top) won the JLPGA season-ender for her fifth title, while Kazuki Higa (bottom) claimed the Dunlop Phoenix for his fourth win of the year on the men's Japan Tour.

op: Ashleigh Buhai, Adrian Meronk and Kipp Popert, all champions at the ISPS Handa Australian Open.
ottom: Thriston Lawrence just held on at Blair Atholl to win his national title at the Investec SA Open.

Jon Rahm won the DP World Tour Championship in Dubai for the third time in four attempts.

Japan LPGA Tour

Youth was again served on the Japan LPGA Tour in 2022. Two players stood out among the plethora of young winners during the season — 20-year-old Mao Saigo in the early months and 21-year-old Miyuu Yamashita, who took full command of the stage during the rest of the season on her way to being crowned the money-winning queen of the year.

Both won five times. Six others posted two wins each — Haruka Kawasaki, 19; Chirei Iwai, 20; Yuna Nishimura, 21; Mone Inami, 22; Minami Katsu, 23, and Sakura Koiwai, 24 – and five more in that age range picked off single victories, including Amiyu Ozeki, another 19-year-old. That adds up to an impressive 27 wins during the 38-tournament season.

Saigo won her five titles in her first 10 starts, beginning with the opening event of the season, her maiden title after seven second places in 2021, and concluding at the Bridgestone Open. She concentrated on the LPGA majors in America and Europe for the next couple of months, finishing in a tie for third at the Amundi Evian Championship, and played well enough when she returned to Japan to finish fifth on the final money list.

But her exploits were overshadowed by Yamashita and her exceptional third season on the tour. Her five victories included the Tour and World Championships, two of the tour's four majors, and a record-setting 60 in the Miyagi Dunlop, and, with four seconds and nine other top-five finishes, she compiled winnings of ¥235,020,967. That record total made her the youngest number one in tour history. Furthermore, Yamashita just missed — by 0.03 of a stroke — setting another record with her 69.97 scoring average.

"I had a lot of fun this year," she said. "I was surprised by the rapid growth in my third year as a professional."

In keeping with the trend, young players won the other two major championships. Katsu, who has been winning tour titles since her first as a 15-year-old, claimed the Japan Women's Open for the second year running, while Kawasaki became the youngest ever winner of the Japan LPGA Championship.

In all, eight players won for the first time in 2022, including Iwai, who then followed up her maiden win at the NEC Karuizawa 72 event with another the following week. The 20-year-old's twin Akie could not quite match her sister, finishing as runner-up to Ayaka Furue at the Fujitsu Ladies. Furue had spent most of the year in America in her rookie season on the US LPGA Tour, although her maiden win on that circuit came at the Trust Golf Scottish Open. Japanese number one Nasa Hataoka continued her winning ways on the LPGA with victory at the Dio Implant LA Open, while success at Q-Series meant Katsu and Nishimura would be joining Hataoka and Furue in America in 2023.

2022 SCHEDULE

Daikin Orchid Ladies	**Mao Saigo**
Meiji Yasuda Ladies Yokohama Tire	**Pei-Ying Tsai (1,2)**
T-Point Eneos Tournament	**Kotone Hori**
AXA Ladies	**Mao Saigo (2)**
Yamaha Ladies Open	**Mao Saigo (3)**
FujiFilm Studio Alice Ladies Open	**Momoko Ueda**
KKT Cup Vantelin Ladies Open	**Nozomi Uetake**
Fujisankei Ladies Classic	**Sayaka Takahasi**
Panasonic Ladies Open	**Mao Saigo (4)**
World Ladies Championship Salonpas Cup	**Miyuu Yamashita**
Hoken no Madoguchi Ladies	**Ayaka Watanabe**
Bridgestone Ladies Open	**Mao Saigo (5)**
Resort Trust Ladies	**Sakura Koiwai**
Richard Mille Yonex Ladies	**Mone Inami**
Ai Miyazato Suntory Ladies Open	**Miyuu Yamashita (2)**
Nichirei Ladies	**Yuna Nishimura**
Earth Mondahmin Cup	**Ayako Kimura**

Shiseido Ladies Open	**Serena Aoki**
Nippon Ham Ladies Classic	**Yuna Nishimura (2)**
Daito Kentaku Eheyanet Ladies	**Erika Kikuchi**
Rakuten Super Ladies	**Minami Katsu**
Hokkaido Meiji Cup	**Min Young Lee[2]**
NEC Karuizawa 72	**Chirei Iwai**
CAT Ladies	**Chirei Iwai (2)**
Nitori Ladies	**Mone Inami (2)**
Golf5 Ladies	**Yuting Seki**
JLPGA Championship Konica Minolta Cup	**Haruka Kawasaki (1,2)**
Sumitomo Life Vitality Ladies Tokai Classic	**Amiyu Ozeki**
Miyagi TV Cup Dunlop Ladies Open	**Miyuu Yamashita (3)**
Japan Women's Open Championship	**Minami Katsu (2)**
Stanley Ladies Honda	**Sakura Koiwai (2)**
Fujitsu Ladies	**Ayaka Furue (1,2)**
Nobuta Ladies Masters	**Haruka Kawasaki (2,3)**
Mitsubishi Electric Hisako Higuchi Ladies	**Kumiko Kaneda**
Toto Japan Classic	**Gemma Dryburgh**
Itoen Ladies	**Miyuu Yamashita (4)**
Daio Paper Elleair Ladies Open	**Saiki Fujita**
JLPGA Tour Championship Ricoh Cup	**Miyuu Yamashita (5)**

Daikin Orchid Ladies

The 2021 season was a lucrative, but at the same time a frustrating one, for Mao Saigo. It all started in the season-opening Daikin Orchid, where the winless 19-year-old shared the lead after the two middle rounds before suffering a bogey on the final hole and dropping into a fourth-place tie. During the rest of the season, Saigo placed second seven times and 18 times was among the top-10 finishers, winding up second to Mone Inami on the final money list with ¥161 million in earnings. Still no victories.

It was a different story for Saigo at the 2022 Daikin Orchid. She lingered off the pace for three days, then came from five strokes back on Sunday, this time parring the 18th hole to notch the elusive maiden win. Her closing 67 for a 10-under-par total of 278 edged Korea's Au-Reum Hwang by a stroke. "Finally, I was relieved. Thank you," expressed Saigo. "I think I've become stronger because I had a lot of regrettable experiences last year. I wanted to have a good year so that I can shed tears of joy."

Saigo's first three rounds of the year at Okinawa's Ryukyu Golf Club (69-73-69) stationed her in a five-way tie for eighth place, five behind co-leaders Ayaka Watanabe and Hwang, whose most recent of five career wins was in the 2019 Stanley tournament. The two had traded the lead the first two days before sharing the top spot at 206. Saigo gained three shots on the leaders on the front nine Sunday and went in front to stay with birdies at the 16th and 17th holes as both Hwang and Watanabe incurred double bogeys on the back nine. The 33-year-old Hwang birdied the last two holes to take second place, a shot ahead of Yuna Nishimura.

Ryukyu Golf Club, Okinawa — March 3-6
Par 72 (36-36); 6,590 yards — Purse: ¥120,000,000

1	**Mao Saigo**	69	73	69	67	278	¥21,600,000
2	**Au-Reum Hwang**	69	67	70	73	279	10,560,000
3	**Yuna Nishimura**	71	69	69	71	280	8,400,000
4	Miyuu Yamashita	72	71	71	67	281	5,550,000
	Nana Yamashiro	69	73	71	68	281	5,550,000
	Minami Katsu	69	73	69	70	281	5,550,000
	Ayaka Watanabe	67	70	69	75	281	5,550,000
8	Ayako Kimura	71	70	69	73	283	3,300,000
	Ai Suzuki	73	69	68	73	283	3,300,000
10	Reika Arakawa (A)	69	75	71	69	284	
	Mayu Hamada	69	70	74	71	284	2,310,000
	Mone Inami	73	69	68	74	284	2,310,000
13	Sakura Koiwai	73	73	70	69	285	1,860,000
	Shina Kanazawa	70	73	69	73	285	1,860,000
	Haruka Morita	70	72	69	74	285	1,860,000
	Miyu Sato	68	75	68	74	285	1,860,000

	Kotone Hori	71	68	71	75	285	1,860,000	26	Yuri Yoshida	75 71 71 71	288	1,020,000	
18	Eri Fukuyama	70	73	72	71	286	1,380,000		Megumi Shimokawa	72 73 70 73	288	1,020,000	
	Sae Ogura	72	74	68	72	286	1,380,000		Teresa Lu	68 72 71 77	288	1,020,000	
	Momoko Kishibe	72	73	69	72	286	1,380,000	29	Rie Tsuji	71 74 71 73	289	912,000	
21	Erika Hara	69	72	74	72	287	1,104,000		Saiki Fujita	71 70 74 74	289	912,000	
	Sumika Nakasone	73	71	74	69	287	1,104,000		Shuri Sakuma	69 75 73 72	289	912,000	
	Hino Shimabukuro (A)	69	73	72	73	287			Kana Nagai	72 74 71 72	289	912,000	
	Maiko Wakabayashi	70	72	72	73	287	1,104,000		Satsuki Oshiro	72 73 70 74	289	912,000	
	Mika Miyazato	72	73	68	74	287	1,104,000		Haruka Kudo	73 72 70 74	289	912,000	

Meiji Yasuda Ladies Yokohama Tire

Pei-Ying Tsai had been coming from Taiwan to play on the Japan LPGA Tour as a pro since 2013, achieving moderate success but no victories, finishing 40th on the 2021 money list in her best showing. Her 2022 season did not get off to a good start either. She missed the cut at the Daikin Orchid badly, shooting 74-79. In an impressive turnaround, she finally broke the ice a week later in the Meiji Yasuda Yokohama Tire tournament when a sparkling final round carried her to a come-from-behind victory.

Four strokes off the lead entering the final round and playing two groups behind the leading threesome, the 30-year-old Taiwanese pro "wondered if it was finally my turn". She had made only two bogeys over the first 36 holes at Tosa Country Club, in Kochi, posting rounds of 68 and 70 as Nozomi Uetake took over first place on Saturday with a pair of 67s, at 134 a shot in front of Mao Saigo (69-66), who had won her first title the previous Sunday in the Daikin Orchid.

The fight for the Yokohama crown was so close at the end that Tsai expected a playoff at best after birdieing four of the last six holes for a bogey-free 65 and 13-under-par 203, finishing ahead of the contenders as the clubhouse leader. But only Uetake managed a birdie on the last two holes and four players — Saigo, Uetake, Rio Ishii and Kotone Hori — wound up in a four-way tie at 204.

Tosa Country Club, Kochi — March 11-13
Par 72 (36-36); 6,228 yards — Purse: ¥80,000,000

1	**Pei-Ying Tsai**	68	70	65	203	¥14,400,000		Mami Fukuda	69	69	71	209	1,176,000
2	**Rio Ishii**	69	69	66	204	5,360,000		Ayaka Watanabe	69	69	71	209	1,176,000
	Kotone Hori	68	68	68	204	5,360,000	19	Karen Tsuruoka	68	72	70	210	816,000
	Mao Saigo	69	66	69	204	5,360,000		Momoko Osato	72	70	68	210	816,000
	Nozomi Uetake	67	67	70	204	5,360,000	21	Saiki Fujita	72	69	70	211	680,000
6	Kana Nagai	67	70	70	207	3,200,000		Erika Hara	71	70	70	211	680,000
7	Momoko Kishibe	71	70	67	208	2,059,200		Nanako Ueno	72	69	70	211	680,000
	Min Young Lee²	72	69	67	208	2,059,200		Akira Yamaji	71	70	70	211	680,000
	Yuna Nishimura	69	71	68	208	2,059,200		Shoko Sasaki	70	70	71	211	680,000
	Shiho Oyama	68	71	69	208	2,059,200		Hiromu Ono	72	70	69	211	680,000
	Rumi Yoshiba	70	69	69	208	2,059,200		Mika Miyazato	71	69	71	211	680,000
12	Hana Lee	69	72	68	209	1,176,000		Lala Anai	72	68	71	211	680,000
	Mao Nozawa	72	68	69	209	1,176,000		Teresa Lu	72	71	68	211	680,000
	Rie Tsuji	74	68	67	209	1,176,000		Asuka Ishikawa	70	73	68	211	680,000
	Kumiko Kaneda	72	67	70	209	1,176,000		Yukiko Nishiki	65	73	73	211	680,000
	Ritsuko Ryu	66	72	71	209	1,176,000							

T-Point Eneos Tournament

Kotone Hori evened things up with her sister when she won the T-Point Eneos tournament in mid-March. Kotone had joined her older sibling, Natsuka, as just the second pair of sisters to both win on the JLPGAT when she captured the Nippon Ham event in 2021. With the T-Point victory, she matched Natsuka's two-win record and remarked: "The sound is different between two wins and one win. I thought one wasn't enough."

The T-Point triumph came a bit easier than that first one (a three-hole playoff). Still, she had to hold off two challengers, Yuna Nishimura and Rumi Yoshiba, to win by a stroke at Kagoshima Takamaki Country Club. After Momoko Ueda opened the tournament on top with her five-under-par 67, Hori took a one-shot lead the second day with 69-68 for seven under par. Ayaka Takahashi, a frequent but frustrated winless contender, was just a shot behind Hori Saturday, but again faltered in the final round.

Instead, Nishimura and Yoshiba put the pressure on Hori, who was comfortably in front until she bogeyed the 10th hole. Ultimately, her birdie on the par-five 16th and a 70 for 207, nine under par, gave her the margin she needed as Nishimura, a three-time winner in 2021, shot a back-nine 32 for 67 and Yoshiba, also a previous winner, closed with a 68.

Kagoshima Takamaki Country Club, Kagoshima — March 18-20
Par 72 (36-36); 6,419 yards — Purse: ¥100,000,000

1	**Kotone Hori**	69	68	70	207	¥18,000,000
2	**Yuna Nishimura**	68	73	67	208	7,900,000
	Rumi Yoshiba	73	67	68	208	7,900,000
4	Kotoko Uchida	70	72	67	209	6,000,000
5	Sayaka Takahashi	71	67	72	210	5,000,000
6	Haruka Morita	73	72	66	211	3,500,000
	Yuri Yoshida	68	75	68	211	3,500,000
	Momoko Ueda	67	73	71	211	3,500,000
9	Sakura Yokomine	70	72	70	212	2,500,000
10	Nana Suganuma	73	72	68	213	1,800,000
	Shina Kanazawa	72	72	69	213	1,800,000
	Mao Saigo	73	71	69	213	1,800,000
	Haruka Kudo	70	74	69	213	1,800,000
	Sakura Koiwai	72	71	70	213	1,800,000
15	Min Young Lee[2]	73	72	69	214	1,300,000
	Serena Aoki	72	73	69	214	1,300,000
	Satsuki Oshiro	70	75	69	214	1,300,000
	Mi-Jeong Jeon	76	70	68	214	1,300,000
	Nanoko Hayashi	74	70	70	214	1,300,000
20	Bo-Mee Lee	73	73	69	215	960,000
	Mayu Hamada	73	71	71	215	960,000
	Minami Katsu	78	69	68	215	960,000
	Mao Nozawa	70	73	72	215	960,000
	Fumika Kawagishi	71	70	74	215	960,000
25	Mami Fukuda	72	73	71	216	820,000
	Momo Yoshikawa	75	69	72	216	820,000
	Yuting Seki	70	74	72	216	820,000
	Shoko Sasaki	73	71	72	216	820,000
	Teresa Lu	74	70	72	216	820,000
	Nanako Ueno	73	73	70	216	820,000
	Karin Takeyama	72	71	73	216	820,000
	Akie Iwai	72	71	73	216	820,000
	Miki Sakai	71	70	75	216	820,000

AXA Ladies

One school of thought is that the second win is the most difficult in professional golf. Young Mao Saigo made that seem doubtful when she won the weather-shortened AXA Ladies tournament in Miyazaki just three weeks after landing her first victory at the Daikin Orchid. It had taken her more than two years to win that first one.

The 20-year-old came from two strokes off the lead for the AXA victory when play resumed at UMK Country Club on Sunday after heavy rain washed out Saturday's play. Her closing 68, for a nine-under-par total of 135, gave her a one-shot victory over Miyuu Yamashita, whose only win came in 2021 in the Vantelin Open. "I'm relieved," the 20-year-old exclaimed. "I was nervous the last few holes."

For good reason. She made her fifth and last birdie at the 13th hole and carried a one-stroke lead through a closing string of five pars with Yamashita and Korea's Seon Woo Bae on her heels. Bogeys at the par-three 16th hole cost both of them their shots at victory, Yamashita taking second place with a 69 and Bae (also 69) tying for third with a disappointed Ai Suzuki, the first-round leader on 65, the week's low round. Suzuki, twice the number one money-winner with 18 career wins on her record, but with only one victory since her seven-win 2019 season, couldn't overcome the double bogey she took at the par-three second hole on Sunday and shot a 72.

UMK Country Club, Miyazaki — March 25-27
Par 72 (36-36); 6,546 yards — Purse: ¥100,000,000

1	**Mao Saigo**	67	68	135	¥13,500,000
2	**Miyuu Yamashita**	67	69	136	6,600,000
3	**Seon Woo Bae**	68	69	137	4,875,000
	Ai Suzuki	65	72	137	4,875,000
5	Sakura Koiwai	71	67	138	2,203,125
	Ayano Yasuda	70	68	138	2,203,125
	Nana Suganuma	70	68	138	2,203,125
	Kana Mikashima	69	69	138	2,203,125
	Satsuki Oshiro	69	69	138	2,203,125
	Nozomi Uetake	69	69	138	2,203,125
	Kotone Hori	68	70	138	2,203,125

	Kotone Hori	68 70	138	2,203,125		Eri Okayama	69 71	140	727,500
	Ayako Kimura	67 71	138	2,203,125		Haruka Morita	72 68	140	727,500
13	Kana Nagai	69 70	139	1,125,000		Sumika Nakasone	69 71	140	727,500
	Seira Oki	67 72	139	1,125,000		Mone Inami	68 72	140	727,500
	Ayaka Watanabe	66 73	139	1,125,000	26	Shuri Sakuma	71 70	141	540,000
16	Haruka Amamoto	71 69	140	727,500		Hana Wakimoto	71 70	141	540,000
	Mizuki Ooide	72 68	140	727,500		Asako Fujimoto	71 70	141	540,000
	Shiho Oyama	70 70	140	727,500		Shoko Sasaki	72 69	141	540,000
	Yuri Yoshida	70 70	140	727,500		Min Young Lee[2]	72 69	141	540,000
	Momoko Ueda	70 70	140	727,500		Miyu Goto	69 72	141	540,000
	Sayaka Takahashi	70 70	140	727,500		Haruka Kudo	72 69	141	540,000

Yamaha Ladies Open

Mao Saigo sort of asked herself a question after scoring her third victory over the first five weeks of the new season. "I'm looking forward to seeing what kind of superstar I will be," the exciting 20-year-old remarked after her one-stroke victory in the Yamaha Ladies Open. It seems that she is well on the way to that status, considering her remarkable start to the year after a splendid, though winless, 2021 when she had seven second-place finishes, 18 top-10s and the runner-up spot on the final money list.

The Yamaha victory on the Yamana course of Katsuragi Golf Club in Shizuoka Prefecture came a bit easier than the earlier ones, both come-from-behind wins, although she nearly blew a five-stroke lead on the miserable rainy Sunday. She hit her final tee shot out of bounds on the 18th hole and took a double bogey for a 76, her eight-under-par 280 just a shot better than that of Kotone Hori, who was also enjoying a strong spring with a victory and a second runner-up finish.

Saigo never trailed at Katsuragi, matching 67-69 scores the first two days with Seon Woo Bae for the lead on eight under, then bolted five strokes ahead Saturday with a four-birdie 68 as Bae slumped to a 73. Mao was rolling comfortably one under par through eight holes Sunday, but made only one birdie amid four bogeys and the final double bogey the rest of the way. Hori, in 12th place after 54 holes, jumped into second place with a 68, supplanting Bae, who shot another 73 and dropped into a tie for third with Nana Suganuma.

Katsuragi Golf Club (Yamana), Shizuoka — March 31-April 3
Par 72 (36-36); 6,590 yards — Purse: ¥100,000,000

1	**Mao Saigo**	67 69 68 76	280	¥18,000,000	18	Kotoko Uchida	68 76 73 72	289	1,050,000
2	**Kotone Hori**	76 68 69 68	281	8,800,000		Yuna Nishimura	72 70 74 73	289	1,050,000
3	**Nana Suganuma**	68 69 73 72	282	6,500,000		Nozomi Uetake	70 70 72 77	289	1,050,000
	Seon Woo Bae	67 69 73 73	282	6,500,000	21	Seira Oki	72 74 73 71	290	780,000
5	Miku Ueta (A)	73 64 75 72	284			Momoko Ueda	72 71 76 71	290	780,000
6	Ayaka Watanabe	70 72 73 70	285	4,166,666		Chae-Young Yoon	68 72 78 72	290	780,000
	Sayaka Takahashi	72 69 71 73	285	4,166,666		Saiki Fujita	72 74 72 72	290	780,000
	Mami Fukuda	72 69 71 73	285	4,166,666		Rumi Yoshiba	68 74 74 74	290	780,000
9	Shuri Sakuma	73 74 71 68	286	2,312,500		Hana Wakimoto	73 73 76 68	290	780,000
	Yuri Yoshida	70 70 72 74	286	2,312,500		Miyuu Yamashita	71 72 72 75	290	780,000
	Mi-Jeong Jeon	69 70 72 75	286	2,312,500		Miki Sakai	72 69 73 76	290	780,000
	Serena Aoki	72 69 69 76	286	2,312,500	29	Eri Okayama	70 73 75 73	291	650,000
13	Miyu Sato	72 71 72 72	287	1,550,000		Yuna Takagi	72 72 76 71	291	650,000
	Aya Kinoshita	76 68 71 72	287	1,550,000		Momoko Osato	72 72 74 73	291	650,000
	Kumiko Kaneda	71 71 72 73	287	1,550,000		Karin Takeyama	75 72 68 76	291	650,000
16	Teresa Lu	73 70 71 74	288	1,300,000		Shina Kanazawa	71 71 71 78	291	650,000
	Simin Feng	68 71 71 78	288	1,300,000					

FujiFilm Studio Alice Ladies Open

Sitting two strokes off the lead of Ai Suzuki, another of the tour's frequent winners, Momoko Ueda was filled with confidence going into the final round of the FujiFilm Studio Alice Open. "I think about various things on the eve of the final day, but this time I will win. I was full of energy and didn't miss a chance," recalled the 35-year-old veteran.

Ueda burst out of the gate on Sunday with an eagle-birdie start to move past Suzuki, who uncharacteristically stumbled to a 78, and two other Momokos, Osato and Kishibe. She rolled to a closing 69 for a nine-under-par total of 207 and a three-stroke triumph. It was the 17th for Ueda, who flashed onto the scene as a 21-year-old who won five times and was the year's money-winning champion in 2007.

Osato had led the first day with a six-under-par 66 at Ishizaka Golf Club in Saitama Prefecture, before Suzuki, the two-time JLPGA number one with 17 wins on her record, took over with 69-67 to be one ahead of Osato (66-71) and two in front of Kishibe (71-67) and Ueda (69-69).

Mone Inami and Mao Saigo, the tour's most recent standouts, came from well off the pace Sunday, both shooting 69s to finish in a second-place tie with Eri Fukuyama (70) and Seira Oki (71), but they never seriously challenged Ueda, who followed the early explosion with two bogeys and two birdies. Saigo had been shooting for a rare three-in-a-row string of victories.

Ishizaka Golf Club, Saitama — April 8-10
Par 72 (36-36); 6,475 yards — Purse: ¥100,000,000

1	**Momoko Ueda**	69	69	69	207	¥18,000,000
2	**Mone Inami**	69	72	69	210	6,700,000
	Mao Saigo	71	70	69	210	6,700,000
	Eri Fukuyama	68	72	70	210	6,700,000
	Seira Oki	69	70	71	210	6,700,000
6	Miyu Goto	70	72	69	211	2,805,000
	Sayaka Takahashi	71	70	70	211	2,805,000
	Asako Fujimoto	71	70	70	211	2,805,000
	Shiho Oyama	68	72	71	211	2,805,000
	Momoko Kishibe	71	67	73	211	2,805,000
	Momoko Osato	66	71	74	211	2,805,000
12	Eri Okayama	74	69	69	212	1,680,000
	Karen Gondo	72	67	73	212	1,680,000
14	Mi-Jeong Jeon	69	74	70	213	1,230,000
	Yuri Yoshida	72	72	69	213	1,230,000
	Serena Aoki	70	72	71	213	1,230,000
	Yuna Nishimura	70	72	71	213	1,230,000
	Asuka Ishikawa	72	70	71	213	1,230,000
	Erika Kikuchi	71	74	68	213	1,230,000
	Akie Iwai	70	70	73	213	1,230,000
21	Haruka Morita	72	72	70	214	870,000
	Mami Fukuda	72	72	70	214	870,000
	Reika Usui	70	71	73	214	870,000
	Hikari Tanabe	71	69	74	214	870,000
	Ai Suzuki	69	67	78	214	870,000
26	Shuri Sakuma	73	70	72	215	760,000
	Mao Nozawa	73	72	70	215	760,000
	Miki Sakai	72	70	73	215	760,000
	Miyuu Yamashita	73	69	73	215	760,000
	Mika Miyazato	72	70	73	215	760,000
	Rumi Yoshiba	70	70	75	215	760,000

KKT Cup Vantelin Ladies Open

The so-called Golden Generation of young winners added its 10th member at the KKT Cup Vantelin Open, but it wasn't easy for Nozomi Uetake. The 23-year-old had to outplay three others through six extra holes to land her first victory less than a year after Hinako Shibuno won the 2021 Stanley on the second hole in the most recent four-way playoff.

Uetake credited a change in her routine as a major factor in the Vantelin victory, which came in her second full season on tour. "Actually, my sister found a note from a TV viewer that I was taking too much time and playing slowly," she revealed. "I changed my putting routine. I feel it became smoother and led to the victory."

She was in contention all week at Kumamoto Kuko Country Club, starting the first day with a 68, two strokes off the pace of Ai Suzuki, who failed to capitalise on a lead for a second straight week. A bogey-free 69 the second day put Nozomi a shot behind leader Yuna Nishimura (67-69) going into the final round. Bogeys at the par-four 17th hole Sunday cost Uetake and Sae Ogura, dropping them into the four-player deadlock after the regulation 54 holes. Yuri Yoshida shot 68, Ogura 69, Uetake 71 and

Nishimura, a three-time winner in 2021, 72 for the matching eight-under-par 208s.

In regulation, none of the four birdied the par-five 18th hole, the site of the subsequent playoff, but birdies abounded there in overtime. Pars took Nishimura out on the first extra hole and Ogura the second. Uetake and Yoshida, seeking her third career win, matched birdies and pars on the next three trips up 18 before Nozomi's seven-foot birdie putt ended the two-hour playoff struggle.

Kumamoto Kuko Country Club, Kumamoto — April 15-17
Par 72 (36-36); 6,499 yards — Purse: ¥100,000,000

1	**Nozomi Uetake**	68	69	71	208	¥18,000,000		Minami Hiruta	69	75	70	214	1,360,000
2	**Yuri Yoshida**	69	71	68	208	7,333,333		Kaori Aoyama	70	72	72	214	1,360,000
	Sae Ogura	69	70	69	208	7,333,333		Seon Woo Bae	70	70	74	214	1,360,000
	Yuna Nishimura	67	69	72	208	7,333,333		Min Young Lee[2]	69	70	75	214	1,360,000
	Uetake won playoff at sixth extra hole						20	Momoko Ueda	69	74	72	215	970,000
5	Sakura Koiwai	70	71	68	209	5,000,000		Aya Kinoshita	70	73	72	215	970,000
6	Saiki Fujita	71	72	67	210	4,000,000		Chae-Young Yoon	70	74	71	215	970,000
7	Ayaka Watanabe	71	68	72	211	3,500,000		Yuka Yasuda	71	71	73	215	970,000
8	Kotone Hori	71	71	70	212	2,500,000		Karin Takeyama	69	71	75	215	970,000
	Shina Kanazawa	71	70	71	212	2,500,000	25	Kotoko Uchida	70	73	73	216	848,571
	Ai Suzuki	66	73	73	212	2,500,000		Mizuki Ooide	71	73	72	216	848,571
11	Nana Suganuma	69	74	70	213	1,810,000		Erika Hara	70	73	73	216	848,571
	Rio Takeda	69	74	70	213	1,810,000		Na-Ri Lee	68	74	74	216	848,571
	Eri Fukuyama	68	74	71	213	1,810,000		Mi-Jeong Jeon	70	74	72	216	848,571
14	Sayaka Takahashi	71	73	70	214	1,360,000		Hikari Tanabe	72	70	74	216	848,571
	Shoko Sasaki	71	73	70	214	1,360,000		Haruka Morita	73	72	71	216	848,571

Fujisankei Ladies Classic

"Can you transform yourself into a Ghostbuster? My biggest enemy is myself." So said Sayaka Takahashi before taking the lead into the final round of the Fujisankei Ladies Classic, referring to the many disheartening Sundays in 2021 when she had her first victory on tour in her sights and failed to convert. Nineteen times the 23-year-old member of the Golden Generation had top-10 finishes, four of them after entering the final round as the tournament leader. Twice she finished second, four times in third place. She had three more top 10s in the weeks before the Fujisankei and finally chased away the ghosts with a two-stroke victory.

She got off to a brilliant start on Friday at the Kawana Hotel Golf Club's Fuji course with an eight-birdie 63, taking a four-stroke lead. But the margin shrank to one Saturday when she shot 69, and unheralded Aya Kinoshita bolted into second place with a bogey-free 63 of her own. The rainy Sunday was adventurous for Takahashi. She bogeyed three of the first five holes but birdied the other two. Kinoshita faded early, but veteran Saiki Fujita staged a strong challenge, actually leading briefly on the back nine before Takahashi ran off three birdies in a four-hole stretch and parred in for another 69 and the winning total of 12-under-par 201.

It was the first wire-to-wire victory in the long history of the tournament. Fujita, 35, the 2010 Japan LPGA champion whose last of five victories was in 2011, also finished with a 69 for 203, three shots ahead of the rest of the field.

Kawana Hotel Golf Club (Fuji), Shizuoka — April 22-24
Par 71 (35-36); 6,447 yards — Purse: ¥80,000,000

1	**Sayaka Takahashi**	63	69	69	201	¥14,400,000		Hikari Tanabe	68	68	71	207	2,600,000
2	**Saiki Fujita**	67	67	69	203	7,200,000		Nozomi Uetake	68	68	71	207	2,600,000
3	**Mayu Hamada**	67	70	69	206	4,800,000		Aya Kinoshita	70	63	74	207	2,600,000
	Miyu Goto	70	67	69	206	4,800,000	10	Nana Suganuma	69	71	68	208	1,525,333
	Yuka Yasuda	68	66	72	206	4,800,000		Mone Inami	71	68	69	208	1,525,333
6	Sakura Koiwai	74	66	67	207	2,600,000		Ayaka Matsumori	67	67	74	208	1,525,333

13	Haruka Amamoto	69	72	68	209	1,288,000		Megumi Kido	72	68	72	212	776,000
	Shiho Kuwaki	69	69	71	209	1,288,000		Mao Nozawa	72	65	75	212	776,000
	Shuri Sakuma	69	68	72	209	1,288,000	25	Kotone Hori	71	71	71	213	704,000
16	Kumiko Kaneda	69	72	69	210	1,128,000		Rio Takeda	72	70	71	213	704,000
17	Kana Nagai	69	72	70	211	968,000		Sae Ogura	69	72	72	213	704,000
	Ayaka Watanabe	69	72	70	211	968,000		Ritsuko Ryu	71	69	73	213	704,000
	Minami Hiruta	68	70	73	211	968,000	29	Rio Ishii	76	66	72	214	636,000
20	Shoko Sasaki	69	72	71	212	776,000		Shiho Oyama	72	69	73	214	636,000
	Erika Kikuchi	71	70	71	212	776,000		Fumika Kawagishi	73	67	74	214	636,000
	Mi-Jeong Jeon	69	71	72	212	776,000		Lala Anai	73	66	75	214	636,000

Panasonic Ladies Open

Nothing was going to slow down Mao Saigo. Not an ailing neck that sidelined her for two weeks. Not one of the JLPGA's most experienced players. In a spectacular run nearly identical to that of Mone Inami a year earlier, Saigo bypassed veteran Teresa Lu and posted her fourth victory in seven starts in the Panasonic Ladies Open at Hamano Golf Club.

The remarkable 20-year-old surged past the 34-year-old Taiwanese pro, a 16-tournament victor but winless on the tour since 2017, on the back nine on Sunday and posted a 68 to take a two-stroke victory with 10-under-par 206. "I was always calm like a veteran," remarked Saigo of her strong finish.

Speaking of veterans, longtime star Jiyai Shin, who hadn't played in Japan since the season-opening Daikin Orchid tournament, returned as the first-round leader with a six-under-par 66, a shot in front of Sayaka Takahashi, the previous week's winner, and two ahead of Lu and three others. Lu took over at the top Saturday with another 68 as Shin astonishingly skied to a 77. Saigo then jumped into second place with 70-68.

Lu seemed to have everything well in hand Sunday, expanding her lead over Saigo to four at the turn. The back nine was a complete turnaround. Lu bogeyed the 10th, Saigo birdied the 12th, Lu bogeyed the 13th. Then, Saigo holed her approach at the par-four 15th for an eagle to take the lead and her birdie at the home hole gave her a 68 and the two-shot win as Lu could do no better than pars on the last five holes, finishing with a 72.

Hamano Golf Club, Chiba — April 29-May1
Par 72 (36-36); 6,660 yards — Purse: ¥80,000,000

1	**Mao Saigo**	70	68	68	206	¥14,400,000		Momoko Kishibe	71	72	70	213	912,000
2	**Teresa Lu**	68	68	72	208	7,040,000		Asuka Kashiwabara	72	70	71	213	912,000
3	**Momoko Ueda**	70	71	68	209	5,200,000		Sumika Nakasone	70	69	74	213	912,000
	Sayaka Takahashi	67	72	70	209	5,200,000	21	Mami Fukuda	72	73	69	214	704,000
5	Kana Mikashima	71	73	66	210	3,600,000		Sakura Koiwai	69	74	71	214	704,000
	Serena Aoki	71	70	69	210	3,600,000		Haruka Amamoto	68	74	72	214	704,000
7	Akie Iwai	70	71	70	211	2,600,000		Ayaka Matsumori	69	73	72	214	704,000
	Miyu Goto	71	70	70	211	2,600,000		Nozomi Uetake	71	71	72	214	704,000
9	Miki Sakai	73	72	67	212	1,451,428	26	Haruka Morita	71	73	71	215	600,000
	Yuna Nishimura	72	72	68	212	1,451,428		Au-Reum Hwang	72	73	70	215	600,000
	Jiyai Shin	66	77	69	212	1,451,428		Chirei Iwai	71	74	70	215	600,000
	Seon Woo Bae	71	72	69	212	1,451,428		Shiho Kuwaki	70	73	72	215	600,000
	Na-Ri Lee	74	69	69	212	1,451,428		Minami Katsu	72	74	69	215	600,000
	Shina Kanazawa	72	70	70	212	1,451,428		Yui Kawamoto	72	70	73	215	600,000
	Kumiko Kaneda	73	69	70	212	1,451,428		Saki Asai	71	70	74	215	600,000
16	Momoko Osato	71	73	69	213	912,000		Saki Nagamine	71	69	75	215	600,000
	Hana Wakimoto	71	73	69	213	912,000							

World Ladies Championship Salonpas Cup

Her recent performances gave no indication that Miyuu Yamashita was about to add a major title to the initial Japan LPGA Tour victory the 20-year-old scored in the 2021 Vantelin Open. She had missed three consecutive cuts coming into the World Ladies Championship for the Salonpas Cup.

In a complete turnaround, Yamashita shot an opening-round 64 on Ibaraki Golf Club's West course, was challenged by veteran Serena Aoki along the way, but rolled ahead in the lead all the way to a three-stroke victory over Aoki with 12-under-par 276. Still, it hadn't come easily according to the winner. "I played in a tremendous amount of tension," she observed.

After the fast start, Yamashita shot 74 on Friday and 29-year-old Aoki, a two-time winner on tour, moved within a stroke of her with a 68. Yamashita bounced back with a six-birdie 67 on Saturday, opening a six-stroke lead over Aoki (72) and Yuka Yasuda (70) and seven ahead of Mone Inami, the 2021 leading money winner. Aoki cut the lead in half with a 33 on the front nine Sunday but never got any closer as Yamashita closed with a 71 and that three-shot margin over Aoki. Inami (70) and Asuka Ishikawa (66) were next, a distant six shots behind the winner.

Ibaraki Golf Club (West), Ibaraki — May 5-8
Par 72 (36-36); 6,680 yards — Purse: ¥120,000,000

1	**Miyuu Yamashita**	64	74	67	71	276	¥24,000,000
2	**Serena Aoki**	71	68	72	68	279	12,000,000
3	**Asuka Ishikawa**	73	73	70	66	282	8,100,000
	Mone Inami	70	71	71	70	282	8,100,000
5	Nana Suganuma	68	73	74	68	283	5,400,000
	Miyu Goto	74	69	72	68	283	5,400,000
7	Miyuki Takeuchi	69	73	71	71	284	3,450,000
	Yuka Yasuda	70	71	70	73	284	3,450,000
9	Momoko Osato	71	73	71	70	285	2,430,000
	Minami Katsu	74	71	68	72	285	2,430,000
11	Min Young Lee2	71	74	72	69	286	2,100,000
12	Saiki Fujita	74	72	71	70	287	1,920,000
	Yuri Yoshida	74	74	69	70	287	1,920,000
14	Mami Fukuda	73	72	72	71	288	1,384,000
	Ritsuko Ryu	74	72	71	71	288	1,384,000
	Seira Oki	69	72	75	72	288	1,384,000
	Shuri Sakuma	74	72	70	72	288	1,384,000
	Yuna Nishimura	71	75	70	72	288	1,384,000
	Nanoko Hayashi	72	75	68	73	288	1,384,000
20	Miyuu Abe	72	78	72	67	289	912,000
	Haruka Amamoto	70	80	69	70	289	912,000
	Eri Okayama	70	72	73	74	289	912,000
23	Sakura Koiwai	72	76	74	68	290	828,000
	Sayaka Takahashi	76	73	71	70	290	828,000
	Mirai Hamasaki	76	73	71	70	290	828,000
	Seon Woo Bae	70	73	75	72	290	828,000
27	Nanako Ueno	73	71	76	71	291	720,000
	Momoko Kishibe	71	74	73	73	291	720,000
	Momoko Ueda	76	74	68	73	291	720,000
	Lala Anai	71	72	74	74	291	720,000
	Kotone Hori	77	70	69	75	291	720,000

Hoken no Madoguchi Ladies

That the putter can compensate for other ills was never more clearly illustrated than with Ayaka Watanabe's overtime victory in the Hoken no Madoguchi Ladies tournament. Wild with her play on the par-five 18th hole at the first extra hole, Watanabe ran in a 17-foot birdie putt to defeat Sayaka Takahashi and score her fifth victory on the Japan LPGA Tour.

The 28-year-old Watanabe, whose most recent victory was in the 2020 Earth Mondahmin, the first tournament played during the pandemic-shortened season, had taken a two-stroke advantage into the final round on the Wajiro course at Fukuoka Country Club. Her pair of five-under-par 67s gave her that margin over three tournament winners — Erika Kikuchi, Erika Hara and Sakura Koiwai. Takahashi, who had finally ended a long string of near-misses with her victory the previous month in the Fujisankei Classic, was another shot back with 68-69.

Watanabe got off to a fast start Sunday with four birdies on the first five holes, but an out-of-bounds double bogey at the eighth hole and a bogey at the 10th put several contenders, particularly Takahashi, back in the game. Pairs of birdies and bogeys the rest of the way for a 71 and 11-under-par 205 were just enough for Watanabe to wind up in a tie with Takahashi, who birdied the last two holes for a 68 to force the playoff.

Fukuoka Country Club (Wajiro), Fukuoka — May 13-15
Par 72 (36-36); 6,299 yards — Purse: ¥120,000,000

1	**Ayaka Watanabe**	67	67	71	205	¥21,600,000
2	**Sayaka Takahashi**	68	69	68	205	10,560,000
	Watanabe won playoff at first extra hole					
3	**Mone Inami**	70	68	69	207	7,800,000
	Sakura Koiwai	66	70	71	207	7,800,000
5	Sae Ogura	69	71	68	208	5,400,000
	Erika Hara	69	67	72	208	5,400,000
7	Jiyai Shin	69	72	68	209	3,900,000
	Erika Kikuchi	66	70	73	209	3,900,000
9	Karen Tsuruoka	70	70	70	210	2,700,000
	Kana Mikashima	72	66	72	210	2,700,000
11	Shuri Sakuma	71	71	69	211	1,716,000
	Au-Reum Hwang	71	71	69	211	1,716,000
	Miki Sakai	69	72	70	211	1,716,000
	Yuna Nishimura	69	72	70	211	1,716,000
	Yuri Yoshida	70	72	69	211	1,716,000
	Mami Fukuda	74	68	69	211	1,716,000
	Serena Aoki	67	75	69	211	1,716,000
	Rie Tsuji	71	70	70	211	1,716,000
	Nozomi Uetake	71	70	70	211	1,716,000
	Mi-Jeong Jeon	68	71	72	211	1,716,000
21	Saiki Fujita	72	70	70	212	1,092,000
	Megumi Kido	70	71	71	212	1,092,000
	Lala Anai	71	70	71	212	1,092,000
	Aya Kinoshita	69	71	72	212	1,092,000
	Yuka Yasuda	69	71	72	212	1,092,000
	Teresa Lu	70	73	69	212	1,092,000
27	Shiho Kuwaki	71	71	71	213	912,000
	Miyuu Abe	71	71	71	213	912,000
	Seira Oki	70	71	72	213	912,000
	Yui Kawamoto	71	70	72	213	912,000
	Nana Suganuma	71	72	70	213	912,000
	Minami Katsu	69	71	73	213	912,000
	Saki Nagamine	71	69	73	213	912,000
	Nanako Ueno	71	69	73	213	912,000
	Sumika Nakasone	66	71	76	213	912,000

Bridgestone Ladies Open

What a turnaround! Mao Saigo's brilliant early season had hit a startling blip. After four wins in her first seven starts, the talented 20-year-old missed two consecutive cuts by sizeable margins. A week later at the Bridgestone Ladies Open, Saigo had a fifth victory on her record. The remarkable start virtually paralleled that of 22-year-old Mone Inami the previous season — five victories in her first 12 starts compared to 10 for Saigo — and, ironically, it was Inami who gave Saigo a run for her money at Sodegaura Country Club.

Saigo (67-70) had moved into a three-way lead with veteran Jiyai Shin and Miyuu Yamashita (both 69-68) the second day and inched into solo first place Saturday with a 69 to be eight under par, a shot ahead of Chie Arimura and Yamashita, two in front of Shin.

Mone, three back going into Sunday's final round, raced into a two-stroke lead with an eagle and two birdies to Saigo's one-bogey 37 on the front nine, only to give it back with successive bogeys at the 12th and the 13th, and fall too far off the pace when Saigo holed a bunker shot at the 16th. She added a second birdie at the 18th for a 69 and a two-stroke victory over Inami, who had her second runner-up finish without a 2022 victory after her sterling 2021 season.

"It was really hard today," Saigo remarked. "But I was inspired because the local people in Chiba supported me a lot."

Sodegaura Country Club (Sodegaura), Chiba — May 19-26
Par 72 (36-36); 6,713 yards — Purse: ¥100,000,000

1	**Mao Saigo**	67	70	69	69	275	¥18,000,000
2	**Mone Inami**	68	72	69	68	277	8,800,000
3	**Serena Aoki**	72	70	71	65	278	6,500,000
	Miyuu Yamashita	69	68	70	71	278	6,500,000
5	Jiyai Shin	69	68	71	71	279	5,000,000
6	Momoko Ueda	72	72	69	68	281	4,000,000
7	Chie Arimura	70	69	68	75	282	3,500,000
8	Au-Reum Hwang	71	73	69	70	283	2,500,000
	Nanoko Hayashi	66	75	70	72	283	2,500,000
	Pei-Ying Tsai	69	72	68	74	283	2,500,000
11	Mami Fukuda	75	70	70	69	284	1,640,000
	Nana Suganuma	70	71	73	70	284	1,640,000
	Yui Kawamoto	69	75	70	70	284	1,640,000
14	Nozomi Uetake	73	71	71	70	285	1,290,000
	Kotone Hori	71	73	70	71	285	1,290,000
	Sakura Yokomine	69	74	70	72	285	1,290,000
	Nanako Ueno	70	72	68	75	285	1,290,000
18	Erika Kikuchi	74	71	70	71	286	888,000
	Sumika Nakasone	74	70	76	66	286	888,000
	Seira Oki	72	73	75	66	286	888,000
	Miki Sakai	71	68	75	72	286	888,000
	Shina Kanazawa	71	70	69	76	286	888,000
23	Asuka Kashiwabara	71	72	74	70	287	740,000
	Fumika Kawagishi	71	72	73	71	287	740,000
	Minami Katsu	75	69	71	72	287	740,000
	Hikaru Yoshimoto	70	73	71	73	287	740,000
	Saiki Fujita	70	71	71	75	287	740,000
28	Yuri Yoshida	72	71	75	70	288	650,000
	Mei Takagi	72	72	72	72	288	650,000
	Ai Suzuki	72	72	72	72	288	650,000
	Saki Baba (A)	75	68	72	73	288	
	Yuna Nishimura	72	72	71	73	288	650,000

Resort Trust Ladies

The saying, "While the cat's away, the mice will play", applied to a degree to the Resort Trust tournament in late May and to Sakura Koiwai in particular. With Mao Saigo, winner of nearly half of the 2022 tournaments, off to play in the US Women's Open and many of the other prominent players skipping the tournament, Koiwai had a less than formidable field to face and she capitalised with her seventh victory on the Japan LPGA Tour.

It had been a disappointing season for the 24-year-old Hokkaido native, who had won four times the year before. In 12 starts she did have four top-10s, but was coming off a missed cut. Rebounding, she was in contention from the start at Maple Point Golf Club in Yamanashi. Tied for fifth place three strokes behind Pei-Ying Tsai and her opening 66, Koiwai climbed into a share of second place on Friday with 69-67, a stroke behind unheralded Minami Hiruta.

The race became pretty much a two-player battle by Saturday's end as Koiwai fired a nine-birdie, one-bogey 64 to be 16 under par and Taiwan's Tsai, the T-Point winner in March, carved out a bogey-free 65 to be 14 under. The rest of the field trailed Koiwai by five shots or more.

After Tsai overtook on the front nine Sunday, Koiwai first got back level and then broke the tie with a 23-foot birdie putt on the 13th hole. She finished with a 71 for a 17-under-par total of 271 on what she called "a really long day". The final margin was two strokes when Tsai bogeyed the 18th for a 71 to share second place with Nana Suganuma (66).

Maple Point Golf Club, Yamanashi — May 26-29
Par 72 (36-36); 6,580 yards — Purse: ¥100,000,000

1	**Sakura Koiwai**	69	67	64	71	271	¥18,000,000
2	**Nana Suganuma**	68	68	71	66	273	7,900,000
	Pei-Ying Tsai	66	71	65	71	273	7,900,000
4	Shiho Kuwaki	69	68	68	69	274	6,000,000
5	Minami Katsu	69	70	69	67	275	3,600,000
	Momoko Osato	70	67	70	68	275	3,600,000
	Rie Tsuji	73	66	68	68	275	3,600,000
	Amiyu Ozeki	69	71	67	68	275	3,600,000
	Miyuu Abe	71	70	66	68	275	3,600,000
10	Kotone Hori	72	68	69	67	276	1,745,000
	Aya Kinoshita	70	68	70	68	276	1,745,000
	Yuri Yoshida	69	70	68	69	276	1,745,000
	Yui Kawamoto	70	70	66	70	276	1,745,000
14	Sayaka Takahashi	68	70	72	67	277	1,360,000
	Shuri Sakuma	72	69	69	67	277	1,360,000
	Minami Hiruta	70	65	71	71	277	1,360,000
17	Saki Nagamine	70	71	68	69	278	1,110,000
	Teresa Lu	71	68	68	71	278	1,110,000
19	Ayako Kimura	71	65	73	70	279	910,000
	Akie Iwai	73	69	66	71	279	910,000
21	Chie Arimura	73	70	71	66	280	790,000
	Mao Nozawa	69	70	71	70	280	790,000
	Mone Inami	73	69	68	70	280	790,000
	Miki Sakai	70	70	68	72	280	790,000
	Rio Ishii	68	70	68	74	280	790,000
	Ayaka Matsumori	69	69	68	74	280	790,000
27	Miyu Sato	76	68	70	67	281	710,000
	Momoko Kishibe	71	72	67	71	281	710,000
29	Haruka Kawasaki	72	70	71	69	282	650,000
	Nanako Ueno	70	69	73	70	282	650,000
	Miyuki Takeuchi	73	68	71	70	282	650,000
	Rumi Yoshiba	74	69	71	68	282	650,000

Richard Mille Yonex Ladies

It took a 14-tournament stretch for Mone Inami to revive her sensational winning ways on tour. Coming off her remarkable eight-victory 2021 when she ran away with the money title, Inami had a pair of runner-up finishes and two thirds but no wins as Mao Saigo virtually duplicated Mone's 2021 accomplishments through the first few months of the new season.

The breakthrough came in the Richard Mille Yonex tournament. The 22-year-old sailed along in first place from the start at Yonex Country Club in Niigata Prefecture as she posted a two-stroke victory with a seven-under-par 209 total. Showing a look of relief after scoring her 11th career win, Inami said: "I'm really happy to be able to hold the winning cup in front of everyone in the gallery."

Inami shared the lead on the first day as she, Nana Suganuma, Yuri Yoshida and Minami Katsu opened with 69s. Her second straight 69 put her two shots in front of Chirei Iwai (73-67), Yoshida and Katsu, who both shot 71s Saturday. A mediocre, one-under-par 71 — three birdies, two bogeys — was good enough for the two-shot win Sunday. Iwai and Saiki Fujita scored 32s on the back nine to jump into a second-place tie at five under.

Yonex Country Club, Niigata — June 3-5
Par 72 (36-36); 6,475 yards — Purse: ¥90,000,000

1	**Mone Inami**	69	69	71	209	¥16,200,000
2	**Saiki Fujita**	73	69	69	211	7,110,000
	Chirei Iwai	73	67	71	211	7,110,000
4	Rio Ishii	71	73	68	212	3,870,000
	Nana Suganuma	69	74	69	212	3,870,000
	Sayaka Takahashi	72	70	70	212	3,870,000
	Lala Anai	73	69	70	212	3,870,000
	Yuri Yoshida	69	71	72	212	3,870,000
9	Serena Aoki	73	74	66	213	2,250,000
10	Miyuu Abe	76	68	70	214	1,755,000
	Akie Iwai	73	71	70	214	1,755,000
12	Shiho Kuwaki	75	68	72	215	1,530,000
	Miyuu Yamashita	73	68	74	215	1,530,000
	Minami Katsu	69	71	75	215	1,530,000
15	Shina Kanazawa	72	73	71	216	1,305,000
	Au-Reum Hwang	73	72	71	216	1,305,000
17	Momoko Osato	74	72	71	217	1,080,000
	Mizuki Ooide	72	73	72	217	1,080,000
	Karin Takeyama	72	72	73	217	1,080,000
20	Yui Kawamoto	74	72	72	218	873,000
	Yuki Ichinose	72	74	72	218	873,000
	Shoko Sasaki	70	74	74	218	873,000
	Asuka Kashiwabara	74	69	75	218	873,000
24	Kana Mikashima	74	72	73	219	747,000
	Aya Kinoshita	71	74	74	219	747,000
	Ayako Kimura	71	75	73	219	747,000
	Mirai Hamasaki	72	73	74	219	747,000
	Eri Okayama	74	71	74	219	747,000
	Miyu Goto	74	71	74	219	747,000
	Hikaru Yoshimoto	72	72	75	219	747,000
	Pei-Ying Tsai	72	72	75	219	747,000
	Miyuki Takeuchi	73	71	75	219	747,000
	Fumika Kawagishi	72	71	76	219	747,000

Ai Miyazato Suntory Ladies Open

The year before, Miyuu Yamashita had a near-miss in the Ai Miyazato Suntory Ladies Open, her closing 67 coming up a stroke short of winner Serena Aoki. "I was a little disappointed," the 21-year-old recalled after rewarding herself with her second victory of the season when she returned to the long-standing tournament in 2022.

The win came at the expense of Saiki Fujita, the 36-year-old former Japan LPGA champion who scored her fifth and most recent victory back in 2011. Fujita had taken a three-stroke lead the second day at Rokko Kokusai Golf Club with her 66-68 and maintained that margin Saturday when she led Amiyu Ozeki and 2021 number one Mone Inami as she followed with a two-under-par 70. Yamashita sat four strokes behind after rounds of 68-71-69.

Fujita motored comfortably with a pair of birdies on the first 10 holes Sunday as the more-threatening move came, not from Yamashita but from 2021 Japan Open champion Minami Katsu, who shot 30 on the front nine. But both of Fujita, incurring four bogeys, and Katsu, with a double bogey and a bogey, faltered on the incoming stretch. That opened the door for Yamashita, who polished off a four-birdie, no-bogey 68 for a 12-under-par total of 276 that gave her a one-shot win when Fujita made her last bogey at the 18th hole.

"I am very happy to be able to play with no bogeys on the final day," observed Yamashita after adding the Suntory to her May victory in the major World Ladies Championship for her third career triumph.

Rokko Kokusai Golf Club, Hyogo — June 9-12
Par 72 (36-36); 6,527 yards — Purse: ¥150,000,000

1	**Miyuu Yamashita**	68	71	69	68	276	¥27,000,000
2	**Saiki Fujita**	66	68	70	73	277	13,200,000
3	**Minami Katsu**	72	68	71	67	278	9,000,000
	Saki Nagamine	69	70	70	69	278	9,000,000
	Mone Inami	68	70	69	71	278	9,000,000
6	Hana Lee	70	68	70	71	279	6,000,000
7	Yuting Seki	70	67	71	72	280	5,250,000
8	Lala Anai	68	73	69	71	281	3,453,750
	Sakura Koiwai	69	69	71	72	281	3,453,750
	Au-Reum Hwang	70	70	68	73	281	3,453,750
	Amiyu Ozeki	72	68	67	74	281	3,453,750
12	Ji-Hee Lee	69	71	72	70	282	2,190,000
	Momoko Kishibe	72	71	68	71	282	2,190,000
	Momoko Osato	68	71	71	72	282	2,190,000
	Kotone Hori	71	68	70	73	282	2,190,000
16	Haruka Morita	71	72	70	71	284	1,380,000
	Momoko Ueda	70	69	74	71	284	1,380,000
	Fumika Kawagishi	72	70	71	71	284	1,380,000
	Serena Aoki	69	73	71	71	284	1,380,000
	Eri Okayama	70	73	69	72	284	1,380,000
	Chae-Young Yoon	70	72	70	72	284	1,380,000
	Ayako Kimura	74	65	71	74	284	1,380,000
	Haruka Kudo	68	69	72	75	284	1,380,000
24	Shiho Kuwaki	69	72	73	71	285	1,050,000
	Erika Hara	73	69	70	73	285	1,050,000
	Maaya Suzuki	73	69	70	73	285	1,050,000
	Rin Yoshida (A)	69	72	70	74	285	
	Yuna Nishimura	65	76	69	75	285	1,050,000
29	Ritsuko Ryu	71	73	69	73	286	918,000
	Momo Yoshikawa	74	71	70	71	286	918,000
	Ayaka Watanabe	72	73	70	71	286	918,000
	Asuka Kashiwabara	74	68	74	70	286	918,000
	Nanoko Hayashi	65	73	73	75	286	918,000

Nichirei Ladies

Coming off her three-victory 2021 season as a 20-year-old, Yuna Nishimura was displeased with her failure to continue on the winning path through the early months of the season. "Even if the shots are in good condition ... I can't win. I was really disappointed to lose in the playoff of the Vantelin Ladies," she remarked.

Things changed brilliantly in June in the Nichirei Ladies after Nishimura made a fruitless trip to America to play in the US Women's Open and switched putters. She staged a bogey-free performance at Sodegaura Country Club in Chiba City and broke open a tight battle with Haruka Morita to win her fifth tour title by three strokes on a 17-under-par total of 199.

With a seven-birdie 65 the first day, Nishimura trailed only Miyu Sato, whose opening 64 included a front-nine 29. The two were joined in a three-way tie at the top Saturday by Morita, 25, a player of Chinese parentage whose mother and father moved to Japan from Shanghai before she was born. She shot 65 to match the 133 totals of Sato (69) and Nishimura, who posted a four-birdie 68.

Although she fell two strokes behind Morita's 32 on the front nine Sunday, Nishimura recalled: "I wasn't impatient. I was waiting for a chance in the second half." She got one stroke back with her third birdie at number 10 and took the lead for keeps when she birdied the 15th as Morita sprayed her approach into the woods and absorbed a crippling bogey. Nishimura then wrapped things up with a birdie-birdie finish to her closing 66. "I'm very happy," she gushed afterward. "It's the first time I've played with no bogeys for three days."

Sodegaura Country Club (Shinsode), Chiba — June 17-19
Par 72 (36-36); 6,563 yards — Purse: ¥100,000,000

1	**Yuna Nishimura**	65	68	66	199	¥18,000,000
2	**Haruka Morita**	68	65	69	202	8,800,000
3	**Miyuu Yamashita**	68	69	67	204	6,500,000
	Mone Inami	68	68	68	204	6,500,000
5	Miyu Sato	64	69	72	205	5,000,000
6	Jiyai Shin	73	67	66	206	3,750,000
	Chie Arimura	66	71	69	206	3,750,000
8	Miyuu Abe	69	69	69	207	2,500,000
	Shina Kanazawa	68	69	70	207	2,500,000
	Shoko Sasaki	70	67	70	207	2,500,000
11	Kana Nagai	70	69	69	208	1,800,000
	Shuri Sakuma	69	69	70	208	1,800,000
13	Nanako Ueno	67	73	69	209	1,550,000
	Saiki Fujita	71	69	69	209	1,550,000
	Pei-Ying Tsai	70	69	70	209	1,550,000
16	Yuri Yoshida	69	71	70	210	1,084,285
	Momoko Osato	70	70	70	210	1,084,285
	Saki Nagamine	74	66	70	210	1,084,285
	Sayaka Takahashi	69	70	71	210	1,084,285
	Miki Sakai	71	68	71	210	1,084,285
	Kotone Hori	72	67	71	210	1,084,285
	Mizuki Ooide	70	73	67	210	1,084,285
23	Min Young Lee[2]	71	70	70	211	830,000
	Seon Woo Bae	68	72	71	211	830,000
	Sakura Koiwai	69	71	71	211	830,000
	Shiho Kuwaki	71	69	71	211	830,000
	Nana Suganuma	69	70	72	211	830,000
	Rie Iwahashi	69	70	72	211	830,000
	Natsuka Hori	68	70	73	211	830,000
30	Mi-Jeong Jeon	73	68	71	212	680,000
	Erika Kikuchi	68	73	71	212	680,000
	Hiromu Ono	71	71	70	212	680,000
	Asuka Ishikawa	70	72	70	212	680,000
	Ai Suzuki	70	72	70	212	680,000
	Seira Oki	73	69	70	212	680,000
	Haruka Kudo	74	69	69	212	680,000
	Miyuki Takeuchi	68	69	75	212	680,000

Earth Mondahmin Cup

Facing the possibility of another playoff, Ayako Kimura had depressing memories of the 2021 Stanley Ladies, when she shot a fine final round ahead of the contenders, had a long wait, then was the first one out of the four-player overtime that followed. "If I lose here, I won't win for the rest of my life," bemoaned the winless veteran of eight seasons on the Japan LPGA Tour after finishing the final round of the Earth Mondahmin Cup with the clubhouse lead after making up a six-stroke deficit with nine contenders still on the course.

Her fears proved unfounded as her closing 69 in windy conditions and her four-under-par 284 total held up for a one-stroke victory over Yuna Nishimura, who was trying for a second straight win, and Shoko Sasaki, the second and third-round leader. "It's like a dream," said the relieved Kimura. "The people around me told me I could win any time, but it took me this long."

After Miyuu Yamashita led the first day with an eight-under-par 64, the top spot belonged to Sasaki the next two days at Camellia Hills Country Club in Sodegaura City. The 26-year-old three-time winner took the lead Friday, by one over Saiki Fujita, Mone Inami and Yamashita, with a par 72 on a day when only three players broke par. A one-under 71 gave her a two-stroke edge over Kumiko Kaneda on Saturday as Kimura struggled with a back-nine 40 for a 75 that put her in a tie for ninth place.

Kimura made up five of the six-shot deficit on the front nine Sunday, bogeyed the 10th, then birdied the 11th and 14th to take the lead and parred in as Sasaki double-bogeyed the 11th hole en route to a 76 and the tie for second with Nishimura (70).

Camellia Hills Country Club, Chiba — June 23-26
Par 72 (36-36); 6,639 yards — Purse: ¥300,000,000

1	**Ayako Kimura**	67	73	75	69	284	¥54,000,000
2	**Yuna Nishimura**	67	77	71	70	285	23,700,000
	Shoko Sasaki	66	72	71	76	285	23,700,000
4	Miyuu Yamashita	64	75	74	73	286	18,000,000
5	Ritsuko Ryu	70	74	74	69	287	13,500,000
	Kana Nagai	72	70	71	74	287	13,500,000
7	Mone Inami	65	74	77	72	288	8,250,000
	Fumika Kawagishi	68	74	72	74	288	8,250,000
	Au-Reum Hwang	71	74	69	74	288	8,250,000
	Kumiko Kaneda	69	73	69	77	288	8,250,000
11	Minami Katsu	71	75	73	70	289	4,230,000
	Miyuu Abe	72	74	73	70	289	4,230,000
	Kotona Izumida	72	76	70	71	289	4,230,000
	Chie Arimura	71	74	73	71	289	4,230,000
	Erika Kikuchi	68	76	72	73	289	4,230,000
16	Momoko Osato	71	74	73	72	290	3,030,000
	Shuri Sakuma	69	76	71	74	290	3,030,000
	Saiki Fujita	68	71	75	76	290	3,030,000
19	Megumi Kido	70	75	75	71	291	2,167,500
	Min Young Lee[2]	70	74	75	72	291	2,167,500
	Mao Nozawa	69	72	77	73	291	2,167,500
	Hikaru Yoshimoto	71	75	70	75	291	2,167,500
23	Lala Anai	69	78	75	70	292	1,980,000
	Jiyai Shin	72	70	75	75	292	1,980,000
	Haruka Morita	71	77	77	67	292	1,980,000
26	Teresa Lu	69	76	75	73	293	1,785,000
	Miki Sakai	72	74	75	72	293	1,785,000
	Seon Woo Bae	72	74	73	74	293	1,785,000
	Momoko Ueda	74	74	74	71	293	1,785,000
	Nozomi Uetake	73	75	74	71	293	1,785,000
	Rie Tsuji	70	77	71	75	293	1,785,000
	Haruka Amamoto	69	77	77	70	293	1,785,000
	Serena Aoki	68	75	74	76	293	1,785,000
	Rie Iwahashi	72	72	72	77	293	1,785,000
	Yumi Narisawa	73	75	76	69	293	1,785,000

Shiseido Ladies Open

Serena Aoki adopted a strong philosophy as she carried a one-stroke lead into the final round of the Shiseido Ladies Open. "Don't be afraid. Fight against invisible enemies," she vowed. The attitude paid off as the 29-year-old veteran carved out her third career victory by two strokes in the new tournament on the JLPGA schedule.

The ¥21 million first-place prize moved Aoki that much closer to a goal she said she has had since elementary-school days — to get closer to Yuri Fudoh, the highly-respected star who reigns as the all-time tour money winner with then career earnings of ¥1,368,935,382 and was still competing at age 45. "I want to be a player who earns one billion yen," stated the diminutive Aoki, one of the shortest players on tour, standing just under five feet tall.

Aoki moved into the lead on Saturday at Totsuka Golf Club, in Yokohama City, after sitting in a 10-player tie, three strokes behind Ji-Hee Lee's 65, the first day. With 68-69, she was a shot back of co-leaders Yuri Yoshida, Hiromu Ono and Mizuki Ooide after Friday's round. Her five-birdie, one-bogey 68 Saturday gave her a one-stroke edge over tour sophomore Yoshida, a two-time winner in 2021, and lesser-known Chae-Young Yoon.

Sunday did not start well for Aoki. She bogeyed the first two holes, but quickly recovered with birdies at the third, fourth and seventh holes. A run of three more following the turn put her in a commanding position and a bogey at the 17th only narrowed her margin of victory. She finished with a 69 and a 14-under-par total of 274. Yoshida shot 70 and tied for second with Erika Kikuchi (68) and Au-Reum Hwang, who raced home with a 64.

Totsuka Country Club, Kanagawa
Par 72 (36-36); 6,570 yards

June 30-July 3
Purse: ¥120,000,000

1	**Serena Aoki**	68	69	68	69	274	¥21,600,000
2	**Au-Reum Hwang**	72	70	70	64	276	8,720,000
	Erika Kikuchi	69	70	69	68	276	8,720,000
	Yuri Yoshida	67	69	70	70	276	8,720,000
5	Mizuki Ooide	67	69	76	65	277	4,320,000
	Minami Katsu	75	67	68	67	277	4,320,000
	Miyuu Yamashita	70	69	70	68	277	4,320,000
	Shoko Sasaki	68	71	68	70	277	4,320,000
	Chae-Young Yoon	72	66	68	71	277	4,320,000
10	Nana Suganuma	69	71	70	68	278	2,238,000
	Shina Kanazawa	68	71	69	70	278	2,238,000
12	Yumi Kudo	68	72	70	69	279	1,896,000
	Ritsuko Ryu	67	70	71	71	279	1,896,000
14	Jiyai Shin	70	70	70	70	280	1,536,000
	Nanoko Hayashi	68	72	69	71	280	1,536,000
	Mao Nozawa	68	69	71	72	280	1,536,000
	Miyu Sato	70	69	69	72	280	1,536,000
18	Ayako Kimura	68	75	70	68	281	1,116,000
	Momoko Kishibe	69	71	71	70	281	1,116,000
	Kotone Hori	72	71	68	70	281	1,116,000
21	Bo-Mee Lee	71	71	71	69	282	888,000
	Momoko Ueda	72	71	71	68	282	888,000
	Erika Hara	71	67	74	70	282	888,000
	Min Young Lee[2]	72	71	69	70	282	888,000
	Hiromu Ono	67	69	75	71	282	888,000
	Mone Inami	67	73	74	68	282	888,000
	Shiho Kuwaki	72	72	71	67	282	888,000
	Seon Woo Bae	66	71	72	73	282	888,000
29	Lala Anai	70	71	72	70	283	713,142
	Yuna Nishimura	70	73	70	70	283	713,142
	Hana Wakimoto	68	73	72	70	283	713,142
	Teresa Lu	71	70	71	71	283	713,142
	Haruka Amamoto	69	71	74	69	283	713,142
	Hana Lee	74	70	70	69	283	713,142
	Amiyu Ozeki	73	70	72	68	283	713,142

Nippon Ham Ladies Classic

Mao Saigo returned to the Japan LPGA Tour after playing in two majors in America on the LPGA Tour, hoping to pick up where she left off when she dominated the early season with five wins and built a commanding lead in the money-list race. However, the 20-year-old had to settle for a modest tie for 19th place in the Nippon Ham Ladies Classic, 12 strokes behind winner Yuna Nishimura, who became her closest challenger with her second win of the year and sixth in her brief three-season career.

Nishimura's victory, as she joined Saigo and Miyuu Yamashita as a multiple 2022 winner, came down to a sand save at the final green of the 72-hole event that gave her a closing two-under-par 70 and a one-stroke triumph over winless Mao Nozawa with an 18-under-par total of 270.

She had taken the lead at Katsura Golf Club at Tomakomai City, Hokkaido, with her second consecutive 67 Friday that featured a hole-in-one at the par-three eighth hole and three birdies in a bogey-free round. She led Seon Woo Bae and Yuri Yoshida by two strokes and edged another shot in front of Nozawa (65) and Mami Fukuda (64) Saturday with a seven-birdie, one-bogey 66.

Trouble in the person of Nozawa loomed on the back nine Sunday when Nishimura absorbed bogeys at the 12th and 13th holes. Nozawa, 159th in the Rolex World Rankings whose best season was in 2020 when she finished 29th on the money list, birdied the 11th and the 12th to overtake Nishimura. But after they both birdied the 14th, Nozawa found water and double-bogeyed the 15th, Nishimura's birdie there giving her a three-stroke margin. Nozawa bounced back with birdies at the 16th and 17th holes before Nishimura knocked a greenside bunker shot two feet from the cup for the deciding save at the last. "I'm really glad I played without giving up," Nishimura summed up the victory.

Katsura Golf Club, Hokkaido
Par 72 (36-36); 6,763 yards

July 7-10
Purse: ¥100,000,000

1	**Yuna Nishimura**	67	67	66	70	270	¥18,000,000
2	**Mao Nozawa**	66	72	65	68	271	8,800,000
3	**Seon Woo Bae**	67	69	68	68	272	7,000,000
4	Miyuu Yamashita	69	68	70	67	274	5,000,000
	Haruka Morita	70	68	66	70	274	5,000,000
	Mami Fukuda	69	70	64	71	274	5,000,000
7	Mone Inami	71	66	71	68	276	3,500,000
8	Megumi Kido	75	67	66	70	278	2,750,000
	Mi-Jeong Jeon	73	70	65	70	278	2,750,000
10	Minami Katsu	76	64	69	70	279	2,000,000
11	Kana Mikashima	70	72	70	68	280	1,690,000
	Momoko Kishibe	70	68	73	69	280	1,690,000
	Kotoko Uchida	70	69	71	70	280	1,690,000
14	Nanoko Hayashi	69	72	71	69	281	1,290,000
	Sakura Koiwai	68	71	72	70	281	1,290,000
	Saiki Fujita	66	75	70	70	281	1,290,000
	Nozomi Uetake	74	68	69	70	281	1,290,000
	Yuri Yoshida	67	69	69	76	281	1,290,000
19	Mao Saigo	70	69	75	68	282	886,000
	Yumi Narisawa	73	71	71	67	282	886,000
	Ji-Hee Lee	71	71	69	71	282	886,000
	Miyu Sato	71	72	67	72	282	886,000

	Asuka Ishikawa	72	67	70	73	282	886,000
24	Aya Kinoshita	74	66	72	71	283	800,000
	Kotone Hori	69	71	70	73	283	800,000
26	Shiho Kuwaki	73	69	71	71	284	710,000
	Haruka Amamoto	74	71	70	69	284	710,000
	Minami Hiruta	70	72	71	71	284	710,000
	Rin Yoshida (A)	73	70	72	69	284	
	Serena Aoki	68	71	72	73	284	710,000
	Chie Arimura	72	70	74	68	284	710,000
	Ayaka Furue	71	73	73	67	284	710,000
	Momoko Osato	74	69	74	67	284	710,000

Daito Kentaku Eheyanet Ladies

Erika Kikuchi didn't quite match three of the previous four victories of her 15-season career in which she led from start to finish, but she came close. The 34-year-old veteran, who has been playing golf since she was six years old, assumed the lead from one stroke back in the second round of the 72-hole Daito Kentaku Eheyanet Ladies tournament in her Hokkaido hometown of Sapporo City and carried it to the fifth victory.

Kikuchi confessed afterwards that the win surprised her. "I wasn't thinking about winning in Hokkaido, but yesterday and the day before yesterday, I had to be aware of it," she said. "I overcame the pressure and won the tournament."

A sparkling 63 the second day at Takino Country Club set things up. Following an opening-day 67, one shot shy of the leading 66s of Mi-Jeong Jeon and Kana Mikashima, the nine-under-par round Friday — with an eagle and seven birdies — staked Kikuchi to a three-stroke advantage over Mikashima (66-67). She took only one bogey over the final 36 holes. She was bogey-free in Saturday's 69, then leading Sakura Koiwai, the Resort Trust winner, by two shots on 17 under. The lone bogey Sunday came on the 13th hole, enabling Mikashima to catch her, but she bounced back immediately with her fourth birdie of the day and rode that one-shot lead to the clubhouse, finishing with a 69 for a 20-under-par total of 268 after matching "very nervous" pars with Mikashima on the final four holes.

Actually, Kikuchi feared a playoff after parring the 18th as she watched as Mikashima, seeking her first tour victory, missed a 15-foot birdie putt for the tie. Koiwai birdied the 18th for 69 and finished third at 270.

Takino Country Club, Hokkaido — July 21-24
Par 72 (36-36); 6,560 yards — Purse: ¥120,000,000

1	**Erika Kikuchi**	67	63	69	69	268	¥21,600,000
2	**Kana Mikashima**	66	67	68	68	269	10,560,000
3	**Sakura Koiwai**	68	66	67	69	270	8,400,000
4	Haruka Morita	67	69	68	68	272	7,200,000
5	Miyuu Yamashita	71	70	68	66	275	5,400,000
	Minami Katsu	69	70	68	68	275	5,400,000
7	Mi-Jeong Jeon	66	71	69	70	276	3,600,000
	Yuri Yoshida	71	69	66	70	276	3,600,000
	Mone Inami	67	68	70	71	276	3,600,000
10	Hana Wakimoto	70	70	68	69	277	2,400,000
11	Chirei Iwai	69	68	71	70	278	2,004,000
	Shina Kanazawa	69	69	70	70	278	2,004,000
	Momoko Osato	70	70	67	71	278	2,004,000
14	Miyu Sato	69	70	72	68	279	1,464,000
	Rio Takeda	69	71	71	68	279	1,464,000
	Ritsuko Ryu	69	71	70	69	279	1,464,000
	Jiyai Shin	67	71	69	72	279	1,464,000
	Hana Lee	73	68	66	72	279	1,464,000
	Ai Suzuki	68	73	66	72	279	1,464,000
20	Seon Woo Bae	70	72	70	68	280	996,000
	Yumi Narisawa	69	71	70	70	280	996,000
	Karen Tsuruoka	71	68	70	71	280	996,000
	Shoko Sasaki	71	69	68	72	280	996,000
	Yui Kawamoto	68	73	67	72	280	996,000
25	Kotone Hori	70	70	72	69	281	888,000
	Serena Aoki	72	70	68	71	281	888,000
	Nanako Ueno	67	73	70	71	281	888,000
	Miyuki Takeuchi	69	72	68	72	281	888,000
29	Hikaru Yoshimoto	70	71	71	70	282	792,000
	Shuri Sakuma	70	70	72	70	282	792,000
	Sayaka Takahashi	69	72	70	71	282	792,000
	Saki Nagamine	70	73	70	69	282	792,000

Rakuten Super Ladies

Minami Katsu added another notable gem to her exceptional career record as she ran away with her seventh tour victory in the Rakuten Super Ladies. Eight years ago, while still a 15-year-old high school amateur, Katsu won the Vantelin Open, becoming the tour's youngest winner ever and launching what became known as the Golden Generation of youthful victors in Japan.

Seven years later, she won the Japan Women's Open, making her just the third player in history to win the four most prestigious titles in Japanese female golf — the Junior, the Women's Amateur and low amateur in the Women's Open, along with the title itself.

Her latest first — playing the 72 holes of the Rakuten Super Ladies tournament without absorbing a single bogey as she eased to a five-stroke victory at Tokyu Grand Oak Golf Club in Kato City. Although starting the final round with a nine-stroke lead, Katsu was feeling the "pressure that I never was aware of the previous three days", referring to the bogey-free situation and her proximation to the 24 under par winning record.

As things turned out, she finished at 266, 22 under and five strokes in front of Mone Inami, who led her by a stroke with a course-record 64 the first day and held second place the rest of the week. Katsu moved in front Friday with a six-birdie 66, taking a four-shot lead over Inami (71) and Yuka Yasuda (66-69). Then, on Saturday, Katsu matched Inami's record 64 — eight birdies — to vault nine shots ahead.

She birdied the third hole Sunday and ran off 15 straight pars the rest of the way for a closing 71 and the five-stroke margin, which surprisingly left her disappointed. "But a win is a win, so I'm honestly happy with the result," she concluded. Inami, who won eight times in 2021 but only once in 2022 until then, conceded that "nobody could win against that kind of play".

Tokyu Grand Oak Golf Club, Hyogo — July 28-31
Par 72 (36-36); 6,616 yards — Purse: ¥100,000,000

1	**Minami Katsu**	65	66	64	71	266	¥18,000,000
2	**Mone Inami**	64	71	69	67	271	8,800,000
3	**Mi-Jeong Jeon**	69	70	69	65	273	6,000,000
	Au-Reum Hwang	70	70	67	66	273	6,000,000
	Sakura Koiwai	67	70	68	68	273	6,000,000
6	Yuri Yoshida	71	69	68	66	274	4,000,000
7	Mao Nozawa	69	68	72	66	275	3,000,000
	Serena Aoki	70	67	68	70	275	3,000,000
	Seon Woo Bae	66	72	67	70	275	3,000,000
10	Kana Nagai	72	67	68	69	276	1,826,666
	Lala Anai	70	67	68	71	276	1,826,666
	Chirei Iwai	69	70	66	71	276	1,826,666
13	Kotoko Uchida	69	69	70	69	277	1,540,000
	Yuka Nii	71	68	69	69	277	1,540,000
15	Nanako Ueno	68	73	67	70	278	1,390,000
16	Eri Okayama	70	71	70	68	279	1,090,000
	Min Young Lee2	70	68	72	69	279	1,090,000
	Miyu Sato	70	70	70	69	279	1,090,000
	Chae-Young Yoon	68	67	71	73	279	1,090,000
	Haruka Amamoto	66	70	70	73	279	1,090,000
21	Ai Suzuki	69	73	69	69	280	820,000
	Erika Kikuchi	68	70	72	70	280	820,000
	Sae Ogura	68	70	72	70	280	820,000
	Momoko Ueda	73	68	69	70	280	820,000
	Karen Tsuruoka	68	72	72	68	280	820,000
	Miyuu Abe	70	66	73	71	280	820,000
27	Maiko Wakabayashi	71	70	70	70	281	690,000
	Akie Iwai	68	72	71	70	281	690,000
	Karen Gondo	71	68	72	70	281	690,000
	Ritsuko Ryu	69	72	69	71	281	690,000
	Yumi Narisawa	68	69	75	69	281	690,000
	Shiho Kuwaki	68	69	75	69	281	690,000
	Na-Ri Lee	69	68	71	73	281	690,000

Hokkaido Meiji Cup

Min Young Lee2 emerged from a heavily bunched field on the final day of the Hokkaido Meiji Cup to score her first victory in three years, an achievement she repeatedly called "unbelievable" in the aftermath. In registering the sixth victory of her consistent six-season career in Japan, Lee2 edged, among others, Sakura Yokomine, who astonishingly had gone without a win since scoring her 23rd in 2014, when she became the tour's second earnings yen billionaire.

Two other experienced winners attracted most of the attention the first two days at Sapporo International Country Club. Ai Suzuki, a 17-time winner but only once since leading the money list for a second time in 2019, led Momoko Ueda and Kotoko Uchida by a shot with a first-round 68. She shared the lead after Saturday's 71 with Ueda (69-70), who won her 17th earlier in the season in the Studio Alice tournament. Lee2 trailed by a stroke with veteran Jiyai Shin and Kokona Sakurai, all with 70-70s.

Yokomine, who had missed seven consecutive cuts and finished last among the four-rounders the previous week, caught fire on the front nine Sunday, running off a five-birdie 31 to eke a shot ahead of Lee^2 and two ahead of Ueda. The 30-year-old Lee^2, who joined the tour in 2017, two years after beating kidney cancer, birdied the 10th and the 11th to take the lead, but wound up on the 18th green where she, Yokomine and Sakurai all faced birdie putts. She made hers from seven feet for the victory as the others missed theirs. She had closed with a 67 for 207, nine under par.

Lee^2 attributed the win to coaching help from her native South Korea. "Thanks to the relaxation of immigration restrictions two weeks ago, I was able to receive guidance in various ways. Thanks to that, I won the championship."

Sapporo International Country Club (Shimamatsu), Hokkaido — August 5-7
Par 72 (36-36); 6,557 yards — Purse: ¥90,000,000

1	**Min Young Lee^2**	70	70	67	207	¥16,200,000
2	**Sakura Yokomine**	72	70	66	208	7,110,000
	Kokona Sakurai	70	70	68	208	7,110,000
4	Momoko Ueda	69	70	70	209	5,400,000
5	Akie Iwai	70	72	68	210	4,050,000
	Ai Suzuki	68	71	71	210	4,050,000
7	Mei Takagi	72	72	67	211	2,925,000
	Jiyai Shin	70	70	71	211	2,925,000
9	Sakura Koiwai	72	71	69	212	2,025,000
	Chirei Iwai	72	69	71	212	2,025,000
11	Ritsuko Ryu	73	71	69	213	1,593,000
	Sae Ogura	72	70	71	213	1,593,000
	Mirai Hamasaki	73	68	72	213	1,593,000
14	Yuri Yoshida	72	72	70	214	1,233,000
	Ayaka Matsumori	73	71	70	214	1,233,000
	Mi-Jeong Jeon	72	71	71	214	1,233,000
	Rumi Yoshiba	74	69	71	214	1,233,000
	Akira Yamaji	72	69	73	214	1,233,000
19	Erika Kikuchi	70	74	71	215	847,285
	Miyu Sato	72	72	71	215	847,285
	Eri Okayama	72	72	71	215	847,285
	Rio Ishii	70	75	70	215	847,285
	Serena Aoki	74	70	71	215	847,285
	Chae-Young Yoon	74	70	71	215	847,285
	Haruka Morita	72	70	73	215	847,285
26	Maiko Wakabayashi	70	74	72	216	747,000
	Asuka Ishikawa	72	71	73	216	747,000
	Nanako Ueno	73	69	74	216	747,000
29	Mone Inami	72	72	73	217	675,000
	Hikaru Yoshimoto	71	74	72	217	675,000
	Mayu Hamada	74	72	71	217	675,000
	Rie Iwahashi	74	72	71	217	675,000
	Aya Kinoshita	74	70	73	217	675,000

NEC Karuizawa 72

The Golden Generation theme that prevailed in recent times on the Japan LPGA Tour got a unique twist at the NEC Karuizawa 72 tournament in early August. Joining the remarkable number of young winners in the 19-to-21 age range was 20-year-old Chirei Iwai, who, with sister Akie, constitute the only twins ever to play on the tour.

Chirei Iwai emerged from a bunched-up group of contenders to eke out a one-stroke victory over six others with a final-round 69 and 13-under-par 203 on Karuizawa 72 Golf's North course in Nagano Prefecture. "I seized one of the rare chances," remarked the young winner, who came into the tournament after successive finishes of 11th, 10th and ninth. Akie tied for fifth that last week. "I'm glad I worked hard. I thought I could win," Chirei added, pointing out that, "Akie has excellent motor skills since she was a child. In contrast, I'm able to do it with hard work."

She was in contention from the start, opening with a 66, tied for second with Hikaru Yoshimoto a stroke behind leader Rio Ishii, then moved into a tie with Yoshimoto as both players shot 68s and led T-Point winner Kotone Hori and Yuri Yoshida by a shot after 36 holes.

Iwai held her own on the front nine Sunday, then went in front to stay with birdies at the 10th, 11th and 13th holes. She took a two-stroke lead to the final green, where a three-putt bogey meant she won by one from Eri Okayama, Nozomi Uetake, Minami Katsu, Yoshida, Hori and Yoshimoto, who made only a single bogey — at the sixth hole Sunday — over the 54 holes as she sought her first tour win. For the record, Akie Iwai tied for 53rd and watched her twin sister seal the victory.

Karuizawa 72 Golf (North), Nagano — August 12-14
Par 72 (36-36); 6,679 yards — Purse: ¥80,000,000

1	**Chirei Iwai**	66	68	69	203	¥14,400,000	16 Rin Yoshida (A)	70	71	67	208	
2	**Eri Okayama**	68	70	66	204	4,573,333	Shina Kanazawa	70	70	68	208	896,000
	Nozomi Uetake	69	69	66	204	4,573,333	Erika Hara	68	71	69	208	896,000
	Minami Katsu	68	69	67	204	4,573,333	Hikari Tanabe	68	70	70	208	896,000
	Yuri Yoshida	68	67	69	204	4,573,333	Kotoko Uchida	67	70	71	208	896,000
	Kotone Hori	68	67	69	204	4,573,333	Karen Tsuruoka	70	67	71	208	896,000
	Hikaru Yoshimoto	66	68	70	204	4,573,333	22 Chia Yen Wu	71	68	70	209	688,000
8	Nana Suganuma	72	69	64	205	2,400,000	Rio Ishii	65	73	71	209	688,000
9	Mirai Hamasaki	69	70	67	206	1,608,000	Miyuu Abe	69	69	71	209	688,000
	Miyu Goto	71	68	67	206	1,608,000	Amiyu Ozeki	69	73	67	209	688,000
	Momoko Ueda	68	70	68	206	1,608,000	Kana Nagai	68	69	72	209	688,000
	Mi-Jeong Jeon	69	68	69	206	1,608,000	27 Chie Arimura	68	72	70	210	616,000
13	Min Young Lee[2]	69	71	67	207	1,216,000	Fumika Kawagishi	71	69	70	210	616,000
	Sumika Nakasone	69	69	69	207	1,216,000	Sayaka Takahashi	69	70	71	210	616,000
	Saki Nagamine	68	69	70	207	1,216,000	Sae Ogura	70	68	72	210	616,000

CAT Ladies

Chirei Iwai quickly showed that her victory in the NEC Karuizawa 72 was no fluke, squeezing out another one-stroke win the following week in the CAT Ladies tournament. In doing so, the 20-year-old become the first player in more than 30 years to go back-to-back off a first victory. "I don't believe I could have done it," remarked the stunned young player.

Typical of the Japan LPGA Tour season, the CAT was the 12th tournament decided by a single stroke, with six others won by two, in addition to a pair of playoffs.

Money-leader Miyuu Yamashita, already a two-time 2022 winner, set up the close finish in the tournament at Diahakone Country Club in Kanagawa Prefecture, following a first-hole, chip-in eagle with six birdies, posting an eight-under-par 64 to take the clubhouse lead at 12 under par. Iwai, with a lone birdie and 15 pars, was 12 under, too, before sinking a 14-foot birdie putt on the par-three 17th hole. A 70 gave her the winning total on 15-under 203.

Iwai trailed by a single stroke after the first round as unheralded Maiko Wakabayashi, Haruka Amamoto and Seira Oki led with 66s, then took sole possession of the lead Saturday with a 66 of her own, sitting a shot ahead of Wakabayashi (69) and two ahead of Minami Katsu (69), who won her seventh title a month earlier in the Rakuten Super tournament. Yamashita was Iwai's only challenger Sunday as, with second money, she increased her lead on the money list over absent Mao Saigo to ¥17 million with ¥117,552,000.

Daihakone Country Club, Kanagawa — August 19-21
Par 72 (36-36); 6,638 yards — Purse: ¥60,000,000

1	**Chirei Iwai**	67	66	70	203	¥10,800,000	Haruka Amamoto	66	73	71	210	744,000
2	**Miyuu Yamashita**	70	70	64	204	5,280,000	Miyu Sato	70	68	72	210	744,000
3	**Rio Takeda**	67	71	68	206	3,900,000	Jiyai Shin	71	67	72	210	744,000
	Minami Katsu	67	69	70	206	3,900,000	20 Mao Saigo	70	72	69	211	552,000
5	Rumi Yoshiba	71	67	69	207	2,700,000	Rie Tsuji	71	71	69	211	552,000
	Erika Hara	69	68	70	207	2,700,000	Seon Woo Bae	74	70	67	211	552,000
7	Hana Lee	68	74	66	208	1,458,000	23 Sumika Nakasone	71	72	69	212	516,000
	Haruka Morita	72	69	67	208	1,458,000	Kotoko Uchida	72	69	71	212	516,000
	Saiki Fujita	71	69	68	208	1,458,000	Kotona Izumida	72	68	72	212	516,000
	Miyu Goto	68	71	69	208	1,458,000	26 Karen Gondo	69	73	71	213	456,000
	Mone Inami	67	71	70	208	1,458,000	Yuting Seki	73	70	70	213	456,000
	Maiko Wakabayashi	66	69	73	208	1,458,000	Ai Suzuki	71	73	69	213	456,000
13	Nana Suganuma	72	70	67	209	954,000	Lala Anai	73	71	69	213	456,000
	Yuri Yoshida	69	72	68	209	954,000	Yuna Nishimura	70	74	69	213	456,000
15	Sayaka Takahashi	73	69	68	210	744,000	Asako Fujimoto	70	70	73	213	456,000
	Shuri Sakuma	70	70	70	210	744,000	Sae Ogura	68	76	69	213	456,000

Nitori Ladies

Although not as dominant as she was during the combined 2020-21 season, Mone Inami maintained her impressive game through the first six months of the 2022 campaign, following up her 11th victory in the Yonex in June with a successful title defence in the Nitori Ladies at the end of August. In between, the 23-year-old had seven top-sevens, including a second and two thirds. The 12th win arrived via the come-from-behind route after Erika Hara, also 23, another member of Japan's Golden Generation of young female winners, led the field at Otaru Country Club in Hokkaido for three rounds.

"It's one of the toughest courses of the season," observed Inami after her final-round 70 carried her to a two-stroke victory over three previous 2022 winners — Yuna Nishimura, Nozomi Uetake and Miyuu Yamashita, the leading money winner. "It's the first time for me to win a tournament back-to-back years. I'm really happy to win." The ¥18 million first prize moved Inami into second place just ¥10 million behind Yamashita on the money list.

Hara racked up nine birdies as she opened the tournament on top with a seven-under-par 65 and a two-stroke lead over Yuri Yoshida. Despite a wild back nine Friday, she maintained her two-shot margin over Yoshida as both players shot 71s. She overcame an early double bogey Saturday and shot another 71, still two strokes in front, but then over five players — Yoshida, Momoko Ueda, Saiki Fujita, Yamashita and Inami, who shot 68 to get into the mix.

Hara suffered another double bogey early in the final round, only made a single birdie and fell out of contention en route to a 76. Yamashita, with an outgoing 33, surged into the lead, but was bypassed by Inami on the way in as Mone closed with a single-birdie back nine for a 70 and 279, 11 under par. Yamashita faltered with three bogeys and no birdies on the back nine and fell into the three-way tie at 281 with Nishimura and Uetake. Hara tied for seventh with Yoshida, who also faded on the last day with a 74.

Otaru Country Club, Hokkaido — August 25-28
Par 72 (36-36); 6,655 yards — Purse: ¥100,000,000

1	**Mone Inami**	69	72	68	70	279	¥18,000,000
2	**Yuna Nishimura**	69	72	71	69	281	7,266,666
	Nozomi Uetake	71	70	70	70	281	7,266,666
	Miyuu Yamashita	72	70	67	72	281	7,266,666
5	Momoko Ueda	68	72	69	73	282	4,500,000
	Saiki Fujita	68	72	69	73	282	4,500,000
7	Yuri Yoshida	67	71	71	74	283	3,250,000
	Erika Hara	65	71	71	76	283	3,250,000
9	Karen Gondo	70	72	72	70	284	2,000,000
	Sayaka Takahashi	70	72	72	70	284	2,000,000
	Miyuki Takeuchi	70	71	72	71	284	2,000,000
	Jiyai Shin	73	68	71	72	284	2,000,000
13	Mei Takagi	70	73	75	67	285	1,250,000
	Akie Iwai	73	72	71	69	285	1,250,000
	Lala Anai	74	69	72	70	285	1,250,000
	Kumiko Kaneda	73	68	73	71	285	1,250,000
	Sakura Koiwai	68	73	72	72	285	1,250,000
	Mirai Hamasaki	70	69	73	73	285	1,250,000
	Hikaru Yoshimoto	72	70	70	73	285	1,250,000
	Ayako Kimura	72	69	70	74	285	1,250,000
21	Kotona Izumida	70	71	75	70	286	860,000
	Nanako Ueno	72	72	71	71	286	860,000
	Serena Aoki	70	69	73	74	286	860,000
24	Ai Suzuki	74	68	74	71	287	800,000
	Miyu Sato	72	71	72	72	287	800,000
	Haruka Kudo	70	71	73	73	287	800,000
27	Kotone Hori	69	73	75	71	288	740,000
	Shiho Kuwaki	72	71	75	70	288	740,000
	Kana Mikashima	73	69	73	73	288	740,000
30	Kana Nagai	71	72	75	71	289	640,000
	Rumi Yoshiba	71	72	74	72	289	640,000
	Yui Kawamoto	74	70	72	73	289	640,000
	Yumi Kudo	70	75	70	74	289	640,000
	Fumika Kawagishi	71	73	76	69	289	640,000
	Shuri Sakuma	73	70	70	76	289	640,000
	Miyuu Abe	72	71	69	77	289	640,000

Golf5 Ladies

It hadn't been much of a year for Yuting Seki, a 24-year-old Chinese national born in Japan who had played sparingly over six winless seasons on the Japan LPGA Tour. Other than a seventh-place finish months earlier, Seki had not placed better than 25th in her 17 starts in 2022 and had missed five cuts.

Abruptly, she became the season's sixth first-time winner when she forced Yuri Yoshida into her fourth runner-up finish of the year, defeating her in the Golf5 Ladies tournament in just the year's third playoff. Ironically, Yoshida, the defending champion, had also won the Golf5 a year earlier in a playoff. "I continue to play with a sense of humility and gratitude," remarked Seki in the aftermath. "Today's victory is also thanks to the sponsors who supported me, the coaches who gave me guidance and my mother."

Minami Katsu, who scored her seventh career win in the Rakuten Super in July, rode first place the first two days at Golf5 Country Oak Village with a blazing, nine-under-par 63 Thursday and 71 Friday. At 10 under par she was a shot ahead of Yoshida, who rallied from an opening 71 with a 64, as Seki, after starting in second place three strokes behind Katsu, dropped four shots back with a 72.

Three front-nine bogeys and a double bogey at the 11th hole crippled Katsu on Sunday as Seki surged in front with an eagle, six birdies and a bogey on the first 13 holes. Seki's bogey, double-bogey on the next two holes enabled Yoshida to edge in front, but Seki bounced back with birdies on the next two holes. Yoshida also birdied the 17th and both parred the final hole, Seki shooting 66 and Yoshida 69 for their 12-under 204s, finishing a stroke ahead of Kotone Hori and Nana Suganuma.

After a shaky first extra hole as both players bogeyed, Seki with an out-of-bounds tee shot and Yoshida with a three-putt, Seki secured the win with a 13-foot birdie putt on the next overtime hole.

Golf5 Country Oak Village Golf Club, Chiba — September 2-4
Par 72 (36-36); 6,465 yards — Purse: ¥100,000,000

1	**Yuting Seki**	66	72	66	204	¥18,000,000
2	**Yuri Yoshida**	71	64	69	204	8,800,000
	Seki won playoff at second extra hole					
3	**Kotone Hori**	68	72	65	205	6,500,000
	Nana Suganuma	69	70	66	205	6,500,000
5	Sakura Koiwai	69	67	70	206	4,500,000
	Minami Katsu	63	71	72	206	4,500,000
7	Amiyu Ozeki	73	68	66	207	3,000,000
	Miyuu Yamashita	71	68	68	207	3,000,000
	Sayaka Takahashi	69	67	71	207	3,000,000
10	Rumi Yoshiba	70	68	70	208	1,833,333
	Miyuu Abe	70	67	71	208	1,833,333
	Erika Hara	67	69	72	208	1,833,333
13	Erika Kikuchi	74	67	68	209	1,400,000
	Momoko Kishibe	71	69	69	209	1,400,000
	Mami Fukuda	67	71	71	209	1,400,000
	Mone Inami	69	69	71	209	1,400,000
	Kana Mikashima	72	66	71	209	1,400,000
18	Maiko Wakabayashi	67	72	71	210	970,000
	Kana Nagai	73	66	71	210	970,000
	Jiyai Shin	67	70	73	210	970,000
	Mao Saigo	70	67	73	210	970,000
22	Yui Kawamoto	72	69	70	211	820,000
	Yuka Nii	71	69	71	211	820,000
	Yumi Kudo	73	69	69	211	820,000
	Hikaru Yoshimoto	70	72	69	211	820,000
	Yuna Nishimura	70	73	68	211	820,000
27	Yuka Yasuda	71	69	72	212	750,000
	Yumi Narisawa	70	66	76	212	750,000
29	Miki Sakai	72	69	72	213	660,000
	Momoko Osato	69	72	72	213	660,000
	Mei Takagi	73	69	71	213	660,000
	Sae Ogura	68	71	74	213	660,000
	Rie Tsuji	70	69	74	213	660,000
	Shoko Sasaki	72	71	70	213	660,000
	Miyu Goto	76	67	70	213	660,000

JLPGA Championship Konica Minolta Cup

The remarkable run of young winners in recent years in Japan continued to an extreme extent at the Japan LPGA Championship as 19-year-old Haruka Kawasaki virtually came out of nowhere to acquire the symbolic Konica Minolta Cup. In so doing, Kawasaki, a tour rookie who had to qualify just to tee up in the championship, became the youngest winner of that major title in its long history, replacing Ai Suzuki, who was 20 when she won in 2014. Only Nasa Hataoka, with her back-to-back victories in the 2016 and 2017 Japan Women's Open at ages 17 and 18, was a younger major winner in Japan. And it all happened in Kawasaki's Kyoto hometown. "It's unbelievable. The reality of my win sank in only after the victory ceremony. I can't believe it. I was surprised," professed the teenaged winner.

There was good reason for that surprise. In 10 starts earlier in her first tour season, Kawasaki missed six cuts and hadn't finished better than a tie for 29th. However, she had won on the Step Up development circuit two weeks before playing at Joyo Country Club. After a 69-69 start, she was three strokes behind three players, including leading money-winner Miyuu Yamashita, and fell four back of Yamashita on Saturday as she shot 70 to Yamashita's 69 for 12 under par.

Kawasaki caught fire, though, on Sunday. After starting quietly with seven pars, she holed a wedge shot for an eagle two at the eighth hole, then birdied six of the last seven on the back nine for an eight-under-par 64 to secure her 16-under-par 272, three strokes ahead of Yamashita, who closed with a 71.

Joyo Country Club, Kyoto — September 8-11
Par 72 (36-36); 6,555 yards — Purse: ¥200,000,000

1	**Haruka Kawasaki**	69	69	70	64	272	¥36,000,000
2	**Miyuu Yamashita**	66	69	69	71	275	17,600,000
3	**Nana Suganuma**	65	70	73	68	276	14,000,000
4	Miyu Sato	71	70	68	68	277	10,000,000
	Shoko Sasaki	73	66	69	69	277	10,000,000
	Haruka Morita	69	68	69	71	277	10,000,000
7	Yuting Seki	71	72	69	66	278	6,000,000
	Seon Woo Bae	68	68	74	68	278	6,000,000
	Mao Saigo	72	71	66	69	278	6,000,000
10	Sae Ogura	69	69	73	68	279	3,166,666
	Erika Kikuchi	71	71	69	68	279	3,166,666
	Min Young Lee[2]	71	72	67	69	279	3,166,666
	Yuri Yoshida	70	70	70	69	279	3,166,666
	Mirai Hamasaki	70	69	69	71	279	3,166,666
	Kana Mikashima	73	67	67	72	279	3,166,666
16	Kana Taneda	66	72	72	70	280	2,200,000
	Akie Iwai	69	70	71	70	280	2,200,000
	Miyuu Abe	68	70	71	71	280	2,200,000
19	Mone Inami	68	71	73	69	281	1,592,000
	Jiyai Shin	68	72	72	69	281	1,592,000
	Yuka Yasuda	71	69	71	70	281	1,592,000
	Momoko Ueda	68	73	70	70	281	1,592,000
	Sakura Koiwai	69	70	70	72	281	1,592,000
24	Hana Wakimoto	69	68	75	70	282	1,360,000
	Megumi Kido	68	72	72	70	282	1,360,000
	Mami Fukuda	68	75	68	71	282	1,360,000
	Kotone Hori	72	69	69	72	282	1,360,000
	Miyu Goto	69	70	70	73	282	1,360,000
29	Chie Arimura	70	74	71	68	283	1,195,000
	Amiyu Ozeki	70	72	68	73	283	1,195,000
	Serena Aoki	69	69	71	74	283	1,195,000
	Asako Fujimoto	68	71	70	74	283	1,195,000

Sumitomo Life Vitality Ladies Tokai Classic

It had to be an all-time first. It seems that never before could two different 19-year-olds have won back-to-back tournaments on any major international tour, male or female. That's what happened at the Sumitomo Life Vitality Ladies Tokai Classic when Amiyu Ozeki squeezed out a one-stroke victory over luckless Yuri Yoshida. "I was inspired by Haruka Kawasaki's victory," said the rookie of the win seven days earlier by another 19-year-old in the Japan LPGA Championship. "I'm really, really happy."

Ozeki started the week at Shin Minami Aichi Country Club's Mihama course two strokes behind little-known Miyu Goto's opening five-under-par 65. Then she took the lead on Saturday with a solid 66 that included an eagle and four birdies. Yoshida also shot 66, her 134 leaving the second-season player a shot off the lead as she sought to get her third career win after enduring four second-place finishes, including two playoff losses, earlier in the 2022 season.

Three bogeys and a pair of Yoshida birdies on the first 11 holes Sunday dropped Ozeki a shot behind, but she staged an impressive finish, birdieing four of the last seven holes, the final one a four-footer on the 18th green for a 70 and a 13-under-par total of 203.

Shin Minami Aichi Country Club (Mihama), Aichi — September 16-18
Par 72 (36-36); 6,502 yards — Purse: ¥100,000,000

1	**Amiyu Ozeki**	67	66	70	203	¥18,000,000
2	**Yuri Yoshida**	68	66	70	204	8,800,000
3	**Miyu Goto**	65	72	69	206	7,000,000
4	Chie Arimura	68	71	68	207	5,500,000
	Kana Nagai	69	70	68	207	5,500,000
6	Nanoko Hayashi	69	69	70	208	3,500,000
	Fumika Kawagishi	68	69	71	208	3,500,000
	Miyuu Yamashita	68	67	73	208	3,500,000
9	Sayaka Takahashi	71	70	68	209	2,133,333
	Jiyai Shin	67	73	69	209	2,133,333
	Min Young Lee[2]	66	71	72	209	2,133,333
12	Erika Hara	69	73	68	210	1,650,000
	Ayako Kimura	71	68	71	210	1,650,000
	Momoko Ueda	68	70	72	210	1,650,000
	Shiho Kuwaki	67	69	74	210	1,650,000
16	Kana Mikashima	73	70	68	211	1,163,333
	Mami Fukuda	69	73	69	211	1,163,333
	Mao Saigo	69	72	70	211	1,163,333
	Haruka Morita	73	68	70	211	1,163,333
	Nozomi Uetake	71	69	71	211	1,163,333
	Asuka Kashiwabara	73	66	72	211	1,163,333
22	Nana Suganuma	71	72	69	212	940,000
	Momoko Osato	68	71	73	212	940,000
	Mone Inami	70	68	74	212	940,000
25	Minami Hiruta	72	71	70	213	870,000
	Miki Sakai	73	70	70	213	870,000
	Sae Ogura	73	71	69	213	870,000
	Mizuki Ooide	73	69	71	213	870,000
29	Hana Lee	67	75	72	214	770,000
	Serena Aoki	74	69	71	214	770,000
	Yuka Yasuda	68	75	71	214	770,000
	Momoko Kishibe	73	71	70	214	770,000
	Akie Iwai	70	74	70	214	770,000
	Miyu Sato	75	69	70	214	770,000

Miyagi TV Cup Dunlop Ladies Open

Miyuu Yamashita expanded her hold on the money list with her third victory of the season in the Miyagi TV Cup Dunlop Ladies Open and set an important new JPGA Tour record in the process. With 12 birdies, including six on the last eight holes and nary a five on the card, the 21-year-old standout opened the tournament at Rifu Golf Club in Miyagi Prefecture with a flawless, 12-under-par 60, one stroke better than the existing mark shared by Korea's Hyo Joo Kim (2012) and Mone Inami (2021). The first prize of ¥12.6 million enriched her with ¥161,518,666, nearly ¥43-million ahead of second placed Inami on the season's earnings list, which she had led since July. In five starts since taking a three-tournament break in August, Yamashita had three second-place finishes and ties for sixth and seventh prior to the Miyagi TV Cup win.

The opening 60 put Yamashita five strokes in front of the field. She followed on Saturday with a bogey-free 67, her 127 total eight strokes better than Kana Mikashima, who shot 64, and yet another young player sparkling on the tour, 19-year-old rookie Rio Takeda (67-68). Yamashita finished off her fourth career win on Sunday with a routine 71 — two birdies and a bogey — her 18-under-par 198 giving her a five-stroke victory over Mikashima and Takeda, who closed with 68s. Yuri Yoshida tied for fourth, her 12th straight tournament with a finish of 14th or better.

"This victory gave me confidence," Yamashita exclaimed. "My style is to play calmly. However, when it comes to the final group on the final day, I get nervous and lose my rhythm." Obviously, not enough to interrupt her success.

Rifu Golf Club, Miyagi — September 23-25
Par 72 (36-36); 6,491 yards — Purse: ¥70,000,000

1	**Miyuu Yamashita**	60	67	71	198	¥12,600,000
2	**Rio Takeda**	67	68	68	203	5,530,000
	Kana Mikashima	71	64	68	203	5,530,000
4	Yuri Yoshida	67	72	67	206	3,850,000
	Nanako Ueno	66	70	70	206	3,850,000
6	Chirei Iwai	72	66	70	208	2,625,000
	Fumika Kawagishi	65	72	71	208	2,625,000
8	Miyuki Takeuchi	68	71	70	209	1,638,000
	Nana Suganuma	68	70	71	209	1,638,000
	Erika Hara	68	70	71	209	1,638,000
	Sayaka Takahashi	69	67	73	209	1,638,000
12	Hana Wakimoto	69	72	69	210	1,127,000
	Sakura Koiwai	68	71	71	210	1,127,000
	Chae-Young Yoon	71	68	71	210	1,127,000
	Asako Fujimoto	71	68	71	210	1,127,000
16	Amiyu Ozeki	68	72	71	211	786,333
	Momoko Osato	72	70	69	211	786,333
	Kana Nagai	72	67	72	211	786,333
	Serena Aoki	67	71	73	211	786,333
	Hana Lee	68	70	73	211	786,333
	Megumi Kido	71	66	74	211	786,333
22	Yuka Yasuda	67	73	72	212	616,000
	Ayaka Watanabe	69	72	71	212	616,000
	Ritsuko Ryu	71	69	72	212	616,000
	Kotone Hori	68	73	71	212	616,000
	Momoko Kishibe	68	74	70	212	616,000
27	Shuri Sakuma	71	70	72	213	504,000
	Yuna Nishimura	71	70	72	213	504,000
	Hitomi Koriyama (A)	72	69	72	213	
	Lala Anai	67	73	73	213	504,000
	Teresa Lu	69	72	72	213	504,000
	Miki Sakai	69	72	72	213	504,000
	Mao Nozawa	68	73	72	213	504,000
	Aoi Ohnishi	69	70	74	213	504,000
	Reika Usui	72	70	71	213	504,000
	Mami Fukuda	70	72	71	213	504,000
	Min Young Lee2	72	70	71	213	504,000
	Shiho Kuwaki	68	69	76	213	504,000

Japan Women's Open Championship

There usually is something unusual about it when Minami Katsu wins a tournament: youngest winner in Japan LPGA Tour history … winning the Japan Women's Open to go along with her Junior and Amateur titles and being low amateur at the national championship … a 72-hole tournament victory without a bogey. This time, it was her second consecutive victory in the Japan Women's Open, something only accomplished in the past by the legendary Hisako Higuchi (1968-71, 1976-77) and Nasa Hataoka (2016-17).

Katsu's one-stroke win at the demanding Sumire course of Murasaki Country Club in Noda, Chiba Prefecture, short-circuited veteran Jiyai Shin's bid for the only missing leg of a JLPGA Grand Slam —

that title to go with her wins in the LPGA and Tour Championships in 2015 and the World in 2018.

"Since the course is different from last year, it doesn't feel like we won back-to-back, but I'm happy to win with a fresh feeling I'm riding," said Katsu, who came from three strokes behind Shin Sunday to score her eighth tour victory and second of the season. "Our goal is to win at least one more game. Two wins in a season is my best. I want to break through that wall and challenge the Q-Series on the US LPGA Tour."

Indicative of the difficulty of the Sumire course, Haruka Morita's leading five-under-par 67 the first day was the week's low round. With her two-under-par 142 (70-72), Ayako Kimura, the Earth Mondahmin winner in June, slipped a stroke in front of Nana Suganuma (72-71) and Morita (76) Friday.

The 34-year-old Shin, whose brilliant international record includes 28 wins in Japan, took over on Saturday with a 69, at two under par a shot in front of the ever-present Yuri Yoshida and three ahead of Katsu (70).

Katsu made up those three strokes early Sunday afternoon with an outgoing, five-birdie 31. The status remained unchanged through the 16th hole. Both players had absorbed a pair of bogeys before a decisive two-shot swing came at the 17th, where Katsu holed a seven-foot birdie putt and Shin took another bogey. The Korean's only birdie on the back nine on the final hole left her a disappointed, one-stroke runner-up, as Katsu parred for a 68 and, on three-under-par 285, the prized title.

Murasaki Country Club (Sumire), Chiba — September 29-October 2
Par 72 (36-36); 6,839 yards — Purse: ¥150,000,000

1	**Minami Katsu**	72	75	70	68	285	¥30,000,000
2	**Jiyai Shin**	72	73	69	72	286	16,500,000
3	**Yuna Nishimura**	72	76	72	68	288	8,450,000
	Miyuu Yamashita	71	76	70	71	288	8,450,000
	Yuri Yoshida	70	75	70	73	288	8,450,000
6	Shuri Sakuma	72	72	75	71	290	5,250,000
7	Seon Woo Bae	72	73	76	71	292	3,637,500
	Kotone Hori	76	72	73	71	292	3,637,500
	Teresa Lu	69	77	74	72	292	3,637,500
	Sakura Koiwai	68	77	74	73	292	3,637,500
11	Saiki Fujita	72	75	74	72	293	2,350,000
	Mami Fukuda	76	74	71	72	293	2,350,000
	Saki Baba (A)	73	73	74	73	293	
	Kotona Izumida	78	69	73	73	293	2,350,000
15	Haruka Kawasaki	72	72	74	76	294	1,890,000
16	Chirei Iwai	72	77	76	70	295	1,545,000
	Mao Nozawa	73	75	75	72	295	1,545,000
	Kana Mikashima	74	76	72	73	295	1,545,000
	Rie Tsuji	74	74	73	74	295	1,545,000
	Ai Suzuki	74	74	72	75	295	1,545,000
	Au-Reum Hwang	72	74	73	76	295	1,545,000
22	Yuting Seki	79	71	75	71	296	1,202,142
	Nana Suganuma	72	71	81	72	296	1,202,142
	Shoko Sasaki	74	76	74	72	296	1,202,142
	Sora Kamiya (A)	73	74	76	73	296	
	Yukari Nishiyama	74	75	74	73	296	1,202,142
	Pei-Ying Tsai	73	72	77	74	296	1,202,142
	Ayako Kimura	70	72	79	75	296	1,202,142
	Momoko Ueda	72	72	76	76	296	1,202,142
30	Hina Arakaki	77	73	77	70	297	1,023,000
	Erika Kikuchi	75	74	77	71	297	1,023,000
	Erika Hara	78	71	74	74	297	1,023,000
	Min Young Lee[2]	70	74	78	75	297	1,023,000
	Haruka Morita	67	76	74	80	297	1,023,000

Stanley Ladies Honda

Sakura Koiwai wasn't about to let it happen again. "I forgot about last year," she said after squeaking out a one-stroke victory in the Stanley Ladies Honda tournament. The reference was to the previous year's Stanley when as a final-round co-leader she shot 77 the last day and plummeted to 24th place. This time the 24-year-old had the lead to herself going into the final round at Tomei Country Club, in Susono City, after shooting a pair of five-under-par 67s. That enabled her to edge a shot in front of veteran Momoko Ueda, the 17-tournament winner who led her and Ayako Kimura by a stroke with a 66 as rain interrupted the opening round and complicated play the rest of the way.

Koiwai then reversed the 2021 finish Sunday with a just-enough 70 for a 12-under-par total of 204. The key was her second birdie of the round when she ran in a 20-foot putt on the 17th green, later pointing out "it wasn't an easy line". That proved to be the deciding moment as she won by one stroke from Kana Nagai, Nana Suganuma and Mao Saigo, who made her best showing since lighting things up with five early-season victories.

"My score was two under par and I didn't improve, so I'm happy that I was able to endure it and win," Sakura observed after clinching her second win of 2022 following the Fujifilm Studio Alice in April, and eighth of her six-season career. Her bogey-free week was the third of the season and 14th since 1990. Money-leader Miyuu Yamashita's run of 12 straight top-10 finishes ended as she tied for 28th.

Tomei Country Club, Shizuoka — October 7-9
Par 72 (36-36); 6,570 yards — Purse: ¥120,000,000

1	**Sakura Koiwai**	67	67	70	204	¥21,600,000
2	**Mao Saigo**	68	69	68	205	8,720,000
	Kana Nagai	69	68	68	205	8,720,000
	Nana Suganuma	68	68	69	205	8,720,000
5	Momoko Osato	71	69	66	206	6,000,000
6	Hana Wakimoto	74	67	66	207	4,800,000
7	Ai Suzuki	70	69	69	208	3,072,000
	Mao Nozawa	71	68	69	208	3,072,000
	Ayako Kimura	67	71	70	208	3,072,000
	Miki Sakai	68	70	70	208	3,072,000
	Momoko Ueda	66	69	73	208	3,072,000
12	Na-Ri Lee	71	67	71	209	1,980,000
	Ritsuko Ryu	70	67	72	209	1,980,000
14	Jiyai Shin	72	70	68	210	1,620,000
	Mone Inami	68	71	71	210	1,620,000
	Sakura Yokomine	68	71	71	210	1,620,000
	Kotoko Uchida	70	67	73	210	1,620,000
18	Nanoko Hayashi	73	68	70	211	1,116,000
	Asuka Kashiwabara	68	72	71	211	1,116,000
	Shiho Kuwaki	73	70	68	211	1,116,000
	Au-Reum Hwang	71	68	72	211	1,116,000
	Lala Anai	73	66	72	211	1,116,000
	Yuri Yoshida	70	67	74	211	1,116,000
24	Amiyu Ozeki	72	69	71	212	948,000
	Miyu Goto	75	67	70	212	948,000
	Haruka Kawasaki	71	71	70	212	948,000
	Momoko Kishibe	73	67	72	212	948,000
28	Rio Takeda	73	68	72	213	780,000
	Hina Arakaki	74	67	72	213	780,000
	Hiromu Ono	76	66	71	213	780,000
	Sae Ogura	70	70	73	213	780,000
	Rie Tsuji	70	70	73	213	780,000
	Serena Aoki	72	67	74	213	780,000
	Kana Mikashima	73	70	70	213	780,000
	Eri Fukuyama	70	67	76	213	780,000
	Chirei Iwai	73	70	70	213	780,000
	Miyuu Yamashita	73	70	70	213	780,000
	Misaki Takagi (A)	73	70	70	213	

Fujitsu Ladies

It wasn't surprising when Ayaka Furue made a triumphant return from America to the Japan Tour by winning the Fujitsu Ladies tournament. After all, she not only was the defending champion, but had also landed the Fujitsu title as a 19-year-old amateur in 2019 immediately before turning pro.

Six more Japan Tour wins followed the next two years before she qualified for the 2022 season on the US-based LPGA Tour, adding further lustre to her record with a course-record 62 final round and victory at the Trust Golf Scottish Open in July.

Mao Saigo, the early-season sensation with five victories, flashed some of that spring brilliance the first day of the Fujitsu at Tokyu Seven Hundred Club in Chiba City. She ran off seven birdies in an eight-hole stretch in the middle of the round, shot 65 and led Furue, Miyuu Abe and Na-Ri Lee by a stroke. Furue matched the 65 Saturday, racking up a pair of front-nine eagles and four birdies to go with a double bogey, and seized first place on 13 under, three strokes ahead of Abe (68) and Minami Hiruta (67). Saigo fell five back with a 71.

As Furue was playing the first 15 holes Sunday in just one under par, Akie Iwai, who was trying to join her 20-year-old twin sister Chirei as a tour tournament winner, raced from five strokes back into the lead with a seventh birdie at the 15th. But Furue was up to the challenge. She birdied the 16th and ran in an 11-footer at the final hole for another birdie, a 69 for 16-under-par 200 and the one-shot victory. Of the deciding stroke, she said afterwards: "I hadn't been that good in putting so far. I didn't want to end up in a playoff."

Tokyu Seven Hundred Club, Chiba — October 14-16
Par 72 (36-36); 6,689 yards — Purse: ¥100,000,000

1	**Ayaka Furue**	66	65	69	200	¥18,000,000
2	**Akie Iwai**	70	66	65	201	8,800,000
3	**Hina Arakaki**	68	67	67	202	7,000,000
4	Mao Saigo	65	71	68	204	5,000,000
	Nana Suganuma	68	68	68	204	5,000,000
	Miyuu Abe	66	68	70	204	5,000,000
7	Miyuu Yamashita	69	69	67	205	3,250,000
	Shiho Kuwaki	74	67	64	205	3,250,000
9	Bo-Mee Lee	72	69	65	206	2,500,000
10	Sakura Koiwai	68	72	67	207	1,657,142
	Teresa Lu	68	71	68	207	1,657,142
	Haruka Morita	70	68	69	207	1,657,142
	Yuting Seki	70	68	69	207	1,657,142
	Lala Anai	68	69	70	207	1,657,142

	Ritsuko Ryu	70	67	70	207	1,657,142		Minami Hiruta	67	67	74	208	1,000,000
	Yuri Yoshida	67	69	71	207	1,657,142	25	Sayaka Takahashi	71	69	69	209	830,000
17	Mone Inami	71	70	67	208	1,000,000		Miki Sakai	73	66	70	209	830,000
	Kana Mikashima	68	71	69	208	1,000,000		Ji-Hee Lee	69	68	72	209	830,000
	Yuri Fudoh	69	70	69	208	1,000,000	28	Ayaka Watanabe	70	70	70	210	750,000
	Jiyai Shin	68	73	67	208	1,000,000		Saki Nagamine	71	70	69	210	750,000
	Ai Suzuki	67	71	70	208	1,000,000		Eri Okayama	73	66	71	210	750,000
	Erika Hara	68	70	70	208	1,000,000		Yuka Yasuda	71	71	68	210	750,000
	Na-Ri Lee	66	70	72	208	1,000,000		Chirei Iwai	69	73	68	210	750,000

Nobuta Ladies Masters

A cool demeanour for a person so young was evident as 19-year-old Haruka Kawasaki eked out the second victory of her rookie season in the Nobuta Ladies Masters. Unlike what happened six weeks earlier when she came from far behind to win the Japan LPGA Championship, Kawasaki prevailed in a down-to-the-wire confrontation with Yui Kawamoto, who, like Kawasaki, won in her first season on the Japan LPGA Tour in 2019.

Kawamoto had been the dominant player all week at Masters Golf Club at Miki City. The 24-year-old opened with 65, tied for the lead with Erika Hara, then spurted three shots in front Friday with a bogey-free 66. Kawasaki caught up the third day. She had followed up an opening 70 with rounds of 68 and 66, overtaking Kawamoto (73) at 12 under.

Kawasaki's composure was challenged immediately on Sunday when she fell two strokes behind after she bogeyed the par-five first and Kawamoto birdied. But Kawasaki cooly regained the tie with a birdie to Kawamoto's bogey at the second hole, and the lead went back and forth until a two-shot swing at the 13th hole gave Kawasaki a one-shot lead. She closed with a 69 for a 15-under-par winning total of 273 when she calmly two-putted the 18th green. Miyu Sato made an exciting final-round charge with a six-birdie, back-nine 30, her 65 coming up a stroke short and tying her with Kawamoto for second place. "I was confident that I didn't drop my score," said Kawasaki. "I'm happy to have another win this year. I want to continue to be a strong golfer."

Masters Golf Club, Hyogo — October 20-23
Par 72 (36-36); 6,585 yards — Purse: ¥200,000,000

1	**Haruka Kawasaki**	70	68	66	69	273	¥36,000,000		Ai Suzuki	71	72	70	67	280	2,420,000
2	**Miyu Sato**	70	70	69	65	274	15,800,000		Lala Anai	69	68	72	71	280	2,420,000
	Yui Kawamoto	65	66	73	70	274	15,800,000		Mi-Jeong Jeon	70	70	68	72	280	2,420,000
4	Jiyai Shin	68	71	70	67	276	11,000,000		Miyuki Takeuchi	68	72	66	74	280	2,420,000
	Yuna Nishimura	70	70	68	68	276	11,000,000	21	Hina Arakaki	70	71	72	68	281	1,820,000
6	Mizuki Ooide	70	72	66	69	277	8,000,000		Ritsuko Ryu	70	68	72	71	281	1,820,000
7	Yuri Yoshida	69	73	71	65	278	7,000,000		Mao Saigo	69	73	68	71	281	1,820,000
8	Minami Katsu	69	71	72	67	279	4,097,142		Chirei Iwai	69	70	68	74	281	1,820,000
	Haruka Morita	71	70	71	67	279	4,097,142	25	Hikaru Yoshimoto	68	70	72	72	282	1,700,000
	Mone Inami	71	70	70	68	279	4,097,142		Sakura Koiwai	68	71	71	72	282	1,700,000
	Rio Takeda	70	70	70	69	279	4,097,142	27	Serena Aoki	71	71	70	71	283	1,540,000
	Nanoko Hayashi	69	68	72	70	279	4,097,142		Yuka Yasuda	69	71	72	71	283	1,540,000
	Ayaka Furue	70	69	70	70	279	4,097,142		Miki Sakai	70	69	72	72	283	1,540,000
	Erika Hara	65	71	72	71	279	4,097,142		Ji-Hee Lee	69	72	72	70	283	1,540,000
15	Yuting Seki	69	71	72	68	280	2,420,000		Erika Kikuchi	68	74	68	73	283	1,540,000
	Teresa Lu	71	72	67	70	280	2,420,000		Miyuu Abe	66	69	73	75	283	1,540,000

Mitsubishi Electric Hisako Higuchi Ladies

To say that Kumiko Kaneda was an unlikely winner of the Mitsubishi Electric Hisako Higuchi event clearly understates the circumstances. Kaneda hadn't won a tournament in 11 years and 189 days — the 2011 Fujisankei in her third season on tour — and she teed off at Musashigaoka Golf Club sitting 63rd on the current money list. What's more, she hadn't finished better than 46th in the last six tournaments, missing two cuts and placing next-to-last in the most recent two events. She had missed eight cuts and withdrew from another of her 22 starts, but did have a pair of top-10 finishes.

"I thought it was like a fairy tale to the fans that, if you don't give up, it will come true," said the teary-eyed 33-year-old after posting her two-stroke victory. "It was a long day, but for me it went by in the blink of an eye." It was the longest victory gap in the modern history of the tour.

Kaneda launched her memorable week with a four-under-par 68, two strokes behind five-time winner Mao Saigo, Fumika Kawagishi and 19-year-old JLPGA champion Haruka Kawasaki, who was coming off a victory the previous Sunday in the Nobuta Masters. Kaneda took a three-stroke lead over Kawasaki (66-72) in the second round, her five-birdie 67 one of only two rounds in the 60s on a windy Saturday when the field was baffled by difficult pin positions. A 72 was enough for Kaneda's win on nine-under-par 211 as scoring was again difficult Sunday with only four players in the 60s. Her round was an up-and-down mix of four birdies and four bogeys, the final birdie at the 17th hole the clincher as Kawasaki shot 71, playing the last seven holes in even par.

Musashigaoka Golf Club, Saitama — October 28-30
Par 72 (36-36); 6,650 yards — Purse: ¥80,000,000

1	**Kumiko Kaneda**	68	67	72	207	¥14,400,000
2	**Haruka Kawasaki**	66	72	71	209	7,040,000
3	**Shuri Sakuma**	69	72	69	210	5,200,000
	Fumika Kawagishi	66	73	71	210	5,200,000
5	Mone Inami	68	73	70	211	3,600,000
	Nana Suganuma	71	69	71	211	3,600,000
7	Kotoko Uchida	68	75	69	212	2,600,000
	Erika Kikuchi	71	70	71	212	2,600,000
9	Hana Lee	73	72	68	213	1,800,000
	Hinako Shibuno	74	71	68	213	1,800,000
11	Chirei Iwai	70	74	70	214	1,224,000
	Erika Hara	73	71	70	214	1,224,000
	Momoko Kishibe	68	75	71	214	1,224,000
	Miyu Goto	68	74	72	214	1,224,000
	Sakura Koiwai	71	76	67	214	1,224,000
	Miyuu Yamashita	69	73	72	214	1,224,000
	Yuka Yasuda	71	70	73	214	1,224,000
18	Amiyu Ozeki	73	72	70	215	800,000
	Mao Saigo	66	77	72	215	800,000
	Ji-Hee Lee	70	73	72	215	800,000
	Yuri Yoshida	70	72	73	215	800,000
22	Hina Arakaki	75	70	71	216	688,000
	Ai Suzuki	70	74	72	216	688,000
	Sae Ogura	73	71	72	216	688,000
	Seon Woo Bae	68	73	75	216	688,000
26	Rio Takeda	69	76	72	217	624,000
	Seira Oki	73	71	73	217	624,000
	Serena Aoki	74	72	71	217	624,000
	Ritsuko Ryu	72	71	74	217	624,000
30	Yuna Nishimura	73	72	73	218	552,000
	Akira Yamaji	72	74	72	218	552,000
	Shoko Sasaki	76	71	71	218	552,000
	Aoi Ohnishi	70	77	71	218	552,000
	Teresa Lu	69	72	77	218	552,000

Toto Japan Classic

For three days the stage of the Toto Japan Classic pretty much belonged to the home players of the Japan LPGA Tour and Momoko Ueda in particular, with a rather thin number of name players from the US LPGA Tour on hand for the co-sanctioned tournament. After 54 holes, eight of the top 10 on the leaderboard were Japanese, mostly accomplished winners.

Come Sunday, though, one of those lesser-knowns from overseas — Scotland's Gemma Dryburgh — dashed the Japanese hopes with a final-round 65 that carried her to a resounding four-stroke victory, her first and just the fourth ever by one from her country on the LPGA Tour. "I was in Korea last week with friends and I said to them, 'I'll mention you in my speech,' as a joke," she recalled. "But it's overwhelming to be honest. It's been a dream of mine for a long time. A lot of hard work has gone into this," added the 29-year-old Tulane University graduate who had never finished better than fifth during her five seasons on the LPGA Tour.

The 35-year-old Ueda, who won the Toto in 2007 and 2011 when it was known as the Mizuno Open, held the lead through three rounds, sharing it with Ai Suzuki, another former Toto champion (2019), the first day. Both opened with seven-under-par 65s at Seta Golf Club in Shiga Prefecture. Prominent Japanese players occupied five of the next six places in the standings at day's end and the home-country dominance continued Friday as Ueda took sole possession of the lead with a 69, a shot in front of Suzuki and Miyuu Yamashita, the JLPGA money-list leader. Dryburgh joined the front ranks, four back at 138 on Friday, then began her major surge towards victory the next day, racing into second place with an eight-birdie 65 to be 13 under par. Ueda shot 68 to maintain a one-shot lead, but expressed some concern about her game, remarking: "I am not comfortable with the rhythm of my swing and also with my putting."

Her worries proved prophetic on Sunday. She slipped a stroke behind the Scot on the front side, then faltered with a back-nine 39, the main blow a double bogey on the par-four 11th hole. At the same time, Dryburgh was pouring in five birdies coming in, finishing with another 65, a 20-under-par total of 268 and a four-stroke margin over Kana Nagai, like the other Japanese contenders during the week a former tour winner. She also shot 65, the day's low round, to grab the runner-up spot, a shot ahead of Ladies European Tour star Linn Grant of Sweden (67).

Seta Golf Club (North), Shiga — November 3-6
Par 72 (35-37); 6,616 yards — Purse: ¥294,000,000

1	**Gemma Dryburgh**	71	67	65	65	268	¥43,821,000
2	**Kana Nagai**	68	70	69	65	272	26,663,325
3	**Linn Grant**	69	70	67	67	273	19,342,297
4	Yuna Nishimura	70	69	67	69	275	14,962,826
5	Ayaka Furue	66	71	70	69	276	10,048,301
	Momoko Ueda	65	69	68	74	276	10,048,301
	Miyuu Yamashita	67	68	69	72	276	10,048,301
8	Minami Katsu	73	70	67	67	277	6,861,200
	Yuri Yoshida	71	69	69	68	277	6,861,200
10	Lilia Vu	75	70	67	66	278	5,320,891
	Atthaya Thitikul	71	67	73	67	278	5,320,891
	Matilda Castren	71	71	69	67	278	5,320,891
	Pajaree Anannarukarn	69	69	69	71	278	5,320,891
14	Carlota Ciganda	69	71	70	69	279	3,936,586
	Wei-Ling Hsu	69	69	71	70	279	3,936,586
	Haruka Morita	71	71	66	71	279	3,936,586
	Jeongeun Lee[6]	69	68	69	73	279	3,936,586
	Sakura Koiwai	66	70	70	73	279	3,936,586
	Saiki Fujita	71	66	69	73	279	3,936,586
20	Hye-Jin Choi	70	71	71	68	280	3,299,137
	Mao Nozawa	71	70	71	68	280	3,299,137
22	Jenny Shin	70	70	73	68	281	2,846,612
	Pauline Roussin	71	72	70	68	281	2,846,612
	Shuri Sakuma	70	72	70	69	281	2,846,612
	Yuting Seki	68	72	71	70	281	2,846,612
	Au-Reum Hwang	73	71	66	71	281	2,846,612
	Mone Inami	70	70	70	71	281	2,846,612
28	Nasa Hataoka	74	71	67	70	282	2,339,311
	Miyu Goto	73	71	68	70	282	2,339,311
	Kana Mikashima	74	67	68	73	282	2,339,311
	Ai Suzuki	65	70	72	75	282	2,339,311
32	Min Young Lee[2]	73	68	73	69	283	1,988,889
	Miyu Sato	71	76	68	68	283	1,988,889
	Pornanong Phatlum	74	72	65	72	283	1,988,889
	Chirei Iwai	70	68	71	74	283	1,988,889
36	Ayaka Watanabe	68	75	71	70	284	1,558,274
	Minjee Lee	72	69	73	70	284	1,558,274
	Mao Saigo	72	72	69	71	284	1,558,274
	Narin An	69	70	75	70	284	1,558,274
	Moriya Jutanugarn	70	71	70	73	284	1,558,274
	Shoko Sasaki	70	75	71	68	284	1,558,274
	Alison Lee	70	72	74	68	284	1,558,274
	Nozomi Uetake	72	74	71	67	284	1,558,274
44	Stephanie Meadow	73	73	70	69	285	1,284,685
45	Mina Harigae	70	71	73	72	286	1,131,312
	Sayaka Takahashi	72	71	69	74	286	1,131,312
	Kelly Tan	71	76	68	71	286	1,131,312
	Erika Kikuchi	75	70	70	71	286	1,131,312
	Emma Talley	71	69	69	77	286	1,131,312
	Chella Choi	74	71	73	68	286	1,131,312
51	Sophia Schubert	71	76	68	72	287	905,049
	Mi-Jeong Jeon	75	71	69	72	287	905,049
	Kotone Hori	68	76	71	72	287	905,049
	Nana Suganuma	71	72	72	72	287	905,049
	Pei-Ying Tsai	75	71	70	71	287	905,049
	Yealimi Noh	72	71	76	68	287	905,049
	Yuka Saso	73	79	70	65	287	905,049
58	Esther Henseleit	70	70	73	75	288	729,911
	Seon Woo Bae	69	74	70	75	288	729,911
	Jiyai Shin	70	72	71	75	288	729,911
	Daniela Darquea	72	70	72	74	288	729,911
	Ayako Kimura	74	71	70	73	288	729,911
	Momoko Osato	74	73	70	71	288	729,911
64	Lindsey Weaver-Wright	69	74	71	75	289	621,381
	Serena Aoki	73	72	70	74	289	621,381
	Nanna Madsen	73	72	70	74	289	621,381
	Mami Fukuda	72	73	71	73	289	621,381
	Hinako Shibuno	75	69	72	73	289	621,381
	Stephanie Kyriacou	72	71	74	72	289	621,381
	Angel Yin	75	70	73	71	289	621,381
	Marina Alex	74	74	72	69	289	621,381
72	Albane Valenzuela	72	75	69	74	290	565,583
	Patty Tavatanakit	71	71	74	74	290	565,583
74	Wichanee Meechai	77	73	68	73	291	554,627
75	Anna Nordqvist	71	77	70	74	292	544,548
	Ariya Jutanugarn	71	72	76	73	292	544,548
77	Maria Fassi	73	71	74	76	294	534,177

Itoen Ladies

Miyuu Yamashita's fourth victory of the Japan LPGA Tour season in the Itoen Ladies tournament brought her more than just the winner's accolades and its ¥18 million first-place prize. It made her the youngest "queen" of the year as leader of the Mercedes point rankings in the history of the tour.

Yamashita was 103 days beyond her 21st birthday when she squeezed out the one-stroke victory at Great Island Club in Chonan, Chiba Prefecture, thereby supplanting Momoko Ueda as the youngest number one. Ueda, who contended and finished third in the Itoen, was 21 years, 156 days old when she was crowned in 2007. Until the current season, the title was determined by money winnings and Ueda, with five wins, ran away at the top that year. The new queen, who stands a mere five feet tall, credited hard work and a careful diet for her solid play in 2022. "I practised for a long time," she said. "Looking at the stats, I analysed the bad points and worked with my father. In order to compete in the full season, maintaining physical fitness is more important than technique."

The Itoen result came down to the final putt. Yamashita had opened the tournament with a six-birdie 66 and a one-stroke lead over Ueda, who won her 17th title in April in the Fujifilm Studio Alice. Number 18 seemed likely when Ueda shot a brilliant 64 — an eagle, seven birdies and a bogey — on Saturday and advanced two shots ahead of Yamashita, who had a solid 67. Lightly-regarded Momoko Kishibe entered the picture another shot back with a 65.

Birdies were hard to come by Sunday at Grand Island. Yamashita ran off 14 straight pars before nailing her first and only birdie at the par-five 15th hole. Ueda lost the lead when she double-bogeyed the 16th hole and Kishibe fell a shot behind with a bogey at the 17th before Yamashita holed a 10-foot par putt on the 18th green for her fifth career victory. She closed with a 71 for 204, 12 under par. Impressively, it was her 20th top-10 finish among 31 starts.

Great Island Club, Chiba — November 11-13
Par 72 (36-36); 6,741 yards — Purse: ¥100,000,000

1	**Miyuu Yamashita**	66	67	71	204	¥18,000,000
2	**Momoko Kishibe**	69	65	71	205	8,800,000
3	**Momoko Ueda**	67	64	75	206	7,000,000
4	Mone Inami	69	69	69	207	6,000,000
5	Nanako Ueno	72	66	70	208	4,500,000
	Haruka Kawasaki	69	67	72	208	4,500,000
7	Min Young Lee[2]	68	71	70	209	2,750,000
	Ji-Hee Lee	68	71	70	209	2,750,000
	Erika Hara	69	70	70	209	2,750,000
	Mao Saigo	68	69	72	209	2,750,000
11	Asuka Kashiwabara	68	71	71	210	1,680,000
	Momoko Osato	71	71	68	210	1,680,000
	Ai Suzuki	71	71	68	210	1,680,000
	Yuting Seki	69	70	71	210	1,680,000
	Yuna Nishimura	67	70	73	210	1,680,000
16	Yuri Yoshida	72	68	71	211	1,230,000
	Saki Nagamine	72	68	71	211	1,230,000
	Au-Reum Hwang	71	68	72	211	1,230,000
	Nana Suganuma	68	69	74	211	1,230,000
20	Mi-Jeong Jeon	69	72	71	212	960,000
	Maiko Wakabayashi	69	69	74	212	960,000
	Amiyu Ozeki	70	68	74	212	960,000
23	Seon Woo Bae	70	71	72	213	860,000
	Hikaru Yoshimoto	68	71	74	213	860,000
	Ayaka Watanabe	72	67	74	213	860,000
	Mami Fukuda	68	70	75	213	860,000
	Yuka Yasuda	74	68	71	213	860,000
	Kotoko Uchida	71	67	75	213	860,000
	Miyuu Abe	70	67	76	213	860,000

Daio Paper Elleair Ladies Open

It had been 11 years and 35 days since Saiki Fujita claimed the last of her five trophies, including the 2010 JLPGA Championship. Three times in 2022 the 36-year-old veteran came within a second-place finish of ending that winless spell, most recently in June when she frittered away a three-stroke lead on the final nine holes of the Suntory Open. Finally, with the season running out, Fujita outlasted Ai Suzuki and landed her sixth win in the Daio Paper Elleair Ladies Open in mid-November, coming from a shot off the lead in one of the year's few 72-hole tournaments to register a one-stroke victory.

She addressed the win simply: "It's been a long time. Thank you."

The 28-year-old Suzuki, with 17 victories and two season number one accolades on her record, had taken the lead from Akie Iwai with opening rounds of 66 and 65 at Elleair Golf Club in Matsuyama City. Her 11-under-par 131 gave her a one stroke lead over little-known Hana Lee and Fujita, who followed up her first-round 67 with a 65.

Suzuki and Fujita left the rest of the field in their dust Saturday, both shooting 64, Suzuki without making a bogey, Fujita with just one. Iwai and Hana, tied for third, were seven strokes off the lead. In the head-to-head duel on Sunday, both leaders were out in 33. Fujita squeezed a stroke in front when Suzuki bogeyed the 11th hole and she birdied the 13th. They both birdied the 15th and Fujita rescued a par with a 15-foot putt at the 16th. Suzuki missed a chance to catch up when she three-putted the par-five 17th and they both parred the final hole, Fujita for a 67 and 21-under-par 263, Suzuki for a 69 and 264.

Elleair Golf Club, Matsuyama, Ehime — November 17-20
Par 71 (35-36); 6,575 yards — Purse: ¥100,000,000

1	**Saiki Fujita**	67	65	64	67	263	¥18,000,000
2	**Ai Suzuki**	66	65	64	69	264	8,800,000
3	**Erika Kikuchi**	70	64	69	66	269	7,000,000
4	Momoko Ueda	69	69	67	66	271	4,625,000
	Mao Nozawa	65	70	69	67	271	4,625,000
	Hana Lee	67	65	70	69	271	4,625,000
	Akie Iwai	64	69	69	69	271	4,625,000
8	Minami Katsu	68	69	68	67	272	3,000,000
9	Mizuki Ooide	66	69	73	66	274	2,250,000
	Fumika Kawagishi	66	71	66	71	274	2,250,000
11	Ayako Kimura	68	69	72	66	275	1,750,000
	Haruka Kawasaki	69	69	70	67	275	1,750,000
	Chirei Iwai	69	71	67	68	275	1,750,000
	Miyuu Yamashita	70	69	67	69	275	1,750,000
15	Saki Baba (A)	69	68	71	68	276	
	Erika Hara	69	70	69	68	276	1,400,000
	Kana Nagai	68	66	72	70	276	1,400,000
	Shuri Sakuma	69	69	68	70	276	1,400,000
19	Mami Fukuda	67	69	73	68	277	1,070,000
	Yuri Yoshida	68	70	70	69	277	1,070,000
	Rio Takeda	67	70	69	71	277	1,070,000
	Kokona Sakurai	70	66	69	72	277	1,070,000
23	Yuting Seki	71	70	68	69	278	920,000
	Asuka Kashiwabara	70	70	69	69	278	920,000
	Eri Okayama	68	71	69	70	278	920,000
	Kana Mikashima	73	67	75	63	278	920,000
	Ritsuko Ryu	69	64	70	75	278	920,000
28	Seon Woo Bae	72	69	68	70	279	850,000
	Rie Tsuji	71	70	70	68	279	850,000
30	Yuna Nishimura	68	70	71	71	280	790,000
	Hikaru Yoshimoto	70	68	71	71	280	790,000
	Haruka Morita	69	70	72	69	280	790,000

JLPGA Tour Championship Ricoh Cup

Miyuu Yamashita put an exclamation point on her splendid season, holing a 26-foot birdie putt on the first hole of a playoff to win the JLPGA Tour Championship, the year's finale. "I wanted to win the season finale," expressed the happy young star. "So I'm glad I did. I had a lot of fun this year. I learned a lot. I was surprised by the rapid growth in my third year as a professional."

Yamashita's victory and season was exceptional in several ways. Not only was she, at 21 years and 103 days, the youngest money-winning champion in the history of the Japan LPGA Tour, but the five victories she amassed during the year, two of them majors — the World and Tour Championships — built that money title to a record ¥235,020,967. Her scoring average of 69.97 was just 0.03 higher than Jiyai Shin's record low in 2019.

Yamashita had her game pretty much in hand all week at Miyazaki Country Club. She opened the championship with a bogey-free, six-under-par 66, a shot in front of five other players, but dropped three strokes behind Min Young Lee[2] (67-66) the second day when she shot 70, tied for second with Yuting Seki (67-69).

Yamashita reclaimed a share of the lead Saturday with 67 as Lee shot 70 for 13 under. On Sunday, while the Korean was dropping from contention with a bogey and a double bogey on the front nine, Minami Katsu was surging into contention. The two-time Japan Women's Open champion produced a sizzling outgoing 31 to pull within a stroke of Yamashita. It stayed that way amid two birdies and a bogey each on the back nine until Katsu birdied the 18th hole for 65 and 15-under-par 273, that total matched minutes later when Yamashita posted a 70. On the two went to the playoff and Yamashita's winning birdie on the first extra hole.

Miyazaki Country Club, Miyazaki — November 24-27
Par 72 (36-36); 6,487 yards — Purse: ¥120,000,000

1	**Miyuu Yamashita**	66	70	67	70	273	¥30,000,000
2	**Minami Katsu**	73	64	71	65	273	18,000,000
	Yamashita won playoff at first extra hole						
3	**Erika Kikuchi**	67	70	67	71	275	12,000,000
4	Yuri Yoshida	69	70	69	69	277	6,180,000
	Ayaka Watanabe	67	72	69	69	277	6,180,000
	Yuna Nishimura	71	68	67	71	277	6,180,000
	Min Young Lee[2]	67	66	70	74	277	6,180,000
8	Yuting Seki	67	69	73	70	279	3,000,000
	Kana Mikashima	68	69	68	74	279	3,000,000
10	Hinako Shibuno	69	72	74	66	281	1,440,000
	Yuka Saso	73	69	72	67	281	1,440,000
	Saiki Fujita	67	73	72	69	281	1,440,000
	Kotone Hori	69	71	71	70	281	1,440,000
14	Erika Hara	72	71	69	70	282	820,000
	Jiyai Shin	68	76	68	70	282	820,000
	Kana Nagai	70	70	71	71	282	820,000
	Haruka Morita	71	70	70	71	282	820,000
	Mao Nozawa	71	68	71	72	282	820,000
	Mone Inami	68	70	71	73	282	820,000
20	Mi-Jeong Jeon	73	71	70	70	284	714,000
	Ai Suzuki	69	70	71	74	284	714,000
22	Ayaka Furue	71	71	73	70	285	690,000
	Seon Woo Bae	74	72	67	72	285	690,000

24	Kumiko Kaneda	70	70	74	72	286	672,000
25	Mami Fukuda	72	70	74	71	287	648,000
	Chirei Iwai	73	71	72	71	287	648,000
	Momoko Ueda	69	73	73	72	287	648,000
28	Shuri Sakuma	70	72	73	73	288	618,000
	Pei-Ying Tsai	71	75	69	73	288	618,000
30	Haruka Kawasaki	71	74	74	72	291	594,000
	Serena Aoki	74	71	71	75	291	594,000

2022 MONEY LIST

1	Miyuu Yamashita	¥235,020,967
2	Yuna Nishimura	149,158,595
3	Mone Inami	139,402,087
4	Minami Katsu	136,776,675
5	Mao Saigo	130,059,607
6	Yuri Yoshida	114,444,959
7	Sakura Koiwai	108,158,103
8	Haruka Kawasaki	92,052,000
9	Nana Suganuma	86,198,649
10	Momoko Ueda	80,605,943

JAPAN STEP UP TOUR

Rashink Ningineer RKB Ladies	**Mayu Hosaka**
Hanasaka Ladies Yanmar Tournament	**Hana Wakimoto**
Fundokin Ladies	**Nao Obayashi**
KCFG Madonoume Cup	**Satsuki Kuwayama**
Twin Field Ladies	**Onnarin Sattayabanphot**
ECC Ladies	**Kokona Sakurai**
Shizuoka Shimbun & SBS Ladies	**Hsuan-Yu Yao**
Castrol Ladies	**Ami Hirai**
San-In Goenmusubi Ladies	**Haruka Kawasaki**
Sanyo Shimbun Ladies Cup	**Kokona Sakurai (2)**
Chugoku Shimbun Chupea Ladies Cup	**Kokona Sakurai (3)**
Sky Ladies ABC Cup	**Misaki Miyazawa**
Kanehide Miyarabi Open	**Kokona Sakurai (4)**
Udon-Ken Ladies	**Kokona Sakurai (5)**
Shishido Hills Ladies Mori Building Cup	**Mana Shinozaki**
Yamaguchi Shunan Ladies Cup	**Miyu Shinkai**
Kyoto Ladies Open	**Hina Arakaki**

WPGA Tour of Australasia

As women's professional golf celebrated 50 years of existence in Australia, Minjee Lee provided an appropriate highlight in 2022 by winning the US Women's Open at Pine Needles. It was the Perth golfer's second major title after she won the Amundi Evian Championship in 2021. It might have been a performance to help her retain the Greg Norman Medal but for the exploits of Cameron Smith in claiming the Claret Jug at St Andrews. But like Smith, Lee enjoyed a homecoming Down Under, showing off the Harton S Semple Trophy around Melbourne ahead of the ISPS Handa Australian Open in December.

The same week there was a celebration of the founding of the Australian LPGA in 1972. South Australian businessmen Alan Gillott and Hugh Bonython, were behind the initiative, feeling it was time women professionals in the country had the opportunity to play in their own tournaments. The first series of events was held in March 1973. "There is no doubt that this was a brave move by both Alan and Hugh, and we will be forever thankful for their vision and commitment," said Karen Lunn, chief executive officer of the WPGA Tour of Australasia.

"We have certainly come a long way since those early days. We have witnessed Australian women Jan Stephenson, Karrie Webb, Hannah Green and Minjee Lee all become major champions and many others win events across all of the world's women's golf tours. We also now have some of the finest female golf coaches, who are inspiring women and girls all across the country every day. I know that every one of our members past and present is grateful not only to Alan and Hugh for having the foresight to start the women's professional tour here in Australia, but truly thankful to the 12 brave founding members who made the transition from amateur golf into the unknown realm of professional golf 50 years ago."

It was also fitting that Lydia Ko, who started out playing on the then ALPG as an amateur, returned to the top of the Rolex Rankings for the first time since 2017. The New Zealander also pipped Lee to the Player of the Year title on the LPGA Tour in America. Yet Lee's magnificent performance at Pine Needles saw the 26-year-old win by four strokes at a venue where Webb also became US Women's Open champion, as did Annika Sorenstam and Cristie Kerr. "It's just super special and such a great honour," said Lee, who broke the championship record previously held by Sorenstam and Juli Inkster. "It's been my dream since I was a little girl. It's the one I always wanted to win. Now I've done it, it's amazing."

Lee had already won the Cognizant Founders Cup and her ball-striking was so good that her proximity-to-the-hole statistics on approach shots was the best in the world, male or female. "My ball-striking has been really good this season, so my woods, long iron shots have been really on the ball," said Lee, who won the season-long Aon Risk Reward Challenge and its $1 million bonus.

On the domestic circuit, Green created history by becoming the first female player to win a mixed event with the men. She had not won on home soil before she claimed the Vic Open and then she followed up the very next week at the Players Series event at Murray River. Green eagled her first hole of the opening round, was six under par for the first six holes and went wire-to-wire, winning by four strokes from Andrew Evans and amateur Hayden Hopewell. Su Oh's third place at the inaugural Players Series event in 2021 had been the previous best result by a woman. Later in the year, Sweden's Linda Grant repeated Green's feat by winning the Scandinavian Mixed on the DP World Tour and the LET.

Green said: "I'm just so grateful that I came. It actually wasn't my plan to play; I was hoping to go back to Perth. Things happen for a reason so I'm really glad that I made it. I wanted to win these two events as soon as I said that I'd enter them. Hopefully it's inspiring the rest of the girls to get their name on a trophy. I don't think this will be the last time these events keep happening. I can easily see 20 on the schedule coming soon hopefully."

For the first time since 2020, the Ladies European Tour held two co-sanctioned events in Australia, with Meghan MacLaren continuing her love affair with the country by winning her third LET title, all of them Down Under, at the Australian Women's Classic, and Sweden's Maja Stark claiming the NSW Women's Open by five strokes.

At the start of the year, the inaugural Australian WPGA Championship was held alongside the men's version at Royal Queensland. Su Oh became the first winner of the Karrie Webb Cup, her first victory since winning the Australian Masters in 2015 in her second start as a professional. "I really wanted to put my name on the Karrie Webb Cup," Oh said. "It's such an honour to put my name there. I can't wait to celebrate with her." Oh paid for dinner when the pair met up in Florida the following week.

At the end of the year, the Australian Women's Open returned to the schedule and for the first time was played "Vic Open" style alongside the men's version, and the All Abilities event, at Victoria Golf Club and Kingston Heath. With the championship not co-sanctioned with the LPGA or LET circuits, the depth of the field was not to the standard of previous years, but the top names all performed with Green and Lee in contention as South Africa's Ashleigh Buhai added to her AIG Women's Open crown by beating former winner Jiyai Shin by one stroke.

Sydney's Grace Kim, 21, was also in contention for her national title after securing her place on the LPGA in America by finishing fifth on the Ascensus Race to the Card standings on the Epson Tour. Kim won once and had four other top-10 finishes. Meanwhile, in Europe, New Zealand's Momoka Kobori won twice on the Access Series to earn her card for the LET in 2023.

2022 SCHEDULE

Fortinet Australian WPGA Championship	**Su Oh**	
Drummond Melbourne International	**Karis Davidson**	
TPS Victoria	**Todd Sinnott**	*See chapter 19*
Vic Open	**Hannah Green**	
TPS Murray River	**Hannah Green (2)**	
TPS Sydney	**Jarryd Felton**	*See chapter 19*
TPS Hunter Valley	**Aaron Pike**	*See chapter 19*
Australian Women's Classic	**Meghan MacLaren**	
Women's NSW Open	**Maja Stark**	
ISPS Handa Australian Open	**Ashleigh Buhai (1,2)**	

Fortinet Australian WPGA Championship

Su Oh did not want to miss out on the chance to be the first winner of the Karrie Webb Cup as the inaugural Fortinet Australian WPGA Championship was played alongside the men's event at Royal Queensland. Oh was in the final group as she and Jediah Morgan congratulated each other on their victories on the 18th green.

Oh, the 25-year-old from Melbourne, had been just 18 when she won her second event as a professional in the 2015 Australian Masters at Royal Pines on the Gold Coast. But even while contemporaries Hannah Green and Minjee Lee had won major titles in recent years, Oh, previously a star amateur, was stuck on one pro win until the opportunity arose to play for a trophy named for Australia's greatest woman player, her friend and mentor. "When I won at Royal Pines, I didn't go into the week trying to win, but this week, when I decided to play, I really wanted to come and win, and hopefully put my name on the Karrie Webb Cup," Oh said. "It's such an honour to put my name there. I can't wait to celebrate with her."

The field was depleted by overseas travel restrictions, while Sarah Kemp and Stephanie Kyriacou had to withdraw on the eve of the event with Covid. Oh, the highest ranked player to tee off, led with an opening 66 before slipping a stroke behind Grace Kim with a second-round 72. But she retook the lead on Saturday and a 68-68 weekend left her on 10-under-par 274, four ahead of Kim, who closed with a 70. Kim, the newly turned professional from Sydney, surged into the lead with five birdies in six holes around the turn, but had a double bogey at the 13th when a chip from off the perched green ran back down to her feet. Oh also missed the green at 13 before holing a putt up a slope and into the cup. "I hit it well but it was also lucky," she said. Oh never relinquished the lead again, with Kim bogeying the 15th and the champion finishing in style with a birdie at the last.

Royal Queensland Golf Club, Brisbane, Queensland — January 13-16
Par 71 (36-35); 6,045 yards — Purse: A$300,000

1	**Su Oh**	66	72	68	68	274	A$180,000
2	**Grace Kim**	69	68	71	70	278	30,000
3	**Sarah Jane Smith**	71	68	69	72	280	15,000
4	Karis Davidson	70	71	72	68	281	10,000
5	Soo Jin Lee	73	71	70	69	283	7,500
6	Julienne Soo	70	73	68	73	284	6,000
7	Kirsten Rudgeley (A)	71	73	73	68	285	
8	Stephanie Bunque	72	72	73	71	288	5,000
9	Kelsey Bennett (A)	73	74	72	70	289	
10	Charlotte Thomas	71	72	77	70	290	3,200
	Min A Yoon	77	74	69	70	290	3,200
	Cassie Porter	72	73	74	71	290	3,200
	Kristalle Blum	71	71	74	74	290	3,200
14	Nicole Garrett	73	73	76	69	291	2,200
	Robyn Choi	75	72	73	71	291	2,200
16	Breanna Gill	75	74	68	76	293	2,100
17	Hanee Song	72	78	69	75	294	2,080
18	Justice Bosio (A)	78	75	70	75	298	
19	Sarah Wilson (A)	70	76	78	75	299	
20	Katelyn Must	77	75	74	74	300	2,060
21	Vicky Uwland	80	74	78	73	305	2,040
22	Tamara Johns	79	75	83	77	314	2,020
23	Paige Stubbs	76	74	83	83	316	2,010
24	Elmay Viking	83	78	81	77	319	1,990

Drummond Melbourne International

On the eve of her rookie season on the LPGA Tour in America, Karis Davidson claimed her first win on the WPGA Tour at the Drummond Melbourne International. Davidson shared the first-round lead on 68 with Breanna Gill in the 36-hole event at Latrobe. A bogey-free 69 the following day gave the 23-year-old from the Gold Coast victory by two strokes from Gill with a seven-under-par total of 137. "This is a great boost to me so early in the year. I had a solid week at the WPGA Championship last week and to get a win under my belt here at Latrobe is amazing," said Davidson, who finished fourth at Royal Queensland.

Gill, 41, birdied the first hole in the second round and twice more found herself a shot ahead until a bogey at the 15th. Davidson, who parred the front nine, had her first birdie of the day at the 10th and then ended in style with birdie fours at the 16th and 18th holes. Gill had a 71 to finish a stroke in front of Coffs Harbour rookie Amelia Mehmet Grohn and England's Charlotte Thomas.

Latrobe Golf Club, Alphington, Victoria — January 24-25
Par 72 (35-37); 5,800 yards — Purse: A$50,000

1	**Karis Davidson**	68	69	137	A$7,500
2	**Breanna Gill**	68	71	139	4,500
3	**Charlotte Thomas**	70	70	140	3,250
	Amelia Mehmet Grohn	70	70	140	3,250
5	Min A Yoon	70	71	141	2,500
6	Stephanie Bunque	70	72	142	2,000
7	Stephanie Na	74	69	143	1,688
	Whitney Hillier	70	73	143	1,688
9	Momoka Kobori	73	71	144	1,438
	Grace Kim	70	74	144	1,438
11	Stacey Peters	71	74	145	1,250
12	Casey Wild	75	71	146	1,063
	Lydia Hall	75	71	146	1,063
14	Kristalle Blum	75	72	147	825
15	Jenna Hunter	75	73	148	800
16	Cassie Porter	77	73	150	763
	Steffanie Vogel	74	76	150	763
18	Georgia Clarke	75	76	151	725
19	Stefanie Hall	78	74	152	663
	Katelyn Must	76	76	152	663
	Elmay Viking	73	79	152	663
	Julienne Soo	72	80	152	663

Vic Open

Hannah Green, one of only four Australian women golfers to win a major championship, claimed her first title on home soil at the Vic Open by six strokes at 13th Beach Links. Green had spent much of the pandemic playing on the LPGA Tour or quarantining in Perth so had not even seen many of her peers let alone played a tournament on home soil for ages. "It's been such a big catch-up week," said the 25-year-old West Australian. "I haven't seen a lot of these people in two years. We'll celebrate pretty well."

Green, the 2019 KPMG Women's PGA champion, had last won at the Portland Classic the same year as her major breakthrough. In her homeland, she had only won a couple of pro-ams in 2017. "The Vic Open was my first ever professional event so it definitely has special memories coming here. Lots of random memories but good memories here," she said. "It's nice to have my name on a proper trophy here."

Green, the top ranked player in the field at 30th in the world, opened 67-70 and then spurted ahead on the front nine on Saturday with four birdies, eventually posting a 68 to lead by five strokes. A slow start on Sunday on the Beach course saw her lead cut to two with her second bogey of the day at the seventh, where Whitney Hillier birdied. "I knew I needed to stay patient. It was a wind direction we haven't had in years. Everyone was going to struggle with lines," Green said.

She responded with birdies at the 12th, 14th and 17th holes for a 71 and a 13-under-par total of 276. "I felt really nervous even with a six-shot lead coming down the last," she admitted. Hillier lost momentum with two bogeys early on the back nine, closing with a 72 to share second place with Karis Davidson (72), two ahead of Su Oh and Cassie Porter.

13th Beach Golf Links (Beach), Barwon Heads, Victoria — February 10-13
Par 72 (36-36); 6,185 yards — Purse: A$410,000
Creek (R1&2) par 73 (36-37); 6,181 yards

1	**Hannah Green**	67	70	68	71	276	A$73,800
2	**Karis Davidson**	66	76	68	72	282	34,850
	Whitney Hillier	67	68	75	72	282	34,850
4	Cassie Porter	71	70	72	71	284	21,525
	Su Oh	71	70	71	72	284	21,525
6	Momoka Kobori	71	72	71	71	285	14,760
7	Kirsten Rudgeley (A)	74	74	71	70	289	
	Soo Jin Lee	72	76	76	65	289	13,120
9	Hanee Song	76	70	74	70	290	12,300
10	Justice Bosio (A)	76	73	71	72	292	
11	Charlotte Thomas	74	72	71	76	293	11,480
12	Robyn Choi	73	74	72	75	294	10,455
	Hannah Park	71	78	73	72	294	10,455
	Sarah Hammett (A)	75	74	72	73	294	
15	Gyu Rin Kim	66	78	75	76	295	8,678
	Julienne Soo	72	74	74	75	295	8,678
	Kelsey Bennett (A)	72	74	74	75	295	
	Stephanie Bunque	74	74	75	72	295	8,678
19	Haruhi Nakatani (A)	73	73	75	75	296	
	Shannon Tan (A)	76	69	72	79	296	
21	Keeley Marx (A)	72	77	75	73	297	
22	Stephanie Kyriacou	73	79	72	74	298	7,380
23	Kristalle Blum	76	71	75	77	299	6,150
	Katelyn Must	72	81	75	71	299	6,150
25	Amelia Mehmet Grohn	74	73	81	72	300	5,125

Murray River

Hannah Green hit her approach at the par-five 10th at Cobram Barooga, her first hole of the tournament, to 10 feet and holed the putt for an eagle. The 25-year-old from Perth led from start to finish in creating history by becoming the first female player to win one of the mixed field Webex Players Series events. Green won by four strokes from Andrew Evans and amateur Hayden Hopewell in the Murray River event played in memory of popular professional Jarrod Lyle, who died at the age of 36 in 2018.

For the second week running, following her first win on home soil at the Vic Open the previous Sunday, Green celebrated with a "shoey", the Australian habit of winners drinking a beverage of choice out of their shoe. "I feel amazing," Green said. "I'm just so grateful that I came. It actually wasn't my plan to play; I was hoping to go back to Perth. Things happen for a reason so I'm really glad that I made it.

"I wanted to win these two events as soon as I said that I'd enter them. Hopefully, it's inspiring the rest of the girls, not only in the juniors, but in the field to try and get their name on a trophy. I don't think this will be the last time these events keep happening. I can easily see 20 on the schedule coming soon hopefully."

Su Oh's third place at the inaugural Players Series event in 2021 was the previous best result by a woman. Grace Kim and New Zealand's Momoko Kobori shared fourth place. The women played off tees at 5,746 yards, compared to the men's 6,809 yards.

Green, after starting with that eagle on Thursday, was six under after six holes and shared the first-round lead with Evans on seven-under 64. She went one ahead of Evans with a 65 the next day but after a 69 on Saturday she was joined at the top of the leaderboard by Evans, Blake Collyer and Matthew Millar. Collyer (75) and Millar (72) slipped back on Sunday, while Green moved one clear of Evans at the turn. Then she eagled the 10th again, this time chipping in from just off the front of the green. She birdied the next and was four clear, the eventual winning margin as a 66 left her on 20-under-par 264. Evans finished with a 70, while Hopewell had set the early clubhouse target with a 65.

Cobram Barooga Golf Club (Old), Barooga, New South Wales — February 17-20
Par 71 (35-36); men 6,809 yards, women 5,746 yards — Purse: A$200,000

1	**Hannah Green**	64 65 69 66	264	A$36,000			
2	**Hayden Hopewell** (A)	68 68 67 65	268				
	Andrew Evans	64 66 68 70	268	20,000			
4	Grace Kim	70 67 64 68	269	12,000			
	Momoka Kobori	67 65 68 69	269	12,000			
6	Austin Bautista	65 69 69 67	270	6,316			
	Aaron Wilkin	68 67 67 68	270	6,316			
	Cassie Porter	66 66 70 68	270	6,316			
	Zach Murray	68 65 66 71	270	6,316			
	Matthew Millar	66 66 66 72	270	6,316			
11	Anthony Quayle	70 67 67 68	272	4,075			
	Nathan Barbieri	67 67 68 70	272	4,075			
13	Max McCardle	70 67 68 68	273	3,010			
	Charlotte Thomas	70 66 69 68	273	3,010			
	James Marchesani	68 67 68 70	273	3,010			
	Blake Collyer	68 67 63 75	273	3,010			
17	Cameron John	70 65 70 69	274	2,460			
18	Charlie Dann	71 68 69 67	275	2,185			
	Dimitrios Papadatos	70 66 69 70	275	2,185			
	Andre Stolz	66 70 69 70	275	2,185			
	Daniel Gale	70 71 63 71	275	2,185			
22	Whitney Hillier	68 64 70 74	276	2,000			
	Douglas Klein	65 69 67 75	276	2,000			
24	Jordan Zunic	68 71 70 68	277	1,840			
	Michael Wright	72 68 69 68	277	1,840			
	David Micheluzzi	76 64 69 68	277	1,840			
	Jarryd Felton	71 70 68 68	277	1,840			
	Jack Buchanan (A)	69 69 70 69	277				
	Louis Dobbelaar	72 68 66 71	277	1,840			
	Hanee Song	66 70 67 74	277	1,840			

Australian Women's Classic

No wonder Meghan MacLaren said, after taking the first round lead at the Australian Women's Classic, of being Down Under once again: "I need to move here. I love it." The 27-year-old Englishwoman's love affair with Australia continued as she went on to a wire-to-wire victory at Bonville, just down the road from Coffs Harbour where MacLaren won the first of two successive NSW Open titles in 2018. All three of her Ladies European Tour victories have come in Australia.

"The people are amazing here and it is a place I feel really comfortable. I'm going to keep coming back here for the rest of my career," she added after birdieing the last hole to win by one stroke from Maja Stark. "It means a lot to win, if a little bit surreal right now. When that putt went in, it was the best feeling in the world."

MacLaren won on the Epson Tour in 2021, but after missing the cut in her first two outings early in 2022 she decided to leave America and return to the LET. This was her third start since making that decision. After an opening 67, she added a 70 split over two days due to heavy rain. The delays meant the tournament was reduced to 54 holes, with MacLaren closing with a 69 for a 10-under-par total of 206.

Stark, runner-up to Sihwan Kim the previous week at the Trust Golf Asian Mixed Stableford, charged into contention on Sunday by going to the turn in 31. But a double bogey at the 13th stalled her challenge although she did respond by birdieing three of the last five holes. MacLaren started the final round slowly with two bogeys in the first six holes, then birdied the seventh and finished with four in the last eight holes. Hannah Burke, Magdalena Simmermacher and Carmen Alonso all finished two behind, with the leading home players being amateurs Justice Bosio and Sarah Hammett in sixth place.

Bonville Golf Resort, Bonville, New South Wales — April 21-24
Par 72 (35-37); 6,249 yards — Purse: A$320,000

1	**Meghan MacLaren**	67 70 69	206	A$48,276
2	**Maja Stark**	70 70 67	207	28,966
3	**Hannah Burke**	72 72 65	209	15,126
	Magdalena Simmermacher	70 70 69	209	15,126
	Carmen Alonso	68 70 71	209	15,126
6	Justice Bosio (A)	70 72 68	210	
	Sarah Hammett (A)	71 70 69	210	
8	Belinda Ji (A)	73 73 65	211	
	Sarah Kemp	71 72 68	211	9,494
	Alice Hewson	69 70 72	211	9,494
11	Jordan O'Brien	71 76 66	213	7,724
	Olivia Mehaffey	69 76 68	213	7,724
	Becky Brewerton	71 71 71	213	7,724
14	Kim Metraux	72 75 68	215	6,184

	Sarah Gee	71 74 70	215	6,184		Johanna Gustavsson	71 73 72	216	5,194
	Kelsey Bennett (A)	74 70 71	215		25	Maria Hernandez	76 71 70	217	4,522
	Moa Folke	70 74 71	215	6,184		Danni Vasquez	72 74 71	217	4,522
	Stephanie Bunque	68 75 72	215	6,184		Amelia Mehmet Grohn	77 73 67	217	4,522
	Lucie Malchirand	71 72 72	215	6,184		Ridhima Dilawari	70 73 74	217	4,522
	Momoka Kobori	73 69 73	215	6,184	29	Kirsten Rudgeley (A)	75 72 71	218	
	Alexandra Swayne	71 71 73	215	6,184		Lydia Hall	74 74 70	218	3,926
22	Mim Sangkapong	75 70 71	216	5,194		Camille Chevalier	73 73 72	218	3,926
	Whitney Hillier	73 77 66	216	5,194		Rosie Davies	72 71 75	218	3,926

Women's NSW Open

After finishing as a runner-up for the previous two weeks, Maja Stark secured her first win of the year with a comfortable five-stroke victory over compatriot Johanna Gustavsson in the Women's NSW Open at Coolangatta & Tweed Heads Golf Club. This was the 22-year-old Swede's third LET title since turning professional in August 2021 and came in the second of two co-sanctioned events. A co-leader after the first round, Stark then kept herself at the head of the leaderboard for the rest of the tournament, scoring 68-69-66-70 for a 15-under-par total of 273. She went four ahead after the third round but struggled to get going on the final day before birdies at the last two holes. Gustavsson went out in 33, cutting her deficit to two shots, and was one back after Stark dropped a shot at the 12th, but three bogeys in a row from the 14th from the chaser provided Stark with some breathing room.

"I am super happy to get my third win on tour after a slow start to the season in the US and then a couple of second places," said Stark. "I started with a birdie on one today, so that helped, but then it was a birdie drought for a long time until I made a bogey. Then I had to get my act together and finish well. I was a bit stressed because Johanna was playing so good. It felt like it could slip away, Johanna was just one shot back for a while, so I don't know if it made me stressed. I didn't feel my heartbeat or my heart racing this round, but I get in my head a lot when I feel like I'm not playing as well as other people and they're catching up. I don't enjoy starting a Sunday with a lead. When I was on 18, it was a perfect ending to a stressful day."

Magdalena Simmermacher was third for the second week running, while Cassie Porter was the leading Australian, sharing fourth place with Michele Thomson.

Coolangatta & Tweed Heads Golf Club, New South Wales — April 28-May 1
Par 72 (36-36); 6,196 yards — Purse: A$280,000

1	**Maja Stark**	68 69 66 70	273	A$42,242		Kelsey Bennett (A)	72 72 68 75	287	
2	**Johanna Gustavsson**	71 70 66 71	278	25,345	19	Whitney Hillier	73 69 72 74	288	5,069
3	**Magdalena Simmermacher**	71 67 70 71	279	16,897	20	Marta Perez	72 75 70 72	289	4,787
4	Michele Thomson	69 72 67 72	280	11,405		Olivia Mehaffey	73 71 72 73	289	4,787
	Cassie Porter	72 68 67 73	280	11,405		Hanee Song	74 69 69 77	289	4,787
6	Hannah Burke	73 70 69 69	281	8,307	23	Lily May Humphreys	73 70 73 74	290	4,435
	Lydia Hall	71 67 70 73	281	8,307		Meghan MacLaren	73 73 70 74	290	4,435
8	Sarah Hammett (A)	70 73 72 67	282		25	Emily Penttila	73 73 70 75	291	4,224
	Alice Hewson	69 70 70 73	282	7,040		Justice Bosio (A)	74 73 69 75	291	
10	Kirsten Rudgeley (A)	74 72 68 69	283		27	Tereza Melecka	72 71 78 71	292	3,661
	Jeneath Wong (A)	73 70 69 71	283			Katja Pogacar	72 74 74 72	292	3,661
12	Virginia Elena Carta	73 71 70 70	284	6,618		Alexandra Swayne	73 69 76 74	292	3,661
	Momoka Kobori	71 71 69 73	284	6,618		Gudrun Bjorgvinsdottir	75 71 72 74	292	3,661
14	Rosie Davies	75 73 68 70	286	6,055		Holly Clyburn	74 71 72 75	292	3,661
	Thalia Martin	76 67 70 73	286	6,055		Becky Brewerton	73 72 72 75	292	3,661
16	Lejan Lewthwaite	77 68 72 70	287	5,491		Genevieve Ling	72 69 70 81	292	3,661
	Maha Haddioui	74 73 70 70	287	5,491					

ISPS Handa Australian Open

What was hoped to be a homecoming for US Women's Open champion Minjee Lee or fellow LPGA star Hannah Green, turned into a double delight for Ashleigh Buhai. The 33-year-old South African added to her breakthrough triumph at the AIG Women's Open at Muirfield in August by claiming the ISPS Handa Australian Open. "It's the cherry on the top, I guess," she said.

But just as at Muirfield, Buhai appeared to be letting her chance slip before salvaging the victory. Three ahead at the turn on a warm and windy Sunday in Melbourne, Buhai had three bogeys in the next seven holes and was in a tie for the lead with young Australian Grace Kim, who graduated from the Epson Tour to join the LPGA in 2023. But Kim, the first-round leader with a new course record of 65 at Kingston Heath on Thursday, had trouble in a fairway bunker at the 18th of Victoria Golf Club and had a double bogey.

Buhai, meanwhile, got up and down for a birdie at the 17th to regain the lead. Former champion Jiyai Shin, the overnight leader, was five over for the day through 15 holes but just missed for an eagle at the 17th and then saw her birdie try at the last roll over the edge of the hole.

The championship, which was not played in 2021, was held alongside the men's and All Abilities versions, with the same prize money as the men although, with the event not co-sanctioned by either the LPGA or Ladies European Tour, the field was reduced to 108 players. Buhai opened with 69s at each of the venues and then went 66-73 over the weekend at Victoria for a 12-under-par total of 277. She won by one from Shin (75), with Green (74) birdieing the last two to take third, Kim in fourth and Lee fifth.

While Buhai's husband David was outside the ropes at Muirfield, he was caddieing this time. "It was a bit easier for him being inside the ropes," Buhai said. "We walked off 16 and by then I was tied for the lead and he said, 'Whatever happens now, I want you to commit to every shot, no matter what the outcome is, that's all you can do'. That's what got the job done at the British this year. I do get a little nervy out there, for sure, but he kept me calm."

Victoria Golf Club, Melbourne, Victoria — December 1-4
Par 72 (36-36); 5,680 yards — Purse: A$1,700,000
Kingston Heath Golf Club (R1&2) par 73 (36-37); 5,928 yards

1	**Ashleigh Buhai**	69	69	66	73	277	A$274,550
2	**Jiyai Shin**	68	68	67	75	278	177,650
3	**Hannah Green**	68	66	71	74	279	101,745
4	Grace Kim	66	72	70	72	280	80,750
5	Minjee Lee	70	70	70	71	281	68,476
6	Jenny Shin	70	73	71	68	282	56,525
7	So Yeon Ryu	69	69	70	75	283	48,450
8	Marina Alex	73	70	69	72	284	38,276
	Stephanie Kyriacou	71	70	71	72	284	38,276
10	Yuri Yoshida	72	69	71	76	288	29,931
	Jennifer Kupcho	72	70	72	74	288	29,931
	Cassie Porter	75	73	67	73	288	29,931
13	Stephanie Bunque	69	78	70	72	289	26,002
14	Xiyu Lin	73	70	72	75	290	23,741
	Chonlada Chayanun	70	78	70	72	290	23,741
	Sarah Jane Smith	73	73	72	72	290	23,741
17	Sarah Kemp	71	72	72	77	292	21,318
	Gabriela Ruffels	72	77	71	72	292	21,318
19	Laura Davies	74	73	75	72	294	19,380
	Momoka Kobori	71	77	75	71	294	19,380
	Sara Kouskova	75	72	72	75	294	19,380
22	Karrie Webb	77	70	72	78	297	18,250
23	Jennifer Chang	78	71	72	77	298	17,765
24	Ya Chun Chang	70	76	77	76	299	17,281

NEW LEVEL
Straight Down

PGA Tour Champions

In only 420 days, Steven Alker rocketed from Tuesday qualifier to Charles Schwab Cup winner, transforming his career and his life. In his first 25 years as a professional, the Kiwi earned around $3 million; in less than two years on the PGA Tour Champions he has accumulated $4,469,632, with an additional $1 million bonus for winning the 2022 Arnold Palmer Trophy. Four victories, including his first major at the KitchenAid Senior PGA Championship, made Alker the number one despite the intensity of leading the standings for the final 21 of the 27-tournament season when respected stars led by Padraig Harrington, Jerry Kelly, Steve Stricker, Miguel Angel Jimenez and Bernhard Langer exerted pressure on him.

Alker's resilience held firm right through to the back nine of the season-ending Charles Schwab Cup Championship when bogeys at the 12th and 13th threatened to derail him. Instead, he immediately hauled himself back on track with birdies at the 14th and 16th to finish third in the tournament and stay ahead of runaway winner Harrington.

For Alker the odyssey began as a 14-year-old at the St Andrews of Hamilton Golf Club overlooking the Waikato River in the city of his birth on New Zealand's North Island. "Steven has always been slight of build so what he didn't have in terms of strength and power he'd make up with finesse, and he had a great instinct for the game. He never lacked any desire," said his first coach, John Griffin.

From working at a petrol station and as a carpet cleaner, Alker set out on a professional pilgrimage during which he won a few times on the PGA Tour of Australasia, and in Canada, plus four times on the Korn Ferry Tour, once after an 11-hole playoff. But in 166 starts on either the PGA Tour or the DP World Tour, there was only one top 10, plus a lot of missed cuts. The support of wife Tanya, often his caddie, was paramount to Alker's resilience and by retaining membership of the Korn Ferry Tour he was able to stay competitive while preparing for his 50th birthday on 28 July 2021.

Alker targeted his Champions Tour debut more than two years out and left little to chance in terms of form and fitness. Los Angeles-based coach Paul Parlane fine-tuned his swing and he enlisted Dr Tyson Marostica, an Arizona chiropractor, to "make sure my body does what I want it to do". Marostica said: "Steven blew me away by how much he wanted to win; how much he wanted to grind."

In August 2021, Alker earned one of four places on offer at a Tuesday qualifier for the Boeing Classic, where he finished seventh. That got him into the Ally Challenge in which he was third. He numbered six straight top-10 finishes, including winning the TimberTech Championship — his first victory since 2014. He approached his first full season with a steely determination and in 23 tournaments recorded four wins — the first three in the Rapiscan Systems Classic, Insperity Invitational and the Senior PGA secured during a five-start span before adding the Dominion Energy Charity Classic in the first event of the playoffs. He also notched four runner-up finishes and four third places.

There were tears in Tanya Alker's eyes as her husband claimed the number one spot in Phoenix with winnings of $3,544,425 in front of a gallery bolstered by family, including children Ben and Skye, and friends, many of whom travelled from the Alker's adopted home town of Fountain Hills less than 40 miles away. "It's a dream come true," Alker said. "We knew it was going to come down to the wire. I was a little nervous teeing off in Phoenix, but it's good to have those butterflies. I've had a bull's eye on my back for six months; I just had to keep the pedal to the metal. It's amazing. My plan, 18 months out, was to get ready for the PGA Tour Champions. I worked hard and I slogged away trying to stay in shape. I stayed competitive playing on the Korn Ferry and I stayed fit.

"It's a combination of everything. The whole change in attitude, a different tour, a new chapter in my career. My game came around at the right time. The secret? Perseverance with a capital 'P'! I've played everywhere. It's been an amazing journey. Where was I a decade ago? I don't know to be honest. I was just trying to survive, basically. Now it's all happened so, so quickly."

Harrington, who pressured Alker by claiming the season-ending Charles Schwab Championship, said: "Steven's a truly deserved winner this year. It's not like he's just some flash in the pan at the end of the season. The pressure has been on him almost right from the start. He had a lead and several of us were catching him. It's very impressive that he's not just held on, but that he won in style."

Harrington's own first full campaign on the tour also brought four victories after he started with three runner-up finishes in his first five events. That he notched his maiden Champions win in a major at the US Senior Open emphasised for a countless time his innate ability to raise his game for the most highly prized titles. He had another runner-up finish at the Senior Open Championship, just pipped by Darren Clarke, who added another jug to his collection after his 2011 Open triumph. Without question Harrington's driving power — he averaged 308 yards against Alker's 287 — is a potent weapon although his powers of recovery were also clearly evident all season. He would win three of the last nine tournaments and his $3,293,255 earnings fell only a little short of those of the New Zealander.

"I'm out here on the Champions Tour to hear the noise," Harrington declared. "I go play the regular PGA Tour and I'm middle of the field. There's no buzz. It's much nicer to be up the business end of things — to be feeling it, feeling under pressure, feeling the nerves, feeling the excitement, to have the buzz of the crowd, to have people watching. This is the big thing about this tour. It gives you a second life with that adrenalin."

While Alker and Harrington were the new kids on the block, 58-year-old Miguel Angel Jimenez added three more wins, while Bernhard Langer won the second tournament of the 2022 schedule and then the penultimate event to extend at the age of 65 years, two months and 10 days his own record as the oldest winner on the Champions Tour. The German's 10th consecutive multi-win season edged him to within one of Hale Irwin's record of 45 triumphs. Langer said: "How long can you keep playing competitive golf full time? That's a good question. I'm getting closer to the point where I'm thinking about it. So far I haven't really thought about it so much."

Fred Couples was compelled to curtail his schedule to eight events due to his familiar back issues, although at the age of 63 he played the "round of my life" to become the first player to shoot his age or better in the final round and win. His success in the SAS Championship — he closed with a 60 with twelve birdies — was his 14th on the Champions Tour, although his first for five years.

Meanwhile, Americans Jerry Kelly and Steve Stricker, both aged 55 and the best of friends, won three and four times respectively. Kelly held high hopes of heading the standings after winning the Principal Charity Classic, Bridgestone Seniors Players Championship and Shaw Charity Classic during a hot two-month spell in the height of summer, although he would eventually finish fourth with $2,364,329, while Stricker ($2,473,725) settled for third place.

Stricker's story was as uplifting as it was unnerving. He surfaced only in late April after battling a mystery illness which had hospitalised him soon after he had led the United States to glory over Europe in the 2021 Ryder Cup. What started with a sore throat and a bad cough evolved into him being diagnosed with pericarditis, an irregular heartbeat, jaundice and high white and red blood cell counts, in addition to a high liver function test. Stricker had no appetite, no strength, no saliva and a fever of 103 degrees. He lost 30 pounds from an already slim build. The doctors could not pinpoint anything, but ruled out Covid-19, cancer and Crohn's disease.

He later admitted: "I didn't really know what to expect when I was starting to come back and hitting it super short. My body felt awful. I was just hoping to play, really, more than anything else. My wife Nicki's thing was, 'Let's take it in two week increments', and that proved to be a saviour because we could see improvement every couple of weeks."

Stricker's return thrilled his family and friends and also the golfing fraternity as he finished runner-up to Alker in the Insperity Invitational. Two weeks later he won the Regions Tradition, the season's first major. Stricker played 12 tournaments in all with his next three wins coming in the space of five tournaments at the Ally Challenge, the Sanford International and the Constellation Furyk & Friends — before hanging out the "Gone Hunting" sign after one of golf's most courageous comebacks.

2022 SCHEDULE

Mitsubishi Electric Championship	**Miguel Angel Jimenez**	
Chubb Classic	**Bernhard Langer**	
Cologuard Classic	**Miguel Angel Jimenez (2)**	
Hoag Classic	**Retief Goosen**	
Rapiscan Systems Classic	**Steven Alker**	
ClubCorp Classic	**Scott Parel**	
Insperity Invitational	**Steven Alker (2)**	
Mitsubishi Electric Classic	**Steve Flesch**	
Regions Tradition	**Steve Stricker**	
KitchenAid Senior PGA Championship	**Steven Alker (3)**	
Principal Charity Classic	**Jerry Kelly**	
American Family Insurance Championship	**Thongchai Jaidee**	
US Senior Open	**Padraig Harrington**	
Bridgestone Senior Players Championship	**Jerry Kelly (2)**	
The Senior Open Presented by Rolex	**Darren Clarke**	*See chapter 28*
Shaw Charity Classic	**Jerry Kelly (3)**	
Boeing Classic	**Miguel Angel Jimenez (3)**	
Dick's Sporting Goods Open	**Padraig Harrington (2)**	
Ally Challenge	**Steve Stricker (2)**	
Ascension Charity Classic	**Padraig Harrington (3)**	
Sanford International	**Steve Stricker (3)**	
Pure Insurance Championship	**Steve Flesch (2)**	
Constellation Furyk & Friends	**Steve Stricker (4)**	
SAS Championship	**Fred Couples**	
Dominion Energy Charity Classic	**Steven Alker (4)**	
TimberTech Championship	**Bernhard Langer (2)**	
Charles Schwab Cup Championship	**Padraig Harrington (4)**	
PNC Championship*	**Vijay Singh/Qass Singh** (A)	*See chapter 10*

**unofficial event*

Mitsubishi Electric Championship

There are times when pony-tailed Miguel Angel Jimenez is simply head and shoulders above his rivals and so it proved as the curtain rose in familiar territory on the Big Island at Hualalai. True, he was taken to a playoff by Steve Alker but with his third victory in eight appearances in this tournament, there was no wonder that he regards this place as "paradise".

Wherever Jimenez had relaxed during the winter there was little change to his pre-round exercise regime which in such surroundings could only be described as exotic. There was, however, a new "kid" on the block with the arrival of 2001 Open champion David Duval. He was eligible to tee up after celebrating his 50th birthday the previous November, and he was not short of confidence. "I expect to succeed," Duval declared.

Coincidentally, the man who succeeded Duval as Open champion, Ernie Els, claimed the first-round honours with a bogey-free 64. Surprisingly, it was the first time in 37 starts on the PGA Tour Champions circuit that the South African had held the solo first-round lead. Els, runner-up in 2020, collected six birdies, including one at the 18th where he struck a beautiful 100-yard bunker shot under the blue skies to 10 feet, and also an eagle from 10 feet at the 14th.

The Jack Nicklaus course, completely renovated in 2020, is a masterpiece, albeit with greens which need some creative reading, and the art is to avoid the dangers that Nicklaus cleverly weaves into his work. This Jimenez achieved with a second-round 66 enabling him to join others, including Alker, on 133 — one behind Els, who now shared the lead with Stephen Ames and Vijay Singh.

Alker and Jimenez wriggled clear of the pack with matching third-round 66s to get to 17-under-par 199 and leave Ames and Singh frustratingly one short of the target. Alker was seeking a second win in only his 11th Champions start following his 50th birthday the previous July. Els slipped back into a tie for sixth; Duval was part of the supporting cast, a closing 70 his best score of the week.

Alker was bunkered at the second extra hole and Jimenez accepted the invitation to celebrate for the second time in 17 days. The Spaniard had turned 58 on January 5 and although he needs no excuse you can be sure as he shook hands with Alker he was relishing the prospect of lighting a Cuban cigar and lifting a large glass of Rioja. Jimenez once explained the secret of his longevity as, "Good food, good wine, good cigars and some exercise". His rivals will tell you it also has much to do with a balanced swing and brilliant temperament.

Hualalai Golf Club, Ka'upulehu-Kona, Hawaii — January 20-22
Par 72 (36-36); 7,107 yards — Purse: $2,000,000

1	**Miguel Angel Jimenez**	67	66	66	199	$340,000
2	**Steven Alker**	66	67	66	199	200,000
	Jimenez won playoff at second playoff					
3	**Stephen Ames**	66	66	68	200	125,000
	Vijay Singh	65	67	68	200	125,000
5	David Toms	67	68	66	201	98,000
6	Ernie Els	64	68	70	202	82,500
	Retief Goosen	66	67	69	202	82,500
8	Jim Furyk	67	66	71	204	63,500
	Brett Quigley	67	66	71	204	63,500
10	Bernhard Langer	66	71	68	205	52,500
	Corey Pavin	69	69	67	205	52,500
12	Shane Bertsch	68	67	71	206	43,500
	Jerry Kelly	71	70	65	206	43,500
14	Doug Barron	69	68	70	207	38,000
	Paul Broadhurst	69	70	68	207	38,000
	Darren Clarke	66	72	69	207	38,000
17	Lee Janzen	68	71	69	208	33,000
	Scott Parel	70	66	72	208	33,000
19	KJ Choi	67	70	72	209	27,750
	Joe Durant	70	73	66	209	27,750
	Ken Tanigawa	71	67	71	209	27,750
	Mike Weir	69	72	68	209	27,750
23	Jeff Maggert	67	70	73	210	24,500
	Jeff Sluman	69	68	73	210	24,500
25	Cameron Beckman	68	72	71	211	22,500
	Rocco Mediate	74	69	68	211	22,500

Chubb Classic

Bernhard Langer could have been forgiven for taking one eye off the Chubb Classic when on the eve of the tournament the news filtered through that a devastating fire had destroyed the sprawling, 100-year-old clubhouse at Oakland Hills, where in 2004 he magnificently captained Europe to an 18½-9½ victory in the Ryder Cup against the United States. The clubhouse housed artefacts of some of golf's greatest stars and Langer said: "So, so sad. Such a waste. A lot of memorabilia in the clubhouse gone, including some of my stuff, and so much history gone."

Langer, however, resumed full concentration the following day, continuing his career-long assault on the record books, and with five straight birdies on the back nine he recorded a pacesetting 64 so shooting his age for the third time. "It's just a fun thing doing that," he quipped. Not so much fun, of course, for his rivals with one of the younger ones only half joking: "I'm glad he's not shooting my age because then we would have no chance. Bernhard is unbelievable."

Ahead by two of Robert Karlsson and Tim Petrovic after that scintillating start, his subsequent pair of 68s for a wire to wire victory afforded the chasing pack little hope. Langer marched majestically to what was without question a record-breaking success. He won at the age of 64 years five months and 24 days so extending his reign as the Tour's oldest winner previously set at the 2021 Dominion Energy Charity Classic (64 years one month 27 days). He became the first four-time winner of the Chubb Classic (2011-13-16-22) — he has made par or better in 40 of his 42 rounds in the tournament — and stretched his run of consecutive seasons with a win on the Champions Tour to 16. Moreover, his 43rd Champions victory put the German only two behind all-time leader Hale Irwin.

"I'm getting closer," said Langer. "Years ago I thought, 'That's almost impossible to reach', but it's in sight. I'm very competitive. I work hard at it." Langer, who previously won the event at The Quarry (twice) and Twin Eagles, had taken an instant liking to Tiburon. "I liked the course when I saw it last year; you've got to be very precise," he said. At 16-under 200, Langer finished three ahead of Petrovic, who was entitled to feel peeved with this being his 10th runners-up finish, and 22nd top 10, through 102 starts on the tour.

Tiburon Golf Club (Black), Naples, Florida — February 18-20
Par 72 (36-36); 6,909 yards — Purse: $1,600,000

1	**Bernhard Langer**	64	68	68	200	$240,000
2	**Tim Petrovic**	66	68	69	203	140,800
3	**Retief Goosen**	67	67	70	204	115,200
4	Brian Gay	70	67	69	206	95,000
5	Steven Alker	71	65	71	207	58,795
	Miguel Angel Jimenez	71	70	66	207	58,795
	Robert Karlsson	66	72	69	207	58,795
	Jerry Kelly	68	68	71	207	58,795
	Scott Parel	70	64	73	207	58,795
10	Ernie Els	69	68	72	209	40,000
	David Toms	71	69	69	209	40,000
12	Colin Montgomerie	72	68	70	210	31,600
	Paul Stankowski	67	72	71	210	31,600
	Kevin Sutherland	73	65	72	210	31,600
	YE Yang	70	67	73	210	31,600
16	Paul Broadhurst	68	73	70	211	26,400
	Wes Short Jr	72	70	69	211	26,400
18	Doug Barron	68	75	69	212	22,560
	Scott Dunlap	68	69	75	212	22,560
	Paul Goydos	69	72	71	212	22,560
21	Joe Durant	69	72	72	213	18,667
	Ken Tanigawa	70	70	73	213	18,667
	Woody Austin	70	68	75	213	18,667
24	Billy Andrade	69	70	75	214	16,400
	Rocco Mediate	68	76	70	214	16,400

Cologuard Classic

Mathematicians can squabble night and day over the odds against holing in one, but one thing is for certain, few bookmakers would take a chance against Miguel Angel Jimenez making an ace. However, even the most parsimonious of bookies might be tempted to take a risk about the Spaniard making two in the same tournament, but that is exactly what he achieved on his way to winning for the second time in three events. Then, again, this was not the first time the magician from Malaga had achieved such a feat, having done so at the 2008 BMW PGA Championship at Wentworth — he holds the record for most aces on the DP World Tour. Coincidentally, 12 months earlier Tim Petrovic made two holes in one at the 2021 Cologuard Classic!

In the shadow of the Sonoran Desert's Santa Catalina Mountains, Jimenez's initial hole in one came in the first round at the 196-yard seventh, which contributed to him sharing the lead on 66 with 64-year-old Jeff Sluman, who won six times in his first seven seasons on the PGA Tour Champions but has not captured a title since 2014. On the second day Jimenez, despite fighting an erratic driver which could have seen him disappear from the leaderboard, demonstrated his powers of recovery. This he emphasised with his escape at his penultimate hole where he drilled his tee-shot into one of the eight sparkling lakes scattered around the parkland Catalina course and still marked a par on his card with a marvellous up and down.

Jimenez's resilience, buoyed by seven birdies, resulted in a 67 for a two-shot lead ahead of tournament host Jerry Kelly and Sluman and, as his two closest rivals faltered, the man nicknamed "The Mechanic" pressed the pedal to the metal and with a 65 for a tournament record total of 18-under 198, he accelerated four shots clear of Woody Austin (66) and Bernhard Langer, who finished with a bogey-free 65. His margin of victory at the end was exactly the strokes he gained with those two aces — the second came with a six-iron at the 188-yard 14th — but that alone does not camouflage the magnificence of his play at the age of 58. He has won at least once in each of his eight seasons on tour, now 12 in all, while not since Loren Roberts in 2006 had a player won two of the first three tournaments of the season.

Omni Tucson National (Catalina), Tucson, Arizona — February 25-27
Par 72 (36-36); 7,123 yards — Purse: $1,800,000

1	**Miguel Angel Jimenez**	66	67	65	198	$270,000
2	**Woody Austin**	67	69	66	202	144,000
	Bernhard Langer	70	67	65	202	144,000
4	Jerry Kelly	68	67	70	205	108,000
5	Scott Parel	71	67	68	206	86,400
6	Robert Karlsson	70	69	68	207	64,533
	Rod Pampling	67	70	70	207	64,533
	Kirk Triplett	69	70	68	207	64,533
9	David Branshaw	71	71	66	208	44,813
	Thongchai Jaidee	72	70	66	208	44,813
	Brandt Jobe	73	65	70	208	44,813
	Tim Petrovic	68	71	69	208	44,813
13	Bob Estes	71	73	65	209	32,400
	Rocco Mediate	73	73	63	209	32,400
	Jeff Sluman	66	69	74	209	32,400
	Kevin Sutherland	72	67	70	209	32,400
	David Toms	71	68	70	209	32,400
18	Paul Broadhurst	74	65	71	210	26,190

	Marco Dawson	70	68	72	210	26,190		Gene Sauers	68	68	75	211	21,132
20	Steven Alker	70	69	72	211	21,132	25	Tom Byrum	71	73	68	212	16,785
	Doug Barron	73	69	69	211	21,132		Jim Furyk	74	69	69	212	16,785
	Alex Cejka	70	69	72	211	21,132		Tom Gillis	70	72	70	212	16,785
	Ernie Els	74	73	64	211	21,132		Dicky Pride	69	70	73	212	16,785

Hoag Classic

A glance at the Champions Board for the Hoag Classic — previously known as the Toshiba Classic — confirmed the 2009 winner to be Eduardo Romero and he was very much in people's hearts as the 26th edition started only 19 days after the popular Argentinian had passed away at the age of 67. Nicknamed "El Gato" ("The Cat"), he won five PGA Tour Champions titles — including two majors — and the last of his amazing career tally of 75 professional wins happened to be his Toshiba Classic triumph on March 8, 2009 when he beat Mark O'Meara and Joey Sindelar by one shot.

Romero richly contributed to the history of this tournament, being one of seven international winners including the defending champion Ernie Els, winner in 2020, and, following a one-year hiatus because of Covid, that number would rise to eight with Retief Goosen following in the footsteps of his South African compatriot. In fact David Frost, another South African, won in 2013 and Els, after following an opening 66 with a 68 to be one clear of Lee Janzen, Cameron Beckman and Goosen, explained why he and his fellow countrymen enjoy the Newport Beach course with its bold stands of aged pine trees and narrow kikuyu fairways leading to small targets.

Els compared the topography and the vegetation as being similar to that back home, especially growing up as he did in a neighbourhood of eucalyptus trees and kikuyu grass, although there was little with which to compare the weather on his own "Sunshine Tour" with biting 25 mph winds testing him and his rivals. Even so, he collected four birdies in the last seven holes to overhaul the impressive Janzen, who went low for the day on 66, and keep alive a successful title defence.

Sunday was Student Day, with those aged 18 and under receiving complimentary entrance, and, although like the rest of the local fans, they missed not seeing local resident and crowd favourite Fred Couples, who withdrew with a back issue, they were treated to a masterclass by Goosen. He was in a unique last group because, like himself, both Els and Janzen own two US Open titles. Goosen, however, eagled the first, birdied the next two and swept clear with an eight-under 63 to win by four on 15-under-par 198, as KJ Choi climbed out of the pack with a 66 for second place. For Goosen, who had undergone shoulder surgery, it was only a second PGA Champions Tour win following the 2019 Bridgestone Senior Players.

Newport Beach Country Club, Newport Beach, California — March 4-6
Par 71 (35-36); 6,612 yards — Purse: $2,000,000

1	**Retief Goosen**	68	67	63	198	$300,000		David Toms	67	69	73	209	44,400
2	**KJ Choi**	69	67	66	202	176,000	15	Paul Broadhurst	68	74	68	210	31,033
3	**Stephen Ames**	68	69	67	204	132,000		YE Yang	68	73	69	210	31,033
	Lee Janzen	69	66	69	204	132,000		Steven Alker	70	74	66	210	31,033
5	Doug Barron	70	69	67	206	88,000		Darren Clarke	66	72	72	210	31,033
	Tim Petrovic	71	68	67	206	88,000		Miguel Angel Jimenez	73	67	70	210	31,033
7	Ernie Els	66	68	73	207	72,000		Robert Karlsson	71	69	70	210	31,033
8	Bernhard Langer	65	73	70	208	60,000	21	Stephen Dodd	65	74	72	211	21,580
	Rocco Mediate	67	72	69	208	60,000		Jerry Kelly	68	72	71	211	21,580
10	Cameron Beckman	64	71	74	209	44,400		Rob Labritz	70	69	72	211	21,580
	Tom Gillis	68	72	69	209	44,400		Tom Lehman	68	71	72	211	21,580
	Rod Pampling	69	70	70	209	44,400		Wes Short Jr	69	73	69	211	21,580
	Tom Pernice Jr	69	72	68	209	44,400		Mike Weir	69	73	69	211	21,580

Rapiscan Systems Classic

Padraig Harrington suggested after a pacesetting first-round 67 that to win on the PGA Tour Champions required an aggressive attitude, and how right he was proved as Steve Alker swung into overdrive, playing his final 40 holes without carding a bogey, and blew the field away to win by six shots at the Rapiscan Systems Classic. Harrington, fast out of the traps with four birdies and an eagle, was seeking a confidence-boosting performance before teeing up the following week in the Masters for the first time since 2015. The winner of three majors was without a win of any description since 2016 and he had elected to compete in Mississippi rather than in Texas on the PGA Tour. "I felt I could better prepare for Augusta by being in contention," he said. Not for the first time he appeared to have made a wise decision considering he had not finished in the top 40 since the 2021 PGA Championship, in which he tied for fourth to earn a Masters return.

Then Harrington turned soothsayer. "These guys on this Tour are shooting 18 under par for three rounds most weeks. That's a lot of birdies. My game has kind of got anti-bogey. I've just got to get used to making a lot of birdies again." Harrington had set the script although it was Alker with a second round of 62 to the Irishman's 72 who would inscribe his name on the trophy with what would eventually be a tournament record total of — yes, you've guessed it — 18 under par! What is more Alker described himself as "just trying to stay aggressive" as he notched no fewer than 10 birdies in taming Jack Nicklaus's Grand Bear design which was hosting the tournament for the first time following 10 editions at Fallen Oak. "I just dialled in my irons and took advantage of the par fives," explained Alker. "Now I have to keep the pedal to the metal!"

The New Zealander, who ended seven years without winning by capturing the TimberTech Championship in November 2021, achieved all that and more in the shadows of the towering pines six miles into the De Soto National Forest. In fact Bob Estes, who has not won a tournament since 2002 on the PGA Tour, tied Alker three times on the front nine. Estes, however, bogeyed the eighth whereas Alker continued to play flawless golf with three birdies in four holes after the turn propelling him clear. "I didn't have my game on the first day but on the next two I just freed it up and let it go." Somehow that seemed to meet with what Harrington had implied was the way forward although to his credit the Irishman was nothing if not aggressive himself with five birdies in an inward 31 to match Alker's closing 65 and tie Alex Cejka (67) for second place.

Grand Bear Golf Club, Coastal Mississippi — April 1-3
Par 72 (36-36); 7,140 yards — Purse: $1,600,000

1	**Steven Alker**	71	62	65	198	$240,000
2	**Alex Cejka**	71	66	67	204	128,000
	Padraig Harrington	67	72	65	204	128,000
4	Bob Estes	70	64	71	205	96,000
5	Rob Labritz	69	70	67	206	66,133
	Retief Goosen	69	67	70	206	66,133
	Brandt Jobe	69	69	68	206	66,133
8	Marco Dawson	74	68	66	208	39,086
	Kent Jones	72	69	67	208	39,086
	David McKenzie	68	71	69	208	39,086
	Stephen Ames	68	70	70	208	39,086
	Paul Broadhurst	69	67	72	208	39,086
	Paul Goydos	69	68	71	208	39,086
	Miguel Angel Jimenez	71	67	70	208	39,086
15	Steve Flesch	72	67	70	209	28,000
	Jerry Kelly	71	69	69	209	28,000
17	YE Yang	72	69	69	210	24,053
	Brian Gay	72	68	70	210	24,053
	Dicky Pride	73	67	70	210	24,053
20	David Branshaw	69	70	72	211	19,840
	Davis Love III	75	70	66	211	19,840
	Rod Pampling	75	67	69	211	19,840
23	Billy Andrade	70	71	71	212	15,337
	Jonathan Kaye	72	71	69	212	15,337
	Doug Barron	70	67	75	212	15,337
	Lee Janzen	73	69	70	212	15,337
	Scott Parel	70	71	71	212	15,337
	Kevin Sutherland	70	69	73	212	15,337
	Kirk Triplett	70	70	72	212	15,337

ClubCorp Classic

Scott Parel worked for 10 years as a programmer and database administrator after graduating from the University of Georgia where he studied computer science, but one statistic haunted him as he shook hands with Steven Alker and Gene Sauers on the 18th tee ahead of settling the inaugural ClubCorp Classic — he had never won a playoff!

Parel, who concentrated on his education in college rather than play golf, turned professional in 1996 at the ripe old age of 31 to chase the dream of becoming a champion. He would endure extra time frustration in the 2012 Rex Hospital Open on the Web.com Tour when he forfeited a fabulous opportunity to win a professional title for the first time although, one year later, he celebrated a three-shot win in the Air Capital Classic in his 161st appearance on that circuit. That victory sparked headlines on an extraordinary story as the Augusta resident — he never played in the Masters and teed up in only two majors, missing the cut both times — won for the first time at the age of 48 years, one month and two days.

What transformed his career — some might say his life — was becoming a member of the PGA Tour Champions because in 2018 he won twice, the Boeing Classic and the Invesco QQQ Championship, and although he would win again in 2020 at the Chubb Classic, he bemoaned the three opportunities he bungled in playoffs.

Parel, at five-foot-five one of the shortest professionals in the game, dismantled the par fives, playing them in 12 under over the three days, so he was buoyed by the knowledge that he was returning to the par-five 18th where he earlier two-putted for a closing 65. Sauers appeared to have momentum, having birdied his last two holes for a closing 63, whereas Alker (68), after seven birdies in nine holes, suddenly hit the buffers with a three-putt bogey at the 13th.

All three drove well at 18 before fortune swung in Parel's favour. Sauers's second shot bounced back into the rocks from where he took a penalty drop. He chipped to eight feet, but the par putt spun out. Alker's long-iron approach from the rough came out heavy and his ball found a watery grave. Parel's par propelled him into playoff ecstasy and he rejoiced: "I'm just glad to win one. I certainly didn't think after those tee shots that par would win, but I played really, really well today."

Las Colinas Country Club, Irving, Texas — April 22-24
Par 71 (36-35); 6,703 yards — Purse: $2,000000

1	**Scott Parel**	67	70	65	202	$300,000
2	**Steven Alker**	68	66	68	202	160,000
	Gene Sauers	67	72	63	202	160,000
	Parel won playoff at first extra hole					
4	Lee Janzen	68	68	67	203	120,000
5	Billy Andrade	69	69	66	204	96,000
6	Jerry Kelly	66	70	69	205	80,000
7	Paul Broadhurst	71	67	68	206	61,000
	Marco Dawson	71	71	64	206	61,000
	Brian Gay	70	69	67	206	61,000
	Rod Pampling	70	70	66	206	61,000
11	Ken Duke	71	69	67	207	44,000
	Tim Petrovic	70	67	70	207	44,000
	Brett Quigley	69	68	70	207	44,000
14	Woody Austin	67	70	71	208	38,000
15	David Branshaw	76	66	67	209	31,100
	KJ Choi	72	67	70	209	31,100
	Scott Dunlap	72	66	71	209	31,100
	Retief Goosen	71	71	67	209	31,100
	Scott Verplank	71	71	67	209	31,100
	Mike Weir	74	69	66	209	31,100
21	Tim Herron	72	65	73	210	22,200
	Jeff Maggert	68	72	70	210	22,200
	Rocco Mediate	74	69	67	210	22,200
	Colin Montgomerie	69	68	73	210	22,200
	Dicky Pride	72	68	70	210	22,200

Insperity Invitational

In the end it was not quite the fairy tale Steve Stricker appeared to be writing on his fabled return to the fairways, but take nothing away from Steve Alker because he continued a storyline which was in its own right every bit as inspiring. This was Stricker's first appearance since succumbing to a mystery illness only weeks after superbly leading the United States to success over Europe in the 2021 Ryder Cup at Whistling Straits in his home state of Wisconsin. He was hospitalised with a soaring white blood cell count and an inflammation around the heart.

Stricker lost 30 pounds and when he teed up in Texas 201 days since his last competitive round he was still 10 pounds lighter than when he tied seventh at the Furyk and Friends Invitational in Florida. Meanwhile, Alker arrived at The Woodlands having won the Rapiscan Systems Classic and finished tied second in the ClubCorp Classic.

So Stricker — "My clubs aren't going as far as they used to" — was making a standing start, whereas Alker had momentum, although at the end of a windy first day they were locked together at the top of the leaderboard with Ernie Els. Stricker honestly admitted: "It was a little up and down, I'm not going to kid you." Els, having birdied all four par fives, looked likely to lead on his own until driving into a hazard at 18. Stricker struck the ball with increasing authority in the second round, although Alker matched his 65 to stay alongside at the head of the field where they were joined by Brandt Jobe, who notched five straight birdies from the 12th for a 64.

The 3M Greats of Golf — a nine-hole fourball scramble, played on the Saturday afternoon of the Insperity — has annually amplified spectator interest and the ninth edition did not disappoint with Jack Nicklaus, aged 82, holing the winning putt at the 18th to celebrate victory with team members Gary Player, Annika Sorenstam and Lee Trevino, but on the final day the focus fell on Alker. The New Zealander watched TV replays during a two-hour rain delay, returned to the course and immediately played a six-hole stretch from the 11th in six under for a closing 66 and a four-shot win on 18-under 198. Nine months earlier he had no status on the PGA Champions Tour; now he was number one in the Charles Schwab Cup standings. "It's been a fun ride," he enthused.

The Woodlands Country Club, The Woodlands, Texas — April 29-May 1
Par 72 (36-36); 7,002 yards — Purse: $2,300,000

1	**Steven Alker**	67	65	66	198	$345,000
2	**Brandt Jobe**	68	64	70	202	184,000
	Steve Stricker	67	65	70	202	184,000
4	Alex Cejka	70	69	66	205	138,000
5	Ken Duke	70	66	70	206	101,200
	Retief Goosen	68	70	68	206	101,200
7	David Toms	71	68	68	207	82,800
8	Bernhard Langer	70	71	67	208	65,933
	Stephen Ames	71	70	67	208	65,933
	Miguel Angel Jimenez	68	70	70	208	65,933
11	Woody Austin	68	69	72	209	50,600
	Kevin Sutherland	70	68	71	209	50,600
	Kirk Triplett	74	68	67	209	50,600
14	Stuart Appleby	72	69	69	210	41,400
	Chris DiMarco	68	70	72	210	41,400
	Paul Goydos	70	68	72	210	41,400
17	Olin Browne	72	70	69	211	29,843
	Fred Couples	69	70	72	211	29,843
	Scott Dunlap	73	68	70	211	29,843
	Joe Durant	69	72	70	211	29,843
	Lee Janzen	71	71	69	211	29,843
	Tim Petrovic	68	71	72	211	29,843
	Scott Verplank	68	72	71	211	29,843
	Mike Weir	71	69	71	211	29,843
25	Ernie Els	67	73	72	212	20,976
	Steve Flesch	74	67	71	212	20,976
	Padraig Harrington	72	70	70	212	20,976
	Tom Lehman	70	68	74	212	20,976
	Rod Pampling	72	70	70	212	20,976

Mitsubishi Electric Classic

A season fast unravelling as the "Story of the Steves" stayed true to script although with Steve Alker taking time out and Steve Stricker switching to the supporting cast, it was Steve Flesch who moved centre-stage.

In truth it was not until the final day that the camera truly focused on the 54-year-old from Cincinnati as a series of sub-plots beguiled the spectators. Clearly David Toms felt at home in Duluth — he won the 2001 US PGA Championship five miles across the suburbs at Atlanta Athletic Club — although times have changed. Toms elected to ride a cart, rare for him, because his two partners were using a similar mode of transportation and also with lightning in the area Toms was mindful of facing a long walk back to the clubhouse on a course calculated to be a nine-mile walk.

Toms, however, was not disrupted by the two-hour rain delay because, despite the gusting conditions on returning to the course, the 55-year-old from Louisiana immediately birdied three in a row to match Ken Duke's opening 65. For Duke it was something of a milestone as for the first time on the PGA Tour Champions he was at the top of the leaderboard albeit sharing that lofty perch with Toms.

Twenty-four hours later Duke was a victim of what can be a cruel game. He faced a 20-foot downhill putt on the 15th green for birdie. He trickled the putt down the slope where, to his astonishment and that of the TV commentators, the ball picked up pace and rolled 35 yards down the fairway. Two indifferent shots later he was facing a similar putt. This time he two-putted but he marked a seven on his card.

Meanwhile, Toms shot 71 to edge two ahead of Duke and four in front of a group of five including Flesch entering the final round when, with the wind finally abating, conditions were ripe for low scoring. Padraig Harrington made five successive birdies from the 10th to match the 18-hole tournament record of 64 and share second place with Fred Couples (66) and Toms (70).

Flesch, similar to Harrington, enjoyed a run of five straight birdies — his came from the second — and after a mid-round blip, he made four more on the back nine, including a 12-foot putt at the 17th, to claim his second Champions title four years after his maiden win which happened to be in this same tournament. Scores of 67-73-65 for 11-under-par 205 left Flesch one in front. "It's been a trying time but, man, this is really, really satisfying," he said.

TPC Sugarloaf, Duluth, Georgia — May 6-8
Par 72 (36-36); 7,179 yards — Purse: $1,800,000

1	**Steve Flesch**	67	73	65	205	$270,000
2	**Fred Couples**	70	70	66	206	132,000
	Padraig Harrington	69	73	64	206	132,000
	David Toms	65	71	70	206	132,000
5	Ernie Els	72	68	67	207	86,400
6	Mark Walker	68	72	68	208	72,000
7	Paul Broadhurst	68	74	68	210	57,600
	Glen Day	69	73	68	210	57,600
	Colin Montgomerie	72	69	69	210	57,600
10	Ken Duke	65	73	73	211	41,400
	Retief Goosen	74	67	70	211	41,400
	Robert Karlsson	68	75	68	211	41,400
	Steve Stricker	68	73	70	211	41,400
14	Stuart Appleby	73	72	67	212	28,058
	Woody Austin	70	74	68	212	28,058
	Doug Barron	72	76	64	212	28,058
	Darren Clarke	79	69	64	212	28,058
	Scott Dunlap	69	73	70	212	28,058
	Jay Haas	71	69	72	212	28,058
	Tom Pernice Jr	69	74	69	212	28,058
	Brett Quigley	72	69	71	212	28,058
22	Miguel Angel Jimenez	70	71	72	213	19,860
	Steve Jones	70	72	71	213	19,860
	Ken Tanigawa	74	71	68	213	19,860
25	Alex Cejka	70	74	70	214	18,000

Regions Tradition

The Cinderella story which started for Steve Stricker 20 days earlier in Houston, Texas, reached its denouement 666 miles east in Hoover, Alabama, when the 55-year-old from Michigan won the 30th edition of the Regions Tradition. Stricker's now well documented recovery from an inexplicable illness — he was hospitalised only weeks after leading the United States to Ryder Cup glory — was given the ultimate shot in the arm as he captured this trophy for a second time to bring his senior major championship haul to four, including the 2019 US Senior Open and 2021 Bridgestone Senior Players Championship.

Stricker, whose wife Nicki caddied for him, said: "It's been a long time. I hate crying but where I was last November and even a couple of months ago to come full circle here means so much. I didn't know what to expect coming out three weeks ago. I didn't know if I could play three weeks in a row. I have a little different perspective after going through what I went through so I'm just enjoying it a little more now. Having Nicki on the bag is fun. We've been enjoying our time together. We're reliving when we first came out on the tour in the mid-1990s. I'm looking forward to getting stronger and healthier and keeping this train rolling."

The Stricker 'train' started rolling Greystone's Founders course with a trailblazing seven-under-par 65 which catapulted him two clear of Miguel Angel Jimenez, the 2018 champion, and Wes Short Jr. Stricker, the 2019 winner who was also runner-up in 2018 and again in 2021, when he lost a playoff to Alex Cejka, notched five of his seven birdies at par fives in a tightly packed group of players with eight finishing on 68 including John Daly, diagnosed with bladder cancer in 2020. He said: "When I found out Steve Stricker was one of the first to call me so I'm just glad he's healthy."

On day two Daly was disqualified for the first time in 102 PGA Champion Tour starts — he did not sign his card after four-putting his final hole in a 72 — but Stricker maintained his two-shot lead with Scott McCarron (65), who had been recovering from an ankle injury and recorded his best score in two years, and Padraig Harrington (66) now his closest pursuers. Stricker ensured by making four of his seven birdies in the last six holes of a Saturday 66 that he would play in the final group on Sunday for the fourth consecutive edition. Indeed, he had spread-eagled the field with Steven Alker shooting 65 to be three back and Jimenez 67 to be five back. Defending champion Cejka shot 66 but he was disqualified for using a yardage book that had not been approved for the competition.

Stricker, on 21-under-par 267, completed a wire-to-wire win — only the second in the history of the tournament — with birdies at the 17th and 18th in a 68 for a fairy-tale victory in the first major of the season. You could say he owns the Founders course. In 20 rounds in five tournaments hosted by Greystone, he has recorded 14 rounds in the 60s and has a scoring average of 67.85. What is more, Stricker and Nicki really enjoyed the walk down 18 as he coasted home by six shots from Harrington, with Alker and Jimenez among the five players tied one shot further back.

Greystone Golf & Country Club (Founders), Birmingham, Alabama — May 12-15
Par 72 (36-36); 7,249 yards — Purse: $2,500,000

1	**Steve Stricker**	65	68	66	68	267	$375,000
2	**Padraig Harrington**	69	66	70	68	273	220,000
3	**Steven Alker**	68	69	65	72	274	128,000
	Stuart Appleby	68	69	68	69	274	128,000
	Ernie Els	68	68	70	68	274	128,000
	Miguel Angel Jimenez	67	70	67	70	274	128,000
	Rod Pampling	68	70	69	67	274	128,000
8	David Branshaw	71	67	70	68	276	80,000
9	Doug Barron	74	68	69	66	277	62,500
	Tim Petrovic	71	68	69	69	277	62,500
	Wes Short Jr	67	73	70	67	277	62,500
	David Toms	69	71	69	68	277	62,500
13	Darren Clarke	72	71	68	67	278	47,500
	Marco Dawson	71	69	69	69	278	47,500
	Jerry Kelly	74	68	70	66	278	47,500
16	Paul Broadhurst	70	72	69	68	279	41,250
	Scott McCarron	70	65	77	67	279	41,250
18	Colin Montgomerie	72	68	69	71	280	36,375
	Ken Tanigawa	68	70	72	70	280	36,375
20	Kevin Sutherland	75	69	71	66	281	33,000
21	Billy Andrade	70	70	69	73	282	27,750
	Shane Bertsch	68	73	71	70	282	27,750
	Glen Day	69	70	67	76	282	27,750
	Joe Durant	69	73	70	70	282	27,750
	Kirk Triplett	71	71	71	69	282	27,750
26	Retief Goosen	69	73	74	67	283	20,786
	Billy Mayfair	72	69	71	71	283	20,786
	David McKenzie	68	76	72	67	283	20,786
	Ken Duke	69	69	74	71	283	20,786
	Steve Flesch	71	67	72	73	283	20,786
	Brandt Jobe	71	74	72	66	283	20,786
	Gene Sauers	71	70	67	75	283	20,786
33	Chris DiMarco	73	75	65	71	284	16,500
	Paul Goydos	75	67	70	72	284	16,500
	Lee Janzen	73	69	72	70	284	16,500
36	KJ Choi	69	73	72	71	285	14,063
	Scott Dunlap	74	73	68	70	285	14,063
	Stephen Leaney	71	71	70	73	285	14,063
	Scott Parel	72	75	71	67	285	14,063
40	John Huston	73	71	71	71	286	11,750
	Jeff Maggert	71	75	68	72	286	11,750
	Rocco Mediate	74	74	68	70	286	11,750
	Brett Quigley	73	70	72	71	286	11,750
	Mike Weir	72	74	73	67	286	11,750
45	Stephen Ames	76	73	72	66	287	10,000
	Woody Austin	73	70	70	74	287	10,000
47	Cameron Beckman	71	71	74	72	288	8,750
	Tom Byrum	72	72	76	68	288	8,750
	Scott Verplank	70	72	70	76	288	8,750
50	Tim Herron	73	70	74	72	289	7,000
	Rob Labritz	72	75	72	70	289	7,000
	Corey Pavin	78	71	74	66	289	7,000
	Jeff Sluman	73	69	73	74	289	7,000
54	Mark O'Meara	74	70	76	70	290	5,750
	Steve Pate	78	69	73	70	290	5,750
	Dicky Pride	70	73	74	73	290	5,750
57	David Frost	75	71	72	73	291	5,000
	Brian Gay	70	69	79	73	291	5,000
	Robert Karlsson	75	72	73	71	291	5,000
60	Jose Maria Olazabal	72	70	80	70	292	4,375
	Joey Sindelar	73	78	71	70	292	4,375
62	Robert Allenby	75	70	70	78	293	4,000
63	Matt Gogel	73	75	72	75	295	3,750
64	Gary Hallberg	72	76	71	77	296	3,375
	Spike McRoy	79	71	72	74	296	3,375
66	David Duval	71	74	76	76	297	2,875
	Kent Jones	78	71	71	77	297	2,875
68	Stephen Dodd	75	73	71	79	298	2,350
	Jim Furyk	75	76	76	71	298	2,350
	Tom Lehman	73	77	75	73	298	2,350
71	Tom Pernice Jr	75	75	76	75	301	2,050
72	John Senden	81	72	76	75	304	1,900
73	Steve Jones	78	78	76	73	305	1,750
74	Larry Mize	80	78	74	74	306	1,650

KitchenAid Senior PGA Championship

The giant Alfred S Bourne Trophy is 42 inches in height and weighs 36 pounds, and Steve Alker's face at the KitchenAid Senior PGA Championship was a picture as he read out some of the names alongside whom his own would now be engraved. "First I saw Arnold Palmer," he enthused. "I'm not sure what year it was, and then you twist the trophy and you see Lee Trevino and you see Jack Nicklaus and you see Tom Watson. It's pretty cool."

Alker's victory in the 82nd edition of senior golf's oldest major is the story of a quite remarkable transformation in fortune. Five-time Champions Tour winner Paul Goydos put it succinctly: "What the hell has he been doing for the first 50 years!"

Talk about the PGA Tour Champions offering a second opportunity. Over three decades it was calculated that the New Zealander had played more than 550 tournaments on six tours. This included 86 PGA Tour events without a single top 10 and with 47 missed cuts, and 80 European Tour events with one top 10 and 42 missed cuts. True, Alker won four times in 304 appearances on the Korn Ferry Tour, but he also missed the cut in nearly half those events. Before turning 50, Alker won $2,318,886; in 19 tournaments since, including the cheque he was now holding, his earnings totalled $2,960,168 with nine top three finishes.

Alker said: "I can't put my finger on one thing exactly. I look back and I go, jeez, did I really have the game or did I have the attitude? I've matured and it's a second wind. Let's stay in shape. Let's keep playing. We have a second career. Let's go for it. It's a great ride. It's just perseverance with a capital 'P'."

Alker came into the tournament with form figures of 1-T2-1-T3 and stayed in the zone with an opening seven-under-par 64 to share the lead with Bob Estes, who carded seven birdies in a blemish-free round. Meanwhile, Steve Stricker's hopes of back-to-back majors disappeared as he was compelled to withdraw with Covid. Day two ushered in squalls of driving rain with 25 mph wind gusts and a serious drop in temperature. Stephen Ames and Scott McCarron defied the difficult conditions to post matching 66s and move to eight under, two ahead of Brian Gay, Mike Weir, Alker (72) and Bernhard Langer. Ames progressed with a third-round 67, as McCarron retreated, to be two ahead of Canadian compatriot Mike Weir and Langer, three in front of Goydos and four clear of defending champion Alex Cejka, Alker (69) and Gay.

Alker made a fast start on Sunday with four straight threes and three birdies in his first five holes. However, Langer, seeking his 12th senior major, powered into the lead with four birdies on the front nine before his challenge was derailed by three straight bogeys from the 12th. "It stopped my momentum," he said. "I was ahead and I didn't close it." Langer's hopes had disappeared by the time he made double bogey at the 18th which enabled Ames to take second place so recording his best finish in a senior major and the best by a Canadian player since the inception of the PGA Tour Champions in 1980. KJ Choi shot a best-of-the-day 65 for a share of fourth place with Miguel Angel Jimenez, Goydos and Weir, but Alker, quite simply, blew the field away.

A closing 63 gave Alker a 16-under-par total of 268 and a three-shot win over Ames. He had bogeyed the seventh but four birdies in a row from the eighth enabled him to join Langer at 14 under. Then he applied the coup de grâce with birdies at the 15th and 16th which secured for him that mind-blowing moment when he was able to wrap his arms around that giant trophy glittering with the greatest names in golf — and now that of Steven Alker.

Harbor Shores Resort, Benton Harbor, Michigan — May 26-29
Par 71 (36-35); 6,852 yards — Purse: $3,250,000

1	**Steven Alker**	64	72	69	63	268	$630,000
2	**Stephen Ames**	68	66	67	70	271	380,000
3	**Bernhard Langer**	68	68	67	71	274	237,500
4	KJ Choi	68	72	70	65	275	128,450
	Paul Goydos	69	68	67	71	275	128,450
	Miguel Angel Jimenez	67	74	65	69	275	128,450
	Mike Weir	65	71	67	72	275	128,450
8	Shane Bertsch	67	72	67	70	276	85,000
	Brian Gay	68	68	69	71	276	85,000
	Mark Hensby	67	75	67	67	276	85,000
	Brandt Jobe	68	71	68	69	276	85,000
	Colin Montgomerie	69	71	68	68	276	85,000
13	Alex Cejka	68	69	68	72	277	70,000
14	Darren Clarke	68	74	68	68	278	61,250
	Ernie Els	67	70	70	71	278	61,250
	Billy Mayfair	70	73	67	68	278	61,250
17	Thongchai Jaidee	70	70	66	73	279	50,000
	Robert Karlsson	66	72	69	72	279	50,000
	Tracy Phillips	69	68	70	72	279	50,000
20	Paul Broadhurst	72	69	71	68	280	35,167
	Bob Estes	64	76	70	70	280	35,167
	Ricardo Gonzalez	69	72	67	72	280	35,167
	Padraig Harrington	68	70	68	74	280	35,167
	Tim Herron	71	71	69	69	280	35,167
	Thomas Levet	67	73	67	73	280	35,167
	Tim Petrovic	69	70	70	71	280	35,167
	Gene Sauers	67	73	66	74	280	35,167
	Charlie Wi	70	73	67	70	280	35,167
29	Woody Austin	67	72	70	72	281	24,250
	Chris DiMarco	67	74	69	71	281	24,250
	Jerry Kelly	69	72	70	70	281	24,250
	Kevin Sutherland	68	71	70	72	281	24,250
33	Retief Goosen	71	74	69	68	282	19,500
	Scott McCarron	68	66	74	74	282	19,500
	Duffy Waldorf	66	74	69	73	282	19,500
	YE Yang	71	71	69	71	282	19,500

37	Michael Allen	68	73	70	72	283	17,000
38	Olin Browne	70	74	71	69	284	16,000
39	Paul Claxton	65	77	73	70	285	13,500
	Glen Day	69	75	72	69	285	13,500
	Jeff Maggert	71	72	70	72	285	13,500
	Rod Pampling	69	68	75	73	285	13,500
43	Thomas Goegele	72	72	76	66	286	9,014
	James Kingston	69	71	73	73	286	9,014
	Tom Lehman	72	71	71	72	286	9,014
	Shaun Micheel	70	68	75	73	286	9,014
	Dicky Pride	67	77	73	69	286	9,014
	Paul Stankowski	70	71	72	73	286	9,014
	Tim Weinhart	73	70	71	72	286	9,014
50	Roger Chapman	70	75	70	72	287	6,920
	Joakim Haeggman	67	74	70	76	287	6,920
	Stephen Leaney	70	75	74	68	287	6,920
	David McKenzie	71	74	70	72	287	6,920
	Omar Uresti	72	70	75	70	287	6,920
55	Michael Campbell	71	70	74	73	288	6,400
	Joe Durant	70	74	75	69	288	6,400
	Peter Fowler	70	72	72	74	288	6,400
	David Frost	73	72	73	70	288	6,400
	Kirk Triplett	70	75	72	71	288	6,400
60	Phillip Price	71	72	73	73	289	6,100
61	Corey Pavin	73	72	73	72	290	5,950
	Brett Quigley	71	73	76	70	290	5,950
63	Gary Wolstenholme	69	74	73	75	291	5,800
64	Harrison Frazar	71	74	73	74	292	5,650
	Jay Haas	72	71	75	74	292	5,650
66	Tim Fleming	71	74	71	77	293	5,475
	Neal Lancaster	74	71	76	72	293	5,475
	Scott Parel	71	74	80	68	293	5,475
	Jeff Sluman	70	73	75	75	293	5,475
70	Stephen Dodd	68	72	80	75	295	5,325
	Bob Sowards	68	74	78	75	295	5,325
72	Billy Andrade	72	72	76	77	297	5,250

Principal Charity Classic

Talk about keeping it in the "family". The week before Steve Stricker was to host the American Family Insurance Championship in which Jerry Kelly sought a third successive victory, so Kelly claimed the Principal Charity Classic courtesy of a putting lesson from ... Stricker.

Kelly and Stricker have been celebrating together since competing at junior level in Wisconsin where they both live now as neighbours in Madison. This win, however, was extra special because as Kelly explained his wife Carol — great friends with Stricker's wife Nicki — had been handling the effects of kidney cancer. "I had to miss Carol's treatments that are going on right now and I wanted to give her something to be happy about," explained Kelly. "Then she gave me the best present possible by having such clean scans on Friday afternoon. Big chills right now — Carol and my son Cooper are the ones that make me stay strong out here even when I'm not strong."

The key to Kelly's triumph in a playoff against Kirk Triplett, seeking a wire-to-wire win, was half-an-hour on the practice putting green with great friend Stricker. "It was a case of getting the set-up again that Steve always wants me to have and it just felt awesome," said Kelly. "I could stroke it down the line and the ball had such a great roll ... the way I used to putt. The stroke felt good all week."

Triplett, aged 60, like Kelly seeking a ninth Champions win and his first since 2019, opened with a nine-under, bogey-free 63 which he described as "a miracle — I haven't shot a low score in a long time!" Triplett, two ahead of Brett Quigley, Ken Tanigawa and Kelly, shot a second-round 68 for a 13-under-par 131, matching his second lowest 36-hole score on the PGA Tour Champions, to stay top of the leaderboard alongside Steve Alker, who played the four par fives in five under for a 64, Kelly and Quigley.

Kelly, who went 65-66 for the first two days, admitted he feared Alker — "the way he's playing you certainly can't let him skate away early" — although it was the dogged Triplett who refused to falter. After a rain delay, he birdied the 16th, but Kelly demonstrated his resilience, not to mention that putting touch, with a birdie two at the short 17th to match Triplett's closing 67 as they tied on 18-under 198, then at the first extra hole he made a four-foot putt for his first win for 357 days.

Wakonda Club, Des Moines, Iowa — June 3-5
Par 72 (36-36); 6,851 yards — Purse: $1,850,000

1	**Jerry Kelly**	65	66	67	198	$277,500
2	**Kirk Triplett**	63	68	67	198	162,800
	Kelly won playoff at first extra hole					
3	**Steven Alker**	67	64	69	200	122,100
	Bernhard Langer	66	66	68	200	122,100
5	Brett Quigley	65	66	70	201	88,800
6	Paul Goydos	68	69	65	202	70,300
	Brandt Jobe	68	67	67	202	70,300
8	Steve Stricker	69	67	67	203	55,500
	Kevin Sutherland	71	65	67	203	55,500
10	Thongchai Jaidee	70	68	66	204	46,250
	Dicky Pride	68	68	68	204	46,250
12	Stephen Ames	71	67	67	205	36,538
	Fred Couples	67	69	69	205	36,538
	Jay Haas	70	69	66	205	36,538
	Ken Tanigawa	65	71	69	205	36,538

16	Stuart Appleby	66 70 70	206	30,525		Ernie Els	70 69 68	207	21,534
	Steve Flesch	69 67 70	206	30,525		Harrison Frazar	72 68 67	207	21,534
18	Doug Barron	69 68 70	207	21,534		Tom Gillis	70 68 69	207	21,534
	David Branshaw	70 68 69	207	21,534		Tim Herron	72 68 67	207	21,534
	Darren Clarke	71 67 69	207	21,534		Mark Walker	68 69 70	207	21,534
	Stephen Dodd	70 71 66	207	21,534		Willie Wood	71 69 67	207	21,534

American Family Insurance Championship

What a weekend for golf! Sweden's Linn Grant became the first female winner on the DP World Tour in the Volvo Car Scandinavian Mixed; Rory McIlroy successfully defended for the first time on the PGA Tour in the RBC Canadian Open; Canadian Brooke Henderson won the ShopRite LPGA Classic on the LPGA Tour; South Africa's Charl Schwartzel captured the inaugural LIV Golf Invitational in England; and Thongchai Jaidee became the first player from Thailand to win on the PGA Tour Champions.

Jaidee, aged 52, closed with a 68 at University Ridge, home course of the University of Wisconsin, to edge out Tom Pernice Jr by one shot. It was also Jaidee's first win on American soil on his 19th career start on the PGA Tour Champions. Pernice fired a superb bogey-free closing 66 while Jerry Kelly, close friend and Madison neighbour of tournament host Steve Stricker, came within a whisker of making history himself. He was chasing a third successive win in this tournament but after a third-round 67 he settled for a share of third place with Marco Dawson, Kirk Triplett and Miguel Angel Jimenez, who led with Jaidee after 36 holes.

Jubilant Jaidee, who earned his place in the tournament with a top-10 finish the previous week, is now exempt on the over-50 circuit through to the end of 2023. "I'm really very happy," he said. "You can't expect to win — sometimes everything has to be perfect. The confidence in my putting helped a lot."

Jaidee, who was in the Thai army and trained as a paratrooper before turning professional aged 30, has made a habit of winning although this was his first since the Open de France in 2016 and his 21st success worldwide including eight on the DP World Tour. Nevertheless, this was a gutsy triumph because, following a first-round pacesetting 65 by Steve Flesch, Jaidee shot a similar score on the second day to join Jimenez in the lead, but appeared to be facing disaster in the final round when at the 16th his ball ricocheted off a tree never to be seen again. A five-iron fourth shot from 215 yards to 25 feet from where he holed for bogey brought calm and a birdie at the short 17th followed by a par at the last sealed the deal on 14-under-par 202.

Pernice, magnanimous in defeat, said: "Thongchai had a little bad break at 16 so to battle back as he did, he deserved to win."

University Ridge Golf Course, Madison, Wisconsin — June 10-12
Par 72 (36-36); 7,083 yards — Purse: $2,400,000

1	**Thongchai Jaidee**	69 65 68	202	$360,000		Alex Cejka	71 68 69	208	38,434
2	**Tom Pernice Jr**	68 69 66	203	211,200		Scott McCarron	74 66 68	208	38,434
3	**Marco Dawson**	71 66 67	204	131,400		David Branshaw	70 66 72	208	38,434
	Miguel Angel Jimenez	66 68 70	204	131,400		Tim Herron	68 69 71	208	38,434
	Jerry Kelly	68 69 67	204	131,400		Colin Montgomerie	66 70 72	208	38,434
	Kirk Triplett	68 68 68	204	131,400	21	Joe Durant	70 70 69	209	27,240
7	Paul Broadhurst	69 66 70	205	86,400		Rocco Mediate	72 70 67	209	27,240
8	John Daly	71 66 69	206	68,800		Dicky Pride	72 69 68	209	27,240
	Paul Goydos	68 67 71	206	68,800		Fran Quinn	70 68 71	209	27,240
	Robert Karlsson	69 68 69	206	68,800	25	Cameron Beckman	74 68 68	210	21,400
11	Doug Barron	70 67 70	207	52,800		Rob Labritz	69 70 71	210	21,400
	Steve Flesch	65 70 72	207	52,800		Jeff Maggert	69 68 73	210	21,400
	Steve Stricker	71 69 67	207	52,800		Corey Pavin	74 69 67	210	21,400
14	Stephen Ames	71 70 67	208	38,434		Paul Stankowski	70 70 70	210	21,400
	Woody Austin	72 70 66	208	38,434		Duffy Waldorf	70 68 72	210	21,400

US Senior Open

Padraig Harrington, the 2021 European Ryder Cup captain, was well aware that sooner or later he would cross swords again with Steve Stricker following the "Walloping at Whistling Straits" where his American counterpart celebrated a record 19-9 victory. What Harrington could not have imagined was that in his pursuit of a first senior major he would be hunted every inch of the way during a titanic final round by the formidably tenacious Stricker, whose willpower examined the Irishman's character to the absolute limit.

The setting was the Old course at Saucon Valley Country Club in Bethlehem, Pennsylvania — less than 1,000 miles virtually due east of Stricker's home state of Wisconsin where the Ryder Cup had unfolded. Harrington, who won three majors prior to turning 50 on 31 August 2021, would need to call on all the skill and strength of character which enabled him to win back-to-back Claret Jugs in 2007 and 2008 to set up a winning opportunity on the Herbert Strong-designed course on which Larry Laoretti and Hale Irwin previously won US Senior Opens in 1992 and 2000 respectively.

There was a hint of irony in that, too, because for Laoretti it marked the only PGA Tour success of his career and for Irwin a second US Senior Open victory on the pathway to a record 45 wins on the PGA Tour Champions. Now Harrington was seeking his first success in his new surroundings and in so doing hoping to light the blue touch paper to, perhaps, one day challenging Irwin's remarkable total. Three runner-up finishes in his last six tournaments indicated that Harrington's game was in the groove and on first sight the Old course, set up to play to a little under 7,000 yards with a par of 71, heightened his confidence for the challenge ahead.

"It was a much stronger test than I expected," explained Harrington. "Way tougher than regular Champions Tour events. I knew this was a big advantage to me, both length-wise and playing from the rough." Nevertheless it was another 50-year-old, Mark Hensby, who shared the first-round lead on 67 with 68-year-old Jay Haas, who for the seventh time on the Champions Tour shot his age or better. This was Haas's 17th US Senior Open appearance, with a best finish of tied third in 2004. Stricker, naturally, was lurking one shot back, alongside Paul Broadhurst, Rocco Mediate and Tim Petrovic, with Harrington off the pace after a 71 which was matched by defending champion Jim Furyk. Harrington, however, had gone out in the morning when heavy rain made life difficult; 10 of the 11 golfers who broke par were in the afternoon wave.

All changed on day two with the temperature rising from the 60s to the 80s and Harrington warming to the challenge with a wonderful 65 which gave him the outright lead for the first time after any round on the Champions Tour. He even overcame a broken driver during the warm-up with six birdies in a bogey-free round which took him one ahead of Stricker (69). "We're halfway home," said Stricker. "It's a jammed-up leaderboard; it's going to take some great golf to come out on top."

So now Harrington and Stricker would look each other in the eyes in round three 278 days on from the last day at Whistling Straits. This time Harrington's own ball did all the talking. He laced a five-wood from 263 yards to six feet for an eagle at 12 and with birdies at three of the last six holes completed a 66 to sweep five shots ahead of Gene Sauers (68) and Rob Labritz (69), who shared second two in front of Ernie Els. Stricker struggled but showed resilience with three closing birdies for a 73 to be eight back, but against all the odds he would in the final round appear in Harrington's rear view mirror.

The American closed the front nine with two birdies, started the back nine with two more at 12 and 14 and frustratingly missed 10-foot chances at the next two. But a tee shot to one foot for a tap-in two at 17 and a 155-yard nine-iron approach to six feet for another birdie at the last gave him a 65 which left Harrington needing to par the last three to hoist the Francis D Ouimet Memorial Trophy and join Arnold Palmer, Gary Player, Lee Trevino and Jack Nicklaus as the only multiple winners of the Open Championship to also win the US Senior Open. He successfully two-putted from 30 feet above the ridge at 16, from 50 feet at 17 by holing a clutch five-footer and from 35 feet across a spine at 18.

"It's special because I've never won a USGA event," said Harrington, whose 72 left him on 10-under-par 274 and one ahead of Stricker. "It's added something to my career." A gracious Stricker confessed: "Hats off to Padraig. He was the better player this week."

Saucon Valley Country Club (Old), Bethlehem, Pennsylvania — June 23-26
Par 71 (36-35); 7,028 yards — Purse: $4,000,000

1	**Padraig Harrington**	71	65	66	72	274	$720,000
2	**Steve Stricker**	68	69	73	65	275	432,000
3	**Mark Hensby**	67	73	71	69	280	267,254
4	Thongchai Jaidee	70	69	72	70	281	160,576
	Rob Labritz	69	69	69	74	281	160,576
	Gene Sauers	72	67	68	74	281	160,576
7	Paul Broadhurst	68	74	70	70	282	107,603
	Jay Haas	67	72	71	72	282	107,603
	Miguel Angel Jimenez	79	64	70	69	282	107,603
	Jerry Kelly	72	71	72	67	282	107,603
11	Steven Alker	72	67	71	73	283	81,554
	David Toms	72	70	69	72	283	81,554
13	Alex Cejka	71	69	71	73	284	65,380
	Ernie Els	72	70	67	75	284	65,380
	Steve Flesch	73	69	73	69	284	65,380
	Rod Pampling	73	70	70	71	284	65,380
17	Doug Barron	72	68	71	74	285	55,333
18	Ken Duke	73	72	68	73	286	44,537
	Brian Gay	72	73	69	72	286	44,537
	Retief Goosen	71	71	75	69	286	44,537
	Rocco Mediate	68	71	74	73	286	44,537
	Ken Tanigawa	75	68	69	74	286	44,537
	YE Yang	74	72	67	73	286	44,537
24	Tracy Phillips	72	69	74	72	287	34,960
25	Stuart Appleby	76	69	71	72	288	31,089
	Markus Brier	71	71	71	75	288	31,089
	Jim Furyk	71	76	66	75	288	31,089
28	Bob Estes	76	71	71	71	289	25,878
	John Huston	72	70	73	74	289	25,878
	Colin Montgomerie	75	71	70	73	289	25,878
	Scott Parel	72	75	70	72	289	25,878
	Kevin Sutherland	72	72	70	75	289	25,878
33	Glen Day	70	74	75	71	290	19,072
	Paul Goydos	69	76	74	71	290	19,072
	Lee Janzen	74	72	72	72	290	19,072
	Davis Love III	76	68	71	75	290	19,072
	Jeff Schmid	75	70	73	72	290	19,072
	Vijay Singh	75	70	72	73	290	19,072
	Jeff Sluman	72	75	71	72	290	19,072
	Charlie Wi	75	69	73	73	290	19,072
41	Cameron Beckman	73	71	71	76	291	12,602
	Jeff Brehaut	75	67	73	76	291	12,602
	Tom Gillis	74	71	73	73	291	12,602
	Andrew Johnson	76	70	74	71	291	12,602
	Robert Karlsson	71	74	74	72	291	12,602
	Michael Muehr	71	73	78	69	291	12,602
	Mark O'Meara	75	72	70	74	291	12,602
	Tim Petrovic	68	75	75	73	291	12,602
49	Richard Green	71	71	73	77	292	9,403
	Scott McCarron	75	72	73	72	292	9,403
51	John Senden	73	72	72	76	293	8,861
	Scott Verplank	74	72	73	74	293	8,861
53	Wes Short Jr	70	73	74	77	294	8,559
	Willie Wood	74	72	74	74	294	8,559
55	Clark Dennis	73	70	77	75	295	8,358
	Phillip Price	74	73	73	75	295	8,358
	Omar Uresti	75	69	74	77	295	8,358
58	James Kingston	71	76	76	73	296	8,157
	Bob May	76	70	77	73	296	8,157
60	Alan McLean	73	73	74	77	297	8,036
61	Jeff Gove	71	76	74	77	298	7,956
62	Gavin Coles	74	73	77	75	299	7,876
63	Peter Baker	74	73	74	79	300	7,795
64	Craig Thomas	74	71	77	84	306	7,717

Bridgestone Senior Players Championship

If it were not for the fact that they are great golfers then you would be forgiven for believing that in another world Madison close neighbours Jerry Kelly and Steve Stricker would have been centre stage as a double act entertaining an altogether different audience similar to Hope and Crosby, Laurel and Hardy, Morecambe and Wise.

On Firestone's famed South course, however, they achieved what they have always done best since growing up together by going head-to-head down the stretch with Kelly eventually prevailing and Stricker confessing: "I was looking to come out on top of this — it's not really what I had in mind."

Kelly, of course, was full of the joys of spring, even if this was mid-summer with the temperature soaring into the high 80s, because by winning the Bridgestone Senior Players Championship for a second time in three years he also earned a place in the 2023 Players Championship. "The first major is awesome but the second brings even more validation," Kelly said. "I'm really excited to go back to Sawgrass for the Players next March. That was a big piece of the desire in winning this tournament. That's one of the great things that we have with our majors that we can get to go play at the high point of golf."

Without question Firestone — this year marked the club's 69th consecutive year of professional golf tournaments initiated by The Rubber City Open in 1954 — has become the perfect stage on which the Kelly and Stricker show has captured the headlines. Kelly won in 2020 – he was also fourth in 2018 – and Stricker pushed Kelly into second place in 2021 ahead of Kelly reversing the one-two in this year's production to win by three shots on 11-under-par 269.

Stricker made an inauspicious start with a level-par 70 whereas Kelly's 67 left him trailing pacesetting Czech-born German Alex Cejka by three. Both Cejka's Champions wins have been majors and his blemish-free 64 put him in contention for another. He retained a share of the lead at halfway with

Charles Schwab Cup leader Steve Alker, who shot a bogey-free 66, Joe Durant (65) and Tim Petrovic (66). "I kind of kept my nose clean," Alker said. "I scrambled nicely."

Stricker's 65 gave him impetus although his third-round 68 left him in a tie for third with Alker (69) as Kelly made his move with a 65 to join Cejka in the lead. "My putter was better today," said Kelly after six birdies and a bogey. Cejka birdied four of his last five for a 67. "Frustrating start with two silly bogeys," said Cejka. "Great finish."

Cejka, however, became part of the supporting cast with a closing 73 as the spotlight fell on Kelly and Stricker. It was touch and go as to who would be playing the starring role as they matched 68s, but Kelly claimed the plaudits with a birdie at 13 and another from 15 feet at the par-five 16th — Stricker had shown him the line — proved the winning act. Stricker provided the final review: "Jerry made the putts when he had to coming down the stretch and, vice versa, I didn't."

Firestone Country Club (South), Akron, Ohio — July 7-10
Par 70 (35-35); 7,248 yards — Purse: $3,000,000

1	**Jerry Kelly**	67	69	65	68	269	$450,000
2	**Steve Stricker**	70	65	68	68	271	264,000
3	**Steven Alker**	68	66	69	69	272	198,000
	Ernie Els	67	68	69	68	272	198,000
5	Stephen Ames	70	71	68	65	274	116,750
	Woody Austin	69	66	71	68	274	116,750
	Alex Cejka	64	70	67	73	274	116,750
	Ken Duke	70	66	72	66	274	116,750
9	David Toms	66	69	70	70	275	84,000
10	Marco Dawson	69	68	68	71	276	78,000
11	Miguel Angel Jimenez	68	68	76	65	277	59,833
	Rod Pampling	73	64	72	68	277	59,833
	KJ Choi	71	69	65	72	277	59,833
	Rob Labritz	70	68	67	72	277	59,833
	Tim Petrovic	68	66	73	70	277	59,833
	Wes Short Jr	71	69	69	68	277	59,833
17	Thongchai Jaidee	71	73	68	66	278	45,000
	Rocco Mediate	68	69	72	69	278	45,000
	YE Yang	70	70	70	68	278	45,000
20	Shane Bertsch	68	70	68	73	279	38,400
	Paul Goydos	69	70	70	70	279	38,400
22	Paul Broadhurst	73	68	71	68	280	33,100
	John Huston	71	69	69	71	280	33,100
	Scott Parel	71	69	72	68	280	33,100
25	Bernhard Langer	72	72	68	69	281	26,667
	Colin Montgomerie	71	70	70	70	281	26,667
	Gene Sauers	74	70	69	68	281	26,667
	Mike Weir	70	68	75	68	281	26,667
	Cameron Beckman	68	73	65	75	281	26,667
	Brandt Jobe	72	70	69	70	281	26,667
31	Michael Allen	69	69	71	73	282	21,150
	Brian Gay	71	74	68	69	282	21,150
	Lee Janzen	70	72	72	68	282	21,150
	Vijay Singh	70	70	69	73	282	21,150
35	Tom Byrum	71	69	71	72	283	18,000
	Joe Durant	69	65	74	75	283	18,000
	Retief Goosen	72	69	68	74	283	18,000
38	Darren Clarke	70	70	72	72	284	15,000
	Glen Day	73	72	71	68	284	15,000
	Bob Estes	68	68	74	74	284	15,000
	Davis Love III	71	66	75	72	284	15,000
	Brett Quigley	71	72	71	70	284	15,000
	Paul Stankowski	76	69	70	69	284	15,000
44	Scott Dunlap	73	75	68	69	285	11,700
	Steve Flesch	72	71	71	71	285	11,700
	Tim Herron	70	68	73	74	285	11,700
	Dicky Pride	71	71	71	72	285	11,700
	Kevin Sutherland	71	70	71	73	285	11,700
49	Ken Tanigawa	72	73	68	73	286	9,900
50	Doug Barron	76	71	68	72	287	8,160
	David McKenzie	76	70	73	68	287	8,160
	Tom Pernice Jr	72	69	75	71	287	8,160
	Duffy Waldorf	70	74	72	71	287	8,160
	Mark Walker	73	68	74	72	287	8,160
55	Kent Jones	74	72	72	70	288	6,600
	Scott McCarron	72	73	73	70	288	6,600
	John Senden	69	74	69	76	288	6,600
58	Billy Andrade	74	73	72	70	289	6,000
59	David Duval	72	69	77	72	290	5,550
	David Frost	75	72	69	74	290	5,550
61	Carlos Franco	71	76	70	74	291	4,800
	Justin Leonard	73	77	70	71	291	4,800
	Corey Pavin	74	75	70	72	291	4,800
64	Jay Haas	70	75	73	74	292	4,200
65	Jeff Maggert	72	76	74	71	293	3,900
66	Mark Hensby	74	72	71	77	294	3,300
	Jesper Parnevik	74	74	68	78	294	3,300
	Joey Sindelar	72	73	74	75	294	3,300
69	Tom Gillis	68	75	73	79	295	2,730
	Billy Mayfair	75	76	72	72	295	2,730
71	David Branshaw	73	73	76	74	296	2,280
	Olin Browne	74	75	75	72	296	2,280
	Fred Funk	75	76	71	74	296	2,280
74	Chris DiMarco	73	74	74	76	297	1,980
75	Kirk Triplett	75	72	77	76	300	1,860
76	Robert Allenby	78	77	76	70	301	1,740
77	Dan Forsman	76	78	79	69	302	1,600
78	Frank Lickliter II	74	80	79	83	316	1,500

Shaw Charity Classic

One by one they challenged Jerry Kelly but at the close of a pulsating afternoon in Calgary only John Huston was capable of matching the score of the 55-year-old from Madison, Wisconsin, as no fewer than five players came up one shot shy. It was, quite simply, a shoot-out in the sunshine as Joe Durant stormed from out of the pack with a sensational 62, one shot outside the Canyon Meadows course record, to initially set the target on eight under with Alex Cejka, Padraig Harrington and Dean Wilson, who all shot 66s, joining him on that mark as did Kirk Triplett with a frustrating 69.

Triplett looked in the mood from the first round when with a 65 he latched on to pacesetting Harrington, who completed a 64 with a long putt for eagle at his last hole as thunderous cheers echoed around the green. The next day Triplett, 10 years older than rookie Harrington, outscored the Irishman by four shots with a 68. At seven under he led by one from Paul Goydos and Kelly and by two from Vijay Singh with Harrington a further shot back tied with Cejka, Huston and Wilson. "This is an exciting opportunity for me to go out and try to win a tournament," said Triplett. Kelly, who progressed with two birdies on each side for a 66, countered: "I wanted to be in the final group. I want to see what's going on. I love being in that atmosphere."

As it happens much of what was going on was happening ahead of him as Durant charged, Cejka, Harrington and Wilson all threatened and Huston set the target at nine-under 201 with a 65. For Florida-based Huston, the winner of seven PGA Tour titles, this was his return to the limelight as his only win on the PGA Tour Champions came in 2011 in the Dick's Sporting Goods Open in only his third appearance after turning 50. Indeed, it seemed that victory might be his when Triplett's four-foot birdie putt at the 585-yard 18th lost speed and lipped out, and Kelly ran his 15 foot putt for birdie four feet past.

Kelly, however, holed out for par and a 67 to tie, then holed for birdie from a similar distance at the first extra hole for his third win of the season. "I love coming to Canada," said Kelly. "To get a win here is something I've always wanted to do." Huston said: "I'm happy the way I played – I haven't played good for a long time. The two worst putts I hit all day were at the last hole in regulation and in the playoff."

Canyon Meadows Golf & Country Club, Calgary, Alberta, Canada — August 5-7
Par 70 (35-35); 7,086 yards — Purse: $2,350,000

1	**Jerry Kelly**	68	66	67	201	$352,500
2	**John Huston**	67	69	65	201	206,800
	Kelly won playoff at first extra hole					
3	**Alex Cejka**	68	68	66	202	120,320
	Joe Durant	70	70	62	202	120,320
	Padraig Harrington	64	72	66	202	120,320
	Kirk Triplett	65	68	69	202	120,320
	Dean Wilson	69	67	66	202	120,320
8	Shane Bertsch	68	69	66	203	70,500
	Marco Dawson	70	70	63	203	70,500
10	Paul Goydos	66	68	70	204	58,750
	Tim Herron	68	70	66	204	58,750
12	Doug Barron	70	68	67	205	46,413
	KJ Choi	71	69	65	205	46,413
	Miguel Angel Jimenez	70	71	64	205	46,413
	Charlie Wi	69	71	65	205	46,413
16	Mark Hensby	68	71	67	206	37,600
	Thongchai Jaidee	68	71	67	206	37,600
	Mario Tiziani	72	66	68	206	37,600
19	Harrison Frazar	69	71	67	207	30,139
	Colin Montgomerie	71	69	67	207	30,139
	Mark O'Meara	73	67	67	207	30,139
	Brett Quigley	71	68	68	207	30,139
23	John Daly	73	68	67	208	20,637
	Steve Flesch	71	70	67	208	20,637
	Mark Walker	72	68	68	208	20,637
	Stephen Ames	69	73	66	208	20,637
	Paul Broadhurst	70	73	65	208	20,637
	Matt Gogel	67	72	69	208	20,637
	Mike Goodes	71	71	66	208	20,637
	Robert Karlsson	66	73	69	208	20,637
	Alan McLean	68	70	70	208	20,637
	Shaun Micheel	71	68	69	208	20,637
	Kevin Sutherland	72	65	71	208	20,637

Boeing Classic

You really had to tip your cap to Miguel Angel Jimenez with the way he once again raised his game, this time in the shadows of the Cascade Mountains, with a performance which typically smacked of class and character. The Spaniard started slower than he hoped, but he played the last 45 holes on the Jack Nicklaus-sculptured course without a blemish, gathering 14 birdies. In fact, the modest Jimenez even impressed himself. "I felt confident with my game," he said. "I felt good from the tee. I felt good with every club in the bag. I played very solid. Very, very solid."

Initially KJ Choi, courtesy of closing his round birdie-eagle-birdie, shared the first-round lead on 67 with Scott Dunlap, Billy Mayfair, Scott McCarron and Tim Petrovic — the most numbers of players tied for the lead after 18 holes this season. Jimenez's opening 70 left him three shots off the pace but all that changed with a fabulous second round of 64 which took him into a share of the lead with Billy Andrade (66), two ahead of Stephen Ames (68), Choi (69) and Gene Sauers, who also shot 64. "Moving day like people say!" said Jimenez. "And we are moving. Bogey free. Very consistent." Andrade matched his low 18-hole score of the season, igniting the prospect following his win in 2015 of following Bernhard Langer (2010, 2016) and Tom Kite (2006, 2008) as a multi-winner of the Boeing Classic, not to mention ending a six-year winless streak.

Those targets disappeared as Jimenez gathered five birdies in the first 12 holes — he parred the last six — of a third-round 67 to finish on 15-under-par 201 and win by two from David McKenzie, the third alternate, whose bogey-free 66 for second place enabled him to match his best finish on tour (runner-up in the 2019 SAS Championship). Ames closed with a 69 to catch Andrade (71) in third, one ahead of Steven Alker (69), although the only hope any of them held of challenging Jimenez — McKenzie actually closed to within one with a birdie at 12 — was when the Spaniard tugged his tee shot at the short 13th. "The only shot I missed in two and a half rounds," said Jimenez. "Very important to save par with a chip to two feet."

The Club at Snoqualmie Ridge, Snoqualmie, Washington — August 12-14
Par 72 (36-36); 7,217 yards — Purse: $2,200,000

1	**Miguel Angel Jimenez**	70	64	67	201		$330,000
2	**David McKenzie**	73	64	66	203		193,600
3	**Stephen Ames**	68	68	69	205		145,200
	Billy Andrade	68	66	71	205		145,200
5	Steven Alker	69	68	69	206		105,600
6	Jerry Kelly	70	69	68	207		88,000
7	Joe Durant	74	63	71	208		79,200
8	Brett Quigley	72	73	64	209		55,733
	David Toms	71	71	67	209		55,733
	Ken Duke	72	68	69	209		55,733
	Thongchai Jaidee	71	68	70	209		55,733
	Rod Pampling	71	70	68	209		55,733
	Gene Sauers	72	64	73	209		55,733
14	KJ Choi	67	69	74	210		39,600
	Padraig Harrington	70	69	71	210		39,600
	Mike Weir	71	68	71	210		39,600
17	Alex Cejka	75	66	70	211		32,065
	Darren Clarke	71	66	74	211		32,065
	Paul Goydos	72	70	69	211		32,065
	John Huston	69	69	73	211		32,065
21	Paul Broadhurst	69	73	70	212		25,025
	Tim Herron	69	72	71	212		25,025
	Brandt Jobe	68	72	72	212		25,025
	Steve Stricker	68	72	72	212		25,025
25	Lee Janzen	73	72	68	213		20,973
	Scott Parel	74	67	72	213		20,973
	Tim Petrovic	67	71	75	213		20,973

Dick's Sporting Goods Open

The news of the passing of Tom Weiskopf, aged 79, filtered amongst the players in the village setting of Endicott some three hours north west of New York City and five hours east of where in 1996 Weiskopf won the last of his 28 professional titles by capturing the Pittsburgh Senior Classic. His CV included, of course, the Open Championship in 1973 though, frustratingly, he finished runner-up no fewer than four times at Augusta National. So it was something of a coincidence that on the day that he died — August 20 — two Masters champions, Mike Weir and Vijay Singh, were jostling for the Dick's Sporting Goods Open title in company with Open champions Ernie Els and Padraig Harrington.

Singh, who started birdie-birdie-eagle, had shared the first round lead on 65 with two other major champions, Darren Clarke and Jim Furyk, returning from an extended break triggered by Covid. "I still don't have a ton of energy," he said. "It's the first time I've ridden a cart in competition." Nevertheless, he packed eight birdies, including a clean sweep of the four par fives, into his round, while Clarke also notched eight birdies with a pair of twos on the back nine.

Weir won the Green Jacket in 2003 since when he had captured only three titles with the last being his maiden PGA Tour Champions win in the 2021 Insperity Classic. The Canadian recorded birdies on seven of eight consecutive holes in a second-round 65 to edge one in front of Harrington (67) and three ahead of Els (68) and Singh (70), with Furyk (71) next on the leaderboard alongside Gene Sauers and Tom Pernice Jr. Harrington, however, began his third round with birdies at the second and the third and he collected three more in bogey-free 67 which catapulted him to 16-under 200 and three clear of Thongchai Jaidee, who eagled the 16th in a 66, and Weir (71), with Furyk (68) and Singh (69) joint fourth.

Harrington said: "Unusually for me there was no drama. Normally, I create some coming home. The greens were awesome. I committed to giving my putts a run all week and I holed my fair share. The golf course suited me. I'm excited to get another win and honestly I've never been more confident with my game. I feel like I've got an advantage with increased power and that feeds into my irons and wedges which are absolutely solid."

En-Joie Golf Club, Endicott, New York — August 19-21
Par 72 (37-35); 6,994 yards — Purse: $2,100,000

1	**Padraig Harrington**	66	67	67	200	$315,000
2	**Thongchai Jaidee**	70	67	66	203	168,000
	Mike Weir	67	65	71	203	168,000
4	Jim Furyk	65	71	68	204	113,400
	Vijay Singh	65	70	69	204	113,400
6	Darren Clarke	65	72	69	206	71,400
	Bernhard Langer	71	67	68	206	71,400
	Gene Sauers	69	67	70	206	71,400
	Ken Tanigawa	69	69	68	206	71,400
10	Shane Bertsch	68	69	70	207	46,620
	Alex Cejka	68	70	69	207	46,620
	Miguel Angel Jimenez	72	69	66	207	46,620
	Brandt Jobe	67	74	66	207	46,620
	Tom Pernice Jr	68	68	71	207	46,620
15	Stuart Appleby	68	70	70	208	29,937
	Ken Duke	70	69	69	208	29,937
	Steve Flesch	69	70	69	208	29,937
	Rocco Mediate	70	69	69	208	29,937
	Scott Parel	70	70	68	208	29,937
	Duffy Waldorf	66	75	67	208	29,937
	Paul Broadhurst	68	69	71	208	29,937
	Ernie Els	67	68	73	208	29,937
	Scott McCarron	68	69	71	208	29,937
24	Doug Barron	69	68	72	209	20,528
	John Daly	72	67	70	209	20,528
	Colin Montgomerie	72	71	66	209	20,528
	Tim Petrovic	73	67	69	209	20,528

Ally Challenge

With an outstretched arm pointing skywards 66-year-old Fred Funk joyously continued a career of proving age is no barrier. His 65 for a one-shot first-round lead over Stephen Ames, Woody Austin and Brett Quigley enabled him to break his age for the first time in competition. "Really cool," Funk said. "I've always wanted to do it out here. A magical day. Pretty amazing because I cannot remember when I last shot a round in the 60s!"

Funk did not win on the PGA Tour until he was 37, was the oldest winner of the Players Championship at 48 in 2005, and two years later at the Mayakoba Golf Classic became the fifth oldest champion in PGA Tour history. Now, after nine Champions wins, Funk was staring at the possibility of becoming the oldest winner on the over-50s circuit.

The prospect of that happening rather disintegrated with a second-round 75 — he would fight back on the third day to finish tied 13th — as Scott Dunlap, aged 59, birdied five of his last six holes for a 63 to set the 36-hole pace at 11 under par with Padraig Harrington (66), Steve Stricker (64) and Quigley (68) one back. Dunlap, whose only previous win on the circuit came in the 2014 Boeing Classic, confessed on this his 171st start: "You never know when something like this is going to happen. But what a joy ... nowadays it's just a case of taking it one day at a time. A little putter change helped."

There would be no birthday celebrations for Bernhard Langer — he turned 65 on the Saturday — as Stricker, benefiting from a putting tip from Jerry Kelly, birdied four holes in a row from the 13th for a 67 to surge to his second win of the season albeit by only one shot in the end from Quigley, who finished eagle-birdie-birdie for a 68. Jeff Maggert sliced through the field with a best-of-the-day 65 for third place, one in front of Dunlap and Harrington. Stricker, however, lifted the trophy one week after caddieing for daughter Bobbi in 100 degrees as she advanced through the first stage of LPGA Qualifying at Mission Hills. "Caddieing for Bobbi was cool, to be part of what she did, seeing the enjoyment and excitement on her face, well, that means a lot to a dad."

One week on he had plenty to celebrate again!

Warwick Hills Golf & Country Club, Grand Blanc, Michigan — August 26-28
Par 72 (36-36); 7,085 yards — Purse: $2,000,000

1	**Steve Stricker**	70	64	67	201	$300,000
2	**Brett Quigley**	66	68	68	202	176,000
3	**Jeff Maggert**	68	70	65	203	144,000
4	Scott Dunlap	70	63	71	204	108,000
	Padraig Harrington	68	66	70	204	108,000
6	Stephen Ames	66	69	70	205	72,000
	Ernie Els	68	67	70	205	72,000
	Rod Pampling	69	68	68	205	72,000
9	Steven Alker	68	68	70	206	54,000
	John Huston	71	68	67	206	54,000
11	Shane Bertsch	68	68	71	207	46,000
	Paul Broadhurst	69	71	67	207	46,000
13	Fred Funk	65	75	68	208	38,000
	Jim Furyk	69	70	69	208	38,000
	David Toms	69	67	72	208	38,000
16	Woody Austin	66	71	72	209	28,371
	Ken Duke	68	70	71	209	28,371
	Joe Durant	69	67	73	209	28,371
	Kent Jones	68	70	71	209	28,371
	Jerry Kelly	70	70	69	209	28,371
	Mario Tiziani	69	68	72	209	28,371
	Duffy Waldorf	69	66	74	209	28,371
23	David Frost	68	74	68	210	20,040
	Lee Janzen	68	75	67	210	20,040
	Rocco Mediate	69	72	69	210	20,040
	Gene Sauers	73	71	66	210	20,040
	Paul Stankowski	69	70	71	210	20,040

Ascension Charity Classic

In a city obsessed by Albert Pujols of the St Louis Cardinals seeking to reach 700 career home runs, Bernhard Langer momentarily moved the focus to another milestone in his pursuit of Hale Irwin's record 45 PGA Tour Champions wins. But Padraig Harrington showed there was little ragged about his rhythm in the city of blues, jazz and ragtime as the Irishman swung his way to his third win of the season, emulating at that time Steven Alker, Jerry Kelly and Miguel Angel Jimenez, and edged closer to Charles Schwab Cup leader Alker.

It was quite like old times from a European Tour standpoint when on the first day Harrington and Langer shared the first-round lead after 65s, with Ernie Els and Jose Maria Olazabal among those one shot behind. Langer, targeting a 44th triumph, shot his age for the second time this season and confessed: "It's fun to be in that position to have a chance to maybe catch Hale. It's not going to be easy but 10 years ago I didn't think it was easy and five years ago I didn't think it was easy and it's still not easy! Hopefully there's a couple more left in the tank."

Langer's prospects remained high with a second-round 67 on the day when Pujols swatted his 696th Major League baseball home run, but Harrington, who celebrated his 51st birthday 10 days earlier, followed his six birdies in round one with another eight in a 66. On 11 under par he led by one from Steve Stricker, who shot 65, and Langer. "It's nice to be the leader," said Harrington. "Traditionally, my whole career I've always been a much better player with my back to the wall. Now I'm finding here on the PGA Tour Champions I'm having to learn how to play when I'm favoured, when I'm out in front, when I'm leading."

Harrington swiftly asserted himself in the final round with birdies at the second and the third, then gave back those gains with a double bogey at the short fourth, before after birdies at the fifth, eighth and ninth, turning two ahead of Stricker. Harrington drove the green at the 300-yard 11th for another birdie and held on despite bogeys at 16 and 18. "Maybe I was looking at the victory speech a little too much," he quipped. A 68 left Harrington on 14-under 199, while YE Yang, with a hat-trick of birdies from 13, overhauled Stricker, who parred his last 13 holes, for second place.

Norwood Hills Country Club (West), St. Louis, Missouri — September 9-11
Par 71 (36-35); 6,992 yards — Purse: $2,000,000

1	**Padraig Harrington**	65	66	68	199	$300,000
2	**YE Yang**	68	66	66	200	176,000
3	**Steve Stricker**	67	65	69	201	144,000
4	Bernhard Langer	65	67	70	202	120,000
5	Steven Alker	66	68	69	203	73,600
	Clark Dennis	68	68	67	203	73,600
	Ernie Els	66	69	68	203	73,600
	Bob Estes	68	67	68	203	73,600
	John Huston	67	66	70	203	73,600
10	Doug Barron	67	68	69	204	50,000
	Kirk Triplett	68	68	68	204	50,000
12	Marco Dawson	71	67	67	205	39,500
	Brandt Jobe	70	66	69	205	39,500
	Scott McCarron	69	71	65	205	39,500
	Tom Pernice Jr	69	66	70	205	39,500
16	Robert Karlsson	67	70	69	206	32,000

	Kevin Sutherland	70	70	66	206	32,000
	David Toms	69	68	69	206	32,000
19	Paul Broadhurst	68	72	67	207	24,920
	Ken Duke	68	69	70	207	24,920
	Joe Durant	67	70	70	207	24,920
	Harrison Frazar	69	69	69	207	24,920
	Justin Leonard	69	69	69	207	24,920
24	Woody Austin	70	71	67	208	19,120
	Darren Clarke	68	67	73	208	19,120
	Chris DiMarco	71	67	70	208	19,120
	Scott Dunlap	69	70	69	208	19,120
	Steve Flesch	66	70	72	208	19,120

Sanford International

Steve Stricker could have been forgiven for not being totally focused on the Sanford International given that he was an assistant to Davis Love III for the Presidents Cup the following week. But, instead, the latest winning American Ryder Cup captain cemented his 10th PGA Tour Champions victory with a stunning pair of 64s over the weekend which rubber-stamped his recovery from the debilitating illness which hospitalised him following his team's victory over Europe at Whistling Straits.

Whether the discussions with Love and fellow assistant Fred Couples concerning the coming match at Quail Hollow were dancing on his mind during an opening 68 are unknown, but Stricker found himself trailing by six shots. Robert Karlsson waltzed to a 62, his lowest round on the Champions Tour, finishing with three straight birdies for identical halves of 31. Perfect weather conditions provided a birdiefest on a course softened by rain 24 hours earlier and no fewer than 51 golfers broke par. Karlsson said: "A fantastic day to play golf. In fact, I've had a couple of good days here before — I really enjoy the people in Sioux Falls."

Jeff Maggert notched five wins including the US Senior Open in his first 19 months on the PGA Tour Champions although with only one win in the last seven years his second round 66 to share the lead on 10 under with Karlsson (68) provided a timely revival for the 58-year-old Texas-based golfer. "The key? Staying patient," Maggert said. "I've been watching my son play a lot of golf lately, we've been feeding off each other and he won his last tournament. I'm kind of learning off him right now."

Stricker, however, had swept into contention with a 64 on Saturday — "I made a few bombs out there with two putts on five and seven totalling 100 feet" — vaulting 32 places up the leaderboard. That second successive 64 on Sunday put him into a tie at 14-under 196 and he sealed the deal with a birdie at the first extra hole to overcome Karlsson. "I was nervous all the way round," admitted Stricker. "I knew I couldn't give any shots away. Make birdies, but no mistakes. I didn't want to mess-up." Then he headed for the airport and Charlotte with Couples and Love, with much to celebrate but also still plenty on his mind.

Minnehaha Country Club, Sioux Falls, South Dakota — September 16-18
Par 70 (34-36); 6,729 yards — Purse: $2,000,000

1	**Steve Stricker**	68	64	64	196	$300,000
2	**Robert Karlsson**	62	68	66	196	176,000
	Stricker won playoff at first extra hole					
3	**Ernie Els**	64	68	66	198	144,000
4	Brandt Jobe	66	69	64	199	98,667
	Paul Stankowski	67	65	67	199	98,667
	Jeff Maggert	64	66	69	199	98,667
7	Steve Flesch	64	68	68	200	61,000
	Thongchai Jaidee	67	65	68	200	61,000
	Miguel Angel Jimenez	66	68	66	200	61,000
	YE Yang	67	67	66	200	61,000
11	Darren Clarke	63	70	68	201	41,200
	Ken Duke	69	65	67	201	41,200
	Padraig Harrington	66	67	68	201	41,200
	Kevin Sutherland	63	71	67	201	41,200
	David Toms	67	68	66	201	41,200
16	Stuart Appleby	71	66	65	202	30,120
	Alex Cejka	66	69	67	202	30,120
	Jerry Kelly	70	69	63	202	30,120
	Scott McCarron	68	68	66	202	30,120
	Dicky Pride	66	67	69	202	30,120
21	Olin Browne	67	69	67	203	21,667
	Harrison Frazar	70	67	66	203	21,667
	Rob Labritz	67	68	68	203	21,667
	Bernhard Langer	64	70	69	203	21,667
	Rocco Mediate	64	67	72	203	21,667
	Tom Pernice Jr	67	66	70	203	21,667

Pure Insurance Championship

Like waiting for a London bus and finding two coming along together, Steve Flesch once went three years without winning on the PGA Tour and then did so twice in 49 days. On the Champions circuit, the 55-year-old from Cincinnati had waited since his maiden victory in 2018, then added to his Mitsubishi Electric Classic win in May with another 140 days later at the Pure Insurance Championship.

A hard-fought triumph by one shot from Ernie Els, Steven Alker and Paul Stankowski began for Flesch with a 66 at Spyglass Hill that tied the lead of Chris DiMarco and Timothy O'Neal, both of whom played at Pebble Beach, with DiMarco covering the back nine in 29. Flesch said: "Always good to get Spyglass out of the way because it's just hard. Not to say Pebble Beach isn't tough, but Spyglass is definitely the harder of the two."

At Spyglass the next day both O'Neal (73) and DiMarco (74) retreated, perhaps giving some credence to Flesch's course comparison, although Flesch himself found scoring more difficult at Pebble. A 71 left him one behind Stankowski, who hit all 14 fairways for a 67 at Spyglass to share the pacesetting with Ken Duke. Stankowski, a native of Oxnard 300 miles south of Pebble on the Californian coast, was also inspired by a sharp short game while Duke posted a 69 at Pebble courtesy of late birdies at 13, 14 and 18.

Els garnered eight birdies in a closing 64 for the field's lowest score of the week. In truth, Flesch set the pace on Sunday with birdies at his first four holes, catapulting him into the lead. After another at the seventh, two bogeys on the back nine allowed the charging Alker (69) to get into pole position. But the New Zealander tugged his tee shot at the short 17th for bogey to fall back into a tie with Els and Flesch. Stankowski (70) also ended up at 10 under, but Flesch struck a superb wedge at the 18th to seven feet, from where he holed for the title.

"It meant so much to me because it's the dream of all professionals to win at Pebble Beach," said Flesch, whose closing 68 put him on 11-under 205. "I hung in there all day. You don't get many opportunities to win." Maybe not but thinking back to those London buses, this was Flesch's ticket to ride.

Pebble Beach Golf Links, Monterey Peninsula, California — September 23-25
Par 72 (36-36); 6,864 yards — Purse: $2,200,000
Spyglass Hill Golf Course (R1&2) par 72 (36-36); 7,003 yards

1	**Steve Flesch**	66	71	68	205	$330,000
2	**Ernie Els**	74	68	64	206	161,333
	Steven Alker	68	69	69	206	161,333
	Paul Stankowski	69	67	70	206	161,333
5	Brian Gay	69	71	67	207	96,800
	Brett Quigley	68	70	69	207	96,800
7	Mario Tiziani	71	70	67	208	70,400
	Rod Pampling	69	70	69	208	70,400
	Ken Duke	67	69	72	208	70,400
10	Thongchai Jaidee	71	72	66	209	57,200
11	Mark Hensby	71	73	66	210	52,800
12	Kirk Triplett	73	70	68	211	39,829
	Doug Barron	70	73	68	211	39,829
	John Huston	71	71	69	211	39,829
	YE Yang	69	71	71	211	39,829
	Paul Goydos	74	72	65	211	39,829
	Lee Janzen	68	70	73	211	39,829
	Charlie Wi	71	67	73	211	39,829
19	Jerry Kelly	73	70	69	212	22,614
	Paul Broadhurst	73	71	68	212	22,614
	Tim Herron	74	70	68	212	22,614
	Rob Labritz	72	71	69	212	22,614
	Joe Durant	73	71	68	212	22,614
	Kevin Sutherland	73	70	69	212	22,614
	Rocco Mediate	68	74	70	212	22,614
	Shane Bertsch	73	68	71	212	22,614
	Marco Dawson	73	72	67	212	22,614
	Harrison Frazar	69	72	71	212	22,614
	Chris DiMarco	66	74	72	212	22,614
	Timothy O'Neal	66	73	73	212	22,614
	Michael Allen	73	74	65	212	22,614

Constellation Furyk & Friends

Steve Stricker won the PGA Tour's Comeback Player of the Year title in both 2006 and 2007, but surely those awards pale into insignificance when compared with his resurgence following a six-month "sabbatical" sprung on him by a mystery ailment. At firm and fast Timuquana Country Club, he broke a five-way tie for most victories this season by winning his fourth by two shots from Monday qualifier Harrison Frazar and by three from tournament host Jim Furyk.

Then, casually as you like, he hung out the "Gone Hunting" sign, most probably leaving Steven Alker and Padraig Harrington to duel for the Charles Schwab Cup, by heading for his beloved Wisconsin woods to follow his passion to hunt white tail deer.

Who could blame Stricker? His recovery from what appeared a life-threatening illness had been nothing less than a dream. Here he was winning for the third time in his last four events with a remarkable sequence of 11 successive rounds in the 60s contributing to a scoring average over that run of 67.

At the event that benefits northeast Florida charities through the Jim & Tabitha Furyk Foundation, Furyk shared the first-round lead by matching the 67s of Pebble Beach winner Steve Flesch and Rob Labritz. After an opening 69, Stricker played his final six holes of the second round in five under for a tournament record eight-under-par 64 and a three-shot lead ahead of Mike Weir, who shot a second successive 68, and Furyk (69). Stricker gave his rivals little cause for hope as he reeled off 46 consecutive bogey-free holes before carding one at his last hole in a closing 69 for a 14-under-par total of 202, which Frazar (65) came closest to reaching following four birdies in his first five holes.

Stricker said: "I didn't make a mistake until the last shot out of the fairway and at that point I figured it was all over. It was a good day, I did all the things I was supposed to do. I think the last month or so I feel like I'm showing better signs. I've been fortunate enough to play a long time, but I still feel like hunting is my passion. There's only really a month of good hunting so I hate to miss this month. It's unfortunate the playoffs are right in that time frame." One suspects Frazar and Furyk wished Stricker had hung out that "Gone Hunting" sign one week earlier.

Timuquana Country Club, Jacksonville, Florida — October 7-9
Par 72 (36-36); 6,949 yards — Purse: $2,000,000

1	**Steve Stricker**	69	64	69	202	$300,000
2	**Harrison Frazar**	71	68	65	204	176,000
3	**Jim Furyk**	67	69	69	205	144,000
4	Thongchai Jaidee	72	65	69	206	108,000
	Bernhard Langer	70	68	68	206	108,000
6	Padraig Harrington	69	69	69	207	80,000
7	Lee Janzen	69	68	71	208	64,000
	Jerry Kelly	70	69	69	208	64,000
	Davis Love III	72	68	68	208	64,000
10	Jay Haas	71	72	67	210	46,000
	Miguel Angel Jimenez	69	72	69	210	46,000
	Rob Labritz	67	71	72	210	46,000
	Gene Sauers	69	71	70	210	46,000
14	Ken Duke	70	68	73	211	34,000
	Bob Estes	71	73	67	211	34,000
	Justin Leonard	75	67	69	211	34,000
	Mario Tiziani	70	71	70	211	34,000
	Mike Weir	68	68	75	211	34,000
19	Doug Barron	69	72	71	212	24,113
	Brett Quigley	69	73	70	212	24,113
	John Daly	71	70	71	212	24,113
	Steve Flesch	67	71	74	212	24,113
	Robert Karlsson	70	70	72	212	24,113
	Ken Tanigawa	68	72	72	212	24,113
25	Stephen Ames	75	70	68	213	18,240
	Ernie Els	73	71	69	213	18,240
	Colin Montgomerie	73	71	69	213	18,240
	Tom Pernice Jr	71	71	71	213	18,240
	YE Yang	74	71	68	213	18,240

SAS Championship

This is all about a 63-year-old golfer pricelessly proving that age is no barrier as, with the 64th professional win at all levels of his illustrious career, Fred Couples "shot the best round I have ever played" with a blistering closing 12-under-par 60 enabling him to capture the SAS Championship, the 24th and final event of the 2022 regular season.

In 2,172 rounds on the PGA Tour and 420 on the Champions Tour, Couples's previous lowest score was a 61 compiled in the 2014 Shaw Charity Classic. He closed the front nine at Prestonwood Country Club with five consecutive birdies and the second nine with seven straight birdies — he played both halves in 30 — to seal his 14th Champions victory by six shots from Charles Schwab Cup leader Steven Alker, in addition to setting a new course record.

Alker, who closed with a 64 to increase his advantage over Padraig Harrington at the top of the standings heading into the playoffs, led the chorus of congratulations for Couples, who finished at 20-under-par 196. Alker said: "What a performance by Freddie. Absolutely fantastic! Insane!"

It all started with a double bogey at his first hole of the week as a 68 put Couples three behind Rocco Mediate. Seeking to end a winless streak of 1,939 days stretching back to the 2017 Family Insurance

Championship, he then shot another 68 to share the lead with YE Yang. A glorious Sunday afternoon in North Carolina was all about the 1992 Masters champion, playing only his eighth event of the season. Couples birdied 12 of his last 14 holes and at 63 years and 13 days became the fourth oldest winner in Champions Tour history. His 60 was the lowest third-round score in the 43-year history of the circuit.

Couples declared: "It was unreal. It's a funky game and today was just one of those days where, honestly, everything got in the way, starting with the hole. Everyone thinks they can win out here; today was my day. My game is trending in the right direction, but this year my back has been so bad I couldn't play until Augusta. And I shouldn't have played there. So now I'll take a month off and hit some balls later in the year."

With that Couples put his clubs away and became a fan headed for the baseball fields. Prior to the tournament, when regular caddie Mark Chaney stayed back home to be with his mother, he needed a fill-in bagman and texted Griffin Flesch, son of fellow Champions Tour player Steve Flesch: "Get to Raleigh on Tuesday and we'll have a good time." They did!

Prestonwood Country Club, Cary, North Carolina — October 14-16
Par 72 (35-37); 7,237 yards — Purse: $2,100,000

1	**Fred Couples**	68	68	60	196	$315,000
2	**Steven Alker**	72	66	64	202	184,800
3	**Jerry Kelly**	68	69	67	204	151,200
4	Rocco Mediate	65	72	68	205	126,000
5	Alex Cejka	70	69	67	206	92,000
	Miguel Angel Jimenez	71	69	66	206	92,000
7	Stephen Ames	72	71	64	207	67,133
	Stuart Appleby	70	69	68	207	67,133
	Colin Montgomerie	68	70	69	207	67,133
10	Ernie Els	71	69	68	208	50,400
	Scott McCarron	68	69	71	208	50,400
	Scott Parel	69	72	67	208	50,400
13	Scott Dunlap	68	72	69	209	39,900
	Jim Furyk	69	69	71	209	39,900
	YE Yang	66	70	73	209	39,900
16	Ken Duke	72	67	71	210	32,603
	Thongchai Jaidee	68	71	71	210	32,603
	Robert Karlsson	68	75	67	210	32,603
	Paul Stankowski	70	68	72	210	32,603
20	Steve Flesch	68	70	73	211	24,654
	Harrison Frazar	70	73	68	211	24,654
	Tom Gillis	67	71	73	211	24,654
	Bernhard Langer	69	69	73	211	24,654
	Corey Pavin	70	70	71	211	24,654
25	Billy Andrade	70	71	71	212	19,152
	Padraig Harrington	70	73	69	212	19,152
	Dicky Pride	71	70	71	212	19,152
	Vijay Singh	70	72	70	212	19,152
	Ken Tanigawa	70	71	71	212	19,152

Dominion Energy Charity Classic

Steve Alker captured three PGA Tour Champions titles in the space of 56 emotion-packed days in April and May, but he waited 147 days to snare his fourth win of the season on the celebrated James River course at The Country Club of Virginia. Alker started the final round two shots behind and sealed victory in the first of three Charles Schwab Cup Playoff events with three birdies in the last four holes.

Alker accurately described a final day when he would increase his lead over Padraig Harrington in the Charles Schwab Cup standings as "something of a dog fight". Jerry Kelly, fourth in the standings, set out on an overcast, drizzly day with that two-shot advantage over Alker, with Harrington and Doug Barron one shot further back. There was little change after nine holes with Kelly and Alker both covering them in level par, but the 10th triggered a swing in fortune with Alker making a birdie to Kelly's bogey. "That freed me up a little," confessed Alker. "It relaxed me. I had struggled on seven, eight and nine."

Nevertheless, Kelly edged back in front by one before Alker, who would miss only two fairways and hit 16 of 18 greens in regulation, pressed the pedal to the metal. First he birdied the 15th — at that point he was tied for the lead with Kelly, Harrington and KJ Choi — then, with the assistance of a silky putter, the 16th and 17th. That changed the landscape so that with a closing 68 he resisted the challenge of Choi, who birdied two of his last three holes for a 67, by one shot on 14-under 202, with Kelly (72) and Harrington (69) sharing third with Barron (69).

"I was trying not to look at the leaderboard because there were so many guys seeking to win the tournament," explained Alker. "Making those clutch birdies at 15 and 16 and especially 17 was huge. It was exciting, nerve-racking but I putted well so it turned out nicely." Kelly, who held the first and second round leads outright, was to an extent a victim of the changing conditions — the temperature dipped into the low 60s with a challenging northerly wind — and Harrington required six birdies to offset three bogeys. Alker found lifting the trophy more of a struggle than winning it, allowing the glass top to clatter to the ground, though happily it remained intact.

The Country Club of Virginia (James River), Richmond, Virginia — October 21-23
Par 72 (36-36); 7,025 yards — Purse: $2,200,000

1	**Steven Alker**	69	65	68	202	$335,000
2	**KJ Choi**	71	65	67	203	194,000
3	**Doug Barron**	68	67	69	204	132,200
	Padraig Harrington	68	67	69	204	132,200
	Jerry Kelly	65	67	72	204	132,200
6	Ernie Els	68	70	67	205	83,850
	Brian Gay	72	64	69	205	83,850
8	Rocco Mediate	71	71	64	206	63,533
	Rod Pampling	69	68	69	206	63,533
	Brett Quigley	69	70	67	206	63,533
11	Stephen Ames	69	68	70	207	48,400
	Jim Furyk	70	69	68	207	48,400
	Kevin Sutherland	69	70	68	207	48,400
14	Bernhard Langer	68	71	69	208	40,700
	David Toms	68	72	68	208	40,700
16	Paul Broadhurst	70	69	70	209	36,300
	Glen Day	67	72	70	209	36,300
18	Shane Bertsch	71	69	70	210	31,020
	Tom Gillis	68	70	72	210	31,020
	Wes Short Jr	70	70	70	210	31,020
21	Scott Parel	74	69	68	211	27,280
22	Stuart Appleby	74	65	73	212	20,702
	David Branshaw	69	70	73	212	20,702
	Scott Dunlap	73	68	71	212	20,702
	Paul Goydos	74	71	67	212	20,702
	Thongchai Jaidee	71	70	71	212	20,702
	Rob Labritz	68	68	76	212	20,702
	Gene Sauers	71	73	68	212	20,702
	Paul Stankowski	71	72	69	212	20,702
	Mario Tiziani	73	67	72	212	20,702
	YE Yang	70	71	71	212	20,702

TimberTech Championship

Bernhard Langer deserved to be headlined in every national paper and on every sports bulletin across the globe after romping to his third TimberTech Championship victory in Boca Raton where he lives with his wife Vikki. Langer recorded the 120th success of his remarkable career and his 44th on the PGA Tour Champions — one shy of Hale Irwin's all-time record.

What is more in once again defying Father Time Langer's second-round nine-under-par score bettered his age by two shots as he extended his own record as the oldest winner on the Champions circuit to 65 years, two months and 10 days. It was his 11th win since turning 60, the most in tour history.

All of which appeared improbable on the first day when, with three holes to play, Langer trailed by six shots. The German, however, birdied each of his last three holes for a 70 to be only three behind pacesetter Miguel Angel Jimenez. And then sounded a lively warning: "I actually hit the ball well, but I didn't make any putts."

Langer would "roll them in from all over the place" during a sensational second-round 63 to take a one-shot lead over Paul Goydos (66) with Rod Pampling (69) three shots further back. Unlike day one there was little wind, the temperature soared into the 80s and Langer notched 10 birdies while restricting himself to 21 putts. "I switched putters," he explained. "Same model, same everything but a little different blade, a little different look. I also just could see the line, feel the pace." It was the sixth time he had shot his age or better on the Champions Tour and the fourth time this season.

For the second successive day Langer carded the lowest score with his closing 66 coasting him home six ahead of Thongchai Jaidee, who sealed his fourth top-three finish of the season with a 67, and Goydos (71), with Padraig Harrington (67) one further back. An ecstatic Langer declared: "It's always awesome to win anywhere in the world, but to win in your home town in front of family and friends is that much more meaningful and special because I have a lot of supporters out there. It's great just to be at home, sleep in your own bed, get some home cooking. We travel all year all over the place so it's very nice to have a tournament at home."

Royal Palm Yacht & Country Club, Boca Raton, Florida — November 4-6
Par 72 (36-36); 7,015 yards — Purse: $2,200,000

1	**Bernhard Langer**	70	63	66	199	$350,000
2	**Paul Goydos**	68	66	71	205	187,500
	Thongchai Jaidee	70	68	67	205	187,500
4	Padraig Harrington	72	67	67	206	150,000
5	Kevin Sutherland	74	66	68	208	110,000
6	Steven Alker	70	68	71	209	84,010
	Robert Karlsson	69	73	67	209	84,010
8	Ken Duke	73	68	70	211	58,080
	John Huston	71	69	71	211	58,080
	Miguel Angel Jimenez	67	72	72	211	58,080
	Rod Pampling	68	69	74	211	58,080
	David Toms	70	70	71	211	58,080
13	Darren Clarke	72	66	74	212	41,800
	Marco Dawson	72	71	69	212	41,800
	Jim Furyk	71	70	71	212	41,800
16	Stephen Ames	70	68	75	213	29,529
	Billy Andrade	74	69	70	213	29,529
	Shane Bertsch	75	67	71	213	29,529
	Paul Broadhurst	70	73	70	213	29,529
	KJ Choi	70	73	70	213	29,529
	Scott Dunlap	73	69	71	213	29,529
	Jerry Kelly	71	71	71	213	29,529
	Colin Montgomerie	70	73	70	213	29,529
	Joe Durant	71	67	75	213	29,529
25	Paul Stankowski	71	72	71	214	22,000

Charles Schwab Cup Championship

In the end Padraig Harrington's admiration for Jack Nicklaus advertised his own affection for the game of golf. With a closing 65 he captured the Charles Schwab Cup Championship by equalling the 72-hole scoring record for the PGA Tour Champions of 27 under par. Nicklaus established that mark at the 1990 Kaulig Companies Championship and Harrington confessed: "Yeah, I didn't realise I'd done that. It's nice to hold the record with Jack Nicklaus. Kind of glad I didn't beat him."

Harrington, however, did more than beat the field in the 2022 season finale. He demolished them. He followed opening rounds of 66-64-62 with that 65 for a total of 257. You needed Lord Nelson's telescope to locate his vanquished rivals — with Alex Cejka and Steven Alker seven and eight shots back respectively. For Alker there was victory in defeat because, if Harrington won, he needed to finish in a two-way tie for fifth or better to clinch the season-long Charles Schwab Cup. His solo third earned for him the number one ranking ahead of Harrington, Jerry Kelly, Steve Stricker and Miguel Angel Jimenez.

"I came into the event knowing I had to win to give myself a chance of the Charles Schwab Cup," said Harrington. "That brings a certain amount of stress and focus. So I'm happy to go out and win the tournament from that position. It brings a bit of confidence going forward. It caps off a great year." Alker, paired with Harrington in the final round, said: "Playing with Padraig was kind of difficult. Do I chase? Do I protect? I just tried to play my game as good as I could, but he played amazing."

Initially Alker and Harrington, first and second in the standings, threatened to turn the event into a duel. Alker went 65-64 to lead by one. What transformed the tournament was Harrington firing his lowest round yet on the circuit. He set the third-round tempo by slotting home an eagle putt at the par-five opener and four straight birdies from the 11th propelled him to a sensational 62. In contrast, while Alker carded his third successive bogey-free round, he found putts difficult to make, settling for a 68. Even with a five-shot lead Harrington was experienced enough to know that there could still be twists and turns, but in taking his tournament birdie haul to 27 — one short of the tour record held by, you've guessed it, Nicklaus — he was able to saunter home.

Phoenix Country Club, Phoenix, Arizona — November 10-13
Par 71 (36-35); 6,860 yards — Purse: $2,500,000

1	**Padraig Harrington**	66	64	62	65	257	$440,000
2	**Alex Cejka**	68	68	63	65	264	250,000
3	**Steven Alker**	65	64	68	68	265	210,000
4	Lee Janzen	67	68	67	66	268	150,417
	Miguel Angel Jimenez	67	66	69	66	268	150,417
	Stephen Ames	65	68	68	67	268	150,417
7	Retief Goosen	68	64	68	70	270	100,000
8	Marco Dawson	68	67	67	69	271	81,250
	Jim Furyk	69	71	66	65	271	81,250
10	Brian Gay	67	65	66	74	272	65,000
11	Paul Broadhurst	68	67	68	70	273	62,500
12	Thongchai Jaidee	67	68	69	70	274	58,750
	Colin Montgomerie	68	66	68	72	274	58,750
14	Doug Barron	70	68	70	67	275	55,000
15	Rocco Mediate	71	67	72	66	276	51,250
	Scott Parel	69	67	71	69	276	51,250
17	John Huston	65	71	72	69	277	44,167
	Jerry Kelly	69	68	71	69	277	44,167
	Bernhard Langer	66	69	70	72	277	44,167
20	Darren Clarke	68	71	70	69	278	32,500
	Brett Quigley	69	68	69	72	278	32,500
22	Ken Duke	70	69	72	68	279	26,250
	Steve Flesch	71	71	65	72	279	26,250
24	Paul Goydos	72	65	74	69	280	23,750
25	Rod Pampling	68	71	70	72	281	22,500

2022 CHARLES SCHWAB CUP

		Points
1	Steven Alker	4,173,435
2	Padraig Harrington	4,015,455
3	Jerry Kelly	2,570,225
4	Steve Stricker	2,473,725
5	Miguel Angel Jimenez	2,461,086
6	Bernhard Langer	2,250,739
7	Thongchai Jaidee	1,903,005
8	Stephen Ames	1,816,071
9	Ernie Els	1,642,269
10	Alex Cejka	1,590,524

European Legends Tour

A single victory rarely brings year-end accolades to a player, but that was enough, allied with a consistently solid season, for James Kingston to claim the Order of Merit and John Jacobs Trophy on the 2022 Legends Tour.

Of course, the limited number of tournaments — 16, including two US majors, played between May and December — had a major bearing on that outcome. Only two men won more often than the 57-year-old South African. Paul Lawrie and Richard Green scored two wins apiece, but neither played a full schedule. Australian Green, a 51-year-old rookie, won the Jersey Legends and the Winston Golf Senior Open in playoffs during six starts early in the year, but didn't play again after the end of July. Lawrie, the 1999 Open champion from Scotland, only teed it up eight times, picking up victories in the two Farmfoods events, the Legends Links and Senior Masters, as well as losing in a playoff against Green in Jersey.

On the other hand, Kingston played in all except the year's opening tournament, had a pair of second-place finishes among seven other top 10s to go with his victory in the Swiss Seniors Open, his second on the Legends Tour and the 19th of his worldwide career. "To think all of this came down to the last tournament, the last round, the last few holes, unbelievable," remarked Kingston. "I am extremely proud of how consistently I have played this whole season, except for last week." His only finish higher than 17th place came in the penultimate event before he wrapped up the title with a runner-up finish in Mauritius.

Darren Clarke, the 2001 Open champion, added The Senior Open presented by Rolex to his splendid 27-win record. "Fulfilling your dreams is a very lucky thing," said the Northern Irishman after nosing out Padraig Harrington, the US Senior Open winner, with a brilliant two-putt on the final green at Gleneagles.

Order of Merit runner-up Adilson Da Silva won the Staysure PGA Seniors Championship, the Legends Tour's other major event in Europe, in a six-stroke runaway. He also won the newly renamed Barry Lane Rookie of the Year award. The Brazilian was one of the circuit's six first-time winners, joining Euan McIntosh, Ricardo Gonzales, Joakim Haeggman, Green and Clarke.

At the start of April, Stephen Dodd was confirmed as winner of the John Jacobs Trophy for 2021 when the MCB Tour Championship — Mauritius was abandoned due to adverse weather on the island. The season-closing event had already been postponed from the previous December due to Covid-19. Welshman Dodd had won The Senior Open at Sunningdale in 2021.

2022 SCHEDULE

MCB Tour Championship — Mauritius		*abandoned*
Riegler & Partner Legends	**Euan McIntosh**	
KitchenAid Senior PGA Championship	**Steven Alker (1,3)**	*See chapter 27*
Jersey Legends	**Richard Green**	
Farmfoods European Legends Links Championship	**Paul Lawrie**	
US Senior Open	**Padraig Harrington**	*See chapter 27*
Swiss Seniors Open	**James Kingston**	
Winston Golf Senior Open	**Richard Green (2)**	
The Senior Open Presented by Rolex	**Darren Clarke**	
JCB Championship	**Alex Cejka**	
Irish Legends	**Phillip Price**	
Staysure PGA Seniors Championship	**Adilson Da Silva**	
WCM Legends Open de France	**Gary Marks**	
Farmfoods European Senior Masters	**Paul Lawrie (2)**	
Italian Senior Open	**Ricardo Gonzalez**	
MCB Tour Championship — Seychelles	**Joakim Haeggman**	
MCB Tour Championship — Mauritius	**Thomas Bjorn**	

Riegler & Partner Legends

The Legends Tour finally got a tournament on the books in early May and a new face emerged as the winner. Originally, the Covid-postponed MCB Championship finale of the 2021 season was to have been played in April, but hazardous weather threatening the African venue on the Indian Ocean led to its cancellation.

Thus, the Riegler and Partner Legends at Murhof in Austria became the year's launchpad for the tour. The first-time winner, 53-year-old Scotsman Euan McIntosh, reached the Legends Tour in unusual fashion. A professional in his early career, McIntosh regained amateur status, feeling that was the best way to prepare for senior tour golf. It worked. He qualified for the Legends Tour in 2019 and became a winner three years later.

The victory didn't come easily. McIntosh shot a one-over-par 73 to finish with a 10-under-par total of 206 in the rain-interrupted final round, barely edging South African James Kingston, an 11-time winner on the Sunshine Tour and the 2021 Senior Italian Open champion, who closed with 67, by one stroke.

"I didn't play very well today," conceded McIntosh. "I was nervous from the start. Everything I tried to do just didn't seem to come off, but I was watching the scoreboard so I knew how to get it over the line."

He didn't make a bogey on the first two days, trailing the first-round leader, Brazilian Adilson Da Silva by four shots with his 69, then surging into a three-stroke lead the second day with an eight-birdie 64 to be 11 under. His closest pursuer then was Gary Wolstenholme, winless on the senior circuit since 2012. Kingston was five back on six under and nearly made up the difference Sunday.

Golf Club Murhof, Frohnleiten, Austria — May 6-8
Par 72 (36-36); 6,701 yards — Purse: €250,000

1	**Euan McIntosh**	69	64	73	206	€37,500
2	**James Kingston**	68	70	69	207	24,750
3	**Joakim Haeggman**	69	72	67	208	13,708
	Marc Farry	67	73	68	208	13,708
	Adilson Da Silva	65	73	70	208	13,708
6	Philip Golding	69	71	69	209	7,979
	Andrew Raitt	69	68	72	209	7,979
	Chris Williams	69	69	71	209	7,979
	Gary Wolstenholme	67	69	73	209	7,979
	Thomas Gogele	69	68	72	209	7,979
11	Magnus P Atlevi	70	72	68	210	5,218
	Mauricio Molina	73	67	70	210	5,218
	Juan Quiros	73	66	71	210	5,218
14	Steen Tinning	72	69	70	211	4,116
	Jean-Francois Remesy	68	72	71	211	4,116
	Timothy Thelen	72	69	70	211	4,116
	Phillip Price	70	70	71	211	4,116
18	Carl Suneson	71	70	71	212	3,260
	Mark Wharton	70	70	72	212	3,260
	Michael Jonzon	74	66	72	212	3,260

Jersey Legends

To nitpick, Richard Green didn't become one of the rare players to win in his or her first start on a recognised tour when he defeated Paul Lawrie in a playoff when the Jersey Legends and La Moye Golf Club returned to senior golf after a six-year hiatus. The 51-year-old Australian actually made his senior debut the week before in the United States in the KitchenAid Senior PGA Championship, which is a tournament on the Legends Tour schedule. He missed the cut in Michigan, but "when I came here, everything kind of fitted into place. I fell in love with La Moye and felt I could really play the golf course. The sequence of holes is beautiful and I was able to play really nicely."

His solid play started the first day, when he joined Lawrie and Phillip Price at 67 in a second-place tie behind Frenchman Christian Cevaer, 52, a two-time winner on the regular DP World Tour, who opened with a bogey-free 64. When Cevaer crashed to a 77 on Saturday, Welshman Price, the 2019 Staysure PGA Seniors champion, assumed the lead with another 67, with Green and Lawrie right on his heels with 68s.

Those two squeezed past Price on Sunday, shooting 71s to his 73 to set up the playoff at 10-under-par 206. Green and Lawrie, the 1999 Open champion, parred the first two playoff holes before Scot Lawrie overshot the green on the third extra hole and Green picked up the victory with his par.

Interestingly, the win gave Green victories in every decade since he turned pro in 1992, beginning with his win in the Dubai Desert Classic in 1997, followed by the BA-CA Open in 2007 and the Portugal Masters in 2010 on the DP World Tour, and the Mastercard Masters in 2004 and the Vic Open in 2015 on the Australasian Tour.

La Moye Golf Club, Jersey
Par 72 (36-36); 6,581 yards

June 10-12
Purse: €300,000

1	**Richard Green**	67	68	71	206	€45,000
2	**Paul Lawrie**	67	68	71	206	29,700
	Green won playoff at third extra hole					
3	**Euan McIntosh**	71	66	70	207	18,000
	Phillip Price	67	67	73	207	18,000
5	Adilson Da Silva	70	70	69	209	13,350
6	Michael Campbell	70	72	68	210	11,850
7	Gary Orr	70	72	69	211	10,050
	Paul Wesselingh	69	69	73	211	10,050
9	Ricardo Gonzalez	68	70	74	212	8,250
10	Markus Brier	73	72	68	213	7,350
	James Kingston	73	69	71	213	7,350
12	Joakim Haeggman	71	73	70	214	6,195
	Gary Wolstenholme	70	72	72	214	6,195
14	Peter Fowler	75	69	71	215	5,310
	Michael Jonzon	72	71	72	215	5,310
	Chris Williams	71	71	73	215	5,310
17	Paul Streeter	71	76	69	216	3,893
	Emanuele Canonica	74	72	70	216	3,893
	Jose Manuel Carriles	71	74	71	216	3,893
	Marc Farry	69	75	72	216	3,893
	Niclas Fasth	68	75	73	216	3,893
	Clark Dennis	71	72	73	216	3,893
	Michael Long	71	72	73	216	3,893
	Christian Cevaer	64	77	75	216	3,893

Farmfoods European Legends Links Championship

Paul Lawrie was honest. "I enjoy the other stuff" — his sports agency, golf centre, foundations involvements — "more than playing ... but when I get a chance to play on this tour I am going to play and if I am going to play, I don't want to play poorly." In fact, the 1999 Open champion played very well two straight weeks on the Legends Tour, reaching a playoff before losing to Richard Green in the Jersey Legends, then leading from wire-to-wire to post a three-stroke victory in the FarmFoods European Legends Links Championship at Trevose in Cornwall, England.

It was Lawrie's second senior victory, almost three years after winning the Scottish Senior Open during his first Legends Tour season in similarly windy conditions in the final round. Despite a double bogey, he shot an eight-under-par 64 the first day, but led only by a stroke over Frenchman Christian Cevaer. Miserable weather raked the second round. "It was a tough day out there. You're just trying to survive really," observed Lawrie, whose 71 established a two-shot lead over England's Paul Streeter (67-70).

Gusty weather prevailed on Sunday as Lawrie staked out a comfortable 70 for an 11-under-par total of 205 and a three-shot margin over fellow Scot Euan McIntosh, the Riegler & Partner Legends winner in May, who closed with a 69, a shot in front of Simon Brown. "Everyone's here to win this week," Lawrie commented. "Only one person can do so. It's nice to be that person."

Trevose Golf & Country Club, Constantine Bay, Cornwall
Par 72 (36-36); 7,045 yards

June 17-19
Purse: €250,000

1	**Paul Lawrie**	64	71	70	205	€50,000
2	**Euan McIntosh**	70	69	69	208	
3	**Simon P Brown**	70	70	69	209	
4	Paul Streeter	67	70	73	210	
5	Michael Jonzon	70	73	69	212	
	Gary Evans	69	73	70	212	
	Philip Golding	71	70	71	212	
	Stuart Little	68	71	73	212	
9	Phillip Archer	70	77	66	213	
	Ricardo Gonzalez	72	72	69	213	
	Chris Williams	68	72	73	213	
	Stephen Dodd	70	69	74	213	
13	Clark Dennis	71	74	69	214	
	James Kingston	69	76	69	214	
	Phillip Price	67	74	73	214	
	Christian Cevaer	65	73	76	214	
17	John Bickerton	70	74	71	215	
18	Peter Wilson	72	73	71	216	
	Carl Suneson	72	72	72	216	
	Paul Eales	68	74	74	216	

Swiss Seniors Open

James Kingston made it clear that he put a serious effort into his play on the Legends Tour after winning his second official victory in the Swiss Seniors Open. "We work all year to try and put ourselves in these positions," observed the 56-year-old South African. "This week I put in the hours. I did the work."

The work particularly paid off for Kingston in the second round at Bad Ragaz when he jumped into a two-stroke lead with a seven-under-par 63, as the first-round leader, Englishman Andrew Raitt (66-69), dropped back. Kingston, who sports a record of 17 wins on the Sunshine, Asia and European Tours in his younger days, was bogey-free for a second straight day in attaining the two-shot margin over former Legends winners Phillip Price and David Shacklady.

Kingston held onto the lead Sunday with an outgoing, one-under-par 35, followed with a birdie-bogey start on the back nine. He ran off solid pars on the next five holes and insured the victory when he holed a long birdie putt on the 17th hole. His final-round 68 for 11-under 199 gave him a three-stroke victory over Price and Shacklady, who both shot 69s. "Obviously delighted to be standing here as the champion," exclaimed Kingston after adding the Swiss title to his Italian Open and unofficial 36-hole Winston Golf Senior Open Invitational wins in 2021.

Golf Club Bad Ragaz, Bad Ragaz, Switzerland — July 8-10
Par 70 (35-35); 6,157 yards — Purse: €350,000

1	**James Kingston**	68	63	68	199	€52,290
2	**David Shacklady**	68	65	69	202	28,683
	Phillip Price	68	65	69	202	28,683
4	Mauricio Molina	69	65	69	203	18,760
5	Phillip Archer	72	66	66	204	13,837
	Steen Tinning	71	65	68	204	13,837
	Peter Baker	67	67	70	204	13,837
8	Philip Golding	70	67	68	205	10,238
	Mark Mouland	68	68	69	205	10,238
10	Jarmo Sandelin	68	73	65	206	7,866
	Ricardo Gonzalez	69	71	66	206	7,866
	Michael Long	71	67	68	206	7,866
	Markus Brier	68	68	70	206	7,866
14	Andre Bossert	74	69	64	207	6,335
	Stephen Dodd	73	64	70	207	6,335
16	Emanuele Canonica	72	69	67	208	4,769
	Joakim Haeggman	71	70	67	208	4,769
	Christian Cevaer	73	68	67	208	4,769
	Steven Richardson	69	71	68	208	4,769
	Carl Suneson	71	68	69	208	4,769
	Euan McIntosh	72	66	70	208	4,769
	Jose Coceres	70	68	70	208	4,769
	Miguel Angel Martin	67	69	72	208	4,769

Winston Golf Senior Open

Ageless Bernhard Langer returned to his homeland from America and the PGA Tour Champions to take another shot at winning the Winston Golf Senior Open and nearly pulled off the 120th professional victory of his splendid career.

The 64-year-old German shared the second-round lead with England's Gary Evans and South Africa's James Kingston at the Winston Golf course in Vorbeck, but neither he nor the others could hang on Sunday. Instead, senior rookie Richard Green became the first multiple winner on the 2022 Legends Tour, again via a playoff, when he defeated Englishman Phillip Archer on the fifth hole of sudden death. "On top of the world. It feels fantastic. I've not won twice in a season before. It's usually taken me a decade to get another win," exclaimed the 51-year-old Australian left-hander, who topped Paul Lawrie in overtime in the Jersey Legends in June to score his first senior win.

Another German, Sven Struver, nailed the first-round Winston lead with 67, a shot in front of Green and Spain's Carl Suneson, before plummeting down the standings with 79-75 rounds on the weekend. Green remained one stroke off the lead Saturday with his 68-70 postings, tied with Spain's Jose Manuel Carriles (71-69) behind Langer (70-69) and Kingston and Evans (both 69-70).

Of his chances Sunday, Langer cautioned: "It's not that there are just two or three of us. There are probably still eight or 10 of us in the hunt." He was right. Green, with 68, and Archer, with 67, emerged atop the board Sunday, tied at eight-under-par 208. Green and Archer matched pars as they played the 18th hole three times, and the 10th hole once, before the Aussie wedged to five feet back on the 18th and holed the birdie putt for the victory.

Winston Golf, Vorbeck, Germany — July 15-17
Par 72 (36-36); 6,810 yards — Purse: €350,000

1	**Richard Green**	68	72	68	208	€52,500
2	**Phillip Archer**	70	71	67	208	34,650
	Green won playoff at fifth extra hole					
3	**Jeev Milkha Singh**	70	73	67	210	21,000
	Gary Evans	69	70	71	210	21,000
5	Bernhard Langer	70	69	72	211	15,575
6	Magnus P Atlevi	70	74	68	212	13,125
	Simon P Brown	71	72	69	212	13,125
8	Christian Cevaer	70	75	68	213	8,709
	Euan McIntosh	74	71	68	213	8,709
	Andrew Raitt	74	70	69	213	8,709
	Peter Wilson	73	71	69	213	8,709
	Thomas Gogele	74	69	70	213	8,709
	James Kingston	69	70	74	213	8,709
14	Paul Wesselingh	72	74	68	214	5,368
	Charlie Wi	71	75	68	214	5,368
	Andrew Oldcorn	73	72	69	214	5,368
	Michael Long	70	74	70	214	5,368
	Carl Suneson	68	74	72	214	5,368
	Phillip Price	69	72	73	214	5,368
	Ricardo Gonzalez	75	68	71	214	5,368
	Jose Manuel Carriles	71	69	74	214	5,368

The Senior Open presented by Rolex

Darren Clarke's clutch finish and victory in The Senior Open presented by Rolex fulfilled a fervent desire: "I've made no secret of the fact that I wanted to win this more than anything," he said. What the genial 53-year-old Northern Irishman had in mind was to add the title to the Open Championship he won 11 years earlier at Royal St George's and join the elite company of Gary Player, Tom Watson and Bob Charles, the only other players to have accomplished that feat. "I am very privileged to get my name on the Claret Jug and to get my name on this one as well, and go beside some legends of the game," Clarke remarked after beating Padraig Harrington by one stroke. "I feel very humbled and very honoured."

Any devotee of the old adage "beware the injured golfer" listening to Clarke a couple of months before the Senior Open may well have taken the view that back in Britain at Gleneagles he was most probably worth a small investment at 66-1 to complete the notable double. At the KitchenAid Senior PGA Championship in late May, Clarke revealed: "All year I've been injured. Every week there's been something wrong with me ... my leg, my back, tendonitis, sore arm. It's been weird because I've gone through my whole career never being injured. I've never been an injured guy. But this year for whatever reason I've just been injured every week. It's been frustrating. I've had ice packs ... I've made surprise visits to the physio truck ... I've taken tablets."

Something worked as Clarke reversed his poor recent form — not a single top 10 on the season to date — just as he did in winning at St George's in 2011. And just as when he became, at 42, the oldest Open champion since 44-year-old Roberto de Vicenzo in 1967, he had a little help from a friend who happens to be one of the world's finest teachers, Pete Cowen. "I was very fortunate to spend some time with him on the range during The Open at St Andrews last week," said Clarke. "Pete helped me to win the main one and now he's helped me to win this one, too." It also helped knowing the King's course from the old days of the Scottish Open, in which Clarke finished fifth in 1994. "I played that tournament a few times," he explained. "And I learned where to hit it and where not to hit it. That was very beneficial. This is one of my favourite places to come and play."

The Northern Irishman clicked from the start on only his third Senior Open appearance — he needed 20, the most of any first time winner, to claim the Claret Jug — with a 65 to trail first-round pacesetters Simon Ames and Glen Day, with Paul Broadhurst, Kent Jones and Jerry Kelly matching his score, and Harrington one shot further back in a group which included Ernie Els. Day used a new set of clubs — his own failed to arrive from the United States — and he eagled the last, but he back-pedalled 24 hours later, whereas Clarke found four back-nine birdies for a 67 in which he demonstrated his course knowledge by playing away from those flags strategically positioned to create havoc for those tempted to fire at them. At halfway Clarke led by two from Scott Parel, but as the American retreated in round three, so Broadhurst, boosted by a hat-trick of birdies from the 13th, swooped with a 66 on an afternoon of heavy rain. Missing a six-foot birdie putt at 18 meant the 2016 champion would only share the lead with Clarke (69), who hit 17 greens in regulation, one ahead of Kelly and Steven Alker, the Kiwi with three wins already on the Champions Tour in 2022.

Harrington, like Clarke, had his own special incentive — he was seeking to complete a rare transatlantic double following his US Senior Open win. Following a near two-hour rain delay on Sunday he took advantage of the softened course by following a double bogey at nine with six birdies in a homeward 30 for a 67. Harrington finished at nine under, one ahead of a large group that included Broadhurst (71), Alker (70) and Els (68). This would eventually leave Clarke needing to two-putt from 100 feet for a birdie at the 18th to reach 10-under-par 270 with a closing 69 and avoid a playoff against Harrington. His first putt was a beauty leaving him one of less than two feet to write another chapter in golf's rich history and declare: "My speed on the greens was a little bit off throughout the week but I did the right thing at 18. When I've won some of my biggest tournaments I've had a sense of calmness and I had that this week. Fulfilling your dreams is a very lucky thing."

Gleneagles Hotel (King's), Auchterarder, Perthshire, Scotland — July 21-24
Par 70 (34-36); 6,859 yards — Purse: $2,500,000

1	**Darren Clarke**	65	67	69	69	270	$432,080
2	**Padraig Harrington**	66	69	69	67	271	288,200
3	**Steven Alker**	68	68	66	70	272	105,747
	Doug Barron	69	71	67	65	272	105,747
	Paul Broadhurst	65	70	66	71	272	105,747
	Ernie Els	66	69	69	68	272	105,747
	Thongchai Jaidee	66	71	67	68	272	105,747
	Mauricio Molina	68	69	70	65	272	105,747
9	Colin Montgomerie	70	66	68	69	273	58,080
10	Paul Lawrie	69	70	69	67	275	49,775
	YE Yang	73	65	68	69	275	49,775
12	Alex Cejka	70	73	64	69	276	41,003
	James Kingston	70	69	66	71	276	41,003
	Bernhard Langer	67	68	70	71	276	41,003
	Charlie Wi	73	66	67	70	276	41,003
16	Mark Brown	72	67	68	70	277	34,870
	Retief Goosen	70	69	70	68	277	34,870
	Simon Khan	66	72	70	69	277	34,870
19	Stuart Appleby	70	67	67	74	278	32,340
20	Stephen Ames	64	71	74	70	279	28,820
	Ken Duke	69	69	71	70	279	28,820
	Kent Jones	65	70	73	71	279	28,820
	Jerry Kelly	65	70	67	77	279	28,820
	Peter O'Malley	71	69	70	69	279	28,820
	Scott Parel	66	68	74	71	279	28,820
	Phillip Price	69	71	68	71	279	28,820
27	Clark Dennis	69	68	69	74	280	24,860
	Prayad Marksaeng	68	71	70	71	280	24,860
29	Carlos Franco	72	71	69	69	281	22,132
	Garry Houston	68	69	71	73	281	22,132
	Miguel Angel Jimenez	69	67	71	74	281	22,132
	Miguel Angel Martin	66	70	73	72	281	22,132
	Ian Woosnam	71	70	68	72	281	22,132
34	Thomas Bjorn	67	74	71	70	282	19,745
	Michael Watson	74	65	71	72	282	19,745
36	Marco Dawson	69	69	70	75	283	17,864
	Glen Day	64	72	77	70	283	17,864
	Harrison Frazar	69	73	69	72	283	17,864
	Tom Gillis	70	70	70	73	283	17,864
	Corey Pavin	69	69	71	74	283	17,864
41	Adilson Da Silva	69	70	71	74	284	15,143
	David Frost	67	68	77	72	284	15,143
	Richard Green	67	72	72	73	284	15,143
	Joakim Haeggman	71	71	74	68	284	15,143
	David Morland IV	71	69	69	75	284	15,143
	Andy Oldcorn	70	71	67	76	284	15,143
47	Woody Austin	70	73	67	75	285	12,210
	Stephen Dodd	69	72	71	73	285	12,210
	Cliff Kresge	72	70	70	73	285	12,210
	Paul McGinley	71	71	69	74	285	12,210
	John Senden	67	71	72	75	285	12,210
	Kirk Triplett	72	70	72	71	285	12,210
53	Markus Brier	67	72	73	74	286	9,735
	Greg Owen	69	72	71	74	286	9,735
	Dicky Pride	66	73	75	72	286	9,735
	Jean-Francois Remesy	69	70	73	74	286	9,735
	John Kemp (A)	73	69	67	77	286	
58	Russ Cochran	73	69	70	75	287	8,415
	Wes Short Jr	72	71	70	74	287	8,415
60	Andre Bossert	70	70	71	77	288	7,645
	Richard Dinsdale	72	71	70	75	288	7,645
	Trevor Foster (A)	71	71	73	73	288	
63	Andrew Butterfield	67	73	72	77	289	6,857
	Paul Streeter	70	71	72	76	289	6,857
	Yoshinobu Tsukada	70	73	72	74	289	6,857
66	Michael Campbell	71	70	72	77	290	6,270
67	Rafael Gomez	76	66	72	77	291	5,885
	Michael Jonzon	71	72	76	72	291	5,885
69	Thomas Levet	69	73	74	79	295	5,500
70	Scott Henderson	69	71	75	81	296	5,170
	Harry Rudolph	73	68	77	78	296	5,170

JCB Championship

For a change, Alex Cejka's win wasn't a major senior championship. Instead, the Czech-born German citizen, whose first two victories after turning 50 were the Tradition and the Senior PGA in America, made off with the JCB Championship, a new tournament on the Legends Tour in England.

The 51-year-old Cejka, whose last victory in Europe was 20 years earlier in the Lancome Trophy in France, had a lot of ground to make up after shooting 69 in the first round as South Africa's James Kingston was grinding out a course-record 62 — eight birdies and a chip-in eagle — at the JCB Golf and Country Club in Uttoxeter. Shooting for his second win of the season to go with his Swiss Senior

Open earlier in July, Kingston led India's Jeev Milkha Singh by two strokes and South Africa's Retief Goosen by four.

Things turned around Saturday as Cejka ran off four birdies and an eagle for 66 as Kingston shot 74 and fell a shot behind Cejka's nine-under lead. With 73, Singh was two back, a stroke in front of Goosen (72) and Paul McGinley, who, along with Senior Open champion Darren Clarke, were Cejka's closest pursuers Sunday.

Cejka never surrendered the lead on the last day, starting birdie-bogey-birdie. He added two more birdies, bogeyed the 13th and parred in for a 70 and an 11-under-par total of 205. McGinley, who was playing in just his second tournament of the year, compiled six birdies, but took three bogeys and posted a 69, to be two back in second place. Clarke (69), Goosen (70) and Kingston (72) were another stroke behind. "I'm super, super happy that I brought it home," Cejka said. "Any win is special no matter where it is on what continent. We had a strong field here. Look at the leaderboard, major champions and Hall-of-Famers right next to each other. It feels great."

JCB Golf & Country Club, Uttoxeter, England — July 28-31
Par 72 (36-36); 6,830 yards — Purse: €600,000

1	**Alex Cejka**	69	66	70	205	825.00
2	**Paul McGinley**	70	68	69	207	544.50
3	**Darren Clarke**	67	72	69	208	301.58
	Retief Goosen	66	72	70	208	301.58
	James Kingston	62	74	72	208	301.58
6	Paul Lawrie	69	71	69	209	206.26
	Vijay Singh	69	70	70	209	206.26
8	Colin Montgomerie	69	74	68	211	162.25
	Christian Cevaer	68	71	72	211	162.25
10	Thongchai Jaidee	71	69	72	212	119.90
	Jarmo Sandelin	73	67	72	212	119.90
	Phillip Price	69	70	73	212	119.90
	Markus Brier	69	70	73	212	119.90
	Mark James	73	66	73	212	119.90
15	Ernie Els	72	72	69	213	91.48
	David Shacklady	73	70	70	213	91.48
	Greg Owen	74	68	71	213	91.48
18	Joakim Haeggman	78	69	67	214	74.39
	Stephen Dodd	71	71	72	214	74.39
	Phillip Archer	74	68	72	214	74.39
	Jose Manuel Carriles	71	70	73	214	74.39

Irish Legends

Phillip Price drew special satisfaction from his survival victory in the Irish Legends a season after losing the title to Thomas Bjorn in a playoff. "I was disappointed last year not winning because I led going into the last day," said the 55-year-old Welshman. "Thomas played great shooting a 66, a worthy champion, but I probably felt I deserved this one."

Playing at Donegal's Rosapenna Hotel & Golf Resort in difficult weather conditions sweeping the Old Tom Morris Links off Sheephaven Bay, Price eked out a one-stroke victory over five other contenders with a 71 and 213 total, even par for the 54 holes. "Well, it was tough out there today," he remarked. "The course was really difficult. I think we were all struggling."

That was the case from the start as Denmark's Steen Tinning, nine years beyond his only two wins on the Legends Tour, led for two days. The 59-year-old mustered a 68 in the opening round — that was to be the lowest round of the week — to stand a shot in front of five others and maintained that margin the second day with a one-over-par 72. Price, tournament host Paul McGinley and Italy's Emanuele Canonica were on his heels.

The Welshman was erratic in the final round as a host of players scrambled for the lead. The 2019 Order of Merit champion cancelled three birdies with four bogeys over the first 14 holes, then birdied the 15th and parred in for the narrow win. Failing to force a playoff and finishing at 214: Sweden's Jarmo Sandelin (birdied 18 for 70); England's Paul Eales (birdie, eagle for 71); England's Peter Baker (birdie, birdie for 71); Tinning (bogey, par for 74) and Canonica (birdie, bogey, par for 73, missing a four-footer on the last hole).

Rosapenna Hotel & Golf Resort (Old Tom Morris), County Donegal, Ireland — August 18-20
Par 71 (35-36); 6,628 yards — Purse: €400,000

1	**Phillip Price**	72	70	71	213	600.00
2	**Jarmo Sandelin**	69	75	70	214	242.40
	Paul Eales	69	74	71	214	242.40
	Peter Baker	73	70	71	214	242.40
	Emanuele Canonica	69	72	73	214	242.40
	Steen Tinning	68	72	74	214	242.40
7	Mauricio Molina	72	73	70	215	126.00
	James Kingston	72	70	73	215	126.00
	Paul McGinley	69	72	74	215	126.00
10	Markus Brier	69	75	72	216	102.00
11	Jose Coceres	72	74	71	217	90.00
	Paul Streeter	71	73	73	217	90.00
13	Thomas Levet	74	73	72	219	74.93
	Simon Khan	72	73	74	219	74.93
	Andrew Oldcorn	71	72	76	219	74.93
16	Magnus P Atlevi	78	72	70	220	57.53
	David Morland IV	75	75	70	220	57.53
	Michael Long	74	74	72	220	57.53
	Rafael Faustino Gomez	72	76	72	220	57.53
	Phillip Archer	76	69	75	220	57.53
	Euan McIntosh	72	70	78	220	57.53

Staysure PGA Seniors Championship

It was quite an impressive performance by a man who recently had misgivings about continuing to play professional golf. Not long after admitting, "me and my wife were considering opening a driving range and that's how things were going," Adilson Da Silva dominated the Staysure PGA Seniors Championship with a six-stroke, wire-to-wire victory.

"I'm glad that we hung in there. She gave me quite a lot of support to try the Legends Tour," pointed out the 50-year-old Brazilian after becoming the first winner from the huge South American country in senior golf. He received an exemption into the season-opening Riegler & Partner Legends, in which he tied for third place, ensuring his place on the tour. Eventually it led him to Formby Golf Club in Merseyside, England, for this second biggest title on the circuit.

Da Silva, who compiled an excellent, 12-victory record on South Africa's Sunshine Tour in his younger days and most recently won on the Asia Tour in 2018, jumped off to a one-stroke lead over Italy's Emanuele Canonica and at least by four over the rest of the field the first day with his eight-birdie 64. Only nine players broke 70.

The Brazilian birdied the last two holes Friday for 69 to edge two strokes ahead of Canonica (65-70) and Sweden's Joakim Haeggman (68-67) and raced to a massive, seven-shot lead Saturday as he went bogey-free a second time with three birdies and a chip-in eagle for a 67 and 16 under par. James Kingston, the Swiss Senior Open winner, moved into second place with 66, a stroke ahead of Haeggman (73) and Michael Jonzon (72) as Canonica fell out of contention with a 76.

Haeggman proved the only threat to Da Silva on Sunday. As Da Silva was coasting with a one-birdie, one-bogey front nine, Haeggman ran off six birdies on the first eight holes to close the gap to three strokes, but a double bogey at the ninth spoiled that charge. Da Silva birdied three of the last five holes for 70 and the winning total of 18-under-par 270, six ahead of Haeggman (68).

Formby Golf Club, Freshfields, Liverpool, England — August 25-28
Par 72 (37-35); 7,031 yards — Purse: €500,000

1	**Adilson Da Silva**	64	69	67	70	270	675.00
2	**Joakim Haeggman**	68	67	73	68	276	445.50
3	**Emanuele Canonica**	65	70	76	69	280	270.00
	Michael Jonzon	69	67	72	72	280	270.00
5	Simon Khan	72	69	71	69	281	179.25
	Phillip Archer	69	70	71	71	281	179.25
	James Kingston	71	70	66	74	281	179.25
8	Christian Cevaer	74	65	77	66	282	141.75
9	Mauricio Molina	73	70	75	65	283	123.75
10	Paul Lawrie	72	72	70	72	286	114.75
11	Paul Streeter	73	72	75	67	287	97.20
	Liam Bond	71	77	71	68	287	97.20
	Carlos Balmaseda Sanchez	70	72	72	73	287	97.20
14	Thomas Gogele	75	71	75	67	288	70.78
	Andrew Oldcorn	73	75	72	68	288	70.78
	Peter Fowler	74	75	70	69	288	70.78
	Thomas Levet	72	72	74	70	288	70.78
	Mark Wharton	70	72	75	71	288	70.78
	Carl Suneson	73	69	74	72	288	70.78
	Jean van de Velde	72	66	75	75	288	70.78

WCM Legends Open de France

Englishman Gary Marks, playing in just his second tournament of the 2022 Legends Tour season, fought off the challenge of 64-year-old Hall-of-Famer Ian Woosnam and two others, scoring a three-stroke victory in the WCM Legends Open de France. The 58-year-old Marks, primarily a club professional who made infrequent forays onto the professional tours, did own a Legends Tour victory — the 2016 Willow Senior Golf Classic — along with the odd wins on Europe's secondary circuits.

Brazil's Adilson Da Silva, coming off his victory the previous Sunday in the Staysure PGA Seniors Championship, got off to a fast start at Saint-Cloud in Paris, his five-under-par 66 giving him a share of the lead with England's Robert Coles. Marks shot 68 and followed up with a strong, lone-bogey 66 Saturday, his eight-under-par 134 moving him a stroke ahead of Woosnam (70-65) and Sweden's Michael Jonzon (69-66) and two in front of Da Silva (70). Marks struggled on the front nine Sunday, going out in 36, but he birdied the 11th and 12th holes to secure his lead, then shot 34 on the back nine. A 70 for nine-under-par 204 gave him a three-stroke victory over Da Silva (71) and four over Woosnam (73) and Denmark's Steen Tinning (71).

Golf de Saint-Cloud, Paris, France — September 15-17
Par 71 (35-36); 6,523 yards — Purse: €250,000

1	**Gary Marks**	68	66	70	204	450.00
2	**Adilson Da Silva**	66	70	71	207	297.00
3	**Steen Tinning**	68	69	71	208	180.00
	Ian Woosnam	70	65	73	208	180.00
5	Phillip Archer	68	72	69	209	126.00
	Michael Jonzon	69	66	74	209	126.00
7	Simon P Brown	70	71	69	210	86.10
	Andrew Raitt	70	71	69	210	86.10
	Michael Long	67	72	71	210	86.10
	Robert Coles	66	72	72	210	86.10
	Phillip Price	67	70	73	210	86.10
12	Miguel Angel Martin	72	70	69	211	56.64
	Jose Manuel Carriles	70	71	70	211	56.64
	Gary Wolstenholme	71	70	70	211	56.64
	Carl Suneson	71	70	70	211	56.64
	Peter Baker	69	71	71	211	56.64
17	James Kingston	70	72	70	212	45.00
	Jonathan S Cheetham	73	67	72	212	45.00
19	Thomas Gogele	75	68	70	213	41.40
20	David Shacklady	69	73	72	214	35.15
	Paul Wesselingh	73	69	72	214	35.15
	Thomas Levet	74	69	71	214	35.15
	Paul Streeter	70	71	73	214	35.15
	Peter Fowler	72	72	70	214	35.15
	Joakim Haeggman	70	74	70	214	35.15

Farmfoods European Senior Masters

Not surprisingly, Paul Lawrie recognised the coincidence after his victory in the Farmfoods European Senior Masters. He had just come from five strokes behind in the final round to pick up his second title of the season and remarked: "I obviously know more than anyone that it's never over until it's over."

He was reminded of the way he landed the most important title of his career — the 1999 Open Championship. He had entered the final round at Carnoustie 10 strokes off the lead and yet wound up clutching the coveted Claret Jug after Frenchman Jean Van de Velde, with victory well in sight, mangled the last hole and, along with American Justin Leonard, lost to Lawrie in the subsequent playoff.

This time it was Sweden's Michael Jonzon who fell apart the last day on La Manga Club's South course in Murcia, Spain, and lost in a playoff to Lawrie, who added the European Masters to his earlier 2022 victory in the European Legends Links, also sponsored by Farmfoods.

Seniors rookie Jonzon, 50, twice a winner on the European Tour, had produced a pair of seven-under-par 66s the first two days for a two-stroke lead over American Clark Dennis, a five-time Legends Tour winner, and seven over Lawrie (71-66) and five others tied for fifth place.

Nothing changed position-wise on the front nine as both Jonzon and Lawrie blazed with six-under-par 31s, but it was a different story after the turn. Jonzon bogeyed the 10th and triple-bogeyed the par-four 11th, then recovered with three birdies on the next six holes, only to lose his ball in the woods at the 18th and finish with a double-bogey seven, 70 and 17-under 202. At the same time, Lawrie was adding two birdies on the back nine, shooting a bogey-free 65.

The subsequent playoff on the par-five 18th ended quickly as the 53-year-old Scot reached the green in two and two-putted from 15 feet for the win as Jonzon missed the green with his second shot and failed to get up and down for a birdie to extend the overtime. "It's unexpected a wee bit, I suppose," exclaimed Lawrie.

La Manga Club (South), Murcia, Spain — October 14-16
Par 73 (37-36); 7,108 yards — Purse: €250,000

1	**Paul Lawrie**	71	66	65	202	450.00
2	**Michael Jonzon**	66	66	70	202	297.00
	Lawrie won playoff at first extra hole					
3	**Clark Dennis**	66	68	71	205	180.00
	Peter Baker	70	65	70	205	180.00
5	Phillip Price	70	68	69	207	119.50
	James Kingston	69	68	70	207	119.50
	Markus Brier	67	70	70	207	119.50
8	Christian Cevaer	72	69	67	208	81.00
	Ricardo Gonzalez	69	71	68	208	81.00
	Robert Coles	69	68	71	208	81.00
	Adilson Da Silva	73	64	71	208	81.00
12	Thomas Gogele	68	68	73	209	64.50
13	Carl Suneson	71	69	70	210	57.75
	Gary Orr	70	68	72	210	57.75
15	Mauricio Molina	71	73	67	211	45.70
	Simon Khan	72	71	68	211	45.70
	Peter Wilson	71	71	69	211	45.70
	Mark Mouland	72	67	72	211	45.70
	Niclas Fasth	72	67	72	211	45.70
	Andre Bossert	69	70	72	211	45.70

Italian Senior Open

Perhaps he was destined to win the Italian Senior Open — Ricardo Gonzalez, an Argentinian, playing the Argentario Golf and Wellness Resort course on Italy's Tuscany coast. Whatever, Gonzalez dealt best with the elements that blasted the field with high winds over the weekend and landed his first Legends Tour title. The fifth first-time winner of the season, he was the only player under par at the end with his two-under 211, three strokes better than runner-up James Kingston, the defending champion.

"I am so happy, so proud. Today is a great day. My first win as a senior," gushed the emotional Gonzalez with his son and caddie, Santi, at his side. "Santi started today saying 'give me a good prize', and the trophy is mine."

Kingston, the Order of Merit leader and winner of the Swiss Seniors in July, got off to a strong start with a first-round 68 and shared the lead at one under with Gonzalez (69-72) at the 36-hole mark. Things looked dark for the Argentinian in the early going Sunday as he struggled with the gales and went out in 40 to Kingston's 35. But he turned things completely around after the turn with birdies at 10, 11 and 12, while the South African was incurring a pair of bogeys.

"The long putt on 15 for birdie was the key to winning this tournament because James hit a three-putt," observed Gonzalez of the two-stroke swing that shifted him two shots in front. He followed with a birdie at the 16th and pars at the last two holes for a 70 and his first European victory since the 2009 SAS Scandinavian Masters. Kingston finished bogey-birdie for a 73.

Argentario Golf Resort & Spa, Porto Ercole, Italy — October 21-23
Par 71 (36-35); 6,839 yards — Purse: €300,000

1	**Ricardo Gonzalez**	69	72	70	211	525.00
2	**James Kingston**	68	73	73	214	346.50
3	**Stephen Dodd**	71	75	70	216	191.92
	Markus Brier	71	73	72	216	191.92
	Gary Wolstenholme	72	71	73	216	191.92
6	Michael Jonzon	71	76	70	217	124.25
	Emanuele Canonica	69	74	74	217	124.25
	Gary Orr	73	70	74	217	124.25
9	Gary Evans	70	78	70	218	89.25
	Adilson Da Silva	71	75	72	218	89.25
	Santiago Luna	71	74	73	218	89.25
12	Chris Williams	74	76	70	220	72.28
	Phillip Price	72	76	72	220	72.28
14	Robert Coles	77	72	72	221	60.03
	Phillip Archer	70	78	73	221	60.03
	Carl Suneson	71	76	74	221	60.03
	Garry Houston	71	75	75	221	60.03
18	Michael Campbell	71	77	74	222	48.42
	Peter Wilson	72	76	74	222	48.42
	Andrew Raitt	70	74	78	222	48.42

MCB Tour Championship — Seychelles

Joakim Haeggman admitted that a nightmare he had experienced in which he shot himself out of contention in a tournament added to the pressure as he sought his first victory on the Legends Tour while playing the final holes of the MCB Tour Championship — Seychelles. However, it turned into a pleasant dream as the 53-year-old Swede shook off two late bogeys and won for the first time in his third season on the circuit, his final-round 66 on the par-70 Constance Lemuria course producing a four-stroke victory. In doing so, Haeggman turned the tables on runner-up Adilson Da Silva, against whom he finished second in the Staysure PGA Seniors earlier in the season in his most recent of several victory bids.

Haeggman had started the two-week finale of the 16-tournament season a shot behind leader Simon Khan's five-under-par 65, and moved into a first-place tie with Austrian Markus Brier with his Saturday 67. Brier, who had started with a modest 70, shot a 63, which included a chip-in eagle. It was the lowest round ever at Constance Lemuria. Haeggman, the Swedish ex-Ryder Cupper, roared three strokes ahead of Brier with an outgoing 30 on Sunday that included an eagle two on the par-four ninth hole. Another birdie followed at the 11th, but Haeggman ran into trouble and felt the pressure with back-to-back bogeys at the 14th and 15th holes.

Undaunted, he birdied the next two holes and took a meaningless six at the home hole for the 66, an 11-under-par 199 total and the four-stroke margin over Da Silva, who closed with a 67. Brier dropped into a fifth-place tie, shooting 73. "I have won golf tournaments all over the world before and knew it was coming, and it happened today," summed up Haeggman, the sixth first-time winner of the season.

Constance Lemuria, Praslin, Seychelles — December 2-4
Par 70 (34-36); 6,135 yards — Purse: €400,000

1	**Joakim Haeggman**	66	67	66	199	675.00
2	**Adilson Da Silva**	68	68	67	203	445.50
3	**Emanuele Canonica**	68	69	67	204	297.00
4	Clark Dennis	68	70	67	205	243.00
5	Jean-Francois Remesy	67	72	67	206	179.25
	Chris Williams	67	71	68	206	179.25
	Markus Brier	70	63	73	206	179.25
8	Simon Khan	65	69	73	207	141.75
9	Gary Wolstenholme	70	68	70	208	123.75
10	Simon P Brown	74	68	67	209	105.75
	Marc Farry	68	71	70	209	105.75
	Liam Bond	67	69	73	209	105.75
13	David Morland IV	70	73	67	210	86.63
	Thomas Gogele	72	70	68	210	86.63
15	Miguel Angel Martin	68	73	70	211	79.65
16	Jarmo Sandelin	68	74	70	212	70.05
	Garry Houston	69	71	72	212	70.05
	Mauricio Molina	71	68	73	212	70.05
19	Magnus P Atlevi	73	71	69	213	58.05
	Peter Baker	71	72	70	213	58.05
	Andrew Raitt	73	69	71	213	58.05
	Jose Manuel Carriles	70	71	72	213	58.05

MCB Tour Championship — Mauritius

Thomas Bjorn put in a rare appearance on the Legends Tour at the year-ending MCB Tour Championship in Mauritius and he certainly made it count. The 51-year-old Dane, whose 17 wins on the European Tour branded him as his country's number one star by far and earned him the Ryder Cup captaincy in 2018, rode a brilliant middle round to a seven-stroke victory in just his second start in 2022 on the senior circuit.

In the tournament's other main storyline, South Africa's James Kingston followed a miserable first-round 74 with a bogey-free 65-64 weekend to secure second place and wrap up the season's Order of Merit title, safely ahead of Brazil's Adilson Da Silva, who was the Barry Lane Rookie of the Year.

Comfortably positioned four strokes and four other players behind leader Jarmo Sandelin's 64 the first day, Bjorn slaughtered Constance Belle Mare Plage's par-five holes Saturday on his way to a course-record 61 and a four-shot lead over Sandelin and Miguel Angel Martin. He racked up two eagles and a pair of birdies on the par fives to go with five other birdies during the bogey-free round.

"I finished nicely yesterday birdieing three of the last four holes and carried that momentum into today," observed Bjorn, whose only previous 2022 start on the Legends Tour was in the Senior Open

Championship. "To shoot 61 is always great."

He shot a less spectacular but steady 67 Sunday, spacing out five birdies nicely over the 18 holes and going without a bogey after the seventh hole the first day to reach the seven-shot final margin. His total of 20-under-par 196 was the lowest winning score of the season. "I didn't have many expectations coming in here," he admitted. "I took advantage of the par fives. They gave me a lot of freedom not to be aggressive with everything else."

Constance Belle Mare Plage, Poste de Flacq, Mauritius — December 9-11
Par 72 (36-36); 6,609 yards — Purse: €500,000

1	**Thomas Bjorn**	68	61	67	196	
2	**James Kingston**	74	65	64	203	371.25
	Simon P Brown	65	70	68	203	371.25
4	Clark Dennis	71	66	67	204	221.63
	Adilson Da Silva	69	66	69	204	221.63
6	Michael Long	71	70	64	205	150.75
	Paul Eales	69	68	68	205	150.75
	Phillip Archer	67	69	69	205	150.75
	Miguel Angel Martin	67	66	72	205	150.75
10	Andrew Raitt	70	66	70	206	110.25
	Joakim Haeggman	65	69	72	206	110.25
12	Thomas Gogele	71	69	67	207	92.93
	Philip Golding	71	69	67	207	92.93
14	David Morland IV	73	69	66	208	81.90
	Jose Manuel Carriles	68	67	73	208	81.90
16	Steen Tinning	74	68	68	210	68.06
	Paul McGinley	70	69	71	210	68.06
	Juan Quiros	68	70	72	210	68.06
	Jarmo Sandelin	64	69	77	210	68.06
20	Euan McIntosh	72	70	69	211	59.40

2022 ORDER OF MERIT

		Points
1	James Kingston	2,844.8
2	Adilson Da Silva	2,253.1
3	Phillip Price	1,937.1
4	Paul Lawrie	1,860.4
5	Joakim Haeggman	1,794.2
6	Euan McIntosh	1,383.8
7	Phillip Archer	1,326.8
8	Mauricio Molina	1,262.2
9	Richard Green	1,189.6
10	Emanuele Canonica	1,185.9

Japan Senior PGA Tour

Mainly while the rest of the golf world understandably wasn't paying attention, a 56-year-old pro from Thailand was accomplishing something on the Japan Senior Tour that hadn't happened anywhere else since Tiger Woods's heydays.

Prayad Marksaeng collected six consecutive victories toward the end of 2022 that made him clearly the season's number one player. He easily topped the money list, his ¥61,281,632 more than ¥21 million ahead of that collected by runner-up Hiroyuki Fujita, the only other multiple winner during the season.

Marksaeng's remarkable run started with victories in the 72-hole Japan Senior Open and PGA Championships. It was the second time he had won both majors, the first time in 2016 when he started his run of 21 victories in just five seasons that carried him past Kiyoshi Murota (20) to become the most successful player in Japan Senior Tour history. Victories in a 54-hole and three 36-hole tournaments followed before Mitsuhiro Watanabe ended the run and became the fifth first-time winner in the season's finale.

One measure of Marksaeng's superiority over the field was his stroke average of 67.89, which was more than half a stroke better than Katsumasa Miyamoto, a 12-time winner on the Japan Tour who was making his debut on the seniors circuit but missed out on a maiden victory. Fujita was the only other player within a stroke and a half of Marksaeng's average over the season.

"I'm very happy to be the money champion for the fourth time," Marksaeng said. "My putting was improving, so the whole play flowed well. After winning the Sasebo Senior, I was able to go for the money king. I was in good shape because I didn't have any pain anywhere in my body. I'd like to get into the new season in good shape for next year."

Fujita was one of those other four initial victors, his first of two in the Starts Senior following three others — Yoshinobu Tsukada, Takashi Kanemoto and Kiyoshi Maita — at the start of the season. A 17-tournament winner on the Japan Tour, Fujita was in his fourth senior season before he scored his first two wins.

2022 SCHEDULE

Kinshu Senior Okinawa Open	**Yoshinobu Tsukada**
Nojima Champions Cup	**Takashi Kanemoto**
Sumaiida Senior Cup	**Kiyoshi Maita**
Starts Senior	**Hiroyuki Fujita**
Fancl Classic	**Toru Suzuki**
Maruhan Cup Taiheiyo Club Senior	**Hiroyuki Fujita (2)**
Komatsu Open	**Keiichiro Fukabori**
Japan Senior Open Championship	**Prayad Marksaeng**
Japan PGA Senior Championship	**Prayad Marksaeng (2)**
Sasebo Senior Trust Group Cup	**Prayad Marksaeng (3)**
ISPS Handa After All Interesting Senior	**Prayad Marksaeng (4)**
Fukuoka Senior Open	**Prayad Marksaeng (5)**
Cosmo Health Senior Cup	**Prayad Marksaeng (6)**
Iwasaki Shiratsuyu Senior	**Mitsuhiro Watanabe**

Kinshu Senior Okinawa Open

Yoshinobu Tsukada thought that being in a comfort zone played a big part in his first Japan Senior Tour victory in the season-opening Kinshu Senior Okinawa Open. "I like the warm climate of Okinawa, which is unique to Asia and is familiar to me on the Asian Tour," observed the 52-year-old Tsukada after posting his one-stroke victory at Kanehide Kise Country Club. The win came nine years after he scored his lone victory on the Japan Tour at the 2013 Token Homemate Cup. "I'm greedy. I want to win some more," he added.

He emerged with the win from a four-way battle in Sunday's final round, which began with Thailand's Thaworn Wiratchant, a five-time winner on the senior circuit, on top with 70-69 for five under par, a shot in front of Tsukada (70-70), Taichi Teshima, the 2019 Okinawa winner, and winless senior Daisuke Maruyama (both 68-72).

Teshima built a two-stroke lead through 13 holes on Sunday, but he double-bogeyed the 15th and fell back into a tie with Tsukada. Then Tsukada birdied the 16th, matched bogeys with Teshima at the 17th and claimed the title with a par at the final hole. His 69 gave Tsukada a seven-under-par total of 209 to edge out Teshima (70) by a shot and Wiratchant (72) by two. Maruyama faded to a 78.

Kanehide Kise Country Club, Okinawa — April 7-9
Par 72 (36-36); 7,193 yards — Purse: ¥32,000,000

1	**Yoshinobu Tsukada**	70	70	69	209	¥5,400,000
2	**Taichi Teshima**	68	72	70	210	2,400,000
3	**Thaworn Wiratchant**	70	69	72	211	1,650,000
4	Masayuki Kawamura	73	71	69	213	1,119,375
	David Smail	73	71	69	213	1,119,375
	Toshimitsu Izawa	70	73	70	213	1,119,375
	Norio Shinozaki	71	70	72	213	1,119,375
8	Toru Taniguchi	73	72	69	214	790,000
	Mitsuhiro Watanabe	73	71	70	214	790,000
	Shigeru Nonaka	70	73	71	214	790,000
11	Toshihiro Aizawa	73	72	70	215	570,000
	Shinichi Yokota	71	74	70	215	570,000
	Kiyoshi Murota	69	75	71	215	570,000
	Takao Nogami	71	71	73	215	570,000
15	Takeshi Kajikawa	72	73	71	216	435,000
	Katsumi Kubo	71	73	72	216	435,000
17	Takashi Kanemoto	73	73	71	217	372,000
	Hirofumi Miyase	73	70	74	217	372,000
	Kazuhiro Takami	70	71	76	217	372,000
20	Katsuhiko Yamazaki	72	77	69	218	303,750
	Toru Suzuki	74	71	73	218	303,750
	Naoki Yazawa	71	74	73	218	303,750
	Daisuke Maruyama	68	72	78	218	303,750

Nojima Champions Cup

Takashi Kanemoto's first victory in the Nojima Champions Cup caught him by surprise. "I wanted to win by the age of 55, but I never thought I could win my first senior victory so quickly," expressed the 51-year-old, second-season pro after his playoff win over Yoichi Shimizu in the 36-hole tournament at Hakone Country Club in Kanagawa Prefecture. Kanemoto won with a par on the first extra hole against the veteran Shimizu, winless as a senior since joining the Japan Senior Tour in 2013, after they matched 65-67 for a 12-under-par total of 132. Playoffs have involved Kanemoto throughout his career. One of his two victories on the Japan Tour came in an overtime event and he lost in two others.

Yoshinobu Tsukada, after his maiden victory in the opening event of the season, led Kanemoto and Shimizu by a shot on the first day, including a pair of eagles in his eight-under-par 64. The three players battled it out Sunday after rain and fog delayed the start. They were tied for the lead through 12 holes. Kanemoto birdied the next two holes and parred in, while Shimizu caught him with a birdie at the 16th hole. A bogey at the par-five 15th cost Tsukada the chance of back-to-back wins, a birdie at the 18th leaving him a stroke short of the playoff.

Hakone Country Club, Kanagawa — April 21-22
Par 72 (36-36); 7,036 yards — Purse: ¥50,000,000

1	**Takashi Kanemoto**	65	67	132	¥10,000,000
2	**Yoichi Shimizu**	65	67	132	5,000,000
	Kanemoto won playoff at first extra hole				
3	**Yoshinobu Tsukada**	64	69	133	2,500,000
4	Hiroaki Iijima	66	68	134	2,020,000
5	Eichi Sato	69	66	135	1,650,000
	Toru Taniguchi	67	68	135	1,650,000
	Toru Suzuki	67	68	135	1,650,000
8	Toshimitsu Izawa	70	66	136	1,250,000
	Tetsuji Hiratsuka	66	70	136	1,250,000
10	Shinichi Yokota	71	66	137	933,333
	Katsunori Kuwabara	71	66	137	933,333
	Prayad Marksaeng	69	68	137	933,333
	Akira Teranishi	68	69	137	933,333
	Tomoyuki Hirano	67	70	137	933,333
	Shinichi Akiba	66	71	137	933,333
16	Naoya Sugiyama	70	68	138	675,000
	Kazuhiko Hosokawa	70	68	138	675,000
	Hirofumi Miyase	68	70	138	675,000
	Takao Nogami	68	70	138	675,000

Sumaiida Senior Cup

His first victory in five years on the Japan Senior Tour had a big emotional impact on Kiyoshi Maita. "I don't want to see the tears of a 62-year-old grandfather, but I'm crying," admitted Maita after squeezing out a one-stroke victory in the Sumaiida Senior Cup at Eastwood Country Club in Tochigi in early June. "I gained a little confidence in the victory after a long absence, but I still have a lot of putts and shots."

Physical ailments had plagued Maita since he scored his sixth senior win in the 2017 Nojima tournament and he had to get through the annual qualifier to compete in 2022. "I haven't had good golf since around 2018. I don't even have a sponsor."

He was one of nine players at 68, one shot off the lead Friday and in a two-way tie for·third place at 136 after 36 holes with Naoyuki Tamura, two behind leader Eichi Sato and one back of Shigeru Nonaka, after a five-birdie run led to his second 68.

A steady, three-birdie 69 on Sunday gave Maita his one-shot victory at 11-under-par 205 as the second-round leaders faded and the challenge came from Yoichi Shimizu, whose closing 68 gave him a second runner-up finish in a row. Maita's eight-foot birdie putt on the par-five 15th hole made the difference as both men parred the last three holes. Hiroo Kawai, with a back-nine 31 for 65, finished third at 207 with Chien-Soon Lu and Katsumi Kubo.

Eastwood Country Club, Tochigi — June 2-4
Par 72 (36-36); 6,862 yards — Purse: ¥50,000,000

1	**Kiyoshi Maita**	68	68	69	205	¥10,000,000
2	**Yoichi Shimizu**	68	70	68	206	5,000,000
3	**Hiroo Kawai**	69	73	65	207	2,066,666
	Chien-Soon Lu	71	68	68	207	2,066,666
	Katsumi Kubo	69	70	68	207	2,066,666
6	Toru Morita	70	72	66	208	1,360,000
	Yoshinobu Tsukada	72	67	69	208	1,360,000
	Shinichi Akiba	68	69	71	208	1,360,000
	Naoyuki Tamura	67	69	72	208	1,360,000
	Shigeru Nonaka	68	67	73	208	1,360,000
11	Kohki Idoki	73	69	67	209	875,000
	Jiro Minamizaki	68	73	68	209	875,000
	Thaworn Wiratchant	70	70	69	209	875,000
	Norio Shinozaki	68	69	72	209	875,000
	Naoki Yazawa	67	70	72	209	875,000
	Eichi Sato	67	67	75	209	875,000
17	Tomoyuki Hirano	68	74	68	210	627,500
	Hisao Ahara	68	72	70	210	627,500
	Naoya Sugiyama	69	70	71	210	627,500
	Prayad Marksaeng	69	70	71	210	627,500

Starts Senior

With two Thailand stars, who between them owned 19 victories on the Japan Senior Tour, among his nearest pursuers, Hiroyuki Fujita knew his three-stroke lead entering the final round of the Starts Senior tournament could be perilous. The winner of 17 tournaments during his fine career on the Japan Tour had gone three pandemic-interrupted years of senior golf without a victory. "I hope I can play like this tomorrow," remarked the 53-year-old after flashing his old form with a 64-66—130 start in the Starts. "Some people will improve their scores and there are Wiratchant and Marksaeng. I don't think I can win the championship unless I improve my score."

He did, as he finished off 54 holes of bogey-free golf at Starts Kasama Golf Club in Ibaraki with a 68, for 18 under par on a total of 198, and a five-stroke victory. Neither Thaworn Wiratchant nor Prayad Marksaeng challenged on Sunday, both shooting 70s that put them into a five-way tie for second place with Suk Joug Yul, David Smail and Tetsuji Hiratsuka, who all closed with 67s.

Fujita had an eagle and six birdies on the first day as he shared the lead at 64 with Wiratchant and Smail, and six birdies the second day. He kept his card clear of bogeys with four birdies in the concluding 68.

Starts Kasama Golf Club, Ibaraki — June 17-19
Par 72 (36-36); 6,972 yards — Purse: ¥60,000,000

1	**Hiroyuki Fujita**	64	66	68	198	¥14,000,000
2	**Suk Joug Yul**	69	67	67	203	3,366,800
	Tetsuji Hiratsuka	68	68	67	203	3,366,800
	David Smail	64	72	67	203	3,366,800
	Prayad Marksaeng	65	68	70	203	3,366,800
	Thaworn Wiratchant	64	69	70	203	3,366,800
7	Kazuhiko Hosokawa	68	66	70	204	1,485,000
8	Satoshi Higashi	72	69	65	206	1,196,666
	Taichi Teshima	69	69	68	206	1,196,666
	Chien-Soon Lu	69	67	70	206	1,196,666
11	Shigeru Nonaka	73	68	66	207	977,000
	Masayoshi Yamazoe	69	70	68	207	977,000
	Hiroaki Iijima	65	72	70	207	977,000
14	Toshimitsu Izawa	71	69	68	208	789,250
	Hirofumi Miyase	71	68	69	208	789,250
	Naoyuki Tamura	69	70	69	208	789,250
	Masahiro Kuramoto	68	68	72	208	789,250
18	Masayoshi Nakayama	70	71	68	209	638,500
	Mamoru Osanai	71	67	71	209	638,500
20	Hisao Ahara	72	67	71	210	537,333
	Katsumi Kubo	71	68	71	210	537,333
	Yutaka Hagawa	72	66	72	210	537,333

Fancl Classic

Toru Suzuki took advantage of a long, Covid-interrupted absence from the Japan Senior Tour to fine-tune his swing and it paid off with his sixth victory on the over-50 circuit in the venerable Fancl Classic.

In the interim between a feeble showing in early June in the Sumaiida Cup and the Fancl Classic in late August, the 56-year-old seasoned pro watched footage that led him to a slower swing. That adjustment set him up to lead from start-to-finish at Susono Country Club in Shizuoka. His final 11-under-par 205 total gave him a comfortable three-stroke victory over the always-dangerous Thaworn Wiratchant, of Thailand.

Suzuki, an eight-time winner on the Japan Tour, opened the week in a three-way tie for the lead at 68 with other former senior winners Katsumi Kubo and Taichi Teshima, then had first place to himself the rest of the way. He went in front alone Saturday with an adventurous 69 — an eagle, four birdies and three bogeys — his 137 placing him two ahead of Wiratchant (69-70) and Teshima (68-71). He was never in trouble on Sunday, racking up five birdies on the first 14 holes, taking his lone bogey at the 15th and parring in for 68 and the three-shot win.

Susono Country Club, Shizuoka — August 19-21
Par 72 (36-36); 7,009 yards — Purse: ¥66,000,000

1	**Toru Suzuki**	68	69	68	205	¥15,000,000
2	**Thaworn Wiratchant**	69	70	69	208	7,200,000
3	**Takashi Kanemoto**	72	69	68	209	3,500,000
4	Tadanori Shibata	72	68	70	210	2,350,000
	Suk Joug Yul	70	70	70	210	2,350,000
6	Mitsutaka Kusakabe	72	69	70	211	1,640,000
	Eichi Sato	71	69	71	211	1,640,000
8	Jeev Milkha Singh	74	69	69	212	1,223,333
	Naoya Sugiyama	73	69	70	212	1,223,333
	Takao Nogami	69	73	70	212	1,223,333
11	Kiyoshi Murota	74	71	68	213	896,000
	Akira Teranishi	72	72	69	213	896,000
	Satoshi Higashi	72	72	69	213	896,000
	Keiichiro Fukabori	72	71	70	213	896,000
	Akio Mizukami (A)	73	68	72	213	
	Takeshi Sakiyama	72	69	72	213	896,000
17	Masayoshi Nakayama	75	68	71	214	647,500
	Tomoyuki Hirano	72	71	71	214	647,500
	Mitsuhiro Watanabe	73	69	72	214	647,500
	Taichi Teshima	68	71	75	214	647,500

Maruhan Cup Taiheiyo Club Senior

Because of his elevated status as a 17-tournment winner over his 30 years on the Japan Tour, 53-year-old Hiroyuki Fujita had his options where to play from week to week — there or on the Japan Senior Tour. "Until now, when regulars and seniors were held on the same week, we have prioritised regulars, but this summer we decided to give priority to seniors," explained Fujita, who had not fared well on the 2022 Japan Tour and, on the other hand, had won his first senior title in the Starts Senior in June. "Sansan KBC Augusta was held in Fukuoka this week and I chose to play here at Gotemba," he remarked as he savoured the decision that led to his one-stroke victory at the Maruhan Cup Taiheiyo Club Senior.

Fujita struggled with his form in an opening 69 — four birdies and a bogey — but was just a stroke off a six-way tie for the lead. His game was much sharper on Sunday, particularly on the back nine. He dropped a four-foot eagle putt at the 11th hole to escape the pack and take the lead, dropped a shot at the 12th, but quickly regained the front-running position with a birdie at the 13th. Another birdie at the 15th and three following pars wrapped up his 66 to win on nine-under 135. Takeshi Sakiyama and Keiichiro Fukabori both birdied the final hole to tie for second place at 136 with Shinichi Akiba, whose closing 65 was the day's best score.

Taiheiyo Club (Gotemba), Shizuoka — August 27-28
Par 72 (36-36); 7,327 yards — Purse: ¥50,000,000

1	**Hiroyuki Fujita**	69	66	135	¥10,000,000
2	**Shinichi Akiba**	71	65	136	3,133,333
	Takeshi Sakiyama	68	68	136	3,133,333
	Keiichiro Fukabori	68	68	136	3,133,333
5	Katsunori Kuwabara	69	68	137	1,800,000
6	Koji Iwasaki	72	66	138	1,650,000
7	Norio Shinozaki	73	66	139	1,350,000
	Kaname Yokoo	68	71	139	1,350,000
	Toru Taniguchi	68	71	139	1,350,000
10	Thaworn Wiratchant	73	67	140	933,333
	Tetsuji Hiratsuka	72	68	140	933,333
	Hidezumi Shirakata	72	68	140	933,333
	Hiroo Kawai	72	68	140	933,333
	Chien-Soon Lu	70	70	140	933,333
	Hirofumi Miyase	68	72	140	933,333
16	Tsukasa Watanabe	72	69	141	652,000
	Prayad Marksaeng	71	70	141	652,000
	Shinichi Yokota	71	70	141	652,000
	Daisuke Maruyama	71	70	141	652,000
	Jeev Milkha Singh	70	71	141	652,000

Komatsu Open

Keiichiro Fukabori, following his runner-up finish in the previous event, credited course strategy as the catalyst after he emerged from a four-way battle down the stretch and a two-hole playoff with victory in the Komatsu Open. "It was good that I was able to devote myself to the management I decided," pointed out the 53-year-old Fukabori after posting his second win in his third season on the Japan Senior Tour, long after the last of his eight victories on the Japan Tour in 2005.

He entered the final round at Komatsu Country Club, Ishikawa Prefecture, tied for the lead at seven under par with Yoshinobu Tsukada and 56-year-old Thai star Prayad Marksaeng, prowling for his 16th win on the circuit. Kenichi Kuboya was just a shot back and was in the thick of things in Saturday's final round until he absorbed a double bogey at the par-four 15th hole. Tsukada's run of pars after his second birdie at the 10th hole dropped him out of contention, making it a two-man duel over the last three holes between Fukabori and Marksaeng, both birdieing the par-five 18th for 66s and matching totals of 13-under-par 203. The playoff went two extra holes, Fukabori winning with a birdie on that par-five 18th hole.

Komatsu Country Club, Ishikawa — September 8-10
Par 72 (36-36); 6,917 yards — Purse: ¥60,000,000

1	**Keiichiro Fukabori**	68	69	66	203	¥12,000,000
2	**Prayad Marksaeng**	70	67	66	203	5,700,000
	Fukabori won playoff at second extra hole					
3	**Kenichi Kuboya**	68	70	68	206	3,225,000
	Yoshinobu Tsukada	68	69	69	206	3,225,000
5	Akira Teranishi	74	67	66	207	2,075,000
	Kazuhiko Hosokawa	71	70	66	207	2,075,000
7	Daisuke Maruyama	71	72	65	208	1,462,500
	Gregory Meyer	71	70	67	208	1,462,500
	Katsumasa Miyamoto	68	73	67	208	1,462,500
	Katsunori Kuwabara	71	68	69	208	1,462,500
11	Yoichi Shimizu	71	71	67	209	1,140,000
	Yoshinori Mizumaki	70	71	68	209	1,140,000
	Kaname Yokoo	70	70	69	209	1,140,000
14	Masahiro Kuramoto	74	72	64	210	870,000
	Toshimitsu Izawa	71	72	67	210	870,000
	Shigeru Nonaka	70	73	67	210	870,000
	Hisao Ahara	69	74	67	210	870,000
	Taichi Teshima	69	71	70	210	870,000
	Hiroyuki Fujita	68	71	71	210	870,000
20	Masayoshi Yamazoe	74	70	67	211	571,666
	Tetsuji Hiratsuka	72	72	67	211	571,666
	Kiyoshi Murota	72	72	67	211	571,666
	David Smail	71	72	68	211	571,666
	Hirofumi Miyase	69	72	70	211	571,666
	Mitsuhiro Tateyama	66	73	72	211	571,666

Japan Senior Open Championship

He's back! Little had been heard from Prayad Marksaeng since 2019 after he dominated the Japan Senior Tour for three years, winning 15 times, including the Japan Senior Open Championship three times. The 56-year-old Thai star made it four when he ended the title drought with a solid, four-stroke victory in a performance that vanquished runner-up Hiroyuki Fujita described as "truly a yokozuna", the supreme ranking in sumo wrestling, Japan's premier sport.

The win, a week after he lost to Keiichiro Fukabori in a playoff in the Komatsu Open, moved Marksaeng a step closer to the record 20 victories of Kiyoshi Murota and, in the case of Senior Open Championships, within one of the great Isao Aoki. "The legend Isao Aoki has won the title five times but, to be honest, I think four titles are enough for me," Prayad remarked with a chuckle, but then added: "If I have the conditions to compete in next year's tournament, I would like to challenge for my fifth title."

The scenario that brought him the fourth came down to a final-round battle with Fujita, twice a winner earlier in the season. The two men had shared the lead at eight-under-par 136 after 36 holes on the West course of Tarao Country Club in Shiga, bypassing Hisao Ahara, the first-round leader with 65. They left the field behind Saturday as Marksaeng inched a stroke ahead of Fujita at 10 under after a 70. Katsumasa Miyamoto was a distant third at four under.

Neither player did much early on Sunday — Marksaeng 37 and Fujita 39 on the front nine — before the Thai stretched his lead to five strokes with back-to-back birdies on the next two holes. Fujita countered with a pair of his own and got within two strokes when Marksaeng bogeyed the 14th hole. However, Marksaeng birdied the 16th and 18th holes for another 70 to finish at 12-under 276 as Fujita finished with a 73.

Tarao Country Club (West), Shiga — September 15-18
Par 72 (36-36); 7,064 yards — Purse: ¥80,000,000

1	**Prayad Marksaeng**	70	66	70	70	276	¥16,000,000
2	**Hiroyuki Fujita**	67	69	71	73	280	8,800,000
3	**Takashi Kanemoto**	73	71	70	68	282	6,160,000
4	Keiichiro Fukabori	70	71	72	70	283	4,000,000
5	Masayoshi Yamazoe	71	71	71	71	284	3,360,000
6	Akira Teranishi	70	74	74	68	286	2,426,666
	Hidezumi Shirakata	73	67	74	72	286	2,426,666
	Katsumasa Miyamoto	70	73	69	74	286	2,426,666
9	Toru Taniguchi	73	70	72	72	287	1,760,000
10	Mitsuhiro Tateyama	72	71	71	74	288	1,520,000
11	Daisuke Maruyama	70	77	72	70	289	1,332,000
	Tetsuji Hiratsuka	73	71	72	73	289	1,332,000
13	Hisao Ahara	65	73	80	72	290	1,052,000
	Naoyuki Tamura	68	74	74	74	290	1,052,000
15	Hitoshi Kato	72	72	77	70	291	888,000
	Shinichi Yokota	71	76	71	73	291	888,000
	Kaname Yokoo	71	70	74	76	291	888,000
18	Jeev Milkha Singh	70	79	73	70	292	760,000
	Mitsunori Harakawa	74	74	73	71	292	760,000
	Gregory Meyer	70	71	76	75	292	760,000

Japan PGA Senior Championship

Prayad Marksaeng's return to prominence and major-tournament dominance on the Japan Senior Tour continued as he won the Japan PGA Senior Championship for a second time just three weeks after he landed his fourth Japan Senior Open Championship in similar runaway fashion.

With the five-stroke victory and acquisition of the Sumitomo Corporation Summit Cup at Summit Golf Club, Ibaraki, the 56-year-old Thai star became the first player in tour history to have won both major titles in the same season twice, duplicating a feat he accomplished in 2016 when he won the Senior PGA and the first of three straight Senior Opens and joined Katsunari Takahashi and Tsuneyuki (Tommy) Nakajima as one of just three players to fit that category. "I did such an amazing thing," he remarked. "I'm surprised that it's as amazing as winning three consecutive Japan Senior Open titles."

Marksaeng said a couple of equipment changes helped him get off to a fast start. He shot a four-under-par 68 that tied him for the lead with 50-year-old senior rookie Katsumasa Miyamoto, a 12-time winner on the Japan Tour. He moved two shots atop the field Friday with a 70 as long-time star Toru Taniguchi fired a bogey-free 66 to be four under, putting him a stroke ahead of Miyamoto, who slipped to 73, and ageless Kiyoshi Murota and his record 20 senior wins. The 67-year-old shot 69.

Things remained tight on Saturday as Marksaeng shot another 70 to be eight under. Murota moved within a stroke with his solid, four-birdie 68 and Miyamoto shot 69 to be a further stroke back. Sunday was a different story. The 56-year-old Thai birdied the first three holes and smiled his way to his 17th tour victory, adding birdies at the 11th, 16th and 18th holes around a lone bogey at 17. A 67 gave him a 13-under-par total of 275 and that five-stroke margin over Miyamoto and six over Taniguchi, as both closed with 70s. Murota ran out of gas, shot 75 and finished fifth.

The victory raised Marksaeng some ¥2.6 million ahead of Hiroyuki Fujita atop the money race, which the Thai had topped at the end of three previous seasons.

Summit Golf Club, Ishioka, Ibaraki — October 6-9
Par 72 (36-36); 7,023 yards — Purse: ¥50,000,000

1	**Prayad Marksaeng**	68	70	70	67	275	¥10,000,000
2	**Katsumasa Miyamoto**	68	73	69	70	280	5,000,000
3	**Toru Taniguchi**	74	66	71	70	281	3,500,000
4	Tetsuji Hiratsuka	72	75	70	66	283	2,500,000
5	Kiyoshi Murota	72	69	68	75	284	2,000,000
6	Eichi Sato	79	70	68	68	285	1,500,000
7	Shinichi Yokota	76	72	69	69	286	1,250,000
	Masayoshi Nakayama	73	71	72	70	286	1,250,000
	Koichi Kokubo	74	70	70	72	286	1,250,000
10	Keiichiro Fukabori	70	76	74	67	287	975,000
	Hiroyuki Fujita	74	74	70	69	287	975,000
	Hiroaki Iijima	73	71	70	73	287	975,000
	Ryoken Kawagishi	71	72	71	73	287	975,000
14	Hiroo Kawai	73	78	66	71	288	775,000
	Katsuyosi Murakami	71	74	72	71	288	775,000
	Yoichi Shimizu	69	74	74	71	288	775,000
	Toshihiro Aizawa	71	74	70	73	288	775,000
18	Mitsutaka Kusakabe	75	76	68	70	289	605,000
	Kazuhiko Hosokawa	73	77	68	71	289	605,000
	Jeev Milkha Singh	72	73	73	71	289	605,000
	Thaworn Wiratchant	71	76	70	72	289	605,000

Sasebo Senior Trust Group Cup

Prayad Marksaeng only had to negotiate two rounds when he romped to his third straight victory on the Japan Senior Tour. On the heels of his 72-hole wins in the Japan Senior Open and PGA, the brilliant Thai pro rolled to a four-stroke victory in the Sasebo Senior Trust Group Cup in his next start.

It marked the second time Marksaeng had won three in a row on the tour. He picked off the Komatsu Open, Japan Senior Open and PGA titles consecutively in 2016. Only Masaru Amano in 1992 accomplished a similar triple. "I wonder if I can make a record of four games in a row," he mused with a chuckle.

Marksaeng attributed much of his success this way: "It's important to be healthy as a professional golfer. I eat well and get enough sleep. Keep smiling."

He had cause for good humour at Sasebo Country Club as he maintained his torrid pace in the opening round with an eagle on the third hole en route to a seven-under-par 65 and a first-place tie with senior rookies Mitsuhiro Watanabe and Katsumasa Miyamoto, the latter in contention for a fourth straight time.

Marksaeng was nearly untouchable on Sunday as he notched his 18th tour title. He ran off five birdies on the first 11 holes and overcame a bogey at 14 with two more birdies to polish off a 66. His 13-under 131 total gave him the four-shot margin over Miyamoto, who suffered a pair of double bogeys amid six birdies in a 70, tying him for second with Hiroo Kawai (67-68) who just turned 50 in August.

Sasebo Country Club, Nagasaki — October 15-16
Par 72 (36-36); 6,783 yards — Purse: ¥20,000,000

1	**Prayad Marksaeng**	65	66	131	¥3,600,000
2	**Hiroo Kawai**	67	68	135	1,500,000
	Katsumasa Miyamoto	65	70	135	1,500,000
4	Koji Iwasaki	66	70	136	880,000
5	Yoshinobu Tsukada	70	68	138	740,000
	Hiroyuki Fujita	70	68	138	740,000
7	Yoichi Shimizu	70	69	139	610,000
	Suk Joug Yul	67	72	139	610,000
9	Kiyoshi Murota	72	68	140	460,000
	Norio Shinozaki	69	71	140	460,000
	Masayoshi Yamazoe	68	72	140	460,000
	Shigeru Nonaka	68	72	140	460,000
13	Gregory Meyer	75	66	141	278,000
	Shinichi Akiba	73	68	141	278,000
	Hiroaki Iijima	72	69	141	278,000
	Shinichi Yokota	72	69	141	278,000
	Masahiro Kuramoto	71	70	141	278,000
	Yoshinori Mizumaki	71	70	141	278,000
	Ryoken Kawagishi	69	72	141	278,000
	Naoyuki Tamura	69	72	141	278,000

ISPS Handa After All Interesting Senior

There was no stopping Prayad Marksaeng. Not only did the talented Thai rack up his fourth victory in a row at the oddly-named ISPS Handa After All Interesting Senior, but again won by a sizeable margin. With his 201 total, at 12 under par, Marksaeng finished three strokes ahead of runner-up Mitsuhiro Watanabe, following victories by four strokes in the Japan Senior Open, by five in the Senior PGA and by four in the 36-hole Sasebo Senior the previous Sunday.

"I didn't miss a chance to win," he stated after polishing off his 19th victory on the Japan Senior Tour, moving within one of Kiyoshi Murota, now 67, who was just a shot off the lead before fading on the final day at the Southern Cross Resort in Ito City. With rounds of 68-67, Marksaeng was tied for the lead after 36 holes at seven-under-par 135 with fellow Thai Thaworn Wiratchant (70-65) and Akira Teranishi (67-68), both multiple senior winners. Nine other players were within three strokes of the top spot.

After bogeying the first hole on Sunday, though, Marksaeng took complete control of the competition. He ran off four birdies in a six-hole stretch in the middle of the round and virtually clinched matters when he holed a 15-yard bunker shot for an eagle on the par-five 12th. He parred in for a 66, while Watanabe jumped into second place with his closing 67.

Southern Cross Resort, Ito, Shizuoka — October 21-23
Par 71 (35-36); 6,439 yards — Purse: ¥38,000,000

1	**Prayad Marksaeng**	68	67	66	201	¥5,400,000
2	**Mitsuhiro Watanabe**	70	67	67	204	3,000,000
3	**Kaname Yokoo**	68	70	67	205	1,875,000
	Takashi Kanemoto	67	71	67	205	1,875,000
5	Naoki Yazawa	71	65	70	206	1,185,000
	Thaworn Wiratchant	70	65	71	206	1,185,000
7	Hiroyuki Fujita	70	71	66	207	885,000
	Takao Nogami	67	70	70	207	885,000
9	Takeshi Sakiyama	64	74	70	208	695,000
	Kiyoshi Murota	71	65	72	208	695,000
	Akira Teranishi	67	68	73	208	695,000
12	Jeev Milkha Singh	69	70	70	209	577,500
	Kazuhiro Takami	72	66	71	209	577,500
14	Chien-Soon Lu	72	70	68	210	495,000
	Hirofumi Miyase	70	68	72	210	495,000
16	Toshimitsu Izawa	73	70	68	211	435,000
	Shinichi Yokota	71	69	71	211	435,000
	Kazuhiko Hosokawa	65	74	72	211	435,000
19	Toru Suzuki	69	76	67	212	360,000
	Norio Shinozaki	71	71	70	212	360,000
	Ikuo Shirahama	71	70	71	212	360,000
	Tetsuji Hiratsuka	70	71	71	212	360,000
	Masayoshi Nakayama	70	71	71	212	360,000
	Kazunori Suzuki	71	68	73	212	360,000
	Yoshinobu Tsukada	71	68	73	212	360,000

Fukuoka Senior Open

Prayad Marksaeng kept finding ways to win, this time when trailing four players going into the final round of a 36-hole tournament. The remarkable Thai star simply conjured up a 68 on the second day of the Fukuoka Senior Open and squeezed out his unprecedented fifth straight victory, a feat that elevated him into a tie with Kiyoshi Murota and his 20 career victories on the Japan Senior Tour, the most in the circuit's history. Furthermore, the ¥7 million first prize and ¥53 million-plus 2022 winnings clinched another money title.

"In Thailand, there were four wins in a row, but five is the first time in my life," admitted the 56-year-old after his seven-under-par 137 total gave him a one-stroke triumph over Hiroyuki Fujita, whose two victories earlier in the season had him in second place on the money list.

Katsumi Kubo and famed 67-year-old Masahiro (Massy) Kuramoto, an eight-time senior winner, opened on top at Fukuoka Country Club's Wajiro course with 67s. Kenichi Kubota and longtime star Toru Taniguchi were at 68, the only others between Marksaeng, Mamoru Osanai and Takeo Nogami (69s) and the lead.

The finish on Sunday turned into a tight battle between Marksaeng and Fujita as Kuramoto shot 72, after birdieing three of the first six holes, and Kubo slipped to 73. Marksaeng eventually faced a 17-foot birdie putt on the par-five 18th hole and thought: "If I make it, I win the championship, but if I do not make it, I can bring it to a playoff." He made it ... and senior tour history.

Fukuoka Country Club (Wajiro), Fukuoka — October 29-30
Par 72 (36-36); 6,607 yards — Purse: ¥35,000,000

1	**Prayad Marksaeng**	69 68	137	¥7,000,000	10	Hiroo Kawai	70 72	142	726,250
2	**Hiroyuki Fujita**	70 68	138	3,325,000		Mamoru Osanai	69 73	142	726,250
3	**Masahiro Kuramoto**	67 72	139	2,380,000	12	Hiroaki Iijima	74 69	143	560,000
4	Taichi Teshima	73 67	140	1,376,666		Kiyoshi Murota	73 70	143	560,000
	Thaworn Wiratchant	72 68	140	1,376,666		Hideki Kase	73 70	143	560,000
	Katsumi Kubo	67 73	140	1,376,666		Takeshi Sakiyama	73 70	143	560,000
7	Masayoshi Nakayama	73 68	141	893,666		Masayuki Kawamura	72 71	143	560,000
	Mitsutaka Kusakabe	70 71	141	893,666		Keiichiro Fukabori	72 71	143	560,000
	Takao Nogami	69 72	141	893,666		Toru Taniguchi	68 75	143	560,000

Cosmo Health Senior Cup

And … the beat went on. Prayad Marksaeng's astonishing run of consecutive victories reached a half dozen when he overcame a slim first-round deficit in a 36-hole tournament for a second straight week and stretched to a three-stroke victory in the Cosmo Health Senior Cup at Hirakawa Country Club in Chiba. With his 21st victory, the talented Thai pro became the most successful player in Japan Senior Tour history, moving a win ahead of Kiyoshi Murota. He achieved this at age 56 despite missing two seasons because of the Covid pandemic.

While attributing much of his success to the absence of three-putts, Marksaeng discounted the importance of keeping the victory string going. "I'm not worried about it. I'm more conscious of my style and play than that," he explained, still conceding: "I think it will go down in history."

The first-round lead belonged to Tomoyuki Hirano, winless in his third season on the senior circuit. Aided by an eagle on the fourth hole and a front-nine 30, Hirano shot 66, two shots ahead of Keiichiro Fukabori and Marksaeng, who had two late bogeys in his 68.

Hirano moved three in front with an early birdie Sunday, but lost it all with a bogey to Marksaeng's birdie-eagle in the middle of the front nine and fell behind for good with another bogey at the 12th hole. Marksaeng then polished things off with a three-birdie run starting at the 14th hole, shooting 67 for nine-under 135 as Hirano closed with a 72.

Hirakawa Country Club, Chiba — November 3-4
Par 72 (36-36); 7,206 yards — Purse: ¥30,000,000

1	**Prayad Marksaeng**	68 67	135	¥5,400,000	11	Takeshi Sakiyama	73 68	141	527,500
2	**Tomoyuki Hirano**	66 72	138	2,700,000		Hiroaki Iijima	73 68	141	527,500
3	**Naoyuki Tamura**	71 68	139	1,370,000		Hisao Ahara	72 69	141	527,500
	Mamoru Osanai	69 70	139	1,370,000		Toru Suzuki	71 70	141	527,500
	Keiichiro Fukabori	68 71	139	1,370,000		Tetsu Nishikawa	71 70	141	527,500
6	Shinichi Yokota	72 68	140	876,000		Yoichi Shimizu	70 71	141	527,500
	Hidezumi Shirakata	71 69	140	876,000	17	Takashi Kanemoto	71 71	142	378,000
	Mitsutaka Kusakabe	70 70	140	876,000		Kiyoshi Murota	70 72	142	378,000
	Koji Iwasaki	69 71	140	876,000	19	Thaworn Wiratchant	73 70	143	333,000
	Jeev Milkha Singh	69 71	140	876,000		Katsuyosi Murakami	71 72	143	333,000

Iwasaki Shiratsuyu Senior

The primary results of the season-ending Iwasaki Shiratsuyu Senior tournament presented a showing of contrasts. The winner, Mitsuhiro Watanabe, was a Japan Senior Tour newcomer without a victory on his record. One of the challenging losers was Prayad Marksaeng, whose remarkable six-in-a-row streak of wins came to an end after he made a strong bid for a 22nd senior title.

Still, although falling two shots short of the playoff that Watanabe won against Hiroaki Iijima, Marksaeng stashed away the money list crown, his ¥61,281,632 more than ¥21 million beyond runner-up Hiroyuki Fujita's winnings.

The two playoff contenders came from two strokes off the pace in the final round on Ibusaki Golf Club's Kaimon course as the three players ahead of them — Yoshinori Mizumaki at 134 and Takashi Kanemoto and Akira Teranishi at 135 — fell back the last day. However, it took an unexpected flameout by Marksaeng on the back nine to set them up for the playoff. He had surged into the lead from four back on the front side with a five-birdie 31, but he bogeyed the 11th hole just as Watanabe was starting a four-birdie run that gave him a two-shot lead.

Marksaeng's chances ended a short time later when he bogeyed the 15th hole and double-bogeyed the 16th as back-to-back bogeys dropped Watanabe back into a tie with Iijima, who was shooting a bogey-free, three-birdie round. Both players parred in for 69s and matching, 11-under-par 205s. Watanabe then holed a three-foot par putt on the first extra hole for the win after Iijima missed his par putt from long range.

"I didn't think I could win," remarked the surprised Watanabe, who had challenged for a win twice earlier in his first senior season. "So, honestly, I haven't thought about anything yet."

Ibusaki Golf Club (Kaimon), Kagoshima — November 25-27
Par 72 (36-36); 7,151 yards — Purse: ¥60,000,000

1	**Mitsuhiro Watanabe**	69	67	69	205	¥12,000,000
2	**Hiroaki Iijima**	66	70	69	205	5,700,000
	Watanabe won playoff at first extra hole					
3	**Koji Iwasaki**	69	69	68	206	3,800,000
4	Prayad Marksaeng	68	70	69	207	2,266,666
	Takashi Kanemoto	67	68	72	207	2,266,666
	Akira Teranishi	67	68	72	207	2,266,666
7	Suk Joug Yul	75	68	66	209	1,462,500
	Keiichiro Fukabori	70	67	72	209	1,462,500
	Katsumasa Miyamoto	67	69	73	209	1,462,500
	Yoshinori Mizumaki	67	67	75	209	1,462,500
11	Tetsuji Hiratsuka	70	69	71	210	1,170,000
	Toru Suzuki	69	69	72	210	1,170,000
13	Masahiro Kuramoto	67	72	72	211	1,080,000
14	Jiro Minamizaki	75	68	69	212	960,000
	Yoshinobu Tsukada	70	72	70	212	960,000
	Shigeru Nonaka	69	71	72	212	960,000
17	Toshimitsu Izawa	73	72	68	213	780,000
	Kazuhiko Hosokawa	72	71	70	213	780,000
	Kenichi Kuboya	68	73	72	213	780,000
20	Naoya Sugiyama	68	76	70	214	645,000
	Naoki Yazawa	72	71	71	214	645,000
	Masayoshi Nakayama	70	71	71	212	360,000
	Kazunori Suzuki	71	68	73	212	360,000
	Yoshinobu Tsukada	71	68	73	212	360,000

2022 MONEY LIST

1	Prayad Marksaeng	¥61,281,632
2	Hiroyuki Fujita	39,930,333
3	Takashi Kanemoto	26,255,073
4	Keiichiro Fukabori	25,662,333
5	Toru Suzuki	20,551,982
6	Thaworn Wiratchant	19,111,143
7	Mitsuhiro Watanabe	18,641,063
8	Yoshinobu Tsukada	16,005,089
9	Yoichi Shimizu	14,779,750
10	Hiroaki Iijima	13,107,250

Legends of the LPGA

One of golf's greatest rivalries was renewed at the Senior LPGA Championship in July when Karrie Webb defeated Annika Sorenstam by four strokes. The pair, both members of the World Golf Hall of Fame and former world number ones, combined for 113 LPGA victories, plus many more worldwide, and shared 17 major titles. "When we play against each other, even if we're going out for a social hit, we'd probably bring the best out of each other," Webb said.

They had not played in the same tournament since Sorenstam retired in 2008 — at least until the previous week at the Dow Great Bay Lakes Invitational with their respective partners. But at Salina Country Club in sweltering Kansas, it was a classic head-to-head battle.

Each was making their debut in the over-45 championship. They played alongside each other all three days, and although they trailed first-round leader Lisa DePaulo by four, Webb took the lead by two from Sorenstam on the second day. In the third and final round, Sorenstam chipped in for an eagle at the first hole and the pair were tied at the turn. An eagle of her own on the back nine and two late bogeys from Sorenstam meant Webb had her first victory since the 2014 Founders Cup. "It's been a long time since I've had to make putts down the stretch to win a golf tournament," said Webb, 47.

Sorenstam, 51, won the US Senior Women's Open in 2021 and said: "I think it was a great head-to-head for most of the day, and I think we both played well. She just came out on top this time."

Perhaps DePaulo, who played with the legends in the final group on Sunday, said it best. "I got to play with the big dogs," she noted. "Does it get any bigger than Annika and Karrie? No, it doesn't. It was awesome. The first hole for Annika to start out eagle, and we're out here having birdies, it was pretty cool. I wish I could have played a little better, but, hey, I paid a $200 entry fee and got the best seat in the house."

If it had been a while for Webb being in contention, it had been an age since Jill McGill had last won — at the 1994 US Women's Amateur Public Links. The 50-year-old from Dallas finally achieved her maiden professional victory at the US Senior Women's Open. "It's been a long time," she said. "It's been a really, really long time."

McGill overcame a host of stars, with the three previous US Senior Women's winners — Laura Davies, Helen Alfredsson and defending champion Sorenstam — all in contention, plus the likes of Catriona Matthew and Juli Inkster. Webb is not yet eligible for the over-50 championship. McGill won by a single stroke from fellow debutant Leta Lindley and joined a stellar cast of those who had won three different USGA Championships — she was also the 1993 US Amateur winner — alongside Arnold Palmer, Jack Nicklaus, Tiger Woods, JoAnne Carner and Carol Semple Thompson. McGill earned an exemption into the US Women's Open in 2023, when it will be played at Pebble Beach for the first time. "I'll have to set my schedule now," said McGill. "I look forward to it. That place is heaven on earth."

In other events on the Legends of the LPGA circuit, Jackie Gallagher-Smith won the 18-hole Legends Tour Challenge at the Country Club of North Carolina in a playoff over Moira Dunn-Bohls. Inkster then defended her title at the 36-hole Land O'Lakes Legends Classic at The Meadows at Mystic Lake with scores of 67-70 for a one-shot win over Lindley, who would go on to be runner-up at the US Senior Women's Open.

It was Inkster's seventh Legends title and came in the year she received the Bob Jones Award from the USGA. "Juli exemplifies the true nature of this award in every way," said Mike Whan, CEO of the USGA. "The game of golf is better because Juli is in it. She has earned respect throughout her impressive playing journey, beginning with three consecutive US Women's Amateur wins all the way through her senior career. But more than that, her mentorship to other players has had a tremendous impact on so many. We are very lucky to have her in the USGA family and are thrilled to honour her with this prestigious award."

Closing the season, Pat Bradley, 71, and Jamie Fischer, 54, returned a 12-under-par 59 to win the BJ's Charity Championship at The Ridge Club by two strokes from the teams of Maria McBride and Michelle McGann, and Trish Johnson and Suzy Whaley. "I was looking forward to my day because I had a youngster with a young heart and a great game on my team," said Hall-of-Famer Bradley. "Jamie was great under pressure. She had my back all day. I know my years are limited now in tournament golf, so to be able to share this day with Jamie and my family and friends and people on the Cape, it's just incredible."

With the Chevron Championship leaving Mission Hills in Rancho Mirage for pastures new after 51 years, a new tournament, the Legends Tour Desert Championship, was announced for the spring of 2023 in the Coachella Valley. The 36-hole team event will celebrate the original tournament's founder, Dinah Shore. "We are thrilled to be able to keep the spirit of the LPGA in the desert with our new event," said Legends of the LPGA board president Cathy Johnston-Forbes. "For over 50 years, the world's best women golfers have competed at Mission Hills Country Club. Many players and champions through the years are now Legends of the LPGA players and are excited about playing in and supporting this new event in the valley."

	2022 SCHEDULE
Legends Tour Challenge	**Jackie Gallagher-Smith**
Senior LPGA Championship	**Karrie Webb**
Land O'Lakes Legends Classic	**Juli Inkster**
US Senior Women's Open	**Jill McGill**
BJ's Charity Championship	**Pat Bradley/Jamie Fischer**

Senior LPGA Championship

Had someone turned back the clocks? Suddenly, it was Karrie Webb versus Annika Sorenstam all over again. Both were making their debuts in the Senior LPGA Championship and despite the high temperatures, golf fans in Kansas turned up at Salina Country Club in large numbers to watch the superstars in action. Webb, 47, wound down her regular tour appearances in 2019, 11 years after Sorenstam, 51, retired. Now, they were going head-to-head one more time.

The last of Webb's 41 LPGA victories — seven major titles included — came in 2014 at the Founders Cup but she had played in three events earlier in the season, making the cut twice, including with Marina Alex at the previous week's Dow Great Bay Lakes Invitational, where the pair finished tied for 15th.

It proved a good warm-up as she scored 69-66-67 for a 14-under-par total of 202 to finish four in front of her old rival, Sorenstam posting 69-68-69. Laura Diaz took third place, three behind the Swede, while Lisa DePaulo, the first round-leader on 65, tied for fourth after her third place in 2021.

"It's been a long time since I've had to make putts down the stretch to win a golf tournament," Webb said. "So the mouth was getting dry and the little putts were seeming a little bit longer. I'm not used to playing golf with adrenaline. It was hard to know how far I was hitting it, so it was a bit of a guessing game, but I think I did pretty good overall with it."

Webb went in front on the second day and took a two-shot advantage over Sorenstam into the final round. The Swede, who won the US Senior Women's Open on her debut in 2021, was not going to make it easy for the Australian and chipped in for an eagle on the first hole. "It was kind of a 'game on' moment," said Webb. "Once that went in, I was, like, 'alright, here we go'. I just knew I had to play my best golf."

The pair were tied at 12 under par at the turn and then Webb eagled the 14th, while Sorenstam slipped back with two late bogeys. "I wish I could have continued that pressure how I started," said Sorenstam. "It would have been fun, but I think I ran out of gas a little bit. It was a great head-to-head for most of the day, and I think we both played well. She just came out on top this time. But it's always nice to have the fans out there cheering and creating a good atmosphere."

Salina Country Club, Salina, Kansas — July 22-24
Par 72 (36-36); 5,863 yards — Purse: $400,000

1	**Karrie Webb**	69	66	67	202	$60,000
2	**Annika Sorenstam**	69	68	69	206	36,507
3	**Laura Diaz**	67	72	70	209	26,483
4	Becky Morgan	69	74	69	212	15,440
	Michele Redman	74	68	70	212	15,440
	Juli Inkster	68	73	71	212	15,440
	Lisa DePaulo	65	73	74	212	15,440
8	Tammie Green	74	71	68	213	7,727
	Christa Johnson	72	71	70	213	7,727
	Catrin Nilsmark	71	72	70	213	7,727
	Jean Bartholomew	71	72	70	213	7,727
	Pat Hurst	71	71	71	213	7,727
	Rosie Jones	71	70	72	213	7,727
	Leta Lindley	69	70	74	213	7,727
15	Moira Dunn-Bohls	69	73	72	214	5,636
	Nicole Jeray	69	72	73	214	5,636
17	Cathy Johnston-Forbes	69	77	69	215	4,789
	Sherry Andonian	74	70	71	215	4,789
	Trish Johnson	72	71	72	215	4,789
	Liselotte Neumann	71	72	72	215	4,789
	Jackie Gallagher-Smith	70	72	73	215	4,789

US Senior Women's Open

Jill McGill turned professional in 1994. She did not win on the LPGA. But on the 50-year-old's debut in the US Senior Women's Open, McGill defeated a trio of former champions on the South course at NCR Country Club in southwest Ohio. McGill finished one ahead of fellow debutant Leta Lindley, and two in front of 2019 winner Helen Alfredsson and Catriona Matthew. Tying in fifth place were the inaugural winner Laura Davies, defending champion Annika Sorenstam and Juli Inkster. "It's been a long time. It's been a really, really long time," McGill said after her maiden professional victory.

McGill, originally from Denver, now a resident of Dallas, had not won since the 1994 US Women's Amateur Public Links, a title she claimed after winning the US Amateur in 1993. This victory put her in rarefied company with victories in three different USGA championships, joining Arnold Palmer, Jack Nicklaus, Tiger Woods, JoAnne Carner and Carol Semple Thompson. On being introduced as the new champion, McGill said: "That sounds amazing. I love the USGA. I've loved it ever since I got spanked in my very first Junior Girls by Brandie Burton. That was a welcome to competitive golf."

Her welcome to the US Senior Women's Open was a one-over-par 74 that put her six strokes behind Tammie Green's 68. Alfredsson took the 36-hole lead after a pair of 70s, with McGill edging a stroke closer after a 71, a score she repeated on Saturday. Now McGill was only a stroke behind Alfredsson and Davies, whose 68 matched Green for the lowest score of the week.

"Well, I don't know if this makes me more nervous or going in for childbirth, one of the two," McGill said of being in contention. "I'm getting my nine-month-old puppies back from military school, so I don't know which one is more challenging at the moment. But it's fun to be in this position."

On the final day McGill was alongside Sorenstam, who birdied the first to tie for the lead. The pair had played together in the final group of the 2002 US Women's Open, when McGill scored 78 and Sorenstam got overtaken by Inkster. This time it was Sorenstam, the eight-stroke winner in 2021, who fell away with a 77 as McGill matched birdies with bogeys on a day when no one broke par.

McGill was two behind Davies at the turn, but the Englishwoman, troubled by a sore right Achilles, saw her bogey-free run of 39 holes end in spectacular fashion at the 12th. Davies drove into the left rough, clipped a tree with her second and went out of bounds. She eventually two-putted for a quadruple-bogey eight and closed with a 78. "I was going really well until the quad," Davies sighed. Of the conditions and pressure down the stretch, Dame Laura added: "About as tough as I've ever known it."

McGill birdied the 14th and 16th holes to give herself a cushion that was required when she bogeyed the last two holes. A 73 gave her a three-under-par total of 289. Lindley closed with a 74, while Matthew and Inkster had 73s. "I knew at the turn I was a couple back, and from that point on, I really had no idea," McGill said. "I knew that I was close when I made a couple of birdies. I was disappointed with that bogey on 17. I tried not to focus on it. All I could do was what I could do, and whatever everybody else was doing was what they were doing."

NCR Country Club (South), Kettering, Ohio — August 25-28
Par 73 (37-36); 6,178 yards — Purse: $1,000,000

1	**Jill McGill**	74	71	71	73	289	$180,000
2	**Leta Lindley**	69	72	75	74	290	108,000
3	**Catriona Matthew**	72	76	70	73	291	58,961
	Helen Alfredsson	70	70	75	76	291	58,961
5	Juli Inkster	76	71	73	73	293	36,010
	Annika Sorenstam	73	70	73	77	293	36,010
	Laura Davies	71	76	68	78	293	36,010
8	Catrin Nilsmark	69	76	76	73	294	28,890
9	Michele Redman	75	74	71	75	295	25,024
	Liselotte Neumann	76	73	71	75	295	25,024
11	Tammie Green	68	76	76	76	296	21,769
12	Trish Johnson	73	73	73	79	298	19,734
13	Stefania Croce	75	75	72	77	299	18,615
14	Pat Hurst	70	78	78	74	300	17,598
15	Patricia Ehrhart (A)	74	75	75	77	301	
	Christa Johnson	75	77	72	77	301	16,123
	Lisa Grimes	76	73	73	79	301	16,123
18	Jackie Gallagher-Smith	74	73	78	77	302	14,750
19	Audra Burks	73	77	77	77	304	13,402
	Jamie Fischer	76	77	72	79	304	13,402